Applied Child and Adolescent Development

CUSTOM EDITION FOR NATIONAL UNIVERSITY

CED 600 Applied Child and Adolescent Development

Taken from:

Development Through the Lifespan, Fifth Edition
by Laura E. Berk

Characteristics of Emotional and Behavioral Disorders of Children and Youth, Ninth Edition
by James M. Kauffman and Timothy J. Landrum

Learning Solutions

New York   Boston   San Francisco
London   Toronto   Sydney   Tokyo   Singapore   Madrid
Mexico City   Munich   Paris   Cape Town   Hong Kong   Montreal

Cover Art: Courtesy of PhotoDisc/Getty Images and EyeWire/Getty Images

Taken from:

Development Through the Lifespan, Fifth Edition
by Laura E. Berk
Copyright © 2010, 2007, 2004, 2001, 1998 by Pearson Education, Inc.
Published by Allyn & Bacon
Boston, Massachusetts 02116

Characteristics of Emotional and Behavioral Disorders of Children and Youth, Ninth Edition
by James M. Kauffman and Timothy J. Landrum
Copyright © 2009, 2005, 2001, 1997, 1993, 1989, 1985, 1977 by Pearson Education, Inc.
Published by Merrill
Upper Saddle River, New Jersey 07458

This special edition published in cooperation with Pearson Learning Solutions.

Pearson Learning Solutions, 501 Boylston Street, Suite 900, Boston, MA 02116
A Pearson Education Company
www.pearsoned.com

Printed in the United States of America

20

000200010270729696

SB

ISBN 10: 0-558-98849-0
ISBN 13: 978-0-558-98849-4

Contents

SECTION **10** (Chapter 7 *in original publication*)
Family Factors   **310**

SECTION **11** (Chapter 8 *in original publication*)
School Factors   **330**

SECTION **12** (Chapter 9 *in original publication*)
Cultural Factors   **358**

SECTION **13** (Chapter 10 *in original publication*)
Attention and Activity Disorders   **385**

Selections from

Development Through the Lifespan

Fifth Edition

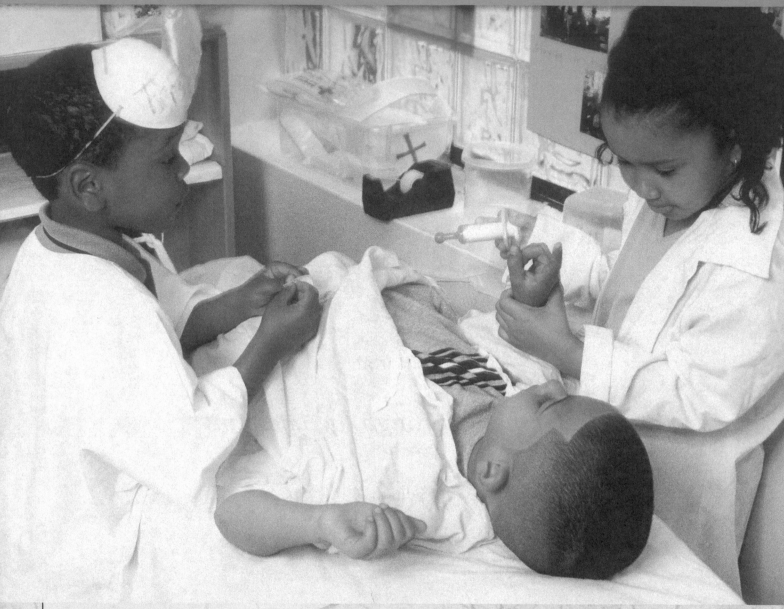

Preschoolers draw on their rich array of everyday experiences when they engage in make-believe play. In turn, their make-believe contributes greatly to their rapidly advancing cognitive and language skills.

Physical and Cognitive Development in Early Childhood

For more than a decade, my fourth-floor office window overlooked the preschool and kindergarten play yard of our university laboratory school. On mild fall and spring mornings, the doors of the classrooms swung open, and sand table, easels, and large blocks spilled out into a small courtyard. Alongside the building was a grassy area with jungle gyms, swings, a playhouse, and a flower garden planted by the children; beyond it, a circular path lined with tricycles and wagons. Each day, the setting was alive with activity.

The years from 2 to 6 are often called "the play years"—aptly so, since play blossoms during this time and supports every aspect of development. Our discussion opens with the physical achievements of early childhood—growth in body size and improvements in motor coordination. We look at biological and environmental factors that support these changes and at their intimate connection with other domains of development.

Then we explore early childhood cognition, beginning with Piaget's pre-operational stage. Recent research, along with Vygotsky's sociocultural theory and information processing, extends our understanding of preschoolers' cognitive competencies. Next, we turn to factors that contribute to early childhood mental development—the home environment, the quality of preschool and child care, and educational media. We conclude with the most awesome achievement of early childhood—language development.

Physical Development

A Changing Body and Brain

In early childhood, body growth tapers off from the rapid rate of the first two years. On average, children add 2 to 3 inches in height and about 5 pounds in weight each year. Boys continue to be slightly larger than girls. As "baby fat" drops off further, children gradually become thinner, although girls retain somewhat more body fat than boys, who are slightly more muscular. As Figure 1.1 shows, by age 5 the top-heavy, bowlegged, potbellied toddler has become a more streamlined, flat-tummied, longer-legged child with body proportions similar to those of adults. Consequently, posture and balance improve—changes that support gains in motor coordination.

Individual differences in body size are even more apparent during early childhood than in infancy and toddlerhood. Speeding around the bike path in the play yard, 5-year-old Darryl—at 48 inches tall and 55 pounds—towered over his kindergarten classmates. (The average North American 5-year-old boy is 43 inches tall and weighs 42 pounds.) Priti, an Asian-Indian child, was unusually small because of genetic factors linked to her cultural ancestry. Lynette and Hal, two Caucasian children with impoverished home lives, were well below average for reasons we will discuss shortly.

PHOTOS OF CHRIS © BOB DAEMMRICH PHOTOGRAPHY; PHOTOS OF MARIEL © JIM WEST PHOTOGRAPHY

Chris at 4½ years

Chris at 3½ years

Chris at 3 years

Chris at 5 years

Mariel at 2½ years

Mariel at 4 years

Mariel at 4½ years

Mariel at 5 years

■ **FIGURE 1.1** ■ **Body growth during early childhood.** During the preschool years, children grow more slowly than in infancy and toddlerhood. Chris and Mariel's bodies became more streamlined, flat-tummied, and longer-legged. Boys continue to be slightly taller, heavier, and more muscular than girls. But generally, the two sexes are similar in body proportions and physical capacities.

Skeletal Growth

The skeletal changes of infancy continue throughout early childhood. Between ages 2 and 6, approximately 45 new *epiphyses*, or growth centers in which cartilage hardens into bone, emerge in various parts of the skeleton. X-rays of these growth centers enable doctors to estimate children's *skeletal age*, or progress toward physical maturity—information helpful in diagnosing growth disorders.

By the end of the preschool years, children start to lose their primary, or "baby," teeth. Genetic factors heavily influence the age at which they do so. For example, girls, who are ahead of boys in physical development, lose teeth earlier. Environmental influences also matter: Prolonged malnutrition delays the appearance of permanent teeth, whereas overweight and obesity accelerate it (Hilgers et al., 2006).

Diseased baby teeth can affect the health of permanent teeth, so preventing decay in primary teeth is essential—by brushing consistently, avoiding sugary foods, drinking fluoridated water, and getting topical fluoride treatments and sealants (plastic coatings that protect tooth surfaces). Another factor is exposure to tobacco smoke, which suppresses children's immune system, including the ability to fight bacteria responsible for tooth decay. Young children in homes with regular smokers are three times as likely as their agemates to have decayed teeth (Shenkin et al., 2004).

Unfortunately, an estimated 30 percent of U.S. preschoolers have tooth decay, a figure that rises to 60 percent by age 18. Causes include poor diet and inadequate health care—factors more likely to affect low-SES children. About 12 percent of U.S. children living in poverty have untreated tooth decay (U.S. Department of Health and Human Services, 2007g).

Brain Development

Between ages 2 and 6, the brain increases from 70 percent of its adult weight to 90 percent. By age 4, many parts of the cerebral cortex have overproduced synapses, and fMRI evidence indicates that cerebral blood flow peaks, signifying a high energy need (Huttenlocher, 2002; Nelson, Thomas, & de Haan, 2006). As *formation of synapses, cell death, myelination*, and *synaptic pruning* occur, preschoolers improve in a wide variety of skills—physical coordination, perception, attention, memory, language, logical thinking, and imagination.

EEG and fMRI measures of neural activity in various cortical regions reveal especially rapid growth from early to middle childhood in frontal-lobe areas devoted to inhibiting impulses and planning and organizing behavior (Bartgis, Lilly, & Thomas, 2003; Diamond, 2004). Furthermore, for most children, the left cerebral hemisphere is especially active between 3 and 6 years and then levels off. In contrast, activity in the right hemisphere increases steadily throughout early and middle childhood (Thatcher, Walker, & Giudice, 1987; Thompson et al., 2000a).

These findings fit nicely with what we know about several aspects of cognitive development. Early childhood is a time of marked gains on tasks that depend on the frontal cortex—ones that require inhibiting impulses and substituting thoughtful responses (Diamond, 2004; Rothbart & Bates, 2006). Further, language skills (typically housed in the left hemisphere) increase at an astonishing pace in early childhood, and they support children's increasing control over behavior. In contrast, spatial skills (usually located in the right hemisphere), such as giving directions, drawing pictures, and recognizing geometric shapes, develop gradually over childhood and adolescence. Differences in rate of development between the two hemispheres suggest that they are continuing to *lateralize* (specialize in cognitive functions). Let's take a closer look at brain lateralization in early childhood by focusing on handedness.

■ **HANDEDNESS.** On one visit to the preschool, I observed 3-year-old Moira drawing pictures, eating a snack, and playing outside. Unlike most of her classmates, Moira does most things—drawing, eating, and zipping her jacket—with her left hand. But she uses her right hand for a few activities, such as throwing a ball. Research on handedness, supports the joint contribution of nature and nurture to brain lateralization.

By age 6 months, infants typically display a smoother, more efficient movement when reaching with their right than their left arm—a difference, believed to be biologically based, that may contribute to the right-hand preference evident in most children by the end of the first year (Hinojosa, Sheu, & Michael, 2003; Rönnqvist & Domellöf, 2006). Gradually, handedness extends to additional skills.

Handedness reflects the greater capacity of one side of the brain—the individual's **dominant cerebral hemisphere**—to carry out skilled motor action. Other important abilities are generally located on the dominant side as well. For right-handed people—in Western nations, 90 percent of the population—language is housed in the left hemisphere with hand control. For the left-handed 10 percent, language is occasionally located

Twins are more likely than ordinary siblings to differ in hand preference, perhaps because twins usually lie in opposite orientations in the uterus.

in the right hemisphere or, more often, shared between the hemispheres (Szaflarski et al., 2002). This indicates that the brains of left-handers tend to be less strongly lateralized than those of right-handers.

Left-handed parents show only a weak tendency to have left-handed children. One genetic theory proposes that most children inherit a gene that *biases* them for right-handedness and a left-dominant cerebral hemisphere, but this bias is not strong enough to overcome experiences that might sway children toward a left-hand preference (Annett, 2002). Even prenatal events may profoundly affect handedness. Both identical and fraternal twins are more likely than ordinary siblings to differ in hand preference, probably because twins usually lie in opposite orientations in the uterus (Derom et al., 1996). The orientation of most singleton fetuses—facing toward the left— is believed to promote greater control over movements on the body's right side (Previc, 1991).

Handedness also involves practice. Newborns' bias in head position causes them to spend more time looking at and using one hand, which contributes to greater skillfulness of that hand (Hinojosa, Sheu, & Michael, 2003). Also, wide cultural differences exist: In Tanzania, Africa, where children are physically restrained and punished for favoring their left hand, less than 1 percent of adults are left-handed (Provins, 1997).

Although left-handedness occurs more frequently among severely retarded and mentally ill people than in the general population, atypical lateralization is probably not responsible for these individuals' problems. Rather, early damage to the left hemisphere may have caused their disabilities while also leading to a shift in handedness. In support of this idea, left-handedness is associated with prenatal and birth difficulties that can result in brain damage, including prolonged labor, prematurity, Rh incompatibility, and breech delivery (O'Callaghan et al., 1993; Powls et al., 1996).

Most left-handers, however, have no developmental problems. In fact, left- and mixed-handed youngsters are more likely than their right-handed agemates to develop outstanding verbal and mathematical talents (Flannery & Liederman, 1995). More even distribution of cognitive functions across both hemispheres may be responsible.

■ OTHER ADVANCES IN BRAIN DEVELOPMENT.
In addition to the cerebral cortex, other parts of the brain make strides during early childhood (see Figure 1.2). All of these changes involve establishing links between parts of the brain, increasing the coordinated functioning of the central nervous system.

At the rear and base of the brain is the **cerebellum,** a structure that aids in balance and control of body movement. Fibers linking the cerebellum to the cerebral cortex grow and myelinate from birth through the preschool years, contributing to dramatic gains in motor coordination: By the end of the preschool years, children can play hopscotch, throw a ball with well-coordinated movements, and print letters of the alphabet. Connections between the cerebellum and cerebral cortex also

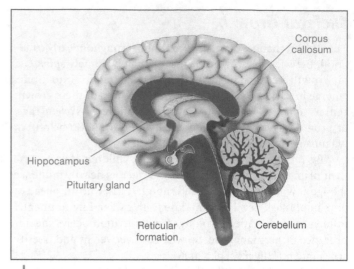

■ **FIGURE 1.2** ■ **Cross-section of the human brain, showing the location of the cerebellum, the reticular formation, the hippocampus, and the corpus callosum.** These structures undergo considerable development during early childhood. Also shown is the pituitary gland, which secretes hormones that control body growth (see page 7).

support thinking (Diamond, 2000): Children with damage to the cerebellum usually display both motor and cognitive deficits, including problems with memory, planning, and language (Noterdaeme et al., 2002; Riva & Giorgi, 2000).

The **reticular formation,** a structure in the brain stem that maintains alertness and consciousness, generates synapses and myelinates throughout childhood and into adolescence. Neurons in the reticular formation send out fibers to the frontal lobes of the cortex, contributing to improvements in sustained, controlled attention.

An inner-brain structure called the **hippocampus,** which plays a vital role in memory and in images of space that help us find our way, undergoes rapid synapse formation and myelination in the second half of the first year, when recall memory and independent movement emerge. Over the preschool and school years, the hippocampus and surrounding areas of the cerebral cortex continue to develop swiftly, establishing connections with one another and with the frontal lobes (Nelson, Thomas, & de Haan, 2006). These changes support the dramatic gains in memory and spatial understanding of early and middle childhood (Nelson, Thomas, & de Haan, 2006).

The **corpus callosum** is a large bundle of fibers connecting the two cerebral hemispheres. Production of synapses and myelination of the corpus callosum peak between 3 and 6 years, then continue more slowly through adolescence (Thompson et al., 2000a). The corpus callosum supports smooth coordination of movements on both sides of the body and integration of many aspects of thinking, including perception, attention, memory, language, and problem solving. The more complex the task, the more essential is communication between the hemispheres.

© ROYALTY-FREE/CORBIS

In early childhood, changes in the corpus callosum and other brain structures enhance communication between parts of the brain, enabling children to perform increasingly complex tasks—like this board game—that require integration of attention, memory, language, and problem solving.

ASK YOURSELF

>> **REVIEW**
What aspects of brain development underlie the tremendous gains in language, thinking, and motor control of early childhood?

>> **APPLY**
Dental checkups revealed a high incidence of untreated tooth decay in a U.S. preschool program serving low-income children. Using findings presented in this section, list possible contributing factors.

>> **CONNECT**
What stand on the nature–nurture issue do findings on development of handedness support? Explain, using research findings.

>> **REFLECT**
How early, and to what extent, did you experience tooth decay in childhood? What factors might have been responsible?

Influences on Physical Growth and Health

As we consider factors affecting growth and health in early childhood, you will encounter some familiar themes. Heredity remains important, but environmental factors—including emotional well-being, good nutrition, relative free-

dom from disease, and physical safety—also are essential. And as the Biology and Environment box on page 8 illustrates, environmental pollutants can threaten children's healthy development. The extent to which low-level lead—one of the most common—undermines children's mental and emotional functioning is the focus of intensive research.

Heredity and Hormones

The impact of heredity on physical growth is evident throughout childhood. Children's physical size and rate of growth are related to those of their parents (Bogin, 2001). Genes influence growth by controlling the body's production of hormones. The **pituitary gland,** located at the base of the brain, plays a critical role by releasing two hormones that induce growth.

The first, **growth hormone (GH),** is necessary for development of all body tissues except the central nervous system and the genitals. Children who lack GH reach an average mature height of only 4 feet, 4 inches. When treated early with injections of GH, such children show catch-up growth and then grow at a normal rate, becoming much taller than they would have without treatment (Saenger, 2003).

A second pituitary hormone, **thyroid-stimulating hormone (TSH),** prompts the thyroid gland in the neck to release *thyroxine,* which is necessary for brain development and for GH to have its full impact on body size. Infants born with a deficiency of thyroxine must receive it at once, or they will be mentally retarded. Once the most rapid period of brain development is complete, children with too little thyroxine grow at a below-average rate, but the central nervous system is no longer affected. With prompt treatment, such children catch up in body growth and eventually reach normal size (Salerno et al., 2001).

Emotional Well-Being

In childhood as in infancy, emotional well-being can profoundly affect growth and health. Children with stressful home lives (due to divorce, financial difficulties, or parental job loss) suffer more respiratory and intestinal illnesses and more unintentional injuries than others (Cohen & Herbert, 1996; Kemeny, 2003).

In addition, high stress suppresses the release of GH (Deltondo et al., 2008). Consequently, extreme emotional deprivation can lead to **psychosocial dwarfism,** a growth disorder that usually appears between ages 2 and 15. Typical characteristics include decreased GH secretion, very short stature, immature skeletal age, and serious adjustment problems, which help distinguish psychosocial dwarfism from normal shortness (Tarren-Sweeney, 2006). Lynette, the 4-year-old mentioned earlier in this section, was diagnosed with this condition. She was placed in foster care after child welfare authorities discovered that she spent most of the day home alone, unsupervised, and might also have been physically abused. When such children are removed from their emotionally inadequate environments, their GH levels quickly return to normal, and they grow rapidly. But if treatment is delayed, the dwarfism can be permanent.

▪ BIOLOGY AND ENVIRONMENT ▪

Low-Level Lead Exposure and Children's Development

Lead is a highly toxic element that, at blood levels exceeding 60 µg/dL (micrograms per deciliter), causes brain swelling and hemorrhaging. Risk of death rises as blood-lead level exceeds 100 µg/dL. Before 1980, lead exposure resulted from use of lead-based paints in residences (where infants and young children often ate paint flakes) and from use of leaded gasoline (car exhaust resulted in a highly breathable form of lead). Laws limiting the lead content of paint and mandating lead-free gasoline led to a sharp decline in children's lead levels, from an average of 15 µg/dL in 1980 to 1.8 µg/dL today (Jones et al., 2009; Meyer et al., 2003).

But in neighborhoods near industries that use lead production processes, or where lead-based paint remains in older homes, children's blood levels are still markedly elevated. About 15 percent of low-income children living in large central cities, and 19 percent of African-American children, have blood-lead levels exceeding 10 µg/dL (the official "level of concern"), warranting immediate efforts to reduce exposure (Jones et al., 2009).

How much lead exposure is too much? Is lead contamination a "silent epidemic," impairing children's mental functioning even in small quantities? Until recently, answers were unclear. Studies reporting a negative relationship between children's current lead levels and cognitive performance often failed to control for factors associated with both blood-lead levels and mental test scores (such as SES, home environmental quality, and nutrition) that might account for the findings.

Over the past two decades, seven longitudinal studies of the developmental consequences of lead have been conducted—three in the United States, two in Australia, one in Mexico City, and one in Yugoslavia. Some focused on inner-city, low-SES minority children; others on middle- and upper-middle-SES suburban children; and one on children living close to a lead smelter. Each tracked children's lead exposure over an extended time and included relevant controls.

Five sites reported negative relationships between lead exposure and children's IQs (Hubbs-Tait et al., 2005). Higher blood levels were also associated with verbal and visual-motor skill deficits, distractibility, overactivity, poor organization, and behavior problems. And an array of findings suggested that persistent childhood lead exposure contributes to antisocial behavior in adolescence (Dietrich et al., 2001; Needleman et al., 2002; Nevin, 2000; Stretesky & Lynch, 2001).

The investigations disagreed on an age period of greatest vulnerability. In some, relationships were strongest in toddlerhood and early childhood; in others, at the most recently studied age—suggesting cumulative effects over time. Still other studies reported similar lead-related cognitive deficits from infancy through adolescence. Overall, poorer mental test scores associated with lead exposure persisted over time and seemed to be permanent. Children given drugs to induce excretion of lead (chelation) did not improve (Dietrich

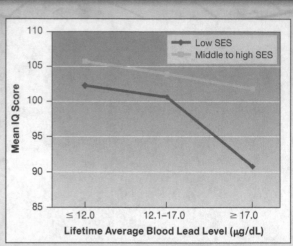

These children play near a factory in Cairo, Egypt, ranked among the world's most polluted cities in levels of lead and other toxins. Studies consistently show lasting negative effects of lead exposure, including learning and behavior problems.

■ FIGURE 1.3 ■ Relationship of lifetime average lead exposure to 11- to-13-year-old IQ by SES. In this study, conducted in the lead-smelting city of Port Pirie, Australia, blood-lead levels of 375 children were measured repeatedly from birth to age 11 to 13. The lead-exposure-related drop in IQ was much greater for low-SES than higher-SES children. (Adapted from Tong, McMichael, & Baghurst, 2000.)

et al., 2004; Rogan et al., 2001). And negative cognitive consequences were evident at all levels of exposure—even below 10 µg/dL (Lamphear et al., 2005).

Although the overall impact of low-level lead exposure on all outcomes is modest, in three longitudinal investigations, cognitive consequences were greatest for low-SES children (see, for example, Figure 1.3) (Bellinger, Leviton, & Sloman, 1990; Ris et al., 2004; Tong, McMichael, & Baghurst, 2000). A stressed, disorganized home life seems to heighten lead-induced damage. Dietary factors can also magnify lead's toxic effects. Iron deficiency, common in low-SES children, increases lead concentration in the blood, whereas iron supplements decrease it. Similarly, exposed children absorb less lead when their diets contain enough zinc (Noonan et al., 2003; Wolf, Jimenez, & Lozoff, 2003; Wright et al., 2003).

In sum, lead impairs learning and contributes to behavior problems. Low-SES children are more likely both to live in lead-contaminated areas and to experience additional risks that magnify lead-induced damage. Because lead is a stable element, its release into the air and soil is difficult to reverse. Therefore, in addition to laws that control lead pollution and limit children's exposure, interventions that reduce the negative impact of lead—through involved parenting, better schools, and dietary enrichment—are vital.

Nutrition

With the transition to early childhood, many children become unpredictable, picky eaters. One father I know wistfully recalled how his son, as a toddler, eagerly sampled Chinese food: "Now, at age 3, the only thing he'll try is the ice cream!"

Preschoolers' appetites decline because their growth has slowed. Their wariness of new foods is also adaptive. If they stick to familiar foods, they are less likely to swallow dangerous substances when adults are not around to protect them (Birch & Fisher, 1995). Parents need not worry about variations in amount eaten from meal to meal. Preschoolers compensate for a meal in which they eat little by eating more at a later meal (Hursti, 1999).

Though they eat less, preschoolers require a high quality diet, including the same foods adults need, but in smaller amounts. Fats, oils, and salt should be kept to a minimum because of their link to high blood pressure and heart disease in adulthood. Foods high in sugar should also be avoided to prevent tooth decay and protect against overweight and obesity.

Children tend to imitate the food choices of people they admire, both adults and peers. For example, in Mexico, where children often see family members enjoying peppery foods, preschoolers enthusiastically eat chili peppers, whereas most North American children reject them (Birch, Zimmerman, & Hind, 1980). Repeated, unpressured exposure to a new food also increases acceptance (Fuller et al., 2005). Serving broccoli or tofu increases children's liking for these healthy foods. In contrast, offering sweet fruit or soft drinks promotes "milk avoidance" (Black et al., 2002).

Although children's healthy eating depends on a wholesome food environment, too much parental control limits children's opportunities to develop self-control. Offering bribes ("Finish your vegetables, and you can have an extra cookie") causes children to like the healthy food less and the treat more (Birch, Fisher, & Davison, 2003).

Finally, as indicated in earlier sections, many children in North America and in developing countries lack access to sufficient high-quality food to support healthy development. Five-year-old Hal rode a bus from a poor neighborhood to our laboratory preschool. His mother's welfare check barely covered her rent, let alone food. Hal's diet was deficient in protein and in essential vitamins and minerals—iron (to prevent anemia), calcium (to support development of bones and teeth), vitamin A (to help maintain eyes, skin, and a variety of internal organs), and vitamin C (to facilitate iron absorption and wound healing). These are the most common deficiencies of the preschool years (Ganji, Hampl, & Betts, 2003). Not surprisingly, Hal was thin, pale, and tired. By the school years, low-SES North American children are, on average, ½ to 1 inch shorter than their economically advantaged counterparts (Cecil et al., 2005; Yip, Scanlon, & Trowbridge, 1993).

Infectious Disease

One day, I noticed that Hal had been absent from the play yard for several weeks, so I asked Leslie, his preschool teacher, what was wrong. "Hal's been hospitalized with the measles," she explained. "He's had difficulty recovering—lost weight when there wasn't much to lose in the first place." In well-nourished children, ordinary childhood illnesses have no effect on physical growth. But when children are poorly fed, disease interacts with malnutrition in a vicious spiral, with potentially severe consequences.

■ **INFECTIOUS DISEASE AND MALNUTRITION.** Hal's reaction to the measles is commonplace in developing nations, where a large proportion of the population lives in poverty and children do not receive routine immunizations. Illnesses such as measles and chicken pox, which typically do not appear until after age 3 in industrialized nations, occur much earlier. Poor diet depresses the body's immune system, making children far more susceptible to disease. Of the 10 million annual deaths of children under age 5 worldwide, 98 percent are in developing countries and 70 percent are due to infectious diseases (World Health Organization, 2008a).

Disease, in turn, is a major contributor to malnutrition, hindering both physical growth and cognitive development. Illness reduces appetite and limits the body's ability to absorb foods, especially in children with intestinal infections. In developing countries, widespread diarrhea, resulting from unsafe water and contaminated foods, leads to growth stunting and nearly two million childhood deaths each year (World Health Organization, 2008a). Studies carried out in the slums and shantytowns of Brazil and Peru reveal that the more persistent diarrhea is in early childhood, the shorter children are in height and the lower they score on mental tests during the school years (Checkley et al., 2003; Niehaus et al., 2002).

This Quechua child of the Peruvian highlands enthusiastically accepts a spoonful of soup made from bitter-tasting potatoes. She has already acquired a taste for the foods that are commonly served in her culture.

Most developmental impairments and deaths due to diarrhea can be prevented with nearly cost-free *oral rehydration therapy (ORT),* in which sick children are given a solution of glucose, salt, and water that quickly replaces fluids the body loses. Since 1990, public health workers have taught nearly half the families in the developing world how to administer ORT. Also, supplements of zinc (essential for immune system functioning), which cost only 30 cents for a month's supply, substantially reduce the incidence of severe diarrhea (Aggarwal, Sentz, & Miller, 2007). Through these interventions, the lives of millions of children are saved each year.

■ **IMMUNIZATION.**   In industrialized nations, childhood diseases have declined dramatically during the past half-century, largely as a result of widespread immunization of infants and young children. Hal got the measles because, unlike classmates from advantaged homes, he did not receive a full program of immunizations. About 23 percent of U.S. preschoolers lack essential immunizations. The rate rises to 26 percent for poverty-stricken children, who do not receive full protection until age 5 or 6, when it is required for school entry (U.S. Department of Health and Human Services, 2007d). In contrast, fewer than 10 percent of preschoolers lack immunizations in Denmark and Norway, and fewer than 7 percent in Great Britain, Canada, the Netherlands, and Sweden (United Nations, 2002; UNICEF, 2008).

Why does the United States lag behind these countries in immunization? As noted in earlier sections, many U.S. children do not have access to the health care they need. In 1994, all medically uninsured children in the United States were guaranteed free immunizations, a program that has led to a steady improvement in immunization rates.

Inability to pay for vaccines is only one cause of inadequate immunization. Parents with stressful daily lives or without health benefits of their own often fail to schedule vaccination appointments, and those without a primary care physician do not want to endure long waits in crowded public health clinics. Some parents have been influenced by media reports suggesting a link between the measles–mumps–rubella vaccine and a rise in the number of children diagnosed with autism, although large-scale studies show no such association (Dales, Hammer, & Smith, 2001; Richler et al., 2006; Stehr-Green et al., 2003). In areas where many parents have refused to immunize their children, disease outbreaks of whooping cough and rubella have occurred, with life-threatening consequences (Kennedy & Gust, 2008; Tuyen & Bisgard, 2003). Public education programs to increase parental knowledge about the importance and safety of timely immunizations are badly needed.

Childhood Injuries

More than any other child in the preschool classroom, 3-year-old Tommy had trouble sitting still and paying attention. Instead, he darted from one place and activity to another. One day, he narrowly escaped serious injury when he put his mother's car into gear while she was outside scraping ice from its windows. The vehicle rolled through a guardrail and over the side

of a 10-foot concrete underpass, where it hung until rescue workers arrived. Police charged Tommy's mother with failure to use a restraint seat for a child younger than age 8.

Unintentional injuries are the leading cause of childhood mortality in industrialized nations. As Figure 1.4 reveals, the United States ranks poorly in these largely preventable events. Nearly 35 percent of U.S. childhood deaths and 50 percent of adolescent deaths result from injuries (Children's Defense Fund, 2008). And among injured children and youths who survive, thousands suffer pain, brain damage, and permanent physical disabilities.

Auto and traffic accidents, drownings, and burns are the most common injuries during early and middle childhood. Motor vehicle collisions are by far the most frequent source of injury across all ages, ranking as the leading cause of death among children more than 1 year old.

■ **FACTORS RELATED TO CHILDHOOD INJURIES.**   The common view of childhood injuries as "accidental" suggests they are due to chance and cannot be prevented (Sleet & Mercy, 2003). In fact, these injuries occur within a complex *ecological system* of individual, family, community, and societal influences—and we can do something about them.

Because of their higher activity level and greater impulsivity and risk taking, boys are 1.5 times more likely to be injured than

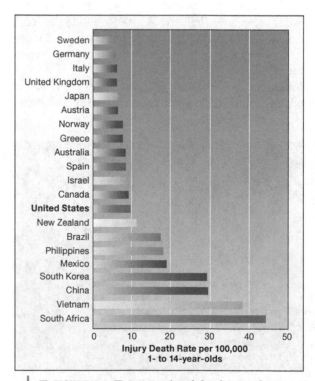

■ **FIGURE 1.4** ■ **International death rates due to unintentional injury among 1- to 14-year-olds.** Compared with other industrialized nations, the United States has a high injury rate, largely because of widespread childhood poverty and shortages of high-quality child care. Injury death rates are many times higher in developing nations, where poverty, rapid population growth, overcrowding in cities, and inadequate safety measures endanger children's lives. (Adapted from World Health Organization, 2008c.)

girls (National Safe Kids Campaign, 2005). Children with certain temperamental and personality characteristics—inattentiveness, overactivity, irritability, defiance, and aggression—are also at greater risk (Ordonana, Caspi, & Moffitt, 2008; Schwebel & Gaines, 2007). These children present child-rearing challenges. They are likely to protest when placed in auto seat restraints or refuse to take a companion's hand when crossing the street— even after repeated instruction and discipline.

Poverty, single parenthood, and low parental education are also strongly associated with injury (Schwebel & Brezausek, 2007; World Health Organization, 2008c). Parents who must cope with many daily stresses often have little energy to monitor the safety of their children. And their rundown homes and neighborhoods pose further risks (Dal Santo et al., 2004).

Broad societal conditions also affect childhood injury. In developing countries, the rate of death from injury before age 15 is five times higher than in developed nations and soon may exceed disease as the leading cause of childhood mortality (World Health Organization, 2008c). Rapid population growth, overcrowding in cities, and heavy road traffic combined with weak safety measures are major causes. Safety devices, such as car safety seats and bicycle helmets, are neither readily available nor affordable.

Childhood injury rates are high in the United States because of extensive poverty, shortages of high-quality child care (to supervise children in their parents' absence), and a high rate of births to teenagers, who are not ready for parenthood. But U.S. children from advantaged families are also at considerably greater risk for injury than children in Western Europe (World Health Organization, 2008c). This indicates that besides reducing poverty and teenage pregnancy and upgrading the status of child care, additional steps are needed to ensure children's safety.

■ **PREVENTING CHILDHOOD INJURIES.** Childhood injuries have many causes, so a variety of approaches are needed to reduce them. Laws prevent many injuries by requiring car safety seats, child-resistant caps on medicine bottles, flameproof clothing, and fencing around backyard swimming pools (the site of 50 percent of early childhood drownings) (Brenner & Committee on Injury, Violence, and Poison Protection, 2003). Communities can help by modifying their physical environments. Playgrounds, a common site of injury, can be covered with protective surfaces (National Safe Kids Campaign, 2005). Free, easily installed window guards can be given to families in high-rise apartment buildings to prevent falls. And media campaigns can inform parents and children about safety issues.

But even though they know better, many parents and children behave in ways that compromise safety. About 40 percent of U.S. parents (like Tommy's mother) fail to place their preschoolers in car safety seats. And when parents do use safety seats, 82 percent either install or use them incorrectly (Howard, 2002; National Safe Kids Campaign, 2005). American parents, especially, seem willing to ignore familiar safety practices, perhaps because of the high value they place on individual rights and personal freedom (Damashek & Peterson, 2002).

Furthermore, many parents begin relying on children's knowledge of safety rules, rather than controlling access to haz-

This Thai family—like many others—rides unprotected on the only form of transportation it has. In developing countries, heavy road traffic and weak safety measures contribute to an injury death rate before age 15 that is five times higher than in developed nations.

ards, as early as 2 or 3 years of age—a premature transition associated with a rise in home injuries (Morrongiello, Ondejko, & Littlejohn, 2004). But even older preschoolers spontaneously recall only about half the safety rules their parents teach them. Even with well-learned rules, they need supervision to ensure they comply (Morrongiello, Midgett, & Shields, 2001).

Parent interventions that highlight risk factors and that model and reinforce safety practices are effective in reducing home hazards and childhood injuries (Kendrick et al., 2008). But such efforts focus narrowly on specific risks. Attention must also be paid to family conditions that can prevent childhood injury: relieving crowding in the home, providing social supports to ease parental stress, and teaching parents to use effective discipline.

ASK YOURSELF

》 REVIEW
How can psychosocial dwarfism caused by extreme emotional deprivation be distinguished from ordinary shortness?

》 APPLY
One day, Leslie prepared a new snack to serve at preschool: celery stuffed with ricotta cheese. The first time she served it, few children touched it. How can Leslie encourage her students to accept the snack? What tactics should she avoid?

》 CONNECT
Using research on malnutrition or on unintentional injuries, show how physical growth and health in early childhood result from a continuous, complex interplay between heredity and environment.

》 REFLECT
Ask a parent or other family member whether, as a preschooler, you were a picky eater, suffered from many infectious diseases, or sustained any serious injuries. In each instance, what factors might have been responsible?

Motor Development

TAKE A MOMENT... Observe several 2- to 6-year-olds at play in a neighborhood park, preschool, or child-care center. You will see that an explosion of new motor skills occurs in early childhood, each of which builds on the simpler movement patterns of toddlerhood.

During the preschool years, children continue to integrate previously acquired skills into more complex, *dynamic systems.* Then they revise each new skill as their bodies grow larger and stronger, their central nervous systems develop, and their environments present new challenges.

Gross-Motor Development

As children's bodies become more streamlined and less top-heavy, their center of gravity shifts downward, toward the trunk. As a result, balance improves greatly, paving the way for new motor skills involving large muscles of the body. By age 2, preschoolers' gaits become smooth and rhythmic—secure enough that soon they leave the ground, at first by running and later by jumping, hopping, galloping, and skipping.

As children become steadier on their feet, their arms and torsos are freed to experiment with new skills—throwing and catching balls, steering tricycles, and swinging on horizontal

As preschoolers' bodies become more streamlined, their balance improves greatly, enabling children to combine upper- and lower-body skills into more refined actions.

bars and rings. Then upper- and lower-body skills combine into more refined actions. Five- and 6-year-olds simultaneously steer and pedal a tricycle and flexibly move their whole body when throwing, catching, hopping, and jumping. By the end of the preschool years, all skills are performed with greater speed and endurance. Table 1.1 provides a closer look at gross-motor development in early childhood.

Fine-Motor Development

Fine-motor skills, too, take a giant leap forward in the preschool years. As control of the hands and fingers improves, young children put puzzles together, build with small blocks, cut and paste, and string beads. To parents, fine-motor progress is most apparent in two areas: (1) children's care of their own bodies, and (2) the drawings and paintings that fill the walls at home, child care, and preschool.

■ **SELF-HELP SKILLS.** As Table 1.1 shows, young children gradually become self-sufficient at dressing and feeding. But parents must be patient about these abilities: When tired and in a hurry, young children often revert to eating with their fingers. And the 3-year-old who dresses himself may end up with his shirt on inside out, his pants on backward, and his left snow boot on his right foot! Perhaps the most complex self-help skill of early childhood is shoe tying, mastered around age 6. Success requires a longer attention span, memory for an intricate series of hand movements, and the dexterity to perform them. Shoe tying illustrates the close connection between motor and cognitive development, as do two other skills: drawing and writing.

■ **DRAWING.** When given crayon and paper, even toddlers scribble in imitation of others. As preschoolers' ability to mentally represent the world expands, marks on the page take on meaning. A variety of factors combine with fine-motor control to influence changes in children's artful representations (Golomb, 2004). These include the realization that pictures can serve as symbols, improved planning and spatial understanding, and the emphasis that the child's culture places on artistic expression.

Typically, drawing progresses through the following sequence:

1. *Scribbles.* At first, children's gestures rather than the resulting scribbles contain the intended representation. For example, one 18-month-old made her crayon hop and, as it produced a series of dots, explained, "Rabbit goes hop-hop" (Winner, 1986).

2. *First representational forms.* Around age 3, children's scribbles start to become pictures. Often children make a gesture with the crayon, notice that they have drawn a recognizable shape, and then label it (Winner, 1986). Few 3-year-olds spontaneously draw so others can tell what their picture represents. But when adults draw with children and point out the resemblances between drawings and objects, preschoolers' pictures become more comprehensible and detailed (Braswell & Callanan, 2003).

■ **TABLE 1.1** ■ *Changes in Gross- and Fine-Motor Skills During Early Childhood*

AGE	GROSS-MOTOR SKILLS	FINE-MOTOR SKILLS
2–3 years	Walks more rhythmically; hurried walk changes to run Jumps, hops, throws, and catches with rigid upper body Pushes riding toy with feet; little steering	Puts on and removes simple items of clothing Zips and unzips large zippers Uses spoon effectively
3–4 years	Walks up stairs, alternating feet, and downstairs, leading with one foot Jumps and hops, flexing upper body Throws and catches with slight involvement of upper body; still catches by trapping ball against chest Pedals and steers tricycle	Fastens and unfastens large buttons Serves self food without assistance Uses scissors Copies vertical line and circle Draws first picture of person, using tadpole image
4–5 years	Walks downstairs, alternating feet Runs more smoothly Gallops and skips with one foot Throws ball with increased body rotation and transfer of weight on feet; catches ball with hands Rides tricycle rapidly, steers smoothly	Uses fork effectively Cuts with scissors following line Copies triangle, cross, and some letters
5–6 years	Increases running speed Gallops more smoothly; engages in true skipping Displays mature throwing and catching patterns Rides bicycle with training wheels	Uses knife to cut soft food Ties shoes Draws person with six parts Copies some numbers and simple words

Sources: Cratty, 1986; Haywood & Getchell, 2005; Malina & Bouchard, 1991.

A major milestone in drawing occurs when children use lines to represent the boundaries of objects, enabling 3- and 4-year-olds to draw their first picture of a person. Fine-motor and cognitive limitations lead the preschooler to reduce the figure to the simplest form that still looks human: a circular shape with lines attached—the universal "tadpole" image shown on the left in Figure 1.5.

3. *More realistic drawings.* Greater realism in drawings develops gradually, as perception, language (ability to describe visual details), memory, and fine-motor capacities improve

(Toomela, 2002). Five- and 6-year-olds create more complex drawings, like the one on the right in Figure 1.5, containing more conventional human and animal figures, with the head and body differentiated. Older preschoolers' drawings still contain perceptual distortions because they have just begun to represent depth (Cox & Littlejohn, 1995). This free depiction of reality makes their artwork look fanciful and inventive. Accomplished artists often must work hard to achieve what they did effortlessly as 5- and 6-year-olds.

■ **FIGURE 1.5** ■ **Examples of young children's drawings.** The universal tadpolelike shape that children use to draw their first picture of a person is shown on the left. The tadpole soon becomes an anchor for greater details that sprout from the basic shape. By the end of the preschool years, children produce more complex, differentiated pictures like the one on the right, drawn by a 6-year-old child. (*Left:* From H. Gardner, 1980, *Artful Scribbles: The Significance of Children's Drawings,* New York: Basic Books, p. 64. Reprinted by permission of Basic Books, a member of Perseus Books Group. *Right:* From E. Winner, "Where Pelicans Kiss Seals," *Psychology Today, 20*[8], August 1986, p. 35. Reprinted by permission from the collection of Ellen Winner.)

■ **CULTURAL VARIATIONS IN DEVELOPMENT OF DRAW-
ING.**   In cultures with rich artistic traditions, children create
elaborate drawings that reflect the conventions of their culture.
Adults encourage young children in drawing activities by offering suggestions, modeling ways to draw, and commenting on
children's pictures (Boyatzis, 2000). Parents and teachers frequently ask children to label their pictures, emphasizing the
representational function of drawing. Peers, as well, discuss one
another's pictures and copy from one another's work (Braswell,
2006). All of these cultural practices enhance young children's
drawing progress.

But in cultures with little interest in art, even older children
and adolescents produce simple forms. In the Jimi Valley, a
remote region of Papua New Guinea with no indigenous picto-
rial art, many children do not attend school and therefore have
little opportunity to develop drawing skills. When a Western
researcher asked nonschooled Jimi 10- to 15-year-olds to draw
a human figure for the first time, most produced nonrepresentational scribbles and shapes or simple "stick" or "contour" images (see Figure 1.6) (Martlew & Connolly, 1996). These forms,
which resemble those of preschoolers, seem to be a universal
beginning in drawing. Once children realize that lines must
evoke human features, they find solutions to figure drawing
that vary somewhat from culture to culture but, overall, follow
the sequence described earlier.

■ **EARLY PRINTING.**   When preschoolers first try to write,
they scribble, making no distinction between writing and drawing. Around age 4, writing shows some distinctive features of
print, such as separate forms arranged in a line on the page. But
children often include picturelike devices—for example, using
a circular shape to write "sun" (Levin & Bus, 2003). Only gradually, between ages 4 and 6, do children realize that writing
stands for language.

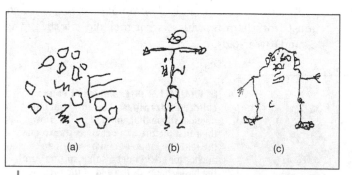

■ **FIGURE 1.6** ■ **Drawings produced by nonschooled 10- to
15-year-olds of the Jimi Valley of Papua New Guinea when
asked to draw a human figure for the first time.**   Many
produced nonrepresentational scribbles and shapes (a), "stick"
figures (b), or "contour" figures (c). Compared with the Western
tadpole form, the Jimi "stick" and "contour" figures emphasize the
hands and feet. Otherwise, the drawings of these older children
resemble those of young preschoolers. (From M. Martlew and
K. J. Connolly, 1996, "Human Figure Drawings by Schooled and
Unschooled Children in Papua New Guinea," *Child Development,
67*, pp. 2750–2751. © The Society for Research in Child Development. Adapted by permission.)

Preschoolers' first attempts to print often involve their
name, generally using a single letter. "How do you make a *D?*"
my older son, David, asked at age 3. When I printed a large uppercase *D*, he tried to copy. "*D* for David," he proclaimed, quite
satisfied with his backward, imperfect creation. By age 5, David
printed his name clearly enough for others to read but, like
many children, continued to reverse some letters until well into
second grade. Until children start to read, they do not find it
useful to distinguish between mirror-image forms, such as *b*
and *d* and *p* and *q* (Bornstein & Arterberry, 1999; Casey, 1986).

Individual Differences in Motor Skills

Wide individual differences exist in the ages at which children
reach motor milestones. A tall, muscular child tends to move
more quickly and to acquire certain skills earlier than a short,
stocky youngster. And as in other domains, parents and teachers
probably provide more encouragement to children with biologically based motor-skill advantages.

Sex differences in motor skills are evident in early childhood.
Boys are ahead of girls in skills that emphasize force and power. By
age 5, they can jump slightly farther, run slightly faster, and throw
a ball about five feet farther. Girls have an edge in fine-motor skills
and in certain gross-motor skills that require a combination of
good balance and foot movement, such as hopping and skipping
(Fischman, Moore, & Steele, 1992; Haywood & Getchell, 2005).
Boys' greater muscle mass and, in the case of throwing, slightly
longer forearms contribute to their skill advantages. And girls'
greater overall physical maturity may be partly responsible for
their better balance and precision of movement.

From an early age, boys and girls are usually encouraged
into different physical activities. For example, fathers are more
likely to play catch with their sons than with their daughters.
Sex differences in motor skills increase with age, but they remain small throughout childhood. This suggests that social
pressures for boys, more than girls, to be active and physically
skilled exaggerate small, genetically based sex differences
(Greendorfer, Lewko, & Rosengren, 1996).

Children master the motor skills of early childhood during
everyday play. Aside from throwing (where direct instruction is
helpful), preschoolers exposed to gymnastics, tumbling, and
other formal lessons do not make faster progress. When children have access to play spaces appropriate for running, climb-
ing, jumping, and throwing and are encouraged to use them,
they respond eagerly to these challenges. Similarly, fine-motor
skills can be supported through daily routines, such as pouring
juice and dressing, and through play that involves puzzles, construction sets, drawing, painting, sculpting, cutting, and pasting.

Finally, the social climate created by adults can enhance or
dampen preschoolers' motor development. When parents and
teachers criticize a child's performance, push specific motor
skills, or promote a competitive attitude, they risk undermining
children's self-confidence and, in turn, their motor progress
(Berk, Mann, & Ogan, 2006). Adults involved in young children's motor activities should focus on fun rather than on winning or perfecting the "correct" technique.

Cognitive Development

One rainy morning, as I observed in our laboratory preschool, Leslie, the children's teacher, joined me at the back of the room for a moment. "Preschoolers' minds are such a blend of logic, fantasy, and faulty reasoning," Leslie reflected. "Every day, I'm startled by the maturity and originality of what they say and do. Yet at other times, their thinking seems limited and inflexible."

Leslie's comments sum up the puzzling contradictions of early childhood cognition. That day, for example, 3-year-old Sammy looked up, startled, after a loud crash of thunder outside. "A magic man turned on the thunder!" he pronounced. Even when Leslie patiently explained that thunder is caused by lightning, not by a person turning it on or off, Sammy persisted: "Then a magic lady did it."

In other respects, Sammy's thinking was surprisingly advanced. At snack time, he accurately counted, "One, two, three, four!" and then got four cartons of milk, one for each child at his table. But when his snack group included more than four children, Sammy's counting broke down. And after Priti dumped out her raisins, scattering them in front of her on the table, Sammy asked, "How come you got lots, and I only got this little bit?" He didn't realize that he had just as many raisins; his were simply all bunched up in a tiny red box.

To understand Sammy's reasoning, we turn first to Piaget's and Vygotsky's theories and evidence highlighting the strengths and limitations of each. Then we consider additional research on young children's cognition, inspired by the information-processing perspective, and look at the dramatic expansion of language in early childhood.

Piaget's Theory: The Preoperational Stage

As children move from the sensorimotor to the **preoperational stage,** which spans the years 2 to 7, the most obvious change is an extraordinary increase in representa-tional, or symbolic, activity. Recall that infants and toddlers have some ability to represent their world. During early childhood, this capacity blossoms.

Mental Representation

Piaget acknowledged that language is our most flexible means of mental representation. By detaching thought from action, language permits far more efficient thinking than was possible earlier. When we think in words, we overcome the limits of our momentary experiences. We can deal with past, present, and future at once and combine concepts in unique ways, as when we imagine a hungry caterpillar eating bananas or monsters flying through the forest at night.

But Piaget did not regard language as the primary ingredient in childhood cognitive change. Instead, he believed that sensorimotor activity leads to internal images of experience, which children then label with words (Piaget, 1936/1952). In support of Piaget's view, that children's first words have a strong sensorimotor basis. In addition, infants and toddlers acquire an impressive range of categories long before they use words to label them. But as we will see, other theorists regard Piaget's account of the link between language and thought as incomplete.

Make-Believe Play

Make-believe play is another excellent example of the development of representation in early childhood. Piaget believed that through pretending, young children practice and strengthen newly acquired representational schemes. Drawing on his ideas, several investigators have traced the development of make-believe during the preschool years.

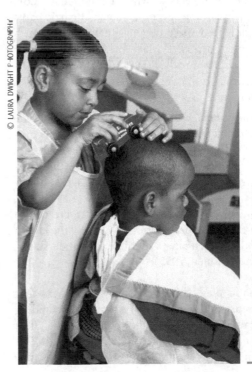

© LAURA DWIGHT PHOTOGRAPHY

Make-believe play increases in sophistication during the preschool years. Children pretend with less realistic toys, so a toy truck can stand for an electric hair clipper. And children increasingly coordinate make-believe roles.

■ **DEVELOPMENT OF MAKE-BELIEVE.**   One day, Sammy's 18-month-old brother, Dwayne, visited the classroom. Dwayne wandered around, picked up a toy telephone receiver, said, "Hi, Mommy," and then dropped it. Next, he found a cup, pretended to drink, and then toddled off again. Meanwhile, Sammy joined Vance and Lynette in the block area for a space shuttle launch.

"That can be our control tower," Sammy suggested, pointing to a corner by a bookshelf. "Countdown!" he announced, speaking into his "walkie-talkie"—a small wooden block. "Five, six, two, four, one, blastoff!" Lynette made a doll push a pretend button, and the rocket was off!

Comparing Dwayne's pretend play with Sammy's, we see three important changes that reflect the preschool child's growing symbolic mastery:

■ *Play detaches from the real-life conditions associated with it.* In early pretending, toddlers use only realistic objects—a toy telephone to talk into, a cup to drink from. Their first pretend acts imitate adults' actions and are not yet flexible. Children younger than age 2, for example, will pretend to drink from a cup but refuse to pretend a cup is a hat (Tomasello, Striano, & Rochat, 1999). They have trouble using an object (cup) that already has an obvious use as a symbol of another object (hat).

After age 2, children pretend with less realistic toys—a block might stand for a telephone receiver. Gradually, they can flexibly imagine objects and events without any support from the real world, as Sammy's imaginary control tower illustrates (O'Reilly, 1995; Striano, Tomasello, & Rochat, 2001).

■ *Play becomes less self-centered.* At first, make-believe is directed toward the self—for example, Dwayne pretends to feed only himself. Soon, children begin to direct pretend actions toward other objects, as when a child feeds a doll. Early in the third year, they become detached participants who make a doll feed itself or (in Lynette's case) push a button to launch a rocket. Make-believe becomes less self-centered as children realize that agents and recipients of pretend actions can be independent of themselves (McCune, 1993).

■ *Play includes more complex combinations of schemes.* Dwayne can pretend to drink from a cup, but he does not yet combine pouring and drinking. Later, children combine schemes with those of peers in **sociodramatic play,** the make-believe with others that is under way around age 2 and increases rapidly during the next few years (Kavanaugh, 2006). Already, Sammy and his classmates can create and coordinate several roles in an elaborate plot. By the end of early childhood, children have a sophisticated understanding of story lines (Göncü, 1993).

In sociodramatic play, children display awareness that make-believe is a representational activity—an understanding that improves steadily over early childhood (Lillard, 2003; Rakoczy, Tomasello, & Striano, 2004; Sobel, 2006). *TAKE A MOMENT...* Listen closely to a group of preschoolers as they assign roles and negotiate make-believe plans: "You *pretend to be* the astronaut, I'll *act like* I'm operating the control tower!" In communicating about pretend, children think about their own and others' fanciful representations—evidence that they have begun to reason about people's mental activities.

■ **BENEFITS OF MAKE-BELIEVE.**   Today, Piaget's view of make-believe as mere practice of representational schemes is regarded as too limited. Play not only reflects but also contributes to children's cognitive and social skills. Compared with social nonpretend activities (such as drawing or putting puzzles together), during sociodramatic play preschoolers' interactions last longer, show more involvement, draw more children into the activity, and are more cooperative (Creasey, Jarvis, & Berk, 1998).

It is not surprising, then, that preschoolers who spend more time at sociodramatic play are seen as more socially competent by their teachers (Connolly & Doyle, 1984). And many studies reveal that make-believe strengthens a wide variety of mental abilities, including sustained attention, memory, logical reasoning, language and literacy skills, imagination, creativity, understanding of emotions, and the ability to reflect on one's own thinking, control one's own behavior, and take another's perspective (Bergen & Mauer, 2000; Berk, Mann, & Ogan, 2006; Elias & Berk, 2002; Hirsh-Pasek et al., 2009; Lindsey & Colwell, 2003; Ruff & Capozzoli, 2003). We will return to the topic of early childhood play in this and the next section.

Symbol–Real-World Relations

To make believe and draw—and to understand other forms of representation, such as photographs, models, and maps—preschoolers must realize that each symbol corresponds to something specific in everyday life. When do children comprehend symbol–real-world relations?

Children who experience a variety of symbols come to understand that one object, such as this play village, can stand for another—a full-sized real village that people live in.

In one study, 2½ - and 3-year-olds watched an adult hide a small toy (Little Snoopy) in a scale model of a room and then were asked to retrieve it. Next, they had to find a larger toy (Big Snoopy) hidden in the room that the model represented. Not until age 3 could most children use the model as a guide to finding Big Snoopy in the real room (DeLoache, 1987). The 2½-year-olds did not realize that the model could be both *a toy room* and *a symbol of another room*. They had trouble with **dual representation**—viewing a symbolic object as both an object in its own right and a symbol. In support of this interpretation, when researchers made the model room less prominent as an object, by placing it behind a window and preventing children from touching it, more 2½-year-olds succeeded at the search task (DeLoache, 2000, 2002).

Recall that in make-believe play, 1½- to 2-year-olds cannot use an object with an obvious use (cup) to stand for another object (hat). Likewise, 2-year-olds do not yet grasp that a drawing—an object in its own right—also represents real-world objects.

How do children grasp the dual representation of symbolic objects? When adults point out similarities between models and real-world spaces, 2½-year-olds perform better on the find-Snoopy task (Peralta de Mendoza & Salsa, 2003). Also, insight into one type of symbol–real world relation helps preschoolers master others. For example, children regard photos and pictures in books as symbols early, around 1½ to 2 years, because a picture's primary purpose is to stand for something; it is not an interesting object in its own right (Preissler & Carey, 2004; Simcock & DeLoache, 2006). And 3-year-olds who can use a model of a room to locate Big Snoopy readily transfer their understanding to a simple map (Marzolf & DeLoache, 1994). In sum, experiences with diverse symbols—photos, picture books, make-believe, and maps—help preschoolers appreciate that one object can stand for another.

Limitations of Preoperational Thought

Aside from gains in representation, Piaget described preschoolers in terms of what they *cannot* understand (Beilin, 1992). As the term *preoperational* suggests, he compared them to older, more competent children who have reached the concrete operational stage. According to Piaget, young children are not capable of *operations*—mental actions that obey logical rules. Rather, their thinking is rigid, limited to one aspect of a situation at a time, and strongly influenced by the way things appear at the moment.

■ **EGOCENTRISM.** For Piaget, the most fundamental deficiency of preoperational thinking is **egocentrism**—failure to distinguish the symbolic viewpoints of others from one's own. He believed that when children first mentally represent the world, they tend to focus on their own viewpoint and simply assume that others perceive, think, and feel the same way they do.

Piaget's most convincing demonstration of egocentrism involves his *three-mountains problem*, described in Figure 1.7. Egocentrism is responsible for preoperational children's **animistic thinking**—the belief that inanimate objects have lifelike qualities, such as thoughts, wishes, feelings, and intentions

■ **FIGURE 1.7** ■ **Piaget's three-mountains problem.** Each mountain is distinguished by its color and by its summit. One has a red cross, another a small house, and the third a snow-capped peak. Children at the preoperational stage respond egocentrically. They cannot select a picture that shows the mountains from the doll's perspective. Instead, they simply choose the photo that reflects their own vantage point.

(Piaget, 1926/1930). Recall Sammy's firm insistence that someone must have turned on the thunder. According to Piaget, because young children egocentrically assign human purposes to physical events, magical thinking is common during the preschool years.

Piaget argued that preschoolers' egocentric bias prevents them from *accommodating,* or reflecting on and revising their faulty reasoning in response to their physical and social worlds. To understand this shortcoming, let's consider some additional tasks that Piaget gave to children.

■ **INABILITY TO CONSERVE.** Piaget's famous conservation tasks reveal a variety of deficiencies of preoperational thinking. **Conservation** refers to the idea that certain physical characteristics of objects remain the same, even when their outward appearance changes. At snack time, Priti and Sammy had identical boxes of raisins, but when Priti spread her raisins out on the table, Sammy was convinced that she had more.

In another conservation task involving liquid, the child is shown two identical tall glasses of water and asked if they contain equal amounts. Once the child agrees, the water in one glass is poured into a short, wide container, changing its appearance but not its amount. Then the child is asked whether or not the amount of water has changed. Preoperational children think the quantity has changed. They explain, "There is less now because the water is way down here" (that is, its level is so low) or, "There is more now because it is all spread out." Figure 1.8 on page 18 illustrates other conservation tasks that you can try with children.

The inability to conserve highlights several related aspects of preoperational children's thinking. First, their understanding is *centered,* or characterized by **centration.** They focus on

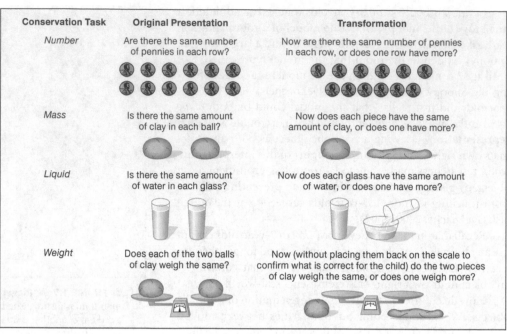

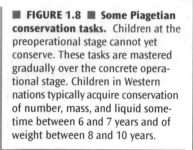

■ FIGURE 1.8 ■ Some Piagetian conservation tasks. Children at the preoperational stage cannot yet conserve. These tasks are mastered gradually over the concrete operational stage. Children in Western nations typically acquire conservation of number, mass, and liquid sometime between 6 and 7 years and of weight between 8 and 10 years.

one aspect of a situation, neglecting other important features. In conservation of liquid, the child *centers* on the height of the water, failing to realize that changes in width compensate for changes in height. Second, children are easily distracted by the *perceptual appearance* of objects. Third, children treat the initial and final states of the water as unrelated events, ignoring the *dynamic transformation* (pouring of water) between them.

The most important illogical feature of preoperational thought is its **irreversibility,** an inability to mentally go through a series of steps in a problem and then reverse direction, returning to the starting point. *Reversibility* is part of every logical operation. After Priti spills her raisins, Sammy cannot reverse by thinking, "I know that Priti doesn't have more raisins than I do. If we put them back in that little box, her raisins and my raisins would look just the same."

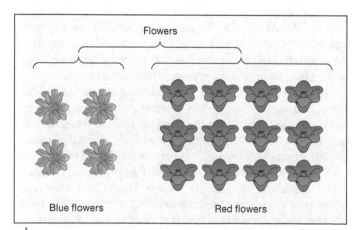

Blue flowers   Red flowers

■ FIGURE 1.9 ■ A Piagetian class inclusion problem. Children are shown 16 flowers, 4 of which are blue and 12 of which are red. Asked, "Are there more red flowers or flowers?" the preoperational child responds, "More red flowers," failing to realize that both red and blue flowers are included in the category "flowers."

■ LACK OF HIERARCHICAL CLASSIFICATION. Preoperational children have difficulty with **hierarchical classification**— the organization of objects into classes and subclasses on the basis of similarities and differences. Piaget's famous *class inclusion problem,* illustrated in Figure 1.9, demonstrates this limitation. Preoperational children center on the overriding feature, red. They do not think reversibly by moving from the whole class (flowers) to the parts (red and blue) and back again.

Follow-Up Research on Preoperational Thought

Over the past three decades, researchers have challenged Piaget's view of preschoolers as cognitively deficient. Because many Piagetian problems contain unfamiliar elements or too many pieces of information for young children to handle at once, preschoolers' responses do not reflect their true abilities. Piaget also missed many naturally occurring instances of effective reasoning by preschoolers.

■ EGOCENTRIC, ANIMISTIC, AND MAGICAL THINKING. Do young children really believe that a person standing elsewhere in a room sees the same thing they see? When researchers adapt the three-mountains problem to include familiar objects and use methods other than picture selection (which is difficult even for 10-year-olds), 4-year-olds show clear awareness of others' vantage points (Borke, 1975; Newcombe & Huttenlocher, 1992). Even 2-year-olds realize that what they see sometimes differs from what another person sees. When asked to help an adult looking for a lost object, 24-month-olds—but not 18-month-olds—handed her a toy resting behind a bucket that was within the child's line of sight but not the adult's (Moll & Tomasello, 2006).

Nonegocentric responses also appear in young children's conversations. For example, preschoolers adapt their speech to fit the needs of their listeners. Four-year-olds use shorter, simpler expressions when talking to 2-year-olds than to agemates or adults (Gelman & Shatz, 1978). And in describing objects, children do not use such words as "big" and "little" in a rigid, egocentric fashion. Rather, they *adjust* their descriptions to allow for context. By age 3, children judge a 2-inch shoe as small when seen by itself (because it is much smaller than most shoes) but as big for a tiny 5-inch-tall doll (Ebeling & Gelman, 1994).

We saw that toddlers have already begun to infer others' intentions. And in his later writings, Piaget (1945/1951) did describe preschoolers' egocentrism as a tendency rather than an inability. As we revisit the topic of perspective taking, we will see that it develops gradually throughout childhood and adolescence.

Piaget also overestimated preschoolers' animistic beliefs. Even young infants have begun to distinguish animate from inanimate, as indicated by their developing categorical distinctions between living and nonliving things. By age 2½, children give psychological explanations ("he likes to"; "she wants to") for people and occasionally for animals, but rarely for objects (Hickling & Wellman, 2001). They do make errors when questioned about vehicles, such as trains and airplanes, which appear to be self-moving and have other lifelike features—for example, headlights that resemble eyes (Gelman & Opfer, 2002). But their responses result from incomplete knowledge, not from a belief that inanimate objects are alive.

The same is true for other fantastic beliefs of the preschool years. Most 3- and 4-year-olds believe in the supernatural powers of fairies, goblins, and other enchanted creatures. They think that magic accounts for events that they cannot explain, as in 3-year-old Sammy's magical explanation of thunder in the opening to this section (Rosengren & Hickling, 2000). Furthermore, older 3-year-olds and 4-year-olds think that violations of physical laws (walking through a wall) and mental laws (turning on the TV just by thinking about it) require magic more than violations of social conventions (taking a bath with shoes on) (Browne & Woolley, 2004). These responses indicate that preschoolers' notions of magic are flexible and appropriate.

Between ages 4 and 8, as children gain familiarity with physical events and principles, their magical beliefs decline. They figure out who is really behind Santa Claus and the Tooth Fairy, and they realize that the antics of magicians are due to trickery (Subbotsky, 2004). Religion and culture also play a role. Jewish children are more likely than their Christian agemates to express disbelief in Santa Claus and the Tooth Fairy. Having learned at home that Santa is unreal, they seem to generalize this attitude to other magical figures (Woolley, 1997). And cultural myths about wishing—for example, the custom of making a wish before blowing out birthday candles—probably underlie the conviction of most 3- to 6-year-olds that by wishing, you can sometimes make your desires come true (Woolley, 2000).

■ **ILLOGICAL THOUGHT.** Many studies show that when preschoolers are given tasks that are simplified and relevant to their everyday lives, they do not display the illogical characteristics that Piaget saw in the preoperational stage. For example, when a conservation-of-number task is scaled down to include only three items instead of six or seven, 3-year-olds perform well (Gelman, 1972). And when preschoolers are asked carefully worded questions about what happens to substances (such as sugar) after they are dissolved in water, they give accurate explanations. Most 3- to 5-year-olds know that the substance is conserved—that it continues to exist, can be tasted, and makes the liquid heavier, even though it is invisible in the water (Au, Sidle, & Rollins, 1993; Rosen & Rozin, 1993).

Preschoolers' ability to reason about transformations is evident on other problems. They can engage in impressive *reasoning by analogy* about physical changes. Presented with the picture-matching problem "Play dough is to cut-up play dough as apple is to . . . ?," even 3-year-olds choose the correct answer (a cut-up apple) from a set of alternatives, several of which (a bitten apple, a cut-up loaf of bread) share physical features with the right choice (Goswami, 1996). These findings indicate that in familiar contexts, preschoolers can overcome appearances and think logically about cause and effect.

Finally, even without detailed biological knowledge, preschoolers understand that the insides of animals are responsible for cause–effect sequences (such as willing oneself to move) that are impossible for nonliving things (Gelman, 2003; Keil & Lockhart, 1999). Preschoolers seem to use illogical reasoning only when grappling with unfamiliar topics, too much information, or contradictory facts that they cannot reconcile (Ruffman, 1999).

■ **CATEGORIZATION.** Although preschoolers have difficulty with Piagetian class inclusion tasks, they organize their everyday knowledge into nested categories at an early age. By the second half of the first year, children have formed a variety of global categories—furniture, animals, vehicles, plants, and kitchen utensils—each of which includes objects varying widely in perceptual features (Mandler, 2004). The objects go together because of their common function or behavior, challenging Piaget's assumption that preschoolers' thinking is wholly governed by appearances. Indeed, 2- to 5-year-olds readily draw inferences about nonobservable characteristics shared by category members (Gopnik & Nazzi, 2003). For example, after being told that a bird has warm blood and that a stegosaurus (dinosaur) has cold blood, preschoolers infer that a pterodactyl (labeled a dinosaur) has cold blood, even though it closely resembles a bird.

During the second and third years, and perhaps earlier, children's global categories differentiate. They form many *basic-level categories*—ones at an intermediate level of generality, such as "chairs," "tables," and "beds." By the third year, children easily move back and forth between basic-level categories and *general categories,* such as "furniture." And they break down basic-level categories into *subcategories,* such as "rocking chairs" and "desk chairs," "bluebirds" and "cardinals" (Mervis, Pani, & Pani, 2003).

© LAURA DWIGHT/PHOTOEDIT

Preschoolers devise many categories based on nonobservable characteristics that members share. This 4-year-old knows that despite wide variations in size and appearance, all dinosaurs share common inner features, such as cold blood.

Preschoolers' rapidly expanding vocabularies and general knowledge support their impressive skill at categorizing (Gelman & Koenig, 2003). As they learn more about their world, they devise ideas about underlying characteristics that category members share—for example, that a combination of physical features, internal organs, and behaviors determines an animal's identity (Gelman & Koenig, 2003). Also, adults label and explain categories to children, and picture-book reading is a rich context for doing so (Gelman & Kalish, 2006). While looking at books, parents make categorical statements ("Penguins live at the South Pole, swim, catch fish, and have thick layers of fat and feathers that help them stay warm") that guide children's construction of categories.

In sum, preschoolers' category systems are not yet very complex. But they already have capacity to classify hierarchically and on the basis of nonobvious properties. And preschoolers use logical, causal reasoning to identify the interrelated features that form the basis of a category and to classify new members.

■ **APPEARANCE VERSUS REALITY.** What happens when preschoolers encounter objects that have two identities—a real one and an apparent one? Can they distinguish appearance from reality? In a series of studies, John Flavell and his colleagues presented children with objects that were disguised in various ways and asked what each "looks like" and what each "is really and truly." Preschoolers had difficulty. For example, when asked whether a candle that looks like a crayon "is really and truly" a

crayon, they often responded, "Yes!" Not until age 6 or 7 did children do well on these tasks (Flavell, Green, & Flavell, 1987).

Younger children's poor performance, however, is not due to a general difficulty in distinguishing appearance from reality, as Piaget suggested. Rather, they have trouble with the *language* of these tasks (Deák, Ray, & Brenneman, 2003). When permitted to solve appearance–reality problems nonverbally, by choosing from an array of objects the one that "really" has a particular identity, most 3-year-olds perform well (Sapp, Lee, & Muir 2000).

Note how the appearance–reality distinction involves an attainment discussed earlier: *dual representation*—the realization that an object can be one thing (a candle) while symbolizing another (a crayon). At first, however, children's understanding is fragile. After putting on a Halloween mask, young preschoolers may be frightened when they see themselves in a mirror. Performing well on verbal appearance–reality tasks signifies a more secure understanding and is related to further progress in representational ability (Bialystok & Senman, 2004).

Evaluation of the Preoperational Stage

Table 1.2 provides an overview of the cognitive attainments of early childhood. **TAKE A MOMENT...** Compare them with Piaget's description of the preoperational child on pages 17–18. The evidence as a whole indicates that Piaget was partly wrong and partly right about young children's cognitive capacities. When given simplified tasks based on familiar experiences, preschoolers show the beginnings of logical thinking, which suggests that they attain logical operations gradually.

Evidence that preschoolers can be trained to perform well on Piagetian problems also supports the idea that operational thought is not absent at one point in time and present at another (Ping & Goldin-Meadow, 2008; Siegler & Svetina, 2006). Over time, children rely on increasingly effective mental (as opposed to perceptual) approaches to solving problems. For example, children who cannot use counting to compare two sets of items do not conserve number (Rouselle, Palmers, & Noël, 2004; Sophian, 1995). Once preschoolers can count, they apply this skill to conservation-of-number tasks involving just a few items. As counting improves, they extend the strategy to problems with more items. By age 6, they understand that number remains the same after a transformation as long as nothing is added or taken away. Consequently, they no longer need to count to verify their answer (Halford & Andrews, 2006).

That logical operations develop gradually poses yet another challenge to Piaget's stage concept, which assumes abrupt change toward logical reasoning around age 6 or 7. Does a preoperational stage really exist? Some no longer think so. According to the information-processing perspective, children work out their understanding of each type of task separately, and their thought processes are basically the same at all ages—just present to a greater or lesser extent.

Other experts think the stage concept is valid but must be modified. For example, some *neo-Piagetian theorists* combine Piaget's stage approach with the information-processing empha-

■ TABLE 1.2 ■ *Some Cognitive Attainments of Early Childhood*

APPROXIMATE AGE	COGNITIVE ATTAINMENTS
2–4 years © ELLEN B. SENISI/THE IMAGE WORKS	Shows a dramatic increase in representational activity, as reflected in the development of language, make-believe play, drawing, understanding of dual representation, and categorization
	Takes the perspective of others in simplified, familiar situations and in everyday, face-to-face communication
	Distinguishes animate beings from inanimate objects; denies that magic can alter everyday experiences
	Grasps conservation, notices transformations, reverses thinking, and understands many cause-and-effect relationships in familiar contexts
	Categorizes objects on the basis of common function and behavior and devises ideas about underlying characteristics that category members share
	Sorts familiar objects into hierarchically organized categories
	Distinguishes appearance from reality
4–7 years © STEVE STARR/CORBIS	Becomes increasingly aware that make-believe (and other thought processes) are representational activities
	Replaces magical beliefs about fairies, goblins, and events that violate expectations with plausible explanations
	Solves verbal appearance–reality problems, signifying a more secure understanding

sis on task-specific change (Case, 1998; Halford & Andrews, 2006). They believe that Piaget's strict stage definition must be transformed into a less tightly knit concept, one in which a related set of competencies develops over an extended time period, depending on brain development and specific experiences. These investigators point to findings indicating that as long as the complexity of tasks and children's exposure to them are carefully controlled, children approach those tasks in similar, stage-consistent ways (Andrews & Halford, 2002; Case & Okamoto, 1996). For example, in drawing pictures, preschoolers depict objects separately, ignoring their spatial arrangement. In understanding stories, they grasp a single story line but have trouble with a main plot plus one or more subplots.

This flexible stage notion recognizes the unique qualities of early childhood thinking. At the same time, it provides a better account of why, as Leslie put it, "Preschoolers' minds are such a blend of logic, fantasy, and faulty reasoning."

Piaget and Education

Three educational principles derived from Piaget's theory continue to have a major impact on both teacher training and classroom practices, especially during early childhood:

■ *Discovery learning.* In a Piagetian classroom, children are encouraged to discover for themselves through spontaneous interaction with the environment. Instead of presenting ready-made knowledge verbally, teachers provide a rich variety of materials designed to promote exploration—art supplies, puzzles, table games, dress-up clothing, building blocks, books, measuring tools, musical instruments, and more.

■ *Sensitivity to children's readiness to learn.* In a Piagetian classroom, teachers introduce activities that build on children's current thinking, challenging their incorrect ways of viewing the world and enabling them to practice newly discovered schemes. But they do not try to hasten development by imposing new skills before children indicate interest or readiness.

■ *Acceptance of individual differences.* Piaget's theory assumes that all children go through the same sequence of development, but at different rates. Therefore, teachers must plan activities for individual children and small groups, not just for the whole class. In addition, teachers evaluate educational progress in relation to the child's previous development, rather than on the basis of normative standards, or average performance of same-age peers.

Like his stages, educational applications of Piaget's theory have met with criticism. Perhaps the greatest challenge has to do with his insistence that young children learn mainly through acting on the environment (Brainerd, 2003). In the next section, we will see that young children also rely on language-based routes to knowledge.

Vygotsky's Sociocultural Theory

Piaget's deemphasis on language as a source of cognitive development brought on yet another challenge, this time from Vygotsky's sociocultural theory, which stresses the social context of cognitive development. During early childhood, rapid growth of language broadens preschoolers' participation in social dialogues with more knowledgeable individuals, who encourage them to master culturally important tasks. Soon children start to communicate with themselves in much the same way they converse with others. This greatly enhances their thinking and ability to control their own behavior. Let's see how this happens.

Private Speech

TAKE A MOMENT... Watch preschoolers as they play and explore the environment, and you will see that they frequently talk out loud to themselves. For example, as Sammy worked a puzzle, he said, "Where's the red piece? Now, a blue one. No, it doesn't fit. Try it here."

Piaget (1923/1926) called these utterances *egocentric speech*, reflecting his belief that young children have difficulty taking the perspectives of others. Their talk, he said, is often "talk for self" in which they express thoughts in whatever form they happen to occur, regardless of whether a listener can understand. Piaget believed that cognitive development and certain social experiences eventually bring an end to egocentric speech. Specifically, through disagreements with peers, children see that others hold viewpoints different from their own. As a result, egocentric speech declines.

Vygotsky (1934/1987) disagreed with Piaget's conclusions. Because language helps children think about their mental activities and behavior and select courses of action, Vygotsky saw it as the foundation for all higher cognitive processes, including controlled attention, deliberate memorization and recall, categorization, planning, problem solving, and self-reflection. In Vygotsky's view, children speak to themselves for self-guidance. As they get older and find tasks easier, their self-directed speech is internalized as silent, *inner speech*—the internal verbal dialogues we carry on while thinking and acting in everyday situations.

Over the past three decades, almost all studies have supported Vygotsky's perspective (Berk & Harris, 2003; Winsler, 2009). As a result, children's self-directed speech is now called **private speech** instead of egocentric speech. Research shows that children use more of it when tasks are appropriately challenging (neither too easy nor too hard), after they make errors, or when they are confused about how to proceed. With age, as Vygotsky predicted, private speech goes underground, changing into whispers and silent lip movements. Furthermore, children who freely use private speech during a challenging activity are more attentive and involved and show better task performance than their less talkative agemates (Al-Namlah, Fernyhough, & Meins, 2006; Berk & Spuhl, 1995; Fernyhough & Fradley, 2005; Winsler, Naglieri, & Manfra, 2006).

© LAURA DWIGHT PHOTOGRAPHY

This 4-year-old talks to himself as he explores a collection of shells, pine cones, and other natural objects. Research supports Vygotsky's theory that children use private speech to guide their own thinking and behavior.

Social Origins of Early Childhood Cognition

Where does private speech come from? Vygotsky believed that children's learning takes place within the *zone of proximal development*—a range of tasks too difficult for the child to do alone but possible with the help of adults and more skilled peers. Consider the joint activity of Sammy and his mother, who helps him put together a difficult puzzle:

Sammy: I can't get this one in. *[Tries to insert a piece in the wrong place.]*

Mother: Which piece might go down here? *[Points to the bottom of the puzzle.]*

Sammy: His shoes. *[Looks for a piece resembling the clown's shoes but tries the wrong one.]*

Mother: Well, what piece looks like this shape? *[Points again to the bottom of the puzzle.]*

Sammy: The brown one. *[Tries it, and it fits; then attempts another piece and looks at his mother.]*

Mother: Try turning it just a little. *[Gestures to show him.]*

Sammy: There! *[Puts in several more pieces while his mother watches.]*

Sammy's mother keeps the puzzle within his zone of proximal development, at a manageable level of difficulty. To do so, she engages in **scaffolding**—adjusting the support offered during a teaching session to fit the child's current level of performance. When the child has little notion of how to proceed, the adult uses direct instruction, breaking the task into manageable units, suggesting strategies, and offering rationales for using them. As the child's competence increases, effective scaffolders gradually and sensitively withdraw support, turning over responsibility to the child. Then children take the language of these dialogues, make it part of their private speech, and use this speech to organize their independent efforts.

What evidence supports Vygotsky's ideas on the social origins of cognitive development? In several studies, children whose parents were effective scaffolders used more private speech, were more successful when attempting difficult tasks on their own, and were advanced in overall cognitive development (Berk & Spuhl, 1995; Conner & Cross, 2003; Mulvaney et al., 2006). Adult cognitive support—teaching in small steps and offering strategies—predicts gains in children's thinking. And adult emotional support—offering encouragement and allowing the child to take over the task—predicts children's effort (Neitzel & Stright, 2003).

Other research shows that although children benefit from working on tasks with same-age peers, their planning and problem solving improve more when their partner is either an "expert" peer (especially capable at the task) or an adult. And peer disagreement (emphasized by Piaget) seems less important in fostering cognitive development than the extent to which children resolve differences of opinion and cooperate (Kobayashi, 1994; Tudge, 1992).

Vygotsky and Education

Both Piagetian and Vygotskian classrooms emphasize active participation and acceptance of individual differences. But a Vygotskian classroom goes beyond independent discovery to promote *assisted discovery*. Teachers guide children's learning, tailoring their interventions to each child's zone of proximal development. Assisted discovery is also aided by *peer collaboration* as children of varying abilities work in groups, teaching and helping one another.

Vygotsky (1933/1978) saw make-believe play as the ideal social context for fostering cognitive development in early childhood. As children create imaginary situations, they learn to follow internal ideas and social rules rather than their immediate impulses. For example, a child pretending to go to sleep follows the rules of bedtime behavior. A child imagining himself as a father and a doll as a child conforms to the rules of parental behavior. According to Vygotsky, make-believe play is a unique, broadly influential zone of proximal development in which children try out a wide variety of challenging activities and acquire many new competencies.

Turn back to page 16 to review findings that make-believe play enhances a diverse array of cognitive and social skills. Pretending is also rich in private speech—a finding that supports its role in helping children bring action under the control of thought (Krafft & Berk, 1998). And preschoolers who spend

© ELLEN B. SENISI PHOTOGRAPHY

In this Vygotsky-inspired classroom, 4- and 5-year-olds benefit from peer collaboration. As they jointly make music, their conductor ensures that each player stays on beat.

▪ CULTURAL INFLUENCES ▪

Children in Village and Tribal Cultures Observe and Participate in Adult Work

In Western societies, the role of equipping children with the skills they need to become competent workers is assigned to school. In early childhood, middle-SES parents' interactions with children dwell on preparing the children for school success through child-focused activities—especially adult–child conversations and play that enhance language, literacy, and other academic knowledge. In village and tribal cultures, children receive little or no schooling, spend their days in contact with adult work, and start to assume mature responsibilities in early childhood (Rogoff et al., 2003). Consequently, parents have little need to rely on conversation and play to teach children.

A study comparing 2- and 3-year-olds' daily lives in four cultures—two U.S. middle-SES suburbs, the Efe hunters and gatherers of the Republic of Congo, and a Mayan agricultural town in Guatemala—documented these differences (Morelli, Rogoff, & Angelillo, 2003). In the U.S. communities, young children had little access to adult work and spent much time conversing and playing with adults. In contrast, the Efe and Mayan children rarely engaged in these child-focused activities. Instead, they spent their days close to—and frequently observing—adult work, which often took place in or near the Efe campsite or the Mayan family home.

An ethnography of a remote Mayan village in Yucatán, Mexico, shows that when young children are legitimate onlookers and participants in a daily life structured around adult work, their competencies differ from those of Western preschoolers (Gaskins, 1999; Gaskins, Haight, & Lancy, 2007). Yucatec Mayan adults are subsistence farmers. Men tend cornfields, aided by sons age 8 and older. Women prepare meals, wash clothes, and care for the livestock and garden, assisted by daughters and by sons too young to work in the fields. Children join in these activities from the second year on. When not participating, they are expected to be self-sufficient. Young children make many nonwork decisions for themselves—how much to sleep and eat, what to wear, and even when to start school. As a result, Yucatec Mayan preschoolers are highly competent at self-care. In contrast, their make-believe play is limited; when it occurs, they usually enact adult work. Otherwise, they watch others—for hours each day.

Yucatec Mayan parents rarely converse or play with preschoolers or scaffold their learning. Rather, when children imitate adult tasks, parents conclude that they are ready for more responsibility. Then they assign chores, selecting tasks the child can do with little help so that adult work is not disturbed. If a child cannot do a task, the adult takes over and the child observes, reengaging when able to contribute.

Expected to be autonomous and helpful, Yucatec Mayan children seldom ask others for something interesting to do. From an early age, they can sit quietly for long periods—through a long religious service or a ride to town. And when an adult directs them to do a chore, they respond eagerly to the type of command that Western children frequently resent. By age 5, Yucatec Mayan children spontaneously take responsibility for tasks beyond those assigned.

A Mayan 3-year-old imitates her mother in balancing a basin of water on her head, while her younger sibling prepares to attempt the skill. Children in Yucatec Mayan culture join in the work of their community from an early age, spending many hours observing adults.

more time engaged in sociodramatic play are better at taking personal responsibility for following classroom rules and at regulating emotion (Berk, Mann, & Ogan, 2006; Lemche et al., 2003). These findings support the role of make-believe in children's increasing self-control.

Evaluation of Vygotsky's Theory

In granting social experience a fundamental role in cognitive development, Vygotsky's theory underscores the vital role of teaching and helps us understand the wide cultural variation in children's cognitive skills. Nevertheless, it has not gone unchallenged. Verbal communication may not be the only means through which children's thinking develops—or even, in some cultures, the most important means. When Western parents scaffold their young children's mastery of challenging tasks, their verbal communication resembles the teaching that takes place in school, where their children will spend years preparing for adult life. In cultures that place less emphasis on schooling and literacy, parents often expect children to take greater responsibility for acquiring new skills through keen observation and participation in community activities (see the Cultural Influences box above).

To account for children's diverse ways of learning through involvement with others, Barbara Rogoff (1998, 2003) suggests the term **guided participation,** a broader concept than scaffolding. It refers to shared endeavors between more expert and less expert participants, without specifying the precise features of communication. Consequently, it allows for variations across situations and cultures.

Finally, Vygotsky's theory says little about how basic motor, perceptual, attention, memory, and problem-solving skills, contribute to socially transmitted higher cognitive processes. For example, his theory does not address how these elementary capacities spark changes in children's social experiences, from which more advanced cognition springs (Miller, 2001; Moll, 1994). Piaget paid far more attention than Vygotsky to the development of basic cognitive processes. It is intriguing to speculate about the broader theory that might exist today if Piaget and Vygotsky—the two twentieth-century giants of cognitive development—had had a chance to meet and weave together their extraordinary accomplishments.

Information Processing

Recall that information processing focuses on *mental strategies* that children use to transform stimuli flowing into their mental systems. During early childhood, advances in representation and in children's ability to guide their own behavior lead to more efficient ways of attending, manipulating information, and solving problems. Preschoolers also become more aware of their own mental life and begin to acquire academically relevant knowledge important for school success.

Attention

As parents and teachers know, preschoolers—compared with school-age children—spend shorter times involved in tasks and are easily distracted. That sustained attention improves in toddlerhood, a trend that continues during the preschool years.

■ **INHIBITION.**   A major reason is a steady gain in children's ability to inhibit impulses and keep their mind on a competing goal. Consider a task in which the child must tap once when the

adult taps twice and tap twice when the adult taps once or must say "night" to a picture of the sun and "day" to a picture of the moon with stars. As Figure 1.10 shows, 3- and 4-year-olds make many errors. But by age 6 to 7, children find such tasks easy (Johnson, Im-Bolter, & Pascual-Leone, 2003; Kirkham, Cruess, & Diamond, 2003; Zelazo et al., 2003). They can resist the "pull" of their attention toward a dominant stimulus—a skill that, as early as age 3 to 5, predicts reading and math achievement from kindergarten through high school (Blair & Razza, 2007; Duncan et al., 2007).

Gains in inhibition are linked to development of the cerebral cortex, especially the frontal lobes (see page 5). But relevant experiences are crucial. In *Tools of the Mind*—a preschool curriculum inspired by Vygotsky's theory—scaffolding of attentional skills is woven into virtually all classroom activities. For example, teachers provide external aids to support attention (a child might hold a drawing of an ear as a reminder to listen during story time); lead games requiring frequent shifts in attention; and encourage make-believe play, which helps children follow rules and use thought to guide behavior (Bodrova & Leong, 2007). When preschoolers from low-income families were randomly assigned to either Tools of the Mind or comparison classrooms, Tools children performed substantially better on end-of-year tasks assessing inhibition and other attentional capacities (Diamond et al., 2007).

■ **PLANNING.**   During early childhood, children also become better at *planning*—thinking out a sequence of acts ahead of time and allocating attention accordingly to reach a goal. As long as tasks are familiar and not too complex, preschoolers can generate and follow a plan. For example, 4-year-olds can search

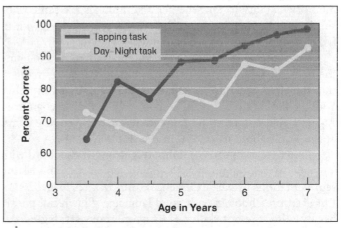

■ **FIGURE 1.10** ■ **Gains between ages 3 and 7 in performance on tasks requiring children to inhibit an impulse and focus on a competing goal.** In the tapping task, children had to tap once when the adult tapped twice and tap twice when the adult tapped once. In the day–night task, children had to say "night" to a picture of the sun and "day" to a picture of the moon with stars. (From A. Diamond, 2004, "Normal Development of Prefrontal Cortex from Birth to Young Adulthood: Cognitive Functions, Anatomy, and Biochemistry," as appeared in D. T. Stuff and R. T. Knight, (Eds.), *Principles of Frontal Lobe Function*, New York: Oxford University Press, p. 474. Reprinted by permission of Adele Diamond.)

for a lost object in a play area systematically if possible locations are few (McColgan & McCormack, 2008). But when asked to compare detailed pictures, preschoolers fail to search thoroughly. And on tasks with several steps, they rarely decide what to do first and what to do next in an orderly fashion (Friedman & Scholnick, 1997; Ruff & Rothbart, 1996).

Children learn much from cultural tools that support planning—directions for playing games, patterns for construction, and recipes for cooking—especially when they collaborate with more expert planners. When 4- to 7-year-olds were observed jointly constructing a toy with their mothers, the mothers provided basic information about the usefulness of plans and how to implement specific steps: "Do you want to look at the picture and see what goes where? What piece do you need first?" After working with their mothers, younger children more often referred to the plan when building on their own (Gauvain, 2004; Gauvain, de la Ossa, & Hurtado-Ortiz, 2001). When parents encourage planning in everyday activities, from loading the dishwasher to packing for a vacation, they help children plan more effectively.

Memory

Unlike infants and toddlers, preschoolers have the language skills to describe what they remember, and they can follow directions on memory tasks. As a result, memory becomes easier to study in early childhood.

■ **RECOGNITION AND RECALL.** *TAKE A MOMENT...* Show a young child a set of 10 pictures or toys. Then mix them up with some unfamiliar items, and ask the child to point to the ones in the original set. You will find that preschoolers' *recognition* memory—ability to tell whether a stimulus is the same as or similar to one they have seen before—is remarkably good. In fact, 4- and 5-year-olds perform nearly perfectly.

Now keep the items out of view, and ask the child to name the ones she saw. This more demanding task requires *recall*— that the child generate a mental image of an absent stimulus. Young children's recall is much poorer than their recognition. At age 2, they can recall no more than one or two of the items, at age 4 only about three or four (Perlmutter, 1984).

Better recall in early childhood is strongly associated with language development, which greatly enhances long-lasting representations of past experiences (Simcock & Hayne, 2003). But even preschoolers with good language skills recall poorly because they are not skilled at using **memory strategies,** deliberate mental activities that improve our chances of remembering. Preschoolers do not yet *rehearse,* or repeat items over and over to remember. Nor do they *organize,* grouping together items that are alike (all the animals together, all the vehicles together) so they can easily retrieve the items by thinking of their similar characteristics—even when they are trained to do so (Gathercole, Adams, & Hitch, 1994).

Why do young children seldom use memory strategies? One reason is that strategies tax their limited working memories. *Digit span* tasks, in which children try to repeat an adult-provided string of numbers, assess the size of working memory, which improves slowly, from an average of two digits at age 2½ to five digits at age 7 (Kail, 2003). With such limits, preschoolers have difficulty holding on to pieces of information and applying a strategy at the same time.

■ **MEMORY FOR EVERYDAY EXPERIENCES.** Think about the difference between your recall of listlike information and your memory for everyday experiences. In remembering lists, you recall isolated bits, reproducing them exactly as you originally learned them. In remembering everyday experiences, you recall complex, meaningful events.

Memory for Familiar Events. Like adults, preschoolers remember familiar, repeated events—what you do when you go to preschool or have dinner—in terms of **scripts,** general descriptions of what occurs and when it occurs in a particular situation. Young children's scripts begin as a structure of main acts. For example, when asked to tell what happens at a restaurant, a 3-year-old might say, "You go in, get the food, eat, and then pay." Although first scripts contain only a few acts, they are almost always recalled in correct sequence (Bauer, 2002a, 2006). With age, scripts become more elaborate, as in this 5-year-old's account of going to a restaurant: "You go in. You can sit in a booth or at a table. Then you tell the waitress what you want. You eat. If you want dessert, you can have some. Then you pay and go home." (Hudson, Fivush, & Kuebli, 1992).

Scripts help children (and adults) organize and interpret everyday experiences. Once formed, they can be used to predict what will happen in the future. Children rely on scripts in make-believe play and when listening to and telling stories. Scripts also support children's earliest efforts at planning by helping them represent sequences of actions that lead to desired goals (Hudson, Sosa, & Shapiro, 1997).

Memory for One-Time Events. We considered a second type of everyday memory—*autobiographical memory,* or representations of personally meaningful, one-time events. As preschoolers' cognitive and conversational skills improve, their descriptions of special events become better organized in time, more detailed, and related to the larger context of their lives (Fivush, 2001).

Adults use two styles to elicit children's autobiographical narratives. In the *elaborative style,* they follow the child's lead, ask varied questions, add information to the child's statements, and volunteer their own recollections and evaluations of events. For example, after a trip to the zoo, the parent might say, "What was the first thing we did?" "Why weren't the parrots in their cages?" "I thought the lion was scary. What did you think?" In contrast, adults who use the *repetitive style* provide little information and keep repeating the same questions, regardless of the child's interest: "Do you remember the zoo? What did we do at the zoo?" Preschoolers who experience the elaborative style recall more information about past events, and they also produce more organized and detailed personal stories when followed up one to two years later (Cleveland & Reese, 2005; Farrant & Reese, 2000).

As she converses with her father about past experiences, this young child in Shanghai builds an autobiographical memory. Perhaps because Asian parents tend to discourage children from talking about themselves, Asian adults' autobiographical memories focus less on their own roles than on the roles of others.

As children talk with adults about the past, they not only improve their autobiographical memory but also create a shared history that strengthens close relationships and self-understanding. Parents and preschoolers with secure attachment bonds engage in more elaborate reminiscing (Bost et al., 2006; Fivush & Reese, 2002). And children of elaborative-style parents describe themselves in clearer, more consistent ways (Bird & Reese, 2006). When, in past-event conversations, a child discovers that she finds swimming, getting together with friends, and going to the zoo fun, she can begin to connect these specific experiences into a general understanding of "what I enjoy," yielding a clearer image of herself (Farrant & Reese, 2000).

Girls produce more organized and detailed narratives than boys. And Western children include more comments about their own thoughts, emotions, and preferences than do Asian children. These differences fit with variations in parent–child conversations. Parents reminisce in more detail with daughters (Bruce, Dolan, & Phillips-Grant, 2000). And collectivist cultural values lead many Asian parents to discourage children from talking about themselves. Chinese parents, for example, engage in less detailed and evaluative past-event dialogues with their preschoolers (Fivush & Wang, 2005; Wang, 2006a). Consistent with these early experiences, women report an earlier age of first memory and more vivid early memories than men. And Western adults' autobiographical memories include earlier, more detailed events that focus more on their own roles than do the memories of Asians, who tend to highlight the roles of others (Wang, 2006b).

The Young Child's Theory of Mind

As representation of the world, memory, and problem solving improve, children start to reflect on their own thought processes. They begin to construct a *theory of mind,* or coherent set of ideas about mental activities. This understanding is also called **metacognition,** or "thinking about thought" (the prefix *meta-* means "beyond" or "higher"). As adults, we have a complex appreciation of our inner mental worlds, which we use to interpret our own and others' behavior and to improve our performance on various tasks. How early are children aware of their mental lives, and how complete and accurate is their knowledge?

■ **AWARENESS OF MENTAL LIFE.**   At the end of the first year, babies view people as intentional beings who can share and influence one another's mental states, a milestone that opens the door to new forms of communication—joint attention, social referencing, preverbal gestures, and spoken language. These interactive skills, in turn, enhance toddlers' mental understandings (Tomasello & Rakoczy, 2003). As they approach age 2, children display a clearer grasp of others' emotions and desires, evident in their realization that people often differ from one another and from themselves in likes, dislikes, wants, needs, and wishes ("Mommy like broccoli. Daddy like carrots. I no like carrots.").

As 2-year-olds' vocabularies expand, their first verbs include such words as *think, remember,* and *pretend* (Wellman, 2002). By age 3, children realize that thinking takes place inside their heads and that a person can think about something without seeing, touching, or talking about it (Flavell, Green, & Flavell, 1995). But 2- to 3-year-olds have only a beginning grasp of the distinction between mental life and behavior. They think that people always behave in ways consistent with their desires and do not understand that less obvious, more interpretive mental states, such as beliefs, also affect behavior.

Between ages 3 and 4, children increasingly refer to their own and others' thoughts and beliefs (Wellman, 2002). And from age 4 on, they realize that both *beliefs* and *desires* determine behavior. Dramatic evidence for this new understanding comes from games that test whether preschoolers realize that *false beliefs*—ones that do not represent reality accurately—can guide people's actions.

TAKE A MOMENT... For example, show a child two small closed boxes—a familiar Band-Aid box and a plain, unmarked box (see Figure 1.11 on page 28). Then say, "Pick the box you think has the Band-Aids in it." Children usually pick the marked container. Next, open the boxes and show the child that, contrary to her own belief, the marked one is empty and the unmarked one contains the Band-Aids. Finally, introduce the child to a hand puppet and explain, "Here's Pam. She has a cut, see? Where do you think she'll look for Band-Aids? Why would she look in there? Before you looked inside, did you think that the plain box contained Band-Aids? Why?" (Bartsch & Wellman, 1995). Only a handful of 3-year-olds can explain Pam's—and their own—false beliefs, but many 4-year-olds can.

Among children of diverse cultural and SES backgrounds, false-belief understanding strengthens after age 3½, becoming

■ **FIGURE 1.11** ■ **Example of a false-belief task.** (a) An adult shows a child the contents of a Band-Aid box and of an unmarked box. The Band-Aids are in the unmarked container. (b) The adult introduces the child to a hand puppet named Pam and asks the child to predict where Pam would look for the Band-Aids and to explain Pam's behavior. The task reveals whether children understand that without having seen that the Band-Aids are in the unmarked container, Pam will hold a false belief.

more secure between ages 4 and 6 (Amsterlaw & Wellman, 2006; Callaghan et al., 2005; Flynn, 2006). During that time, it becomes a powerful tool for understanding one-self and others and a good predictor of social skills (Harwood & Farrar, 2006; Watson et al., 1999). It is also associated with early reading ability, probably because it helps children comprehend story narratives (Astington & Pelletier, 2005).

■ **FACTORS CONTRIBUTING TO PRESCHOOLERS' THEORY OF MIND.** How do children develop a theory of mind at such a young age? Language, cognitive abilities, make-believe play, and social experiences all contribute.

Understanding the mind requires the ability to reflect on thoughts, which language makes possible. Many studies indicate that language ability strongly predicts preschoolers' grasp of false belief (Milligan, Astington, & Dack, 2007). Children who spontaneously use, or who are trained to use, complex sentences with mental-state words are especially likely to pass false-belief tasks (de Villiers & de Villiers, 2000; Hale & Tager-Flusberg, 2003). Among the Quechua of the Peruvian highlands, whose language lacks mental-state terms, children have difficulty with false-belief tasks for years after children in industrialized nations have mastered them (Vinden, 1996). Chinese languages, in contrast, have verb markers that can label the word *believe* as decidedly false. When adults use those markers within false-belief tasks, Chinese preschoolers perform better (Tardif, Wellman, & Cheung, 2004).

The ability to inhibit inappropriate responses, think flexibly, and plan fosters mastery of false belief (Hughes, 1998; Sabbagh et al., 2006). Gains in inhibition are strongly related to mastery of false belief, perhaps because to do well on false-belief tasks, children must suppress an irrelevant response—the tendency to assume that others share their own knowledge and beliefs (Birch & Bloom, 2003; Carlson, Moses, & Claxton, 2004).

Social experience also promotes understanding of the mind. In longitudinal research, mothers of securely attached babies were more likely to comment appropriately on their infants' mental states: "Do you *remember* Grandma?" "You really *like* that swing!" These mothers continued to describe their children, when they reached preschool age, in terms of mental characteristics: "She's got a mind of her own!" This maternal "mind-mindedness" was positively associated with later performance on false-belief and other theory-of-mind tasks (Meins et al., 1998, 2003; Ruffman et al., 2006). Secure attachment is also related to more elaborative parent–child narratives, including discussions of mental states—conversations that expose preschoolers to concepts and language that help them think about their own and others' mental lives (Ontai & Thompson, 2008; Taumoepeau & Ruffman, 2006).

Also, preschoolers with siblings who are children (but not infants)—especially older siblings or two or more siblings—tend to be more aware of false belief because they are exposed to more family talk about others' perspectives (Jenkins et al., 2003; McAlister & Peterson, 2006, 2007). Similarly, preschool friends who often engage in mental-state talk—as children do during make-believe play—are ahead in false-belief understanding (de Rosnay & Hughes, 2006). Interacting with more mature members of society contributes, too. In a study of Greek preschoolers, daily contact with many adults and older children predicted mastery of false belief (Lewis et al., 1996). All these encounters offer extra opportunities to observe different viewpoints and talk about inner states.

Core knowledge theorists believe that to profit from the social experiences just described, children must be biologically prepared to develop a theory of mind. They claim that children with *autism,* for whom mastery of false belief is either greatly delayed or absent, are deficient in the brain mechanism that enables humans to detect mental states. See the Biology and Environment box on the following page to find out more about the biological basis of reasoning about the mind.

■ **LIMITATIONS OF PRESCHOOLERS' UNDERSTANDING OF MENTAL LIFE.** Though surprisingly advanced, preschoolers' awareness of mental activities is far from complete. For example, 3- and 4-year-olds are unaware that people continue to think while they wait, look at pictures, listen to stories, or read books—when there are no obvious cues that they are thinking (Flavell, Green, & Flavell, 1993, 1995, 2000). And children younger than age 6 pay little attention to the *process* of thinking. When asked about subtle distinctions between mental states, such as *know* and *forget,* they express confusion (Lyon & Flavell, 1994). And they believe that all events must be directly observed to be known. They do not understand that *mental inferences* can be a source of knowledge (Miller, Hardin, & Montgomery, 2003).

These findings suggest that preschoolers view the mind as a passive container of information. Consequently, they greatly

■ BIOLOGY AND ENVIRONMENT ■

"Mindblindness" and Autism

Michael stood at the water table in Leslie's classroom, repeatedly filling a plastic cup and dumping out its contents—dip–splash, dip–splash—until Leslie came over and redirected his actions. Without looking at Leslie's face, Michael moved to a new repetitive pursuit: pouring water from one cup into another and back again. As other children entered the play space and conversed, Michael hardly noticed.

Michael has *autism* (a term that means "absorbed in the self"), the most severe behavior disorder of childhood. Like other children with autism, by age 3 he displayed deficits in three core areas of functioning. First, he had only limited ability to engage in nonverbal behaviors required for successful social interaction, such as eye gaze, facial expressions, gestures, and give-and-take. Second, his language was delayed and stereotyped. He used words to echo what others said and to get things he wanted, not to exchange ideas. Third, he engaged in much less make-believe play than other children (Frith, 2003; Walenski, Tager-Flusberg, & Ullman, 2006). And Michael showed another typical feature of autism: His interests were narrow and overly intense. For example, one day he sat for more than an hour spinning a toy Ferris wheel.

Researchers agree that autism stems from abnormal brain functioning, usually due to genetic or prenatal environmental causes. From the first year on, children with the disorder have larger-than-average brains, perhaps due to massive overgrowth of synapses and lack of synaptic pruning, which accompanies normal development of cognitive and language skills (Courchesne, Carper, & Akshoomoff, 2003). Furthermore, fMRI studies reveal that autism is associated with reduced activity in areas of the cerebral cortex known to mediate emotional and social responsiveness and thinking about mental activities, including mirror neurons (Mundy, 2003; Théoret et al., 2005).

Growing evidence reveals that children with autism have a deficient theory of mind. Long after they reach the intellectual level of an average 4-year-old, they have great difficulty with false-belief tasks. Most find it hard to attribute mental states to themselves or others (Steele, Joseph, & Tager-Flusberg, 2003). They rarely use mental-state words, such as *believe, think, know, feel,* and *pretend*.

As early as the second year, children with autism show deficits in capacities believed to contribute to an understanding of mental life. Compared with other children, they less often establish joint attention, engage in social referencing, or imitate an adult's novel behaviors (Mundy & Stella, 2000; Vivanti et al., 2008). Furthermore, they are relatively insensitive to eye gaze as a cue to what a speaker is talking about. Instead, they often assume that another person's language refers to what they themselves are looking at— a possible reason for their frequent nonsensical expressions (Baron-Cohen, Baldwin, & Crowson, 1997).

Do these findings indicate that autism is due to impairment of an innate, core brain function, which leaves the child "mindblind" and therefore deficient in human sociability? Some researchers think so (Baron-Cohen & Belmonte, 2005; Scholl & Leslie, 2000). But others point out that individuals with mental retardation but not autism also do poorly on tasks assessing mental understanding (Yirmiya et al., 1998). This suggests that some kind of general intellectual impairment may be involved.

One conjecture is that children with autism are impaired in *executive processing* (refer to the *central executive* in the information-processing model). This leaves them deficient in skills involved in flexible, goal-oriented thinking, including shifting attention to relevant aspects of a situation, inhibiting irrelevant responses, applying strategies to hold

This child, who has autism, is barely aware of his teacher and classmates. Researchers disagree on whether the "mindblindness" accompanying autism results from a specific deficit in social understanding or a general impairment in executive processing.

information in working memory, and generating plans (Geurts et al., 2004; Joseph & Tager-Flusberg, 2004). Another possibility is that children with autism display a peculiar style of information processing, preferring to process the parts of stimuli over patterns and coherent wholes (Frith & Happé, 1994). Deficits in thinking flexibly and in holistic processing of stimuli would each interfere with understanding the social world, since social interaction requires quick integration of information from various sources and evaluation of alternative possibilities.

It is not clear which of these hypotheses is correct. Some research suggests that impairments in social awareness, flexible thinking, processing coherent wholes, and verbal ability contribute independently to autism (Morgan, Maybery, & Durkin, 2003; Pellicano et al., 2006). Perhaps several biologically based deficits underlie the tragic social isolation of children like Michael.

underestimate the amount of mental activity that people engage in and are poor at inferring what people know or are thinking about. In contrast, older children view the mind as an active, constructive agent—a change we will consider further.

Early Childhood Literacy

One week, Leslie's students created a make-believe grocery store. They brought empty food boxes from home, placed them on shelves in the classroom, labeled items with prices, and made paper money for use at the cash register. A sign at the entrance announced the daily specials: "APLS BNS 5¢" ("apples bananas 5¢").

As such play reveals, preschoolers understand a great deal about written language long before they learn to read or write in conventional ways. This is not surprising: Children in industrialized nations live in a world filled with written symbols. Each day, they observe and participate in activities involving storybooks, calendars, lists, and signs and, while doing so, try to figure out how written symbols convey meaning. Children's active efforts to construct literacy knowledge through informal experiences are called **emergent literacy.**

Young preschoolers search for units of written language as they "read" memorized versions of stories and recognize familiar signs, such as "PIZZA." But they do not yet understand the symbolic function of the elements of print (Bialystok & Martin, 2003). Many preschoolers think that a single letter stands for a whole word or that each letter in a person's signature represents a separate name. Children revise these ideas as their cognitive capacities improve, as they encounter writing in many contexts, and as adults help them with written communication. Gradually, they notice more features of written language and depict writing that varies in function, as in the "story" and "grocery list" in Figure 1.12.

Eventually, children figure out that letters are parts of words and are linked to sounds in systematic ways, as seen in the invented spellings that are typical between ages 5 and 7. At first, children rely on sounds in the names of letters, as in "ADE LAFWTS KRMD NTU A LAVATR" ("eighty elephants crammed into a[n] elevator"). Over time, they grasp sound–letter correspondences and learn that some letters have more than one common sound (McGee & Richgels, 2008).

Literacy development builds on a broad foundation of spoken language and knowledge about the world. Over time, children's language and literacy progress facilitate one an-

Preschoolers acquire literacy knowledge informally through participating in everyday activities involving written symbols. Here a young chef "jots down" a phone order for a take-out meal.

other. **Phonological awareness**—the ability to reflect on and manipulate the sound structure of spoken language, as indicated by sensitivity to changes in sounds within words, to rhyming, and to incorrect pronunciation—is a strong predictor of emergent literacy knowledge (Dickinson et al., 2003; Paris & Paris, 2006). When combined with sound–letter knowledge, it enables children to isolate speech segments and link them with their written symbols. Vocabulary and grammatical skills are also influential.

The more informal literacy-related experiences young children have, the better their language and emergent literacy development and their later reading skills (Dickinson & McCabe, 2001; Speece et al., 2004). Pointing out letter–sound correspondences and playing language–sound games enhance children's awareness of the sound structure of language and how it is represented in print (Foy & Mann, 2003). *Interactive* reading, in which adults discuss storybook content with preschoolers, promotes many aspects of language and literacy development. And adult-supported writing activities that focus on narrative, such as preparing a letter or a story, also have wide-ranging benefits (Purcell-Gates, 1996; Wasik & Bond, 2001).

Preschoolers from low-SES families have fewer home and preschool language and literacy learning opportunities—a major reason that they are behind in reading achievement throughout the school years (Foster et al., 2005; Foster & Miller, 2007). In a program that "flooded" child-care centers with children's books and provided training to caregivers on how to get 3- and 4-year-olds to spend time with books, children showed much greater gains in emergent literacy than a no-intervention control group (Neuman, 1999). Providing low-SES parents with children's books, along with guidance in how to stimulate literacy learning in preschoolers, greatly enhances literacy activities in the home (High et al., 2000).

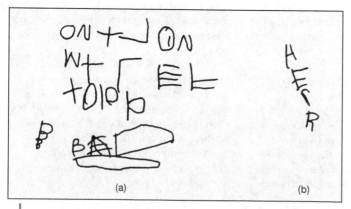

(a)   (b)

■ **FIGURE 1.12** ■ **A story (a) and a grocery list (b) written by a 4-year-old child.** This child's writing has many features of real print. It also reveals an awareness of different kinds of written expression. (From L. M. McGee & D. J. Richgels, *Literacy's Beginnings: Supporting Young Readers and Writers, 4/e.* Published by Allyn and Bacon, Boston, MA. Copyright © 2004 by Pearson Education. Reprinted by permission of the publisher.)

Young Children's Mathematical Reasoning

Mathematical reasoning, like literacy, builds on informally acquired knowledge. Between 14 and 16 months, toddlers display a beginning grasp of **ordinality**, or order relationships between quantities—for example, that 3 is more than 2, and 2 is more than 1. Soon they attach verbal labels (*lots, little, big, small*) to amounts and sizes. Sometime in the third year, they begin to count. By the time children turn 3, most can count rows of about five objects, although they do not yet know exactly what the words mean. For example, when asked for *one*, they give one item, but when asked for *two, three, four*, or *five*, they usually give a larger, but incorrect, amount. Nevertheless, 2½- to 3½-year-olds realize that a number word refers to a unique quantity—that when a number label changes (for example, from *five* to *six*), the number of items should also change (Sarnecka & Gelman, 2004).

By age 3½ to 4, most children have mastered the meaning of numbers up to ten, count correctly, and grasp the vital principle of **cardinality**—that the last number in a counting sequence indicates the quantity of items in a set (Geary, 2006a). Mastery of cardinality increases the efficiency of children's counting.

Around age 4, children use counting to solve arithmetic problems. At first, their strategies are tied to the order of numbers as presented; to add 2 + 4, they count on from 2 (Bryant & Nunes, 2002). But soon they experiment with other strategies and eventually arrive at the most efficient, accurate approach—in this example, beginning with the higher digit. Around this time, children realize that subtraction cancels out addition. Knowing, for example, that 4 + 3 = 7, they can infer without counting that 7 − 3 = 4 (Rasmussen, Ho, & Bisanz, 2003). Grasping basic arithmetic rules facilitates rapid computation, and with enough practice, children recall answers automatically.

When adults provide many occasions for counting, comparing quantities, and talking about number concepts, children acquire these understandings sooner (Ginsburg, Lee, & Boyd, 2008; Klibanoff et al., 2006). In an early childhood math curriculum, called *Building Blocks*, materials that promote math concepts and skills through three types of media—computers, manipulatives, and print—enable teachers to weave math into many preschool daily activities, from building blocks to art and stories. Compared with agemates randomly assigned to other preschool programs, low-SES preschoolers experiencing Building Blocks showed substantially greater year-end gains in math concepts and skills, including counting, sequencing, arithmetic computation, and geometric shapes (Clements & Sarama, 2008). Solid, secure early childhood math knowledge is essential for the wide variety of mathematical skills children will be taught in school.

© SALLY AND RICHARD GREENHILL/ALAMY

Preschoolers construct basic arithmetic understandings sooner when they have many opportunities to count, compare quantities, and talk about number concepts.

ASK YOURSELF

》 **REVIEW**
Describe a typical 4-year-old's understanding of mental activities, noting both strengths and limitations.

》 **APPLY**
Lena, mother of 4-year-old Gregor, wonders why his preschool teacher provides extensive playtime in learning centers instead of formal lessons in literacy and math skills. Explain to Lena why adult-supported play is the best way for preschoolers to develop academically.

》 **CONNECT**
Cite evidence on the development of preschoolers' memory, theory of mind, and literacy and mathematical understanding that is consistent with Vygotsky's sociocultural theory.

》 **REFLECT**
Describe informal experiences important for literacy and math development that you experienced while growing up. How do you think those experiences contributed to your academic progress in school?

Individual Differences in Mental Development

Five-year-old Hal sat in a testing room while Sarah gave him an intelligence test. Some of Sarah's questions were *verbal*. For example, she showed him a picture of a shovel and said, "Tell me what this is"—an item measuring vocabulary. She tested his memory by asking him to repeat sentences and lists of numbers back to her. To assess Hal's spatial reasoning, Sarah

Applying What We Know

Features of a High-Quality Home Life for Preschoolers: The HOME Early Childhood Subscales

Subscale	Sample Item
Cognitive stimulation through toys, games, and reading material	Home includes toys that teach colors, sizes, and shapes.
Language stimulation	Parent teaches child about animals through books, games, and puzzles.
Organization of the physical environment	All visible rooms are reasonably clean and minimally cluttered.
Emotional support	Parent spontaneously praises child's qualities or behavior twice during observer's visit. Parent caresses, kisses, or hugs child at least once during observer's visit.
Stimulation of academic behavior	Child is encouraged to learn colors.
Modeling and encouragement of social maturity	Parent introduces interviewer to child.
Opportunities for variety in daily stimulation	Family member takes child on one outing at least every other week (picnic, shopping).
Avoidance of physical punishment	Parent neither slaps nor spanks child during observer's visit.

Sources: Bradley, 1994; Bradley et al., 2001.

used *nonverbal* tasks: Hal copied designs with special blocks, figured out the pattern in a series of shapes, and indicated what a piece of paper folded and cut would look like when unfolded (Roid, 2003; Wechsler, 2002).

Sarah knew that Hal came from an economically disadvantaged family. When low-SES and certain ethnic minority preschoolers are bombarded with questions by an unfamiliar adult, they sometimes react with anxiety. Also, such children may not define the testing situation in achievement terms. Instead, they may look for attention and approval from the adult and may settle for lower performance than their abilities allow. Sarah spent time playing with Hal before she began testing and encouraged him while testing was in progress. Under these conditions, low-SES preschoolers improve in performance (Bracken, 2000).

The questions Sarah asked Hal tap knowledge and skills that not all children have equal opportunity to learn. In Section 3, we will take up the hotly debated issue of *cultural bias* in mental testing. For now, keep in mind that intelligence tests do not sample all human abilities, and performance is affected by cultural and situational factors (Sternberg, 2005). Nevertheless, test scores remain important: By age 6 to 7, they are good predictors of later IQ and academic achievement, which are related to vocational success in industrialized societies. Let's see how the environments in which preschoolers spend their days—home, preschool, and child care—affect mental test performance.

Home Environment and Mental Development

A special version of the *Home Observation for Measurement of the Environment (HOME)*, assesses aspects of 3- to 6-year-olds' home lives that support mental development (see Applying

What We Know above). Preschoolers who develop well intellectually have homes rich in educational toys and books. Their parents are warm and affectionate, stimulate language and academic knowledge, and arrange interesting outings. They also make reasonable demands for socially mature behavior—for example, that the child perform simple chores and behave courteously toward others. And these parents resolve conflicts with reason instead of physical force and punishment (Bradley & Caldwell, 1982; Espy, Molfese, & DiLalla, 2001; Roberts, Burchinal, & Durham, 1999).

These characteristics are less often seen in poverty-stricken families. When low-SES parents manage, despite daily pressures, to obtain high HOME scores, their preschoolers do substantially better on tests of intelligence and emergent literacy skills (Foster et al., 2005; Klebanov et al., 1998). And in a study of low-SES African-American 3- and 4-year-olds, HOME cognitive stimulation and emotional support subscales predicted reading achievement four years later (Zaslow et al., 2006). These findings highlight the vital role of home environmental quality in children's mental development.

Preschool, Kindergarten, and Child Care

Children between ages 2 and 6 spend even more time away from their homes and parents than infants and toddlers do. Largely because of the rise in maternal employment, over the past several decades the number of young children enrolled in preschool or child care has steadily increased to more than 60 percent in the United States (U.S. Census Bureau, 2009b).

A *preschool* is a program with planned educational experiences aimed at enhancing the development of 2- to 5-year-olds. In contrast, *child care* refers to a variety of arrangements for supervising children. With age, children tend to shift from home-based to center programs. Many children, however, experience several types of arrangements at once (Federal Interagency Forum on Child and Family Statistics, 2008).

The line between preschool and child care is fuzzy. Responding to the needs of employed parents, many U.S. preschools, as well as public school kindergartens, have increased their hours from half to full days (U.S. Department of Education, 2009). At the same time, good child care means more than simply keeping children safe and adequately fed. It should provide the same high-quality educational experiences that an effective preschool does.

■ **TYPES OF PRESCHOOL AND KINDERGARTEN.** Preschool and kindergarten programs range along a continuum, from child-centered to teacher-directed. In **child-centered programs,** teachers provide a variety of activities from which children select, and much learning takes place through play. In contrast, in **academic programs,** teachers structure children's learning, teaching letters, numbers, colors, shapes, and other academic skills through formal lessons, often using repetition and drill.

Despite evidence that formal academic training in early childhood undermines motivation and emotional well-being, preschool and kindergarten teachers have felt increased pressure to take this approach. Preschoolers and kindergartners who spend much time passively sitting and completing worksheets display more stress behaviors (such as wiggling and rocking), have less confidence in their abilities, prefer less challenging tasks, and are less advanced in motor, academic, language, and social skills at the end of the school year (Marcon, 1999a; Stipek et al., 1995). Follow-ups reveal lasting effects through elementary school in poorer study habits and achievement (Burts et al., 1992; Hart et al., 1998, 2003). These outcomes are strongest for low-SES children.

A special type of child-centered approach is Montessori education, devised a century ago by Italian physician and child development researcher Maria Montessori, who originally applied her method to poverty-stricken children. Features of Montessori schooling include materials designed to promote exploration and discovery, child-chosen activities, and equal emphasis on academic and social development (Lillard, 2007). In an evaluation of public preschools serving mostly urban minority children in Milwaukee, researchers compared students randomly assigned to either Montessori or other classrooms (Lillard & Else-Quest, 2006). Five-year-olds who had completed two years of Montessori education outperformed controls in literacy and math skills, false-belief understanding, concern with fairness in solving conflicts with peers, and cooperative play with classmates.

■ **EARLY INTERVENTION FOR AT-RISK PRESCHOOLERS.** In the 1960s, as part of the "War on Poverty" in the United States, many intervention programs for low-SES preschoolers were initiated in an effort to address learning problems before formal schooling begins. The most extensive of these federal programs, **Project Head Start,** began in 1965. A typical Head Start center provides children with a year or two of preschool,

along with nutritional and health services. Parent involvement is central to the Head Start philosophy. Parents serve on policy councils, contribute to program planning, work directly with children in classrooms, attend special programs on parenting and child development, and receive services directed at their own emotional, social, and vocational needs. Currently, more than 18,000 U.S. Head Start centers serve about 908,000 children (Head Start Bureau, 2008).

More than two decades of research have established the long-term benefits of preschool intervention. The most extensive of these studies combined data from seven interventions implemented by universities or research foundations. Results showed that poverty-stricken children who attended programs scored higher in IQ and achievement than controls during the first two to three years of elementary school. After that, differences declined (Lazar & Darlington, 1982). But on real-life measures of school adjustment, children and adolescents who had received intervention remained ahead. They were less likely to be placed in special education or retained in grade, and a greater number graduated from high school.

A separate report on one program—the High/Scope Perry Preschool Project—revealed benefits lasting well into adulthood. Two years' exposure to cognitively enriching preschool was associated with increased employment and reduced pregnancy and delinquency rates in adolescence. At age 27, those who had attended preschool were more likely than no-preschool controls to have graduated from high school and college, have higher earnings, be married, and own their own home—and less likely to have been involved with the criminal justice system (see Figure 1.13 on page 34) (Weikart, 1998). In the most recent follow-up, at age 40, the intervention group

Project Head Start provides preschoolers from poverty-stricken families with preschool education and nutritional and health services. High-quality, early educational intervention has benefits lasting into adulthood.

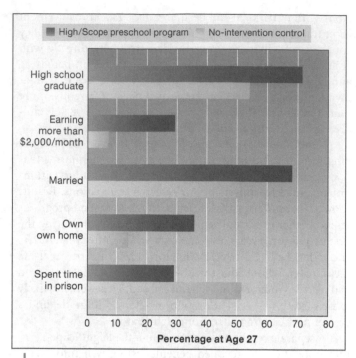

■ **FIGURE 1.13** ■ **Some outcomes of the High/Scope Perry Preschool Project on follow-up at age 27.** Although two years of a cognitively enriching preschool program did not eradicate the effects of growing up in poverty, children who received intervention were advantaged over no-intervention controls on all measures of life success when they reached adulthood. (Adapted from Schweinhart et al., 2005.)

sustained its advantage on all measures of life success, including education, income, family life, and law-abiding behavior (Schweinhart et al., 2005).

Do the effects of these well-designed and well-delivered programs generalize to Head Start and other community-based preschool interventions? Gains are similar, though not as strong. Head Start preschoolers, who are more economically disadvantaged than children in other programs, have more severe learning and behavior problems. And quality of services is more variable across community programs (Barnett, 2004; NICHD Early Child Care Research Network, 2001). But interventions of high quality are associated with diverse favorable outcomes, including greater year-end gains in academic skills and—in the long term—higher rates of high school graduation and college enrollment and lower rates of adolescent drug use and delinquency (Garces, Thomas, & Currie, 2002; Love et al., 2006; Mashburn, 2008).

A consistent finding is that gains in IQ and achievement test scores from attending Head Start and other interventions quickly dissolve. These children typically enter inferior public schools in poverty-stricken neighborhoods, an experience that undermines the benefits of preschool education (Brooks-Gunn, 2003; Ramey, Ramey, & Lanzi, 2006). An exception is the Chicago Child–Parent Centers—a program emphasizing literacy intervention and parent involvement that began at age 3 and continued through third grade—in which gains in academic achievement were still evident in junior high school (Reynolds & Temple, 1998).

Still, the gains in school adjustment that result from attending a one- or two-year Head Start program are impressive. Program effects on parents may contribute: The more involved parents are in Head Start, the better their child-rearing practices and the more stimulating their home learning environments—factors positively related to preschoolers' task persistence and year-end academic, language, and social skills (Marcon, 1999b; McLoyd, Aikens, & Burton, 2006; Parker et al., 1999).

Head Start is highly cost-effective when compared with the cost of providing special education, treating criminal behavior, and supporting unemployed adults. Economists estimate a lifetime return to society of more than $250,000 on an investment of $15,000 per preschool child—a potential savings of many billions of dollars if every poverty-stricken preschooler in the United States were enrolled (Heckman & Masterov, 2004; Temple & Reynolds, 2006). Because of funding shortages, however, many eligible children do not receive services.

■ **CHILD CARE.** We have seen that high-quality early intervention can enhance the development of economically disadvantaged children. However, much U.S. child care lacks quality. Preschoolers exposed to substandard child care, especially for long hours, score lower in cognitive and social skills and higher in behavior problems (Belsky, 2006; Lamb & Ahnert, 2006; NICHD Early Child Care Research Network, 2003b, 2006). Psychological well-being also declines when children experience the instability of several child-care settings. The emotional problems of temperamentally difficult preschoolers worsen considerably (De Schipper, van IJzendoorn, & Tavecchio, 2004; De Schipper et al., 2004).

In contrast, good child care enhances cognitive, language, and social development, especially for low-SES children—effects that persist into the early school years (Lamb & Ahnert, 2006; NICHD Early Child Care Research Network, 2006; Peisner-Feinberg et al., 2001). In an investigation that followed very-low-income children over the preschool years, center-based care was more strongly associated with cognitive gains than were other child-care arrangements, probably because centers are more likely to provide a systematic educational program. At the same time, better-quality experiences in all types of child care predicted modest improvements in cognitive, emotional, and social development (Loeb et al., 2004).

Applying What We Know on the following page summarizes characteristics of high-quality early childhood programs, based on standards for developmentally appropriate practice devised by the U.S. National Association for the Education of Young Children. These standards offer a set of worthy goals as the United States strives to upgrade child-care and educational services for young children.

Educational Media

Besides home and preschool, young children spend much time in another learning environment: electronic media, including both television and computers. In the United States and other industrialized nations, nearly all homes have at least one televi-

Applying What We Know

Signs of Developmentally Appropriate Early Childhood Programs

Program Characteristics	Signs of Quality
Physical setting	Indoor environment is clean, in good repair, and well-ventilated. Classroom space is divided into richly equipped activity areas, including make-believe play, blocks, science, math, games and puzzles, books, art, and music. Fenced outdoor play space is equipped with swings, climbing equipment, tricycles, and sandbox.
Group size	In preschools and child-care centers, group size is no greater than 18 to 20 children with two teachers.
Caregiver–child ratio	In child-care centers, teacher is responsible for no more than eight to ten children. In child-care homes, caregiver is responsible for no more than six children.
Daily activities	Children mainly work individually or in small groups, selecting many of their own activities and learning through experiences relevant to their own lives. Teachers facilitate children's involvement, accept individual differences, and adjust expectations to children's developing capacities.
Interactions between adults and children	Teachers move among groups and individuals, asking questions, offering suggestions, and adding more complex ideas. Teachers use positive guidance techniques, such as modeling and encouraging expected behavior and redirecting children to more acceptable activities.
Teacher qualifications	Teachers have college-level specialized preparation in early childhood development, early childhood education, or a related field.
Relationships with parents	Parents are encouraged to observe and participate. Teachers talk frequently with parents about children's behavior and development.
Licensing and accreditation	Child-care setting, whether a center or a home, is licensed by the state or province. In the United States, voluntary accreditation by the National Academy of Early Childhood Programs (www.naeyc.org/accreditation) or the National Association for Family Child Care (www.nafcc.org) is evidence of a high-quality program.

Source: Copple & Bredekamp, 2009.

sion set, and most have two or more. And about 85 percent of U.S. children live in homes with one or more computers, two-thirds of which have an Internet connection (Roberts, Foehr, & Rideout, 2005; U.S. Census Bureau, 2009b).

■ **EDUCATIONAL TELEVISION.** Sammy's favorite TV program, *Sesame Street*, uses lively visual and sound effects to stress basic literacy and number concepts and puppet and human characters to teach general knowledge, emotional and social understanding, and social skills. Today, *Sesame Street* is broadcast in more than 120 countries, making it the most widely viewed children's program in the world (Sesame Workshop, 2008).

Time devoted to watching children's educational programs is associated with gains in early literacy and math skills and academic progress in elementary school (Ennemoser & Schneider, 2007; Linebarger et al., 2004; Wright et al., 2001). Consistent with these findings, one study reported a link between preschool viewing of *Sesame Street* and other similar educational programs and getting higher grades, reading more books, and placing more value on achievement in high school (Anderson et al., 2001). In recent years, *Sesame Street* has modified its rapid-paced format in favor of more leisurely episodes with a clear story line. Watching children's programs with slow-paced action and easy-to-follow narratives, such as *Barney and Friends*, leads to more elaborate make-believe play than viewing programs that present quick, disconnected bits of information (Singer & Singer, 2005).

Despite the spread of computers, television remains the dominant form of youth media, with children first becoming viewers in early infancy. About 40 percent of U.S. 3-month-olds regularly watch either TV or videos, a figure that rises to 90 percent by age 2 (Zimmerman, Christakis, & Meltzoff, 2007). The average U.S 2- to 6 year old watches TV programs and videos from 1½ to 2 hours a day. In middle childhood, viewing time increases to an average of 3½ hours a day, then declines slightly in adolescence (Rideout & Hamel, 2006; Scharrer & Comstock, 2003).

Low-SES children are more frequent viewers, perhaps because few alternative forms of entertainment are available in their neighborhoods or affordable for their parents. Also, parents with limited education are more likely to engage in practices that heighten TV viewing, including eating family meals in front of the set and failing to limit children's TV access (Hesketh et al., 2007). About one-third of U.S. preschoolers and two-thirds of school-age children and adolescents have a TV set in their bedroom; these children spend from 40 to 90 more minutes per day watching than agemates without one (Rideout & Hamel, 2006). And if parents watch a lot of TV, their children do, too.

Does extensive TV viewing take children away from worthwhile activities? The more preschool and school-age children watch prime-time shows and cartoons, the less time they spend reading and interacting with others and the poorer their academic skills (Ennemoser & Schneider, 2007; Huston et al., 1999; Wright et al., 2001). Whereas educational programs can be beneficial, watching entertainment TV—especially heavy viewing—detracts from children's school success and social experiences.

■ **LEARNING WITH COMPUTERS.** Because computers can have rich educational benefits, many early childhood class-rooms include computer learning centers. Word-processing programs can support emergent literacy, enabling preschool and young school-age children to experiment with letters and words without having to struggle with handwriting and to easily revise their text and check their spelling. When children worry less about making mistakes, their written products tend to be longer and of higher quality (Clements & Sarama, 2003).

Simplified computer languages that children can use to make designs or build structures introduce them to program-ming skills. As long as adults support children's efforts, com-puter programming promotes improved problem solving and metacognition because children must plan and reflect on their thinking to get their programs to work. Furthermore, while programming, children are especially likely to help one another and to persist in the face of challenge (Nastasi & Clements, 1994; Resnick & Silverman, 2005).

As with television, children spend much time using com-puters for entertainment purposes, especially game playing. Both media are rife with gender stereotypes and violence. We will consider their impact on emotional and social develop-ment in the next section.

ASK YOURSELF

>> **REVIEW**
What findings indicate that child-centered rather than academic preschools and kindergartens are better suited to fostering academic development?

>> **APPLY**
Your senator has heard that IQ gains resulting from Head Start do not last, so he plans to vote against additional funding. Write a letter explaining why he should support Head Start.

>> **CONNECT**
Compare outcomes resulting from preschool intervention programs with those from interventions beginning in infancy. Which are more likely to lead to lasting cognitive gains? Explain.

>> **REFLECT**
How much and what kinds of TV viewing and computer use did you engage in as a child? How do you think your home media environment influenced your development?

Language Development

Language is intimately related to virtually all the cog-nitive changes discussed in this section. Between ages 2 and 6, children make momentous advances in language. Their remark-able achievements, as well as their mistakes along the way, reveal their active, rule-oriented approach to mastering language.

Vocabulary

At age 2, Sammy had a spoken vocabulary of 200 words. By age 6, he will have acquired around 10,000 words (Bloom, 1998). To accomplish this feat, Sammy will learn about five new words each day. How do children build their vocabularies so quickly? Research shows that they can connect new words with their un-derlying concepts after only a brief encounter, a process called **fast-mapping.** Preschoolers can even fast-map two or more new words encountered in the same situation (Wilkinson, Ross, & Diamond, 2003).

■ **TYPES OF WORDS.** Children in many Western and non-Western language communities fast-map labels for objects es-pecially rapidly because these refer to concepts that are easy to perceive. When adults point to, label, and talk about an object, they help the child figure out the word's meaning (Gershoff-Stowe & Hahn, 2007). Soon children add verbs (*go, run, broke*), which require more complex understandings of relationships between objects and actions. Children learning Chinese, Japa-nese, and Korean—languages in which nouns are often omitted from adult sentences, while verbs are stressed—acquire verbs especially quickly (Kim, McGregor, & Thompson, 2000; Tardif, 2006). Gradually, preschoolers add modifiers (*red, round, sad*). Among those that are related in meaning, general distinctions (which are easier) appear before specific ones. Thus, children first acquire *big–small*, then *tall–short, high–low,* and *wide–narrow* (Stevenson & Pollitt, 1987).

To fill in for words they have not yet learned, children as young as age 3 coin new words using ones they already know—for example, "plant-man," for a gardener, "crayoner" for a child using crayons. Preschoolers also extend language meanings through metaphor—like the 3-year-old who described a stom-achache as a "fire engine in my tummy" (Winner, 1988). Young preschoolers' metaphors involve concrete sensory comparisons: "Clouds are pillows," "Leaves are dancers." Once vocabulary and general knowledge expand, children also appreciate nonsensory comparisons: "Friends are like magnets," "Time flies by" (Keil, 1986; Özçaliskan, 2005). As a result, young children sometimes communicate in amazingly vivid and memorable ways.

■ **STRATEGIES FOR WORD LEARNING.** Preschoolers figure out the meanings of new words by contrasting them with words they already know. But exactly how they discover which concept each word picks out is not yet fully understood. One specula-tion is that early in vocabulary growth, children adopt a *mutual exclusivity bias;* they assume that words refer to entirely sepa-rate (nonoverlapping) categories (Markman, 1992). Consistent with this idea, when 2-year-olds hear the labels for two distinct novel objects (for example, *clip* and *horn*), they assign each word correctly, to the whole object and not just a part of it (Waxman & Senghas, 1992).

Indeed, children's first several hundred nouns refer mostly to objects well-organized by shape. And learning of nouns based on the perceptual property of shape heightens young children's attention to the distinctive shapes of other objects

(Smith et al., 2002; Yoshida & Smith, 2003). This *shape bias* helps preschoolers master additional names of objects, and vocabulary accelerates.

But mutual exclusivity and object shape cannot account for preschoolers' remarkably flexible responses when objects have more than one name. In these instances, children often call on other components of language. According to one proposal, they figure out many word meanings by observing how words are used in the structure of sentences (Gleitman et al., 2005; Naigles & Swenson, 2007). Consider an adult who says, "This is a *citron* one," while showing the child a yellow car. Two- and 3-year-olds conclude that a new word used as an adjective for a familiar object (car) refers to a property of that object (Hall & Graham, 1999; Imai & Haryu, 2004). As preschoolers hear the word in various sentence structures ("That lemon is bright *citron*"), they refine its meaning.

Young children also take advantage of the rich social information that adults frequently provide when they introduce new words. For example, they often draw on their expanding ability to infer others' intentions, desires, and perspectives (Akhtar & Tomasello, 2000). In one study, an adult performed an action on an object and then used a new label while looking back and forth between the child and the object, as if inviting the child to play. Two-year-olds concluded that the label referred to the action, not the object (Tomasello & Akhtar, 1995). By age 3, children can even use a speaker's recently expressed desire (which of two novel objects the adult said she liked) to figure out a word's meaning ("I really want to play with the *riff*") (Saylor & Troseth, 2006).

Young children rely on any useful information available to add to their vocabularies. As his father prepares a hook, this 3-year-old attends to a variety of perceptual, social, and linguistic cues to grasp the meanings of unfamiliar fishing words, such as bait, line, bobber, and sinker.

Adults also inform children directly about which of two or more words to use—by saying, for example, "You can call it a sea creature, but it's better to say *dolphin*." Parents who provide such clarifying information have preschoolers whose vocabularies grow more quickly (Callanan & Sabbagh, 2004).

■ **EXPLAINING VOCABULARY DEVELOPMENT.** Children acquire vocabulary so efficiently and accurately that some theorists believe that they are innately biased to induce word meanings using certain principles, such as mutual exclusivity (Lidz, Gleitman, & Gleitman, 2004; Woodward & Markman, 1998). But critics point out that a small set of built-in, fixed principles cannot account for the varied, flexible manner in which children master vocabulary (Deák, 2000). And many word-learning strategies cannot be innate because children acquiring different languages use different approaches to mastering the same meanings.

An alternative perspective is that vocabulary growth is governed by the same cognitive strategies that children apply to nonlinguistic information. According to one account, children draw on a *coalition* of cues—perceptual, social, and linguistic—which shift in importance with age (Golinkoff & Hirsh-Pasek, 2006). Infants rely solely on perceptual features. Toddlers and young preschoolers, while still sensitive to perceptual features (such as object shape), increasingly attend to social cues—the speaker's direction of gaze, gestures, and expressions of desire and intention (Hollich, Hirsh-Pasek, & Golinkoff, 2000; Pruden et al., 2006). And as language develops further, linguistic cues—sentence structure and intonation (stress, pitch, and loudness)—play larger roles.

Preschoolers are most successful at figuring out new word meanings when several kinds of information are available (Saylor, Baldwin, & Sabbagh, 2005). Researchers have just begun to study the multiple cues that children use for different kinds of words and how their combined strategies change with development.

Grammar

Between ages 2 and 3, English-speaking children use simple sentences that follow a subject–verb–object word order. Children learning other languages adopt the word orders of the adult speech to which they are exposed.

■ **BASIC RULES.** Studies of children acquiring diverse languages reveal that their first use of grammatical rules is piecemeal—limited to just a few verbs. As children listen for familiar verbs in adults' speech, they expand their own utterances containing those verbs, relying on adult speech as their model (Gathercole, Sebastián, & Soto, 1999; Lieven, Pine, & Baldwin, 1997). Sammy, for example, added the preposition *with* to the verb *open* ("You open with scissors") but not to the word *hit* ("He hit me stick").

To test preschoolers' ability to generate novel sentences that conform to basic English grammar, researchers had them use a new verb in the subject–verb–object form after hearing it in a different construction, such as passive: "Ernie is getting *gorped* by the dog." The percentage of children who, when asked what the dog was doing, could respond, "He's *gorping* Ernie," rose steadily with age. But not until 3½ to 4 could the majority of children apply the subject–verb–object structure broadly, to newly acquired verbs (Tomasello, 2003, 2006).

As soon as children form three-word sentences, they make small additions and changes to words that enable them to express meanings flexibly and efficiently. For example, they add *-s* for plural *(cats),* use prepositions *(in* and *on),* and form various tenses of the verb *to be (is, are, were, has been, will).* All English-speaking children master these grammatical markers in a regular sequence, starting with those that involve the simplest meanings and structures (Brown, 1973; de Villiers & de Villiers, 1973).

Once children acquire these markers, they sometimes overextend the rules to words that are exceptions—a type of error called **overregularization.** "My toy car *breaked*" and "We each have two *feets*" are expressions that appear between ages 2 and 3 (Maratsos, 2000; Marcus, 1995).

■ **COMPLEX STRUCTURES.** Gradually, preschoolers master more complex grammatical structures, although they do make mistakes. In first creating questions, 2- to 3-year-olds use many formulas: "Where's *X?*" "Can I *X?*" (Dabrowska, 2000; Tomasello, 1992, 2003). Question asking remains variable for the next couple of years. An analysis of one child's questions revealed that he inverted the subject and verb when asking certain questions but not others ("What she will do?" "Why he can go?") The correct expressions were the ones he heard most often in his mother's speech (Rowland & Pine, 2000). And sometimes children produce errors in subject–verb agreement ("Where does the dogs play?") and in subject case ("Where can me sit?") (Rowland, 2007).

Similarly, children have trouble with some passive sentences. When told, "The car was pushed by the truck," young preschoolers often make a toy car push a truck. By age 5, they understand such expressions, but full mastery of the passive form is not complete until the end of middle childhood (Horgan, 1978; Lempert, 1990).

Nevertheless, preschoolers' grasp of grammar is remarkable. By age 4 to 5, they form embedded sentences ("I think *he will come*"), tag questions ("Dad's going to be home soon, *isn't he?*"), and indirect objects ("He showed *his friend* the present"). As the preschool years draw to a close, children use most of the grammatical constructions of their language competently (Tager-Flusberg & Zukowski, 2009).

■ **EXPLAINING GRAMMATICAL DEVELOPMENT.** Evidence that grammatical development is an extended process has raised questions about Chomsky's nativist theory. Some experts believe that grammar is a product of general cognitive development—children's tendency to search consistencies and patterns of all sorts (Bloom, 1999; Chang, Dell, & Bock, 2006; Tomasello, 2003). These *information-processing theorists* believe that children notice which words appear in the same positions in sentences and are similarly combined with other words. Over time, they group words into grammatical categories and use them appropriately in sentences.

Still other theorists, while also focusing on how children process language, agree with Chomsky that children are specially tuned to acquire grammar. One idea proposes that the grammatical categories into which children group word meanings are innate—present at the outset (Pinker, 1999). But critics point out that children's early word combinations do not show a grasp of grammar. According to another view, rather than starting with innate knowledge, children have built-in procedures for analyzing language that support discovery of grammatical regularities (Slobin, 1985, 1997). Controversy persists over whether a universal language-processing device exists or whether children hearing different languages devise unique strategies (Lidz, 2007; Marchman & Thal, 2005).

Conversation

Besides acquiring vocabulary and grammar, children must learn to engage in effective and appropriate communication. This practical, social side of language is called **pragmatics,** and preschoolers make considerable headway in mastering it.

As early as age 2, children are skilled conversationalists. In face-to-face interaction, they take turns and respond appropriately to their partners' remarks (Pan & Snow, 1999). With age, the number of turns over which children can sustain interaction and their ability to maintain a topic over time increase. By age 4, children adjust their speech to fit the age, sex, and social status of their listeners. For example, in acting out roles with hand puppets, they use more commands when playing socially dominant and male roles (teacher, doctor, father) but speak more politely and use more indirect requests when playing less dominant and female roles (student, patient, mother) (Anderson, 2000).

Preschoolers' conversational skills occasionally do break down—for example, when talking on the phone. Here is an

Preschool children are skilled conversationalists. In face-to-face interaction, they take turns and respond appropriately to their partners' remarks.

excerpt from one 4-year-old's phone conversation with his grandfather:

Grandfather: How old will you be?

John: Dis many. *[Holding up four fingers.]*

Grandfather: Huh?

John: Dis many. *[Again holding up four fingers.]* (Warren & Tate, 1992, pp. 259–260)

Young children's conversations appear less mature in highly demanding situations in which they cannot see their listeners' reactions or rely on typical conversational aids, such as gestures and objects to talk about. But when asked to tell a listener how to solve a simple puzzle, 3- to 6-year-olds give more specific directions over the phone than in person, indicating that they realize the need for more verbal description on the phone (Cameron & Lee, 1997). Between ages 4 and 8, both conversing and giving directions over the phone improve greatly. Telephone talk provides yet another example of how preschoolers' competencies depend on the demands of the situation.

Supporting Language Development in Early Childhood

How can adults foster preschoolers' language development? As in toddlerhood, interaction with more skilled speakers is vital. Conversational give-and-take with adults, either at home or in preschool, is consistently related to language progress (Hart & Risley, 1995; NICHD Early Child Care Research Network, 2000b).

Sensitive, caring adults use additional techniques that promote early language skills. When children use words incorrectly or communicate unclearly, they give helpful, explicit feedback, such as, "I can't tell which ball you want. Do you mean the large red one?" But they do not overcorrect, especially when children make grammatical mistakes. Criticism discourages children from freely using language in ways that lead to new skills.

Instead, adults often provide indirect feedback about grammar by using two strategies, often in combination: **recasts**—restructuring inaccurate speech into correct form, and **expansions**—elaborating on children's speech, increasing its complexity (Bohannon & Stanowicz, 1988; Chouinard & Clark, 2003). For example, if a child says, "I gotted new red shoes," the parent might respond, "Yes, you got a pair of new red shoes." In one study, after such corrective input, 2- to 4-year-olds often shifted to correct forms—improvements still evident several months later (Saxton, Backley, & Galloway, 2005). However, the impact of such feedback has been challenged. The techniques are not used in all cultures and, in a few investigations, had no impact on children's grammar (Strapp & Federico, 2000; Valian, 1999). Rather than eliminating errors, perhaps expansions and recasts model grammatical alternatives and encourage children to experiment with them.

Do the findings just described remind you once again of Vygotsky's theory? In language, as in other aspects of intellectual growth, parents and teachers gently prompt children to take the next step forward. Children strive to master language because they want to connect with other people. Adults, in turn, respond to children's desire to become competent speakers by listening attentively, elaborating on what children say, modeling correct usage, and stimulating children to talk further. In the next section, we will see that this combination of warmth and encouragement of mature behavior is at the heart of early childhood emotional and social development as well.

ASK YOURSELF

>> **REVIEW**
Provide a list of recommendations for supporting language development in early childhood, noting research that supports each.

>> **APPLY**
Sammy's mother explained to him that the family would take a vacation in Miami. The next morning, Sammy announced, "I gotted my bags packed. When are we going to Your-ami?" What explains Sammy's error?

>> **CONNECT**
Explain how children's strategies for word learning support the interactionist perspective on language development.

Summary

PHYSICAL DEVELOPMENT

A Changing Body and Brain

Describe body growth and brain development during early childhood.

>> Children grow more slowly in early childhood than they did in the first two years, and they become longer and leaner. New growth centers appear in the skeleton, and by the end of early childhood, children start to lose their primary teeth.

>> Frontal-lobe areas of the cerebral cortex devoted to planning and organizing behavior develop rapidly. The left cerebral hemisphere shows more neural activity than the right, supporting preschoolers' expanding language skills.

>> Hand preference strengthens during early and middle childhood, indicating that lateralization is increasing. Handedness reflects an individual's **dominant cerebral hemisphere.** One theory proposes that most children are genetically biased for right-handedness but that experience can sway them toward a left-hand preference.

>> In early childhood, fibers linking the **cerebellum** to the cerebral cortex myelinate, enhancing balance, motor control, and thinking. The **reticular formation,** responsible for alertness and consciousness; the **hippocampus,** which plays a vital role in memory and spatial orientation; and the **corpus callosum,** connecting the two cerebral hemispheres, also develop rapidly.

Influences on Physical Growth and Health

Describe the effects of heredity, emotional well-being, nutrition, and infectious disease on physical growth in early childhood.

>> Heredity influences physical growth by controlling the release of hormones from the **pituitary gland.** Two hormones are especially influential: **growth hormone (GH)** and **thyroid-stimulating hormone (TSH).**

>> Emotional well-being continues to influence body growth. An emotionally inadequate home life can lead to a disorder called **psychosocial dwarfism.**

>> As growth rate slows, preschoolers' appetites decline, and many become picky eaters. Repeated exposure to new foods and a positive mealtime atmosphere encourages healthy, varied eating.

© MARC GARANGER/CORBIS

>> Dietary deficiencies, especially in protein, vitamins and minerals, can affect growth and resistance to disease. In the developing world, disease often contributes to malnutrition and growth stunting, especially when intestinal infections cause persistent diarrhea.

>> Immunization rates are lower in the United States than in other industrialized nations because many economically disadvantaged children lack access to health care. Parental stress and misconceptions about vaccine safety also contribute.

What factors increase the risk of unintentional injuries, and how can childhood injuries be prevented?

>> Unintentional injuries are the leading cause of childhood mortality in industrialized countries. Injury victims are more likely to be boys; to be temperamentally irritable, inattentive, and negative; and to be growing up in stressed, poverty-stricken inner-city families.

>> Effective injury prevention includes reducing poverty and other sources of family stress; passing laws that promote child safety; creating safer home, travel, and play environments; improving public education; and changing parent and child behaviors.

Motor Development

Cite major milestones of gross- and fine-motor development in early childhood.

>> As the child's center of gravity shifts toward the trunk, balance improves, paving the way for many gross-motor achievements. Preschoolers run, jump, hop, gallop, eventually skip, throw and catch, and generally become better coordinated.

>> Increasing control of the hands and fingers leads to dramatic improvements in fine-motor skills. Preschoolers gradually become self-sufficient at dressing and using a knife and fork.

>> By age 3, children's scribbles become pictures. With age, their drawings increase in complexity and realism, influenced by schooling and by their culture's artistic traditions. Preschoolers also try to print alphabet letters and, later, words.

>> Body build and opportunity for physical play affect motor development. Sex differences that favor boys in skills requiring force and power and girls in skills requiring balance and fine movements are partly genetic, but environmental pressures exaggerate them. Children master the motor skills of early childhood through informal play experiences.

COGNITIVE DEVELOPMENT

Piaget's Theory: The Preoperational Stage

Describe cognitive advances and limitations during the preoperational stage.

>> Rapid advances in mental representation mark the beginning of Piaget's **preoperational stage.** With age, make-believe becomes increasingly complex, evolving into **sociodramatic play** with others. Preschoolers' make-believe supports many aspects of development. Gradually, children become capable of **dual representation**— viewing a symbolic object as both an object in its own right and a symbol.

>> Piaget also described preoperational children as egocentric, often failing to imagine others' perspectives. **Egocentrism** contributes to **animistic thinking, centration,** a focus on perceptual appearances, and **irreversibility.** These difficulties cause preschoolers to fail **conservation** and **hierarchical classification** tasks.

What does follow-up research reveal about the accuracy of Piaget's preoperational stage?

>> When young children are given simplified problems relevant to their everyday lives, their performance appears more mature than Piaget assumed. Preschoolers recognize differing perspectives, distinguish animate from inanimate objects, reason by analogy about physical transformations, understand cause-and-effect relationships, and organize knowledge into hierarchical categories, including categories based on nonobvious features.

>> Evidence that operational thinking develops gradually over the preschool years challenges Piaget's stage concept. Some theorists propose a more flexible view of stages.

What educational principles can be derived from Piaget's theory?

>> A Piagetian classroom promotes discovery learning, sensitivity to children's readiness to learn, and acceptance of individual differences.

Vygotsky's Sociocultural Theory

Explain Vygotsky's perspective on children's private speech, describe applications of his theory to education, and note how cross-cultural research has expanded his ideas.

>> Unlike Piaget, Vygotsky regarded language as the foundation for all higher cognitive processes. According to Vygotsky, **private speech,** or language used for self-guidance, emerges out of social communication as adults and more skilled peers help children master challenging tasks. Private speech is gradually internalized as inner, verbal thought. **Scaffolding** is a form of social interaction that promotes the transfer of cognitive processes to children.

>> A Vygotskian classroom emphasizes assisted discovery—verbal guidance from teachers and peer collaboration. Make-believe play is a vital zone of proximal development that promotes many competencies.

© ELLEN B. SENISI PHOTOGRAPHY

>> **Guided participation,** a broader term than scaffolding, recognizes cultural and situational variations in adult support of children's efforts.

Information Processing

How do attention and memory change during early childhood?

>> Attention gradually becomes more sustained, and planning improves. Nevertheless, compared with older children, preschoolers spend relatively short periods involved in tasks and are less systematic in planning.

- Preschoolers' recognition memory is very accurate, but their recall for listlike information is poor because they use **memory strategies** less effectively than older children.

- Like adults, preschoolers remember recurring experiences in terms of **scripts,** which become more elaborate with age. When adults use an elaborative style of conversing with children about the past, their autobiographical memory becomes better organized and detailed.

Describe the young child's theory of mind.

- Preschoolers begin to construct a theory of mind, indicating that they are capable of **metacognition.** Around age 4, they understand that people can hold false beliefs. Language, cognitive abilities, make-believe play, and diverse social experiences with adults, siblings, and peers all contribute to the development of a theory of mind. Preschoolers regard the mind as a passive container of information rather than as an active, constructive agent.

Summarize children's literacy and mathematical knowledge during early childhood.

- Young children in industrialized nations attempt to figure out how written symbols convey meaning—an active effort known as **emergent literacy.** Preschoolers gradually revise incorrect ideas about the meaning of written symbols as their cognitive and language capacities improve, as they encounter writing in many different contexts, and as adults help them with written communication. **Phonological awareness** is a strong predictor of emergent literacy knowledge.

- In the second year, children have a beginning grasp of **ordinality.** Soon they discover additional mathematical principles, including **cardinality,** and experiment with counting strategies to solve arithmetic problems, eventually arriving at the most efficient, accurate techniques. Many occasions for counting, comparing quantities, and talking about number promote mathematical knowledge.

© SALLY AND RICHARD GREENHILL/ALAMY

Individual Differences in Mental Development

Describe early childhood intelligence tests and the impact of home, educational programs, child care, and media on preschoolers' mental development.

- By age 5 to 6, intelligence test scores are good predictors of later IQ and academic achievement. Children growing up in warm, stimulating homes with parents who make reasonable demands for mature behavior score higher on mental tests.

- Preschool and kindergarten programs include both **child-centered programs,** in which much learning takes place through play, and **academic programs,** in which teachers train children in academic skills, often through repetition and drill. Emphasizing formal academic instruction undermines young children's motivation and negatively influences later school achievement.

- **Project Head Start** is the largest U.S. federally funded preschool program for low-income children. High-quality preschool intervention results in immediate IQ and achievement gains and long-term improvements in school adjustment. The more parents are involved in Head Start, the higher children's year-end academic, language, and social skills. Regardless of SES, poor-quality child care undermines preschoolers' cognitive and social development.

- Children pick up many cognitive skills from educational television programs. Programs with slow-paced action and easy-to-follow story lines foster more elaborate make-believe play. But heavy viewing of prime-time shows and cartoons takes children away from reading and interacting with others and is related to weaker academic skills.

- Computer word-processing programs can support preschoolers' emergent literacy. Introducing young children to simplified computer languages fosters problem solving and metacognition.

Language Development

Trace the development of vocabulary, grammar, and conversational skills in early childhood.

- Supported by **fast-mapping,** preschoolers' vocabularies grow dramatically. On hearing a new word, children contrast it with words they know and often assume that words refer to entirely separate categories. When adults call an object by more than one name, preschoolers figure out word meanings from diverse cues—perceptual, social, and linguistic. They also extend language meanings by coining new words and creating metaphors.

- Between ages 2 and 3, children adopt the basic word order of their language. As they master grammatical rules, they sometimes overextend them in a type of error called **overregularization.** By the end of early childhood, children have acquired complex grammatical forms.

- **Pragmatics** refers to the practical, social side of language. Two-year-olds are already skilled conversationalists in face-to-face interaction. By age 4, children adapt their speech to their listeners in culturally accepted ways.

Cite factors that support language learning in early childhood.

- Conversational give-and-take with more skilled speakers fosters language progress. Adults often provide explicit feedback on the clarity of children's language and indirect feedback about grammar through **recasts** and **expansions.**

Important Terms and Concepts

academic programs (p. 33)
animistic thinking (p. 17)
cardinality (p. 31)
centration (p. 17)
cerebellum (p. 6)
child-centered programs (p. 33)
conservation (p. 17)
corpus callosum (p. 6)
dominant cerebral hemisphere (p. 5)
dual representation (p. 17)
egocentrism (p. 17)
emergent literacy (p. 30)

expansions (p. 39)
fast-mapping (p. 36)
growth hormone (GH) (p. 7)
guided participation (p. 24)
hierarchical classification (p. 18)
hippocampus (p. 6)
irreversibility (p. 18)
memory strategies (p. 26)
metacognition (p. 27)
ordinality (p. 31)
overregularization (p. 38)
phonological awareness (p. 30)

pituitary gland (p. 7)
pragmatics (p. 38)
preoperational stage (p. 15)
private speech (p. 22)
Project Head Start (p. 33)
psychosocial dwarfism (p. 7)
recasts (p. 39)
reticular formation (p. 6)
scaffolding (p. 23)
scripts (p. 26)
sociodramatic play (p. 18)
thyroid-stimulating hormone (TSH) (p. 7)

During the preschool years, children make great strides in understanding the thoughts and feelings of others, and they build on these skills as they form first friendships—special relationships marked by attachment and common interests.

SECTION 2

Emotional and Social Development in Early Childhood

A
s the children in Leslie's classroom moved through the preschool years, their personalities took on clearer definition. By age 3, they voiced firm likes and dislikes as well as new ideas about themselves. "Stop bothering me," Sammy said to Mark, who had reached for Sammy's beanbag as Sammy aimed it toward the mouth of a large clown face. "See, I'm great at this game," Sammy announced with confidence, an attitude that kept him trying, even though he missed most of the throws.

The children's conversations also revealed early notions about morality. Often they combined adults' statements about right and wrong with forceful attempts to defend their own desires. "You're 'posed to share," stated Mark, grabbing the beanbag out of Sammy's hand.

"I was here first! Gimme it back," demanded Sammy, pushing Mark. The two boys struggled until Leslie intervened, provided another beanbag, and showed them how both could play.

As the interaction between Sammy and Mark reveals, preschoolers quickly become complex social beings. Young children argue, grab, and push, but cooperative exchanges are far more frequent. Between ages 2 and 6, first

© ELLEN B. SENSI/ PHOTOGRAPHY

friendships form, in which children converse, act out complementary roles, and learn that their own desires for companionship and toys are best met when they consider others' needs and interests.

The children's developing understanding of their social world was especially evident in their growing attention to the dividing line between male and female. While Lynette and Karen cared for a sick baby doll in the housekeeping area, Sammy, Vance, and Mark transformed the block corner into a busy intersection. "Green light, go!" shouted police officer Sammy as Vance and Mark pushed large wooden cars and trucks across the floor. Already, the children preferred same-sex peers and, in their play, mirrored their culture's gender stereotypes.

This section is devoted to the many facets of early childhood emotional and social development. We begin with Erik Erikson's theory, which provides an overview of personality change in the preschool years. Then we consider children's concepts of themselves, their insights into their social and moral worlds, their gender typing, and their increasing ability to manage their emotional and social behaviors. Finally, we ask, What is effective child rearing? And we discuss the complex conditions that support good parenting or lead it to break down.

Erikson's Theory: Initiative versus Guilt

Erikson (1950) described early childhood as a period of "vigorous unfolding." Once children have a sense of autonomy, they become less contrary than they were as toddlers. Their energies are freed for tackling the psychological conflict of the preschool years: **initiative versus guilt.** As the word *initiative* suggests, young children have a new sense of purposefulness. They are eager to tackle new tasks, join in activities with peers, and discover what they can do with the help of adults. They also make strides in conscience development.

Erikson regarded play as a means through which young children learn about themselves and their social world. Play permits preschoolers to try out new skills with little risk of criticism and failure. It also creates a small social organization of children who must cooperate to achieve common goals. Around the world, children act out family scenes and highly visible occupations—police officer, doctor, and nurse in Western societies, rabbit hunter and potter among the Hopi Indians, hut

This 3-year-old in India pretends to do the laundry on the washing stone outside her family's home. Around the world, young children act out family scenes and highly visible occupations, developing a sense of initiative as they gain insight into what they can do.

builder and spear maker among the Baka of West Africa (Göncü, Patt, & Kouba, 2004).

Recall that Erikson's theory builds on Freud's psychosexual stages. In Freud's Oedipus and Electra conflicts, to avoid punishment and maintain the affection of parents, children form a *superego,* or conscience, by identifying with the same-sex parent. As a result, they adopt the moral and gender-role standards of their society. Each time the child disobeys standards of conscience, painful feelings of guilt occur. For Erikson, the negative outcome of early childhood is an overly strict superego that causes children to feel too much guilt because they have been threatened, criticized, and punished excessively by adults. When this happens, preschoolers' exuberant play and bold efforts to master new tasks break down.

Although Freud's ideas are no longer accepted as satisfactory explanations of conscience development, Erikson's image of initiative captures the diverse changes in young children's emotional and social lives. Early childhood is, indeed, a time when children develop a confident self-image, more effective control over their emotions, new social skills, the foundations of morality, and a clear sense of themselves as boy or girl.

Self-Understanding

The development of language enables young children to talk about their own subjective experience of being. In Section 1, we noted that young children acquire a vocabulary for talking about their inner mental lives and refine their understanding of mental states. As self-awareness strengthens, preschoolers focus more intently on qualities that make the self unique. They begin to develop a **self-concept,** the set of attributes, abilities, attitudes, and values that an individual believes defines who he or she is.

Foundations of Self-Concept

Ask a 3- to 5-year-old to tell you about himself, and you are likely to hear something like this: "I'm Tommy. See, I got this new red T-shirt. I'm 4 years old. I can wash my hair all by myself. I have a new Tinkertoy set, and I made this big, big tower." Preschoolers' self-concepts are very concrete. Usually, they mention observable characteristics, such as their name, physical appearance, possessions, and everyday behaviors (Harter, 2006; Watson, 1990).

By age 3½, preschoolers also describe themselves in terms of typical emotions and attitudes—"I'm happy when I play with my friends"; "I don't like being with grownups"—suggesting a beginning understanding of their unique psychological characteristics (Eder & Mangelsdorf, 1997). Furthermore, when given a trait label ("shy" or "mean"), 4-year-olds infer appropriate motives and feelings. For example, they know that a shy person doesn't like to be with unfamiliar people (Heyman & Gelman, 1999). But preschoolers do not say, "I'm helpful" or "I'm shy." Direct references to personality traits must wait for greater cognitive maturity.

■ CULTURAL INFLUENCES ■

Cultural Variations in Personal Storytelling: Implications for Early Self-Concept

Preschoolers of many cultural backgrounds participate in personal storytelling with their parents. Striking cultural differences exist in parents' selection and interpretation of events in these narratives, affecting the way children view themselves.

In one study, researchers spent hundreds of hours studying the storytelling practices of six middle-SES Irish-American families in Chicago and six middle-SES Chinese families in Taiwan. From extensive videotapes of adults' conversations with 2½-year-olds, the investigators identified personal stories and coded them for content, quality of their endings, and evaluation of the child (Miller, Fung, & Mintz, 1996; Miller et al., 1997).

Parents in both cultures discussed pleasurable holidays and family excursions in similar ways and with similar frequency. But Chinese parents more often told long stories about the child's misdeeds—using impolite language, writing on the wall, or playing in an overly rowdy way. These narratives were conveyed with warmth and caring, stressed the impact

of misbehavior on others ("You made Mama lose face"), and often ended with direct teaching of proper behavior ("Saying dirty words is not good"). By contrast, in the few instances in which Irish-American stories referred to transgressions, parents downplayed their seriousness, attributing them to the child's spunk and assertiveness.

Early narratives about the child launch preschoolers' self-concepts on culturally distinct paths (Miller, Fung, & Koven, 2007). Influenced by Confucian traditions of strict discipline and social obligations, Chinese parents integrated these values into their stories, affirming the importance of not disgracing the family and explicitly conveying expectations in the story's conclusion. Although Irish-American parents disciplined their children, they rarely dwelt on misdeeds in storytelling. Rather, they cast the child's shortcomings in a positive light, perhaps to promote self-esteem.

Whereas most North Americans believe that favorable self-esteem is crucial for healthy development, Chinese adults generally see it as unimportant or even negative—as impeding the child's willingness to listen and be corrected (Miller et al., 2002). Consistent with this view, the Chinese parents did little to cultivate their child's individuality. Instead, they used storytelling to guide the child toward socially

A Chinese mother speaks gently to her children about proper behavior. Chinese parents often tell preschoolers stories that point out the negative impact on others of the child's misdeeds. The Chinese child's self-concept, in turn, emphasizes social obligations.

responsible behavior. Hence, the Chinese child's self-image emphasizes obligations to others, whereas the North American child's is more autonomous.

In fact, very young preschoolers' concepts of themselves are so bound up with specific possessions and actions that they spend much time asserting their rights to objects ("Mine!"), as Sammy did in the beanbag incident at the beginning of this section. The stronger children's self-definition, the more possessive they tend to be (Fasig, 2000; Levine, 1983). A firmer sense of self also enables children to cooperate in resolving disputes over objects, playing games, and solving simple problems (Brownell & Carriger, 1990; Caplan et al., 1991). Accordingly, when trying to promote friendly peer interaction, parents and teachers can accept young children's possessiveness as a sign of self-assertion ("Yes, that's your toy") and then encourage compromise ("but in a little while, would you give someone else a turn?"), rather than simply insisting on sharing.

Recall from that adult–child conversations about personally experienced events contribute to the development of an autobiographical memory—a life-story narrative that is more coherent and lasting than the isolated memories of the first few years (see page 26). In one study, the richness of mothers' emotional communication about the past (evaluations of positive events, explanations of children's negative feelings and their resolution) helped children understand themselves: It predicted greater consistency in 5- and 6-year-olds' reports of their personal characteristics (Bird & Reese, 2006).

And as early as age 2, parents use these narratives to impart rules, standards for behavior, evaluative information about the child: "You added the milk when we made the mashed potatoes. That's a very important job!" (Nelson, 2003). As the Cultural Influences box above reveals, these self-evaluative narratives are a major means through which caregivers imbue the young child's self-concept with cultural values.

As they talk about personally significant events and as their cognitive skills advance, preschoolers gradually come to view themselves as persisting over time. Around age 4, children first become certain that a video image of themselves replayed a few minutes after it was filmed is still "me" (Povinelli, 2001). Similarly, when researchers asked 3- to 5-year-olds to imagine a future event (walking next to a waterfall) and to envision a future personal state by choosing from three items (a raincoat, money, a blanket) the one they would need to bring with them, performance—along with future-state justifications ("I'm gonna get wet")—increased sharply from age 3 to 4 (Atance & Meltzoff, 2005).

Emergence of Self-Esteem

Another aspect of self-concept emerges in early childhood: **self-esteem,** the judgments we make about our own worth and the feelings associated with those judgments. **TAKE A MOMENT...** Make a list of your own self-judgments. Notice that, besides a global appraisal of your worth as a person, you have a variety of separate self-evaluations concerning how well you perform at different activities. These evaluations are among the most important aspects of self-development because they affect emotional experiences, future behavior, and long-term psychological adjustment.

By age 4, preschoolers have several self-judgments—for example, about learning things in school, making friends, getting along with parents, and treating others kindly (Marsh, Ellis, & Craven, 2002). But because preschoolers cannot distinguish between their desired and their actual competence, they usually

A preschooler proudly displays a string of beads she has assembled. Her high self-esteem contributes greatly to her initiative in mastering many new skills.

rate their own ability as extremely high and underestimate task difficulty, as when Sammy asserted, despite his many misses, that he was great at beanbag throwing (Harter, 2003, 2006).

High self-esteem contributes greatly to preschoolers' initiative during a period in which they must master many new skills. By age 3, children with a history of parental criticism of their worth and performance give up easily when faced with a challenge and express shame and despondency after failing (Kelley, Brownell, & Campbell, 2000). When preschool nonpersisters use dolls to act out an adult's reaction to failure, they anticipate disapproval—saying, for example, "He's punished because he can't do the puzzle." They also report that their parents berate them for small mistakes (Burhans & Dweck, 1995; Heyman, Dweck, & Cain, 1992). Adults can avoid promoting these self-defeating reactions by adjusting their expectations to children's capacities, scaffolding children's attempts at difficult tasks (see Section 1, page 23), and pointing out effort and improvement in children's behavior.

Emotional Development

Gains in representation, language, and self-concept support emotional development in early childhood. Between ages 2 and 6, children make strides in emotional abilities that, collectively, researchers refer to as *emotional competence* (Halberstadt, Denham, & Dunsmore, 2001; Saarni et al., 2006). First, preschoolers gain in emotional understanding, becoming better able to talk about feelings and to respond appropriately to others' emotional signals. Second, they become better at emotional self-regulation—in particular, at coping with intense negative emotion. Finally, preschoolers more often experience *self-conscious emotions* and *empathy,* which contribute to their developing sense of morality.

Parenting strongly influences preschoolers' emotional competence. Emotional competence, in turn, is vital for successful peer relationships and overall mental health.

Understanding Emotion

Early in the preschool years, children refer to causes, consequences, and behavioral signs of emotion, and over time their understanding becomes more accurate and complex (Stein & Levine, 1999). By age 4 to 5, children correctly judge the causes of many basic emotions ("He's happy because he's swinging very high"; "He's sad because he misses his mother"). Preschoolers' explanations tend to emphasize external factors over internal states, a balance that changes with age (Levine, 1995). After age 4, children better understand that both desires and beliefs motivate behavior (see page 27 in Section 1). Then their grasp of how internal factors can trigger emotion expands.

Preschoolers can also predict what a playmate expressing a certain emotion might do next. Four-year-olds know that an angry child might hit someone and that a happy child is more likely to share (Russell, 1990). And they realize that thinking and feeling are interconnected—that a person reminded of a previous sad experience is likely to feel sad (Lagattuta, Wellman, & Flavell, 1997). Furthermore, they come up with effective ways to relieve others' negative feelings, such as hugging to reduce sadness (Fabes et al., 1988). Overall, preschoolers have an impressive ability to interpret, predict, and change others' feelings.

At the same time, preschoolers have difficulty interpreting situations that offer conflicting cues about how a person is feeling. When shown a picture of a happy-faced child with a broken bicycle, 4- and 5-year-olds tended to rely on the emotional expression: "He's happy because he likes to ride his bike." Older children more often reconciled the two cues: "He's happy because his father promised to help fix his broken bike" (Gnepp, 1983; Hoffner & Badzinski, 1989). As in their approach to Piagetian tasks, preschoolers focus on the most obvious aspect of an emotional situation to the neglect of other relevant information.

Preschoolers whose parents frequently acknowledge their emotional reactions and talk about diverse emotions are better able to judge others' emotions when tested at later ages (Denham & Kochanoff, 2002). In one study, mothers who explained feelings and who negotiated and compromised during conflicts with their 2½-year-olds had children who, at age 3, were advanced in emotional understanding and used similar strategies to resolve disagreements (Laible & Thompson, 2002). Furthermore, 3- to 5-year-olds who are securely attached to their mothers better understand emotion. Attachment security is related to warmer and more elaborative parent–child narratives, including discussions of feelings that highlight the emotional significance of events (Laible, 2004; Laible & Song, 2006; Raikes & Thompson, 2006).

As preschoolers learn about emotion from interacting with adults, they engage in more emotion talk with siblings and friends, especially during make-believe play (Brown, Donelan-McCall, & Dunn, 1996; Hughes & Dunn, 1998). Make-believe, in turn, contributes to emotional understanding, especially when children play with siblings (Youngblade & Dunn, 1995). The intense nature of the sibling relationship, combined with frequent acting out of feelings, makes pretending an excellent context for learning about emotions. Also, the more preschoolers refer to feelings when interacting with playmates, the better liked they are by their peers (Fabes et al., 2001). Children seem to recognize that acknowledging others' emotions and explaining their own enhance the quality of relationships.

Emotional Self-Regulation

Language also contributes to preschoolers' improved *emotional self-regulation*. By age 3 to 4, children verbalize a variety of strategies for adjusting their emotional arousal to a more comfortable level. For example, they know they can blunt emotions by restricting sensory input (covering their eyes or ears to block out a scary sight or sound), talking to themselves ("Mommy said she'll be back soon"), or changing their goals (deciding that they don't want to play anyway after being excluded from a game) (Thompson & Goodvin, 2007). As children use these strategies, emotional outbursts decline. *Effortful control*—in particular, inhibiting impulses and shifting attention—also continues to

be vital in managing emotion during early childhood. Three-year-olds who can distract themselves when frustrated tend to become cooperative school-age children with few problem behaviors (Gilliom et al., 2002a).

Temperament affects the development of emotional self-regulation. Children who experience negative emotion intensely find it harder to inhibit feelings and shift attention away from disturbing events. They are more likely to be anxious and fearful, respond with irritation to others' distress, react angrily or aggressively when frustrated, and get along poorly with teachers and peers (Chang et al., 2003; Denham et al., 2002; Eisenberg et al., 2005).

To avoid social difficulties, emotionally reactive children must develop effective emotion-regulation strategies (Rothbart & Bates, 2006). By watching parents manage their feelings, children learn strategies for regulating their own. When parents rarely express positive emotion, dismiss children's feelings as unimportant, and have difficulty controlling their own anger, children have continuing problems managing emotion (Gilliom et al., 2002; Katz & Windecker-Nelson, 2004). And because emotionally reactive children become increasingly difficult to rear, they are often targets of ineffective parenting, which compounds their poor self-regulation.

Adults' conversations with preschoolers also foster emotional self-regulation (Thompson, 2006). Parents who prepare children for difficult experience by describing what to expect and ways to handle anxiety offer strategies that children can apply. Preschoolers' vivid imaginations and incomplete grasp of the distinction between appearance and reality make fears common in early childhood. Consult Applying What We Know on page 48 for ways adults can help young children manage fears.

Self-Conscious Emotions

One morning in Leslie's classroom, a group of children crowded around for a bread-baking activity. Leslie asked them to wait patiently while she got a baking pan. But Sammy reached over to feel the dough, and the bowl tumbled off the table. When Leslie returned, Sammy looked at her, then covered his eyes with his hands and said, "I did something bad." He felt ashamed and guilty.

As their self-concepts develop, preschoolers become increasingly sensitive to praise and blame or to the possibility of such feedback. They more often experience *self-conscious emotions*—feelings that involve injury to or enhancement of their sense of self. By age 3, self-conscious emotions are clearly linked to self-evaluation (Stipek, 1995; Thompson, Meyer, & McGinley, 2006). But because preschoolers are still developing standards of excellence and conduct, they depend on the messages of parents, teachers, and others who matter to them to know *when* to feel proud, ashamed, or guilty, often viewing adult expectations as obligatory rules ("Dad said you're 'posed to take turns") (Stipek, 1995; Thompson, Meyer, & McGinley, 2006).

When parents repeatedly comment on the worth of the child and her performance ("That's a bad job! I thought you were a good girl!"), children experience self-conscious emotions

Applying What We Know

Helping Children Manage Common Fears of Early Childhood

Fear	Suggestion
Monsters, ghosts, and darkness	Reduce exposure to frightening stories in books and on TV until the child is better able to sort out appearance from reality. Make a thorough "search" of the child's room for monsters, showing him that none are there. Leave a night-light burning, sit by the child's bed until he falls asleep, and tuck in a favorite toy for protection.
Preschool or child care	If the child resists going to preschool but seems content once there, then the fear is probably separation. Provide a sense of warmth and caring while gently encouraging independence. If the child fears being at preschool, find out what is frightening—the teacher, the children, or perhaps a crowded, noisy environment. Provide extra support by accompanying the child and gradually lessening the amount of time you are present.
Animals	Do not force the child to approach a dog, cat, or other animal that arouses fear. Let the child move at her own pace. Demonstrate how to hold and pet the animal, showing the child that when treated gently, the animal is friendly. If the child is larger than the animal, emphasize this: "You're so big. That kitty is probably afraid of you!"
Intense fears	If a child's fear is intense, persists for a long time, interferes with daily activities, and cannot be reduced in any of the ways just suggested, it has reached the level of a *phobia*. Sometimes phobias are linked to family problems, and counseling is needed to reduce them. At other times, phobias diminish without treatment as the child's capacity for emotional self-regulation improves.

intensely—more shame after failure, more pride after success. In contrast, parents who focus on how to improve performance ("You did it this way; now try doing it that way") induce moderate, more adaptive levels of shame and pride and greater persistence on difficult tasks (Kelley, Brownell, & Campbell, 2000; Lewis, 1998).

Among Western children, intense shame is associated with feelings of personal inadequacy ("I'm stupid"; "I'm a terrible person") and with maladjustment—withdrawal and depression as well as intense anger and aggression toward those who participated in the shame-evoking situation (Lindsay-Hartz, de Rivera, & Mascolo, 1995; Mills, 2005). In contrast, guilt—when it occurs in appropriate circumstances and is not accompanied by shame—is related to good adjustment. Guilt helps children resist harmful impulses, and it motivates a misbehaving child to repair the damage and behave more considerately (Mascolo & Fischer, 2007; Tangney, 2001).

The consequences of shame for children's adjustment, however, may vary across cultures. As illustrated in the Cultural Influences box on page 45, people in Asian collectivist societies, who define themselves in relation to their social group, view shame as an adaptive reminder of an interdependent self and of the importance of others' judgments (Bedford, 2004).

Empathy

In early childhood, another emotional capacity, *empathy,* becomes more common and serves as an important motivator of **prosocial,** or **altruistic, behavior**—actions that benefit another person without any expected reward for the self (Eisenberg, Fabes, & Spinrad, 2006). Compared with toddlers, preschoolers rely more on words to communicate empathic feelings, a change that indicates a more reflective level of empa-

thy. And as the ability to take another's perspective improves, empathic responding increases. When a 4-year-old received a Christmas gift that she hadn't included on her list for Santa, she assumed it belonged to another little girl and pleaded with her parents, "We've got to give it back—Santa's made a big mistake. I think the girl's crying 'cause she didn't get her present!"

Yet empathy—*feeling with* another person and responding emotionally in a similar way—does not always yield acts of kindness and helpfulness. For some children, empathizing with an upset adult or peer escalates into personal distress. In trying to reduce these feelings, the child focuses on his own anxiety rather than the person in need. As a result, empathy does not lead to **sympathy**—feelings of concern or sorrow for another's plight.

As children's language skills and ability to take the perspective of others improve, empathy also increases, motivating prosocial, or altruistic, behavior.

Temperament plays a role in whether empathy prompts sympathetic, prosocial behavior or self-focused personal distress. Children who are sociable, assertive, and good at regulating emotion are more likely to help, share, and comfort others in distress. But poor emotion regulators less often display sympathetic concern and prosocial behavior (Bengtsson, 2005; Eisenberg et al., 1998). When faced with someone in need, they react with facial and physiological distress—frowning, lip biting, a rise in heart rate, and a sharp increase in EEG brain-wave activity in the right cerebral hemisphere (which houses negative emotion)—indications that they are overwhelmed by their feelings (Jones, Field, & Davalos, 2000; Pickens, Field, & Nawrocki, 2001).

As with emotional self-regulation, parenting affects empathy and sympathy. When parents are warm, encourage emotional expressiveness, and show sensitive, empathic concern for their preschoolers' feelings, children are likely to react in similar fashion to others' distress—relationships that persist into adolescence and early adulthood (Koestner, Franz, & Weinberger, 1990; Michalik et al., 2007; Strayer & Roberts, 2004). Besides modeling sympathy, parents can teach children the importance of kindness and can intervene when they display inappropriate emotion—strategies that predict high levels of sympathetic responding (Eisenberg, 2003).

In contrast, angry, punitive parenting disrupts empathy and sympathy at an early age (Valiente et al., 2004). In one study, physically abused preschoolers at a child-care center rarely expressed concern at a peer's unhappiness but, rather, reacted with fear, anger, and physical attacks (Klimes-Dougan & Kistner, 1990). The children's behavior resembled their parents' insensitive responses to the suffering of others.

Peer Relations

As children become increasingly self-aware and better at communicating and understanding the thoughts and feelings of others, their skill at interacting with peers improves rapidly. Peers provide young children with learning experiences they can get in no other way. Because peers interact on an equal footing, children must keep a conversation going, cooperate, and set goals in play. With peers, children form friendships—special relationships marked by attachment and common interests. Let's look at how peer interaction changes over the preschool years.

Advances in Peer Sociability

Mildred Parten (1932), one of the first to study peer sociability among 2- to 5-year-olds, noticed a dramatic rise with age in joint, interactive play. She concluded that social development proceeds in a three-step sequence. It begins with **nonsocial activity**—unoccupied, onlooker behavior and solitary play. Then it shifts to **parallel play,** in which a child plays near other children with similar materials but does not try to influence their behavior. At the highest level are two forms of true social interaction. In **associative play,** children engage in separate activities but exchange toys and comment on one another's behavior. Finally, in **cooperative play,** a more advanced type of interaction, children orient toward a common goal, such as acting out a make-believe theme.

■ **FOLLOW-UP RESEARCH ON PEER SOCIABILITY.** Longitudinal evidence indicates that these play forms emerge in the order suggested by Parten but that later-appearing ones do not replace earlier ones in a developmental sequence (Rubin, Bukowski, & Parker, 2006). Rather, all types coexist in early childhood.

TAKE A MOMENT... Watch preschoolers move from one type of play to another in a play group or preschool classroom, and you will see that they often transition from onlooker to parallel to cooperative play and back again (Robinson et al., 2003). Preschoolers seem to use parallel play as a way station—a respite from the demands of complex social interaction and a crossroad to new activities. And although nonsocial activity declines with age, it is still the most frequent form among 3- to 4-year-olds and accounts for a third of kindergartners' free-play

These 4-year-olds (left) engage in parallel play. Cooperative play (right) develops later than parallel play, but preschool children continue to move back and forth between the two types of sociability, sometimes using parallel play as a respite from the complex demands of cooperation.

■ **TABLE 2.1** ■ *Developmental Sequence of Cognitive Play Categories*

PLAY CATEGORY	DESCRIPTION	EXAMPLES
Functional play	Simple, repetitive motor movements with or without objects, especially common during the first two years	Running around a room, rolling a car back and forth, kneading clay with no intent to make something
Constructive play	Creating or constructing something, especially common between 3 and 6 years	Making a house out of toy blocks, drawing a picture, putting together a puzzle
Make-believe play	Acting out everyday and imaginary roles, especially common between 2 and 6 years	Playing house, school, or police officer; acting out storybook or television characters

Source: Rubin, Fein, & Vandenberg, 1983.

time. Also, both solitary and parallel play remain fairly stable from 3 to 6 years, accounting for as much of the child's play as cooperative interaction (Rubin, Fein, & Vandenberg, 1983).

We now understand that the *type,* not the amount, of solitary and parallel play changes in early childhood. In studies of preschoolers' play in Taiwan and the United States, researchers rated the *cognitive maturity* of nonsocial, parallel, and cooperative play, using the categories shown in Table 2.1 above. Within each play type, older children displayed more cognitively mature behavior than younger children (Pan, 1994; Rubin, Watson, & Jambor, 1978).

Often parents wonder if a preschooler who spends much time playing alone is developing normally. But only *certain types* of nonsocial activity—aimless wandering, hovering near peers, and functional play involving repetitive motor action—are cause for concern. Children who watch peers without playing are usually temperamentally inhibited—high in social fearfulness (Coplan et al., 2004; Rubin, Burgess, & Hastings, 2002). And preschoolers who engage in solitary, repetitive behavior (banging blocks, making a doll jump up and down) tend to be immature, impulsive children who find it difficult to regulate anger and aggression (Coplan et al., 2001). In the classroom, both reticent and impulsive children are at risk for rejection by their peers.

But most preschoolers with low rates of peer interaction simply like to play alone, and their solitary activities are positive and constructive. Children who prefer solitary play with art materials, puzzles, and building toys are typically well-adjusted youngsters who, when they do play with peers, show socially skilled behavior (Rubin & Coplan, 1998). Still, a few preschoolers who engage in such age-appropriate solitary play (mostly boys) are rebuffed by peers. Perhaps because their behavior is inconsistent with the "masculine" gender role, boys who play quietly are at risk for negative reactions from both parents and peers and, eventually, for adjustment problems (Coplan et al., 2001, 2004).

■ **CULTURAL VARIATIONS.** Peer sociability in collectivist societies, which stress group harmony, differs from that in individualistic cultures. For example, children in India generally play in large groups that require high levels of cooperation. Much of their behavior is imitative, occurs in unison, and in-

volves close physical contact. In a game called Bhatto Bhatto, children act out a script about a trip to the market, touching one another's elbows and hands as they pretend to cut and share a tasty vegetable (Roopnarine et al., 1994).

Furthermore, unlike North American preschoolers, who tend to reject reticent classmates, Chinese preschoolers are more willing to include a quiet, reserved child in play (Chen et al., 2006). We saw that until recently, collectivist values, which discourage self-assertion, led to a positive attitude toward shyness in China. Apparently, this benevolent stance is still evident in the play behaviors of Chinese young children.

© DORANNE JACOBSON

Village children in India, varying widely in age, play a "circle tapping" game to help one another learn that requires high levels of cooperation. The child in the center recites a poem, the alphabet, or numbers, then walks around the outside of the circle, saying, "Whomever I tap, whomever I tap, it will be their turn." The tapped child moves to the center to recite.

Cultural beliefs about the importance of play also affect early peer associations. Adults who view play as mere entertainment are less likely to provide props or to encourage pretend than those who value its cognitive and social benefits (Farver & Wimbarti, 1995). Preschoolers of Korean-American parents, who emphasize task persistence as vital for learning, spend less time than Caucasian-American children in joint make-believe and more time unoccupied and in parallel play (Farver, Kim, & Lee, 1995).

Recall the description of children's daily lives in village and tribal cultures, described on page 24 in Section 1. Mayan parents, for example, do not promote children's play—yet Mayan children are socially competent (Gaskins, 2000). Perhaps Western-style sociodramatic play, with its elaborate materials and wide-ranging themes, is particularly important for social development in societies where child and adult worlds are distinct. It may be less crucial when children participate in adult activities from an early age.

First Friendships

As preschoolers interact, first friendships form that serve as important contexts for emotional and social development. To adults, friendship is a mutual relationship involving companionship, sharing, understanding of thoughts and feelings, and caring for one another in times of need. In addition, mature friendships endure over time and survive occasional conflicts.

Preschoolers understand something about the uniqueness of friendship. They say that a friend is someone "who likes you" and with whom you spend a lot of time playing. Yet their ideas about friendship are far from mature. Four- to 7-year-olds regard friendship as pleasurable play and sharing of toys. As yet, friendship does not have a long-term, enduring quality based on mutual trust (Damon, 1988a; Hartup, 2006). Indeed, Sammy would declare, "Mark's my best friend," on days when the boys got along well. But when a dispute arose, he would reverse himself: "Mark, you're not my friend!"

Nevertheless, interactions between young friends are unique. Preschoolers give far more reinforcement—greetings, praise, and compliance—to children they identify as friends and also receive more from them. Friends are more emotionally expressive—talking, laughing, and looking at each other more often than nonfriends do (Hartup, 2006; Vaughn et al., 2001). Furthermore, children who begin kindergarten with friends in their class or readily make new friends adjust to school more favorably (Ladd, Birch, & Buhs, 1999; Ladd & Price, 1987). Perhaps the company of friends serves as a secure base from which to develop new relationships, enhancing children's feelings of comfort in the new classroom.

The ease with which kindergartners make new friends and are accepted by their classmates predicts cooperative participation in classroom activities and self-directed completion of learning tasks—behaviors linked to gains in achievement (Ladd, Birch, & Buhs, 1999; Ladd, Buhs, & Seid, 2000). The capacity to form friendships enables kindergartners to integrate themselves into classroom environments in ways that foster both academic and social competence. In a longitudinal follow-up of more than 900 4-year-olds, children of average intelligence but with above-average social skills fared better in academic achievement in first grade than children of equal mental ability who were socially below average (Konold & Pianta, 2005).

Because social maturity in early childhood contributes to later academic performance, a growing number of experts propose that kindergarten readiness be assessed in terms of not just academic skills but also social skills (Ladd, Herald, & Kochel, 2006; Thompson & Raikes, 2007). Preschool interventions, too, should attend to these vital social prerequisites.

Parental Influences on Early Peer Relations

Children first acquire skills for interacting with peers within the family. Parents influence children's peer sociability both *directly*, through attempts to influence children's peer relations, and *indirectly*, through their child-rearing practices and play behaviors (Ladd & Pettit, 2002; Rubin et al., 2005).

Parents influence preschoolers' peer interaction skills by offering advice, guidance, and examples of how to behave. These children receive a lesson in how to greet a friend by shaking hands.

© MICHAEL NEWMAN/PHOTOEDIT

■ **DIRECT PARENTAL INFLUENCES.** Preschoolers whose parents frequently arrange informal peer play activities tend to have larger peer networks and to be more socially skilled (Ladd, LeSieur, & Profilet, 1993). In providing play opportunities, parents show children how to initiate their own peer contacts. And parents' skillful suggestions for entering play groups and managing conflict are associated with preschoolers' social competence and peer acceptance (Mize & Pettit, 1997; Parke et al., 2004b).

■ **INDIRECT PARENTAL INFLUENCES.** Many parenting behaviors not directly aimed at promoting peer sociability nevertheless influence it. For example, secure attachments to parents are linked to more responsive, harmonious peer interaction, larger peer networks, and warmer, more supportive friendships during the preschool and school years (Laible, 2007; Lucas-Thompson & Clarke-Stewart, 2007; Wood, Emmerson, & Cowan, 2004). The sensitive, emotionally expressive communication that contributes to attachment security may be responsible.

Parent–child play is a particularly effective context for promoting peer-interaction. During play, parents interact with their child on a "level playing field," much as peers do. And perhaps because parents play more with children of their own sex, mothers' play is more strongly linked to daughters' competence, fathers' play to sons' competence (Lindsey & Mize, 2000; Pettit et al., 1998).

Some preschoolers already have great difficulty with peer relations. In Leslie's classroom, Robbie was one of them. Wherever he happened to be, comments like "Robbie ruined our block tower" and "Robbie hit me for no reason" could be heard. As we take up moral development in the next section, you will learn more about how parenting contributed to Robbie's peer problems.

ASK YOURSELF

>> **REVIEW**
Among children who spend much time playing alone, what factors distinguish those who are likely to have adjustment difficulties from those who are well-adjusted and socially skilled?

>> **APPLY**
Three-year-old Ben lives in the country, with no other preschoolers nearby. His parents wonder whether it is worth driving Ben into town once a week to participate in a peer play group. What advice would you give Ben's parents, and why?

>> **CONNECT**
How does emotional self-regulation affect the development of empathy and sympathy? Why are these emotional capacities vital for positive peer relations?

>> **REFLECT**
What did your parents do, directly and indirectly, that might have influenced your earliest peer relationships?

Foundations of Morality

Children's conversations and behavior provide many examples of their developing moral sense. By age 2, they use words to evaluate behavior as "good" or "bad" and react with distress to acts that are aggressive or that otherwise might do harm (Kochanska, Casey, & Fukumoto, 1995). And we have seen that children of this age share toys, help others, and cooperate in games—early indicators of considerate, responsible prosocial attitudes.

Adults everywhere take note of this budding capacity to distinguish right from wrong. Some cultures have special terms for it. The Utku Indians of Hudson Bay say the child develops *ihuma* (reason). The Fijians believe that *vakayalo* (sense) appears. In response, parents hold children more responsible for their behavior (Dunn, 2005). By the end of early childhood, children can state many moral rules: "Don't take someone's things without asking!" "Tell the truth!" In addition, they argue over matters of justice: "You sat there last time, so it's my turn." "It's not fair. He got more!"

All theories of moral development recognize that conscience begins to take shape in early childhood. And most agree that at first, the child's morality is *externally controlled* by adults. Gradually, it becomes regulated by *inner standards*. Truly moral individuals do not do the right thing just to conform to others' expectations. Rather, they have developed compassionate concerns and principles of good conduct, which they follow in many situations.

Each major theory emphasizes a different aspect of morality. Psychoanalytic theory stresses the *emotional side* of conscience development—in particular, identification and guilt as motivators of good conduct. Social learning theory focuses on how *moral behavior* is learned through reinforcement and modeling. Finally, the cognitive-developmental perspective emphasizes *thinking*—children's ability to reason about justice and fairness.

The Psychoanalytic Perspective

Recall that according to Freud, young children form a *superego*, or conscience, by *identifying* with the same-sex parent, whose moral standards they adopt. Children obey the superego to avoid *guilt*, a painful emotion that arises each time they are tempted to misbehave. Moral development, Freud believed, is largely complete by 5 to 6 years of age.

Today, most researchers disagree with Freud's view of conscience development. In his theory (see page 44), fear of punishment and loss of parental love motivate conscience formation and moral behavior (Tellings, 1999). Yet children whose parents frequently use threats, commands, or physical force tend to violate standards often and feel little guilt, whereas parental warmth and responsiveness predict greater guilt following transgressions (Kochanska et al., 2002, 2005, 2008). And if a parent withdraws love after misbehavior—for example, refuses to speak to or states a dislike for the child—children often respond with high levels of self-blame, thinking "I'm no good," or "Nobody loves me." Eventually, to protect themselves from overwhelming guilt, these children may deny the emotion and, as a result, also develop a weak conscience (Kochanska, 1991; Zahn-Waxler et al., 1990).

■ **INDUCTIVE DISCIPLINE.** In contrast, conscience formation is promoted by a type of discipline called **induction,** in which an adult helps the child notice feelings by pointing out the effects of the child's misbehavior on others. For example, a parent might say, "She's crying because you won't give back her doll" (Hoffman, 2000). When generally warm parents provide explanations that match the child's capacity to understand while firmly insisting that the child listen and comply, induction is effective as early as age 2. Preschoolers whose parents use it are more likely to refrain from wrongdoing, confess and repair damage after misdeeds, and display prosocial behavior (Kerr et al., 2004; Zahn-Waxler, Radke-Yarrow, & King, 1979).

The success of induction may lie in its power to motivate children's active commitment to moral standards. Induction gives children information about how to behave that they can use in future situations. By emphasizing the impact of the child's actions on others, it encourages empathy and sympathy (Krevans & Gibbs, 1996). And giving children reasons for changing their behavior encourages them to adopt moral standards because they make sense.

In contrast, discipline that relies too heavily on threats of punishment or withdrawal of love makes children so anxious and frightened that they cannot think clearly enough to figure out what they should do. As a result, these practices do not get children to internalize moral rules (Eisenberg, Fabes, & Spinrad, 2006).

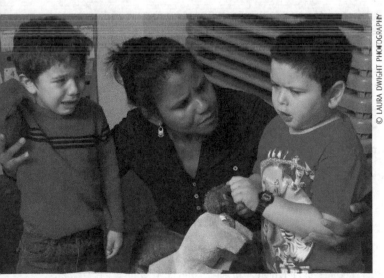

This teacher uses inductive discipline to explain to a child the impact of his transgression on others. She indicates how the child should behave, encouraging empathy and sympathetic concern.

© LAURA DWIGHT PHOTOGRAPHY

■ **THE CHILD'S CONTRIBUTION.** Although good discipline is crucial, children's characteristics also affect the success of parenting techniques. Twin studies suggest a modest genetic contribution to empathy (Knafo & Plomin, 2006; Zahn-Waxler et al., 2001). More empathic children require less power assertion and are more responsive to induction.

Temperament is also influential. Mild, patient tactics—requests, suggestions, and explanations—are sufficient to prompt guilt reactions in anxious, fearful preschoolers (Kochanska et al., 2002). But with fearless, impulsive children, gentle discipline has little impact. Power assertion also works poorly. It undermines the child's capacity for effortful control, which strongly predicts good conduct, empathy, sympathy, and prosocial behavior (Kochanska & Aksan, 2006; Kochanska & Knaack, 2003). Parents of impulsive children can foster conscience development by ensuring a secure attachment relationship and combining firm correction with induction (Kochanska, Aksan, & Joy, 2007). When children are so low in anxiety that parental disapproval causes them little discomfort, a close parent–child bond motivates them to listen to parents as a means of preserving an affectionate, supportive relationship.

■ **THE ROLE OF GUILT.** Although little support exists for Freudian ideas about conscience development, Freud was correct that guilt is an important motivator of moral action. Inducing *empathy-based guilt* (expressions of personal responsibility and regret, such as "I'm sorry I hurt him") by explaining that the child is harming someone and has disappointed the parent is a means of influencing children without using coercion. Empathy-based guilt reactions are associated with stopping harmful actions, repairing damage caused by misdeeds, and engaging in future prosocial behavior (Baumeister, 1998). At the same time, parents must help children deal with guilt feelings constructively—by guiding them to make up for immoral behavior rather than minimizing or excusing it.

But contrary to what Freud believed, guilt is not the only force that compels us to act morally. Nor is moral development complete by the end of early childhood. Rather, it is a gradual process, extending into adulthood.

Social Learning Theory

According to social learning theory, morality does not have a unique course of development. Rather, moral behavior is acquired just like any other set of responses: through reinforcement and modeling.

■ **THE IMPORTANCE OF MODELING.** Operant conditioning—reinforcement for good behavior, in the form of approval, affection, and other rewards—is not enough for children to acquire moral responses. To be reinforced, a behavior must first occur spontaneously. Yet many prosocial acts, such as sharing, helping, or comforting an unhappy playmate, occur so rarely at first that reinforcement cannot explain their rapid development in early childhood. Rather, social learning theorists believe that children learn to behave morally largely through *modeling*—observing and imitating people who demonstrate appropriate behavior (Bandura, 1977; Grusec, 1988). Once children acquire a moral response, such as sharing or telling the truth, reinforcement in the form of praise increases its frequency (Mills & Grusec, 1989).

Many studies show that having helpful or generous models increases young children's prosocial responses. And certain characteristics of models affect children's willingness to imitate:

- *Warmth and responsiveness.* Preschoolers are more likely to copy the prosocial actions of a warm, responsive adult than those of a cold, distant adult (Yarrow, Scott, & Waxler, 1973). Warmth seems to make children more attentive and receptive to the model and is itself an example of a prosocial response.

- *Competence and power.* Children admire and therefore tend to imitate competent, powerful models—especially older peers and adults (Bandura, 1977).

- *Consistency between assertions and behavior.* When models say one thing and do another—for example, announce that "it's important to help others" but rarely engage in helpful acts—children generally choose the most lenient standard of behavior that adults demonstrate (Mischel & Liebert, 1966).

Models are most influential in the early years. In one study, toddlers' eager, willing imitation of their mothers' behavior predicted moral conduct (not cheating in a game) and guilt following transgressions at age 3 (Forman, Aksan, & Kochanska, 2004). At the end of early childhood, children who have had consistent exposure to caring adults have internalized prosocial rules and follow them whether or not a model is present (Mussen & Eisenberg-Berg, 1977).

■ **THE EFFECTS OF PUNISHMENT.** Many parents know that yelling at, slapping, and spanking children for misbehavior are ineffective disciplinary tactics. A sharp reprimand or physical force to restrain or move a child is justified when immediate obedience is necessary—for example, when a 3-year-old is about to run into the street. In fact, parents are most likely to use forceful methods under these conditions. But to foster long-term goals, such as acting kindly toward others, they tend to rely on warmth and reasoning (Kuczynski, 1984). And in response to very serious transgressions, such as lying and stealing, they often combine power assertion with reasoning (Grusec, 2006; Grusec & Goodnow, 1994).

Frequent punishment, however, promotes only immediate compliance, not lasting changes in behavior. For example, Robbie's parents often hit, criticized, and shouted at him. But as soon as they were out of sight, Robbie usually engaged in the unacceptable behavior again. The more harsh threats, angry physical control, and physical punishment children experience, the more likely they are to develop serious, lasting mental health problems. These include weak internalization of moral rules;

depression, aggression, antisocial behavior, and poor academic performance in childhood and adolescence; and depression, alcohol abuse, criminality, and partner and child abuse in adulthood (Afifi et al., 2006; Bender et al., 2007; Gershoff, 2002a; Kochanska, Aksan, & Nichols, 2003; Lynch et al., 2006).

Parents with conflict-ridden marriages and with mental health problems (who are depressed or aggressive) are more likely to be punitive and also to have hard-to-manage children, whose disobedience evokes more parental harshness (Erath et al., 2006; Knafo & Plomin, 2006). These parent–child similarities suggest that heredity contributes to the link between punitive discipline and children's adjustment difficulties. But heredity is not a complete explanation. To review findings indicating that good parenting can shield children who are genetically at risk for aggression and antisocial activity from developing those behaviors. Furthermore, parental harshness and corporal punishment predict emotional and behavior problems in children of diverse temperaments (Mulvaney & Mebert, 2007). Negative outcomes are simply more pronounced among temperamentally difficult children.

In view of these findings, the widespread use of corporal punishment by American parents is cause for concern. A survey of a nationally representative sample of U.S. households revealed that although corporal punishment increases from infancy to age 5 and then declines, it is high at all ages (see Figure 2.1) (Straus & Stewart, 1999). Repeated use of physical punishment is more common with toddlers and preschoolers. And more than onefourth of physically punishing parents report having used a hard object, such as a brush or a belt (Gershoff, 2002b).

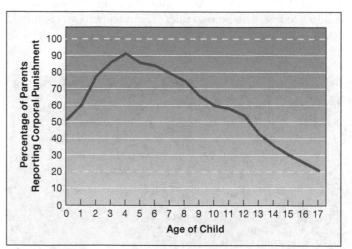

■ **FIGURE 2.1** ■ **Prevalence of corporal punishment by children's age.** Estimates are based on the percentage of parents in a nationally representative U.S. sample of nearly 1,000 reporting one or more instances of spanking, slapping, pinching, shaking, or hitting with a hard object in the past year. Physical punishment increases sharply during early childhood and then declines, but it is high at all ages. (From M. A. Straus & J. H. Stewart, 1999, "Corporal Punishment by American Parents: National Data on Prevalence, Chronicity, Severity, and Duration, in Relation to Child and Family Characteristics," *Clinical Child and Family Psychology Review, 2,* p. 59. Adapted with kind permission from Springer Science and Business Media and Murray Straus.)

▪ CULTURAL INFLUENCES ▪

Ethnic Differences in the Consequences of Physical Punishment

In an African-American community, six elders, who had volunteered to serve as mentors for parents facing child-rearing challenges, met to discuss parenting issues at a social service agency. Their attitudes toward discipline were strikingly different from those of the white social workers who had brought them together. Each elder argued that successful child rearing required the use of appropriate physical tactics. At the same time, they voiced strong disapproval of screaming or cursing at children, calling such out-of-control parental behavior "abusive." Ruth, the oldest and most respected member of the group, characterized good parenting as a complex combination of warmth, teaching, talking nicely, and disciplining physically. She related how an older neighbor advised her to handle her own children when she was a young parent:

> She said to me says, don't scream . . . you talk to them real nice and sweet and when they do something ugly . . . she say you get a nice little switch and you won't have any trouble with them and from that day that's the way I raised 'em. (Mosby et al., 1999, pp. 511–512)

Use of physical punishment is highest among low-SES ethnic minority parents, who are more likely than middle-SES white parents to advocate slaps and spankings (Pinderhughes et al., 2000; Straus & Stewart, 1999). And although corporal punishment is linked to a wide array of negative child outcomes, exceptions do exist.

In one longitudinal study, researchers followed several hundred families for 12 years, collecting information from mothers on disciplinary strategies in early and middle childhood and from both mothers and their children on youth problem behaviors in adolescence. Even after many child and family characteristics were controlled, the findings were striking: In Caucasian-American families, physical punishment was positively associated with adolescent aggression and antisocial behavior. In African-American families, by contrast, the more mothers had disciplined physically in childhood, the less their teenagers displayed angry, acting-out behavior and got in trouble at school and with the police (Lansford et al., 2004).

African-American and Caucasian-American parents seem to mete out physical punishment differently. In black families, such discipline is typically culturally approved, mild, delivered in a context of parental warmth, and aimed at helping children become responsible adults. White parents, in contrast, typically consider physical punishment to be wrong, so when they resort to it, they are often highly agitated and rejecting of the child (Dodge, McLoyd, & Lansford, 2006). As a result, most black children may view spanking as a practice carried out with their best interests in mind, whereas white children may regard it as an "act of personal aggression" (Gunnoe & Mariner, 1997, p. 768).

In support of this view, when several thousand ethnically diverse children were followed from the preschool through the early school years, spanking was associated with a rise in behavior problems if parents were cold and rejecting, but not if they were warm and supportive (McLoyd & Smith, 2002). And in another study, spanking predicted depressive symptoms only among a minority of African-American children whose mothers disapproved of the practice and, as a result, tended to use it when they were highly angry and frustrated (McLoyd et al., 2007).

These findings are not an endorsement of physical punishment. Other forms of discipline, including time out, withdrawal of privileges, and the positive strategies listed on page 56, are far more effective. But it is noteworthy that the meaning and impact of physical discipline vary sharply with cultural context.

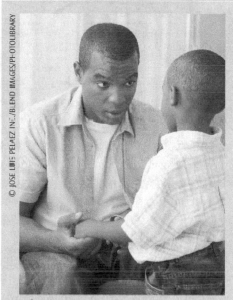

In African-American families, physical discipline is typically culturally approved, mild, and delivered in a context of parental warmth. As a result, African-American children may view spanking as a practice carried out with their best interests in mind, not as an act of aggression.

A prevailing North American belief is that corporal punishment, if implemented by caring parents, is harmless, perhaps even beneficial. But as the Cultural Influences box above reveals, this assumption is valid only under conditions of limited use in certain social contexts.

Repeated harsh punishment has wide-ranging, undesirable side effects:

- Parents often spank in response to children's aggression (Holden, Coleman, & Schmidt, 1995). Yet the punishment itself models aggression!

- Harshly treated children develop a chronic sense of being personally threatened, which prompts a focus on their own distress rather than a sympathetic orientation to others' needs.

- Children who are frequently punished soon learn to avoid the punishing adult, who, as a result, has little opportunity to teach desirable behaviors.

- By stopping children's misbehavior temporarily, harsh punishment gives adults immediate relief. For this reason, a punitive adult is likely to punish with greater frequency over time, a course of action that can spiral into serious abuse.

- Adults whose parents used corporal punishment are more accepting of such discipline (Bower-Russa, Knutson, & Winebarger, 2001; Deater-Deckard et al., 2003). In this way, use of physical punishment may transfer to the next generation.

Applying What We Know

Using Positive Discipline

Strategy	Explanation
Use transgressions as opportunities to teach.	When a child engages in harmful or unsafe behavior, intervene firmly, and then use induction, which motivates children to make amends and behave prosocially.
Reduce opportunities for misbehavior.	On a long car trip, bring back-seat activities that relieve children's restlessness. At the supermarket, converse with children and let them help with shopping. As a result, children learn to occupy themselves constructively when options are limited.
Provide reasons for rules.	When children appreciate that rules are fair to all concerned, not arbitrary, they strive to follow the rules because these are reasonable and rational.
Arrange for children to participate in family routines and duties.	By joining with adults in preparing a meal, washing dishes, or raking leaves, children develop a sense of responsible participation in family and community life and acquire many practical skills.
When children are obstinate, try compromising and problem solving.	When a child refuses to obey, express understanding of the child's feelings ("I know it's not fun to clean up"), suggest a compromise ("You put those away, I'll take care of these"), and help the child think of ways to avoid the problem in the future. Responding firmly but kindly and respectfully increases the likelihood of willing cooperation.
Encourage mature behavior.	Express confidence in children's capacity to learn and appreciation for effort and cooperation, as in "You gave that your best!" "Thanks for helping!" Adult encouragement fosters pride and satisfaction in succeeding, thereby inspiring children to improve further.

■ **ALTERNATIVES TO HARSH PUNISHMENT.** Alternatives to criticism, slaps, and spankings can reduce the side effects of punishment. A technique called **time out** involves removing children from the immediate setting—for example, by sending them to their rooms—until they are ready to act appropriately. When a child is out of control, a few minutes in time out can be enough to change behavior while also giving angry parents a cooling-off period. Another approach is *withdrawal of privileges,* such as watching a favorite TV program. Like time out, removing privileges allows parents to avoid harsh techniques that can easily intensify into violence.

When parents decide to use punishment, they can increase its effectiveness in three ways:

■ *Consistency.* Permitting children to act inappropriately on some occasions but scolding them on others confuses them, and the unacceptable act persists (Acker & O'Leary, 1996).

■ A *warm parent–child relationship.* Children of involved, caring parents find the interruption in parental affection that accompanies punishment especially unpleasant. They want to regain parental warmth and approval as quickly as possible.

■ *Explanations.* Providing reasons for mild punishment helps children relate the misdeed to expectations for future behavior. This approach leads to a far greater reduction in misbehavior than using punishment alone (Larzelere et al., 1996).

■ **POSITIVE DISCIPLINE.** The most effective forms of discipline encourage good conduct—by building a mutually respectful bond with the child, letting the child know ahead of time how to act, and praising mature behavior (Zahn-Waxler & Robinson, 1995). When sensitivity, cooperation, and shared positive emotion are evident in joint activities between parents and preschoolers, children show firmer conscience development—expressing empathy after transgressions, playing fairly in games, and considering others' welfare (Kochanska et al., 2005, 2008). Parent–child closeness leads children to heed parental demands because the child feels a sense of commitment to the relationship.

Consult Applying What We Know above for ways to discipline positively. Parents who use these strategies focus on long-

© STOCK4B/GETTY IMAGES

Parents who engage in positive discipline encourage good conduct and reduce opportunities for misbehavior. By bringing along toys and joining in his make-believe, this mother helps her young child behave appropriately during a long wait at the airport.

term social and life skills—cooperation, problem solving, and consideration for others. As a result, they greatly reduce the need for punishment.

The Cognitive-Developmental Perspective

The psychoanalytic and behaviorist approaches to morality focus on how children acquire ready-made standards of good conduct from adults. In contrast, the cognitive-developmental perspective regards children as *active thinkers* about social rules. As early as the preschool years, children make moral judgments, deciding what is right or wrong on the basis of concepts they construct about justice and fairness (Gibbs, 2010; Turiel, 2006).

Young children have some well-developed ideas about morality. As long as researchers emphasize people's intentions, 3-year-olds say that a person with bad intentions—someone who deliberately frightens, embarrasses, or otherwise hurts another—is more deserving of punishment than a well-intentioned person (Helwig, Zelazo, & Wilson, 2001; Jones & Thompson, 2001). Around age 4, children know that a person who expresses an insincere intention—says, "I'll come over and help you rake leaves" but doesn't intend to do so—is lying (Maas, 2008). And 4-year-olds approve of telling the truth and disapprove of lying, even when a lie remains undetected (Bussey, 1992).

Furthermore, preschoolers distinguish **moral imperatives,** which protect people's rights and welfare, from two other types of rules and expectations: **social conventions,** customs determined solely by consensus, such as table manners and politeness rituals (saying "please," "thank you"); and **matters of personal choice,** such as choice of friends, hairstyle, and leisure activities, which do not violate rights and are up to the individual (Killen, Margie, & Sinno, 2006; Nucci, 1996; Smetana, 2006). Interviews with 3- and 4-year-olds reveal that they judge moral violations (stealing an apple) as more wrong than violations of social conventions (eating ice cream with your fingers). And preschoolers' concern with personal choice, conveyed through such statements as "I'm gonna wear *this* shirt," serves as the springboard for moral concepts of individual rights, which will expand greatly in middle childhood and adolescence (Nucci, 2005).

Within the moral domain, however, preschool and young school-age children tend to reason *rigidly,* making judgments based on salient features and consequences while neglecting other important information. For example, they are more likely than older children to claim that stealing and lying are always wrong, even when a person has a morally sound reason for engaging in these acts (Lourenco, 2003). They view inflicting physical damage (breaking a peer's toy) as a more serious transgression than treating others unfairly (not sharing) (Nucci, 2002). And their focus on outcomes means that they fail to realize that a promise is still a promise, even if it is unfulfilled (Maas, 2008; Maas & Abbeduto, 2001).

Still, preschoolers' ability to distinguish moral imperatives from social conventions is impressive. How do they do so? According to cognitive-developmental theorists, they *actively make sense* of their experiences (Turiel, 2006). They observe that after a moral offense, peers respond with strong negative emotion, describe their own injury or loss, tell another child to stop, or retaliate. And an adult who intervenes is likely to call attention to the rights and feelings of the victim. In contrast, violations of social convention elicit less intense peer reactions. And in these situations, adults usually demand obedience without explanation or point to the importance of keeping order.

Cognition and language support preschoolers' moral understanding, but social experiences are vital. Disputes with siblings and peers over rights, possessions, and property allow preschoolers to negotiate, compromise, and work out their first ideas about justice and fairness (Killen & Nucci, 1995). Children also learn by observing the way adults handle rule violations and discuss moral issues. Children who are advanced in moral thinking tend to have parents who adapt their communications about fighting, honesty, and ownership to what their children can understand, tell stories with moral implications, encourage prosocial behavior, and gently stimulate the child to think further, without being hostile or critical (Janssens & Deković, 1997; Walker & Taylor, 1991a).

Preschoolers who verbally and physically assault others, often with little or no provocation, are already delayed in moral reasoning (Helwig & Turiel, 2004; Sanderson & Siegal, 1988). Without special help, such children show long-term disruptions in moral development, deficits in self-control, and ultimately an antisocial lifestyle.

The Other Side of Morality: Development of Aggression

Beginning in late infancy, all children display aggression at times. As interactions with siblings and peers increase, so do aggressive outbursts (Dodge, Coie, & Lynam, 2006; Tremblay, 2004). By the second year, two general types of aggression emerge. Initially, the most common is **proactive** (or *instrumental*) **aggression,** in which children act to fulfill a need or desire—obtain an object, privilege, space, or social reward, such as adult or peer attention—and unemotionally attack a person to achieve their goal. The other type, **reactive** (or *hostile*) **aggression,** is an angry, defensive response to provocation or a blocked goal and is meant to hurt another person (Dodge, Coie, & Lynam, 2006; Little et al., 2003).

Proactive and reactive aggression come in three forms, which are the focus of the majority of research:

- **Physical aggression** harms others through physical injury—pushing, hitting, kicking, or punching others or destroying another's property.
- **Verbal aggression** harms others through threats of physical aggression, name-calling, or hostile teasing.
- **Relational aggression** damages another's peer relationships through social exclusion, malicious gossip, or friendship manipulation.

Although verbal aggression is always direct, physical and relational aggression can be either *direct* or *indirect.* For example, hitting injures a person directly, whereas destroying property indirectly inflicts physical harm. Similarly, saying, "Do what I say, or I won't be your friend," conveys relational aggression directly, while spreading rumors, refusing to talk to a peer, or manipulating friendships by saying behind someone's back, "Don't play with her; she's a nerd," does so indirectly.

In early childhood, verbal aggression gradually replaces physical aggression (Alink et al., 2006; Tremblay et al., 1999). And proactive aggression declines as preschoolers' improved capacity to delay gratification enables them to avoid grabbing others' possessions. But reactive aggression in verbal and relation forms tends to rise over early and middle childhood (Côté et al., 2007; Tremblay, 2000). Older children are better able to recognize malicious intentions and, as a result, more often respond in hostile ways.

By age 17 months, boys are more physically aggressive than girls—a difference found throughout childhood in many cultures (Baillargeon et al., 2007; Card et al., 2008). The sex difference is due in part to biology—in particular, to male sex hormones (androgens) and temperamental traits (activity level, irritability, impulsivity) on which boys score higher. Gender-role conformity is also important. As soon as preschoolers are aware of gender stereotypes—that males and females are expected to behave differently—physical aggression drops off more sharply in girls than in boys (Fagot & Leinbach, 1989). Parents also respond far more negatively to physical fighting in girls (Arnold, McWilliams, & Harvey-Arnold, 1998).

Although girls have a reputation for being both more verbally and relationally aggressive than boys, the sex difference is small (Crick et al., 2004, 2006; Crick, Ostrov, & Werner, 2006). Beginning in the preschool years, girls concentrate most of their aggressive acts in the relational category. Boys inflict harm in more variable ways: Physically and verbally aggressive boys also tend to be relationally aggressive (Card et al., 2008). Therefore, boys display overall rates of aggression that are much higher than girls'.

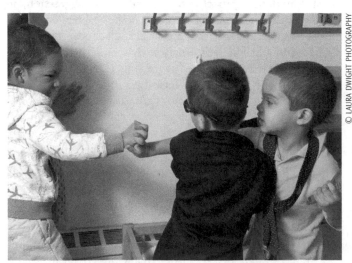

As early as 17 months of age, boys are more physically aggressive than girls—a difference found throughout childhood in many cultures.

At the same time, girls more often use indirect relational tactics that—in disrupting intimate bonds especially important to girls—can be particularly mean. Whereas physical attacks are usually brief, acts of indirect relational aggression may extend for hours, weeks, or even months (Nelson, Robinson, & Hart, 2005; Underwood, 2003). In one instance, a 6-year-old girl formed a "pretty-girls club" and—for nearly an entire school year—convinced its members to exclude several classmates by saying they were "dirty and smelly."

An occasional aggressive exchange between preschoolers is normal. But children who are emotionally negative, impulsive, and disobedient are prone to early, high rates of physical or relational aggression (or both) that often persist, resulting in serious conduct problems in middle childhood and adolescence (Côté et al., 2007; Vaillancourt et al., 2003). These negative outcomes, however, depend on child-rearing conditions.

■ **THE FAMILY AS TRAINING GROUND FOR AGGRESSIVE BEHAVIOR.** "I can't control him, he's impossible," Robbie's mother, Nadine, complained to Leslie one day. When Leslie asked if Robbie might be troubled by something happening at home, she discovered that his parents fought constantly and resorted to harsh, inconsistent discipline. The same child-rearing practices that undermine moral internalization—love withdrawal, power assertion, physical punishment, and inconsistency—are linked to aggression from early childhood through adolescence, in children of both sexes and in many cultures, with most of these practices predicting both physical and relational forms (Bradford et al., 2003; Côté et al., 2007; Nelson et al., 2006a; Rubin et al., 2003; Yang et al., 2004).

In families like Robbie's, anger and punitiveness quickly create a conflict-ridden family atmosphere and an "out-of-control" child. The pattern begins with forceful discipline, which occurs more often with stressful life experiences, a parent with an unstable personality, or a difficult child (Dodge, Coie, & Lynam, 2006). Typically, the parent threatens, criticizes, and punishes, and the child whines, yells, and refuses until the parent "gives in." As these cycles become more frequent, they generate anxiety and irritability among other family members, who soon join in the hostile interactions. Compared with siblings in typical families, preschool siblings who have critical, punitive parents are more aggressive to one another. Destructive sibling conflict, in turn, quickly spreads to peer relationships, contributing to poor impulse control and antisocial behavior by the early school years (Garcia et al., 2000; Ostrov, Crick, & Stauffacher, 2006).

Boys are more likely than girls to be targets of harsh, inconsistent discipline because they are more active and impulsive and therefore harder to control. Children who are products of these family processes come to view the world from a violent perspective, seeing hostile intent where it does not exist (Lochman & Dodge, 1998; Orbio de Castro et al., 2002). As a result, they make many unprovoked attacks and soon conclude that aggression "works" to control others.

Highly aggressive children tend to be rejected by peers, to fail in school, and (by adolescence) to seek out deviant peer groups that lead them toward violent delinquency and adult criminality. We will consider this life-course path of antisocial activity.

■ **VIOLENT MEDIA AND AGGRESSION.** In the United States, 57 percent of television programs between 6 A.M. and 11 P.M. contain violent scenes, often portraying repeated aggressive acts that go unpunished. TV victims of violence are rarely shown experiencing serious harm, and few programs condemn violence or depict other ways of solving problems. Violent content is 9 percent above average in children's programming, and cartoons are the most violent (Center for Communication and Social Policy, 1998).

Reviewers of thousands of studies have concluded that TV violence increases the likelihood of hostile thoughts and emotions and of verbally, physically, and relationally aggressive behavior (Comstock & Scharrer, 2006; Ostrov, Gentile, & Crick, 2006). And a growing number of studies show that playing violent video and computer games has similar effects (Anderson, 2004). Although young people of all ages are susceptible, preschool and young school-age children are especially likely to imitate TV violence because they believe much TV fiction is real and accept what they see uncritically.

Violent programming not only creates short-term difficulties in parent and peer relations but also has lasting negative consequences. In several longitudinal studies, time spent watching TV in childhood and adolescence predicted aggressive behavior in adulthood, after other factors linked to TV viewing (such as prior child and parent aggression, IQ, parent education, family income, and neighborhood crime) were controlled (see Figure 2.2) (Graber et al., 2006; Huesmann, 1986; Huesmann et al., 2003; Johnson et al., 2002). Aggressive children and adolescents have a

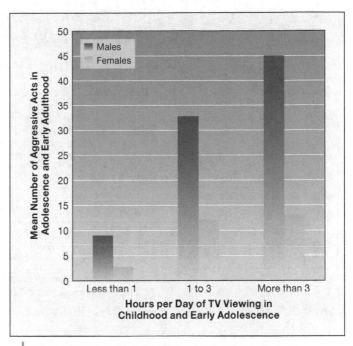

■ **FIGURE 2.2** ■ **Relationship of television viewing in childhood and early adolescence to aggressive acts in adolescence and early adulthood.** Interviews with more than 700 parents and youths revealed that the more TV watched in childhood and early adolescence, the greater the annual number of aggressive acts committed by the young person, as reported in follow-up interviews at ages 16 and 22. (Adapted from Johnson et al., 2002.)

greater appetite for violent TV and computer games. And boys devote more time to violent media than girls, in part because of male-oriented themes of conquest and adventure and use of males as lead characters. But even in nonaggressive children, violent TV sparks hostile thoughts and behavior; its impact is simply less intense (Bushman & Huesmann, 2001).

Furthermore, media violence "hardens" children to aggression. Viewers quickly habituate, responding with reduced arousal to real-world instances and tolerating more aggression in others (Anderson et al., 2003). Heavy viewers believe that there is much more violence in society than actually exists—an effect that is especially strong for children who perceive media violence to be relevant to their own lives (Donnerstein, Slaby, & Eron, 1994). As these responses indicate, exposure to violent media modifies children's attitudes toward social reality so they increasingly match media images.

The ease with which television and computer games can manipulate children's beliefs and behavior has led to strong public pressure to improve its content. In the United States, the First Amendment right to free speech has hampered efforts to regulate TV content. Instead, all programs must be rated for violent and sexual content, and all new TV sets are required to contain the V-chip, which allows parents to block undesired material. In contrast, Canada's nationwide broadcasting code bans from children's shows realistic scenes of violence that minimize

TV violence increases the likelihood of hostile thoughts and emotions and tolerance of real-world aggression. And playing violent video and computer games has similar effects.

Applying What We Know

Regulating TV and Computer Use

Strategy	Description
Limit TV viewing and computer use.	Provide clear rules limiting what children can view on TV and do on the computer, and stick to them. Avoid using the TV or the computer as a babysitter for children. Do not place a TV or a computer in a child's bedroom; doing so substantially increases use and makes the child's activity hard to monitor.
Avoid using TV or computer time as a reward.	When TV or computer access is used to reward or withheld as a punishment, children become increasingly attracted to it.
When possible, watch TV with children.	When adults raise questions about realism in TV depictions, express disapproval of on-screen behavior, and encourage discussion, they help children understand and evaluate TV content.
Link TV content to everyday learning experiences.	Parents can extend TV learning in ways that encourage children to engage actively with their surroundings. For example, a program on animals might spark a trip to the zoo, a visit to the library for a book about animals, or new ways of observing and caring for the family pet.
Model good TV and computer practices.	Parents' media behavior—avoiding excessive TV and computer use and limiting exposure to harmful content—influences their children's media behavior.

consequences and cartoons with violence as the central theme. Further, violent programming intended for adults cannot be shown on Canadian channels before 9 P.M. (Canadian children, however, can access violent TV fare on U.S. channels.)

At present, parents bear most responsibility for regulating their children's exposure to media violence and other inappropriate content. Besides TV and computer games, the Internet poses risks. As with the V-chip for TV, parents can control children's Internet access by using filters or programs that monitor website visits. Yet surveys of U.S. parents indicate that 20 to 30 percent of preschoolers and 40 percent of school-age children experience no limits on TV or computer use at home. Some children begin accessing websites without parental supervision as early as age 4 (Rideout & Hamel, 2006; Roberts, Foehr, & Rideout, 2005; Varnhagen, 2007). Applying What We Know above lists strategies parents can use to protect their children from undesirable TV and computer fare.

■ **HELPING CHILDREN AND PARENTS CONTROL AGGRES-SION.** Treatment for aggressive children is best begun early, before their antisocial behavior becomes well-practiced and difficult to change. Breaking the cycle of hostilities between family members and promoting effective ways of relating to others are crucial.

Leslie suggested that Robbie's parents see a family therapist, who observed their inept practices and coached them in alternatives. They learned not to give in to Robbie, to pair commands with reasons, and to replace verbal insults and harsh physical punishment with more effective strategies, such as time out and withdrawal of privileges. After several weeks of such training, children's aggression declines, and parents view their children more positively—benefits still evident one to four years later (Kazdin, 2003; Patterson & Fisher, 2002).

Leslie also began coaching Robbie in emotional competence (see page 46) and in how to interact successfully with

peers. When opportunities arose, she encouraged Robbie to talk about a playmate's feelings and to express his own. As Robbie practiced taking the perspective of others and feeling sympathetic concern, his angry lashing out at peers declined (Izard et al., 2004). Robbie participated in social problem-solving training as well. Over several months, he met with Leslie and a small group of classmates to act out common conflicts using puppets, discuss alternatives for resolving disputes, and practice successful strategies. Children who receive such training show gains in social competence still present several months later (Shure & Aberson, 2005).

Finally, Robbie's parents sought counseling for their marital problems. When parents receive help in coping with stressors in their own lives, interventions aimed at reducing children's aggression are even more effective (Kazdin & Whitley, 2003).

ASK YOURSELF

>> **REVIEW**
What experiences help children differentiate moral imperatives, social conventions, and matters of personal choice?

>> **APPLY**
Alice and Wayne want their two children to become morally mature, caring individuals. List some parenting practices they should use and some they should avoid.

>> **CONNECT**
What must parents do to foster conscience development in fearless, impulsive children? Does this remind you of the concept of goodness of fit? Explain.

>> **REFLECT**
Which types of punishment for a misbehaving preschooler do you endorse, and which types do you reject? Why?

Gender Typing

Gender typing refers to any association of objects, activities, roles, or traits with one sex or the other in ways that conform to cultural stereotypes (Liben & Bigler, 2002). In Leslie's classroom, girls spent more time in the housekeeping, art, and reading corners, while boys gathered more often in spaces devoted to blocks, woodworking, and active play. Already, the children had acquired many gender-linked beliefs and preferences and tended to play with peers of their own sex.

The same theories that provide accounts of morality have been used to explain children's gender typing: *social learning theory*, with its emphasis on modeling and reinforcement, and *cognitive-developmental theory*, with its focus on children as active thinkers about their social world. We will see that neither is adequate by itself. *Gender schema theory*, a third perspective that combines elements of both, has gained favor. In the following sections, we consider the early development of gender typing.

Gender-Stereotyped Beliefs and Behavior

Even before children can label their own sex consistently, they have begun to acquire common associations with gender— men as rough and sharp, women as soft and round. In one study, 18-month-olds linked such items as fir trees and hammers with males, although they had not yet learned comparable feminine associations (Eichstedt et al., 2002). Around age 2, children use such words as *boy*, *girl*, *lady*, and *man* appropriately. As soon as gender categories are established, children sort out what they mean in terms of activities and behavior.

Preschoolers associate toys, articles of clothing, tools, household items, games, occupations, colors (blue and pink), and behaviors (physical and relational aggression) with one sex or the other (Giles & Heyman, 2005; Poulin-Dubois et al., 2002; Ruble, Martin, & Berenbaum, 2006). And their actions reflect their beliefs, not only in play preferences but in personality traits as well. As we have seen, boys tend to be more active, impulsive, assertive, and physically aggressive. Girls tend to be more fearful, dependent, emotionally sensitive, compliant, advanced in effortful control, and skilled at understanding self-conscious emotions and at inflicting indirect relational aggression (Bosacki & Moore, 2004; Else-Quest et al., 2006; Underwood, 2003).

During early childhood, children's gender-stereotyped beliefs strengthen—so much so that many children apply them as blanket rules rather than as flexible guidelines. When children were asked whether gender stereotypes could be violated, half or more of 3- and 4-year-olds answered "no" to clothing, hairstyle, and play with certain toys (such as Barbie dolls and GI Joes) (Blakemore, 2003). Furthermore, most 3- to 6-year-olds are firm about not wanting to be friends with a child who violates a gender stereotype (a boy who wears nail polish, a girl who plays with trucks) or to attend a school where such violations are allowed (Ruble et al., 2007).

The rigidity of preschoolers' gender stereotypes helps us understand some commonly observed everyday behaviors. When Leslie showed her class a picture of a Scottish bagpiper wearing a kilt, the children insisted, "Men don't wear skirts!" During free play, they often exclaimed that girls can't be police officers and boys don't take care of babies. These one-sided judgments are a joint product of gender stereotyping in the environment and young children's cognitive limitations (Trautner et al., 2005). Most preschoolers do not yet realize that characteristics *associated with* being male or female—activities, toys, occupations, hairstyle, and clothing—do not *determine* a person's sex.

Genetic Influences on Gender Typing

The sex differences just described appear in many cultures around the world (Munroe & Romney, 2006; Whiting & Edwards, 1988). Certain ones—male activity level and physical aggression, female emotional sensitivity, and preference for same-sex playmates—are widespread among mammalian species (de Waal, 1993, 2001). According to an evolutionary perspective, the adult life of our male ancestors was largely oriented toward competing for mates, that of our female ancestors toward rearing children. Therefore, males became genetically primed for dominance and females for intimacy, responsiveness, and cooperativeness. Evolutionary theorists claim that family and cultural forces can influence the intensity of biologically based sex differences. But experience cannot eradicate those aspects of gender typing that served adaptive functions in human history (Geary, 1999; Maccoby, 2002).

© LAURA DWIGHT PHOTOGRAPHY

Early in the preschool years, gender typing is well under way. Girls tend to play with girls and are drawn to toys and activities that emphasize nurturance, cooperation, and physical attractiveness.

Experiments with animals reveal that prenatally administered androgens increase active play and aggression and suppress maternal caregiving in both male and female mammals (Sato et al., 2004). Eleanor Maccoby (1998) argues that hormones also affect human play styles, leading to rough, noisy movements among boys and calm, gentle actions among girls. Then, as children interact with peers, they choose partners whose interests and behaviors are compatible with their own. Preschool girls increasingly seek out other girls and like to play in pairs because they share a preference for quieter activities involving cooperative roles. Boys come to prefer larger-group play with other boys, who share a desire to run, climb, play-fight, compete, and build up and knock down (Fabes, Martin, & Hanish, 2003). At age 4, children spend three times as much time with same-sex as with other-sex playmates. By age 6, this ratio has climbed to 11 to 1 (Martin & Fabes, 2001).

Even stronger support for the role of biology in human gender typing comes from research on girls exposed prenatally to high levels of androgens, due either to normal variation in hormone levels or to a genetic defect. In both instances, these girls showed more "masculine" behavior—a preference for trucks and blocks over dolls, for active over quiet play, and for boys as playmates—even when parents encouraged them to engage in gender-typical play (Cohen-Bendahan, van de Beek, & Berenbaum, 2005; Pasterski et al., 2005).

And additional evidence for the role of biology in gender typing comes from a case study of a boy who experienced serious sexual-identity and adjustment problems because his biological makeup and sex of rearing were at odds. Turn to the Lifespan Vista box on the following page to find out about David's development.

Environmental Influences on Gender Typing

In a study following almost 14,000 British children from ages 2½ to 8, gender-typed behavior rose steadily over early childhood, with the most gender-typed young preschoolers showing the sharpest increase (Golombok et al., 2008). A wealth of evidence reveals that environmental forces—at home, at school, and in the community—build on genetic influences to promote vigorous gender typing in early childhood.

■ **PARENTS.**   Beginning at birth, parents have different expectations of sons than of daughters. Many parents prefer that their children play with "gender-appropriate" toys. And they tend to describe achievement, competition, and control of emotion as important for sons and warmth, "ladylike" behavior, and closely supervised activities as important for daughters (Brody, 1999; Turner & Gervai, 1995).

Actual parenting practices reflect these beliefs. Parents give their sons toys that stress action and competition (guns, cars, tools, footballs) and their daughters toys that emphasize nurturance, cooperation, and physical attractiveness (dolls, tea sets, jewelry) (Leaper, 1994; Leaper & Friedman, 2007). Parents also actively reinforce independence in boys and closeness and

dependency in girls. For example, parents react more positively when a son plays with cars and trucks, demands attention, runs and climbs, or tries to take toys from others. When interacting with daughters, they more often direct play activities, provide help, encourage participation in household tasks, make supportive statements (approval, praise, and agreement), and refer to emotions (Clearfield & Nelson, 2006; Fagot & Hagan, 1991; Kuebli, Butler, & Fivush, 1995; Leaper et al., 1995). Gender-typed play contexts amplify these communication differences. For example, when playing housekeeping, mothers engage in high rates of supportive, emotion talk with girls (Leaper, 2000).

Furthermore, parents provide children with indirect cues about gender categories and stereotypes through the language they use. In one study, researchers observed mothers talking about picture books with their 2- to 6-year-olds (Gelman, Taylor, & Nguyen, 2004). Mothers often labeled gender, even when they did not have to do so ("That's a boy." "Is that a she?"). And they frequently expressed *generic utterances,* which referred to many, or nearly all, males or females as alike, ignoring exceptions: "Boys can be sailors." "Most girls don't like trucks." As Figure 2.3 shows, with age, both mothers and children produced more of these generic statements. At age 2, mothers introduced these sweeping generalizations nearly three times as often as children. By age 6, children were producing these generics more often than mothers, suggesting that children picked up many of these expressions from parental speech. And 4- to 6-year-olds frequently made stereotyped generic statements, which their mothers often affirmed (*Child:* "Only boys can drive trucks." *Mother:* "OK.").

Of the two sexes, boys are more gender-typed. Fathers, especially, are more insistent that boys conform to gender roles. They place more pressure to achieve on sons than on daughters

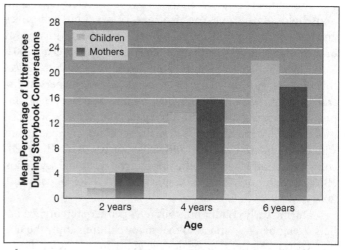

■ **FIGURE 2.3** ■ **Mothers' and children's use of generic reference to gender during storybook conversations.** Mothers' and children's use of generics increased dramatically between ages 2 and 6. At age 2, mothers produced more generics than children. By age 6, children produced more generics than mothers. (From S. A. Gelman, M. G. Taylor, & S. P. Nguyen, "Mother–Child Conversations About Gender," *Monographs of the Society for Research in Child Development,* 69[1, Serial No. 275], p. 46. Reprinted by permission of Wiley-Blackwell Publishers.)

■ A LIFESPAN VISTA: Looking Forward, Looking Back ■

David: A Boy Who Was Reared as a Girl

As a married man and father in his mid-thirties, David Reimer talked freely about his everyday life: his problems at work and the challenges of child rearing. But when asked about his first 15 years, he distanced himself, speaking as if the child of his early life were another person. In essence, she was.

David—named Bruce at birth—underwent the first infant sex reassignment ever reported on a genetically and hormonally normal child. To find out about David's development, researchers interviewed him intensively and studied his medical and psychotherapy records (Colapinto, 2001; Diamond & Sigmundson, 1999).

When Bruce was 8 months old, his penis was accidentally severed during circumcision. Soon afterward, his desperate parents heard about psychologist John Money's success in assigning a sex to children born with ambiguous genitals. They traveled from their home in Canada to Johns Hopkins University in Baltimore, where, under Money's oversight, 22-month-old Bruce had surgery to remove his testicles and sculpt his genitals to look like those of a girl. The operation complete, Bruce's parents named their daughter Brenda.

Brenda's upbringing was tragic. From the outset, she resisted her parents' efforts to steer her in a "feminine" direction. A dominant, rough-and-tumble child, Brenda picked fights with other children and usually won. Brian (Brenda's identical twin brother) recalled that Brenda looked like a delicate, pretty girl—until she moved or spoke: "She walked like a guy. Sat with her legs apart. She talked about guy things. . . . She played with my toys: Tinkertoys, dump trucks" (Colapinto, 2001, p. 57).

At school, Brenda's boyish behavior led classmates to taunt and tease her. When she played with girls, she tried organizing large-group, active games, but they weren't interested. Friendless and uncomfortable as a girl, Brenda increasingly displayed behavior problems. During periodic medical follow-ups, she drew pictures of herself as a boy and refused additional surgery to create a vagina.

As adolescence approached, Brenda's parents moved her from school to school and from therapist to therapist in an effort to help her fit in socially and accept a female identity—pressures that only increased Brenda's anxiety and conflict with her parents. At puberty, when Brenda's shoulders broadened and her body added muscle, her parents

Because of a medical accident when he was a baby, David Reimer underwent the first sex reassignment on a genetically and hormonally normal child. He was reared as a girl. David's case shows the overwhelming impact of biology on gender identity. At age 36, as shown here, he was a married man and father. But two years later, the troubled life that sprang from David's childhood ended tragically, in suicide.

insisted that she begin estrogen therapy to feminize her appearance. Soon she grew breasts and added fat around her waist and hips. Repelled by her feminizing shape, Brenda began overeating to hide it. Her classmates reacted to her confused appearance with stepped-up brutality.

At last, Brenda was transferred to a therapist who recognized her despair and encouraged her parents to tell her about her infancy. When Brenda was 14, her father explained the circumcision accident. David recalled reacting with relief. Deciding to return to his biological sex immediately, he chose for himself the name David, after the biblical lad who slew a giant and overcame adversity. David soon started injections of the androgen hormone testosterone to masculinize his body, and he underwent surgery to remove his breasts and to construct a penis. Although his adolescence continued to be troubled, in his twenties he fell in love with Jane, a single mother of three children, and married her.

David's case confirms the impact of genetic sex and prenatal hormones on a person's sense of self as male or female. His gender reassignment failed because his male biology overwhelmingly demanded a consistent sexual identity. At the same time, his childhood highlights the importance of experience. David expressed outrage at adult encouragement of dependency in girls—after all, he had experienced it firsthand.

Although David tried to surmount his tragic childhood, the troubled life that sprang from it persisted. When David was in his mid-thirties, his twin brother, Brian, committed suicide. Then, after David had lost his job and had been swindled out of his life savings in a shady investment deal, his wife left him, taking the children with her. Grief-stricken, David sank into a deep depression. On May 4, 2004, at age 38, he shot himself.

and are less tolerant of "cross-gender" behavior in sons—more concerned when a boy acts like a "sissy" than when a girl acts like a "tomboy" (Sandnabba & Ahlberg, 1999; Wood, Desmarais, & Gugula, 2002). Parents who hold nonstereotyped values and consciously avoid behaving in these ways have children who are less gender-typed (Tenenbaum & Leaper, 2002; Weisner & Wilson-Mitchell, 1990).

■ **TEACHERS.** Teachers often act in ways that extend gender-role learning. Several times, Leslie caught herself emphasizing gender distinctions when she called out, "Will the girls line up on one side and the boys on the other?" or pleaded, "Boys, I wish you'd quiet down like the girls!"

Like parents, preschool teachers give girls more encouragement to participate in adult-structured activities. Girls frequently cluster around the teacher, following directions, while boys are attracted to areas of the classroom where teachers are minimally involved (Campbell, Shirley, & Candy, 2004; Powlishta, Serbin, & Moller, 1993). As a result, boys and girls engage in different social behaviors. Compliance and bids for help occur more often in adult-structured contexts; assertiveness, leadership, and creative use of materials in unstructured pursuits.

Gender-typed behavior rises steadily over early childhood, due to a mix of genetic and environmental forces. On the environmental side, fathers, especially, are more insistent that boys conform to gender roles. This father shows his son how to cut shavings of wood for kindling a campfire.

Teachers also use more disapproval and controlling discipline with boys. When girls misbehave, teachers tend to negotiate, coming up with a joint plan to improve behavior (Erden & Wolfgang, 2004). Teachers seem to expect boys to misbehave more often—a belief based partly on boys' actual behavior and partly on gender stereotypes.

■ **PEERS.** Children's same-sex peer associations make the peer context a potent source of gender-role learning. The more preschoolers play with same-sex partners, the more their behavior becomes gender-typed—in toy choices, activity level, aggression, and adult involvement (Martin & Fabes, 2001). By age 3, same-sex peers positively reinforce one another for gender-typed play by praising, imitating, or joining in. In contrast, when preschoolers engage in "cross-gender" activities—for example, when boys play with dolls or girls with cars and trucks—peers criticize them. Boys are especially intolerant of cross-gender play in other boys (Fagot, 1984). A boy who frequently crosses gender lines is likely to be ignored by other boys even when he does engage in "masculine" activities!

Children also develop different styles of social influence in gender-segregated peer groups. To get their way in large-group play, boys often rely on commands, threats, and physical force. Girls' preference for playing in pairs leads to greater concern with a partner's needs, evident in girls' use of polite requests, persuasion, and acceptance. Girls soon find that these tactics succeed with other girls but not with boys, who ignore their courteous overtures (Leaper, 1994; Leaper, Tenenbaum, & Shaffer, 1999). Boys' unresponsiveness gives girls another reason to stop interacting with them.

Over time, children come to believe in the "correctness" of gender-segregated play, which further strengthens gender segregation and gender-stereotyped activities (Martin et al., 1999).

As boys and girls separate, *in-group favoritism*—more positive evaluations of members of one's own gender—becomes another factor that sustains the separate social worlds of boys and girls, resulting in "two distinct subcultures" of knowledge, beliefs, interests, and behaviors (Maccoby, 2002).

■ **THE BROADER SOCIAL ENVIRONMENT.** Finally, although children's everyday environments have changed to some degree, they continue to present many examples of gender-typed behavior—in occupations, leisure activities, media portrayals, and achievements of men and women. As we will see next, children soon come to view not just their social surroundings but also themselves through a "gender-biased lens"—a perspective that can seriously restrict their interests and learning opportunities.

Gender Identity

As adults, each of us has a **gender identity**—an image of oneself as relatively masculine or feminine in characteristics. By middle childhood, researchers can measure gender identity by asking children to rate themselves on personality traits. A child or adult with a "masculine" identity scores high on traditionally masculine items (such as *ambitious, competitive,* and *self-sufficient*) and low on traditionally feminine items (such as *affectionate, cheerful,* and *soft-spoken*). Someone with a "feminine" identity does the reverse. And a substantial minority (especially females) have a gender identity called **androgyny**, scoring high on both masculine and feminine personality characteristics.

Gender identity is a good predictor of psychological adjustment. "Masculine" and androgynous children and adults have higher self-esteem than "feminine" individuals, perhaps because many typically feminine traits are not highly valued by society (Boldizar, 1991; Bronstein, 2006; Harter, 2006). Also, androgynous individuals are more adaptable—able to show masculine independence or feminine sensitivity, depending on the situation (Huyck, 1996; Taylor & Hall, 1982). The existence of an androgynous identity demonstrates that children can acquire a mixture of positive qualities traditionally associated with each gender—an orientation that may best help them realize their potential.

■ **EMERGENCE OF GENDER IDENTITY.** How do children develop a gender identity? According to *social learning theory*, behavior comes before self-perceptions. Preschoolers first acquire gender-typed responses through modeling and reinforcement and only later organize these behaviors into gender-linked ideas about themselves. In contrast, *cognitive-developmental theory* maintains that self-perceptions come before behavior. Over the preschool years, children acquire a cognitive appreciation of the permanence of their sex. They develop **gender constancy**—a full understanding of the biologically based permanence of their gender, including the realization that sex remains the same even if clothing, hairstyle, and play activities change. Then children use this knowledge to guide their behavior (Kohlberg, 1966).

Children younger than age 6 who watch an adult dress a doll in "other-gender" clothing typically insist that the doll's sex has also changed (Chauhan, Shastri, & Mohite, 2005; Fagot, 1985). Attainment of gender constancy is strongly related to ability to pass Piagetian conservation and verbal appearance–reality tasks (see page 20 in Section 1) (De Lisi & Gallagher, 1991; Trautner, Gervai, & Nemeth, 2003). Indeed, gender constancy tasks can be considered a type of appearance–reality problem, in that children must distinguish what a person looks like from who he or she really is.

In many cultures, young children do not have access to basic biological knowledge about gender because they rarely see members of the other sex naked. But giving preschoolers information about genital differences does not result in gender constancy. Preschoolers who have such knowledge usually say changing a doll's clothing will not change its sex, but when asked to justify their responses, they do not refer to sex as an innate, unchanging quality of people (Szkrybalo & Ruble, 1999). This suggests that cognitive immaturity, not social experience, is responsible for preschoolers' difficulty grasping the permanence of sex.

Is cognitive-developmental theory correct that gender constancy is responsible for children's gender-typed behavior? Evidence for this assumption is weak. "Gender-appropriate" behavior appears so early in the preschool years that its initial appearance must result from modeling and reinforcement, as social learning theory suggests. Although outcomes are not entirely consistent, some evidence suggests that gender constancy actually contributes to the emergence of more flexible gender-role attitudes during the school years (Ruble et al., 2007). But overall, the impact of gender constancy on gender typing is not

great. As research in the following section reveals, gender-role adoption is more powerfully affected by children's beliefs about how close the connection must be between their own gender and their behavior.

■ **GENDER SCHEMA THEORY.**   **Gender schema theory** is an information-processing approach to gender typing that combines social learning and cognitive-developmental features. It explains how environmental pressures and children's cognitions work together to shape gender-role development (Martin & Halverson, 1987; Martin, Ruble, & Szkrybalo, 2002). At an early age, children pick up gender-typed preferences and behaviors from others. At the same time, they organize their experiences into *gender schemas,* or masculine and feminine categories, that they use to interpret their world. As soon as preschoolers can label their own sex, they select gender schemas consistent with it ("Only boys can be doctors" or "Cooking is a girl's job") and apply those categories to themselves. Their self-perceptions then become gender-typed and serve as additional schemas that children use to process information and guide their own behavior.

We have seen that individual differences exist in the extent to which children endorse gender-typed views. Figure 2.4 shows different cognitive pathways for children who often apply gender schemas to their experiences and those who rarely do (Liben & Bigler, 2002). Consider Billy, who encounters a doll. If Billy is a *gender-schematic child,* his *gender-salience filter* immediately makes gender highly relevant. Drawing on his prior learning, he asks himself, "Should boys play with dolls?" If he answers "yes" and the toy interests him, he will approach

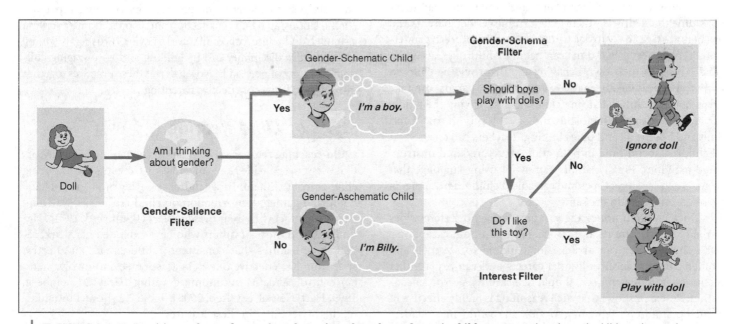

■ **FIGURE 2.4** ■ **Cognitive pathways for gender-schematic and gender-aschematic children.** In *gender-schematic children,* the gender-salience filter immediately makes gender highly relevant: Billy sees a doll and thinks, "I'm a boy. Should boys play with dolls?" Drawing on his experiences, he answers "yes" or "no." If he answers "yes" and the doll interests him, he plays with the doll. If he answers "no," he avoids the "gender-inappropriate" toy. *Gender-aschematic children* rarely view the world in gender-linked terms: Billy simply asks, "Do I like this toy?" and responds on the basis of his interests. (Reprinted by permission of Rebecca Bigler.)

it, explore it, and learn more about it. If he answers "no," he will respond by avoiding the "gender-inappropriate" toy. But if Billy is a *gender-aschematic child*—one who seldom views the world in gender-linked terms—he simply asks himself, "Do I like this toy?" and responds on the basis of his interests.

Gender schemas are powerful: When children see others behaving in "gender-inconsistent" ways, they often cannot remember the information or distort it to make it "gender-consistent." For example, when shown a picture of a male nurse, they may remember him as a doctor (Liben & Signorella, 1993; Martin & Ruble, 2004). And because gender-schematic preschoolers typically conclude, "What I like, children of my own sex will also like," they often use their own preferences to add to their gender biases! For example, a girl who dislikes oysters may conclude that only boys like oysters even though she has never actually been given information promoting such a stereotype (Liben & Bigler, 2002).

Reducing Gender Stereotyping in Young Children

How can we help young children avoid rigid gender schemas that restrict their behavior and learning opportunities? No easy recipe exists. Biology clearly affects children's gender typing, channeling boys toward active, competitive play and girls toward quieter, more intimate interaction. But most aspects of gender typing are not built into human nature (Maccoby, 2000). Furthermore, a long human childhood ensures that experiences can greatly influence biologically based sex differences (Ruble, Martin, & Berenbaum, 2006).

Because young children's cognitive limitations lead them to assume that cultural practices determine gender, parents and teachers are wise to try to delay preschoolers' exposure to gender-stereotyped messages. Adults can begin by limiting traditional gender roles in their own behavior and by providing children with nontraditional alternatives. For example, parents can take turns making dinner, bathing children, and driving the family car, and they can give their sons and daughters both trucks and dolls and both pink and blue clothing. Teachers can ensure that all children spend time in both adult-structured and unstructured activities. Finally, adults can avoid using language that conveys gender stereotypes and can shield children from media presentations that do the same.

Once children notice the vast array of gender stereotypes in their society, parents and teachers can point out exceptions. For example, they can arrange for children to see men and women pursuing nontraditional careers and can explain that interests and skills, not sex, should determine a person's occupation. Research shows that such reasoning is highly effective in reducing children's tendency to view the world in a gender-biased fashion. By middle childhood, children who hold flexible beliefs about what boys and girls can do are more likely to notice instances of gender discrimination (Bigler & Liben, 1992; Brown & Bigler, 2004). And, as we will see next, a rational

approach to child rearing promotes healthy, adaptable functioning in many other areas as well.

ASK YOURSELF

>> **REVIEW**
Explain how the social environment and young children's cognitive limitations contribute to rigid gender stereotyping in early childhood.

>> **APPLY**
List findings indicating that language and communication—between parents and children, between teachers and children, and between peers—powerfully affect children's gender typing. What recommendations would you make to counteract these influences?

>> **CONNECT**
What other cognitive changes are associated with gender constancy? What do these attainments have in common?

>> **REFLECT**
Would you describe your own gender identity as "masculine," "feminine," or androgynous? What biological and social factors might have influenced your gender identity?

Child Rearing and Emotional and Social Development

In this and previous sections, we have seen how parents can foster children's competence—by building a parent–child relationship based on affection and cooperation, by serving as models and reinforcers of mature behavior, by using reasoning and inductive discipline, and by guiding and encouraging children's mastery of new skills. Now let's put these practices together into an overall view of effective parenting.

Styles of Child Rearing

Child-rearing styles are combinations of parenting behaviors that occur over a wide range of situations, creating an enduring child-rearing climate. In a landmark series of studies, Diana Baumrind gathered information on child rearing by watching parents interact with their preschoolers (Baumrind, 1971). Her findings, and those of others who have extended her work, reveal three features that consistently differentiate an effective style from less effective ones: (1) acceptance and involvement, (2) control, and (3) autonomy granting (Gray & Steinberg, 1999; Hart, Newell, & Olsen, 2003). Table 2.2 shows how child-rearing styles differ in these features.

■ **AUTHORITATIVE CHILD REARING.** The **authoritative child-rearing style**—the most successful approach—involves high acceptance and involvement, adaptive control techniques,

■ **TABLE 2.2** ■ *Features of Child-Rearing Styles*

CHILD-REARING STYLE	ACCEPTANCE AND INVOLVEMENT	CONTROL	AUTONOMY GRANTING
Authoritative	Is warm, responsive, attentive, patient, and sensitive to the child's needs	Makes reasonable demands for maturity and consistently enforces and explains them	Permits the child to make decisions in accord with readiness Encourages the child to express thoughts, feelings, and desires When parent and child disagree, engages in joint decision making when possible
Authoritarian	Is cold and rejecting and frequently degrades the child	Makes many demands coercively, using force and punishment Often uses psychological control, withdrawing love and intruding on the child's individuality	Makes decisions for the child Rarely listens to the child's point of view
Permissive	Is warm but overindulgent or inattentive	Makes few or no demands	Permits the child to make many decisions before the child is ready
Uninvolved	Is emotionally detached and withdrawn	Makes few or no demands	Is indifferent to the child's decision making and point of view

and appropriate autonomy granting. Authoritative parents are warm, attentive, and sensitive to their child's needs. They establish an enjoyable, emotionally fulfilling parent–child relationship that draws the child into close connection. At the same time, authoritative parents exercise firm, reasonable control. They insist on mature behavior, give reasons for their expectations, and use disciplinary encounters as "teaching moments" to promote the child's self-regulation. Finally, authoritative parents engage in gradual, appropriate autonomy granting, allowing the child to make decisions in areas where he is ready to do so (Kuczynski & Lollis, 2002; Russell, Mize, & Bissaker, 2004).

Throughout childhood and adolescence, authoritative parenting is linked to many aspects of competence—an upbeat mood, self-control, task persistence, cooperativeness, high self-esteem, social and moral maturity, and favorable school performance (Amato & Fowler, 2002; Aunola, Stattin, & Nurmi, 2000; Gonzalez & Wolters, 2006; Mackey, Arnold, & Pratt, 2001; Milevsky et al., 2007; Steinberg, Darling, & Fletcher, 1995).

■ **AUTHORITARIAN CHILD REARING.** The **authoritarian child-rearing style** is low in acceptance and involvement, high in coercive control, and low in autonomy granting. Authoritarian parents appear cold and rejecting. To exert control, they yell, command, criticize, and threaten. "Do it because I said so!" is their attitude. They make decisions for their child and expect the child to accept their word unquestioningly. If the child resists, authoritarian parents resort to force and punishment.

Children of authoritarian parents are anxious, unhappy, and low in self-esteem and self-reliance. When frustrated, they tend to react with hostility and, like their parents, resort to force when they do not get their way. Boys, especially, show high rates of anger and defiance. Although girls also engage in acting-out behavior, they are more likely to be dependent, lacking interest in exploration, and overwhelmed by challenging tasks (Hart,

Newell, & Olsen, 2003; Nix et al., 1999; Thompson, Hollis, & Richards, 2003). Children and adolescents exposed to the authoritarian style typically do poorly in school, but because of their parents' concern with control, they tend to achieve better and to commit fewer antisocial acts than peers with undemanding parents—that is, whose parents use one of the type styles we will consider next (Steinberg, Blatt-Eisengart, & Cauffman, 2006).

In addition to unwarranted direct control, authoritarian parents engage in a more subtle type called **psychological control**—behaviors that intrude on and manipulate children's verbal expression, individuality, and attachments to parents. In an attempt to decide virtually everything for the child, these parents frequently interrupt or put down the child's ideas, decisions, and choice of friends. When they are dissatisfied, they withdraw love, making their affection or attention contingent on the child's compliance. They also hold excessively high expectations that do not fit the child's developing capacities. Children and adolescents subjected to psychological control exhibit adjustment problems involving both anxious, withdrawn and defiant, aggressive behaviors (Barber & Harmon, 2002; Silk et al., 2003).

■ **PERMISSIVE CHILD REARING.** The **permissive child-rearing style** is warm and accepting but uninvolved. Permissive parents are either overindulging or inattentive and, thus, engage in little control. Instead of gradually granting autonomy, they allow children to make many of their own decisions at an age when they are not yet capable of doing so. Their children can eat meals and go to bed whenever they wish and can watch as much television as they want. They do not have to learn good manners or do any household chores. Although some permissive parents truly believe in this approach, many others simply lack confidence in their ability to influence their child's behavior (Oyserman et al., 2005).

Children of permissive parents are impulsive, disobedient, and rebellious. Compared with children whose parents exert more control, they are also overly demanding and dependent on adults, and they show less persistence on tasks, poorer school achievement, and more antisocial behavior. The link between permissive parenting and dependent, nonachieving behavior is especially strong for boys (Barber & Olsen, 1997; Baumrind, 1971; Steinberg, Blatt-Eisengart, & Cauffman, 2006).

■ **UNINVOLVED CHILD REARING.** The **uninvolved child-rearing style** combines low acceptance and involvement with little control and general indifference to issues of autonomy. Often these parents are emotionally detached and depressed, so overwhelmed by life stress that they have little time and energy for children. At its extreme, uninvolved parenting is a form of child maltreatment called *neglect*. Especially when it begins early, it disrupts virtually all aspects of development. Even with less extreme parental disengagement, children and adolescents display many problems—poor emotional self-regulation, school achievement difficulties, and antisocial behavior (Aunola, Stattin, & Nurmi, 2000; Kurdek & Fine, 1994).

What Makes Authoritative Child Rearing Effective?

Like all correlational findings, the relationship between the authoritative style and children's competence is open to interpretation. Perhaps parents of well-adjusted children are authoritative because their youngsters have especially cooperative dispositions. But longitudinal research indicates that authoritative child rearing promotes maturity and adjustment in children of diverse temperaments (Hart, Newell, & Olson, 2003; Olson et al., 2000; Rubin, Burgess, & Coplan, 2002). It seems to create a positive emotional context for parental influence in the following ways:

■ Warm, involved parents who are secure in the standards they hold for their children provide models of caring concern as well as confident, self-controlled behavior.

■ Children are far more likely to comply with and internalize control that appears fair and reasonable, not arbitrary.

■ By making demands and engaging in autonomy granting that matches children's ability to take responsibility for their own behavior, authoritative parents let children know that they are competent individuals who can do things successfully for themselves. In this way, parents foster favorable self-esteem and cognitive and social maturity.

■ Supportive aspects of the authoritative style, including parental acceptance, involvement, and rational control, help protect children from the negative effects of family stress and poverty (Beyers et al., 2003).

Over time, the relationship between parenting and children's attributes becomes increasingly bidirectional (Kuczynski, 2003). When parents intervene patiently but firmly, they promote favorable adjustment, setting the stage for a positive parent–child relationship.

Cultural Variations

Although authoritative child rearing is broadly advantageous, ethnic groups often have distinct parenting beliefs and practices that reflect cultural values. Let's take some examples.

Compared with Western parents, Chinese parents describe their parenting as more controlling. They are more directive in teaching and scheduling their children's time, as a way of fostering self-control and high achievement. Chinese parents may appear less warm than Western parents because they withhold praise, which they believe results in self-satisfied, poorly motivated children (Chao, 1994; Chen et al., 2001). Chinese parents report expressing affection and using induction and other reasoning-oriented discipline as much as North American parents do, but they more often shame a misbehaving child (see page 45), withdraw love, and use physical punishment (Jose et al., 2000; Shwalb et al., 2004; Wu et al., 2002). When these practices become excessive, Chinese children display the same negative outcomes seen in Western children: anxiety, depression, and aggression (Nelson et al., 2005, 2006a, 2006b; Wang, Pomerantz, & Chen, 2007).

In Hispanic families, Asian Pacific Island families, and Caribbean families of African and East Indian origins, firm insistence on respect for parental authority is paired with high parental warmth—a combination suited to promoting competence and family loyalty (Harrison et al., 1994; Roopnarine & Evans, 2007). Hispanic fathers typically spend much time with their children and are warm and sensitive (Cabrera & Garcia-Coll, 2004; Jambunathan, Burts, & Pierce, 2000). In Caribbean

© GERI ENGBERG/THE IMAGE WORKS

This father encourages his daughter to help with recycling. By letting children know they are competent individuals, authoritative parents foster high self-esteem and social maturity.

families that have immigrated to the United States, fathers' authoritativeness—but not mothers—predicted preschoolers' literacy and math skills, probably because Caribbean fathers take a larger role in guiding their children's academic progress (Roopnarine et al., 2006).

Although wide variation exists, low-SES African-American parents tend to expect immediate obedience, regarding strictness as fostering self-control and a watchful attitude in risky surroundings. Consistent with these beliefs, African-American parents who use more controlling strategies tend to have more cognitively and socially competent children (Brody & Flor, 1998). Recall, also, that a history of physical punishment is associated with a reduction in antisocial behavior among African-American youths but with an increase among Caucasian Americans (see page 55). Most African-American parents who use strict, "no-nonsense" discipline use physical punishment sparingly and combine it with warmth and reasoning.

These cultural variations remind us that child-rearing styles must be viewed in their larger context. As we have seen, many factors contribute to good parenting: personal characteristics of the child and parent, SES, access to extended family and community supports, cultural values and practices, and public policies.

As we turn to the topic of child maltreatment, our discussion will underscore, once again, that effective child rearing is sustained not just by the desire of mothers and fathers to be good parents. Almost all want to be. Unfortunately, when vital supports for parenting break down, children—as well as parents—can suffer terribly.

Child Maltreatment

Child maltreatment is as old as human history, but only recently has the problem been widely acknowledged and research aimed at understanding it. Perhaps public concern has increased because child maltreatment is especially common in large indus-

trialized nations. In the most recently reported year, 905,000 U.S. children (12 out of every 1,000) were identified as victims (U.S. Department of Health and Human Services, 2008e). Most cases go unreported, so the true figures are much higher.

Child maltreatment takes the following forms:

- *Physical abuse:* Assaults, such as kicking, biting, shaking, punching, or stabbing, that inflict physical injury
- *Sexual abuse:* Fondling, intercourse, exhibitionism, commercial exploitation through prostitution or production of pornography, and other forms of exploitation
- *Neglect:* Failure to meet a child's basic needs for food, clothing, medical attention, or supervision
- *Emotional abuse:* Acts that could cause serious mental or behavioral disorders, including social isolation, repeated unreasonable demands, ridicule, humiliation, intimidation, or terrorizing

Parents commit more than 80 percent of abusive incidents. Other relatives account for about 7 percent. The remainder are perpetrated by parents' unmarried partners, school officials, camp counselors, and other adults. Mothers engage in neglect more often than fathers, whereas fathers engage in sexual abuse more often than mothers. Maternal and paternal rates of physical and emotional abuse are fairly similar. Infants and young preschoolers are at greatest risk for neglect, preschool and school-age children for physical, emotional, and sexual abuse (Trocomé & Wolfe, 2002; U.S. Department of Health and Human Services, 2008e). Because most sexual abuse victims are identified in middle childhood, we will pay special attention to this form of maltreatment.

■ **ORIGINS OF CHILD MALTREATMENT.** Early findings suggested that child maltreatment was rooted in adult psychological disturbance (Kempe et al., 1962). But although child maltreatment is more common among disturbed parents, no

Our future is in their hands.

Care, don't scare. Love don't shove. Smile to your child.
STOP child abuse. And make our future a little brighter..

Each year, fourth to sixth graders across Los Angeles County enter a poster contest to celebrate Child Abuse Prevention Month. This 2008 winner appeals to parents to treat children with warmth and caring. (Lisa Valicente and Madeline Zauss, 6th Grade, Jefferson Elementary School, Redondo Beach, CA. Courtesy ICAN Associates, Los Angeles County InterAgency Council on Child Abuse & Neglect, ican4kids.org.)

■ **TABLE 2.3** ■ *Factors Related to Child Maltreatment*

FACTOR	DESCRIPTION
Parent characteristics	Psychological disturbance; alcohol and drug abuse; history of abuse as a child; belief in harsh, physical discipline; desire to satisfy unmet emotional needs through the child; unreasonable expectations for child behavior; young age (most under 30); low educational level
Child characteristics	Premature or very sick baby; difficult temperament; inattentiveness and overactivity; other developmental problems
Family characteristics	Low income; poverty; homelessness; marital instability; social isolation; physical abuse of mother by husband or boyfriend; frequent moves; large families with closely spaced children; overcrowded living conditions; disorganized household; lack of steady employment; other signs of high life stress
Community	Characterized by violence and social isolation; few parks, child-care centers, preschool programs, recreation centers, or religious institutions to serve as family supports
Culture	Approval of physical force and violence as ways to solve problems

Sources: Wekerle & Wolfe, 2003; Whipple, 2006.

single "abusive personality type" exists. Parents who were abused as children do not necessarily become abusers (Buchanan, 1996; Simons et al., 1991). And sometimes even "normal" parents harm their children!

For help in understanding child maltreatment, researchers turned to ecological systems theory. They discovered that many interacting variables—at the family, community, and cultural levels—contribute. The more risks present, the greater the likelihood of abuse or neglect (see Table 2.3 above).

The Family. Within the family, children whose characteristics make them more challenging to rear are more likely to become targets of abuse. These include premature or very sick babies and children who are temperamentally difficult, are inattentive and overactive, or have other developmental problems (Sidebotham et al., 2003). But whether such children actually are maltreated depends on parents' characteristics.

Maltreating parents are less skillful than other parents in handling discipline confrontations. They also suffer from biased thinking about their child. For example, they often attribute their baby's crying or their child's misdeeds to a stubborn or bad disposition, evaluate child transgressions as worse than they are, and feel powerless in parenting—perspectives that lead them to move quickly toward physical force (Bugental & Happaney, 2004; Crouch et al., 2008).

Once abuse begins, it quickly becomes part of a self-sustaining relationship. The small irritations to which abusive parents react—a fussy baby, a preschooler who knocks over her milk, a child who will not mind immediately—soon become bigger ones. Then the harshness increases. By the preschool years, abusive and neglectful parents seldom interact with their children. When they do, the communication is almost always negative (Wolfe, 2005).

Most parents have enough self-control not to respond with abuse to their child's misbehavior or developmental problems. Other factors combine with these conditions to prompt an extreme response. Abusive parents react to stressful situations with high emotional arousal. And low income, low education (less than a high school diploma), unemployment, young maternal age, alcohol and drug use, marital conflict, overcrowded living conditions, frequent moves, and extreme household disorganization are common in abusive homes (Wekerle & Wolfe, 2003; Wekerle et al., 2007). These conditions increase the chances that parents will be too overwhelmed to meet basic child-rearing responsibilities or will vent their frustrations by lashing out at their children.

The Community. The majority of abusive and neglectful parents are isolated from both formal and informal social supports. Because of their life histories, many have learned to mistrust and avoid others and are poorly skilled at establishing and maintaining positive relationships. Also, maltreating parents are more likely to live in unstable, rundown neighborhoods that provide few links between family and community, such as parks, child-care centers, preschool programs, recreation centers, and religious institutions (Coulton et al., 2007; Zielinski & Bradshaw, 2006). They lack "lifelines" to others and have no one to turn to for help during stressful times.

The Larger Culture. Cultural values, laws, and customs profoundly affect the chances that child maltreatment will occur when parents feel overburdened. Societies that view violence as an appropriate way to solve problems set the stage for child abuse.

Although the United States has laws to protect children from maltreatment, widespread support exists for use of physical force with children (refer back to page 54). Many countries—including Austria, Croatia, Cyprus, Denmark, Finland, Germany, Israel, Italy, Latvia, Norway, and Sweden—have outlawed physical punishment, a measure that dampens both physical discipline and abuse (Bugental & Grusec, 2006). Furthermore, every industrialized nation except the United States and Canada now prohibits corporal punishment in schools (Center for Effective Discipline,

2005). The U.S. Supreme Court has twice upheld the right of school officials to use corporal punishment. Fortunately, some U.S. states and Canadian provinces have passed laws that ban it.

■ **CONSEQUENCES OF CHILD MALTREATMENT.** The family circumstances of maltreated children impair the development of emotional self-regulation, empathy and sympathy, self-concept, social skills, and academic motivation. Over time, these youngsters show serious learning and adjustment problems, including academic failure, severe depression, aggressive behavior, peer difficulties, substance abuse, and delinquency, including violent crime (Cicchetti & Toth, 2006; Shonk & Cicchetti, 2001; Wolfe et al., 2001).

How do these damaging consequences occur? Think back to our earlier discussion of hostile cycles of parent–child interaction. For abused children, these are especially severe. Indeed, a family characteristic strongly associated with child abuse is partner abuse (Cox, Kotch, & Everson, 2003). Clearly, the home lives of abused children overflow with opportunities to learn to use aggression as a way of solving problems.

Furthermore, demeaning parental messages, in which children are ridiculed, humiliated, rejected, or terrorized, result in low self-esteem, high anxiety, self-blame, depression, and efforts to escape from extreme psychological pain—at times severe enough to lead to attempted suicide in adolescence (Wolfe, 2005). At school, maltreated children present serious discipline problems. Their noncompliance, poor motivation, and cognitive immaturity interfere with academic achievement, further undermining their chances for life success (Wekerle & Wolfe, 2003).

Finally, repeated abuse is associated with central nervous system damage, including abnormal EEG brain-wave activity, fMRI-detected reduced size and impaired functioning of the cerebral cortex and corpus callosum, and atypical production of the stress hormone cortisol—initially too high but, after months of abuse, often too low. Over time, the massive trauma of persistent abuse seems to blunt children's normal physiological response to stress (Cicchetti, 2007; Teicher et al., 2004; Watts-English et al., 2006). These effects increase the chances that cognitive and emotional problems will endure.

■ **PREVENTING CHILD MALTREATMENT.** Because child maltreatment is embedded in families, communities, and society as a whole, efforts to prevent it must be directed at each of these levels. Suggested approaches include teaching high-risk parents effective child-rearing strategies, providing direct experience with children in high school child development courses, and developing broad social programs aimed at improving economic conditions for low-SES families.

We have seen that providing social supports to families is effective in easing parental stress. This approach sharply reduces child maltreatment. A trusting relationship with another person is the most important factor in preventing mothers with childhood histories of abuse from repeating the cycle with their own children (Egeland, Jacobvitz, & Sroufe, 1988). Parents Anonymous, a U.S. organization with affiliate programs around the world, helps child-abusing parents learn constructive parenting practices, largely through social supports. Its local sections offer self-help group meetings, daily phone calls, and regular home visits to relieve social isolation and teach child-rearing skills.

Early intervention aimed at strengthening both child and parent competencies can reduce child maltreatment substantially. Healthy Families America, a program that began in Hawaii and has spread to 440 sites across the United States and Canada, identifies at-risk families during pregnancy or at birth. Each receives three years of home visitation, in which a trained worker helps parents manage crises, encourages effective child rearing, and puts parents in touch with community services (PCA America, 2009). In an evaluation its effectiveness, Healthy Families home visitation alone reduced only neglect, not abuse (Duggan et al., 2004). But adding a *cognitive component* dramatically increased its impact. When home visitors helped parents change negative appraisals of their children—by countering inaccurate interpretations (for example, that the baby is behaving with malicious intent) and by working on solving child-rearing problems—physical punishment and abuse dropped sharply after one year of intervention (Bugental et al., 2002).

Even with intensive treatment, some adults persist in their abusive acts. An estimated 1,500 U.S. children, most of them infants and preschoolers, die from maltreatment each year (U.S. Department of Health and Human Services, 2008e). When parents are unlikely to change their behavior, the drastic step of separating parent from child and legally terminating parental rights is the only justifiable course of action.

Child maltreatment is a sad note on which to end our discussion of a period of childhood that is so full of excitement, awakening, and discovery. But there is reason to be optimistic. Great strides have been made over the past several decades in understanding and preventing child maltreatment.

ASK YOURSELF

≫ **REVIEW**
Summarize findings on ethnic variations in child-rearing styles. Is the concept of authoritative parenting useful for understanding effective parenting across cultures? Explain.

≫ **APPLY**
Chandra heard a news report about ten severely neglected children, living in squalor in an inner-city tenement. She wondered, "Why would parents mistreat their children?" How would you answer Chandra?

≫ **CONNECT**
Which child-rearing style is most likely to be associated with inductive discipline, and why?

≫ **REFLECT**
How would you classify your parents' child-rearing styles? What factors might have influenced their approach to parenting?

Summary

Erikson's Theory: Initiative versus Guilt

What personality changes take place during Erikson's stage of initiative versus guilt?

>> Erikson's image of **initiative versus guilt** captures the emotional and social changes of early childhood. A healthy sense of initiative depends on exploring the social world through play, forming a conscience through identification with the same-sex parent, and receiving supportive child rearing.

Self-Understanding

Describe preschoolers' self-concepts and self-esteem.

>> As preschoolers think more intently about themselves, they construct a **self-concept,** or set of beliefs about their own characteristics, that consists largely of observable characteristics and typical emotions and attitudes. Their increasing self-awareness underlies struggles over objects as well as first efforts to cooperate.

>> During early childhood, high **self-esteem** contributes to a mastery-oriented approach to the environment. But even a little adult disapproval can undermine a young child's self-esteem and enthusiasm for learning.

Emotional Development

Cite changes in understanding and expression of emotion during early childhood, along with factors that influence those changes.

>> Preschoolers have an impressive understanding of the causes, consequences, and behavioral signs of basic emotions, supported by secure attachment and conversations about feelings. By age 3 to 4, children are aware of various

strategies for emotional self-regulation. Temperament and parental modeling influence preschoolers' capacity to handle negative emotion.

>> As their self-concepts develop, preschoolers experience self-conscious emotions more often. Parental messages affect the intensity of these emotions and the situations in which they occur. Empathy also becomes more common. Temperament and parenting affect the extent to which empathy leads to **sympathy** and to **prosocial,** or **altruistic, behavior.**

Peer Relations

Describe peer sociability and friendship in early childhood, along with cultural and parental influences on early peer relations.

>> During early childhood, peer interaction increases, as children move from **nonsocial activity** to **parallel play,** then to **associative** and **cooperative play.** But even as associative and cooperative play increase, both solitary and parallel play remain common.

>> In collectivist societies, play occurs in large groups and is highly cooperative. Sociodramatic play seems especially important in societies where child and adult worlds are distinct.

>> Preschoolers view friendship in concrete, activity-based terms. Parents affect peer sociability both directly, through attempts to influence their child's peer relations, and indirectly, through their child-rearing practices.

Foundations of Morality

What are the central features of psychoanalytic, social learning, and cognitive-developmental approaches to moral development?

>> Psychoanalytic and social learning approaches to morality focus on how children acquire ready-made standards held by adults. Contrary to the claims of Freud's psychoanalytic theory, discipline based on fear of punishment and loss of parental love does not foster conscience development. Instead, **induction** is far more effective in encouraging self-control and prosocial behavior.

>> Social learning theory regards reinforcement and modeling as the basis for moral action. Adults who are warm, powerful, and practice what they preach provide effective models of morality. Alternatives such as **time out** and withdrawal of privileges can help parents avoid the undesirable side effects of harsh punishment. Punishment is more effective when parents are consistent, have a warm relationship with the child, and offer explanations.

>> The cognitive-developmental perspective views children as active thinkers about social rules. Although preschoolers tend to reason rigidly about moral matters, by age 4 they can consider people's intentions in making moral judgments and can distinguish truthfulness from lying. Preschoolers also distinguish **moral imperatives** from **social conventions** and **matters of personal choice.**

Describe the development of aggression in early childhood, including family and television as major influences.

>> Aggression first appears by the second year. During early childhood, **proactive aggression** declines, while **reactive aggression** increases. Proactive and reactive aggression come in at least three forms: **physical aggression, verbal aggression,** and **relational aggression.** Preschoolers gradually replace physical with verbal aggression. By the second year, boys are more physically aggressive than girls.

>> Ineffective discipline and a conflict-ridden family atmosphere promote and sustain aggression in children. Media violence, both on TV and in computer games, also triggers childhood aggression. Teaching parents effective child-rearing practices, providing children with social problem-solving training, reducing family hostility, and shielding children from violent media can reduce aggressive behavior.

Gender Typing

Discuss genetic and environmental influences on preschoolers' gender-stereotyped beliefs and behavior.

>> **Gender typing** is well under way in the preschool years. Prenatal male sex hormone (androgen) levels contribute to sex differences in play styles and, in turn, to preference for same-sex peers. But parents, teachers, peers, and the broader social environment also encourage many gender-typed responses.

Describe and evaluate the accuracy of major theories that explain the emergence of gender identity.

>> Although most people have a traditional **gender identity,** some exhibit **androgyny,** combining both masculine and feminine characteristics. Masculine and androgynous identities are linked to better psychological adjustment.

>> According to social learning theory, preschoolers first acquire gender-typed responses through modeling and reinforcement and then organize them into gender-linked ideas about themselves. Cognitive-developmental theory suggests that **gender constancy** must precede gender-typed behavior, though evidence for this assumption is weak.

>> **Gender schema theory** combines features of social learning and cognitive-developmental perspectives. As children acquire gender-stereotyped preferences and behaviors, they form masculine and feminine categories that they apply to themselves and use to interpret their world.

Child Rearing and Emotional and Social Development

Describe the impact of child-rearing styles on children's development, and note cultural variations in child rearing.

>> Three features distinguish major **child-rearing styles:** (1) acceptance and involvement, (2) control, and (3) autonomy granting. In contrast to the **authoritarian, permissive,** and **uninvolved** styles, the **authoritative style** promotes cognitive, emotional, and social competence. Warmth, explanations, and reasonable demands for mature behavior account for the effectiveness of this style.

>> Certain ethnic groups, including Chinese, Hispanic, Asian Pacific Island, and African-American, combine parental warmth with high levels of control. But when control becomes harsh and excessive, it impairs academic and social competence.

Discuss the multiple origins of child maltreatment, its consequences for development, and effective prevention.

>> Maltreating parents use ineffective discipline, hold a negatively biased view of their child, and feel powerless in parenting. Unmanageable parental stress and social isolation greatly increase the chances of abuse and neglect. Societal approval of physical force as a means of solving problems promotes child abuse.

>> Maltreated children are impaired in emotional self-regulation, empathy and sympathy, self-concept, social skills, and academic motivation. The trauma of repeated abuse is associated with central nervous system damage and serious adjustment problems. Successful prevention requires efforts at the family, community, and societal levels.

Important Terms and Concepts

androgyny (p. 64)
associative play (p. 49)
authoritarian child-rearing style (p. 67)
authoritative child-rearing style (p. 66)
child-rearing styles (p. 66)
cooperative play (p. 49)
gender constancy (p. 64)
gender identity (p. 64)
gender schema theory (p. 65)
gender typing (p. 61)

induction (p. 53)
initiative versus guilt (p. 44)
matters of personal choice (p. 57)
moral imperatives (p. 57)
nonsocial activity (p. 49)
parallel play (p. 49)
permissive child-rearing style (p. 67)
physical aggression (p. 57)
proactive aggression (p. 57)
prosocial, or altruistic, behavior (p. 48)

psychological control (p. 67)
reactive aggression (p. 57)
relational aggression (p. 57)
self-concept (p. 44)
self-esteem (p. 46)
social conventions (p. 57)
sympathy (p. 40)
time out (p. 56)
uninvolved child-rearing style (p. 68)
verbal aggression (p. 57)

Milestones
Development in Early Childhood

2 years

PHYSICAL

- Throughout early childhood, height and weight increase more slowly than in toddlerhood. (4)
- Balance improves; walks more rhythmically; hurried walk changes to run. (12, 13)
- Jumps, hops, throws, and catches with rigid upper body. (12, 13)
- Puts on and removes simple items of clothing. (12, 13)
- Uses spoon effectively. (13)
- First drawings are gestural scribbles. (12)

COGNITIVE

- Make-believe becomes less dependent on realistic objects, less self-centered, and more complex. (16); sociodramatic play increases. (16)
- Understands the symbolic function of photos and pictures in books. (17)
- Takes the perspective of others in simplified, familiar situations and in face-to-face communication. (18–19)

- Recognition memory is well-developed. (26)
- Shows awareness of the distinction between inner mental and outer physical events. (27)
- Begins to count. (31)

LANGUAGE

- Vocabulary increases rapidly. (36)
- Uses a coalition of cues—perceptual and, increasingly, social and linguistic—to figure out word meanings. (37)
- Speaks in simple sentences that follow basic word order of native language. (37)
- Adds grammatical markers. (38)
- Displays effective conversational skills. (38)

EMOTIONAL/SOCIAL

- Understands causes, consequences, and behavioral signs of basic emotions. (46)
- Begins to develop self-concept and self-esteem. (44–46)
- Shows early signs of developing moral sense—verbal evaluations of own and others' actions and distress at harmful behaviors. (52)
- May display proactive (instrumental) aggression. (57)
- Gender-stereotyped beliefs and behavior increase. (61)

3–4 years

PHYSICAL

- Running, jumping, hopping, throwing, and catching become better coordinated. (13)

- Galloping and one-foot skipping appear. (13)
- Pedals and steers tricycle. (13)
- Uses scissors. (13)
- Fastens and unfastens large buttons. (13)
- Uses fork effectively. (13)
- Draws first picture of a person, using tadpole image. (13)

COGNITIVE

- Understands the symbolic function of drawings and of models of real-world spaces. (17)
- Grasps conservation, reasons about transformations, reverses thinking, and understands cause-and-effect relationships in familiar contexts. (19)
- Distinguishes appearance from reality. (20)
- Sorts familiar objects into hierarchically organized categories. (21)
- Uses private speech to guide behavior during challenging tasks. (22)
- Sustained attention and planning improve. (25–26)
- Uses scripts to recall familiar experiences. (26)
- Understands that both beliefs and desires determine behavior. (27)
- Knows meaning of numbers up to ten, counts correctly, grasps principle of cardinality. (31)

Note: Numbers in parentheses indicate the page or pages on which each milestone is discussed.

LANGUAGE

- Aware of some meaningful features of written language. (30)
- Coins new words based on known words; extends language meanings through metaphor. (36)
- Masters increasingly complex grammatical structures. (38)
- Occasionally overextends grammatical rules to exceptions. (38)
- Adjusts speech to fit the age, sex, and social status of listeners. (38)

EMOTIONAL/SOCIAL

- Describes self in terms of observable characteristics and typical emotions and attitudes. (44)
- Has several self-esteems, such as learning things in school, making friends, and getting along with parents. (46)
- Emotional self-regulation improves. (47)
- Experiences self-conscious emotions more often. (47)
- Relies more on language to express empathy. (48)
- Engages in associative and cooperative play with peers, in addition to parallel play. (49)
- Forms first friendships, based on pleasurable play and sharing of toys. (51)

- Distinguishes truthfulness from lying. (57)
- Distinguishes moral imperatives from social conventions and matters of personal choice. (57)
- Proactive aggression declines, while reactive aggression (verbal and relational) increases. (58)
- Preference for same-sex playmates strengthens. (62)

5–6 years

PHYSICAL

- Starts to lose primary teeth. (5)
- Increases running speed, gallops more smoothly, and engages in true skipping. (12, 13)
- Displays mature throwing and catching patterns. (13)

- Uses knife to cut soft foods. (13)
- Ties shoes. (12, 13)
- Draws more complex pictures. (13)
- Copies some numbers and simple words. (13)

COGNITIVE

- Magical beliefs decline. (19, 21)
- Ability to distinguish appearance from reality improves. (20)
- Attention and planning continue to improve. (25–26)
- Recognition, recall, scripted memory, and autobiographical memory improve. (26–27)

- Understanding of false belief strengthens. (27–28)

LANGUAGE

- Understands that letters and sounds are linked in systematic ways. (30)
- Uses invented spellings. (30)
- By age 6, vocabulary reaches about 10,000 words. (36)
- Uses most grammatical constructions competently. (38)

EMOTIONAL/SOCIAL

- Emotional understanding (ability to interpret, predict, and influence others' emotional reactions) improves. (46–47)
- Empathic responding increases. (48)
- Has acquired many morally relevant rules and behaviors. (53–54)
- Gender-stereotyped beliefs and behavior and preference for same-sex playmates continue to strengthen. (61–62)
- Understands gender constancy. (64)

On a bird-watching field trip, fourth-grade classmates collaborate to identify an unfamiliar species. An improved capacity to remember, reason, and reflect on one's own thinking makes middle childhood a time of dramatic advances in academic learning and problem solving.

Physical and Cognitive Development in Middle Childhood

"**I**'m on my way, Mom!" hollered 10-year-old Joey as he stuffed the last bite of toast into his mouth, slung his book bag over his shoulder, dashed out the door, jumped on his bike, and headed down the street for school. Joey's 8-year-old sister Lizzie followed, kissing her mother good-bye and pedaling furiously until she caught up with Joey. Rena, the children's mother and one of my colleagues at the university, watched from the front porch as her son and daughter disappeared in the distance.

"They're branching out," Rena told me over lunch that day, as she described the children's expanding activities and relationships. Homework, household chores, soccer teams, music lessons, scouting, friends at school and in the neighborhood, and Joey's new paper route were all part of the children's routine. "It seems as if the basics are all there. I don't have to monitor Joey and Lizzie constantly anymore. Being a parent is still very challenging, but it's more a matter of refinements—helping them become independent, competent, and productive individuals."

Joey and Lizzie have entered middle childhood—the years from 6 to 11. Around the world, children of this age are assigned new responsibilities. For children in industrialized nations, middle childhood is often called the "school years" because its onset is marked by the start of formal schooling. In village and tribal cultures, the school may be a field or a jungle. But universally, children in this period are guided by mature members of society toward real-world tasks that increasingly resemble those they will perform as adults.

This section focuses on physical and cognitive development in middle childhood. By age 6, the brain has reached 90 percent of its adult weight, and the body continues to grow slowly. In this way, nature gives school-age children the mental powers to master challenging tasks as well as added time to acquire the knowledge and skills essential for life in a complex social world.

We begin by reviewing typical growth trends, gains in motor skills, and special health concerns. Then we return to Piaget's theory and the information-processing approach for an overview of cognitive changes during the school years. Next, we examine the genetic and environmental roots of IQ scores, which often enter into educational decisions. Our discussion continues with the further blossoming of language. Finally, we turn to the importance of schools in children's learning and development.

Physical Development

Body Growth

Physical growth during the school years continues at the slow, regular pace of early childhood. At age 6, the average North American child weighs about 45 pounds and is 3½ feet tall. Over the next few years, children add about 2 to 3 inches in height and 5 pounds in weight each year (see Figure 3.1). Between ages 6 and 8, girls are slightly shorter and lighter than boys. By age 9, this trend reverses as girls approach the dramatic adolescent growth spurt, which occurs two years earlier in girls than in boys.

Because the lower portion of the body is growing fastest, Joey and Lizzie appeared longer-legged than they had in early childhood. They grew out of their jeans more quickly than their jackets and frequently needed larger shoes. As in early childhood, girls have slightly more body fat and boys more muscle. After age 8, girls begin accumulating fat at a faster rate, and they will add even more during adolescence (Siervogel et al., 2000).

During middle childhood, the bones of the body lengthen and broaden. But ligaments are not yet firmly attached to bones, and this, combined with increasing muscle strength, gives children the unusual flexibility needed to perform cartwheels and handstands. As their bodies become stronger, many children experience a greater desire for physical exercise. Nighttime "growing pains"—stiffness and aches in the legs—are common as muscles adapt to an enlarging skeleton (Evans & Scutter, 2004).

Between ages 6 and 12, all 20 primary teeth are lost and replaced by permanent ones, with girls losing their teeth slightly earlier than boys. For a while, the permanent teeth seem much too large. Gradually, growth of facial bones, especially the jaw and chin, causes the child's face to lengthen and mouth to widen, accommodating the newly erupting teeth.

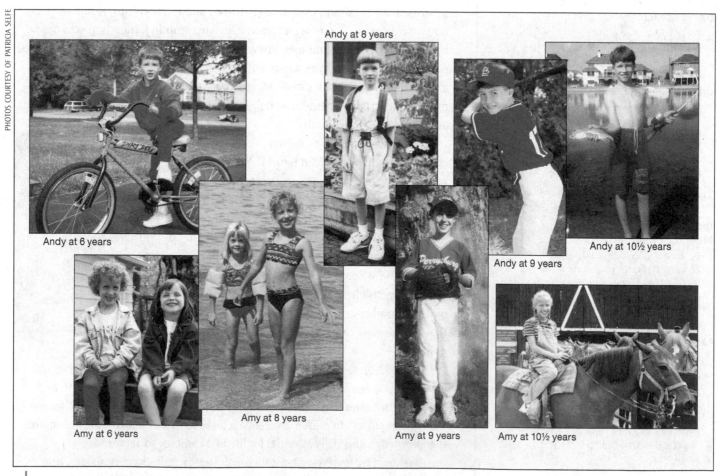

PHOTOS COURTESY OF PATRICIA SELFE

Andy at 6 years

Andy at 8 years

Andy at 9 years

Andy at 10½ years

Amy at 6 years

Amy at 8 years

Amy at 9 years

Amy at 10½ years

■ **FIGURE 3.1** ■ **Body growth during middle childhood.** School-age children continue the slow, regular pattern of growth they showed in early childhood. But around age 9, girls begin to grow at a faster rate than boys. At age 10½, Amy was taller, heavier, and more mature looking than Andy.

Common Health Problems

Children from economically advantaged homes, like Joey and Lizzie, are at their healthiest in middle childhood, full of energy and play. The cumulative effects of good nutrition, combined with rapid development of the body's immune system, offer greater protection against disease. At the same time, growth in lung size permits more air to be exchanged with each breath, so children are better able to exercise vigorously without tiring.

Not surprisingly, poverty continues to be a powerful predictor of ill health during the school years. Because economically disadvantaged U.S. families often lack health insurance (see Section 1), many children do not have regular access to a doctor. A substantial number also lack such basic necessities as a comfortable home and regular meals.

Vision and Hearing

The most common vision problem in middle childhood is *myopia,* or nearsightedness. By the end of the school years, it affects nearly 25 percent of children—a rate that rises to 60 percent by early adulthood. Heredity plays a role: Identical twins are more likely than fraternal twins to share the condition (Pacella et al., 1999). And worldwide, it occurs far more frequently in Asian than in Caucasian populations (Feldkämper & Schaeffel, 2003). Early biological trauma also can induce

© LAURA DWIGHT PHOTOGRAPHY

Heredity contributes to myopia, or nearsightedness—the most common vision problem in middle childhood. Identical twins are more likely than fraternal twins to share the condition.

myopia. School-age children with low birth weights show an especially high rate, believed to result from immaturity of visual structures, slower eye growth, and a greater incidence of eye disease (O'Connor et al., 2002).

When parents warn their children not to read in dim light or sit too close to the TV or computer screen, their concern ("You'll ruin your eyes!") is well-founded. In diverse cultures, the more time children spend reading, writing, using the computer, and doing other close work, the more likely they are to be myopic (Mutti et al., 2002; Rose et al., 2008). Consequently, myopia is one of the few health conditions to increase with SES. Fortunately, it can be overcome easily with corrective lenses.

During middle childhood, the Eustachian tube (canal that runs from the inner ear to the throat) becomes longer, narrower, and more slanted, preventing fluid and bacteria from traveling so easily from the mouth to the ear. As a result, middle-ear infections, common in infancy and early childhood, become less frequent. Still, about 3 to 4 percent of the school-age population, and as many as 20 percent of low-SES children, develop permanent hearing loss as a result of repeated infections (Ryding et al., 2002). With regular screening for both vision and hearing, defects can be corrected before they lead to serious learning difficulties.

Nutrition

School-age children need a well-balanced, plentiful diet to provide energy for successful learning in school and increased physical activity. With their increasing focus on play, friendships, and new activities, many children spend little time at the table, and the percentage who eat dinner with their families drops sharply between ages 9 and 14. Family dinnertimes have waned in general over the past two decades. Yet eating an evening meal with parents leads to a diet higher in fruits and vegetables and lower in fried foods and soft drinks (Fiese & Schwartz, 2008; Neumark-Sztainer et al., 2003).

School-age children say that they "feel better" and "focus better" after eating healthy foods and that they feel sluggish, "like a blob," after eating junk foods (O'Dea, 2003). Consistent with these informal reports, even mild nutritional deficits can affect cognitive functioning. Among school-age children from middle- to high-SES families, insufficient dietary iron and folate predicted slightly lower mental test performance (Arija et al., 2006).

As we saw in earlier sections, many poverty-stricken children in developing countries and in North America suffer from serious and prolonged malnutrition. Unfortunately, malnutrition that persists from infancy or early childhood into the school years usually leads to permanent physical and mental damage (Grantham-McGregor, Walker, & Chang, 2000; Liu et al., 2003). Government-sponsored supplementary food programs from the early years through adolescence can prevent these effects. In studies carried out in Egypt, Kenya, and Mexico, quality of food (protein, vitamin, and mineral content) strongly predicted favorable cognitive development in middle childhood (Sigman, 1995; Watkins & Pollitt, 1998).

Obesity

Mona, a very heavy child in Lizzie's class, often watched from the sidelines during recess. When she did join in games, she was slow and clumsy, the target of unkind comments: "Move it, Tubs!" Most afternoons, she walked home from school alone while the other children gathered in groups, talking, laughing, and chasing. At home, Mona sought comfort in high-calorie snacks.

Mona suffers from **obesity,** a greater-than-20-percent increase over healthy weight, based on *body mass index (BMI)*—a ratio of weight to height associated with body fat. (A BMI above the 85th percentile for a child's age and sex is considered overweight, a BMI above the 95th percentile obese.) During the past several decades, a rise in overweight and obesity has occurred in many Western nations, with large increases in Canada, Finland, Greece, Great Britain, Ireland, New Zealand, and the United States. Today, 32 percent of U.S. children and adolescents are overweight, and 11 percent are obese (Ogden, Carroll, & Flegal, 2008; Shields, 2005).

Obesity rates are also increasing rapidly in developing countries, as urbanization shifts the population toward sedentary lifestyles and diets high in meats and refined foods (World Press Review, 2004; Wrotniak et al., 2004). In China, for example, where obesity was nearly nonexistent a generation ago, today 15 percent of children and adolescents are overweight, and 3 percent are obese—a fourfold increase over the past two decades, with boys affected more than girls (Wu, 2006). In addition to lifestyle changes, a prevailing belief in Chinese culture that excess body fat signifies prosperity and health—carried over from a half-century ago, when famine caused millions of deaths—has contributed to this alarming upsurge. High valuing of sons may induce Chinese parents to offer boys especially generous portions of energy-dense foods that were once scarce but now are widely available.

Overweight rises with age, from 24 percent among U.S. preschoolers to nearly 34 percent among teenagers (Ogden, Carroll, & Flegal, 2008). More than 80 percent of affected children become overweight adults. Besides serious emotional and social difficulties, obese children are at risk for lifelong health problems. Symptoms that begin to appear in the early school years—high blood pressure, high cholesterol levels, respiratory abnormalities, and insulin resistance—are powerful predictors of heart disease, circulatory difficulties, type 2 diabetes, gallbladder disease, sleep and digestive disorders, many forms of cancer, and early death (Krishnamoorthy, Hart, & Jelalian, 2006; World Cancer Research Fund, 2007). Furthermore, obesity has caused a dramatic rise in cases of diabetes in children, sometimes leading to early, severe complications, including stroke, kidney failure, and circulatory problems that heighten the risk of eventual blindness and leg amputation (Hannon, Rao, & Arslanian, 2005).

■ **CAUSES OF OBESITY.** Not all children are equally at risk for excessive weight gain. Overweight children tend to have overweight parents, and identical twins are more likely to share the disorder than fraternal twins. But heredity accounts only for a *tendency* to gain weight (Salbe et al., 2002). The importance of environment is seen in the consistent relationship of low SES to obesity in industrialized nations, especially among ethnic minorities, including African-American, Hispanic, and Native-American children and adults (Anand et al., 2001; Ogden et al., 2006). Factors responsible include lack of knowledge about healthy diet; a tendency to buy high-fat, low-cost foods; and family stress, which can prompt overeating. Recall, also, that children who were malnourished in their early years are at increased risk for becoming overweight later.

Parental feeding practices also play a role. Some parents anxiously overfeed, interpreting almost all their child's discomforts as a desire for food. Others are overly controlling, restricting when, what, and how much their child eats and constantly worrying about weight gain (Moens, Braet, & Soetens, 2007). Both types of parents fail to help children learn to regulate their own energy intake. Also, parents of overweight children often use high-fat, sugary foods to reinforce other behaviors—a practice that leads children to attach greater value to treats (Sherry et al., 2004).

Because of these experiences, obese children soon develop maladaptive eating habits. They are more responsive than normal-weight individuals to external stimuli associated with food—taste, sight, smell, time of day, and food-related words—and less responsive to internal hunger cues (Jansen et al., 2003; Temple et al., 2007). They also eat faster and chew their food less thoroughly, a behavior pattern that appears as early as 18 months of age (Drabman et al., 1979).

Another behavior pattern implicated in weight gain involves sleep. A follow-up of more than 2,000 U.S. 3- to 12-year-olds revealed that children who got less nightly sleep were more likely to be overweight five years later (Snell, Adam, & Duncan,

These children consume a snack of cheesy fries with joyous abandon. High-calorie, fatty foods are prominent in the family diets provided by overweight parents, leaving their children at high risk for excessive weight gain.

© JEFF GREENBERG/THE IMAGE WORKS

2007). Reduced sleep may increase time available for eating, leave children too fatigued for physical activity, or disrupt the brain's regulation of hunger and metabolism.

Overweight children are less physically active than their normal-weight peers. Inactivity is both cause and consequence of excessive weight gain. Research reveals that the rise in childhood obesity is due in part to the many hours U.S. children spend watching television. In a study that tracked children's TV viewing from ages 4 to 11, the more TV children watched, the more body fat they added: Children who devoted more than 3 hours per day to TV accumulated 40 percent more fat than those devoting less than 1¾ hours (see Figure 3.2) (Proctor et al., 2003). Watching TV reduces time spent in physical exercise, and TV ads encourage children to eat fattening, unhealthy snacks. Children permitted to have a TV in their bedroom—a practice linked to especially high TV viewing—are at even further risk for overweight (Adachi-Mejia et al., 2007).

Finally, the broader food environment affects the incidence of obesity. Compared with a half-century ago, new communities today are designed for automobile use, with fewer sidewalks and other walkways—a change that has contributed to reduced physical activity (Krishnamoorthy, Hart, & Jelalian, 2006). And over the past two to three decades, the number of families who frequently eat meals outside the home has risen dramatically. Eating in restaurants or at relatives', neighbors', or friends' homes, as opposed to at home, substantially increases children's overall food consumption, including high-calorie drinks and snacks, and risk of weight gain (Ayala et al., 2008; French, Story, & Jeffrey, 2001).

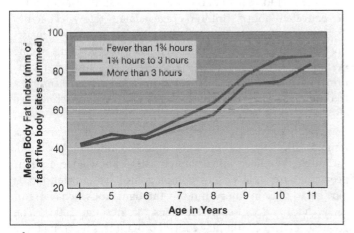

■ **FIGURE 3.2** ■ **Relationship of television viewing to gains in body fat from ages 4 to 11.** Researchers followed more than 100 children longitudinally, collecting information on hours per day of television viewing and on body fat, measured in millimeters of skinfold thickness at five body sites (upper arms, shoulders, abdomen, trunk, and thighs). The more TV children watched, the greater the gain in body fat. At ages 10 to 11, the difference between children watching fewer than 1¾ hours and those watching more than 3 hours had become large. (From M. H. Proctor et al., 2003, "Television Viewing and Change in Body Fat from Preschool to Early Adolescence: The Framingham Children's Study," *International Journal of Obesity, 27,* p. 831. © 2003 Nature Publishing Group. Adapted by permission of Macmillan Publishers, Ltd.)

■ **CONSEQUENCES OF OBESITY.** Unfortunately, physical attractiveness is a powerful predictor of social acceptance. In Western societies, both children and adults rate obese youngsters as less likable than other children, stereotyping them as lazy, sloppy, ugly, stupid, self-doubting, and deceitful (Kilpatrick & Sanders, 1978; Penny & Haddock, 2007; Tiggemann & Anesbury, 2000). By middle childhood, obese children are often socially isolated, and they report more emotional, social, and school difficulties and display more behavior problems than normal-weight agemates. Persistent obesity from childhood into adolescence predicts serious disorders, including defiance, aggression, and severe depression (Schwimmer, Burwinkle, & Varni, 2003; Young-Hyman et al., 2006). As we will see in Section 7, these psychological consequences combine with continuing discrimination to result in reduced life chances in close relationships and employment.

■ **TREATING OBESITY.** In Mona's case, the school nurse suggested that Mona and her obese mother enter a weight-loss program together. But Mona's mother, unhappily married for many years, had her own reasons for overeating and rejected this idea. In one study, only one-fourth of overweight parents judged their overweight children to have a weight problem (Jeffrey, 2004). Consistent with these findings, fewer than 20 percent of obese children get any treatment.

The most effective interventions are family-based and focus on changing behaviors (Kitzmann & Beech, 2006). In one program, both parent and child revised eating patterns, exercised daily, and reinforced each other with praise and points for progress, which they exchanged for special activities and times together. The more weight parents lost, the more their children lost (Wrotniak et al., 2004). Follow-ups after five and ten years showed that children maintained their weight loss more effectively than adults, a finding that underscores the importance of early intervention (Epstein, Roemmich, & Raynor, 2001). Treatment programs that focus on diet and lifestyle can yield substantial, long-lasting weight reduction among children and adolescents. But these interventions work best when parents' and children's weight problems are not severe (Eliakim et al., 2004; Nemet et al., 2005).

Children consume one-third of their daily caloric intake at school. Therefore, schools can also help reduce obesity by serving healthier meals, ensuring regular physical activity, and offering weight reduction programs.

Illnesses

Children experience a somewhat higher rate of illness during the first two years of elementary school than later because of exposure to sick children and an immune system that is still developing. About 15 to 20 percent of North American children have chronic diseases and conditions (including physical disabilities). By far the most common—accounting for about one-third of childhood chronic illness and the most frequent cause of school absence and childhood hospitalization—is *asthma,* in which the bronchial tubes (passages that connect the throat and lungs) are highly sensitive (Bonilla et al., 2005). In response to a variety of stimuli, such as cold weather, infection, exercise, allergies, and emotional stress, they fill with mucus and contract, leading to coughing, wheezing, and serious breathing difficulties.

During the past three decades, the number of children with asthma has more than doubled, and asthma-related deaths have also risen. Although heredity contributes to asthma, researchers believe that environmental factors are necessary to spark the illness. Boys, African-American children, and children who were born underweight, whose parents smoke, or who live in poverty are at greatest risk (Federico & Liu, 2003; Pearlman et al., 2006). For African-American and poverty-stricken youngsters, pollution in inner-city areas (which triggers allergic reactions), stressful home lives, and lack of access to good health care are implicated. Childhood obesity is also related to asthma in middle childhood, perhaps due to high levels of blood-circulating inflammatory substances associated with body fat (Saha, Riner, & Liu, 2005).

About 2 percent of North American youngsters have more severe chronic illnesses, such as sickle cell anemia, cystic fibrosis, diabetes, arthritis, cancer, and AIDS. Painful medical treatments, physical discomfort, and changes in appearance often disrupt the sick child's daily life, making it difficult to concentrate in school and separating the child from peers. As the illness worsens, family stress increases (LeBlanc, Goldsmith, & Patel, 2003). For these reasons, chronically ill children are at risk for academic, emotional, and social difficulties.

A strong link between good family functioning and child well-being exists for chronically ill children, just as it does for physically healthy children (Drotar et al., 2006). Interventions that foster positive family relationships help parent and child cope with the disease and improve children's adjustment. These include health education, counseling, social support, and disease-specific summer camps, which teach children self-help skills and give parents time off from the demands of caring for a chronically ill youngster.

Unintentional Injuries

As we conclude our discussion of threats to school-age children's health, let's return to the topic of unintentional injuries (discussed in detail in Section 1). As Figure 3.3 shows, injury fatalities increase from middle childhood into adolescence, with rates for boys rising considerably above those for girls.

Motor vehicle accidents, involving children as passengers or pedestrians, continue to be the leading cause of injury, followed by bicycle accidents (U.S. Department of Health and Human Services, 2008d). Pedestrian injuries most often result from midblock dart-outs, bicycle accidents from disobeying traffic signals and rules. When many stimuli impinge on them at once, young school-age children often fail to think before they act (Tuchfarber, Zins, & Jason, 1997). They need frequent reminders, supervision, and prohibitions against venturing into busy traffic on their own—especially as they begin to range farther from home.

Effective school-based intervention programs use extensive modeling and rehearsal of safety practices, give children

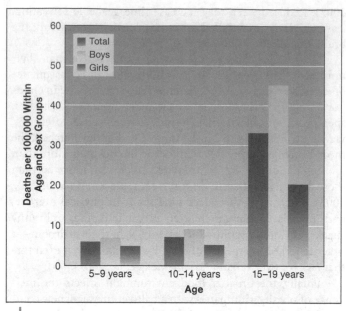

■ **FIGURE 3.3** ■ **U.S. rates of injury mortality from middle childhood to adolescence.** Injury fatalities increase with age, and the gap between boys and girls expands. Motor vehicle (passenger and pedestrian) accidents are the leading cause, with bicycle injuries next in line. (From U.S. Department of Health and Human Services, 2008d.)

feedback about their performance along with praise and tangible rewards for acquiring safety skills, and provide occasional booster sessions (Zins et al., 1994). Parents, who often overestimate their child's safety knowledge and physical abilities, must be educated about children's age-related safety capacities (Schwebel & Bounds, 2003). One vital safety measure is insisting that children wear protective helmets while bicycling, in-line skating, skateboarding, or using scooters. This simple precaution leads to an 85 percent reduction in risk of head injury, a leading cause of permanent disability and death in school-age children (Schieber & Sacks, 2001).

Highly active, impulsive children, many of whom are boys, remain especially susceptible to injury in middle childhood. Although they have just as much safety knowledge as their peers, they are far less likely to implement it. Parents tend to be particularly lax in intervening in the dangerous behaviors of such children (Schwebel, Hodgens, & Sterling, 2006). The greatest challenge for injury control programs is reaching these children and reducing their exposure to hazardous situations.

Motor Development and Play

TAKE A MOMENT... Visit a park on a pleasant weekend afternoon, and watch several preschool and school-age children at play. You will see that gains in body size and muscle strength support improved motor coordination in middle childhood. And greater cognitive and social maturity enables older children to use their new motor skills in more complex ways. A major change in children's play takes place at this time.

Gross-Motor Development

During the school years, running, jumping, hopping, and ball skills become more refined. Third to sixth graders burst into sprints as they race across the playground, jump quickly over rotating ropes, engage in intricate hopscotch patterns, kick and dribble soccer balls, bat at balls pitched by their classmates, and balance adeptly as they walk heel-to-toe across narrow ledges. These diverse skills reflect gains in four basic motor capacities:

- *Flexibility.* Compared with preschoolers, school-age children are physically more pliable and elastic, a difference that can be seen as they swing bats, kick balls, jump over hurdles, and execute tumbling routines.

- *Balance.* Improved balance supports many athletic skills, including running, hopping, skipping, throwing, kicking, and the rapid changes of direction required in many team sports.

- *Agility.* Quicker and more accurate movements are evident in the fancy footwork of dance and cheerleading and in the forward, backward, and sideways motions used to dodge opponents in tag and soccer.

- *Force.* Older youngsters can throw and kick a ball harder and propel themselves farther off the ground when running and jumping than they could at earlier ages (Haywood & Getchell, 2005).

Along with body growth, more efficient information processing plays a vital role in improved motor performance. During middle childhood, the capacity to react only to relevant information increases. And steady gains in reaction time occur, with 11-year-olds responding twice as quickly as 5-year-olds (Band et al., 2000; Kail, 2003). Because 6- and 7-year-olds are seldom successful at batting a thrown ball, T-ball is more appropriate than baseball at this age. Likewise, handball, foursquare, and kickball should precede instruction in tennis, basketball, and football.

Fine-Motor Development

Fine-motor development also improves over the school years. On rainy afternoons, Joey and Lizzie experimented with yo-yos, built model airplanes, and wove potholders on small looms. Like many children, they took up musical instruments, which demand considerable fine-motor control.

By age 6, most children can print the alphabet, their first and last names, and the numbers from 1 to 10 with reasonable clarity. Their writing is large, however, because they make strokes with the entire arm rather than just the wrist and fingers. Children usually master uppercase letters first because their horizontal and vertical motions are easier to control than the small curves of the lowercase alphabet. Legibility of writing gradually increases as children produce more accurate letters

A fancy twist of the rope following each revolution complicates this game of jump rope. During the school years, improved physical flexibility, balance, agility, and force combine with more efficient information processing to promote gains in many gross motor skills.

with uniform height and spacing. These improvements prepare children for mastering cursive writing by third grade.

Children's drawings show dramatic gains in middle childhood. By the end of the preschool years, children can accurately copy many two-dimensional shapes, and they integrate these into their drawings. Some depth cues have also begun to appear, such as making distant objects smaller than near ones (Braine et al., 1993). Around 9 to 10 years, the third dimension is clearly evident through overlapping objects, diagonal placement, and converging lines. Furthermore, as Figure 3.4 on page 84 shows, school-age children not only depict objects in considerable detail but also relate them to one another as part of an organized whole (Case, 1998; Case & Okamoto, 1996).

Sex Differences

Sex differences in motor skills that appeared during the preschool years extend into middle childhood and, in some instances, become more pronounced. Girls have an edge in fine-motor skills of handwriting and drawing and in gross-motor capacities that depend on balance and agility, such as hopping and skipping. But

■ FIGURE 3.4 ■ Increase in organization, detail, and depth cues in school-age children's drawings. *TAKE A MOMENT...* Compare both drawings to the one by a 6-year-old on page 13. In the drawing on the left, an 8-year-old represents her family at the dinner table. Notice how all parts are depicted in relation to one another, and with greater detail. Integration of depth cues increases dramatically over the school years, as shown in the drawing on the right, by a 10-year-old artist from Singapore. Here, depth is indicated by overlapping objects, diagonal placement, and converging lines, as well as by making distant objects smaller than near ones.

boys outperform girls on all other gross-motor skills and, in throwing and kicking, the gender gap is large (Cratty, 1986; Haywood & Getchell, 2005).

School-age boys' genetic advantage in muscle mass is not large enough to account for their gross-motor superiority. Rather, the social environment plays a larger role. Research confirms that parents hold higher expectations for boys' athletic performance, and children readily absorb these messages. From first through twelfth grades, girls are less positive than boys about the value of sports and their own sports ability—differences explained in part by parental beliefs (Fredricks & Eccles, 2002). In one study, boys more often stated that it was vital to their parents that they participate in athletics. These attitudes affected children's self-confidence and behavior. Girls saw themselves as having less talent at sports and, by sixth grade, devoted less time than boys to athletics (Eccles & Harold, 1991). But girls and older school-age children regard boys' advantage in sports as unjust. They indicate, for example, that coaches should spend equal time with children of each sex and that female sports should command just as much media attention as male sports (Solomon & Bredemeier, 1999).

Educating parents about the minimal differences between school-age boys' and girls' physical capacities and sensitizing them to unfair biases against promotion of girls' athletic ability may help increase girls' self-confidence and participation in athletics. And greater emphasis on skill training for girls, along with increased attention to their athletic achievements, is also likely to help. As a positive sign, compared with a generation ago, many more girls now participate in individual and team sports such as gymnastics and soccer (National Council of Youth Sports, 2008). Middle childhood is a crucial time to encourage girls' sports participation because during this time, children start to discover what they are good at and make some definite skill commitments.

Games with Rules

The physical activities of school-age children reflect an important advance in the quality of their play: Games with rules become common. Children around the world engage in an enormous variety of informally organized games, including variants on popular sports such as soccer, baseball, and basketball. In addition to the best-known childhood games, such as tag, jacks, and hopscotch, children have also invented hundreds of other games, including red rover, statues, leapfrog, kick the can, and prisoner's base (Kirchner, 2000).

Gains in perspective taking—in particular, the ability to understand the roles of several players in a game—permit this transition to rule-oriented games. These play experiences, in turn, contribute greatly to emotional and social development. Child-invented games usually rely on simple physical skills and a sizable element of luck. As a result, they rarely become contests of individual ability. Instead, they permit children to try out different styles of cooperating, competing, winning, and losing with little personal risk. Also, in their efforts to organize a game, children discover why rules are necessary and which ones work well. As we will see in Section 4, these experiences help children construct more mature concepts of fairness and justice.

Partly because of parents' concerns about safety and because of the attractions of TV, video games, and the Internet,

Applying What We Know

Providing Developmentally Appropriate Organized Sports in Middle Childhood

Suggestion	Description
Build on children's interests.	Permit children to select from among appropriate activities the ones that suit them best. Do not push children into sports they do not enjoy.
Teach age-appropriate skills.	For children younger than age 9, emphasize basic skills, such as kicking, throwing, and batting, and simplified games that grant all participants adequate playing time.
Emphasize enjoyment.	Permit children to progress at their own pace and to play for the fun of it, whether or not they become expert athletes.
Limit the frequency and length of practices.	Adjust practice time to children's attention spans and need for unstructured time with peers, with family, and for homework. Two practices a week, each no longer than 30 minutes for younger school-age children and 60 minutes for older school-age children, are sufficient.
Focus on personal and team improvement.	Emphasize effort, skill gains, and teamwork rather than winning. Avoid criticism for errors and defeat, which promotes anxiety and avoidance of athletics.
Discourage unhealthy competition.	Avoid all-star games and championship ceremonies that recognize individuals. Instead, acknowledge all participants.
Permit children to contribute to rules and strategies.	Involve children in decisions aimed at ensuring fair play and teamwork. To strengthen desirable responses, reinforce compliance rather than punishing noncompliance.

today's children devote less time to informal outdoor play. At the same time, organized sports, such as Little League baseball and soccer and hockey leagues, have expanded tremendously, filling many hours that children used to devote to spontaneous play. About half of U.S. children—66 percent of boys and 37 percent of girls—participate in organized sports at some time between ages 5 and 18 (National Council of Youth Sports, 2008).

For most children, playing on a community athletic team is associated with increased self-esteem and social competence (Daniels & Leaper, 2006; Fletcher, Nickerson, & Wright, 2003). And children who view themselves as good at sports are more

© SW PRODUCTIONS/BRAND X/CORBIS

With their coach's encouragement, these young softball players are likely to evaluate their own sports ability positively and to continue playing, thereby narrowing the gender gap in athletic participation.

likely to continue playing on teams in adolescence, which predicts greater participation in sports and other physical fitness activities in early adulthood (Marsh et al., 2007; McHale et al., 2005).

In some cases, though, the arguments of critics—that youth sports overemphasize competition and substitute adult control for children's natural experimentation with rules and strategies—are valid. Children who join teams so early that the necessary skills are beyond their abilities soon lose interest. Coaches and parents who criticize rather than encourage and who react angrily to defeat can prompt intense anxiety in some children, setting the stage for emotional difficulties and early athletic dropout, not elite performance (Tofler, Knapp, & Drell, 1998; Wall & Côté, 2007). See Applying What We Know above for ways to ensure that athletic leagues provide children with positive learning experiences.

Shadows of Our Evolutionary Past

TAKE A MOMENT... While watching children in your neighborhood park, notice how they sometimes wrestle, roll, hit, and run after one another, alternating roles while smiling and laughing. This friendly chasing and play-fighting is called **rough-and-tumble play.** It emerges in the preschool years and peaks in middle childhood, and children in many cultures engage in it with peers whom they like especially well (Pellegrini, 2004).

Children's rough-and-tumble play resembles the social behavior of many other young mammals. It seems to originate in parents' physical play with babies, especially fathers with sons. And it is more common among boys, probably because prenatal exposure to androgens (male sex hormones) predisposes boys toward active play (see Section 2).

SOCIAL ISSUES

School Recess—A Time to Play, a Time to Learn

When 7-year-old Whitney's family moved to a new city, she left a school with three daily recess periods for one with just a single 15-minute break per day, which her second-grade teacher cancelled if any child misbehaved. Whitney, who had previously enjoyed school, complained daily of headaches and an upset stomach. Her mother, Jill, thought, "My child is stressing out because she can't move all day!" After Jill and other parents successfully appealed to the school board to add a second recess period, Whitney's symptoms vanished (Rauber, 2006).

In recent years, recess—with its rich opportunities for child-organized play and peer interaction—has diminished or disappeared in many U.S. elementary schools (Pellegrini, 2005; Pellegrini & Holmes, 2006). Under the assumption that extra time for academics will translate into achievement gains, 7 percent of U.S. schools no longer provide recess to students as young as second grade. And over half

of schools that do have recess now schedule it just once a day (U.S. Department of Education, 2009).

Yet rather than subtracting from classroom learning, recess periods boost it! Research dating back more than a century confirms that distributing cognitively demanding tasks over a longer time by introducing regular breaks, rather than consolidating intensive effort within one period, enhances attention and performance at all ages. Such breaks are particularly important for children. In a series of studies, elementary school students were more attentive in the classroom after recess than before it—an effect that was greater for second than fourth graders (Pellegrini, Huberty, & Jones, 1995).

In other research, kindergartners' and first graders' engagement in peer conversation and games during recess predicted gains in academic achievement, even after other factors that might explain the relationship (such as previous achievement) were controlled (Pellegrini, 1992; Pellegrini et al., 2002). Recall from Section 2 that children's social maturity contributes substantially to academic competence. Recess is one of the few remaining contexts

Recess offers rich opportunities for child-organized play and games that promote academic achievement and social competence.

devoted to child-organized games that provide practice in vital social skills—cooperation, leadership, followership, and inhibition of aggression—under adult supervision rather than adult direction. As children transfer these skills to the classroom, they may participate in discussions, collaborate, follow rules, and enjoy academic pursuits more—factors that enhance motivation and achievement.

In our evolutionary past, rough-and-tumble play may have been important for developing fighting skill (Power, 2000). It also helps children form a **dominance hierarchy**—a stable ordering of group members that predicts who will win when conflict arises. Observations of arguments, threats, and physical attacks between children reveal a consistent lineup of winners and losers that becomes increasingly stable in middle childhood, especially among boys. Once school-age children

establish a dominance hierarchy, hostility is rare (Pellegrini & Smith, 1998; Roseth et al., 2007). Children seem to use play-fighting as a safe context to assess the strength of a peer before challenging that peer's dominance.

As children reach puberty, individual differences in strength become apparent, and rough-and-tumble play declines. When it does occur, its meaning changes: Adolescent boys' rough-and-tumble is linked to aggression (Pellegrini, 2003). Unlike children, teenage rough-and-tumble players "cheat," hurting their opponent. In explanation, boys often say that they are retaliating, apparently to reestablish dominance. Thus, a play behavior that limits aggression in childhood becomes a context for hostility in adolescence.

Physical Education

Physical activity supports many aspects of children's development—health, sense of self-worth, and the cognitive and social skills necessary for getting along with others. Yet to devote more time to academic instruction, U.S. elementary schools have cut back on recess, despite its contribution to all domains of development (see the Social Issues box above). Similarly, only 15 percent of U.S. elementary and middle schools provide students with physical education at least three days a week, a figure that drops to 3 percent in high school (Lee et al., 2007). Not surpris-

On an Alaskan beach, these 6- and 7-year-old brothers engage in rough-and-tumble play, which can be distinguished from aggression by its good-natured quality.

ingly, physical inactivity among school-age children is pervasive: Only 42 percent of boys and 11 percent of girls are active enough for good health—that is, engage in at least moderate-intensity exercise for one hour or more per day (Metcalf et al., 2008).

Many experts believe that schools should not only offer more frequent physical education classes but also change the content of these programs. Training in competitive sports, often a high priority, is unlikely to reach the least physically fit youngsters, who avoid activities demanding a high level of skill. Instead, programs should emphasize enjoyable, informal games and individual exercise—pursuits most likely to endure.

Physically fit children tend to become active adults who reap many benefits (Dennison et al., 1998; Tammelin et al., 2003). These include greater physical strength, resistance to many illnesses (from colds and flu to cancer, diabetes, and heart disease), enhanced psychological well-being, and a longer life.

ASK YOURSELF

>> **REVIEW**
Explain the adaptive value of rough-and-tumble play and dominance hierarchies.

>> **APPLY**
Nine-year-old Allison thinks she isn't good at sports, and she doesn't like physical education class. Suggest some strategies her teacher can use to improve her pleasure and involvement in physical activity.

>> **CONNECT**
Select one of the following health problems of middle childhood: myopia, obesity, asthma, or unintentional injuries. Explain how both genetic and environmental factors contribute to it.

>> **REFLECT**
Did you participate in organized sports as a child? If so, what kind of climate for learning did coaches and parents create? What impact do you think your experiences had on your development?

Cognitive Development

"Finally!" 6-year-old Lizzie exclaimed the day she entered first grade. "Now I get to go to real school, just like Joey!" Lizzie walked into her classroom confidently, pencils, crayons, and writing pad in hand, ready for a more disciplined approach to learning than she had experienced in early childhood.

Lizzie was entering a whole new world of challenging mental activities. In a single morning, she and her classmates wrote in journals, met in reading groups, worked on addition and subtraction, and sorted leaves gathered for a science project. As Lizzie and Joey moved through the elementary school grades, they tackled increasingly complex tasks and became more accomplished at reading, writing, math skills, and general knowledge of the world. To understand the cognitive attain-

ments of middle childhood, we turn to research inspired by Piaget's theory and by the information-processing perspective. And we look at expanding definitions of intelligence that help us appreciate individual differences. Our discussion continues with language, which blossoms further in these years. Finally, we consider the role of schools in children's development.

Piaget's Theory: The Concrete Operational Stage

When Lizzie visited my child development class as a 4-year-old, Piaget's conservation problems confused her (see Section 1, page 17). For example, when water was poured from a tall, narrow container into a short, wide one, she insisted that the amount of water had changed. But when Lizzie returned at age 8, she found these tasks easy. "Of course it's the same!" she exclaimed. "The water's shorter, but it's also wider. Pour it back," she instructed the college student who was interviewing her. "You'll see, it's the same amount!"

Concrete Operational Thought

Lizzie has entered Piaget's **concrete operational stage,** which extends from about 7 to 11 years and marks a major turning point in cognitive development. Thought is far more logical, flexible, and organized than it was earlier.

■ **CONSERVATION.** The ability to pass *conservation tasks* provides clear evidence of *operations*—mental actions that obey logical rules. Notice how Lizzie is capable of *decentration*, focusing on several aspects of a problem and relating them, rather than centering on just one. Lizzie also demonstrates **reversibility,** the capacity to think through a series of steps and then mentally reverse direction, returning to the starting point. Recall from Section 1 that reversibility is part of every logical operation. It is solidly achieved in middle childhood.

■ **CLASSIFICATION.** Between ages 7 and 10, children pass Piaget's *class inclusion problem* (see page 18). This indicates that they are more aware of classification hierarchies and can focus on relations between a general category and two specific categories at the same time—that is, on three relations at once (Hodges & French, 1988; Ni, 1998). Collections—stamps, coins, baseball cards, rocks, and bottle caps—become common in middle childhood. At age 10, Joey spent hours sorting and resorting his baseball cards, grouping them first by league and team, then by playing position and batting average. He could separate the players into a variety of classes and subclasses and easily rearrange them.

■ **SERIATION.** The ability to order items along a quantitative dimension, such as length or weight, is called **seriation.** To test for it, Piaget asked children to arrange sticks of different lengths from shortest to longest. Older preschoolers can put the sticks in a row, but they do so haphazardly, making many errors. In

An improved ability to categorize underlies children's interest in collecting objects during middle childhood. Here, an 8-year-old sorts and organizes buttons in her extensive collection.

contrast, 6- to 7-year-olds create the series efficiently, moving in an orderly sequence from the smallest stick, to the next largest, and so on.

The concrete operational child can also seriate mentally, an ability called **transitive inference.** In a well-known transitive inference problem, Piaget showed children pairings of sticks of different colors. From observing that Stick A is longer than Stick B and Stick B is longer than Stick C, children must infer that A is longer than C. Like Piaget's class inclusion task, transitive inference requires children to integrate three relations at once—in this instance, A–B, B–C, and A–C. When researchers take steps to ensure that children remember the premises (A–B and B–C), 7-year-olds can grasp transitive inference (Andrews & Halford, 1998; Wright, 2006).

■ **SPATIAL REASONING.** Piaget found that school-age children's understanding of space is more accurate than that of preschoolers. Let's consider children's **cognitive maps**—their mental representations of familiar large-scale spaces, such as their neighborhood or school. Drawing a map of a large-scale space requires considerable perspective-taking skill. Because the entire space cannot be seen at once, children must infer its overall layout by relating its separate parts.

Preschoolers and young school-age children include *landmarks* on the maps they draw, but their arrangement is not always accurate. They do better when asked to place stickers showing the location of desks and people on a map of their classroom. But if the map is rotated to a position other than the orientation of the classroom, they have difficulty (Liben & Downs, 1993).

Around age 8 to 10, maps become better organized, showing landmarks along an *organized route of travel*. At the same time, children become able to give clear, well-organized instructions for getting from one place to another by using a "mental walk" strategy—imagining another person's movements along a route (Gauvain & Rogoff, 1989). At the end of middle childhood, children form an *overall view of a large-scale space*. And they readily draw and read maps, even when the orientation of the map and the space it represents do not match (Liben, 1999). Ten- to 12-year-olds also grasp the notion of *scale*—the proportional relation between a space and its representation on a map (Liben, 2006).

Cultural frameworks influence children's map making. In many non-Western communities, people rarely use maps for way-finding but rely on information from neighbors, street vendors, and shopkeepers. Also, compared to their Western agemates, non-Western children less often ride in cars and more often walk, which results in intimate neighborhood knowledge. When a researcher had older school-age children in small cities in India and in the United States draw maps of their neighborhoods, the Indian children represented a rich array of landmarks and aspects of social life, such as people and vehicles, in a small area surrounding their home. The U.S. children, in contrast, drew a more formal, extended space, highlighting main streets and key directions (north–south, east–west) but including few landmarks (see Figure 3.5) (Parameswaran, 2003). Although the U.S. children's maps scored higher in cognitive maturity, this difference reflected cultural interpretations of the task. When asked to create a map to "help people find their way," the Indian children drew spaces as far-reaching and organized as the U.S. children's.

Limitations of Concrete Operational Thought

As the name of this stage suggests, concrete operational thinking suffers from one important limitation: Children think in an organized, logical fashion only when dealing with concrete information they can perceive directly. Their mental operations work poorly with abstract ideas—ones not apparent in the real world. Consider children's solutions to transitive inference problems. When shown pairs of sticks of unequal length, Lizzie easily engaged in transitive inference. But she had difficulty with a hypothetical version of this task: "Susan is taller than Sally, and Sally is taller than Mary. Who is the tallest?" Not until age 11 or 12 can children solve this problem.

That logical thought is at first tied to immediate situations helps account for a special feature of concrete operational reasoning: School-age children master concrete operational tasks step by step, not all at once. For example, they usually grasp conservation of number first, followed by conservation of length, liquid, and mass, and then weight. This *continuum of acquisition* (or gradual mastery) of logical concepts is another indication of

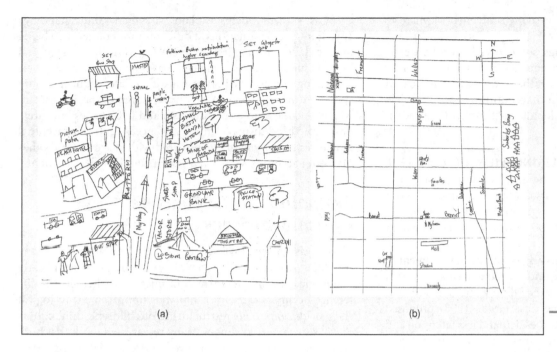

(a)   (b)

■ **FIGURE 3.5** ■ **Maps drawn by older school-age children from India and the United States.** (a) The Indian child depicted many landmarks and features of social life in a small area near her home. (b) The U.S. child drew a more extended space and highlighted main streets and key directions but included few landmarks and people. (From G. Parameswaran, 2003, "Experimenter Instructions as a Mediator in the Effects of Culture on Mapping One's Neighborhood," *Journal of Environmental Psychology, 23,* pp. 415–416. Copyright © 2003, reprinted with permission from Elsevier.)

the limitations of concrete operational thinking (Fischer & Bidell, 1991). Rather than coming up with general logical principles that they apply to all relevant situations, school-age children seem to work out the logic of each problem separately.

Follow-Up Research on Concrete Operational Thought

According to Piaget, brain development combined with experience in a rich and varied external world should lead children everywhere to reach the concrete operational stage at about the same time. Yet recent evidence indicates that specific cultural and school practices have much to do with mastery of Piagetian tasks (Rogoff, 2003; Rogoff & Chavajay, 1995). And information-processing research helps explain the gradual mastery of logical concepts in middle childhood.

■ **THE IMPACT OF CULTURE AND SCHOOLING.** In tribal and village societies, conservation is often delayed. For example, among the Hausa of Nigeria, who live in small agricultural settlements and rarely send their children to school, even the most basic conservation tasks—number, length, and liquid—are not understood until age 11 or later (Fahrmeier, 1978). This suggests that taking part in relevant everyday activities helps children master conservation and other Piagetian problems. Joey and Lizzie, for example, think of fairness in terms of equal distribution—a value emphasized in their culture. They frequently divide materials, such as crayons or treats, equally among their friends. Because they often see the same quantity arranged in different ways, they grasp conservation early.

The very experience of going to school seems to promote mastery of Piagetian tasks. When children of the same age are tested, those who have been in school longer do better on transitive inference problems (Artman & Cahan, 1993). Opportunities

to seriate objects, to learn about order relations, and to remember the parts of complex problems are probably responsible. Yet certain informal nonschool experiences can also foster operational thought. Around age 7 to 8, Zinacanteco Indian girls of southern Mexico, who learn to weave elaborately designed fabrics as an alternative to schooling, engage in mental transformations to figure out how a warp strung on a loom will turn out as woven cloth—reasoning expected at the concrete operational stage. North American children of the same age, who do much better than Zinacanteco children on Piagetian tasks,

This Zinacanteco Indian girl of southern Mexico learns the centuries-old practice of backstrap weaving, which requires complex mental transformations. Although North American children perform better on Piaget's tasks, Zinacanteco children are far more adept at figuring out how to transform warp strung on a loom into woven cloth.

have great difficulty with these weaving problems (Maynard & Greenfield, 2003).

On the basis of such findings, some investigators have concluded that the forms of logic required by Piagetian tasks do not emerge spontaneously but, rather, are heavily influenced by training, context, and cultural conditions. Does this view remind you of Vygotsky's sociocultural theory, discussed in earlier sections?

■ **AN INFORMATION-PROCESSING VIEW OF CONCRETE OPERATIONAL THOUGHT.** The gradual mastery of logical concepts in middle childhood raises a familiar question about Piaget's theory: Is an abrupt stagewise transition to logical thought the best way to describe cognitive development in middle childhood?

Some *neo-Piagetian theorists* argue that the development of operational thinking can best be understood in terms of gains in information-processing speed rather than a sudden shift to a new stage. For example, Robbie Case (1996, 1998) proposed that, with practice, cognitive schemes demand less attention and become more automatic. This frees up space in *working memory* so children can focus on combining old schemes and generating new ones. For instance, the child who sees water poured from one container to another recognizes that the height of the liquid changes. As this understanding becomes routine, the child notices that the width of the water changes as well. Soon children coordinate these observations, and they conserve liquid. Then, as this logical idea becomes well-practiced, the child transfers it to more demanding situations.

Once the schemes of a Piagetian stage are sufficiently automatic, enough working memory is available to integrate them into an improved representation. As a result, children acquire *central conceptual structures*—networks of concepts and relations that permit them to think more effectively about a wide range of situations (Case, 1996, 1998). The central conceptual structures that emerge from integrating concrete operational schemes are broadly applicable principles that result in increasingly complex, systematic reasoning, which we will discuss in Section 14 in the context of formal operational thought.

Case and his colleagues—along with other information-processing researchers—have examined children's performance on a wide variety of tasks, including solving arithmetic problems, understanding stories, drawing pictures, and interpreting social situations. In each task, preschoolers typically focus on only one dimension. In understanding stories, for example, they grasp only a single story line. In drawing pictures, they depict objects separately. By the early school years, children coordinate two dimensions—two story lines in a single plot and drawings that show both the features of objects and their relationships. Around 9 to 11 years, children integrate multiple dimensions (Case, 1998; Halford & Andrews, 2006). Children tell coherent stories with a main plot and several subplots. And their drawings follow a set of rules for representing perspective and, therefore, include several points of reference, such as near, midway, and far.

Case's theory helps explain why many understandings appear in specific situations at different times rather than being mastered all at once. First, different forms of the same logical insight, such as the various conservation tasks, vary in their processing demands, with those acquired later requiring more space in working memory. Second, children's experiences vary widely. A child who often listens to and tells stories but rarely draws pictures displays more advanced central conceptual structures in storytelling. Compared with Piaget's, Case's theory better accounts for unevenness in cognitive development.

Evaluation of the Concrete Operational Stage

Piaget was correct that school-age children approach many problems in organized, rational ways not possible in early childhood. But disagreement continues over whether this difference occurs because of *continuous* improvement in logical skills or *discontinuous* restructuring of children's thinking (as Piaget's stage idea assumes). Many researchers think that both types of change may be involved (Carey, 1999; Case, 1998; Demetriou et al., 2002; Fischer & Bidell, 2006; Halford & Andrews, 2006).

During the school years, children apply logical schemes to many more tasks. In the process, their thought seems to undergo qualitative change—toward a comprehensive grasp of the underlying principles of logical thought. Piaget himself seems to have recognized this possibility in evidence for gradual mastery of conservation and other tasks. So perhaps some blend of Piagetian and information-processing ideas holds the greatest promise for understanding cognitive development in middle childhood.

ASK YOURSELF

>> **REVIEW**
Children's performance on conservation tasks illustrates a continuum of acquisition of logical concepts. Review the preceding sections, and list additional examples of gradual development of logical reasoning.

>> **APPLY**
Nine-year-old Adrienne spends many hours helping her father build furniture in his woodworking shop. How might this experience facilitate Adrienne's performance on Piagetian seriation problems?

>> **CONNECT**
Explain how advances in perspective taking contribute to school-age children's improved ability to draw and use maps.

>> **REFLECT**
Which aspects of Piaget's description of the concrete operational child do you accept? Which do you doubt? Explain, citing research evidence.

Information Processing

In contrast to Piaget's focus on overall cognitive change, the information-processing perspective examines separate aspects of thinking. Attention and memory, which underlie every act of cognition, are central concerns in middle childhood, just as they were during infancy and the preschool years. Advances in metacognition and opportunities for self-regulation aid development. Also, increased understanding of how school-age children process information is being applied to their academic learning—in particular, to reading and mathematics.

Researchers believe that brain development contributes to the following basic changes in information processing that facilitate diverse aspects of thinking:

■ *Increases in information-processing speed and capacity.* Time needed to process information on a wide variety of cognitive tasks declines rapidly between ages 6 and 12 (Kail & Park, 1992, 1994). This suggests a biologically based gain in speed of thinking, possibly due to myelination and synaptic pruning in the brain (Kail, 2003). Some researchers believe this greater efficiency contributes to more complex, effective thinking because a faster thinker can hold on to and operate on more information in working memory (Halford & Andrews, 2006; Luna et al., 2004). Indeed, *digit span,* which assesses the basic capacity of working memory (see page 26), improves from about five digits at age 7 to seven digits at age 12 (Kail, 2003).

■ *Gains in inhibition.* As indicated in earlier sections, inhibition—the ability to control internal and external distracting stimuli—improves from infancy on. But additional strides occur in middle childhood as the frontal lobes of the cerebral cortex develop further (Luna et al., 2004; Nelson, Thomas, & de Haan, 2006). Individuals skilled at inhibition can prevent their minds from straying to irrelevant thoughts, an ability that supports many information-processing skills by preserving space in working memory for the task at hand (Dempster & Corkill, 1999; Klenberg, Korkman, & Lahti-Nuuttila, 2001).

Besides brain development, strategy use contributes to more effective information processing. As we will see, school-age children think far more strategically than preschoolers.

Attention

In middle childhood, attention becomes more selective, adaptable, and planful. First, children become better at deliberately attending to just those aspects of a situation that are relevant to their goals. Researchers study this increasing selectivity of attention by introducing irrelevant stimuli into a task and seeing how well children attend to its central elements. Performance improves sharply between ages 6 and 10 (Goldberg, Maurer, & Lewis, 2001; Gomez-Perez & Ostrosky-Solis, 2006; Tabibi & Pfeffer, 2007).

Second, older children flexibly adapt their attention to task requirements. When asked to sort cards with pictures that vary in both color and shape, children age 5 and older can switch their basis of sorting from color to shape when asked to do so; younger children typically persist in sorting in just one way (Brooks et al., 2003; Zelazo, Frye, & Rapus, 1996). And when studying for a spelling test, 10-year-old Joey was much more likely than Lizzie to devote most attention to the words he knew least well (Masur, McIntyre, & Flavell, 1973).

Finally, planning improves greatly in middle childhood (Gauvain, 2004; Scholnick, 1995). School-age children scan detailed pictures and written materials for similarities and differences more thoroughly than preschoolers. And on tasks with many parts, they make decisions about what to do first and what to do next in an orderly fashion. As Section 1 revealed, children learn much about planning by collaborating with more expert planners. In one study of family interactions, discussions involving planning at ages 4 and 9 predicted planning competence in adolescence (Gauvain & Huard, 1999). The demands of school tasks—and teachers' explanations of how to plan—also contribute to gains in planning.

The attentional strategies just considered are crucial for success in school. Unfortunately, some children have great difficulty paying attention. See the Biology and Environment box on pages 92–93 for a discussion of the serious learning and behavior problems of children with attention-deficit hyperactivity disorder.

Memory Strategies

As attention improves, so do *memory strategies,* deliberate mental activities we use to store and retain information. When Lizzie had a list of things to learn—for example, the state capitals of the United States—she immediately used **rehearsal**—repeating the information to herself. This memory strategy first appears in the early grade school years. Soon after, a second strategy becomes common: **organization**—grouping related items together (for example, all state capitals in the same part of the country), an approach that improves recall dramatically (Schneider, 2002).

Perfecting memory strategies requires time and effort. Eight-year-old Lizzie rehearsed in a piecemeal fashion. After being given the word *cat* in a list of items, she said, "Cat, cat, cat." But 10-year-old Joey used a more effective approach: He combined previous words with each new item, saying, "Desk, man, yard, cat, cat" (Kunzinger, 1985). Joey also organized more skillfully, grouping items into fewer categories. And he used organization in a wide range of memory tasks, whereas Lizzie used it only when categorical relations among items were obvious (Bjorklund et al., 1994).

Furthermore, Joey often combined several strategies—for example, organizing items, then stating the category names, and finally rehearsing. The more strategies children apply simultaneously and consistently, the better they remember (Hock, Park, & Bjorklund, 1998; DeMarie et al., 2004). Younger

▪ BIOLOGY AND ENVIRONMENT ▪

Children with Attention-Deficit Hyperactivity Disorder

While the other fifth graders worked quietly at their desks, Calvin squirmed, dropped his pencil, looked out the window, and fiddled with his shoelaces. "Hey Joey," he yelled across the room, "wanna play ball after school?" But the other children weren't eager to play with Calvin, who was physically awkward and failed to follow the rules of the game. He had trouble taking turns at bat. In the outfield, he tossed his mitt up in the air and looked elsewhere when the ball came his way. Calvin's desk was a chaotic mess. He often lost pencils, books, and other school materials, and he had difficulty remembering assignments and due dates.

Symptoms of ADHD

Calvin is one of 3 to 6 percent of school-age children with **attention-deficit hyperactivity disorder (ADHD)**, which involves inattention, impulsivity, and excessive motor activity resulting in academic and social problems (American Psychiatric Association, 1994; Barkley, 2006). Boys are diagnosed about four times as often as girls. However, many girls with ADHD seem to be overlooked, either because their symptoms are less flagrant or because of a gender bias: A

disruptive boy is more likely to be referred for treatment (Abikoff et al., 2002; Biederman et al., 2005).

Children with ADHD cannot stay focused on a task requiring mental effort for more than a few minutes. They often act impulsively, ignoring social rules and lashing out with hostility when frustrated. Many, though not all, are *hyperactive,* exhausting parents and teachers and irritating other children with their excessive motor activity. For a child to be diagnosed with ADHD, these symptoms must have appeared before age 7 as a persistent problem.

Because of their difficulty concentrating, children with ADHD score 7 to 15 points lower than other children on intelligence tests (Barkley, 2002a). Researchers agree that deficient executive processing underlies ADHD symptoms. According to one view, children with ADHD are impaired in capacity to inhibit action in favor of thought (Barkley, 2003a). Another hypothesis is that ADHD results from a cluster of executive processing problems that interfere with ability to guide one's own actions (Brown, 2005, 2006). Research confirms that children with ADHD do poorly on tasks requiring sustained attention; find it hard to ignore irrelevant information; have difficulty with memory, planning, reasoning, and problem solving in academic and social situations; and often fail to manage

frustration and intense emotion (Barkley, 2003b, 2006).

Origins of ADHD

ADHD runs in families and is highly heritable: Identical twins share it more often than fraternal twins (Rasmussen et al., 2004; Rietvelt et al., 2004). Children with ADHD show abnormal brain functioning, including reduced electrical and blood-flow activity and structural abnormalities in the frontal lobes of the cerebral cortex and in other areas involved in attention, inhibition of behavior, and other aspects of motor control (Mackie et al., 2007; Sowell et al., 2003). Also, the brains of children with ADHD grow more slowly and are about 3 percent smaller in overall volume than those of unaffected agemates (Durston et al., 2004; Shaw et al., 2007). Several genes affecting neural communication have been implicated in the disorder (Biederman & Spencer, 2000; Quist & Kennedy, 2001).

At the same time, ADHD is associated with environmental factors. Prenatal teratogens—particularly those involving long-term exposure, such as illegal drugs, alcohol, and tobacco—are linked to inattention and hyperactivity (Milberger et al., 1997). Furthermore, children with ADHD are more likely to come from homes in which marriages are unhappy and family stress is high (Bernier & Siegel, 1994). But a stressful home life rarely causes

---

school-age children often try out various memory strategies, but they use them less systematically and with less success than older children. Still, the tendency to experiment allows younger children to discover which strategies work best and how to combine them effectively. Indeed, children experiment with strategies when faced with many cognitive challenges—an approach that enables them to gradually "home in" on the most effective techniques (Siegler, 1996, 2007).

By the end of middle childhood, children start to use **elaboration**—creating a relationship, or shared meaning, between two or more pieces of information that do not belong to the same category. For example, if two of the words you must learn are *fish* and *pipe,* you might generate the verbal statement or mental image, "The fish is smoking a pipe." This highly effective memory technique, which requires considerable effort and space in working memory, becomes increasingly common in adolescence and early adulthood (Schneider & Pressley, 1997).

Because organization and elaboration combine items into *meaningful chunks,* they permit children to hold onto much more information and, as a result, further expand working memory. In addition, when children link a new item to information

they already know, they can *retrieve* it easily by thinking of other items associated with it. As we will see, this also contributes to improved memory during the school years.

The Knowledge Base and Memory Performance

During middle childhood, the long-term knowledge base grows larger and becomes organized into increasingly elaborate, hierarchically structured networks. This rapid growth of knowledge helps children use strategies and remember (Schneider, 2002). In other words, knowing more about a topic makes new information more meaningful and familiar so it is easier to store and retrieve.

To test this idea, researchers classified fourth graders as either experts or novices in knowledge of soccer, then gave both groups lists of soccer and nonsoccer items to learn. Experts remembered far more items on the soccer list (but not on the nonsoccer list) than novices. And during recall, experts' listing of items was better organized, as indicated by clustering of items into categories (Schneider & Bjorklund, 1992). This better

ADHD. Rather, these children's behaviors can contribute to family problems, which intensify the child's preexisting difficulties.

Treating ADHD

Calvin's doctor eventually prescribed stimulant medication, the most common treatment for ADHD. As long as dosage is carefully regulated, these drugs reduce symptoms in 70 percent of children who take them (Greenhill, Halperin, & Abikoff, 1999). Stimulant medication seems to increase activity in the frontal lobes, thereby improving the child's capacity to sustain attention and to inhibit off-task behavior.

In 2006, an advisory panel convened by the U.S. Food and Drug Administration warned that stimulants might impair heart functioning, even causing sudden death in a few individuals, and advocated warning labels describing these potential risks. Debate over the safety of medication for ADHD is likely to intensify. In any case, medication is not enough. Drugs cannot teach children to compensate for inattention and impulsivity. The most effective treatment approach combines medication with interventions that model and reinforce appropriate academic and social behavior (American Academy of Pediatrics, 2005a; Smith, Barkley, & Shapiro, 2006).

Family intervention is also important. Inattentive, overactive children strain the patience of parents, who are likely to react punitively and inconsistently—a child-rearing style that strengthens defiant, aggressive behavior. In fact, in 45 to 65 percent of cases, these two sets of behavior problems occur together (Barkley, 2002b).

Some media reports suggest that the number of U.S. children diagnosed with ADHD has increased greatly. But two large surveys yielded similar overall prevalence rates 20 years ago and today. Nevertheless, the incidence of ADHD is much higher in some communities than others. At times, children are overdiagnosed and unnecessarily medicated because their parents and teachers are impatient with inattentive, active behavior within normal range. In Hong Kong, where academic success is particularly prized, children are diagnosed at more than twice the rate seen in North America. But in Great Britain, where doctors are hesitant to label a child with ADHD or to prescribe medication, children are underdiagnosed and often do not receive the treatment they need (Taylor, 2004).

ADHD is usually a lifelong disorder. Affected individuals are at risk for persistent antisocial behavior, depression, and other problems (Kessler et al., 2005, 2006). Adults with ADHD continue to need help in structuring their environments, regulating negative emotion, selecting appropriate careers, and understanding their condition as a biological deficit rather than a character flaw.

This child frequently engages in disruptive behavior at school. Children with ADHD have great difficulty staying on task and often act impulsively, ignoring social rules.

organization at retrieval suggests that highly knowledgeable children organize information in their area of expertise with little or no effort. Consequently, experts can devote more working-memory resources to using recalled information for reasoning and problem solving (Bjorklund & Douglas, 1997).

But knowledge is not the only important factor in children's strategic memory processing. Children who are expert in an area are usually highly motivated. As a result, they not only acquire knowledge more quickly but also *actively use what they know* to add more. In contrast, academically unsuccessful children fail to ask how previously stored information can clarify new material. This, in turn, interferes with the development of a broad knowledge base (Schneider & Bjorklund, 1998). So by the end of the school years, extensive knowledge and use of memory strategies support one another.

Culture, Schooling, and Memory Strategies

Rehearsal, organization, and elaboration are techniques that people usually use when they need to remember information for its own sake. On many other occasions, memory occurs as a natural byproduct of participation in daily activities (Rogoff, 2003).

A repeated finding is that people in non-Western cultures who lack formal schooling do not use or benefit from instruction in memory strategies because they see no practical reason to use these techniques (Rogoff & Chavajay, 1995). Tasks that require children to recall isolated bits of information, which are common in classrooms, strongly motivate use of memory strategies. In fact, Western children get so much practice with this type of learning that they do not refine techniques relying on cues available in everyday life, such as spatial location and arrangement of objects. For example, Guatemalan Mayan 9-year-olds do slightly better than their North American agemates when told to remember the placement of 40 familiar objects in a play scene. North American children often rehearse object names when it would be more effective to keep track of spatial relations (Rogoff & Wadell, 1982). The development of memory strategies, then, is not just a product of a more competent information-processing system. It also depends on task demands and cultural circumstances.

A mother and daughter of the Colombian U'wa people, who have no written tradition, make "cocara" leaf hats, which girls wear from puberty until marriage. Although this child demonstrates keen memory for how to select, cut, and assemble the leaves, she may have difficulty recalling the isolated bits of information that school tasks often require.

The School-Age Child's Theory of Mind

During middle childhood, children's *theory of mind,* or set of ideas about mental activities, becomes more elaborate and refined. Recall from Section 1 that this awareness of thought is often called *metacognition.* School-age children's improved ability to reflect on their own mental life is another reason that their thinking advances.

Unlike preschoolers, who view the mind as a passive container of information, older children regard it as an active, constructive agent that selects and transforms information (Kuhn, 2000). Consequently, they have a much better understanding of cognitive processes and the impact of psychological

factors on performance. School-age children, for example, know that doing well on a task depends on focusing attention—concentrating and exerting effort (Miller & Bigi, 1979). With age, they also become increasingly aware of effective memory strategies and why they work (Alexander et al., 2003). And children gradually grasp relationships between mental activities—for example, that remembering is crucial for understanding and that understanding strengthens memory (Schwanenflugel, Henderson, & Fabricius, 1998).

Furthermore, school-age children's understanding of sources of knowledge expands. They realize that people can extend their knowledge not just by directly observing events and talking to others but also by making *mental inferences* (Miller, Hardin, & Montgomery, 2003). This grasp of inference enables knowledge of *false belief* to expand. In several studies, researchers told children complex stories involving one character's belief about a second character's belief. Then the children answered questions about what the first character thought the second character would do (see Figure 3.6). By age 7, children were aware that people form beliefs about other people's beliefs and that these second-order beliefs can be wrong! Appreciation of *second-order false belief* enables children to pinpoint the reasons that another person arrived at a certain belief (Astington, Pelletier, & Homer, 2002; Naito & Seki, 2009). This assists them greatly in understanding others' perspectives.

School-age children's capacity for more complex thinking contributes greatly to their more reflective, process-oriented view of the mind. But experiences that foster awareness of mental activities are also involved. In a study of rural children of Cameroon, Africa, those who attended school performed much better on theory-of-mind tasks (Vinden, 2002). In school, teachers often call attention to the workings of the mind when they remind children to pay attention, remember mental steps, and evaluate their reasoning. And as children engage in reading,

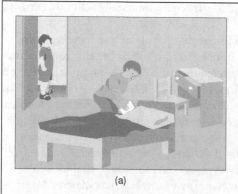

(a)

Jason has a letter from a friend. Lisa wants to read the letter, but Jason doesn't want her to. Jason puts the letter under his pillow.

(b)

Jason leaves the room to help his mother.

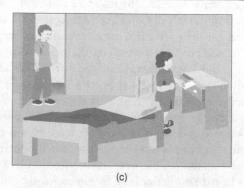

(c)

While Jason is gone, Lisa takes the letter and reads it. Jason returns and watches Lisa, but Lisa doesn't see Jason. Then Lisa puts the letter in Jason's desk.

■ **FIGURE 3.6** ■ **A second-order false-belief task.** After relating the story in the sequence of pictures, the researcher asks a second-order false-belief question: "Where does Lisa think Jason will look for the letter? Why?" Around age 7, children answer correctly—that Lisa thinks Jason will look under his pillow because Lisa doesn't know that Jason saw her put the letter in the desk. (Adapted from Astington, Pelletier, & Homer, 2002.)

writing, and math, they often use *private speech,* at first speaking out loud and then silently to themselves. As they "hear themselves think," they probably detect many aspects of mental life.

Cognitive Self-Regulation

Although metacognition expands, school-age children often have difficulty putting what they know about thinking into action. They are not yet good at **cognitive self-regulation,** the process of continuously monitoring progress toward a goal, checking outcomes, and redirecting unsuccessful efforts. For example, Lizzie knows she should group items when memorizing and that she should reread a complicated paragraph to make sure she understands. But she does not always engage in these activities.

To study cognitive self-regulation, researchers sometimes look at the impact that children's awareness of memory strategies has on how well they remember. By second grade, the more children know about memory strategies, the more they recall— a relationship that strengthens over middle childhood (Pierce & Lange, 2000). And when children apply a strategy consistently, their knowledge of strategies strengthens, resulting in a bidirectional association between metacognition and strategy use that enhances self-regulation (Schlagmüller & Schneider, 2002).

Why does cognitive self-regulation develop gradually? Monitoring learning outcomes is cognitively demanding, requiring constant evaluation of effort and progress. By adolescence, self-regulation is a strong predictor of academic success (Joyner & Kurtz-Costes, 1997). Students who do well in school know when their learning is going well. If they encounter obstacles, they take steps to address them—for example, organize the learning environment, review confusing material, or seek support from more expert adults or peers. This active, purposeful approach contrasts sharply with the passive orientation of students who achieve poorly (Zimmerman & Risemberg, 1997).

Parents and teachers can foster self-regulation. In one study, researchers observed parents helping their children with problem solving during the summer before third grade. Parents who patiently pointed out important features of the task and suggested strategies had children who, in the classroom, more often discussed ways to approach problems and monitored their own performance (Stright et al., 2002). Explaining the effectiveness of strategies is particularly helpful because it provides a rationale for future action.

Children who acquire effective self-regulatory skills develop a sense of *academic self-efficacy*—confidence in their own ability, which supports future self-regulation (Schunk & Pajares, 2005). Unfortunately, some children receive messages from parents and teachers that seriously undermine their academic self-esteem and self-regulatory skills. We will consider these *learned-helpless* children, along with ways to help them, in Section 4.

Applications of Information Processing to Academic Learning

Fundamental discoveries about the development of information processing have been applied to children's learning of reading and mathematics. Researchers are identifying the cognitive ingredients of skilled performance, tracing their development, and pinpointing differences in cognitive skills between good and poor readers. They hope, as a result, to design teaching methods that will improve children's learning.

■ **READING.** Reading makes use of many skills at once, taxing all aspects of our information-processing systems. Joey and Lizzie must perceive single letters and letter combinations, translate them into speech sounds, recognize the visual appearance of many common words, hold chunks of text in working memory while interpreting their meaning, and combine the meanings of various parts of a text passage into an understandable whole. And because reading is so demanding, most or all of these skills must be done automatically. If one or more are poorly developed, they will compete for space in our limited working memories, and reading performance will decline.

As children make the transition from emergent literacy to conventional reading, *phonological awareness* continues to facilitate their progress (see page 30 in Section 1). Other information-processing activities also contribute. Gains in processing speed foster children's rapid conversion of visual symbols into sounds (McBride-Chang & Kail, 2002). And visual scanning and discrimination are also important and improve with reading experience (Rayner, Pollatsek, & Starr, 2003). Performing all these skills efficiently releases working memory for higher-level activities involved in comprehending the text's meaning.

Until recently, researchers were involved in an intense debate over how to teach beginning reading. Those who took a **whole-language approach** argued that reading should be taught in a way that parallels natural language learning. From the beginning, children should be exposed to text in its complete form—stories, poems, letters, posters, and lists—so that they can appreciate the communicative function of written language. According to this view, as long as reading is kept whole and meaningful, children will be motivated to discover the specific skills they need (Watson, 1989). Other experts advocated a **phonics approach,** believing that children should first be coached on *phonics*—the basic rules for translating written symbols into sounds. Only after mastering these skills should they get complex reading material (Rayner & Pollatsek, 1989).

Many studies show that, in fact, children learn best with a mixture of both approaches. In kindergarten, first, and second grades, teaching that includes phonics boosts reading scores, especially for children who lag behind in reading progress (Stahl & Miller, 2006; Xue & Meisels, 2004). And when teachers combine real reading and writing with teaching of phonics and engage in other excellent teaching practices—encouraging children to tackle reading challenges and integrating reading into all school subjects—first graders show far greater literacy progress (Pressley et al., 2002).

Why might combining phonics with whole language work best? Learning relationships between letters and sounds enables children to decipher words they have never seen before. Consequently, it promotes children's belief that they can succeed at challenging reading tasks (Tunmer & Chapman, 2002). Yet too much emphasis on basic skills may cause children to lose sight of the goal of reading: understanding. Children who read aloud fluently without registering meaning know little about effective reading strategies—for example, that they must read more carefully if they will be tested than if they are reading for pleasure, or that explaining a passage in their own words is a good way to assess comprehension. Providing instruction aimed at increasing knowledge and use of reading strategies enhances reading performance from third grade on (Paris & Paris, 2006; Van Keer, 2004).

■ **MATHEMATICS.** Mathematics teaching in elementary school builds on and greatly enriches children's informal knowledge of number concepts and counting. Written notation systems and formal computational procedures enhance children's ability to represent numbers and compute. Over the early elementary school years, children acquire basic math facts through a combination of frequent practice, experimentation with diverse computational procedures (through which they discover faster, more accurate techniques), reasoning about number concepts, and teaching that conveys effective strategies (Alibali, 1999; Siegler, 2007). For example, when first graders realize that regardless of the order in which two sets are combined, they yield the same result (2 + 6 = 8 and 6 + 2 = 8), they more often start with the higher digit (6) and count on (7, 8), a strategy that minimizes the work involved. Eventually children retrieve answers automatically and apply this knowledge to more complex problems.

Arguments about how to teach mathematics resemble those about reading, pitting drill in computing against "number sense," or understanding. Again, a blend of both approaches is most beneficial. In learning basic math, poorly performing students use cumbersome techniques or try to retrieve answers from memory too soon. They have not sufficiently experimented with strategies to see which are most effective and to reorganize their observations in logical, efficient ways—for example, noticing that multiplication problems involving 2 (2 × 8) are equivalent to addition doubles (8 + 8). On tasks that assess their understanding of math concepts, their performance is weak (Canobi, 2004; Canobi, Reeve, & Pattison, 2003). This suggests that encouraging students to apply strategies and making sure they understand why certain strategies work well are essential for solid mastery of basic math.

A similar picture emerges for more complex skills, such as carrying in addition, borrowing in subtraction, and operating with decimals and fractions. When taught by rote, children cannot apply the procedure to new problems. Instead, they persistently make mistakes, following a "math rule" that they recall incorrectly because they do not understand it (Carpenter et al., 1999). Consider the following subtraction errors:

$$
\begin{array}{r} 427 \\ -\ 138 \\ \hline 311 \end{array}
\qquad
\begin{array}{r} 7{,}002 \\ -\ 5{,}445 \\ \hline 1{,}447 \end{array}
$$

In the first problem, the child subtracts a smaller from a larger digit, regardless of which is on top. In the second, the child skips

Arguments about how to teach mathematics pit drill in computing against "number sense," or understanding. A blend of both approaches is most beneficial, including opportunities to experiment with problem solving, grasp the reasons behind strategies, and evaluate solution techniques.

columns with zeros in a borrowing operation, and the bottom digit is written as the answer.

Children who are given rich opportunities to experiment with problem solving, to grasp the reasons behind strategies, and to evaluate solution techniques seldom make such errors. In one study, second graders taught in these ways not only mastered correct procedures but even invented their own successful strategies, some of which were superior to standard, school-taught methods (Fuson & Burghard, 2003).

In Asian countries, students receive a variety of supports for acquiring mathematical knowledge and often excel at math computation and reasoning. Use of the metric system helps Asian children grasp place value. The consistent structure of number words in Asian languages (*ten-two* for 12, *ten-three* for 13) also makes this idea clear (Miura & Okamoto, 2003). And because Asian number words are shorter and more quickly pronounced, more digits can be held in working memory at once, increasing the speed of thinking. Furthermore, Chinese parents provide their preschoolers with extensive practice in counting and adding—experiences that contribute to the superiority of Chinese over U.S. children's math knowledge even before school entry (Siegler & Mu, 2008; Zhou et al., 2006). Finally, as we will see later in this section, compared with lessons in North America, those in Asian classrooms devote more time to exploring math concepts and less to drill and repetition.

ASK YOURSELF

>> **REVIEW**
Cite evidence that school-age children view the mind as an active, constructive agent.

>> **APPLY**
After viewing a slide show on endangered species, second and fifth graders were asked to remember as many animals as they could. Explain why fifth graders recalled much more than second graders.

>> **APPLY**
Lizzie knows that if you have difficulty learning part of a task, you should devote extra attention to that part. But she plays each of her piano pieces from beginning to end instead of practicing the hard parts. What explains Lizzie's failure to engage in cognitive self-regulation?

>> **REFLECT**
In your own elementary school math education, how much emphasis was placed on computational drill and how much on understanding of concepts? How do you think that balance affected your interest and performance in math?

Individual Differences in Mental Development

Around age 6, IQ becomes more stable than it was at earlier ages, and it correlates moderately well with academic achievement, typically around .50 to .60. And children with higher IQs are more likely when they grow up to attain higher levels of education and enter more prestigious occupations (Brody, 1997; Deary et al., 2007). Because IQ predicts school performance and educational attainment, it often enters into educational decisions. Do intelligence tests accurately assess the school-age child's ability to profit from academic instruction? Let's look closely at this controversial issue.

Defining and Measuring Intelligence

Virtually all intelligence tests provide an overall score (the IQ), which represents *general intelligence,* or reasoning ability, along with an array of separate scores measuring specific mental abilities. But intelligence is a collection of many capacities, not all of which are included on currently available tests (Carroll, 2005; Sternberg, 2005). Test designers use a complicated statistical technique called *factor analysis* to identify the various abilities that intelligence tests measure. It identifies which sets of test items cluster together, meaning that test-takers who do well on one item in a cluster tend to do well on the others. Distinct clusters are called *factors,* each of which represents an ability. See Figure 3.7 for items typically included in intelligence tests for children.

The intelligence tests given from time to time in classrooms are *group-administered tests.* They permit large numbers of students to be tested at once and are useful for instructional planning and for identifying children who require more extensive evaluation with *individually administered tests.* Unlike group tests, which teachers can give with minimal training, individually administered tests demand considerable training and experience to give well. The examiner not only considers the child's answers but also observes the child's behavior, noting such reactions as attention to and interest in the tasks and wariness of the adult. These observations provide insight into whether the test results accurately reflect the child's abilities. Two individual tests—the Stanford-Binet and the Wechsler—

■ FIGURE 3.7 ■ Test items like those on commonly used intelligence tests for children. The verbal items emphasize culturally loaded, fact-oriented information. The perceptual- and spatial-reasoning, working-memory, and processing-speed items emphasize aspects of information processing and are assumed to assess more biologically based skills.

are often used to identify highly intelligent children and to diagnose children with learning problems.

The modern descendant of Alfred Binet's first successful intelligence test is the *Stanford-Binet Intelligence Scales,* Fifth Edition, for individuals from age 2 to adulthood. It assesses general intelligence and five intellectual factors: knowledge, quantitative reasoning, visual–spatial processing, working memory, and basic information processing (such as speed of analyzing information). Each factor includes both a verbal mode and a nonverbal mode of testing, yielding 10 subtests in all (Roid, 2003). The nonverbal subtests, which do not require spoken language, are especially useful when assessing individuals with limited English, hearing impairments, or communication disorders. The knowledge and quantitative reasoning factors emphasize culturally loaded, fact-oriented information, such as vocabulary and arithmetic problems. In contrast, the visual–spatial processing, working-memory, and basic information-processing factors are assumed to be less culturally biased because they require little specific information (see the spatial visualization item in Figure 3.7).

The *Wechsler Intelligence Scale for Children (WISC-IV)* is the fourth edition of a widely used test for 6- through 16-year-olds (Wechsler, 2003). It measures general intelligence and four broad factors: verbal reasoning, perceptual (or visual–spatial) reasoning, working memory, and processing speed. Each factor is made up of two or three subtests, yielding 10 separate scores in all. The WISC-IV was designed to downplay culturally dependent knowledge, which is emphasized on only one factor (verbal reasoning). According to the test designers, the result is the most "culture-fair" intelligence test available (Williams, Weis, & Rolfhus, 2003). The WISC was also the first test to be standardized on children representing the total population of the United States, including ethnic minorities.

Recent Efforts to Define Intelligence

As we have seen, mental tests now tap important aspects of information processing. In line with this trend, some researchers are combining the mental testing approach to defining intelligence with the information-processing approach. They believe that once we identify the processing skills that separate individuals who test well from those who test poorly, we will know more about how to intervene to improve performance. These investigators conduct *componential analyses* of children's test scores. This means that they look for relationships between aspects (or components) of information processing and children's intelligence test scores.

Measures of basic working-memory capacity (such as digit span) correlate well with mental test scores (de Ribaupierre & Lecerf, 2006). And processing speed, assessed in terms of reaction time on diverse cognitive tasks, is moderately related to IQ (Deary, 2001; Li et al., 2004). Individuals whose nervous systems function efficiently, permitting them to take in more information and manipulate it quickly, appear to have an edge in intellectual skills.

But flexible attention, memory, and reasoning strategies are as important as efficient thinking in predicting IQ, and they explain some of the association between response speed and good test performance (Lohman, 2000; Miller & Vernon, 1992). Children who apply strategies effectively acquire more knowledge and can retrieve it rapidly—advantages that carry over to mental test performance. Similarly, recall that available space in working memory depends in part on effective inhibition (see page 91). Inhibition and sustained and selective attention are among a wide array of attentional skills that are good predictors of IQ (Schweizer, Moosbrugger, & Goldhammer, 2006).

The componential approach has one major shortcoming: It regards intelligence as entirely due to causes within the child. Yet throughout this book, we have seen how cultural and situational factors affect children's thinking. Robert Sternberg has expanded the componential approach into a comprehensive theory that regards intelligence as a product of inner and outer forces.

■ **STERNBERG'S TRIARCHIC THEORY OF SUCCESSFUL INTELLIGENCE.** As Figure 3.8 shows, Sternberg's (2001, 2002, 2005) **triarchic theory of successful intelligence** identifies three broad, interacting intelligences: (1) *analytical intelligence,* or information-processing skills; (2) *creative intelligence,* the capacity to solve novel problems; and (3) *practical intelligence,* application of intellectual skills in everyday situations. Intelligent behavior involves balancing all three intelligences to achieve success in life according to one's personal goals and the requirements of one's cultural community.

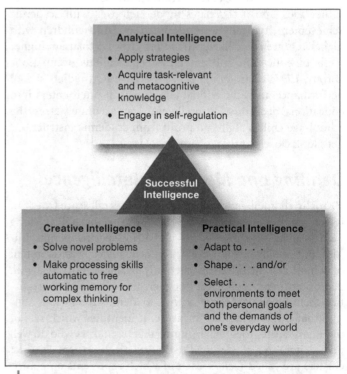

■ **FIGURE 3.8** ■ **Sternberg's triarchic theory of successful intelligence.** People who behave intelligently balance three interrelated intelligences—analytical, creative, and practical—to achieve success in life, defined by their personal goals and the requirements of their cultural communities.

Analytical Intelligence. *Analytical intelligence* consists of the information-processing components that underlie all intelligent acts: applying strategies, acquiring task-relevant and metacognitive knowledge, and engaging in self-regulation. On mental tests, however, processing skills are used in only a few of their potential ways, resulting in a far too narrow view of intelligent behavior. As we have seen, children in tribal and village societies do not necessarily perform well on measures of "school" knowledge but thrive when processing information in out-of-school situations that most Westerners would find highly challenging.

Creative Intelligence. In any context, success depends not only on processing familiar information but also on generating useful solutions to new problems. People who are *creative* think more skillfully than others when faced with novelty. Given a new task, they apply their information-processing skills in exceptionally effective ways, rapidly making these skills automatic so that working memory is freed for more complex aspects of the situation. Consequently, they quickly move to high-level performance. Although all of us are capable of some creativity, only a few individuals excel at generating novel solutions.

Practical Intelligence. Finally, intelligence is a *practical,* goal-oriented activity aimed at *adapting to, shaping,* or *selecting environments.* Intelligent people skillfully *adapt* their thinking to fit with both their desires and the demands of their everyday worlds. When they cannot adapt to a situation, they try to *shape,* or change, it to meet their needs. If they cannot shape it, they *select* new contexts that better match their skills, values, or goals. Practical intelligence reminds us that intelligent behavior is never culture-free. Children with certain life histories do well at the behaviors required for success on intelligence tests and adapt easily to the testing conditions. Others, with different backgrounds, may misinterpret or reject the testing context. Yet such children often display sophisticated abilities in daily life—for example, telling stories, engaging in complex artistic activities, or interacting skillfully with other people.

The triarchic theory highlights the complexity of intelligent behavior and the limitations of current intelligence tests in assessing that complexity. For example, out-of-school, practical forms of intelligence are vital for life success and help explain why cultures vary widely in the behaviors they regard as intelligent (Sternberg et al., 2000). When researchers asked ethnically diverse parents to describe an intelligent first grader, Caucasian Americans mentioned cognitive traits. In contrast, ethnic minorities (Cambodian, Filipino, Vietnamese, and Mexican immigrants) identified noncognitive capacities—motivation, self-management, and social skills (Okagaki & Sternberg, 1993). According to Sternberg, mental tests can easily underestimate, and even overlook, the intellectual strengths of some children, especially ethnic minorities.

■ **GARDNER'S THEORY OF MULTIPLE INTELLIGENCES.** In yet another view of how information-processing skills underlie intelligent behavior, Howard Gardner's (1983, 1993, 2000) **theory of multiple intelligences** defines intelligence in terms of distinct sets of processing operations that permit individuals to engage in a wide range of culturally valued activities. Dismissing the idea of general intelligence, Gardner proposes at least eight independent intelligences (see Table 3.1).

■ **TABLE 3.1** ■ *Gardner's Multiple Intelligences*

INTELLIGENCE	PROCESSING OPERATIONS	END-STATE PERFORMANCE POSSIBILITIES
Linguistic	Sensitivity to the sounds, rhythms, and meaning of words and the functions of language	Poet, journalist
Logico-mathematical	Sensitivity to, and capacity to detect, logical or numerical patterns; ability to handle long chains of logical reasoning	Mathematician
Musical	Ability to produce and appreciate pitch, rhythm (or melody), and aesthetic quality of the forms of musical expressiveness	Instrumentalist, composer
Spatial	Ability to perceive the visual–spatial world accurately, to perform transformations on those perceptions, and to re-create aspects of visual experience in the absence of relevant stimuli	Sculptor, navigator
Bodily-kinesthetic	Ability to use the body skillfully for expressive as well as goal-directed purposes; ability to handle objects skillfully	Dancer, athlete
Naturalist	Ability to recognize and classify all varieties of animals, minerals, and plants	Biologist
Interpersonal	Ability to detect and respond appropriately to the moods, temperaments, motivations, and intentions of others	Therapist, salesperson
Intrapersonal	Ability to discriminate complex inner feelings and to use them to guide one's own behavior; knowledge of one's own strengths, weaknesses, desires, and intelligences	Person with detailed, accurate self-knowledge

Sources: Gardner, 1993, 1998a, 2000.

According to Gardner, children are capable of at least eight distinct intelligences. As this child learns pottery skills under the guidance of an expert potter, she enriches her spatial intelligence.

Gardner believes that each intelligence has a unique biological basis, a distinct course of development, and different expert, or "end-state," performances. At the same time, he emphasizes that a lengthy process of education is required to transform any raw potential into a mature social role (Connell, Sheridan, & Gardner, 2003). Cultural values and learning opportunities affect the extent to which a child's intellectual strengths are realized and the ways they are expressed.

Gardner's list of abilities has yet to be firmly grounded in research. Neurological evidence for the independence of his abilities is weak. Some exceptionally gifted individuals have abilities that are broad rather than limited to a particular domain (Goldsmith, 2000). And research with mental tests suggests that several of Gardner's intelligences (linguistic, logico-mathematical, and spatial) have common features. Nevertheless, Gardner calls attention to several abilities not measured by intelligence tests. For example, his interpersonal and intrapersonal intelligences include a set of capacities for dealing with people and understanding oneself. As the Lifespan Vista box on the following page indicates, researchers are attempting to define, measure, and foster these abilities, which are vital for a satisfying, successful life.

Explaining Individual and Group Differences in IQ

When we compare individuals in terms of academic achievement, years of education, and occupational status, it quickly becomes clear that certain sectors of the population are advantaged over others. In trying to explain these differences, researchers have compared the IQ scores of ethnic and SES groups. American black children score, on average, 12 to 13 IQ points below American white children, although the difference has been shrinking (Dickens & Flynn, 2006; Edwards & Oakland, 2006; Hedges & Nowell, 1998). Hispanic children fall midway between black and white children (Ceci, Rosenblum, & Kumpf, 1998).

The IQ gap between middle-SES and low-SES children— about 9 points—accounts for some of the ethnic differences in IQ, but not all. When black children and white children are matched on parental education and income, the black–white IQ gap is reduced by a third to a half (Brooks-Gunn et al., 2003; Smith, Duncan, & Lee, 2003). Of course, considerable variation exists within each ethnic and SES group. Still, these group differences in IQ are large enough and their consequences serious enough that they cannot be ignored.

In the 1970s, the IQ nature–nurture controversy escalated after psychologist Arthur Jensen (1969) published a controversial monograph entitled, "How Much Can We Boost IQ and Scholastic Achievement?" Jensen argued—and still maintains—that heredity is largely responsible for individual, ethnic, and SES variations in intelligence (Jensen, 1998, 2001; Rushton & Jensen, 2005, 2006). His work sparked an outpouring of research studies and responses, including ethical challenges reflecting deep concern that his conclusions would fuel social prejudices. Richard Herrnstein and Charles Murray rekindled the controversy with *The Bell Curve* (1994). Like Jensen, they argued that heredity contributes substantially to individual and SES differences in IQ, and they implied that heredity plays a sizable role in the black–white IQ gap. Let's look closely at some important evidence.

■ **NATURE VERSUS NURTURE.** We introduced the *heritability estimate*. Recall that heritabilities are obtained from *kinship studies*, which compare family members. The most powerful evidence on the role of heredity in IQ involves twin comparisons. The IQ scores of identical twins (who share all their genes) are more similar than those of fraternal twins (who are genetically no more alike than ordinary siblings). On the basis of this and other kinship evidence, researchers estimate that about half the differences in IQ among children can be traced to their genetic makeup.

Recall, however, that heritabilities risk overestimating genetic influences and underestimating environmental influences. Although these measures offer convincing evidence that genes contribute to IQ, disagreement persists over how large the role of heredity really is (Grigorenko, 2000; Plomin, 2003). And heritability estimates do not reveal the complex processes through which genes and experiences influence intelligence as children develop.

Compared with heritabilities, adoption studies offer a wider range of information. Findings consistently reveal that when young children are adopted into caring, stimulating homes, their IQs rise substantially compared with the IQs of nonadopted children who remain in economically deprived families (van IJzendoorn, Juffer, & Poelhuis, 2005). But adopted children benefit to varying degrees. In one investigation, children of two extreme groups of biological mothers—those with

▪ A LIFESPAN VISTA: Looking Forward, Looking Back ▪

Emotional Intelligence

During recess, Muriel handed a birthday party invitation to every fifthgrade girl except Claire, who looked on sadly as her classmates chattered about the party. But one of Muriel's friends, Jessica, looked troubled. Pulling Muriel aside, she exclaimed, "Why'd you do that? You hurt Claire's feelings—you embarrassed her! If you bring invitations to school, you've got to give everybody one!" And after school, Jessica comforted Claire, saying, "If you aren't invited, I'm not going, either!"

Jessica's IQ is only slightly above average, but she excels at *emotional intelligence*—a term that has captured public attention because of popular books suggesting that it is an overlooked set of skills that can greatly improve life success (Goleman, 1995, 1998). According to one influential definition, **emotional intelligence** refers to a set of emotional abilities that enable individuals to process and adapt to emotional information (Salovey & Pizzaro, 2003). To measure it, researchers have devised items tapping emotional skills that enable people to manage their own emotions and interact competently with others. One test requires people to identify and rate the strength of emotions expressed in photographs of faces (emotional perception), to reason about emotions in social situations (emotional understanding), to identify which emotions promote certain thoughts and activities (emotional facilitation),

and to evaluate the effectiveness of strategies for controlling negative emotions (emotion regulation). Factor analyses of the scores of hundreds of test-takers identified several emotional capacities as well as a higher-order general factor (Mayer, Salovey, & Caruso, 2003).

Emotional intelligence is modestly related to IQ. And in school-age children, adolescents, and adults, it is positively associated with self-esteem, empathy, prosocial behavior, cooperation, leadership skills, and life satisfaction and negatively related to drug and alcohol use, dependency, depression, and aggressive behavior (Brackett, Mayer, & Warner, 2004; Mavroveli et al., 2007; Petrides et al., 2006). In the workplace, emotional intelligence predicts many aspects of success, including managerial effectiveness, productive co-worker relationships, and job performance (Mayer, Roberts, & Barsade, 2008; Mayer, Salovey, & Caruso, 2008).

Only a few assessments of emotional intelligence are available for children. These require careful training of teachers in observing and recording children's emotional skills during everyday activities, gathering information from parents, and taking ethnic backgrounds into account (Denham, 2005; Denham & Burton, 2003). As more and better measures are devised, they may help identify children with weak social and emotional competencies who would

profit from intervention (Denham, 2006; Stewart-Brown & Edmunds, 2007).

The concept of emotional intelligence has increased teachers' awareness that providing experiences that meet students' social and emotional needs can improve their adjustment. Lessons that teach emotional understanding, respect and caring for others, strategies for regulating emotion, and resistance to unfavorable peer pressure—using active learning techniques that provide skill practice both in and out of the classroom—are becoming more common (Goetz et al., 2005).

The 7-year-old on the right displays high emotional intelligence as she accurately reads her friend's sadness and offers comfort.

IQs below 95 and those with IQs above 120—were adopted at birth by parents who were well above average in income and education. During the school years, the children of the low-IQ biological mothers scored above average in IQ, indicating that test performance can be greatly improved by an advantaged home life. But they did not do as well as children of high-IQ biological mothers placed in similar adoptive families (Loehlin, Horn, & Willerman, 1997). Adoption research confirms that heredity and environment contribute jointly to IQ.

Adoption research also sheds light on the black–white IQ gap. In two studies, African-American children adopted into economically well-off white homes during the first year of life scored high on intelligence tests, attaining mean IQs of 110 and 117 by middle childhood—20 to 30 points higher than the typical scores of children growing up in low-income black communities (Moore, 1986; Scarr & Weinberg, 1983). In one investigation, the IQs of black adoptees declined in adoles-

cence, perhaps because of the challenges faced by minority teenagers in forming an ethnic identity that blends birth and adoptive backgrounds (DeBerry, Scarr, & Weinberg, 1996). When this process is filled with emotional turmoil, it can dampen motivation on tests and in school. Still, the black adoptees remained above the IQ average for low-SES African Americans.

Adoption findings do not completely resolve questions about ethnic differences in IQ. Nevertheless, the IQ gains of black children "reared in the culture of the tests and schools" are consistent with a wealth of evidence that poverty severely depresses the intelligence of ethnic minority children.

■ **CULTURAL INFLUENCES.** A controversial question raised about ethnic differences in IQ has to do with whether they result from *test bias*. If a test samples knowledge and skills that not all groups of children have had equal opportunity to learn, or if the testing situation impairs the performance of some groups but not others, then the resulting score is a biased, or unfair, measure.

Some experts reject the idea that intelligence tests are biased, claiming that they are intended to represent success in the common culture. According to this view, because IQ predicts academic achievement equally well for majority and minority children, IQ tests are fair to both groups (Edwards & Oakland, 2006; Jensen, 2002). Others believe that lack of exposure to certain communication styles and knowledge, along with negative stereotypes about the test-taker's ethnic group, can undermine children's performance (Ceci & Williams, 1997; Sternberg, 2005). Let's look at the evidence.

Communication Styles. Ethnic minority families often foster unique language skills that do not match the expectations of most classrooms and testing situations. In one study, a researcher spent many hours observing in low-SES black homes in a southeastern U.S. city (Heath, 1990). She found that African-American parents rarely asked their children the knowledge-training questions typical of middle-SES white parents and of tests and classrooms ("What color is it?" "What's this story about?"). Instead, the black parents asked only "real" questions, ones they themselves could not answer. Often these were analogy questions ("What's that like?") or story-starter questions ("Didja hear Miss Sally this morning?") that called for elaborate responses about everyday events and had no "right" answer.

These experiences lead low-SES black children to develop complex verbal skills at home, such as storytelling and exchanging quick-witted remarks. But their language emphasizes emotional and social concerns rather than facts about the world. Not surprisingly, black children may be confused by the "objective" questions they encounter on tests and in classrooms.

Furthermore, many ethnic minority parents without extensive schooling prefer a *collaborative style of communication* when completing tasks with children. They work together in a coordinated, fluid way, each focused on the same aspect of the problem. This pattern of adult–child engagement has been observed in Native-American, Canadian Inuit, Hispanic, and Guatemalan Mayan cultures (Chavajay & Rogoff, 2002; Crago, Annahatak, & Ningiuruvik, 1993; Delgado-Gaitan, 1994). With increasing education, parents establish a *hierarchical style of communication,* like that of classrooms and tests. The parent directs each child to carry out an aspect of the task, and children work independently (Greenfield, Suzuki, & Rothstein-Fish, 2006). This sharp discontinuity between home and school practices may contribute to low-SES minority children's lower IQ and school performance.

Test Content. Many researchers argue that IQ scores are affected by specific information acquired as part of majority-culture upbringing. Consistent with this view, low-SES African-American children often miss vocabulary words on mental tests that have alternative meanings in their cultural community—for example, interpreting the word *frame* as

"physique" and *wrapping* as "rapping," a popular style of music (Champion, 2003a).

Unfortunately, attempts to change tests by eliminating verbal, fact-oriented items and relying only on spatial reasoning tasks (believed to be less culturally loaded) have not raised the scores of low-SES minority children much (Reynolds & Kaiser, 1990). Yet even these nonverbal test items depend on learning opportunities. For example, using small blocks to duplicate designs and playing video games increase success on spatial tasks (Dirks, 1982; Maynard, Subrahmanyam, & Greenfield, 2005). Low-income minority children, who often grow up in more "people-oriented" than "object-oriented" homes, may lack toys and games that promote certain intellectual skills.

Furthermore, the sheer amount of time a child spends in school predicts IQ. When children of the same age enrolled in different grades are compared, those who have been in school longer score higher on intelligence tests (Ceci, 1991, 1999). Taken together, these findings indicate that children's exposure to the factual knowledge and ways of thinking valued in classrooms has a sizable impact on their intelligence test performance.

Stereotypes. Imagine trying to succeed at an activity when the prevailing attitude is that members of your group are incompetent. **Stereotype threat**—the fear of being judged on the basis of a negative stereotype—can trigger anxiety that interferes with performance (Steele, 1997). Mounting evidence confirms that stereotype threat undermines test taking in children and adults. For example, researchers gave African-American, Hispanic-American, and Caucasian 6- to 10-year-olds verbal tasks. Some children were told that the tasks were "not a test." Others were told they were "a test of how good children are at school problems" (McKown & Weinstein, 2003). Among children who were aware of ethnic stereotypes (such as "black people aren't smart"), African Americans and Hispanics performed far

School-age children become increasingly conscious of ethnic stereotypes, and those from stigmatized groups are especially mindful of them. The fear of being judged on the basis of a negative stereotype may be behind this child's hands-off attitude toward his schoolwork.

© ELLEN B. SENISI PHOTOGRAPHY

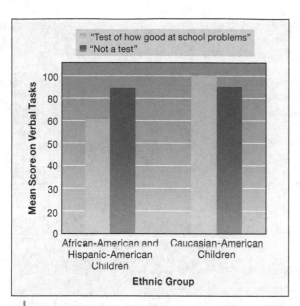

■ FIGURE 3.9 ■ Effect of stereotype threat on test performance. Among African-American and Hispanic-American children who were aware of ethnic stereotypes, being told that verbal tasks were a "test of how good children are at school problems" led to far worse performance than being told the tasks were "not a test." These statements had little impact on the performance of Caucasian-American children. (Adapted from McKown & Weinstein, 2003.)

worse in the "test" condition than in the "not a test" condition. Caucasian children, in contrast, performed similarly in both conditions (see Figure 3.9).

Over middle childhood, children become increasingly conscious of ethnic stereotypes, and those from stigmatized groups are especially mindful of them. By junior high school, many low-SES minority students start to say that doing well in school is not important to them (Major et al., 1998; Osborne, 1994). Self-protective disengagement, sparked by stereotype threat, may be responsible. This weakening of motivation can have serious, long-term consequences. Research shows that self-discipline—effort and delay of gratification—predicts school performance at least as well as, and sometimes better than, IQ does (Duckworth & Seligman, 2005).

Reducing Cultural Bias in Testing. Although not all experts agree, many acknowledge that IQ scores can underestimate the intelligence of culturally different children. A special concern exists about incorrectly labeling minority children as slow learners and assigning them to remedial classes, which are far less stimulating than regular school experiences. To avoid this danger, test scores need to be combined with assessments of children's adaptive behavior—their ability to cope with the demands of their everyday environments. The child who does poorly on an intelligence test yet plays a complex game on the playground or figures out how to rewire a broken TV is unlikely to be mentally deficient.

In addition, culturally relevant testing procedures enhance minority children's test performance. In an approach called **dynamic assessment,** an innovation consistent with Vygotsky's

zone of proximal development, an adult introduces purposeful teaching into the testing situation to find out what the child can attain with social support. Research shows that children's receptivity to teaching and their capacity to transfer what they have learned to novel problems contribute substantially to gains in test performance (Lidz, 2001; Sternberg & Grigorenko, 2002). In one study, Ethiopian 6- and 7-year-olds who had recently immigrated to Israel scored well below their Israeli-born agemates on spatial reasoning tasks. The Ethiopian children had little experience with this type of thinking. After several dynamic assessment sessions in which the adult suggested effective strategies, the Ethiopian children's scores rose sharply, nearly equaling those of the Israeli-born children (Tzuriel & Kaufman, 1999). They also transferred their learning to new test items.

But rather than adapting testing to support ethnic minority children's learning needs, North American education is placing greater emphasis on traditional test scores. To upgrade the academic achievement of poorly performing students, a *high-stakes testing* movement has arisen, making progress through school contingent on test performance. As the Social Issues box on pages 104–105 indicates, this stepped-up emphasis on passing standardized tests has narrowed the focus of instruction, and it may widen SES and ethnic differences in educational attainment.

In view of its many problems, should intelligence testing in schools be suspended? Most experts reject this solution. Without testing, important educational decisions would be based only on subjective impressions, perhaps increasing discriminatory placement of minority children. Intelligence tests are useful when interpreted carefully by psychologists and educators who are sensitive to cultural influences on test performance. And despite their limitations, IQ scores continue to be fairly accurate measures of school learning potential for the majority of Western children.

This teacher uses dynamic assessment, tailoring instruction to students' individual needs—an approach that reveals what a child can learn with social support.

SOCIAL ISSUES

High-Stakes Testing

To better hold schools accountable for educating students, during the past two decades many U.S. states have mandated that students pass exams for high school graduation. As these high-stakes achievement tests spread, schools stepped up their testing programs, extending them downward to elementary school. Some states and school districts also made grade promotion (in New York City, as early as the third grade) and secondary-school academic course credits contingent on test scores (Gootman, 2005).

The U.S. No Child Left Behind Act, authorized by Congress in 2002, broadens high-stakes testing to the identification of "passing" and "failing" schools. The law mandates that each state evaluate every public school's performance through annual achievement testing and publicize the results. Schools that consistently perform poorly (have a high percentage of failing students) must give parents options for upgrading their children's education, such as transfers to nearby, higher-performing schools or enrollment in remedial classes. Some states offer schoolwide rewards for high scores, including official praise and financial bonuses to school staff. Penalties imposed for low scores include withdrawal of accreditation, state takeover, and closure.

Proponents of high-stakes testing believe that it introduces greater rigor into classroom teaching, improves student motivation and achievement, and either turns around poor-performing schools or protects students from being trapped in them. But accumulating evidence indicates that high-stakes testing often undermines, rather than upgrades, the quality of education.

In a Canadian study, researchers examined the impact of requiring students to pass a high school exit exam on eighth-, tenth-, and twelfth-grade science teaching. They found that twelfth-grade teachers narrowed the scope of what they taught to strings of facts to be memorized for the test. As a result, eighth and tenth graders, in some respects, were doing more advanced work than twelfth graders—conducting more experiments, exploring topics in greater depth, and engaging in more critical thinking (Wideen et al., 1997).

Because the main goal of high-stakes testing is to upgrade the test performance of poorly performing students, low-income and ethnic minority children are especially likely to be exposed to narrowly focused, regimented teaching. Simultaneously, the education needs of gifted students are neglected (Mondoza, 2006).

An additional concern is that high-stakes testing promotes fear—a poor motivator for upgrading teaching and learning. Principals

In many U.S. classrooms, high-stakes testing has narrowed the focus of the curriculum to test preparation and promoted a one-size-fits-all education.

and teachers worry about losing funding and their jobs if students do poorly—punishments that have sparked unprecedented levels of adult cheating and other educationally detrimental behaviors. These range from giving students answers, changing students' scores,

---

ASK YOURSELF

》 REVIEW
Using Sternberg's triarchic theory and Gardner's theory of multiple intelligences, explain the limitations of current intelligence tests in assessing the diversity of human intelligence.

》 APPLY
Josefina, a Hispanic fourth grader, does well on homework assignments. But when her teacher announces, "It's time for a test to see how much you've learned," Josefina usually does poorly. How might stereotype threat explain this inconsistency?

》 CONNECT
Explain how dynamic assessment is consistent with Vygotsky's zone of proximal development and with scaffolding. (See Section 1, page 23.)

》 REFLECT
Do you think that intelligence tests are culturally biased? What observations and evidence influenced your conclusions?

Language Development

Vocabulary, grammar, and pragmatics continue to develop in middle childhood, although less obviously than at earlier ages. In addition, school-age children's attitude toward language undergoes a fundamental shift. They develop language awareness.

Schooling contributes greatly to these language competencies. Reflecting on language is extremely common during reading instruction. And fluent reading is a major new source of language learning (Ravid & Tolchinsky, 2002). In the following sections, we will see how an improved ability to reflect on language grows out of literacy and supports language skills.

Vocabulary

During the elementary school years, vocabulary increases fourfold, eventually exceeding 40,000 words. On average, children learn about 20 new words each day, a rate of growth exceeding that in early childhood. In addition to the word-learning strategies discussed in Section 1, school-age children add to their

and offering students rewards (money, sweets, and expensive toys) for earning high scores to suspending or expelling students likely to perform poorly just before test administration (Nichols & Berliner, 2007).

Furthermore, many students who get passing school grades, even high grades, fail exams because a time-limited test can tap only a small sample of skills covered in the classroom (Hursh, 2007). Students most likely to score poorly are minority youths living in poverty. When they are punished with course failure and grade retention, their self-esteem and motivation drop sharply. Research confirms that high-stakes testing requirements have contributed to the high U.S. dropout rates among inner-city minority youths (Balfanz et al., 2007; Hursh, 2007).

The trend toward teaching to tests induced by high-stakes testing contrasts sharply with the emphasis on teaching for deeper understanding in countries that rank at the top in cross-cultural comparisons of academic achievement (see pages 112–113). Even after hundreds of hours of class time devoted to test preparation, tens of thousands of U.S. students fail school-exit exams and do not graduate. Although most retake these exams, some fail repeatedly, with potentially dire consequences for the course of their lives.

Clearly, serious issues remain for lawmakers and educators to resolve about the use of high-stakes tests. These include their questionable power to spark school reforms that make students better learners.

vocabularies by analyzing the structure of complex words. From *happy* and *decide,* they quickly derive the meanings of *happiness* and *decision* (Larsen & Nippold, 2007). They also figure out many more word meanings from context (Nagy & Scott, 2000).

As at earlier ages, children benefit from conversation with more expert speakers, especially when their partners use complex words and explain them (Weizman & Snow, 2001). But because written language contains a far more diverse and complex vocabulary than spoken language, reading contributes enormously to vocabulary growth in middle childhood and adolescence. Children who engage in as little as 21 minutes of independent reading per day are exposed to nearly 2 million words per year (Cunningham & Stanovich, 1998).

As their knowledge expands and becomes better organized, older school-age children think about and use words more precisely. In addition to the verb *fall,* for example, they also use *topple, tumble,* and *plummet* (Berman, 2007). Word definitions also illustrate this change. Five- and 6-year-olds offer concrete descriptions referring to functions or appearance: *knife:* "when you're cutting carrots"; *bicycle:* "it's got wheels, a chain, and handlebars." By the end of elementary school, synonyms and explanations of categorical relationships appear—for example, *knife:* "something you could cut with. A saw is like a knife. It could also be a weapon" (Wehren, De Lisi, & Arnold, 1981). This advance reflects older children's ability to deal with word meanings on an entirely verbal plane. They can add new words to their vocabulary simply by being given a definition.

School-age children's more reflective and analytical approach to language permits them to appreciate the multiple meanings of words—to recognize, for example, that many words, such as *cool* or *neat,* have psychological as well as physical meanings: "What a cool shirt!" or "That movie was really neat!" This grasp of double meanings permits 8- to 10-year-olds to comprehend subtle metaphors, such as "sharp as a tack" and "spilling the beans" (Nippold, Taylor, & Baker, 1996; Wellman & Hickling, 1994). It also leads to a change in children's humor. Riddles and puns that alternate between different meanings of a key word are common: "Hey, did you take a bath?" "Why, is one missing?"

Grammar

During the school years, mastery of complex grammatical constructions improves. For example, English-speaking children use the passive voice more frequently, and they more often extend it from an abbreviated form ("It broke") into full statements ("The glass was broken by Mary") (Israel, Johnson, & Brooks, 2000; Tomasello, 2006). Although the passive form is challenging, language input makes a difference. When adults speak a language that emphasizes full passives, such as Inukitut (spoken by the Inuit people of Arctic Canada), children produce them earlier (Allen & Crago, 1996).

Another grammatical achievement of middle childhood is advanced understanding of infinitive phrases—the difference between "John is eager to please" and "John is easy to please" (Chomsky, 1969). Like gains in vocabulary, appreciation of these subtle grammatical distinctions is supported by an improved ability to analyze and reflect on language.

Pragmatics

Improvements in *pragmatics,* the communicative side of language, also occur. Conversational strategies become more refined. For example, school-age children are better at phrasing things to get their way. When an adult refuses to hand over a desired object, 9-year-olds, but not 5-year-olds, state their second requests more politely (Axia & Baroni, 1985).

Furthermore, as a result of improved memory and ability to take the perspective of listeners, children's narratives increase in organization, detail, and expressiveness. A typical 4- or 5-year-old's narrative states what happened: "We went to the lake. We fished and waited. Paul caught a huge catfish." Six- and 7-year-olds, in contrast, include orienting information (time, place, and participants) and many connectives that lend coherence to the story ("next," "then," "so," "finally"). Gradually, narratives lengthen into a *classic form* in which events not only build to a high point but resolve: "After Paul reeled in the catfish, Dad cleaned and cooked it. Then we ate it all up!" And evaluative comments rise dramatically, becoming common by age 8 to 9:

In families who regularly eat meals together, children are advanced in language and literacy development. Mealtimes offer many opportunities to relate complex, extended personal stories.

"The catfish tasted great. Paul was so proud!" (Melzi & Ely, 2009; Ukrainetz et al., 2005).

Because children pick up the narrative styles of significant adults in their lives, their narrative forms vary widely across cultures. For example, instead of the *topic-focused style* of most North American school-age children, who describe an experience from beginning to end, African-American children often use a *topic-associating style* in which they blend several similar anecdotes. One 9-year-old related having a tooth pulled, then described seeing her sister's tooth pulled, next told how she had removed one of her baby teeth, and concluded, "I'm a pullin-teeth expert . . . call me, and I'll be over" (McCabe, 1997, p. 164). As a result, African-American children's narratives are usually longer and more complex than those of white children (Champion, 2003b).

The ability to generate clear oral narratives enhances reading comprehension and prepares children for producing longer, more explicit written narratives. In families who regularly eat meals together, children are advanced in language and literacy development because mealtimes offer many opportunities to relate complex, extended personal stories (Snow & Beals, 2006).

Learning Two Languages at a Time

Joey and Lizzie speak only one language—English, their native tongue. Yet throughout the world, many children grow up *bilingual,* learning two languages, and sometimes more than two, in childhood. An estimated 15 percent of U.S. children—6 million in all—speak a language other than English at home (U.S. Census Bureau, 2009b).

■ **BILINGUAL DEVELOPMENT.**   Children can become bilingual in two ways: (1) by acquiring both languages at the same time in early childhood or (2) by learning a second language after mastering the first. Children of bilingual parents who teach them both languages in infancy and early childhood separate the language systems from the start and attain early language milestones according to a typical timetable (Bosch & Sebastian-Galles, 2001;

Conboy & Thal, 2006; Holowka, Brosseau-Lapré, & Petitto, 2002). When school-age children acquire a second language after they already speak a first language, they generally take five to seven years to attain speaking and writing skills on a par with those of native-speaking agemates (Paradis, 2007).

As with first-language development, a *sensitive period* for second-language development exists. Mastery must begin sometime in childhood for most second-language learners to attain full proficiency. But a precise age cutoff for a decline in second-language learning has not been established (Hakuta, Bialystok, & Wiley, 2003). Rather, a continuous age-related decrease from childhood to adulthood occurs.

A large body of research shows that bilingualism has positive consequences for development. Children who are fluent in two languages do better than others on tests of selective attention, analytical reasoning, concept formation, and cognitive flexibility (Bialystok, 2001; Bialystok & Martin, 2004). They are also advanced in certain aspects of language awareness, such as detection of errors in grammar and meaning. And children readily transfer their phonological awareness skills in one language to the other (Bialystok, McBride-Chang, & Luk, 2005; Snow & Kang, 2006). These capacities, as noted earlier, enhance reading achievement.

■ **BILINGUAL EDUCATION.**   The advantages of bilingualism provide strong justification for bilingual education programs in schools. In Canada, about 7 percent of elementary school students are enrolled in *language immersion programs,* in which English-speaking children are taught entirely in French for several years. This strategy has been successful in developing children who are proficient in both languages and who, by grade 6, achieve as well in reading, writing, and math as their counterparts in the regular English program (Harley & Jean, 1999; Holobow, Genesee, & Lambert, 1991; Turnbull, Hart, & Lapkin, 2003).

In the United States, fierce disagreement exists over the question of how best to educate ethnic minority children with limited English proficiency. Some believe that time spent communicating in the child's native tongue detracts from English-language achievement, which is crucial for success in school and at work. Other educators, committed to developing minority children's native language while fostering mastery of English, note that providing instruction in the native tongue lets minority children know that their heritage is respected. In addition, it prevents inadequate proficiency in both languages. Minority children who gradually lose the first language as a result of being taught the second end up limited in both languages for a time (Ovando & Collier, 1998). This circumstance leads to serious academic difficulties and is believed to contribute to high rates of school failure and dropout among low-SES Hispanic young people, who make up 50 percent of the U.S. language-minority population.

At present, public opinion and educational practice favor English-only instruction. Many U.S. states have passed laws declaring English to be their official language, creating conditions in which schools have no obligation to teach minority students in languages other than English. Yet in classrooms where

© ROBIN SACHS/PHOTOEDIT

In this English–Spanish bilingual classroom, children are more involved in learning, participate more actively in class discussions, and acquire the second language more easily.

both languages are integrated into the curriculum, minority children are more involved in learning and acquire the second language more easily. In contrast, when teachers speak only in a language children can barely understand, minority children display frustration, boredom, and withdrawal (Crawford, 1997).

Supporters of U.S. English-only education often point to the success of Canadian language immersion programs, in which classroom lessons are conducted in the second language. But Canadian parents enroll their children in immersion classrooms voluntarily, and both French and English are majority languages that are equally valued in Canada. For American non-English-speaking minority children, whose native languages are not valued by the larger society, a different strategy seems necessary: one that promotes children's native language skills while they learn English.

ASK YOURSELF

>> **REVIEW**
Cite examples of how language awareness fosters school-age children's language progress.

>> **APPLY**
Ten-year-old Shana arrived home from soccer practice and remarked, "I'm wiped out!" Megan, her 5-year-old sister, looked puzzled. "What did'ya wipe out, Shana?" Megan asked. Explain Shana's and Megan's different understandings of this expression.

>> **CONNECT**
How can bilingual education promote ethnic minority children's cognitive and academic development?

>> **REFLECT**
Did you acquire a second language at home or study one in school? When did you start, and how proficient are you in the second language? Considering research on bilingualism, what changes would you make in your own second-language learning, and why?

Learning in School

Evidence cited throughout this section indicates that schools are vital forces in children's cognitive development. How do schools exert such a powerful influence? Research looking at schools as complex social systems—class size, educational philosophies, teacher–student relationships, and larger cultural context—provides important insights. As you read about these topics, refer to Applying What We Know on page 108, which summarizes characteristics of high-quality education in elementary school.

Class Size

As each school year began, Rena telephoned the principal's office to ask, "How large will Joey's and Lizzie's classes be?" Her concern is well-founded. In a large field experiment, more than 6,000 Tennessee kindergartners were randomly assigned to three class types: "small" (13 to 17 students), "regular" (22 to 25 students) with only a teacher, and regular with a teacher plus a full-time teacher's aide. These arrangements continued into third grade. Small-class students—especially ethnic minority children—scored higher in reading and math achievement each year (Mosteller, 1995). Placing teacher's aides in regular-size classes had no impact. Rather, being in small classes from kindergarten through third grade predicted substantially higher achievement from fourth through ninth grades, after children had returned to regular-size classes. It also predicted greater likelihood of graduating from high school (Finn, Gerber, & Boyd-Zaharias, 2005; Nye, Hedges, & Konstantopoulos, 2001).

Why is small class size beneficial? With fewer children, teachers spend less time disciplining and more time teaching and giving individual attention. Also, children who learn in smaller groups show better concentration, higher-quality class participation, and more favorable attitudes toward school (Blatchford et al., 2003, 2007; Blatchford, Bassett, & Brown, 2005).

Educational Philosophies

Each teacher brings to the classroom an educational philosophy that plays a major role in children's learning. Two philosophical approaches have received most research attention. They differ in what children are taught, the way they are believed to learn, and how their progress is evaluated.

■ **TRADITIONAL VERSUS CONSTRUCTIVIST CLASSROOMS.** In a **traditional classroom,** the teacher is the sole authority for knowledge, rules, and decision making and does most of the talking. Students are relatively passive—listening, responding when called on, and completing teacher-assigned tasks. Their progress is evaluated by how well they keep pace with a uniform set of standards for their grade.

A **constructivist classroom,** in contrast, encourages students to *construct* their own knowledge. Although constructivist approaches vary, many are grounded in Piaget's theory,

Applying What We Know

Signs of High-Quality Education in Elementary School

Classroom Characteristics	Signs of Quality
Class size	Optimum class size is no larger than 18 children.
Physical setting	Space is divided into richly equipped activity centers—for reading, writing, playing math or language games, exploring science, working on construction projects, using computers, and engaging in other academic pursuits. Spaces are used flexibly for individual and small-group activities and whole-class gatherings.
Curriculum	The curriculum helps children both achieve academic standards and make sense of their learning. Subjects are integrated so that children apply knowledge in one area to others. The curriculum is implemented through activities responsive to children's interests, ideas, and everyday lives, including their cultural backgrounds.
Daily activities	Teachers provide challenging activities that include opportunities for small-group and independent work. Groupings vary in size and makeup of children, depending on the activity and on children's learning needs. Teachers encourage cooperative learning and guide children in attaining it.
Interactions between teachers and children	Teachers foster each child's progress and use intellectually engaging strategies, including posing problems, asking thought-provoking questions, discussing ideas, and adding complexity to tasks. They also demonstrate, explain, coach, and assist in other ways, depending on each child's learning needs.
Evaluations of progress	Teachers regularly evaluate children's progress through written observations and work samples, which they use to enhance and individualize teaching. They help children reflect on their work and decide how to improve it. They also seek information and perspectives from parents on how well children are learning and include parents' views in evaluations.
Relationship with parents	Teachers forge partnerships with parents. They hold periodic conferences and encourage parents to visit the classroom anytime, to observe and volunteer.

Source: Copple & Bredekamp, 2009.

which views children as active agents who reflect on and coordinate their own thoughts rather than absorbing those of others. A glance inside a constructivist classroom reveals richly equipped learning centers, small groups and individuals solving self-chosen problems, and a teacher who guides and supports in response to children's needs. Students are evaluated by considering their progress in relation to their own prior development.

In the United States, the pendulum has swung back and forth between these two views. In the 1960s and early 1970s, constructivist classrooms gained in popularity. Then, as concern arose over the academic progress of children and youths, a "back-to-basics" movement arose. Classrooms returned to traditional instruction, a style still prevalent today.

Although older elementary school children in traditional classrooms have a slight edge in achievement test scores, constructivist settings are associated with many other benefits—gains in academic motivation, critical thinking, social and moral maturity, and positive attitudes toward school (DeVries, 2001; Rathunde & Csikszentmihalyi, 2005; Walberg, 1986). And as noted in Section 1, when teacher-directed instruction is emphasized in preschool and kindergarten, it actually undermines academic motivation and achievement, especially in low-SES children.

The heavy emphasis on knowledge absorption as early as kindergarten has contributed to a growing trend among parents to delay their child's school entry—especially if the child is a boy with a birth date close to the cutoff for kindergarten enrollment. But research has not revealed any long-term benefits, either academic or social (Lincove & Painter, 2006; Stipek, 2002). To the contrary, younger first graders reap achievement gains from on-time enrollment, outperforming same-age children a year behind them (Stipek & Byler, 2001). An alternative perspective is that school readiness can be cultivated through classroom experiences that foster children's individual progress.

■ **NEW PHILOSOPHICAL DIRECTIONS.** New approaches to education, grounded in Vygotsky's sociocultural theory, capitalize on the rich social context of the classroom to spur children's learning. In these **social-constructivist classrooms,** children participate in a wide range of challenging activities with teachers and peers, with whom they jointly construct understandings. As children acquire knowledge and strategies from working together, they become competent, contributing members of their classroom community and advance in cognitive and social development (Bodrova & Leong, 2007; Palincsar, 2003). Vygotsky's emphasis on the social origins of higher cognitive processes has inspired the following educational themes:

■ *Teachers and children as partners in learning.* A classroom rich in both teacher–child and child–child collaboration transfers culturally valued ways of thinking to children.

- *Experiences with many types of symbolic communication in meaningful activities.* As children master reading, writing, and mathematics, they become aware of their culture's communication systems, reflect on their own thinking, and bring it under voluntary control. ***TAKE A MOMENT…*** Can you identify research presented earlier in this section that supports this theme?

- *Teaching adapted to each child's zone of proximal development.* Assistance that both responds to current understandings and encourages children to take the next step helps ensure that each child makes the best progress possible.

According to Vygotsky, besides teachers, more expert peers can spur children's learning, as long as they adjust the help they provide to fit the less mature child's zone of proximal development. Consistent with this idea, mounting evidence confirms that peer collaboration promotes development only under certain conditions. A crucial factor is **cooperative learning,** in which small groups of classmates work toward common goals—by resolving differences of opinion, sharing responsibilities, and providing one another with sufficient explanations to correct misunderstandings. And children profit more when their peer partner is an "expert"—especially capable at the task. When older or more expert students assist younger or less expert students, both benefit in achievement and self-esteem (Ginsburg-Block, Rohrbeck, & Fantuzzo, 2006; Renninger, 1998).

Because Western cultural-majority children regard competition and independent work as natural, they typically require extensive guidance to succeed at cooperative learning. In several studies, groups of students trained in collaborative processes displayed more cooperative behavior, gave clearer explanations, and enjoyed learning more than did untrained groups (Gillies, 2000, 2003; Terwel et al., 2001). In other research,

These children attending a rural school in India cooperate easily while completing a reading assignment. Their Western cultural-majority agemates, in contrast, typically require extensive guidance to succeed at cooperative learning.

the quality of children's collaborative discussions predicted gains in diverse cognitive skills that persisted for weeks beyond the cooperative learning experience (Fleming & Alexander, 2001). Notice how teaching through cooperative learning broadens Vygotsky's concept of the zone of proximal development, from a single child collaborating with an expert partner (adult or peer) to multiple partners with diverse expertises, stimulating and encouraging one another.

Teacher–Student Interaction

Elementary school students describe good teachers as caring, helpful, and stimulating—behaviors associated with gains in motivation, achievement, and positive peer relations (Daniels, Kalkman, & McCombs, 2001; Hughes & Kwok, 2006, 2007; Hughes, Zhang, & Hill, 2006). But too many U.S. teachers emphasize repetitive drill over higher-level thinking, such as grappling with ideas and applying knowledge to new situations (Sacks, 2005). In a longitudinal investigation of middle-school students, those in more academically demanding classrooms showed better attendance and larger gains in math achievement over the following two years (Phillips, 1997).

Of course, teachers do not interact in the same way with all children. Well-behaved, high-achieving students typically get more encouragement and praise, whereas unruly students have more conflicts with teachers and receive more criticism from them (Henricsson & Rydell, 2004). Caring teacher–student relationships have an especially strong impact on the achievement and social behavior of low-SES minority students (Baker, 2006; Crosno, Kirkpatrick, & Elder, 2004). But overall, higher-SES students—who tend to be higher-achieving and to have fewer discipline problems—have more supportive relationships with teachers (Pianta, Hamre, & Stuhlman, 2003).

Unfortunately, once teachers' attitudes toward students are established, they can become more extreme than is warranted by students' behavior. Of special concern are **educational self-fulfilling prophecies:** Children may adopt teachers' positive or negative views and start to live up to them. This effect is especially strong when teachers emphasize competition and publicly compare children, regularly favoring the best students (Kuklinski & Weinstein, 2001; Weinstein, 2002).

Teacher expectations have a greater impact on low achievers than high achievers (Madon, Jussim, & Eccles, 1997). When a teacher is critical, high achievers can fall back on their history of success. Low-achieving students' sensitivity to self-fulfilling prophecies can be beneficial when teachers believe in them. But biased teacher judgments are usually slanted in a negative direction. In one study, African-American children were especially responsive to negative teacher expectations in reading, and girls were especially responsive to negative teacher expectations in math (McKown & Weinstein, 2002). Recall our discussion of *stereotype threat.* A child in the position of confirming a negative stereotype may respond with anxiety and reduced motivation, increasing the likelihood of a negative self-fulfilling prophecy.

These second and third graders learn together during a visit to their school library. Compared to children in single-grade classrooms, children in multigrade classrooms are usually advantaged in academic achievement, self-esteem, and attitudes toward school.

Grouping Practices

In many schools, students are assigned to *homogeneous groups* or classes, in which children of similar ability levels are taught together. Homogeneous grouping can be a potent source of self-fulfilling prophecies. Low-group students—who as early as first grade are more likely to be low-SES, minority, and male—get more drill on basic facts and skills, engage in less discussion, and progress at a slower pace. Gradually, they decline in self-esteem and motivation (Chorzempa & Graham, 2006; Condron, 2007; Trautwein et al., 2006). Not surprisingly, homogeneous grouping widens the gap between high and low achievers (Ross & Harrison, 2006).

Partly because of this finding, some schools have increased the *heterogeneity* of classes by combining two or three adjacent grades. In *multigrade classrooms,* academic achievement, self-esteem, and attitudes toward school are usually more favorable than in the single-grade arrangement (Lloyd, 1999; Ong, Allison, & Haladyna, 2000). Perhaps multigrade grouping decreases competition and promotes *cooperative learning,* which also fosters these positive outcomes (see page 109).

Teaching Children with Special Needs

We have seen that effective teachers flexibly adjust their teaching strategies to accommodate students with a wide range of characteristics. These adjustments are especially challenging at the very low and high ends of the ability distribution. How do schools serve children with special learning needs?

■ **CHILDREN WITH LEARNING DIFFICULTIES.** U.S. legislation mandates that schools place children who require special supports for learning in the "least restrictive" (as close to normal as possible) environments that meet their educational needs. In **inclusive classrooms,** students with learning difficulties are placed in regular classrooms for all or part of the school day, a practice designed to prepare them for participation in society and to combat prejudices against individuals with disabilities (Kugelmass & Ainscow, 2004). Largely as the result of parental pressures, an increasing number of students experience *full inclusion*—full-time placement in regular classrooms.

Some students in inclusive classrooms have *mild mental retardation:* Their IQs fall between 55 and 70, and they also show problems in adaptive behavior, or skills of everyday living (American Psychiatric Association, 1994). But the largest number—5 to 10 percent of school-age children—have **learning disabilities,** great difficulty with one or more aspects of learning, usually reading. As a result, their achievement is considerably behind what would be expected on the basis of their IQ. Sometimes deficits express themselves in other ways—for example, as severe inattention, which depresses both IQ and achievement (recall our discussion of ADHD on page 304). The problems of students with learning disabilities cannot be traced to any obvious physical or emotional difficulty or to environmental disadvantage. Instead, subtle deficits in brain functioning seem to be involved (Berninger, 2006). In many instances, the cause is unknown.

Although some included students benefit academically, many do not. Achievement gains depend on both the severity of the disability and the support services available (Klingner et al., 1998). Furthermore, children with disabilities are often rejected by regular-classroom peers. Students with mental retardation are overwhelmed by the social skills of their classmates; they cannot interact adeptly in a conversation or game. And the processing deficits of some students with learning disabilities lead to problems in social awareness and responsiveness (Kelly & Norwich, 2004; Sridhar & Vaughn, 2001).

Does this mean that students with special needs cannot be served in regular classrooms? Not necessarily. Often these children do best when they receive instruction in a resource room for part of the day and in the regular classroom for the remainder (Weiner & Tardif, 2004). In the resource room, a special education teacher works with students on an individual and small-group basis. Then, depending on their progress, children join regular classmates for different subjects and amounts of time.

Special steps must to be taken to promote peer relations in inclusive classrooms. Cooperative learning and peer-tutoring experiences in which teachers guide children with learning difficulties and their classmates in working together lead to friendly interaction, improved peer acceptance, and achievement gains (Fuchs et al., 2002a, 2002b). Teachers can also prepare their class for the arrival of a student with special needs. Under these conditions, inclusion may foster emotional sensitivity and prosocial behavior among regular classmates.

In this inclusive second-grade classroom, a teacher encourages a special-needs child to listen to his classmate read a story. The child is likely to do well if he receives support from a special education teacher and if his classroom teacher minimizes comparisons and promotes cooperative learning.

■ **GIFTED CHILDREN.** In Joey and Lizzie's school, some children are **gifted,** displaying exceptional intellectual strengths. One or two students in every grade have IQ scores above 130, the standard definition of giftedness based on intelligence test performance (Gardner, 1998b). High-IQ children, as we have seen, have keen memories and an exceptional capacity to solve challenging academic problems. Yet recognition that intelligence tests do not sample the entire range of human mental skills has led to an expanded conception of giftedness.

Creativity and Talent. **Creativity** is the ability to produce work that is original yet appropriate—something others have not thought of that is useful in some way (Lubart, 2003; Sternberg, 2003b). A child with high potential for creativity can be designated as gifted. Tests of creative capacity tap **divergent thinking**—the generation of multiple and unusual possibilities when faced with a task or problem. Divergent thinking contrasts with **convergent thinking,** which involves arriving at a single correct answer and is emphasized on intelligence tests (Guilford, 1985).

Because highly creative children (like high-IQ children) are often better at some tasks than others, a variety of tests of divergent thinking are available (Runco, 1992; Torrance, 1988). A verbal measure might ask children to name uses for common objects (such as a newspaper). A figural measure might ask them to create drawings based on a circular motif (see Figure 3.10). A "real-world problem" measure requires students to suggest solutions to everyday problems. Responses can be scored for the number of ideas generated and their originality.

Yet critics point out that these measures are poor predictors of creative accomplishment in everyday life because they tap only one of the complex cognitive contributions to creativity. Also involved are defining new and important problems, evaluating divergent ideas, choosing the most promising, and calling on relevant knowledge to understand and solve problems (Sternberg, 2003b; Guignard & Lubart, 2006).

Consider these ingredients, and you will see why people usually demonstrate creativity in only one or a few related areas. Even individuals designated as gifted by virtue of high IQ often show uneven ability across academic subjects. Partly for this reason, definitions of giftedness have been extended to include **talent**—outstanding performance in a specific field. Case studies reveal that excellence in writing, mathematics, science, music, visual arts, athletics, or leadership has roots in specialized interests and skills that first appear in childhood (Moran & Gardner, 2006; Winner, 2003). Highly talented children are biologically prepared to master their domain of interest, and they display a passion for doing so.

But talent must be nurtured. Studies of the backgrounds of talented children and highly accomplished adults often reveal parents who are warm and sensitive, provide a stimulating home life, are devoted to developing their child's abilities, and provide models of hard work. These parents are reasonably demanding but not driving or overambitious (Winner, 1996, 2000). They arrange for caring teachers while the child is young and for more rigorous master teachers as the talent develops.

Many gifted children and adolescents are socially isolated, partly because their highly driven, nonconforming, and

■ **FIGURE 3.10** ■ **Responses of an 8-year-old who scored high on a figural measure of divergent thinking.** This child was asked to make as many pictures as she could from the circles on the page. The titles she gave her drawings, from left to right, are as follows: "Dracula," "one-eyed monster," "pumpkin," "Hula-Hoop," "poster," "wheelchair," "earth," "stop-light," "planet," "movie camera," "sad face," "picture," "beach ball," "the letter O," "car," "glasses." Tests of divergent thinking tap only one of the complex cognitive contributions to creativity. (Reprinted by permission of Laura Berk.)

independent styles leave them out of step with peers and partly because they enjoy solitude, which is necessary to develop their talents. Still, gifted children desire gratifying peer relationships, and some—more often girls than boys—try to become better liked by hiding their abilities. Compared with their ordinary agemates, gifted youths, especially girls, report more emotional and social difficulties, including low self-esteem and depression (Reis, 2004; Winner, 2000).

Finally, whereas many talented youths become experts in their fields, few become highly creative. Rapidly mastering an existing field requires different skills than innovating in that field (Moran & Gardner, 2006). The world, however, needs both experts and creators.

Educating the Gifted. Debate about the effectiveness of school programs for the gifted typically focuses on factors irrelevant to giftedness—whether to provide enrichment in regular classrooms, pull children out for special instruction (the most common practice), or advance brighter students to a higher grade. Overall, gifted children fare well academically and socially within each of these models (Moon & Feldhusen, 1994). Yet the extent to which programs foster creativity and talent depends on opportunities to acquire relevant skills.

Gardner's theory of multiple intelligences has inspired several model programs that provide enrichment to all students in diverse disciplines. Meaningful activities, each tapping a specific intelligence or set of intelligences, serve as contexts for assessing strengths and weaknesses and, on that basis, teaching new knowledge and original thinking (Gardner, 1993, 2000). For example, linguistic intelligence might be fostered through storytelling or playwriting; spatial intelligence through drawing, sculpting, or taking apart and reassembling objects; and kinesthetic intelligence through dance or pantomime.

Evidence is still needed on how effectively these programs nurture children's talent and creativity. But they have already succeeded in one way—by highlighting the strengths of some students who previously had been considered unexceptional or even at risk for school failure (Kornhaber, 2004). Consequently, they may be especially useful in identifying talented, low-SES ethnic minority children, who are underrepresented in school programs for the gifted (McBee, 2006).

How Well-Educated Are North American Children?

Our discussion of schooling has largely focused on how teachers can support the education of children. Yet many factors—both within and outside schools—affect children's learning. Societal values, school resources, quality of teaching, and parental encouragement all play important roles. Nowhere are these multiple influences more apparent than when schooling is examined in cross-cultural perspective.

In international studies of reading, mathematics, and science achievement, young people in Hong Kong, Korea, Japan, and Taiwan are consistently top performers. Among Western nations, Canada, Finland, Netherlands, and Switzerland are also

in the top tier. But U.S. students typically perform at the international average, and sometimes below it (see Figure 3.11) (Programme for International Student Assessment, 2003, 2006).

Why do U.S. youths fall behind in academic accomplishment? In the Programme for International Student Assessment, which periodically assesses academic achievement of 15-year-olds in many countries, students were asked about their study habits. Compared with students in the top-achieving nations, many more U.S. students reported studying by memorizing rather than by relating information to previously acquired knowledge. Also, achievement varies much more among U.S. schools, suggesting that the United States is less equitable in the quality of education it provides (Programme for International Student Assessment, 2005).

Researchers have conducted in-depth research on learning environments in Asian nations, such as Japan, Korea, and

	Country	Average Math Achievement Score
High-Performing Nations	Taiwan	549
	Finland	548
	Hong Kong	547
	Korea, Republic of	547
	Netherlands	531
	Switzerland	530
	Canada	527
	Macao, China	525
	Japan	523
	New Zealand	522
	Belgium	520
	Australia	520
Intermediate-Performing Nations	Denmark	513
	Czech Republic	510
	Iceland	506
	Austria	505
	Germany	504
	Sweden	502
International Average = 498	Ireland	501
	France	496
	United Kingdom	495
	Poland	495
	Hungary	491
	Luxembourg	491
	Norway	490
	Spain	480
	United States	**474**
Low-Performing Nations	Portugal	466
	Italy	462
	Greece	459
	Turkey	424

■ **FIGURE 3.11** ■ **Average mathematics scores of 15-year-olds by country.** The Programme for International Student Assessment measured achievement in many nations around the world. Taiwan, Hong Kong, Korea, and Japan were among the top performers in mathematics, whereas the United States performed below the international average. Similar outcomes occurred in reading and science. (Adapted from Programme for International Student Assessment, 2006.)

Taiwan, to clarify the factors that support high achievement. A variety of social forces combine to foster a strong commitment to learning in Asian families and schools:

- *Emphasis on effort.* Whereas North American parents and teachers tend to regard native ability as key to academic success, Japanese, Korean, and Taiwanese parents and teachers believe that all children can succeed academically with enough effort. Asian parents devote many more hours to helping their children with homework (Stevenson, Lee, & Mu, 2000). Furthermore, Asian youths, influenced by collectivist values, typically view striving to achieve as a moral obligation—a responsibility to family and community. North American young people view working hard in individualistic terms—as a personal choice (Bempechat & Drago-Severson, 1999).

- *High-quality education for all.* Ability grouping is absent from Japanese, Korean, and Taiwanese elementary schools. All students receive the same nationally mandated, high-quality education, delivered by teachers who are better paid than in the United States (U.S. Department of Education, 2008). Academic lessons are particularly well-organized and presented in ways that capture children's attention and encourage high-level thinking (Grow-Maienza, Hahn, & Joo, 2001). And Japanese elementary school teachers are three times as likely as U.S. teachers to work outside class with students who need extra help (Woodward & Ono, 2004).

- *More time devoted to instruction.* In Japan, Hong Kong, and Taiwan, the school year is more than 50 days longer than in the United States (World Education Services, 2007). And on a day-to-day basis, Asian teachers devote much more time to academic pursuits (Stevenson, Lee, & Mu, 2000). Yet Asian schools are not regimented: An eight-hour school day allows time for extra recesses as well as field trips and extracurricular activities, which contribute to children's capacity to learn (see page 86).

The Asian examples underscore the need for families, schools, and the larger society to work together to upgrade education. Currently, the United States is investing more tax dollars in elementary and secondary education and strengthening teacher preparation. In addition, many schools are taking steps to increase parent involvement. Children whose parents create stimulating learning environments at home, monitor their child's academic progress, help with homework, and communicate often with teachers consistently show superior achievement (Hill & Taylor, 2004; Jeynes, 2005). The results of these efforts can be seen in recent national assessments of educational progress (U.S Department of Education, 2003, 2005). After two decades of decline, U.S. students' overall academic achievement has risen, although not enough to enhance their standing internationally.

Summary

PHYSICAL DEVELOPMENT

Body Growth

Describe major trends in body growth during middle childhood.

» Gains in body size during middle childhood continue at a slow, regular pace. Bones lengthen and broaden, and permanent teeth replace all 20 primary teeth. By age 9, girls overtake boys in physical size.

Common Health Problems

What vision and hearing problems are common in middle childhood?

» The most common vision problem is myopia, or nearsightedness. It is influenced by heredity, early biological trauma, and time spent doing close work. Myopia is one of the few health conditions that increase with SES.

» Middle-ear infections become less frequent. But repeated infections lead to permanent hearing loss in as many as 20 percent of low-SES children.

Describe the causes and consequences of serious nutritional problems in middle childhood, giving special attention to obesity.

» Many poverty-stricken children in developing countries and North America continue to suffer from serious and prolonged malnutrition, which can permanently impair physical and mental development.

>> Overweight and **obesity** are growing problems in Western and developing nations, posing long-term health risks. Although heredity contributes to obesity, reduced sleep, parental feeding practices, maladaptive eating habits, and lack of exercise also play important roles.

>> Obese children are rated as less likable by peers and adults and have serious adjustment problems. Family-based interventions to change parents' and children's eating patterns and lifestyles are the most effective treatment approaches.

What factors contribute to illness during the school years, and how can these health problems be reduced?

>> Children experience more illnesses during the first two years of elementary school than later because of exposure to sick children and an immature immune system.

>> The most common cause of school absence and childhood hospitalization is asthma. Although heredity contributes to asthma, environmental factors—pollution, stressful home lives, lack of access to good health care, and the rise in childhood obesity—have led to an increase in the disease, especially among African-American and poverty-stricken children.

>> Children with severe chronic illnesses are at risk for academic, emotional, and social difficulties, but positive family relationships improve adjustment.

Describe changes in unintentional injuries in middle childhood.

>> Unintentional injuries increase over middle childhood and adolescence, especially for boys, with auto and bicycle accidents accounting for most of the rise. School-based programs that use modeling, rehearsal, and rewards for following safety practices help prevent injuries.

Motor Development and Play

Cite major changes in motor development and play during middle childhood.

>> Gains in flexibility, balance, agility, and force, along with more efficient information processing, contribute to school-age children's improved motor performance.

>> Fine-motor development also improves. Children's writing becomes more legible, and

their drawings increase in organization, detail, and representation of depth.

>> While girls outperform boys in fine-motor skills, boys outperform in all gross-motor skills except those requiring balance and agility. Higher expectations by parents for boys' athletic performance play a large role.

>> Games with rules become common during the school years, contributing to emotional and social development. Children, especially boys, also engage in **rough-and-tumble play,** friendly play-fighting that helps establish a **dominance hierarchy** among group members.

>> Most U.S. school-age children are not active enough for good health. With cutbacks in recess and physical education, they do not reap the health and social benefits of physical fitness.

COGNITIVE DEVELOPMENT

Piaget's Theory: The Concrete Operational Stage

What are the major characteristics of concrete operational thought?

>> Children in the **concrete operational stage** can reason logically about concrete, tangible information. Mastery of conservation demonstrates **reversibility** in thinking. School-age youngsters are also better at hierarchical classification and **seriation,** including **transitive inference.** Their spatial reasoning improves, as seen in their ability to give directions and to create **cognitive maps** representing familiar large-scale spaces.

>> School-age children master logical ideas gradually, not all at once. Concrete operational thought is limited in that children do not come up with general logical principles.

Discuss follow-up research on concrete operational thought.

>> Specific cultural practices, especially those associated with schooling, affect children's mastery of Piagetian tasks.

>> Some researchers attribute the gradual development of operational thought to gains in information-processing speed. According to Case's neo-Piagetian theory, with practice, cognitive schemes demand less attention and become more automatic, freeing up space in working memory for combining old schemes and generating new ones. Eventually, children consolidate schemes into highly efficient, central conceptual structures, becoming increasingly able to coordinate and integrate multiple dimensions.

Information Processing

Cite basic changes in information processing, and describe the development of attention and memory in middle childhood.

>> Brain development contributes to increases in processing speed and capacity and to gains

in inhibition, which facilitate many aspects of thinking.

>> During the school years, attention becomes more selective, adaptable, and planful. The serious symptoms of **attention-deficit hyperactivity disorder (ADHD)** lead to both academic and social problems.

>> Memory strategies also improve. **Rehearsal** appears first, followed by **organization** and then **elaboration.** With age, children combine memory strategies.

>> Development of the long-term knowledge base makes new information easier to store and retrieve. Children's motivation to use what they know also contributes to memory development. Memory strategies are promoted by learning activities in school.

Describe the school-age child's theory of mind and capacity to engage in self-regulation.

>> Metacognition expands over middle childhood. School-age children regard the mind as an active, constructive agent, and they develop an integrated theory of mind. **Cognitive self-regulation**—putting what one knows about thinking into action—develops slowly over middle childhood and adolescence. It improves with instructions to monitor cognitive activity.

Discuss current controversies in teaching reading and mathematics to elementary school children.

>> Skilled reading draws on all aspects of the information-processing system. Research showing that a mixture of **whole language** and **phonics** is most effective in teaching beginning reading has resolved a long-standing debate. Teaching that blends practice in basic

Individual Differences in Mental Development

Describe major approaches to defining and measuring intelligence.

>> Most intelligence tests yield an overall score as well as scores for separate intellectual factors. During the school years, IQ becomes more

stable, and it correlates moderately well with academic achievement.

>> The componential approach to defining intelligence seeks to identify the inner, information-processing skills that contribute to mental test performance. Memory span, speed of thinking, and effective strategy use are positively related to IQ.

>> Sternberg's **triarchic theory of successful intelligence** views intelligence as an interaction of inner and outer forces—analytical intelligence (information-processing skills), creative intelligence (capacity to solve novel problems), and practical intelligence (ability to succeed in one's everyday world).

>> Gardner's **theory of multiple intelligences** identifies at least eight mental abilities, each with a distinct biological basis and course of

Describe evidence indicating that both heredity and environment contribute to intelligence.

>> Heritability estimates and adoption research indicate that intelligence is a product of both heredity and environment. Studies of black children adopted into well-to-do homes during the first year of life indicate that the black–white IQ gap is substantially influenced by environment.

>> IQ scores are affected by cultural forces, including exposure to certain communication styles and knowledge and ways of thinking sampled by the test. Among children aware of ethnic stereotypes, **stereotype threat** can trigger anxiety that interferes with test performance. **Dynamic**

assessment helps many minority children perform more competently on mental tests.

Language Development

Describe changes in school-age children's vocabulary, grammar, and pragmatics, and cite the advantages of bilingualism for development.

>> During middle childhood, vocabulary continues to grow rapidly, and children have a more precise and flexible understanding of word meanings. They also use more complex grammatical constructions and conversational strategies, and their narratives increase in organization, detail, and expressiveness. Language awareness contributes to school-age children's language progress.

>> Mastery of a second language must begin in childhood for full proficiency to occur. Bilingualism has positive consequences for cognitive development and certain aspects of language awareness. In Canada, language immersion programs are highly successful in making children proficient in both English and French. In the United States, bilingual education that combines instruction in the native tongue and in English supports ethnic minority children's academic learning.

Learning in School

Describe the impact of class size and educational philosophies on children's motivation and academic achievement.

>> Smaller classes in the early elementary grades promote lasting gains in academic achievement. Older elementary school students in **traditional classrooms** have a slight edge in academic achievement over those in **constructivist classrooms,** who gain in academic motivation, critical thinking, social and moral maturity, and positive attitudes toward school.

>> Students in **social-constructivist classrooms** benefit from working collaboratively in meaningful activities and from teaching adapted to

each child's zone of proximal development. **Cooperative learning** promotes achievement and self-esteem.

Discuss the role of teacher–student interaction and grouping practices in academic achievement.

>> Caring, helpful, and stimulating teaching fosters children's motivation, academic achievement, and peer relations. **Educational self-fulfilling prophecies** have a greater impact on low than high achievers and are especially likely to occur in classrooms that emphasize competition and public evaluation. Heterogeneous grouping in multigrade classrooms promotes favorable self-esteem and school attitudes and higher achievement.

Under what conditions is placement of children with learning difficulties in regular classrooms successful?

>> Students with mild mental retardation and **learning disabilities** are often placed in **inclusive classrooms.** The success of regular-classroom placement depends on meeting individual learning needs and positive peer relations.

Describe the characteristics of gifted children and current efforts to meet their educational needs.

>> **Giftedness** includes high IQ, **creativity,** and **talent.** Tests of creativity that tap **divergent** rather than **convergent thinking** focus on only one of the ingredients of creativity. Highly talented children have parents and teachers who nurture their exceptional abilities. Gifted children are best served by educational programs that build on their special strengths.

How well are North American children achieving compared with children in other industrialized nations?

>> In international studies, young people in Asian nations are consistently top performers, whereas American students typically display an average or below-average performance. Asian parents and teachers emphasize effort over native ability, and Asian schools provide the same high-quality education to all students and devote more time to instruction.

Important Terms and Concepts

attention-deficit hyperactivity disorder (ADHD) (p. 92)
cognitive maps (p. 88)
cognitive self-regulation (p. 95)
concrete operational stage (p. 87)
constructivist classroom (p. 107)
convergent thinking (p. 111)
cooperative learning (p. 109)
creativity (p. 111)
divergent thinking (p. 111)
dominance hierarchy (p. 86)

dynamic assessment (p. 103)
educational self-fulfilling prophecies (p. 109)
elaboration (p. 92)
emotional intelligence (p. 101)
gifted (p. 111)
inclusive classrooms (p. 110)
learning disabilities (p. 110)
obesity (p. 80)
organization (p. 91)
phonics approach (p. 95)
rehearsal (p. 91)

reversibility (p. 87)
rough-and-tumble play (p. 85)
seriation (p. 87)
social-constructivist classroom (p. 108)
stereotype threat (p. 102)
talent (p. 111)
theory of multiple intelligences (p. 99)
traditional classroom (p. 107)
transitive inference (p. 88)
triarchic theory of successful intelligence (p. 98)
whole-language approach (p. 95)

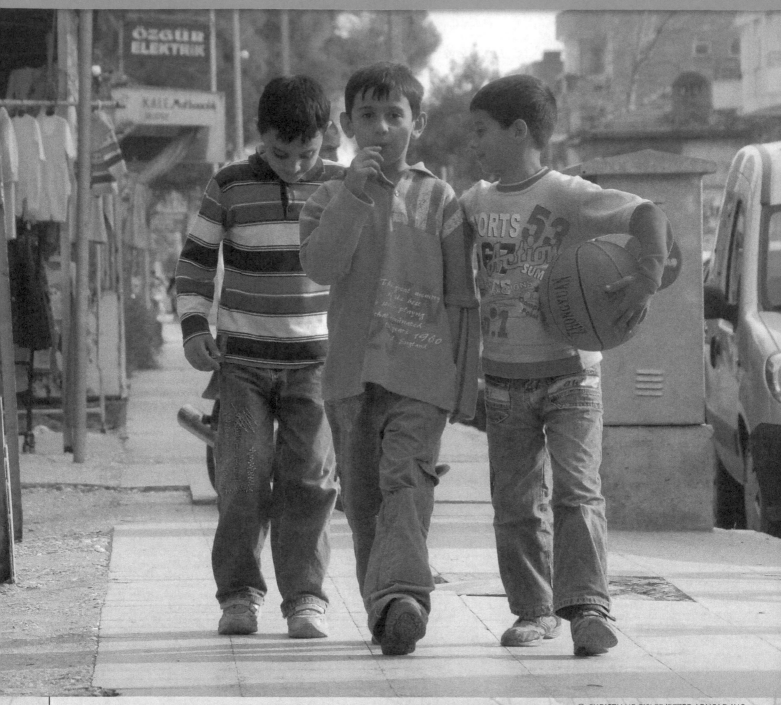

Social understanding expands greatly in middle childhood. Like others their age around the world, these Turkish children select friends based on personal qualities, and they become more responsive to one another's needs and desires.

Emotional and Social Development in Middle Childhood

ate one afternoon, Rena heard her son Joey burst through the front door, run upstairs, and phone his best friend Terry. "Terry, gotta talk to you," Joey pleaded breathlessly. "Everything was going great until that word I got—*porcupine*," Joey went on, referring to the fifth-grade spelling bee at school that day. "Just my luck! *P-o-r-k*, that's how I spelled it! I can't believe it. Maybe I'm not so good at social studies," Joey confided, "but I *know* I'm better at spelling than that stuck-up Belinda Brown. I knocked myself out studying those spelling lists. Then *she* got all the easy words. If I *had* to lose, why couldn't it be to a nice person?"

Joey's conversation reflects his new emotional and social capacities. By entering the spelling bee, he shows *industriousness,* the energetic pursuit of meaningful achievement in his culture—a major change of middle childhood. Joey's social understanding has also expanded: He can size up strengths, weaknesses, and personality character-istics. Furthermore, friendship means something different to Joey than it did earlier—he counts on his best friend, Terry, for understanding and emotional support.

For an overview of personality change in middle childhood, we return to Erikson's theory. Then we look at children's views of themselves and of others, their moral understanding, and their peer relationships. Each increases in complexity as children reason more effectively and spend more time in school and with agemates.

Despite changing parent–child relationships, the family remains powerfully influential in middle childhood. Today, family lifestyles are more diverse than ever before. Through Joey and his younger sister Lizzie's experiences with parental divorce, we will see that family functioning is far more important than family structure in ensuring children's well-being. Finally, we look at some common emotional problems of middle childhood.

Erikson's Theory: Industry versus Inferiority

According to Erikson (1950), children whose previous experiences have been positive enter middle childhood prepared to redirect their energies from the make-believe of early childhood into realistic accomplishment. Erikson believed that the combination of adult expectations and children's drive toward mastery sets the stage for the psychological conflict of middle childhood, **industry versus inferiority,** which is resolved positively when children develop a sense of competence at useful skills and tasks. In cultures everywhere, adults respond to children's improved physical and cognitive capacities by making new demands, and children are ready to benefit from those challenges.

In industrialized nations, the beginning of formal schooling marks the transition to middle childhood. With it comes literacy training, which prepares children for a vast array of specialized careers. In school, children discover their own and others' unique capacities, learn the value of division of labor, and develop a sense of moral commitment and responsibility. The danger at this stage is *inferiority,* reflected in the pessimism of children who have little confidence in their ability to do things well. This sense of inadequacy can develop when family life has not prepared children for school life or when teachers and peers destroy children's feelings of competence and mastery with negative responses.

Erikson's sense of industry combines several developments of middle childhood: a positive but realistic self-concept, pride in accomplishment, moral responsibility, and cooperative participation with agemates. How do these aspects of self and social relationships change over the school years?

The industriousness of middle childhood involves mastery of useful skills. As these young musicians participate in their school orchestra, they gain awareness of others' unique capacities and come to view themselves as responsible, capable, and cooperative.

© TOM & DEE ANN MCCARTHY/CORBIS

Self-Understanding

In middle childhood, children become able to describe themselves in terms of psychological traits, to compare their own characteristics with those of their peers, and to speculate about the causes of their strengths and weaknesses. These transformations in self-understanding have a major impact on children's self-esteem.

Self-Concept

During the school years, children refine their self-concept, organizing their observations of behaviors and internal states into general dispositions. A major change takes place between ages 8 and 11, as the following self-description by an 11-year-old illustrates:

> My name is A. I'm a human being. I'm a girl. I'm a truthful person. I'm not pretty. I do so-so in my studies. I'm a very good cellist. I'm a very good pianist. I'm a little bit tall for my age. I like several boys. I like several girls. I'm old-fashioned. I play tennis. I am a very good swimmer. I try to be helpful. I'm always ready to be friends with anybody. Mostly I'm good, but I lose my temper. I'm not well-liked by some girls and boys. I don't know if I'm liked by boys or not. (Montemayor & Eisen, 1977, pp. 317–318)

Instead of specific behaviors, this child emphasizes competencies: "I'm a very good cellist" (Damon & Hart, 1988). She also describes her personality, mentioning both positive and negative traits: "truthful" but short-tempered. Older school-age children are far less likely than younger children to describe themselves in extreme, all-or-none ways (Harter, 2003, 2006).

These evaluative self-descriptions result from school-age children's frequent **social comparisons**—judgments of their appearance, abilities, and behavior in relation to those of others. For example, Joey observed that he was "better at spelling" than his peers but "not so good at social studies." Whereas 4- to 6-year-olds can compare their own performance to that of one peer, older children can compare multiple individuals, including themselves (Butler, 1998; Harter, 2006).

What factors account for these revisions in self-concept? Cognitive development affects the changing *structure* of the self. School-age children, as we saw in Section 3, can better coordinate several aspects of a situation in reasoning about their physical world. Similarly, in the social realm, they combine typical experiences and behaviors into psychological dispositions, blend positive and negative characteristics, and compare their own characteristics with those of many peers (Harter, 2003, 2006).

The changing *content* of self-concept is a product of both cognitive capacities and feedback from others. Sociologist George Herbert Mead (1934) proposed that a well-organized psychological self emerges when children adopt a view of the self that resembles others' attitudes toward the child. Mead's ideas indicate that *perspective-taking skills*—in particular, an improved ability to infer what other people are thinking—are crucial for developing a self-concept based on personality traits. School-age children become better at "reading" others' messages and internalizing their expectations. As they do so, they form an *ideal self* that they use to evaluate their real self. As we will see shortly, a large discrepancy between the two can undermine self-esteem.

In middle childhood, children look to more people beyond the family for information about themselves as they enter a wider range of settings in school and community. And self-descriptions now include frequent reference to social groups: "I'm a Boy Scout, a paperboy, and a Prairie City soccer player," said Joey. And as children move into adolescence, although parents and other adults remain influential, self-concept is increasingly vested in feedback from close friends (Oosterwegel & Oppenheimer, 1993).

But recall that the content of self-concept varies from culture to culture. In earlier sections, we noted that Asian parents stress harmonious interdependence, whereas Western parents stress independence and self-assertion. When asked to recall personally significant past experiences (their last birthday, a time their parent scolded them), U.S. children gave longer accounts including more personal preferences, skills, and opinions. Chinese children, in contrast, more often referred to social interactions and to others. Similarly in their self-descriptions, U.S. children listed more personal attributes ("I'm smart," "I like hockey"), Chinese children more attributes involving group

membership and relationships ("I'm in second grade," "My friends are crazy about me") (Wang, 2004, 2006b).

Development of Self-Esteem

Recall that most preschoolers have extremely high self-esteem. But as children enter school and receive much more feedback about how well they perform compared with their peers, self-esteem differentiates and also adjusts to a more realistic level.

■ **A HIERARCHICALLY STRUCTURED SELF-ESTEEM.** Researchers have asked children to indicate the extent to which statements such as "I am good at homework" or "I'm usually the one chosen for games" are true of themselves. By age 6 to 7, children have formed at least four broad self-evaluations—academic competence, social competence, physical/athletic competence, and physical appearance. Within these are more refined categories that become increasingly distinct with age (Marsh, 1990; Marsh & Ayotte, 2003; Van den Bergh & De Rycke, 2003). Furthermore, the capacity to view the self in terms of stable dispositions permits school-age children to combine their separate self-evaluations into a general psychological image of themselves—an overall sense of self-esteem (Harter, 2003, 2006). As a result, self-esteem takes on the hierarchical structure shown in Figure 4.1.

Children attach greater importance to certain self-evaluations than to others. Although individual differences exist, during

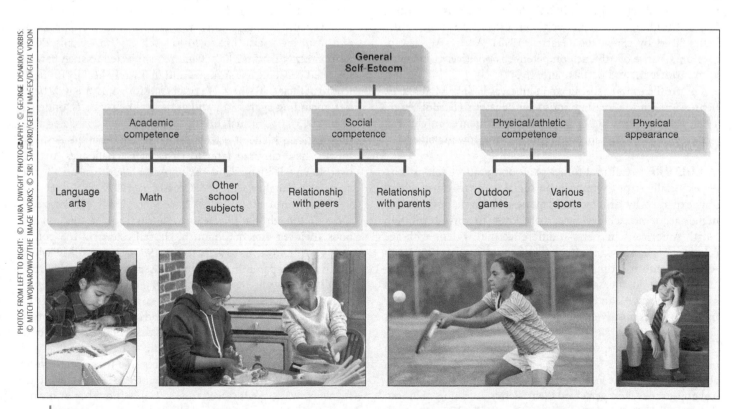

■ **FIGURE 4.1** ■ **Hierarchical structure of self-esteem in the mid-elementary school years.** From their experiences in different settings, children form at least four separate self-esteems: academic competence, social competence, physical/athletic competence, and physical appearance. These differentiate into additional self-evaluations and combine to form a general sense of self-esteem.

childhood and adolescence, perceived physical appearance correlates more strongly with overall self-worth than any other self-esteem factor (Klomsten, Skaalvik, & Espnes, 2004; Shapka & Keating, 2005). Emphasis on appearance, in the media and in society, has major implications for young people's overall satisfaction with themselves.

■ **CHANGES IN LEVEL OF SELF-ESTEEM.** Self-esteem declines during the first few years of elementary school as children evaluate themselves in various areas (Marsh, Craven, & Debus, 1998; Wigfield et al., 1997). Typically, the drop is not great enough to be harmful. Most (but not all) children appraise their characteristics and competencies realistically while maintaining an attitude of self-respect. Then, from fourth grade on, self-esteem rises for the majority of young people, who feel especially good about their peer relationships and athletic capabilities (Cole et al., 2001; Twenge & Campbell, 2001).

Influences on Self-Esteem

From middle childhood on, individual differences in self-esteem become increasingly stable (Trzesniewski, Donnellan, & Robins, 2003). And positive relationships among self-esteem, valuing of various activities, and success at those activities emerge and strengthen. Academic self-esteem predicts how important, useful, and enjoyable children judge school subjects to be, their willingness to try hard, and their achievement (Denissen, Zarrett, & Eccles, 2007; Valentine, DuBois, & Cooper, 2004). Children with high social self-esteem are consistently better-liked by classmates (Harter, 1999). And as we saw in Section 3, sense of athletic competence is positively associated with investment and performance in sports.

A profile of low self-esteem in all areas is linked to anxiety, depression, and increasing antisocial behavior (DuBois et al., 1999; Robins et al., 2001). What social influences might lead self-esteem to be high for some children and low for others?

■ **CULTURE.** Cultural forces profoundly affect self-esteem. An especially strong emphasis on social comparison in school may explain why Chinese and Japanese children, despite their higher academic achievement, score lower in self-esteem than North American children—a difference that widens with age (Harter, 2006; Hawkins, 1994; Twenge & Crocker, 2002). In Asian classrooms, competition is tough and achievement pressure is high. At the same time, because their culture values social harmony, Asian children tend to be reserved about judging themselves positively but generous in their praise of others (Falbo et al., 1997).

Gender-stereotyped expectations also affect self-esteem. In one study, the more 5- to 8-year-old girls talked with friends about the way people look, watched TV shows focusing on physical appearance, and perceived their friends as valuing thinness, the lower their physical self-esteem and overall self-worth a year later (Dohnt & Tiggemann, 2006). In academic self-judgments, girls score higher in language arts self-esteem, whereas boys have

higher math, science, and physical/athletic self-esteem—even when children of equal skill levels are compared (Fredricks & Eccles, 2002; Jacobs et al., 2002; Tennenbaum & Leaper, 2003). At the same time, girls exceed boys in self-esteem dimensions of close friendship and social acceptance. And despite a widely held assumption that boys' overall self-worth is much higher than girls', the difference is slight (Marsh & Ayotte, 2003; Young & Mroczek, 2003). Girls may think less well of themselves because they internalize this negative cultural message.

Compared with their Caucasian agemates, African-American children tend to have slightly higher self-esteem, possibly because of warm, extended families and a stronger sense of ethnic pride (Gray-Little & Hafdahl, 2000). Finally, children and adolescents who attend schools or live in neighborhoods where their SES and ethnic groups are well-represented feel a stronger sense of belonging and have fewer self-esteem problems (Gray-Little & Carels, 1997).

■ **CHILD-REARING PRACTICES.** Children whose parents use an *authoritative* child-rearing style (see Section 2) feel especially good about themselves (Carlson, Uppal, & Prosser, 2000; Rudy & Grusec, 2006; Wilkinson, 2004). Warm, positive parenting lets children know that they are accepted as competent and worthwhile. And firm but appropriate expectations, backed up with explanations, help them evaluate their own behavior against reasonable standards.

Controlling parents—those who too often help or make decisions for their child—communicate a sense of inadequacy to children. Having parents who are repeatedly disapproving and insulting is also linked to low self-esteem (Kernis, 2002; Pomerantz & Eaton, 2000). Children subjected to such parenting need constant reassurance, and many rely heavily on peers to affirm their self-worth—a risk factor for adjustment difficulties, including aggression and antisocial behavior (Donnellan et al., 2005). In contrast, indulgent parenting is correlated with unrealistically high self-esteem, which also undermines development. These children tend to lash out at challenges to their overblown self-images and, thus, are also likely to be hostile and aggressive (Hughes, Cavell, & Grossman, 1997).

American cultural values have increasingly emphasized a focus on the self that may lead parents to indulge children and boost their self-esteem too much. The self-esteem of U.S. youths rose sharply from the 1970s to the 1990s—a period in which much popular parenting literature advised promoting children's self-esteem (Twenge & Campbell, 2001). Yet compared with previous generations, American youths are achieving less well and displaying more antisocial behavior and other adjustment problems (Berk, 2005). Research confirms that children do not benefit from compliments ("You're terrific") that have no basis in real attainment (Damon, 1995). Rather, the best way to foster a positive, secure self-image is to encourage children to strive for worthwhile goals. Over time, a bidirectional relationship emerges: Achievement fosters self-esteem, which contributes to further effort and gains in performance (Gest, Domitrovich, & Welsh, 2005; Guay, Marsh, & Boivin, 2003).

What can adults do to promote, and to avoid undermining, this mutually supportive relationship between motivation and self-esteem? Some answers come from research on the precise content of adults' messages to children in achievement situations. Let's look first at the meanings children assign to their successes and failures.

■ **MAKING ACHIEVEMENT-RELATED ATTRIBUTIONS.** *Attributions* are our common, everyday explanations for the causes of behavior—our answers to the question, "Why did I or another person do that?" Notice how Joey, in talking about the spelling bee at the beginning of this section, attributes his disappointing performance to *luck* (Belinda got all the easy words) and his usual success to *ability* (he *knows* he's a better speller than Belinda). Joey also appreciates that *effort* matters: "I knocked myself out studying those spelling lists."

Cognitive development permits school-age children to separate all these variables in explaining performance (Dweck, 2002). Those who are high in academic self-esteem and motivation make **mastery-oriented attributions,** crediting their successes to ability—a characteristic they can improve through trying hard and can count on when facing new challenges. And they attribute failure to factors that can be changed or controlled, such as insufficient effort or a very difficult task (Heyman & Dweck, 1998). So whether these children succeed or fail, they take an industrious, persistent approach to learning.

In contrast, children who develop **learned helplessness** attribute their failures, not their successes, to ability. When they succeed, they conclude that external factors, such as luck, are responsible. Unlike their mastery-oriented counterparts, they believe that ability is fixed and cannot be improved by trying hard (Cain & Dweck, 1995). When a task is difficult, these children experience an anxious loss of control—in Erikson's terms, a pervasive sense of inferiority. They give up without really trying.

Children's attributions affect their goals. Mastery-oriented children seek information on how best to increase their ability through effort. Hence, their performance improves over time (Blackwell, Trzesniewski, & Dweck, 2007). In contrast, learned-helpless children focus on obtaining positive and avoiding negative evaluations of their fragile sense of ability. Over time, their ability no longer predicts how well they do (Pomerantz & Saxon, 2001). Because they fail to connect effort with success, learned-helpless children do not develop the metacognitive and self-regulatory skills necessary for high achievement (see Section 3). Lack of effective learning strategies, reduced persistence, low performance, and a sense of loss of control sustain one another in a vicious cycle (Chan & Moore, 2006).

■ **INFLUENCES ON ACHIEVEMENT-RELATED ATTRIBUTIONS.** What accounts for the different attributions of mastery-oriented and learned-helpless children? Adult communication plays a key role. Children with a learned-helpless style often have parents who believe that their child is not very capable and must work harder than others to succeed. When the child fails, the parent might say, "You can't do that, can you? It's OK if you

Mastery-oriented children credit their successes to ability, and they seek information on how best to increase their ability through effort. Hence, their performance improves over time.

quit" (Hokoda & Fincham, 1995). After the child succeeds, the parent might give feedback that evaluates the child's traits ("You're so smart"). Trait statements promote a fixed view of ability, leading children to question their competence in the face of setbacks and to retreat from challenge (Mueller & Dweck, 1998).

Teachers' messages also affect children's attributions. Teachers who are caring and helpful and emphasize learning over getting good grades tend to have mastery-oriented students (Anderman et al., 2001). In contrast, students with unsupportive teachers often regard their performance as externally controlled (by teachers or luck), withdraw from learning activities, and decline in achievement—outcomes that lead children to doubt their ability (Skinner, Zimmer-Gembeck, & Connell, 1998).

For some children, performance is especially likely to be undermined by adult feedback. Despite their higher achievement, girls more often than boys blame poor performance on ability. Girls tend to receive messages from teachers and parents that their ability is at fault when they do not do well, and negative stereotypes (for example, that girls are weak at math) reduce their interest and effort (Bleeker & Jacobs, 2004; Cole et al., 1999). And as Section 3 revealed, low-SES ethnic minority students often receive less favorable feedback from teachers, especially when assigned to homogeneous groups of poorly achieving students—conditions that result in a drop in academic self-esteem and achievement (Harris and Graham, 2007).

Finally, cultural values affect the likelihood that children will develop learned helplessness. Because of the high value their

Applying What We Know

Fostering a Mastery-Oriented Approach to Learning

Strategy	Description
Provision of tasks	Select tasks that are meaningful, responsive to a diversity of student interests, and appropriately matched to current competence so that the child is challenged but not overwhelmed.
Parent and teacher encouragement	Communicate warmth, confidence in the child's abilities, the value of achievement, and the importance of effort in success.
	Model high effort in overcoming failure.
	(For teachers) Communicate often with parents, suggesting ways to foster children's effort and progress.
	(For parents) Monitor schoolwork; provide scaffolded assistance that promotes knowledge of effective strategies and self-regulation.
Performance evaluations	Make evaluations private; avoid publicizing success or failure through wall posters, stars, privileges for "smart" children, or prizes for "best" performance.
	Emphasize individual progress and self-improvement.
School environment	Offer small classes, which permit teachers to provide individualized support for mastery.
	Provide for cooperative learning and peer tutoring, in which children assist one another; avoid ability grouping, which makes evaluations of children's progress public.
	Accommodate individual and cultural differences in learning styles.
	Create an atmosphere that values academics and sends a clear message that all students can learn.

Sources: Hilt, 2004; Wigfield et al., 2006.

culture places on effort and self-improvement, Asians attend more to failure than to success, because failure indicates where corrective action is needed. Americans, in contrast, focus more on success because it enhances self-esteem. When researchers observed U.S. and Chinese mothers' responses to their fourth and fifth graders' puzzle solutions, the U.S. mothers offered more praise after success, whereas the Chinese mothers more often pointed out the child's inadequate performance. And regardless of success or failure, Chinese mothers made more task-relevant statements aimed at ensuring that children exerted sufficient effort to do well ("You concentrated on it": "You got only 6 out of 12"). When children continued with the task after mothers left the room, the Chinese children showed greater gains in performance (Ng, Pomerantz, & Lam, 2007).

■ **FOSTERING A MASTERY-ORIENTED APPROACH.** Attribution research suggests that well-intended messages from adults sometimes undermine children's competence. An intervention called *attribution retraining* encourages learned-helpless children to believe that they can overcome failure by exerting more effort. Children are given tasks difficult enough that they will experience some failure, followed by repeated feedback that helps them revise their attributions: "You can do it if you try harder." After they succeed, children receive additional feedback—"You're really good at this" or "You really tried hard on that one"—so that they attribute their success to both ability and effort, not chance. Another approach is to encourage low-effort students to focus less on grades and more on mastering a

task for its own sake (Hilt, 2004; Horner & Gaither, 2004). Instruction in effective strategies and self-regulation is also vital, to compensate for development lost in this area and to ensure that renewed effort pays off (Wigfield et al., 2006).

Attribution retraining is best begun early, before children's views of themselves become hard to change. An even better approach is to prevent learned helplessness, using the strategies summarized in Applying What We Know above.

ASK YOURSELF

» REVIEW
How does level of self-esteem change in middle childhood, and what accounts for these changes?

» APPLY
Should parents promote children's self-esteem by telling them they're "smart" or "wonderful"? Are children harmed if they do not feel good about everything they do? Why or why not?

» CONNECT
What cognitive changes, described in Section 3, support the transition to a self-concept emphasizing competencies, personality traits, and social comparisons?

» REFLECT
Recall your own attributions for academic successes and failures when you were in elementary school. What are those attributions like now? What messages from others may have contributed to your attributions?

Emotional Development

Greater self-awareness and social sensitivity support gains in emotional competence in middle childhood. Changes take place in experience of self-conscious emotions, emotional understanding, and emotional self-regulation.

Self-Conscious Emotions

In middle childhood, the self-conscious emotions of pride and guilt become clearly governed by personal responsibility. Children experience pride in a new accomplishment and guilt over a transgression, even when no adult is present (Harter & Whitesell, 1989). Also, children no longer report guilt for any mishap, as they did earlier, but only for intentional wrongdoing, such as ignoring responsibilities, cheating, or lying (Ferguson, Stegge, & Damhuis, 1991).

Pride motivates children to take on further challenges, whereas guilt prompts them to make amends and to strive for self-improvement. But harsh, insensitive reprimands from adults ("Everyone else can do it! Why can't you?") can lead to intense shame, which (as noted in Section 2) is particularly destructive. A shame-induced, sharp drop in self-esteem can trigger withdrawal, depression, and intense anger at those who participated in the shame-evoking situation (Lindsay-Hartz, de Rivera, & Mascolo, 1995; Mills, 2005).

Emotional Understanding

School-age children's understanding of mental activity means that, unlike preschoolers, they are likely to explain emotion by referring to internal states, such as happy or sad thoughts, than to external events (Flavell, Flavell, & Green, 2001). Also, around age 8, children become aware that they can experience more than one emotion at a time, each of which may be positive or negative and differ in intensity (Pons et al., 2003). For example, recalling the birthday present he received from his grandmother, Joey reflected, "I was very happy that I got something but a little sad that I didn't get just what I wanted."

Appreciating mixed emotions helps children realize that people's expressions may not reflect their true feelings (Misailidi, 2006; Saarni, 1999). It also fosters awareness of self-conscious emotions. For example, between ages 6 and 7, children improve sharply in ability to distinguish pride from happiness and surprise (Tracy, Robins, & Lagattuta, 2005). And 8- and 9-year-olds understand that pride combines two sources of happiness—joy in accomplishment and joy that a significant person recognized that accomplishment (Harter, 1999). Furthermore, children of this age can reconcile contradictory facial and situational cues in figuring out another's feelings (see page 47 in Section 2). And they can use information about "what might have happened" to predict how people will feel in a new situation—realizing, for example, that someone will feel a sense of relief when an actual outcome is more favorable than what could have occurred (Guttentag & Ferrell, 2004).

These 8-year-old twin brothers raised over $5,000 for victims of the devastating tsunami of 2005. Their gains in emotional understanding and perspective taking enable them to respond with empathy to people's immediate distress as well as to their general life condition.

As with self-understanding, gains in emotional understanding are supported by cognitive development and social experiences, especially adults' sensitivity to children's feelings and willingness to discuss emotions. Together, these factors lead to a rise in empathy as well. As children move closer to adolescence, advances in perspective taking permit an empathic response not just to people's immediate distress but also to their general life condition (Hoffman, 2000). As Joey and Lizzie imagined how people who are chronically ill or hungry feel and evoked those emotions in themselves, they gave part of their allowance to charity and joined in fundraising projects through school, community center, and scouting.

Emotional Self-Regulation

Rapid gains in emotional self-regulation occur in middle childhood. As children engage in social comparison and care more about peer approval, they must learn to manage negative emotion that threatens their self-esteem.

By age 10, most children shift adaptively between two general strategies for managing emotion. In **problem-centered coping,** they appraise the situation as changeable, identify the difficulty, and decide what to do about it. If problem solving does not work, they engage in **emotion-centered coping,** which is internal, private, and aimed at controlling distress when little can be done about an outcome (Kliewer, Fearnow, & Miller, 1996;

Lazarus & Lazarus, 1994). For example, when faced with an anxiety-provoking test or an angry friend, older school-age children view problem solving and seeking social support as the best strategies. But when outcomes are beyond their control—for example, after receiving a bad grade—they opt for distraction or try to redefine the situation: "Things could be worse. There'll be another test." School-age children's improved ability to reflect on thoughts and feelings means that, compared with preschoolers, they more often use these internal strategies to manage emotion (Brenner & Salovey, 1997).

Furthermore, through interacting with parents, teachers, and peers, school-age children become more knowledgeable about socially approved ways to display negative emotion. They increasingly prefer verbal strategies ("Please stop pushing and wait your turn") to crying, sulking, or aggression (Shipman et al., 2003). Young school-age children justify these more mature displays of emotion by mentioning avoidance of punishment or adult approval but, by third grade, they begin to emphasize concern for others' feelings. Children with this awareness are rated as especially helpful, cooperative, and socially responsive by teachers and as better-liked by peers (Garner, 1996; McDowell & Parke, 2000).

When emotional self-regulation has developed well, school-age children acquire a sense of *emotional self-efficacy*—a feeling of being in control of their emotional experience (Saarni, 2000). This fosters a favorable self-image and an optimistic outlook, which further help children face emotional challenges. As at younger ages, school-age children whose parents respond sensitively and helpfully when the child is distressed are emotionally well-regulated—generally upbeat in mood and also empathic and prosocial. In contrast, poorly regulated children often experience hostile, dismissive parental reactions to distress (Davidov & Grusec, 2006; Zeman, Shipman, & Suveg, 2002). These children are overwhelmed by negative emotion, a response that interferes with empathy and prosocial behavior.

Understanding Others: Perspective Taking

We have seen that middle childhood brings major advances in **perspective taking,** the capacity to imagine what other people may be thinking and feeling. These changes support self-concept and self-esteem, understanding of others, and a wide variety of social skills. Robert Selman's five-stage sequence describes changes in perspective-taking skill, based on children's and adolescents' responses to social dilemmas in which characters have differing information and opinions about an event.

As Table 4.1 indicates, at first children have only a limited idea of what other people might be thinking and feeling. Over time, they become more aware that people can interpret the same event quite differently. Soon, they can "step into another person's shoes" and reflect on how that person might regard their own thoughts, feelings, and behavior, as when they say something like, "I *thought you would think* I was just kidding when I said that." (Note the similarity between this level of perspective taking and second-order false belief, described on page 94 in Section 3.) Finally, older children and adolescents can evaluate two people's perspectives simultaneously, at first from the vantage point of a disinterested spectator and later by referring to societal values (Gurucharri & Selman, 1982). The following explanation reflects this ability: "I know why Joey hid the stray kitten in the basement, even though his mom was against keeping it. He believes in not hurting animals. If you put the kitten outside or give it to the pound, it might die."

Experiences in which adults and peers explain their viewpoints contribute greatly to children's perspective taking. Good perspective takers, in turn, are more likely to display empathy and sympathy and to handle difficult social situations effectively—among the reasons they are better-liked by peers (FitzGerald & White, 2003). Children with poor social skills, especially the angry, aggressive styles discussed in Section 2, have great

■ TABLE 4.1 ■ *Selman's Stages of Perspective Taking*

STAGE	APPROXIMATE AGE RANGE	DESCRIPTION
Level 0: Undifferentiated perspective taking	3–6	Children recognize that self and other can have different thoughts and feelings, but they frequently confuse the two.
Level 1: Social-informational perspective taking	4–9	Children understand that different perspectives may result because people have access to different information.
Level 2: Self-reflective perspective taking	7–12	Children can "step into another person's shoes" and view their own thoughts, feelings, and behavior from the other person's perspective. They also recognize that others can do the same.
Level 3: Third-party perspective taking	10–15	Children can step outside a two-person situation and imagine how the self and other are viewed from the point of view of a third, impartial party.
Level 4: Societal perspective taking	14–adult	Individuals understand that third-party perspective taking can be influenced by one or more systems of larger societal values.

Sources: Selman, 1976; Selman & Byrne, 1974.

difficulty imagining others' thoughts and feelings. They often mistreat adults and peers without feeling the guilt and remorse prompted by awareness of another's viewpoint. Interventions that provide coaching and practice in perspective taking help reduce antisocial behavior and increase empathy and prosocial responding (Chalmers & Townsend, 1990).

Moral Development

Recall from Section 2 that preschoolers pick up many morally relevant behaviors through modeling and reinforcement. By middle childhood, they have had time to internalize rules for good conduct: "It's good to help others in trouble" or "It's wrong to take something that doesn't belong to you." This change leads children to become considerably more independent and trustworthy.

In Section 2, we also saw that children do not just copy their morality from others. As the cognitive-developmental approach emphasizes, they actively think about right and wrong. An expanding social world, the capacity to consider more information when reasoning, and perspective taking lead moral understanding to advance greatly in middle childhood.

Moral and Social-Conventional Understanding

During the school years, children construct a flexible appreciation of moral rules. By age 7 to 8, they no longer say truth telling is always good and lying is always bad but also consider prosocial and antisocial intentions. They evaluate certain types of truthfulness very negatively—for example, bluntly telling a classmate that you don't like her drawing (Bussey, 1999). And although both Chinese and North American schoolchildren consider lying about antisocial acts "very naughty," Chinese children—influenced by collectivist values—more often rate lying favorably when the intention is modesty, as when a student who has thoughtfully picked up litter from the playground says, "I didn't do it" (Lee et al., 1997, 2001). Similarly, Chinese children are more likely to favor lying to support the group at the expense of the individual (saying you're sick so, as a poor singer, you won't harm your class's chances of winning a singing competition). In contrast, North American children more often favor lying to support the individual at the expense of the group (claiming that a friend who is a poor speller is actually a good speller because he wants to participate in a spelling competition) (Fu et al., 2007).

As children's ideas about justice take into account an increasing number of variables, they clarify and link moral imperatives and social conventions. School-age children, for example, distinguish social conventions with a clear *purpose* (not running in school hallways to prevent injuries) from ones with no obvious justification (crossing a "forbidden" line on the playground). They regard violations of purposeful social conventions as closer to moral transgressions (Buchanan-Barrow & Barrett, 1998).

School-age children recognize that certain social conventions have a clear purpose—such as separating recyclables from trash to prevent waste. And they regard violations of these kinds of conventions as closer to moral transgressions.

With age, they also realize that people's *intentions* and the *contexts* of their actions affect the moral implications of violating a social convention. In one study, 8- to 10-year-olds stated that because of a flag's symbolic value, burning it to express disapproval of a country or to start a cooking fire is worse than burning it accidentally. But they recognized that flag burning is a form of freedom of expression, and most agreed that it would be acceptable in a country that treated its citizens unfairly (Helwig & Prencipe, 1999).

Children in Western and non-Western cultures reason similarly about moral and social-conventional concerns (Neff & Helwig, 2002; Nucci, 2002, 2005). When a directive is fair and caring, such as telling children to stop fighting or to share candy, school-age children view it as right, regardless of who states it—a principal, a teacher, or a child with no authority. In contrast, even in Korean culture, which places a high value on deference to authority, 7- to 11-year-olds evaluate negatively a teacher's or principal's order to engage in immoral acts, such as stealing or refusing to share—a response that strengthens with age (Kim, 1998; Kim & Turiel, 1996).

Understanding Individual Rights

When children in diverse cultures challenge adult authority, they typically do so within the personal domain. As their grasp of moral imperatives and social conventions strengthens, so does their conviction that certain choices, such as hairstyle, friends, and leisure activities, are up to the individual. A Colombian child illustrated this passionate defense of personal control when asked if a teacher had the right to tell a student where to sit during circle time. In the absence of a moral reason from the teacher, the child declared, "She should be able to sit wherever she wants" (Ardila-Rey & Killen, 2001, p. 249).

Notions of personal choice, in turn, enhance children's moral understanding. As early as age 6, children view freedom of speech and religion as individual rights, even if laws exist that deny those rights (Helwig, 2006). And they regard laws that discriminate against individuals—for example, denying certain people access to medical care or education—as wrong and worthy of violating (Helwig & Jasiobedzka, 2001). In justifying their responses, children appeal to personal privileges and, by the end of middle childhood, to the importance of individual rights for maintaining a fair society.

At the same time, older school-age children place limits on individual choice. Fourth graders faced with conflicting moral and personal concerns—such as whether or not to befriend a classmate of a different race or gender—typically decide in favor of kindness and fairness (Killen et al., 2002). Partly for this reason, prejudice usually declines in middle childhood.

Understanding Diversity and Inequality

By the early school years, children associate power and privilege with white people and poverty and inferior status with people of color. They do not necessarily acquire these views directly from parents or friends (Aboud & Doyle, 1996). Rather, they seem to pick up prevailing societal attitudes from implicit messages in the media and elsewhere in their environments.

■ **IN-GROUP AND OUT-GROUP BIASES: DEVELOPMENT OF PREJUDICE.** Studies in diverse Western nations confirm that by age 5 to 7, white children generally evaluate their own racial group favorably and other racial groups less favorably or negatively (Aboud, 2003; Nesdale et al., 2004). Many minority children of this age, in a reverse pattern, assign positive characteristics to the privileged white majority and negative characteristics to their own group (Averhart & Bigler, 1997; Corenblum, 2003).

But recall that with age, children pay more attention to inner traits. The capacity to classify the social world in multiple ways enables school-age children to understand that people who look different need not think, feel, or act differently (Aboud & Amato, 2001). Consequently, voicing of negative attitudes toward minorities declines. After age 7 or 8, both majority and minority children express in-group favoritism, and white children's prejudice against out-group members often weakens (Nesdale et al., 2005; Ruble et al., 2004).

Yet even in children aware of the injustice of discrimination, prejudice may operate unintentionally and without awareness—as it does in many white adults (Dunham, Baron, & Banaji, 2006). Consider a study in which white school-age children were asked to divide fairly among three child artists—two white and one black—money that had been earned from selling the children's art. In each version of the task, one artist

was labeled "productive" (making more art works), one as "the oldest," and one as "poor and needing money for lunch." By age 8 to 9, most children recognize that special consideration should be given to children who either perform exceptionally or are at a disadvantage. But racial stereotypes interfered with fourth graders' evenhanded application of these principles. They gave more money to a productive black artist (who countered the racial stereotype of "low achiever") than to a productive white artist and less money to a needy black artist (who conformed to the racial stereotype of "poor") than to a needy white artist (see Figure 4.2) (McGillicuddy-De Lisi, Daly, & Neal, 2006).

Nevertheless, the extent to which children hold racial and ethnic biases varies, depending on the following factors:

■ *A fixed view of personality traits.* Children who believe that people's personality traits are fixed rather than changeable often judge others as either "good" or "bad." Ignoring motives and circumstances, they readily form prejudices on the basis of limited information. For example, they might infer that "a new child at school who tells a lie to get other kids to like her" is simply a bad person (Levy & Dweck, 1999).

■ *Overly high self-esteem.* Children (and adults) with very high self-esteem are more likely to hold racial and ethnic prejudices (Baumeister et al., 2003; Bigler, Brown, & Markell, 2001). These individuals seem to belittle disadvantaged individuals or groups to justify their own extremely favorable

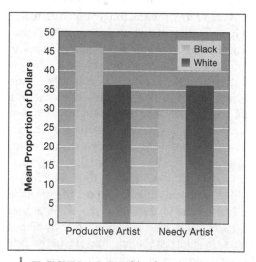

■ **FIGURE 4.2** ■ **White fourth graders' racially biased distribution of money to child artists.** When dividing money earned from selling children's art among three child artists—two white and one black—the fourth graders gave more money to a productive black artist (who countered a stereotype) than to a productive white artist and less money to a needy black artist (who conformed to a stereotype) than to a needy white artist. In both instances, the fourth graders seemed to engage in subtle, unintentional prejudice. (From A. V. McGillicuddy-De Lisi, M. Daly, & A. Neal, 2006, "Children's Distributive Justice Judgments: Aversive Racism in Euro-American Children?" *Child Development, 77,* p. 1072. © The Society for Research in Child Development, Inc. Adapted by permission of Blackwell Publishing Ltd. and A. V. McGillicuddy-De Lisi.)

© MICHAEL J. DOOLITTLE/THE IMAGE WORKS

Children perform a Polynesian song on the playground of their culturally diverse school. Collaboration with members of other ethnic groups and traditions can reduce the tendency to classify the social world on the basis of race and ethnicity and to view one's own group positively and other groups negatively.

self-evaluation. Furthermore, children who say their own ethnicity makes them feel especially "good"—and thus perhaps socially superior—are more likely to display in-group favoritism and out-group prejudice (Pfeifer et al., 2007).

■ *A social world in which people are sorted into groups.* The more adults highlight group distinctions for children and the less interracial contact children experience, the more likely white children are to display prejudice (Bigler, Brown, & Markell, 2001; McGlothlin & Killen, 2006).

■ **REDUCING PREJUDICE.** Research confirms that an effective way to reduce prejudice is through intergroup contact, in which racially and ethnically different children work toward common goals and become personally acquainted (Tropp & Pettigrew, 2005). Children assigned to cooperative learning groups with peers of diverse backgrounds, for example, form more cross-race friendships. Sharing thoughts and feelings with close, cross-race friends, in turn, reduces even subtle, unintentional prejudices (Turner, Hewstone, & Voci, 2007). But these positive effects seem not to generalize to relationships beyond the group.

Long-term contact and collaboration in neighborhoods, schools, and communities may be the best way to reduce prejudice. Classrooms that expose children to ethnic diversity, teach them to value those differences, directly address the damage caused by prejudice, and encourage perspective taking and empathy both prevent children from forming negative biases and reduce already acquired biases (Pfeifer, Brown, & Juvonen, 2007).

Finally, inducing children to view others' traits as changeable, by discussing with them the many possible influences on

those traits, is helpful. The more children believe that people can change their personalities, the more they report liking and perceiving themselves as similar to members of disadvantaged groups. Furthermore, children who believe in the changeability of human attributes spend more time volunteering to help the needy (Karafantis & Levy, 2004). Volunteering, in turn, may promote a changeable view of others by helping children take the perspective of the underprivileged and appreciate the social conditions that lead to disadvantage.

ASK YOURSELF

>> **REVIEW**
How does emotional self-regulation improve in middle childhood? What implications do these changes have for children's self-esteem?

>> **APPLY**
Ten-year-old Marla says her classmate Bernadette will never get good grades because she's lazy. Jane believes that Bernadette tries but can't concentrate because her parents are divorcing. Why is Marla more likely than Jane to develop prejudices?

>> **CONNECT**
Cite examples of how older children's capacity to take more information into account enhances their emotional and moral understanding.

>> **REFLECT**
Did you attend an integrated elementary school? Why is school integration vital for reducing racial and ethnic prejudice?

Peer Relations

In middle childhood, the society of peers becomes an increasingly important context for development. Peer contact, as we have seen, contributes to perspective taking and understanding of self and others. These developments, in turn, enhance peer interaction. Compared with preschoolers, school-age children resolve conflicts more effectively, using persuasion and compromise (Mayeux & Cillessen, 2003). Sharing, helping, and other prosocial acts also increase. In line with these changes, aggression declines. But the drop is greatest for physical attacks (Côté et al., 2007; Tremblay, 2000). As we will see, verbal and relational aggression continue as children form peer groups.

Peer Groups

TAKE A MOMENT... Watch children in the schoolyard or neighborhood, and notice how often they gather in groups of three to a dozen or more. In what ways are members of the same group noticeably alike?

By the end of middle childhood, children display a strong desire for group belonging. They form **peer groups,** collectives that generate unique values and standards for behavior and a social structure of leaders and followers. Peer groups organize on the basis of proximity (being in the same classroom) and similarity in sex, ethnicity, popularity, and aggression (Rubin, Bukowski, & Parker, 2006).

The practices of these informal groups lead to a "peer culture" that typically consists of a specialized vocabulary, dress code, and place to "hang out." As children develop these exclusive associations, the codes of dress and behavior that grow out of them become more broadly influential. Schoolmates who deviate—by "kissing up" to teachers, wearing the wrong kind of shirt or shoes, or tattling on classmates—are often rebuffed, becoming targets of critical glances and comments. These customs bind peers together, creating a sense of group identity. Within the group, children acquire many social skills—cooperation, leadership, followership, and loyalty to collective goals.

Most school-age children believe a group is wrong to exclude a peer (Killen, Crystal, & Watanabe, 2002). Nevertheless, children do exclude, often using relationally aggressive tactics. Peer groups—at the instigation of their leaders, who can be skillfully aggressive—frequently oust no longer "respected" children. Some, whose own previous behavior toward outsiders reduces their chances of being included elsewhere, turn to other low-status peers with poor social skills (Werner & Crick, 2004). Socially anxious children, when ousted, often become increasingly peer-avoidant and thus more isolated (Gazelle & Rudolph, 2004). In either case, opportunities to acquire socially competent behavior diminish.

School-age children's desire for group membership can also be satisfied through formal group ties such as scouting, 4-H, and religious youth groups. Adult involvement holds in check the negative behaviors associated with children's informal peer

These girls have probably established a peer-group structure of leaders and followers as they gather for joint activities. Their relaxed body language and similar way of dressing suggest their strong sense of group belonging.

groups. And through working on joint projects and helping in their communities, children gain in social and moral maturity (Vandell & Shumow, 1999).

Friendships

Whereas peer groups provide children with insight into larger social structures, friendships contribute to the development of trust and sensitivity. During the school years, friendship becomes more complex and psychologically based. Consider the following 8-year-old's ideas:

> *Why is Shelly your best friend?* Because she helps me when I'm sad, and she shares. . . . *What makes Shelly so special?* I've known her longer, I sit next to her and got to know her better. . . . *How come you like Shelly better than anyone else?* She's done the most for me. She never disagrees, she never eats in front of me, she never walks away when I'm crying, and she helps me with my homework. . . . *How do you get someone to like you?* . . . If you're nice to [your friends], they'll be nice to you. (Damon, 1988b, pp. 80–81)

As these responses show, friendship has become a mutually agreed-on relationship in which children like each other's personal qualities and respond to one another's needs and desires. And once a friendship forms, *trust* becomes its defining feature. School-age children state that a good friendship is based on acts of kindness that signify that each person can be counted on to support the other (Hartup & Abecassis, 2004; Selman, 1980). Consequently, older children regard violations of trust, such as not helping when others need help, breaking promises, and gossiping behind the other's back, as serious breaches of friendship.

Because of these features, school-age children's friendships are more selective. Whereas preschoolers say they have lots of friends, by age 8 or 9, children name only a handful of good friends. Girls, who demand greater closeness than boys, are more exclusive in their friendships (Markovitz, Benenson, & Dolensky, 2001).

In addition, children tend to select friends similar to themselves in age, sex, race, ethnicity, and SES. Friends also resemble one another in personality (sociability, aggression), popularity, academic achievement, prosocial behavior, and judgments (including biased perceptions) of other people (Hartup, 2006; Mariano & Harton, 2005). But friendship opportunities offered by children's environments also affect their choices. As noted earlier, in integrated classrooms with mixed-race collaborative learning groups, students form more cross-race friendships.

Over middle childhood, friendships remain fairly stable, with about 50 to 70 percent enduring over a school year, and some for several years (Berndt, 2004). Through them, children come to realize that close relationships can survive disagreements if friends are secure in their liking for one another (Rose & Asher, 1999). In this way, friendship provides an important context in which children learn to tolerate criticism and resolve disputes.

Yet the impact of friendships on children's development depends on the nature of those friends. Children who bring kindness and compassion to their friendships strengthen each

School-age children tend to select friends similar to themselves in age, sex, race, ethnicity, and SES. However, in integrated classrooms with mixed-race collaborative learning groups, students form more cross-race friendships.

other's prosocial tendencies and form more lasting ties. When aggressive children make friends, the relationship is often riddled with hostile interaction and is at risk for breakup, especially when just one member of the pair is aggressive (Ellis & Zarbatany, 2007). Aggressive girls' friendships are high in exchange of private feelings but full of jealousy, conflict, and betrayal (Werner & Crick, 2004). Aggressive boys' friendships involve frequent expressions of anger, coercive statements, physical attacks, and enticements to rule-breaking behavior (Bagwell & Coie, 2004; Crick & Nelson, 2002; Dishion, Andrews, & Crosby, 1995). These findings indicate that the social problems of aggressive children operate within their closest peer ties.

Peer Acceptance

Peer acceptance refers to likability—the extent to which a child is viewed by a group of agemates, such as classmates, as a worthy social partner. Unlike friendship, likability is not a mutual relationship but a one-sided perspective, involving the group's view of an individual. Nevertheless, certain social skills that contribute to friendship also enhance peer acceptance. Better-accepted children tend to have more friends and more positive relationships with them (Lansford et al., 2006).

To assess peer acceptance, researchers usually use self-reports that measure *social preferences*—for example, asking children to identify classmates whom they "like very much" or "like very little." Another approach assesses *social prominence*—children's judgments of whom most of their classmates admire. The class-

mates children identify as prominent (looked up to by many others) show only moderate correspondence with those they say they personally prefer (LaFontana & Cillessen, 1999).

Children's self-reports yield four general categories of peer acceptance:

- **Popular children,** who get many positive votes (are well-liked)
- **Rejected children,** who get many negative votes (are disliked)
- **Controversial children,** who get a large number of positive and negative votes (are both liked and disliked)
- **Neglected children,** who are seldom mentioned, either positively or negatively

About two-thirds of students in a typical elementary school classroom fit one of these categories (Coie, Dodge, & Coppotelli, 1982). The remaining one-third, who do not receive extreme scores, are *average* in peer acceptance.

Peer acceptance is a powerful predictor of psychological adjustment. Rejected children, especially, are anxious, unhappy, disruptive, and low in self-esteem. Both teachers and parents rate them as having a wide range of emotional and social problems. Peer rejection in middle childhood is also strongly associated with poor school performance, absenteeism, dropping out, substance use, depression, antisocial behavior, and delinquency in adolescence and with criminality in early adulthood (Laird et al., 2001; Parker et al., 1995; Rubin, Bukowski, & Parker, 2006).

However, earlier influences—children's characteristics combined with parenting practices—may largely explain the link between peer acceptance and adjustment. School-age children with peer-relationship problems are more likely to have experienced family stress due to low income, insensitive child rearing, and coercive discipline (Cowan & Cowan, 2004). Nevertheless, as we will see, rejected children evoke reactions from peers that contribute to their unfavorable development.

■ **DETERMINANTS OF PEER ACCEPTANCE.** Why is one child liked while another is rejected? A wealth of research reveals that social behavior plays a powerful role.

Popular Children. The majority of **popular-prosocial children** combine academic and social competence, performing well in school and communicating with peers in sensitive, friendly, and cooperative ways (Cillessen & Bellmore, 2004). But other popular children are admired for their socially adept yet belligerent behavior. This smaller subtype, **popular-antisocial children,** includes "tough" boys—athletically skilled but poor students who cause trouble and defy adult authority—and relationally aggressive boys and girls who enhance their own status by ignoring, excluding, and spreading rumors about other children (Cillessen & Mayeux, 2004; Rodkin et al., 2000; Rose, Swenson, & Waller, 2004).

Despite their aggressiveness, peers view these youths as "cool," perhaps because of their athletic ability and sophisticated but devious social skills. Although peer admiration gives these children some protection against lasting adjustment difficulties, their antisocial acts require intervention (Prinstein & La Greca, 2004; Rodkin et al., 2006). With age, peers like these high-status, aggressive youths less and less, a trend that is stronger for relationally aggressive girls. The more socially prominent and controlling these girls become, the more they engage in relational aggression (Cillessen & Mayeux, 2004). Eventually peers condemn their nasty tactics and reject them.

Rejected Children. Rejected children display a wide range of negative social behaviors. Most are **rejected-aggressive children,** who show high rates of conflict, physical and relational aggression, and hyperactive, inattentive, and impulsive behavior. These children are also deficient in perspective taking and emotion regulation. For example, they tend to misinterpret the innocent behaviors of peers as hostile and to blame others for their social difficulties (Crick, Casas, & Nelson, 2002; Dodge, Coie, & Lynam, 2006; Hoza et al., 2005). Compared with popular-aggressive children, they are more extremely antagonistic. In contrast, **rejected-withdrawn children,** a smaller subtype, are passive and socially awkward. These timid children are overwhelmed by social anxiety, hold negative expectations for treatment by peers, and worry about being scorned and attacked (Hart et al., 2000; Ladd & Burgess, 1999; Troop-Gordon & Asher, 2005).

Rejected children are excluded by peers as early as kindergarten. Soon their classroom participation declines, their feelings of loneliness rise, their academic achievement falters, and they want to avoid school (Buhs & Ladd, 2001). Most have few friends, and some have none—a circumstance that predicts severe adjustment difficulties (Ladd & Troop-Gordon, 2003).

Both types of rejected children are at risk for peer harassment. But as the Biology and Environment box on the following page reveals, rejected-aggressive children also act as bullies, and rejected-withdrawn children are especially likely to be victimized (Putallaz et al., 2007; Sandstrom & Cillessen, 2003).

Controversial and Neglected Children. Consistent with the mixed peer opinion they engender, controversial children display a blend of positive and negative social behaviors. They are hostile and disruptive, but they also engage in positive, prosocial acts. Even though some peers dislike them, they have qualities that protect them from social exclusion. They have as many friends as popular children and are happy with their peer relationships (Newcomb, Bukowski, & Pattee, 1993). But like their popular-antisocial counterparts, they often bully others and engage in calculated relational aggression to sustain their dominance (DeRosier & Thomas, 2003; Putallaz et al., 2007).

Perhaps the most surprising finding is that neglected children, once thought to be in need of treatment, are usually well-adjusted. Although they engage in low rates of interaction, most are just as socially skilled as average children. They do not report feeling lonely or unhappy, and when they want to, they can break away from their usual pattern of playing by themselves (Harrist et al., 1997; Ladd & Burgess, 1999). Neglected

children remind us that an outgoing, gregarious personality style is not the only path to emotional well-being.

■ **HELPING REJECTED CHILDREN.** A variety of interventions exist to improve the peer relations and psychological adjustment of rejected children. Most involve coaching, modeling, and reinforcing positive social skills, such as how to initiate interaction with a peer, cooperate in play, and respond to another child with friendly emotion and approval. Several of these programs have produced lasting gains in social competence and peer acceptance (Asher & Rose, 1997; DeRosier, 2007). Combining social-skills training with other treatments increases their effectiveness. Rejected children are often poor students, whose low academic self-esteem magnifies negative reactions to teachers and classmates. Intensive academic tutoring improves both school achievement and social acceptance (O'Neill et al., 1997).

Still another approach focuses on training in perspective taking and in solving social problems. But many rejected-aggressive children are unaware of their poor social skills and do not take responsibility for their social failures (Mrug, Hoza, & Gerdes, 2001). Rejected-withdrawn children, in contrast, are likely to develop a *learned-helpless* approach to peer difficulties—concluding, after repeated rebuffs, that they will never be liked (Wichmann, Coplan, & Daniels, 2004). Both types of children need help attributing their peer difficulties to internal, changeable causes.

Finally, because rejected children's socially incompetent behaviors often originate in harsh, intrusive, authoritarian parenting, interventions that focus on the child alone may not be sufficient (Rubin, Bukowski, & Parker, 2006). If parent–child interaction does not change, children may soon return to their old behavior patterns.

Gender Typing

Children's understanding of gender roles broadens in middle childhood, and their gender identities (views of themselves as relatively masculine or feminine) change as well. We will see that development differs for boys and girls, and it can vary considerably across cultures.

Gender-Stereotyped Beliefs

Research in many countries reveals that stereotyping of personality traits increases steadily in middle childhood, becoming adultlike around age 11 (Best, 2001; Heyman & Legare, 2004). For example, children regard "tough," "aggressive," "rational," and "dominant" as masculine and "gentle," "sympathetic," and "dependent" as feminine (Serbin, Powlishta, & Gulko, 1993).

Children derive these distinctions from observing sex differences in behavior as well as from adult treatment. When helping a child with a task, for example, parents (especially fathers) behave in a more mastery-oriented fashion with sons, setting higher

▪ BIOLOGY AND ENVIRONMENT ▪

Bullies and Their Victims

Follow the activities of aggressive children over a school day, and you will see that they reserve their hostilities for certain peers. A particularly destructive form of interaction is **peer victimization,** in which certain children become targets of verbal and physical attacks or other forms of abuse. What sustains these repeated assault–retreat cycles between pairs of children?

About 10 to 20 percent of children are bullies, while 15 to 30 percent are repeatedly victimized. Most bullies are boys who use both physical and verbal attacks, but girls sometimes bombard a vulnerable classmate with verbal and relational hostility (Rigby, 2004). And in a study of several hundred middle school students, about one in four reported experiencing "cyberbullying" through text messages, e-mail, or other electronic tools (Li, 2006).

Some bullies are high-status youngsters who may be liked for their leadership or athletic abilities. But most are disliked, or become so, because of their cruelty (Vaillancourt, Hymel, & McDougall, 2003). Nevertheless, peers rarely intervene to help victims, and about 20 to 30 percent of onlookers actually encourage bullies, even joining in (Salmivalli & Voeten, 2004).

Chronic victims tend to be passive when active behavior is expected. On the playground, they hang around chatting or wander on their own. When bullied, they give in, cry, and assume defensive postures (Boulton, 1999). Biologically based traits—an inhibited temperament and a frail physical appearance—contribute to victimization. But victims also have histories of resistant attachment, overly controlling child rearing, and maternal overprotection—parenting that prompts anxiety,

low self-esteem, and dependency, resulting in a fearful demeanor that marks these children as vulnerable (Snyder et al., 2003). Persistent bullying, in turn, further impairs victims' emotional self-regulation and social skills—outcomes that heighten victimization (Hoglund & Leadbeater, 2007; Rosen, Milich, & Harris, 2007). Victims' adjustment problems include depression, loneliness, poor school performance, disruptive behavior, and school avoidance (Paul & Cillessen, 2003).

Aggression and victimization are not polar opposites. One-third to one-half of victims are also aggressive. Occasionally, they retaliate against powerful bullies, who respond by abusing them again—a cycle that sustains their victim status (Kochenderfer-Ladd, 2003). Among rejected children, these bully/victims are the most despised. They often have histories of extremely maladaptive parenting, including child abuse. This combination of highly negative home and peer experiences places them at severe risk for maladjustment (Schwartz, Proctor, & Chien, 2001).

Interventions that change victimized children's negative opinions of themselves and that teach them to respond in nonreinforcing ways to their attackers are helpful. Another way to assist victimized children is to help them form and maintain a gratifying friendship. When children have a close friend to whom they can turn for help, bullying episodes usually end quickly. Anxious, withdrawn

children with a best friend have fewer adjustment problems than victims with no close friends (Bollmer et al., 2005; Fox & Boulton, 2006).

Although modifying victimized children's behavior can help, this does not mean they are to blame. The best way to reduce bullying is to change youth environments (including school, sports programs, recreation centers, and neighborhoods), promoting prosocial attitudes and behaviors. Effective approaches include developing school and community codes against bullying, teaching child bystanders to intervene, enlisting parents' assistance in changing bullies' behaviors, and (if necessary) moving socially prominent bullies to another class or school (Leadbeater & Hoglund, 2006; Smith, Ananiadou, & Cowie, 2003).

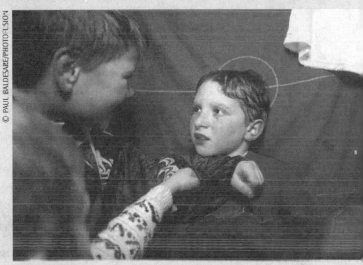

Some bullies are high-status youngsters, but most are disliked, or become so, because of their cruelty. Chronic victims tend to be physically weak, rejected by peers, and afraid to defend themselves—characteristics that make them easy targets.

---

standards, explaining concepts, and pointing out important features of tasks—particularly during gender-typed pursuits, such as science activities (Tenenbaum & Leaper, 2003; Tenenbaum et al., 2005). Furthermore, parents less often encourage girls to make their own decisions. And both parents and teachers more often praise boys for knowledge and accomplishment, girls for obedience (Good & Brophy, 2003; Leaper, Anderson, & Sanders, 1998; Pomerantz & Ruble, 1998).

Also in line with adult stereotypes, school-age children quickly figure out which academic subjects and skill areas are "masculine" and which are "feminine." They often regard reading,

spelling, art, and music as more for girls and mathematics, athletics, and mechanical skills as more for boys (Eccles, Jacobs, & Harold, 1990; Jacobs & Weisz, 1994). These attitudes influence children's preferences for and sense of competence at certain subjects. For example, boys tend to feel more competent than girls at math and science, whereas girls feel more competent than boys at language arts—even when children of equal skill level are compared (Bhanot & Jovanovic, 2005; Freedman-Doan et al., 2000; Hong, Veach, & Lawrenz, 2003). As we will see in Section 5, these beliefs become realities for many young people in adolescence.

Although school-age children are aware of many stereotypes, they also develop a more open-minded view of what males and females *can do* (Trautner et al., 2005). As with racial stereotypes (see page 126), the ability to classify flexibly underlies this change. School-age children realize that a person can belong to more than one social category—for example, be a "boy" yet "like to play house" (Bigler, 1995). By the end of middle childhood, children regard gender typing as socially rather than biologically influenced (Taylor, 1996). Nevertheless, acknowledging that people *can* cross gender lines does not mean that children always *approve* of doing so. They take a harsh view of certain violations—boys playing with dolls and wearing girls' clothing, girls acting noisily and roughly. They are especially intolerant when boys engage in "cross-gender" acts, which children regard as nearly as bad as moral transgressions (Blakemore, 2003; Levy, Taylor, & Gelman, 1995).

Gender Identity and Behavior

From third to sixth grade, boys strengthen their identification with "masculine" personality traits, whereas girls' identification with "feminine" traits declines. Girls often describe themselves as having some "other-gender" characteristics (Serbin, Powlishta, & Gulko, 1993). Whereas boys usually stick to "masculine" pursuits, girls now experiment with a wider range of options—from cooking and sewing to sports and science fairs—and more often consider traditionally male future work roles, such as firefighter or astronomer (Liben & Bigler, 2002).

These changes are due to a mixture of cognitive and social forces. School-age children of both sexes are aware that society

© PETER HVIZDAK/THE IMAGE WORKS

This 9-year-old girl enjoys karate lessons. Whereas school-age boys usually stick to "masculine" pursuits, girls experiment with a wider range of options.

attaches greater prestige to "masculine" characteristics. For example, they rate "masculine" occupations as having higher status than "feminine" occupations (Liben, Bigler, & Krogh, 2001). Messages from adults and peers are also influential. In Section 2, we saw that parents (especially fathers) are far less tolerant when sons, as opposed to daughters, cross gender lines. Similarly, a tomboyish girl can make her way into boys' activities without losing the approval of her female peers, but a boy who hangs out with girls is likely to be ridiculed and rejected.

As school-age children make social comparisons and characterize themselves in terms of stable dispositions, their gender identity expands to include the following self-evaluations, which greatly affect their adjustment:

- *Gender typicality*—the degree to which the child feels similar to others of the same gender. Although children need not be highly gender-typed to view themselves as gender-typical, their psychological well-being depends, to some degree, on feeling that they "fit in" with their same-sex peers (Egan & Perry, 2001).

- *Gender contentedness*—the degree to which the child feels satisfied with his or her gender assignment, which also promotes happiness.

- *Felt pressure to conform to gender roles*—the degree to which the child feels parents and peers disapprove of his or her gender-related traits. Because such pressure reduces the likelihood that children will explore options related to their interests and talents, children who feel strong gender-typed pressure are often distressed.

In a longitudinal study of third through seventh graders, *gender-typical* and *gender-contented* children gained in self-esteem over the following year. In contrast, children who were *gender-atypical* and *gender-discontented* declined in self-worth. Furthermore, gender-atypical children who reported *intense pressure to conform to gender roles* experienced serious difficulties—withdrawal, sadness, disappointment, and anxiety (Yunger, Carver, & Perry, 2004).

Clearly, how children feel about themselves in relation to their gender group becomes vitally important in middle childhood, and those who experience rejection because of their gender-atypical traits suffer profoundly. ***TAKE A MOMENT...*** Return to the case of David, the boy who was reared as a girl, on page 63 in Section 2. Note how David's dissatisfaction with his gender assignment joined with severe peer condemnation to severely impair his adjustment.

Currently, researchers and therapists are debating how best to help children who feel gender-atypical. Some advocate making them more gender-typical, through therapy that reinforces such children for engaging in traditional gender-role activities so they will feel more compatible with same-sex peers (Zucker, 2006). Others oppose this approach on grounds that it is likely to heighten felt pressure to conform (which predicts maladjustment) and—for children who fail to change—may result in parental rejection. These experts advocate intervening with parents and peers to help them become more accepting of children's gender-atypical interests and behaviors (Bigler, 2007; Conway, 2007; Crawford, 2003). *TAKE A MOMENT...* In view of what you have learned about the development of children's gender typing, which approach do you think would be more successful, and why?

ASK YOURSELF

>> **REVIEW**
How does friendship change in middle childhood?

>> **APPLY**
What changes in parent–child relationships are probably necessary to help rejected children?

>> **CONNECT**
Return to page 64 in Section 2, and review the concept of androgyny. Which of the two sexes is more androgynous in middle childhood, and why?

>> **REFLECT**
As a school-age child, did you have classmates you would classify as popular-aggressive? What were they like, and why do you think peers admired them?

Family Influences

As children move into school, peer, and community contexts, the parent–child relationship changes. At the same time, children's well-being continues to depend on the quality of family interaction. In the following sections, we will see that contemporary changes in families—high rates of divorce, remarriage, and maternal employment—can have positive as well as negative effects on children. In later sections, we take up other family structures, including gay and lesbian families, never-married single-parent families, and the increasing numbers of grandparents rearing grandchildren.

Parent–Child Relationships

In middle childhood, the amount of time children spend with parents declines dramatically. The child's growing independence means that parents must deal with new issues. "I've struggled with how many chores to assign, how much allowance to give, whether their friends are good influences, and what to do about problems at school," Rena remarked. "And then there's the challenge of keeping track of them when they're out—or even when they're home and I'm not there to see what's going on."

Despite these new concerns, child rearing becomes easier for those parents who established an authoritative style in the early years. Reasoning is more effective with school-age children because of their greater capacity for logical thinking and their increased respect for parents' expert knowledge (Collins, Madsen, & Susman-Stillman, 2002).

As children demonstrate that they can manage daily activities and responsibilities, effective parents gradually shift control

from adult to child. They do not let go entirely but, rather, engage in **coregulation,** a form of supervision in which parents exercise general oversight while letting children take charge of moment-by-moment decision making. Coregulation grows out of a warm, cooperative relationship between parent and child based on give-and-take and mutual respect. Parents must guide and monitor from a distance and effectively communicate expectations when they are with their children. And children must inform parents of their whereabouts, activities, and problems so parents can intervene when necessary (Maccoby, 1984). Coregulation supports and protects children while preparing them for adolescence, when they will make many important decisions themselves.

As at younger ages, mothers spend more time than fathers with school-age children. Mothers also are more knowledgeable about children's everyday activities. Still, fathers are often highly involved. Each parent, however, tends to devote more time to children of their own sex (Crouter et al., 1999; Lamb & Lewis, 2004). In parents' separate activities with children, mothers are more concerned with caregiving and ensuring that children meet responsibilities in homework, after-school lessons, and chores. Fathers, especially those with sons, focus on achievement related and recreational pursuits (Collins & Russell, 1991). But when both parents are present, fathers engage in as much caregiving as mothers.

Although school-age children often press for greater independence, they know how much they need their parents' continuing support. In one study, fifth and sixth graders described parents as the most influential people in their lives (Furman & Buhrmester, 1992). They often turned to mothers and fathers for affection, advice, enhancement of self-worth, and assistance with everyday problems.

Siblings

In addition to parents and friends, siblings continue to be important sources of support. Yet sibling rivalry tends to increase in middle childhood. As children participate in a wider range of activities, parents often compare siblings' traits and accomplishments. The child who gets less parental affection, more disapproval, or fewer material resources is likely to be resentful (Dunn, 2004; Tamrouti-Makkink et al., 2004).

For same-sex siblings who are close in age, parental comparisons are more frequent, resulting in more quarreling and antagonism and poorer adjustment. This effect is particularly strong when parents are under stress as a result of financial worries, marital conflict, or single parenthood (Jenkins, Rasbash, & O'Connor, 2003). Parents whose energies are drained become less careful about being fair.

To reduce this rivalry, siblings often strive to be different from one another. For example, two brothers I know deliberately selected different athletic pursuits and musical instruments. If the older one did especially well at an activity, the younger one did not want to try it. Parents can limit these effects by making an effort not to compare children, but some feedback about their competencies is inevitable. As siblings

Although sibling rivalry tends to increase in middle childhood, siblings also provide one another with emotional support and help with difficult tasks.

strive to win recognition for their own uniqueness, they shape important aspects of each other's development.

Although conflict rises, school-age siblings continue to rely on each other for companionship and assistance. When researchers asked siblings about shared daily activities, children mentioned that older siblings often helped younger siblings with academic and peer challenges. And both offered each other help with family issues (Tucker, McHale, & Crouter, 2001).

But for siblings to reap these benefits, parental encouragement of warm, considerate sibling ties is vital. Providing parents with training in mediation—how to get siblings to lay down ground rules, clarify their points of disagreement and common ground, and discuss possible solutions—increases siblings' awareness of each other's perspectives and reduces animosity (Smith & Ross, 2007). When siblings get along well, the older sibling's academic and social competence tends to "rub off on" the younger sibling, fostering more favorable achievement and peer relations (Brody & Murry, 2001; Lamarche et al., 2006). But older siblings with conflict-ridden peer relations tend to transmit their physically or relationally aggressive styles to their younger brothers and sisters (Ostrov, Crick, & Staffacher, 2006).

Only Children

Although sibling relationships bring many benefits, they are not essential for healthy development. Contrary to popular belief, only children are not spoiled, and in some respects, they are advantaged. U.S. children growing up in one-child and multichild families do not differ in self-rated personality traits (Mottus, Indus, & Allik, 2008). And compared to children with siblings, only children are higher in self-esteem and achievement motivation, do better in school, and attain higher levels of education. One reason may be that only children have somewhat closer relationships with parents, who may exert more pressure for mastery and accomplishment (Falbo, 1992). However, only children tend to be less well-accepted in the peer group, perhaps because they have not had opportunities to learn effective conflict-resolution strategies through sibling interaction (Kitzmann, Cohen, & Lockwood, 2002).

Favorable development also characterizes only children in China, where a one-child family policy has been strictly enforced in urban areas for more than two decades to control population growth (Yang, 2008). Compared with agemates who have siblings, Chinese only children are advanced in cognitive development and academic achievement. They also feel more emotionally secure, perhaps because government disapproval promotes tension in families with more than one child (Falbo & Poston, 1993; Jiao, Ji, & Jing, 1996; Yang et al., 1995). Chinese mothers usually ensure that their children have regular contact with first cousins (who are considered siblings). Perhaps as a result, Chinese only children do not differ from agemates with siblings in social skills and peer acceptance (Hart, Newell, & Olsen, 2003). The next generation of Chinese only children, however, will have no first cousins.

In China, a one-child family policy has been strictly enforced in urban areas for more than two decades to control population growth. However, Chinese only children do not differ from agemates with siblings in social skills and peer acceptance.

Divorce

Children's interactions with parents and siblings are affected by other aspects of family life. Joey and Lizzie's relationship, Rena told me, had been particularly negative only a few years before. Joey pushed, hit, and taunted Lizzie and called her names. Although she tried to retaliate, she was no match for Joey's larger size. The arguments usually ended with Lizzie running in tears to her mother. Joey and Lizzie's fighting coincided with their parents' growing marital unhappiness. When Joey was 8 and Lizzie 5, their father, Drake, moved out.

Between 1960 and 1985, divorce rates in Western nations rose dramatically before stabilizing in most countries. The United States has the highest divorce rate in the world (see Figure 4.3). Of the 45 percent of American marriages that end in divorce, half involve children. At any given time, one-fourth of U.S. children live in single-parent households. Although most reside with their mothers, the percentage in father-headed households has increased steadily, to about 12 percent (Federal Interagency Forum on Child and Family Statistics, 2008).

Children of divorce spend an average of five years in a single-parent home—almost a third of childhood. For many, divorce leads to new family relationships. About two-thirds of divorced parents marry again. Half their children eventually experience a third major change—the end of a parent's second marriage (Hetherington & Kelly, 2002).

These figures reveal that divorce is not a single event in the lives of parents and children. Instead, it is a transition that leads to a variety of new living arrangements, accompanied by changes in housing, income, and family roles and responsibilities. Since the 1960s, many studies have reported that marital breakup is stressful for children. But the research also reveals great individual differences (Hetherington, 2003). How well children fare depends on many factors: the custodial parent's psychological health, the child's characteristics, and social supports within the family and surrounding community.

■ **IMMEDIATE CONSEQUENCES.** "Things were worst during the period Drake and I decided to separate," Rena reflected. "We fought over division of our belongings and the custody of the children, and the kids suffered. Sobbing, Lizzie told me she was 'sorry she made Daddy go away.' Joey kicked and threw things at home and didn't do his work at school. In the midst of everything, I could hardly deal with their problems. We had to sell the house; I couldn't afford it alone. And I needed a better-paying job."

Family conflict often rises in newly divorced households as parents try to settle disputes over children and possessions. Once one parent moves out, additional events threaten supportive interactions between parents and children. Mother-headed households typically experience a sharp drop in income. In the United States, the majority of single mothers with young children live in poverty, getting less than the full amount of child support from the absent father or none at all (Children's Defense Fund, 2009). They often have to move to lower-cost housing, reducing supportive ties to neighbors and friends.

The transition from marriage to divorce typically leads to high maternal stress, depression, and anxiety and to a disorganized family situation. Declines in well-being are greatest for mothers of young children (Williams & Dunne-Bryant, 2006). "Meals and bedtimes were at all hours, the house didn't get cleaned, and I stopped taking Joey and Lizzie on weekend outings," said Rena. As children react with distress and anger to their less secure home lives, discipline may become harsh and inconsistent. Contact with noncustodial fathers often decreases over time (Hetherington & Kelly, 2002). Fathers who see their children only occasionally are inclined to be permissive and indulgent, making the mother's task of managing the child even more difficult.

The more parents argue and fail to provide children with warmth, involvement, and consistent guidance, the poorer children's adjustment. About 20 to 25 percent of children in divorced families display severe problems, compared with about 10 percent in nondivorced families (Gerard, Krishnakumar, & Buehler, 2006; Strohschein, 2005). At the same time, reactions vary with children's age, temperament, and sex.

Children's Age. Five-year-old Lizzie's fear that she had caused her father to leave is not unusual. Preschool and young school-age children often blame themselves for a marital breakup and fear that both parents may abandon them (Pryor & Rodgers, 2001). Even many older children, with the cognitive maturity to understand that they are not responsible for their parents' divorce, react strongly, declining in school performance, becoming unruly, and escaping into undesirable peer activities, especially when family conflict is high and supervision

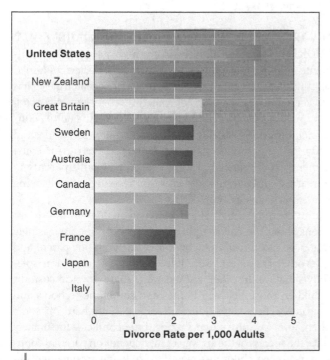

■ **FIGURE 4.3** ■ **Divorce rates in ten industrialized nations.** The U.S. divorce rate is the highest in the industrialized world, far exceeding divorce rates in other countries. (Adapted from U.S. Census Bureau, 2008c; United Nations, 2002.)

Divorce Rate per 1,000 Adults

United States, New Zealand, Great Britain, Sweden, Australia, Canada, Germany, France, Japan, Italy

of children is low (D'Onofrio et al., 2006; Lansford et al., 2006). But some older children—especially the oldest child in the family—display more mature behavior, willingly taking on extra family and household tasks as well as emotional support of a depressed, anxious mother. But if these demands are too great, these children may eventually become resentful, withdraw from the family, and engage in angry, acting-out behavior (Hetherington, 1999).

Children's Temperament and Sex. Exposure to stressful life events and inadequate parenting magnifies the problems of temperamentally difficult children. In contrast, easy children are less often targets of parental anger and also cope more effectively with adversity.

These findings help explain sex differences in response to divorce. Girls sometimes respond as Lizzie did, with internalizing reactions such as crying, self-criticism, and withdrawal. More often, children of both sexes show demanding, attention-getting, acting-out behavior. But in mother-custody families, boys are at greater risk for serious adjustment problems (Amato, 2001). Recall from Section 2 that boys are more active and noncompliant—behaviors that increase with exposure to parental conflict and inconsistent discipline. Coercive maternal behavior and defiance on the part of sons are common in divorcing households.

Perhaps because their behavior is so unruly, boys receive less emotional support from mothers, teachers, and peers. And as Joey's behavior toward Lizzie illustrates, the coercive cycles of interaction between boys and their divorced mothers soon spread to sibling relationships, compounding adjustment difficulties (Hetherington & Kelly, 2002; Sheehan et al., 2004). After divorce, children who are challenging to rear generally get worse.

■ **LONG-TERM CONSEQUENCES.** Rena eventually found better-paying work and gained control over the daily operation of the household. Her own feelings of anger and rejection also declined. And after several meetings with a counselor, Rena and Drake realized the harmful impact of their quarreling on Joey and Lizzie. Drake visited regularly and handled Joey's unruliness with firmness and consistency. Soon Joey's school performance improved, his behavior problems subsided, and both children seemed calmer and happier.

Most children show improved adjustment by two years after divorce. Yet overall, children and adolescents of divorced parents continue to score slightly lower than children of continuously married parents in academic achievement, self-esteem, and social competence and emotional adjustment (Amato, 2001). Children with difficult temperaments are especially likely to drop out of school, to be depressed, and to display antisocial behavior. And divorce is linked to problems with adolescent sexuality and development of intimate ties. Young people who experienced parental divorce—especially more than once—display higher rates of early sexual activity and adolescent parenthood (Wolfinger, 2000). Some experience other lasting difficulties—reduced educational attainment, troubled romantic relationships and marriages, divorce in adulthood, and unsatisfying parent–child

relationships (Amato, 2006; Amato & Cheadle, 2005; Wallerstein & Lewis, 2004).

The overriding factor in positive adjustment following divorce is effective parenting—shielding the child from family conflict and using authoritative child rearing (Leon, 2003; Wolchik et al., 2000). Where the custodial parent is the mother, contact with fathers is important. The more paternal contact and the warmer the father–child relationship, the less children react with defiance and aggression (Dunn et al., 2004). For girls, a good father–child relationship protects against early sexual activity and unhappy romantic involvements. For boys, it seems to affect overall psychological well-being. In fact, several studies indicate that outcomes for sons are better when the father is the custodial parent (Clarke-Stewart & Hayward, 1996; McLanahan, 1999). Fathers' greater economic security and image of authority seem to help them engage in effective parenting with sons. And boys in father-custody families may benefit from greater involvement of both parents because noncustodial mothers participate more than noncustodial fathers in their children's lives.

Although divorce is painful for children, remaining in an intact but high-conflict family is much worse than making the transition to a low-conflict, single-parent household (Greene et al., 2003; Strohschein, 2005). Divorcing parents who set aside their disagreements and support each other in their child-rearing roles greatly improve their children's chances of growing up competent, stable, and happy. Caring extended-family members, teachers, siblings, and friends also reduce the likelihood that divorce will result in long-term difficulties (Hetherington, 2003; Lussier et al., 2002).

■ **DIVORCE MEDIATION, JOINT CUSTODY, AND CHILD SUPPORT.** Awareness that divorce is highly stressful for children and families has led to community-based services aimed at helping them through this difficult time. One such service is **divorce mediation,** a series of meetings between divorcing adults and a trained professional aimed at reducing family conflict, including legal battles over property division and child custody. Research reveals that mediation increases out-of-court settlements, cooperation and involvement of both parents in child rearing, and parents' and children's feelings of well-being (Emery, Sbarra, & Grover, 2005).

Joint custody, which grants parents equal say in important decisions about the child's upbringing, is becoming increasingly common. In most instances, children reside with one parent and see the other on a fixed schedule, similar to the typical sole-custody situation. In other cases, parents share physical custody, and children move between homes and sometimes schools and peer groups. These transitions can be especially hard on some children. Joint-custody parents report little conflict—fortunately so, since the success of the arrangement depends on parental cooperation. And their children—regardless of living arrangements—tend to be better-adjusted than children in sole-maternal-custody homes (Bauserman, 2002).

Finally, many single-parent families depend on child support from the noncustodial parent to relieve financial strain. All

Applying What We Know

Helping Children Adjust to Their Parents' Divorce

Suggestion	Rationale
Shield children from conflict.	Witnessing intense parental conflict is very damaging to children. If one parent insists on expressing hostility, children fare better if the other parent does not respond in kind.
Provide children with as much continuity, familiarity, and predictability as possible.	Children adjust better during the period surrounding divorce when their lives have some stability—for example, the same school, bedroom, babysitter, playmates, and daily schedule.
Explain the divorce, and tell children what to expect.	Children are more likely to develop fears of abandonment if they are not prepared for their parents' separation. They should be told that their parents will not be living together anymore, which parent will be moving out, and when they will be able to see that parent. If possible, parents should explain the divorce together. Parents should provide a reason for the divorce that the child can understand and assure children that they are not to blame.
Emphasize the permanence of the divorce.	Fantasies of parents getting back together can prevent children from accepting the reality of their current life. Children should be told that the divorce is final and that they cannot change this fact.
Respond sympathetically to children's feelings.	Children need a supportive and understanding response to their feelings of sadness, fear, and anger. For children to adjust well, their painful emotions must be acknowledged, not denied or avoided.
Engage in authoritative parenting.	Parents should provide children with affection and acceptance, reasonable demands for mature behavior, and consistent, rational discipline. Parents who engage in authoritative parenting greatly reduce their children's risk of maladjustment following divorce.
Promote a continuing relationship with both parents.	When parents disentangle their lingering hostility toward the former partner from the child's need for a continuing relationship with the other parent, children adjust well. Grandparents and other extended-family members can help by not taking sides.

Source: Teyber, 2001.

U.S. states have procedures for withholding wages from parents who fail to make these payments. Although child support is usually not enough to lift a single-parent family out of poverty, it can ease its burdens substantially. Noncustodial fathers who have generous visitation schedules and who often see their children are more likely to pay child support regularly (Amato & Sobolewski, 2004). Applying What We Know above summarizes ways to help children adjust to their parents' divorce.

Blended Families

"If you get married to Wendell, and Daddy gets married to Carol," Lizzie wondered aloud to Rena, "then I'll have two sisters and one more brother. And let's see, how many grandmothers and grandfathers? A lot!" exclaimed Lizzie.

About 60 percent of divorced parents remarry within a few years. Others *cohabit,* or share a sexual relationship and a residence with a partner outside of marriage. Parent, stepparent, and children form a new family structure called the **blended, or reconstituted, family.** For some children, this expanded family network is positive, bringing more adult attention. But most have more problems than children in stable, first-marriage families. Switching to stepparents' new rules and expectations can be stressful, and children often view steprelatives as intruders. How well they adapt is, again, related to the quality of family functioning (Hetherington & Kelly, 2002). This depends on which parent forms a new relationship, the child's age and sex,

and the complexity of blended-family relationships. As we will see, older children and girls seem to have the hardest time.

■ **MOTHER–STEPFATHER FAMILIES.** Because mothers generally retain custody of children, the most common form of blended family is a mother–stepfather arrangement. Boys tend to adjust quickly, welcoming a stepfather who is warm, who refrains from exerting his authority too quickly, and who offers relief from coercive cycles of mother–son interaction. Mothers' friction with sons also declines as a result of greater economic security, another adult to share household tasks, and an end to loneliness (Visher, Visher, & Pasley, 2003). Stepfathers who marry rather than cohabit are more involved in parenting, perhaps because men who choose to marry a mother with children are more interested in and skilled at child rearing (Hofferth & Anderson, 2003). Girls, however, often have difficulty with their custodial mother's remarriage. Stepfathers disrupt the close ties many girls have established with their mothers, and girls often react with sulky, resistant behavior (Bray, 1999).

But age affects these findings. Older school-age children and adolescents of both sexes display more irresponsible, acting-out behavior than their peers not in stepfamilies (Hetherington & Stanley-Hagan, 2000). Some parents are warmer and more involved with their biological children than with their stepchildren. Older children are more likely to notice and challenge unfair treatment. And adolescents often view the new stepparent as a threat to their freedom, especially if they experienced little

Adapting to life in a blended family can be stressful for children. But the transition can be eased if stepparents move into their new roles gradually, first building warm relationships with children.

© ARIEL SKELLEY/GETTY IMAGES/BLEND IMAGES

parental monitoring in the single-parent family. Still, when teenagers have affectionate, cooperative relationships with their mothers, many eventually develop good relations with their step-fathers—a circumstance linked to better adjustment (Yuan & Hamilton, 2006).

■ **FATHER–STEPMOTHER FAMILIES.** Remarriage of non-custodial fathers often leads to reduced contact with their bio-logical children, as these fathers tend to withdraw from their "previous" families (Dunn, 2002). When fathers have custody, children typically react negatively to remarriage. One reason is that children living with fathers often start out with more prob-lems. Perhaps the biological mother could no longer handle the difficult child (usually a boy), so the father and his new partner are faced with a youngster who has behavior problems. In other instances, the father has custody because of a very close rela-tionship with the child, and his remarriage disrupts this bond (Buchanan, Maccoby, & Dornbusch, 1996).

Girls, especially, have a hard time getting along with their stepmothers, either because the remarriage threatens the girl's bond with her father or because she becomes entangled in loy-alty conflicts between the two mother figures. But the longer girls live in father–stepmother households, the more positive their interaction with stepmothers becomes (Hetherington & Jodl, 1994). With time and patience, most girls benefit from the support of a second mother figure.

■ **SUPPORT FOR BLENDED FAMILIES.** Family life educa-tion and therapy can help parents and children adapt to the com-plexities of blended families. Effective approaches encourage stepparents to move into their new roles gradually by first build-

ing a warm relationship with the child (Visher, Visher, & Pasley, 2003). Counselors can help couples form a cooperative "parent-ing coalition" to limit loyalty conflicts and provide consistency in child rearing. This allows children to benefit from the increased diversity that stepparent relationships bring to their lives.

Unfortunately, the divorce rate for second marriages is even higher than for first marriages. Parents with antisocial tendencies and poor child-rearing skills are particularly likely to have sev-eral divorces and remarriages. And the more marital transitions children experience, the greater their difficulties (Dunn, 2002). These families usually require prolonged, intensive therapy.

Maternal Employment and Dual-Earner Families

Today, U.S. single and married mothers are in the labor market in nearly equal proportions, and more than three-fourths of those with school-age children are employed (U.S. Census Bureau, 2009a). In previous sections, we saw that the impact of maternal employment on early development depends on the quality of child care and the continuing parent–child relation-ship. The same is true in middle childhood.

■ **MATERNAL EMPLOYMENT AND CHILD DEVELOPMENT.** Children whose mothers enjoy their work and remain commit-ted to parenting show favorable adjustment—higher self-esteem, more positive family and peer relations, less gender-stereotyped beliefs, and better grades in school. Girls, especially, profit from the image of female competence. Regardless of SES, daughters of employed mothers perceive women's roles as involving more freedom of choice and satisfaction and are more achievement- and career-oriented (Hoffman, 2000).

Parenting practices contribute to these benefits. Employed mothers who value their parenting role are more likely to use authoritative child rearing and coregulation. Also, children in dual-earner households devote more daily hours to doing homework under parental guidance and participate more in household chores. And maternal employment leads fathers—especially those who believe in the importance of the paternal role and who feel successful at parenting—to take on greater child-rearing responsibilities, with a small but increasing num-ber staying home full-time (Gottfried, Gottfried, & Bathurst, 2002; Jacobs & Kelley, 2006). Paternal involvement is associated with higher intelligence and achievement, more mature social behavior, and a flexible view of gender roles in childhood and adolescence, and with generally better mental health in adult-hood (Coltrane, 1996; Pleck & Masciadrelli, 2004).

But when employment places heavy demands on a mother's schedule or is stressful for other reasons, children are at risk for ineffective parenting. Working many hours or experiencing a negative workplace atmosphere is associated with reduced parental sensitivity, fewer joint parent–child activities, and poorer cognitive development in children throughout childhood and adolescence (Brooks-Gunn, Han, & Waldfogel, 2002; Bumpus,

Crouter, & McHale, 2006; Strazdins et al., 2006). Negative consequences are magnified when low-SES mothers spend long days at low-paying, physically exhausting jobs—conditions linked to maternal depression and harsh, inconsistent discipline (Raver, 2003). In contrast, part-time employment and flexible work schedules are associated with good child adjustment (Frederiksen-Goldsen & Sharlach, 2000; Hill et al., 2006). By preventing work–family role conflict, these arrangements help parents meet children's needs.

■ **SUPPORT FOR EMPLOYED PARENTS AND THEIR FAMILIES.** In dual-earner families, the father's willingness to share responsibilities is a crucial factor. If he helps little or not at all, the mother carries a double load, at home and at work, leading to fatigue, distress, and little time and energy for children.

Employed mothers and dual-earner parents need assistance from work settings and communities in their child-rearing roles. Part-time employment, flexible schedules, job sharing, and paid leave when children are ill help parents juggle the demands of work and child rearing. Equal pay and employment opportunities for women are also important. Because these policies enhance financial status and morale, they improve the way mothers feel and behave when they arrive home at the end of the working day.

■ **CHILD CARE FOR SCHOOL-AGE CHILDREN.** High-quality child care is vital for parents' peace of mind and children's well-being, even in middle childhood. An estimated 7 million 5- to 13-year-olds in the United States are **self-care children,** who are without adult supervision for some period of time after school (Durlak & Weissberg, 2007). Self-care increases with age and also with SES, perhaps because of the greater safety of higher-income neighborhoods. But when lower-SES parents lack alternatives to self-care, their children spend more hours on their own (Casper & Smith, 2002).

Some studies report that self-care children suffer from adjustment problems, whereas others show no such effects. Children's maturity and the way they spend their time seem to explain these contradictions. Among younger school-age children, those who spend more hours alone have more emotional and social difficulties (Vandell & Posner, 1999). As children become old enough to look after themselves, those who have a history of authoritative child rearing, are monitored by parental telephone calls, and have regular after-school chores appear responsible and well-adjusted. In contrast, children left to their own devices are more likely to bend to peer pressures and engage in antisocial behavior (Coley, Morris, & Hernandez, 2004; Vandell et al., 2006).

Before age 8 or 9, most children need supervision because they are not yet competent to handle emergencies (Galambos & Maggs, 1991). But throughout middle childhood, attending after-school programs with well-trained staffs, generous adult–child ratios, and skill-building activities is linked to good school performance and emotional and social adjustment (Durlak & Weissberg, 2007; Granger, 2008). Low-SES children

In this after-school program, children learn about fossils from an AmeriCorps volunteer. Attending high-quality after-school programs is linked to good school performance and emotional and social adjustment.

who participate in "after-care" programs offering academic assistance and enrichment activities (scouting, music and art lessons, clubs) show special benefits. They exceed their self-care counterparts in classroom work habits, academic achievement, and prosocial behavior and display fewer behavior problems (Lauer et al., 2006; Vandell et al., 2006).

Unfortunately, good after-care is in especially short supply in low-income neighborhoods (Afterschool Alliance, 2004). A special need exists for well-planned programs in these areas—ones that provide safe environments, warm relationships with adults, and enjoyable, goal-oriented activities.

ASK YOURSELF

REVIEW
Describe and explain changes in sibling relationships during middle childhood.

APPLY
Steve and Marissa are in the midst of an acrimonious divorce. Their 9-year-old son Dennis has become hostile and defiant. How can Steve and Marissa help Dennis adjust?

CONNECT
How does each level in Bronfenbrenner's ecological systems theory—microsystem, mesosystem, exosystem, and macrosystem—contribute to the effects of maternal employment on children's development?

REFLECT
What after-school child-care arrangements did you experience in elementary school? How do you think they influenced your development?

Some Common Problems of Development

We have considered a variety of stressful experiences that place children at risk for future problems. Next, we address two more areas of concern: school-age children's fears and anxieties and the consequences of child sexual abuse. Finally, we sum up factors that help children cope effectively with stress.

Fears and Anxieties

Although fears of the dark, thunder and lightning, and supernatural beings persist into middle childhood, older children's anxieties are also directed toward new concerns. As children begin to understand the realities of the wider world, the possibility of personal harm (being robbed, stabbed, or shot) and media events (war and disasters) often trouble them. Other common worries include academic failure, parents' health, physical injuries, and peer rejection (Muris et al., 2000; Weems & Costa, 2005).

Children in Western nations mention exposure to negative information in the media as the most common source of their fears, followed by direct exposure to frightening events (Muris et al., 2001). Nevertheless, as we saw in Section 2, many parents have no rules about their children's TV viewing or computer use, including Internet access.

As long as fears are not too intense, most children handle them constructively, using the more sophisticated emotional regulation strategies that develop in middle childhood. Consequently, fears decline with age, especially for girls, who express more fears than boys throughout childhood and adolescence (Gullone, 2000). But about 5 percent of school-age children develop an intense, unmanageable fear called a **phobia.** Children with inhibited temperaments are at high risk, displaying phobias five to six times more often than other children (Ollendick, King, & Muris, 2002).

For example, in *school phobia*, children feel severe apprehension about attending school, often accompanied by physical complaints (dizziness, nausea, stomachaches, and vomiting). About one-third of children with school phobia are 5- to 7-year-olds for whom the real fear is maternal separation. Family therapy helps these children, whose difficulty can often be traced to parental overprotection (Elliott, 1999). Most cases of school phobia appear around age 11 to 13. These children usually find a particular aspect of school frightening—an overcritical teacher, a school bully, or too much parental pressure to achieve. A change in school environment or parenting practices may be needed. Firm insistence that the child return to school, along with training in how to cope with difficult situations, is also helpful (Silverman & Pina, 2008).

Severe childhood anxieties may arise from harsh living conditions. In inner-city ghettos and in war-torn areas of the world, large numbers of children live in the midst of constant danger, chaos, and deprivation. As the Lifespan Vista box on the following page reveals, these youngsters are at risk for long-term emotional distress and behavior problems. Finally, as we saw in our discussion of child abuse in Section 2, too often violence and other destructive acts become part of adult–child relationships. During middle childhood, child sexual abuse increases.

Child Sexual Abuse

Until recently, child sexual abuse was considered rare, and adults often dismissed children's claims of abuse. In the 1970s, efforts by professionals and media attention led to recognition of child sexual abuse as a serious and widespread problem. About 90,000 cases in the United States were confirmed in the most recently reported year (U.S. Department of Health and Human Services, 2008e).

■ **CHARACTERISTICS OF ABUSERS AND VICTIMS.** Sexual abuse is committed against children of both sexes, but more often against girls. Most cases are reported in middle childhood, but for some victims, abuse begins early in life and continues for many years (Hoch-Espada, Ryan, & Deblinger, 2006; Trickett & Putnam, 1998).

Typically, the abuser is male—a parent or someone the parent knows well—a father, stepfather, or live-in boyfriend, somewhat less often an uncle or older brother. But in about 25 percent of cases, mothers are the offenders, more often with sons (Boroughs, 2004). If the abuser is a nonrelative, the person is usually someone the child has come to know and trust. However, the Internet and mobile phones have become avenues through which other adults commit sexual abuse—for example, by exposing children and adolescents to pornography and online sexual advances as a way of "grooming" them for sexual acts offline (Wolak et al., 2008).

Abusers make the child comply in a variety of distasteful ways, including deception, bribery, verbal intimidation, and physical force. You may wonder how any adult—especially a parent or close relative—could violate a child sexually. Many offenders deny their own responsibility, blaming the abuse on the willing participation of a seductive youngster. Yet children are not capable of making a deliberate, informed decision to enter into a sexual relationship! Even older children and adolescents are not free to say yes or no. Rather, the responsibility lies with abusers, who tend to have characteristics that predispose them toward sexual exploitation of children. They have great difficulty controlling their impulses and may suffer from psychological disorders, including alcohol and drug abuse. Often they pick out children who are unlikely to defend themselves or to be believed—those who are physically weak, emotionally deprived, socially isolated, or affected by disabilities (Bolen, 2001).

Reported cases of child sexual abuse are linked to poverty, marital instability, and resulting weakening of family ties. Children who live in homes with a constantly changing cast of characters—repeated marriages, separations, and new partners—are especially vulnerable. But children in economically advantaged, stable families are also victims, although their abuse is more likely to escape detection (Putnam, 2003).

■ A LIFESPAN VISTA: Looking Forward, Looking Back ■

Impact of Ethnic and Political Violence on Children

Around the world, many children live with armed conflict, terrorism, and other acts of violence stemming from ethnic and political tensions. Some children may participate in fighting, either because they are forced or because they want to please adults. Others are kidnapped, assaulted, and tortured. Those who are bystanders often come under direct fire and may be killed or physically maimed. And many watch in horror as family members, friends, and neighbors flee, are wounded, or die. In the past decade, wars have left 6 million children physically disabled, 20 million homeless, and more than 1 million separated from their parents (Ursano & Shaw, 2007; Wexler, Branski, & Kerem, 2006)

When war and social crises are temporary, most children can be comforted and do not show long-term emotional difficulties. But chronic danger requires children to make substantial adjustments that can seriously disrupt their psychological functioning. Many children of war lose their sense of safety, become desensitized to violence, are haunted by terrifying memories, are impaired in moral reasoning, and build a pessimistic view of the future. Anxiety and depression increase, as do aggression and antisocial behavior—outcomes seen in every war zone studied, from Bosnia, Angola, Rwanda, and the Sudan to the West Bank, Afghanistan, and Iraq (Barenbaum, Ruchkin, & Schwab Stone, 2004; Klingman, 2006).

Parental affection and reassurance are the best protection against lasting problems. When parents offer security and serve as role models of calm emotional strength, most children can withstand even extreme war-related violence (Smith et al., 2001). Children who are separated from parents must rely on help from their communities. Orphans in Eritrea who were placed in residential settings where they could form close emotional ties with an adult showed less emotional stress five years later than orphans placed in impersonal settings (Wolff & Fesseha, 1999). Education and recreation programs are powerful safeguards, too, providing children with consistency in their lives along with teacher and peer supports.

With the September 11, 2001, terrorist attacks on the World Trade Center, some U.S. children experienced extreme wartime violence firsthand. Children in Public School 31 in Brooklyn, New York, for example, watched through classroom windows as the planes struck the towers and were engulfed in flames and as the towers crumbled. Many worried about the safety of family members, and some lost them. In the aftermath, most expressed intense fears—for example, that terrorists were infiltrating their neighborhoods and that planes flying overhead might smash into nearby buildings.

Unlike many war-traumatized children in the developing world, Public School 31 students received immediate intervention—a "trauma curriculum" in which they expressed their emotions through writing, drawing, and discussion and participated in experiences aimed at restoring trust and tolerance (Lagnado, 2001). Older children learned about the feelings of their Muslim classmates, the dire condition of children in Afghanistan, and ways to help victims as a means of overcoming a sense of helplessness.

When wartime drains families and communities of resources, international organizations must step in and help children. Efforts to preserve children's physical, psychological, and educational well-being may be the best way to stop transmission of violence to the next generation.

A trauma counselor comforts a child standing amid the rubble of her neighborhood in the Gaza Strip. Many children of war lose their sense of safety, and without special support from caring adults, they are likely to have lasting emotional problems.

■ **CONSEQUENCES.** The adjustment problems of child sexual abuse victims—including anxiety, depression, low self-esteem, mistrust of adults, and anger and hostility—are often severe and can persist for years after the abusive episodes. Younger children frequently react with sleep difficulties, loss of appetite, and generalized fearfulness. Adolescents may run away and show suicidal reactions, substance abuse, and delinquency. At all ages, persistent abuse accompanied by force, violence, and a close relationship to the perpetrator (incest) has a greater impact (Feiring, Taska, & Lewis, 1999; Wolfe, 2006). And repeated sexual abuse, like physical abuse, is associated with central nervous system damage (Cicchetti, 2007).

Sexually abused children frequently display precocious sexual knowledge and behavior. In adolescence, abused young people often become promiscuous, and as adults, they show increased arrest rates for sex crimes (mostly against children) and prostitution (Salter et al., 2003; Whipple, 2006). Furthermore, women who were sexually abused are likely to choose partners who abuse them and their children. As mothers, they often engage in irresponsible and coercive parenting, including child abuse and neglect (Pianta, Egeland, & Erickson, 1989). In all these ways, the harmful impact of sexual abuse is transmitted to the next generation.

■ **PREVENTION AND TREATMENT.** Because sexual abuse typically appears in the midst of other serious family problems, long-term therapy with both children and parents is usually needed (Olafson & Boat, 2000). The best way to reduce

Keeping Ourselves Safe is New Zealand's school-based child abuse prevention program. It involves teachers, police officers, and parents in protecting children by teaching them to recognize and respond to abusive adult behaviors.

COURTESY OF THE NEW ZEALAND POLICE

the suffering of victims is to prevent sexual abuse from continuing. Today, courts are prosecuting abusers more vigorously and taking children's testimony more seriously (see the Social Issues box on the following page).

Educational programs that teach children to recognize inappropriate sexual advances and whom to turn to for help reduce the risk of abuse (Hebert & Tourigny, 2004). Yet because of controversies over educating children about sexual abuse, few schools offer these interventions. New Zealand is the only country with a national, school-based prevention program targeting sexual abuse. In Keeping Ourselves Safe, children and adolescents learn that abusers are rarely strangers. Parent involvement ensures that home and school collaborate in teaching children self-protection skills. Evaluations reveal that virtually all New Zealand parents and children support the program and that it has helped many children avoid or report abuse (Sanders, 2006).

Fostering Resilience in Middle Childhood

Throughout middle childhood—and other periods of development—children encounter challenging and sometimes threatening situations that require them to cope with psychological stress. In this and the previous section, we have considered such topics as chronic illness, learning disabilities, achievement expectations, divorce, wartime trauma, and sexual abuse. Each taxes children's coping resources, creating serious risks for development.

Nevertheless, only a modest relationship exists between stressful life experiences and psychological disturbance in child-

hood (Masten & Reed, 2002). The long-term consequences of birth complications, we noted that some children manage to overcome the combined effects of birth trauma, poverty, and troubled family life. The same is true for school difficulties, family transitions, and child maltreatment. That four broad factors protect against maladjustment: (1) the child's personal characteristics, including an easy temperament and a mastery-oriented approach to new situations; (2) a warm parental relationship; (3) an adult outside the immediate family who offers a support system; and (4) community resources, such as good schools, social services, and youth organizations and recreation centers (Commission on Children at Risk, 2008; Wright & Masten, 2005).

Any one of these ingredients of resilience can account for why one child fares well and another poorly. Usually, however, personal and environmental factors are interconnected: Each resource favoring resilience strengthens others. For example, safe, stable neighborhoods with family-friendly community services reduce parents' daily hassles and stress, thereby promoting good parenting (Pinderhughes et al., 2001). In contrast, unfavorable home and neighborhood experiences increase the chances that children will act in ways that expose them to further hardship. And when negative conditions pile up, such as marital discord, poverty, crowded living conditions, neighborhood violence, and abuse, the rate of maladjustment multiplies (Wright & Masten, 2005).

Rather than a preexisting attribute, *resilience* is a capacity that develops, enabling children to use internal and external resources to cope with adversity (Roberts & Masten, 2004; Yates, Egeland, & Sroufe, 2003). Throughout our discussion, we have seen how families, schools, communities, and society as a whole can enhance or undermine school-age children's supportive relationships and sense of competence. As the next two sections will reveal, young people whose childhood experiences helped them learn to overcome obstacles, strive for self-direction, and respond considerately and sympathetically to others meet the challenges of the next period—adolescence—quite well.

SOCIAL ISSUES

Children's Eyewitness Testimony

Increasingly, children are being called on to testify in court cases involving child abuse and neglect, child custody, and similar matters. The experience can be difficult and traumatic, requiring children to report on highly stressful events and sometimes to speak against a parent or other relative to whom they feel loyal. In some family disputes, they may fear punishment for telling the truth. In addition, child witnesses are faced with an unfamiliar situation—at the very least an interview in the judge's chambers and at most an open courtroom with judge, jury, spectators, and the possibility of unsympathetic cross-examination. Not surprisingly, these conditions can compromise the accuracy of children's recall.

Age Differences

Until recently, children younger than age 5 were rarely asked to testify, and not until age 10 were they assumed fully competent to do so. As a result of societal reactions to rising rates of child abuse and the difficulty of prosecuting perpetrators, legal requirements for child testimony have been relaxed in the United States (Sandler, 2006). Children as young as age 3 frequently serve as witnesses.

Compared with preschoolers, school age children are better at giving accurate, detailed narrative accounts of past experiences and correctly inferring others' motives and intentions. Older children are also more resistant to misleading questions that attorneys may ask when probing for more information or, in cross-examination, trying to influence the child's response (Roebers & Schneider, 2001). But when properly questioned, even 3-year-olds can recall recent events accurately (Peterson & Rideout, 1998).

Suggestibility

Court testimony, however, often involves repeated interviews. When biased adults lead witnesses by suggesting incorrect "facts," interrupt children's denials, reinforce them for giving desired answers, or use a confrontational questioning style, they increase the likelihood of incorrect reporting by preschoolers and school-age children alike (Bruck & Ceci, 2004; Owen-Kostelnik, Rappucci, & Meyer, 2006).

In one study, 4- to 7-year-olds were asked to recall details about a visitor who had come to their classroom a week earlier. Half the children received a low-pressure interview containing leading questions that implied abuse ("He took your clothes off, didn't he?"). The other half received a high-pressure interview in which an adult told the child that her friends had said "yes" to the leading questions, praised the child for agreeing ("You're doing great"), and, if the child did not agree, repeated the question. Children were far more likely to give false information—even to fabricate quite fantastic events—in the high-pressure condition (Finnilä et al., 2003).

By the time children appear in court, weeks, months, or even years have passed since the target events. When a long delay is combined with biased interviewing and with stereotyping of the accused ("He's in jail because he's been bad"), children can easily be misled into giving false information (Gilstrap & Ceci, 2005; Quas et al., 2007). The more distinctive and personally relevant an event is, the more likely children are to recall it accurately over time. For example, a year later, even when exposed to misleading information, children correctly reported details of an injury that required emergency room treatment (Peterson, Parsons, & Dean, 2004).

In many sexual abuse cases, anatomically correct dolls are used to prompt children's recall. Although this method helps older children provide more detail about experienced events, it increases the suggestibility of preschoolers, who report physical and sexual contact that never happened (Goodman et al., 1999).

Interventions

Adults must prepare child witnesses so they understand the courtroom process and know what to expect. In some places, "court schools" take children through the setting and give them an opportunity to role-play court activities. Practice interviews—in which children learn to provide the most accurate, detailed information possible and to admit not knowing

rather than agreeing or guessing—are helpful (Saywitz, Goodman, & Lyon, 2002).

At the same time, legal professionals must use interviewing procedures that increase children's accurate reporting. Unbiased, open-ended questions that prompt children to disclose details—"Tell me what happened" or "You said there was a man; tell me about the man"—reduce suggestibility (Holliday, 2003). Also, a warm, supportive interview tone fosters accurate recall, perhaps by easing children's fears so they feel freer to disagree with an interviewer's false suggestions (Ceci, Bruck, & Battin, 2000).

If children are likely to experience emotional trauma or later punishment (as in a family dispute), courtroom procedures can be adapted to protect them. For example, children can testify over closed-circuit TV so they do not have to face an abuser. When it is not wise for a child to participate directly, impartial expert witnesses can provide testimony that reports on the child's psychological condition and includes important elements of the child's story.

When interviewed for their eyewitness accounts, school-age children are better able than preschoolers to give accurate, detailed descriptions and correctly infer others' motives and intentions. This police officer can promote accurate recall by using a warm, supportive tone and avoiding leading questions.

Summary

Erikson's Theory: Industry versus Inferiority

What personality changes take place during Erikson's stage of industry versus inferiority?

>> According to Erikson, children who successfully resolve the psychological conflict of **industry versus inferiority** develop a sense of competence at skills and tasks, a positive but realistic self-concept, pride in accomplishment, moral responsibility, and the ability to work cooperatively with agemates.

© TOM & DEE ANN MCCARTHY/CORBIS

Self-Understanding

Describe school-age children's self-concept and self-esteem and how they make achievement-related attributions.

>> During middle childhood, children's self-concepts include competencies, personality traits, and **social comparisons.**

>> Self-esteem differentiates further and becomes hierarchically organized and more realistic. Authoritative parenting is linked to favorable self-esteem.

>> Children who make **mastery-oriented attributions** credit success to ability and failure to controllable factors, such as insufficient effort. In contrast, children who receive negative feedback about their ability are likely to develop **learned helplessness,** attributing success to external factors, such as luck, and failure to low ability.

Emotional Development

Cite changes in self-conscious emotions and in understanding and management of emotion in middle childhood.

>> In middle childhood, the self-conscious emotions of pride and guilt become clearly governed by personal responsibility. Experiencing intense shame can shatter self-esteem.

>> School-age children recognize that people can experience more than one emotion at a time. They also reconcile contradictory cues in interpreting another's feelings. Empathy increases and includes sensitivity to both people's immediate distress and their general life condition.

>> By age 10, most children can shift adaptively between **problem-centered** and **emotion-centered coping** in regulating emotion. Emotionally well-regulated children are upbeat, empathic, and prosocial.

Understanding Others: Perspective Taking

How does perspective taking change in middle childhood?

>> As Selman's five-stage sequence indicates, **perspective taking,** the capacity to imagine others' thoughts and feelings, improves greatly, supported by cognitive maturity and experiences in which others explain their viewpoints. Good perspective takers have more positive social skills.

Moral Development

Describe changes in moral understanding during middle childhood.

>> By middle childhood, children have internalized rules for good conduct. They clarify and link moral imperatives and social conventions, considering the purpose of the rule, people's intentions, and the context of their actions. They also better understand individual rights.

© JEFF GREENBERG/ALAMY

>> Though children of all races pick up prevailing societal attitudes about race and ethnicity, school-age children understand that people who look different need not think, feel, or act differently, and prejudice typically declines. Children most likely to hold biases are those who believe that personality traits are fixed, who have inflated self-esteem, and who live in a social world that highlights group distinctions. Long-term, intergroup contact is most effective at reducing prejudice.

Peer Relations

How do peer sociability and friendship change in middle childhood?

>> In middle childhood, prosocial acts increase while physical aggression declines. By the end of the school years, children organize themselves into **peer groups.**

>> Friendships develop into mutual relationships based on trust. Children tend to select friends similar to themselves in many ways.

Describe categories of peer acceptance and ways to help rejected children.

>> On measures of **peer acceptance, popular children** are well-liked by many agemates; **rejected children** are actively disliked; **controversial children** are both liked and disliked; and **neglected children** are seldom chosen, either positively or negatively.

>> Two subtypes of popular children exist: **popular-prosocial children,** who are academically and socially competent, and **popular-antisocial children,** who are aggressive but admired. Rejected children also divide into two subtypes: **rejected-aggressive children,** who are especially high in conflict and hostility, and **rejected-withdrawn children,** who are passive, socially awkward, and at risk for **peer victimization.**

>> Rejected children often experience lasting adjustment difficulties. Interventions involving coaching in social skills, academic tutoring, and training in perspective taking and solving social problems produce gains in social competence and peer acceptance.

Gender Typing

What changes in gender-stereotyped beliefs and gender identity occur during middle childhood?

≫ School-age children extend their awareness of gender stereotypes to personality traits and academic subjects. But they also develop a more open-minded view of what males and females can do.

≫ Boys strengthen their identification with the masculine role, whereas girls often experiment with "other-gender" activities. Gender identity includes self-evaluations based on typicality, contentedness, and felt pressure to conform to gender roles, each of which affects adjustment.

Family Influences

How do parent–child communication and sibling relationships change in middle childhood?

≫ Despite declines in time spent with parents, effective **coregulation** allows parents to exercise general oversight over children, who increasingly make their own decisions.

≫ Sibling rivalry tends to increase with greater participation in diverse activities and more frequent parental comparisons. Only children do not differ from children with siblings in self-rated personality traits and are higher in self-esteem, school performance, and educational attainment.

What factors influence children's adjustment to divorce and remarriage?

≫ Although marital breakup is often quite stressful for children, individual differences exist based on parental psychological health, child characteristics (age, temperament, and sex), and social supports. Boys and children with difficult temperaments are at greater risk for adjustment problems. In both sexes, divorce is linked to early sexual activity, adolescent parenthood, and relationship difficulties.

≫ The overriding factor in positive adjustment following divorce is effective parenting. Positive father–child relationships have protective value, as do extended-family supports.

≫ **Divorce mediation** can be beneficial in the period surrounding divorce. The success of **joint custody** depends on a cooperative relationship between divorcing parents.

≫ When divorced parents enter new relationships and form **blended,** or **reconstituted, families,** girls, older children, and children in father–stepmother families display the greatest adjustment problems. Stepparents who move into their roles gradually and form a "parenting coalition" help children adjust.

How do maternal employment and life in dual-earner families affect school-age children?

≫ When mothers enjoy their work and remain committed to parenting, their children benefit from higher self-esteem, more positive family and peer relations, less gender-stereotyped beliefs, and better school grades. In dual-earner families, the father's willingness to share in household responsibilities is linked to many positive child outcomes Workplace supports help parents in their child-rearing roles.

≫ Authoritative child rearing, parental monitoring, and regular after-school chores lead **self-care children** to be responsible and well-adjusted. Good "after-care" programs also aid school performance and emotional and social adjustment.

Some Common Problems of Development

Cite common fears and anxieties in middle childhood.

≫ School-age children's fears are directed toward new concerns, including personal harm, media events, academic failure, parents' health, and peer rejection. Children with inhibited temperaments are at higher risk of developing a **phobia.** Harsh living conditions can also cause severe anxiety.

Discuss factors related to child sexual abuse and its consequences for children's development.

≫ Child sexual abuse is generally committed by male family members, more often against girls than boys. Abusers have characteristics that predispose them toward sexual exploitation of children. Reported cases are strongly associated with poverty and marital instability. Abused children often have severe adjustment problems.

Cite factors that foster resilience in middle childhood.

≫ Overall, only a modest relationship exists between stressful life experiences and psychological disturbance in childhood. The child's personal characteristics, a warm parental relationship, other supportive adults, and community resources predict resilience. But when negative factors pile up, the rate of maladjustment multiplies.

Important Terms and Concepts

blended, or reconstituted, families (p. 137)
controversial children (p. 129)
coregulation (p. 133)
divorce mediation (p. 136)
emotion-centered coping (p. 123)
industry versus inferiority (p. 118)
joint custody (p. 136)
learned helplessness (p. 121)

mastery-oriented attributions (p. 121)
neglected children (p. 129)
peer acceptance (p. 129)
peer group (p. 127)
peer victimization (p. 131)
perspective taking (p. 124)
phobia (p. 140)
popular children (p. 129)

popular-antisocial children (p. 129)
popular-prosocial children (p. 129)
problem-centered coping (p. 123)
rejected children (p. 129)
rejected-aggressive children (p. 130)
rejected-withdrawn children (p. 130)
self-care children (p. 139)
social comparisons (p. 118)

Milestones
Development in Middle Childhood

6–8 years

PHYSICAL

- Slow gains in height and weight continue until adolescent growth spurt. (78)
- Permanent teeth gradually replace primary teeth. (78)
- Legibility of writing increases, preparing children to master cursive writing. (83)
- Drawings become more organized and detailed and include some depth cues. (83)
- Games with rules and rough-and-tumble play become common. (84, 85–86)
- Dominance hierarchies become more stable, especially among boys. (86)

COGNITIVE

- Thought becomes more logical, as shown by the ability to pass Piagetian conservation, class inclusion, and seriation problems. (87–88)

- Spatial reasoning improves; gives clear, well-organized directions and draws coherent cognitive maps. (88)
- Attention becomes more selective, adaptable, and planful. (91)
- Uses memory strategies of rehearsal and then organization. (91)
- Views the mind as an active, constructive agent, capable of transforming information. (94)
- Awareness of memory strategies and the impact of psychological factors (such as focusing attention) on task performance improves. (94)
- Appreciates second-order false beliefs. (94)
- Uses informal knowledge of number concepts and counting to master more complex mathematical skills. (96)

LANGUAGE

- Vocabulary increases rapidly throughout middle childhood, eventually exceeding 40,000 words. (104)
- Word definitions are concrete, referring to functions and appearance. (105)
- Narratives increase in organization, detail, and expressiveness. (105)
- Transitions from emergent literacy to conventional reading. (95)
- Language awareness improves. (104)
- Conversational strategies become more refined. (105)

EMOTIONAL/SOCIAL

- Self-concept begins to include personality traits and social comparisons. (118)
- Self-esteem differentiates, becomes hierarchically organized, and declines to a more realistic level. (119–120)
- Self-conscious emotions of pride and guilt are governed by personal responsibility. (123)
- Understands that people may have different perspectives because they have access to different information. (124)
- Recognizes that individuals can experience more than one emotion at a time and that people's expressions may not reflect their true feelings. (123)
- Empathy increases. (123)
- Reconciles contradictory facial and situational cues in understanding another's feelings. (123)

- Becomes more independent and trustworthy. (125)
- Constructs a flexible appreciation of moral rules, taking prosocial and antisocial intentions into account. (125)
- Physical aggression declines; verbal and relational aggression continue. (127)
- Resolves conflicts more effectively. (127)

9–11 years

PHYSICAL

- Adolescent growth spurt begins two years earlier in girls than in boys. (78)
- Executes gross motor skills of running, jumping, throwing, catching, kicking, batting, and dribbling more quickly and with better coordination. (83)

Note: Numbers in parentheses indicate the page or pages on which each milestone is discussed.

- Steady gains in reaction time contribute to improved motor performance. (83)
- Representation of depth in drawings expands. (83)

COGNITIVE

- Continues to master Piagetian tasks in a step-by-step fashion. (87)
- Spatial reasoning further improves; readily draws and reads maps, and grasps the notion of scale. (88)
- Selective attention and planning improve further. (91)
- Uses memory strategies of rehearsal and organization more effectively. (91)

- Applies several memory strategies simultaneously; begins to use elaboration. (91–92)
- Long-term knowledge base grows larger and becomes better organized. (92)
- Theory of mind becomes more elaborate and refined. (94)
- Cognitive self-regulation improves. (95)

LANGUAGE

- Thinks about and uses words more precisely; word definitions emphasize synonyms and categorical relations. (105)
- Grasps double meanings of words, as reflected in comprehension of metaphors and humor. (105)
- Continues to master complex grammatical constructions. (105)
- Continues to refine conversational strategies. (105)

- Narratives lengthen, become more coherent, and include more evaluative comments. (105–106)

EMOTIONAL/SOCIAL

- Self-esteem tends to rise (120)
- Distinguishes ability, effort, and external factors in attributions for success and failure. (121)
- Becomes more knowledgeable about socially approved ways to display negative emotion. (123–124)
- Empathic responding extends to general life conditions. (123)

- Shifts adaptively between problem-centered and emotion-centered strategies in regulating emotion. (123–124)
- Can "step into another's shoes" and view the self from that person's perspective; later, can view the relationship between self and other from the perspective of a third, impartial party. (124)

- Clarifies and links moral rules and social conventions. (125–126)
- Convictions about matters of personal choice strengthen, and understanding of individual rights expands. (126)

- Friendships become more selective and are based on mutual trust. (128)
- Peer groups emerge. (127)
- Becomes aware of more gender stereotypes, including personality traits and achievement, but has a flexible appreciation of what males and females can do. (131–132)
- Gender identity expands to include self-evaluations of typicality, contentedness, and pressure to conform. (132–133)
- Sibling rivalry tends to increase. (133)

Adolescence brings momentous advances. A flood of biological events leads to an adult-sized body and sexual maturity. Cognitive changes allow teenagers to grasp complex scientific principles, grapple with political issues, and detect the deep meaning of a poem or story.

Physical and Cognitive Development in Adolescence

On Sabrina's eleventh birthday, her friend Joyce gave her a surprise party, but Sabrina seemed somber during the celebration. Although Sabrina and Joyce had been close friends since third grade, their relationship was faltering. Sabrina was a head taller and some 20 pounds heavier than most girls in her sixth-grade class. Her breasts were well-developed, her hips and thighs had broadened, and she had begun to menstruate. In contrast, Joyce still had the short, lean, flat-chested body of a school-age child.

Ducking into the bathroom while the other girls put candles on the cake, Sabrina frowned at her image in the mirror. "I'm so big and heavy," she whispered. At church youth group on Sunday evenings, Sabrina broke away from Joyce and joined the eighth-grade girls. Around them, she didn't feel so large and awkward.

Once a month, parents gathered at Sabrina's and Joyce's school to discuss child-rearing concerns. Sabrina's parents, Franca and Antonio, attended whenever they could. "How you know they are becoming teenagers is this," volunteered Antonio. "The bedroom door is closed, and they want to be alone. Also, they contradict and disagree. I tell Sabrina, 'You have to go to Aunt Gina's on Saturday for dinner with the family.' The next thing I know, she is arguing with me."

Sabrina has entered **adolescence**, the transition between childhood and adulthood. In industrialized societies, the skills young people must master are so complex and the choices confronting them so diverse that adolescence is greatly extended. But around the world, the basic tasks of this period are much the same. Sabrina must accept her full-grown body, acquire adult ways of thinking, attain greater independence from her family, develop more mature ways of relating to peers of both sexes, and begin to construct an identity—a secure sense of who she is in terms of sexual, vocational, moral, ethnic, religious, and other life values and goals.

The beginning of adolescence is marked by **puberty**, a flood of biological events leading to an adult-sized body and sexual maturity. As Sabrina's reactions suggest, entry into adolescence can be an especially trying time for some young

© DAVID YOUNG-WOLFF/PHOTOEDIT

people. In this section, we trace the events of puberty and take up a variety of health concerns—physical exercise, nutrition, sexual activity, substance abuse, and other problems affecting teenagers who encounter difficulties on the path to maturity.

Adolescence also brings with it vastly expanded powers of reasoning. Teenagers can grasp complex scientific and mathematical principles, grapple with social and political issues, and delve deeply into the meaning of a poem or story. The second part of this section traces these extraordinary changes from both Piaget's and the information-processing perspective. Next, we examine sex differences in mental abilities. Finally, we turn to the main setting in which adolescent thought takes shape: the school.

Physical Development

Conceptions of Adolescence

Why is Sabrina self-conscious, argumentative, and in retreat from family activities? Historically, theorists explained the impact of puberty on psychological development by resorting to extremes—either a biological or a social explanation. Today, researchers realize that biological and social forces jointly determine adolescent psychological change.

The Biological Perspective

TAKE A MOMENT... Ask several parents of young children what they expect their sons and daughters to be like as teenagers. You will probably get answers like these: "Rebellious and irresponsible," "Full of rages and tempers" (Buchanan & Holmbeck, 1998). This widespread storm-and-stress view dates back to major early-twentieth-century theorists. The most influential, G. Stanley Hall, based his ideas about development on Darwin's theory of evolution. Hall (1904) described adolescence as a period so turbulent that it resembled the era in which humans evolved from savages into civilized beings. Similarly, Anna Freud (1969), who expanded the focus on adolescence of her father Sigmund Freud's theory, viewed the teenage years as a biologically based, universal "developmental disturbance." In Freud's *genital stage,* sexual impulses reawaken, triggering psychological conflict and volatile behavior. As adolescents find intimate partners, inner forces gradually achieve a new, mature harmony, and the stage concludes with marriage, birth, and child rearing. In this way, young people fulfill their biological destiny: sexual reproduction and survival of the species.

The Social Perspective

Contemporary research suggests that the storm-and-stress notion of adolescence is exaggerated. Certain problems, such as eating disorders, depression, suicide, and lawbreaking, do occur more often than earlier (Farrington, 2004; Graber, 2004). But the overall rate of psychological disturbance rises only slightly, by about 3 percent, from childhood to adolescence, when it is nearly the same as in the adult population—about 15 percent (Roberts, Attkisson, & Rosenblatt, 1998). Although some teenagers encounter serious difficulties, emotional turbulence is not routine.

The first researcher to point out the wide variability in adolescent adjustment was anthropologist Margaret Mead (1928). She returned from the Pacific islands of Samoa with a startling conclusion: Because of the culture's relaxed social relationships and openness toward sexuality, adolescence "is perhaps the pleasantest time the Samoan girl (or boy) will ever know" (p. 308). Mead offered an alternative view in which the social environment is entirely responsible for the range of teenage experiences, from erratic and agitated to calm and stress-free. Later researchers found that Samoan adolescence was not as untroubled as Mead had assumed (Freeman, 1983). Still, she showed that to understand adolescent development, researchers must pay greater attention to social and cultural influences.

A Balanced Point of View

Today we know that biological, psychological, and social forces combine to influence adolescent development (Magnusson, 1999; Susman & Rogol, 2004). Biological changes are universal—found in all primates and all cultures. These internal stresses and the social expectations accompanying them—that the young person give up childish ways, develop new interpersonal relationships, and take on greater responsibility—are likely to prompt moments of uncertainty, self-doubt, and disappointment in all teenagers. Adolescents' prior and current experiences affect their success in surmounting these challenges.

At the same time, the length of adolescence and its demands and pressures vary substantially among cultures. Most tribal and village societies have only a brief intervening phase between childhood and full assumption of adult roles (Schlegel & Barry, 1991; Weisfield, 1997). In industrialized nations, young people face prolonged dependence on parents and postponement of sexual gratification while they prepare for a productive work life. As a result, adolescence is greatly extended—so much so that researchers commonly divide it into three phases:

1. *Early adolescence* (11–12 to 14 years): This is a period of rapid pubertal change.
2. *Middle adolescence* (14 to 16 years): Pubertal changes are now nearly complete.
3. *Late adolescence* (16 to 18 years): The young person achieves full adult appearance and anticipates assumption of adult roles.

The more the social environment supports young people in achieving adult responsibilities, the better they adjust. For all the biological tensions and uncertainties about the future that teenagers feel, most negotiate this period successfully. With this in mind, let's look closely at puberty, the dawning of adolescent development.

Sex differences in pubertal growth are obvious among these sixth graders. Although the children are the same age, the boy is much shorter and less mature looking than the girls.

Puberty: The Physical Transition to Adulthood

The changes of puberty are dramatic: Within a few years, the body of the school-age child is transformed into that of a full-grown adult. Genetically influenced hormonal processes regulate pubertal growth. Girls, who have been advanced in physical maturity since the prenatal period, reach puberty, on average, two years earlier than boys.

Hormonal Changes

The complex hormonal changes that underlie puberty occur gradually and are under way by age 8 or 9. Secretions of *growth hormone (GH)* and *thyroxine* (see Section 1, page 7) increase, leading to tremendous gains in body size and to attainment of skeletal maturity.

Sexual maturation is controlled by the sex hormones. Although we think of *estrogens* as female hormones and *androgens* as male hormones, both types are present in each sex but in different amounts. The boy's testes release large quantities of the androgen *testosterone*, which leads to muscle growth, body and facial hair, and other male sex characteristics. Androgens (especially testosterone for boys) also contribute greatly to gains in body size. Because the testes secrete small amounts of estrogen as well, 50 percent of boys experience temporary breast enlargement. In both sexes, estrogens also increase GH secretion, adding to the growth spurt and, in combination with androgens, stimulating gains in bone density, which continue into early adulthood (Cooper, Sayer, & Dennison, 2006; Styne, 2003).

Estrogens released by girls' ovaries cause the breasts, uterus, and vagina to mature, the body to take on feminine proportions, and fat to accumulate. Estrogens also contribute to regulation of the menstrual cycle. *Adrenal androgens,* released from the adrenal glands on top of each kidney, influence girls' height spurt and stimulate growth of underarm and pubic hair. They have little impact on boys, whose physical characteristics are influenced mainly by androgen and estrogen secretions from the testes.

As you can see, pubertal changes are of two broad types: (1) overall body growth and (2) maturation of sexual characteristics. We have seen that the hormones responsible for sexual maturity also affect body growth, making puberty the time of greatest sexual differentiation since prenatal life.

Body Growth

The first outward sign of puberty is the rapid gain in height and weight known as the **growth spurt.** On average, it is under way for North American girls shortly after age 10, for boys around age 12½. Because estrogens trigger and then restrain GH secretion more readily than androgens, the typical girl is taller and heavier during early adolescence (Archibald, Graber, & Brooks-Gunn, 2006; Bogin, 2001). At age 14, however, she is surpassed by the typical boy, whose adolescent growth spurt has now started, whereas hers is almost finished. Growth in body size is complete for most girls by age 16 and for boys by age 17½, when the epiphyses at the ends of the long bones close completely (see Section 1, page 5). Altogether, adolescents add 10 to 11 inches in height and 50 to 75 pounds—nearly 50 percent of adult body weight. Figure 5.1 on page 152 illustrates pubertal changes in general body growth.

■ **BODY PROPORTIONS.** During puberty, the cephalocaudal growth trend of infancy and childhood reverses. The hands, legs, and feet accelerate first, followed by the torso, which accounts for most of the adolescent height gain (Sheehy et al., 1999). This pattern helps explain why early adolescents often appear awkward and out of proportion—long-legged, with giant feet and hands.

Large sex differences in body proportions also appear, caused by the action of sex hormones on the skeleton. Boys' shoulders broaden relative to the hips, whereas girls' hips broaden relative to the shoulders and waist. Of course, boys also end up larger than girls, and their legs are longer in relation to the rest of the body—mainly because boys have two extra years of preadolescent growth, when the legs are growing the fastest.

■ **MUSCLE–FAT MAKEUP AND OTHER INTERNAL CHANGES.** Sabrina worried about her weight because compared with her later-developing girlfriends, she had accumulated much more fat. Around age 8, girls start to add fat on their arms, legs, and trunk, a trend that accelerates between ages 11 and 16. In

Kate at 13

Kate at 17

Kate at 11

Steven at 13

Steven at 16

Steven at 18

■ **FIGURE 5.1** ■ **Body growth during adolescence.**   Because the pubertal growth spurt takes place earlier for girls than for boys, Kate reached her adult body size earlier than Steven. During puberty, adolescents show large sex differences in body proportions.

contrast, arm and leg fat decreases in adolescent boys. Although both sexes gain in muscle, this increase is much greater in boys, who develop larger skeletal muscles, hearts, and lung capacity (Rogol, Roemmich, & Clark, 2002). Also, the number of red blood cells—and therefore the ability to carry oxygen from the lungs to the muscles—increases in boys but not in girls. Altogether, boys gain far more muscle strength than girls, a difference that contributes to teenage boys' superior athletic performance (Ramos et al., 1998).

Motor Development and Physical Activity

Puberty brings steady improvement in gross motor performance, but the pattern of change differs for boys and girls. Girls' gains are slow and gradual, leveling off by age 14. In contrast, boys show a dramatic spurt in strength, speed, and endurance that continues through the teenage years. By midadolescence, few girls perform as well as the average boy in running speed, broad jump, and throwing distance, and practically no boys score as low as the average girl (Haywood & Getchell, 2005; Malina & Bouchard, 1991).

Because girls and boys are no longer well-matched physically, gender-segregated physical education usually begins in middle or junior high school. At the same time, athletic options for both sexes expand as new sports—including track and field, wrestling, tackle football, weight lifting, floor hockey, archery, tennis, and golf—are added to the curriculum.

Among boys, athletic competence is strongly related to peer admiration and self-esteem. Some adolescents are so obsessed with physical prowess that they turn to performance-enhancing drugs. In recent large-scale studies, about 8 percent of U.S. high school seniors, mostly boys, reported using creatine, an over-the-counter substance that enhances short-term muscle power but carries a risk of serious side effects, including muscle tissue disease, brain seizures, and heart irregularities (Castillo & Comstock, 2007). About 2 percent of seniors, again mostly boys, have taken anabolic steroids or a related substance, androstenedione—powerful prescription medications that boost muscle mass and strength (Johnston et al., 2007). Teenagers usually obtain steroids illegally, ignoring side effects, which range from acne, excess body hair, and high blood pressure to mood swings, aggressive behavior, and damage to the liver, circulatory system, and reproductive organs (Casavant et al., 2007).

AP IMAGES/THE ALBUQUERQUE JOURNAL, MARLA BROSE

Although high school girls' participation in sports has increased, it still falls far short of boys'. Yet intraschool and intramural athletics yield many benefits—not just gains in motor skills but important lessons in teamwork, problem solving, assertiveness, and competition.

Coaches and health professionals should inform teenagers of the dangers of these performance-enhancing substances.

In 1972, the U.S. federal government required schools receiving public funds to provide equal opportunities for males and females in all educational programs, including athletics. Since then, high school girls' sports participation has increased, although it still falls far short of boys'. According to a recent survey of all 50 U.S. state high school athletic associations, 41 percent of sports participants are girls, 59 percent boys (National Federation of State High School Associations, 2008). In Section 3, we saw that girls get less encouragement and recognition for athletic achievement, a pattern that starts early and clearly persists into the teenage years (see page 84).

Furthermore, when researchers followed a large, representative sample of U.S. youths from ages 9 to 15, physical activity declined by about 40 minutes per day each year until, at age 15, less than one-third met the U.S. government recommendation of at least 60 minutes of moderate to strenuous physical activity per day (see Figure 5.2) (Nader et al., 2008). In high school, only 58 percent of U.S. boys and 49 percent of girls are enrolled in any physical education, with less than 30 percent of all students experiencing a daily physical education class (U.S. Department of Health and Human Services, 2008k).

Besides improving motor performance, sports and exercise influence cognitive and social development. Interschool and intramural athletics provide important lessons in teamwork, problem solving, assertiveness, and competition. And regular, sustained physical activity—which required physical education can ensure—is associated with lasting health benefits and enjoyment of sports and exercise. In one study, participating in team or individual sports at age 14 at least once a week for girls and twice a week for boys predicted high physical activity rates at age 31. Endurance sports, such as running and cycling—activities that do not require expensive equipment or special facilities—were especially likely to continue into adulthood (Tammelin et al., 2003). And adolescent exertion during exercise, defined as sweating and breathing heavily, is one of the best predictors of adult physical exercise, perhaps because it fosters high *physical self-efficacy*—belief in one's ability to sustain an exercise program (Motl et al., 2002; Telama et al., 2005).

Sexual Maturation

Accompanying rapid body growth are changes in physical features related to sexual functioning. Some, called **primary sexual characteristics,** involve the reproductive organs (ovaries, uterus, and vagina in females; penis, scrotum, and testes in males). Others, called **secondary sexual characteristics,** are visible on the outside of the body and serve as additional signs of sexual maturity (for example, breast development in females and the appearance of underarm and pubic hair in both sexes). As Table 5.1 on page 154 shows, these characteristics develop in a fairly standard sequence, although the ages at which each begins and is completed vary greatly. Typically, pubertal development takes about four years, but some adolescents complete it in two years, whereas others take five to six years.

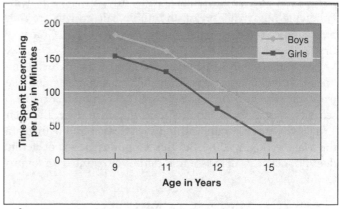

■ **FIGURE 5.2** ■ **Decline in physical activity from ages 9 to 15 among U.S. boys and girls.** In a large representative sample of youths followed over six years, time spent exercising dropped sharply until, at age 15, most youths did not meet government recommendations of at least 60 minutes of moderate to vigorous physical activity per day. At all ages, boys spent more time exercising than girls. (Adapted from Nader et al., 2008.)

■ **TABLE 5.1** ■ *Pubertal Development in North American Girls and Boys*

GIRLS	AVERAGE AGE ATTAINED	AGE RANGE	BOYS	AVERAGE AGE ATTAINED	AGE RANGE
Breasts begin to "bud"	10	(8–13)	Testes begin to enlarge	11.5	(9.5–13.5)
Height spurt begins	10	(8–13)	Pubic hair appears	12	(10–15)
Pubic hair appears	10.5	(8–14)	Penis begins to enlarge	12	(10.5–14.5)
Peak strength spurt	11.6	(9.5–14)	Height spurt begins	12.5	(10.5–16)
Peak height spurt	11.7	(10–13.5)	Spermarche (first ejaculation) occurs	13.5	(12–16)
Menarche (first menstruation) occurs	12.5	(10.5–14)	Peak height spurt	14	(12.5–15.5)
Peak weight spurt	12.7	(10–14)	Peak weight spurt	14	(12.5–15.5)
Adult stature reached	13	(10–16)	Facial hair begins to grow	14	(12.5–15.5)
Pubic hair growth completed	14.5	(14–15)	Voice begins to deepen	14	(12.5–15.5)
Breast growth completed	15	(10–17)	Penis and testes growth completed	14.5	(12.5–16)
			Peak strength spurt	15.3	(13–17)
			Adult stature reached	15.5	(13.5–17.5)
			Pubic hair growth completed	15.5	(14–17)

Sources: Chumlea et al., 2003; Herman-Giddens, 2006; Rogol, Roemmich, & Clark, 2002; Wu, Mendola, & Buck, 2002.

Photos: (left) © David Young-Wolff/PhotoEdit; (right) © Rob Melnychuk/Getty Images/Taxi

■ **SEXUAL MATURATION IN GIRLS.** Female puberty usually begins with the budding of the breasts and the growth spurt. **Menarche,** or first menstruation, typically occurs around age 12½ for North American girls, 13 for Western Europeans. But the age range is wide, from 10½ to 15½ years. Following menarche, breast and pubic hair growth are completed, and underarm hair appears (Archibald, Graber, & Brooks-Gunn, 2006).

Notice in Table 5.1 that nature delays sexual maturity until the girl's body is large enough for childbearing; menarche takes place after the peak of the height spurt. As an extra measure of security, for 12 to 18 months following menarche, the menstrual cycle often occurs without the release of an ovum from the ovaries (Bogin, 2001). But this temporary period of sterility does not occur in all girls, and it cannot be counted on for protection against pregnancy.

■ **SEXUAL MATURATION IN BOYS.** The first sign of puberty in boys is the enlargement of the testes (glands that manufacture sperm), accompanied by changes in the texture and color of the scrotum. Pubic hair emerges soon after, about the same time the penis begins to enlarge (Rogol, Roemmich, & Clark, 2002).

As Table 5.1 reveals, the growth spurt occurs much later in the sequence of pubertal events for boys than for girls. When it reaches its peak around age 14, enlargement of the testes and penis is nearly complete, and underarm hair appears. So do facial and body hair, which increase gradually for several years. Another landmark of male physical maturity is the deepening of the voice as the larynx enlarges and the vocal cords lengthen. (Girls' voices also deepen slightly.) Voice change usually takes place at the peak of the male growth spurt and is often not complete until puberty is over (Archibald, Graber, & Brooks-Gunn, 2006).

While the penis is growing, the prostate gland and seminal vesicles (which together produce semen, the fluid containing sperm) enlarge. Then, around age 13½, **spermarche,** or first ejaculation, occurs (Rogol, Roemmich, & Clark, 2002). For a while, the semen contains few living sperm. So, like girls, boys have an initial period of reduced fertility.

Individual Differences in Pubertal Growth

Heredity contributes substantially to the timing of pubertal changes: Identical twins are more similar than fraternal twins in attainment of most pubertal milestones (Eaves et al., 2004; Mustanski et al., 2004). Nutrition and exercise also make a difference. In females, a sharp rise in body weight and fat may trigger sexual maturation. Fat cells release a protein called *leptin,* which is believed to signal the brain that a girl's energy stores are sufficient for puberty—a likely reason that breast and pubic hair growth and menarche occur earlier for heavier and, especially, obese girls. In contrast, girls who begin rigorous athletic training at an early age or who eat very little (both of which reduce the percentage of body fat) usually experience later puberty (Anderson, Dallal, & Must, 2003; Lee et al., 2007; Slyper, 2006).

Variations in pubertal growth also exist among regions of the world and among SES and ethnic groups. Physical health plays a major role. In poverty-stricken regions where malnutrition and infectious disease are common, menarche is greatly delayed, occurring as late as age 14 to 16 in many parts of Africa. Within developing countries, girls from higher-income families reach menarche 6 to 18 months earlier than those living in economically disadvantaged homes (Parent et al., 2003).

But in industrialized nations where food is abundant, the joint roles of heredity and environment in pubertal growth are apparent. For example, breast and pubic hair growth begin, on average, around age 9 in African-American girls—a year earlier than in Caucasian-American girls. And African-American girls reach menarche about six months earlier, around age 12. Although widespread overweight and obesity in the black population contribute, a genetically influenced faster rate of physical maturation is also involved. Black girls usually reach menarche before white girls of the same age and body weight (Anderson, Dallal, & Must, 2003; Chumlea et al., 2003; Herman-Giddens, 2006).

Early family experiences may also affect pubertal timing. One theory suggests that humans have evolved to be sensitive to the emotional quality of their childhood environments. When children's safety and security are at risk, it is adaptive for them to reproduce early. Research indicates that girls and (less consistently) boys with a history of family conflict, harsh parenting, or parental separation tend to reach puberty early. In contrast, those with warm, stable family ties reach puberty relatively late (Belsky et al., 2007; Bogaert, 2005; Ellis, 2004; Ellis & Essex, 2007; Mustanski et al., 2004; Tremblay & Frigon, 2005). But critics offer an alternative explanation—that mothers who reached puberty early are more likely to bear children earlier, which increases the risk of marital conflict and separation (Mendle et al., 2006). Children of these mothers also inherit a genetic tendency toward early puberty.

In the research we have considered, threats to emotional health accelerate puberty, whereas threats to physical health delay it. A **secular trend,** or generational change, in pubertal timing lends added support to the role of physical well-being in pubertal development. In industrialized nations, age of menarche declined steadily—by about three to four months per decade—from 1900 to 1970, a period in which nutrition, health care, sanitation, and control of infectious disease improved greatly. Boys, too, have reached puberty earlier in recent decades (Karpati et al., 2002). In North America and a few European countries, soaring rates of overweight and obesity are responsible for a modest, continuing trend toward earlier menarche (Kaplowitz, 2006; Parent et al., 2003). A worrisome

consequence is that girls who reach sexual maturity at age 10 or 11 will feel pressure to act much older than they are. As we will see shortly, early-maturing girls are at risk for unfavorable peer involvements, including sexual activity.

Brain Development

The physical transformations of adolescence include major changes in the brain. Brain-imaging research reveals continued pruning of unused synapses in the cerebral cortex, especially in the frontal lobes—the "governor" of thought and action. In addition, growth and myelination of stimulated neural fibers accelerate, strengthening connections among various brain regions. In particular, linkages between the two cerebral hemispheres through the corpus callosum, and between the frontal lobes and other brain areas, expand and attain rapid communication (Blakemore & Choudhury, 2006; Keating, 2004; Lenroot & Giedd, 2006). This sculpting of the adolescent brain supports diverse cognitive skills, including improved processing speed, attention, memory, planning, capacity to integrate information, and self-regulation.

In addition, sensitivity of neurons to certain chemical messages changes. In humans and other mammals, neurons become more responsive to excitatory neurotransmitters during puberty. As a result, adolescents react more strongly to stressful events and experience pleasurable stimuli more intensely—but have not yet acquired the capacity to control these powerful impulses (Casey, Getz, & Galvan, 2008; Spear, 2004, 2008). These changes probably contribute to teenagers' drive for novel experiences, including drug taking, especially among those who engage in reward seeking to counteract chronic emotional pain. Alterations in neurotransmitter activity may also be involved in adolescents' increased susceptibility to certain disorders, such as depression and eating disturbances.

During puberty, neurons become more responsive to excitatory neurotransmitters. As a result, adolescents react more strongly to stressful events, such as disagreements with parents. This mother must try to be patient with her son, despite his intense resistance.

To what extent are the hormonal changes of puberty responsible for adolescent brain growth and reorganization? Researchers do not yet have a ready answer. But the transformations that occur—much greater than previously thought—enhance our understanding of both the cognitive advances and the troubling behaviors of adolescence, along with teenagers' need for adult patience, oversight, and guidance.

Changing States of Arousal

At puberty, revisions occur in the way the brain regulates the timing of sleep, perhaps because of increased neural sensitivity to evening light. As a result, adolescents go to bed much later than they did as children. Yet they need almost as much sleep as they did in middle childhood—about nine hours. When the school day begins early, their sleep needs are not satisfied.

This sleep "phase delay" strengthens with pubertal growth. But today's teenagers often have evening social activities and part-time jobs, as well as TVs, computers, and phones in their bedrooms. As a result, they get much less sleep than teenagers of previous generations (Carskadon, Acebo, & Jenni, 2004; Carskadon et al., 2002). Sleep-deprived adolescents perform especially poorly on cognitive tasks during morning hours. And they are more likely to achieve less well in school, suffer from depressed mood, and engage in high-risk behaviors, including drinking and reckless driving (Dahl & Lewin, 2002; Hansen et al., 2005). Sleep rebound on weekends sustains the pattern by leading to difficulty falling asleep on subsequent evenings (Laberge et al., 2001). Later school start times ease but do not eliminate sleep loss. Educating teenagers about the importance of sleep is vital.

The Psychological Impact of Pubertal Events

TAKE A MOMENT... Think back to your late elementary and middle school days. As you reached puberty, how did your feelings about yourself and your relationships with others change? Research reveals that pubertal events affect adolescents' self-image, mood, and interaction with parents and peers. Some outcomes are a response to dramatic physical change, whenever it occurs. Others have to do with pubertal timing.

Reactions to Pubertal Changes

Two generations ago, menarche was often traumatic. Today, girls commonly react with "surprise," undoubtedly due to the sudden onset of the event. Otherwise, they typically report a mixture of positive and negative emotions (DeRose & Brooks-Gunn, 2006). Yet wide individual differences exist that depend on prior knowledge and support from family members, which in turn are influenced by cultural attitudes toward puberty and sexuality.

For girls who have no advance information, menarche can be shocking and disturbing. In the 1950s, up to 50 percent

received no prior warning, and of those who did, many were given "grin-and-bear-it" messages (Costos, Ackerman, & Paradis, 2002; Shainess, 1961). Today, few girls are uninformed, a shift that is probably due to parents' greater willingness to discuss sexual matters and to the spread of health education classes (Omar, McElderry, & Zakharia, 2003). Almost all girls get some information from their mothers. And some evidence suggests that compared with Caucasian-American families, African-American families may better prepare girls for menarche, treat it as an important milestone, and express less conflict over girls reaching sexual maturity—factors that lead African-American girls to react more favorably (Martin, 1996; Scott et al., 1989).

Like girls' reactions to menarche, boys' responses to spermarche reflect mixed feelings. Virtually all boys know about ejaculation ahead of time, but many say that no one spoke to them before or during puberty about physical changes (Omar, McElderry, & Zakharia, 2003). Usually they get their information from reading material. Even boys who had advance information often say that their first ejaculation occurred earlier than they expected and that they were unprepared for it. As with girls, boys who feel better prepared tend to react more positively (Stein & Reiser, 1994). But whereas almost all girls eventually tell a friend that they are menstruating, far fewer boys tell anyone about spermarche (DeRose & Brooks-Gunn, 2006; Downs & Fuller, 1991). Overall, boys get much less social support than girls for the physical changes of puberty. They might benefit, especially, from opportunities to ask questions and discuss feelings with a sympathetic parent or health professional.

Many tribal and village societies celebrate the onset of puberty with an *initiation ceremony,* a ritualized announcement to the community that marks an important change in privilege and responsibility. Consequently, young people know that reaching puberty is valued in their culture. In contrast, Western societies grant little formal recognition to movement from childhood to adolescence or from adolescence to adulthood. Ceremonies such as the Jewish bar or bat mitzvah and the *quinceañera* in Hispanic communities (celebrating a 15-year-old girl's sexual maturity and marriage availability), resemble initiation ceremonies, but only within the ethnic or religious subculture. They do not mark a significant change in social status in the larger society.

Instead, Western adolescents are granted partial adult status at many different ages—for example, an age for starting employment, for driving, for leaving high school, for voting, and for drinking. And in some contexts (at home and at school), they may still be regarded as children. The absence of a widely accepted marker of physical and social maturity makes the process of becoming an adult more confusing.

Pubertal Change, Emotion, and Social Behavior

A common belief is that puberty has something to do with adolescent moodiness and the desire for greater physical and

In Hispanic communities, the *quinceañera,* celebrated at age 15, is a rite of passage honoring a girl's journey from childhood to maturity. It usually begins with a mass in which the priest blesses gifts presented to the girl.

monitored by having them carry electronic pagers. Over a one-week period, they were beeped at random intervals and asked to write down what they were doing, whom they were with, and how they felt.

As expected, adolescents reported less favorable moods than school-age children and adults (Larson et al., 2002; Larson & Lampman-Petraitis, 1989). But negative moods were linked to a greater number of negative life events, such as difficulty getting along with parents, disciplinary actions at school, and breaking up with a boyfriend or girlfriend. Negative events increased steadily from childhood to adolescence, and teenagers also seemed to react to them with greater emotion than children (Larson & Ham, 1993). (Recall that stress reactivity is heightened by changes in brain neurotransmitter activity during adolescence.)

Compared with the moods of older adolescents and adults, those of younger adolescents (ages 12 to 16) were less stable, often shifting from cheerful to sad and back again. These mood swings were strongly related to situational changes. High points of adolescents' days were times spent with peers and in self-chosen leisure activities. Low points tended to occur in adult-structured settings—class, job, and religious services. Furthermore, emotional highs coincided with Friday and Saturday evenings, especially in high school (see Figure 5.3). Going out with friends and romantic partners increases so dramatically during adolescence that it becomes a "cultural script" for what is *supposed* to happen. Consequently, teenagers who spend weekend evenings at home often feel profoundly lonely (Larson & Richards, 1998).

In sum, biological, psychological, and social forces combine to make adolescence a time of deeper valleys and higher peaks in emotional experience. This explanation is consistent with the balanced view presented earlier in this section.

psychological separation from parents. Let's see what research says about these relationships.

■ **ADOLESCENT MOODINESS.** Higher pubertal hormone levels are linked to greater moodiness, but only modestly so (Buchanan, Eccles, & Becker, 1992; Graber, Brooks-Gunn, & Warren, 2006). What other factors might contribute? In several studies, the moods of children, adolescents, and adults were

■ **PARENT–CHILD RELATIONSHIPS.** Sabrina's father noticed that as his children entered adolescence, they kept their bedroom doors closed, resisted spending time with the family, and became more argumentative. Sabrina and her mother squabbled over Sabrina's messy room ("It's *my* room, Mom. You don't have to live in it!"). And Sabrina resisted the family's regular weekend visit to Aunt Gina's ("Why do I have to go *every* week?"). Research in cultures as diverse as the United

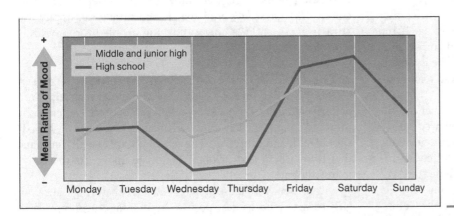

■ **FIGURE 5.3** ■ **Younger and older adolescents' emotional experiences across the week.** Adolescents' reports revealed that emotional high points are on Fridays and Saturdays. Mood drops on Sunday, before returning to school, and during the week, as students spend much time in adult-structured settings in school. (From R. Larson & M. Richards, 1998, "Waiting for the Weekend: Friday and Saturday Night as the Emotional Climax of the Week," in A. C. Crouter & R. Larson (Eds.), *Temporal Rhythms in Adolescence: Clocks, Calendars, and the Coordination of Daily Life.* San Francisco: Jossey-Bass, p. 41. Reprinted with permission from John Wiley & Sons, Inc.)

States and Turkey shows a rise in parent–child conflict at puberty (Gure, Ucanok, & Sayil, 2006; Laursen, Coy, & Collins, 1998; Steinberg & Morris, 2001). Frequency of arguing is surprisingly similar across North American subcultures, occurring as often in families of European descent as in immigrant Asian and Hispanic families whose traditions emphasize respect for parental authority (Fuligni, 1998).

Why should a youngster's more adultlike appearance trigger these disputes? The association may have adaptive value. Among nonhuman primates, the young typically leave the family group around the time of puberty. The same is true in many nonindustrialized cultures (Caine, 1986; Schlegel & Barry, 1991). Departure of young people discourages sexual relations between close blood relatives. But adolescents in industrialized nations, who are still economically dependent on parents, cannot leave the family. Consequently, a modern substitute seems to have emerged: psychological distancing.

As children become physically mature, they demand to be treated in adultlike ways. And as we will see, adolescents' new powers of reasoning may also contribute to a rise in family tensions. Parent–adolescent disagreements focus largely on everyday matters such as driving, dating partners, and curfews (Adams & Laursen, 2001). But beneath these disputes lie serious concerns: parental efforts to protect teenagers from substance use, auto accidents, and early sex. The larger the gap between parents' and adolescents' views of teenagers' readiness for new responsibilities, the more quarreling (Deković, Noom, & Meeus, 1997).

Parent–daughter conflict tends to be more intense than conflict with sons, perhaps because parents place more restrictions on girls (Allison & Schultz, 2004). But this gender disparity varies with culture; for example, it is less evident in Canada than in Italy, where gender-role attitudes are more traditional (Claes et al., 2003). But most disputes are mild. Parents and teenagers display both conflict and affection, and they usually agree on important values, such as honesty and the importance of education. Although separation from parents is adaptive, both generations benefit from warm, protective family bonds throughout the lifespan.

Pubertal Timing

"All our children were early maturers," said Franca during the parents' discussion group. "The three boys were tall by age 12 or 13, but it was easier for them. They felt big and important. Sabrina was skinny as a little girl, but now she says she is too fat and needs to diet. She thinks about boys and doesn't concentrate on her schoolwork."

Findings of several studies match the experiences of Sabrina and her brothers. Both adults and peers viewed early-maturing boys as relaxed, independent, self-confident, and physically attractive. Popular with agemates, they tended to hold leadership positions in school and to be athletic stars. In contrast, both adults and peers viewed late-maturing boys as anxious, overly talkative, and attention-seeking (Brooks-Gunn,

African-American early-maturing girls seem to escape the adjustment difficulties commonly associated with early pubertal timing. Their families and friends tend to be welcoming of menarche, and they are more likely to report a positive body image than their Caucasian counterparts.

1988; Clausen, 1975). However, early-maturing boys, though viewed as well-adjusted, report slightly more psychological stress and problem behaviors (sexual activity, smoking, drinking, delinquency) than their later-maturing agemates (Ge, Conger, & Elder, 2001; Huddleston & Ge, 2003).

In contrast, early-maturing girls were unpopular, withdrawn, lacking in self-confidence, anxious, and prone to depression, and they held few leadership positions (Ge, Conger, & Elder, 1996; Graber et al., 1997; Graber, Brooks-Gunn, & Warren, 2006; Jones & Mussen, 1958). They were more involved in deviant behavior (getting drunk, participating in early sexual activity) and achieved less well in school (Caspi et al., 1993; Dick et al., 2000; Ge et al., 2006). In contrast, their later-maturing counterparts were regarded as physically attractive, lively, sociable, and leaders at school. In one study of several hundred eighth graders, however, negative effects were not evident among early-maturing African-American girls, whose families—and perhaps friends as well—tend to be more unconditionally welcoming of menarche (see page 156) (Michael & Eccles, 2003).

Two factors largely account for these trends: (1) how closely the adolescent's body matches cultural ideals of physical attractiveness, and (2) how well young people fit in physically with their peers.

■ **THE ROLE OF PHYSICAL ATTRACTIVENESS.** *TAKE A MOMENT...* Flip through your favorite popular magazine. You will see evidence of our society's view of an attractive female as thin and long-legged and a good-looking male as tall, broad-shouldered, and muscular. The female image is a girlish shape that favors the late developer. The male image fits the early-maturing boy.

Consistent with these preferences, early-maturing Caucasian girls tend to report a less positive **body image**—conception of and attitude toward their physical appearance—than their on-time and late-maturing agemates. Compared with African-American and Hispanic girls, Caucasian girls are more likely to have internalized the cultural ideal of female attractiveness: Most want to be thinner (Rosen, 2003; Stice, Presnell, & Bearman, 2001; Williams & Currie, 2000). Although boys are less consistent, early, rapid maturers are more likely to be satisfied with their physical characteristics (Alsaker, 1995; Sinkkonen, Anttila, & Siimes, 1998).

Body image is a strong predictor of young people's self-esteem (Harter, 2006). But the negative effects of pubertal timing on body image and—as we will see next—emotional adjustment are greatly amplified when accompanied by other stressors (Stice, 2003).

■ **THE IMPORTANCE OF FITTING IN WITH PEERS.** Physical status in relation to peers also explains differences in adjustment between early and late maturers. From this perspective, early-maturing girls and late-maturing boys have difficulty because they fall at the extremes of physical development and feel "out of place" when with their agemates. Not surprisingly, adolescents feel most comfortable with peers who match their own level of biological maturity (Stattin & Magnusson, 1990).

Because few agemates of the same pubertal status are available, early-maturing adolescents of both sexes seek out older companions, who often encourage them into activities they are not ready to handle emotionally, including sexual activity, drug and alcohol use, and minor delinquent acts (Ge et al., 2002). Perhaps as a result, early maturers of both sexes report feeling emotionally stressed and show declines in academic performance (Graber, 2003; Mendle, Turkheimer, & Emery, 2007).

At the same time, the young person's context greatly increases the likelihood that early pubertal timing will lead to negative outcomes. Early maturers in economically disadvantaged neighborhoods are especially vulnerable to establishing ties with deviant peers, which heightens their defiant, hostile behavior. And because families in such neighborhoods tend to be exposed to chronic, severe stressors and to have few social supports, these early maturers are also more likely to experience harsh, inconsistent parenting, which predicts both deviant peer associations and antisocial behavior (Conger et al., 2002; Ge et al., 2002).

■ **LONG-TERM CONSEQUENCES.** Do the effects of pubertal timing last? Follow-ups reveal that early-maturing girls, especially, are prone to lasting difficulties. In one study, depression subsided by age 13 in early-maturing boys but tended to persist in early-maturing girls (Ge et al., 2003). In another study, which followed young people from ages 14 to 24, early-maturing boys again showed good adjustment. But early-maturing girls reported poorer-quality relationships with family and friends, smaller social networks, and lower life satisfaction into early adulthood than their on-time counterparts (Graber et al., 2004).

Recall that childhood family conflict and harsh parenting are linked to earlier pubertal timing, more so for girls than for boys (see page 155). Perhaps many early-maturing girls enter adolescence with emotional and social difficulties. As the stresses of puberty interfere with school performance and lead to unfavorable peer pressures, poor adjustment extends and deepens (Graber, 2003). Clearly, interventions that target at-risk early-maturing youths are needed. These include educating parents and teachers and providing adolescents with counseling and social supports so they will be better prepared to handle the emotional and social challenges of this transition.

Health Issues

The arrival of puberty brings new health issues related to the young person's efforts to meet physical and psychological needs. As adolescents attain greater autonomy, their personal decision making becomes important, in health as well as other areas. Yet none of the health concerns we are about to discuss can be traced to a single cause. Rather, biological, psychological, family, peer, and cultural factors jointly contribute.

Nutritional Needs

When their sons reached puberty, Franca and Antonio reported a "vacuum cleaner effect" in the kitchen as the boys routinely emptied the refrigerator. Rapid body growth leads to a dramatic rise in food intake. During the growth spurt, boys require about 2,700 calories a day and much more protein than they did earlier, girls about 2,200 calories but somewhat less protein than boys because of their smaller size and muscle mass (Cortese & Smith, 2003).

This increase in nutritional requirements comes at a time when the diets of many young people are the poorest. Of all age groups, adolescents are the most likely to skip breakfast (a practice linked to obesity), eat on the run, and consume empty calories rather than nutrient-rich fruits and vegetables

(Stockman et al., 2005; Striegel-Moore & Franko, 2006). Fast-food restaurants, where teenagers often gather, have begun to offer some healthy menu options. But adolescents need guidance in choosing these alternatives. Eating fast food and school purchases from snack bars and vending machines is strongly associated with consumption of high-fat foods and soft drinks, indicating that teenagers often make unhealthy food choices (Bowman et al., 2004; Kubik et al., 2003).

The most common nutritional problem of adolescence is iron deficiency. Iron requirements increase to a maximum during the growth spurt and remain high among girls because of iron loss during menstruation. A tired, irritable teenager may be suffering from anemia rather than unhappiness and should have a medical checkup. Most teenagers get too little calcium and are also deficient in riboflavin (vitamin B_2) and magnesium, both of which support metabolism (Cavadini, Siega-Riz, & Popkin, 2000).

Frequency of family meals is strongly associated with greater intake of fruits, vegetables, grains, and calcium-rich foods and reduced soft drink consumption by teenagers (Fiese & Schwartz, 2008). But compared to families with younger children, those with adolescents eat fewer meals together. In addition to their other benefits (see page 106 in Section 3), family meals can greatly improve teenagers' diets.

Adolescents—especially girls concerned about their weight—tend to be attracted to fad diets. Unfortunately, most are too limited in nutrients and calories to be healthy for fast-growing, active teenagers (Donatelle, 2009). Parents should encourage young people to consult a doctor or dietitian before trying any special diet.

Eating Disorders

Sabrina's desire to lose weight worried Franca. She explained to her daughter that Sabrina was really quite average in build for an adolescent girl and reminded her that her Italian ancestors had considered a plump female body more beautiful than a thin one. Girls who reach puberty early, who are very dissatisfied with their body image, and who grow up in homes where concern with weight and thinness is high are at risk for serious eating problems. Severe dieting is the strongest predictor of the onset of an eating disorder in adolescence (Lock & Kirz, 2008). The two most serious are anorexia nervosa and bulimia nervosa.

■ **ANOREXIA NERVOSA. Anorexia nervosa** is a tragic eating disturbance in which young people starve themselves because of a compulsive fear of getting fat. About 1 percent of North American and Western European teenage girls are affected. During the past half-century, cultural admiration of female thinness has fueled a sharp increase in cases. Anorexia nervosa is equally common in all SES groups, but Asian-American, Caucasian-American, and Hispanic girls are at greater risk than African-American girls, who tend to be more satisfied with their size and shape (Fairburn & Harrison, 2003; Granillo, Jones-Rodriguez, & Carvajal, 2005; Steinhausen,

Aiva, age 16, an anorexia nervosa patient, is shown at left on the day she entered treatment. She weighed just 77 pounds—69 percent of her normal body weight. At right, Aiva appears 10 weeks later, on her last day of treatment. Only about 50 percent of young people with anorexia fully overcome the disorder.

2006). Boys account for about 10 percent of cases of anorexia; about half of these are homosexual or bisexual young people who are uncomfortable with a strong, muscular appearance (Robb & Dadson, 2002).

Anorexics have an extremely distorted body image. Even after they have become severely underweight, they see themselves as too heavy. Most go on self-imposed diets so strict that they struggle to avoid eating in response to hunger. To enhance weight loss, they exercise strenuously.

In their attempt to reach "perfect" slimness, anorexics lose between 25 and 50 percent of their body weight. Because a normal menstrual cycle requires about 15 percent body fat, either menarche does not occur or menstrual periods stop. Malnutrition causes pale skin, brittle discolored nails, fine dark hairs all over the body, and extreme sensitivity to cold. If it continues, the heart muscle can shrink, the kidneys can fail, and irreversible brain damage and loss of bone mass can occur. About 6 percent of anorexics die of the disorder, as a result of either physical complications or suicide (Katzman, 2005).

Forces within the person, the family, and the larger culture give rise to anorexia nervosa. Identical twins share the disorder more often than fraternal twins, indicating a genetic influence. Abnormalities in neurotransmitters in the brain, linked to anxiety and impulse control, may make some individuals more susceptible (Kaye, 2008; Lock & Kirz, 2008). Many anorexics have extremely high standards for their own behavior and performance, are emotionally inhibited, and avoid intimate ties outside the family. Consequently, they are often excellent students who are responsible and well-behaved. But as we have also seen, the societal image of "thin is beautiful" contributes to the poor body image of many girls—especially early-maturing girls, who are at greatest risk for anorexia nervosa (Tyrka, Graber, & Brooks-Gunn, 2000).

In addition, parent–adolescent interactions reveal problems related to adolescent autonomy. Often the mothers of these girls have high expectations for physical appearance, achievement, and social acceptance and are overprotective and controlling. Fathers tend to be emotionally distant. These parental attributes may contribute to anorexic girls' persistent anxiety and fierce pursuit of perfection in achievement, respectable behavior, and thinness (Kaye, 2008). Nevertheless, it remains unclear whether maladaptive parent–child relationships precede the disorder, emerge in response to it, or both.

Because anorexic girls typically deny or minimize the seriousness of their disorder, treating it is difficult (Couturier & Lock, 2006). Hospitalization is often necessary to prevent life-threatening malnutrition. The most successful treatment is family therapy and medication to reduce anxiety and neurotransmitter imbalances (Fairburn, 2005; Treasure & Schmidt, 2005). Still, only about 50 percent of anorexics fully recover. For many, eating problems continue in less extreme form. About 10 percent show signs of a less severe, but nevertheless debilitating, disorder: bulimia nervosa.

■ **BULIMIA NERVOSA.** When Sabrina's 16-year-old brother, Louis, brought his girlfriend Cassie to the house, Sabrina admired her good figure. "What willpower!" Sabrina thought. "Cassie hardly touches food. But what's the matter with her teeth?"

Cassie's secret was not willpower. She actually had great difficulty controlling her appetite. Cassie suffered from **bulimia nervosa,** an eating disorder in which young people (again, mainly girls, but gay and bisexual boys are also vulnerable) engage in strict dieting and excessive exercise accompanied by binge eating, often followed by deliberate vomiting and purging with laxatives (Herzog, Eddy, & Beresin, 2006; Wichstrøm, 2006). When she was alone, Cassie often felt anxious and unhappy. She responded with eating rampages, consuming thousands of calories in an hour or two, followed by vomiting that eroded the enamel on her teeth. In some cases, life-threatening damage to the throat and stomach occurs.

Bulimia is more common than anorexia nervosa, affecting about 2 to 4 percent of teenage girls, only 5 percent of whom have previously been anorexic. Twin studies show that bulimia, like anorexia, is influenced by heredity (Klump, Kaye, & Strober, 2001). Overweight and early menarche increase the risk. Some bulimics, like anorexics, are perfectionists. But most are impulsive, sensation-seeking young people who lack self-control in many areas, engaging in petty shoplifting, alcohol abuse, and other risky behaviors (Kaye, 2008). And although bulimics share with anorexics pathological anxiety about gaining weight, they may have experienced their parents as disengaged and emotionally unavailable rather than controlling (Fairburn & Harrison, 2003).

Unlike anorexics, bulimics usually feel depressed and guilty about their abnormal eating habits and desperately want help. As a result, bulimia is usually easier to treat than anorexia, through support groups, nutrition education, training in changing eating habits, and anti-anxiety, antidepressant, and appetite-control medication (Hay & Bacaltchuk, 2004).

Sexuality

Louis and Cassie hadn't planned to have intercourse—it "just happened." But before and after, a lot of things passed through their minds. After they had dated for three months, Cassie began to wonder, "Will Louis think I'm normal if I don't have sex with him? If he wants to and I say no, will I lose him?" Both young people knew their parents wouldn't approve. In fact, when Franca and Antonio noticed how attached Louis was to Cassie, they talked to him about the importance of waiting and the dangers of pregnancy. But that Friday evening, Louis and Cassie's feelings for each other seemed overwhelming. "If I don't make a move," Louis thought, "will she think I'm a wimp?"

With the arrival of puberty, hormonal changes—in particular, the production of androgens in young people of both sexes—lead to an increase in sex drive (Halpern, Udry, & Suchindran, 1997). In response, adolescents become very concerned about managing sexuality in social relationships. New cognitive capacities involving perspective taking and self-reflection affect

Adolescence is an especially important time for the development of sexuality, as these two young people demonstrate. But North American teenagers receive contradictory and confusing messages about the appropriateness of sex.

Applying What We Know

Communicating with Adolescents About Sexual Issues

Strategy	Explanation
Foster open communication.	Let the teenager know you are a willing and trustworthy resource by stating that you are available when questions arise and will answer fully and accurately.
Use correct terms for body parts.	Correct vocabulary gives the young person a basis for future discussion and also indicates that sex is not a secretive topic.
Use effective discussion techniques.	Listen, encourage the adolescent to participate, ask open-ended rather than yes/no questions, and give supportive responses. Avoid dominating and lecturing, which cause teenagers to withdraw.
Reflect before speaking.	When the adolescent asks questions or offers opinions about sex, remain nonjudgmental. If you differ with the teenager's views, convey your perspective in a nonthreatening manner, emphasizing that although you disagree, you are not attacking his or her character. Trying to dictate the young person's behavior generally results in alienation.
Keep conversations going.	Many parents regard their job as finished once they have had the "big talk" in early adolescence. But young people are more likely to be influenced by an accumulation of smaller discussions. If open communication is sustained, the teenager is more likely to return with thoughts and questions.

Source: Berkowitz, 2004.

their efforts to do so. Yet like the eating behaviors we have just discussed, adolescent sexuality is heavily influenced by the young person's social context.

■ **THE IMPACT OF CULTURE.** *TAKE A MOMENT...* When did you first learn the "facts of life"—and how? Was sex discussed openly in your family, or was it treated with secrecy? Exposure to sex, education about it, and efforts to limit the sexual curiosity of children and adolescents vary widely around the world.

Despite the prevailing image of sexually free adolescents, sexual attitudes in North America are relatively restrictive. Typically, parents provide little or no information about sex, discourage sex play, and rarely talk about sex in children's presence. When young people become interested in sex, only about half report getting information from parents about intercourse, pregnancy prevention, and sexually transmitted disease. Many parents, fearing embarrassment or concerned that their teenager will not take them seriously, avoid meaningful discussions about sex. Yet warm, open give-and-take, as described in Applying What We Know above, is associated with teenagers' adoption of parents' views and with reduced sexual risk taking (Jaccard, Dodge, & Dittus, 2003; Miller, Forehand, & Kotchick, 1999).

Adolescents who do not get information about sex from their parents are likely to learn from friends, books, magazines, movies, TV, and the Internet (Jaccard, Dodge, & Dittus, 2002; Sutton et al., 2002). On prime-time TV shows, which adolescents watch more than other TV offerings, 80 percent of programs contain sexual content. Most depict partners as spontaneous and passionate, taking no steps to avoid preg-

nancy or sexually transmitted disease, and experiencing no negative consequences (Roberts, Henriksen, & Foehr, 2004). In several studies, media exposure to sexual content predicted teenagers' current sexual activity, intentions to be sexually active in the future, and subsequent pregnancies, even after many other relevant factors were controlled (Chandra et al., 2008; Friedman, 2006; Pardum, L'Engle, & Brown, 2005).

The Internet is an especially hazardous "sex educator." In a survey of a large sample of U.S. 10- to 17-year-old Web users, 42 percent said they had viewed online pornographic websites (images of naked people or people having sex) while surfing the Internet in the past 12 months. Of these, 66 percent indicated they had encountered the images accidentally and did not want to view them. Youths who felt depressed, had been bullied by peers, or were involved in delinquent activities had more encounters with Internet pornography, which may have intensified their adjustment problems (Wolak, Mitchell, & Finkelhor, 2007).

Consider the contradictory messages young people receive. On one hand, adults express disapproval of sex at a young age and outside of marriage. On the other hand, the broader social environment extols the excitement and romanticism of sex. North American teenagers are left bewildered, poorly informed about sexual facts, and with little sound advice on how to conduct their sex lives responsibly.

■ **ADOLESCENT SEXUAL ATTITUDES AND BEHAVIOR.** Although differences between subcultural groups exist, sexual attitudes of U.S. adolescents and adults have become more liberal over the past 40 years. Compared with a generation ago, more people believe that sexual intercourse before marriage is all right, as long as two people are emotionally committed to each other (ABC News, 2004; Michael et al., 1994). During the past decade, adolescents have swung back slightly toward more conservative sexual beliefs, largely in response to the risk of sexually transmitted disease, especially AIDS, and to teenage sexual abstinence programs sponsored by schools and religious organizations (Ali & Scelfo, 2002; Cope-Farrar & Kunkel, 2002).

Trends in adolescents' sexual behavior are consistent with their attitudes. Rates of extramarital sex among U.S. young people rose for several decades but have recently declined (U.S. Department of Health and Human Services, 2008k). Nevertheless, as Figure 5.4 illustrates, a substantial percentage of U.S. young people are sexually active quite early, by ninth grade (ages 14 to 15). Males tend to have their first intercourse earlier than females.

Overall teenage sexual activity rates are similar in the United States and other Western countries: About half of adolescents have had intercourse. But quality of sexual experiences differs. U.S. youths become sexually active earlier than their Canadian and European counterparts (Boyce et al., 2006; U.S. Department of Health and Human Services, 2008k). And about 18 percent of adolescent boys in the United States—more than twice the percentage in Canada, France, and Great Britain—have had sexual relations with three or more partners in the past year (Alan Guttmacher Institute, 2004). Most teenagers, however, have had only one or two sexual partners by the end of high school.

■ CHARACTERISTICS OF SEXUALLY ACTIVE ADOLESCENTS.

Early and frequent teenage sexual activity is linked to personal, family, peer, and educational characteristics. These include childhood impulsivity, weak sense of personal control over life events, early pubertal timing, parental divorce, single-parent and stepfamily homes, large family size, little or no religious involvement, weak parental monitoring, disrupted parent–child communication, sexually active friends and older siblings, poor school performance, lower educational aspirations, and tendency to engage in norm-violating acts, including alcohol and drug use and delinquency (Crockett, Raffaelli, & Shen, 2006; Howard & Wang, 2004; Manlove et al., 2006; Siebenbruner, Zimmer-Gembeck, & Egeland, 2007; Silver & Bauman, 2006).

Because many of these factors are associated with growing up in a low-income family, it is not surprising that early sexual activity is more common among young people from economically disadvantaged homes. Living in a neighborhood high in physical deterioration, crime, and violence also increases the likelihood that teenagers will be sexually active (Ge et al., 2002). In such neighborhoods, social ties are weak, adults exert little oversight and control over adolescents' activities, and negative peer influences are widespread. In fact, the high rate of sexual activity among African-American teenagers—67 percent report having had sexual intercourse, compared with 48 percent of all U.S. young people—is largely accounted for by widespread poverty in the black population (Darroch, Frost, & Singh, 2001; U.S. Department of Health & Human Services, 2008k).

■ CONTRACEPTIVE USE.

Although adolescent contraceptive use has increased in recent years, about 20 percent of sexually active teenagers in the United States are at risk for unintended pregnancy because they do not use contraception consistently (see Figure 5.5 on page 164) (Alan Guttmacher Institute, 2002, 2005). Why do so many fail to take precautions? Typically, teenagers respond, "I wasn't planning to have sex," or, "I didn't want to spoil the moment." As we will see when we take up adolescent cognitive development, although adolescents can consider multiple possibilities when faced with a problem, they often fail to apply this reasoning to everyday situations.

One reason is that advances in perspective taking lead teenagers, for a time, to be extremely concerned about others' opinions of them. Recall how Cassie and Louis each worried about what the other would think if they decided not to have sex. Furthermore, in the midst of everyday social pressures, adolescents often overlook the consequences of engaging in risky behaviors (Beyth-Marom & Fischhoff, 1997). And many teenagers—especially those from troubled, low-SES families—do not have realistic expectations about the impact of early parenthood on their current and future lives (Stevens-Simon, Sheeder, & Harter, 2005).

As these findings suggest, the social environment also contributes to teenagers' reluctance to use contraception. Those without the rewards of meaningful education and work are especially likely to engage in irresponsible sex, sometimes within relationships characterized by exploitation. About 11 percent of U.S. girls and 5 percent of boys say they were pressured to have intercourse when they were unwilling (U.S. Department of Health and Human Services, 2008k).

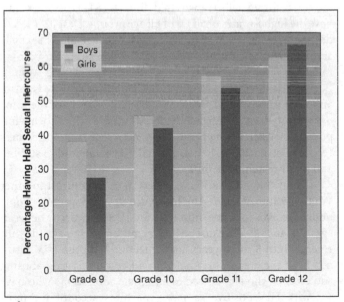

■ **FIGURE 5.4** ■ **U.S. adolescents who report ever having had sexual intercourse.** Many young adolescents are sexually active—more than in other Western nations. Boys tend to have their first intercourse earlier than girls. By the end of high school, rates of boys and girls having had sexual intercourse are similar. (From U.S. Department of Health and Human Services, 2008k.)

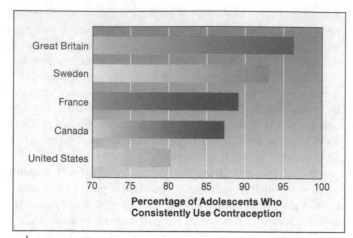

■ FIGURE 5.5 ■ Adolescent contraceptive use in five industrialized nations. Sexually active U.S. teenagers are less likely to use contraception consistently than teenagers in other industrialized nations. (Adapted from Darroch, Frost, & Singh, 2001; U.S. Department of Health and Human Services, 2008k.)

In contrast, teenagers who report good relationships with parents and who talk openly with them about sex and contraception are more likely to use birth control (Henrich et al., 2006; Kirby, 2002a). But few adolescents believe their parents would be understanding and supportive. School sex education classes, as well, often leave teenagers with incomplete or incorrect knowledge. Some do not know where to get birth control counseling and devices; those who do often worry that a doctor or family planning clinic might not keep their visits confidential. About 20 percent of adolescents using health services say that if their parents were notified, they would still have sex, but without contraception (Jones et al., 2005).

■ SEXUAL ORIENTATION. So far, we have focused only on heterosexual behavior. About 2 to 3 percent of young people identify as lesbian, gay, or bisexual (Bailey, Dunne, & Martin, 2000; Savin-Williams & Diamond, 2004). An unknown number experience same-sex attraction but have not come out to friends or family (see the Social Issues box on the following page). Adolescence is an equally crucial time for the sexual development of these young people, and societal attitudes, again, loom large in how well they fare.

Heredity makes an important contribution to homosexuality: Identical twins of both sexes are much more likely than fraternal twins to share a homosexual orientation; so are biological (as opposed to adoptive) relatives (Kendler et al., 2000; Kirk et al., 2000). Furthermore, male homosexuality tends to be more common on the maternal than on the paternal side of families, suggesting that it might be X-linked. Indeed, one gene-mapping study found that among 40 pairs of homosexual brothers, 33 (82 percent) had an identical segment of DNA on the X chromosome. One or several genes in that region might predispose males to become homosexual (Hamer et al., 1993).

How might heredity lead to homosexuality? According to some researchers, certain genes affect the level or impact of prenatal sex hormones, which modify brain structures in ways that induce homosexual feelings and behavior (Bailey et al., 1995; LeVay, 1993). Keep in mind, however, that environmental factors can also alter prenatal hormones. Girls exposed prenatally to very high levels of androgens or estrogens—either because of a genetic defect or from drugs given to the mother to prevent miscarriage—are more likely to become homosexual or bisexual (Meyer-Bahlburg et al., 1995). Furthermore, homosexual men tend to be later in birth order and to have a higher-than-average number of older brothers (Blanchard & Bogaert, 2004). Perhaps mothers with several male children sometimes produce antibodies to androgens, which reduces the prenatal impact of male sex hormones on the brains of later-born boys.

Stereotypes and misconceptions about homosexuality persist. For example, contrary to common belief, most homosexual adolescents are not "gender-deviant" in dress or behavior. And attraction to members of the same sex is not limited to gay, lesbian, and bisexual teenagers. About 50 to 60 percent of adolescents who report having engaged in homosexual acts identify as heterosexual (Savin-Williams & Diamond, 2004).

The evidence to date suggests that genetic and prenatal biological influences are largely responsible for homosexuality. In our evolutionary past, homosexuality may have served the adaptive function of reducing aggressive competition for other-sex mates (Rahman & Wilson, 2003).

Sexually Transmitted Diseases

Sexually active adolescents, both homosexual and heterosexual, are at risk for sexually transmitted diseases (STDs). Adolescents have the highest rates of STDs of all age groups. Despite a recent decline in STDs in the United States, one out of six sexually active teenagers contracts one of these illnesses each year—a rate three or more times as high as that of Canada and Western Europe (Health Canada, 2006; U.S. Centers for Disease Control and Prevention, 2007). Teenagers at greatest risk are the same ones most likely to engage in irresponsible sexual behavior: poverty-stricken young people who feel a sense of hopelessness (Niccolai et al., 2004). Left untreated, STDs can lead to sterility and life-threatening complications.

By far the most serious STD is AIDS. In contrast to other Western nations, where the incidence of AIDS among people under age 30 is low, one-fifth of U.S. AIDS cases occur between ages 20 and 29. Because AIDS symptoms typically do not emerge until 8 to 10 years after infection with the HIV virus, nearly all these cases originated in adolescence. Drug-abusing adolescents who share needles and male adolescents who have sex with HIV-positive same-sex partners account for most cases, but heterosexual spread of the disease remains high, especially among teenagers with more than one partner in the previous 18 months (Kelley et al., 2003). It is at least twice as easy for a male to infect a female with any STD, including HIV, as for a female to infect a male. Currently, females account for about 37 percent of new U.S. cases among adolescents and young adults (Rangel et al., 2006).

SOCIAL ISSUES

Gay, Lesbian, and Bisexual Youths: Coming Out to Oneself and Others

Cultures vary as much in their acceptance of homosexuality as in their approval of extramarital sex. In North America, homosexuals are stigmatized, as shown by the degrading language often used to describe them. This makes forming a sexual identity a much greater challenge for gay, lesbian, and bisexual youths than for their heterosexual counterparts.

Wide variations in sexual identity formation exist, depending on personal, family, and community factors. Yet interviews with gay and lesbian adolescents and adults reveal that many (though not all) move through a three-phase sequence in coming out to themselves and others.

Feeling Different

Many gay men and lesbians recall feeling different from other children when they were young. Typically, this first sense of their biologically determined sexual orientation appears between ages 6 and 12, in play interests more like those of the other gender (Rahman & Wilson, 2003). Boys may find that they are less interested in sports, more drawn to quieter activities, and more emotionally sensitive than other boys; girls may find that they are more athletic and active than other girls.

By age 10, many of these children start to engage in *sexual questioning*—wondering why the typical heterosexual orientation does not apply to them. Often, they experience their sense of being different as deeply distressing. Compared with children who are confident of their homosexuality, sexual-questioning children report greater anxiety about peer relationships and greater dissatisfaction with their biological gender over time (Carver, Egan, & Perry, 2004).

Confusion

With the arrival of puberty, feeling different clearly encompasses feeling sexually different. In research on ethnically diverse gay, lesbian, and bisexual youths, awareness of a same-sex physical attraction occurred, on average, between ages 11 and 12 for boys and 14 and 15 for girls, perhaps because adolescent social pressures toward heterosexuality are particularly intense for girls (D'Augelli, 2006; Diamond, 1998).

Realizing that homosexuality has personal relevance generally sparks additional confusion. A few adolescents resolve their discomfort by crystalizing a gay, lesbian, or bisexual identity quickly, with a flash of insight into their sense of being different. But most experience an inner struggle and a deep sense of isolation—outcomes intensified by lack of role models and social support (D'Augelli, 2002; Safren & Pantalone, 2006).

Some throw themselves into activities they associate with heterosexuality. Boys may go out for athletic teams; girls may drop softball and basketball in favor of dance. And many homosexual youths (more females than males) try heterosexual dating, sometimes to hide their sexual orientation and at other times to develop intimacy skills that they later apply to same-sex relationships (D'Augelli, 2006; Dubé, Savin-Williams, & Diamond, 2001). Those who are extremely troubled and guilt-ridden may escape into alcohol, drugs, and suicidal thinking. Suicide attempts are unusually high among gay, lesbian, and bisexual young people (McDaniel, Purcell, & D'Augelli, 2001; Morrow, 2006).

Self-Acceptance

By the end of adolescence, the majority of gay, lesbian, and bisexual teenagers accept their sexual identity. But they face another crossroad: whether to tell others. Powerful stigma against their sexual orientation leads some to decide that disclosure is impossible: While self-defining as gay, they otherwise "pass" as heterosexual (Savin-Williams, 2001). When homosexual youths do come out, they often face intense hostility. In a study of over 500 gay, lesbian, and bisexual youths in Canada, New Zealand, and the United States, 75 percent reported being verbally abused, and 15 percent physically attacked, because of their sexual orientation (D'Augelli, 2002).

Nevertheless, many young people eventually acknowledge their sexual orientation publicly, usually by telling trusted friends first. Once teenagers establish a same-sex sexual or romantic relationship, many come out to parents. Few parents respond with severe rejection; most are either positive or slightly negative and disbelieving (Savin-Williams & Ream, 2003a). Parental understanding is the strongest predictor of favorable adjustment—including

These teens prepare to celebrate ALLY week, designed to encourage students to be allies against anti-lesbian, gay, bisexual, and transgender language, bullying, and harassment in America's schools. When peers react with acceptance, coming out strengthens the young person's view of homosexuality as a valid and fulfilling identity.

reduced *internalized homophobia,* or societal prejudice turned against the self (D'Augelli, Grossman, & Starks, 2005; Savin-Williams, 2003).

When people react positively, coming out strengthens the young person's view of homosexuality as a valid, meaningful, and fulfilling identity. Contact with other gays and lesbians is important for reaching this phase, and changes in society permit many adolescents in urban areas to attain it earlier than their counterparts did a decade or two ago. Gay and lesbian communities exist in large cities, but teenagers in small towns and rural areas may have difficulty meeting other homosexuals and finding a supportive environment. These adolescents have a special need for caring adults and peers who can help them find self- and social acceptance.

Gay, lesbian, and bisexual youths who succeed in coming out to themselves and others integrate their sexual orientation into a broader sense of identity, a process we will address in Section 6. As a result, they no longer need to focus so heavily on their homosexual self, and energy is freed for other aspects of psychological growth. In sum, coming out can foster many aspects of adolescent development, including self-esteem, psychological well-being, and relationships with family and friends.

COURTESY OF GLSEN.ORG

As the result of school courses and media campaigns, about 60 percent of U.S. middle-school students and 90 percent of high school students are aware of basic facts about AIDS. But most have limited understanding of other STDs, underestimate their own susceptibility, and are poorly informed about how to protect themselves (Coholl et al., 2001; Ethier et al., 2003). Furthermore, high school students report engaging in oral sex much more often than intercourse, and with more partners. But few report consistently using STD protection during oral sex, which is a significant mode of transmission of several STDs (Prinstein, Meade, & Cohen, 2003). Concerted efforts are needed to educate young people about the full range of STDs and risky sexual behaviors.

Adolescent Pregnancy and Parenthood

Cassie didn't get pregnant after having sex with Louis, but some of her classmates were less fortunate. An estimated 750,000 to 850,000 teenage girls in the United States—20 percent of those who have sexual intercourse—become pregnant annually, about 25,000 of them younger than age 15. Despite a steady decline since 1991, the U.S. adolescent pregnancy rate is much higher than that of any other industrialized country (see Figure 5.6). Three factors heighten the incidence of adolescent pregnancy: (1) Effective sex education reaches too few teenagers; (2) convenient, low-cost contraceptive services for adolescents are scarce; and (3) many families live in poverty, which encourages young people to take risks without considering the future implications of their behavior.

Because 40 percent of U.S. adolescent pregnancies end in abortion, the number of American teenage births is actually lower than it was 50 years ago (U.S. Department of Health and

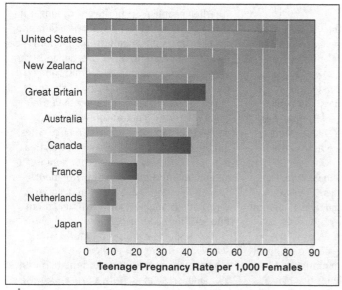

■ **FIGURE 5.6** ■ **Pregnancy rates among 15- to 19-year-olds in eight industrialized nations.** U.S. teenagers have the highest pregnancy rate. (Adapted from Alan Guttmacher Institute, 2001, 2006.)

Human Services, 2007a). But teenage parenthood is a much greater problem today because adolescents are far less likely to marry before childbirth. In 1960, only 15 percent of teenage births were to unmarried females, compared with 86 percent today (Child Trends, 2008). Increased social acceptance of single motherhood, along with the belief of many teenage girls that a baby might fill a void in their lives, means that very few girls give up their infants for adoption.

■ **CORRELATES AND CONSEQUENCES OF ADOLESCENT PARENTHOOD.** Becoming a parent is especially challenging for adolescents, who have not yet established a clear sense of direction for their own lives. Both life conditions and personal attributes jointly contribute to adolescent childbearing and also interfere with teenagers' capacity to parent effectively (Jaffee et al., 2001).

Teenage parents are far more likely to be poor than agemates who postpone parenthood. Their backgrounds often include low parental warmth and involvement, domestic violence and child abuse, repeated parental divorce and remarriage, adult models of early unmarried parenthood, and residence in neighborhoods where other adolescents also display these risks. Girls at risk for early pregnancy do poorly in school, engage in alcohol and drug use, have a childhood history of aggressive and antisocial behavior, associate with deviant peers, and experience high rates of depression (Elfenbein & Felice, 2003; Hillis et al., 2004; Luster & Haddow, 2005). A high percentage of out-of-wedlock births are to low-income ethnic minority teenagers. Many turn to early parenthood as a way to move into adulthood when educational and career avenues are unavailable.

After a baby is born, adolescents' lives often worsen in several respects:

- *Educational attainment.* Giving birth before age 18 reduces the likelihood of finishing high school. Only about 70 percent of U.S. adolescent mothers graduate, compared with 95 percent of girls who wait to become parents (National Women's Law Center, 2007).

- *Marital patterns.* Teenage motherhood reduces the chances of marriage and, for those who do marry, increases the likelihood of divorce compared with peers who delay childbearing (Moore & Brooks-Gunn, 2002). Consequently, teenage mothers spend more of their parenting years as single parents. About 35 percent become pregnant again within two years. Of these, about half go on to deliver a second child (Child Trends, 2008).

- *Economic circumstances.* Because of low educational attainment, marital instability, and poverty, many teenage mothers are on welfare. Limited education restricts many others to unsatisfying, low-paid jobs. Many adolescent fathers, too, are unemployed or work at unskilled jobs, usually earning too little to provide their children with basic necessities (Bunting & McAuley, 2004). And an estimated 50 percent have committed illegal offenses resulting in imprisonment (Elfenbein & Felice, 2003).

Because many pregnant teenage girls have inadequate diets, smoke, use alcohol and other drugs, and do not receive early prenatal care, their babies often experience prenatal and birth complications—especially low birth weight (Dell, 2001). And compared with adult mothers, adolescent mothers know less about child development, have unrealistically high expectations of infants, perceive their babies as more difficult, and interact less effectively with them (Moore & Florsheim, 2001; Pomerleau, Scuccimarri, & Malcuit, 2003). Their children tend to score low on intelligence tests, achieve poorly in school, and engage in disruptive social behavior.

Furthermore, teenage parents tend to pass on their personal attributes as well as create unfavorable child-rearing conditions. Consequently, their offspring are at risk for irresponsible sexual activity when they reach puberty. As the Lifespan Vista box on page 168 indicates, adolescent parenthood frequently is repeated in the next generation (Brooks-Gunn, Schley, & Hardy, 2002). Even when children born to teenage mothers do not become early child bearers, their development is often compromised, in terms of likelihood of high school graduation, financial independence in adulthood, and long-term physical and mental health (Moore, Morrison, & Green, 1997; Pogarsky, Thornberry, & Lizotte, 2006).

Still, outcomes vary widely. If a teenage parent finishes high school, secures gainful employment, avoids additional births, and finds a stable marriage partner, long-term disruptions in her own and her child's development will be less severe.

■ **PREVENTION STRATEGIES.** Preventing teenage pregnancy means addressing the many factors underlying early sexual activity and lack of contraceptive use. Too often, sex education courses are given late (after sexual activity has begun), last only a few sessions, and are limited to a catalog of facts about anatomy and reproduction. Sex education that goes beyond this minimum does not encourage early sex, as some opponents claim (Kirby, 2002c). It does improve awareness of sexual facts—knowledge that is necessary for responsible sexual behavior.

Knowledge, however, is not enough: Sex education must also help teenagers build a bridge between what they know and what they do. Effective sex education programs combine several key elements:

- They teach techniques for handling sexual situations—including refusal skills for avoiding risky sexual behaviors and communication skills for improving contraceptive use—through role-playing and other activities.

- They deliver clear, accurate messages that are appropriate in view of participating adolescents' culture and sexual experiences.

- They last long enough to have an impact.

- They provide specific information about contraceptives and ready access to them.

Many studies show that sex education with these components can delay the initiation of sexual activity, increase contraceptive use, change attitudes (for example, strengthen future orientation), and reduce pregnancy rates (Kirby, 2002b; Manlove et al., 2006; Thomas & Dimitrov, 2007).

Proposals to increase access to contraceptives are the most controversial aspect of adolescent pregnancy prevention. Many adults argue that placing birth control pills or condoms in the hands of teenagers is equivalent to approving of early sex. Yet sex education programs focusing on abstinence have little or no impact on delaying teenage sexual activity or on preventing pregnancy (Bennett & Assefi, 2005; Underhill, Montgomery, & Operario, 2007). And in Canada and Western Europe, where community- and school-based clinics offer adolescents contraceptives and where universal health insurance helps pay for them, teenage sexual activity is no higher than in the United States—but pregnancy, childbirth, and abortion rates are much lower (Schalet, 2007). Radio and TV campaigns promoting contraceptive use—used widely in Africa, Europe, India, and South America—are associated with a reduction in early sexual activity and with an increase in teenagers' use of birth control (Keller & Brown, 2002).

Efforts to prevent adolescent pregnancy and parenthood must go beyond improving sex education and access to contraception to build academic and social competence (Allen, Seitz, & Apfel, 2007). In one study, researchers randomly assigned at-risk high school students either to a year-long community service class, called Teen Outreach, or to regular classroom experiences in health or social studies. In Teen Outreach, adolescents spent at least 20 hours per week in volunteer work tailored to their interests. They returned to school for discussions that focused on enhancing their community service skills and their ability to cope with everyday challenges. At the end of the school year, pregnancy, school failure, and school suspension were substantially lower among participants in Teen Outreach, which fostered social skills, connection to the community, and self-respect (Allen et al., 1997).

Finally, teenagers who look forward to a promising future are far less likely to engage in early and irresponsible sex. By expanding educational, vocational, and employment opportunities, society can give young people good reasons to postpone childbearing.

■ **INTERVENING WITH ADOLESCENT PARENTS.** The most difficult and costly way to deal with adolescent parenthood is to wait until it happens. Young parents need health care, encouragement to stay in school, job training, instruction in parenting and life-management skills, and high-quality, affordable child care. Schools that provide these services reduce the incidence of low-birth-weight babies, increase educational success, and prevent additional childbearing (Barnet et al., 2004; Seitz & Apfel, 2005).

Adolescent mothers also benefit from relationships with family members who are sensitive to their developmental needs. Older teenage mothers display more effective parenting when they establish their own residence with the help of relatives—an arrangement that offers a balance of autonomy and support

■ A LIFESPAN VISTA: Looking Forward, Looking Back ■

Like Parent, Like Child: Intergenerational Continuity in Adolescent Parenthood

Does adolescent parenthood increase the chances of teenage childbearing in the next generation? To find out, researchers have conducted several unique studies of mothers (first generation)—some who gave birth as teenagers and some who postponed parenting—and their children (second generation), who were followed longitudinally for several decades (Barber, 2001b; Campa & Eckenrode, 2006; Hardy et al., 1998; Manlove, 1997).

First-generation mothers' age at first childbirth strongly predicted the age at which second-generation young people—both daughters and sons—became parents. Yet becoming a second-generation teenage parent is not inevitable for individuals born to an adolescent mother. Rather, adolescent parenthood is linked to a set of related, unfavorable family conditions and personal characteristics, which negatively influence development over an extended time and, therefore, often transfer to the next generation:

■ *Home environmental quality and parenting skills.* The long-term poverty and unstable marital patterns linked to adolescent parenthood reduce the quality of the home environment—in terms of organization, play and learning materials, and parental warmth, encouragement, verbal stimula-

tion, and acceptance of the child (as opposed to punitiveness and abuse). Compared with daughters in other families, the daughters of unmarried adolescent mothers live in families that obtain lower early childhood HOME scores (see page 32 in Section 1), even after mothers' prebirth SES is controlled (Campa & Eckenrode, 2006). Low HOME scores are associated with poorer language and IQ scores, which, in turn, contribute to the poor school performance and decision making associated with early sexual activity, laxity in use of contraceptives, and adolescent childbearing.

■ *Intelligence and education.* Younger mothers' cognitive deficits and reduced educational attainment contribute to the likelihood their children will experience long-term, poor-quality home environments and, thus, in adolescence will engage in the maladaptive behaviors just mentioned (Barber, 2001b; Hardy et al., 1998).

■ *Father absence.* In several studies, intergenerational continuity in adolescent parenthood—especially for daughters—was far greater when teenage mothers remained unmarried (Barber, 2001b; Campa & Eckenrode, 2006). Marriage may limit the negative impact of teenage childbearing on development by strengthening parental financial resources and involvement and reducing family stress. It may be particularly protective for girls because unmarried fathers are less likely

Will the child of this teenage mother also become an adolescent parent? Negative family conditions and personal characteristics associated with early childbearing increase the likelihood that adolescent parenthood will recur in the next generation.

to remain in regular contact with daughters than with sons. Recall from Section 4 that a warm, involved noncustodial father is linked to reduced early sexual activity in girls (see page 136).

In sum, a life course of adversity—poverty, depleted and disorganized home environments, poor parenting, father absence, intellectual deficits, poor academic performance, and limited educational opportunities—contributes to intergenerational continuity in adolescent pregnancy and parenthood.

(East & Felice, 1996). In one study, African-American teenage mothers who had a long-term "mentor" relationship—an aunt, neighbor, or teacher who provided emotional support and guidance—were far more likely than those without a mentor to stay in school and graduate (Klaw, Rhodes, & Fitzgerald, 2003).

Programs focusing on fathers attempt to increase their financial and emotional commitment to the baby. Although nearly half of young fathers visit their children during the first few years, contact usually diminishes. By the time the child starts school, fewer than one-fourth have regular paternal contact. As with teenage mothers, support from family members helps fathers stay involved (Bunting & McAuley, 2004). Teenage mothers who receive financial and child-care assistance and emotional support from their child's father are less

distressed and more likely to sustain a relationship with him (Cutrona et al., 1998; Gee & Rhodes, 2003). And infants with lasting ties to their teenage fathers show better long-term adjustment (Florsheim & Smith, 2005; Furstenberg & Harris, 1993).

Substance Use and Abuse

At age 14, Louis waited until he was alone at home, took some cigarettes from his uncle's pack, and smoked. At an unchaperoned party, he and Cassie drank several cans of beer and lit up marijuana joints. Louis got little physical charge out of these experiences. A good student, who was well-liked by peers and got along well with his parents, he did not need drugs as an escape valve. But he knew of other teenagers who started with

Encouragement from friends contributes to teenagers' alcohol and drug use and—among young people with family difficulties—increases the risk of drug abuse.

alcohol and cigarettes, moved on to harder substances, and eventually were hooked.

Teenage alcohol and drug use is pervasive in industrialized nations. According to the most recent, nationally representative survey of U.S. high school students, by tenth grade, 40 percent of U.S. young people have tried cigarette smoking, 63 percent drinking, and 38 percent at least one illegal drug (usually marijuana). At the end of high school, 17 percent smoke cigarettes regularly, 28 percent have engaged in heavy drinking during the past two weeks, and 40 percent have experimented with illegal drugs. About 20 percent have tried at least one highly addictive and toxic substance, such as amphetamines, cocaine, phencyclidine (PCP), Ecstasy (MDMA), inhalants, heroin, sedatives (including barbiturates), or OxyContin (a narcotic painkiller) (Johnston et al., 2008).

These figures represent a substantial decline since the mid-1990s, probably resulting from greater parent, school, and media focus on the hazards of drug use. But use of inhalants, sedatives, and OxyContin has risen in recent years (Johnston et al., 2008). Other drugs, such as LSD, PCP, and Ecstasy, have made a comeback as adolescents' knowledge of their risks faded.

In part, drug taking reflects the sensation seeking of the teenage years. But adolescents also live in drug-dependent cultural contexts. They see adults relying on caffeine to stay alert, alcohol and cigarettes to cope with daily hassles, and other remedies to relieve stress, depression, and physical discomfort. And compared to a decade or two ago, today doctors more often prescribe—and parents frequently seek—medication to treat children's problems (Brody, 2006). In adolescence, these young people may readily "self-medicate" when stressed. Furthermore, over 90 percent of teenagers say they are aware of cigarette and alcohol ads specifically targeting them, and most say these ads influence their behavior (Alcohol Concern, 2007).

The majority of teenagers who dabble in alcohol, tobacco, and marijuana are not headed for a life of addiction. These *minimal experimenters* are usually psychologically healthy, sociable, curious young people (Shedler & Block, 1990). As Figure 5.7 shows, tobacco and alcohol use is somewhat greater among European than U.S. adolescents, perhaps because European adults more often smoke and drink. But illegal drug use is far more prevalent among U.S. teenagers (Hibell, 2001). A greater percentage of American young people live in poverty, which is linked to family and peer contexts that promote illegal drug use. At the same time, use of diverse drugs is lower among African Americans than among Hispanic and Caucasian Americans; Native-American youths rank highest in drug taking (Johnston et al., 2008; Wallace et al., 2003). Researchers have yet to explain these variations.

Adolescent experimentation with any drug should not be taken lightly. Because most drugs impair perception and thought processes, a single heavy dose can lead to permanent injury or death. And a worrisome minority of teenagers move from substance use to abuse—taking drugs regularly, requiring increasing amounts to achieve the same effect, moving on to harder substances, and using enough to interfere with their ability to meet daily responsibilities.

■ **CORRELATES AND CONSEQUENCES OF ADOLESCENT SUBSTANCE ABUSE.** Unlike experimenters, drug abusers are seriously troubled young people. Their impulsive, disruptive, hostile style is often evident in early childhood, and they are inclined to express their unhappiness through antisocial acts. Compared with other young people, their drug taking starts

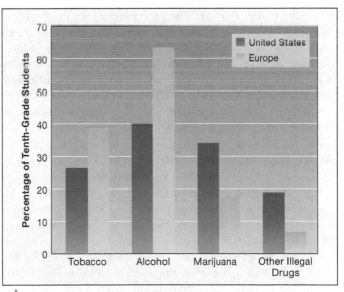

■ **FIGURE 5.7** ■ **Tenth-grade students in the United States and Europe who have used various substances.** Rates for tobacco and alcohol are based on any use in the past 30 days. Rates for marijuana and other illegal drugs are based on any lifetime use. Tobacco use and alcohol use are greater for European adolescents, whereas illegal drug use is greater for U.S. adolescents. (Adapted from Hibell, 2001; Johnston et al., 2008.)

earlier and may have genetic roots (Chassin et al., 2004; Ellickson et al., 2005). But environmental factors also contribute. These include low SES, family mental health problems, parental and older sibling drug abuse, lack of parental warmth and involvement, physical and sexual abuse, and poor school performance. Especially among teenagers with family difficulties, encouragement from friends who use and provide drugs increases substance abuse (Goldstein, Davis-Kean, & Eccles, 2005; Prinstein, Boergers, & Spirito, 2001).

Teenagers who depend on alcohol and hard drugs to deal with daily stresses fail to learn responsible decision-making skills and alternative coping techniques. They show serious adjustment problems, including chronic anxiety, depression, and antisocial behavior, that are both cause and consequence of heavy drug taking (Kassel et al., 2005; Simons-Morton & Haynie, 2003). And they often enter into marriage, childbearing, and the work world prematurely and fail at them—painful outcomes that further promote addictive behavior.

■ **PREVENTION AND TREATMENT.** School and community programs that reduce drug experimentation typically combine several components:

- They promote effective parenting, including monitoring of teenagers' activities.
- They teach skills for resisting peer pressure.
- They reduce the social acceptability of drug taking by emphasizing health and safety risks.
- They get adolescents to commit to not using drugs (Cuijpers, 2002; Griffin et al., 2003).

But because some drug taking seems inevitable, interventions that prevent teenagers from harming themselves and others when they do experiment are essential. Many communities offer weekend on-call transportation services that any young person can contact for a safe ride home, with no questions asked.

Because drug abuse has different roots than occasional use, different prevention strategies are required. One approach is to work with parents early, reducing family adversity and improving parenting skills, before children are old enough for drug involvement (Velleman, Templeton, & Copello, 2005). Programs that teach at-risk teenagers effective strategies for handling life stressors and that build competence through community service reduce alcohol and drug abuse, just as they reduce teenage pregnancy.

When an adolescent becomes a drug abuser, family and individual therapy are generally needed to treat maladaptive parent–child relationships, impulsivity, low self-esteem, anxiety, and depression. Academic and vocational training to improve life success also helps. But even comprehensive programs have alarmingly high relapse rates—from 35 to 85 percent (Brown & Ramo, 2005; Waldron, Turner, & Ozechowski, 2005). One recommendation is to start treatment gradually, through support-group sessions that focus on reducing drug taking (Myers et al., 2001). Modest improvements may increase young people's motivation to make longer-lasting changes through intensive treatment.

ASK YOURSELF

>> **REVIEW**
Compare risk factors for anorexia nervosa and bulimia nervosa. How do treatments and outcomes differ for the two disorders?

>> **APPLY**
After 17-year-old Veronica gave birth to Ben, her parents told her they didn't have room for the baby. Veronica dropped out of school and moved in with her boyfriend, who soon left. Why are Veronica and Ben likely to experience long-term hardships?

>> **CONNECT**
What unfavorable life experiences do teenagers who engage in early and frequent sexual activity have in common with those who abuse drugs?

>> **REFLECT**
Describe your experiences with peer pressure to experiment with alcohol and drugs. What factors influenced your response?

Cognitive Development

One mid-December evening, a knock at the front door announced the arrival of Franca and Antonio's oldest son, Jules, home for vacation after the fall semester of his sophomore year at college. The family gathered around the kitchen table. "How did it all go, Jules?" asked Antonio as he served slices of apple pie.

"Well, physics and philosophy were awesome," Jules responded with enthusiasm. "The last few weeks, our physics prof introduced us to Einstein's theory of relativity. Boggles my mind, it's so incredibly counterintuitive."

"Counter-what?" asked 11-year-old Sabrina.

"Counterintuitive. Unlike what you'd normally expect," explained Jules. "Imagine you're on a train, going unbelievably fast, like 160,000 miles a second. The faster you go, approaching the speed of light, the slower time passes and the denser and heavier things get relative to on the ground. The theory revolutionized the way we think about time, space, matter—the entire universe."

Sabrina wrinkled her forehead, baffled by Jules's otherworldly reasoning. "Time slows down when I'm bored, like right now, not on a train when I'm going somewhere exciting. No speeding train ever made me heavier, but this apple pie will if I eat any more of it," Sabrina announced, leaving the table.

Sixteen-year-old Louis reacted differently. "Totally cool, Jules. So what'd you do in philosophy?"

"It was a course in philosophy of technology. We studied the ethics of futuristic methods in human reproduction. For example, we argued the pros and cons of a world in which all embryos develop in artificial wombs."

"What do you mean?" asked Louis. "You order your kid at the lab?"

"That's right. I wrote my term paper on it. I had to evaluate it in terms of principles of justice and freedom. I can see some advantages but also lots of dangers...."

As this conversation illustrates, adolescence brings with it vastly expanded powers of reasoning. At age 11, Sabrina finds it difficult to move beyond her firsthand experiences to a world of possibilities. Over the next few years, her thinking will acquire the complex qualities that characterize the cognition of her older brothers. Jules considers multiple variables simultaneously and thinks about situations that are not easily detected in the real world or that do not exist at all. As a result, he can grasp advanced scientific and mathematical principles and grapple with social and political issues. Compared with school-age children's thinking, adolescent thought is more enlightened, imaginative, and rational.

Systematic research on adolescent cognitive development began with testing of Piaget's ideas (Keating, 2004). Recently, information-processing research has greatly enhanced our understanding.

Piaget's Theory: The Formal Operational Stage

According to Piaget, around age 11 young people enter the **formal operational stage,** in which they develop the capacity for abstract, systematic, scientific thinking. Whereas concrete operational children can "operate on reality," formal operational adolescents can "operate on operations." They no longer require concrete things and events as objects of thought. Instead, they can come up with new, more general logical rules through internal reflection (Inhelder & Piaget, 1955/1958). Let's look at two major features of the formal operational stage.

Hypothetico-Deductive Reasoning

Piaget believed that at adolescence, young people first become capable of **hypothetico-deductive reasoning.** When faced with a problem, they start with a *hypothesis,* or prediction about variables that might affect an outcome, from which they *deduce* logical, testable inferences. Then they systematically isolate and combine variables to see which of these inferences are confirmed in the real world. Notice how this form of problem solving begins with possibility and proceeds to reality. In contrast, concrete operational children start with reality—with the most obvious predictions about a situation. When these are not confirmed, they usually cannot think of alternatives and fail to solve the problem.

Adolescents' performance on Piaget's famous *pendulum problem* illustrates this approach. Suppose we present several school-age children and adolescents with strings of different lengths, objects of different weights to attach to the strings, and

■ **FIGURE 5.8** ■ **Piaget's pendulum problem.** Adolescents who engage in hypothetico-deductive reasoning think of variables that might possibly affect the speed with which a pendulum swings through its arc. Then they isolate and test each variable, as well as testing the variables in combination. Eventually they deduce that the weight of the object, the height from which it is released, and how forcefully it is pushed have no effect on the speed with which the pendulum swings through its arc. Only string length makes a difference.

a bar from which to hang the strings (see Figure 5.8). Then we ask each of them to figure out what influences the speed with which a pendulum swings through its arc.

Formal operational adolescents hypothesize that four variables might be influential: (1) the length of the string, (2) the weight of the object hung on it, (3) how high the object is raised before it is released, and (4) how forcefully the object is pushed. By varying one factor at a time while holding the other three constant, they test each variable separately and, if necessary, also in combination. Eventually they discover that only string length makes a difference.

In contrast, concrete operational children cannot separate the effects of each variable. They may test for the effect of string length without holding weight constant—comparing, for example, a short, light pendulum with a long, heavy one. Also, they typically fail to notice variables that are not immediately suggested by the concrete materials of the task—for example, how high the object is raised or how forcefully it is released.

Propositional Thought

A second important characteristic of Piaget's formal operational stage is **propositional thought**—adolescents' ability to evaluate the logic of propositions (verbal statements) without referring to real-world circumstances. In contrast, children can evaluate the logic of statements only by considering them against concrete evidence in the real world.

In Piaget's formal operational stage, adolescents engage in propositional thought. As these students discuss problems in a science class, they show that they can reason with symbols that do not necessarily represent objects in the real world.

In a study of propositional reasoning, a researcher showed children and adolescents a pile of poker chips and asked whether statements about the chips were true, false, or uncertain (Osherson & Markman, 1975). In one condition, the researcher hid a chip in her hand and presented the following propositions:

"*Either* the chip in my hand is green or it is not green."
"The chip in my hand is green *and* it is not green."

In another condition, the experimenter made the same statements while holding either a red or a green chip in full view.

School-age children focused on the concrete properties of the poker chips. When the chip was hidden, they replied that they were uncertain about both statements. When it was visible, they judged both statements to be true if the chip was green and false if it was red. In contrast, adolescents analyzed the logic of the statements. They understood that the "either-or" statement is always true and the "and" statement is always false, regardless of the chip's color.

Although Piaget did not view language as playing a central role in children's cognitive development (see Section 1), he acknowledged its importance in adolescence. Formal operations require language-based and other symbolic systems that do not stand for real things, such as those in higher mathematics. Secondary school students use such systems in algebra and geometry. Formal operational thought also involves verbal reasoning about abstract concepts. Jules was thinking in this way when he pondered relationships among time, space, and matter in physics and wondered about justice and freedom in philosophy.

Follow-Up Research on Formal Operational Thought

Research on formal operational thought poses questions similar to those we discussed with respect to Piaget's earlier stages: Does formal operational thinking appear earlier than Piaget

expected? Do all individuals reach formal operations during their teenage years?

■ **ARE CHILDREN CAPABLE OF HYPOTHETICO-DEDUCTIVE AND PROPOSITIONAL THINKING?** School-age children show the glimmerings of hypothetico-deductive reasoning, although they are less competent at it than adolescents. In simplified situations—ones involving no more than two possible causal variables—6-year-olds understand that hypotheses must be confirmed by appropriate evidence (Ruffman et al., 1993). But school-age children cannot sort out evidence that bears on three or more variables at once. And as we will see when we take up information-processing research, children have difficulty explaining why a pattern of observations supports a hypothesis, even when they recognize the connection between the two.

With respect to propositional thought, when a simple set of premises defies real-world knowledge ("All cats bark. Rex is a cat. Does Rex bark?"), 4- to 6-year-olds can reason logically in make-believe play. To justify their answer, they are likely to say, "We can pretend cats bark!" (Dias & Harris, 1988, 1990). But in an entirely verbal mode, children have great difficulty reasoning from premises that contradict reality or their own beliefs.

Consider this set of statements: "If dogs are bigger than elephants and elephants are bigger than mice, then dogs are bigger than mice." Children younger than 10 judge this reasoning to be false because some of the relations specified do not occur in real life (Moshman & Franks, 1986; Pillow, 2002). They have more difficulty than adolescents inhibiting activation of well-learned knowledge ("Elephants are larger than dogs") that casts doubt on the truthfulness of the premises (Klaczynski, Schuneman, & Daniel, 2004; Simoneau & Markovits, 2003). Partly for this reason, they fail to grasp the *logical necessity* of propositional reasoning—that the accuracy of conclusions drawn from premises rests on the rules of logic, not on real-world confirmation.

As with hypothetico-deductive reasoning, in early adolescence, young people become better at analyzing the *logic* of propositions irrespective of their *content*. And as they get older, they handle problems requiring increasingly complex mental operations. In justifying their reasoning, they more often explain the logical rules on which it is based (Müller, Overton, & Reese, 2001; Venet & Markovits, 2001). But these capacities do not appear suddenly at puberty. Rather, gains occur gradually from childhood on—findings that call into question the emergence of a discrete new stage of cognitive development at adolescence (Keating, 2004; Kuhn & Franklin, 2006; Moshman, 2005).

■ **DO ALL INDIVIDUALS REACH THE FORMAL OPERATIONAL STAGE?** *TAKE A MOMENT...* Try giving one or two of the formal operational tasks just described to your friends. How well do they do? Even many well-educated adults fail hypothetico-deductive tasks and have difficulty reasoning with sets of propositions that contradict real-world facts (Keating, 1979; Markovits & Vachon, 1990).

Why are so many adults not fully formal operational? One reason is that people are most likely to think abstractly and systematically on tasks in which they have had extensive guidance and practice in using such reasoning. This conclusion is supported by evidence that taking college courses leads to improvements in formal reasoning related to course content. Math and science prompt gains in propositional thought, social science in methodological and statistical reasoning (Lehman & Nisbett, 1990). Like concrete reasoning in children, formal operations do not emerge in all contexts at once but are specific to situation and task (Keating, 1990, 2004).

Individuals in tribal and village societies rarely master formal operational tasks (Cole, 1990). Piaget acknowledged that without the opportunity to solve hypothetical problems, people in some societies might not display formal operations. Still, these findings raise further questions about Piaget's stage sequence. Does formal operational thought largely result from children's and adolescents' independent efforts to make sense of their world, as Piaget claimed? Or is it a culturally transmitted way of thinking that is specific to literate societies and taught in school? In an Israeli study of middle school students, after controlling for participants' age, researchers found that years of schooling fully accounted for gains in propositional thought (Artman, Cahan, & Avni-Babad, 2006). School tasks, the investigators speculated, provide crucial experiences in setting aside the "if . . . then" logic of everyday conversations that is often used to convey intentions, promises, and threats ("If you don't do your chores, then you won't get your allowance") but that conflicts with the logic of academic reasoning. In school, then, adolescents encounter rich opportunities to realize their neurological potential to think more effectively.

An Information-Processing View of Adolescent Cognitive Development

Information-processing theorists refer to a variety of specific mechanisms, supported by brain development and experience, that underlie cognitive change in adolescence. Each was discussed in previous sections (Case, 1998; Kuhn & Franklin, 2006; Luna et al., 2004). Now let's draw them together:

- *Attention* becomes more selective (focused on relevant information) and better-adapted to the changing demands of tasks.

- *Inhibition*—both of irrelevant stimuli and of well-learned responses in situations where they are inappropriate—improves, supporting gains in attention and reasoning.

- *Strategies* become more effective, improving storage, representation, and retrieval of information.

- *Knowledge* increases, easing strategy use.

- *Metacognition* (awareness of thought) expands, leading to new insights into effective strategies for acquiring information and solving problems.

- *Cognitive self-regulation* improves, yielding better moment-by-moment monitoring, evaluation, and redirection of thinking.

- *Speed of thinking* and *processing capacity* increase. As a result, more information can be held at once in working memory and combined into increasingly complex, efficient representations, "opening possibilities for growth" in the capacities just listed and also improving as a result of gains in those capacities (Demetriou et al., 2002, p. 97).

As we look at influential findings from an information-processing perspective, we will see some of these mechanisms of change in action. And we will discover that researchers regard one of them—*metacognition*—as central to adolescent cognitive development.

Scientific Reasoning: Coordinating Theory with Evidence

During a free moment in physical education class, Sabrina wondered why more of her tennis serves and returns passed the net and dropped into her opponent's court when she used a particular brand of balls. "Is it something about their color or size?" she asked herself. "Hmm . . . or maybe it's their surface texture—that might affect their bounce."

The heart of scientific reasoning is coordinating theories with evidence. Deanna Kuhn (2002) has conducted extensive research into the development of scientific reasoning, using problems that, like Piaget's tasks, involve several variables that might affect an outcome. In one series of studies, third, sixth, and ninth graders and adults were first given evidence—sometimes consistent and sometimes conflicting with theories—and then questioned about the accuracy of each theory.

For example, participants were given a problem much like the one Sabrina posed. They were asked to theorize about which of several features of sports balls—size (large or small), color (light or dark), texture (rough or smooth), or presence or absence of ridges on the surface—influences the quality of a player's serve. Next, they were told about the theory of Mr. (or Ms.) S, who believes that the ball's size is important, and the theory of Mr. (or Ms.) C, who thinks color makes a difference. Finally, the interviewer presented evidence by placing balls with certain characteristics in two baskets, labeled "good serve" and "bad serve" (see Figure 5.9 on page 174).

The youngest participants often ignored conflicting evidence or distorted it in ways consistent with their preferred theory. Instead of viewing evidence as separate from and bearing on a theory, children often blend the two into a single representation of "the way things are." They are especially likely to overlook evidence that does not match their prior beliefs when a causal variable is implausible (like color affecting the performance of a sports ball) and when task demands (number of variables to be evaluated) are high (Zimmerman, 2005, 2007). The ability to distinguish theory from evidence and to use logical rules to examine their relationship improves steadily from childhood into adolescence, continuing into adulthood (Kuhn & Dean, 2004; Kuhn & Pearsall, 2000).

■ **FIGURE 5.9** ■ **Which features of these sports balls—size, color, surface texture, or presence or absence of ridges— influence the quality of a player's serve?** This set of evidence suggests that color might be important, since light-colored balls are largely in the good-serve basket and dark-colored balls in the bad-serve basket. But the same is true for texture! The good-serve basket has mostly smooth balls; the bad-serve basket, rough balls. Since all light-colored balls are smooth and all dark-colored balls are rough, we cannot tell whether color or texture makes a difference. But we can conclude that size and presence or absence of ridges are not important, since these features are equally represented in the good-serve and bad-serve baskets. (Adapted from Kuhn, Amsel, & O'Loughlin, 1988.)

How Scientific Reasoning Develops

What factors support skill at coordinating theory with evidence? Greater working-memory capacity, permitting a theory and the effects of several variables to be compared at once, is vital. Adolescents also benefit from exposure to increasingly complex problems and to teaching that highlights critical features of scientific reasoning—for example, why a scientist's expectations in a particular situation are inconsistent with everyday beliefs and experiences (Chinn & Malhotra, 2002). This explains why scientific reasoning is strongly influenced by years of schooling, whether individuals grapple with traditional scientific tasks (like the sports-ball problem) or engage in informal reasoning—for example, justifying a theory about what causes children to fail in school (Amsel & Brock, 1996).

Researchers believe that sophisticated *metacognitive understanding* is vital for scientific reasoning (Kuhn, 1999; Moshman, 1999). When adolescents regularly pit theory against evidence over many weeks, they experiment with various strategies, reflect on and revise them, and become aware of the nature of logic. Then they apply their appreciation of logic to an increasingly wide variety of situations. The ability to *think about* theories, *deliberately isolate* variables, and *actively seek* disconfirming evidence is rarely present before adolescence (Kuhn, 2000; Moshman, 1998).

But adolescents and adults vary widely in scientific reasoning skills. Many continue to show a self-serving bias, applying logic more effectively to ideas they doubt than to ideas they favor (Klaczynski, 1997; Klaczynski & Narasimham, 1998). Reasoning scientifically requires the metacognitive capacity to evaluate one's objectivity—to be fair-minded rather than self-serving (Moshman, 1999). As we will see in Section 6, this flexible, open-minded approach is not just a cognitive attainment

but a personality trait—one that assists teenagers greatly in forming an identity and developing morally.

Adolescents develop scientific reasoning skills in a similar step-by-step fashion on different types of tasks. In a series of studies, 10- to 20-year-olds were given sets of problems graded in difficulty. One set consisted of quantitative-relational tasks like the pendulum problem in Figure 5.8. Another contained propositional tasks like the poker chip problem on page 172. Still another set were causal-experimental tasks like the sports-ball problem in Figure 5.9 (Demetriou et al., 1993, 1996, 2002).

In each type of task, adolescents mastered component skills in sequential order by expanding their metacognitive awareness. For example, on causal-experimental tasks, they first became aware of the many variables that—separately and in combination—could influence an outcome. This enabled them to formulate and test hypotheses. Over time, adolescents combined separate skills into a smoothly functioning system, constructing a general model that they could apply to many instances of a given type of problem. In the researcher's words, young people seem to form a "hypercognitive system," or super-system, that understands, organizes, and influences other aspects of cognition (Demetriou & Kazi, 2001).

Piaget underscored the role of metacognition in formal operational thought when he spoke of "operating on operations" (see page 171). But information-processing findings confirm that scientific reasoning does not result from an abrupt, stagewise change. Instead, it develops gradually out of many specific experiences that require children and adolescents to match theories against evidence and reflect on and evaluate their thinking.

Consequences of Adolescent Cognitive Changes

The development of increasingly complex, effective thinking leads to dramatic revisions in the way adolescents see themselves, others, and the world in general. But just as adolescents are occasionally awkward in using their transformed bodies, they initially falter in their abstract thinking. Teenagers' self-concern, idealism, criticism, and indecisiveness, though perplexing to adults, are usually beneficial in the long run. Applying What We Know on the following page suggests ways to handle the everyday consequences of teenagers' newfound cognitive capacities.

Self-Consciousness and Self-Focusing

Adolescents' ability to reflect on their own thoughts, combined with physical and psychological changes, leads them to think more about themselves. Piaget believed that a new form of egocentrism arises, in which adolescents again have difficulty distinguishing their own and others' perspectives (Inhelder & Piaget, 1955/1958). Piaget's followers suggest that two distorted images of the relation between self and other appear.

Applying What We Know

Handling Consequences of Teenagers' New Cognitive Capacities

Thought expressed as . . .	Suggestion
Sensitivity to public criticism	Refrain from finding fault with the adolescent in front of others. If the matter is important, wait until you can speak to the teenager alone.
Exaggerated sense of personal uniqueness	Acknowledge the adolescent's unique characteristics. At opportune times, encourage a more balanced perspective by pointing out that you had similar feelings as a teenager.
Idealism and criticism	Respond patiently to the adolescent's grand expectations and critical remarks. Point out positive features of targets, helping the teenager see that all societies and people are blends of virtues and imperfections.
Difficulty making everyday decisions	Refrain from deciding for the adolescent. Model effective decision making and offer diplomatic suggestions about the pros and cons of alternatives, the likelihood of various outcomes, and learning from poor choices.

The first is called the **imaginary audience,** adolescents' belief that they are the focus of everyone else's attention and concern (Elkind & Bowen, 1979). As a result, they become extremely self-conscious. When Sabrina woke up one Sunday morning with a large pimple on her chin, her first thought was, "I can't possibly go to church! Everyone will notice how ugly I look." The imaginary audience helps explain why adolescents spend long hours inspecting every detail of their appearance and why they are so sensitive to public criticism. To teenagers, who believe that everyone is monitoring their performance, a critical remark from a parent or teacher can be mortifying.

A second cognitive distortion is the **personal fable.** Certain that others are observing and thinking about them, teenagers develop an inflated opinion of their own importance—a feeling that they are special and unique. Many adolescents view themselves as reaching great heights of omnipotence and also sinking to unusual depths of despair—experiences that others cannot possibly understand (Elkind, 1994). One teenager wrote in her diary, "My parents' lives are so ordinary, so stuck in a rut. Mine will be different. I'll realize my hopes and ambitions." Another, upset when a boyfriend failed to return her affections, rebuffed her mother's comforting words: "Mom, you don't know what it's like to be in love!"

Although imaginary-audience and personal-fable ideation is common in adolescence, these distorted visions of the self do not result from egocentrism, as Piaget suggested. Rather, they are partly an outgrowth of advances in perspective taking, which cause young teenagers to be more concerned with what others think (Vartanian & Powlishta, 1996).

In fact, certain aspects of the imaginary audience may serve positive, protective functions. When asked why they worry about the opinions of others, adolescents responded that others' evaluations have important *real* consequences—for self-esteem, peer acceptance, and social support (Bell & Bromnick, 2003). The idea that others care about their appearance and behavior also has emotional value, helping teenagers hold onto important relationships as they struggle to establish an independent sense of self (Vartanian, 1997).

With respect to the personal fable, in a study of sixth through tenth graders, sense of omnipotence predicted self-esteem and overall positive adjustment. Viewing the self as highly capable and influential may help young people cope with challenges of adolescence. In contrast, sense of personal uniqueness was modestly associated with depression and suicidal thinking (Aalsma, Lapsley, & Flannery, 2006). Focusing on the distinctiveness of one's own experiences may interfere with forming close, rewarding relationships, which provide social support in stressful times. And when combined with a sensation-seeking personality, the personal fable seems to contribute to adolescent risk taking by reducing teenagers' sense of vulnerability. Young people with high personal-fable and sensation-seeking scores tend to take more sexual risks, more often use drugs, and commit more delinquent acts than their agemates (Greene et al., 2000).

© STUART HUGHS/GETTY IMAGES/STONE

The personal fable leads adolescents to view themselves as special and unique. When combined with a sensation-seeking personality, it seems to reduce teenagers' sense of vulnerability and contribute to risky behaviors.

Idealism and Criticism

Adolescents' capacity to think about possibilities opens up the world of the ideal. Teenagers can imagine alternative family, religious, political, and moral systems, and they want to explore them. They often construct grand visions of a world with no injustice, discrimination, or tasteless behavior. The disparity between teenagers' idealism and adults' greater realism creates tension between parent and child. Envisioning a perfect family against which their parents and siblings fall short, adolescents become fault-finding critics.

Overall, however, teenage idealism and criticism are advantageous. Once adolescents come to see other people as having both strengths and weaknesses, they have a much greater capacity to work constructively for social change and to form positive and lasting relationships (Elkind, 1994).

Decision Making

Adolescents handle many cognitive tasks more effectively than they did when younger. But in their everyday decision making, they often do not think rationally: (1) identifying the pros and cons of each alternative, (2) assessing the likelihood of various outcomes, (3) evaluating their choice in terms of whether their goals were met and, if not, (4) learning from the mistake and making a better future decision. In one study of decision making, researchers gave adolescents and adults hypothetical dilemmas—whether to have cosmetic surgery, which parent to live with after divorce—and asked them to explain how they would decide. Adults outperformed adolescents, more often considering alternatives, weighing benefits and risks, and suggesting advice seeking (Halpern-Felsher & Cauffman, 2001).

Furthermore, in making decisions, adolescents, more often than adults (who also have difficulty), fall back on well-learned intuitive judgments (Jacobs & Klaczynski, 2002). Consider a hypothetical problem requiring a choice, on the basis of two arguments, between taking a traditional lecture class and taking a computer-based class. One argument contains large-sample information: course evaluations from 150 students, 85 percent of whom liked the computer class. The other argument contains small-sample personal reports: complaints of two honor-roll students who both hated the computer class and enjoyed the traditional class. Most adolescents, even those who knew that selecting the large-sample argument was "more intelligent," based their choice on the small-sample argument, which resembled the informal opinions they depend on in everyday life (Klaczynski, 2001).

Why is decision making so challenging for adolescents? As "first-timers" at many experiences, they do not have sufficient knowledge to predict potential outcomes. They also face many complex situations involving competing goals, such as how to maintain social status while avoiding getting drunk at a party. In unfamiliar circumstances and when making a good decision would mean inhibiting "feel-good" behavior (smoking, overeating, unsafe sex), adolescents are far more likely than adults

These high school students attending a college fair will face many choices over the next few years. In unfamiliar situations, teenagers are more likely than adults to fall back on intuitive judgments rather than to use sound decision-making strategies.

to emphasize short-term over long-term goals (Amsel et al., 2005; Boyer, 2006; Reyna & Farley, 2006). Furthermore, teenagers often feel overwhelmed by their expanding range of options—abundant school courses, extracurricular activities, social events, and material goods. As a result, their efforts to choose frequently break down, and they resort to habit, act on impulse, or postpone decisions.

Over time, young people learn from their successes and failures, gather information from others about factors that affect decision making, and reflect on the decision-making process (Byrnes, 2003; Jacobs & Klaczynski, 2002). Consequently, their confidence and performance improve. Still, errors in decision making remain common in adulthood.

ASK YOURSELF

>> **REVIEW**
Describe research findings that challenge Piaget's notion of a new, discrete stage of cognitive development at adolescence.

>> **APPLY**
Clarissa, age 14, is convinced that no one appreciates how hurt she feels at not being invited to the homecoming dance. Meanwhile, 15-year-old Justine, alone in her room, pantomimes being sworn in as student body president with her awestruck parents looking on. Which aspect of the personal fable is each girl displaying? Which girl is more likely to be well-adjusted, which poorly adjusted? Explain.

>> **CONNECT**
How does evidence on adolescent decision making help us understand teenagers' risk taking in sexual activity and drug use?

>> **REFLECT**
Do you recall engaging in idealistic thinking or poor decision making as a teenager? Cite examples.

Sex Differences in Mental Abilities

Sex differences in mental abilities have sparked almost as much controversy as the ethnic and SES differences in IQ considered in Section 3. Although boys and girls do not differ in general intelligence, they do vary in specific mental abilities.

Verbal Abilities

Throughout the school years, girls attain higher scores in reading achievement and account for a lower percentage of children referred for remedial reading instruction. Girls continue to score slightly higher on tests of verbal ability in middle childhood and adolescence in every country in which assessments have been conducted (Halpern, 2000, 2004; Mullis et al., 2007). And when verbal tests are heavily weighted with writing, girls' advantage is large (Halpern et al., 2007).

A special concern is that girls' advantage in reading and writing achievement increases in adolescence, with boys doing especially poorly in writing—trends evident in the United States and other industrialized nations (see Figure 5.10) (OECD, 2008a; Statistics Canada, 2006a; U.S. Department of Education, 2007c, 2007d). These differences are believed to be major contributors to a widening gender gap in college enrollments. Thirty years ago, males accounted for 60 percent of North American undergraduate students; today, they are in the minority, at 42 percent (Statistics Canada, 2006a; U.S. Department of Education, 2009).

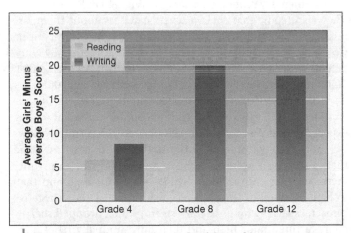

■ FIGURE 5.10 ■ Reading and writing achievement score gaps favoring girls at grades 4, 8, and 12. Findings are based on the U.S. National Assessment of Educational Progress. The bars represent the average girls' score minus the average boys' score. Thus, the height of the bar indicates the extent to which girls outperform boys, a difference that increases in adolescence. By grades 8 and 12, girls have an especially large advantage in writing skill. Similar trends are evident in other industrialized nations. (Adapted from U.S. Department of Education, 2007c, 2007d.)

That girls show a biological advantage in earlier development of the left hemisphere of the cerebral cortex, where language is usually localized. And fMRI research indicates that in tackling language tasks (such as deciding whether two spoken or written words rhyme), 9- to 15-year-old girls show concentrated activity in language-specific brain areas. Boys, in contrast, display more widespread activation—in addition to language areas, considerable activity in auditory and visual areas, depending on how words are presented (Burman, Bitan, & Booth, 2007). This suggests that girls are more efficient linguistic processors than boys, who rely heavily on sensory brain regions and process spoken and written words differently.

Girls also receive more verbal stimulation from mothers from the preschool years through adolescence (Peterson & Roberts, 2003). Furthermore, children view language arts as a "feminine" subject. And as a result of the high-stakes testing movement, students today spend more time at their desks being taught in a regimented way—an approach particularly at odds with boys' higher activity level, assertiveness, and incidence of learning problems.

Finally, high divorce and out-of-wedlock birth rates mean that more children today grow up without the continuous presence of a father who models and encourages good work habits and skill at reading and writing. Both maternal and paternal involvement contributes to the achievement and educational attainment of adolescents of both genders (Flouri & Buchanan, 2004). But some research suggests that high-achieving African-American boys are particularly likely to come from homes in which fathers are warm, verbally communicative, and demanding of achievement (Grief, Hrabowski, & Maton, 1998). Clearly, reversing boys' weakening literacy skills is a high priority, requiring a concerted effort by families, schools, and communities.

Mathematics

Studies of mathematical abilities in the early school grades are inconsistent. Some find no sex differences, others slight disparities depending on the skill assessed (Lachance & Mazzocco, 2006). Girls tend to be advantaged in arithmetic computation, perhaps because of their better verbal skills and more methodical approach to problem solving. But around early adolescence, when math concepts become more abstract and spatial, boys start to outperform girls. The difference is especially evident on tests of complex reasoning and geometry (Bielinski & Davison, 1998). In science achievement, too, boys' advantage increases as problems become more difficult (Penner, 2003).

This male advantage is evident in virtually every country where males and females have equal access to secondary education, but the gap is small and has diminished over the past 30 years (Bussière, Knighton, & Pennock, 2007; Halpern, Wai, & Saw, 2005; U.S. Department of Education, 2007a). Among the most capable, however, the gender gap is greater. In widely publicized research on more than 100,000 bright seventh and eighth graders invited to take the Scholastic Assessment Test (SAT), boys outscored girls on the mathematics subtest year after year. Yet even this disparity has been shrinking. A quarter-century ago, 13 times as many boys as girls scored over 700 (out of a possible 800) on the math portion of the SAT; today, the ratio is 2.8 to 1 (Benbow & Stanley, 1983; Monastersky, 2005).

Some researchers believe that heredity contributes substantially to the gender gap in math, especially to the tendency for more boys to be extremely talented. Accumulating evidence indicates that boys' advantage originates in two skill areas: (1) their more rapid numerical memory, which permits them to devote more energy to complex mental operations; and (2) their superior spatial reasoning, which enhances their mathematical problem solving (Geary et al., 2000; Halpern et al., 2007). (See the Biology and Environment box on the following page for discussion of this issue.)

Social pressures are also influential. Long before sex differences in math achievement appear, many children view math as a "masculine" subject. Also, many parents think boys are better at it—an attitude that encourages girls to blame their errors on lack of ability and to consider math less useful for their future lives. These beliefs, in turn, reduce girls' confidence and interest in math and their willingness to consider math- or science-related careers (Bhanot & Jovanovic, 2005; Bleeker & Jacobs, 2004; Kenney-Benson et al., 2006). Furthermore, *stereotype threat*—fear of being judged on the basis of a negative stereotype (see page 102 in Section 3)—causes females to do worse than their abilities allow on difficult math problems (Ben-Zeev et al., 2005; Muzzatti & Agnoli, 2007). As a result of these influences, even girls who are highly talented are less likely to develop effective math reasoning skills.

A positive sign is that today, boys and girls reach advanced levels of high school math and science study in equal proportions—a crucial factor in reducing sex differences in knowledge and skill (Gallagher & Kaufman, 2005). But boys spend more time than girls with computers, and they tend to use them differently. Whereas girls typically focus on e-mail, instant messaging, and gathering information for homework assignments, boys more often write computer programs, analyze data, and use graphics programs (Freeman, 2004; Looker & Thiessen, 2003). As a result, boys acquire more specialized computer knowledge.

Clearly, extra steps must be taken to promote girls' interest in and confidence at math and science. When parents hold nonstereotyped beliefs, daughters are less likely to avoid math and science and more likely to achieve well (Updegraff, McHale, & Crouter, 1996). And a math curriculum beginning in kindergarten that teaches children how to apply effective spatial strategies—drawing diagrams, mentally manipulating visual images, searching for numerical patterns, and graphing—is vital (Nuttal, Casey, & Pezaris, 2005). Because girls are biased toward verbal processing, they may not realize their math and science potential unless they are taught how to think spatially.

Learning in School

In complex societies, adolescence coincides with entry into secondary school. Most young people move into either a middle or a junior high school and then into a high school. With each change, academic achievement increasingly determines higher education options and job opportunities. In the following sections, we take up various aspects of secondary school life.

School Transitions

When Sabrina started junior high, she left a small, intimate, self-contained sixth-grade classroom for a much larger school. "I don't know most of the kids in my classes, and my teachers don't know me," Sabrina complained to her mother at the end of the first week. "Besides, there's too much homework. I get assignments in all my classes at once. I can't do all this!" she shouted, bursting into tears.

■ **IMPACT OF SCHOOL TRANSITIONS.** As Sabrina's reactions suggest, school transitions can create adjustment problems. With each school change—from elementary to middle or junior high and then to high school—adolescents' grades decline. The drop is partly due to tighter academic standards. At the same time, the transition to secondary school often means less personal attention, more whole-class instruction, and less chance to participate in classroom decision making (Seidman, Aber, & French, 2004).

It is not surprising, then, that students rate their middle or junior high school learning experiences less favorably than their elementary school experiences (Wigfield & Eccles, 1994). They also report that their teachers care less about them, are less friendly, grade less fairly, and stress competition more. Consequently, many young people feel less academically competent, and their motivation declines (Barber & Olsen, 2004; Gutman & Midgley, 2000; Otis, Grouzet, & Pelletier, 2005).

Inevitably, students must readjust their feelings of self-confidence and self-worth as they encounter revised academic expectations and a more complex social world. A study following more than 300 students from sixth to tenth grade revealed that grade point average declined and feelings of anonymity increased after each school change—to junior high and then to high school. But the earlier transition had a more negative impact, especially on girls' self-esteem, which dropped sharply after starting junior high and then only gradually rebounded (Simmons & Blyth, 1987). Girls fared less well, the researchers argued, because movement to junior high tended to coincide with other life changes: the onset of puberty and dating. Adolescents facing added strains—family disruption, poverty, low parental involvement, or learned helplessness on academic tasks—are at greatest risk for self-esteem and academic difficulties (de Bruyn, 2005; Rudolph et al., 2001; Seidman et al., 2003).

■ BIOLOGY AND ENVIRONMENT ■

Sex Differences in Spatial Abilities

Spatial skills are a key focus of researchers' efforts to explain sex differences in mathematical reasoning. The gender gap favoring males is large for *mental rotation tasks,* in which individuals must rotate a three-dimensional figure rapidly and accurately inside their heads (see Figure 5.11). Males also do considerably better on *spatial perception tasks,* in which people must determine spatial relationships by considering the orientation of the surrounding environment. Sex differences on *spatial visualization tasks,* involving analysis of complex visual forms, are weak or nonexistent. Because many strategies can be used to solve these tasks, both sexes may come up with effective procedures (Collaer & Hill, 2006; Voyer, Voyer, & Bryden, 1995).

Sex differences in spatial abilities emerge in early childhood, persist throughout the lifespan, and are evident in many cultures (Levine et al., 1999; Silverman, Choi, & Peters, 2007). The pattern is consistent enough to suggest a biological explanation. One hypothesis is that heredity, perhaps through exposure to androgen hormones, enhances right hemispheric functioning, giving males a spatial advantage. (Recall that for most people, spatial skills are housed in the right hemisphere of the cerebral cortex.) In support of this idea, girls and women whose prenatal androgen levels were abnormally high show superior performance on spatial rotation tasks (Berenbaum, 2001; Halpern & Collaer, 2005). And in some studies, spatial performance varies with daily and annual androgen levels in both men and women (Temple & Carney, 1995; Van Goozen et al., 1995).

Why might a biologically based sex difference in spatial abilities exist? Evolutionary theorists point out that mental rotation skill predicts rapid, accurate map drawing and interpretation, areas in which boys and men do better than girls and women. Over the course of human evolution, the cognitive abilities of males became adapted for hunting, which required generating mental representations of large-scale spaces to find one's way (Jones, Braithwaite, & Healy, 2003). But this explanation is controversial: Critics point out that female gatherers also needed to travel long distances to find fruits and vegetables that ripened in different seasons (Newcombe, 2007).

Experience also contributes to males' superior spatial performance. Children who engage in manipulative activities, such as block play, model building, and carpentry, do better on spatial tasks (Baenninger & Newcombe, 1995). Furthermore, playing video games that require rapid mental rotation of visual images enhances spatial scores (Subrahmanyam & Greenfield, 1996; Terlecki

When provided with the necessary encouragement and educational experiences, girls are capable of top-level achievement in math and science. In 2007, high school senior Isha Jain won first prize in the prestigious Siemens Competition in Math, Science, and Technology for her breakthrough discovery of a cellular mechanism that underlies bone growth spurts. She aspires to lead a research lab focusing on biology and math.

& Newcombe, 2005). Boys spend far more time than girls at these pursuits.

In studies of middle and high school students, *both* spatial abilities and self-confidence at doing math were related to performance on complex math problems, with spatial skills being the stronger predictor (Casey, Nuttall, & Pezaris, 1997, 2001). Boys are advantaged in both spatial performance and math self-confidence. Still, spatial skills respond readily to training, with improvements often larger than the sex differences themselves. But because boys and girls show similar training effects, sex differences persist (Newcombe & Huttenlocher, 2006). In sum, biology and environment *jointly* explain variations in spatial and math performance—both within and between the sexes.

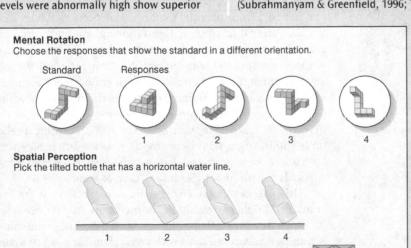

Mental Rotation
Choose the responses that show the standard in a different orientation.

Standard   Responses

1   2   3   4

Spatial Perception
Pick the tilted bottle that has a horizontal water line.

1   2   3   4

Spatial Visualization
Find the figure embedded in this complex shape.

■ **FIGURE 5.11** ■ **Types of spatial tasks.** Large sex differences favoring males appear on mental rotation, and males do considerably better than females on spatial perception. In contrast, sex differences on spatial visualization are weak or nonexistent. (From M. C. Linn & A. C. Petersen, 1985, "Emergence and Characterization of Sex Differences in Spatial Ability: A Meta-Analysis," *Child Development, 56,* pp. 1482, 1483, 1485. © The Society for Research in Child Development. Reprinted with permission.)

Distressed young people whose school performance either remains low or drops sharply after school transition often show a persisting pattern of poor self-esteem, motivation, and achievement. In another study, researchers compared "multiple-problem" youths (those having both academic and mental health problems), youths having difficulties in just one area (either academic or mental health), and well-adjusted youths (those doing well in both areas) across the transition to high school. Although all groups declined in grade point average, well-adjusted students continued to get high marks and multiple-problem youths low marks, with the others falling in between. And as Figure 5.12 shows, the multiple-problem youths showed a far greater rise in truancy and out-of-school problem behaviors (Roeser, Eccles, & Freedman-Doan, 1999). For some, school transition initiates a downward spiral in academic performance and school involvement that leads to dropping out.

■ HELPING ADOLESCENTS ADJUST TO SCHOOL TRANSITIONS.
As these findings reveal, school transitions often lead to environmental changes that fit poorly with adolescents' developmental needs (Eccles, 2004). They disrupt close relationships with teachers at a time when adolescents need adult support. They emphasize competition during a period of heightened self-focusing. They reduce decision making and

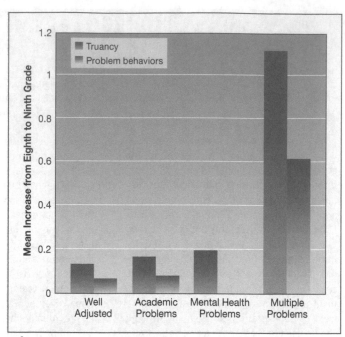

■ **FIGURE 5.12** ■ **Increase in truancy and out-of-school problem behaviors across the transition to high school in four groups of students.** Well-adjusted students, students with only academic problems, and students with only mental health problems showed little change. (Good students with mental health problems actually declined in problem behaviors, so no purple bar is shown for them.) In contrast, multiple-problem students—with both academic and mental health difficulties—increased sharply in truancy and problem behaviors after changing schools from eighth to ninth grade. (Adapted from Roeser, Eccles, & Freedman-Doan, 1999.)

This seventh grader hurries at his locker so he won't be late for class at his new middle school. Moving from a small, self-contained elementary school classroom to a large, impersonal secondary school is stressful for adolescents.

© DWIGHT CENDROWSKI, WWW.CENDROWSKI.COM

choice as the desire for autonomy is increasing. And they interfere with peer networks as young people become more concerned with peer acceptance.

Support from parents, teachers, and peers can ease these strains. Parental involvement, monitoring, gradual autonomy granting, and emphasis on mastery rather than merely good grades are associated with better adjustment (Grolnick et al., 2000; Gutman, 2006). Adolescents with close friends are more likely to sustain these friendships across the transition, which increases social integration and academic motivation in the new school (Aikens, Bierman, & Parker, 2005). Forming smaller units within larger schools promotes closer relationships with both teachers and peers and—as we will see later—greater extracurricular involvement (Seidman, Aber, & French, 2004).

Other, less extensive changes are also effective. In the first year after a school transition, homerooms can be provided in which teachers offer academic and personal counseling. Assigning students to classes with several familiar peers or a constant group of new peers strengthens emotional security and social support. In schools that took these steps, students were less likely to decline in academic performance or display other

Applying What We Know

Supporting High Achievement During Adolescence

Factor	Description
Child-rearing practices	Authoritative parenting
	Joint parent–adolescent decision making
	Parent involvement in the adolescent's education
Peer influences	Peer valuing of and support for high achievement
School characteristics	Teachers who are warm and supportive, develop personal relationships with parents, and show them how to support their teenager's learning
	Learning activities that encourage high-level thinking
	Active student participation in learning activities and classroom decision making
Employment schedule	Job commitment limited to less than 15 hours per week
	High-quality vocational education for non-college-bound adolescents

adjustment problems, including low self-esteem, substance abuse, delinquency, and dropping out (Felner et al., 2002).

Finally, teenagers' perceptions of the sensitivity and flexibility of their school learning environments contribute substantially to successful school transitions. When schools minimize competition and differential treatment based on ability, middle school students are less likely to feel angry and depressed, to be truant, or to show declines in academic values, self-esteem, and achievement (Roeser, Eccles, & Sameroff, 2000).

Academic Achievement

Adolescent achievement is the result of a long history of cumulative effects. Early on, positive educational environments, both family and school, lead to personal traits that support achievement—intelligence, confidence in one's own abilities, the desire to succeed, and high educational aspirations. Nevertheless, improving an unfavorable environment can foster resilience among poorly performing young people. See Applying What We Know above for a summary of environmental factors that enhance achievement during the teenage years.

■ **CHILD-REARING PRACTICES.** Authoritative parenting is linked to higher grades in school among adolescents varying widely in SES, just as it predicts mastery-oriented behavior in childhood. In contrast, authoritarian and permissive styles are associated with lower grades (Collins & Steinberg, 2006; Vazsonyi, Hibbert, & Snider, 2003). Uninvolved parenting (low in both warmth and maturity demands) predicts the poorest grades and worsening school performance over time (Glasgow et al., 1997; Kaisa, Stattin, & Nurmi, 2000).

The link between authoritative parenting and adolescents' academic competence has been confirmed in countries with diverse value systems, including Argentina, Australia, China, Hong Kong, Pakistan, and Scotland (de Bruhn, Deković, & Meijnen, 2003; Steinberg, 2001). In Section 2, we noted that authoritative parents adjust their expectations to children's capacity to take responsibility for their own behavior. Adolescents whose parents engage in joint decision making, gradually permitting more autonomy with age, achieve especially well (Spera, 2005; Wang, Pomerantz, & Chen, 2007). Warmth, open discussion, firmness, and monitoring of the adolescents' whereabouts and activities make young people feel cared about and valued, encourage reflective thinking and self-regulation, and increase awareness of the importance of doing well in school. These factors, in turn, are related to mastery-oriented attributions, effort, achievement, and high educational aspirations (Aunola, Stattin, & Nurmi, 2000; Gregory & Weinstein, 2004; Trusty, 1999).

■ **PARENT–SCHOOL PARTNERSHIPS.** High-achieving students typically have parents who keep tabs on their child's progress, communicate with teachers, and make sure that their child is enrolled in challenging, well-taught classes. These efforts are just as important during middle and high school as they were earlier (Hill & Taylor, 2004). In a large, nationally representative sample of U.S. adolescents, parents' school involvement in eighth grade strongly predicted students' grade point average in tenth grade, beyond the influence of SES and previous academic achievement. This relationship held for each ethnic group included—black, white, Native-American, and Asian (Keith et al., 1998). Parents who are in frequent contact with the school send their teenager a message about the value of educa-

This parent is involved in his adolescent son's schooling. By keeping tabs on his progress, the father sends a message to his child about the importance of education and teaches skills for solving academic problems.

tion, model constructive solutions to academic problems, and promote wise educational decisions.

The daily stresses of living in low-income, high-risk neighborhoods reduce parents' energy for school involvement (Bowen, Bowen, & Ware, 2002). Yet stronger home–school links could relieve some of this stress. Schools can build parent–school partnerships by strengthening personal relationships between teachers and parents, tapping parents' talents to improve the quality of school programs, and including parents in school governance so they remain invested in school goals.

■ **PEER INFLUENCES.** Peers play an important role in adolescent achievement, in a way that relates to both family and school. Teenagers whose parents value achievement generally choose friends who share those values (Rubin, Bukowski, & Parker, 2006). For example, when Sabrina began to make new friends in junior high, she often studied with her girlfriends. Each girl wanted to do well and reinforced this desire in the others.

Peer support for high achievement also depends on the overall climate of the peer culture, which, for ethnic minority youths, is powerfully affected by the surrounding social order. In one study, integration into the school peer network predicted higher grades among Caucasians and Hispanics but not among Asians and African Americans (Faircloth & Hamm, 2005). Asian cultural values stress respect for family and teacher expectations over close peer ties (Chao & Tseng, 2002; Chen, 2005). African-American minority adolescents may observe that their ethnic group is worse off than the white majority in educational attainment, jobs, income, and housing. And discriminatory treatment by teachers and peers, often resulting from stereotypes that they are "not intelligent," triggers anger,

anxiety, self-doubt, declines in achievement, association with peers who are not interested in school, and increases in problem behaviors (Wong, Eccles, & Sameroff, 2003).

Yet not all economically disadvantaged minority students respond this way. Case studies of inner-city, poverty-stricken African-American adolescents who were high-achieving and optimistic about their future revealed that they were intensely aware of oppression but believed in striving to alter their social position (O'Connor, 1997). How did they develop this sense of agency? Parents, relatives, and teachers had convinced them through discussion and example that injustice should not be tolerated and that, together, African Americans could overcome it—a perspective that encouraged both strong ethnic identity and high academic motivation, even in the face of peer pressures against excelling academically.

■ **SCHOOL CHARACTERISTICS.** Adolescents need school environments that are responsive to their expanding powers of reasoning and their emotional and social needs. Without appropriate learning experiences, their cognitive potential is unlikely to be realized.

Classroom Learning Experiences. As noted earlier, in large, departmentalized secondary schools, many adolescents report that their classes lack warmth and supportiveness—a circumstance that dampens their motivation. One study tracked changes in students' academic orientation in math classes from seventh to eighth grade. Those who entered classrooms high in teacher support, encouragement of student interaction about academic work, and promotion of mutual respect among classmates gained in academic motivation and cognitive self-regulation (reflected in whether they understood concepts and in their willingness to check their work). In classrooms emphasizing competition and public comparison of students, declines in motivation and self-regulation occurred (Ryan & Patrick, 2001).

Of course, an important benefit of separate classes in each subject is that adolescents can be taught by experts, who are more likely to encourage high-level thinking, teach effective learning strategies, and emphasize content relevant to students' experiences—factors that promote interest, effort, and achievement (Eccles, 2004). But many secondary school classrooms do not consistently provide interesting, challenging teaching. Because of the uneven quality of instruction, many seniors graduate from high school deficient in basic academic skills. Although the achievement gap separating African-American, Hispanic, and Native-American students from white students has declined since the 1970s, mastery of reading, writing, mathematics, and science by low-SES ethnic minority students remains disappointing (U.S. Department of Education, 2007b, 2007c, 2007d). Too often these young people attend underfunded schools with rundown buildings, outdated equipment, and textbook shortages. In some, crime and discipline problems receive more attention than teaching and learning. By middle school, many low-SES minority students have been placed in low academic tracks, compounding their learning difficulties.

Tracking. Ability grouping, as we saw in Section 3, is detrimental during the elementary school years. At least into middle or junior high school, mixed-ability classes are desirable. They effectively support the motivation and achievement of students who vary widely in academic progress (Gillies, 2003; Gillies & Ashman, 1996).

By high school, some grouping is unavoidable because certain aspects of education must dovetail with the young person's future educational and vocational plans. In the United States, high school students are counseled into college preparatory, vocational, or general education tracks. Unfortunately, low-SES minority students are assigned in large numbers to noncollege tracks, perpetuating educational inequalities of earlier years.

Longitudinal research following thousands of U.S. students from eighth to twelfth grade reveals that assignment to a college preparatory track accelerates academic progress, whereas assignment to a vocational or general education track decelerates it (Hallinan & Kubitschek, 1999). Even in secondary schools with no formal tracking program, low-SES minority students tend to be assigned to lower course levels in most or all academic subjects, resulting in *de facto* (unofficial) *tracking* (Lucas & Behrends, 2002).

Breaking out of a low academic track is difficult. Track or course enrollment is generally based on past performance, which is limited by placement history. Interviews with African-American students in one high school revealed that many thought their previous performance did not reflect their ability. Yet teachers and counselors, overburdened with other responsibilities, had little time to reconsider individual cases (Ogbu, 2003). And compared to students in higher tracks, those in low tracks exert substantially less effort—a difference due in part to less stimulating classroom experiences (Carbonaro, 2005).

High school students are separated into academic and vocational tracks in virtually all industrialized nations. In China, Japan, and most Western European countries, students' placement in high school is determined by their performance on a national exam. The outcome usually fixes the young person's future possibilities. In the United States, students who are not assigned to a college preparatory track or who do poorly in high school can still attend college. Ultimately, however, many young people do not benefit from the more open U.S. system. By adolescence, SES differences in quality of education and academic achievement are greater in the United States than in most other industrialized countries (Marks, Cresswell, & Ainley, 2006). And the United States has a higher percentage of young people who see themselves as educational failures and drop out of high school (see Figure 5.13).

■ **PART-TIME WORK.** In high school, nearly half of U.S. adolescents are employed—a greater percentage than in other developed countries (Bowlby & McMullen, 2002; Children's Defense Fund, 2008). Most are middle-SES adolescents in pur-

suit of spending money rather than vocational exploration and training. Low-income teenagers who need to contribute to family income or to support themselves find it harder to get jobs (U.S. Department of Education, 2009).

Adolescents typically hold jobs that involve low-level, repetitive tasks and provide little contact with adult supervisors. A heavy commitment to such jobs is harmful. The more hours students work, the poorer their school attendance, the lower their grades, the less likely they are to participate in extracurricular activities, and the more likely they are to drop out (Marsh & Kleitman, 2005). Students who spend many hours at such jobs also tend to feel more distant from their parents and report more drug and alcohol use and delinquent acts (Kouvonen & Kivivuori, 2001; Staff & Uggen, 2003).

In contrast, participation in work–study programs or other jobs that provide academic and vocational learning opportunities is related to positive school and work attitudes, improved achievement, and reduced delinquency (Hamilton & Hamilton, 2000; Staff & Uggen, 2003). Yet high-quality vocational preparation for non-college-bound U.S. adolescents is scarce. Unlike some European nations, the United States has no widespread training system to prepare youths for skilled business and industrial occupations and manual trades. Although U.S. federal and state governments support some job-training programs, most are too brief to make a difference. Poorly skilled adolescents need intensive training and academic remediation before they are ready to enter the job market. And at present, these programs serve only a small minority of young people who need assistance.

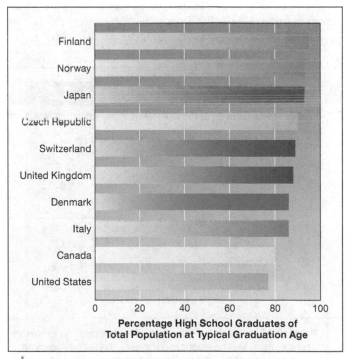

Finland
Norway
Japan
Czech Republic
Switzerland
United Kingdom
Denmark
Italy
Canada
United States

0   20   40   60   80   100

**Percentage High School Graduates of
Total Population at Typical Graduation Age**

■ **FIGURE 5.13** ■ **High school graduation rates in ten industrialized nations.** The United States ranks below many other developed countries. (From OECD, 2008a.)

Dropping Out

Across the aisle from Louis in math class sat Norman, who day-dreamed, crumpled his notes into his pocket after class, and rarely did his homework. On test days, he twirled a rabbit's foot for good luck but left most questions blank. Louis and Norman had been classmates since fourth grade, but they had little to do with each other. To Louis, who was quick at schoolwork, Norman seemed to live in another world. Once or twice a week, Norman cut class; one spring day, he stopped coming altogether.

Norman is one of about 10 percent of U.S. 16- to 24-year-olds who dropped out of high school and remain without a diploma or a GED (U.S. Department of Education, 2009). The dropout rate is higher among boys than girls and is particularly high among low-SES ethnic minority youths, especially Native-American and Hispanic teenagers (see Figure 5.14). The decision to leave school has dire consequences. Youths without upper secondary education have much lower literacy scores than high school graduates; they lack the skills employers value in today's knowledge-based economy. Consequently, dropouts have much lower employment rates than high school graduates. Even when employed, dropouts are far more likely to remain in menial, low-paying jobs and to be out of work from time to time.

■ **FACTORS RELATED TO DROPPING OUT.** Although many dropouts achieve poorly and show high rates of norm-violating acts, a substantial number are like Norman—young people with few behavior problems who simply experience academic difficulties and quietly disengage from school (Janosz et al., 2000; Newcomb et al., 2002). The pathway to dropping out starts early. Risk factors in first grade predict dropout nearly as well as risk factors in secondary school (Entwisle, Alexander, & Olson, 2005).

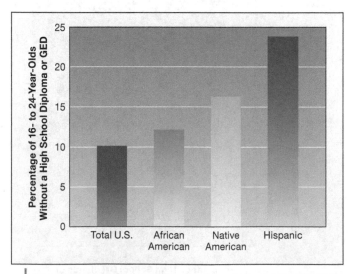

■ **FIGURE 5.14** ■ **U.S. high school dropout rates by ethnicity.** Because many African-American, Hispanic, and Native-American young people come from low-income and poverty-stricken families and attended underfunded, poor-quality schools, their dropout rates are above the national average. Rates for Native-American and Hispanic youths are especially high. (From U.S. Department of Education, 2009.)

Norman had a long history of marginal-to-failing school grades and low academic self-esteem. Faced with a challenging task, he gave up, relying on luck—his rabbit's foot—to get by. As Norman got older, he attended class less regularly, paid little attention when he was there, and rarely did his homework. He didn't join school clubs or participate in sports. As a result, few teachers or students got to know him well. By the day he left, Norman felt alienated from all aspects of school life.

As with other dropouts, Norman's family background contributed to his problems. Compared with other students, even those with the same grade profile, dropouts are more likely to have parents who are uninvolved in their teenager's education and engage in little monitoring of their youngster's daily activities. Many are single parents, never finished high school themselves, and are unemployed (Englund, Egeland, & Collins, 2008; Pagani et al., 2008).

Academically marginal students who drop out often have school experiences that undermine their chances for success: grade retention, which marks them as academic failures; large, impersonal secondary schools; and classes with unsupportive teachers and few opportunities for active participation (Hardre & Reeve, 2003; Lee & Burkam, 2003). In such schools, rule breaking is common and often results in suspension, which—by excluding students from classes—contributes further to academic failure (Christie, Jolivette, & Nelson, 2007). Recent reports indicate that over 60 percent of adolescents in some U.S. inner-city high schools do not graduate. Students in general education and vocational tracks, where teaching tends to be the least stimulating, are three times as likely to drop out as those in a college preparatory track (U.S. Department of Education, 2009).

■ **PREVENTION STRATEGIES.** Among the diverse strategies available for helping teenagers at risk of dropping out, several common themes are related to success:

- *Remedial instruction and counseling that offer personalized attention.* Most potential dropouts need intensive remedial instruction in small classes that foster warm, caring teacher–student relationships. To overcome the negative psychological effects of repeated school failure, academic assistance must be combined with social support (Christenson & Thurlow, 2004). In one successful approach, at-risk students are matched with retired adults, who serve as tutors, mentors, and role models in addressing academic and vocational needs (Prevatt, 2003).

- *High-quality vocational training.* For many marginal students, the real-life nature of vocational education is more comfortable and effective than purely academic work. To work well, vocational education must carefully integrate academic and job-related instruction so students see the relevance of classroom experiences to their future goals (Harvey, 2001).

- *Efforts to address the many factors in students' lives related to leaving school early.* Programs that strengthen parent involvement, offer flexible work–study arrangements, and provide on-site child care for teenage parents can make staying in school easier for at-risk adolescents.

AP IMAGES/CAROLYN KASTER

A baking and pastry student puts the finishing touches on a cake at a technical high school in Pennsylvania. High-quality vocational education, integrated with academic instruction, helps students at risk for dropping out see the relevance of school learning to their future goals.

■ *Participation in extracurricular activities.* Another way of helping marginal students is to draw them into the community life of the school. The most powerful influence on extracurricular involvement is small school size (Barker & Gump, 1964; Feldman & Matjasko, 2007). In high schools of 500 to 700 students or less, potential dropouts are far more likely to be needed to help staff and operate school activities. In large schools, creation of smaller "schools within schools" has the same effect.

Participation focusing on the arts, community service, and vocational development promotes diverse aspects of adjustment, including improved academic performance, reduced antisocial behavior, more favorable self-esteem and initiative, and increased peer acceptance (Fredricks & Eccles, 2005, 2006; Mahoney, 2000). Adolescents with academic, emotional, and social problems are especially likely to benefit (Marsh & Kleitman, 2002).

As we conclude our discussion of academic achievement, let's place the school dropout problem in historical perspective. Over the past half-century, the percentage of U.S. young people completing high school by age 24 increased steadily, from less than 50 percent to 90 percent. College attendance also rose during this period: Today, nearly 40 percent of U.S. young people earn college degrees. Despite the worrisome decline in male college enrollment noted earlier, U.S. higher education rates continue to rank among the highest in the world (U.S. Department of Education, 2007a).

Finally, although many dropouts get caught in a vicious cycle in which their lack of self-confidence and skills prevents them from seeking further education and training, about one-third return to finish their secondary education within a few years (U.S. Department of Education, 2008). And some extend their schooling further, realizing how essential education is for a rewarding job and a satisfying adult life.

ASK YOURSELF

>> **REVIEW**
List ways that parents can promote their adolescent's academic achievement. Explain why each is effective.

>> **APPLY**
Tanisha is finishing sixth grade. She can either continue in her current school through eighth grade or switch to a much larger seventh- to ninth-grade middle school. Which choice would you suggest, and why?

>> **CONNECT**
How are educational practices that prevent school dropout similar to those that improve learning for adolescents in general?

>> **REFLECT**
Describe your own experiences in making the transition to middle or junior high school and then to high school. What did you find stressful? What helped you adjust?

Summary

PHYSICAL DEVELOPMENT

Conceptions of Adolescence

How have conceptions of adolescence changed over the past century?

>> **Adolescence** is the period of transition between childhood and adulthood. Early theorists viewed adolescence as either a biologically determined period of storm and stress or entirely influenced by the social

environment. Contemporary research shows that adolescence is a product of biological, psychological, and social forces.

Puberty: The Physical Transition to Adulthood

Describe pubertal changes in body size, proportions, motor performance, and sexual maturity.

>> Hormonal changes beginning in middle childhood initiate **puberty,** on average,

two years earlier for girls than for boys. The first outward sign is the **growth spurt.** As the body enlarges, girls' hips and boys' shoulders broaden. Girls add more fat, boys more muscle. Puberty brings improvement in gross motor performance—slow and gradual for girls, more dramatic for boys. Nevertheless, the number of adolescents participating in regular physical activity declines sharply with age.

AP IMAGES/THE ALBUQUERQUE JOURNAL, MARLA BROSE

>> At puberty, changes in **primary** and **secondary sexual characteristics** accompany rapid body growth. **Menarche** occurs late in the girl's sequence of pubertal events, after the growth spurt peaks. In boys, the peak in growth occurs later, preceded by enlargement of the sex organs and **spermarche.**

What factors influence the timing of puberty?

>> Heredity, nutrition, exercise, and overall physical health contribute to pubertal timing. A **secular trend** toward earlier menarche has occurred in industrialized nations as physical well-being increased.

What changes in the brain take place during adolescence?

>> Pruning of unused synapses in the cerebral cortex continues in adolescence, and growth and myelination of stimulated neural fibers accelerate, supporting cognitive advances. Also, neurons become more responsive to excitatory neurotransmitters, a change that probably contributes to teenagers' drive for novel experiences.

>> Changes also occur in brain regulation of sleep timing, leading to a sleep "phase delay." Sleep deprivation increases, contributing to poorer achievement, depressed mood, and behavior problems.

The Psychological Impact of Pubertal Events

Explain adolescents' reactions to the physical changes of puberty.

>> Girls generally react to menarche with mixed emotions, although those who receive advance information and support from family members respond more positively. Although boys usually know ahead of time about spermarche, they also react with mixed feelings. Boys receive less social support for pubertal changes than girls.

>> Besides higher hormone levels, negative life events and adult-structured situations are associated with adolescents' negative moods. In contrast, teenagers feel upbeat when with peers and in self-chosen leisure activities.

>> Psychological distancing between parent and child accompanies puberty. It may be a modern substitute for physical departure from the family, which typically occurs at sexual maturity in primate species.

Describe the impact of pubertal timing on adolescent adjustment, noting sex differences.

>> Early-maturing boys and late-maturing girls, whose appearance closely matches cultural standards of physical attractiveness, have a more positive **body image** and usually adjust well in adolescence. In contrast, early-maturing girls and late-maturing boys, who fit in least well with peers, experience emotional and social difficulties, which—for girls—persist into early adulthood.

Health Issues

Describe nutritional needs during adolescence, and cite factors that contribute to eating disorders.

>> Nutritional requirements increase with rapid body growth. Poor eating habits lead to vitamin and mineral deficiencies in many adolescents. Frequency of family meals is associated with healthy eating.

>> Early puberty, certain personality traits, maladaptive family interactions, and societal emphasis on thinness heighten risk of eating disorders such as **anorexia nervosa** and **bulimia nervosa.**

Discuss factors that influence adolescent sexual attitudes and behavior.

>> North American attitudes toward adolescent sex remain relatively restrictive, and the social environment—parents, schools, and mass media—delivers contradictory messages. Compared with a generation ago, U.S. adolescents' sexual attitudes and behavior have become more liberal, with a slight swing back recently.

© JEFF GREENBERG/PHOTOEDIT

>> Early, frequent sexual activity is linked to factors associated with economic disadvantage. Many sexually active teenagers do not practice contraception consistently. Adolescent cognitive processes and a lack of social support for responsible sexual behavior, including access

to birth control, underlie this failure to take precautions against pregnancy.

>> Biological factors, including heredity and prenatal hormone levels, play an important role in homosexuality. Lesbian and gay teenagers face special challenges in developing a positive sexual identity.

>> Early sexual activity combined with inconsistent contraceptive use results in high rates of sexually transmitted diseases (STDs) among U.S. adolescents.

Discuss factors related to adolescent pregnancy and parenthood.

>> Adolescent pregnancy and parenthood rates are higher in the United States than in any other industrialized nation. Life conditions linked to economic disadvantage, along with personal attributes, contribute to adolescent childbearing. Adolescent parenthood is associated with school dropout, reduced chances of marriage, greater likelihood of divorce, and poverty.

>> Effective sex education, access to contraceptives, and programs that build academic and social competence help prevent early pregnancy. Adolescent mothers need school programs that provide job training, instruction in life-management skills, child care, and family support that is sensitive to their needs. When teenage fathers stay involved, children develop more favorably.

What personal and social factors are related to adolescent substance use and abuse?

>> Teenage alcohol and drug use is pervasive in industrialized nations, reflecting the sensation seeking of adolescence as well as a drug-dependent cultural context. The minority who move to substance abuse often start drug-taking early, display other antisocial behaviors, and come from families with mental health problems. Effective prevention programs work with parents early, to reduce family adversity and strengthen parenting skills, and build teenagers' competence.

COGNITIVE DEVELOPMENT

Piaget's Theory: The Formal Operational Stage

What are the major characteristics of formal operational thought?

>> During Piaget's **formal operational stage,** adolescents engage in **hypothetico-deductive reasoning.** When faced with a problem, they start with a hypothesis about variables that might affect an outcome, deduce logical, testable inferences, and systematically isolate and combine variables to see which inferences are confirmed.

>> **Propositional thought** also develops. Adolescents can evaluate the logic of verbal statements apart from real-world circumstances.

Discuss follow-up research on formal operational thought and its implications for the accuracy of Piaget's formal operational stage.

>> Adolescents and adults are most likely to think abstractly and systematically in situations in which they have had extensive guidance and practice in using such reasoning. Individuals in tribal and village societies rarely master formal operational tasks. Piaget's highest stage seems to depend on specific learning opportunities made available in school.

An Information-Processing View of Adolescent Cognitive Development

How do information-processing researchers account for cognitive changes in adolescence?

>> Information-processing researchers believe that a variety of specific mechanisms underlie cognitive gains in adolescence: improved attention and inhibition, more effective strategies, greater knowledge, improved cognitive self-regulation, gains in speed of thinking and processing capacity, and, especially, advances in metacognition.

>> Research on scientific reasoning indicates that the ability to coordinate theory with evidence improves as adolescents solve increasingly complex problems and reflect on their thinking, acquiring more mature metacognitive understanding.

Consequences of Adolescent Cognitive Changes

Describe typical reactions of adolescents that result from their advancing cognition.

>> As adolescents reflect on their own thoughts, they think more about themselves, and two distorted images of the relation between self and other appear—the **imaginary audience** and the **personal fable.** Teenagers' capacity to think about possibilities prompts idealistic visions at odds with everyday reality, and they often become fault-finding critics.

>> Compared with adults, adolescents have difficulty with decision making. They more often fall back on well-learned, intuitive judgments and emphasize short-term over long-term goals.

© BOB DAEMMRICH/THE IMAGE WORKS

Sex Differences in Mental Abilities

What factors contribute to sex differences in mental abilities during adolescence?

>> Girls score slightly better than boys on tests of verbal ability, and their advantage in reading and writing achievement increases, probably due to earlier development of the left hemisphere of the cerebral cortex and greater maternal verbal stimulation. Gender-stereotyping of language arts as "feminine" and regimented teaching may weaken boys' literacy skills.

>> Boys surpass girls in complex mathematical reasoning. Overall, the gender difference is small, but it is greater among the most capable students. Boys' biologically based superior spatial skills enhance their mathematical problem solving. Gender stereotyping of math as "masculine" and self-confidence and interest in doing math contribute to boys' spatial and math advantages.

Learning in School

Discuss the impact of school transitions on adolescent adjustment.

>> Girls experience more adjustment difficulties than boys after transitioning to middle or

junior high school because other life changes (puberty and the beginning of dating) also occur at that time. Teenagers coping with added stresses—especially those with both academic and mental health difficulties—are at greatest risk for adjustment problems following school transition.

Discuss family, peer, school, and employment influences on academic achievement during adolescence.

>> Authoritative parenting and parents' school involvement promote high achievement. Teenagers whose parents encourage achievement are likely to choose friends from similar families.

>> Warm, supportive learning environments with activities that emphasize high-level thinking enable adolescents to reach their academic potential.

>> By high school, separate educational tracks that dovetail with students' future plans are necessary. But high school tracking in the United States often extends the educational inequalities of earlier years.

>> The more hours students devote to a part-time job, the poorer their school attendance, academic performance, and extracurricular participation. In contrast, work–study programs that provide academic and vocational learning opportunities predict positive school and work attitudes and better academic achievement among non-college-bound teenagers.

What factors increase the risk of high school dropout?

>> About 10 percent of U.S. young people leave high school and remain without a diploma, many of whom are low-SES minority youths. Contributing factors include a long history of poor school performance, lack of parental support for academic achievement, large impersonal classes, and unstimulating teaching.

Important Terms and Concepts

adolescence (p. 149)
anorexia nervosa (p. 160)
body image (p. 158)
bulimia nervosa (p. 161)
formal operational stage (p. 171)
growth spurt (p. 151)

hypothetico-deductive reasoning (p. 171)
imaginary audience (p. 175)
menarche (p. 154)
personal fable (p. 175)
primary sexual characteristics (p. 153)

propositional thought (p. 171)
puberty (p. 149)
secondary sexual characteristics (p. 153)
secular trend (p. 155)
spermarche (p. 154)

As adolescents spend less time with family, peer groups become more tightly knit into cliques. Mixed-sex cliques provide boys and girls with models of how to interact and a chance to do so without having to be intimate.

Emotional and Social Development in Adolescence

Louis sat on the grassy hillside overlooking the high school, waiting for his best friend, Darryl, to arrive from his fourth-period class. The two boys often met at noontime and had lunch together. Watching as hundreds of students poured onto the school grounds, Louis reflected on what he had learned in government class that day. "Suppose I *had* been born in the People's Republic of China. I'd be sitting here, speaking a different language, being called by a different name, and thinking about the world in different ways. Wow," Louis pondered. "I am who I am through some quirk of fate."

Louis awoke from his thoughts with a start to see Darryl standing in front of him. "Hey, dreamer! I've been shouting and waving from the bottom of the hill for five minutes. How come you're so spaced out lately, Louis?"

"Oh, just wondering about stuff—what I want, what I believe in. My older brother Jules—I envy him. He seems to know more about where he's going. I'm up in the air about it. You ever feel that way?"

"Yeah, a lot," Darryl admitted, looking at Louis seriously. "I wonder, what am I really like? Who will I become?"

Louis and Darryl's introspective remarks are signs of a major reorganization of the self at adolescence: the development of identity. Both young people are attempting to formulate who they are—their personal values and the directions they will pursue in life.

We begin this section with Erikson's account of identity development and the research it has stimulated on teenagers' thoughts and feelings about themselves. The quest for identity extends to many aspects of development. We will see how a sense of cultural belonging, moral understanding, and masculine and feminine self-images are refined during adolescence. And as parent–child relationships are revised and young people become increasingly independent of the family, friendships and peer networks become crucial contexts for bridging the gap between childhood and adulthood. Our section concludes with a discussion of several serious adjustment problems of adolescence: depression, suicide, and delinquency.

© MARY KATE DENNY/PHOTOEDIT

Erikson's Theory: Identity versus Role Confusion

Erikson (1950, 1968) was the first to recognize **identity** as the major personality achievement of adolescence and as a crucial step toward becoming a productive, content adult. Constructing an identity involves defining who you are, what you value, and the directions you choose to pursue in life. One expert described it as an explicit theory of oneself as a rational agent—one who acts on the basis of reason, takes responsibility for those actions, and can explain them (Moshman, 2005). This search for what is true and real about the self drives many choices—vocation, interpersonal relationships, community involvement, ethnic-group membership, and expression of one's sexual orientation, as well as moral, political, and religious ideals.

Although the seeds of identity formation are planted early, not until late adolescence and early adulthood do young people become absorbed in this task. According to Erikson, in complex societies, teenagers experience an *identity crisis*—a temporary period of distress as they experiment with alternatives before settling on values and goals. They go through a process of inner soul-searching, sifting through characteristics that defined the self in childhood and combining them with emerging traits, capacities, and commitments. Then they mold these into a solid inner core that provides a mature identity—a sense of self-continuity as they move through various roles in daily life. Once formed, identity continues to be refined in adulthood as people reevaluate earlier commitments and choices.

Erikson called the psychological conflict of adolescence **identity versus role confusion.** If young people's earlier conflicts were resolved negatively or if society limits their choices to ones that do not match their abilities and desires, they may appear shallow, directionless, and unprepared for the challenges of adulthood.

Current theorists agree with Erikson that questioning of values, plans, and priorities is necessary for a mature identity, but they no longer describe this process as a "crisis" (Grotevant, 1998; Kroger, 2005). For most young people, identity development is not traumatic and disturbing but, rather, a process of *exploration* followed by *commitment*. As young people try out life possibilities, they gather important information about themselves and their environment and move toward making enduring decisions. In doing so, they forge an organized self-structure (Arnett, 2000, 2006; Moshman, 2005). In the following sections, we will see that adolescents go about the task of defining the self in ways that closely match Erikson's description.

Self-Understanding

During adolescence, the young person's vision of the self becomes more complex, well-organized, and consistent. Compared with younger children, adolescents have more or less positive feelings about an increasing variety of aspects of the self. Over time, they form a balanced, integrated representation of their strengths and limitations (Harter, 2003, 2006). Changes in self-concept and self-esteem set the stage for developing a unified personal identity.

Changes in Self-Concept

Recall that by the end of middle childhood, children can describe themselves in terms of personality traits. In early adolescence, they unify separate traits ("smart," "talented") into more abstract descriptors ("intelligent"). But these generalizations are not interconnected and are often contradictory. For example, 12- to 14-year-olds might mention opposing traits—"intelligent" and "dork," "shy" and "outgoing." These disparities result from the expansion of adolescents' social world, which creates pressure to display different selves in different contexts—self with mother, father, close friends, and romantic partner; self as student, athlete, and employee. As teenagers become increasingly aware of inconsistencies, they agonize over "which is the real me" (Harter, 1998, 2003, 2006).

From middle to late adolescence, cognitive changes enable teenagers to combine their traits into an organized system. Their use of qualifiers ("I have a *fairly* quick temper," "I'm not *thoroughly* honest") reveals their awareness that psychological qualities can vary from one situation to the next. Older adolescents also add integrating principles that make sense out of formerly troublesome contradictions. "I'm very adaptable," said one young person. "When I'm around my friends, who think what I say is important, I'm talkative; but around my family I'm quiet because they're never interested enough to really listen to me" (Damon, 1990, p. 88).

Compared with school-age children, teenagers place more emphasis on social virtues, such as being friendly, considerate, kind, and cooperative—traits that reflect adolescents' increasing concern with being viewed positively by others. Among older adolescents, personal and moral values also appear as key themes. As young people revise their views of themselves to include enduring beliefs and plans, they move toward the unity of self that is central to identity development.

Changes in Self-Esteem

Self-esteem, the evaluative side of self-concept, continues to differentiate in adolescence. Teenagers add several new dimensions of self-evaluation—close friendship, romantic appeal, and job competence—to those of middle childhood (see Section 4, page 119) (Harter, 1999, 2003, 2006).

Level of self-esteem also changes. Though some adolescents experience temporary or persisting declines after school transitions (see Section 5, pages 178 and 180), self-esteem rises for most young people, who report feeling especially good about their peer relationships and athletic capabilities (Cole et al., 2001; Twenge & Campbell, 2001). Teenagers often assert that they have become more mature, capable, personable, and attractive than in the past. In a study of adolescents in 13 industrialized nations, most were optimistic, felt a sense of control over their personal and vocational futures, and expressed

During adolescence, self-esteem rises for most young people, who feel especially good about their peer relationships and athletic capabilities.

confidence in their ability to cope with life's problems (Grob & Flammer, 1999).

At the same time, individual differences in self-esteem become increasingly stable in adolescence (Trzesniewski, Donnellan, & Robins, 2003). And positive relationships among self-esteem, valuing of various activities, and success at those activities strengthen. For example, academic self-esteem is a powerful predictor of teenagers' judgments of the importance and usefulness of school subjects, willingness to exert effort, achievement, and eventual career choice (Bleeker & Jacobs, 2004; Denissen, Zarrett, & Eccles, 2007; Valentine, DuBois, & Cooper, 2004; Whitesell et al., 2009).

Across SES and ethnic groups, individuals with mostly favorable self-esteem profiles tend to be well-adjusted, sociable, and conscientious. In contrast, low self-esteem in all areas is linked to adjustment difficulties (DuBois et al., 1999; Robins et al., 2001). But certain self-esteem factors are more strongly related to adjustment. Teenagers who feel highly dissatisfied with parental relationships often are aggressive and antisocial. Those with poor academic self-esteem tend to be anxious and unfocused. And those with negative peer relationships are likely to be anxious and depressed (Marsh, Parada, & Ayotte, 2004; Rudolph, Caldwell, & Conley, 2005).

In adolescence as in childhood, authoritative parenting predicts high self-esteem, as does encouragement from teachers (Carlson, Uppal, & Prosser, 2000; McKinney, Donnelly, & Renk, 2008; Wilkinson, 2004). In contrast, teenagers whose parents are critical and insulting have unstable and generally low self-esteem (Kernis, 2002). Feedback that is negative, inconsistent, or not contingent on performance triggers, at best, uncertainty

about the self's capacities and, at worst, a sense of being incompetent and unloved. Teenagers who experience such parenting tend to rely only on peers, not on adults, to affirm their self-esteem—a risk factor for adjustment difficulties (DuBois et al., 1999, 2002).

Paths to Identity

Adolescents' well-organized self-descriptions and differentiated sense of self-esteem provide the cognitive foundation for forming an identity. Using a clinical interviewing procedure devised by James Marcia (1980) or briefer questionnaire measures, researchers commonly evaluate progress in identity development on two key criteria derived from Erikson's theory: *exploration* and *commitment*. Their various combinations yield four *identity statuses*, summarized in Table 6.1 on page 192: **identity achievement,** commitment to values, beliefs, and goals following a period of exploration; **identity moratorium,** exploration without having reached commitment; **identity foreclosure,** commitment in the absence of exploration; and **identity diffusion,** an apathetic state characterized by lack of both exploration and commitment.

Identity development follows many paths. Some young people remain in one status, whereas others experience many status transitions. And the pattern often varies across *identity domains*, such as sexual orientation, vocation, and religious and political values. Most young people change from "lower" statuses (foreclosure or diffusion) to higher ones (moratorium or achievement) between their mid-teens and mid-twenties, but some move in the reverse direction (Kroger, 2001, 2005; Meeus, 1996).

Because attending college provides opportunities to explore career options and lifestyles, college students make more identity progress than they did in high school (Montgomery & Côté, 2003). After college, they often sample a broad range of life experiences before choosing a life course. Those who go to work immediately after high school graduation settle on a self-definition earlier. But if they encounter obstacles to realizing their occupational goals because of lack of training or vocational choices, they are at risk for identity foreclosure or diffusion (Cohen et al., 2003; Eccles et al., 2003).

At one time, researchers thought that adolescent girls postponed establishing an identity and instead focused on Erikson's next stage, intimacy development. Some girls do show more sophisticated reasoning than boys in identity domains related to intimacy, such as sexuality and family versus career priorities. Otherwise, adolescents of both sexes typically make progress on identity concerns before experiencing genuine intimacy in relationships (Berman et al., 2006; Kroger, 2000).

Identity Status and Psychological Well-Being

A wealth of research verifies that both identity achievement and moratorium are psychologically healthy routes to a mature self-definition. Long-term foreclosure and diffusion, in contrast, are maladaptive.

■ TABLE 6.1 ■ *The Four Identity Statuses*

IDENTITY STATUS	DESCRIPTION	EXAMPLE
Identity achievement	Having already explored alternatives, identity-achieved individuals are committed to a clearly formulated set of self-chosen values and goals. They feel a sense of psychological well-being, of sameness through time, and of knowing where they are going.	When asked how willing she would be to give up going into her chosen occupation if something better came along, Lauren responded, "Well, I might, but I doubt it. I've thought long and hard about law as a career. I'm pretty certain it's for me."
Identity moratorium	*Moratorium* means "delay or holding pattern." These individuals have not yet made definite commitments. They are in the process of exploring—gathering information and trying out activities, with the desire to find values and goals to guide their lives.	When asked whether he had ever had doubts about his religious beliefs, Ramón said, "Yes, I guess I'm going through that right now. I just don't see how there can be a God and yet so much evil in the world."
Identity foreclosure	Identity-foreclosed individuals have committed themselves to values and goals without exploring alternatives. They accept a ready-made identity chosen for them by authority figures—usually parents but sometimes teachers, religious leaders, or romantic partners.	When asked if she had ever reconsidered her political beliefs, Hillary answered, "No, not really, our family is pretty much in agreement on these things."
Identity diffusion	Identity-diffused individuals lack clear direction. They are neither committed to values and goals nor actively trying to reach them. They may never have explored alternatives or may have found the task too threatening and overwhelming.	When asked about his attitude toward nontraditional gender roles, Joel responded, "Oh, I don't know. It doesn't make much difference to me. I can take it or leave it."

Adolescents in moratorium resemble identity-achieved individuals in using an active, *information-gathering cognitive style* when making personal decisions and solving problems: They seek out relevant information, evaluate it carefully, and critically reflect on and revise their views (Berzonsky, 2003; Berzonsky & Kuk, 2000). Young people who are identity-achieved or exploring have higher self-esteem, feel more in control of their own lives, are more likely to view school and work as feasible avenues for realizing their aspirations, and are more advanced in moral reasoning (Adams & Marshall, 1996; Kroger, 2007; Serafini & Adams, 2002).

Adolescents stuck in either foreclosure or diffusion are passive in the face of identity concerns and have adjustment difficulties. Foreclosed individuals display a *dogmatic, inflexible cognitive style,* internalizing the values and beliefs of parents and others without deliberate evaluation and resisting information that threatens their position (Berzonsky & Kuk, 2000). Most fear rejection by people on whom they depend for affection and self-esteem. A few foreclosed teenagers who are alienated from their families and society may join cults or other extremist groups, uncritically adopting a way of life different from their past.

Long-term diffused individuals are the least mature in identity development. They typically use a *diffuse-avoidant cognitive style* in which they avoid dealing with personal decisions and problems and, instead, allow current situational pressures to dictate their reactions (Berzonsky & Kuk, 2000; Krettenauer, 2005). Taking an "I don't care" attitude, they entrust themselves to luck or fate and tend to go along with the crowd. As a result, they experience time management and academic difficulties and, of all young people, are most likely to use and abuse drugs (Archer & Waterman, 1990; Schwartz et al., 2005). Often at the heart of their apathy is a sense of hopelessness about the future.

Factors Affecting Identity Development

Adolescent identity formation begins a lifelong, dynamic process in which a change in either the individual or the context opens up the possibility of reformulating identity (Kunnen & Bosma, 2003). A wide variety of factors influence identity development.

Identity status, as we have just seen, is both cause and consequence of personality characteristics. Adolescents who assume that absolute truth is always attainable tend to be foreclosed, while those who doubt that they will ever feel certain about anything are more often identity-diffused. Young people who appreciate that they can use rational criteria to choose among alternatives are likely to be in a state of moratorium or identity achievement (Berzonsky & Kuk, 2000; Boyes & Chandler, 1992).

Teenagers' identity development is enhanced when their families serve as a "secure base" from which they can confidently move out into the wider world. Adolescents who feel attached to their parents but also free to voice their own opinions tend to be in a state of moratorium or identity achievement (Berzonsky, 2004; Luyckx, Goossens, & Soenens, 2006; Schwartz et al., 2005). Foreclosed teenagers usually have close bonds with parents but lack opportunities for healthy separation. And diffused young people report the lowest levels of parental support and of warm, open communication (Reis & Youniss, 2004; Zimmerman & Becker-Stoll, 2002).

Interaction with diverse peers through school and community activities encourages adolescents to explore values and role possibilities (Barber et al., 2005). And close friends, like parents, can act as a secure base, providing emotional support, assistance, and models of identity development. In one study, 15-year-olds with warm, trusting peer ties were more involved

Applying What We Know

Supporting Healthy Identity Development

Strategy	Explanation
Engage in warm, open communication.	Provides both emotional support and freedom to explore values and goals
Initiate discussions that promote high-level thinking at home and at school.	Encourages rational and deliberate selection among beliefs and values
Provide opportunities to participate in extracurricular activities and vocational training programs.	Permits young people to explore the real world of adult work
Provide opportunities to talk with adults and peers who have worked through identity questions.	Offers models of identity achievement and advice on how to resolve identity concerns
Provide opportunities to explore ethnic heritage and learn about other cultures in an atmosphere of respect.	Fosters identity achievement in all areas and ethnic tolerance, which supports the identity explorations of others

in exploring relationship issues—for example, thinking about what they valued in close friends and in a life partner (Mccus, Oosterwegel, & Vollebergh, 2002). In another study, young people's attachment to friends predicted progress in choosing a career (Felsman & Blustein, 1999).

Identity development also depends on schools and communities that offer rich and varied opportunities for exploration. Supportive experiences include classrooms that promote high-level thinking, extracurricular activities that enable teenagers to take on responsible roles, teachers and counselors who encourage low-SES students to go to college, and vocational training that immerses young people in the real world of adult work (Coatsworth et al., 2005; McIntosh, Metz, & Youniss, 2005).

Culture strongly influences an aspect of mature identity not captured by the identity-status approach: constructing a sense of self-continuity despite major personal changes. In one

This adolescent feels attached to her father but also free to voice her own opinions—circumstances that foster healthy identity development.

study, researchers asked Native Canadian and cultural-majority 12- to 20-year-olds to describe themselves in the past and in the present and then to justify why they were the same continuous person (Lalonde & Chandler, 2005). Most cultural-majority adolescents used an individualistic approach: They described an *enduring personal essence,* a core self that remained the same despite change. In contrast, Native Canadian youths took an interdependent approach that emphasized a *constantly transforming self,* resulting from new roles and relationships. They typically constructed a *coherent narrative* in which they linked together various time slices of their life with a thread that explained how they had changed in meaningful ways.

Finally, societal forces also are responsible for the special challenges faced by gay, lesbian, and bisexual youths (see Section 5) and by ethnic minority adolescents in forming a secure identity (see the Cultural Influences box on page 194). Applying What We Know above summarizes ways that adults can support adolescents in their quest for identity.

ASK YOURSELF

>> REVIEW
List personal and contextual factors that promote identity development.

>> APPLY
Return to the conversation between Louis and Darryl in the opening of this section. Which identity status best characterizes each of the two boys, and why?

>> CONNECT
Explain the close link between adolescent identity development and cognitive processes.

>> REFLECT
Does your identity status vary across the domains of sexuality, close relationships, vocation, religious beliefs, and political values? Describe factors that may have influenced your identity development in an important domain.

▪ CULTURAL INFLUENCES ▪

Identity Development Among Ethnic Minority Adolescents

Most adolescents are aware of their cultural ancestry but relatively unconcerned about it. However, for teenagers who are members of minority groups, **ethnic identity**—a sense of ethnic-group membership and attitudes and feelings associated with that membership—is central to the quest for identity. As they develop cognitively and become more sensitive to feedback from the social environment, minority youths become painfully aware that they are targets of discrimination and inequality. This discovery complicates their efforts to develop a sense of cultural belonging and a set of personally meaningful goals.

In many immigrant families from collectivist cultures, adolescents' commitment to obeying their parents and fulfilling family obligations lessens the longer the family has been in the immigrant-receiving country—a circumstance that induces **acculturative stress,** psychological distress resulting from conflict between the minority and the host culture (Phinney, Ong, & Madden, 2000). When immigrant parents tightly restrict their teenagers through fear that assimilation into the larger society will undermine their cultural traditions, their youngsters often rebel, rejecting aspects of their ethnic background.

At the same time, discrimination can interfere with the formation of a positive ethnic identity. In one study, Mexican-American youths who had experienced more discrimination were less likely to explore their ethnicity and to report feeling good about it. Those with low ethnic pride showed a sharp drop in self-esteem in the face of discrimination (Romero & Roberts, 2003).

With age, some ethnic minority young people progress from ethnic-identity diffusion or foreclosure through moratorium to ethnic-identity achievement. But because the process of forging an ethnic identity can be painful and confusing, others show no change, and still others regress (Seaton, Scottham, & Sellers, 2006). Young people with parents of different ethnicities face extra challenges. In a large survey of high school students, part-black biracial teenagers reported as much discrimination as their monoracial black counterparts, yet they felt less positively

about their ethnicity. And compared with monoracial minorities, many biracials—including black–white, black–Asian, white–Asian, black–Hispanic, and white–Hispanic—regarded ethnicity as less central to their identities (Herman, 2004). Perhaps these adolescents encountered fewer opportunities in their homes and communities to forge a strong sense of belonging to either culture.

When family members encourage adolescents to disprove ethnic stereotypes of low achievement or antisocial behavior, young people typically surmount the threat that discrimination poses to a favorable ethnic identity. These young people manage experiences of unfair treatment effectively, by seeking social support and engaging in direct problem solving (Phinney & Chavira, 1995; Scott, 2003). Also, adolescents whose families taught them the history, traditions, values, and language of their ethnic group and who frequently interact with same-ethnicity peers are more likely to forge a favorable ethnic identity (Hughes et al., 2006; McHale et al., 2006).

How can society help minority adolescents resolve identity conflicts constructively? Here are some relevant approaches:

- Promote effective parenting, in which children and adolescents benefit from family ethnic pride yet are encouraged to explore the meaning of ethnicity in their own lives.
- Ensure that schools respect minority youths' native languages, unique learning styles, and right to high-quality education.
- Foster contact with peers of the same ethnicity, along with respect between ethnic groups (García Coll & Magnuson, 1997).

A strong, secure ethnic identity is associated with higher self-esteem, optimism, and sense of mastery over the environment, and with more positive attitudes toward one's ethnicity (St. Louis & Liem, 2005; Umana-Taylor

& Updegraff, 2007; Worrell & Gardner-Kitt, 2006). For these reasons, adolescents with a positive connection to their ethnic group are better adjusted. They cope more effectively with stress, show higher achievement in school, and have fewer emotional and behavior problems than agemates who identify only weakly with their ethnicity (Greene, Way, & Pahl, 2006; Seaton, Scottham, & Sellers, 2006; Umana-Taylor & Alfaro, 2006; Yip, Seaton, & Sellers, 2006).

Forming a **bicultural identity**—by exploring and adopting values from both the adolescent's subculture and the dominant culture—offers additional benefits. Biculturally identified adolescents tend to be achieved in other areas of identity as well and to have especially favorable relations with members of other ethnic groups (Phinney, 2007; Phinney et al., 2001). In sum, achievement of ethnic identity enhances many aspects of emotional and social development.

© DAVID GROSSMAN/THE IMAGE WORKS

These adolescents celebrate their cultural heritage by participating in a Filipino parade in New York City. When minority youths encounter respect for their ethnic heritage in schools and communities, they are more likely to retain ethnic values and customs as an important part of their identity.

Moral Development

Eleven-year-old Sabrina sat at the kitchen table reading the Sunday newspaper, her eyes wide with interest. "You gotta see this," she said to 16-year-old Louis, who sat munching cereal. Sabrina held up a page of large photos showing a 70-year-old woman standing in her home. The floor and furniture were piled with stacks of newspapers, cardboard boxes, tin cans, glass containers, food, and clothing. The accompanying article described crumbling plaster on the walls, frozen pipes, and nonfunctioning sinks, toilet, and furnace. The headline read: "Loretta Perry: My Life Is None of Their Business."

"Look what they're trying to do to this poor lady," exclaimed Sabrina. "They wanna throw her out of her house and tear it down! Those city inspectors must not care about anyone. Here it says, 'Mrs. Perry has devoted much of her life to doing favors for people.' Why doesn't someone help *her*?"

"Sabrina, you're missing the point," Louis responded. "Mrs. Perry is violating 30 building code standards. The law says you're supposed to keep your house clean and in good repair."

"But Louis, she's old, and she needs help. She says her life will be over if they destroy her home."

"The building inspectors aren't being mean, Sabrina. Mrs. Perry is stubborn. She's refusing to obey the law. And she's not just a threat to herself—she's a danger to her neighbors, too. Suppose her house caught on fire. You can't live around other people and say your life is nobody's business."

"You don't just knock someone's home down," Sabrina replied angrily. "Why aren't her friends and neighbors over there fixing up that house? You're just like those building inspectors, Louis. You've got no feelings!"

As Louis and Sabrina's disagreement over Mrs. Perry's plight illustrates, cognitive development and expanding social experiences permit adolescents to better understand larger social structures—societal institutions and law-making systems—that govern moral responsibilities. As their grasp of social arrangements expands, adolescents construct new ideas about what should be done when the needs and desires of people conflict. As a result, they move toward increasingly just, fair, and balanced solutions to moral problems.

Kohlberg's Theory of Moral Development

Early work by Piaget on the moral judgment of the child inspired Lawrence Kohlberg's more comprehensive cognitive-developmental theory of moral understanding. Kohlberg used a clinical interviewing procedure in which he presented a sample of 10- to 16-year-old boys with hypothetical *moral dilemmas*—stories presenting a conflict between two moral values—and asked them what the main actor should do and why. Then he followed the participants longitudinally, reinterviewing them at 3- to 4-year intervals over the next 20 years. The best known of Kohlberg's dilemmas, the "Heinz dilemma," pits the value of obeying the law (not stealing) against the value of human life (saving a dying person):

In Europe a woman was near death from cancer. There was one drug the doctors thought might save her. A druggist in the same town had discovered it, but he was charging ten times what the drug cost him to make. The sick woman's husband, Heinz, went to everyone he knew to borrow the money, but he could only get together half of what it cost. The druggist refused to sell the drug for less or let Heinz pay later. So Heinz became desperate and broke into the man's store to steal the drug for his wife. Should Heinz have done that? Why or why not? (paraphrased from Colby et al., 1983, p. 77)

Kohlberg emphasized that it is *the way an individual reasons* about the dilemma, not *the content of the response* (whether or not to steal), that determines moral maturity. Individuals who believe Heinz should take the drug and those who think he should not can be found at each of Kohlberg's first four stages. Only at the two highest stages do moral reasoning and content come together in a coherent ethical system (Kohlberg, Levine, & Hewer, 1983). Given a choice between obeying the law and preserving individual rights, the most advanced moral thinkers support individual rights (in the Heinz dilemma, stealing the drug to save a life). **TAKE A MOMENT...** Does this remind you of adolescents' efforts to formulate a sound, well-organized set of personal values in constructing an identity? According to some theorists, the development of identity and moral understanding are part of the same process (Bergman, 2004; Blasi, 1994).

■ **KOHLBERG'S STAGES OF MORAL UNDERSTANDING.** Kohlberg organized moral development into three levels, each with two stages, yielding six stages in all. He believed that moral understanding is promoted by the same factors Piaget thought were important for cognitive development: (1) actively grappling with moral issues and noticing weaknesses in one's current reasoning, and (2) gains in perspective taking, which permit individuals to resolve moral conflicts in more effective ways. **TAKE A MOMENT...** As we examine Kohlberg's developmental sequence in light of possible responses to the Heinz dilemma, look for changes in perspective taking that each stage assumes.

The Preconventional Level. At the **preconventional level,** morality is externally controlled. Children accept the rules of authority figures and judge actions by their consequences. Behaviors that result in punishment are viewed as bad, those that lead to rewards as good.

■ *Stage 1: The punishment and obedience orientation.* Children at this stage find it difficult to consider two points of view in a moral dilemma. As a result, they overlook people's intentions. Instead, they focus on fear of authority and avoidance of punishment as reasons for behaving morally.

> *Prostealing:* "If you let your wife die, you will . . . be blamed for not spending the money to help her and there'll be an investigation of you and the druggist for your wife's death." (Kohlberg, 1969, p. 381)

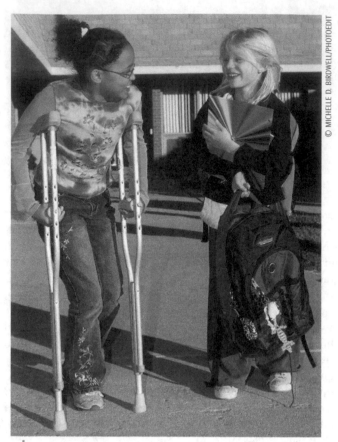

If the 12-year-old on the right expects a favor in return for carrying her injured friend's backpack, she is at Kohlberg's preconventional level. If she is guided by the Golden Rule, "Do unto others as you would have them do unto you," then she understands ideal reciprocity and has advanced to the conventional level.

Antistealing: "You shouldn't steal the drug because you'll be caught and sent to jail if you do. If you do get away, [you'd be scared that] the police would catch up with you any minute." (Kohlberg, 1969, p. 381)

■ *Stage 2: The instrumental purpose orientation.* Children become aware that people can have different perspectives in a moral dilemma, but at first this understanding is concrete. They view right action as flowing from self-interest and understand reciprocity as equal exchange of favors: "You do this for me and I'll do that for you."

Prostealing: "[I]f Heinz decides to risk jail to save his wife, it's his life he's risking; he can do what he wants with it. And the same goes for the druggist; it's up to him to decide what he wants to do." (Rest, 1979, p. 26)

Antistealing: "[Heinz] is running more risk than it's worth [to save a wife who is near death]." (Rest, 1979, p. 27)

The Conventional Level. At the **conventional level,** individuals continue to regard conformity to social rules as important, but not for reasons of self-interest. They believe that actively maintaining the current social system ensures positive relationships and societal order.

■ *Stage 3: The "good boy–good girl" orientation, or the morality of interpersonal cooperation.* The desire to obey rules because they promote social harmony first appears in the context of close personal ties. Stage 3 individuals want to maintain the affection and approval of friends and relatives by being a "good person"—trustworthy, loyal, respectful, helpful, and nice. The capacity to view a two-person relationship from the vantage point of an impartial, outside observer supports this new approach to morality. At this stage, individuals understand *ideal reciprocity:* They express the same concern for the welfare of another as they do for themselves—a standard of fairness summed up by the Golden Rule: "Do unto others as you would have them do unto you."

Prostealing: "No one will think you're bad if you steal the drug, but your family will think you're an inhuman husband if you don't. If you let your wife die, you'll never be able to look anyone in the face again." (Kohlberg, 1969, p. 381)

Antistealing: "It isn't just the druggist who will think you're a criminal, everyone else will too. . . . [Y]ou'll feel bad thinking how you've brought dishonor on your family and yourself." (Kohlberg, 1969, p. 381)

■ *Stage 4: The social-order-maintaining orientation.* At this stage, the individual takes into account a larger perspective—that of societal laws. Moral choices no longer depend on close ties to others. Instead, rules must be enforced in the same evenhanded fashion for everyone, and each member of society has a personal duty to uphold them. The Stage 4 individual believes that laws should never be disobeyed because they are vital for ensuring societal order and cooperative relations between individuals.

Prostealing: "Heinz has a duty to protect his wife's life; it's a vow he took in marriage. But it's wrong to steal, so he would have to take the drug with the idea of paying the druggist for it and accepting the penalty for breaking the law later."

Antistealing: "Even if his wife is dying, it's still [Heinz's] duty as a citizen to obey the law. . . . If everyone starts breaking the law in a jam, there'd be no civilization, just crime and violence." (Rest, 1979, p. 30)

The Postconventional or Principled Level. Individuals at the **postconventional level** move beyond unquestioning support for their own society's rules and laws. They define morality in terms of abstract principles and values that apply to all situations and societies.

■ *Stage 5: The social contract orientation.* At Stage 5, individuals regard laws and rules as flexible instruments for furthering human purposes. They can imagine alternatives to their own social order, and they emphasize fair procedures for interpreting and changing the law. When laws are consistent with individual rights and the interests of the majority, each person follows them because of a *social* contract orientation—free and willing participation in the system because it brings about more good for people than if it did not exist.

> *Prostealing:* "Although there is a law against stealing, the law wasn't meant to violate a person's right to life. . . . If Heinz is prosecuted for stealing, the law needs to be reinterpreted to take into account situations in which it goes against people's natural right to keep on living."

- **Stage 6: The universal ethical principle orientation.** At this highest stage, right action is defined by self-chosen ethical principles of conscience that are valid for all people, regardless of law and social agreement. These values are abstract, not concrete moral rules like the Ten Commandments. Stage 6 individuals typically mention such principles as respect for the worth and dignity of each person.

> *Prostealing:* "It doesn't make sense to put respect for property above respect for life itself. [People] could live together without private property at all. Respect for human life and personality is absolute and accordingly [people] have a mutual duty to save one another from dying." (Rest, 1979, p. 37)

■ **RESEARCH ON KOHLBERG'S STAGE SEQUENCE.** Kohlberg's original research and other longitudinal studies provide the most convincing evidence for his stage sequence. With few exceptions, individuals move through the first four stages in the predicted order (Colby et al., 1983; Dawson, 2002; Walker & Taylor, 1991b). Moral development is slow and gradual: Reasoning at Stages 1 and 2 decreases in early adolescence, while Stage 3 increases through midadolescence and then declines. Stage 4 reasoning rises over the teenage years until, by early adulthood, it is the typical response.

Few people move beyond Stage 4. In fact, postconventional morality is so rare that no clear evidence exists that Kohlberg's Stage 6 actually follows Stage 5. This poses a key challenge to Kohlberg's theory: If people must reach Stages 5 and 6 to be considered truly morally mature, few individuals anywhere would measure up! According to one reexamination of Kohlberg's stages, moral maturity can be found in a revised understanding of Stages 3 and 4 (Gibbs, 1991, 2010). These stages are not "conventional"—based on social conformity—as Kohlberg assumed. Rather, they require profound moral constructions—an understanding of ideal reciprocity as the basis for relationships (Stage 3) and for widely accepted moral standards, set forth in rules and laws (Stage 4). In this view, "postconventional" morality is a highly reflective endeavor limited to a handful of people who have attained advanced education, usually in philosophy.

TAKE A MOMENT... Think of an actual moral dilemma you faced recently. How did you solve it? Did your reasoning fall at the same stage as your thinking about Heinz? Real-life conflicts often elicit moral reasoning below a person's actual capacity because they involve practical considerations and mix cognition with intense emotion (Carpendale, 2000). Although

adolescents and adults mention reasoning as their most frequent strategy for resolving these dilemmas, they also refer to other strategies—talking through issues with others, relying on intuition, and calling on notions of religion and spirituality. And they report feeling drained, confused, and torn by temptation—an emotional side of moral judgment not tapped by hypothetical situations, which evoke the upper limits of moral thought because they allow reflection without the interference of personal risk (Walker, 2004).

The influence of situational factors on moral judgments indicates that like Piaget's cognitive stages, Kohlberg's moral stages are loosely organized and overlapping. Rather than developing in a neat, stepwise fashion, people draw on a range of moral responses that vary with context. With age, this range shifts upward as less mature moral reasoning is gradually replaced by more advanced moral thought.

Are There Sex Differences in Moral Reasoning?

As we have seen, real-life moral dilemmas often highlight the role of emotion in moral judgment. In the discussion at the beginning of this section, notice how Sabrina's moral argument focuses on caring and commitment to others.

Carol Gilligan (1982) is the best-known of those who have argued that Kohlberg's theory—originally formulated on the basis of interviews with males—does not adequately represent the morality of girls and women. Gilligan believes that feminine morality emphasizes an "ethic of care" that Kohlberg's system devalues. Sabrina's reasoning falls at Stage 3 because it is based on mutual trust and affection, whereas Louis's is at Stage 4 because he emphasizes following the law. According to Gilligan, a concern for others is a *different* but no less valid basis for moral judgment than a focus on impersonal rights.

Many studies have tested Gilligan's claim that Kohlberg's approach underestimates the moral maturity of females, and most do not support it (Turiel, 2006; Walker, 2006). On hypothetical dilemmas as well as everyday moral problems, adolescent and adult females display reasoning at the same stage as their male agemates and often at a higher stage. Themes of justice and caring appear in the responses of both sexes, and when girls do raise interpersonal concerns, they are not downgraded in Kohlberg's system (Jadack et al., 1995; Kahn, 1992; Walker, 1995). These findings suggest that although Kohlberg emphasized justice rather than caring as the highest moral ideal, his theory taps both sets of values.

Still, Gilligan makes a powerful claim that research on moral development has been limited by too much attention to rights and justice (a "masculine" ideal) and too little to care and responsiveness (a "feminine" ideal). Some evidence shows that although the morality of males and females taps both orientations, females do tend to emphasize care, whereas males either stress justice or focus equally on justice and care (Jaffee & Hyde, 2000; Wark & Krebs, 1996; Weisz & Black, 2002). This difference in emphasis, which appears more often in real-life dilemmas than in hypothetical ones, may reflect women's greater involvement in daily activities involving care and concern for others.

Indeed, both cultural and situational contexts profoundly affect use of a care orientation. In one study, U.S. and Canadian 17- to 26-year-old females exceeded their male counterparts in complex reasoning about care issues. But Norwegian males were just as advanced as Norwegian females in care-based understanding (Skoe, 1998). Perhaps Norwegian culture, which explicitly endorses gender equality, induces boys and men to think deeply about interpersonal obligations. And in an Australian investigation, researchers presented 18- to 38-year-old university students with one of three versions of a moral dilemma, in which the main character varied in familiarity: (1) a close friend in class, (2) a person "known only vaguely" from class, or (3) a classmate whose relationship was unspecified (Ryan, David, & Reynolds, 2004). When asked whether they would permit the character, who was in danger of failing the course, to borrow a copy of their recently completed assignment despite risk of cheating, both males and females gave more care responses when considering a close friend than a socially distant classmate. As Figure 6.1 shows, gender differences emerged only in the unspecified condition, where women—who tend to forge closer relationships—may have assumed greater familiarity.

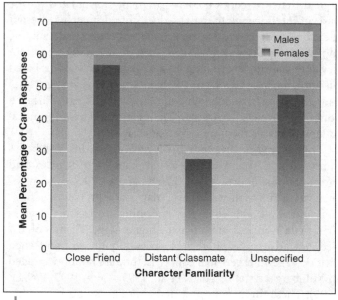

■ **FIGURE 6.1** ■ **Relationship of familiarity of the main character in a moral dilemma to care responses.** Australian university students were presented with one of three versions of a moral dilemma in which familiarity of the main character varied: close friend, distant classmate, and unspecified. Both male and female participants gave more care responses when considering a close friend than a distant classmate. Sex differences appeared only in the unspecified condition, where females may have assumed greater familiarity. (From M. K. Ryan, B. David, & K. J. Reynolds, 2004, "Who Cares? The Effect of Gender and Context on the Self and Moral Reasoning," *Psychology of Women Quarterly, 28,* 246–255. Copyright © 2004 by the American Psychological Association. Reprinted with permission of the American Psychological Association.)

Coordinating Moral, Social-Conventional, and Personal Concerns

Adolescents' moral advances are also evident in their reasoning about situations that raise competing moral, social-conventional, and personal issues. In diverse Western and non-Western cultures, teenagers express great concern with matters of personal choice—a reflection of their quest for identity and strengthening independence (Neff & Helwig, 2002; Nucci, 2002). More firmly than at younger ages, they assert that dress, hairstyle, diary records, and friendships are solely the province of the individual and not subject to control by authority figures (such as parents) (Nucci, 2001, 2005). As adolescents enlarge the range of issues they regard as personal, they think more intently about conflicts between personal choice and community obligation—for example, whether, and under what conditions, it is permissible for laws to restrict speech, religion, marriage, childbearing, group membership, and other individual rights (Helwig, 1995; Wainryb, 1997).

Teenagers display more subtle thinking than school-age children on such issues. When asked if it is OK to exclude a child from a peer group on the basis of race or gender, fourth graders usually say exclusion is always unfair. But by tenth grade, young people, though increasingly mindful of fairness, indicate that under certain conditions—within friendship more often than peer groups, and on the basis of gender more often than race—exclusion is OK (Killen et al., 2002). In explaining, they mention the right to personal choice as well as concerns about effective group functioning. Justifying her opinion that members of an all-boys music club need not let a girl join, one tenth grader said, "It's not nice . . . but it's their club." Another commented, "[The girl and the boys] probably wouldn't relate on very many things" (p. 62).

As adolescents integrate personal rights with ideal reciprocity, they demand that protections they want for themselves extend to others. For example, with age, adolescents are more likely to defend the government's right to limit the personal right to engage in risky health behaviors such as smoking and drinking, in the interest of the larger public good (Flanagan, Stout, & Gallay, 2008). Similarly, they are increasingly mindful of the overlap between moral imperatives and social conventions. Eventually they realize that violating strongly held conventions—showing up at a wedding in a T-shirt, talking out of turn at a student council meeting—can harm others, either by inducing distress or by undermining fair treatment. Over time, as their grasp of fairness deepens, young people realize that many social conventions have moral implications: They are vital for maintaining a just and peaceful society (Nucci, 2001). Notice how this understanding is central to Kohlberg's Stage 4, which is typically attained as adolescence draws to a close.

Influences on Moral Reasoning

Many factors influence moral understanding, including child-rearing practices, schooling, peer interaction, and culture. Growing evidence suggests that, as Kohlberg believed, these

These teenagers are making signs for an anti-war demonstration. Adolescent moral development involves thinking more intently about conflicts between personal choice and community obligation—for example, whether, and under what conditions, it is permissible to challenge a decision by one's country to go to war.

experiences work by presenting young people with cognitive challenges, which stimulate them to think about moral problems in more complex ways.

■ **PARENTING PRACTICES.** As in childhood, parenting practices associated with moral maturity in adolescence combine warmth, exchange of ideas, and appropriate demands for maturity. Adolescents who gain most in moral understanding have parents who engage in moral discussions, encourage prosocial behavior, and create a supportive atmosphere by listening sensitively, asking clarifying questions, and presenting higher-level reasoning (Pratt, Skoe, & Arnold, 2004; Wyatt & Carlo, 2002). In one study, 11-year-olds were asked what they thought an adult would say to justify a moral rule, such as not lying, stealing, or breaking a promise. Those with warm, demanding, communicative parents were far more likely than their agemates to point to the importance of ideal reciprocity: "You wouldn't like it if I did it to you" (Leman, 2005). In contrast, when parents lecture, use threats, or make sarcastic remarks, adolescents show little or no change in moral reasoning over time (Walker & Taylor, 1991a).

■ **SCHOOLING.** Years of schooling is a powerful predictor of movement to Kohlberg's Stage 4 or higher (Dawson et al., 2003; Gibbs et al., 2007). Higher education introduces young people to social issues that extend beyond personal relationships to entire political or cultural groups. Consistent with this idea, college students who report more perspective-taking opportunities (for example, classes that emphasize open discussion of opinions, friendships with others of different cultural backgrounds) and who indicate that they have become more aware of social diversity tend to be advanced in moral reasoning (Comunian & Gielen, 2006; Mason & Gibbs, 1993a, 1993b).

■ **PEER INTERACTION.** Interaction among peers who present differing viewpoints promotes moral understanding. When young people negotiate and compromise with agemates, they realize that social life can be based on cooperation between equals rather than authority relations (Killen & Nucci, 1995). Teenagers who report more close friendships and who more often participate in conversations with their friends are advanced in moral reasoning (Schonert-Reichl, 1999). The mutuality and intimacy of friendship, which fosters decisions based on consensual agreement, may be particularly important for moral development.

Peer discussions and role playing of moral problems have provided the basis for interventions aimed at improving high school and college students' moral understanding. For these discussions to be effective, young people must be highly engaged—confronting, critiquing, and attempting to clarify one another's viewpoints, as Sabrina and Louis did when they argued over Mrs. Perry's plight (Berkowitz & Gibbs, 1983; Comunian & Gielen, 2006). And because moral development occurs gradually, many peer interaction sessions over weeks or months typically are needed to produce moral change.

■ **CULTURE.** Individuals in industrialized nations move through Kohlberg's stages more quickly and advance to a higher level than individuals in village societies, who rarely move beyond Stage 3. One explanation of these cultural differences is that in village societies, moral cooperation is based on direct relations between people and does not allow for the development of advanced moral understanding (Stages 4 to 6), which depends on appreciating the role of larger social structures, such as laws and government institutions (Gibbs et al., 2007).

A second possible reason for cultural variation is that responses to moral dilemmas in collectivist cultures (including village societies) are often more other-directed than in Western Europe and North America (Miller, 2006). In both village and industrialized cultures that highly value interdependency, statements portraying the individual as vitally connected to the social group are common. In one study, Japanese male and female adolescents, who almost always integrated caring and justice-based reasoning, placed greater weight on caring, which they regarded as a communal responsibility (Shimizu, 2001). Similarly, in research conducted in India, even highly educated people (expected to have attained Kohlberg's Stages 4 and 5) viewed solutions to moral dilemmas as the responsibility of the entire society, not of a single person (Miller & Bersoff, 1995).

These findings raise the question of whether Kohlberg's highest level represents a culturally specific way of thinking—one limited to Western societies that emphasize individualism

Growing up in a small village in the Pamir Mountains of China, these adolescents view moral cooperation as based on direct relations between people. Consequently, their moral reasoning is unlikely to advance beyond Kohlberg's Stage 3.

and an appeal to an inner, private conscience. At the same time, a review of over 100 studies confirmed an age-related trend consistent with Kohlberg's Stages 1 to 4 across diverse societies (Gibbs et al., 2007). A common justice morality is clearly evident in the dilemma responses of people from vastly different cultures.

Moral Reasoning and Behavior

A central assumption of the cognitive-developmental perspective is that moral understanding should affect moral action. According to Kohlberg, mature moral thinkers realize that behaving in line with their beliefs is vital for creating and maintaining a just social world (Gibbs, 2010). Consistent with this idea, higher-stage adolescents more often act prosocially by helping, sharing, and defending victims of injustice (Carlo et al., 1996; Comunian & Gielen, 2000, 2006). Also, they less often engage in cheating, aggression, and other antisocial behaviors (Gregg, Gibbs, & Fuller, 1994; Raaijmakers, Engels, & Van Hoof, 2005; Stams et al., 2006).

Yet the connection between mature moral reasoning and action is only modest. As we have seen, moral behavior is influenced by many factors besides cognition, including the emotions of empathy, sympathy, and guilt; individual differences in temperament; and a long history of experiences that affect moral decision making. **Moral self-relevance**—the degree to which morality is central to self-concept—also affects moral behavior (Walker, 2004). In a study of low-SES African-American and Hispanic teenagers, those who emphasized moral traits and goals in their self-descriptions displayed exceptional levels of community service (Hart & Fegley, 1995). But they did not differ from their agemates in moral reasoning.

Research has yet to identify the origins of a sense of moral self-relevance, or just how thought combines with other influences to foster moral commitment. Close relationships with parents, teachers, and friends may play a vital role by modeling prosocial behavior and fostering morally relevant emotions of empathy and guilt, which combine with moral cognition to powerfully motivate moral action (Arsenio, 2006; Hoffman, 2000). Another possibility is that *just educational environments*—in which teachers guide students in democratic decision making and rule setting, resolving disputes civilly, and taking responsibility for others' welfare—are influential (Atkins, Hart, & Donnelly, 2004). A compassionate and just school climate may be particularly important for poverty-stricken ethnic minority students. For many, meaningful participation in their school community may be crucial in preventing them from concluding that prejudice and diminished opportunity are so pervasive in society as to be insurmountable (Hart & Atkins, 2002).

Schools may also foster students' moral self-relevance by expanding opportunities for civic engagement. As the Social Issues box on the following page reveals, encouraging civic responsibility in young people can help them see the connection between their personal interests and the public interest—an insight that may foster all aspects of morality.

Religious Involvement and Moral Development

Recall that in resolving real-life moral dilemmas, many people voice notions of religion and spirituality. Religion is especially important in U.S. family life. In recent national polls, nearly two-thirds of Americans reported being religious, compared with one-half of those in Canada, one-third of those in Great Britain and Italy, and even fewer elsewhere in Europe (Gallup News Service, 2006; Jones, 2003). People who regularly attend religious services include many parents with children. But as adolescents search for a personally meaningful identity, formal religious involvement declines—for U.S. youths, from 55 percent at ages 13 to 15 to 40 percent at ages 17 to 18 (Donahue & Benson, 1995; Kerestes & Youniss, 2003).

Nevertheless, teenagers who remain part of a religious community are advantaged in moral values and behavior. Compared with nonaffiliated youths, they are more involved in community service activities aimed at helping the less fortunate (Kerestes, Youniss, & Metz, 2004). And religious involvement promotes responsible academic and social behavior and discourages misconduct (Dowling et al., 2004). It is associated with lower levels of drug and alcohol use, early sexual activity, and delinquency (Regnerus, Smith, & Fritsch, 2003).

A variety of factors probably contribute to these favorable outcomes. In a study of inner-city high school students, religiously involved young people were more likely to report trusting relationships with parents, other adults, and friends who hold similar worldviews. The more activities they shared with this network, the higher they scored in empathy and prosocial behavior (King & Furrow, 2004). Furthermore, religious

SOCIAL ISSUES

Development of Civic Responsibility

On Thanksgiving Day, Jules, Louis, and Sabrina joined their parents at a soup kitchen to serve a holiday dinner to poverty-stricken people. Throughout the year, Sabrina volunteered on Saturday mornings at a nursing home, conversing with bedridden elders. During a congressional election campaign, all three adolescents raised questions about issues at special youth meetings with candidates. At school, Louis and his girlfriend, Cassie, formed an organization devoted to promoting ethnic and racial tolerance.

These young people show a strong sense of *civic responsibility*—a complex combination of cognition, emotion, and behavior. Civic responsibility involves knowledge of political issues, a desire to make a difference in the community, and skills for achieving civic goals, such as how to resolve differing views fairly and conduct meetings so all participants have a voice (Flanagan & Faison, 2001).

When young people engage in community service that exposes them to people in need or to public issues, they are especially likely to express a commitment to future service. And youth volunteers—who tend to be advanced in moral reasoning—gain further in moral maturity as a result of participating (Gibbs et al., 2007; Hart, Atkins, & Donnelly, 2006). Family, school, and community experiences contribute to adolescents' civic responsibility.

Family Influences

Teenagers whose parents encourage their children to form opinions about controversial issues are more knowledgeable about civic issues and better able to see them from more than one perspective (Santoloupo & Pratt, 1994). Also, adolescents whose parents engage in community service and stress compassion for the less fortunate tend to hold socially responsible values. When asked what causes unemployment or poverty, they more often mention situational and societal factors (lack of education, government policies, or the state of the economy) than individual factors (low intelligence or personal problems). Youths who endorse situational and societal causes, in turn, have more altruistic life goals, such as working to eradicate poverty or to preserve the earth for future generations (Flanagan &

Tucker, 1999). And they engage in more civic activities into early adulthood (Zaff, Malanchuk, & Eccles, 2008).

School and Community Influences

A democratic climate at school in which teachers promote discussion of controversial issues, while insisting that students listen to and respect one another, fosters critical analysis of political issues and commitment to social causes (Flanagan & Faison, 2001). Participation in extracurricular activities at school and in youth organizations is also associated with civic commitment that persists into adulthood (Obradović & Masten, 2007).

Two aspects of these involvements seem to account for their lasting impact. First, they introduce adolescents to the vision and skills required for mature civic engagement. Within student government, clubs, teams, and other groups, young people see how their actions affect the wider school and community. They realize that collectively they can achieve results greater than any one person can achieve alone. And they learn to work together, balancing strong convictions with compromise (Atkins, Hart, & Donnelly, 2004; Youniss, McLellan, & Yates, 1997). Second, while producing a weekly newspaper or implementing a service project, young people explore political and moral ideals. Often they redefine their identities to include a responsibility to combat others' misfortunes (Wheeler, 2002).

The power of family, school, and community to promote civic responsibility may lie in discussions, educational practices, and activities that jointly foster moral thought, emotion, and behavior. In a comparison of nationally representative samples of 14-year-olds in 28 nations, U.S. young people excelled at community service, with 50 percent of students reporting membership in organizations devoted to volunteering (Torney-Purta, 2002).

Currently, 66 percent of U.S. public schools provide students with community service opportunities. Nearly half of these have *service-learning programs,* which integrate service activities into the academic curriculum, and about one-third of students enroll. High school students who are required to serve their communities express as strong a desire to remain engaged as do students who volunteer. And when they reach early adulthood,

they are equally likely to vote and participate in community organizations (Hart et al., 2007; Metz & Youniss, 2005).

Still, most U.S. schools offering service learning do not have policies encouraging or mandating such programs (Scales & Roehlkepartain, 2004). Furthermore, low-SES, inner-city youths—although they express high interest in contributing to society—score substantially lower than higher-SES youths in civic knowledge and participation (Balsano, 2005). A broad societal commitment to fostering civic character must pay special attention to supportive school and community experiences for these young people, so their eagerness to make a difference can be realized.

Adolescents paint a mural on a wall once filled with graffiti in a low-income, inner-city neighborhood. Family, school, and community experiences contribute to their sense of civic responsibility.

These teenagers gather with other religious groups to voice their support for world peace. Involvement in a religious community promotes teens' moral values and behavior, encouraging responsible academic work and community service.

education and youth activities directly teach concern for others and provide opportunities for moral discussions and civic engagement. And adolescents who feel connected to a higher being may develop certain inner strengths, including moral self-relevance and prosocial values, that help them translate their thinking into action (Hardy & Carlo, 2005; Sherrod & Spiewak, 2008).

Because most teenagers, regardless of formal affiliation, identify with a religious denomination and say they believe in a higher being, religious institutions may be uniquely suited to foster moral and prosocial commitments. For inner-city youths with few alternative sources of social support, outreach by religious institutions can lead to life-altering involvement (Jang & Johnson, 2001). An exception is seen in religious cults, where rigid indoctrination into the group's beliefs, suppression of individuality, and estrangement from society all work against moral maturity (Richmond, 2004).

Further Challenges to Kohlberg's Theory

Although much evidence is consistent with the cognitive-developmental approach to morality, Kohlberg's theory has faced major challenges. The most radical opposition comes from researchers who—referring to wide variability in moral reasoning across situations—claim that Kohlberg's stage sequence inadequately accounts for morality in everyday life (Krebs and Denton, 2005). These investigators favor abandoning Kohlberg's stages for a *pragmatic approach to morality*. They assert that each person makes moral judgments at varying levels of maturity, depending on the individual's current context and motivations: Conflict over a business deal is likely to evoke Stage 2 (instrumental purpose) reasoning, a friendship or romantic dispute Stage 3 (ideal reciprocity) reasoning, and a breach of contract Stage 4 (social-order-maintaining) reasoning (Krebs et al., 1991).

According to the pragmatic view, everyday moral judgments—rather than being efforts to arrive at just solutions—

are practical tools that people use to achieve their goals. To benefit personally, they often must advocate cooperation with others. But people often act first and then invoke moral judgments to rationalize their actions, regardless of whether their behavior is self-centered or prosocial (Haidt, 2001). And sometimes people use moral judgments for immoral purposes—for example, to excuse their transgressions.

Is the pragmatic approach correct that people strive to resolve moral conflicts fairly only when they themselves have nothing to lose? Supporters of the cognitive-developmental perspective point out that people frequently rise above self-interest to defend others' rights. For example, moral leaders in business—rather than resorting to Stage 2 reasoning—endorse trust, integrity, good faith, and just laws and codes of conduct (Damon, 2004; Gibbs, 2006). Also, when presented with moral justifications varying in maturity, adolescents and adults are well aware of the greater adequacy of higher-stage thinking, which some people act on despite highly corrupt environments. Furthermore, individuals who engage in sudden altruistic action may have previously considered relevant moral issues so thoroughly that their moral judgment activates automatically, triggering an immediate response (Gibbs et al., 2009a; Pizzaro & Bloom, 2003). In these instances, people who appear to be engaging in after-the-fact moral justification are actually behaving with great forethought.

In sum, the cognitive-developmental approach to morality has done much to clarify our profound moral potential. And despite opposition, Kohlberg's central assumption—that with age, humans everywhere construct a deeper understanding of fairness and justice that guides moral action—remains powerfully influential.

Gender Typing

As Sabrina entered adolescence, she began to place more emphasis on excelling in literature, art, and music—traditionally feminine subjects. When with peers, she worried about walking, talking, eating, dressing, laughing, and competing in ways consistent with gender roles.

Early adolescence is a period of **gender intensification**—increased gender stereotyping of attitudes and behavior and movement toward a more traditional gender identity (Basow & Rubin, 1999; Galambos, Almeida, & Petersen, 1990). Both sexes experience gender intensification, but it is stronger for girls, who feel less free to experiment with "other-gender" activities and behavior than they did in middle childhood (Huston & Alvarez, 1990).

What accounts for gender intensification? Biological, social, and cognitive factors are involved. As puberty magnifies sex differences in appearance, teenagers spend more time thinking about themselves in gender-linked ways. Pubertal changes also prompt gender-typed pressures from others. Parents—especially those with traditional gender-role beliefs—may encourage "gender-appropriate" activities and behavior more than they did earlier (Crouter, Manke, & McHale, 1995;

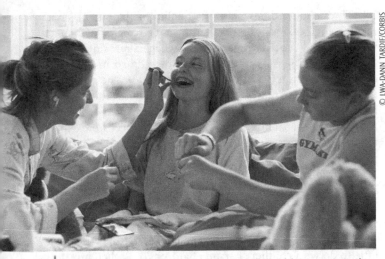

In early adolescence, young people, especially girls, move toward more traditional gender identities. By the late teens, gender intensification declines, especially among adolescents encouraged to explore non-gender-typed options.

Shanahan et al., 2007). And when adolescents start to date, they often become more gender typed as a way of increasing their attractiveness (Maccoby, 1998). Finally, cognitive changes—in particular, greater concern with what others think—make young teenagers more responsive to gender-role expectations.

Gender intensification declines by middle to late adolescence, but not all young people move beyond it to the same degree. Teenagers who are encouraged to explore non-gender-typed options and to question the value of gender stereotypes for themselves and society are more likely to build an androgynous gender identity (see Section 2, page 64). Overall, androgynous adolescents, especially girls, tend to be psychologically healthier—more self-confident, more willing to speak their own mind, better liked by peers, and identity-achieved (Bronstein, 2006; Dusek, 1987; Harter, 2006).

ASK YOURSELF

>> **REVIEW**
How does an understanding of ideal reciprocity contribute to moral development? Why are Kohlberg's Stages 3 and 4 morally mature constructions?

>> **APPLY**
Tam grew up in a small village culture, Lydia in a large industrial city. At age 15, Tam reasons at Kohlberg's Stage 3, Lydia at Stage 4. What factors might account for the difference?

>> **CONNECT**
How might the exploration of values and goals associated with healthy identity development contribute to the eventual decline in adolescent gender intensification?

>> **REFLECT**
Do you favor a cognitive-developmental or a pragmatic approach to morality, or both? What research evidence and personal experiences influenced your viewpoint?

The Family

Franca and Antonio remember their son Louis's freshman year of high school as a difficult time. Because of a demanding project at work, Franca was away from home many evenings and weekends. In her absence, Antonio took over, but when business declined and he had to cut costs at his hardware store, he, too, had less time for the family. That year, Louis and two friends used their computer know-how to crack the code of a long-distance telephone service. From the family basement, they made calls around the country. Louis's grades fell, and he often left the house without saying where he was going. Franca and Antonio began to feel uncomfortable about the long hours Louis was spending in the basement and their lack of contact with him. Finally, when the telephone company traced the illegal calls to their phone number, they knew they had cause for concern.

Development at adolescence involves striving for **autonomy**—a sense of oneself as a separate, self-governing individual. Teenagers strive to rely more on themselves and less on parents for decision making (Collins & Laursen, 2004; Steinberg & Silk, 2002). Nevertheless, parent–child relationships remain vital for helping adolescents become autonomous, responsible individuals.

Parent–Child Relationships

A variety of changes within the adolescent support autonomy. In Section 5, we saw that puberty triggers psychological distancing from parents. In addition, as young people look more mature, parents give them more independence and responsibility. Cognitive development also paves the way toward autonomy: Gradually, adolescents solve problems and make decisions more effectively. And an improved ability to reason about social relationships leads teenagers to *deidealize* their parents, viewing them as "just people." Consequently, they no longer bend as easily to parental authority as they did when younger.

Yet as Franca and Antonio's episode with Louis reveals, teenagers still need guidance and, at times, protection from dangerous situations. In diverse ethnic groups, SES levels, nations, and family structures (including single-parent, two-parent, and stepparent), warm, supportive parent–adolescent ties that permit young people to explore ideas and social roles foster autonomy, predicting high self-reliance, work orientation, academic competence, favorable self-esteem, and ease of separation in the transition to college (Bean, Barber, & Crane, 2007; Eisenberg et al., 2005b; Vazsonyi, Hibbert, & Snider, 2003; Wang, Pomerantz, & Chen, 2007). Conversely, parents who are coercive or psychologically controlling interfere with the development of autonomy. These tactics are consistently linked to low self-esteem, depression, drug and alcohol use, and antisocial behavior among teenagers—outcomes that often persist into early adulthood (Barber, Stolz, & Olsen, 2005; Bronte-Tinkew, Moore, & Carrano, 2006; Wissink, Deković, & Meijer, 2006).

We described the family as a *system* that must adapt to changes in its members. The rapid physical and psychological changes of adolescence trigger conflicting expectations in

This teenager and his father share an affectionate moment. Adolescents may resist parental authority, especially in matters of personal choice such as dress. But most maintain close family ties, particularly when parents give them the freedom to explore ideas and social roles.

parent–child relationships—a major reason that many parents find rearing teenagers to be stressful.

Earlier we noted that interest in making choices about personal matters strengthens in adolescence. Yet parents and teenagers—especially young teenagers—differ sharply on the appropriate age for granting certain privileges, such as control over clothing, school courses, going out with friends, and dating (Smetana, 2002). Consistent parental monitoring of the young person's daily activities, through a cooperative relationship in which the adolescent willingly discloses information, is linked to a variety of positive outcomes—prevention of delinquency, reduction in sexual activity, improved school performance, and positive psychological well-being (Crouter & Head, 2002; Jacobson & Crockett, 2000).

Parents' own development can also lead to friction with teenagers. While their children face a boundless future and a wide array of choices, middle-aged parents must accept the fact that their own possibilities are narrowing (Holmbeck, 1996). Often they can't understand why the adolescent wants to skip family activities to be with peers. And teenagers fail to appreciate that parents want the family to spend as much time together as possible because an important period in their adult life—child rearing—will soon end.

Immigrant parents from cultures that highly value family closeness and obedience to authority have greater difficulty adapting to their teenagers' push for autonomy, often reacting more strongly to adolescent disagreement (Phinney & Ong, 2001). And as adolescents acquire the host culture's language and are increasingly exposed to its individualistic values, immigrant parents may become even more critical, causing teenagers to rely less on the family network for social support. The resulting acculturative stress is associated with a rise in deviant behavior, including alcohol use and delinquency (Crane et al., 2005; Warner et al., 2006).

Throughout adolescence, the quality of the parent–child relationship is the single most consistent predictor of mental health. In well-functioning families, teenagers remain attached to parents and seek their advice, but they do so in a context of greater freedom (Collins & Steinberg, 2006). The mild conflict that arises facilitates adolescent identity and autonomy by helping family members express and tolerate disagreement. Conflicts also inform parents of teenagers' changing needs and expectations, signaling a need for adjustments in the parent–child relationship.

By middle to late adolescence, most parents and children achieve this mature, mutual relationship, and harmonious interaction is on the rise. The reduced time that Western teenagers spend with parents—for U.S. youths, a drop from 33 percent of waking hours in fifth grade to 14 percent in twelfth grade—has little to do with conflict (Larson et al., 1996). Rather, it results from the large amount of unstructured time available to teenagers in North America and Western Europe—on average, nearly half their waking hours (Larson, 2001). Young people tend to fill these hours with activities that take them away from home—part-time jobs, leisure and volunteer pursuits, and time with friends.

But this drop in family time is not universal. In one study, urban low- and middle-SES African-American youths showed no decline in hours spent with family—a pattern typical in cultures with collectivist values (Larson et al., 2001). Furthermore, teenagers living in risky neighborhoods tend to have more trusting relationships with parents and adjust more favorably when parents maintain tighter control and pressure them not to engage in worrisome behaviors (McElhaney & Allen, 2001). In harsh surroundings, young people seem to interpret more measured granting of autonomy as a sign of parental caring.

Family Circumstances

As Franca and Antonio's experience with Louis reminds us, adult life stress can interfere with warm, involved parenting and, in turn, with children's adjustment at any period of development. But parents who are financially secure, not overloaded with job pressures, and content with their marriages usually find it easier to grant teenagers appropriate autonomy and experience less conflict with them (Cowan & Cowan, 2002; Crouter & Bumpass, 2001). When Franca and Antonio's work stress eased and they recognized Louis's need for more involvement and guidance, his problems subsided.

Less than 10 percent of families with adolescents have seriously troubled relationships. Of these, most have difficulties that began in childhood (Collins & Laursen, 2004). Table 6.2 summarizes family conditions considered in earlier sections that pose challenges for adolescents. Teenagers who develop well despite family stresses continue to benefit from factors that fostered resilience in earlier years: an appealing, easy-going disposition; a parent who combines warmth with high expectations; and (especially if parental supports are lacking) bonds with prosocial adults outside the family who care deeply about the adolescent's well-being (Masten, 2001; Masten & Shaffer, 2006).

■ **TABLE 6.2** ■ *Family Circumstances with Implications for Adolescent Adjustment*

FAMILY CIRCUMSTANCE	TO REVIEW, TURN TO . . .
TYPE OF FAMILY	
Adoptive	
Divorced single-parent	Section 4, pages 135–137
Blended	Section 4, pages 139–144
Employed mother and dual-earner	Section 4, pages 138–139
FAMILY CONDITIONS	
Economic hardship	
Child maltreatment	Section 2, pages 69–71
	Section 4, pages 140–142
Adolescent parenthood	Section 5, pages 166–168

Siblings

Like parent–child relationships, sibling interactions adapt to development at adolescence. As younger siblings become more self-sufficient, they accept less direction from their older brothers and sisters, and sibling influence declines. Also, as teenagers become more involved in friendships and romantic relationships, they invest less time and energy in siblings, who are part of the family from which they are trying to establish autonomy. As a result, sibling relationships often become less intense, in both positive and negative feelings (Hetherington, Henderson, & Reiss, 1999; Kim et al., 2006).

Nevertheless, attachment between siblings remains strong for most young people. Brothers and sisters who established a positive bond in early childhood continue to express affection and caring—an outcome linked to more favorable emotional and social adjustment (Branje et al., 2004; Kim et al., 2007). Also, mild sibling differences in perceived parental affection no longer trigger jealousy but, instead, predict greater sibling warmth (Feinberg et al., 2003). Perhaps adolescents interpret a unique relationship with parents, as long as it is generally accepting, as a gratifying sign of their own individuality.

Peer Relations

As adolescents spend less time with family members, peers become increasingly important. In industrialized nations, young people spend most of each weekday with agemates in school. Teenagers also spend much out-of-class time together, more in some cultures than others. For example, U.S. young people have about 50 hours of free time per week, Europeans about 45 hours, and East Asians about 33 hours (Larson, 2001). A shorter school year and less demanding academic standards, which lead American youths to devote much less time to schoolwork, account for this difference.

In the following sections, we will see that adolescent peer relations can be both positive and negative. At their best, peers serve as critical bridges between the family and adult social roles.

Friendships

Number of "best friends" declines from about four to six in early adolescence to one or two in adulthood (Hartup & Stevens, 1999). At the same time, the nature of the relationship changes.

■ **CHARACTERISTICS OF ADOLESCENT FRIENDSHIPS.** When asked about the meaning of friendship, teenagers stress three characteristics. The most important is *intimacy,* or psychological closeness, which is supported by *mutual understanding* of each other's values, beliefs, and feelings. In addition, more than younger children, teenagers want their friends to be *loyal*—to stick up for them and not to leave them for somebody else (Buhrmester, 1996; Hartup & Abecassis, 2004).

As frankness and faithfulness increase, *self-disclosure* (sharing of private thoughts and feelings) between friends rises steadily over the adolescent years (see Figure 6.2 on page 206). As a result, teenage friends get to know each other better as personalities. In addition to the many characteristics that school-age friends share (see page 128 in Section 4), adolescent friends tend to be alike in identity status, educational aspirations, political beliefs, and willingness to try drugs and engage in lawbreaking acts. Over time, they become more similar in these ways (Akers, Jones, & Coyl, 1998; Berndt & Murphy, 2002). Occasionally, however, teenagers choose friends with differing attitudes and values, which permits them to explore new perspectives within the security of a compatible relationship.

During adolescence, cooperation and mutual affirmation between friends increase—changes that reflect greater skill at preserving the relationship and sensitivity to a friend's needs and desires (Phillipsen, 1999). Adolescents also are less possessive of their friends than they were in childhood (Parker et al., 2005). Desiring a certain degree of autonomy for themselves, they recognize that friends need this, too.

■ **SEX DIFFERENCES IN FRIENDSHIPS.** *TAKE A MOMENT...* Ask several adolescents to describe their close friendships. You are likely to find a consistent sex difference: Emotional closeness is more common between girls than between boys (Markovits, Benenson, & Dolensky, 2001). Girls frequently get together to "just talk," and their interactions contain more self-disclosure and supportive statements. In contrast, boys more often gather for an activity—usually sports and competitive games. Boys' discussions usually focus on accomplishments and involve more competition and conflict (Brendgen et al., 2001; Rubin, Bukowski, & Parker, 2006).

Because of gender-role expectations, girls' friendships typically focus on communal concerns, boys' on achievement and status. Boys do form close friendship ties, but the quality of their friendships is more variable. Gender identity plays a role:

■ **FIGURE 6.2** ■ **Age changes in reported self-disclosure to parents and peers, based on findings of several studies.**
Self-disclosure to friends increases steadily during adolescence, reflecting intimacy as a major basis of friendship. Self-disclosure to romantic partners also rises. However, not until the college years does it surpass intimacy with friends. Self-disclosure to parents declines in early adolescence, a time of mild parent–child conflict. As family relationships readjust to the young person's increasing autonomy, self-disclosure to parents rises. (From D. Buhrmester, 1996, "Need Fulfillment, Interpersonal Competence, and the Developmental Contexts of Early Adolescent Friendship," in W. M. Bukowski, A. F. Newcomb, & W. W. Hartup (Eds.), *The Company They Keep: Friendship During Childhood and Adolescence,* New York: Cambridge University Press, p. 168. Reprinted with the permission of Cambridge University Press.)

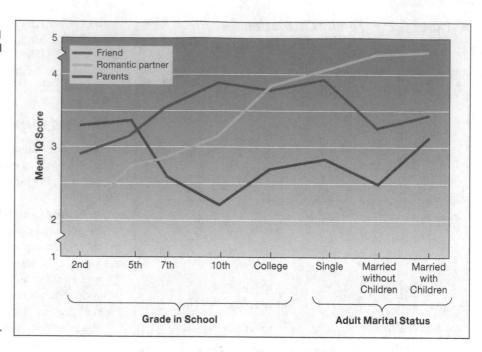

Androgynous boys are just as likely as girls to form intimate same-sex ties, whereas highly "masculine" boys are less likely to do so (Jones & Dembo, 1989).

Friendship closeness, though usually beneficial, can have costs. When focusing on deeper thoughts and feelings, adolescent friends tend to *coruminate,* or repeatedly mull over problems and negative emotions. Corumination, while contributing to high friendship quality, also triggers anxiety and depression—symptoms more common among girls than among boys (Rose, Carlson, & Waller, 2007). And when conflicts arise between intimate friends, more potential exists for one party to harm the other through relational aggression—for example, by divulging sensitive personal information to outsiders. For this reason, girls' closest same-sex friendships tend to be of shorter duration than boys' (Benenson & Christakos, 2003).

Compared to boys, girls place a higher value on emotional closeness, engaging in more self-disclosure and mutually supportive statements with friends.

■ **FRIENDSHIPS ON THE INTERNET.** Teenagers frequently use the Internet to communicate with friends. Instant messaging—their preferred means of online interaction—seems to support friendship closeness. As amount of instant messaging between preexisting friends increases, so do young people's perceptions of intimacy in the relationship and feelings of well-being (Hu et al., 2004; Valkenburg & Peter, 2007a, 2007b).

Although mostly communicating with friends they know, teenagers are also drawn to meeting new people over the Internet. Chat rooms, blogs, message boards, and social networking sites such as MySpace open up vast alternatives beyond their families, schools, and communities. Through these online ties, young people explore central adolescent issues—sexuality, challenges in parent and peer relationships, and attitudes and values—in contexts that may feel less threatening than similar everyday conversations (Subrahmanyam, Smahel, & Greenfield, 2006). Online interactions with strangers also offer some teenagers vital social support. Young people suffering from eating disorders, depression, and other problems can access message boards where participants provide mutual assistance, including a sense of group belonging and acceptance (Whitlock, Powers, & Eckenrode, 2006).

But online communication also poses dangers. In unmonitored chat rooms, teenagers are likely to encounter degrading racial and ethnic slurs and sexually obscene and harassing remarks (Tynes, Reynolds, & Greenfield, 2004). Furthermore, in a survey of a nationally representative sample of U.S. 10- to 17-year-olds, 14 percent reported online close friendships or romances (Wolak, Mitchell, & Finkelhor, 2003). Although some well-adjusted adolescents formed these bonds, many were youths who reported high levels of conflict with parents, peer victimization, depression, and delinquency, and who spent extensive time on the Internet (see Figure 6.3). They also more often had been asked by online friends for face-to-face meetings and had attended those meetings—without telling their parents.

© MYRLEEN FERGUSON CATE/PHOTOEDIT

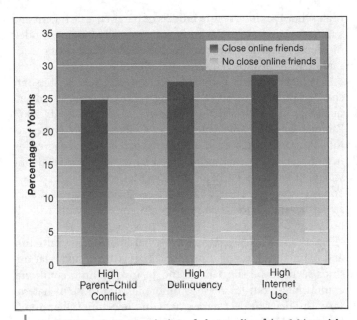

■ **FIGURE 6.3** ■ **Association of close online friendships with parent–child conflict, delinquency, and high Internet use.** In this survey of a nationally representative sample of 1,500 U.S. Internet-using 10- to 17-year-olds, those who reported that they had formed close online friendships or romances were more likely to be troubled youths who spent much time on the Internet. (Adapted from Wolak, Mitchell, & Finkelhor, 2003.)

The Internet's value for enabling convenient and satisfying communication among teenage friends must be weighed against its potential for facilitating harmful social experiences. Parents are wise to point out the risks of Internet communication, including harassment and exploitation, and to insist that teenagers follow Internet safety rules (see *www.safeteens.com*).

■ **FRIENDSHIPS AND ADJUSTMENT.** As long as adolescent friendships are not characterized by jealousy, relational aggression, or attraction to antisocial behavior, they are related to many aspects of psychological health and competence into early adulthood (Bagwell et al., 2001; Bukowski, 2001), for several reasons:

■ *Close friendships provide opportunities to explore the self and develop a deep understanding of another.* Through open, honest communication, friends become sensitive to each other's strengths and weaknesses, needs and desires—a process that supports the development of self-concept, perspective taking, and identity.

■ *Close friendships provide a foundation for future intimate relationships.* Recall from Figure 6.2 that self-disclosure to friends precedes disclosure to romantic partners. Conversations with teenage friends about sexuality and romance, along with the intimacy of friendship itself, may help adolescents establish and work out problems in romantic partnerships (Connolly & Goldberg, 1999).

■ *Close friendships help young people deal with the stresses of adolescence.* By enhancing sensitivity to and concern for another, supportive friendships promote empathy, sympa-

thy, and prosocial behavior. As a result, friendships contribute to involvement in constructive youth activities, avoidance of antisocial acts, and psychological well-being (Lansford et al., 2003; Wentzel, Barry, & Caldwell, 2004).

■ *Close friendships can improve attitudes toward and involvement in school.* When teenagers enjoy interacting with friends at school, they may begin to view all aspects of school life more positively (Berndt & Murphy, 2002).

Cliques and Crowds

In early adolescence, *peer groups* (see Section 4) become increasingly common and tightly knit. They are organized into **cliques,** groups of about five to seven members who are friends and, therefore, usually resemble one another in family background, attitudes, and values. At first, cliques are limited to same-sex members. Among girls but not boys, being in a clique predicts academic and social competence. Clique membership is more important to girls, who use it as a context for expressing emotional closeness (Henrich et al., 2000). By midadolescence, mixed-sex cliques are common.

Often several cliques with similar values form a larger, more loosely organized group called a **crowd.** Unlike the more intimate clique, membership in a crowd is based on reputation and stereotype, granting the adolescent an identity within the larger social structure of the school. Prominent crowds in a typical high school might include "brains" (nonathletes who enjoy academics), "jocks" (who are very involved in sports), "populars" (class leaders who are highly social and involved in activities), "partyers" (who value socializing but care little about schoolwork), "nonconformists" (who like unconventional clothing and music), and "burnouts" (who cut school and get into trouble) (Kinney, 1999; Stone & Brown, 1999).

What influences the sorting of teenagers into cliques and crowds? Crowd affiliations are linked to strengths in adolescents' self-concepts, which reflect their abilities and interests (Prinstein & La Greca, 2002). Family factors are important, too. In a study of 8,000 ninth to twelfth graders, adolescents who described their parents as authoritative were members of "brain," "jock," and "popular" groups that accepted both adult and peer reward systems. In contrast, boys with permissive parents aligned themselves with the "partyers" and "burnouts," suggesting lack of identification with adult reward systems (Durbin et al., 1993).

These findings indicate that many peer-group values are extensions of ones acquired at home. Once adolescents join a clique or crowd, it can modify their beliefs and behavior. But the positive impact of having academically and socially skilled peers is greatest for teenagers whose own parents are authoritative. And the negative impact of having antisocial, drug-using friends is strongest for teenagers whose parents use less effective child-rearing styles (Mounts & Steinberg, 1995). In sum, family experiences affect the extent to which adolescents become like their peers over time.

As interest in dating increases, boys' and girls' cliques come together. Mixed-sex cliques provide boys and girls with models of how to interact and a chance to do so without having to be

Members of this Ultimate Frisbee team form a crowd. Unlike the more intimate clique, the larger, more loosely organized crowd grants the adolescent an identity within the larger social structure of the school.

intimate (Connolly et al., 2004). By late adolescence, when boys and girls feel comfortable enough about approaching each other directly, the mixed-sex clique disappears (Connolly & Goldberg, 1999).

Crowds also decline in importance. As adolescents settle on personal values and goals, they no longer feel a need to broadcast, through dress, language, and activities, who they are. From tenth to twelfth grade, about half of young people switch crowds, mostly in favorable directions (Strouse, 1999). "Brains" and "normal" crowds grow and deviant crowds lose members as teenagers focus more on their future.

Dating

The hormonal changes of puberty increase sexual interest, but cultural expectations determine when and how dating begins. Asian youths start dating later and have fewer dating partners than young people in Western societies, which tolerate and even encourage romantic involvements from middle school on (see Figure 6.4). At age 12 to 14, these relationships last only briefly, but by age 16 they continue, on average, for nearly two years (Carver, Joyner, & Udry, 2003). Young adolescents tend to mention recreation and achieving peer status as reasons for dating. By late adolescence, as young people are ready for greater psychological intimacy, they look for someone who offers companionship, affection, and social support (Brown, 2004; Collins & van Dulmen, 2006c).

The achievement of intimacy between dating partners typically lags behind that between friends. According to ethological theory, early attachment bonds lead to an *internal working model*, or set of expectations about attachment figures, that guides later close relationships. Consistent with this idea, secure attachment to parents in infancy and childhood—together with recollections of that security in adolescence—predicts quality of teenagers' friendship and romantic ties (Collins & van Dulmen, 2006a; Weimer, Kerns, & Oldenburg, 2004). And in a study of

high school seniors, secure models of parental attachment and supportive interactions with parents predicted secure models of friendship, which, in turn, were related to the security of romantic relationships (Furman et al., 2002).

Perhaps because early adolescent dating relationships are shallow and stereotyped, early dating is related to drug use, delinquency, and poor academic achievement (Eaton et al., 2007; Zimmer-Gembeck, Siebenbruner, & Collins, 2001). These factors, along with a history of uninvolved parenting and aggression in family and peer relationships, increase the likelihood of dating violence (Arriaga & Foshee, 2004; Cyr, McDuff, & Wright, 2006). Young teenagers are better off sticking with group activities, such as parties and dances, before becoming involved with a steady boyfriend or girlfriend.

Gay and lesbian youths face special challenges in initiating and maintaining visible romances. Their first dating relationships seem to be short-lived and to involve little emotional commitment, but for reasons different from those of heterosexuals: They fear peer harassment and rejection (Diamond & Lucas, 2004). Recall from Section 5 that because of intense prejudice, homosexual adolescents often retreat into heterosexual dating. In addition, many have difficulty finding a same-sex partner because their homosexual peers have not yet come out. Often their first contacts with other sexual minority youths occur in support groups, where they are free to date publicly and can discuss concerns about coming out (Diamond, 2003).

As long as it does not begin too soon, dating provides lessons in cooperation, etiquette, and dealing with people in a wide range of situations. Among older teenagers, close romantic ties promote sensitivity, empathy, self-esteem, social support, and identity development (Collins, 2003; Furman & Shaffer, 2003). Still, about half of first romances do not survive high school graduation, and those that do usually become less

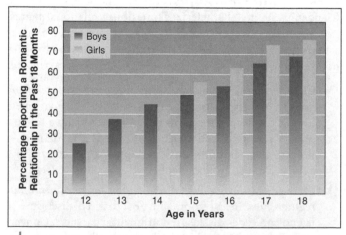

■ **FIGURE 6.4** ■ **Increase in romantic relationships in adolescence.** More than 16,000 U.S. youths responded to an interview in which they indicated whether they had been involved in a romantic relationship during the past 18 months. At age 12, about one-fourth of young people reported them, a figure that rose to about three-fourths at age 18. (Adapted from Carver, Joyner, & Udry, 2003.)

As long as dating does not begin too soon, it extends the benefits of adolescent friendships. Besides being fun, dating promotes sensitivity, empathy, and identity development as teenagers relate to someone whose needs differ from their own.

satisfying (Shaver, Furman, & Buhrmester, 1985). Because young people are still forming their identities, high school couples often find that they have little in common later.

Peer Conformity

When Franca and Antonio discovered Louis's lawbreaking during his freshman year of high school, they began to worry about the negative side of adolescent peer networks. Although conformity to peer pressure is greater during adolescence than in childhood or early adulthood, it is a complex process, varying with the young person's age, current situation, need for social approval, and culture.

A study of several hundred U.S. youths revealed that adolescents felt greatest pressure to conform to the most obvious aspects of the peer culture—dress, grooming, and participation in social activities. Peer pressure to engage in proadult behavior, such as cooperating with parents and getting good grades, was also strong (Brown, Lohr, & McClenahan, 1986). Many teenagers said that their friends actively discouraged antisocial acts. In research conducted in Singapore, a culture that emphasizes family loyalty, outcomes were similar, except that peer pressure to meet family and school obligations exceeded pressure to join in peer-culture pursuits (Sim & Koh, 2003). As these findings show, peers and parents often act in concert, toward desirable ends!

Perhaps because of greater concern with what their friends think of them, early adolescents are more likely than younger or older individuals to give in to peer pressure to engage in drug taking and delinquent acts (Brown, Clasen, & Eicher, 1986; McIntosh, MacDonald, & McKeganey, 2006). But although peers exert more influence on teenagers' day-to-day personal choices, parents have more impact on basic life values and educational plans (Steinberg, 2001). And young people who feel

competent and worthwhile are less likely to fall in line behind peers.

Finally, authoritative child rearing is related to resistance to peer pressure. When parents are supportive and exert appropriate oversight, teenagers respect them and, therefore, usually follow their rules and consider their advice. In contrast, adolescents whose parents exert either too much or too little control tend to be highly peer-oriented (Allen, Porter, & McFarland, 2006). They more often rely on friends for advice about their personal lives and future and are more willing to break their parents' rules, ignore their schoolwork, and engage in other problem behaviors.

ASK YOURSELF

>> **REVIEW**
Describe the distinct positive functions of friendships, cliques, and crowds in adolescence. What factors lead some friendships and peer-group ties to be harmful?

>> **APPLY**
Thirteen-year-old Mattie's parents are warm, firm in their expectations, and consistent in monitoring her activities. At school, Mattie met some girls who want her to tell her parents she's going to a friend's house and then, instead, join them at the beach for a party. Is Mattie likely to comply? Explain.

>> **CONNECT**
How might gender intensification contribute to the shallow quality of early adolescent dating relationships?

>> **REFLECT**
How did family experiences influence your crowd membership in high school? How did your crowd membership influence your behavior?

Problems of Development

Most young people move through adolescence with little disturbance. But as we have seen, some encounter major disruptions in development, such as early parenthood, substance abuse, and school failure. In each instance, biological and psychological changes, families, schools, peers, communities, and culture combine to yield particular outcomes. Serious difficulties rarely occur in isolation but are usually interrelated as is apparent in three additional problems of the teenage years: depression, suicide, and delinquency.

Depression

Depression—feeling sad, frustrated, and hopeless about life, accompanied by loss of pleasure in most activities and disturbances in sleep, appetite, concentration, and energy—is the most common psychological problem of adolescence. About 15 to 20 percent of teenagers have had one or more major depressive episodes, a rate comparable to that of adults. From 2 to 8 percent are chronically depressed—gloomy and self-critical for many months and sometimes years (Rushton, Forcier, & Schectman, 2002).

Serious depression affects only 1 to 2 percent of children, many of whom remain depressed in adolescence. In addition, depression increases sharply from ages 12 to 16 in industrialized nations, with many more girls than boys displaying adolescent onset. Teenage girls are twice as likely as boys to report persistent depressed mood—a difference sustained throughout the lifespan (Dekker et al., 2007; Hankin & Abela, 2005; Nolen-Hoeksema, 2002). If allowed to continue, depression seriously impairs social, academic, and vocational functioning. Unfortunately, the stereotypical view of adolescence as a period of "storm and stress" leads many adults to minimize the seriousness of adolescent depression, misinterpreting it as just a passing phase.

■ **FACTORS RELATED TO DEPRESSION.**   The precise combination of biological and environmental factors leading to depression varies from one individual to the next. Kinship studies reveal that heredity plays an important role (Glowinski et al., 2003). Genes can induce depression by affecting the balance of neurotransmitters in the brain, the development of brain regions involved in inhibiting negative emotion, or the body's hormonal response to stress.

But experience can also activate depression, promoting any of these biological changes. A high incidence of depression and other psychological disorders is seen in parents of depressed children and adolescents. Although a genetic risk may be passed from parent to child, in earlier sections we saw that depressed or otherwise stressed parents often engage in maladaptive parenting. As a result, their child's emotional self-regulation, attachment, and self-esteem may be impaired, with serious consequences for many cognitive and social skills (Abela et al., 2005; Yap, Allen, & Ladouceur, 2008). Depressed youths usually display a learned-helpless attributional style (see Section 4) (Graber, 2004). In a vulnerable young person, numerous events can spark depression—for example, failing at something important, parental divorce, or the end of a close friendship or romantic partnership.

■ **SEX DIFFERENCES.**   Why are girls more prone to depression than boys? Biological changes associated with puberty cannot be responsible because the gender difference is limited to industrialized nations. In developing countries, rates of depression are similar for males and females and occasionally higher in males (Culbertson, 1997). Even when females do exceed males in depression, the size of the difference varies. For example, it is smaller in China than in North America, perhaps because of decades of efforts by the Chinese government to eliminate gender inequalities (Greenberger et al., 2000).

Instead, stressful life events and gender-typed coping styles seem to be responsible. Early-maturing girls are especially prone to depression (see Section 5). And the gender intensification of early adolescence often strengthens girls' passivity, dependency, and tendency to ruminate on their anxieties and problems—maladaptive approaches to tasks expected of teenagers in complex cultures. Consistent with this explanation, adolescents who identify strongly with "feminine" traits

In industrialized nations, stressful life events and gender-typed coping styles—passivity, dependency, and rumination—make adolescent girls more susceptible to depression than boys.

ruminate more and are more depressed, regardless of their sex (Broderick & Korteland, 2004; Papadakis et al., 2006). Girls who repeatedly feel overwhelmed develop an overly reactive physiological stress response and cope more poorly with future challenges (Nolen-Hoeksema, 2006). In this way, stressful experiences and stress reactivity feed on one another, sustaining depression. Profound depression can lead to suicidal thoughts, which all too often are translated into action.

Suicide

The suicide rate increases over the lifespan, from childhood to old age, but it jumps sharply at adolescence. Currently, suicide is the third-leading cause of death among American youths (after motor vehicle collisions and homicides) (U.S. Census Bureau, 2009b). Perhaps because U.S. teenagers experience more stress and fewer supports than in the past, the adolescent suicide rate tripled between the mid-1960s and mid-1990s, followed by a slight decline (Spirito & Esposito-Smythers, 2006). At the same time, rates of adolescent suicide vary widely among industrialized nations—low in Greece, Italy, the Netherlands, and Spain; intermediate in Australia, Canada, Japan, and the United States; and high in Finland, New Zealand, and Singapore (Bridge, Goldstein, & Brent, 2006). These international differences remain unexplained.

■ **FACTORS RELATED TO ADOLESCENT SUICIDE.**   Despite girls' higher rates of depression, the number of boys who kill themselves exceeds the number of girls by a ratio of 3 or 4 to 1. Girls make more unsuccessful suicide attempts and use methods from which they are more likely to be revived, such as a sleeping pill overdose. In contrast, boys tend to choose techniques that lead to instant death, such as firearms or hanging. Gender-role expectations may contribute; less tolerance exists for feelings of helplessness and failed efforts in males than in females (Canetto & Sakinofsky, 1998).

Perhaps because of greater extended-family support, African Americans and Hispanics have lower suicide rates than

Caucasian Americans. Recently, however, suicide has risen among African-American adolescent males; the current rate approaches that of Caucasian-American males. And Native-American youths commit suicide at rates two to six times national averages (U.S. Census Bureau, 2009b). High rates of profound family poverty, school failure, alcohol and drug use, and depression probably underlie these trends.

Gay, lesbian, and bisexual youths are also at high risk, attempting suicide three times as often as other adolescents. Those who have tried to kill themselves report more family conflict over their gender-atypical behavior, inner turmoil about their sexuality, and peer victimization due to their sexual orientation (D'Augelli et al., 2005).

Suicide tends to occur in two types of young people. The first group includes adolescents who are highly intelligent but solitary, withdrawn, and unable to meet their own standards or those of important people in their lives. Members of a second, larger group show antisocial tendencies and express their un-happiness through bullying, fighting, stealing, increased risk taking, and drug abuse (Evans, Hawton, & Rodham, 2004). Besides being hostile and destructive, they turn their anger and disappointment inward.

Suicidal adolescents often have a family history of emotional and antisocial disorders. In addition, they are likely to have experienced multiple stressful life events, including economic disadvantage, parental divorce, frequent parent–child conflict, and abuse and neglect. Stressors typically increase during the period preceding a suicide attempt or completion (Beautrais, 2003; Pfeffer, 2006). Triggering events include parental blaming of the teenager for family problems, the breakup of an important peer relationship, or the humiliation of having been caught engaging in antisocial acts.

Public policies resulting in cultural disintegration have amplified suicide rates among Native-American youths. From the late 1800s to the 1970s, Native-American families were forced to enroll their children in government-run residential boarding schools designed to erase tribal affiliations. From the moment children arrived, they were not allowed to "be Indian" in any way—culturally, linguistically, artistically, or spiritually (Goldston et al., 2008). These repressive schools left many young people academically unprepared and emotionally scarred, contributing to family and community disorganization in current and succeeding generations. Consequently, youth crime and suicide rates increased (Barnes, Josefowitz, & Cole, 2006; Howell & Yuille, 2004).

Why does suicide increase in adolescence? One factor seems to be teenagers' improved ability to plan ahead. Although some act impulsively, many young people take purposeful steps toward killing themselves. Other cognitive changes also contribute. Belief in the personal fable leads many depressed young people to conclude that no one could possibly understand their intense pain. As a result, their despair and hopelessness deepen.

■ **PREVENTION AND TREATMENT.** To prevent suicides, parents and teachers must be trained to pick up on the signals that a troubled teenager sends (see Table 6.3). Schools and

■ **TABLE 6.3** ■ *Warning Signs of Suicide*

Efforts to put personal affairs in order—smoothing over troubled relationships, giving away treasured possessions

Verbal cues—saying goodbye to family members and friends, making direct or indirect references to suicide ("I won't have to worry about these problems much longer"; "I wish I were dead")

Feelings of sadness, despondency, "not caring" anymore

Extreme fatigue, lack of energy, boredom

No desire to socialize; withdrawal from friends

Easily frustrated

Emotional outbursts—spells of crying or laughing, bursts of energy

Inability to concentrate, distractible

Decline in grades, absence from school, discipline problems

Neglect of personal appearance

Sleep change—loss of sleep or excessive sleepiness

Appetite change—eating more or less than usual

Physical complaints—stomachaches, backaches, headaches

recreational and religious organizations can provide counseling and support (Spirito et al., 2003). Once a teenager takes steps toward suicide, staying with the young person, listening, and expressing compassion and concern until professional help can be obtained are essential.

Treatments for depressed and suicidal adolescents range from antidepressant medication to individual, family, and group therapy. Until the adolescent improves, removing weapons, knives, razors, scissors, and drugs from the home is vital. On a broader scale, gun-control legislation that limits adolescents' access to the most frequent and deadly suicide method in the United States would greatly reduce both the number of suicides and the high teenage homicide rate (Commission on Adolescent Suicide Prevention, 2005).

After a suicide, family and peer survivors need support to help them cope with grief, anger, and guilt over not having been able to help the victim. Teenage suicides often occur in clusters, with one death increasing the likelihood of others among depressed peers who knew the young person or heard about the suicide through the media (Bearman & Moody, 2004; Gould, Jamieson, & Romer, 2003). In view of this trend, a watchful eye must be kept on vulnerable adolescents after a suicide happens. Restraint by journalists in publicizing teenage suicides also aids prevention.

Delinquency

Juvenile delinquents are children or adolescents who engage in illegal acts. Although youth crime has declined in the United States since the mid-1990s, 12- to 17-year-olds account for about 15 percent of police arrests, although they constitute only

8 percent of the population (U.S. Department of Justice, 2008). When asked directly and confidentially about lawbreaking, almost all teenagers admit to having committed some sort of offense—usually a minor crime, such as petty stealing or disorderly conduct (Flannery et al., 2003).

Both police arrests and self-reports show that delinquency rises over the early teenage years, remains high in middle adolescence, and then declines (Farrington, 2004; U.S. Department of Justice, 2008). Recall that among young teenagers, antisocial behavior increases as a result of desire for peer approval. Over time, peers become less influential, moral reasoning improves, and young people enter social contexts (such as higher education, work, marriage, and career) that are less conducive to lawbreaking.

For most adolescents, a brush with the law does not forecast long-term antisocial behavior. But repeated arrests are cause for concern. Teenagers are responsible for 18 percent of violent offenses in the United States (U.S. Department of Justice, 2008). A small percentage become recurrent offenders, who commit most of these crimes, and some enter a life of crime. As the Lifespan Vista box on the following page reveals, childhood-onset conduct problems are far more likely to persist than conduct problems that first appear in adolescence.

■ FACTORS RELATED TO DELINQUENCY.

In adolescence, the gender gap in physical aggression widens (Chesney-Lind, 2001). Although girls account for about one in five adolescent arrests for violence, their offenses are largely limited to simple assault (such as pushing or spitting). Violent crime is mostly the domain of boys (Dahlberg & Simon, 2006). SES and ethnicity are strong predictors of arrests but only mildly related to teenagers' self-reports of antisocial acts. The difference is due to the tendency to arrest, charge, and punish low-SES ethnic minority youths more often than their higher-SES white and Asian counterparts (Farrington, 2004; U.S. Department of Justice, 2008).

Difficult temperament, low intelligence, poor school performance, peer rejection in childhood, and association with antisocial peers are linked to delinquency (Laird et al., 2005). How do these factors fit together? One of the most consistent findings about delinquent youths is that their families are low in warmth, high in conflict, and characterized by harsh, inconsistent discipline and low monitoring (Barnes et al., 2006; Capaldi et al., 2002a). Because marital transitions often contribute to family discord and disrupted parenting, boys who experience parental separation and divorce are especially prone to delinquency (Farrington, 2004). And youth crime peaks on weekdays between 2:00 and 8:00 P.M., when many teenagers are unsupervised (U.S. Department of Justice, 2008).

Our discussion on page 58 in Section 2 explained how ineffective parenting can promote and sustain children's aggression. Boys are more likely than girls to be targets of angry, inconsistent discipline because they are more active and impulsive and therefore harder to control. When children who are extreme in these characteristics are exposed to emotionally negative, inept parenting, aggression rises during childhood, leads to violent offenses in adolescence, and persists into adulthood (again, see the Lifespan Vista box).

Delinquency rises during the early teen years and remains high during middle adolescence. Although most of the time it involves petty stealing and disorderly conduct, a small percentage of young people engage in repeated, serious offenses and are at risk for a life of crime.

Teenagers commit more crimes in poverty-stricken neighborhoods with limited recreational and employment opportunities and high adult criminality (Kroneman, Loeber, & Hipwell, 2004). In such neighborhoods, adolescents have easy access to deviant peers, drugs, and firearms and are likely to be recruited into antisocial gangs, whose members commit the vast majority of violent delinquent acts. Furthermore, schools in these locales typically fail to meet students' developmental needs (Flannery et al., 2003). Large classes, weak instruction, and lax enforcement of rules increase teenagers' inclination toward aggression and violence.

■ PREVENTION AND TREATMENT.

Because delinquency has roots in childhood and results from events in several contexts, prevention must start early and take place at multiple levels (Frey et al., 2009). Positive family relationships, authoritative parenting, high-quality teaching in schools, and communities with healthy economic and social conditions go a long way toward reducing adolescent antisocial acts.

Lacking resources for effective prevention, many U.S. schools have implemented *zero tolerance policies*, which severely punish all disruptive and threatening behavior, major and minor, usually with suspension or expulsion. Yet often they are implemented inconsistently: Low-SES minority students are two to three times as likely to be punished, especially for minor misbehaviors (Goode & Goode, 2007; Skiba & Rausch, 2006). No evidence exists that zero tolerance achieves its objective of reducing youth aggression and other forms of misconduct (Stinchcomb, Bazemore, & Riestenberg, 2006). To the contrary, some studies find that by excluding students from school, zero tolerance heightens high school dropout and antisocial behavior.

■ A LIFESPAN VISTA: Looking Forward, Looking Back ■

Two Routes to Adolescent Delinquency

Persistent adolescent delinquency follows two paths of development, one involving a small number of youths with an onset of conduct problems in childhood, the second a larger number with an onset in adolescence. The early-onset type is far more likely to lead to a life-course pattern of aggression and criminality (Moffitt, 2006). The late-onset type usually does not persist beyond the transition to early adulthood.

Both childhood-onset and adolescent-onset youths engage in serious offenses; associate with deviant peers; participate in substance abuse, unsafe sex, and dangerous driving; and spend time in correctional facilities. Why does antisocial activity more often continue and escalate into violence in the first group? Longitudinal studies yield similar answers to this question. Most research has focused on boys, but several investigations report that girls who were physically aggressive in childhood are also at risk for later problems—occasionally violent delinquency but more often other norm-violating behaviors and psychological disorders (Broidy et al., 2003; Chamberlain, 2003).

Early-Onset Type

Early-onset youngsters seem to inherit traits that predispose them to aggressiveness (Pettit, 2004). For example, violence-prone boys are emotionally negative, restless, willful, and physically aggressive as early as age 2. They also show subtle deficits in cognitive functioning that seem to contribute to disruptions in the development of language, memory, and cognitive and emotional self-regulation (Moffitt, 2006; Shaw et al., 2003). Some have attention-deficit hyperactivity disorder (ADHD), which compounds their learning and self-control problems (see Section 3, page 92).

Yet these biological risks are not sufficient to sustain antisocial behavior: Most early-onset boys decline in aggression over time. Among those who follow the life-course path, inept parenting transforms their undercontrolled style into defiance and persistent aggression (Brame, Nagin, & Tremblay, 2001; Broidy et al., 2003). As they fail academically and are rejected by peers, they befriend other deviant youths, who facilitate one another's violent behavior while relieving loneliness (see Figure 6.5) (Lacourse et al., 2003). Limited cognitive and social skills result in high rates of school dropout and unemployment, contributing further to antisocial involvements. Often these boys experience their first arrest before age 14—a good indicator that they will be chronic offenders by age 18 (Patterson & Yoerger, 2002).

Preschoolers high in relational aggression also tend to be hyperactive and frequently in conflict with peers and adults (Willoughby, Kupersmidt, & Bryant, 2001). As these behaviors trigger peer rejection, relationally aggressive girls befriend other girls high in relational hostility, and their relational aggression rises (Werner & Crick, 2004). Adolescents high in relational aggression are often angry, vengeful, and defiant of adult rules. Among teenagers who combine physical and relational hostility, these oppositional reactions intensify, increasing the likelihood of serious antisocial activity (Harachi et al., 2006; Prinstein, Boergers, & Vernberg, 2001).

Late-Onset Type

Other youths first display antisocial behavior around the time of puberty, gradually increasing their involvement. Their conduct problems arise from the peer context of early adolescence, not from biological deficits and a history of unfavorable development. For some, quality of parenting may decline for a time, perhaps due to family stresses or the challenges of disciplining an unruly teenager (Moffitt, 2006). When age brings gratifying adult privileges, these youths draw on prosocial skills mastered before adolescence and abandon their antisocial ways.

A few late-onset youths do continue to engage in antisocial acts. The seriousness of their adolescent offenses seems to trap them in situations that close off opportunities for responsible behavior. Being employed or in school and forming positive, close relationships predict an end to criminal offending by age 20 to 25 (Clingempeel & Henggeler, 2003; Stouthamer-Loeber et al., 2004). In contrast, the longer antisocial young people spend in prison, the more likely they are to sustain a life of crime.

These findings suggest a need for a fresh look at policies aimed at stopping youth crime. Keeping youth offenders locked up for many years disrupts their vocational lives and access to social support during a crucial period of development, condemning them to a bleak future.

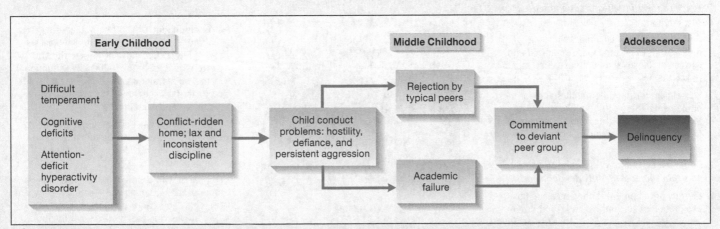

■ **FIGURE 6.5** ■ **Path to chronic delinquency for adolescents with childhood-onset antisocial behavior.** Difficult temperament and cognitive deficits characterize many of these youths in early childhood; some have attention-deficit hyperactivity disorder. Inept parenting transforms biologically based self-control difficulties into hostility and defiance.

Treating serious offenders requires an intensive, often lengthy approach, also directed at the multiple determinants of delinquency. The most effective methods include training parents in communication, monitoring, and discipline strategies and providing youths with experiences that improve cognitive and social skills, moral reasoning, and anger management and other aspects of emotional self-regulation (Gibbs et al., 2009b; Heilbrun, Lee, & Cottle, 2005).

Yet even these multidimensional treatments can fall short if young people remain embedded in hostile home lives, antisocial peer groups, and fragmented neighborhoods. In a program called *multisystemic therapy,* counselors combined family intervention with integrating violent youths into positive school, work, and leisure activities and disengaging them from deviant peers. Compared with conventional services or individual therapy, the intervention led to greater improvement in parent–child relations and school performance and a dramatic and sustained drop in number of arrests (Borduin, 2007; Henggeler, Sheidow, & Lee, 2007). Efforts to create nonaggres-

sive environments—at the family, community, and cultural levels—are needed to help delinquent youths and to foster healthy development of all young people.

ASK YOURSELF

>> REVIEW

Why are adolescent girls at greater risk for depression and adolescent boys at greater risk for suicide?

>> APPLY

Zeke had been well-behaved in elementary school, but at age 13 he started spending time with the "wrong crowd." At age 16, he was arrested for property damage. Is Zeke likely to become a long-term offender? Why or why not?

>> CONNECT

Reread the sections on adolescent pregnancy and substance abuse in Section 5. What factors do these problems have in common with suicide and delinquency?

Summary

Erikson's Theory: Identity versus Role Confusion

According to Erikson, what is the major personality achievement of adolescence?

>> Erikson's theory regards **identity** as the major personality achievement of adolescence. Young people who successfully resolve the psychological conflict of **identity versus role confusion** construct a solid self-definition consisting of self-chosen values and goals.

Self-Understanding

Describe changes in self-concept and self-esteem during adolescence.

>> Cognitive changes lead adolescents' self-descriptions to become more organized and consistent. Personal and moral values appear as key themes.

>> Self-esteem further differentiates and, for most adolescents, rises. Authoritative parenting and schools and neighborhoods that respect the young person's ethnicity support positive self-esteem.

Describe the four identity statuses, along with factors that promote identity development.

>> Identity development is often measured by exploration of alternatives and commitment to self-chosen values and goals. **Identity achievement** (commitment, preceded by exploration) and **identity moratorium** (exploration without having reached commitment) are psychologically healthy identity statuses.

>> Long-term **identity foreclosure** (commitment without exploration) and **identity diffusion** (lack of both exploration and commitment) are related to adjustment difficulties.

>> An information-gathering cognitive style, healthy parental attachment, interaction with diverse peers, close friendships, and schools and communities that provide rich and varied opportunities promote healthy identity development. Similarly, supportive parents, peers, and schools can foster a strong, secure **ethnic identity** among minority adolescents. A **bicultural identity** offers additional emotional and social benefits.

© DAVID GROSSMAN/THE IMAGE WORKS

Moral Development

Describe Kohlberg's theory of moral development, and evaluate its accuracy.

>> According to Kohlberg, moral reasoning develops gradually through three levels, each of which contains two stages: At the **preconventional level**, morality is externally controlled by rewards, punishments, and authority figures; at the **conventional level,** conformity to laws and rules preserves positive human relationships and societal order; and at the **postconventional level,** morality is defined by abstract, universal principles of justice.

>> A reexamination of Kohlberg's stages suggests that moral maturity can be found at Stages 3 and 4; few people move beyond to the postconventional level. The influence of situational factors on moral judgment suggests that Kohlberg's moral stages are best viewed as loosely organized and overlapping.

>> Contrary to Gilligan's claim, Kohlberg's theory does not underestimate the moral reasoning of females but instead taps both justice and caring moralities.

>> Compared with children, teenagers display more subtle reasoning about conflicts between personal choice and community obligation. They are also increasingly aware of the moral implications of following social conventions.

Describe influences on moral reasoning and its relationship to moral behavior.

» Experiences contributing to moral maturity include warm, rational child-rearing practices, years of schooling, and peer discussions of moral issues. In village societies, where moral cooperation is based on direct relations between people, moral reasoning rarely moves beyond Kohlberg's Stage 3. In collectivist cultures, dilemma responses often are more other-directed than in Western societies.

» Maturity of moral reasoning is only modestly related to moral behavior. Moral action is also influenced by the individual's empathy and guilt, temperament, history of morally relevant experiences, and **moral self-relevance.**

» Despite declines in formal religious involvement in adolescence, most religiously affiliated teenagers are advantaged in moral values and behavior.

Gender Typing

Why is early adolescence a period of gender intensification?

» Biological, social, and cognitive factors jointly contribute to **gender intensification.** As pubertal changes occur and concern with what others think strengthens, teenagers focus on gender-linked attributes. Also, parents and dating partners encourage gender-appropriate behavior.

The Family

Discuss changes in parent–child and sibling relationships during adolescence.

» In their quest for **autonomy,** adolescents strive to rely more on themselves and less on parents for decision making. As teenagers deidealize their parents, they often question parental authority. During a time of major life transitions, adolescents and parents approach situations with conflicting expectations and from different perspectives. Warm, supportive parenting and consistent monitoring predict favorable outcomes, even in the face of reduced time spent with parents.

» Sibling relationships become less intense as adolescents separate from the family and turn toward peers. Still, attachment to siblings remains strong for most young people.

Peer Relations

Describe adolescent friendships, peer groups, and dating relationships and their consequences for development.

» Adolescent friendships are based on greater intimacy, mutual understanding, and loyalty and contain more self-disclosure. Girls' friendships place greater emphasis on emotional closeness, boys' on shared activities and accomplishments.

» As long as they are not characterized by jealousy, relational aggression, or attraction to antisocial behavior, adolescent friendships promote self-concept, perspective taking, identity, and the capacity for intimate relationships. They also help young people deal with stress and can improve attitudes toward school.

» Adolescent peer groups are organized into more intimate **cliques,** particularly important to girls, and **crowds,** which grant teenagers an identity within the larger social structure of the school. Parenting styles influence the assortment of teenagers into cliques and crowds. With interest in dating, mixed-sex cliques grow in importance and then decline. Crowds also diminish, as teenagers settle on personal values and goals.

» Intimacy in dating relationships lags behind that of same-sex friendships. Positive relationships with parents and friends contribute to secure romantic ties, which enhance emotional and social development in older teenagers.

Discuss conformity to peer pressure in adolescence.

» Peer conformity is greater during adolescence than earlier or later. Young teenagers are most likely to give in to peer pressure for antisocial behavior. Yet most peer pressure is not in conflict with important adult values. Authoritative parenting is related to resistance to unfavorable peer pressure.

Problems of Development

What factors are related to adolescent depression and suicide?

» Depression is the most common psychological problem of the teenage years, with girls at greater risk in industrialized nations. Various combinations of biological and environmental factors are implicated—heredity, maladaptive parenting, learned-helpless attributional style, and negative life events.

» The suicide rate increases dramatically at adolescence. Boys account for most teenage deaths by suicide, while girls make more unsuccessful suicide attempts. Teenagers at risk for suicide may be intelligent, solitary, and withdrawn, but more often, they are antisocial. Family turmoil is common in the backgrounds of suicidal adolescents.

Discuss factors related to delinquency.

» Although almost all teenagers engage in some delinquent activity, only a few are serious repeat offenders. Most are boys with a childhood history of conduct problems.

» A consistent factor related to delinquency is a family environment low in warmth, high in conflict, and characterized by inconsistent discipline and low monitoring. Poverty-stricken neighborhoods with high crime rates and ineffective schools also promote lawbreaking.

Important Terms and Concepts

acculturative stress (p. 194)
autonomy (p. 203)
bicultural identity (p. 194)
clique (p. 207)
conventional level (p. 196)
crowd (p. 207)

ethnic identity (p. 194)
gender intensification (p. 202)
identity (p. 190)
identity achievement (p. 191)
identity diffusion (p. 191)
identity foreclosure (p. 191)

identity moratorium (p. 191)
identity versus role confusion (p. 190)
moral self-relevance (p. 200)
postconventional level (p. 196)
preconventional level (p. 195)

Milestones
Development in Adolescence

Early Adolescence: 11–14

PHYSICAL

- If a girl, reaches peak of growth spurt. (151)
- If a girl, adds more body fat than muscle. (151–152)
- If a girl, starts to menstruate. (154)
- If a boy, begins growth spurt. (151)
- If a boy, starts to ejaculate seminal fluid. (154)
- Is likely to be aware of sexual orientation. (164)
- If a girl, motor performance increases gradually, leveling off by age 14. (152)
- Shows heightened stress response and novelty-seeking. (155)

COGNITIVE

- Shows gains in hypothetico-deductive reasoning and propositional thought. (171–172)
- Improves in scientific reasoning—coordinating theory with evidence—on complex, multivariable tasks. (173)
- Becomes more self-conscious and self-focused. (174–175)

- Becomes more idealistic and critical. (176)
- Metacognition and self-regulation continue to improve. (173)

EMOTIONAL/SOCIAL

- Self-concept includes abstract descriptors unifying separate personality traits, but these are are often contradictory and not interconnected. (190)
- Shows gender intensification—increased gender stereotyping of attitudes and behavior. (202)
- In striving for autonomy, spends less time with parents and siblings, more time with peers. (205)
- Friendships decline in number and are based on intimacy, mutual understanding, and loyalty. (205)
- Peer groups become organized around same-sex cliques. (207)
- Cliques with similar values form crowds. (207–208)
- Conformity in response to peer pressure increases. (209)

Middle Adolescence: 14–16

PHYSICAL

- If a girl, completes growth spurt. (151)
- If a boy, reaches peak of growth spurt. (151)
- If a boy, voice deepens. (154)
- If a boy, adds muscle while body fat declines. (152)
- If a boy, motor performance improves dramatically. (152)
- May have had sexual intercourse. (163)

COGNITIVE

- Continues to improve in hypothetico-deductive reasoning and propositional thought. (171–172)

Note: Numbers in parentheses indicate the page or pages on which each milestone is discussed.

- Continues to improve in scientific reasoning, following a similar sequential order on different types of tasks. (174)
- Becomes less self-conscious and self-focused. (175)
- Improves in everyday decision making. (176)

EMOTIONAL/SOCIAL

- Combines features of the self into an organized self-concept. (190)
- Self-esteem differentiates further and tends to rise. (190–191)

- In most cases, begins to move from "lower" to "higher" identity statuses. (191–192)
- Is likely to engage in societal perspective taking. (124, 196)
- Increasingly emphasizes ideal reciprocity and societal laws as the basis for resolving moral dilemmas. (196)
- Engages in more subtle reasoning about conflicts between moral, social-conventional, and personal-choice issues. (198)
- Gender intensification declines. (203)
- Mixed-sex cliques become common. (207–208)
- Has probably started dating. (208)
- Conformity to peer pressure may decline. (209)

Late Adolescence: 16–18

PHYSICAL

- If a boy, completes growth spurt. (151)
- If a boy, gains in motor performance continue. (152)

COGNITIVE

- Continues to improve in metacognition, scientific reasoning, and decision making. (173–174, 176)

EMOTIONAL/SOCIAL

- Self-concept emphasizes personal and moral standards. (190)
- Continues to construct an identity, typically moving to higher identity statuses. (191–193)
- Continues to advance in maturity of moral reasoning. (195–197)
- Cliques and crowds decline in importance. (207–208)
- Seeks psychological intimacy in romantic ties, which last longer. (208)

Early adulthood brings momentous changes—
among them, selecting a vocation, starting full-time
work, and attaining economic independence.
Once young adults embark on a career path, as
this young Guatemalan archaeologist has, strong
ties with mentors are vital for success.

SECTION 7

Physical and Cognitive Development in Early Adulthood

The back seat and trunk piled high with belongings, 23-year-old Sharese hugged her mother and brother goodbye, jumped in the car, and headed toward the interstate with a sense of newfound freedom mixed with apprehension. Three months earlier, the family had watched proudly as Sharese received her bachelor's degree in chemistry from a small university 40 miles from her home. Her college years had been a time of gradual release from economic and psychological dependency on her family. She returned home periodically on weekends and lived there during the summer months. Her mother supplemented Sharese's loans with a monthly allowance. But this day marked a turning point. She was moving to her own apartment in a city 800 miles away, with

plans to work on a master's degree. With a teaching assistantship and a student loan, Sharese felt more "on her own" than at any previous time in her life.

During her college years, Sharese made lifestyle changes and settled on a vocational direction. Overweight throughout high school, she lost 20 pounds in her sophomore year, revised her diet, and began an exercise regimen by joining the university's Ultimate Frisbee team, eventually becoming its captain. A summer spent as a counselor at a camp for chronically ill children helped convince Sharese to apply her background in science to a career in public health.

Still, two weeks before she was to leave, Sharese confided in her mother that she was having doubts about her decision. "Sharese," her mother advised, "we never know if our life choices are going to suit us just right, and most times they aren't perfect. It's what we make of them—how we view and mold them— that turns them into successes." So Sharese embarked on her journey and found herself face-to-face with a multitude of exciting challenges and opportunities.

In this section, we take up the physical and cognitive sides of early adulthood, which extends from about age 18 to 40. The adult years are difficult to divide into discrete periods because the timing of important milestones varies greatly among individuals—much more so than in childhood and adolescence. But for most people, early adulthood involves a common set of tasks: leaving home, completing education, beginning full-time work, attaining economic

219

independence, establishing a long-term sexually and emotionally intimate relationship, and starting a family. These are energetic decades filled with momentous decisions that—more than any other time of life—offer the potential for living to the fullest.

Physical Development

We have seen that throughout childhood and adolescence, the body grows larger and stronger, coordination improves, and sensory systems gather information more effectively. Once body structures reach maximum capacity and efficiency, **biological aging,** or **senescence,** begins—genetically influenced declines in the functioning of organs and systems that are universal in all members of our species. Like physical growth, however, biological aging varies widely across parts of the body, and individual differences are great—variation that the *lifespan perspective* helps us understand. A host of contextual factors—including each person's unique genetic makeup, lifestyle, living environment, and historical period—influence biological aging, each of which can accelerate or slow age-related declines (Arking, 2006). As a result, the physical changes of the adult years are, indeed, *multidimensional* and *multidirectional*.

In the following sections, we examine the process of biological aging. Then we turn to physical and motor changes already under way in early adulthood. As you will see, biological aging is not fixed and immutable. It can be modified substantially through behavioral and environmental interventions. Over the past century, improved nutrition, medical treatment, sanitation, and safety have added 25 to 30 years to *average life expectancy* in industrialized nations.

Biological Aging Is Under Way in Early Adulthood

At an intercollegiate tournament, Sharese dashed across the playing field for hours, leaping high to catch Frisbees sailing her way. In her early twenties, she is at her peak in strength, endurance, sensory acuteness, and immune system responsiveness. Yet over the next two decades, she will age and, as she moves into middle and late adulthood, will show more noticeable declines.

Biological aging is the combined result of many causes, some operating at the level of DNA, others at the level of cells, and still others at the level of tissues, organs, and the whole organism. Hundreds of theories exist, indicating that our understanding is still in an early stage (Arking, 2006). For example, one popular idea—the *"wear-and-tear" theory*—is that the body wears out from use. But no relationship exists between physical activity and early death. To the contrary, regular,

This rock climber, in her early twenties, is at her peak in strength, endurance, sensory acuteness, and immune system responsiveness.

moderate-to-vigorous exercise predicts a healthier, longer life for people differing widely in SES and ethnicity (Cockerham et al., 2004; Stessman et al., 2005). We now know that this "wear-and-tear" theory is an oversimplification.

Aging at the Level of DNA and Body Cells

Current explanations of biological aging at the level of DNA and body cells are of two types: (1) those that emphasize the *programmed effects of specific genes* and (2) those that emphasize the *cumulative effects of random events* that damage genetic and cellular material. Support for both views exists, and a combination may eventually prove to be correct.

Genetically programmed aging receives some support from kinship studies indicating that longevity is a family trait. People whose parents had long lives tend to live longer themselves. And greater similarity exists in the lifespans of identical than fraternal twins. But the heritability of longevity is modest, ranging from .15 to .25 for age at death and from .27 to .57 for various measures of current biological age, such as strength of hand grip, respiratory capacity, blood pressure, and bone density (Cevenini et al., 2008; Kerber et al., 2001; Mitchell et al., 2001). Rather than inheriting longevity directly, people probably

■ BIOLOGY AND ENVIRONMENT ■

Telomere Length: A New Marker of the Impact of Life Circumstances on Biological Aging

In the not-too-distant future, your annual physical exam may include an assessment of the length of your *telomeres*—DNA at the ends of chromosomes, which safeguard the stability of your cells. Telomeres shorten with each cell duplication; when they drop below a critical length, the cell can no longer divide and becomes senescent. Although telomeres shorten with age, the rate at which they do so varies greatly. An enzyme called *telomerase* prevents shortening and can even reverse the trend, causing telomeres to lengthen and, thus, protecting the aging cell.

Over the past decade, research examining the influence of life circumstances on telomere length has exploded. A well-established finding is that chronic illnesses, such as cardiovascular disease and cancer, hasten telomere shortening in white blood cells, which play a vital role in the immune response (see page 225). Telomere shortening, in turn, predicts more rapid disease progression and earlier death (Fuster & Andres, 2006).

Accelerated telomere shortening has been linked to a variety of unhealthy behaviors, including cigarette smoking and the physical inactivity and overeating that lead to obesity and to insulin resistance, which often precedes type 2 diabetes (Epel et al., 2006; Gardner et al., 2005). Unfavorable health conditions may alter telomere length as early as the prenatal period, with possible long-term negative consequences for biological aging. In research on rats, poor maternal nutrition during pregnancy resulted in low birth weight and development of shorter telomeres in kidney and heart tissue (Jennings et al., 1999; Tarry-Adkins et al., 2008). In a related human investigation, preschoolers who had been low-birth-weight as infants had shorter telomeres in their white blood cells than did their normal-birth-weight agemates (Raqib et al., 2007).

Persistent psychological stress—parenting a child with a chronic illness, caring for an elder with dementia, or severe depression—is linked to reduced telomerase activity and telomere shortness in white blood cells (Damjanovic et al., 2007; Epel et al., 2004; McEwen, 2007; Simon et al., 2006). Can stress actually modify telomeres? In a laboratory experiment, researchers exposed human white blood cells to the stress hormone cortisol. The cells responded by decreasing production of telomerase (Choi, Fauce, & Effros, 2008).

Fortunately, when adults make positive lifestyle changes, telomeres seem to respond accordingly. In one study, declines in psychological stress were associated with telomere lengthening in white blood cells (Epel et al., 2009). In another investigation of men with low-risk prostate cancer, three months of intensive improvement in diet and exercise

Accelerated telomere shortening has been linked to a variety of unhealthy behaviors. Fortunately, positive lifestyle changes, including healthy diet and exercise, seem to trigger a positive response in telomeres.

led to decreased blood cholesterol and psychological stress, along with increased white cell telomerase activity (Ornish et al., 2008).

Currently, researchers are working on identifying sensitive periods of telomere change—times when telomeres are most susceptible to modification. Early intervention—for example, enhanced prenatal care and interventions to reduce obesity in childhood—may be particularly powerful. But telomeres are changeable well into late adulthood (Epel et al., 2009). As our understanding of predictors and consequences of telomere length expands, it may become an important index of health and aging throughout life.

---

inherit one or more risk factors, which influence their chances of dying earlier or later.

One "genetic programming" theory proposes the existence of "aging genes" that control certain biological changes, such as menopause, gray hair, and deterioration of body cells. The strongest evidence for this view comes from research showing that human cells allowed to divide in the laboratory have a lifespan of 50 divisions, plus or minus 10 (Hayflick, 1998). With each duplication, a special type of DNA called **telomeres**—located at the ends of chromosomes, serving as a "cap" to protect the ends from destruction—shortens. Eventually, so little remains that the cells no longer duplicate at all. Telomere shortening acts as a brake against somatic mutations (such as those involved in cancer), which become more likely as cells duplicate (Wright & Shay, 2005). But an increase in the number of senescent cells (ones with short telomeres) also contributes to age-related disease, loss of function, and earlier mortality (Epel et al., 2009; Shin et al., 2006). As the Biology and Environment box above reveals, researchers have begun to identify health behaviors and psychological states that accelerate telomere shortening—powerful biological evidence that certain life circumstances compromise longevity.

According to an alternative, "random events" theory, DNA in body cells is gradually damaged through spontaneous or externally caused mutations. As these accumulate, cell repair and replacement become less efficient, and abnormal cancerous cells are often produced. Animal studies confirm an increase in DNA breaks and deletions and damage to other cellular material with age. Similar evidence is accruing for humans (Schumacher, Garinis, & Hoeijmakers, 2007).

Kinship studies indicate that longevity is a family trait. In addition to favorable heredity, these grandsons will likely benefit from the model of a fit, active grandfather who buffers stress by enjoying life.

One probable cause of age-related DNA and cellular abnormalities is the release of **free radicals**—naturally occurring, highly reactive chemicals that form in the presence of oxygen. (Radiation and certain pollutants and drugs can trigger similar effects.) When oxygen molecules break down within the cell, the reaction strips away an electron, creating a free radical. As it seeks a replacement from its surroundings, it destroys nearby cellular material, including DNA, proteins, and fats essential for cell functioning. Free radicals are thought to be involved in more than 60 disorders of aging, including cardiovascular disease, neurological disorders, cancer, cataracts, and arthritis (Barja, 2004; Cutler & Mattson, 2006). Although our bodies produce substances that neutralize free radicals, some harm occurs, and it accumulates over time.

Animal species with longer life expectancies display slower rates of free-radical damage to DNA (Sanz, Pamplona, & Barja, 2006). Some researchers believe that genes for longevity work by defending against free radicals. In this way, a programmed genetic response may limit random DNA and cellular deterioration. Foods rich in vitamins C and E and beta-carotene also forestall free-radical damage—a reason that improved diet contributes to gains in life expectancy (Milbury & Richer, 2008).

Aging at the Level of Tissues and Organs

What consequences might the DNA and cellular deterioration just described have for the structure and functioning of organs and tissues? There are many possibilities. Among those with clear support is the **cross-linkage theory of aging.** Over time, protein fibers that make up the body's connective tissue form bonds, or links, with one another. When these normally separate fibers cross-link, tissue becomes less elastic, leading to many negative outcomes, including loss of flexibility in the skin and other organs, clouding of the lens of the eye, clogging of arteries, and damage to the kidneys. Like other aspects of aging, cross-linking can be reduced by external factors, including regular exercise and a vitamin-rich, low-fat diet (Schneider, 1992; Wickens, 2001).

Gradual failure of the endocrine system, which produces and regulates hormones, is yet another route to aging. An obvious example is decreased estrogen production in women, which culminates in menopause. Because hormones affect many body functions, disruptions in the endocrine system can have widespread effects on health and survival. For example, a gradual drop in growth hormone (GH) is associated with loss of muscle and bone mass, addition of body fat, thinning of the skin, and decline in cardiovascular functioning. In adults with abnormally low levels of GH, hormone therapy can slow these symptoms, but it has serious side effects, including increased risk of fluid retention in tissues, muscle pain, and cancer (Harman & Blackman, 2004; Toogood, 2004). So far, diet and physical activity are safer ways to limit these aspects of biological aging.

Finally, declines in immune system functioning contribute to many conditions of aging, including increased susceptibility to infectious disease and cancer and changes in blood vessel walls associated with cardiovascular disease. Decreased vigor of the immune response seems to be genetically programmed, but other aging processes we have considered (such as weakening of the endocrine system) can intensify it (Hawkley & Cacioppo, 2004; Malaguarnera et al., 2001). Indeed, combinations of theories—the ones just reviewed as well as others—are needed to explain the complexities of biological aging. With this in mind, let's turn to physical signs and other characteristics of aging.

Physical Changes

During the twenties and thirties, changes in physical appearance and declines in body functioning are so gradual that most are hardly noticeable. Later, they will accelerate. The physical changes of aging are summarized in Table 7.1. We will examine several in detail here and take up others in later sections. Before we begin, let's note that these trends are derived largely from cross-sectional studies. Because younger cohorts have experienced better health care and nutrition, cross-sectional evidence can exaggerate impairments associated with aging. Fortunately, longitudinal evidence is expanding, helping to correct this picture.

Cardiovascular and Respiratory Systems

During her first month in graduate school, Sharese pored over research articles on cardiovascular functioning. In her African-American extended family, her father, an uncle, and three aunts had died of heart attacks in their forties and fifties. These tragedies prompted Sharese to reconsider her own health-related behaviors. She also decided to enter the field of public health in hopes of finding ways to relieve health problems among black Americans. *Hypertension,* or high blood pressure, occurs 12 percent more often in the U.S. black than in the U.S. white population;

■ **TABLE 7.1** ■ *Physical Changes of Aging*

ORGAN OR SYSTEM	TIMING OF CHANGE	DESCRIPTION
Sensory		
Vision	From age 30	As the lens stiffens and thickens, ability to focus on close objects declines. Yellowing of the lens, weakening of muscles controlling the pupil, and clouding of the vitreous (gelatin-like substance that fills the eye) reduce light reaching the retina, impairing color discrimination and night vision. Visual acuity, or fineness of discrimination, decreases, with a sharp drop between ages 70 and 80.
Hearing	From age 30	Sensitivity to sound declines, especially at high frequencies but gradually extending to all frequencies. Change is more than twice as rapid for men as for women.
Taste	From age 60	Sensitivity to the four basic tastes—sweet, salty, sour, and bitter—is reduced. This may be due to factors other than aging, since number and distribution of taste buds do not change.
Smell	From age 60	Loss of smell receptors reduces ability to detect and identify odors.
Touch	Gradual	Loss of touch receptors reduces sensitivity on the hands, particularly the fingertips.
Cardiovascular	Gradual	As the heart muscle becomes more rigid, maximum heart rate decreases, reducing the heart's ability to meet the body's oxygen requirements when stressed by exercise. As artery walls stiffen and accumulate plaque, blood flow to body cells is reduced.
Respiratory	Gradual	Under physical exertion, respiratory capacity decreases and breathing rate increases. Stiffening of connective tissue in the lungs and chest muscles makes it more difficult for the lungs to expand to full volume.
Immune	Gradual	Shrinking of the thymus limits maturation of T cells and disease-fighting capacity of B cells, impairing the immune response.
Muscular	Gradual	As nerves stimulating them die, fast-twitch muscle fibers (responsible for speed and explosive strength) decline in number and size to a greater extent than slow-twitch fibers (which support endurance). Tendons and ligaments (which transmit muscle action) stiffen, reducing speed and flexibility of movement.
Skeletal	Begins in the late thirties, accelerates in the fifties, slows in the seventies	Cartilage in the joints thins and cracks, leading bone ends beneath it to erode. New cells continue to be deposited on the outer layer of the bones, and mineral content of bone declines. The resulting broader but more porous bones weaken the skeleton and make it more vulnerable to fracture. Change is more rapid in women than in men.
Reproductive	In women, accelerates after age 35; in men, begins after age 40	Fertility problems (including difficulty conceiving and carrying a pregnancy to term) and risk of having a baby with a chromosomal disorder increase.
Nervous	From age 50	Brain weight declines as neurons lose water content and die, mostly in the cerebral cortex, and as ventricles (spaces) within the brain enlarge. Development of new synapses and limited generation of new neurons can, in part, compensate for these declines.
Skin	Gradual	Epidermis (outer layer) is held less tightly to the dermis (middle layer); fibers in the dermis and hypodermis (inner layer) thin; fat cells in the hypodermis decline. As a result, the skin becomes looser, less elastic, and wrinkled. Change is more rapid in women than in men.
Hair	From age 35	Grays and thins.
Height	From age 50	Loss of bone strength leads to collapse of disks in the spinal column, leading to a height loss of as much as 2 inches by the seventies and eighties.
Weight	Increases to age 50; declines from age 60	Weight change reflects a rise in fat and a decline in muscle and bone mineral. Since muscle and bone are heavier than fat, the resulting pattern is weight gain followed by loss. Body fat accumulates on the torso and decreases on the extremities.

Sources: Arking, 2006; Whalley, 2001; Whitbourne, 1996.

the rate of death from heart disease among African Americans is 30 percent higher (American Heart Association, 2009).

Sharese was surprised to learn that fewer age-related changes occur in the heart than we might expect, given that heart disease is a leading cause of death throughout adulthood,

responsible for as many as 10 percent of U.S. male and 5 percent of U.S. female deaths between ages 20 and 34—figures that more than double in the following decade and, thereafter, continue to rise steadily with age (Lloyd-Jones et al., 2009). In healthy individuals, the heart's ability to meet the body's oxygen requirements under typical conditions (as measured by heart rate in relation to volume of blood pumped) does not change during adulthood. Only during stressful exercise does heart performance decline with age—a change due to a decrease in maximum heart rate and greater rigidity of the heart muscle (Arking, 2006). Consequently, the heart has difficulty delivering enough oxygen to the body during high activity and bouncing back from strain.

One of the most serious diseases of the cardiovascular system is *atherosclerosis*, in which heavy deposits of plaque containing cholesterol and fats collect on the walls of the main arteries. If present, it usually begins early in life, progresses during middle adulthood, and culminates in serious illness. Atherosclerosis is multiply determined, making it hard to separate the contributions of biological aging from individual genetic and environmental influences. The complexity of causes is illustrated by animal research indicating that before puberty, a high-fat diet produces only fatty streaks on the artery walls (Olson, 2000). In sexually mature adults, however, it leads to serious plaque deposits, suggesting that sex hormones may heighten the insults of a high-fat diet.

Heart disease has decreased considerably since the mid-twentieth century, with a larger drop in the last 20 years due to a decline in cigarette smoking, to improved diet and exercise among at-risk individuals, and to better medical detection and treatment of high blood pressure and cholesterol (American Heart Association, 2008). And as longitudinal research on more than 17,000 Chicago-area 18- to 39-year-olds revealed, young adults at low risk for heart disease—defined by not smoking, absence of diabetes, and normal blood cholesterol, blood pressure, and body weight—had much lower death rates than their higher-risk agemates over the succeeding three decades (Daviglus et al., 2004; Stamler et al., 1999). Later, when we consider health and fitness, we will see why heart attacks were so common in Sharese's family—and why they occur at especially high rates in the African-American population.

Like the heart, the lungs show few age-related changes in functioning at rest, but during physical exertion, respiratory volume decreases and breathing rate increases with age. Maximum vital capacity (amount of air that can be forced in and out of the lungs) declines by 10 percent per decade after age 25 (Mahanran et al., 1999). Connective tissue in the lungs, chest muscles, and ribs stiffens with age, making it more difficult for the lungs to expand to full volume (Smith & Cotter, 2008). Fortunately, under normal conditions, we use less than half our vital capacity. Nevertheless, aging of the lungs contributes to older adults' difficulty in meeting the body's oxygen needs while exercising.

Motor Performance

Declines in heart and lung functioning under conditions of exertion, combined with gradual muscle loss, lead to changes in motor performance. In most people, the impact of biological aging on motor skills is difficult to separate from decreases in motivation and practice. Therefore, researchers study outstanding athletes, who try to attain their very best performance in real

life (Tanaka & Seals, 2003). As long as athletes continue intensive training, their attainments at each age approach the limits of what is biologically possible.

Many athletic skills peak between ages 20 and 35, then gradually decline. In several investigations, the mean ages for best performance of Olympic and professional athletes in a variety of sports were charted over time. Absolute performance in most events improved over the past century. Athletes continually set new world records, suggesting improved training methods. But ages of best performance remained relatively constant. Athletic tasks that require speed of limb movement, explosive strength, and gross-motor coordination—sprinting, jumping, and tennis—typically peak in the early twenties. Those that depend on endurance, arm–hand steadiness, and aiming—long-distance running, baseball, and golf—usually peak in the late twenties and early thirties. Because these skills require either stamina or precise motor control, they take longer to perfect (Schulz & Curnow, 1988).

Research on outstanding athletes tells us that the upper biological limit of motor capacity is reached in the first part of early adulthood. How quickly do athletic skills weaken in later years? Longitudinal research on master runners reveals that as long as practice continues, speed drops only slightly from the mid-thirties into the sixties, when performance falls off at an accelerating pace (see Figure 7.1) (Tanaka & Higuchi, 1998; Trappe, 2007). In the case of long-distance swimming—a non-weight-bearing exercise with a low incidence of injury—the decline in speed is even more gradual: The accelerating performance drop-off is delayed until the seventies (Tanaka & Seals, 1997).

© BRYN LENNON/GETTY IMAGES

In 2009, 37-year-old Lance Armstrong attempted the near-impossible by going for an eighth victory in the Tour de France, the world's toughest cycling race. He scored an impressive third place; first and second place went to cyclists more than ten years younger. Sustained training leads to adaptations in body structures that minimize motor decline into the sixties.

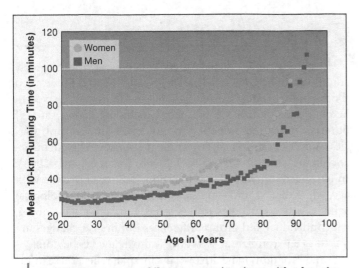

■ **FIGURE 7.1** ■ **Ten-kilometer running times with advancing age, based on longitudinal performances of hundreds of master athletes.** Runners maintain their speed into the mid-thirties, followed by modest increases in running times into the sixties, with a progressively steeper increase thereafter. (From H. Tanaka & D. R. Seals, 2003, "Dynamic Exercise Performance in Masters Athletes: Insight into the Effects of Primary Human Aging on Physiological Functional Capacity," *Journal of Applied Physiology, 5,* p. 2153. Adapted with permission of The American Physiological Society.)

Indeed, sustained training leads to adaptations in body structures that minimize motor decline. For example, vital capacity is one-third greater in both younger and older people who participate actively in sports than in healthy inactive agemates (Pimentel et al., 2003; Tanaka et al., 1997). Training also slows muscle loss, increases speed and force of muscle contraction, and leads fast-twitch muscle fibers to be converted into slow-twitch fibers, which support excellent long-distance running performance and other endurance skills (Faulkner et al., 2007; Trappe, 2001).

In sum, although athletic skills are at their best in early adulthood, biological aging accounts for only a small part of age-related decline until advanced old age. Lower levels of performance by healthy people into their sixties and seventies largely reflect reduced capacities resulting from adaptation to a less physically demanding lifestyle.

Immune System

The immune response is the combined work of specialized cells that neutralize or destroy antigens (foreign substances) in the body. Two types of white blood cells play vital roles. *T cells,* which originate in the bone marrow and mature in the thymus (a small gland located in the upper part of the chest), attack antigens directly. *B cells,* manufactured in the bone marrow, secrete antibodies into the bloodstream that multiply, capture antigens, and permit the blood system to destroy them. Since receptors on their surfaces recognize only a single antigen, T and B cells come in great variety. They join with additional cells to produce immunity.

The capacity of the immune system to offer protection against disease increases through adolescence and declines after age 20. The trend is partly due to changes in the thymus, which is largest during the teenage years, then shrinks until it is barely detectable by age 50. As a result, production of thymic hormones is reduced, and the thymus is less able to promote full maturity and differentiation of T cells. Because B cells release far more antibodies when T cells are present, the immune response is compromised further (Weng, 2008).

Withering of the thymus is not the only reason that the body gradually becomes less effective in warding off illness. The immune system interacts with the nervous and endocrine systems. For example, psychological stress can weaken the immune response (Coe & Laudenslager, 2007; Larbi et al., 2008). During final exams, for example, Sharese was less resistant to colds. And in the month after her father died, she had great difficulty recovering from the flu. Divorce, caring for an ill aging parent, sleep deprivation, and chronic depression can also reduce immunity (Hamer, Wolvers, & Albers, 2004; Robles & Kiecolt-Glaser, 2003). And physical stress—from pollution, allergens, poor nutrition, and rundown housing—undermines immune functioning throughout adulthood. When physical and psychological stress combine, the risk of illness is magnified (Friedman & Lawrence, 2002).

The link between stress and illness makes sense when we consider that stress hormones mobilize the body for action, whereas the immune response is fostered by reduced activity. But this also means that increased difficulty coping with physical and psychological stress can contribute to age-related declines in immune system functioning.

Reproductive Capacity

Sharese was born when her mother was in her early twenties. At the same age a generation later, Sharese was still single and entering graduate school. Many people believe that pregnancy during the twenties is ideal, not only because of lower risk of miscarriage and chromosomal disorders but also because younger parents have more energy to keep up with active children. As Figure 7.2 on page 226 reveals, however, first births to women in their thirties have increased greatly over the past three decades. Many people are delaying childbearing until their education is complete, their careers are well-established, and they know they can support a child.

Nevertheless, reproductive capacity does decline with age. Fertility problems among women increase from age 15 to 50. Between ages 15 and 29, 8 percent of U.S. women surveyed report difficulties, a figure that rises to 14 percent among 30- to 34-year-olds and 18 percent among 35- to 44-year-olds, when the success of reproductive technologies drops sharply (U.S. Department of Health and Human Services, 2009a). Since the uterus shows no consistent changes from the late thirties through the forties, the decline in female fertility is largely due to reduced number and quality of ova. In many mammals, including humans, a certain level of reserve ova in the ovaries is necessary for conception. Some women have normal menstrual cycles but do not conceive because their reserve of ova is too low—the major cause of the female age-related decline in fertility (Djahanbakhch, Ezzati, & Zosmer, 2007).

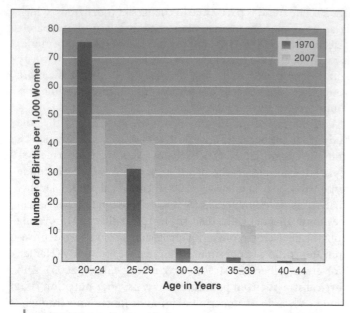

■ FIGURE 7.2 ■ First births to American women of different ages in 1970 and 2007. The birthrate decreased during this period for women 20 to 24 years of age, whereas it increased for women 25 years of age and older. For women in their thirties, the birthrate more than doubled. Similar trends have occurred in other industrialized nations. (From U.S. Census Bureau, 2009b.)

In males, semen volume, sperm motility, and percentage of normal sperm decrease gradually after age 35, contributing to reduced fertility rates in older men (Lambert, Masson, & Fisch, 2006). Although there is no best time in adulthood to begin parenthood, individuals who postpone childbearing until their late thirties or their forties risk having fewer children than they desired or none at all.

ASK YOURSELF

≫ REVIEW
How does research on life conditions that accelerate telomere shortening illustrate the joint influence of heredity and environment on biological aging?

≫ APPLY
Penny is a long-distance runner for her college track team. She wonders what her running performance will be like 30 years from now. What factors will affect Penny's future athletic skill?

≫ CONNECT
How do heredity and environment jointly contribute to age-related changes in cardiovascular, respiratory, and immune system functioning?

≫ REFLECT
Before reading this section, had you thought of early adulthood as a period of aging? Why is it important for young adults to be conscious of factors that contribute to biological aging?

Health and Fitness

Figure 7.3 displays leading causes of death in early adulthood in the United States. Death rates for all causes exceed those of other industrialized nations—a difference believed to be due to a combination of factors, including higher rates of poverty and extreme obesity, more lenient gun-control policies, and lack of universal, government-sponsored health insurance in the United States (OECD, 2008b; Torrey & Haub, 2004). In later sections, we will see that homicide rates decline with age, while disease and physical disability rates rise. Biological aging clearly contributes to this trend. But, as we have noted, wide individual and group differences in physical changes are linked to environmental risks and health-related behaviors.

SES variations in health over the lifespan reflect these influences. Income, education, and occupational status show strong and continuous relationships with almost every disease and health indicator (Adler & Newman, 2002; Alwin & Wray, 2005; Geiger, 2007). Furthermore, when a nationally representative sample of 3,600 Americans were asked about health-related limitations on their daily lives, SES differences widened over early and middle adulthood but contracted during old age, when individuals in the poorest health had died (see Figure 7.4) (House, Lantz, & Herd, 2005). Longitudinal evidence confirms these trends: Economically advantaged and well-educated individuals sustain better health over most of their adult lives, whereas the health of lower-income individuals with limited education steadily declines (Lantz et al., 1998, 2001).

SES differences in health-related circumstances and habits—stressful life events, crowding, pollution, diet, exercise, overweight and obesity, substance abuse, jobs with numerous health risks, availability of supportive social relationships, and (in the United States) access to affordable health care—are largely responsible (Brand et al., 2007; Evans & Kantrowitz, 2002; Wray, Alwin, & McCammon, 2005). Further, poor health in childhood, which is linked to low SES, affects health in adulthood. The overall influence of childhood factors lessens if SES improves. But in most instances, child and adult SES remain fairly consistent, exerting a cumulative impact that amplifies SES health disparities with age (Luo & Waite, 2005; Strand & Kunst, 2007).

Why are SES disparities in health and mortality larger in the United States than in other industrialized nations (Mackenbach, 2002)? Besides the lack of universal health insurance, poverty-stricken U.S. families have lower incomes than those classified as poor in other countries. In addition, SES groups are more likely to be segregated by neighborhood in the United States, resulting in greater inequalities in environmental factors that affect health, such as housing, pollution, education, and community services.

These findings reveal, once again, that the living conditions that nations and communities provide combine with those that people create for themselves to affect physical aging. Because the incidence of health problems is much lower during the twenties and thirties than later on, early adulthood is an excellent time to

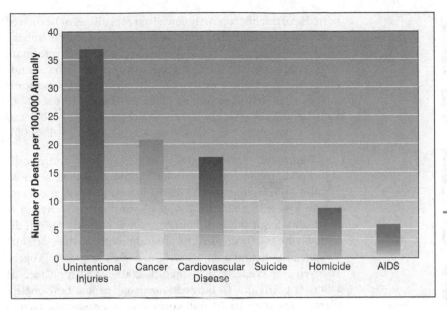

■ **FIGURE 7.3** ■ **Leading causes of death between 25 and 44 years of age in the United States.** Nearly half of unintentional injuries are motor vehicle accidents. As later sections will reveal, unintentional injuries remain a leading cause of death at older ages, rising sharply in late adulthood. Rates of cancer and cardiovascular disease rise steadily over middle and late adulthood. (Adapted from U.S. Census Bureau, 2009b.)

prevent later problems. In the following sections, we take up a variety of major health concerns—nutrition, exercise, substance abuse, sexuality, and psychological stress.

Nutrition

Bombarded with advertising claims and an extraordinary variety of food choices, adults find it increasingly difficult to make wise dietary decisions. An abundance of food, combined with a heavily scheduled life, means that most Americans eat because they feel like it or because it is time to do so rather than to maintain the body's functions (Donatelle, 2009). As a result, many eat the wrong types and amounts of food. Overweight and obesity and a high-fat diet are widespread nutritional problems with long-term consequences for health in adulthood.

■ **OVERWEIGHT AND OBESITY.** In Section 3, we noted that obesity (a greater than 20 percent increase over average body weight, based on age, sex, and physical build) has increased dramatically in many Western nations. Among adults, a body mass index (BMI) of 25 to 29 constitutes overweight, a BMI of 30 or greater (amounting to 30 or more excess pounds) constitutes obesity. Today, 34 percent of U.S. adults are obese. The rate rises to 35 percent among Native Americans, 36 percent among Hispanics, and 45 percent among African Americans. In the United States and Western Europe, 5 to 7 percent more women than men suffer from obesity (Tjepkema, 2005; U.S. Department of Health and Human Services, 2009a, 2009c).

Overweight—a less extreme but nevertheless unhealthy condition—affects an additional 33 percent of Americans. Combine the rates of overweight and obesity and the total,

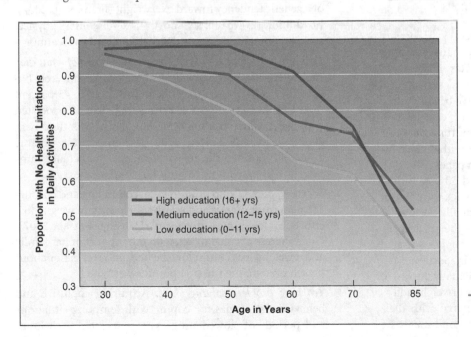

■ **FIGURE 7.4** ■ **Age differences in self-reported health status by socioeconomic status (SES), as indexed by education.** The figure shows cross-sectional trends. In longitudinal research as well, SES differences in health increase over early and middle adulthood and then contract in old age as people in the poorest health die earlier. Environmental risks and poor health habits contribute to earlier declining health among low-SES adults. (From J. S. House, P. M. Lantz, & P. Herd, 2005, "Continuity and Change in the Social Stratification of Aging and Health Over the Life Course: Evidence from a Nationally Representative Longitudinal Study from 1986 to 2001/2002," *Journal of Gerontology, 60B*, p. 16. Copyright © 2005 The Gerontological Society of America. Adapted by permission of Oxford University Press and James S. House.)

© SHIFT FOTO/CORBIS

Overweight adults suffer enormous social discrimination. Which of these two young career women is more likely to find a mate, successfully vie for a new job, and be treated kindly by others?

67 percent, makes Americans the heaviest people in the world. **TAKE A MOMENT...** Notice in these figures that the U.S. obesity rate now exceeds its rate of overweight, a blatant indicator of the growing severity of the problem.

Recall from Section 3 that overweight children are very likely to become overweight adults. But a substantial number of people show large weight gains in adulthood, most often between ages 25 and 40. And young adults who were already overweight or obese typically get heavier, leading obesity rates to rise steadily between ages 20 and 60 (Tjepkema, 2005; U.S. Department of Health and Human Services, 2009a).

Causes and Consequences. As noted in Section 3, heredity makes some people more vulnerable to obesity than others. But environmental pressures underlie the rising rates of obesity in industrialized nations: With the decline in need for physical labor in the home and workplace, our lives have become more sedentary. Meanwhile, the average number of calories and amount of sugar and fat consumed by Americans rose over most of the twentieth and early twenty-first century, with a sharp increase after 1970 (see the Lifespan Vista box on pages 230–231).

Adding some weight between ages 25 and 50 is a normal part of aging because **basal metabolic rate (BMR),** the amount of energy the body uses at complete rest, gradually declines as the number of active muscle cells (which create the greatest energy demand) drops off. But excess weight is strongly associated with serious health problems (see page 80 in Section 3)—including type 2 diabetes, heart disease, and many forms of cancer—and with early death. Furthermore, overweight adults suffer enormous social discrimination. Compared with their normal-weight agemates, they are less likely to find mates, be

rented apartments, receive financial aid for college, or be offered jobs. And they report frequent mistreatment by family members, peers, co-workers, and health professionals (Carr & Friedman, 2005; Puhl & Brownell, 2006). From the mid-1990s to the mid-2000s, discrimination experienced by overweight Americans increased, perhaps because of greater attention to obesity in national news coverage, which typically frames the problem as simply a personal choice (Andreyeva, Puhl, & Brownell, 2008).

Treatment. Because obesity climbs in early and middle adulthood, treatment for adults should begin as soon as possible—preferably in the early twenties. Even moderate weight loss reduces health problems substantially (Orzano & Scott, 2004). But successful intervention is difficult. Most individuals who start a weight-loss program return to their original weight, and often to a higher weight, within two years (Vogels, Diepvens, & Westerterp-Plantenga, 2005). The high rate of failure is partly due to limited knowledge of just how obesity disrupts the complex neural, hormonal, and metabolic factors that maintain a normal body-weight set point. Until more information is available, researchers are examining the features of treatments and participants associated with greater success. The following elements promote lasting behavior change:

- *A well-balanced diet lower in calories and fat, plus exercise.* To lose weight, Sharese sharply reduced calories, sugar, and fat in her diet and exercised regularly. The precise balance of dietary protein, carbohydrates, and fats that best helps adults lose weight is a matter of heated debate. Although scores of diet books offer different recommendations, no clear-cut evidence exists for the long-term superiority of one approach over others (Tsai & Wadden, 2005). Research does confirm that a lifestyle alteration that restricts calorie intake and fat (to no more than 20 to 30 percent of calories) and increases physical activity is essential for reducing the impact of a genetic tendency toward overweight (Franz et al., 2007). In addition (as we will see shortly), exercise offers physical and psychological benefits that help prevent overeating.

- *Training participants to keep an accurate record of what they eat.* About 30 to 35 percent of obese people sincerely believe they eat less than they do, and from 25 to 45 percent report problems with binge eating—a behavior associated with weight-loss treatment failure (Blaine & Rodman, 2007; Wadden & Foster, 2000). When Sharese became aware of how often she ate when she was not actually hungry, she was better able to limit her food intake.

- *Social support.* Group or individual counseling and encouragement from friends and relatives help sustain weight-loss efforts by fostering self-esteem (Dansinger et al., 2007). Once Sharese decided to act, with the support of her family and a weight-loss counselor, she began to feel better about herself even before the first pounds were shed.

- *Teaching problem-solving skills.* Acquiring cognitive and behavioral strategies for coping with tempting situations and periods of slowed progress is associated with long-term change. Weight-loss maintainers are more likely than individuals who relapse to be conscious of their behavior, to use social support, and to confront problems directly (Cooper & Fairburn, 2002).

■ *Extended intervention.* Longer treatments (from 25 to 40 weeks) that include the components listed here grant people time to develop new habits.

Although many Americans on weight-reduction diets are overweight, about one-third are within normal range (Mokdad et al., 2001). Recall from Section 5 that the high value placed on thinness creates unrealistic expectations about desirable body weight and contributes to anorexia and bulimia, dangerous eating disorders that remain common in early adulthood (see pages 160–161). Throughout adulthood, both underweight and obesity are associated with increased mortality (Flegal et al., 2005). A sensible body weight—neither too low nor too high—predicts physical and psychological health and longer life.

■ **DIETARY FAT.** During college, Sharese altered the diet of her childhood and adolescent years, sharply limiting red meat, eggs, butter, and fried foods. U.S. national dietary recommendations include reducing dietary fat to 30 percent of total caloric intake, with no more than 10 percent made up of saturated fat, which generally comes from meat and dairy products and is solid at room temperature (U.S. Department of Health and Human Services, 2009a). Many researchers believe that fat consumption plays a role in breast cancer and (when it includes large amounts of red meat) is linked to colon cancer (Blackburn & Wang, 2007; Kono, 2004). But the main reasons for limiting dietary fat are the strong connection of total fat with obesity and of saturated fat with cardiovascular disease

© TIM PLATT/GETTY IMAGES/ICONICA

A balanced, low-fat diet promotes physical and psychological well-being and contributes to a normal body weight.

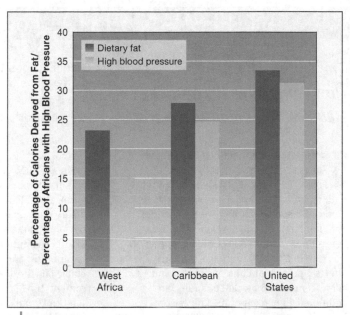

■ **FIGURE 7.5** ■ **Dietary fat and prevalence of high blood pressure among Africans in West Africa, the Caribbean, and the United States.** The three regions represent the historic path of the slave trade and, therefore, have genetically similar populations. As dietary fat increases, high blood pressure and heart disease rise. Both are particularly high among African Americans. (Adapted from Luke et al., 2001.)

(Bruner et al., 2007). Nevertheless, despite a slight drop in fat consumption, most American adults eat too much.

Moderate fat consumption is essential for normal body functioning. But when we consume too much fat, especially saturated fat, some is converted to cholesterol, which accumulates as plaque on the arterial walls in atherosclerosis. Earlier in this section, we noted that atherosclerosis is determined by multiple biological and environmental factors. But excess fat consumption (along with other societal conditions) is a major contributor to the high rate of heart disease in the U.S. black population. When researchers compare Africans in West Africa, the Caribbean, and the United States (the historic path of the slave trade), dietary fat increases, and so do high blood pressure and heart disease (see Figure 7.5) (Luke et al., 2001). Indeed, West Africans have one of the lowest rates of heart disease in the world.

The best rule of thumb is to eat less fat of all kinds and to substitute unsaturated fat, which is derived from vegetables or fish and liquid at room temperature, for saturated fat when possible. Furthermore, regular exercise can reduce the harmful influence of dietary fat because it creates chemical byproducts that help eliminate cholesterol from the body.

Exercise

Three times a week, over the noon hour, Sharese delighted in running, making her way to a wooded trail that cut through a picturesque area of the city. Regular exercise kept her fit and slim, and she noticed that she caught fewer respiratory illnesses than in the days when she had been sedentary and overweight. As

■ A LIFESPAN VISTA: Looking Forward, Looking Back ■

The Obesity Epidemic: How Americans Became the Heaviest People in the World

In the late 1980s, obesity in the United States started to soar. As the maps in Figure 7.6 show, it quickly engulfed the nation and has continued to expand. The epidemic also spread to other Western nations and, more recently, to developing countries. For example, as noted in Section 3, obesity was rare in China 30 years ago, but today it affects 3 percent of Chinese children and adolescents and 6 percent of adults; an additional 23 percent of the Chinese population is overweight (Levine, 2007). Yet China is a low-prevalence country! Worldwide, over-weight afflicts more than 1 billion adults, 300 million of whom are obese. Samoa leads the globe in overweight and obesity, with more than 75 percent of people affected (World Health Organization, 2009b). Among industrialized nations, no country matches the United States in prevalence of this life-threatening condition.

A Changing Food Environment and Lifestyle

Several societal factors have encouraged wide-spread rapid weight gain:

■ *Availability of cheap commercial fat and sugar.* The 1970s saw two massive changes in the U.S. food economy: (1) the discovery and mass production of high-fructose corn syrup, a sweetener six times as sweet as or-dinary sugar, and therefore far less expen-sive; and (2) the importing from Malaysia of large quantities of palm oil, which is lower in cost and tastier than other veg-etable oils because of its high saturated fat content. Use of corn syrup and palm oil in soft drinks and calorie-dense convenience foods lowered production costs for these items, inaugurating a new era of "cheap, abundant, and tasty calories" (Critser, 2003).

■ *Portion supersizing.* Fast-food chains dis-covered a successful strategy for attracting customers: increasing portion sizes sub-stantially and prices just a little for foods that had become inexpensive to produce. Customers thronged to buy "value meals," jumbo burgers and burritos, and 20-ounce Cokes (Critser, 2003). And research revealed

that when presented with larger portions, individuals 2 years and older increased their intake, on average, by 25 to 30 per-cent (Fisher, Rolls, & Birch, 2003; Rolls, Morris, & Roe, 2002).

■ *Increasingly busy lives.* Between the 1970s and 1990s, women entered the labor force in record numbers, and the average amount of time Americans worked in-creased by 15 percent, or about 350 hours per year (Higgins & Duxbury, 2002; Schor, 2002). As time became scarce, eating out increased. In addition, Americans became frequent snackers, aided by a growing diversity of high-calorie snack foods on supermarket shelves. During this period, the number of calories Americans con-sumed away from home nearly doubled, and dietary fat increased from 19 to 38 percent. Overall, average daily food intake rose by almost 200 calories—enough to add an extra pound every 20 days (Nielsen & Popkin, 2003).

■ *Declining rates of physical activity.* During the 1980s, physical activity, which had risen since the 1960s, started to fall as Americans spent more time in sedentary transportation and jobs—driving to and

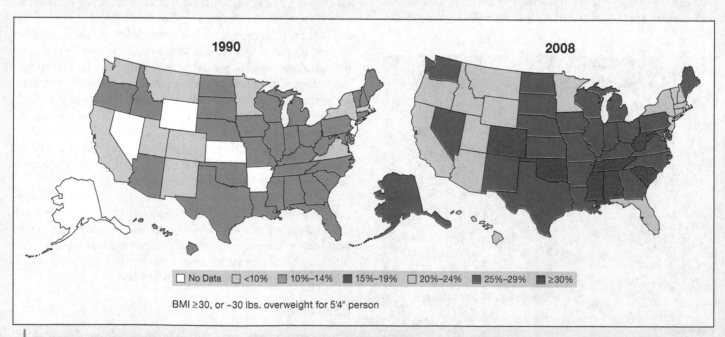

No Data □   <10% □   10%–14% ■   15%–19% ■   20%–24% □   25%–29% ■   ≥30% ■

BMI ≥30, or ~30 lbs. overweight for 5'4" person

■ **FIGURE 7.6** ■ **Obesity trends among U.S. adults, 1990 and 2008.** The maps show that obesity has increased sharply. In 2008, only one state (Colorado) had an obesity rate less than 20 percent. Thirty-two states had rates equal to or greater than 25 percent; six of these states (Alabama, Mississippi, Oklahoma, South Carolina, Tennessee, and West Virginia) had rates equal to or greater than 30 percent. (CDC Behavioral Risk Factor Surveillance System, U.S. Department of Health and Human Services, 2009e.)

from work and sitting throughout the work day, often behind a computer. At home, a rise in TV viewing to an average of more than four hours per day has been linked to weight gain in adults and children alike (Foster, Gore, & West, 2006).

Combating the Obesity Epidemic

Obesity is responsible for $150 billion in health expenditures and 300,000 premature deaths per year in the United States alone (Levine, 2007; Manson et al., 2004). Broad societal efforts are needed to combat this epidemic. Suggestions include

- Government funding to support massive public education about healthy eating and physical activity
- A high priority placed on building parks and recreation centers in low-income neighborhoods, where overweight and obesity are highest

- Laws that mandate prominent posting of the calorie, sugar, and fat content of foods sold in restaurants, movie theaters, and convenience stores
- A special tax on foods high in calories, sugar, or fat
- Incentives to schools and workplaces for promoting healthy eating and daily exercise and for offering weight-management programs

---

Sharese explained to a friend, "Exercise gives me a positive outlook and calms me down. Afterward, I feel a burst of energy that gets me through the day. If I don't do it, I get tired in the afternoon."

Although most Americans are aware of the health benefits of exercise, only 30 percent engage in at least moderate leisure-time physical activity for 20 minutes or more at least five times a week. And about 40 percent are inactive, with no regular brief sessions of even light activity (U.S. Department of Health and Human Services, 2009a). More women than men are inactive. And inactivity is greater among low-SES adults, who live in less safe neighborhoods, have more health problems, experience less social support for exercising regularly, and feel less personal control over their health (Grzywacz & Marks, 2001; Wilson et al., 2004).

Besides reducing body fat and building muscle, exercise fosters resistance to disease. Frequent bouts of moderate-intensity exercise enhance the immune response, lowering the risk of colds or flu and promoting faster recovery from these illnesses (Donatelle, 2009). Furthermore, in several longitudinal studies extending over 10 to 20 years, physical activity was linked to reduced incidence of cancer at all body sites except the skin, with the strongest findings for cancer of the rectum and colon (Albanes, Blair, & Taylor, 1989; Tardon et al., 2005; Wannamethee, Shaper, & Macfarlane, 1993). Physically active people are also less likely to develop diabetes and cardiovascular disease (Bassuk & Manson, 2005). If they do, these illnesses typically occur later and are less severe than among their inactive agemates.

How does exercise help prevent these serious illnesses? First, it reduces the incidence of obesity—a risk factor for heart disease, diabetes, and several forms of cancer. In addition, people who exercise probably adopt other healthful behaviors, thereby lowering the risk of diseases associated with high-fat diets, alcohol consumption, and smoking. In animal studies, exercise directly inhibits growth of cancerous tumors—beyond the impact of diet, body fat, and the immune response (de Lima et al., 2008). Exercise also promotes cardiovascular functioning by strengthening the heart muscle, decreasing blood pressure, and producing a form of "good cholesterol" (high-density lipoproteins, or HDLs) that helps remove "bad cholesterol" (low-density lipoproteins, or LDLs) from the artery walls (Donatelle, 2009).

Yet another way that exercise may guard against illness is through its mental health benefits. Physical activity reduces anxiety and depression and improves mood, alertness, and energy.

Regular, moderate-to-vigorous exercise predicts a healthier, longer life. Participants in this kickboxing class reap both physical and mental health benefits.

Furthermore, as EEG and fMRI evidence indicates, exercise enhances neural activity in the cerebral cortex and improves overall cognitive functioning (Hillman, Erickson, & Kramer, 2008; Johnson & Krueger, 2007; Mutrie & Faulkner, 2004; Penedo & Dahn, 2005). The impact of exercise on a "positive outlook" as Sharese expressed it, is most obvious just after a workout and can last for several hours (Chollar, 1995). The stress-reducing properties of exercise undoubtedly strengthen immunity to disease. And as physical activity enhances cognitive functioning and psychological well-being, it promotes on-the-job productivity, self-esteem, ability to cope with stress, and life satisfaction.

When we consider the evidence as a whole, it is not surprising that physical activity is associated with substantially lower death rates from all causes. The contribution of exercise to longevity cannot be accounted for by preexisting illness in inactive people. In a Danish longitudinal study of a nationally representative sample of 7,000 healthy 20- to 79-year-olds followed over several decades, mortality was lower among those who increased their leisure-time physical activity from low to either moderate or high than among those who remained consistently inactive (Schnohr, Scharling, & Jensen, 2003).

How much exercise is recommended for a healthier, happier, and longer life? Moderately intense physical activity—for example, 30 minutes of brisk walking—on most days leads to health benefits for previously inactive people. Adults who exercise at greater intensity—enough to build up a sweat—derive even greater protection against cardiovascular disease, diabetes, colon cancer, and obesity (Hu & Manson, 2001; Yu et al., 2003). Currently, the U.S. government recommends 30 minutes of moderate-intensity physical activity on five or more days per week or 20 or more minutes of vigorous-intensity exercise (for example, jogging, biking uphill, fast swimming) on three or more days per week (U.S. Department of Health and Human Services, 2009d).

Substance Abuse

Drug taking peaks among U.S. 19- to 22-year-olds and then declines over the decade of the twenties. Eager to try a wide range of experiences before settling down to the responsibilities of adulthood, young people of this age are more likely than younger or older individuals to smoke cigarettes, chew tobacco, use marijuana, and take stimulants to enhance cognitive or physical performance (U.S. Department of Health and Human Services, 2009b). Binge drinking and experimentation with prescription drugs (such as OxyContin, a highly addictive painkiller) and "party drugs" (such as LSD and MDMA, or Ecstasy) also increase, at times with tragic consequences. Risks include brain damage, lasting impairments in mental functioning, and unintentional injury and death (Burgess, O'Donohoe, & Gill, 2000; Montoya et al., 2002).

Furthermore, when alcohol and drug taking become chronic, they intensify the psychological problems that under-

lie addiction. As many as 20 percent of U.S. 21- to 25-year-olds are substance abusers (U.S. Department of Health and Human Services, 2009b). Return to Section 5, pages 169–170, to review the factors that lead to alcohol and drug abuse in adolescence. The same personal and situational conditions are predictive in the adult years. Cigarette smoking and alcohol consumption are the most commonly abused substances.

■ **CIGARETTE SMOKING.** Dissemination of information on the harmful effects of cigarette smoking has helped reduce its prevalence among U.S. adults from 40 percent in 1965 to 24 percent in 2007 (U.S. Department of Health and Human Services, 2009b). Still, smoking has declined very slowly, and most of the drop is among college graduates, with very little change for those who did not finish high school. Furthermore, although more men than women smoke, the gender gap is much smaller today than in the past, reflecting a sharp increase in smoking among young women who did not finish high school. Smoking among college students has also risen—for students of both sexes and of diverse ethnicities. More than 90 percent of men and 85 percent of women who smoke started before age 21 (U.S. Department of Health and Human Services, 2009b). And the earlier people start smoking, the greater their daily cigarette consumption and likelihood of continuing, an important reason that preventive efforts with adolescents and young adults are vital.

The ingredients of cigarette smoke—nicotine, tar, carbon monoxide, and other chemicals—leave their damaging mark throughout the body. As smokers inhale, oxygen delivery to tissues is reduced, and heart rate and blood pressure rise. Over time, exposure to toxins and insufficient oxygen result in damage to the retina of the eye; skin abnormalities, including premature aging, poor wound healing, and hair loss; a decline in bone mass; a decrease in reserve ova and earlier menopause in women; and a reduced sperm count and higher rate of sexual impotence in men (American Society for Reproductive Medicine, 2004; Freiman et al., 2004; Thornton et al., 2005). Other deadly outcomes include increased risk of heart attack, stroke, acute leukemia, melanoma, and cancer of the mouth, throat, larynx, esophagus, lungs, stomach, pancreas, kidneys, and bladder.

Cigarette smoking is the single most important preventable cause of death in industrialized nations. One of every three young people who become regular smokers will die from a smoking-related disease (U.S. Department of Health and Human Services, 2008a). The chances of premature death rise with the number of cigarettes consumed. At the same time, the benefits of quitting include return of most disease risks to nonsmoker levels within three to eight years. Although millions of people have stopped smoking without help, those who enter treatment programs or use cessation aids (for example, nicotine gum, nasal spray, or patches, designed to reduce dependency gradually) often fail: After one year, 70 to 90 percent start smoking again (Ludvig, Miner, & Eisenberg, 2005). Unfortunately, too few treatments last long enough or teach skills for avoiding relapse.

■ **ALCOHOL.** National surveys reveal that about 11 percent of men and 3 percent of women in the United States are heavy drinkers (U.S. Department of Health and Human Services, 2009b). About one-third of this group are *alcoholics*—people who cannot limit their alcohol use. In men, alcoholism usually begins in the teens and early twenties and worsens over the following decade. In women, its onset is typically later, in the twenties and thirties, and its course is more variable. Many alcoholics are also addicted to other drugs. About 80 percent are heavy cigarette smokers (John et al., 2003).

Twin studies support a genetic contribution to alcoholism (Tsuang et al., 2001). But whether a person comes to deal with life's problems through drinking is greatly affected by personal characteristics and circumstances: Half of hospitalized alcoholics have no family history of problem drinking (Hawkins, Catalano, & Miller, 1992). Alcoholism crosses SES and ethnic lines but is higher in some groups than others. In cultures where alcohol is a traditional part of religious or ceremonial activities, people are less likely to abuse it. Where access to alcohol is carefully controlled and viewed as a sign of adulthood, dependency is more likely—factors that may, in part, explain why college students drink more heavily than young people not enrolled in college (Slutske et al., 2004). Poverty and hopelessness also promote excessive drinking (Donatelle, 2009; U.S. Department of Health and Human Services, 2009b).

Alcohol acts as a depressant, impairing the brain's ability to control thought and action. In a heavy drinker, it relieves anxiety at first but then induces it as the effects wear off, so the alcoholic drinks again. Chronic alcohol use does widespread physical damage. Its best-known complication is liver disease, but it is also linked to cardiovascular disease, inflammation of the pancreas, irritation of the intestinal tract, bone marrow problems, disorders of the blood and joints, and some forms of cancer. Over time, alcohol causes brain damage, leading to confusion, apathy, inability to learn, and impaired memory (Brun & Andersson, 2001). The costs to society are enormous. About 40 percent of fatal motor vehicle crashes in the United States involve drivers who have been drinking (Pickrell, 2006). Nearly half of convicted felons are alcoholics, and about half of police activities in large cities involve alcohol-related offenses (McKim, 2002). Alcohol frequently plays a part in sexual coercion, including date rape, and in domestic violence.

The most successful treatments combine personal and family counseling, group support, and aversion therapy (use of medication that produces a physically unpleasant reaction to alcohol, such as nausea and vomiting). Alcoholics Anonymous, a community support approach, helps many people exert greater control over their lives through the encouragement of others with similar problems. Nevertheless, breaking an addiction that has dominated a person's life is difficult; about 50 percent of alcoholics relapse within a few months (Volpicelli, 2001).

Sexuality

At the end of high school, about 65 percent of U.S. young people have had sexual intercourse; by age 25, nearly all have done so, and the gender and SES differences that were apparent in adolescence (see page 163 in Section 5) have diminished (U.S. Department of Health and Human Services, 2008k). Compared with earlier generations, contemporary adults display a wider range of sexual choices and lifestyles, including cohabitation, marriage, extramarital experiences, and orientation toward a heterosexual or homosexual partner. In this section, we explore the attitudes, behaviors, and health concerns that arise as sexual activity becomes a regular event in young people's lives. In Section 8, we focus on the emotional side of close relationships.

■ **HETEROSEXUAL ATTITUDES AND BEHAVIOR.** One Friday evening, Sharese accompanied her roommate Heather to a young singles bar. Shortly after they arrived, two young men joined them. Faithful to her boyfriend, Ernie, whom she had met in college and who worked in another city, Sharese remained aloof for the next hour. In contrast, Heather was talkative and gave one of the men, Rich, her phone number. The next weekend, Heather went out with Rich. On the second date, they had intercourse, but the romance lasted only a few weeks. Aware of Heather's more adventurous sex life, Sharese wondered whether her own was normal. Only after several months of dating exclusively had she and Ernie slept together.

Since the 1950s, public display of sexuality in movies, newspapers, magazines, and books has steadily increased, fostering the impression that Americans are more sexually active than ever before. What are contemporary adults' sexual attitudes and behaviors really like? Answers were difficult to find until the National Health and Social Life Survey, the first in-depth study of U.S. adults' sex lives based on a nationally representative sample, was carried out in the early 1990s. Nearly four out of

In cultures where alcohol is a traditional part of religious or ceremonial activities, people are less likely to abuse it. This Jewish grandfather teaches his grandson the customs of the Passover Seder, which include blessing and drinking wine.

© BILL ARON/PHOTOEDIT

Sexual partners tend to be similar in age, education, ethnicity, and religion. And those who establish lasting relationships usually meet through family members or friends, or at work, school, or social events where people similar to themselves congregate.

five randomly chosen 18- to 59-year-olds agreed to participate—3,400 in all. Findings were remarkably similar to those of surveys conducted at about the same time in France, Great Britain, and Finland, and to a more recent U.S. survey (Langer, 2004; Laumann et al., 1994; Michael et al., 1994).

Recall from Section 5 that the sex lives of most teenagers do not dovetail with exciting media images. The same is true of adults in Western nations. Although their sexual practices are diverse, they are far less sexually active than we have come to believe. Monogamous, emotionally committed couples like Sharese and Ernie are more typical (and more satisfied) than couples like Heather and Rich.

Sexual partners, whether dating, cohabiting, or married, usually do not select each other arbitrarily. They tend to be similar in age (within five years), education, ethnicity, and (to a lesser extent) religion. In addition, people who establish lasting relationships usually meet in conventional ways—either through family members or friends, or at work, school, or social events where people similar to themselves congregate. The powerful influence of social networks on sexual choice is adaptive. Sustaining an intimate relationship is easier when adults share interests and values and people they know approve of the match.

Over the past decade, Internet dating services have become an increasingly popular and widely accepted way to initiate relationships. According to one estimate, over 40 percent of single U.S. adults visit these matchmaking websites (Mazzarella, 2007). By creating a personal profile and describing the type of person they want to meet, users hope to find a compatible partner quickly. Although success rates are lower than with conventional strategies, adults who form an online relationship and then meet face-to-face often go on to see each other again, with 18 percent of such ties lasting for more than a year (Gavin, Scott, & Duffield, 2005).

Consistent with popular belief, Americans today have more sexual partners over their lifetimes than they did a generation ago. For example, one-third of adults over age 50 have had five or more partners, whereas half of 30- to 50-year-olds have accumulated that many in much less time. And although women are more opposed to casual sex then men, after excluding a small number of men (less than 3 percent) with a great many sexual partners, contemporary men and women differ little in average number of lifetime sexual partners (Langer, 2004). Why is this so? From an evolutionary perspective, contemporary effective contraception has permitted sexual activity with little risk of pregnancy, enabling women to have as many partners as men without risking the welfare of their offspring.

But when adults of any age are asked how many partners they have had in the past year, the usual reply (for about 70 percent) is one. What explains the trend toward more relationships in the context of sexual commitment? In the past, dating several partners was followed by marriage. Today, dating more often gives way to cohabitation, which leads either to marriage or to breakup. In addition, people are marrying later, and the divorce rate remains high. Together, these factors create more opportunities for new partners. Still, surveys of college students reveal that almost all want to settle down with a mutually exclusive sexual partner eventually (Pedersen et al., 2002). In line with this goal, most people spend the majority of their lives with one partner.

How often do Americans have sex? Not nearly as frequently as the media would suggest. One-third of 18- to 59-year-olds have intercourse as often as twice a week, another third have it a few times a month, and the remaining third have it a few times a year or not at all. Three factors affect frequency of sexual activity: age, whether people are cohabiting or married, and how long the couple has been together. Single people have more partners, but this does not translate into more sex! Sexual activity increases through the twenties as people either cohabit or marry. Then, around age 30, it declines, even though hormone levels have not changed much. The demands of daily life—working, commuting, taking care of home and children—are probably responsible. Despite the common assumption that sexual practices vary greatly across social groups, the patterns just described are unaffected by education, SES, or ethnicity.

Most adults say they are happy with their sex lives. For those in committed relationships, more than 80 percent report feeling "extremely physically and emotionally satisfied," a figure that rises to 88 percent for married couples. In contrast, as number of sex partners increases, satisfaction declines sharply. These findings challenge two stereotypes—that marriage is sexually dull and that people with many partners have the "hottest" sex.

Only a minority of adults—women more often than men—report persistent sexual problems. For women, the two most frequent difficulties are lack of interest in sex (33 percent) and inability to achieve orgasm (24 percent); for men, climaxing too early (29 percent) and anxiety about performance (16 percent). Sexual difficulties are linked to low SES and psychological stress, and are more common among people who are not married, have had more than five partners, and have experienced sexual abuse during childhood or (for women) sexual coercion in adulthood (Laumann, Paik, & Rosen, 1999). As these findings suggest, a history of unfavorable personal relationships and sexual experiences increases the risk of sexual dysfunction.

But overall, a completely untroubled physical experience is not essential for sexual happiness. Surveys of adults repeatedly show that satisfying sex involves more than technique; it is attained in the context of love, affection, and fidelity. In sum, happiness with partnered sex is linked to an emotionally fulfilling relationship, good mental health, and overall contentment with life (Bancroft, 2002; Santtila et al., 2008).

■ **HOMOSEXUAL ATTITUDES AND BEHAVIOR.** The majority of Americans support civil liberties and equal employment opportunities for gay men, lesbians, and bisexuals (Brooks, 2000). And attitudes toward sexual relations between two adults of the same sex have gradually become more accepting: In one survey, 55 to 65 percent of U.S. 18- to 65-year-olds agreed "it is OK" (Langer, 2004). Homosexuals' political activism and greater openness about their sexual orientation have contributed to slow gains in acceptance. Exposure and interpersonal contact reduce negative attitudes. But perhaps because they are especially concerned with gender-role conformity, heterosexual men judge homosexuals (and especially gay men) more harshly than do heterosexual women (Kite & Whitley, 2003; Lim, 2002).

In the National Health and Social Life Survey, 2.8 percent of men and 1.4 percent of women identified themselves as homosexual or bisexual—figures similar to those of other national surveys conducted in the United States, France, and Great Britain (Black, Gates, & Sanders, 2000; Mercer et al., 2007; Mosher, Chandra, & Jones, 2005; Spira, 1992). But an estimated 30 percent of same-sex couples do not report themselves as such in survey research. This unwillingness to answer questions, engendered by a climate of persecution, has limited researchers' access to information about the sex lives of gay men and lesbians. The little evidence available indicates that homosexual sex follows many of the same rules as heterosexual sex: People tend to seek out partners similar in education and background to themselves; partners in committed relationships have sex more often and are more satisfied; and the overall frequency of sex is modest (Laumann et al., 1994; Michael et al., 1994).

Homosexuals tend to live in large cities, where many others share their sexual orientation, or in college towns, where attitudes are more accepting. Living in small communities where prejudice is intense and no social network exists through which to find compatible homosexual partners is isolating, lonely, and predictive of mental health problems (Meyer, 2003).

People who identify themselves as gay or lesbian also tend to be well-educated (Black, Gates, & Sanders, 2000; Mercer et al., 2007). In the National Health and Social Life Survey, twice as many college-educated as high-school-educated men and eight times as many college-educated as high-school-educated women

stated they were homosexual. Although the reasons for these findings are not clear, they probably reflect greater social and sexual liberalism among the more highly educated and therefore greater willingness to disclose homosexuality.

■ **SEXUALLY TRANSMITTED DISEASES.** In the United States, one in every four individuals is likely to contract a sexually transmitted disease (STD) at some point in life (U.S. Department of Health and Human Services, 2009a). Although the incidence is highest in adolescence, STDs continue to be prevalent in early adulthood. During the teens and twenties, people accumulate most of their sexual partners, and they often do not take appropriate precautions to prevent the spread of STDs (see page 164 in Section 5). The overall rate of STDs is higher among women than men because it is at least twice as easy for a man to infect a woman with any STD, including AIDS, than for a woman to infect a man.

Although AIDS, the most deadly STD, remains concentrated among gay men and intravenous drug abusers, many homosexuals have responded to its spread by changing their sexual practices—limiting number of sexual partners, choosing partners more carefully, and using latex condoms consistently and correctly. Heterosexuals at high risk due to a history of many partners have done the same. As a result, the number of infections is lower among gay and heterosexual men today than it was in the early 1980s. Still, AIDS remains the sixth-leading cause of death among U.S. young adults (refer to Figure 7.3 on page 227). The incidence of HIV-positive adults is higher in the United States than in any other industrialized nation (OECD, 2008b). AIDS is spreading most rapidly through heterosexual contact in poverty-stricken minority groups, among whom high rates of intravenous drug abuse coexist with poor health, inadequate education, high life stress, and hopelessness. People overwhelmed by these problems are least likely to take preventive measures (Capaldi et al., 2002b).

Yet AIDS can be contained and reduced—through sex education extending from childhood into adulthood and through access to health services, condoms, and clean needles and syringes for high-risk individuals. In view of the dramatic rise in AIDS among women, who currently account for one-fourth of cases in North America, Western Europe, and East Asia, one-third in Latin America, and slightly over half in Africa, a special need exists for female-controlled preventive measures (Quinn & Overbaugh, 2005). A recent redesign of the female condom for comfort and ease of use offers some promise. But it is more expensive than the male condom, and its effectiveness and acceptability are not yet established.

■ **SEXUAL COERCION.** After a long day of classes, Sharese flipped on the TV and caught a talk show discussion on sex without consent. Karen, a 25-year-old woman, described her husband Mike pushing, slapping, verbally insulting, and forcing her to have sex. "It was a control thing," Karen explained tearfully. "He complained that I wouldn't always do what he wanted. I was confused and blamed myself. I didn't leave because I was sure he'd come after me and get more violent."

One day, as Karen was speaking long distance to her mother on the phone, Mike grabbed the receiver and shouted, "She's not the woman I married! I'll kill her if she doesn't shape up!" Alarmed, Karen's parents arrived by plane the next day to rescue her, then helped her start divorce proceedings and get treatment.

An estimated 15 to 20 percent of U.S. women have endured *rape*, legally defined as intercourse by force, by threat of harm, or when the victim is incapable of giving consent (because of mental illness, mental retardation, or alcohol consumption). From 22 to 57 percent of women have experienced other forms of sexual aggression. The majority of victims (eight out of ten) are under age 30 (Schewe, 2007; Testa et al., 2003; U.S. Department of Health and Human Services, 2009a). Women are vulnerable to partners, acquaintances, and strangers, but in most instances their abusers are men they know well. Sexual coercion crosses SES and ethnic lines; people of all walks of life are offenders and victims.

Personal characteristics of the man with whom a woman is involved are far better predictors of her chances of becoming a victim than her own characteristics. Men who engage in sexual assault tend to believe in traditional gender roles, approve of violence against women, and accept rape myths (for example, "Women really want to be raped"). Perpetrators also tend to interpret women's social behavior inaccurately, viewing friendliness as seductiveness, assertiveness as hostility, and resistance as desire. Frequently reasoning that "she brought it on herself," they express little remorse (Abbey & McAuslan, 2004; Scully & Marolla, 1998). Furthermore, sexual abuse in childhood, promiscuity in adolescence, and alcohol abuse in adulthood are associated with sexual coercion. Approximately half of all sexual assaults take place while people are intoxicated (Abbey et al., 2004; Kalof, 2000).

Cultural forces also contribute. When men are taught from an early age to be dominant, competitive, and aggressive and women to be submissive, cooperative, and passive, the themes of rape are reinforced. Under these conditions, men may view a date not as a chance to get to know a partner but as a potential sexual conquest. Societal acceptance of violence also sets the stage for rape, which typically occurs in relationships in which other forms of aggression are commonplace. Exposure to sexually aggressive pornography and other media images, which portray women desiring and enjoying the assault, also promote sexual coercion by dulling sensitivity to its harmful consequences.

About 15 to 30 percent of U.S. young adult samples report female-initiated coercive sexual behavior against men, with 3 to 10 percent of male respondents indicating threats of physical force or actual force. Victimized men often say that women who committed these acts encouraged them to get drunk and threatened to end the relationship unless they complied (Anderson & Savage, 2005). Unfortunately, authorities rarely recognize female-initiated forced sex as illegal, and few men report these crimes.

Consequences. Women's psychological reactions to rape resemble those of survivors of extreme trauma. Immediate responses—shock, confusion, withdrawal, and psychological numbing—eventually give way to chronic fatigue, tension, disturbed sleep, depression, substance abuse, social anxiety, and suicidal thoughts (Schewe, 2007; Stein et al., 2004). Victims of ongoing sexual coercion may fall into a pattern of extreme passivity and fear of taking any action. A woman who has a history of sexual abuse or who received negative feedback after trying to tell someone is more likely to blame herself, which strengthens helpless reactions (Briere & Jordan, 2004).

One-third to one-half of female rape victims are physically injured. From 4 to 30 percent contract sexually transmitted diseases, and pregnancy results in 5 to 20 percent of cases. Furthermore, women victimized by rape (and other crimes) report more symptoms of illness across almost all body systems. And they are more likely to engage in negative health behaviors, including smoking and alcohol use (McFarlane et al., 2005; Schewe, 2007).

Like their female counterparts, some male victims report psychological and physical consequences, including long-term depression (Struckman-Johnson & Struckman-Johnson, 1998). But female-initiated coercion and its effects are far less often studied.

Prevention and Treatment. Many female rape victims are less fortunate than Karen because anxiety about provoking another attack keeps them from confiding even in trusted family members and friends. If they seek help for other problems, conflict over issues surrounding sexuality may lead a sensitive health professional to detect a possible rape. A variety of community services, including safe houses, crisis hotlines, support groups, and legal assistance, exist to help women take refuge from abusive partners, but most are underfunded and cannot reach out to everyone in need. Practically no services are available for victimized men, who are often too embarrassed to come forward (Anderson & Savage, 2005).

The trauma induced by rape is severe enough that therapy is important—both individual treatment to reduce anxiety and depression and group sessions where contact with other survivors

© GERI ENGBERG/THE IMAGE WORKS

A counselor and client talk at a rape crisis center. A variety of community services, including safe houses, crisis hotlines, and support groups, help women take refuge from abusive partners.

Applying What We Know

Preventing Sexual Coercion

Suggestion	Description
Reduce gender stereotyping and gender inequalities.	The roots of men's sexual coercion of women lie in the historically subordinate status of women. Unequal educational and employment opportunities keep many women economically dependent on men and therefore poorly equipped to avoid partner violence. At the same time, there is a need for increased public awareness that women sometimes commit sexually aggressive acts.
Mandate treatment for men and women who physically or sexually assault their partners.	Ingredients of effective intervention include combating rape myths and inducing personal responsibility for violent behavior; teaching social awareness, social skills, and anger management; and developing a support system to prevent future attacks.
Expand interventions for children and adolescents who have witnessed violence between their parents.	Although most child witnesses to parental violence do not become involved in abusive relationships as adults, they are at increased risk.
Teach both men and women to take precautions that lower the risk of sexual assault.	Risk of sexual assault can be reduced by communicating sexual limits clearly to a date and, among women, developing neighborhood ties to other women; increasing the safety of the immediate environment (for example, installing deadbolt locks, checking the back seat of the car before entering); avoiding deserted areas; not walking alone after dark; and leaving parties where alcohol use is high.
Broaden definitions of rape to be gender-neutral.	In some U.S. states, where the definition of rape is limited to vaginal or anal penetration, a woman legally cannot rape a man. A broader definition is needed to encompass women as both receivers and perpetrators of sexual aggression.

Sources: Anderson & Savage, 2005; Schewe, 2007.

helps counter isolation and self-blame (Neville & Heppner, 2002). Other critical features that foster recovery include

- *Routine screening for victimization* during health-care visits to ensure referral to community services and protection from future harm
- *Validation of the experience*, by acknowledging that many others have been physically and sexually assaulted by intimate partners; that such assaults lead to a wide range of persisting symptoms, are illegal and inappropriate, and should not be tolerated; and that the trauma can be overcome
- *Safety planning*, even when the abuser is no longer present, to prevent recontact and reassault. This includes information about how to obtain police protection, legal intervention, a safe shelter, and other aid should a rape survivor be at risk again.

Finally, many steps can be taken at the level of the individual, the community, and society to prevent sexual coercion. Some are listed in Applying What We Know above.

■ **MENSTRUAL CYCLE.** The menstrual cycle is central to women's lives and presents unique health concerns. Although almost all women experience some discomfort during menstruation, others have more severe difficulties. **Premenstrual syndrome (PMS)** refers to an array of physical and psychological symptoms that usually appear six to ten days prior to menstruation. The most common are abdominal cramps, fluid retention, diarrhea, tender breasts, backache, headache, fatigue, tension, irritability, and depression; the precise combination varies from

person to person. Nearly 40 percent of women have some form of PMS, usually beginning sometime after age 20. For most, symptoms are mild, but for 10 to 20 percent, PMS is severe enough to interfere with academic, occupational, and social functioning. PMS affects women of all SES levels and is a worldwide phenomenon—just as common in Italy and the Islamic nation of Bahrain as it is in the United States (Brody, 1992; Halbreich, 2004).

The causes of PMS are not well-established, but evidence for a genetic predisposition is accumulating. Identical twins are twice as likely as fraternal twins to share the syndrome (Freeman & Halbreich, 1998; Treloar, Heath, & Martin, 2002). PMS is related to hormonal changes that follow ovulation and precede menstruation. But hormone therapy is not consistently effective, suggesting that sensitivity of brain centers to these hormones, rather than the hormones themselves, is probably responsible (Dickerson, Mazyck, & Hunter, 2003; Indusekhar, Usman, & O'Brien, 2007). Common treatments include analgesics for pain, antidepressant medication, diuretics for fluid buildup, limiting caffeine intake (which can intensify symptoms), a low-fat, high-fiber diet, vitamin/mineral supplements, exercise, and other strategies for reducing stress. Although each of these approaches is helpful in certain cases, no method has been devised for curing PMS.

Psychological Stress

A final health concern, threaded throughout previous sections, has such a broad impact that it merits a comment of its own. Psychological stress, measured in terms of adverse social conditions,

Applying What We Know

Fostering a Healthy Adult Life

Suggestion	Description
Engage in healthy eating behavior.	Educate yourself and those with whom you live about the makeup of a healthy diet. Eat in moderation, and learn to distinguish true hunger from eating due to boredom or stress.
Maintain a reasonable body weight.	If you need to lose weight, make a commitment to a lifelong change in the way you eat, not just a temporary diet. Select a sensible, well-balanced dietary plan, and exercise regularly.
Keep physically fit.	Choose a specific time to exercise, and stick with it. To help sustain physical activity and make it more enjoyable, exercise with your partner or a friend, and encourage each other. Set reasonable expectations, and allow enough time to reach your fitness goals; many people become exercise dropouts because their expectations were too high.
Control alcohol intake and do not smoke cigarettes.	Drink moderately or not at all. Do not allow yourself to feel you must drink to be accepted or to enjoy a social event. If you smoke, choose a time that is relatively stress-free to quit. Seek the support of your partner or a friend.
Engage in responsible sexual behavior.	Identify attitudes and behaviors that you need to change to develop a healthy intimate relationship. Educate yourself about sexual anatomy and functioning so you can make sound decisions about contraception and protect yourself against sexually transmitted disease.
Manage stress.	Seek a reasonable balance among work, family, and leisure. Become more aware of stressors, and identify effective ways of coping with them so you are better-prepared when they arise. Engage in regular exercise, and find time each day for relaxation and quiet reflection.

Source: Donatelle, 2009.

negative life events, or daily hassles, is related to a wide variety of unfavorable health outcomes—both unhealthy behaviors and clear physical consequences.

Chronic stress resulting from economic hardship and inner-city living is consistently linked to hypertension, a relationship that contributes to the high incidence of heart disease in low-income groups, especially African Americans. As it mobilizes the body for action, stress elevates blood pressure. Compared with higher-SES individuals, low-SES adults show a stronger cardiovascular response to stress, perhaps because they more often perceive stressors as unsolvable (Almeida et al., 2005; Carroll et al., 2007). Earlier we mentioned that psychological stress interferes with immune system functioning, a link that may underlie its relationship to several forms of cancer. And by reducing digestive activity as blood flows to the brain, heart, and extremities, stress can cause gastrointestinal difficulties, including constipation, diarrhea, colitis, and ulcers (Donatelle, 2009).

The many challenging tasks of early adulthood make it a particularly stressful time of life. Young adults more often report depressive feelings than middle-aged people, many of whom have attained vocational success and financial security and are enjoying more free time as parenting responsibilities decline (Schieman, Gundy, & Taylor, 2001; Wade & Cairney, 1997). Middle-aged adults are better than young adults at coping with stress (Aldwin & Levenson, 2002). Because of their longer life experience and greater sense of personal control over their lives, they are more likely to engage in problem-centered coping when stressful conditions can be changed and emotion-centered coping when nothing can be done.

In previous sections, we repeatedly noted the stress-buffering effect of social support, which continues throughout life. Helping stressed young adults establish and maintain satisfying social ties is as important a health intervention as any we have mentioned. Before we turn to the cognitive side of early adulthood, consult Applying What We Know above for strategies that foster a healthy adult life.

ASK YOURSELF

>> **REVIEW**
List as many factors as you can that may have contributed to heart attacks and early death among Sharese's African-American relatives.

>> **REVIEW**
Why are people in committed relationships likely to be more sexually active and satisfied than those who are dating several partners?

>> **APPLY**
Tom had been going to a health club three days a week after work, but job pressures convinced him that he no longer had time for regular exercise. Explain to Tom why he should keep up his exercise regimen, and suggest ways to fit it into his busy life.

>> **CONNECT**
Describe history-graded influences that have contributed to the obesity epidemic. (To review this aspect of the lifespan perspective.)

Cognitive Development

The cognitive changes of early adulthood are supported by further development of the cerebral cortex, especially the frontal lobes. Pruning of synapses along with growth and myelination of stimulated neural fibers continue, though at a slower pace than in adolescence (Nelson, Thomas, & De Haan, 2006). As we will see, cognitive advances (and underlying brain growth) are promoted by major life events, including attaining higher education, establishing a career, and grappling with the demands of marriage and child rearing. fMRI evidence reveals that as young adults become increasingly proficient in a field of endeavor, cortical regions specialized for those activities undergo further *experience-dependent brain growth*. In addition to functioning more efficiently, structural changes may occur as skill refinement results in increased cortical tissue devoted to the task and, at times, reorganization of brain areas governing the activity (Hill & Schneider, 2006).

How does cognition change in early adulthood? Lifespan theorists have examined this question from three familiar vantage points. First, they have proposed transformations in the structure of thought—new, qualitatively distinct ways of thinking that extend the cognitive-developmental changes of childhood and adolescence. Second, adulthood is a time of attaining advanced knowledge in a particular area, an accomplishment that has important implications for information processing and creativity. Finally, researchers have been interested in the extent to which the diverse mental abilities assessed by intelligence tests remain stable or change during the adult years.

Changes in the Structure of Thought

Sharese described her first year in graduate school as a "cognitive turning point." As part of her internship in a public health clinic, she observed firsthand the many factors that affect human health-related behaviors. For a time, the realization that everyday dilemmas did not have clear-cut solutions made her intensely uncomfortable. "Working in this messy reality is so different from the problem solving I did in my undergraduate classes," she told her mother over the phone one day.

Piaget (1967) acknowledged the possibility that important advances in thinking follow the attainment of formal operations. He observed that adolescents prefer an idealistic, internally consistent perspective on the world to one that is vague, contradictory, and adapted to particular circumstances (see Section 5, page 176). Sharese's reflections fit the observations of researchers who have studied **postformal thought**—cognitive development beyond Piaget's formal operations. To clarify how thinking is restructured in adulthood, let's look at some influential theories, along with supportive research. Together, they show how personal effort and social experiences spark increasingly rational, flexible, and practical ways of thinking that accept uncertainties and vary across situations.

Perry's Theory: Epistemic Cognition

The work of William Perry (1981, 1970/1998) provided the starting point for an expanding research literature on the development of *epistemic cognition*. *Epistemic* means "of or about knowledge," and **epistemic cognition** refers to our reflections on how we arrived at facts, beliefs, and ideas. When mature, rational thinkers reach conclusions that differ from those of others, they consider the justifiability of their conclusions. When they cannot justify their approach, they revise it, seeking a more balanced, adequate route to acquiring knowledge.

■ **DEVELOPMENT OF EPISTEMIC COGNITION.**   Perry wondered why young adults respond in dramatically different ways to the diversity of ideas they encounter in college. To find out, he interviewed Harvard University undergraduates at the end of each of their four years, asking "what stood out" during the previous year. Responses indicated that students' reflections on knowing changed as they experienced the complexities of university life and moved closer to adult roles—findings confirmed in many subsequent studies (King & Kitchener, 1994, 2002; Magolda, 2002; Moore, 2002).

Younger students regarded knowledge as made up of separate units (beliefs and propositions), whose truth could be determined by comparing them to objective standards—standards that exist apart from the thinking person and his or her situation.

When college students challenge one another's reasoning while tackling realistic, ambiguous problems, they are likely to gain in epistemic cognition.

As a result, they engaged in **dualistic thinking,** dividing information, values, and authority into right and wrong, good and bad, we and they. As one college freshman stated, "When I went to my first lecture, what the man said was just like God's word. I believe everything he said because he is a professor . . . and this is a respected position" (Perry, 1981, p. 81). And when asked, "If two people disagree on the interpretation of a poem, how would you decide which one is right?" a sophomore replied, "You'd have to ask the poet. It's his poem" (Clinchy, 2002, p. 67).

Older students, in contrast, had moved toward **relativistic thinking**—viewing all knowledge as embedded in a framework of thought. Aware of a diversity of opinions on many topics, they gave up the possibility of absolute truth in favor of multiple truths, each relative to its context. As a result, their thinking became more flexible and tolerant. As one college senior put it, "Just seeing how [famous philosophers] fell short of an all-encompassing answer, [you realize] that ideas are really individualized. And you begin to have respect for how great their thought could be, without its being absolute" (Perry, 1970/1998, p. 90). Relativistic thinking leads to the realization that one's own beliefs are often subjective, since several frameworks may satisfy the criterion of internal logical consistency (Moore, 2002; Sinnott, 2003). Thus, the relativistic thinker is acutely aware that each person, in arriving at a position, creates her own "truth."

Eventually, the most mature individuals progress to **commitment within relativistic thinking.** Instead of choosing between opposing views, they try to formulate a more satisfying perspective that synthesizes contradictions. When considering which of two theories studied in a college course is better, or which of several movies most deserves an Oscar, the individual moves beyond the stance that everything is a matter of opinion and generates rational criteria against which options can be evaluated (Moshman, 2003, 2005). Few college students reach this extension of relativism. Adults who attain it generally display a more sophisticated approach to learning, in which they actively seek out differing perspectives to advance their knowledge and understanding.

■ **IMPORTANCE OF PEER INTERACTION AND REFLECTION.** Advances in epistemic cognition depend on further gains in metacognition, which are likely to occur in situations that challenge young peoples' perspectives and induce them to consider the rationality of their thought processes (Moshman, 2005). In a study of the college learning experiences of seniors who scored low and high in Perry's scheme, high-scoring students frequently reported activities that encouraged them to struggle with realistic but ambiguous problems in a supportive environment, in which faculty offered encouragement and guidance. For example, an engineering major, describing an airplane-design project that required advanced epistemic cognition, noted his discovery that "you can design 30 different airplanes and each one's going to have its benefits and there's going to be problems with each one" (Marra & Palmer, 2004, p. 116). The low-scoring students rarely mentioned such experiences.

When students tackle challenging, ill-structured problems, interaction among individuals who are roughly equal in knowledge and authority is beneficial because it prevents acceptance of another's reasoning simply because of greater power or expertise. When college students were asked to devise the most effective solution to a difficult logical problem, only 3 out of 32 students (9 percent) in a "work alone" condition succeeded. But in an "interactive" condition, 15 out of 20 small groups (75 percent) arrived at the correct solution following extensive discussion (Moshman & Geil, 1998). Whereas few students working alone reflected on their solution strategies, most groups engaged in a process of "collective rationality" in which members challenged one another to justify their reasoning and collaborated in working out the most defensible strategy.

Of course, reflection on one's own thinking can also occur individually. But peer interaction fosters the necessary type of individual reflection: arguing with oneself over competing ideas and strategies and coordinating opposing perspectives into a new, more effective structure. ***TAKE A MOMENT...*** Return to page 109 in Section 3 to review how peer collaboration fosters cognitive development in childhood. It remains a highly effective basis for education in early adulthood.

Perry's theory and the research it stimulated are based on samples of highly educated young adults. These investigators acknowledge that movement from dualism to relativism is probably limited to people confronting the multiplicity of viewpoints typically encountered during a college education, and that the most advanced attainment—commitment within relativism—may require advanced graduate study (King & Kitchener, 2002). But the underlying theme—thought less constrained by the need to find one answer to a question and more responsive to its context—is also evident in another theory of adult cognition.

Labouvie-Vief's Theory: Pragmatic Thought and Cognitive-Affective Complexity

Gisella Labouvie-Vief's (1980, 1985) portrait of adult cognition echoes features of Perry's theory. Adolescents, she points out, operate within a world of possibility. Adulthood involves movement from hypothetical to **pragmatic thought,** a structural advance in which logic becomes a tool for solving real-world problems.

According to Labouvie-Vief, the need to specialize motivates this change. As adults select one path out of many alternatives, they become more aware of the constraints of everyday life. And in the course of balancing various roles, they accept contradictions as part of existence and develop ways of thinking that thrive on imperfection and compromise. Sharese's friend Christy, a student and mother of two young children, illustrates:

> I've always been a feminist, and I wanted to remain true to my beliefs in family and career. But this is Gary's first year of teaching high school, and he's saddled with four preparations and coaching the school's basketball team. At least

for now, I've had to settle for "give-and-take feminism"—going to school part-time and shouldering most of the responsibility for the kids while he gets used to his new job. Otherwise, we'd never make it financially.

Labouvie-Vief (2003, 2006) also points out that young adults' enhanced reflective capacities alter the dynamics of their emotional lives: They become more adept at integrating cognition with emotion and, in doing so, again make sense of discrepancies. Examining the self-descriptions of several hundred 10- to 80-year-olds diverse in SES, Labouvie-Vief found that from adolescence through middle adulthood, people gained in **cognitive-affective complexity**—awareness of positive and negative feelings and coordination of them into a complex, organized structure (see Figure 7.7) (Labouvie-Vief, 2008; Labouvie-Vief et al., 1995; Labouvie-Vief, DeVoe, & Bulka, 1989). For example, one 34-year-old combined roles, traits, and diverse emotions into this coherent self-description: "With the recent birth of our first child, I find myself more fulfilled than ever, yet struggling in some ways. My elation is tempered by my gnawing concern over meeting all my responsibilities in a satisfying way while remaining an individualized person with needs and desires."

Cognitive-affective complexity promotes greater awareness of one's own and others' perspectives and motivations. As Labouvie-Vief (2003) notes, it is a vital aspect of adult *emotional intelligence* (see page 101 in Section 3) and is valuable in solving many pragmatic problems. Individuals high in cognitive-affective complexity view events and people in a tolerant, open-minded fashion. And because cognitive-affective complexity involves accepting and making sense of both positive and negative feelings, it helps people regulate intense emotion and, therefore, think rationally about real-world dilemmas, even those that are laden with negative information (Labouvie-Vief & Gonzalez, 2004).

Awareness of multiple truths, integration of logic with reality, and cognitive-affective complexity sum up qualitative transformations in thinking under way in early adulthood (Sinnott, 1998, 2003, 2008). As we will see next, adults' increasingly specialized and context-bound thought, although it closes off certain options, opens new doors to higher levels of competence.

Expertise and Creativity

In Section 3, we noted that children's expanding knowledge improves their ability to remember new information related to what they already know. For young adults, **expertise**—acquisition of extensive knowledge in a field or endeavor—is supported by the specialization that begins with selecting a college major or an occupation, since it takes many years for a person to master any complex domain. Once attained, expertise has a profound impact on information processing.

Compared with novices, experts remember and reason more quickly and effectively. The expert knows more domain-specific concepts and represents them in richer ways—at a deeper and more abstract level and as having more features that can be linked to other concepts. As a result, unlike novices, whose understanding is superficial, experts approach problems with underlying principles in mind. For example, a highly trained physicist notices when several problems deal with conservation of energy and can therefore be solved similarly. In contrast, a beginning physics student focuses only on surface features—whether the problem contains a disk, a pulley, or a coiled spring (Chi, 2006; Chi, Glaser, & Farr, 1988). Experts can use what they know to arrive at many solutions automatically—through quick and easy remembering. And when a problem is challenging, they tend to plan ahead, systematically analyzing and categorizing elements and selecting the best from many possibilities, while the novice proceeds more by trial and error.

Expertise is necessary for creativity as well as problem solving (Weissberg, 2006). The creative products of adulthood differ from those of childhood in that they are not just original but also directed at a social or aesthetic need. Mature creativity requires a unique cognitive capacity—the ability to formulate new, culturally meaningful problems and to ask significant questions that have not been posed before. According to Patricia Arlin (1989), movement from *problem solving* to *problem finding* is a core feature of postformal thought evident in highly accomplished artists and scientists.

Case studies support the 10-year rule in development of master-level creativity—a decade between initial exposure to a

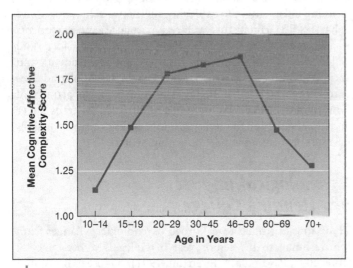

■ **FIGURE 7.7** ■ **Changes in cognitive-affective complexity from adolescence to late adulthood.** Performance, based on participants' descriptions of their roles, traits, and emotions, increased steadily from adolescence through early adulthood, peaked in middle age, and fell off in late adulthood when (as we will see in later sections) basic information-processing skills decline. (From G. Labouvie-Vief, 2004, "Dynamic Integration: Affect, Cognition, and the Self in Adulthood," *Current Directions in Psychological Science, 12,* p. 203. Reprinted by permission of Blackwell Publishing Ltd.)

field and sufficient expertise to produce a creative work (Simonton, 2000; Winner, 2003). Furthermore, a century of research reveals that creative accomplishment rises in early adulthood, peaks in the late thirties or early forties, and gradually declines, though rarely so substantially as to turn a creative person into a noncreative person (Dixon, 2003). And exceptions to this pattern exist. Those who get an early start in creativity tend to peak and drop off sooner, whereas "late bloomers" reach their full stride at older ages. This suggests that creativity is more a function of "career age" than of chronological age.

The course of creativity also varies across disciplines (Simonton, 1991, 2006). For example, artists and musicians typically show an early rise in creativity, perhaps because they do not need extensive formal education before they begin to produce. Academic scholars and scientists, who must earn higher academic degrees and spend years doing research to make worthwhile contributions, usually display their achievements later and over a longer time.

Though creativity is rooted in expertise, not all experts are creative. Creativity also requires other qualities—an innovative thinking style, tolerance of ambiguity, a special drive to succeed, and a willingness to experiment and try again after failure (Lubart, 2003; Sternberg & Lubart, 1996). And creativity demands time and energy. For women especially, it may be postponed or disrupted by child rearing, divorce, or an unsupportive partner (Vaillant & Vaillant, 1990). In sum, creativity is multiply determined. When personal and situational factors jointly promote it, creativity can continue for many decades, well into old age.

A sculptor works on a statue to honor those who died in the Asian tsunami of 2004. The creative products of adulthood differ from those of childhood in that they are not just original but also directed at a social or aesthetic need.

© BORDERLANDS/ALAMY

The College Experience

Looking back at the trajectory of their lives, many people view the college years as formative—more influential than any other period of adulthood. This is not surprising. College serves as a "developmental testing ground," a time for devoting full attention to exploring alternative values, roles, and behaviors. To facilitate this exploration, college exposes students to a form of "culture shock"—encounters with new ideas and beliefs, new freedoms and opportunities, and new academic and social demands. About two-thirds of U.S. high school graduates enroll in an institution of higher education (U.S. Department of Education, 2009). Besides offering a route to a high-status career and its personal and monetary rewards, colleges and universities have a transforming impact on young people.

Psychological Impact of Attending College

Thousands of studies reveal broad psychological changes from the freshman to the senior year of college (Montgomery & Côté, 2003; Pascarella & Terenzini, 1991). As research inspired by Perry's theory indicates, students become better at reasoning about problems that have no clear solution, identifying the strengths and weaknesses of opposing sides of complex issues, and reflecting on the quality of their thinking. Their attitudes and values also broaden. They show increased interest in literature, the performing arts, and philosophical and historical issues and greater tolerance for ethnic and cultural diversity. Also, as noted in Section 6, college leaves its mark on moral reasoning by fostering concern with individual rights and human welfare.

Interacting with other college students in academic and extracurricular settings yields rich benefits. Residence hall living in particular predicts cognitive change because it maximizes involvement in the educational and social systems of the institution.

Finally, exposure to multiple worldviews encourages young people to look more closely at themselves. During the college years, students develop greater self-understanding, enhanced self-esteem, and a firmer sense of identity.

How do these interrelated changes come about? The type of four-year institution attended—public versus private, highly selective versus relatively open in enrollment—makes little difference in psychological outcomes or even in ultimate career success and earnings (Montgomery & Côté, 2003). And cognitive growth is just as great at two-year community colleges as at four-year institutions (Bohr et al., 1994).

Rather, the impact of college is jointly influenced by the person's involvement in academic and nonacademic activities and the richness and diversity of the campus environment. The more students interact with peers in academic and extracurricular settings, the more they benefit. Residence hall living is one of the most consistent predictors of cognitive change because it maximizes involvement in the educational and social systems of the institution (Terenzini, Pascarella, & Blimling, 1999). These findings underscore the importance of programs that integrate commuting students into out-of-class campus life. Quality of academic experiences also affects college outcomes. Psychological benefits increase with students' effort and willingness to participate in class and with challenging teaching that integrates learning in separate courses, offers extensive contact with faculty, and connects course work with real workplace activities (Franklin, 1995).

Dropping Out

Completing a college education has enduring effects on people's postcollege opportunities and worldview. Yet 45 percent of U.S. students at two-year institutions and 30 percent of students at four-year institutions drop out, most within the first year and many within the first six weeks (ACT, 2008). Dropout rates are higher in colleges with less selective admission requirements; in some, first-year dropout approaches 50 percent. And ethnic minority students from low-SES families are at increased risk for dropping out (Montgomery & Côté, 2003).

Both personal and institutional factors contribute to college leaving. Most entering freshmen have high hopes for college life but find the transition difficult. Those who have trouble adapting—because of lack of motivation, poor study skills, financial pressures, or emotional dependence on parents—quickly develop negative attitudes toward the college environment. Often these exit-prone students do not meet with their advisers or professors. At the same time, colleges that do little to help high-risk students, through developmental courses and other support services, have a higher percentage of dropouts (Moxley, Najor-Durack, & Dumbrigue, 2001). And when students report experiencing "disrespect" on campus because of their ethnicity or religion, their desire to continue plummets (Zea et al., 1997).

Beginning to prepare young people in early adolescence with the necessary visions and skills can do much to improve college success. In a study that followed up nearly 700 young people from sixth grade until two years after high school graduation, a set of factors—grade point average, academic self-concept, persistence in the face of challenge, parental SES and valuing of a college education, and the individual's plans to attend college—predicted college enrollment at age 20 (Eccles, Vida, & Barber, 2004). Although parental SES is difficult to modify, improving parents' attitudes and behaviors and students' academic motivation and educational aspirations is within reach, through a wide array of strategies considered in Section 5 and 6.

Once young people enroll in college, reaching out to them, especially during the early weeks and throughout the first year, is crucial. Programs that forge bonds between teachers and students and that provide academic support, part-time work opportunities, and meaningful extracurricular roles increase retention. Membership in campus-based social and religious organizations is especially helpful in strengthening minority students' sense of belonging (Fashola & Slavin, 1998). Young people who feel that they have entered a college community that is concerned about them as individuals are far more likely to graduate.

Vocational Choice

Young adults, college-bound or not, face a major life decision: the choice of a suitable work role. Being a productive worker calls for many of the same qualities as being an active citizen and a nurturant family member—good judgment, responsibility, dedication, and cooperation. What influences young people's decisions about careers? What is the transition from school to work like, and what factors make it easy or difficult?

Selecting a Vocation

In societies with an abundance of career possibilities, occupational choice is a gradual process that begins long before adolescence. Major theorists view the young person as moving through several periods of vocational development (Gottfredson, 2005; Super, 1990, 1994):

1. The **fantasy period:** In early and middle childhood, children gain insight into career options by fantasizing about them. Their preferences, guided largely by familiarity, glamour, and excitement, bear little relation to the decisions they will eventually make.

2. The **tentative period:** Between ages 11 and 16, adolescents think about careers in more complex ways, at first in terms of their *interests,* and soon—as they become more aware of personal and educational requirements for different vocations—in terms of their *abilities* and *values.* "I like science and the process of discovery," Sharese thought as she neared high school graduation. "But I'm also good with people, and I'd like to do something to help others. So maybe teaching or medicine would suit my needs."

3. The **realistic period:** By the late teens and early twenties, with the economic and practical realities of adulthood just around the corner, young people start to narrow their options. A first step is often further *exploration*—gathering more information about possibilities that blend with their personal characteristics. In the final phase, *crystallization,* they focus on a general vocational category and experiment for a time before settling on a single occupation. As a college sophomore, Sharese pursued her interest in science, but she had not yet selected a major. Once she decided on chemistry, she considered whether to pursue teaching, medicine, or public health.

Factors Influencing Vocational Choice

Most, but not all, young people follow this pattern of vocational development. A few know from an early age just what they want to be and follow a direct path to a career goal. Some decide and later change their minds, and still others remain undecided for an extended period. College students are granted added time to explore various options. In contrast, the life conditions of many low-SES youths restrict their range of choices.

Making an occupational choice is not simply a rational process in which young people weigh abilities, interests, and values against career options. Like other developmental milestones, it is the result of a dynamic interaction between person and environment (Gottfredson & Duffy, 2008). A great many influences feed into the decision, including personality, family, teachers, and gender stereotypes, among others.

■ **PERSONALITY.**   People are attracted to occupations that complement their personalities. John Holland (1985, 1997) identified six personality types that affect vocational choice:

- The *investigative person,* who enjoys working with ideas, is likely to select a scientific occupation (for example, anthropologist, physicist, or engineer).

- The *social person,* who likes interacting with people, gravitates toward human services (counseling, social work, or teaching).

- The *realistic person,* who prefers real-world problems and working with objects, tends to choose a mechanical occupation (construction, plumbing, or surveying).

- The *artistic person,* who is emotional and high in need for individual expression, looks toward an artistic field (writing, music, or the visual arts).

- The *conventional person,* who likes well-structured tasks and values material possessions and social status, has traits well-suited to certain business fields (accounting, banking, or quality control).

- The *enterprising person,* who is adventurous, persuasive, and a strong leader, is drawn to sales and supervisory positions or to politics.

TAKE A MOMENT... Does one of these personality types describe you? Or do you have aspects of more than one type? Research confirms a relationship between personality and vocational choice in diverse cultures, but it is only moderate. Many people are blends of several personality types and can do well at more than one kind of occupation (Holland, 1997; Spokane & Cruza-Guet, 2005). Furthermore, career decisions are made in the context of family influences, educational opportunities, and current life circumstances. For example, Sharese's friend Christy scored high on Holland's investigative dimension. But when she married and had children early, she postponed her dream of becoming a college professor and chose a human services career that required fewer years of education. As Christy's case illustrates, personality takes us only partway in understanding vocational choice.

■ **FAMILY INFLUENCES.**   Young people's vocational aspirations correlate strongly with their parents' jobs. Individuals who grew up in higher-SES homes are more likely to select high-status, white-collar occupations, such as doctor, lawyer, scientist, or engineer. In contrast, those with lower-SES backgrounds tend to choose less prestigious, blue-collar careers—for example, plumber, construction worker, food service employee, or secretary. Parent–child vocational similarity is partly a function of similarity in personality, intellectual abilities, and—especially—educational attainment (Ellis & Bonin, 2003; Schoon & Parsons, 2002). More today than in past generations, number of years of schooling completed powerfully predicts occupational status.

Other factors also promote family resemblance in occupational choice. Higher-SES parents are more likely to give their children important information about the world of work and to have connections with people who can help the young person obtain a high-status position (Kalil, Levine, & Ziol-Guest, 2005). In a study of African-American mothers' influence on their

This young man has followed his father's career path to become an emergency medical technician. Parent–child vocational similarity is partly a function of similarity in personality, intellectual abilities, and—especially—educational attainment.

daughters' academic and career goals, college-educated mothers engaged in a wider range of strategies to promote their daughters' progress, including gathering information on colleges and areas of study and identifying knowledgeable professionals who could help (Kerpelman, Shoffner, & Ross-Griffin, 2002). Parenting practices also shape work-related values. Higher-SES parents tend to promote curiosity and self-direction, which are required in many high-status careers. Lower-SES parents, in contrast, are more likely to emphasize conformity and obedience. Eventually, young people may choose careers that dovetail with these differences.

Still, parents can foster higher aspirations. Parental pressure to do well in school and encouragement toward high-status occupations predict vocational attainment beyond SES (Bryant, Zvonkovic, & Reynolds, 2006).

■ **TEACHERS.** Young adults preparing for or in careers requiring extensive education often report that teachers influenced their choice (Bright et al., 2005; Reddin, 1997). High school students who say that most of their teachers are caring and accessible, interested in their future, and expect them to work hard feel more confident about choosing a personally suitable career and succeeding at it (Metheny, McWhirter, & O'Neil, 2008). College-bound high school students tend to have closer relationships with teachers than do other students—relationships that are especially likely to foster high career aspirations in young women (Wigfield et al., 2002).

These findings provide yet another reason to promote positive teacher–student relations, especially for high school students from low-SES families. The power of teachers in offering encouragement and acting as role models can serve as an important source of resilience for these young people.

■ **GENDER STEREOTYPES.** Over the past three decades, young women have expressed increasing interest in occupations largely held by men (Gottfredson, 2005). Changes in gender-role attitudes, along with a dramatic rise in numbers of employed mothers who serve as career-oriented models for their daughters, are common explanations for women's attraction to nontraditional careers.

But women's progress in entering and excelling at male-dominated professions has been slow. As Table 7.2 shows, although the percentage of women engineers, lawyers, doctors, and business executives increased between 1983 and 2007 in the United States, it still falls far short of equal representation. Women remain concentrated in less well-paid, traditionally feminine professions, such as writing, social work, education, and nursing (U.S. Census Bureau, 2009b). In virtually all fields, their achievements lag behind those of men, who write more books, make more discoveries, hold more positions of leadership, and produce more works of art.

Ability cannot account for these dramatic sex differences. Recall from Section 5 that girls are advantaged in reading and writing achievement, and the gender gap favoring boys in math is small. Rather, gender-stereotyped messages play a key role. Although girls earn higher grades than boys, they reach secondary school less confident of their abilities, more likely to underestimate their achievement, and less likely to express interest in math and science careers (Wigfield et al., 2002). In college, the career aspirations of many women decline further as they question their capacity and opportunities to succeed in male-dominated fields and worry about combining a highly

■ **TABLE 7.2** ■ *Percentage of Women in Various Professions in the United States, 1983 and 2007*

PROFESSION	1983	2007
Engineer	5.8	9.7
Lawyer	15.8	32.6
Doctor	15.8	30.0
Business executive	32.4	37.5[a]
Author, artist, entertainer	42.7	47.1
Social worker	64.3	82.0
Elementary or middle school teacher	93.5	80.9
Secondary school teacher	62.2	56.9
College or university professor	36.3	46.2
Librarian	84.4	83.2
Registered nurse	95.8	91.7
Psychologist	57.1	64.4

Source: U.S. Census Bureau, 2009b.

[a]This percentage includes executives and managers at all levels. Women make up only 25 percent of chief executive officers at large corporations, although that figure represents a sixfold increase over the past 25 years.

SOCIAL ISSUES

Masculinity at Work: Men Who Choose Nontraditional Careers

Ross majored in engineering through his sophomore year of college, when he startled his family and friends by switching to nursing. "I've never looked back," Ross said. "I love the work." He noted some benefits of being a male in a female work world, including the high regard of women colleagues and rapid advancement. "But as soon as they learn what I do," Ross remarked with disappointment, "guys on the outside question my abilities and masculinity."

What factors influence the small but increasing number of men who, like Ross, enter careers dominated by women? Compared to their traditional-career counterparts, these men are less gender-typed, less focused on the social status of their work, and more interested in working with people (Dodson & Borders, 2006; Jome, Surething, & Taylor,

2005). When several hundred men were assessed in their first year of college and again four years later, those who chose traditionally feminine occupations had more liberal social attitudes, including attitudes about gender roles, than those who chose traditionally masculine occupations. They also less often rated occupational prestige as important in their choice and were less likely to aspire to graduate education (Lease, 2003). Perhaps these men's gender-stereotype flexibility allowed them to choose occupations they found satisfying, even if those jobs were not typically regarded as appropriate for men.

In one study, 40 men who were primary school teachers, nurses, airline stewards, or librarians, when asked how they arrived at their choice, described diverse pathways (Simpson,

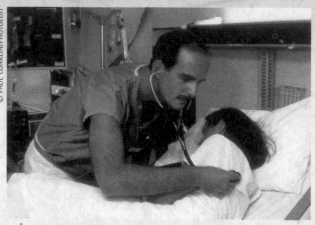

© PAUL CONKLIN/PHOTOEDIT

This nurse exemplifies the increasing number of men entering careers dominated by women. Compared with his traditional-career counterparts, he is likely to be less gender-typed, less focused on the social status of his work, and more interested in working with people.

2005). Some actively sought the career, others happened on it while exploring possibilities, and still others first spent time in another occupation (usually male-dominated), found

---

demanding career with family responsibilities (Chhin, Bleeker, & Jacobs, 2008; Wigfield et al., 2006). Research indicates that many mathematically talented college women settle on non-science majors. And those who remain in the sciences more often choose medicine or another health profession and less often choose engineering or a math or physical science career, than their male counterparts (Benbow et al., 2000; Halpern et al., 2007).

These findings reveal a pressing need for programs that sensitize high school and college personnel to the special problems women face in developing and maintaining high vocational aspirations and selecting nontraditional careers. Young women's aspirations rise in response to career guidance that encourages them to set goals that match their abilities, interests, and values. Those who continue to achieve usually have four experiences in common:

- A college environment that values women's accomplishments and attempts to enhance women's experiences in its curriculum

- Frequent interaction with faculty and professionals in their chosen fields

- The opportunity to test their abilities in a supportive environment

- Models of accomplished women who have successfully dealt with family–career role conflict (Swanson & Fouad, 1999; Zeldin & Pajares, 2000)

Compared to women, men have changed little in their interest in nontraditional occupations. See the Social Issues box above for research on the motivations and experiences of men who do choose female-dominated careers.

Vocational Preparation of Non-College-Bound Young Adults

Sharese's younger brother Leon graduated from high school in a vocational track. Like approximately one-third of American young people with a high school diploma, he had no current plans to go to college. While in school, Leon held a part-time job selling candy at the local shopping mall. He hoped to work in data processing after graduation, but six months later he was still a part-time sales clerk at the candy store. Although Leon had filled out many job applications, he got no interviews or offers. He soon despaired of discovering any relationship between his schooling and a career.

Leon's inability to find a job other than the one he held as a student is typical for U.S. non-college-bound high school graduates. Although they are more likely to find employment than youths who drop out, they have fewer work opportunities than high school graduates of several decades ago. About 20 percent of recent high school graduates who do not continue their education are unemployed (U.S. Department of Education, 2009). When they do find work, most hold low-paid, unskilled jobs. In addition, they have few alternatives for vocational counseling

it unsatisfying, and then settled into their current career.

The men also confirmed Ross's observations: Because of their male minority status, co-workers often assumed they were more knowledgeable than they actually were. They also had opportunities to move quickly into supervisory positions, although many did not seek advancement (Simpson, 2004). As one teacher commented, "I just want to be a good classroom teacher. What's wrong with that?" Furthermore, while in training and on the job,

virtually all the men reported feeling socially accepted—relaxed and comfortable working with women.

But when asked to reflect on how others reacted to their choice, many men expressed anxiety about being stigmatized—by other men, not by women, whom they reported as generally accepting. To reduce these feelings, the men frequently described their job in ways that minimized its feminine image. Several librarians emphasized technical requirements by referring to their title as

"information scientist" or "researcher." The teachers often highlighted the sports aspect of their work. And nurses sometimes distanced themselves from a feminine work identity by specializing in "adrenalin-charged" areas such as accident or emergency.

Despite these tensions, the men uniformly derived enjoyment and self-esteem from their nontraditional career choice. As with Ross, their high level of private comfort seemed to prevail over uneasiness about the feminine public image of their work.

---

and job placement as they transition from school to work (Shanahan, Mortimer, & Krüger, 2002).

American employers regard recent high school graduates as poorly prepared for skilled business and industrial occupations and manual trades. And there is some truth to this impression. As noted in Section 5, unlike European nations, the United States has no widespread training system for non-college-bound youths. As a result, most graduate without work-related skills and experience a "floundering period" that lasts for several years.

In Germany, young people who do not go to a Gymnasium (college-preparatory high school) have access to one of the most successful work–study apprenticeship systems in the world for entering business and industry. About two-thirds of German youths participate. After completing full-time schooling at age 15 or 16, they spend the remaining two years of compulsory education in the Berufsschule, combining part-time vocational courses with an apprenticeship that is jointly planned by educators and employers. Students train in work settings for more than 350 blue- and white-collar occupations (Deissinger, 2007). Apprentices who complete the program and pass a qualifying examination are certified as skilled workers and earn union-set wages. Businesses provide financial support because they know that the program guarantees a competent, dedicated work force (Heinz, 1999; Kerckhoff, 2002). Many apprentices are hired into well-paid jobs by the firms that train them. And young employees who excel are eligible for government financial aid to extend their vocational education in special promotion programs (Buchman, 2002).

The success of the German system—and of similar systems in Austria, Denmark, Switzerland, and several East European countries—suggests that a national apprenticeship program would improve the transition from high school to work for U.S. young people. The many benefits of bringing together the worlds of schooling and work include helping non-college-bound young people establish productive lives right after graduation, motivating at-risk youths to stay in school, and contributing to the nation's economic growth. Nevertheless, implementing an apprenticeship system poses major challenges: overcoming the reluctance of employers to assume part of the responsibility for

vocational training, ensuring cooperation between schools and businesses, and preventing low-SES youths from being concentrated in the lowest-skilled apprenticeship placements, an obstacle that Germany itself has not yet fully overcome (Hamilton & Hamilton, 2000). Currently, small-scale school-to-work projects in the United States are attempting to solve these problems and build bridges between learning and working.

Although vocational development is a lifelong process, adolescence and early adulthood are crucial periods for defining occupational goals and launching a career. Young people who are well-prepared for an economically and personally satisfying work life are much more likely to become productive citizens, devoted family members, and contented adults. The support of families, schools, businesses, communities, and society as a whole can contribute greatly to a positive outcome. In Section 8, we will take up the challenges of establishing a career and integrating it with other life tasks.

ASK YOURSELF

>> **REVIEW**
What student and college-environment characteristics contribute to favorable psychological changes during the college years?

>> **APPLY**
Diane, a high school senior, knows that she wants to "work with people" but doesn't yet have a specific career in mind. Diane's father is a chemistry professor, her mother a social worker. What steps can Diane's parents take to broaden her awareness of the world of work and help her focus on an occupational goal?

>> **CONNECT**
What have you learned in previous sections about development of gender stereotypes that helps explain why women's progress in entering and excelling at male-dominated professions has been slow? (*Hint:* See Section 4, pages 130–131 and Section 5, page 178.)

>> **REFLECT**
Describe your progress in choosing a vocation. What personal and environmental factors have been influential?

Summary

PHYSICAL DEVELOPMENT

Biological Aging Is Under Way in Early Adulthood

Describe current theories of biological aging, including those at the level of DNA and body cells and those at the level of tissues and organs.

» Once body structures reach maximum capacity and efficiency in the teens and twenties, **biological aging,** or **senescence,** begins.

» The programmed effects of specific genes may control certain age-related biological changes in DNA and body cells. For example, **telomere** shortening results in senescent cells, which contribute to disease and loss of function.

» DNA may also be damaged as random mutations accumulate, leading to less efficient cell repair and replacement and to abnormal cancerous cells. Release of highly reactive **free radicals** is a likely cause of age-related DNA and cellular damage.

» Genetic and cellular deterioration affects tissues and organs. The **cross-linkage theory of aging** suggests that over time, protein fibers form links and become less elastic, producing negative changes in many organs. Declines in the endocrine and immune systems may also contribute to aging.

Physical Changes

Describe the physical changes of aging, paying special attention to the cardiovascular and respiratory systems, motor performance, the immune system, and reproductive capacity.

» Gradual physical changes take place in early adulthood and later accelerate. Declines in heart and lung performance are evident during exercise. Heart disease is a leading cause of death in adults, although it has decreased considerably since the mid-twentieth century due to lifestyle changes and medical advances. Atherosclerosis is a serious, multiply determined cardiovascular disease involving fatty deposits on artery walls.

» Athletic skills requiring speed, strength, and gross-motor coordination peak in the early twenties; those requiring endurance, arm–hand steadiness, and aiming peak in the late twenties and early thirties. Less active lifestyles rather than biological aging account for most of the age-related decline in athletic skill and motor performance.

» The immune response declines after age 20. This trend is due to shrinking of the thymus gland and increased difficulty coping with physical and psychological stress.

» Women's reproductive capacity declines with age due to reduced quality and quantity of ova. Men show a gradual decrease in semen volume and sperm quality after age 35.

Health and Fitness

Describe the impact of SES, nutrition, and exercise on health, and discuss obesity in adulthood.

» Economically advantaged, well-educated adults tend to sustain good health, whereas the health of lower-income individuals with limited education declines. Health-related living conditions and habits are largely responsible.

» Today, Americans are the heaviest people in the world. Sedentary lifestyles and diets high in sugar and fat contribute to obesity, which is associated with serious health problems, social discrimination, and early death.

» Some weight gain between ages 25 and 50 results from a decrease in **basal metabolic rate (BMR),** but many young adults show large increases. Treatments for obesity involve a reduced-calorie, low-fat diet plus exercise, recording of food consumption, social support, and teaching problem-solving skills.

» Regular exercise reduces body fat, builds muscle, helps prevent illness (including cardiovascular disease), and enhances psychological well-being. Moderately intense exercise on most days leads to health benefits, which increase with greater intensity of exercise.

What are the two most commonly abused substances, and what health risks may result?

» Cigarette smoking and alcohol consumption are the two most common substance abuses. Smokers, most of whom began before age 21, are at increased risk for many health problems, including eye and skin abnormalities, decline in bone mass, heart attack, stroke, and numerous cancers.

» About one-third of heavy drinkers suffer from alcoholism, to which both heredity and environment contribute. Alcohol is implicated in liver and cardiovascular disease, certain cancers, numerous other physical disorders, and highway fatalities, crime, and sexual coercion.

Describe sexual attitudes and behavior of young adults, and discuss sexually transmitted diseases, sexual coercion, and premenstrual syndrome.

» Most adults are less sexually active than popular media images suggest, but they display a wider range of sexual choices and lifestyles and have had more sexual partners than earlier generations.

» Adults in committed relationships report high satisfaction with their sex lives. Only a minority of adults report persistent sexual problems—difficulties linked to low SES and stress.

» Attitudes toward same-sex couples have gradually become more accepting. Homosexual relationships, like heterosexual relationships, are characterized by similarity between partners in education and background, greater satisfaction in committed relationships, and modest frequency of sexual activity.

» One-quarter of Americans are likely to contract a sexually transmitted disease (STD) during their lifetime; women are more vulnerable than men. Although AIDS remains concentrated among gay men and intravenous drug abusers, the incidence among homosexuals is declining. Currently, the disease is spreading most rapidly through heterosexual contact in poverty-stricken minority groups, with women at high risk.

>> Most rape victims are under age 30 and have been harmed by men they know well. Men who commit sexual assault typically hold traditional gender roles, approve of violence against women, accept rape myths, and have difficulty interpreting women's social behavior accurately. Cultural acceptance of strong gender typing and of violence contributes to sexual coercion, which leads to psychological trauma. Female-initiated coercive sexual behavior also occurs, although it is less often reported and recognized by the legal system.

>> Nearly 40 percent of women experience **premenstrual syndrome (PMS),** usually in mild form. For some, PMS is severe enough to interfere with daily life. Evidence for a genetic predisposition to PMS is accumulating.

How does psychological stress affect health?

>> Chronic psychological stress induces physical responses that contribute to heart disease, several types of cancer, and gastrointestinal problems. Because the many challenges of early adulthood make it a highly stressful time of life, interventions that help stressed young people form supportive social ties are especially important.

COGNITIVE DEVELOPMENT

Changes in the Structure of Thought

Describe characteristics of adult thought, and explain how thinking changes in adulthood.

>> Cognitive development beyond Piaget's formal operations is known as **postformal thought.** Adult cognition typically reflects an awareness of multiple truths, integrates logic with reality, and tolerates the gap between the ideal and the real.

>> According to Perry's theory of **epistemic cognition,** college students move from **dualistic thinking,** dividing information into right and wrong, to **relativistic thinking,** awareness of multiple truths. Eventually, the most mature individuals progress to **commitment within relativistic thinking,** a perspective that synthesizes contradictions.

>> Advances in epistemic cognition depend on gains in metacognition. Peer collaboration on challenging, ill-structured problems is especially beneficial.

>> According to Labouvie-Vief's theory, the need to specialize motivates adults to progress from the ideal world of possibilities to **pragmatic thought,** which uses logic as a tool to solve real-world problems and accepts contradiction, imperfection, and the need to compromise. As a result of enhanced reflective capacities, adults also gain in **cognitive-affective complexity**—coordination of positive and negative feelings into a complex, organized structure.

Expertise and Creativity

What roles do expertise and creativity play in adult thought?

>> Specialization in college and in an occupation leads to **expertise,** which enhances problem solving and is necessary for creativity. Mature creativity involves formulating meaningful new problems and questions. Although creativity tends to rise in early adulthood and to peak in the late thirties or early forties, its development varies across disciplines and individuals. In addition to expertise, diverse personal and situational factors jointly promote creativity.

The College Experience

Describe the impact of a college education on young people's lives, and discuss the problem of dropping out.

>> Through involvement in academic programs and campus life, college students engage in exploration that produces gains in knowledge and reasoning ability, revised attitudes and values, enhanced self-understanding and self-esteem, and preparation for a high-status career.

>> Dropout rates are higher in less selective colleges and for ethnic minority students from low-SES families. Personal and institutional factors contribute to college leaving, which is especially likely during the freshman year. High-risk students benefit from interventions that show concern for them as individuals.

Vocational Choice

Trace the development of vocational choice, and cite factors that influence it.

>> Vocational choice moves through a **fantasy period,** in which children explore career options by fantasizing about them; a **tentative period,** in which teenagers weigh different careers against their interests, abilities, and values; and a **realistic period,** in which young people settle on a vocational category and then a specific occupation.

>> Vocational choice is influenced by personality; parents' provision of educational opportunities, vocational information, and encouragement; and close relationships with teachers. Women's progress in male-dominated professions has been slow, and their achievements lag behind those of men in virtually all fields. Gender-stereotyped messages play a key role. Although some men choose careers in female-dominated fields, this is still uncommon.

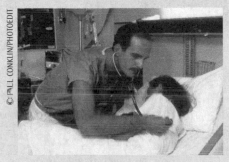

What problems do U.S. non-college-bound young people face in preparing for a vocation?

>> U.S. non-college-bound high school graduates are poorly prepared for skilled business and industrial occupations and manual trades. Most are limited to low-paid, unskilled jobs, and too many are unemployed. Youth apprenticeships, like those widely available in European countries, would address the need for vocational training and improve the transition from school to work for these young people.

Important Terms and Concepts

basal metabolic rate (BMR) (p. 228)
biological aging, or senescence (p. 220)
cognitive-affective complexity (p. 241)
commitment within relativistic thinking (p. 240)
cross-linkage theory of aging (p. 222)
dualistic thinking (p. 240)

epistemic cognition (p. 239)
expertise (p. 241)
fantasy period (p. 244)
free radicals (p. 222)
postformal thought (p. 239)
pragmatic thought (p. 240)

premenstrual syndrome (PMS) (p. 237)
realistic period (p. 244)
relativistic thinking (p. 240)
telomeres (p. 221)
tentative period (p. 244)

For many young people in industrialized nations, the transition to early adulthood is a time of prolonged exploration of attitudes, values, and life possibilities. This young adult has interrupted his education to volunteer for Clowns Without Borders, an organization that brings joy to children living in refugee camps and conflict zones. Here he entertains a Sudanese audience, most of whom have lost family members and been left homeless due to ongoing civil war.

SECTION 8

Emotional and Social Development in Early Adulthood

After completing her master's degree at age 26, Sharese returned to her hometown, where she and Ernie would soon be married. During their year-long engagement, Sharese had vacillated about whether to follow through. At times, she looked with envy at Heather, still unattached and free to choose from an array of options before her. After graduating from college, Heather accepted a Peace Corps assignment in a remote region of Ghana, forged a romance with another Peace Corps volunteer that she ended at the conclusion of her tour of duty, and then traveled for eight months before returning to the United States to contemplate next steps.

Sharese also pondered the life circumstances of Christy and her husband, Gary—married their junior year in college and parents of two children born within the next few years. Despite his good teaching performance, Gary's relationship with the high school principal deteriorated, and he quit his job at the end of his first year. Financial pressures and the demands of parenthood had put Christy's education and career plans on hold. Sharese wondered whether it was really possible to combine family and career.

As her wedding approached, Sharese's ambivalence intensified, and she admitted to Ernie that she didn't feel ready to marry. Ernie's admiration for Sharese had strengthened over their courtship, and he reassured her of his love. His career had been under way for two years, he recently had received a company promotion, and at age 28, he looked forward to marriage and starting a family. Uncertain and conflicted, Sharese felt swept toward the altar as relatives, friends, and gifts began to arrive. On the appointed day, she walked down the aisle.

In this section, we take up the emotional and social sides of early adulthood. Notice that Sharese, Ernie, and Heather moved toward adult roles slowly, at times vacillating along the way. Not until their mid- to late twenties did they make lasting career and romantic choices and attain full economic independence— broadly accepted markers of adulthood that young people of previous generations reached considerably earlier. Each of these young people received financial and other forms of support from parents and other family members, which

251

enabled them to postpone taking on adult roles. We consider whether prolonged exploration of life options has become so widespread that we must posit a new developmental period—*emerging adulthood*—to describe and understand it.

Recall from Section 6 that identity development continues to be a central focus from the late teens into the mid-twenties (see page 191). As they achieve a secure identity and independence from parents, young adults seek close, affectionate ties. Yet the decade of the twenties is accompanied by a sharp rise in the extent to which people feel they are personally in control of events in their lives. Indeed, 20- to 29-year-olds report a greater sense of control than they ever will again (Grob, Krings, & Bangerter, 2001). Perhaps for this reason, like Sharese, they often fear losing their freedom. Once this struggle is resolved, early adulthood leads to new family units and parenthood, accomplished in the context of diverse lifestyles. At the same time, young adults must master the skills and tasks of their chosen career.

Our discussion will reveal that identity, love, and work are intertwined. In negotiating these arenas, young adults do more choosing, planning, and changing course than any other age group. When their decisions are in tune with themselves and their social and cultural worlds, they acquire many new competencies, and life is full and rewarding.

A Gradual Transition: Emerging Adulthood

TAKE A MOMENT... Think about your own development. Do you consider yourself to have reached adulthood? When a large sample of American 18- to 25-year-olds was asked this question, the majority gave an ambiguous answer: "yes and no" (see Figure 8.1). Only after reaching their late twenties and early thirties did most feel that they were truly adult—findings evident in a wide range of industrialized nations, including Argentina, Canada, the Czech Republic, Finland, Germany, Israel, Italy, and Spain (Arnett, 1997, 2001, 2003, 2007a; Buhl & Lanz, 2007; Macek, Bejček, & Vaníčková, 2007). The life pursuits and subjective judgments of many contemporary young people indicate that the transition to adult roles has become so delayed and prolonged that it has spawned a new transitional period, extending from the late teens to the mid-twenties, called **emerging adulthood**.

Unprecedented Exploration and Advances in Identity

The late teens and early twenties are a time of great challenge and uncertainty. Emerging adults have left adolescence but are

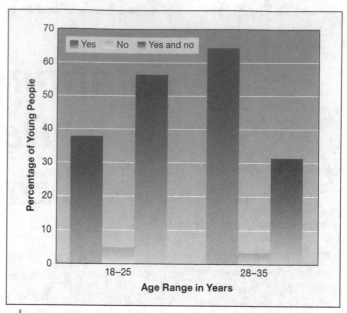

■ **FIGURE 8.1** ■ American young people's responses to the question, "Do you feel that you have reached adulthood?" Between ages 18 and 25, the majority answered "yes and no," reflecting their view that they had left adolescence but were not yet fully adult. Even in their late twenties and early thirties, about one-third of young people judged that they had not completed the transition to adulthood. (Adapted from Arnett, 2001.)

some distance from taking on adult responsibilities, and their parents agree: In a survey of parents of a large sample of ethnically and religiously diverse U.S. undergraduate and graduate students, most viewed their children as not yet fully adult (Nelson et al., 2007). Rather, young people who have the economic resources to do so explore alternatives in education, work, personal beliefs and values, and love more intensively than they did as teenagers (Arnett, 2006, 2007b).

Notice how emerging adulthood greatly prolongs identity development. Released from the oversight of parents but not yet immersed in adult roles, 18- to 25-year-olds can engage in activities of the widest possible scope. Because so little is normative, or socially expected, routes to adult responsibilities are highly diverse in timing and order across individuals (Côté, 2006). For example, many more college students than in past generations pursue their education in a drawn-out, nonlinear way—changing majors as they explore career options, taking courses while working part-time, or interrupting school to work or travel. About one-third of U.S. college graduates enter graduate school, taking still more years to settle into their desired career track (U.S. Department of Education, 2009).

As a result of these experiences, young people's attitudes and values broaden. They express increased interest in philosophical, historical, and political issues and greater tolerance for ethnic and cultural diversity. And as discussed in Section 6, college leaves its mark on moral reasoning by fostering greater concern with individual rights and human welfare, sometimes expressed in political activism. Furthermore, exposure to multiple viewpoints encourages young people to look more closely at themselves. As a result, they develop a more complex self-concept that includes awareness of their own changing traits and values over time, along with enhanced self-esteem (Galambos, Barker, & Krahn, 2006; Labouvie-Vief, 2006; Montgomery & Côté, 2003). Together, these changes contribute to advances in identity.

During the college years, young people refine their approach to constructing an identity. Besides exploring in *breadth* (weighing multiple possibilities), they also explore in *depth*—evaluating existing commitments (Luyckx et al., 2006). For example, if you have not yet selected your major, you may be taking classes in a broad array of disciplines. Once you choose a major, you are likely to embark on an in-depth evaluation of your choice—reflecting on your interest, motivation, and performance and on your career prospects as you take additional classes in that field. Depending on the outcome of your evaluation, either your commitment to your major strengthens, or you return to a broad exploration of options.

In a longitudinal study extending over the first two years of college, most students cycled between making commitments and evaluating commitments in various identity domains. Fluctuations in students' certainty about their commitments sparked movement between these two states (Luyckx, Goossens, &

Identity development during the college years involves exploring in depth—evaluating current commitments. As these archaeology majors excavate a Mayan site in Belize, they mull over their interest, motivation, and career prospects as future archaeologists.

Soenens, 2006). ***TAKE A MOMENT...*** Consider your own identity progress. Does it fit this *dual-cycle model,* in which identity formation is a lengthy process of feedback loops? Notice how the model helps explain the movement between identity statuses displayed by many young people, described in Section 6. College students who move toward exploration in depth and certainty of commitment are better-adjusted, academically and socially. Those who spend much time exploring in breadth without making commitments tend to be poorly adjusted—depressed and higher in drug use (Luyckx et al., 2006).

Many aspects of the life course that were once socially structured—marriage, parenthood, religious beliefs, and career paths—are increasingly left to individuals to decide on their own. During the college years, for example, attendance at religious services drops to its lowest level—about 30 percent in the United States—as young people continue to evaluate the beliefs they acquired in their families against alternatives. Many emerging adults work on constructing their own individualistic faith, often weaving together beliefs and practices from a variety of sources, including Eastern and Western religious traditions, science, and popular culture (Shipman et al., 2002).

Identity progress in emerging adulthood requires a sense of purpose, self-efficacy (belief in one's ability to succeed), determination to overcome obstacles, and responsibility for outcomes. Among young people of diverse ethnicities and SES levels, this set of qualities—called *personal agency*—is positively related to an information-gathering cognitive style and identity exploration and commitment, and negatively related to identity diffusion (Schwartz, Côté, & Arnett, 2005).

Cultural Change, Cultural Variation, and Emerging Adulthood

Rapid cultural change explains the recent appearance of this rich, complex bridge between adolescence and assumption of adult responsibilities. First, entry-level positions in many fields require more education than in the past, prompting young adults to seek higher education in record numbers and thus delaying financial independence and career commitment. Second, wealthy nations with longer-lived populations have no pressing need for young people's labor, freeing 18- to 25-year-olds for the extended exploration of emerging adulthood.

Indeed, emerging adulthood is limited to cultures that postpone entry into adult roles until the twenties. In developing nations such as China and India, only a privileged few—usually those from wealthier families who are admitted to universities—experience emerging adulthood, often for a shorter time span than their Western counterparts (Badger, Nelson, & Barry, 2006; Nelson & Chen, 2007). Furthermore, the overwhelming majority of young people in traditional non-Western countries—those who have few economic resources or who remain in rural regions where they grew up—have no "emerging adulthood." With limited education, they typically enter marriage, parenthood, and lifelong work early (UNICEF, 2009).

In industrialized countries, where many benefit from these transitional years, young people nevertheless vary in their beliefs about what it means to become an adult. Reflecting on the self-searching of these years, respondents from diverse cultures, ethnicities, and religious backgrounds emphasize psychological qualities, especially self-sufficiency—accepting responsibility for one's actions, deciding on personal beliefs and values, establishing an equal relationship with parents, and becoming financially independent (Facio & Micocci, 2003; Mayseless & Sharf, 2003; Nelson et al., 2007). Youths from collectivist minority groups also attach great importance to becoming more considerate of others, to attaining certain roles, and to self-control.

For example, African-American and Hispanic young people point to supporting and caring for a family as a major marker of adulthood (Arnett, 2003). Mormon college students believe that becoming less self-oriented and conducting oneself responsibly are as important as self-sufficiency, and they rate family commitments a close second (Nelson, 2003). And in a survey of Canadian Aboriginal university students (which includes Native Canadian and Inuit peoples, as well as Métis, or mixed blood people of both Native Canadian and European descent), those who identified strongly with their cultural heritage regarded "good control over emotions" and "capable of supporting parents financially" as more important than did those with less cultural identification. And both groups of Aboriginal students placed greater weight on financial self-sufficiency and on interdependent qualities (such as making life-long commitments to others) than did Canadian white students (Cheah & Nelson, 2004).

Nevertheless, for low-SES young people in Western nations who are burdened by early parenthood, do not finish high school, are otherwise academically unprepared for college, or do not have access to vocational training, emerging adulthood is limited or nonexistent (see Section 5 and 7). Instead of excitement and personal expansion, these individuals encounter a "floundering period," during which they alternate between unemployment and dead-end, low-paying jobs (Cohen et al., 2003; Eccles et al., 2003).

As the Cultural Influences box on the following page indicates, because of its strong association with SES and higher education, some researchers reject the notion of emerging adulthood as a distinct period of development. Others disagree, predicting that emerging adulthood will become increasingly common as *globalization*—the exchange of ideas, information, trade, and immigration among nations—accelerates. Contact between industrialized and developing countries fosters economic progress. It also heightens awareness of events, lifestyles, and practices in faraway places. As globalization proceeds, gains in financial security and higher education and the formation of a common "global identity" among young people may lead to rapid spread of emerging adulthood (Arnett, 2007a; Nelson & Chen, 2007). Eventually, proponents claim, this period may become a typical experience on the path to adult life around the world.

Risk and Resilience in Emerging Adulthood

In grappling with momentous choices, emerging adults play a more active role in their own development than at any earlier time. They must choose and coordinate demanding life roles and acquire the skills necessary to succeed in those roles (Arnett, 2006; Eccles et al., 2003). As they experiment, they often encounter disappointments in love and work that require them to adjust, and sometimes radically change, their life path.

Emerging adults' vigorous explorations also extend earlier risks, including unprotected sexual activity, substance use, and hazardous driving behavior. And certain risks increase. For example, drug taking peaks between ages 19 and 22 (see Section 7). And as we will see later in this section, feelings of loneliness are higher than at any other time of life. As they move through school and employment settings, emerging adults must constantly separate from friends and forge new relationships.

Longitudinal research shows that the personal attributes and social supports listed in Applying What We Know on page 256 foster successful passage through these years, as indicated by completing a college education, forging a warm, stable intimate relationship, finding and keeping a well-paying job, and volunteering in one's community (Benson et al., 2006; Eccles & Gootman, 2002). Notice how factors in the table overlap with ones discussed in previous sections that promote development through *resilience*, the capacity to overcome challenge and adversity. Young people with more of these resources—and with resources in all three categories—probably make an especially smooth transition to adulthood. But many emerging adults with only a few resources also fare well.

As in childhood, certain resources strengthen others. Relationships with parents have an especially wide-ranging influence. A secure, affectionate parent–emerging adult bond that extends the balance of connection and separation established in adolescence promotes many aspects of adaptive functioning: favorable self-esteem, identity progress, successful transition to college life, higher academic achievement, more rewarding friendships and romantic ties, and reduced anxiety, depression, loneliness, and drug abuse (Aquilino, 2006).

In addition, emerging adults who feel securely attached to parents and who view them as having used an authoritative child-rearing style are more likely to have integrated their parents' religious or spiritual beliefs into their own personal world view (Okagaki, Hammond, & Seamon, 1999). Then, as young people seek their place in an increasingly complex, ever-changing world, a religious or spiritual ideology helps anchor them. It serves as a reminder of social injustices, motivating—as it did in adolescence—community service. It also offers a transcendent system through which they can view stressful, confusing events and an image of ideal character traits toward which they can strive (Kerestes & Youniss, 2003).

■ CULTURAL INFLUENCES ■

Is Emerging Adulthood Really a Distinct Period of Development?

Although broad consensus exists that cultural change has prolonged the transition to adult roles for many young people, disagreement exists over whether these years of "emergence" merit the creation of a new developmental period (Hendry & Kloep, 2007). Critics of the concept of emerging adulthood offer the following arguments.

First, burgeoning higher education enrollment, delayed career entry, and later marriage and parenthood are cultural trends that began as early as the 1970s in industrialized nations, only gradually becoming more conspicuous. At no time has adulthood in complex societies been attained at a distinct moment. Rather, young people have in the past and continue today to reach adult status earlier in some domains, later in others. And they may reverse direction. For example, after finishing college or being laid off from a job, they might move back to the parental home to get their bearings (Cohen et al., 2003). In accord with the lifespan perspective, development is multidimensional and multidirectional, for 18- to 25-year-olds as it is for adults of all ages. Transitions occur during all periods of the lifespan, with societal conditions heavily influencing their length and complexity.

Second, emerging adulthood fails to describe the experiences of most of the world's youths (Bynner, 2005). In many developing countries, young people—particularly women—are limited in education and marry

and have children early. According to one estimate, nearly 1.5 billion individuals—86 percent of young people—follow this traditional route to adulthood, with no prospect of alternatives (Lloyd, 2005). And as we have seen, many low-SES young people in industrialized nations lack the academic preparation and financial resources to experience an emerging adulthood.

Third, research on emerging adulthood largely emphasizes its personal and societal benefits. But the extended exploration that defines this period, though opening opportunities, might be risky for those without the personal agency to make effective choices and acquire adult skills (Levine, 2005). These young people may remain uncommitted for too long—an outcome that would impede the focused learning required for a successful work life. A favorable emerging adulthood, then, depends on whether it is used effectively to acquire the competencies needed for modern living.

Proponents of emerging adulthood as a distinct developmental period respond that, though not universal, it applies to most young people in industrialized societies and is spreading rapidly in developing nations that play major roles in our global economy (Arnett, 2007a). Furthermore, the concept reminds us that the lives of many people in their early twenties differ vastly from those in their thirties, and of the need to clarify the contextual factors that contribute to

This married man and father living in a rural region of India has few economic resources. Like the majority of young people in developing countries, he has no emerging adulthood.

their experiences. But—as skeptics note—age-graded influences have declined in favor of nonnormative influences throughout contemporary adulthood (Hendry & Kloep, 2007). In their view, rather than being unique, emerging adults are part of a general trend toward blurring of age-related expectations, yielding multiple transitions and increased diversity in development across the adult years.

As one reviewer of research concluded, "What seems advantageous for emerging adults' achievement of independence is feeling connected, secure, understood, and loved in their families, and having the willingness to call on parental resources" (Aquilino, 2006, p. 201). In contrast, exposure to multiple negative life events—family conflict, abusive intimate relationships, repeated romantic breakups, academic or employment difficulties, and financial strain—undermines development, even in emerging adults whose childhood and adolescence prepared them well for this transition (Cui & Vaillant, 1996).

In sum, supportive family, school, and community environments are crucial, just as they were at earlier ages. The overwhelming majority of young people with access to these resources are highly optimistic about their future (Arnett, 2000, 2006). Although they worry about grim aspects of their world, such as crime, war, environmental destruction, and persistent economic recession, they remain convinced that they will eventually arrive at where they want to be in life: secure enough financially and happy in work and close relationships. Now let's turn to theories of psychosocial development in early adulthood.

Applying What We Know

Resources That Foster Resilience in Emerging Adulthood

Type of Resource	Description
Cognitive attributes	Effective planning and decision making
	Information-gathering cognitive style
	Good school performance
	Knowledge of vocational options and skills
Emotional and social attributes	Positive self-esteem
	Good emotional self-regulation and flexible coping strategies
	Good conflict-resolution skills
	Confidence in one's ability to reach one's goals
	Sense of personal responsibility for outcomes
	Persistence and good use of time
	Healthy identity development—movement toward exploration in depth and commitment certainty
	Strong moral character
	Sense of meaning and purpose in life, engendered by religion, spirituality, or other sources
	Desire to contribute meaningfully to one's community
Social supports	Positive relationships with parents, peers, teachers, and mentors
	Sense of connection to social institutions, such as school, church, workplace, and community center

Sources: Benson et al., 2006; Eccles and Gootman, 2002.

ASK YOURSELF

>> **REVIEW**
What cultural changes have led to the emergence of the period known as emerging adulthood?

>> **APPLY**
List supports that your college environment offers emerging adults in its health and counseling services, academic advising, residential living, and extracurricular activities. How does each help young people master the challenges of this period?

>> **CONNECT**
How are resources that foster resilience in emerging adulthood similar to those that promote resilience in childhood and adolescence? (See page 142 in Section 4, and page 204 in Section 6.)

>> **REFLECT**
Should emerging adulthood be considered a distinct developmental period? Why or why not?

Erikson's Theory: Intimacy versus Isolation

Erikson's vision has influenced all contemporary theories of adult personality development. His psychological conflict of early adulthood is **intimacy versus isolation,** reflected in the young person's thoughts and feelings about making a permanent commitment to an intimate partner.

As Sharese discovered, establishing a mutually gratifying close relationship is challenging. Most young adults are still grappling with identity issues. Yet intimacy requires that they give up some of their independent self and redefine their identity to include both partners' values and interests. Those in their teens and early twenties frequently say they don't feel ready for a lasting tie (Collins & van Dulmen, 2006b). During their first year of marriage, Sharese separated from Ernie twice as she tried to reconcile her desire for self-determination with her desire for intimacy. Maturity involves balancing these forces. Without intimacy, young adults face the negative outcome of Erikson's early adulthood stage: loneliness and self-absorption. Ernie's patience and stability helped Sharese realize that committed love requires generosity and compromise but not total surrender of the self.

Research confirms that—as Erikson emphasized—a secure identity fosters attainment of intimacy. Commitment to personally meaningful values and goals prepares young adults for interpersonal commitments, which increase as early adulthood progresses (Kroger, 2007). Among large samples of college students, identity achievement was positively correlated with fidelity (loyalty in relationships) and love, for both men and women. In contrast, identity moratorium—a state of searching prior to commitment—was negatively associated with fidelity and love (Markstrom et al., 1997; Markstrom & Kalmanir, 2001). Other studies show that advanced identity development strongly predicts involvement in a deep, committed love partnership or readiness to establish such a partnership (Craig-Bray, Adams, & Dobson, 1988; Montgomery, 2005). Still, the coordination of identity and intimacy is more complex for women, who are more likely than men to consider the impact of their personal goals on important relationships (Archer, 2002).

In friendships and work ties, too, young people who have achieved intimacy are cooperative, tolerant, and accepting of differences in background and values. In contrast, people with a sense of isolation hesitate to form close ties because they fear loss of their own identity, tend to compete rather than cooperate, are not accepting of differences, and are easily threatened when others get too close (Hamachek, 1990; Marcia, 2002).

Erikson believed that successful resolution of intimacy versus isolation prepares the individual for the middle adulthood stage, which focuses on *generativity*—caring for the next generation and helping to improve society. But as noted previously, few adults follow a fixed series of tasks tied neatly to age. Some aspects of generativity—childbearing and child rearing, as well as contributions to society through work—are under way in the twenties and thirties. And many combinations of intimate partnership, parenting, and career exist, each with a unique pattern of timing and commitment.

In sum, identity, intimacy, and generativity are concerns of early adulthood, with shifts in emphasis that differ among individuals. Recognizing that Erikson's theory provides only a broad sketch of adult personality development, other theorists have expanded and modified his stage approach, adding detail and flexibility.

Other Theories of Adult Psychosocial Development

In the 1970s, growing interest in adult development led to several widely read books on the topic. Daniel Levinson's *The Seasons of a Man's Life* (1978) and George Vaillant's *Adaptation to Life* (1977) and *Aging Well* (2002) present psy-chosocial theories in the tradition of Erikson. Each is summarized in Table 8.1.

Levinson's Seasons of Life

Seeking an underlying order to the life course, Levinson (1978) conducted in-depth biographical interviews with 40 35- to 45-year-old men from four occupational subgroups: hourly workers in industry, business executives, university biologists, and novelists. Later he interviewed 45 women, also 35 to 45 years of age, from three subgroups: homemakers, business executives, and university professors. His results and those of others suggest a common path of change within which men and women approach developmental tasks in somewhat different ways (Levinson, 1996; Roberts & Newton, 1987).

Like Erikson, Levinson (1978, 1996) saw development as a sequence of qualitatively distinct eras (stages or seasons). Each begins with a *transition,* followed by a stable phase during which individuals build a life structure aimed at harmonizing inner personal and outer societal demands to enhance quality of life. Eventually people question the current structure, and a new transition ensues.

The **life structure,** a key concept in Levinson's theory, is the underlying design of a person's life, consisting of relationships with significant others—individuals, groups, and institutions. Of its many components, usually only a few, relating to marriage/family and occupation, are central. But wide individual differences exist in the weight of central and peripheral components.

Men's and women's accounts of their lives offer support for Levinson's description. They also reveal that early adulthood is the era of "greatest energy and abundance, contradiction and stress" (Levinson, 1986, p. 5). These years can bring rich satisfaction in love, sexuality, occupational advancement, family life, and realization of life goals. But they also involve serious decisions about work, marriage, children, and lifestyle before many people have enough experience to choose wisely.

■ TABLE 8.1 ■ *Theories of Adult Psychosocial Development*

PERIOD OF DEVELOPMENT	ERIKSON	LEVINSON	VAILLANT
Early adulthood (18–40 years)	Intimacy versus isolation	Early adult transition: 17–22 years	Intimacy
		Entry life structure for early adulthood: 22–28 years	
		Age-30 transition: 28–33 years	Career consolidation
		Culminating life structure for early adulthood: 33–40 years	
Middle adulthood (40–65 years)	Generativity versus stagnation	Midlife transition: 40–45 years	Generativity
		Entry life structure for middle adulthood: 45–50 years	
		Age-50 transition: 50–55 years	Keeper of meaning
		Culminating life structure for middle adulthood: 55–60 years	
Late adulthood (65 years–death)	Ego integrity versus despair	Late adult transition: 60–65 years	Ego integrity
		Late adulthood: 65 years–death	

Although both of these young scientists are deeply committed to their careers, their images of their future lives may differ. Men more often see themselves as independent achievers in their occupational role, whereas women tend to have "split dreams" involving both marriage and career.

Levinson reported that during the early adult transition, most young people construct a *dream*—an image of themselves in the adult world that guides their decision making. For men, the dream usually emphasizes an independent achiever in an occupational role. In contrast, most career-oriented women display "split dreams" involving both marriage and career. Also, women's dreams tend to define the self in terms of relationships with husband, children, and colleagues. Men's dreams are usually more individualistic: They view significant others, especially wives, as vital supporters of their goals and less often see themselves as supporting others' goals.

Young adults also form a relationship with a *mentor* who facilitates realization of their dream—often a senior colleague at work but occasionally a more experienced friend, neighbor, or relative. As we will see when we take up vocational development, finding a supportive mentor is easier for men than for women. According to Levinson, men oriented toward high-status careers spend their twenties acquiring professional skills, values, and credentials. Although some women follow this path, for many others (and for men who serve as primary caregivers of their children), career development extends into middle age (Kogan & Vacha-Haase, 2002; Levinson, 1978, 1996).

During the age-30 transition, young people who had been preoccupied with career and are still single usually focus on finding a life partner, while women who had emphasized marriage and motherhood often develop more individualistic goals. For example, Christy, who had dreamed of becoming a professor, finally earned her doctoral degree in her mid-thirties and secured a college teaching position. Married women tend to demand that their husbands recognize and accommodate their interests and aspirations beyond the home. For young people without a satisfying intimate tie or vocational direction, this can be a time of crisis. For others who question the per-

sonal meaning of their life structure, it can bring considerable conflict and instability.

To create the culminating life structure of early adulthood, men usually "settle down" by focusing on certain relationships and aspirations, setting others aside. Their goal is to establish a stable niche in society that is consistent with their values, whether those be wealth, prestige, artistic or scientific achievement, or forms of family or community participation. In his thirties, Sharese's husband, Ernie, expanded his knowledge of real estate accounting, became a partner in his firm, coached his son's soccer team, and was elected treasurer of his church. He paid less attention to golf, travel, and playing the guitar than he had in his twenties.

Many women, however, remain unsettled in their thirties, often because they have added an occupational or relationship commitment. When her two children were born, Sharese felt torn between her research position in the state health department and her family. She took three months off after the arrival of each baby. When she returned to work, she did not pursue attractive administrative openings that required travel and time away from home. And shortly after Christy began teaching, she and Gary divorced. Becoming a single parent while starting her professional life introduced new strains. Not until middle age do many women attain the stability typical of men in their thirties—reaching career maturity and taking on more authority in the community (Levinson, 1996).

Vaillant's Adaptation to Life

Vaillant (1977) examined the development of nearly 250 men born in the 1920s, selected for study while they were students at a highly competitive liberal arts college, and followed as many as possible over the lifespan. In college, the participants underwent extensive interviews. During each succeeding decade, they answered lengthy questionnaires. Then Vaillant (2002) interviewed the men at ages 47, 60, and 70 about work, family, and physical and mental health.

Other than denying a strict age-related schedule of change, Vaillant's theory is compatible with Levinson's. Both agree that quality of relationships with important people shape the life course. In studying how the men altered themselves and their social world to adapt to life, Vaillant confirmed Erikson's stages but filled gaps between them. After a period in their twenties devoted to intimacy concerns, the men focused on career consolidation in their thirties. During their forties, they pulled back from individual achievement and became more generative—giving to and guiding others. In their fifties and sixties, they became "keepers of meaning," or guardians of their culture, expressing concern about the values of the younger generation and the state of their society. Many felt a deep need to preserve and pass on cultural traditions by teaching others what they had learned from life experience (Vaillant & Koury, 1994). Finally, in their seventies, the men became more spiritual and reflective, contemplating the meaning of life and accepting its finiteness.

Although Vaillant initially studied only men, eventually he examined the development of a sample of bright, well-educated women who were participants in another lifelong study. His findings, and those of others, suggest that women undergo a series of changes similar to those just described (Block, 1971; Oden & Terman, 1968; Vaillant, 2002).

Limitations of Levinson's and Vaillant's Theories

The patterns Levinson and Vaillant identified are based largely on interviews with people born in the first few decades of the twentieth century. As our discussion of emerging adulthood illustrates, young adults' development is more variable today than in past generations. Furthermore, Levinson's sample included only a few non-college-educated, low-income adults, and low-SES women remain almost entirely uninvestigated. Examining longitudinal archives on low-SES men who had grown up in the 1940s, Vaillant (1993) reported evidence for his stage sequence. Still, he acknowledged that the sample was limited.

Finally, Levinson's participants, interviewed in middle age, might not have remembered all aspects of their early adulthoods accurately. Studies of new generations—both men and women, of diverse backgrounds—are needed to discern the extent to which the developmental paths just described apply to most or all young people.

The Social Clock

As we have seen, changes in society from one generation to the next can affect the life course. Bernice Neugarten (1968a, 1979) identified an important cultural and generational influence on adult development: the **social clock**—age-graded expectations for major life events, such as beginning a first job, getting married, birth of the first child, buying a home, and retiring. All societies have such timetables. Being on time or off time can affect self-esteem because adults (like children and adolescents) make social comparisons, measuring their progress against that of agemates.

Conformity to or departure from the social clock can be a major source of adult personality change. In a study of college women born in the 1930s who were followed up at ages 27 and 43, researchers determined how closely participants followed a "feminine" social clock (marriage and parenthood in the early or mid-twenties) or a "masculine" one (entry into a high-status career and advancement by the late twenties). Those who started families on time became more responsible, self-controlled, tolerant, and caring but declined in self-esteem and felt more vulnerable as their lives progressed. Those who followed a "masculine" occupational timetable became more dominant, sociable, independent, and intellectually effective, a trend also found in a cohort born a decade later (Vandewater & Stewart, 1997). And women who had neither married nor begun a career by age 30 suffered from self-doubt, feelings of incompetence, and loneliness (Helson, 1992; Helson, Mitchell, & Moane, 1984).

As noted earlier, age-graded expectations for appropriate behavior have become increasingly flexible. Still, many adults experience psychological distress when they are substantially behind in timing of life events (Antonucci & Akiyama, 1997; Rook, Catalano, & Dooley, 1989). Following a social clock of some kind seems to foster confidence during early adulthood because it guarantees that young people will engage in the work of society, develop skills, and gain in understanding of the self and others (Helson, 1997; Hendry & Kloep, 2007). As Neugarten (1979) suggested, the stability of society depends on having people committed to social-clock patterns. With this in mind, let's take a closer look at how young men and women traverse the major tasks of young adulthood.

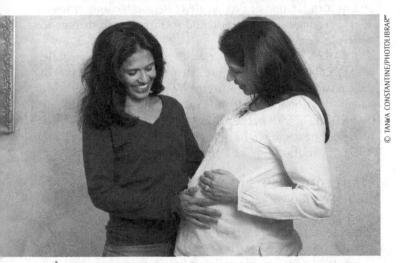

© TANYA CONSTANTINE/PHOTOLIBRARY

Being on time or off time for major life events, such as parenthood, can affect self-esteem because adults make social comparisons, measuring their progress against that of agemates.

ASK YOURSELF

>> **REVIEW**
According to Levinson, how do the life structures of men and women differ?

>> **APPLY**
Using the concept of the social clock, explain Sharese's conflicted feelings about marrying Ernie after she finished graduate school.

>> **CONNECT**
Return to page 191 in Section 6 and review the contributions of exploration and commitment to a mature identity. Using the two criteria, explain why identity achievement is positively related to attainment of intimacy (fidelity and love), whereas identity moratorium is negatively predictive.

>> **REFLECT**
Describe your early adulthood dream. Then ask a friend or classmate of the other gender to describe his or her dream, and compare the two. Are they consistent with Levinson's findings?

Close Relationships

To establish an intimate tie to another person, people must find a partner and build an emotional bond that they sustain over time. Although young adults are especially concerned with romantic love, the need for intimacy can also be satisfied through other relationships involving mutual commitment—with friends, siblings, and co-workers.

Romantic Love

At a party during her junior year of college, Sharese fell into conversation with Ernie, a senior and one of the top students in her government class. Sharese had already noticed Ernie in class, and as they talked, she discovered that he was as warm and interesting as he had seemed from a distance. Ernie found Sharese to be lively, intelligent, and attractive. By the end of the evening, the two realized that they had similar opinions on important social issues and liked the same leisure activities. They began dating steadily. Six years later, they married.

Finding a life partner is a major milestone of early adult development, with profound consequences for self-concept and psychological well-being (Meeus et al., 2007). As Sharese and Ernie's relationship reveals, it is also a complex process that unfolds over time and is affected by a variety of events.

■ **SELECTING A MATE.** Recall from Section 7 that intimate partners generally meet in places where they find people of their own age, ethnicity, SES, and religion or (somewhat less often) connect through Internet dating services. People usually select partners who resemble themselves in other ways—attitudes, personality, educational plans, intelligence, physical attractiveness, and even height (Keith & Schafer, 1991; Simpson & Harris, 1994). Romantic partners sometimes have complementary traits—for example, one more gregarious, the other more reserved. As long as these differences permit each person to satisfy personal preferences and goals, they can contribute to compatibility (Dryer & Horowitz, 1997). But overall, little support exists for the idea that "opposites attract." In fact, many studies confirm that the more similar partners are, the more satisfied they tend to be with their relationship and the more likely they are to stay together (Blackwell & Lichter, 2004; Lucas et al., 2004).

Nevertheless, in choosing a long-term partner, men and women differ in the importance they place on certain characteristics. In research carried out in diverse industrialized and developing countries, women assign greater weight to intelligence, ambition, financial status, and moral character, whereas men place more emphasis on physical attractiveness and domestic skills. In addition, women prefer a same-age or slightly older partner, men a younger partner (Buunk, 2002; Cramer, Schaefer, & Reid, 2003; Stewart, Stinnett, & Rosenfeld, 2000).

Evolutionary theory helps us understand these findings. Recall from Section 7 that because their capacity to reproduce is limited, women seek a mate with traits, such as earning power and emotional commitment, that help ensure children's survival and well-being. In contrast, men look for a mate with traits that signal youth, health, sexual pleasure, and ability to give birth to and care for offspring. As further evidence for this difference, men often want a relationship to move quickly toward physical intimacy, while women typically prefer to take the time to achieve psychological intimacy first (Buss, 2008).

From an alternative, social learning perspective, gender roles profoundly influence criteria for mate selection. Beginning in childhood, men learn to be assertive and independent—behaviors needed for success in the work world. Women acquire nurturant behaviors, which facilitate caregiving. Then each sex learns to value traits in the other that fit with a traditional division of labor (Eagly & Wood, 1999; Wood & Eagly, 2000). In support of this theory, in cultures and in younger generations experiencing greater gender equity, men and women are more alike in their mate preferences. For example, compared with men in China and Japan, American men place more emphasis on their mate's financial prospects, less on her domestic skills. Also, when either male or female young adults are asked to imagine themselves as a future homemaker, their preferences for a good provider and an older partner strengthen (Eagly, Eastwick, & Johannesen-Schmidt, 2009).

But neither men nor women put good looks, earning power, and mate's age relative to their own at the top of their wish list. They place a higher value on mutual attraction, caring, dependability, emotional maturity, and a pleasing disposition—that is, on relationship satisfaction (Buss et al., 2001; Toro-Morn & Sprecher, 2003). Nevertheless, men continue to value physical attractiveness more than women do, and women continue to value earning capacity more than men do. Furthermore, these gender differences—along with gender similarity in desire for a caring, sensitive partner—also characterize homosexual men and women (Impett & Peplau, 2006; Regan, Medina, & Joshi, 2001). In sum, both biological and social forces contribute to mate selection.

As the Lifespan Vista box on the following page reveals, young people's choice of an intimate partner and the quality of their relationship also are affected by memories of their early parent–child bond. Finally, for romance to lead to a lasting partnership, it must happen at the right time. Two people may be right for each other, but if one or both do not feel ready to marry, the relationship is likely to dissolve.

■ **THE COMPONENTS OF LOVE.** How do we know that we are in love? Robert Sternberg's (1988, 2000, 2006) **triangular theory of love** identifies three components—intimacy, passion, and commitment—that shift in emphasis as romantic relationships develop. *Intimacy,* the emotional component, involves warm, tender communication, expressions of concern about the other's well-being, and a desire for the partner to reciprocate. *Passion,* the desire for sexual activity and romance, is the physical- and psychological-arousal component. *Commitment*

■ A LIFESPAN VISTA: Looking Forward, Looking Back ■

Childhood Attachment Patterns and Adult Romantic Relationships

According to Bowlby's ethological theory of attachment, the early attachment bond leads to construction of an *internal working model*, or set of expectations about attachment figures, that serves as a guide for close relationships throughout life. Adults' evaluations of their early attachment experiences are related to their parenting behaviors—specifically, to the quality of attachments they build with their children. Additional evidence indicates that recollections of childhood attachment patterns strongly predict romantic relationships in adulthood.

In studies carried out in Australia, Israel, and the United States, researchers asked people about their early parental bonds (attachment history), their attitudes toward intimate relationships (internal working model), and their actual experiences with romantic partners. In a few studies, investigators also observed couples' behaviors. Consistent with Bowlby's theory, adults' memories and interpretations of childhood attachment patterns were good indicators of internal working models and relationship experiences.

Secure Attachment

Adults who described their attachment history as secure (warm, loving, and supportive parents) had internal working models that reflected this security. They viewed themselves as likable and easy to get to know, were comfortable with intimacy, and rarely worried about abandonment. They characterized their most important love relationship in terms of trust, happiness, and friendship (Cassidy, 2001). Their behaviors toward their partner were empathic and supportive and their conflict resolution strategies constructive. They were also at ease in turning to their partner for comfort and assistance and reported mutually initiated, enjoyable sexual activity (Collins et al., 2006; Creasey, 2002; Creasey & Ladd, 2004; Roisman et al., 2002).

Avoidant Attachment

Adults who reported an avoidant attachment history (demanding, disrespectful, and critical parents) displayed internal working models that stressed independence, mistrust of love partners, and anxiety about people getting too close. They were convinced that others disliked them and that romantic love is hard to find and rarely lasts. Jealousy, emotional distance, lack of support in response to their partner's distress, and little enjoyment of physical contact pervaded their most important love relationship (Collins et al., 2006). Avoidant adults often deny attachment needs through excessive work and brief sexual encounters and affairs (Feeney, 1998). They endorse many unrealistic beliefs about relationships—for example, that partners cannot change, that males' and females' needs differ, and that "mind reading" is expected (Stackert & Bursik, 2003).

Resistant Attachment

Adults recalling a resistant attachment history (parents who responded unpredictably and unfairly) presented internal working models in which they sought to merge completely with another person and fall in love quickly (Cassidy, 2001). At the same time, they worried that their intense feelings would overwhelm others, who really did not love them and would not want to stay with them. Their most important love relationship was riddled with jealousy, emotional highs and lows, and desperation about whether the partner would return their affection (Feeney, 1999). Resistant adults, though offering support, do so in ways that fit poorly with their partner's needs (Collins et al., 2006). They are also quick to express fear and anger, and they disclose information about themselves at inappropriate times (Brennan & Shaver, 1995).

Are adults' descriptions of their childhood attachment experiences accurate, or are they distorted or even completely invented? In several longitudinal studies, quality of parent–child interactions, observed or assessed through family interviews 5 to 23 years earlier, were good predictors of internal working models and romantic-relationship quality in early adulthood (Allen & Hauser, 1996; Donnellan, Larsen-Rife, & Conger, 2005; Ogawa et al., 1997; Roisman et al., 2001). These findings suggest that adult recollections bear some resemblance to actual parent–child experiences. However, quality of attachment to parents is not the only factor that influences later internal working models and intimate ties. Characteristics of the partner and current life conditions also are important. In one study, adults with an inner sense of security fostered security in their partners as well as in their adolescent and young adult children (Cook, 2000).

In sum, negative parent–child experiences can be carried forward into adult relationships. At the same time, internal working models are continuously "updated." When adults with unhappy love lives have a chance to form more satisfying intimate ties, they may revise their internal working models. As the new partner approaches the relationship with a secure state of mind and sensitive, supportive behavior, the insecure partner reappraises her expectations and responds in kind. This reciprocity creates a feedback loop through which a revised, more favorable internal working model, along with mutually gratifying interaction, is sustained over time.

How might the internal working model constructed by this baby, held tenderly by his father, have influenced the relationship he forged as a young adult with his wife? Research indicates that early attachment pattern is one among several factors that predicts the quality of later intimate ties.

COURTESY OF CAROL LIPER

Applying What We Know

Keeping Love Alive in a Romantic Partnership

Suggestion	Description
Make time for your relationship.	To foster relationship satisfaction and a sense of being "in love," plan regular times to be together.
Tell your partner of your love.	Express affection and caring, including the powerful words "I love you," at appropriate times. These messages increase perceptions of commitment and encourage your partner to respond in kind.
Be available to your partner in times of need.	Provide emotional support, giving of yourself when your partner is distressed.
Communicate constructively and positively about relationship problems.	When you or your partner is dissatisfied, suggest ways of overcoming difficulties and ask your partner to collaborate in choosing and implementing a course of action. Avoid the four enemies of a gratifying, close relationship: criticism, contempt, defensiveness, and stonewalling.
Show an interest in important aspects of your partner's life.	Ask about your partner's work, friends, family, and hobbies and express appreciation for his or her special abilities and achievements. In doing so, you grant your partner a sense of being valued.
Confide in your partner.	Share innermost feelings, keeping intimacy alive.
Forgive minor offenses and try to understand major offenses.	Whenever possible, overcome feelings of anger through forgiveness. In this way, you acknowledge unjust behavior but avoid becoming preoccupied with it.

Sources: Donatelle, 2009; McCarthy & McCarthy, 2004.

is the cognitive component, leading partners to decide that they are in love and to maintain that love.

At the beginning of a relationship, **passionate love**— intense sexual attraction—is strong. Gradually, passion declines in favor of intimacy and commitment, which form the basis for **companionate love**—warm, trusting affection and caregiving (Acker & Davis, 1992; Fehr, 1994). Each aspect of love, however, helps sustain the relationship. Early passionate love is a strong predictor of whether partners keep dating. But without the quiet intimacy, predictability, and shared attitudes and values of companionate love, most romances eventually break up (Hendrick & Hendrick, 2002).

An ongoing relationship requires effort from both partners. Research on newlyweds' feelings and behavior over the first year of marriage reveals that husbands and wives gradually felt less "in love" and less pleased with married life. A variety of factors contributed, including a sharp drop in time spent talking to each other and doing things that brought each other pleasure (for example, saying "I love you" or making the other person laugh). Joint leisure pursuits gave way to more household tasks and chores and, therefore, fewer enjoyable times together. Also, when discussing areas of conflict, partners declined in accurate reading of each other's thoughts and feelings. Perhaps after an increasing number of such interactions, they tried less hard to grasp the other's point of view and resorted to well-established habits, such as giving in or withdrawing (Huston, McHale, & Crouter, 1986; Kilpatrick, Bissonnette, & Rusbult, 2002).

But couples whose relationships endure generally report that they love each other more than they did earlier (Sprecher, 1999). In the transformation of romantic involvements from passionate to companionate, *commitment* may be the aspect of

love that determines whether a relationship survives. Communicating that commitment—through warmth, attentiveness, empathy, caring, acceptance, and respect—strongly predicts relationship maintenance (Rusbult et al., 2006). For example, Sharese's doubts about getting married subsided largely because of Ernie's expressions of commitment. In the most dramatic of these, he painted a large sign, reading "I LOVE SHARESE," and placed it in their front yard on her birthday. Sharese returned Ernie's sentiments, and the intimacy of their bond deepened.

Intimate partners who consistently express their commitment report higher-quality and longer-lasting relationships (Fitzpatrick & Sollie, 1999). An important feature of their communication is constructive conflict resolution—directly expressing wishes and needs, listening patiently, asking for clarification, compromising, accepting responsibility, forgiving their partner, and avoiding the escalation of negative interaction sparked by criticism, contempt, defensiveness, and stonewalling (Johnson et al., 2005; Schneewind & Gerhard, 2002). In a longitudinal study, newlyweds' negative behavior and, especially, sharp rise in blood levels of stress hormones during conflict predicted eventual marital dissatisfaction and divorce over the following decade (Kiecolt-Glaser et al., 2003). Couples whose relationships dissolved did not show greater initial physiological reactivity. Rather, poor problem solving altered their stress hormone levels, which often remained elevated throughout the day.

How men handle conflict is particularly important because they tend to be less skilled than women at negotiating it, often avoiding discussion (Gayle, Preiss, & Allen, 2002). Applying What We Know above lists ways to help keep the embers of love aglow in a romantic partnership.

■ **CULTURE AND THE EXPERIENCE OF LOVE.** Passion and intimacy, which form the basis for romantic love, became the dominant basis for marriage in twentieth-century Western nations as the value of individualism strengthened. From this vantage point, mature love is based on autonomy, appreciation of the partner's unique qualities, and intense emotion. Trying to satisfy dependency needs through an intimate bond is regarded as immature (Hatfield, Rapson, & Martel, 2007).

This Western view contrasts sharply with the perspectives of Eastern cultures. In Japan, for example, lifelong dependency is accepted and viewed positively. The Japanese word *amae*, or love, means "to depend on another's benevolence." The traditional Chinese collectivist view defines the self through role relationships—son or daughter, brother or sister, husband or wife. Feelings of affection are distributed across a broad social network, reducing the intensity of any one relationship.

In choosing a mate, Chinese and Japanese young people are expected to consider obligations to others, especially parents. As one writer summarized, "An American asks, 'How does my heart feel?' A Chinese asks, 'What will other people say?'" (Hsu, 1981, p. 50). College students of Asian heritage are less likely than those of American or European descent to endorse a view of love based solely on physical attraction and deep emotion (Hatfield, Rapson, & Martel, 2007; Hatfield & Sprecher, 1995). Instead, compared to Westerners, they place greater weight on companionship and practical matters—similarity of background, career promise, and likelihood of being a good parent. Similarly, compared with American couples, dating couples in China report less passion but equally strong feelings of intimacy and commitment (Gao, 2001).

Still, even in countries where arranged marriages are still fairly common (including China, India, and Japan), parents and prospective brides and grooms consult one another before moving forward (Goodwin & Pillay, 2006). If parents try to force their children into an unappealing marriage, sympathetic extended family members may come to children's defense. In a study in which college students in diverse nations were asked if they were willing to marry someone they did not love, those from more affluent industrialized nations (such as Japan) said no. Only in developing countries were students willing to compromise on love (Levine et al., 1995). In sum, today young people in many countries consider love to be a prerequisite for marriage, though Westerners assign greater importance to it—especially its passionate component.

Friendships

Like romantic partners and childhood friends, adult friends are usually similar in age, sex, and SES—factors that contribute to common interests, experiences, and needs and therefore to the pleasure derived from the relationship. As in earlier years, friends in adulthood enhance self-esteem through affirmation and acceptance and provide support in times of stress (Bagwell et al., 2005; Collins & Madsen, 2006). Friends also make life more interesting by expanding social opportunities and access to knowledge and points of view.

Trust, intimacy, and loyalty continue to be important in adult friendships, as they were in middle childhood and adolescence. Sharing thoughts and feelings is sometimes greater in friendship than in marriage, although commitment is less strong as friends come and go over the life course. Even so, some adult friendships continue for many years, at times throughout life. Female friends see one another more often, which contributes to greater friendship continuity for women (Sherman, de Vries, & Lansford, 2000).

■ **SAME-SEX FRIENDSHIPS.** Throughout life, women have more intimate same-sex friendships than men. Extending a pattern evident in childhood and adolescence, female friends often say they prefer to "just talk," whereas male friends say they like to "do something" such as play sports (see Section 6, page 205). Barriers to intimacy between male friends include competitiveness, which may make men unwilling to disclose weaknesses, and concern that if they tell about themselves, their friends will not reciprocate (Reid & Fine, 1992). Because a balance of power and give-and-take is basic to a good friendship, women generally evaluate their same-sex friendships more positively than men do (Veniegas & Peplau, 1997).

Of course, individual differences in friendship quality exist. The longer-lasting men's friendships are, the closer they become and the more they involve disclosure of personal information (Sherman, de Vries, & Lansford, 2000). Furthermore, involvement in family roles affects reliance on friends. For

In this Hindu wedding ceremony, a relative symbolizes the marriage knot by tying the groom's scarf to the bride's dress. Although arranged marriages are still common in India, parents and prospective brides and grooms usually consult one another before moving forward.

single adults, friends are the preferred companions and confidants. The more intimate young adults' same-sex friendships are in terms of warmth, exchange of social support, and self-disclosure, the more satisfying and longer-lasting the relationship and the greater its contribution to psychological well-being (Sanderson, Rahm, & Beigbeder, 2005; Sherman, Lansford, & Volling, 2006). Gay and lesbian romantic relationships often develop out of close same-sex friendships, with lesbians, especially, forging compatible friendships based on gratifying communication before becoming involved romantically (Diamond, 2006).

As they develop romantic ties and marry, young adults—especially men—direct more of their disclosures toward their partners (Carbery & Buhrmester, 1998; Kito, 2005). Still, friendships continue to be vital contexts for personal sharing throughout adulthood. Turn back to Figure 12.2 on page 206 to view developmental trends in self-disclosure to romantic partners and friends.

■ **OTHER-SEX FRIENDSHIPS.** During the college years, other-sex friendships are as common as romantic relationships. After marriage, they decline with age for men but increase for women, who tend to form them in the workplace. Highly educated, employed women have the largest number of other-sex friends. Through these relationships, young adults often gain in companionship and self-esteem and learn a great deal about masculine and feminine styles of intimacy (Bleske & Buss, 2000). Because men confide especially easily in their female friends, such friendships offer them a unique opportunity to broaden their expressive capacity. And women sometimes say male friends offer objective points of view on problems and situations—perspectives not available from female friends (Monsour, 2002).

Many people try to keep other-sex friendships platonic to safeguard their integrity (Messman, Canary, & Hause, 2000). Still, about half of college students engage in sexual activity with an other-sex friend whom they have no intention of dating. Men are more likely than women to feel sexually attracted to an other-sex friend (Kaplan & Keys, 1997). If these feelings persist, the relationship often changes into a romantic bond. Some friends sustain a platonic friendship that includes sexuality. Others find the platonic and sexual aspects incompatible, and the friendship disintegrates (Afifi & Faulkner, 2000). When a solid other-sex friendship does evolve into a romance, it may be more stable and enduring than a romantic relationship formed without a foundation in friendship (Hendrick & Hendrick, 1993).

■ **SIBLINGS AS FRIENDS.** Whereas intimacy is essential to friendship, commitment—willingness to maintain a relationship and care about the other—is the defining characteristic of family ties. As young people marry and invest less time in developing a romantic partnership, siblings—especially sisters whose earlier bond was positive—become more frequent companions than in adolescence. Often, friend and sibling roles

As young people marry and invest less time in developing romantic partnerships, siblings—especially sisters whose earlier bond was positive—become more frequent companions than in adolescence. Often, friend and sibling roles merge.

merge. For example, Sharese described Heather's practical assistance—helping with moving and running errands during an illness—in kinship terms: "She's like a sister to me. I can always turn to her." And adult sibling ties resemble friendships, in which the main concerns are staying in contact, offering social support, and enjoying being together (O'Connor, 1992).

A childhood history of intense parental favoritism and sibling rivalry can disrupt sibling bonds in adulthood (Panish & Stricker, 2002). But when family experiences have been positive, relationships between adult same-sex siblings can be especially close. A shared background promotes similarity in values and perspectives and the possibility of deep mutual understanding.

Warm sibling relationships in adulthood are important sources of psychological well-being (Sherman, Lansford, & Volling, 2006). In Vaillant's (1977) study of well-educated men, a close sibling tie in early adulthood was the single best predictor of emotional health at age 65.

Loneliness

Young adults are at risk for **loneliness**—unhappiness resulting from a gap between the social relationships we currently have and those we desire—when they either do not have an intimate partner or lack gratifying friendships. Though both situations give rise to similar emotions, they are not interchangeable. For example, even though she had several enjoyable friendships, Heather sometimes felt lonely because she was not dating someone she cared about. And although Sharese and Ernie

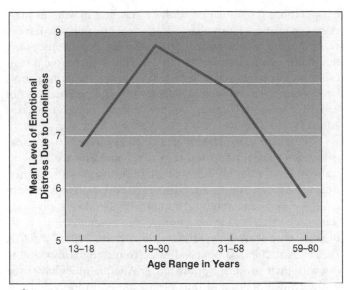

■ FIGURE 8.2 ■ Changes in emotional distress due to loneliness from adolescence to late adulthood. More than 700 Canadian 13- to 80-year-olds responded to a questionnaire assessing the extent to which they experienced emotional distress due to loneliness. Loneliness rose sharply from the early teens to the late teens and early twenties and then declined. (Adapted from Rokach, 2001.)

were happily married, they felt lonely after moving to a new town where they did not know anyone.

Loneliness peaks in the late teens and early twenties, then declines steadily into the seventies. Figure 8.2 shows this trend, based on a large Canadian sample ranging in age from 13 to 80 (Rokach, 2001). The rise in loneliness during early adulthood is understandable. As young people move through school

Loneliness peaks in the late teens and early twenties as young people frequently change school and employment settings. But loneliness can be used for positive ends—to deepen self-understanding.

and employment settings, they must constantly develop new relationships. Also, young adults may expect more from their intimate ties than older adults, who have learned to live with imperfections. With age, people become better at accepting loneliness and using it for positive ends—to sharpen awareness of their personal fears and needs (Rokach, 2003).

Loneliness is intense after loss of an intimate tie: Separated, divorced, or widowed adults are lonelier than their married, co-habiting, or single counterparts. Men not involved in a romantic relationship feel lonelier than women, perhaps because they have fewer alternatives for satisfying intimacy needs (Stroebe et al., 1996). And immigrants from collectivist cultures report higher levels of loneliness than people born in the United States and Canada (DiTommaso, Brannen, & Burgess, 2005). Leaving a large, close-knit family system for an individualistic society seems to prompt intense feelings of isolation.

Personal characteristics also contribute to loneliness. Young adults who are socially anxious or who have insecure working models of attachment to parents are more often intensely lonely (Jackson et al., 2002). When extreme loneliness persists, it is associated with a wide variety of self-defeating attitudes and behaviors. Lonely people evaluate themselves and others more negatively, tend to be socially unresponsive and insensitive, and are slow to develop intimacy because they are reluctant to tell others about themselves (Jones, 1990). These responses, whether cause or consequence of loneliness, promote further isolation.

As long as loneliness is not overwhelming, it can motivate young people to reach out to others. It can also encourage them to find ways to be comfortably alone and to use this time to understand themselves better (Rokach & Neto, 2006). Healthy personality development involves striking this balance between gratifying relationships with others and contentment within ourselves.

ASK YOURSELF

≫ REVIEW
Describe gender differences in traits usually desired in a long-term partner. What findings indicate that *both* biological and social forces contribute to those differences?

≫ APPLY
After dating for two years, Mindy and Graham reported greater love and relationship satisfaction than during their first few months of dating. What features of communication probably deepened their bond, and why is it likely to endure?

≫ CONNECT
How might recollections and evaluations of childhood attachment history, discussed on page 473, affect intimate partners' readiness to develop companionate love?

≫ REFLECT
Do you have a nonromantic, close other-sex friendship? If so, how has it enhanced your emotional and social development?

The Family Life Cycle

For most young people, the life course takes shape within the **family life cycle**—a sequence of phases characterizing the development of most families around the world. In early adulthood, people typically live on their own, marry, and bear and rear children. In middle age, as their children leave home, their parenting responsibilities diminish. Late adulthood brings retirement, growing old, and (more often for women) death of one's spouse (Carter & McGoldrick, 2005).

But we must be careful not to view the family life cycle as a fixed progression. Today, wide variations exist in the sequence and timing of its phases—high rates of out-of-wedlock births, delayed marriage and childbearing, divorce, and remarriage, among others. And some people, voluntarily or involuntarily, do not experience all family life-cycle phases. Still, the family life-cycle model is useful. It offers an organized way of thinking about how the family system changes over time and the impact of each phase on the family unit and the individuals within it.

Leaving Home

During her first semester of college, Sharese noticed a change in how she related to her mother. She found it more enjoyable to discuss daily experiences and life goals, sought advice and listened with greater openness, and expressed affection more freely. Looking around her childhood bedroom before she moved out permanently, Sharese felt nostalgia for the warmth and security of her childhood days, coupled with a sense of pride at being on her own.

Departure from the parental home is a major step toward assuming adult responsibilities. The average age of leaving has decreased in recent years as more young people live independently before marriage. In 1940, over 80 percent of Americans in their twenties resided with their parents; today, only about 50 percent of 18- to 25-year-olds do. Residential independence rises steadily with age—a trend evident in most industrialized nations (Cohen et al., 2003).

Departures for education tend to occur at earlier ages, those for full-time work and marriage later. Because the majority of U.S. young adults enroll in higher education, many leave home around age 18. Other young people leave early to escape family friction (Stattin & Magnusson, 1996). Those from divorced, single-parent homes tend to be early leavers, perhaps because of family stress (Cooney & Mortimer, 1999). Compared with the previous generation, fewer North American and Western European young people leave home to marry; more do so just to be "independent"—to express their adult status. But difficult job markets and high housing costs mean that many must take undesirable work or remain financially dependent on parents (Lindsay, Almey, & Normand, 2002).

Nearly half of young adults return home for a brief time after initial leaving. Those who left to marry are least likely to return. But single, independent living is a fragile arrangement. As people encounter unexpected twists and turns on the road to independence, the parental home offers a safety net and base of operations for launching adult life. Failures in work or marriage can prompt a move back. Also, young people who left because of family conflict often return—largely because they were not ready for independent living. Usually, though, role transitions, such as the end of college or military service, bring people back. Contrary to popular belief, returning home usually is not a sign of weakness but a common event among unmarried adults (Ward & Spitze, 2007).

The extent to which young people live on their own before marriage varies with SES and ethnicity. Those who are economically well-off are more likely to establish their own residence. Among African-American, Hispanic, and Native-American groups, poverty and a cultural tradition of extended family living lead to lower rates of leaving home, even among young people in college or working (De Marco & Berzin, 2008; Fussell & Furstenberg, 2005). Unmarried Asian young adults also tend to live with their parents. But the longer Asian families have lived in the United States and thus been exposed to individualistic values, the more likely young people are to move out after finishing high school (Goldscheider & Goldscheider, 1999).

When young adults are prepared for independence and feel securely attached to their parents, departure from the home is linked to more satisfying parent–child interaction and successful transition to adult roles, even among ethnic minorities that strongly emphasize family loyalty and obligations. In a study of middle-SES African-American 17- to 20-year-olds, girls who had moved out of the home to attend college reported fewer negative interactions with their mothers than girls still living at home or in transition to independent living (Smetana, Metzger, & Campione-Barr, 2004). African-American boys (unlike their Caucasian counterparts in other studies) showed no systematic change in frequency of conflict with mothers as a result of autonomous living, perhaps because in adolescence, they had been granted considerably more freedom than teenagers of other ethnic groups (Bulcroft, Carmody, & Bulcroft, 1996).

Finally, leaving home very early can contribute to long-term disadvantage because it is associated with job seeking rather than education and with lack of parental financial and social support. Not surprisingly, non-college-bound youths who move out in their late teens have less successful marriages and work lives (White, 1994).

Joining of Families in Marriage

The average age of first marriage in the United States has risen from about 20 for women and 23 for men in 1950 to 25½ for women and 27½ for men today. The number of first and second marriages has declined over the last few decades as more people stay single, cohabit, or do not remarry after divorce. Still, nearly 90 percent of Americans marry at least once. At present, 58 percent of U.S. adults live together as married couples (U.S. Census Bureau, 2009b).

Same-sex marriages are recognized nationwide in Belgium, Canada, the Netherlands, Norway, South Africa, Spain, and Sweden. In the United States, Connecticut, Iowa, Massachusetts, and Vermont have legalized same-sex marriage. California,

Hawaii, Maine, New Hampshire, New Jersey, Washington, and the District of Columbia grant people in same-sex unions the same legal status as married couples. Because legalization is so recent, research on same-sex couples in the context of marriage is scant. But evidence on cohabiting same-sex couples suggests that the same factors that contribute to happiness in other-sex marriages do so in same-sex unions (Diamond, 2006).

Marriage is more than the joining of two individuals. It also requires that two systems—the spouses' families—adapt and overlap to create a new subsystem. Consequently, marriage presents complex challenges. This is especially so today because husband–wife roles have only recently moved in the direction of a true partnership—educationally, occupationally, and in emotional connectedness. Among same-sex couples, acceptance of the relationship by parents, inclusion of the partner in family events, and living in a supportive community where they can be open about their bond benefit relationship satisfaction and durability (Diamond, 2006; Elizur & Mintzer, 2003; Rostosky et al., 2007).

■ **MARITAL ROLES.** Their honeymoon over, Sharese and Ernie turned to a multitude of issues that they had previously decided individually or that their families of origin had prescribed—from everyday matters (when and how to eat, sleep, talk, work, relax, have sex, and spend money) to family traditions and rituals (which to retain, which to work out for themselves). And as they related to their social world as a couple, they modified relationships with parents, siblings, extended family, friends, and co-workers.

Contemporary alterations in the context of marriage, including changing gender roles and living farther away from family members, mean that couples must work harder than in the past to define their relationships. Although partners are usually similar in religious and ethnic background, "mixed" marriages are increasingly common today. For example, nearly half of American Jews who marry today select a non-Jewish spouse (Fishman, 2004). And other-race unions now account for nearly 4 percent of the married population in the United States (U.S. Census Bureau, 2009b). Couples whose backgrounds differ greatly face extra challenges in making the transition to married life.

Because many couples live together before marriage, it has become less of a turning point in the family life cycle. Still, defining marital roles can be difficult. Age of marriage is the most consistent predictor of marital stability. Young people who marry in their teens and early twenties are far more likely to divorce than those who marry later (Heaton, 2002). Most of those who marry early have not developed a secure identity or sufficient independence to form a mature marital bond. Both early marriage followed by childbirth and the reversal of family life-cycle events (childbirth before marriage) are more common among low-SES adults (Leonard & Roberts, 1998; U.S. Census Bureau, 2009b). This acceleration of family formation complicates adjustment to life as a couple.

Despite progress in the area of women's rights, **traditional marriages,** involving a clear division of husband's and wife's

In an egalitarian marriage, husband and wife share power and authority. Both are equally concerned with the balance between work, children, and their relationship.

roles, still exist in Western nations. The man is the head of household; his primary responsibility is the economic well-being of his family. The woman devotes herself to caring for her husband and children and to creating a nurturant, comfortable home. In recent decades, however, these marriages have changed, with many women who focused on motherhood while their children were young returning to the work force later.

In **egalitarian marriages,** partners relate as equals, sharing power and authority. Both try to balance the time and energy they devote to their occupations, their children, and their relationship. Most well-educated, career-oriented women expect this form of marriage. And college-student couples who eventually intend to marry often plan in advance how they will coordinate work and family roles, especially if the woman intends to enter a male-dominated career (Botkin, Weeks, & Morris, 2000; Peake & Harris, 2002).

In Western nations, men in dual-earner marriages participate much more in child care than in the past. U.S. fathers in such marriages put in 85 percent as much time as mothers do. But housework—cleaning, shopping, cooking, laundry, picking up clutter—reveals a different story. Recent surveys indicate that women in the United States and Canada spend nearly twice as much time as men on housework, women in Australia nearly three times as much (see Figure 8.3 on page 268). In Sweden, which places a high value on gender equality, men do more than in other nations. In contrast, men typically do little housework or child care in Japan, where corporate jobs typically demand long work hours (Institute for Social Research, 2002; Shwalb et al., 2004). In sum, true equality in marriage is still rare, and couples who strive for it usually attain a form of marriage in between traditional and egalitarian.

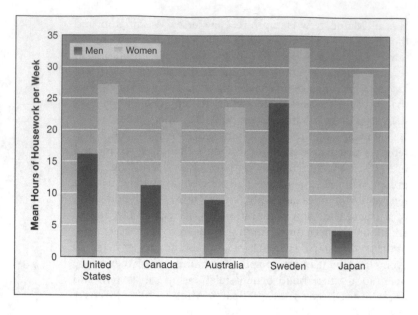

■ **FIGURE 8.3** ■ **Average hours per week of housework reported by men and women in five nations.** In each nation, women devote considerably more time than men to housework. Men's participation is greater in Sweden, which places a high value on gender equality. In Japan, where traditional gender roles prevail, men devote the least time to housework. (Data for the United States, Sweden, and Japan from Institute for Social Research, 2002; for Canada from Statistics Canada, 2006b; for Australia from Baxter, Hewett, & Haynes, 2008.)

■ **MARITAL SATISFACTION.** Despite its rocky beginnings, Sharese and Ernie's marriage grew to be especially happy. In contrast, Christy and Gary became increasingly discontented. What distinguishes satisfying marriages from less successful partnerships? Differences between these two couples mirror the findings of a large body of research on personal and contextual factors, summarized in Table 8.2.

Christy and Gary had a brief courtship, married and had children early, and struggled financially. Gary's negative, critical personality led him to get along poorly with Christy's parents and to feel threatened when he and Christy disagreed. Christy tried to offer Gary encouragement and support, but her own needs for nurturance and individuality were not being met. Gary felt threatened by Christy's career aspirations. As she came closer to attaining them, the couple grew further apart. In contrast, Sharese and Ernie married later, after their educations were complete. They postponed having children until their careers were under way and they had built a sense of togetherness that allowed each to thrive as an individual. Patience, caring, common values, enjoyment of each other's company, sharing of personal experiences through conversation, cooperating in household responsibilities, and good conflict-resolution skills contributed to their compatibility.

Men tend to report feeling slightly happier with their marriages than women do (Dillaway & Broman, 2001; Kurdek, 2005). In the past, quality of the marital relationship had a greater impact on women's psychological well-being, but today it predicts mental health similarly for both genders (Kurdek, 2005; Williams, 2003). Women, however, feel particularly dissatisfied with marriage when the demands of husband, children, housework, and career are overwhelming (Forry, Leslie, & Letiecq, 2007; Saginak & Saginak, 2005). Research in both Western and non-Western industrialized nations reveals that equal power in the relationship and sharing of family responsibilities usually enhance both men's and women's satisfaction, largely by strengthening marital harmony (Amato & Booth, 1995; Xu & Lai, 2004).

At their worst, marital relationships can become contexts for intense opposition, dominance–submission, and emotional and physical violence. As the Social Issues box on pages 270–271 explains, although women are more often targets of severe partner abuse, both men and women play both roles: perpetrator and victim.

■ **MARITAL EXPECTATIONS AND MYTHS.** In a study in which 50 happily married couples were interviewed about their marriages, each participant reported both good times and bad, and many admitted to having moments when they wanted out (Wallerstein & Blakeslee, 1995). Clearly, marital happiness was no "rose garden." Rather, it was grounded in mutual respect, pleasure and comfort in each other's company, and joint problem solving. All couples emphasized the need to reshape their relationship in response to new circumstances and to each partner's changing needs and desires.

Yet many young people have a mythical image of marital bliss, based more on TV romantic comedies and dramas than on reality (Segrin & Nabi, 2002). For example, a substantial number of young adults endorse these beliefs, all unsupported by facts:

- The best single predictor of marital satisfaction is the quality of a couple's sex life.
- If my spouse loves me, he or she should instinctively know what I want and need to be happy.
- No matter how I behave, my spouse should love me simply because he or she is my spouse. (Larson, 1988, p. 5; McCarthy & McCarthy, 2004)

As these myths are overturned, couples react with disappointment, and marriage becomes less satisfying and more conflict-ridden. Interestingly, young people who hold a religious view of marriage as sacred are less likely to enter it with unrealistic expectations and better able to cope with disagreement (Mahoney et al., 1999). Perhaps because of their reverence for the marital bond, they are highly invested in forging a well-functioning

■ **TABLE 8.2** ■ *Factors Related to Marital Satisfaction*

FACTOR	HAPPY MARRIAGE	UNHAPPY MARRIAGE
Family backgrounds	Partners similar in SES, education, religion, and age	Partners very different in SES, education, religion, and age
Age at marriage	After age 23	Before age 23
Length of courtship	At least six months	Less than six months
Timing of first pregnancy	After first year of marriage	Before or within first year of marriage
Relationship to extended family	Warm and positive	Negative; wish to maintain distance
Marital patterns in extended family	Stable	Unstable; frequent separations and divorces
Financial and employment status	Secure	Insecure
Family responsibilities	Shared; perception of fairness	Largely the woman's responsibility; perception of unfairness
Personality characteristics	Emotionally positive; good conflict-resolution skills	Emotionally negative and impulsive; poor conflict-resolution skills

Note: The more factors present, the greater the likelihood of marital happiness or unhappiness.

Sources: Bradbury, Fincham, & Beach, 2000; Johnson et al., 2005; Waldinger et al., 2004.

relationship, engaging in more verbal collaboration and less conflict than other couples.

In view of its long-term implications, it is surprising that most couples spend little time before their wedding day reflecting on the decision to marry. High school and college courses in family life education can help dispel marital myths and promote better mate selection. And counseling aimed at helping couples discuss their desires openly and use positive, respectful conflict-resolution strategies are highly effective in easing adjustment to marriage and enhancing relationship quality (Christensen & Heavey, 1999, Gordon, Temple, & Adams, 2005).

Parenthood

For many adults, the decision to have children used to be "a biological given or an unavoidable cultural demand" (Michaels, 1988, p. 23). Today, in Western industrialized nations, parenthood is a matter of true individual choice. Effective birth control techniques enable adults to avoid having children in most instances. And changing cultural values allow people to remain childless with less fear of social criticism and rejection than a generation or two ago.

In 1950, 78 percent of American married couples were parents. Today, 70 percent bear children, and they tend to be older when they have their first child. Consistent with this pattern of delayed childbearing and with the decision of most women to divide their energies between family and work, family size in industrialized nations has declined. In 1950, the average number of children per couple was 3.1. Currently, it is 1.8 in the United States and Canada; 1.7 in Australia, Great Britain, and Sweden; 1.4 in Japan and Germany; and 1.3 in Italy (U.S. Census Bureau, 2009a, 2009b). Nevertheless, the vast majority of married people continue to embrace parenthood as one of life's most meaningful experiences. Why do they do so, and how do the challenges of child rearing affect the adult life course?

■ **THE DECISION TO HAVE CHILDREN.** The choice of parenthood is affected by a complex array of factors, including financial circumstances, personal and religious values, and health conditions. Women with traditional gender identities usually decide to have children. Whether a woman is employed has less impact on childbearing than her occupation. Women with high-status, demanding careers less often choose parenthood and, when they do, more often delay it than women with less consuming jobs (Barber, 2001a; Tangri & Jenkins, 1997).

When Americans are asked about their desire to have children, they mention a variety of advantages and disadvantages, listed in Table 8.3 on page 270. Some ethnic and regional differences exist, but in all groups, the most important reasons for having children include the warm, affectionate relationship and the stimulation and fun that children provide. Also frequently mentioned are growth and learning experiences that children bring to the lives of adults, the desire to have someone carry on after one's own death, and feelings of accomplishment and creativity that come from helping children grow (Cowan & Cowan, 2000; O'Laughlin & Anderson, 2001).

Most young adults also realize that having children means years of extra burdens and responsibilities. Among disadvantages of parenthood, they cite "loss of freedom" most often, followed by "financial strain." According to a conservative estimate, new parents in the United States today will spend about $200,000 to rear a child from birth to age 18, and many will incur substantial additional expense for higher education and financial dependency during emerging adulthood (U.S. Department of Agriculture, 2007).

Greater freedom to choose whether and when to have children makes family planning more challenging today than in the past. With each partner expecting an equal say, childbearing often becomes a matter of delicate negotiation (Cowan & Cowan, 2000). Yet carefully weighing the pros and cons of parenthood

SOCIAL ISSUES

Partner Abuse

Violence in families is a widespread health and human rights issue, occurring in all cultures and SES groups. Often one form of domestic violence is linked to others. Recall the story of Karen in Section 7. Her husband, Mike, not only assaulted her sexually and physically but also abused her psychologically—isolating, humiliating, and demeaning her (Dutton, 2007; Dutton & Nicholls, 2005). Violent adults also break their partner's favorite possessions, punch holes in walls, or throw objects. If children are present, they may become victims.

Partner abuse in which husbands are perpetrators and wives are physically injured is the type most likely to be reported to authorities. But many acts of family violence are not reported. When researchers ask American couples about fights that led to acts of hostility, men and women report similar rates of assault (Archer, 2002; Dutton, 2007). Women victims are more often physically injured, but sex differences in severity of abuse are not great (Archer, 2002; Ehrensaft, Moffitt, & Caspi, 2004). Partner abuse occurs at about the same rate in same-sex relationships as in heterosexual relationships (Schwartz & Waldo, 2004).

Although self-defense is a frequently reported cause of domestic assault by women,

American men and women are equally likely to "strike first" (Carrado et al., 1996; Currie, 1999). "Getting my partner's attention," "gaining control," and "expressing anger" are reasons that partners typically give for abusing each other (Dutton, 2007).

Factors Related to Partner Abuse

In abusive relationships, dominance–submission sometimes proceeds from husband to wife, sometimes from wife to husband. In about one-third to one-half of cases, both partners are violent (Dutton, Nicholls, & Spidel, 2005). Marvin's and Pat's relationship helps us understand how partner abuse escalates. Shortly after their wedding, Pat began complaining about the demands of Marvin's work and insisted that he come home early to spend time with her. When he resisted, she hurled epithets, threw objects, and slapped him. One evening, Marvin became so angry at Pat's hostilities that he smashed a dish against the wall, threw his wedding ring at her, and left the house. The next morning, Pat apologized and promised not to attack again. But her outbursts became more frequent and desperate.

These violence–remorse cycles, in which aggression escalates, characterize many abusive relationships. Why do they occur? Personality and developmental history, family circumstances, and cultural factors combine to make

partner abuse more likely (Dixon & Browne, 2003).

Many abusers are overly dependent on their spouses as well as jealous, possessive, and controlling. For example, the thought of Karen ever leaving induced such high anxiety in Mike that he monitored all her activities. Depression, anxiety, and low self-esteem also characterize abusers. And because they have great difficulty managing anger, trivial events—such as an unwashed shirt or a late meal—can trigger abusive episodes. When asked to explain their offenses, they attribute greater blame to their partner than to themselves (Henning, Jones, & Holdford, 2005).

A high proportion of spouse abusers grew up in homes where parents engaged in hostile interactions, used coercive discipline, and were abusive toward their children (Bevan & Higgins, 2002; Ehrensaft, Cohen, & Johnson, 2006). Perhaps this explains why conduct problems in childhood and violent delinquency in adolescence also predict partner abuse (Dutton, 2007). Adults with childhood exposure to domestic violence are not doomed to repeat it. But their parents provided them with negative expectations and behaviors that they often transfer to their close relationships. Stressful life events, such as job loss or financial difficulties, increase the likelihood of partner abuse (Emery & Laumann-Billings,

---

means that many more couples are making informed and personally meaningful choices—a trend that should increase the chances that they will have children when ready and will find parenting an enriching experience.

■ **TRANSITION TO PARENTHOOD.** The early weeks after a baby enters the family are full of profound changes: constant caregiving, added financial responsibilities, and less time for the couple's relationship. These demands usually cause the gen-

---

■ **TABLE 8.3** ■ *Advantages and Disadvantages of Parenthood Mentioned by Contemporary Couples*

ADVANTAGES	DISADVANTAGES
Giving and receiving warmth and affection	Loss of freedom, being tied down
Experiencing the stimulation and fun that children add to life	Financial strain
Being accepted as a responsible and mature member of the community	Role overload—not enough time for both family and work responsibilities
Experiencing new growth and learning opportunities that add meaning to life	Interference with mother's employment opportunities
Having someone carry on after one's own death	Risks of bringing up children in a world plagued by crime, war, and pollution
Gaining a sense of accomplishment and creativity from helping children grow	Worries over children's health, safety, and well-being
Learning to become less selfish and to sacrifice	Reduced time to spend with partner
Having offspring who help with parents' work or add their own income to the family's resources	Loss of privacy
	Fear that children will turn out badly, through no fault of one's own

Source: Cowan & Cowan, 2000; O'Laughlin & Anderson, 2001.

1998). Because of widespread poverty, African Americans and Native Americans report high rates of partner violence (Hoff, 2001). Alcohol abuse is another related factor.

At a societal level, cultural norms that endorse male dominance and female submissiveness promote partner abuse (World Health Organization, 2000, 2005). As Figure 8.4 shows, in countries with widespread poverty that also sanction gender inequality, partner violence against women is especially high, affecting nearly half or more of the female population.

Victims are chronically anxious and depressed and experience frequent panic attacks (Stuart et al., 2006). Why don't they simply leave these destructive relationships? A variety of situational factors discourage them from leaving. A victimized wife may depend on her husband's earning power or fear even worse harm to herself or her children. Extreme assaults, including homicide, tend to occur after partner separation. And victims of both sexes, but especially men, are deterred by the embarrassment of going to the police. Also, victims may falsely believe that their partner will change (Straus, 1999).

Intervention and Treatment

Community services available to battered women include crisis telephone lines that provide anonymous counseling and social support and shelters that offer protection and treatment (see page 236). Because many women return to their abusive partners several times before making their final move, community agencies usually offer therapy to male batterers. Most rely on several months to a year of group sessions that confront rigid gender stereotyping; teach communication, problem solving, and anger control; and use social support to motivate behavior change (Whitaker, Baker, & Arias, 2007).

Although existing treatments are better than none, most are not effective at dealing with relationship difficulties or alcohol abuse. Consequently, many treated perpetrators repeat their violent behavior with the same or a new partner (Schwartz & Waldo, 2004; Stuart, 2005). At present, few interventions acknowledge that men also are victims. Yet ignoring their needs perpetuates domestic violence. When victims do not want to separate from a violent partner, a whole-family treatment approach that focuses on changing partner interaction and reducing high life stress is crucial.

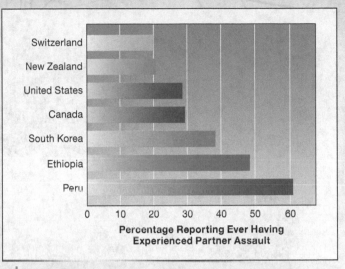

■ **FIGURE 8.4** ■ **Assaults by intimate partners against women in seven nations.** In each country, samples of women were asked to indicate whether they had ever experienced partner physical abuse. The incidence, always underreported, is high in all nations. It is especially high in countries that endorse traditional gender roles and suffer from widespread poverty. (From World Health Organization, 2000, 2005.)

der roles of husband and wife to become more traditional—even for couples like Sharese and Ernie who are strongly committed to gender equality (Cowan & Cowan, 2000; Salmela-Aro et al., 2001).

First and Second Births. For most new parents, however, the arrival of a baby does not cause significant marital strain. Marriages that are gratifying and supportive tend to remain so (Feeney et al., 2001; Miller, 2000). But troubled marriages usually become more unhappy and distressed (Houts et al., 2008; Kluwer & Johnson, 2007). In a study of newlyweds who were interviewed annually for six years, the husband's affection, expression of "we-ness" (values and goals similar to his wife's), and awareness of his wife's daily life predicted mothers' stable or increasing marital satisfaction after childbirth. In contrast, the husband's negativity and the couple's out-of-control conflict predicted a drop in mothers' satisfaction (Shapiro, Gottman, & Carrere, 2000). When expectant couples anticipate lack of partner support in parenting, their prediction generally becomes reality, yielding an especially difficult post-birth adjustment (McHale & Rotman, 2007).

Violated expectations about division of labor in the home powerfully affect new parents' well-being. In dual-earner marriages, the larger the difference in men's and women's caregiving responsibilities, the greater the decline in marital satisfaction after childbirth, especially for women—with negative consequences for parent–infant interaction. In contrast, sharing caregiving predicts greater parental happiness and sensitivity to the baby (McHale et al., 2004; Moller, Hwang, & Wickberg, 2008). An exception exists, however, for employed lower-SES women who endorse traditional gender roles. When their husbands take on considerable child-care responsibilities, these mothers tend to report more distress, perhaps because of disappointment at being unable to fulfill their desire to do most of the caregiving (Goldberg & Perry-Jenkins, 2003).

Postponing childbearing until the late twenties or thirties, as more couples do today, eases the transition to parenthood. Waiting permits couples to pursue occupational goals, gain life experience, and strengthen their relationship. Under these circumstances, men are more enthusiastic about becoming fathers and therefore more willing to participate. And women whose careers are well under way and whose marriages are happy are

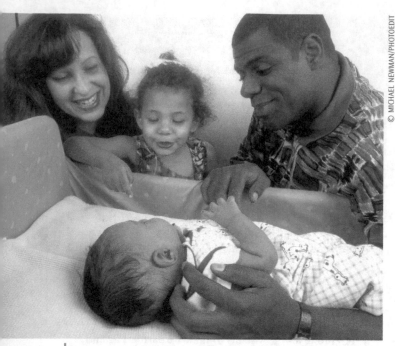

© MICHAEL NEWMAN/PHOTOEDIT

Compared to a first birth, a second birth typically requires that fathers become more actively involved in parenting, sharing in the high demands of tending to both a baby and a young child.

more likely to encourage their husbands to share housework and child care, which fosters fathers' involvement (Lee & Dougherty, 2007; Schoppe-Sullivan et al., 2008).

A second birth typically requires that fathers take an even more active role in parenting—by caring for the firstborn while the mother is recuperating and by sharing in the high demands of tending to both a baby and a young child. Consequently, well-functioning families with a newborn second child typically pull back from the traditional division of responsibilities that occurred after the first birth. In a study that tracked parents from the end of pregnancy through the first year after their second child's birth, fathers' willingness to place greater emphasis on the parenting role was strongly linked to mothers' adjustment after the arrival of a second baby (Stewart, 1990). And the support of family, friends, and spouse are crucial for fathers' well-being.

Interventions. Couples' groups led by counselors are highly effective in easing the transition to parenthood. In one program, first-time expectant couples gathered once a week for six months to discuss their dreams for the family and changes in relationships sparked by the baby's arrival. Eighteen months after the program ended, participating fathers described themselves as more involved with their child than did fathers in a no-intervention condition. Perhaps because of fathers' caregiving assistance, participating mothers maintained their prebirth satisfaction with family and work roles. Three years after the birth, the marriages of participating couples were intact and just as happy as they had been before parenthood. In contrast, 15 percent of couples receiving no intervention had divorced (Cowan & Cowan,

1997; Schulz, Cowan, & Cowan, 2006). For high-risk parents struggling with poverty or the birth of a child with disabilities, interventions must be more intensive, focusing on enhancing social support and parenting skills (Cowan & Cowan, 1995).

Generous, paid employment leave—widely available in industrialized nations but not in the United States—is crucial for parents of newborns. But financial pressures mean that many new mothers who are eligible for unpaid work leave take far less than they are guaranteed by U.S. federal law, while new fathers take little or none (Han & Waldfogel, 2003). When favorable workplace policies exist and parents take advantage of them, couples are more likely to support each other and experience family life as gratifying (Feldman, Sussman, & Zigler, 2004). As a result, the stress caused by the birth of a baby stays at manageable levels.

■ **FAMILIES WITH YOUNG CHILDREN.**   A year after the birth of their first child, Sharese and Ernie received a phone call from Heather, who asked how they liked parenthood: "Is it a joy, a dilemma, a stressful experience—how would you describe it?"

Chuckling, Sharese and Ernie responded in unison, "All of the above!"

In today's complex world, men and women are less certain about how to rear children than in previous generations. Clarifying child-rearing values and implementing them in warm, involved, and appropriately demanding ways are crucial for the welfare of the next generation and society. Yet cultures do not always place a high priority on parenting, as indicated by the lack of many societal supports for children and families. Furthermore, changing family forms mean that the lives of today's parents differ substantially from those of past generations.

In previous sections, we discussed a wide variety of influences on child-rearing styles, including personal characteristics of children and parents, SES, and ethnicity. The couple's relationship is also vital. Parents who work together as a *coparenting team,* cooperating and showing solidarity and respect for each other in parenting roles, are more likely to gain in warm marital interaction, feel competent as parents, use effective child-rearing practices, and have children who are developing well (McHale et al., 2002; Schoppe-Sullivan et al., 2004). When parents forge this coparenting alliance within the first few months after childbirth, it is more likely to persist (Fivaz-Depeursinge & Corboz-Warnery, 1999).

For employed parents, a major struggle is finding good child care and, when their child is ill or otherwise in need of emergency care, taking time off from work or making other urgent arrangements. The younger the child, the greater parents' sense of risk and difficulty—especially low-income parents, who must work longer hours to pay bills; who often, in the United States, have no workplace benefits (health insurance or paid sick leave); and who typically cannot afford the cost of child care (Halpern, 2005b). When competent, convenient child care is not available, the woman usually faces added pressures. She must either curtail or give up her work, with profound financial consequences in low-income families, or endure unhappy children, missed workdays, and constant searches for new arrangements.

Despite its challenges, rearing young children is a powerful source of adult development. Parents report that it expands their emotional capacities and enriches their lives. For example, Ernie remarked that through sharing in child rearing, he felt "rounded out" as a person. Other involved parents say that parenthood helped them tune in to others' feelings and needs, required that they become more tolerant, self-confident, and responsible, and broadened their extended family, friendship, and community ties (Knoester & Eggebeen, 2006; Nomaguchi & Milkie, 2003).

■ **FAMILIES WITH ADOLESCENTS.** Adolescence brings sharp changes in parental roles. In Section 5 and 6, we noted that parents must establish a revised relationship with their adolescent children—blending guidance with freedom and gradually loosening control. As adolescents gain in autonomy and explore values and goals in their search for identity, parents often complain that their teenager is too focused on peers and no longer cares about being with the family. Heightened parent–child bickering over everyday issues takes a toll, especially on mothers, who do most of the negotiating with teenagers.

Overall, children seem to navigate the challenges of adolescence more easily than parents, many of whom report a dip in marital and life satisfaction. More people seek family therapy during this period of the family life cycle than during any other (Steinberg & Silk, 2002).

■ **PARENT EDUCATION.** In the past, family life changed little from one generation to the next, and adults learned what they needed to know about parenting through modeling and direct experience. Today's world confronts adults with a host of factors that impinge on their ability to succeed as parents.

Contemporary parents eagerly seek information on child rearing. New mothers often regard popular parenting books and magazines as particularly valuable. They also reach out to a network of other women for knowledge and assistance. Fathers, by contrast, rarely have social networks through which they can learn about child care and child rearing. Consequently, they frequently turn to mothers to figure out how to relate to their child, especially if they have a close, confiding marriage (Lamb & Lewis, 2004; McHale, Kuersten-Hogan, & Rao, 2004). Marital harmony fosters both parents' positive engagement with babies, but it is especially important for fathers.

Parent education courses exist to help parents clarify child-rearing values, improve family communication, understand how children develop, and apply more effective parenting strategies. A variety of programs yield positive outcomes, including enhanced knowledge of effective parenting practices, improved parent–child interaction, and heightened

© JOHN BIRDSALL/THE IMAGE WORKS

Contemporary parents eagerly seek information on child rearing, and women often reach out to a network of friends for knowledge and assistance.

awareness by parents of their role as educators of their children (Bert, Ferris, & Borkowski, 2008; Smith, Perou, & Lesesne, 2002). Another benefit is social support—opportunities to discuss concerns with experts and other dedicated parents, who share the view that no job is more important to the future of society than child rearing.

ASK YOURSELF

>> **REVIEW**
What strategies can couples use to ease the transition to parenthood?

>> **APPLY**
After her wedding, Sharese was convinced she had made a mistake. Cite factors that sustained her marriage and led it to become especially happy.

>> **CONNECT**
What aspects of adolescent development make rearing teenagers stressful for parents, leading to a dip in marital and life satisfaction? (See Section 5, pages 157–158 and 176, and Section 6, pages 203–204.)

>> **REFLECT**
Do you live with your parents or on your own? What factors contributed to your current living arrangements? If you live independently, has your relationship with your parents changed in ways that match the findings of research?

The Diversity of Adult Lifestyles

The current array of adult lifestyles dates back to the 1960s, when young people began to question the conventional wisdom of previous generations and to ask, "How can I find happiness? What kinds of commitments should I make to live a full and rewarding life?" As the public became more accepting of diverse lifestyles, choices such as staying single, cohabiting, remaining childless, and divorcing seemed more available.

Today, nontraditional family options have penetrated the American mainstream. Many adults experience not just one but several. As we will see, some adults make a deliberate decision to adopt a lifestyle, whereas others drift into it. The lifestyle may be imposed by society, as is the case for cohabiting same-sex couples in the United States, who cannot marry legally in most states. Or people may choose a certain lifestyle because they feel pushed away from another, such as a marriage gone sour. In sum, the adoption of a lifestyle can be within or beyond the person's control.

Singlehood

On finishing her education, Heather joined the Peace Corps and spent four years in Ghana. Though open to a long-term relationship, she had only fleeting romances. After she returned to the United States, she accepted a management position with an insurance company. Professional challenge and travel preoccupied her. At age 35, over lunch with Sharese, she reflected on her life: "I was open to marriage, but after my career took off, it would have interfered. Now I'm so used to independence that I question whether I could adjust to living with another person. I like being able to pick up and go where I want, when I want, without having to ask anyone or think about caring for anyone. But there's a tradeoff: I sleep alone, eat most of my meals alone, and spend a lot of my leisure time alone."

Singlehood—not living with an intimate partner—has increased in recent years, especially among young adults. For example, rates of never-married American 30- to 34-year-olds have risen sixfold since 1970, to about one-third of males and one-fourth of females. More people marry later or not at all, and divorce has added to the numbers of single adults. In view of these trends, it is likely that most Americans will spend a substantial part of their adult lives single, and a growing minority—about 8 to 10 percent—will stay that way (U.S. Census Bureau, 2009b).

Because they marry later, more young adult men than women are single. But women are far more likely than men to remain single for many years or their entire life. With age, fewer men are available with characteristics that most women seek in a mate—the same age or older, equally or better educated, and professionally successful. In contrast, men can choose partners from a large pool of younger unmarried women. Because of the tendency for women to "marry up" and men to "marry down," men in blue-collar occupations and women in prestigious careers are overrepresented among singles after age 30.

Compared with single men, single women more easily come to terms with their lifestyle, in part because of the greater social support available to women through intimate same-sex friendships.

Ethnic differences also exist. For example, the percentage of never-married African Americans is nearly twice as great as that of Caucasian Americans in early adulthood. As we will see later, high unemployment among black men interferes with marriage. Many African Americans eventually marry in their late thirties and forties, a period in which black and white marriage rates come closer together (U.S. Census Bureau, 2009b).

Singlehood can have a variety of meanings. At one extreme are people who choose it deliberately; at the other those who see themselves as single because of circumstances beyond their control. Most, like Heather, are in the middle—adults who wanted to marry but made choices that took them in a different direction. In interview studies of never-married women, some said they focused on occupational goals instead of marriage. Others reported that they found singlehood preferable to their disappointing intimate relationships. And still others commented that they just did not meet "the right person" (Baumbusch, 2004; Lewis, 2000).

The most commonly mentioned advantages of singlehood are freedom and mobility. But singles also recognize drawbacks—loneliness, the dating grind, limited sexual and social life, reduced sense of security, and feelings of exclusion from the world of married couples. Single men have more physical and mental health problems than single women, who more easily come to terms with their lifestyle, in part because of the greater social support available to women through intimate same-sex friendships (Pinquart, 2003). But overall, people who have always been single are content with their lives. Though not quite as happy as married people, they report feeling considerably happier than people recently widowed or divorced (Lucas et al., 2003; DePaulo & Morris, 2005).

Nevertheless, many single people go through a stressful period in their late twenties, when most of their friends have married. Widespread veneration of marriage, along with negative stereotyping of singles as socially immature and self-centered, probably contributes (DePaulo & Morris, 2006). For single women, the mid-thirties is another trying time, as the biological deadline for childbearing approaches. A few decide to become parents through artificial insemination or a love affair. And an increasing number are adopting, often from overseas countries.

Cohabitation

Cohabitation refers to the lifestyle of unmarried couples who have a sexually intimate relationship and who share a residence. Until the 1960s, cohabitation in Western nations was largely limited to low-SES adults. Since then, it has increased in all groups, with an especially dramatic rise among well-educated, economically advantaged young people. Today's young adults are much more likely than those of a generation ago to form their first conjugal union through cohabitation. Among Americans in their twenties, cohabitation is now the preferred mode of entry into a committed intimate partnership, chosen by more than 50 percent of couples (U.S. Census Bureau, 2009b). Cohabitation rates are even higher among adults with failed marriages. Half of cohabiting relationships in the United States involve at least one partner who is separated or divorced; one-third of these households include children (Cohan & Kleinbaum, 2002).

For some couples, cohabitation serves as *preparation for marriage*—a time to test the relationship and get used to living together. For others, however, it is an *alternative to marriage*, offering the rewards of sexual intimacy and companionship along with the possibility of easy departure if satisfaction declines. It is not surprising, then, that cohabiters vary greatly in the extent to which they share money and possessions and take responsibility for each other's children.

Although Americans are more open to cohabitation than in the past, their attitudes are not yet as positive as those of Western Europeans. In the Netherlands, Norway, and Sweden, cohabitation is thoroughly integrated into society. From 70 to 90 percent of young people cohabit in their first intimate partnership, and cohabiters are nearly as devoted to each other as married people (Fussell & Gauthier, 2005; Ramsøy, 1994). Whereas about 50 percent of American cohabiting unions break up within two years, only 6 to 16 percent dissolve in Western Europe (Brown, 2000; Kiernan, 2002). When they decide to marry, Dutch, Norwegian, and Swedish cohabiters more often do so to legalize their relationships, especially for the sake of children. American cohabiters typically marry to confirm their love and commitment—sentiments that Western Europeans attach to cohabitation.

Furthermore, American couples who cohabit before they are engaged to be married are more prone to divorce than couples who wait to live together until after they have made a commitment to each other. But this association is less strong or absent in Western European nations (Kiernan, 2001, 2002; Kline et al., 2004; Rhoades, Stanley, & Markman, 2006). U.S. young people who cohabit prior to engagement tend to have less conventional values. They have had more sexual partners and are more politically liberal, less religious, and more androgynous. In addition, a larger number have parents who divorced (Axinn & Barber, 1997; Cunningham & Antill, 1994; Kurdek, 2006).

These personal characteristics may contribute to the negative outcomes associated with cohabitation. But the cohabitation experience itself also plays a role. Cohabiters are less likely than married people to pool finances or jointly own a house. In addition, both preengagement cohabiters and formerly cohabiting married couples have poorer-quality relationships (Cohan & Kleinbaum, 2002; Kline et al., 2004). Perhaps the open-ended nature of the cohabiting relationship reduces motivation to develop effective conflict-resolution skills. When cohabiters carry negative communication into marriage, it undermines marital satisfaction. Finally, a history of parental divorce may increase cohabiters' willingness to dissolve a union when it becomes less satisfying.

Certain couples, however, are exceptions to the trends just described. People who cohabit after separation or divorce often test a new relationship carefully to prevent another failure, especially when children are involved. As a result, they cohabit longer and are less likely to move toward marriage (Smock & Gupta, 2002). Similarly, cohabitation is often an alternative to marriage among low-SES couples. Many regard their earning power as too uncertain for marriage and continue living together, sometimes giving birth to children and marrying when their financial status improves (Jayakody & Cabrera, 2002).

In the Netherlands, cohabitation is thoroughly integrated into society. Most Dutch young people cohabit in their first intimate partnership, and cohabiters are nearly as devoted to each other as married people.

Finally, cohabiting gay and lesbian couples report strong commitment, equal to that of married people. When their relationships become difficult, they end more often than marriages only because of fewer barriers to separating, including children in common, financial dependence on a partner, or concerns about the costs of divorce (Kurdek, 1998, 2006). In a study in which same-sex couples in Vermont were followed over three years, cohabiters were more likely than couples in civil unions to have ended their relationships (Balsam et al., 2008). Civil unions were as stable as heterosexual marriages.

For people not ready for marriage, cohabitation combines the rewards of a close relationship with the opportunity to avoid the legal obligations of marriage. But cohabiting couples can encounter difficulties precisely because they do not have these obligations (Mahoney, 2002). Bitter fights over property, money, rental contracts, and responsibility for children are the rule rather than the exception when unmarried couples split up.

Childlessness

At work, Sharese got to know Beatrice and Daniel. Married for seven years and in their mid-thirties, they did not have children and were not planning any. To Sharese, their relationship seemed especially caring and affectionate. "At first, we were open to becoming parents," Beatrice explained, "but eventually we decided to focus on our marriage."

Some people are *involuntarily childless* because they did not find a partner with whom to share parenthood or their efforts at fertility treatments did not succeed. Beatrice and Daniel are in another category—men and women who are *voluntarily childless*.

Childlessness in the United States has increased steadily, from 9 percent of women between ages 20 and 44 in 1975 to about 20 percent in the mid-2000s, with similar trends occurring in other Western nations (Rowland, 2007; Sewall & Burns, 2006). Current figures vary somewhat, perhaps because voluntary childlessness is not always a permanent condition. A few people decide early that they do not want to be parents and stick to their plans. But most, like Beatrice and Daniel, make their decision after they are married and have developed a lifestyle they do not want to give up. Later, some change their minds.

Besides marital satisfaction and freedom from child-care responsibilities, common reasons for not having children include the woman's career and economic security. Consistent with these motives, the voluntarily childless are usually college-educated, have prestigious occupations, and are highly committed to their work (Amba & Martinez, 2006; Kemkes-Grottenhaler, 2003).

Negative stereotypes of nonparenthood—as a sign of self-indulgence and irresponsibility—have weakened in Western nations as people have become more accepting of diverse lifestyles (Dykstra & Hagestad, 2007). Acceptance is greatest among highly educated women, who—while not necessarily embracing childlessness—may be more attuned to the demands of parenthood, which are still borne mostly by women (Koropeckyj-Cox & Pendell, 2007).

In line with this trend, voluntarily childless adults are just as content with their lives as parents who have warm relationships with their children. But adults who cannot overcome infertility are likely to be dissatisfied—some profoundly disappointed, others more ambivalent, depending on compensations in other areas of their lives (Letherby, 2002; Nichols & Pace-Nichols, 2000). Childlessness interferes with adjustment and life satisfaction only when it is beyond a person's control.

Divorce and Remarriage

Divorce rates have stabilized since the mid-1980s, partly because of rising age of marriage, which is linked to greater financial stability and marital satisfaction. In addition, the increase in cohabitation has curtailed divorce: Many relationships that once would have been marriages now break up before marriage (Bumpass, 2004; Heaton, 2002). Still, 45 percent of U.S. marriages dissolve. Because most divorces occur within seven years of marriage, many involve young children. Divorces are also common during the transition to midlife, when people have adolescent children— a period (as noted earlier) of reduced marital satisfaction.

About two-thirds of divorced people remarry. But marital failure is even greater during the first few years of second marriages—10 percent above that for first marriages. Afterward, the divorce rates for first and second marriages are similar (Coleman, Ganong, & Fine, 2000; U.S. Census Bureau, 2009b).

■ **FACTORS RELATED TO DIVORCE.** Why do so many marriages fail? As Christy and Gary's divorce illustrates, the most obvious reason is a disrupted husband–wife relationship. Christy and Gary did not argue more than Sharese and Ernie. But their problem-solving style was ineffective, and it weakened their attachment to each other. When Christy raised concerns, Gary reacted with contempt, resentment, defensiveness, and retreat—a demand–withdraw pattern found in many partners who split up (Haltzman, Holstein, & Moss, 2007). Another

© NOEL HENDRICKSON/PHOTODISC RED/GETTY IMAGES

An ineffective problem-solving style can lead to divorce. Many partners who split up follow a pattern in which one partner raises concerns, and the other reacts with resentment, anger, and retreat.

typical style involves little conflict, but partners increasingly lead separate lives because they have different expectations of family life and few shared interests, activities, or friends (Gottman & Levenson, 2000).

What problems underlie these maladaptive communication patterns? In a nine-year longitudinal study, researchers asked a U.S. national sample of 2,000 married people about marital problems and followed up three, six, and nine years later to find out who had separated or divorced (Amato & Rogers, 1997). Wives reported more problems than husbands, with the gender difference largely involving the wife's emotions, such as anger and hurt feelings. Husbands seemed to have difficulty sensing their wife's distress, which contributed to her view of the marriage as unhappy. Regardless of which spouse reported the problem or was judged responsible for it, the strongest predictors of divorce during the following decade were infidelity, spending money foolishly, drinking or using drugs, expressing jealousy, engaging in irritating habits, and moodiness.

Background factors that increase the chances of divorce are younger age at marriage, not attending religious services, being previously divorced, and having parents who had divorced—all of which are linked to marital difficulties. For example, couples who married at younger ages are more likely to report infidelity and jealousy. Low religious involvement subtracts an influential context for instilling positive marital attitudes and behaviors. And research following families over two decades reveals that parental divorce elevates risk of divorce in at least two succeeding generations, in part because it promotes child adjustment problems and reduces commitment to the norm of lifelong marriage (Amato & Cheadle, 2005; Wolfinger, 2005). As a result, when adult children marry, they are more likely to engage in inconsiderate behaviors and to have conflict-ridden relationships and less likely to try to work through these difficulties or (if they do try) to have the skills to do so. Marriage to a caring spouse from a stable family background reduces these negative outcomes.

Poorly educated, economically disadvantaged couples who suffer multiple life stresses are especially likely to split up (Clarke-Stewart & Brentano, 2006). But Christy's case represents another trend—rising marital breakup among well-educated, career-oriented, economically independent women. When a woman's workplace status and income exceed her husband's, the risk of divorce increases—an association explained by differing gender-role beliefs between the spouses. A husband's lack of support for his wife's career can greatly heighten her unhappiness and, therefore, the chances that she will end the marriage (Popenoe, 2006). Overall, women are twice as likely as men to initiate divorce proceedings.

■ **CONSEQUENCES OF DIVORCE.** When Sharese learned that Christy and Gary's marriage had dissolved, she felt as if "someone had died." Her description is fitting: Divorce involves the loss of a way of life and therefore a part of the self sustained by that way of life. As a result, it provides opportunities for both positive and negative change.

Immediately after separation, both men and women experience disrupted social networks, a decline in social support, and

increased anxiety, depression, and impulsive behavior (Amato, 2000). For most, these reactions subside within two years. Nonworking women who organized their identities around their husbands have an especially hard time. And some noncustodial fathers feel disoriented and rootless as a result of decreased contact with their children. Others distract themselves with a frenzy of social activity (Coleman, Ganong, & Leon, 2006).

Finding a new partner contributes most to the life satisfaction of divorced adults (Forste & Heaton, 2004; Wang & Amato, 2000). But it is more crucial for men, who adjust less well than women to living on their own. Despite loneliness and a drop in income (see Section 4), women tend to bounce back more easily from divorce. Christy, for example, developed new friendships and a sense of self-reliance that might not have emerged had she remained married to Gary. However, a few women—especially those who are anxious and fearful, who remain strongly attached to their ex-spouses, or who lack education and job skills—experience a drop in self-esteem and persistent depression and sometimes enter into unsuccessful relationships repeatedly (Amato, 2000; Coleman, Ganong, & Leon, 2006). Job training, continued education, career advancement, and social support from family and friends play vital roles in the economic and psychological well-being of many divorced women.

■ **REMARRIAGE.** On average, people remarry within four years of divorce, men somewhat faster than women. As noted earlier, remarriages are especially vulnerable to breakup, for several reasons. Practical matters—financial security, help in rearing children, relief from loneliness, and social acceptance—figure more heavily into a second marriage than a first. These concerns do not provide a sound footing for a lasting partnership. Second, some people transfer the negative patterns of interaction and problem solving learned in their first marriage to the second. Third, people with a failed marriage behind them are more likely to view divorce as an acceptable solution when marital difficulties resurface. Finally, remarried couples experience more stress from stepfamily situations (Coleman, Ganong, & Leon, 2006). As we will see, stepparent–stepchild ties are powerful predictors of marital happiness.

Blended families generally take three to five years to develop the connectedness and comfort of intact biological families (Ihinger-Tallman & Pasley, 1997). Family life education, couples counseling, and group therapy can help divorced and remarried adults adapt to the complexities of their new circumstances (Whiteside, 2006).

Variant Styles of Parenthood

Diverse family forms result in varied styles of parenthood. Each type of family—blended, never-married, gay or lesbian, among others—presents unique challenges to parenting competence and adult psychological well-being.

■ **STEPPARENTS.** Whether stepchildren live in the household or visit only occasionally, stepparents are in a difficult position. Stepparents enter the family as outsiders and, too often, move into their new parental role too quickly. Lacking a warm attachment bond to build on, their discipline is usually ineffective. Stepparents frequently criticize the biological parent for being too lenient, while the biological parent may view the stepparent as too harsh (Ganong & Coleman, 2004). Compared with first-marriage parents, remarried parents typically report higher levels of tension and disagreement, most centering on child-rearing issues. When both adults have children from prior marriages, rather than only one, more opportunities for conflict exist and relationship quality is poorer (Coleman, Ganong, & Fine, 2000).

Stepmothers are especially likely to experience conflict. Those who have not previously been married and had children may have an idealized image of family life, which is quickly shattered. Expected to be in charge of family relationships, stepmothers quickly find that stepparent–stepchild ties do not develop instantly. After divorce, biological mothers are frequently jealous, uncooperative, and possessive of their children. Even when their husbands do not have custody, stepmothers feel stressed. As stepchildren go in and out of the home, stepmothers find life easier without resistant children and then feel guilty about their "unmaternal" feelings (Church, 2004; MacDonald & DeMaris, 1996). No matter how hard a stepmother tries to build a close parent–child bond, her efforts are probably doomed to failure in the short run.

Stepfathers with children of their own tend to establish positive bonds with stepchildren relatively quickly, perhaps because they are experienced in building warm parent–child ties and feel less pressure than stepmothers to plunge into parenting. And stepchildren generally respond favorably to stepfathers' efforts to connect with them through enjoyable activities (Ganong et al., 1999). But stepfathers without biological children (like their stepmother counterparts) can have unrealistic expectations. Or their wives may push them into the father role, sparking negativity from children. After making several overtures that are ignored or rebuffed, these stepfathers often withdraw from parenting (Hetherington & Clingempeel, 1992).

A caring husband–wife relationship, cooperation from the biological parent, and children's willingness to accept their parent's new spouse are crucial for stepparent adjustment. Over time, many couples strengthen their relationship and build a coparenting partnership that improves interactions with stepchildren (Church, 2004). But because stepparent–stepchild bonds are hard to establish, the divorce rate is higher for remarried couples with stepchildren than for those without them.

■ **NEVER-MARRIED SINGLE PARENTS.**   About 10 percent of U.S. children live with a single parent who has never married and does not have a partner. Of these parents, about 85 percent are mothers, 15 percent fathers (U.S. Census Bureau, 2009b). In recent years, more single women over age 30 in high-status occupations have become parents. But they are still few in number, and little is known about how they and their children fare.

In the United States, African-American young women make up the largest group of never-married parents. Over 60 percent of births to black mothers in their twenties are to women without a partner, compared with 13 percent of births to white women (U.S. Census Bureau, 2009b). African-American women postpone marriage more and childbirth less than women in other U.S. ethnic groups. Job loss, persisting unemployment, and consequent inability of many black men to support a family have contributed to the postponement of marriage.

Never-married black mothers tap the extended family, especially their own mothers and sometimes male relatives, for help in rearing their children (Gasden, 1999; Jayakody & Kalil, 2002). For about one-third, marriage—not necessarily to the child's biological father—occurs within nine years after birth of the first child (Wu, Bumpass, & Musick, 2001). These couples function much like other first-marriage parents. Their children are often unaware that the father is a stepfather, and parents do not report the child-rearing difficulties typical of blended families (Ganong & Coleman, 1994).

Still, for low-SES women, never-married parenthood generally increases financial hardship. Nearly 50 percent of white mothers and 60 percent of black mothers have a second child while unmarried. And they are far less likely than divorced mothers to receive paternal child support payments, although child support enforcement both reduces financial stress and increases father involvement (Huang, 2006).

Children of never-married mothers who lack father involvement achieve less well in school and display more antisocial behavior than children in low-SES, first-marriage families—problems that make life more difficult for mothers (Coley, 1998). But marriage to the child's biological father benefits children only when the father is a reliable source of economic and emotional support. When a mother pairs up with an antisocial father, her child is at greater risk for conduct problems than if she had reared the child alone (Jaffee et al., 2003). Strengthening social support, education, and employment opportunities for low-SES parents would greatly enhance the well-being of unmarried mothers and their children.

■ **GAY AND LESBIAN PARENTS.**   Several million American gay men and lesbians are parents, most through previous heterosexual marriages, some through adoption, and a growing number through reproductive technologies (Ambert, 2005; Patterson, 2002). In the past, because of laws assuming that homosexuals could not be adequate parents, those who divorced a heterosexual partner lost custody of their children. Today, some U.S. states hold that sexual orientation by itself is irrelevant to custody. A few U.S. states, however, ban gay and lesbian couples from adopting children.

Most research on homosexual parents and children is limited to volunteer samples. Findings of these investigations indicate that gay and lesbian parents are as committed to and effective at child rearing as heterosexual parents and sometimes more so (Bos, van Balen, & van den Boom, 2007; Tasker, 2005). Also, whether born to or adopted by their parents or conceived through donor insemination, children in gay and lesbian families did not differ from the children of heterosexuals in mental health, peer relations, or gender identity (Allen & Burrell, 1996; Flaks et al., 1995; Golombok & Tasker, 1996). Two additional studies, which surmounted the potential bias associated with a volunteer sample by including all lesbian-mother families who had conceived children at a fertility clinic, also reported that children were developing favorably (Brewaeys et al., 1997; Chan, Raboy, & Patterson, 1998). Likewise, among participants drawn from a representative sample of British mothers and their 7-year-olds, children reared in lesbian-mother families did not differ from children reared in heterosexual families in adjustment and gender-role preferences (Golombok et al., 2003). Furthermore, children of gay and lesbian parents do not differ from other children in sexual orientation; the large majority are heterosexual (Tasker, 2005).

When extended-family members have difficulty accepting them, homosexual mothers and fathers often build "families of choice" through friends, who assume the roles of relatives. Usually, however, parents of gays and lesbians cannot endure a permanent rift (Fisher, Easterly, & Lazear, 2008). With time, interactions between homosexual parents and their families of origin become more positive and supportive.

Homosexual couples' joint involvement in parenting varies with the way children entered the family. When partners choose parenthood through adoption or reproductive technologies, they report fairly even division of child-care and household tasks (Chan, Raboy, & Patterson, 1998). When children resulted from a previous heterosexual relationship, the biological parent typically assumes a larger parenting role (Hare & Richards, 1993).

A major concern of gay and lesbian parents is that their children will be stigmatized by their parents' sexual orientation. Most studies indicate that incidents of teasing or bullying are rare because parents and children carefully manage the information they reveal to others (Tasker, 2005). But in an Australian study, even though most third to tenth graders were guarded about

Gay and lesbian parents are as committed to and effective at child rearing as heterosexual parents. Overall, families headed by same-sex partners can be distinguished from other families only by issues related to living in a nonsupportive society.

discussing their parents' relationship with peers, nearly half reported harassment (Ray & Gregory, 2001). Overall, families headed by homosexuals can be distinguished from other families only by issues related to living in a nonsupportive society.

ASK YOURSELF

>> **REVIEW**
Why is never-married single parenthood especially high among African Americans? What conditions affect parent and child well-being in these families?

>> **APPLY**
After dating for a year, Wanda and Scott decided to live together. Their parents worried that cohabitation would reduce the couple's chances for a successful marriage. Is this fear justified? Why or why not?

>> **CONNECT**
Return to Section 4, pages 135–136, and review the impact of divorce and remarriage on children and adolescents. How do those findings resemble outcomes for adults? What might account for the similarities?

>> **REFLECT**
Do your own experiences or those of your friends match research findings on cohabitation, singlehood, never-married parents, or gay and lesbian parents? Select one instance and discuss.

Career Development

Besides family life, vocational life is a vital domain of social development in early adulthood. After choosing an occupation, young people must learn how to perform its tasks well, get along with co-workers, respond to authority, and protect their own interests. When work experiences go well, adults develop new competencies, feel a sense of personal accomplishment, make new friends, and become financially independent and secure. And as we have seen, especially for women but also for men who support their partner's career development, aspirations and accomplishments in the workplace and the family are interwoven.

Establishing a Career

Our discussion of Levinson's and Vaillant's theories highlighted diverse paths and timetables for career development. *TAKE A MOMENT...* Consider, once again, the wide variations among Sharese, Ernie, Christy, and Gary. Notice that, as is typical for men, Ernie's and Gary's career lives were long and *continuous,* from completion of formal education to retirement. Sharese and Christy, like many women, had *discontinuous* career paths—ones that were interrupted or deferred by child rearing and other family needs (Huang & Sverke, 2007; Moen & Roehling, 2005). Furthermore, not all people embark on the vocation of their dreams. In an Australian study that followed 1,200 young people after they finished their schooling, at any given time during the next seven years, only 20 percent were working in a field consistent with their greatest interest (Athanasou, 2002).

Even for those who enter their chosen field, initial experiences can be discouraging. At the health department, Sharese discovered that committee meetings and paperwork consumed much of her day. Because each project had a deadline, the pressure of productivity weighed heavily on her. Adjusting to unanticipated disappointments in salary, supervisors, and co-workers is difficult. As new workers become aware of the gap between their expectations and reality, resignations are common. On average, people in their twenties move to a new job every two years; five or six changes are not unusual (Petersen & Gonzales, 1999).

After a period of evaluation and adjustment, young adults generally settle into their work. In careers with opportunities for promotion, high aspirations must often be revised downward because the structure of most work settings resembles a pyramid, with few high-level executive and supervisory jobs. In a longitudinal study of more than 400 lower-level male managers at AT&T, the importance of work in men's lives varied with career advancement and age (Howard & Bray, 1988). For men who advanced very little, "work disengagement" occurred early; family, recreation, and community service assumed greater importance by the early thirties. Men with average levels of career success emphasized nonwork roles at a later age. In contrast, men who were highly successful became more involved in their jobs over time. Although the desire for advancement tends to decline with age, most people still seek challenges and find satisfaction in their work roles.

Besides opportunity, personal characteristics affect career progress. As we will see, a sense of self-efficacy is influential. Young people who are very anxious about on-the-job failure tend to set their career aspirations either too high or too low. When they encounter obstacles, they quickly conclude that career tasks are too hard and give up (Lent & Brown, 2002). As a result, they achieve far less than their abilities would permit.

Recall from our discussion of Levinson's theory that career success often depends on the quality of a mentoring relationship. Access to an effective mentor—a person with advanced experience and knowledge who is emotionally invested in the junior person's development and who fosters a bond of trust—is jointly affected by the availability of willing people and the individual's capacity to select an appropriate individual (Ramaswami & Dreher, 2007). The best mentors are seldom top executives, who tend to be preoccupied and therefore less helpful and sympathetic. Usually, young adults fare better with lower-level mentors—more experienced co-workers or members of their professional associations (Allen & Finkelstein, 2003).

Women and Ethnic Minorities

Although women and ethnic minorities have penetrated nearly all professions, their talents often are not developed to the fullest. Women, especially those who are members of economically disadvantaged minorities, remain concentrated in occupations that offer little opportunity for advancement, and they are underrepresented in executive and managerial roles (see Section 7,

page 245). And although the overall difference between men's and women's earnings is smaller today than 30 years ago, it remains considerable. U.S. government surveys following 9,000 U.S. college-educated workers for a decade revealed that a year after receiving their bachelor's degrees, women working full time earned just 80 percent as much as men. The difference was largely (but not entirely) due to gender differences in college majors: Women more often chose education and service fields, men higher-paying scientific and technical fields. Ten years after graduation, the gender pay gap had widened: Women's pay was only 69 percent of men's, and in no profession did women's earnings equal men's (Dey & Hill, 2007). Gender disparities in career development accounted for about 90 percent of the gap, with the remaining 10 percent attributed to on-the-job discrimination.

Especially for women in traditionally feminine occupations, career planning is often short-term and subject to change. Many enter and exit the labor market several times as they give birth to and rear children. Between ages 18 and 34, the typical woman has been out of the labor force 26 percent of the time, in contrast to 11 percent for the typical man (Furchtgott-Roth, 2009; U.S. Department of Labor, 2004). Time away from a career greatly hinders advancement—a major reason that women in prestigious, male-dominated careers tend to delay or avoid childbearing (Blair-Loy & DeHart, 2003). Yet an increasing number of accomplished professional women are leaving their jobs to devote themselves full-time to child rearing—a trend that has generated much media attention along with mistaken, gender-stereotyped interpretations of their "choice" (see the Social Issues box on the following page).

Ethnic minority women, such as this scientist, must surmount combined gender and racial discrimination to realize their career potential. Those who succeed often display an unusually high sense of self-efficacy.

SOCIAL ISSUES

Women in "Fast-Track" Careers Who Opt to Stay Home

Although the vast majority are employed, women with professional degrees opt out of the labor force at three to four times the rate of similarly accomplished men. In one national survey, ten years after graduation, 12 percent of women but only 4 percent of men in the field of law were not working. The figures for MDs were 11 versus 3 percent, for MBAs 8 versus 2 percent (Baker, 2002). Women often said they left their careers to attend to family responsibilities.

The apparent contradiction between these women's achievements and their decision to stay home has made them the focus of a growing number of newspaper and magazine features and on-air programs. Often their transformation into full-time mothers is interpreted in gender-stereotyped terms, as the exercise of a personal preference for a traditional role. In fact, it is almost always an agonizing decision—the outcome of multiple constraints in their lives.

In-depth interviews with 43 women—all of whom had left prestigious, well-paid careers after being employed for an average of 13 years to focus full time on their families revealed that over 90 percent were ambivalent about quitting (Stone & Lovejoy, 2004). Giving up a solid career identity, pride in accomplishment, and the intrinsic pleasure they derived from work was a painful, protracted process.

Two-thirds of the women had excelled in male-dominated professions such as law, business, medicine, or the sciences. Others had high-powered careers in publishing, marketing, banking, or health. Even though they were professionally and financially successful, a mix of work-, spouse-, and child-related factors led them to hand in their resignations.

Work

For 86 percent, work environments were the most significant reason for leaving. Many, with work weeks of 60 hours or more, had faced extreme time pressures even before they had children. And economic restructuring of their industries—mergers, takeovers, and expansions—often disrupted their existing work–family equilibrium. One former company executive commented after a merger: "I had to travel before, but this was just on a scale like [gesturing with her hands and making sounds to indicate a nuclear explosion]" (p. 71).

More than one-third, citing pervasive workplace inflexibility, characterized their jobs as "all or nothing." Requests to cut back to part-time were often denied. Of those who arranged part-time work, most ended up with part-time positions in name only: Their actual hours expanded. In workplaces where part-time employment was rare, women reported being labeled as on the "mommy track," losing interesting responsibilities, and watching their chances for promotion evaporate. They wondered, "Is this worth it?" and ultimately concluded, "No."

Spouses and Children

Because most participants were married to men in "high-octane" careers like their own, their husbands were usually minimally involved in child care and housework. But despite their own success, few entertained the possibility that their husbands would agree to cut back. Rather, these women implicitly assumed that when the pressures of the dual-earner lifestyle became excessive, they would need to sacrifice. Their husbands, while usually stating, "It's your choice," concurred.

Almost all the women had the financial means to hire in-home help. Yet having worked for a decade or more and (in many

© ROYALTY-FREE/CORBIS

Women in fast-track careers may opt out of the labor force because their workplace thwarts their efforts to balance work with family. Requests to work part-time or spend some days working from home are often denied.

instances) postponed childbearing, they felt uncomfortable, sometimes anguished, about being away from their children. Several who had become first-time mothers in their early forties felt a strong desire to experience motherhood because they did not expect to have more children. Others wanted to be available to support their school-age children's increasingly complex lives—homework, lessons, sports, and other activities—or simply worried about "missing out." But though the pull of family was intense, for most, work-related issues cemented their decision.

Other investigations confirm that few professionally successful women freely chose to step off the career track (Rubin & Wooten, 2007). Rather, their highly demanding, inflexible workplaces thwart their efforts to balance work and family.

In addition, low self-efficacy with respect to male-dominated fields limits women's career progress. Women who pursue nontraditional careers usually have "masculine" traits—high achievement orientation, self-reliance, and belief that their efforts will result in success. But even those with high self-efficacy are less certain than their male counterparts that they can overcome barriers to career success (Lindley, 2005). In a study of women scientists on university faculties, those reporting a sexist work climate (sexual harassment or discrimination in salary, promotion, or resources) were less satisfied with their jobs and less productive (Settles et al., 2006). Gender-stereotyped images of women as followers rather than leaders slow advancement into top-level management positions. And because men dominate high-status fields, fewer women are available to serve as mentors (Stewart & Lavaque-Manty, 2008). Although amount of mentor support is similar in same-sex and other-sex mentoring relationships, women with female mentors tend to be more productive (O'Neill, Horton, & Crosby, 1999). Perhaps female mentors are more likely to be perceived as role models and to provide guidance on the unique problems women encounter in the workplace.

Despite laws guaranteeing equal opportunity, racial bias in the labor market remains strong. In one study, researchers responded to more than 1,300 help-wanted newspaper ads with fictitious résumés, some containing higher qualifications and some lower qualifications. Half the résumés were assigned a white-sounding name (Emily Walsh, Brendan Baker) and half a black-sounding name (Lakisha Washington, Jamal Jones). At all job levels, from clerical work to top management, résumés with "white" names evoked 50 percent more callbacks than résumés with "black" names. And although whites received substantially more callbacks in response to high-quality than to low-quality résumés, having a high-quality résumé made little difference for blacks (see Figure 8.5). As the researchers noted, "Discrimination appears to bite twice, making it harder for African Americans to find a job and to improve their employability" (Bertrand & Mullainathan, 2004, p. 3). Consistent with this conclusion, African Americans spend more time searching for work, experience less stable employment, and acquire less work experience than Caucasian Americans with equivalent job qualifications (Pager & Shepherd, 2008).

Ethnic minority women must surmount combined gender and racial discrimination to realize their career potential. Those who succeed often display an unusually high sense of self-efficacy, attacking problems head-on despite repeated obstacles

to achievement (Byars & Hackett, 1998). In an interview study of African-American women who had become leaders in diverse fields, all reported intense persistence, fueled by supportive relationships with other women, including teachers, colleagues, and friends who countered their sense of professional isolation. Many described their mothers as inspiring role models who had set high standards for them. Others felt empowered by a deep sense of connection to their African-American communities (Richie et al., 1997).

Despite obstacles to success, young and middle-aged women who have developed rewarding careers generally report higher levels of psychological well-being and life satisfaction (Burke, 2001). This finding suggests that some of the discontent frequently expressed by married women may not be due to marriage per se but, rather, to lack of a gratifying work life. Consistent with this idea, most women prefer to blend work and family (Barnett & Hyde, 2001). And those in financially stressed families must do so.

Combining Work and Family

Whether women work because they want to or have to (or both), the dominant family form today is the dual-earner marriage. Most dual-earner couples are also parents, since the majority of women with children are in the work force (see page 138 in Section 4). But many more women than men experience moderate to high levels of stress in trying to meet both work and family responsibilities (Cinamon & Rich, 2002).

TAKE A MOMENT... Think about a dual-earner family you know well. What are the main sources of strain? When Sharese returned to her job after her children were born, she felt a sense of *role overload*, or conflict between work and family responsibilities. In addition to a demanding career, she also (like most employed women) shouldered most of the household and child-care tasks. And both Sharese and Ernie felt torn between the desire to excel at their jobs and the desire to spend more time with each other, their children, and their friends and relatives. Role overload is linked to increased psychological stress, poorer marital relations, less effective parenting, and child behavior problems (Perry-Jenkins, Repetti, & Crouter, 2000; Saginak & Saginak, 2005).

Role overload is greater for women than for men, especially for women in low-status work roles with rigid schedules and little autonomy (Marshall, 1997). Couples in prestigious careers have more control over both work and family domains. For example, Sharese and Ernie devised ways to spend more time with their children. They picked them up at child care early one day a week, compensating by doing certain occupational tasks on evenings and weekends. Like other career-oriented mothers, Sharese eased role pressures by setting priorities: She decreased the amount of time she spent on household chores, not child rearing (Institute for Social Research, 2002).

As Sharese and Ernie's strategies indicate, workplace supports can greatly reduce role overload, yielding substantial payoffs for employers. Among a large, nationally representative sample of U.S. working adults, the greater the number of time-flexible policies available in their work settings (for example,

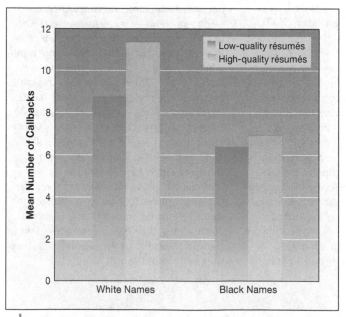

■ **FIGURE 8.5** ■ **Relationship of ethnicity of job applicant's name to employer callbacks.** Researchers responded to help-wanted newspaper ads with fictitious résumés, some having white-sounding names and others black-sounding names. Résumés with "white" names evoked many more callbacks than résumés with "black" names. When résumés were high in quality, callbacks to whites increased, but those to blacks showed little change. (Adapted from Bertrand & Mullainathan, 2004.)

Applying What We Know

Strategies That Help Dual-Earner Couples Combine Work and Family Roles

Strategy	Description
Devise a plan for sharing household tasks.	As soon as possible in the relationship, discuss relative commitment to work and family and division of household responsibilities. Decide who does a particular chore on the basis of who has the needed skill and time, not on the basis of gender. Schedule regular times to rediscuss your plan.
Begin sharing child care right after the baby's arrival.	For fathers, strive to spend equal time with the baby early. For mothers, refrain from imposing your standards on your partner. Instead, share the role of "child-rearing expert" by discussing parenting values and concerns often. Attend a parent education course together.
Talk over conflicts about decision making and responsibilities.	Face conflict through communication. Clarify your feelings and needs and express them to your partner. Listen and try to understand your partner's point of view. Then be willing to negotiate and compromise.
Establish a balance between work and family.	Critically evaluate the time you devote to work in view of your values and priorities. If it is too much, cut back.
Make sure your relationship receives regular loving care.	See Applying What We Know on page 262.
Press for workplace and public policies that assist dual-earner-family roles.	Difficulties faced by dual-earner couples are partly due to lack of workplace and societal supports. Encourage your employer to provide benefits that help combine work and family, such as flexible work hours, parental leave with pay, and on-site high-quality, affordable child care. Communicate with lawmakers and other citizens about improving public policies for children and families.

time off to care for a sick child, choice in start and stop times, and opportunities to work from home), the better their work performance (Halpern, 2005a). Employees with several time-flexible options missed fewer days of work, less often arrived at work late or left early, felt more committed to their employer, and worked harder. They also reported fewer stress-related health symptoms.

Effectively balancing work and family brings many benefits—a better standard of living, improved work productivity, enhanced psychological well-being, greater self-fulfillment, and happier marriages. Ernie took great pride in Sharese's career

accomplishments, which contributed to his view of her as an interesting, capable helpmate. Multiple roles also granted both young people expanded contexts for experiencing success and greater similarity in everyday experiences, which fostered gratifying communication (Barnett & Hyde, 2001). Applying What We Know above lists strategies that help dual-earner couples combine work and family roles in ways that promote mastery and pleasure in both spheres of life.

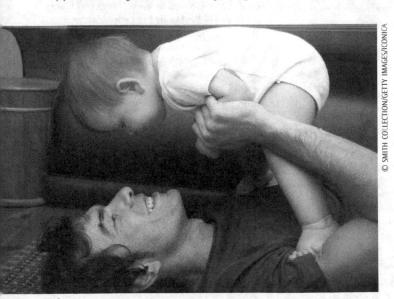

Dual-earner couples can better balance work and family if they share both the pleasures and the burdens of child rearing.

ASK YOURSELF

≫ REVIEW
Why do professionally accomplished women, especially those who are members of economically disadvantaged minorities, typically display high self-efficacy?

≫ APPLY
Heather climbed the career ladder of her company quickly, reaching a top-level executive position by her early thirties. In contrast, Sharese and Christy did not attain managerial roles in early adulthood. What factors might account for this disparity in career progress?

≫ CONNECT
Work and family life are inseparably intertwined. Explain how this is so in early adulthood.

≫ REFLECT
Contact a major employer in your area and ask about its policies for helping employees combine work and family roles. What improvements would you suggest? Why are family-friendly policies "win-win" situations for both workers and employers?

© SMITH COLLECTION/GETTY IMAGES/ICONICA

Summary

A Gradual Transition: Emerging Adulthood

What is emerging adulthood, and how has cultural change contributed to it?

>> In **emerging adulthood,** young adults from about age 18 to 25 have not yet taken on adult roles. During these years, they prolong identity development as they explore alternatives in breadth and depth.

>> Increased education required for entry-level positions in many fields, gains in economic prosperity, reduced need for young people's labor, and globalization have prompted the appearance and spread of emerging adulthood.

>> In trying out possibilities, emerging adults must adjust to disappointments in love and work, and their explorations also extend risky behaviors of adolescence. A wide array of personal attributes and social supports foster resilience.

Erikson's Theory: Intimacy versus Isolation

According to Erikson, what personality changes take place during early adulthood?

>> In Erikson's theory, young adults must resolve the conflict of **intimacy versus isolation** as they form a close relationship with a partner. The negative outcome is loneliness and self-absorption.

>> Young people also focus on aspects of generativity, including parenting and contributions to society through work.

Other Theories of Adult Psychosocial Development

Describe and evaluate Levinson's and Vaillant's psychosocial theories of adult personality development.

>> Levinson described a series of eras, each consisting of a transition and a stable phase, in which people revise their **life structure.** Young adults usually construct a dream, typically involving career for men and both marriage and career for women, and form a relationship with a mentor to help them realize their dream. In their thirties, men tend to settle down, whereas many women remain unsettled into middle adulthood.

>> Vaillant refined Erikson's stages, portraying the twenties as devoted to intimacy, the thirties to career consolidation, the forties to generativity, and the fifties and sixties to cultural values.

>> The patterns Levinson and Vaillant identified are based on limited samples of people born in the first few decades of the twentieth century. Young adults' development is more variable today than in past generations.

What is the social clock, and how does it affect personality in adulthood?

>> Conformity to or departure from the **social clock**—age-graded expectations for major life events—can be a major source of personality change in adulthood. Following a social clock grants confidence to young adults; deviating from it can bring psychological distress.

Close Relationships

Describe factors affecting mate selection and the role of romantic love in the young adult's quest for intimacy.

>> Establishing an intimate bond is a major milestone of adult development. Romantic partners tend to resemble one another in age, ethnicity, SES, religion, and various personal and physical attributes.

>> According to evolutionary theory, women seek a mate with traits that help ensure children's survival, while men look for characteristics signaling sexual pleasure and ability to bear offspring. An alternative, social learning perspective emphasizes that gender roles profoundly influence criteria for mate selection. Research suggests that both biological and social forces are involved.

>> According to the **triangular theory of love,** the balance among intimacy, passion, and commitment changes as romantic relationships move from the intense sexual attraction of **passionate love** toward more settled **companionate love.** Commitment is key to a satisfying, enduring relationship. The Western emphasis on romantic love in mate selection does not characterize all cultures.

Describe adult friendships and sibling relationships, and the role of loneliness in adult development.

>> Adult friendships have characteristics and benefits similar to earlier friendships and are based on trust, intimacy, and loyalty. Women's same-sex friendships tend to be more intimate than men's. After college, other-sex friendships decline with age for men but increase for highly educated, employed women, who tend to form them in the workplace. Adult sibling relationships often resemble friendships, especially among sisters with positive early experiences.

>> Young adults are vulnerable to **loneliness,** which declines with age as they form satisfying intimate ties. As long as it is not too intense, loneliness can encourage young people to reach out to others and better understand themselves.

The Family Life Cycle

Trace phases of the family life cycle that are prominent in early adulthood, and cite factors that influence these phases today.

>> Wide variations exist in the sequence and timing of phases of the **family life cycle.** Leaving home is a major step in assuming adult responsibilities. Departures for education occur earlier than those for full-time work and marriage. SES and ethnicity influence the likelihood that a young person will live independently before marriage. Many unmarried young adults return home for a period of time.

>> Nearly 90 percent of Americans marry, at later ages than in the past. Today, couples must work harder to define their marital roles. Both **traditional marriages** and **egalitarian marriages** are affected by women's participation in the work force. Even in dual-earner marriages, North American women spend nearly twice as much time as men on housework.

>> Quality of the marital relationship predicts mental health similarly for both men and women. Women, however, feel particularly dissatisfied when the combined demands of work and family roles are overwhelming. Many young people enter marriage with unrealistic expectations.

>> Effective birth control techniques and changing cultural values make parenthood a matter of choice in Western industrialized nations. Although most couples become parents, they do so at a later age and have fewer children than in the past.

>> The arrival of a child requires couples to adjust to increased responsibilities and often prompts a shift to more traditional roles, though this may reverse after the birth of a second child. Marriages that are gratifying and supportive tend to remain so after childbirth, but troubled marriages usually become more distressed. Shared caregiving predicts greater parental happiness and positive parent–infant interaction.

>> Families with young children face challenges of clarifying and implementing child-rearing values. Couples who work together as a coparenting team are more likely to gain in warm marital interaction, feel competent as parents, use effective child-rearing practices, and have children who are developing well.

>> In families with adolescents, parents must establish new relationships with their increasingly autonomous teenagers, blending guidance with freedom and gradually loosening control. Marital satisfaction often declines in this phase.

>> Parent education programs can help parents clarify their child-rearing values and use more effective strategies.

The Diversity of Adult Lifestyles

Discuss the diversity of adult lifestyles, focusing on singlehood, cohabitation, and childlessness.

>> Singlehood has risen in recent years because of a trend toward later marriage and a high divorce rate. Despite certain drawbacks, singles appreciate their freedom and mobility. Women tend to adjust more favorably than men.

>> **Cohabitation** has risen dramatically, especially among well-educated, economically advantaged young adults, for whom it is the preferred mode of entry into a committed intimate partnership. Cohabitation rates are especially high among separated and divorced adults. Compared with their Western European counterparts, American cohabiters tend to be less conventional in values and behavior and less committed to their partner, and their subsequent marriages are more likely to fail. However, gay and lesbian couples who cohabit because they cannot marry report commitment equal to that of married couples.

>> Voluntarily childless adults tend to be well-educated and career-oriented and are as satisfied with their lives as parents who have good relationships with their children. But when childlessness is beyond a person's control, it interferes with adjustment and life satisfaction.

Discuss today's high rates of divorce and remarriage, and cite factors that contribute to them.

>> Nearly half of U.S. marriages dissolve, often while children are at home. About two-thirds of divorced people remarry, and many divorce again. Maladaptive communication patterns, younger ages at marriage, a family history of divorce, poverty, and the changing status of women all contribute to divorce.

>> Finding a new partner is important to many divorced adults, especially men. Remarriages break up for several reasons, including the prominence of practical concerns rather than love in the decision to remarry, the persistence of negative styles of communication, the acceptance of divorce as a solution to marital difficulties, and problems adjusting to a stepfamily.

Discuss the challenges associated with variant styles of parenthood, including stepparents, never-married parents, and gay and lesbian parents.

>> Establishing stepparent–stepchild ties is difficult, especially for stepmothers and for stepfathers without children of their own. A caring husband–wife relationship, cooperation from the biological parent, and children's acceptance are crucial for stepparent adjustment.

>> Never-married single parenthood is especially high among low-income African-American women in their twenties. Unemployment among black men contributes to this trend. Although these mothers often receive help from extended family members, they find it difficult to overcome poverty.

>> Gay and lesbian parents are as committed to and effective at child rearing as heterosexual parents, and their children are as well-adjusted as those reared by heterosexual parents.

Career Development

Discuss patterns of career development, and cite difficulties faced by women, ethnic minorities, and couples seeking to combine work and family.

>> Men's career paths are usually continuous, whereas women's are often discontinuous because of child rearing and other family needs. After adjusting to the realities of the work world, young adults settle into an occupation. Their progress is affected by opportunities for promotion, personal characteristics such as self-efficacy, and access to an effective mentor.

>> Women and ethnic minorities have penetrated nearly all professions but have made limited progress in career advancement. Women are hampered by time away from the labor market, low self-efficacy and lack of mentoring in traditionally male-dominated fields, and gender stereotypes of women as followers rather than leaders. Racial bias in the labor market remains strong, and ethnic minority women who succeed display an unusually high sense of self-efficacy.

>> Couples, particularly women, in dual-earner marriages often experience role overload. Effectively balancing work and family brings a better standard of living, enhanced psychological well-being, and happier marriages. Time-flexible workplace policies reduce stress while augmenting work performance.

Important Terms and Concepts

cohabitation (p. 275)
companionate love (p. 262)
egalitarian marriage (p. 267)
emerging adulthood (p. 252)

family life cycle (p. 266)
intimacy versus isolation (p. 256)
life structure (p. 257)
loneliness (p. 264)

passionate love (p. 262)
social clock (p. 259)
traditional marriage (p. 267)
triangular theory of love (p. 260)

Milestones
Development in Early Adulthood

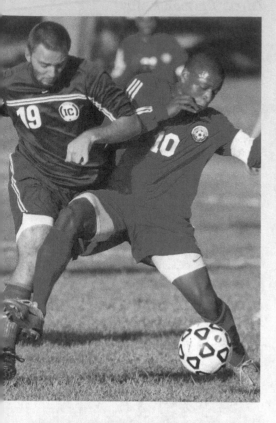

PHYSICAL

- Athletic skills that require speed of limb movement, explosive strength, and gross motor coordination peak early in this decade, then decline. (224)
- Athletic skills that depend on endurance, arm–hand steadiness, and aiming peak at the end of this decade, then decline. (224)
- Declines in touch sensitivity, cardiovascular and respiratory capacity, immune system functioning, and skin elasticity begin and continue throughout adulthood. (223)

- As basal metabolic rate declines, gradual weight gain begins in the middle of this decade and continues through middle adulthood. (227–228)
- Sexual activity increases. (233–235)

COGNITIVE

- If college educated, dualistic thinking declines in favor of relativistic thinking. (240)

- Moves from hypothetical to pragmatic thought. (240)
- Narrows vocational options and settles on a specific career. (244)
- Shows gains in cognitive–affective complexity, which continue through middle adulthood. (241)

- Develops expertise in a field of endeavor, which enhances problem solving. (241)

- May increase in creativity. (241–242)

EMOTIONAL/SOCIAL

- In the first half of this decade, if life circumstances permit, may engage in the extended exploration that characterizes emerging adulthood. (252–253)
- Feels increasingly in control of life events. (252)
- Is likely to achieve a personally meaningful identity. (253)
- Leaves the parental home permanently. (266)

- Strives to make a permanent commitment to an intimate partner. (256–257, 260)
- Usually constructs a dream—an image of the self in the adult world that guides decision making. (258)

Note: Numbers in parentheses indicate the page or pages on which each milestone is discussed.

- Typically forms a relationship with a mentor. (258)
- If in a high-status career, acquires professional skills, values, and credentials. (258)
- Begins to develop mutually gratifying adult friendships and work ties. (263–264)
- May cohabit, marry, and bear children. (266–267, 269–272)

- Sibling relationships become more companionate. (264)
- Loneliness peaks early in this decade, then declines steadily throughout adulthood. (265)

30–40 years

PHYSICAL

- Declines in vision, hearing, and the skeletal system begin and continue throughout adulthood. (223)
- In women, reproductive capacity continues to decline, and fertility problems increase sharply after the middle of this decade. (225)

- In men, semen volume, sperm motility, and percentage of normal sperm decrease gradually in the second half of this decade. (226)
- Hair begins to gray and thin in the middle of this decade. (223)
- Sexual activity declines, probably as a result of the demands of daily life. (234)

COGNITIVE

- May develop commitment within relativistic thinking. (240)
- Creative accomplishment often peaks in the second half of this decade, although this varies across disciplines. (241–242)

EMOTIONAL/SOCIAL

- Reevaluates life structure and tries to change components that are inadequate. (257–258)
- Establishes a stable niche in society through family, occupation, and community activities. (For women, career maturity and authority in the community may be delayed.) (258)

Selections from

Characteristics of Emotional and Behavioral Disorders of Youth and Children

Ninth Edition

SECTION 9
BIOLOGICAL FACTORS

As you read this section, keep these guiding questions in mind:

- Why do biological factors have such great appeal as explanations of deviant behavior?

- Under what conditions is it most likely that a person will develop schizophrenia?

- What can one conclude about the relationship between brain damage or dysfunction and emotional or behavioral disorders?

- What is temperament, and how might it affect pupil–teacher interactions?

- What are the primary implications of biological causes of emotional or behavioral disorders for educators?

APPEAL OF BIOLOGICAL FACTORS AS CAUSAL EXPLANATIONS

A biological view of emotional or behavioral disorders has particular appeal. On the one hand, psychological models of behavior cannot account for all behavioral variations in children (Pinker, 2002). On the other hand, advances in genetics, physiology, and medical technologies such as imaging and medications make the suggestion of a biological basis for all emotional or behavioral disorders seem plausible (see Weiner, 1999; Wilson, 1998). Moreover, research suggests that a high percentage of students with serious EBD have neuropsychological problems (Mattison, Hooper, & Carlson, 2006).

Completion of the Human Genome Project was announced on April 14, 2003 (Collins, 2003; Collins, Green, Guttmacher, & Guyer, 2003). That is, the "mapping" of all the genes in human DNA was completed. This accomplishment may well allow preventive medicine to make great progress and even have benefits for the prediction and early treatment of certain mental disorders. It was said by its director to have "great potential to revolutionize medicine throughout the world" (Collins, 2003, p. A19). However, enthusiasm for advances in understanding genetic codes has to be tempered with the understanding that genes alone do not determine the way people behave.

The central nervous system is undeniably involved in all behavior, and all behavior involves neurochemical activity. Furthermore, scientists long ago established that genetic factors alone are potentially sufficient to explain all variation in human behavior (Eiduson, Eiduson, & Geller, 1962; see also Weiner, 1999). It may seem reasonable to believe, therefore, that disordered emotion or behavior always implies a genetic accident, bacterial or viral disease, brain injury, brain dysfunction, allergy, or some other biochemical imbalance (Linnoila, 1997). And we can find cases in which serious antisocial behavior is attributable to such neurological problems as brain tumors (e.g., Burns & Swerdlow, 2003), or biological factors provide a predisposition to develop antisocial behavior (Dodge & Pettit, 2003; see also Earley, 2006; Sedgwick, 2007).

As attractive as biological explanations may appear on the surface, however, the assumption that disorders are simply a result of biological misfortune is misleading, as is the suggestion that disorders are simply a result of social or cultural conditioning. Although biological processes have a pervasive influence on behavior, they affect behavior only in interaction with environmental factors (see Jensen et al., 2001; Leve, Winebarger, Fagot, Reid, & Goldsmith, 1998; Pinker, 2002; Plomin, 1995; Rutter, 1995). In the case of genetics, Plomin (1995) noted, "Twenty years ago, the message from behavioural genetics research was that genetic factors play a major role in behavioural/dimensions and disorders. The message today is that these same data provide strong evidence for the importance of environmental factors as well as genetic factors" (p. 34). Research in cloning in the 21st century underscores Plomin's observation. An identical genetic code does not result in identical behavior, simply because environment also shapes behavior (see Pinker, 2002).

Knowing that a disorder has a biological cause does not always lead to a prescription for treatment. This does not mean that biologically based disorders are untreatable; it means that scientists may not be able to devise a biological treatment designed to reverse the cause but may only be able to treat its effects, the symptoms of the biological process. Furthermore, because biological and environmental processes are interactive, sometimes the best treatment for a biological disorder is an alteration of the environment—arrangement of the social environment to ameliorate the effects of the biologically based disorder. For example, Tourette's disorder, a neurological disorder with symptoms including tics and often accompanied by obsessions, compulsions, hyperactivity, distractibility, and impulsivity, may be treated with a combination of medication and cognitive-behavioral approaches involving changes in the social environment. The social environment may have significant effects on the symptoms of Tourette's disorder, although the basic cause of the disorder is neurological. Medication may be the single most effective treatment alternative for most children with attention deficit–hyperactivity disorder (ADHD), but for many, especially those showing defiant and disruptive behavior in addition to ADHD, the combination of medication and psychosocial intervention (behavior therapy) works better (Jensen et al., 2001).

The biological processes involved in behavioral deviance are extremely complex, and new discoveries are being made rapidly. Moreover, nearly every type of biological factor has been suggested as a possible cause of nearly every type of psychopathology (see Klorman, 1995; Werry, 1986a). We may conclude that the effects of biological factors on behavioral development are considerable but frequently neither demonstrable nor simple. And although biological factors influence behavior, environmental conditions modify biological processes. Knowledge of biological causes may carry significant implications for prevention or medical treatment, but such knowledge usually has few direct implications for the work of educators. Educators work almost exclusively with environmental influences, relying on biological scientists and medical personnel to diagnose and treat the physiological aspects of emotional or behavioral disorders. Thus, educators should have basic information about biological factors but focus primarily on how the environmental conditions they may be able to control might affect students' behavior.

With these points in mind, we discuss several biological factors that may contribute to the development of disordered emotions or behavior: genetics, brain injury or dysfunction, malnutrition and allergies, and temperament. We cannot discuss the role of every possible biological factor in every type of disorder. Clearly, such things as the mother's substance abuse during pregnancy *can* contribute to emotional or behavioral problems in children. However, our discussion is brief and focused on representative examples of known or presumed biological causes and disorders in which such factors may play a role.

GENETICS

Children inherit more than physical characteristics from their parents; they also inherit predispositions to certain behavioral characteristics. Not surprisingly, genes have been suggested as causal factors in every kind of emotional or behavioral difficulty, including criminality, attention deficits, hyperactivity, schizophrenia, depression,

Tourette's disorder, autism, and anxiety (see Asarnow & Asarnow, 2003; Levy & Hay, 2001). Research indicates that, indeed, genes have a strong influence on the development of all types of behavior, both desirable and undesirable (see Leve et al., 1998; McGuffin & Thapar, 1997; Pinker, 2002; Weiner, 1999). In fact, the evidence that there are significant genetic influences on behavior is now so overwhelming that "genetic studies are moving away from establishing the *fact* of heritability and toward explaining the *how* of heritability" (Carey & Goldman, 1997, p. 250, emphasis in original).

Genes linked to some specific diseases or vulnerabilities have been identified, but gene therapy, in which genes are manipulated, has been oversold by some scientists and the news media. However, genetically determined differences in children's behavior are observed by scientists not only in their research but also in their everyday lives. Compare the following quotation from the eminent biologist Seymour Benzer, who saw dramatic differences in the behavior of his two daughters, Barbie and Martha, to the personal reflections of Dixie Jordan at the end of section 10:

> "When you have one child, it behaves like a child," Benzer told a lecture audience not long ago, accepting the Crafoord Prize in Stockholm for his work on genes and behavior. "But as soon as you have a second child you realize from Day One that this one is different from the other." (Weiner, 1999, p. 65)

In the early 21st century, we are learning that cloned animals (and, by extension, humans) do not necessarily have the same behavior as their genetic match. The same is true for identical twins (naturally occurring clones). Scientists have very good reason to understand that behavioral characteristics are not determined solely by genes. Environmental factors, particularly social learning, play an important role in modifying inherited emotional or behavioral predispositions.

Furthermore, at the level of specific behaviors, social learning is nearly always far more important than genetics. Little or no evidence supports the suggestion that specific behaviors are genetically transmitted; however, some type of genetic influence obviously contributes to the major psychiatric disorders of children and adolescents and to many other disorders as well. What is inherited is a predisposition to behave in certain ways, a tendency toward certain types of behavior that may be made stronger or weaker by environmental conditions. The predisposition is created by a very complex process involving multiple genes. Seldom do emotional or behavioral disorders involve a single gene or an identifiable chromosomal anomaly. Moreover, comorbidity—multiple disorders involving complex gene interactions—is common (Hay & Levy, 2001).

Genetic factors are suspected in a wide variety of disorders. However, a disorder in which genetic transmission is particularly well recognized is schizophrenia. The onset of schizophrenia occurs only rarely in young children, but onset in middle and late adolescence is not uncommon (Asarnow & Asarnow, 2003; Remschmidt, Schulz, Martin, Warnke, & Trott, 1994). In most cases, the first symptoms of schizophrenia are observed in people ranging from 15 to 45 years of age. The features of schizophrenia are similar in children and adults, although onset in childhood may be associated with a severe form of the disorder (Alaghband-Rad et al., 1995; Russell, 1994; Spencer & Campbell, 1994). The major characteristics are delusions, hallucinations, disorganized

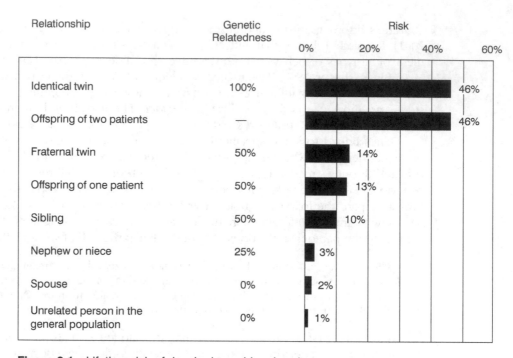

Figure 9.1   Lifetime risk of developing schizophrenia

Source: Nicol, S. E., & Gottesman, I. (1983). Clues to the genetics and neurobiology of schizophrenia. *American Scientist, 71,* 399. Used with permission.

speech, and thought disorders (see the case of Chad in the accompanying case book for further discussion).

The exact genetic mechanisms responsible for a predisposition to schizophrenia and other disorders such as depression and bipolar disorder (formerly called manic depression) are still unknown, but research decades old clearly shows an increase in risk for schizophrenia and schizophreniclike behavior (often called *schizoid or schizophrenic spectrum behavior*) in the relatives of schizophrenics. More recent research has not overturned the basic findings of a genetic link. The closer the genetic relationship between the child and a schizophrenic relative, the higher the risk that the child will develop the condition. Heightened risk cannot be attributed to the social environment or interpersonal factors alone. Figure 9.1 shows the long-known increased level of risk that goes with increasingly close genetic relatedness to a person who has schizophrenia. Having an identical twin who has schizophrenia increases an individual's risk of developing schizophrenia by a factor of 46; having a sibling with schizophrenia carries 10 times the risk of the general population (see also Pinker, 2002).

Many people misunderstand the implications of increased risk for schizophrenia or other disorders. Does a heightened genetic risk for schizophrenia mean a person will necessarily develop the disorder? Do the genetic factors in schizophrenia mean that prevention is impossible? The answer to both questions is no. "Not all people with the genetic potential to become schizophrenic will actually develop the clinical disorder" (Nicol & Erlenmeyer-Kimling, 1986, p. 33). Plomin (1995) pointed out that although genetic relatedness increases risk for schizophrenia dramatically, the chance that someone will develop schizophrenia is less than 50%, even for those at highest genetic risk—those having an identical twin or both parents with schizophrenia (see also Pinker, 2002; see Sedgwick, 2007, for a family tree and description of personal history involving depression). Furthermore, risk factors can be lowered by altering the social environment and avoiding circumstances that might trigger the disorder.

The causes of schizophrenia are likely multiple and complex, with genetic factors being only one predisposing factor. However, schizoid behavior or full-blown schizophrenia can apparently be triggered by a bad drug trip as well as environmental stressors. Those at highest risk for schizophrenia (i.e., those with close blood relatives with the disorder) would be well advised to avoid experimenting with drugs (Gottesman, 1987, 1991).

Implications of Genetic Factors

A common misperception is that disorders arising from genetic accidents are not treatable—that once the genetic code is set, the related deviant behavior is immutable. But this is not necessarily the case (Gottesman, 1991; Hay & Levy, 2001; Plomin, 1995; Wilson, 1998). As with schizophrenia, environmental as well as biological factors are involved in the causation of deviant behavior. When the biochemical mechanisms underlying genetic transmission are discovered, there is hope that effective interventions will be found to prevent or alter the course of behavioral development.

Genetic factors are known to contribute to a variety of emotional and behavioral disorders, perhaps even to most (see Pinker, 2002; Weiner, 1999; Wilson, 1998). In some severe disorders, such as schizophrenia, the level of the genetic contribution is clear, but how the gene system works remains obscure. For most types of emotional or behavioral disorders, the genetic contributions remain unclear, and environmental factors appear to be far more important for educators (see Leve et al., 1998).

Evolutionary biology strongly suggests that many behaviors are influenced by genetic makeup and the mixing of genes from unrelated individuals. Genetic mixing ordinarily helps species perpetuate their kind. However, genetic mutations—random changes or errors in genes—also occur (Batshaw, 2002b; Judson, 2002). Sometimes these are destructive and do not help a species survive. We do not really know which emotional or behavioral disorders are mutations and which, if any, help to perpetuate *Homo sapiens.*

BRAIN DAMAGE OR DYSFUNCTION

The brain can be traumatized in several different ways before, during, or after birth, and such damage may contribute substantially to antisocial behavior (Batshaw, 2002a; Dell Orto & Power, 2000). Physical insult during an accident or during the birth process may destroy brain tissue. Prolonged high fever, infectious disease, and toxic chemicals (such as drugs or poisons taken by the child or by a woman during pregnancy) may also damage the brain. A frequently suspected or known cause of brain damage in children, however, is *hypoxia* (also known as *anoxia*), a seriously reduced supply of oxygen. Hypoxia often occurs during birth but can also occur during accidents or as a result of disease or respiratory disorders later in life.

The brain may function improperly for a variety of reasons. Tissue damage from traumatic injury may cause dysfunction. In the case of traumatic brain injury (TBI), we know that the brain's function has been impaired by documented damage at a specific location or locations. However, the brain may not function properly because of structural anomalies (i.e., malformation of certain parts of the brain) that are present at birth or are part of a disease process or because of a neurochemical imbalance resulting from a disease or drugs. In some cases, scientists do not know exactly why the brain is not working as it should, although it obviously is not. For example, schizophrenia has been clearly established as a brain disorder, but we do not yet know exactly what is wrong with the brain of a person who has schizophrenia.

A very wide range of emotional or behavioral disorders has been attributed to known or suspected brain damage or dysfunction (Light, McCleary, Asarnow, Zaucha, & Lewis, 1998). Learning disabilities and the related problems of hyperactivity, impulsivity, and inattention have historically been assumed to be caused by brain injury or dysfunction, although the exact nature of the injury or dysfunction has not been demonstrated (Hallahan, Lloyd, Kauffman, Weiss, & Martinez, 2005). Subtle brain injury before, during, or shortly after birth is an important contributing cause of serious juvenile delinquency and adult criminality, according to some researchers (Bower, 1995). Other researchers have found neuropsychological problems involving language and attention in a high percentage of students with serious EBD (Mattison et al., 2006).

Nearly every sort of serious emotional or behavioral problem could be hypothesized to be, at some level, a matter of structural or chemical problems of the brain. For purposes of illustration, consider a category of acquired disability that was made a separate special education category under federal law in 1990: traumatic brain injury.

Traumatic Brain Injury

Synonymous terms for the same general type of neurological damage include *traumatic head injury, cerebral trauma,* or *craniocerebral trauma*. However, *traumatic brain injury* (TBI) is the term used in federal laws related to special education. TBI is not a new type of disability, it was made a separate category for special education because it is an increasingly frequent cause of neurological impairment in children and youth (Hallahan, Kauffman, & Pullen, 2009; Stichter, Conroy, & Kauffman, 2008). Furthermore, it presents unique educational problems that have been poorly understood and often mismanaged, and recent medical advances have greatly improved its diagnosis and treatment. The return of soldiers injured in war has often prompted the recognition and treatment of disabilities among children and youth. Because TBI is one of the most common injuries suffered by soldiers in Iraq and Afghanistan, the public might become more aware of and demand better treatment of youngsters with TBI.

TBI does not include all types of brain damage. The term means the following:

- There is injury to the brain caused by an external force.
- The injury is not caused by a degenerative or congenital condition.
- There is a diminished or altered state of consciousness.
- Neurological or neurobehavioral dysfunction results from the injury.

TBI may involve open head injuries from causes such as a fall, a gunshot wound, an assault, a vehicular accident, or surgery; there is a penetrating head wound. TBI may also involve closed head injuries, which may be caused by a variety of events, including a fall, an accident, or abuse such as violent shaking; there is no open head wound, but the brain is damaged by internal compression, stretching, or other shearing motion of neural tissues within the head.

The educational definition of TBI focuses on impairments in one or more areas that are important for learning, such as cognition, language, speech, memory, information processing, attention, reasoning, abstract thinking, judgment, problem solving, perceptual abilities, psychosocial behavior, or physical abilities. The various *sequelae* (consequences) of TBI create a need for special education; the injury itself is a medical problem.

The effects of TBI depend on a variety of factors, including the part(s) of the brain damaged; the severity of the damage; the age of the individual when the damage occurs; and the medical, psychological, and educational treatment the student receives. The effects may range from very mild to profound and be temporary or permanent. Sometimes all the effects are immediately apparent, but some effects may not be seen at all immediately after the injury; some may appear months or even years afterward. About half of the children and youth who experience serious TBI will require special education, and those who return to regular classes will almost certainly require modifications if they are to be successful (Allison, 1992; Tyler & Mira, 1999).

The effects of TBI may be misattributed to other causes if the brain injury is not diagnosed and understood. In many cases, violence and other disturbing behavior cannot be connected to brain damage, and it is important not to attribute such behavior to brain damage in the absence of medical evidence of damage. However, we also know that TBI can cause violent aggression, hyperactivity, impulsivity, inattention, and a wide range of other emotional or behavioral problems, depending on just what parts of the brain are damaged. The possible effects of TBI include a long list of other psychosocial problems, some of which we list here:

- Inappropriate manners or mannerisms
- Failure to understand humor or read social situations
- Becoming easily tired, frustrated, or angered
- Unreasonable fear or anxiety
- Irritability
- Sudden, exaggerated mood swings

- Depression
- Perseveration (getting stuck on one thought or behavior)

The emotional and behavioral effects of TBI are determined by more than the physical damage. These effects also depend on the student's age at the time of injury and the social environment before and after the injury occurs. Home, community, or school environments that foster misbehavior of any child or youth—disorganization, lack of adult supervision, dangerous circumstances, lack of safety precautions, for example—are known to be associated with higher risk for acquiring TBI. Such environments also are extremely likely to make any emotional or behavioral problem resulting from TBI worse.

Creating an environment that is conducive to and supportive of appropriate behavior is one of the great challenges of dealing effectively with the sequelae of brain injury (Best, Heller, & Bigge, 2005). Medical treatment usually cannot undo the effects of TBI. Emotional or behavioral problems may be known to have resulted from brain injury, but these problems must be addressed primarily through environmental modifications—changing other people's demands, expectations, and responses to behavior.

TBI often shatters an individual's sense of self. Recovering one's identity may require a long period of rehabilitation and may be a painstaking process requiring multidisciplinary efforts (see Crimmins, 2000). Effective education and treatment often require not only classroom behavior management but also family therapy, medication, cognitive training, and communication training.

Brain damage or dysfunction can produce a wide variety of emotional and behavioral disorders. Brain damage or dysfunction is not the only cause of such disorders, however, and it is important to remember that environmental factors can make a significant difference in the effects of brain injury on behavior.

MALNUTRITION, ALLERGIES, AND OTHER HEALTH-RELATED ISSUES

We have known for decades that severe malnutrition can have catastrophic effects on children's cognitive and physical development. Malnutrition is especially devastating to the development of very young children. It reduces the child's responsiveness to stimulation and produces apathy. The eventual result of serious malnutrition (especially severe protein deficiency) is retardation in brain growth, irreversible brain damage, mental retardation, or some combination of these effects. Apathy, social withdrawal, and school failure are expected long-term outcomes if children are severely malnourished. Furthermore, it is well recognized that hunger and inadequate nutrition interfere with the ability to concentrate on academic and social learning. Thus, the concern for children's adequate nutrition in poor families is well justified (Tanner & Finn-Stevenson, 2002).

The belief that less-severe nutritional inadequacies (such as not enough vitamins or minerals) or excesses (such as too much sugar or caffeine) cause children to misbehave has been popular for many years (see Pescara-Kovach & Alexander, 1994; Wolraich, Wilson, & White, 1995). Disorders ranging from hyperactivity to depression to autism to delinquency have been attributed by some to what young-sters eat or do not eat. Hypoglycemia (low blood sugar), vitamin or mineral defi-ciencies, and allergies can influence behavior, and teachers should be aware of these potential problems (McLoughlin & Nall, 1994). However, the role of specific foods and allergies in causing cognitive, emotional, or behavioral problems has often been exaggerated.

Although we know that some children are allergic to certain foods and a variety of other substances (e.g., medications, pollens, dust, insect stings), there is little evi-dence that these allergies are often causes of emotional or behavioral problems. However, teachers, like parents, may prefer the belief that diet is a major factor in causing misbehavior (McLoughlin & Nall, 1994, p. 206).

Nutrition and allergies can affect behavior, but there is little evidence that they play a major role in causing emotional or behavioral disorders except in extreme cases. Biases and expectations appear to maintain the superstition that foods and allergies often cause behavioral or emotional problems. Adequate nutrition is crucial; excluding or severely restricting certain food substances seldom is.

A wide variety of other health-related disorders are found in the child population, including obesity, sleep disorders, injuries, and diseases (Peterson, Reach, & Grabe, 2003). In some cases, these involve emotional or behavioral disorders as well as health problems. However, it is important not to assume that all health-related prob-lems are created by emotional or behavioral disorders.

TEMPERAMENT

Beginning in the 1960s, researchers began to explore the centuries-old notion of *temperament*. The definition and measurement of temperament and the stability or continuity of temperament across time are matters of considerable controversy (Bates & Wachs, 1994; Garrison & Earls, 1987; Kagan, Gibbons, Johnson, Reznick, & Snidman, 1990; Keogh, 2003; Rimm-Kaufman & Kagan, 2005; Teglasi, 1998). Tempera-ment has been variously defined as "behavioral style," or the "how" rather than the "what" and "how well" of behavior; as the "active and reactive qualities" of infant behavior; and as "measurable behavior" during infancy. It has been measured by questionnaires given to parents or teachers and by direct observation of children's behavior. Despite differences in the ways in which researchers define and measure it, we can describe the concept of temperament in general terms: Individuals tend to have consistent, predictable reactions to certain types of circumstances or events, and their typical way of responding—their temperament—is partly determined by basic biological processes as well as environmental factors (see Carey, 1998; Keogh, 2003).

The point is that infants begin life with an inborn tendency to behave in certain ways. The newborn has a behavioral style that is determined predominantly by bio-logical factors, and how a baby behaves at birth and in the first weeks and months thereafter will influence how others respond. But temperament can be changed by the environment in which the child develops; what the child experiences and how the child is managed may change temperament for better or worse (Bates & Wachs, 1994; Carey, 1998; Chess & Thomas, 2003; Keogh, 2003; Nelson, Stage, Duppong-Hurley, Synhorst, & Epstein, 2007). A difficult temperament may increase the child's risk for emotional or behavioral disorders. However, temperament is an initial behavioral style that may change in interaction with environmental influences. Based on their now classic longitudinal study, Thomas, Chess, and Birch, (1968) described nine categories of temperamental characteristics (see also Garrison & Earls, 1987; Keogh, 2003):

1. *Activity level:* how much the child moves about during activities such as feeding, bathing, sleeping, and playing
2. *Rhythmicity:* the regularity or predictability with which the child eats, sleeps, eliminates, and so on
3. *Approach or withdrawal:* how the child responds initially to new events such as people, places, toys, and foods
4. *Adaptability:* how quickly the child becomes accustomed to or modifies an initial reaction to new situations or stimuli
5. *Intensity of reaction:* the amount of energy expended in reacting (positively or negatively) to situations or stimuli
6. *Threshold of responsiveness:* the amount or intensity of stimulation required to elicit a response from the child
7. *Quality of mood:* the amount of pleasant, joyful, and friendly behavior compared with unpleasant, crying, and unfriendly behavior exhibited by the child
8. *Distractibility:* the frequency with which extraneous or irrelevant stimuli interfere with the ongoing behavior of the child in a given situation
9. *Attention span and persistence:* the length of time a child will spend on a given activity and the tendency to maintain an activity in the face of obstacles to performance.

Thomas et al. (1968) found that children with any kind of temperament might develop emotional or behavioral disorders, depending on the child-rearing practices of their parents and other adults. Besides the characteristics listed, other more inclusive or general temperaments have been described. As Keogh (2003) pointed out, some children may be described as "easy." An easy temperament is characterized by regularity, adaptability, and positive response to new stimuli, mild or moderate intensity of response, positive mood. Children with "difficult" temperaments are more likely to develop troublesome behavior. A difficult temperament is characterized by irregularity in biological functioning, mostly negative (withdrawing) responses to new stimuli, slow adaptation to changes in the environment, frequent displays of negative mood, and mostly intense reactions. Some children can be described as "slow-to-warm-up" in temperament. Other temperament types include "undercontrolled," "inhibited," "confident," "sluggish," and "well adjusted."

Keogh (2003) pointed out that the "difficulty" of a child depends on the social context in which the child is behaving—the particular situation or circumstances and the cultural expectations. The key point is that what is perceived as a "difficult" temperament may elicit negative responses from a child's caretakers: A baby with a difficult temperament is not easy to care for and may increase parents' irritability, negative mood, and tendency to ignore or punish the child. If infant and parents adopt a pattern of mutual irritation, their negative interactions may increase the probability that the youngster will exhibit inappropriate or undesirable behavior in future years. Longitudinal research by other investigators also points to the potential for temperament to partially explain or predict later behavior. For example, inhibited and uninhibited temperamants in infancy have been shown to be associated with differences in observed kindergarten behavior (Rimm-Kaufman & Kagan, 2005); difficult temperament at an early age has been shown to be predictive of behavioral problems in adolescence (Caspi, Henry, McGee, Moffitt, & Silva, 1995); an easy or positive temperament has been found to be associated with children's resilience in responding to stress (Keogh, 2003; Smith & Prior, 1995); and temperament interacts with parenting behavior to place children at risk (Nelson et al., 2007).

The concept of difficult temperament has its critics (see Garrison & Earls, 1987). Some suggest that what researchers believe are inborn biological characteristics of infants are merely the subjective interpretations of mothers' reports. That is, "difficult temperament" reflects social perceptions of an infant's behavior and may not be within-the-individual characteristics. A baby is said to have a difficult temperament on the basis of the mother's report rather than more objective evaluations; therefore, the mother's perceptions (and the researcher's) are being assessed rather than a biological characteristic of the baby. Thomas, Chess, and Korn (1982), Keogh (2003), and others, however, interpret their research as confirming the reality of inborn behavioral characteristics or temperaments that are altered by environmental conditions (see Rutter, 1995). Carey and McDevitt (1995) noted the consensus regarding the interaction of environmental and inborn factors in shaping children's behavior:

1. Environmental effects such as family dysfunction, neighborhood violence, poor schools, and other unfortunate conditions are responsible for a substantial proportion of children's behavioral disorders.
2. Intrinsic factors explain some disorders formerly thought to be caused by the social environment. We now understand, for example, that autism and learning disabilities and perhaps other problems such as obesity are caused primarily by biological processes. These disorders are likely to exist under a wide range of environmental conditions.
3. A poor fit between a child's normal temperament and the values and expectations of the child's caregivers can cause stress leading to emotional or behavioral disorder.

Both environmental and intrinsic, biological factors contribute to emotional or behavioral disorders. Environmental and intrinsic factors combine to shape temperament. Moreover, a mismatch of social environment and the child's behavioral style can exacerbate a difficult temperament. A difficult temperament may increase a child's risk of exhibiting an emotional or behavioral disorder, but the risk may be either heightened further or lowered by the way in which parents and teachers manage the child's behavior (Henderson & Fox, 1998; Keogh, 2003; Kochanska, 1995; Nelson et al., 2007).

A few researchers have investigated teachers' ratings of children's temperaments in the classroom (see Keogh, 2003, for a review). Their general findings are that children do exhibit a consistent behavioral style or temperament in the classroom and that teachers tend to take children's temperaments into account in planning, instruction, and management. Moreover, teachers have a temperament, which may be a good or bad fit with the child's temperament.

Temperament may play a significant role in the development of emotional or behavioral disorders, but it does so only in interaction with environmental conditions. A consistent behavioral disposition or temperament such as irritability or impulsivity may heighten the risk for emotional or behavioral disorders. Research does not indicate that temperament is the direct or exclusive result of biological factors, but it does suggest that students exhibit a consistent behavioral style that teachers recognize and should consider in instruction and accommodation of behavioral diversity among students (Henderson & Fox, 1998; Keogh, 2003; Martin, 1992).

IMPLICATIONS FOR EDUCATORS

The biological factors that may have a significant negative effect on behavior are many and complex. It is important for educators to understand how genetics, parental neglect or abuse, malnutrition, and neurological damage may be linked to school failure and impulsive or antisocial behavior. Biological and social risk factors together offer the best explanations of the causes of antisocial behavior, and the same applies to other forms of emotional and behavioral disorders. Genetic predisposition, neglect, abuse, malnutrition, and brain injury all are more likely to be significant contributors to maladaptive behavior when they are accompanied by inconsistent or ill-suited behavior management at home and school.

However, it is erroneous to assume that all emotional or behavioral disorders have a biological origin and that therefore all such disorders are best handled by medical intervention. Not only is the tie between many of these disorders and specific biological causative factors tenuous, but also a biological cause may have no direct implications for change in educational methodology. Educators should work with other professionals to obtain the best possible medical care, nutrition, and physical environment for their students. However, educators cannot provide medical intervention, and they have only very limited influence over their students' physical health. Although teachers should be aware of possible biological factors and refer students for evaluation by other professionals when appropriate, they must not allow speculation regarding biological etiologies to excuse them from teaching appropriate behavior when they can—the academic and social skills that will enable students to be happy and successful in everyday environments.

Pharmacological treatment of many emotional and behavioral disorders is becoming more common, systematic, and effective (Forness, 2005; Forness & Beard, 2007; Forness, Freeman, & Paparella, 2006; Forness, Kavale, Sweeney, & Crenshaw, 1999; Hallfors, Fallon, & Watson, 1998; Konopasek & Forness, 2004;

Kutcher, 2002; Pomeroy & Gadow, 1998; Sweeney, Forness, Kavale, & Levitt, 1997). Medications can be extremely helpful in controlling some emotional or behavioral disorders (see Earley, 2006 for a description of its importance in managing schizophrenia and other serious mental disorders). Unfortunately, there appears to be a strong antimedication bias among many educators. Part of this bias may be because of teachers' lack of awareness of the purposes and possible benefits of medications and to their failure to understand that careful monitoring of classroom behavior is necessary to determine whether the drug is working, should be discontinued, or needs a dosage adjustment to obtain maximum benefits with minimum side effects.

Although the teacher is not able to prescribe medications or adjust dosages, the teacher's observations provide critical information for the physician. Teachers should be aware of the major types of drugs that may be prescribed for their students and the possible effects and side effects those drugs may have on classroom behavior and performance. Table 9.1 provides examples of four major types of medication and some of their possible effects. The generic (chemical) name is shown in parentheses under the brand or trade name for each example listed.

Table 9.1 Four Types of Psychotropic Medication and Some Possible Classroom Effects

Class of Drugs	Examples	Possible Classroom Effects
Stimulants[a]	Ritalin (methylphenidate) Adderall (mixed amphetamine salts) Dexedrine (dextroamphetamine)	Increased attention and decreased need for teacher control; effects usually evident within the first hour after ingestion; effects may last for up to 10 hours with time-release capsules; possible side effects include headaches, stomachaches, or increased irritability; too high of a dosage can decrease learning.
Antipsychotics (neuroleptics or major tranquilizers)	Risperdal (risperidone) Seroquel (quetiapine) Abilify (aripiprazole)	Effects usually gradual; decreased aggression or agitation and decreased hallucination within days; increased socialization within 3 to 4 weeks; decreased thought disorder within 2 months; side effects may include tremors, drowsiness, decreased attention, weight gain.
Antidepressants	Prozac (fluoxetine) Zoloft (sertraline) Wellbutrin (buproprion) Effexor (venlafaxine)	Classroom effects not yet extensively studied; improved sad affect; may increase communication and attention to tasks, decrease disruptiveness; effects may not be seen for 2 to 3 weeks; side effects vary widely with drug, but do include rare increase in suicide symptoms with SSRIs.
Mood stabilizers	Lithium Depakote (divalproex) Topamax (topirimate) Lamictal (lamotrigine)	Decreased mood lability and extremes of anger; side effects vary with drug; all but lithium are also used as anticonvulsants.

[a]Nonstimulant medications that are also used to treat attention deficit–hyperactivity disorder include Strattera (atomoxetine), Catapress (clonidine), and Tenex (guanfacine).

Source: We are grateful to Richard Mattison, M.D. for the information in this table.

Table 9.1 provides only a limited amount of information. Teachers should seek additional facts relevant to particular cases. There are many other categories and subcategories of psychotropic drugs, new drugs are constantly being introduced, and the effects and side effects of a given drug may vary greatly depending on the dosage level and the individual. The teacher should consult a nurse, physician, or professional publications for more detailed information about specific drugs and dosages (e.g., Forness et al., 1999; Konopasek, 1996; Konopasek & Forness, 2004; Sweeney et al., 1997). A student's parents or physician should inform the teacher that the student is taking a particular medication and ask the teacher to monitor its effects on the student's classroom behavior and academic performance. If the teacher is not so informed and is not asked to participate in evaluating the drug's classroom effects but becomes aware that the student is taking a psychotropic medication, he or she should approach the parents or the school nurse about monitoring the way in which the student is responding to the drug.

SUMMARY

Biological factors have special appeal because all behavior involves biochemical, neurological activity. Among the many biological factors that may contribute to the origins of emotional or behavioral disorders are genetics, brain damage or dysfunction, malnutrition or allergies, and temperament.

Genetic factors have been suggested as the causes of nearly every type of disorder. Genetics are known to be involved in causing schizophrenia, but little is known about how the gene system that causes the disorder works. Environmental factors appear to trigger schizophrenia in individuals who are genetically vulnerable. The fact that a disorder has a genetic cause does not mean that the disorder is untreatable.

Brain damage or dysfunction has been suggested as a cause of nearly every type of emotional or behavioral disorder. Traumatic brain injury involves known damage to the brain and may cause a wide variety of emotional and behavioral problems. Schizophrenia is now recognized as a biological disorder, although neither the exact nature nor the reason for the brain dysfunction are known. In both TBI and schizophrenia, environmental conditions can be significant in managing the disorder.

Severe malnutrition has devastating effects on young children's development. However, the popular notion that many emotional or behavioral disorders are caused by diet or allergies has not been supported by a consistent body of research. Teachers should be aware of possible dietary problems and allergies of students, but concern for these possible causes should not distract attention from instructional procedures.

Temperament is a consistent behavioral style or predisposition to respond in certain ways to one's environment. Although temperament may have a biological basis, it is also shaped by environmental factors. Skillful management by parents and teachers can lower the risk of emotional or behavioral disorders associated with difficult temperament.

When biological factors contribute to emotional or behavioral disorders, they do not operate in isolation from or independently of environmental (psychological) forces. The most tenable view at this time is that biological and environmental factors interact with one another to cause disorders. It seems reasonable to propose a continuum of biological causes ranging from minor, undetectable, organic faults to profound accidents of nature and a related continuum of emotional or behavioral disorders, ranging from mild to profound, to which these biological accidents contribute. Implications of biological factors for the day-to-day work of teachers may in some cases be nil, but teachers should be aware of possible biological causes and refer students to other professionals when appropriate. Teachers should be aware of the possible effects and side effects of psychotropic medications and be involved in monitoring drug effects.

CASE FOR DISCUSSION

She Goes On and On
Elizabeth

Sometimes I go on and on when I talk, and people have a hard time understanding what I am talking about. My family is always saying to me, "You're going on and on." This is supposed to be a clue to me to stop talking, or that nobody is understanding what I am talking about. My brother says that nobody wants to hear all the things I have to say, but brothers talk that way to sisters all the time.

Actually that was one of the first clues my doctor had as to what was wrong with me. I had lots of problems, but they didn't have a name. My first psychiatrist thought I had attention deficit disorder because I had so much trouble paying attention and getting my work done. But one time when I was going on and on, my mother said that the listener had to share the experience with me to be able to understand what I was talking about, and even then it was hard. My doctor said that was a serious symptom and then he asked if I was hearing voices. When I said yes, he said I needed to be hospitalized for evaluation, and that was a very serious problem. My parents were scared out of their wits.

I still go on and on. I have trouble writing too. I leave words out of sentences, or I don't finish writing a word. Then, of course, the sentences don't make any sense. Sometimes my sentences get really long. I guess I go on and on in writing too. I cannot write more than one or two paragraphs because I get really confused.

Source: This case is taken from Anonymous (1994), p. 589.

Questions About the Case

1. Imagine that Elizabeth is in your 10th-grade class. Would knowing that she has schizophrenia and is taking medication for it make a difference in how you respond to her going on and on? If not, why not? If so, how?

2. As her teacher, what strategies might you try to help Elizabeth learn to converse more normally (i.e., not to go on and on)?

3. If Elizabeth were a student in a regular 10th-grade class, how would you help her classmates respond kindly and helpfully to her when she goes on and on?

Biological Factors

Richard E. Mattison, M.D., is professor of (child) psychiatry and director of school consultation in the Department of Psychiatry and Behavioral Science at the State University of New York at Stony Brook.

What emotional or behavioral disorders have a known biological cause?

Although science is progressively learning the neurobiology of psychiatric disorders, most causes are still to be determined. Advances in methodologies to study the brain have brought us a long way from early observations that stimulated research into brain-disorder connections, such as the observed association of frontal lobe injuries with rages, impulsivity, decreased cognitive function, mood dyscontrol, reduced attention, loss of social skills, or all of these symptoms. The general neurobiology of several psychiatric disorders has now been outlined, especially the important brain regions and neurotransmitters.

The majority of child and adolescent diagnoses that occur most commonly in special education students classified with emotional or behavioral disorders (EBDs) have candidate brain regions or systems, neurotransmitters, or genes. For example, for the most frequent disorder in these students, attention deficit–hyperactivity disorder (ADHD), converging studies point to the frontal lobe and the basal ganglia of the brain as primary candidate regions, which are rich in the neurotransmitter dopamine. In turn, suspect single genes have been identified that affect dopamine neurotransmission, although a polygenic (multiple genes) solution will be the probable outcome, as is likely in most psychiatric disorders. However, these guideposts represent only an early stage in deciphering the complex neurobiology of this disorder.

Advances in the study of the brain from several disciplines have contributed to our progressive understanding of the neurobiology of psychiatric disorders, at times in ways that might surprise EBD teachers. Most impressive have been the contributions from brain imaging. First, magnetic resonance imaging (MRI) allowed scientists to identify structural differences in greater detail between children with and without a specific psychiatric disorder. More recently, functional MRI (fMRI) has shown differences

between such groups of children in the real-time metabolism of brain systems (interconnected regions) that operate as children perform carefully designed tasks that represent specific brain functions. Thus, "malfunctioning" brain regions or systems are gradually being identified, which can then be investigated for a variety of causative factors. Potential etiologies for such deficits might include structural or neuronal damage from some trauma during prenatal neurodevelopment, as well as genetic defects that disrupt the production of neurotransmitters. Or, intriguingly, neuroscience has also begun to show that environmental experiences may skew the neurobiology of brain function. For example, abuse has been demonstrated to affect the underlying neurobiology of children's stress response, which can in part explain much of the clinical picture that EBD teachers observe in many of their students who have been physically abused.

This advanced understanding of the neurobiology of psychiatric disorders has also led to treatment discoveries with interesting implications for EBD teachers. For example, obsessive-compulsive disorder (OCD) is especially associated with dysfunction in the right caudate nucleus. When a person with OCD takes a selective serotonin reuptake inhibitor (SSRI) medication such as fluoxetine (i.e., Prozac), brain imaging shows that the abnormal hypermetabolism of that brain area decreases. Moreover, the same neuroradiological improvement also occurs after a course of specific behavioral therapy. Thus, brain change in this disorder is accomplished directly by medication and indirectly by a psychotherapeutic intervention. Not surprisingly, more lasting improvement often results from a combination of both therapies. Such findings will quite likely hold true for a variety of disorders in students with EBDs: Not only will therapeutic brain changes require medication, but such changes will also be dependent on consistent cognitive-behavioral intervention by their teachers.

Thus, as science has begun to establish the neurobiology of brain function and thereby psychiatric disorders, our understanding of nature–nurture interaction has also matured. EBD teachers may at one time have been leery that the discovery of neurobiological causes for emotional and behavioral disorders would lead to biological treatments that would make their work less relevant. In fact, much the opposite is being found.

What are the most important signs that a child's parents should be encouraged to obtain a neurological examination or consider medication?

Parents should not initially worry whether their child has problems that may require a neurological examination or medication, which may unfortunately deter them from seeking necessary help. Rather, the first step a parent should take if they are concerned that their child may have a behavioral or emotional disorder is to honestly consider how much dysfunction the child is experiencing with family or friends or at school—is he or she suffering or are other people around him suffering during their interaction with the child? If the answer is yes, then an evaluation should be sought.

Parents who have reached this conclusion should begin with an evaluation by a clinician who specializes in such disorders or, at the least, talk to their pediatrician or family doctor. That professional can then determine whether a neurological examination is necessary, which primarily occurs if there is very noteworthy history like an unusual headache pattern for the child or deterioration of already acquired skills, for example, loss of language or motor abilities. Children with most psychiatric disorders rarely require neurological examinations—a review of their medical and neurological history by the clinician will usually suffice. However, a more intensive medical and neurological investigation is appropriate for a few uncommon child psychiatric disorders, such as autism and psychosis.

Similarly, a parent need not initially consider whether their child has a condition that requires medication. Such a discussion should take place after the evaluation. Even if a parent seeks initial evaluation for their child's psychopathology with a nonphysician clinician, at the end of the evaluation the parents should expect the mental health professional's diagnosis or explanation for the child's psychopathology and if or when medication might be indicated. In this day and age, all clinicians should be quite proficient at addressing such questions since medications are indicated for several child psychiatric disorders, either as an initial treatment component or as a subsequent addition if nonmedication therapy is not successful.

If a parent is concerned that their child has ADHD and may require a medication, then the parent should contact a physician in their community who specializes in treating such children. Such a referral can be gained from the family doctor or pediatrician, or often schools or parent groups such as CHADD will know which doctors in the community treat ADHD children well. When medication is indicated for non-ADHD psychiatric disorders, especially where depression, anxiety, or anger outbursts are severe or chronic, then a parent may wish to seek further evaluation or consultation by a child psychiatrist, that is, the specialist with the widest knowledge and experience of medications used for child or adolescent psychiatric disorders. If indicated, the child psychiatrist may begin an initial prescription and establish a beneficial dosage, with the plan that the medicine can subsequently be prescribed and monitored by the child's pediatrician with consultation backup, if the psychiatrist and pediatrician are both comfortable that this is within the pediatrician's ability. Such consultation arrangements are common because the various pediatric specialists are usually few in number; for example, the number of practicing child psychiatrists in our nation is fewer than 8,000.

Finally, parents should realize that in most cases medication is only part of the treatment plan. Medications do not cure child psychiatric disorders, but at this point only stabilize their symptoms. At a minimum, parents will require thorough education about the disorder and practical understanding of how to handle typical accompanying problems. Furthermore, parents of EBD students should expect that combination treatment is especially necessary for their children who usually have complicated, serious, or chronic disorders.

If a student is taking medication, what are the responsibilities of the teacher?

During their training, EBD teachers should be taught an appropriate working knowledge of psychiatric disorders, including medications that are commonly used for specific disorders and both the positive effects that can be expected from specific medications as well as the most common side effects. For example, if a parent or a community physician informs a teacher that a student is being started on an SSRI for a depressive disorder, then the teacher should be able to monitor depressive symptomology in school for change. The teacher should be aware that no positive effect may be observed for 2 or more weeks with SSRIs. Finally, worsening irritability or agitation should be reported to the parent or doctor immediately, as should any abrupt reversal of mood toward silliness.

When an EBD teacher first meets the parent(s) of a new student, the teacher should make clear that he or she wishes to help any community therapist or physician who evaluates or treats the child by supplying observations about the student's functioning in school. If the new child is currently receiving treatment, then the teacher should have the parent sign a consent form (established by the special education agency) for the teacher to provide information to the community professional. If the community clinician does not contact the teacher after the student's next appointment to request information in some form, then the teacher should contact the professional to initiate collaboration.

I realize this view is aggressive. However, students with EBDs will very frequently require medication(s) as part of their overall treatment plan for their common ADHD, depressive, or conduct (aggressive) disorders. Furthermore, they often have comorbid disorders that additionally complicates medication decision making, and once they are on more than one medication (polypharmacy) the issue of side effects mimicking symptoms increases. Therefore, EBD teachers can increase the chances that their students are on the best possible regimen of medication by proactively ensuring that prescribing physicians (both psychiatrists and nonpsychiatrist physicians) have sufficient school data to make well-informed medication decisions. Otherwise, in my experience as well as the literature, community physicians will too often make medicine decisions with no input from teachers, or with only feedback about school from parents who may not be sufficiently aware of their child's true status at school.

The most common method that prescribing physicians use to gain information from teachers is behavior checklists (both general and specific). Such instruments can objectively supplement differential diagnosis and outcome assessment, and can provide effective communication (to replace phone tag). The more working knowledge that teachers have about a student's diagnosis and prescribed medication, the more helpful they can be with their ratings and also through their written comments, which are typically encouraged at the end of such instruments. If a teacher is not contacted about a student, I would encourage her or him to mail to the treating clinician a preselected general behavior checklist (chosen with the help of the school psychologist or psychiatric consultant).

Finally, EBD teachers should be able to work appropriately with parents about medication. Parents are more likely to ask the EBD teacher about medication ("Is it necessary?" and "Is it working?") than the doctor treating their child because they often have a more established relationship with the teacher. As part of their professional role, EBD teachers should also be able to raise with parents the issue of diagnoses that may need medication. Their handling of such situations can be crucial to a student's progress. If a teacher does not feel adequately trained to deal with such parental interaction, he or she should refer such questions to the family's doctor or psychiatrist, or seek coaching from a consultant psychiatrist on how to answer such questions most constructively.

Are there other points you would like to make about the topic?

My career has offered me a unique viewpoint. I am a child psychiatrist with a "minor" in special education. Both my clinical and research careers have focused on students with EBD. As a school consultant to EBD staffs, I have continually dealt with making psychiatric knowledge relevant and practical for special educators. They have taught me much about this issue, which has greatly influenced my answers to the preceding questions.

As a researcher, I have investigated characteristics of students with EBDs from a modern psychiatric perspective, their function and outcome over time in EBD classes, and predictors of their educational outcome. I have been adapting methodology from my research training in child psychiatry, and simultaneously I have become conversant in techniques used by EBD researchers. Most striking to me is how both fields avoid the other, like the proverbial two ships passing in the night, despite the growing relevancy of one for the other.

Consequently, I would also point out that, much as advances in the neurobiology of brain function and psychiatric disorders have increased meaning and implications for EBD teachers (as I have already described), the same holds true for EBD researchers. Thus, they must more actively determine what advances need to become more common research variables in their work. For example, they could ask such questions as: What psychiatric diagnosis, medication use, or environmental stresses affect children's neurobiological function? Also, EBD researchers should increasingly both design and participate in collaborative research with allied disciplines, to which they must more aggressively contribute their invaluable expertise about student function in school, combined with their skills at objective observation and specific intervention plans. Otherwise, the situation is much as I've described between community physicians and EBD teachers. For example, a child psychiatrist researcher who is examining the effect of a new medication or combination therapy may either not measure school function or not do it adequately. The participation of a well-trained EBD researcher could make the difference in whether or not the true effectiveness of the intervention is ascertained. Unfortunately, this situation is an ongoing problem in medication research for non-ADHD disorders.

Furthermore, teachers will increasingly look toward researchers and trainers of EBD teachers for guidance on how to incorporate neurobiological advances. Such progress by other disciplines can no longer be dismissed as irrelevant, nor can special education depend on other disciplines to make the case for such advances. Their value for EBD teachers must be translated by EBD researchers and trainers of teachers, and EBD researchers must more proactively help to set a collaborative research agenda that includes relevance for EBD teachers.

QUESTIONS FOR FURTHER REFLECTION

1. How can a teacher best stay abreast of developments in brain imaging and medication?
2. What are the greatest advantages and disadvantages of medication for emotional or behavioral disorders?
3. How should knowledge of a biological cause of a student's behavior affect the way you work with that student as a teacher?

SECTION 10
FAMILY FACTORS

As you read this section, keep these guiding questions in mind:

- What are the implications of an interactional–transactional model of family influence for families with abused children?

- How could one characterize the most and least desirable types of parental discipline?

- What is a negative reinforcement trap?

- How are coercive family interactions related to the development of antisocial behavior?

- How can parents foster school success or school failure?

APPEAL OF FAMILY FACTORS AS CAUSAL EXPLANATIONS

When youngsters misbehave, a natural tendency may be to blame parental misman-agement or family disintegration. Given the primacy of family relations in children's social development, it is understandable that we have sought the origins of emotional and behavioral disorders in the structure, composition, and interactions of family units. These elements do not, however, provide a straightforward recipe for predict-ing emotional or behavioral disorders. Like other causal factors, those related to the family are complex and influenced by genetic factors as well as a wide variety of envi-ronmental events (Pinker, 2002; Plomin, 1995). We must guard against adopting facile explanations of "familial determinants" of emotional and behavioral disorders and rely instead on those factors that researchers have reliably identified as predictors of child psychopathology.

Family characteristics appear to predict emotional and behavioral development only in complex interactions with other factors, such as socioeconomic status, sources of support outside the family, and the child's age, sex, and temperamental characteristics. The concept of *risk* is important here: The idea is that in examining causal factors we are dealing with probabilities and that particular events or condi-tions may increase the probability that there will be a particular outcome for the child, such as an emotional or behavioral disorder. When several risk factors occur together—for example, poverty, parental antisocial behavior, community violence, and difficult temperament—their effects are not merely additive but multiplicative, more than doubling the probability that a child will develop a disorder. If a third fac-tor is added, the chance of disorder is several times higher yet (Garmezy, 1987; Quinn & McDougal, 1998; Seeley, Rohde, Lewinsohn, & Clarke, 2002).

Rutter's reviews of research on maternal deprivation (1979) and attachment (1995) and Plomin's (1995) and Pinker's (2002) reviews of the role of genetics in chil-dren's experiences in the family highlight some of the complexities in family influ-ences. For example, it is not always the case that separation of the child from one or both parents impairs a child's psychological and behavioral development. In an intact family, parental discord may exert a more pernicious influence than parental separa-tion. A good relationship with one parent may sustain a child, even in the face of parental discord or separation. The interaction of the child's constitutional or tem-peramental characteristics with parental behavior may be more important than parental separation or disharmony. In addition, factors outside the home (school, for instance) may lessen or heighten the negative influence of family factors.

For some reason, some children do not succumb to extreme disruption or disin-tegration of their families. We do not know precisely why some children are vulnera-ble and others invulnerable to negative family influences. A positive, or easy, child temperament (recall our discussion of temperament in section 9) and maternal warmth appear to be factors that may heighten resilience, but these factors may be insufficient to buffer children against psychopathology in violent families (McCloskey, Figueredo, & Koss, 1995). Research also suggests that high cognitive skills, curiosity, enthusiasm, ability to set goals for oneself, and high self-esteem are associated with resilience (Hanson & Carta, 1996). Many intervention programs now focus on reducing risk factors and fostering resilient behaviors in at-risk children (Beardslee, Versage, Van de Velde, Swatling, & Hoke, 2002; Olsson, Bond, Burns, Vella-Brodrick, & Sawyer, 2003; Place, Reynolds, Cousins, & O'Neill, 2002).

Conversely, we know that certain features of family relationships, especially parental deviance and discord, harsh and unpredictable parental discipline, and lack of emotional support, increase children's risk for developing emotional or behavioral disorders (Reid & Eddy, 1997). Yet a family environment that creates high risk does not necessarily cause a child to have a disorder. Causation is more complex than that (see the cases of Sylvain and Jack in the accompanying case book for illustrations of family involvement in emotional and behavioral disorders).

The concept of *heightened risk,* as opposed to a simple cause–effect relationship, is important in disordered behavior. What happens in families in which risk of emotional or behavioral disorder is high? We can answer this question in general terms, but we cannot make confident predictions of outcomes for individual children for two reasons. First, each child is affected individually by the family environment. A younger, more compliant child may experience her family quite differently than her older, more disobedient brother. Second, whether life circumstances or environmental conditions are positive or negative for a child, and whether they heighten or reduce the child's risk of emotional or behavioral disorders, depends on the processes involved. Processes or mechanisms—not merely the presence of risk variables but how children cope with degrees and patterns of exposure to those variables—determine how vulnerable or resilient a child will be. The shared family context simply does not offer uniform experiences to all children in the family (Jenkins, Rasbash, & O'Connor, 2003; Pinker, 2002).

We understand little about the processes involved in producing vulnerability and resilience, but a key ingredient for each individual appears to be the pattern, sequence, and intensity of exposure to stressful circumstances. We do know that the accumulation of stressful life events is an important factor in determining how a child will be able to cope. Stressful life events may occur within the family, but they are related to the larger social environment in which the family itself must function as a unit. Therefore, it is important to consider both the interpersonal transactions that occur between the child and other family members and the external pressures on the family that may affect those interactions.

Whereas the research of 30 years ago tended to focus on the general processes thought to be the basis for the development of child psychopathology, recent research has examined more specific, focused interactions that may contribute to causing or exacerbating emotional or behavioral disorders (Dadds, 2002). The empirical evidence increasingly points to *social learning* as the basis for many emotional and behavioral disorders; research suggests that parental *modeling, reinforcement,* and *punishment* of specific types of behavior hold the keys to how families influence children's behavioral development. For example, researchers have documented that children who demonstrate high levels of anxiety often have families in which caution and avoidance are modeled and reinforced (Dadds, 2002). In such instances parents may reward avoidance of risk and social disengagement and thereby foster the development and expression of fear and anxiety.

Evidence from longitudinal studies increasingly points to families as critical factors, but not the only factors in the development of antisocial and delinquent behavior. In a sample of approximately 1,500 boys, Loeber, Farrington, Stouthamer-Loeber, and Van Kammen (1998a) found a correlation between early onset of behavioral problems and deviant parental behavior. However, these authors also argued that such findings demonstrated a clear need for interventions aimed at introducing protective factors in the lives of these at-risk youth. Thus, familial factors may be critical, but they are not sufficiently powerful to set a child's fate.

The structure and interaction patterns in families clearly influence children's success or failure at school and, ultimately, in life. In turn, family interactions may be shaped by external influences; we consider in particular the potentially powerful influences of factors such as poverty and parental employment. We also discuss the implications for educators of what we know about families, especially families of children with emotional or behavioral disorders. The scope and complexity of family-related research are enormous, however, and we reiterate that this overview highlights only a few dimensions of this complex topic and only scratches the surface of this vast literature.

FAMILY DEFINITION AND STRUCTURE

Although the intact mother–father–children concept of family remains the ideal for many in mainstream American culture, a variety of diverse family forms fit the realities of contemporary life. The essential functions of families are to

- Provide care and protect children
- Regulate and control children's behavior
- Convey knowledge and skills important for understanding and coping with the physical and social worlds
- Give affective meaning to interactions and relationships
- Facilitate children's self-understanding

Regardless of how families define themselves, the key elements of the definition of family are that "the members of the unit see themselves as a family, are affiliated with one another, and are committed to caring for one another" (Hanson & Lynch, 1992, p. 285). Given these considerations, it may be important to examine whether or to what extent family structure affects children's behavior.

The effects of family size and birth order on behavioral development have been studied extensively, but such elements of family configuration are far outweighed by factors related to divorce and other circumstances resulting in single-parent homes or other nontraditional family structures (Zigler & Finn-Stevenson, 1997). Family composition or configuration may have an effect on children's behavior, but other factors involving interactions among family members and the social contexts in which they live appear to be far more important contributors to behavior problems than family structure alone. However, we briefly examine the effects of single-parent families and substitute care (e.g., foster care, adoption, care by relatives other than parents) on children's behavior.

Single-Parent Families

A substantial proportion of children are now reared in single-parent families, usually because of divorce but also often because of out-of-wedlock births or military assignment. Census data from the year 2000 indicated that nearly one fourth of U.S. families with children under the age of 18 were headed by single parents. Thus, we must ask whether the presence of only one parent in a family puts children at risk for emotional or behavioral disorders. We begin by considering the effects of divorce on children's behavior.

Divorce is traumatic, not only for parents and children but also for extended family and friends. The lasting psychological pain and fear felt by many children whose parents divorce are well known (Bolgar, Zweig-Frank, & Paris, 1995; Wallerstein, 1987). Yet overwhelming evidence shows that most children adjust to divorce and go on with their lives without developing chronic emotional or behavioral problems. "Most children manifest some disturbances—often a combination of anger, anxiety, depression, dependency, and noncompliance—in thé immediate aftermath of divorce; however, most children and adults also recover and adjust to their new life situation by about three years after divorce" (Hetherington & Martin, 1986, p. 340).

How children adjust to divorce depends on factors beyond family dissolution. These factors are numerous and include concerns such as the child's age when the divorce occurs, characteristics of the custodial parent, and the child's cognitive and affective characteristics related to coping with stress (see Johnson, 1986; Zigler & Finn-Stevenson, 1997). There is no general formula for predicting child psychopathology following divorce, but it is clear that many children and adolescents whose parents are divorced have lower scholastic aptitude, perform less well in school, and have less confidence in their academic abilities than do youngsters from intact families (Watt, Moorehead-Slaughter, Japzon, & Keller, 1990).

The absence of fathers in homes and families is a distressing feature of contemporary life, particularly as it affects African Americans (see King, 1999). Boys in families headed by mothers alone may be at risk for developing aggressive behavior (Vaden-Kiernan, Ialongo, Pearson, & Kellam, 1995). Among the family configurations found by Achenbach et al. (1991) to be significantly related to higher behavioral problem ratings of children were "fewer adults in the household; more unrelated adults in the household; parents who were separated, divorced, or never married to each other" (p. 92). These findings are of concern, but far more important are the conditions accompanying a household headed by a single parent, which is typically the mother.

Economic hardship or impoverishment carry a number of attendant deprivations, including higher levels of parental substance abuse or criminality, interpersonal conflict and violence, and lack of parental supervision and nurturing. These factors appear to shape children's behavior significantly, regardless of whether the family contains one parent or two (Baumrind, 1995; Ellwood & Stolberg, 1993). Rutter (1995) noted

> Early writings on the risks associated with parental divorce and family break-up focused on the role of "loss" because that had received such an emphasis in early writings on attachment. Empirical findings have made clear, however, that the main

risks do not stem from loss as such but rather from the discordant and disrupted relationships that tend to precede or follow the loss. . . . Loss is a risk indicator but it is not the major player in most risk mechanisms. (pp. 563–564)

Substitute Care

Children in foster care and those living with relatives who are not their parents appear to be at high risk for emotional or behavioral disorders and school-related problems (Pilowsky, 1995; Smucker, Kauffman, & Ball, 1996; Stein, Raegrant, Ackland, & Avison, 1994). Sheehan's (1993a, 1993b) description of foster care in New York City provides graphic details about the stresses many foster children and foster parents face. Researchers are only beginning to examine the specific nature of stress and strain on nonparental caregivers of students with identified emotional or behavioral disorders (e.g., Taylor-Richardson, Heflinger, & Brown, 2006).

Some children are placed in substitute care because of the death or incapacitation of their parents, but the great majority—and an increasing percentage—are placed under the care of the child protection system because of their parents' neglect and abuse. Virtually never are children placed in any form of substitute care unless they have suffered trauma that is highly likely to result in at least short-term emotional or behavioral problems (except in the case of adopted infants). Abused children are known to have more behavioral problems than those who are not maltreated (Feldman et al., 1995). Yet much remains unknown about why and how children are placed in protective care.

A major problem in providing substitute care is finding or training caregivers who are highly motivated and skilled in child rearing. Many foster parents have little or no training for the task, and few are well trained in dealing with difficult children. Although long-term foster care has demonstrated positive outcomes (Minty, 1999; Reddy & Pfeiffer, 1997), many foster children are placed for short periods in many different foster homes, and the risk for negative behavioral and emotional outcomes appears to increase with the number of different placements (see Smucker et al., 1996). The lack of stability, continuity, attachment, and nurturing that goes with numerous foster placements and unskilled foster parents is likely to promote emotional or behavioral disorders (Clark et al., 1994).

Adoptive families, like biological families, have a variety of structures. The influence of adoptive families on children's emotional and behavioral development can be predicted to parallel the influence of biological families. Controversy sometimes arises regarding the adequacy of adoption by single parents or adoptive families that involve differences in sexual orientation (e.g., gay fathers or lesbian mothers) or differences in the color or ethnicity of children and parents (e.g., Caucasian parents adopting children of color). Here, too, we might expect familial determinants to function as they do in any other family structure. For example, Tasker and Golombok (1995) found that being raised by a lesbian mother did not necessarily cause children to be maladjusted or to become gay or lesbian.

Research clearly suggests that family form by itself has relatively little affect on children's emotional and behavioral development. Although children reared in single-parent families may be at heightened risk, the risk factors appear to be conditions associated with a single-parent family structure, not single parenting itself. Being reared by substitutes for one's biological parents may be associated with heightened risk but only insofar as abuse, neglect, or other traumatic circumstances affect children before they are removed from their biological parents or after they enter foster care. In short, family structure is far less important than what happens in the family—the interactions among family members—regardless of how the family is constituted.

FAMILY INTERACTION

When we think of family factors, our tendency is to ask: What kinds of families produce children with emotional or behavioral disorders? However, it is also reasonable to ask: What kinds of families do children with emotional or behavioral disorders produce?

Child developmentalists now realize that children's influence on their parents' behavior is significant in determining family interactions. A child from a broken family may well exhibit behavioral characteristics that would break nearly any family (see Pinker, 2002). Researchers found decades ago that undesirable parenting behavior and negative family interactions are in part a reaction of family members to a deviant youngster (e.g., Bell, 1968; Bell & Harper, 1977; Martin, 1981; Patterson, 1982, 1986a, 1986b; Patterson, Reid, & Dishion, 1992; Reid & Eddy, 1997; Sameroff & Chandler, 1975). Reciprocity of influence can be observed from the earliest parent–child interactions, strengthening and manifesting in all subsequent interactions. This dynamic is especially evident in child management and child abuse.

Child Management

Parental management or discipline comes up as a topic in almost every discussion of children's emotional or behavioral disorders. We shall return to family interactions as potential causal factors in each of the section. Here, we review general findings on parental management of children but focus on the role of family interactions in causing the disorder people usually consider first in discussions of family factors: the impulsive, aggressive, acting-out behavior generally known as *conduct disorder*. In fact, we know more about the effects of parental discipline on disruptive, oppositional, aggressive behavior than we do about the effects of parental behavior on children's anxiety, fear, and depression (Ehrensaft et al., 2003; O'Leary, 1995).

The effects of discipline techniques are complex and not highly predictable without considering both the parents' and the child's general behavioral characteristics and ongoing stress in the family. Nevertheless, we can suggest some general guidelines for discipline that can help parents avoid the types of interactions that research strongly suggests are mistakes, and these principles may hold across all cultural groups. For example, O'Leary (1995) identified three types of mistakes typically made by mothers of 2- to 4-year-old children: laxness, overreactivity, and verbosity. "Laxness includes giving in, not enforcing rules, and providing positive reinforcement for misbehavior. Overreactivity includes anger, meanness, and irritability. Verbosity involves the propensity to engage in lengthy verbal interactions about misbehavior even when the talking is ineffective" (O'Leary, 1995, p. 12). Parents can be very "nice" to their children but ineffective in discipline because they are unable or unwilling to set consistent, firm, unambiguous limits. These parents may use long, delayed, gentle (but imprudent) reprimands that actually make the child's behavior worse. Others may make the mistake of using harsh reprimands for misbehavior, but paying little attention to the child when he or she is behaving well.

Baumrind (1995) reviewed what decades of research on parental discipline in nonabusive middle-class families has shown (see also Campbell, 1995; Stichter et al., 2008). Researchers describe two primary dimensions of discipline: *responsiveness* (which involves warmth, reciprocity, and attachment) and *demandingness* (involving monitoring, firm control, and positive and negative consequences for behavior). Parents who provide optimal management of their children are both highly responsive and highly demanding; they are highly invested in their children (Baumrind, 1996). More specifically, parents who discipline most effectively are sensitive to their children's needs, empathic, and attentive. They establish a pattern of mutually positive, reciprocal interactions with their children, and their warmth and reciprocity form the basis for emotional attachment or adult–child bonding. These parents are also demanding of their children. They monitor their children's behavior, providing appropriately close supervision for the child's age. They confront their children's misbehavior directly and firmly rather than attempting to manipulate or coerce their children. They provide unambiguous instructions and demands in a firm but nonhostile manner and consistently follow through with negative but nonabusive consequences for misbehavior. They provide positive reinforcement in the form of praise, approval, encouragement, and other rewards for their children's desirable behavior.

Parental discipline that is both demanding and responsive is sometimes referred to as *authoritative* (as opposed to *authoritarian* discipline, which is demandingness without responsiveness) and is typically found to have the best effects on children's behavioral development. Researchers have even found a relationship between authoritative parenting and decreased tobacco and alcohol usage among children and youth, decreased violence among adolescents, and decreased levels of anger and alienation among middle-school students (Adamczyk-Robinette, Fletcher, & Wright, 2002; Jackson, Henriksen, & Foshee, 1998). Authoritative discipline balances what is asked of the child with what is offered to the child, and this balance may be the key characteristic of effective parental discipline in various cultures (Abrams, 1995). It may be, in fact, the key to effective discipline by all caretakers of children, but it is not the pattern of interaction typically found in families of children who exhibit antisocial behavior.

The work of Patterson and his colleagues gives insight into the characteristics of interactions in the families of antisocial youngsters (Patterson, 1973, 1980, 1982, 1986a, 1986b; Patterson, Reid, Jones, & Conger, 1975; Patterson et al., 1992; Reid & Eddy, 1997). His research group's methods involve direct observation of parents' and children's behavior in the home, revealing an identifiable family pattern. They show that interaction in families with aggressive children is characterized by exchange of negative, hostile behaviors, whereas the interaction in families with nonaggressive children tends to be mutually positive and gratifying for parents and children. In families with aggressive children, not only do the children behave in ways that are highly irritating and aversive to their parents, but also the parents rely primarily on aversive methods (hitting, shouting, threatening, and so forth) to control their children. Thus, children's aggression in the family seems both to produce counteraggression and to be produced by punitive parenting techniques.

Decades ago, Patterson (1980) studied mutually aversive interactions between mothers and children, and his findings have not been overturned by new data (go to www.oslc.org to see many research citations and reports of research at the Oregon Social Learning Center). Patterson's research group focused on families of aggressive children and found that many of the undesirable behaviors are maintained by negative reinforcement. *Negative reinforcement* involves escape from or avoidance of an unpleasant condition, which is rewarding (negatively reinforcing) because it brings relief from psychological or physical pain or anxiety.

An example of negative reinforcement in mother–child interactions is shown in Table 10.1. Patterson calls these interactions *negative reinforcement traps* because they set the stage for greater conflict and coercion; each person in the trap tends to reciprocate the other's aversive behavior and to escalate attempts to use *coercion*—controlling someone by negative reinforcement. Patterson and his colleagues have found that, unlike normal children, children with conduct problems tend to increase their disruptive behavior in response to parental punishment. Predictably, therefore,

Table 10.1 Some Reinforcement Traps

Negative Reinforcement Arrangement			
Neutral Antecedent:	**Time Frame 1**	**Time Frame 2**	**Time Frame 3**
Behavior:	**Mother ("clean your room")**	**Child (whine)**	**Mother (stops asking)**
	Short-Term Effect		Long-Term Effect
Mother	The pain (child's Whine) stops		Mother will be more likely to give in when child whines
Child	The pain (mother's Nag) stops		Given a messy room, mother less likely to ask him to clean it up in the future
Overall	The room was not cleaned		Child more likely to use whine to turn off future requests to clean room

Explanation: The child's room is messy, an aversive condition for the mother. When the mother asks the child to clean the room, the child whines. The child's whining is painfully aversive to the mother, so the mother stops asking or nagging. The mother's nagging is painfully aversive to the child, who finds that his or her whining will stop the mother's nagging. In the short run, both mother and child escape pain—child stops whining and the mother stops nagging—but the child's room is not cleaned. In the long run, the mother avoids asking the child to clean the room, and the child learns to use whining to stop the mother's nagging. Both mother and child are negatively reinforced by the avoidance of or escape from aversive consequences. However, the problem condition (the messy room) still exists as potential source of future negative interactions.

Source: Patterson, G. R. (1980). Mothers: The unacknowledged victims. *Monographs of the Society for Research in Child Development, 45*(5, Serial No. 186), 5. (c) 1980 by the University of Chicago Press. Reprinted by permission.

the families of aggressive children seem to foster undesirable child behavior—to encourage and even teach the very behavior they find problematic.

In effect, the members of families with aggressive children "train" each other to be aggressive. Although the major training occurs in transactions between an aggressive child and parent(s), it spills over to include siblings. Patterson (1986b) reported that siblings of an aggressive child are no more aggressive toward their parents than are children in families without an aggressive child. Interactions between siblings in families of antisocial youngsters, however, are more aggressive than those in families without an aggressive child. Coercive exchanges between aggressive children and their parents appear to teach siblings to be coercive with each other. Not surprisingly, these children then tend to be more aggressive in other social contexts, such as school. In fact, school conflict and school failure are frequently associated with antisocial behavior at home (cf. Kazdin, 1998; Kerr & Nelson, 2006; Patterson, 1986b; Stevenson-Hinde, Hinde, & Simpson, 1986; Walker, Ramsey, & Gresham, 2004).

It is difficult to delineate the development of overt behavioral disorders; however, the model emerging from Patterson's research group suggests that they arise from "failure by parents to effectively punish garden-variety, coercive behaviors" (Patterson, 1986b, p. 436). The child begins winning battles with the parents, and parents become increasingly punitive but ineffective in responding to coercion. Coercive exchanges escalate in number and intensity, increasing sometimes to hundreds per day and progressing from whining, yelling, and temper tantrums to hitting and other forms of physical assault. The child continues to win a high percentage of the battles with parents; parents continue to use ineffective punishment, setting the stage for another round of conflict. This coercive family process may occur in concert with other conditions associated with high risk for psychopathology: social and economic disadvantage, substance abuse, and a variety of other stressors such as parental discord and separation or divorce. During the process, the child receives little or no parental warmth and is often rejected by peers. School failure is another typical concomitant of the process. Understandably, the child usually develops a poor self-image (Patterson & Capaldi, 1990).

Patterson's suggestion that parents of aggressive children do not punish their children effectively does not mean he believes punishment should be the focus of parental discipline. Instead, his work suggests that parents need to set clear limits for children's behavior, provide a warm and loving home environment, provide positive attention and approval for appropriate behavior, and follow through with nonhostile and nonphysical punishment for coercive conduct.

Patterson and other researchers have shown that the pattern of coercive exchanges characterizing families of antisocial children can be identified early (e.g., Reid & Eddy, 1997; Shaw & Winslow, 1997). In addition, these and other findings suggest that children with conduct disorders are at risk from an early age, partly because they are infants with difficult temperaments and have parents who may lack coping skills (cf. Campbell, 1995; Kazdin, 1998; Nelson, Stage, Duppong-Hurley, Synhorst, & Epstein, 2007; Patterson, 1986b). For children demonstrating disordered behaviors, inconsistent discipline and family conflict often become the norm. Although data do not support the conclusion that punitive parents cause their children to become aggressive—the relationship does not appear that direct—researchers have observed that parent education can, in some circumstances, modify children's aggression (Patterson et al., 1975, 1992; Reid, 1993; Serbin et al., 2002).

Child Abuse

We may now know something about how coercive interactions begin and are sustained in families of aggressive children and how parents sometimes provide ineffective or counterproductive discipline. However, we must not forget the old and repeatedly confirmed wisdom that "there are probably many routes to becoming a 'good parent' which vary with the personality of both the parents and children and with pressures in the environment with which one must learn to cope" (Becker, 1964, p. 202). When is ineffective child management abusive or neglectful? This question is not easily answered (Baumrind, 1997; Haugaard, 1992). Much depends on the developmental level of the child, specific circumstances, professional and legal judgments, and cultural norms. If there is a consensus about how to define *child abuse,* it likely is centered on parental behavior that seriously endangers or delays the normal development of the child (Baumrind, 1995; Cicchetti & Toth, 1995; Janko, 1994; Widom, 1997). Azar and Wolfe (1998) suggested that for treatment purposes, child abuse and neglect be defined "in terms of the *degree to which a parent uses aversive or inappropriate control strategies with his or her child and/or fails to provide minimal standards of caregiving and nurturance*" (p. 502, italics in original).

Given the difficulty in defining *abuse,* it is not surprising that reliable estimates of child abuse and family violence are difficult to find (Cicchetti & Toth, 1995). Nevertheless, without belaboring the issue, we may conclude that family violence and child abuse—physical, psychological, and sexual—are problems of great magnitude; it very likely involves more than a million children per year in the United States (Azar & Wolfe, 1998; Baumrind, 1995; Cicchetti & Toth, 1995; Wolfe, 1998). Although abuse of all types is serious and has important sequelae, we focus our discussion here on physical abuse.

Most people give little thought to children's and parents' interactive effects on each other in cases of abuse. Child abuse is often seen as a problem of parental behavior alone, and intervention has often been directed only at changing parents' responses to their children. The *interactional–transactional model* considers abused children's influence on their parents and suggests that intervention deal directly with the abused child's undesirable behavior as well as with the parents' abusive responses (see Patterson, 1980, 1982; Walker et al., 2004; Zirpoli, 1986). This perspective is valuable even when the child is not initially an instigator of abuse but has been drawn into an abusive relationship and is exhibiting inappropriate behavior. Intervention typically needs to be directed toward the entire family and its social context (Baumrind, 1995; Janko, 1994; see also Reppucci, Britner, & Woodard, 1997).

One hypothesis about parent–child interaction in child abuse is that their children's responses to punishment inadvertently "teach" parents to become increasingly punitive (recall our prior discussion of how family members may train each other to be aggressive). For example, if the child exhibits behavior that is aversive to the parent (perhaps whining), the parent may punish the child (perhaps by slapping). If the punishment is successful and the child stops the aversive behavior, then the parent is negatively reinforced by the consequence; the parent is, in effect, rewarded by the child's stopping the aversive behavior. The next time the child whines, the parent is more likely to try slapping to get relief from the whining. If at first the child does not stop whining, the parent may slap harder or more often to try to make the child be quiet. Thus, the parent's punishment becomes increasingly harsh as a means of dealing with the child's increasingly aversive behavior. Although abusive parents are not usually successful in punishing their child, they continue to escalate punishment. They seem not to understand or be able to use alternative means of control. Although abused children suffer in the bargain, they often hold their own in the battle with their parents; they may stubbornly refuse to knuckle under to parental pressure. Parent and child are trapped in a mutually destructive, coercive cycle in which they cause and are caused physical or psychological pain (see Shaw & Winslow, 1997).

The negative reinforcement trap can escalate behavior to the level of abuse. Such a coercive struggle is characteristic of conduct disorder, and the developmental consequences for children are severe (Patterson et al., 1992; Walker et al., 2004). Moreover, if abuse is transmitted across generations, it is likely through such processes because children with conduct disorder are likely to become parents with antisocial behavior and poor child management skills. For example, Serbin et al. (2002) conducted a longitudinal study spanning approximately 25 years and documented that "the more aggressive a mother was as a child, the more aggressive her child was observed to be" (p. 57). Of course, such observations could also confirm genetic tendencies (see Pinker, 2002).

The conclusion that the child's behavior is always a reciprocal causal factor in an abusive relationship with a parent is not warranted, however. Abusive relationships are extremely varied, both in abusive behaviors and in abused–abuser relations. Sexual abuse in families, for example, takes many forms and may involve incestuous relationships between siblings, parent and child, or other family members (for example, stepparent or grandparent) and child. Because it is a social problem surrounded by many taboos, sexual abuse is a difficult, yet not impossible, topic to research. Existing research studies have failed to demonstrate that children contribute to their sexual victimizaton, particularly when the abused child is very young. A history of sexual abuse or observation of overt sexual behavior may cause some children to be sexually provocative, which may contribute to, but not cause, their further abuse.

Much has been written about the characteristics of abusive parents, and stereotypes abound. One stereotype is that they are socially isolated; another is that they themselves were abused as children; still another is that they are mentally ill. Although all three impressions hold for some cases, none is supported by research as an abusive parent prototype (cf. Baumrind, 1995; Thompson & Wilcox, 1995). Nevertheless, we can point to several psychological characteristics that frequently accompany abusive parenting. For example, abusive parents tend to exhibit deficits in empathy, role taking, impulse control, and self-esteem, and an external locus of control (Baumrind, 1995).

Children who are abused by their parents have been shown by research to be at risk for the full range of emotional and behavioral disorders, including both internalizing problems such as depression and externalizing problems such as conduct disorder (Cicchetti & Toth, 1995; Widom, 1997). Teachers, parents, and peers are all likely to see higher levels of behavioral problems in physically abused than in nonmaltreated children (Feldman et al., 1995). Bolger, Patterson, and Kupersmidt (1998) found that type of maltreatment was related to the nature of the child's maladjustment. For example, sexual abuse predicted low self-esteem, and emotional abuse predicted difficulties in peer relationships. The negative effects of abuse may be compounded further if the child already has an emotional or behavioral problem (Levendosky, Okun, & Parker, 1995).

In devising intervention programs for abused children and youth, it is important to recognize that their behavior may be directly related to family violence and that attempting merely to modify their behavior in school may be insufficient. Teachers, as well as others with responsibility for children's welfare, must report suspected abuse and work toward comprehensive services that meet all the student's needs. These individuals can play pivotal roles in cultivating the resilience of children suffering from abuse (Doyle, 2003).

FAMILY INFLUENCES ON SCHOOL SUCCESS AND FAILURE

Because the responsibility for children's learning is regularly delegated to schools, the family's contribution to school performance often plays a secondary role. Parents nevertheless contribute to or detract from their child's success at school in several ways: their expressed attitudes toward education, their own school experience, and their attitudes toward appropriate school-related behaviors, such as attending regularly, completing homework, reading, and studying. Gesten, Scher, and Cowen (1978) found long ago that "homes characterized by lack of educational stimulation appear to produce children who are prone to learning problems" (p. 254). In addition, the social training children receive at home may be an important factor in determining school success. Moreover, poor peer relations in school, especially rejection by peers, is highly predictive of academic problems (DeRosier, Kupersmidt, & Patterson, 1995; Reid & Eddy, 1997; Walker et al., 2004; Wentzel & Asher, 1995).

Parental discipline, parent–school relations, and parent–child relationships play important roles in school success and school failure. The authoritative parental discipline described previously (both responsive and demanding) is likely to support students' achievement (cf. Baumrind, 1995; Campbell, 1995; Rutter, 1995). Parents who are positively involved with their child's education tend to have youngsters who perform at a higher academic level. Conversely, families in which a coercive process is at work are likely to send students to school unprepared to comply with teachers' instructions, to complete homework assignments, or to relate well to their peers.

Unprepared for the demands of school, these students are virtually certain to fail to meet reasonable expectations for academic performance and social interaction (Patterson et al., 1992; Walker et al., 2004).

EXTERNAL PRESSURES AFFECTING FAMILIES

Family interactions are influenced by external conditions that put stress on parents and children. Poverty, unemployment, underemployment, homelessness, community violence—it is not surprising that these conditions influence the ability of families to cope from day to day, of parents to nurture children, and of children to behave well at home and perform well in school (Pungello, Kupersmidt, Burchinal, & Patterson, 1996; Walker et al., 2004). Homelessness affects not only entire families but, in some cases, adolescents alienated from their families, sometimes because of external influences that destroyed parent–child bonds.

Poverty is perhaps the most critical problem undermining families (see Fujiura & Yamaki, 2000). Severe economic hardship is known to be associated with abusive or neglectful parental behavior and children's maladaptive behavior (Achenbach et al., 1991; Bolger et al., 1998; Felner et al., 1995; Janko, 1994). Poverty often means that families live in inadequate or dangerous housing (if they are not homeless) in neighborhoods rife with substance abuse and violence. These neighborhood conditions often contribute to parents and children being victimized and to their feelings of inadequacy, depression, and hopelessness (DuRant, Getts, Cadenhead, Emans, & Woods, 1995).

Predictably, there is a substantial link between poverty and risk of disability (Fujiura & Yamaki, 2000). Neighborhoods characterized by low family income, high unemployment, transient populations, high concentrations of children living in single-parent families, and high rates of violence and substance abuse are places in which families are at high risk of dysfunction and disintegration, and children are at high risk for psychopathology and school failure (Fitzgerald, Davies, & Zucker, 2002). Violent victimization, whether by family members or others, puts children and youth at risk for emotional and behavioral disorders and school problems of wide variety. Furthermore, in communities characterized by danger of victimization, restrictive parenting may be adaptive (Jackson, 1995; Zayas, 1995).

A common misperception of poor families is that the parents typically are unemployed or uninterested in work. Although unemployment and lack of work skills are problems of a substantial percentage of poor parents, the majority of poor parents are workers. Parental unemployment is a stressor of enormous proportions, but parental employment that does not pay a decent wage is not far behind in its effects. Employment of both parents places stress on middle-class families and requires extraordinary parental efforts to provide adequate monitoring and nurturing for children, but when such employment does not allow the family to escape poverty, the stress is multiplied. Poverty and the social and personal problems stemming from it are issues our society must address more effectively if we wish to reduce family stress and child psychopathology (Freedman, 1993; Knitzer & Aber, 1995).

IMPLICATIONS FOR EDUCATORS

We must begin with a strong cautionary note. In their national survey of behavioral problems and competencies of children, Achenbach et al. (1991) found higher ratings on behavioral problem scales for children living in homes in which a family member was receiving mental health services. This should not be interpreted to mean that all children with behavioral problems have parents with mental illness, nor that all parents with mental illness have children with behavioral problems. Familial factors in behavioral problems are multiple, complex, and interactive—they are seldom direct and straightforward (Pinker, 2002).

With what we know about the family's role in children's emotional or behavioral disorders, educators would be foolish to ignore the influence of home conditions on school performance and conduct. Still, blaming parents of troubled students is unjustified. Very good parents can have children with very serious emotional or behavioral disorders. The teacher must realize that the parents of a youngster with an emotional or behavioral disorder have undergone a great deal of disappointment and frustration and that they, too, would like to see the child's behavior improve, both at home and at school. We find the strongest indicators for family causal contributions to antisocial behavior. However, even for conduct disorder and delinquency, we should not assume that parents are usually the primary cause.

Educators must be careful not to become entangled in the same coercive process that may characterize the antisocial student's family life. Harsh, hostile, verbal, or physical punishment at school is likely to function as a new challenge for antisocial students who may have been trained, albeit inadvertently, by their parents to step up their own aversive behavior in response to punishment. To win the battle with such students, school personnel must employ the same strategies that are recommended for parents: clearly state expectations for behavior, emphasize positive attention for appropriate conduct, and punish misbehavior in a calm, firm, nonhostile, and reasoned manner (Kauffman, Mostert, Trent, & Pullen, 2006; Pullen, 2004; Walker, 1995; Walker et al., 2004). Teachers need to be both responsive and demanding. They must not allow their student's disadvantaged home lives to become an excuse for poor teaching.

For far too long, educators, and many others in our society as well, have not only blamed parents for students' emotional or behavioral difficulties but viewed parents as likely adversaries rather than potential sources of support for their troubled children. More positive views of parents and their role in helping their children is in large measure a result of effective parent advocacy. The organization of the Federation of Families for Children's Mental Health in 1989 brought parents together to advocate more effectively for mental health and special education programs for their children. Parent groups in many states have established resource centers that provide information and guidance for parents who want to become more actively involved in seeing that their children get appropriate education and mental health services (e.g., Friesen

& Stephens, 1998; Jordan, 1995; Jordan, Goldberg, & Goldberg, 1991). Hanson and Carta (1996) suggested that teachers enlist the help and support of other professionals to do the following:

- Provide critical positive interactions with students and demonstrate these for parents
- Find and support the strengths of individual families
- Help families find and use informal sources of support from friends, neighbors, coworkers, or others in the community
- Become competent in understanding and valuing cultural differences in families
- Provide a broad spectrum of coordinated services so that families receive comprehensive, flexible, and usable services that address their needs.

SUMMARY

Although many look to the family as a likely source of deviant behavior, the factors that account for children's disordered behavior are multiple and complex. Some family factors, notably conflict and coercion, are known to increase a youngster's risk for developing an emotional or behavioral disorder. We do not fully understand why some children are more vulnerable to risk factors than others.

Families are best defined by their function. They provide protection, regulation, knowledge, affect, and self-understanding to children. Family structure, by itself, appears to have negligible effects. Divorce does not usually produce chronic disorders in children, although we can expect temporary negative effects. Children living in single-parent families may be at risk for behavioral problems, but we do not know precisely why. When children are cared for by substitutes for their biological parents, any negative effects stem primarily from traumas experienced before their separation or from a continuation of dysfunctional parenting.

An interactional–transactional model of family influence suggests that children and parents exert reciprocal effects; children affect their parents' behavior as surely as parents affect their children's. Parental discipline is a significant factor in behavioral development. Discipline that is authoritative—characterized by high levels of responsiveness and demandingness—usually produces the best outcomes. Ineffective discipline often involves lax supervision, harshness, and inconsistency.

We can view both conduct disorder and child abuse in terms of the interactions and transactions of parents and their children. In both cases, parent and child become involved in an aversive cycle of negative reinforcement, escalating aversive behavior and obtaining reinforcement through coercion. A child's difficult temperament and a parent's lack of coping skills may contribute to the initial difficulty; the coercive process then grows from nagging, whining, and yelling to more serious and assaultive behavior such as hitting.

Parental behaviors affect children's school performance and conduct. External factors such as poverty and employment may have substantial effects on family functioning. Many children grow up in poverty, even if their parents work, and their living conditions put them at risk for a variety of emotional and behavioral disorders.

Educators should be concerned about the family's influence on children's conduct at school, but they must not blame parents for children's misbehavior. School personnel must avoid becoming enmeshed in the same coercive process that antisocial students are probably experiencing at home and should use the same intervention strategies that are recommended for parents. Educators must work with other professionals to obtain comprehensive services for families.

CASE FOR DISCUSSION

He's Our Son, You Know
Weird Nick

Earlier in the day I had taken Nick to the principal's office because he had refused to restore the classroom computer password. He was a genius at computers, and it had taken no time at all for him to discover the school password and replace it with one only he knew. He liked the power this action had given him, knowing it had infuriated me. He loved it when people took his bait, as I had, whether it was in the form of a bomb threat, a detailed drawing of a stabbing, or his consistent proclamation that "Satan rules!"

Nick had sat quietly in the principal's office. He looked the part of a satanic cultist in his black jeans, black shirt, and black shoes. His black hair hung in stringy curls over his pale face. His fingers were busily drawing a pentagram. Was this just the image building of a middle school student plagued by self-doubt, or was it really an expression of belief in the occult?

I remembered how Nick seemed to get a special kick out of leaving the school building, forcing support staff to track him visually, walkie-talkies in hand. He knew that leaving the school grounds would necessitate our calling the police, so he would walk the perimeter of the property, running ahead if an adult came too close. All the other kids were afraid of "Weird Nick," as they called him. They kept their distance from this tall, powerful loner. And he distanced himself from his family, his classmates, and his teachers, unable to connect with anyone. All of us on the staff shared the concern that someday we would be hearing about Nick on the evening news.

Now his mother sat with me and the principal in my classroom after school, nervously twisting her gloves as if wringing out a rag, staring out the window at the freezing rain and growing darkness. "I just don't know what to do with him. I take him to church with me every chance I get. You know I go to church every day. Why is he doing this to me? He knows that his fascination with satanism hurts us deeply. Is he going to hurt us? He's our son, you know. What are we supposed to do?"

Questions About the Case

1. If you were Nick's teacher, how would you respond to his mother's obvious distress?
2. Given Nick's pattern of behavior, what focus would you suggest for his school program? That is, what would be your primary concerns and teaching or management strategies?
3. Would you advise Nick's teacher and principal to make special efforts to work with Nick's parents? Why or why not? If so, how?

■ PERSONAL REFLECTIONS

Family Factors

Dixie Jordan is the parent of a son with an emotional and behavioral disorder. She is director of the Families and Advocates Partnership for Education at the PACER Center in Minneapolis (a resource center for parents of children with disabilities) and is a founding member of the Federation of Families for Children's Mental Health. She is also a Systems of Care coach for Four Directions Consulting.

Why do you think there is such a strong tendency to hold parents responsible for their children's emotional or behavioral disorders?

I am the parent of two children, the younger of which has emotional and behavioral problems. When my firstborn and I were out in public, strangers often commented on what a "good" mother I was to have such an obedient, well-behaved, and compliant child. Frankly, I enjoyed the comments and really believed that those parents whose children were throwing tantrums and generally demolishing their environments were simply not very skilled in child rearing. I recall casting my share of reproachful glances in those days and thinking with some arrogance that raising children should be left to those of us who knew how to do it well. Several years later, my second child and I were on the business end of such disdain, and it was a lesson in humility that I shall never forget. Very little that I had learned in the previous 3 years as a parent worked with this child; he was neurologically different, hyperactive, inattentive, and noncompliant even when discipline was consistently applied. His doctors, his neurologist, and finally his teachers referred me to parenting classes as though the experiences I had had with my older child were nonexistent; his elementary principal even said that there was nothing wrong that a good spanking wouldn't cure. I expected understanding that this was a very difficult child to raise, but the unspoken message was that I lacked competence in basic parenting skills, the same message that I sent to similarly situated parents just a few years earlier.

Most of us in the world today are parents. The majority of us have children who do not have emotional or behavioral problems. Everything in our experience suggests that when our children are successful and obedient, it is because of our parenting.

We are reinforced socially for having a well-behaved child from friends, grandparents, even strangers. It makes sense, then, to attribute less-desirable behaviors in children to the failure of their parents to provide appropriate guidance or to set firm limits. Many parents have internalized that sense of responsibility or blame for causing their child's emotional problems, even when they are not able to identify what they might have done or be doing wrong. It is a very difficult attitude to shake, especially when experts themselves cannot seem to agree on causation. With most children, the "cause" of an emotional or behavioral disorder is more likely a complex interplay of multiple factors than it is parenting styles, biology, or environmental influences as discrete entities; but it is human nature to latch onto a simple explanation—and inadequate parenting is, indeed, a simple explanation. When systems blame parents for causing their child's emotional or behavioral disorders, the focus is no longer on services to help the child learn better adaptive skills or appropriate behaviors but on rationalizing why such services may not work. When parents feel blamed, their energies shift from focusing on the needs of their child to defending themselves. In either instance, the child is less well served.

Another reason people hold parents responsible for their children's emotional or behavioral disorders is that parents may be under such unrelenting stress from trying to manage their child's behavior that they may resort to inappropriate techniques because of the failure of more conventional methods. A parent whose 8-year-old hyperactive child smashes out his bedroom window while taking time-out for another problem may know that tying the child to a chair is not a good way to handle the crisis, but that parent may be out of alternatives. It may not have been the "right" thing for the parent to do, but it is not what was responsible for causing the child's problems in the first place. It would be a mistake to attribute the incidence of abuse or neglect as "causing" most emotional or behavioral disorders without consideration that difficult children are perhaps more likely to be abused because of their noncompliant or otherwise difficult behaviors.

What are the most important things for teachers to understand about being the parent of a child with emotional or behavioral disorders?

Teachers need to try to understand the isolation that many families may feel when raising a child with emotional or behavioral problems. Parents may not have amicable relationships with their extended families or with the neighbors because of their child and may not have a single person with whom they can freely discuss their child's problems or seek solutions to them. They may not have a sitter to watch their child for a few hours in the evening so they can take a break. They may on occasion feel physically threatened by their own child. Raising a child with an emotional or behavioral disorder is hard work—exhausting work—and families in many instances operate as little islands in their communities, cut off by their child's behavior from extended families, friends, or community supports.

Parents of children with emotional or behavioral disorders bring with them a historical perspective not only of their child's problems but perhaps of the failure of other systems to adequately address those problems before the child ever gets into school. By the time their children are enrolled in elementary school, many parents have lost confidence in any system to truly help them. They may be suspicious and distrustful of schools. When personalized, this leads to suspicion and distrust of teachers. Innocuous comments such as "What is going on at home with your child?" may be interpreted as "What are you doing wrong at home with your child?" It can be difficult for teachers to understand that the anger parents sometimes direct toward schools may stem from a frustration with systems in general and not with a specific program or person.

Teachers also need to understand that not all parents will be able to help their child with homework or school activities, especially if homework causes a great deal of stress or anxiety for the child. When the problem gets to be one of providing either academic support or emotional support because providing both is not possible, it may become more important to parents to support the child emotionally and to skip the homework. This should be negotiated with each family and based on the needs and abilities of each child, but the inability to help a child with homework should not be automatically viewed as lack of parental concern or involvement.

What key steps can teachers take in working more effectively with parents who have children with emotional or behavioral disorders?

One of the greatest fears expressed by parents regarding their child's school program is that if they disagree with any part of the program, the teachers will take it out on their child. If I were a special education teacher, my first step each year would be to call each parent and let them know that I am interested in their child and need their help in developing a program. I would explain to them that we might not always agree about what to do, but that they could call me and know that I would listen, and that no matter what they said, I would never punish any child for the parents' displeasure with the program. As an advocate, I must say that fear of complaining is the single most important reason—according to the parents I've heard from—that they do not openly disagree with their child's school program, even when they believe it does not meet their child's needs.

A second key to building trust with parents is being honest with them about their child's needs. Parents may opt for a special education program with the expectation that it is for a few weeks or months, although the teacher knows or is at least reasonably sure that the placement may be for a few years and that the goal of total remediation of academic and behavioral deficits may never be achieved. Many parents, especially of younger children, may not see their child's problems as a disability but as a transitory phase of development. Although that certainly may be true for some children, there are many others for whom an educated guess would be that their problems will be chronic and of long duration. If parents have an understanding of the longitudinal nature of their child's disability and of the possibility of the long-term need for special education services, they will be less apt to get discouraged or angry when their child continues to need services.

Many parents report that the only time they hear from their child's teacher is when there is trouble at school. It is very important for teachers to communicate regularly with parents. There is no easier or more effective way to establish a relationship of trust and open communication with families than with frequent (and at least 50% positive) communication.

Another suggestion for teachers is to learn to apologize when a mistake has been made. Most parents expect that teachers and other school professionals will make mistakes from time to time in dealing with their child, but it is the wise teacher who is ready with an apology for wrongly accusing or for misunderstanding a situation in which the child was disciplined unfairly.

Most teachers truly do not understand how stressful IEP (individualized education program) planning meetings can be for parents. Attention at such meetings is generally focused on the problems a child is having, and parents are nearly always outnumbered by professional educators. A common occurrence at such meetings is for the teachers to refer to the parents as "Dad" or "Mom," which many parents report interpreting as denigrating or disrespectful. Careful planning of such meetings with an eye to the comfort and ease of parents can help increase their participation and their sense of power.

Parents are the true experts on their child, and the information they bring, if it can be tapped, can be invaluable in planning an appropriate program. Parents may not be specialists in behavior management, but they know their child across years and across environments, and if they do not know what techniques will work with a particular child, they at least know what has *not* worked. It can be helpful for teachers to consider the honorable intentions when they are dealing with angry or uncooperative parents. Why are the parents upset? What are they trying to convey (regardless of how inappropriately) about the needs of their child? It is human nature to become defensive, but many such stalemates are resolved by teachers who recognize first that an angry parent is one who is concerned about his or her child's school program, the teacher can then respond to the concern and not the anger. Recognizing honorable intentions, especially in forced relationships such as those at IEP planning meetings, can greatly facilitate open communication between parents and teachers.

QUESTIONS FOR FURTHER REFLECTION

1. How would you talk with parents whom you suspect are abusive toward their child?
2. How could you best express empathy for parents whose child is exhibiting behavior that is troublesome to you?
3. How would you approach parents who do not see their child as exhibiting troublesome behavior, although you see their child's behavior as very worrisome?

SECTION 11
SCHOOL FACTORS

As you read this section, keep these guiding questions in mind:

- Why should educators consider how the school might contribute to the development of disordered behavior?

- With what academic skill levels should teachers of students with emotional or behavioral disorders be prepared to deal?

- What characteristics of student behavior are most likely to be associated with success in

school? What are those associated with school failure?

- How might inconsistent management in the classroom produce results similar to those produced by a coercive family process?

- How does ineffective instruction in critical academic and social skills contribute to emotional and behavioral problems?

THE APPEAL OF SCHOOL FACTORS AS CAUSAL EXPLANATIONS

Besides the family, the school is probably the most important socializing influence on children and youth. In our culture, success or failure in school is tantamount to success or failure as a person; school is the occupation of all children and youth in our society—and sometimes it is their preoccupation. As high-stakes testing becomes a great obsession of the standards movement in school reform, especially the federal No Child Left Behind Act (NCLB) and related state laws, school performance becomes even more a matter of concern. Little wonder that the demands of school should precipitate extreme anxiety in some students.

Academic success is fundamentally important for social development and opportunities outside school. As nearly any student, teacher, or parent can tell you, certain types of behavior are unacceptable in school. Yet many people, including many educators, seem to be unaware of how the school environment can inadvertently foster the very behavior that teachers, parents, and students find objectionable.

The school environment is the causal factor over which teachers and principals have direct control. Some youngsters develop behavior problems before they begin school, and some develop problems because of events outside school. Even so, educators should consider how the school might either ameliorate the problem or make it worse. And because many youngsters do not exhibit emotional or behavioral disorders until after they enter school, educators must recognize the possibility that the school experience could be a significant causal factor.

An ecological approach to understanding behavior includes the assumption that all aspects of a youngster's environment are interconnected; changes in one element of the ecology have implications for the other elements. Success or failure at school affects behavior at home and in the community; effects of school performance ripple outward. Consequently, success at school assumes even greater importance if a youngster's home and community environments are disastrous. Furthermore, prereferral strategies, required before a student is evaluated for special education, imply that the current classroom environment might be involved as a cause. Most special educators recognize the importance of eliminating possible school contributions to misconduct before labeling the student as having a disability.

Before discussing social–interpersonal behavior and its school and classroom contexts, we must consider the characteristics of students with emotional or behavioral disorders that are relevant to a central mission of the school: academic learning. Intelligence and academic achievement are the two characteristics most closely linked to the way in which students respond to the expectations and demands of the school.

INTELLIGENCE

Intelligence tests are most reasonably viewed as tests of general learning in areas that are important to academic success. IQ refers only to performance on an intelligence test. IQs are moderately good predictors of how students will perform academically and how they will adapt to the demands of everyday life. Standardized tests are the best single means we have to measure general intelligence, even though performance on a test is not the only indicator of intelligence and may not tap abilities in specific areas that are important in everyday life (see Hallahan, Kauffman, & Pullen, 2009; Gould, 1996).

The definition and measurement of intelligence are controversial issues, with implications for the definition of giftedness, mental retardation, and other exceptionalities for which special education may be needed (see Hallahan, Kauffman, & Pullen, 2009; Reschly, 1997). Psychologists agree that intelligence is comprised of a variety of abilities, both verbal and nonverbal. The ability to direct and sustain attention, process information, think logically, perceive social circumstances accurately, and understand abstractions, for example, are distinguishable parts of what makes a person "smart." But scholars continue to debate the merits of the concept of *general intelligence* versus the idea of *multiple intelligences* (e.g., Chan, 2006; Gardner & Hatch, 1989; Sternberg, 1991; White & Breen, 1998). Some have called the theory of multiple intelligences "scientifically untenable" (e.g., Lloyd & Hallahan, 2007) and question practices based on it, but debating these issues is beyond the scope of this book (see also Willingham, 2004 for a critique; Google educationnext.org, click on Hoover Institution-Education Next, and search for Willingham to find the online article and controversy about it). Although the theory of multiple intelligences is widely held to be legitimate, there are no (or very few) proven applications of it to teaching (see Lloyd & Hallahan, 2007). We do not intend to imply that intelligence can be reduced to a single score or performance, but we do suggest that the idea of *many* intelligences remains unproven.

Goleman (1995) popularized the notion of *emotional intelligence,* which refers broadly to individuals' awareness of their own and other's emotions, and the impact of that awareness—or lack of awareness—on their thinking and behavior (Salovey & Mayer, 1990). The definition and measurement of emotional intelligence is also controversial (e.g., Davies, Stankov, & Roberts, 1998).

Intelligence of Students with Emotional or Behavioral Disorders

Authorities on emotional and behavioral disorders have traditionally assumed that students with such disorders fall within the normal range of intelligence. If the IQ falls below 70, the student is considered to have mental retardation, even when behavioral problems are a major concern. Occasionally, however, students with IQs in the retardation range are said to have emotional or behavioral disorders or learning disabilities rather than mental retardation, on the presumption that emotional or perceptual disorders prevent them from performing to their true capacity (cf. Hallahan, Lloyd, Kauffman, Weiss, & Martinez, 2005).

The average IQ for most students with emotional or behavioral disorders is in the low normal range, with a dispersion of scores from the severe mental retardation range to the highly gifted level. Over the past 40 years, numerous studies have yielded the same general finding: Average tested IQ for these students is in the low 90s (e.g., Bortner & Birch, 1969; Bower, 1981; Duncan, Forness, & Hartsough, 1995;

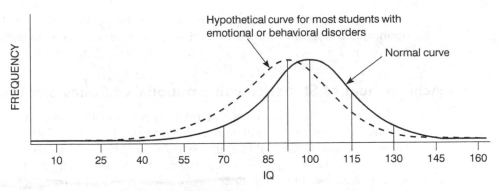

Figure 11.1 Hypothetical frequency distributions of IQ for students with emotional or behavioral disorders as compared to a normal frequency distribution

Graubard, 1964; Kauffman, Cullinan, & Epstein, 1987; Lyons & Powers, 1963; Motto & Wilkins, 1968; Rubin & Balow, 1978). We have accumulated enough research on these students' intelligence to draw this conclusion. Although the majority fall only slightly below average in IQ, a disproportionate number, compared to the normal distribution, score in the lower end of the normal range and the range generally associated with mild mental retardation, and relatively few fall in the upper ranges. Research findings suggest a distribution like that in Figure 11.1. The hypothetical curve for most students with emotional or behavioral disorders shows a mean of about 90 to 95 IQ, with more students falling at the lower IQ levels and fewer at the higher levels than in the normal distribution. If this hypothetical distribution of intelligence is correct, then we can expect a greater than normal frequency of academic failure and socialization difficulties for these students

Implications of Low IQ

Research clearly suggests that students with emotional or behavioral disorders tend to be lower than normal in IQ and that the most severely disabled students also tend to be the lowest in IQ. The correlation between intelligence and level of disorder, however, does not imply a causal relationship. The predictive power of IQ for achievement and future social adjustment of students with emotional and behavioral disorders probably approximates the predictive power of IQ for students in the normal distribution: significant but far from perfect.

ACADEMIC ACHIEVEMENT

Although academic achievement is usually assessed by standardized achievement tests, it is dangerous to place too much confidence in them because they are not highly accurate measures of academic aptitude nor highly precise measures of the academic attainment of the individual student (Reschly, 1997). Scores on achievement tests do, however, allow comparisons between the performances of normative and nonnormative groups, which are valuable in assessing and predicting students' school success.

Achievement of Students with Emotional or Behavioral Disorders

The academic achievement of students with emotional or behavioral disorders and juvenile delinquents has been studied for many years (Bower, 1981; Graubard, 1964; Motto & Wilkins, 1968; Rubin & Balow, 1978; Silberberg & Silberberg, 1971; Stone & Rowley, 1964; Tamkin, 1960; Trout, Nordness, Pierce, & Epstein, 2003; see also Walker, Ramsey, & Gresham, 2004). Collectively, research leads to the conclusion that most such students are academically deficient, even taking into account their mental ages, which are typically slightly below those of their chronological age-mates. Although some students with emotional or behavioral disorders work at grade level and a very few are academically advanced, most function a year or more below grade level in most academic areas (Lane, 2004).

Implications of Academic Underachievement

Low achievement and behavior problems go hand in hand; they are highly related risk factors (Kupersmidt & Patterson, 1987; Lane, 2004). In most cases, it is not clear whether disordered behavior causes underachievement or vice versa. Sometimes the weight of evidence may be more on one side of the issue than the other, but in the majority of instances the precise nature of the relationship is elusive. As we will see, there is reason to believe that underachievement and disordered behavior affect each other reciprocally. Disordered behavior apparently makes academic achievement less likely, and underachievement produces social consequences that are likely to foster inappropriate behavior (Bower, 1995; Lane, 2004; Walker et al., 2004). In any case, we have known for a long time that the effects of educational failure on future opportunity should cause alarm for the plight of students with emotional or behavioral disorders. As researchers explained decades ago:

> Educational attainment and opportunity are linked in many ways. Abundant evidence supports the view that education affects income, occupational choice, social and economic mobility, political participation, social deviance, etc. Indeed, educational attainment is related to opportunity in so many ways that the two terms seem inextricably intertwined in the mind of the layman and in the findings of the social scientist. (Levin, Guthrie, Kleindorfer, & Stout, 1971, p. 14)

SOCIAL SKILLS

Interest in the social skills that make people attractive to others and enable them to cope effectively with difficult interpersonal circumstances is many decades, if not centuries, old. Obviously, people who are considered to have emotional or behavioral disorders lack certain critical social skills. However, it is often not so obvious just what those skills are, and how to teach people the skills they lack is even less apparent (see Blake, Wang, Cartlege, & Gardner, 2000; Hallahan et al., 2005; Kavale, Mathur, & Mostert, 2004; Maag, 2006).

Social skills related to schooling may be those that allow a student to establish and maintain positive interpersonal relationships, be accepted by peers, and get along well in the larger social environment (Walker et al., 2004). Students with emotional or behavioral disorders often do not know how to make and keep friends. They frequently behave in ways that anger and disappoint their teachers and classmates. They find it difficult or impossible to adjust to changing expectations when they move from one social environment to another (cf. Farmer & Hollowell, 1994; Guevremont & Dumas, 1994; Hundert, 1995; Kavale et al., 2004; Walker, Schwarz, Nippold, Irvin, & Noell, 1994).

A list of the most important social skills encompasses many that are necessary for academic and social success in school. They include listening to others, taking turns in conversations, greeting others, joining in ongoing activities, giving compliments, expressing anger in socially acceptable ways, offering help to others, following rules, being adequately organized and focused, and doing high-quality work. Knowing what these skills are is important; assessing the extent to which individual students have mastered them is critical in dealing effectively with antisocial behavior (Kavale et al., 2004; Walker et al., 2004).

At the heart of social skills is the ability to communicate verbally and nonverbally—to use language competently. In fact, a large percentage of students with emotional or behavioral disorders is known to have language disorders (Rogers-Adkinson & Griffith, 1999). Although these students may have problems in any area of language competence (e.g., they may have difficulty with word sounds, word forms, grammar, and so on), they tend to be particularly deficient in *pragmatics*—the practical, social uses of language. Acting-out youngsters may know how to use language very effectively to irritate, intimidate, and coerce others, but they do not have skills in using language effectively for positive, constructive social purposes. A functional analysis of their language skills is likely to indicate that they need to learn to use language to obtain desired consequences in ways that are socially acceptable. Withdrawn students lack the sophisticated language repertoires their normal peers have for engaging others in discourse. We may conclude that a lack of social skills, especially pragmatic language skills, may underlie many of the behavior problems that are predictive of school failure. Students with emotional or behavioral disorders may need instruction in specific language-based social skills such as these:

- Identifying, labeling, and expressing needs, wants, and feelings
- Describing and interpreting emotions of oneself and others
- Recognizing incipient emotions, providing control over them, and integrating them into appropriate social behavior.

Instruction in the pragmatics of language can improve the language skills of students with EBD (Hyter, Rogers-Adkinson, Self, & Jantz, 2002).

Behavior Predictive of School Success and Failure

Educational researchers are interested in identifying the classroom behavior associated with academic accomplishment in the hope that teachers can teach those behaviors. For instance, if attentiveness is found to be positively correlated with achievement, then teaching students to pay better attention might improve academic performance. Similarly, if achievement correlates negatively with certain dependence behaviors, then reducing dependency behaviors might be successful. Implicit here is the assumption that the identified behavioral characteristics will have more than a correlational relationship to achievement; there will be a causal link between certain overt behaviors and achievement.

The causal relationship between classroom behavior and academic success or failure is not entirely clear. Although a frequent strategy of teachers and educational researchers has been to modify behavior (such as task attention) in the hope of improving performance on academic tasks, direct modification of academic skills has proved most effective in preventing failure or remediating deficits (Lloyd, Hallahan, Kauffman, & Keller, 1998). For decades, we have known that in some cases direct reinforcement of academic performance eliminates classroom behavior problems (Kauffman, Mostert, Trent, & Pullen, 2006). Increasing a student's correct academic responses is often effective in reducing classroom behavior problems (Gunter, Hummel, & Conroy, 1998; Trout, Epstein, Mickelson, Nelson, & Lewis, 2003). Nevertheless, classroom success or failure is determined by more than academic competence; doing the academic work is critical, but it is not the whole story (see Walker & McConnell, 1988).

Success and failure in school correlate with a variety of academic and social characteristics. Students who are low achieving and socially unsuccessful tend to exhibit

- Behavior requiring teacher intervention or control, such as teasing, annoying, or interfering with others
- Dependence on the teacher for direction
- Difficulty paying attention and concentrating
- Becoming upset under pressure
- Sloppy, impulsive work
- Low self-confidence

High-achieving and popular students, on the other hand, tend to exhibit

- Rapport with the teacher, including friendly conversation before and after class and responsiveness in class
- Appropriate verbal interaction, asking relevant questions, volunteering, and participating in class discussions
- Doing more than the minimum work required, taking care to understand directions and to master all details
- Originality and reasoning ability, quickness to grasp new concepts and apply them
- Sensitivity to the feelings of others.

However, we must also consider the teacher's expectations and responses to students' behavior. Sometimes, as we shall discuss further, the mismatch between a student's and teacher's temperaments seems to be the primary reason for academic failure (Keogh, 2003).

School Failure and Later Adjustment

Low IQ and academic failure often foretell difficulty for students. A higher proportion of those with low IQ and achievement than of students with high IQ and achievement will experience adjustment difficulties as adults; those with low IQ are disproportionately represented among people who commit criminal acts (Bower, 1995). A high proportion of schizophrenic and antisocial adults are known to have exhibited low academic achievement as children (Bower, Shellhammer, & Daily, 1960; Kazdin, 1998; Robins, 1966, 1986; Watt, Stolorow, Lubensky, & McClelland, 1970).

However, low IQ and achievement alone do not spell disaster for later adjustment. Most youngsters with mild mental retardation, whose achievement may lag behind even their mental ages, do not turn into social misfits, criminals, or institutional residents in adult life; they are considered problems only during their school years (Edgerton, 1984). The same can be said of most youngsters with learning disabilities, whose academic retardation usually marks them as school failures (see Hallahan et al., 2005). Even among children and youth with emotional or behavioral disorders, the prognosis is not necessarily poor just because the student has a low IQ or fails academically.

When school failure is accompanied by serious and persistent antisocial behavior—conduct disorder—the risk for mental health problems in adulthood is most grave (Fergusson & Horwood, 1995; Kazdin, 1998; Walker et al., 2004). And the earlier the onset and the greater the number of antisocial behaviors, the greater the risk. Even when conduct disorder is accompanied by low intelligence and low achievement, we must be careful in drawing causal inferences; if a causal connection does exist between achievement and antisocial behavior, however, then it has implications for education, as we have long understood·

> It is well known . . . that children with antisocial behavior are usually seriously retarded in academic performance. We do not know at this point whether academic failure usually preceded or followed the onset of antisocial behavior. If experiencing academic failure contributes to the occurrence of antisocial behavior disorders, then it is clear that preventive efforts should include efforts to forestall failure through programs such as those currently endeavoring to improve the IQs and academic success of disadvantaged children either by educating their parents to stimulate them as infants or through a variety of educationally oriented daycare and preschool programs. (Robins, 1974, p. 455)

To reiterate, low IQ and school failure alone are not as highly predictive of adult psychopathology as when they are combined with conduct disorder. The outlook for a youngster is particularly grim when he or she is at once relatively unintelligent, underachieving, and highly aggressive or extremely withdrawn. If conduct disorder is fostered by school failure, then programs to prevent school failure may also contribute to prevention of antisocial behavior.

INTELLIGENCE, ACHIEVEMENT, AND ANTISOCIAL BEHAVIOR

Given that antisocial behavior (for example, hostile aggression, theft, incorrigibility, running away from home, truancy, vandalism, sexual misconduct), low intelligence, and low achievement are interrelated in a complex way, it may be important to clarify their apparent interrelationship. Figure 11.2 shows a hypothetical relationship among the three characteristics. The various shaded areas in the diagram represent the approximate (hypothesized) proportions in which various combinations of the three characteristics occur. The diagram illustrates the hypothesis that relatively few youngsters who exhibit antisocial behavior are above average in IQ and achievement (area A), most are below average in IQ and achievement (area D), and a few are below average in only IQ (area B) or only achievement (area C). Whereas the majority of underachieving youngsters are low in IQ (areas D and G), they are usually not antisocial (area G is much larger than area D). Some youngsters are low in IQ but not achievement (areas B and E) or vice versa (areas C and F), but relatively few of these youngsters are antisocial (area E is much larger than area B, and area F is much larger than area C).

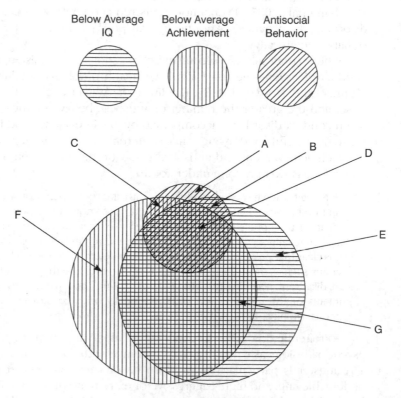

Figure 11.2 Hypothetical relationships among below-average IQ, below-average achievement, and antisocial behavior

Keep in mind that additional factors enter the picture to determine the adult outcome for children and youth with a given combination of characteristics. The severity of the antisocial behavior, the parents' behavioral characteristics, and perhaps parental socioeconomic circumstances influence the probability that behavioral difficulties will persist into adulthood. To the extent that youngsters exhibit many antisocial behaviors in a variety of settings and at high frequency, have parents who are themselves antisocial or abusive, and come from a lower social class, they have a greater chance of being hospitalized as mentally ill or incarcerated as a criminal when they become adults (Bower, 1995; Loeber, 1982; Robins, 1979; Walker et al., 2004). Also, remember that many children and youth who are low in intelligence, low in achievement, high in antisocial behavior, or some combination of these do not exhibit serious behavioral disorders as adults. Any prediction of adult behavior based on childhood behavioral characteristics is subject to substantial error in prediction for the individual case.

SCHOOL'S CONTRIBUTION TO EMOTIONAL AND BEHAVIORAL DISORDERS

The demands of school and the student's social and academic repertoire probably affect each other reciprocally. For decades, we have known that a circular reaction occurs between the student and the social context of the classroom (Glidewell, 1969; Glidewell, Kantor, Smith, & Stringer, 1966; Keogh, 2003). Students who are healthy, intelligent, upper-middle class, high achieving, high in self-esteem, and adroit in interpersonal skills (likely to be perceived as "easy" and "teachable" by a teacher) enter the classroom at a distinct advantage. They are likely to make positive approaches to others, who in turn are likely to respond positively, and these advantaged students will be sensitive to others' responses toward them and be able to use their intelligence to further enhance their personal power and social status. Intelligence and achievement beget social acceptability, self-esteem, accurate social perception, and status, all of which in turn induce positive social responses from others and facilitate achievement. This perspective on the student's reciprocal interaction with the social ecology of the classroom is entirely consistent with research (cf. Colvin, Greenberg, & Sherman, 1993; Haager & Vaughn, 1997; Hess & Holloway, 1984; Keogh, 2003; Wong & Donahue, 2002). Moreover, the same coercive process found in families of antisocial boys (Patterson, 1986a, 1986b) can be found in schools (Walker et al., 2004). Educators (like parents) and classroom peers (like siblings) can become entangled in escalating contests of aversiveness, in which the individual who causes greater pain is the winner, obtaining negative reinforcement and digging in for the next round of conflict.

The same type of interaction between the student's temperament and the parents' child-rearing techniques appears to occur between the student's temperament and the school's social and academic demands. The student who is slow to approach others, has irregular work habits, is slow to adapt to new situations, and is predominantly negative in mood is most likely to have difficulty in school, although any temperamental characteristic is susceptible to modification with proper handling (Carey, 1998; Keogh, 2003; Martin, 1992; Thomas, Chess, & Birch, 1968).

The school, like the family and biological factors, does not operate unilaterally to determine students' emotional and behavioral development. However, we can identify classroom conditions and teacher reactions to pupil behavior that make behavioral difficulties more likely or could be changed to reduce the likelihood of acting out and other emotional or behavioral problems (Keogh, 2003; Kerr & Nelson, 2006; Walker, 1995). The school might contribute to disordered behavior and academic failure in one or more of the following ways:

1. Insensitivity to students' individuality
2. Inappropriate expectations for students
3. Inconsistent management of behavior
4. Instruction in nonfunctional and irrelevant skills
5. Ineffective instruction in critical skills
6. Destructive contingencies of reinforcement
7. Undesirable models of school conduct

Besides these factors, others such as crowded and deteriorated schools and classrooms are associated with aggression and other problems. The physical conditions under which students are taught will surely affect their behavior for better or worse.

Insensitivity to Students' Individuality

Special educators of all persuasions recognize the necessity of meeting pupils' individual needs. Some speculate, in fact, that a large proportion of the schoolchildren identified as having learning and behavioral disorders reflect the failure of the education system to accommodate individual differences. Although not making reasonable accommodations to individual needs undoubtedly contributes to some students' failures or maladjustment, reasonable requirements for conformity to rules and standards clearly do not account for the failure or deviance of many others. In fact, just the opposite may be the case for some students; they may fail and behave antisocially because reasonable rules and expectations for conformity to standards of achievement and civility are not made clear (cf. Kauffman, Mostert et al., 2006; Landrum & Kauffman, 2006; Walker, 1995; Walker et al., 2004).

However, rigidity and failure to tolerate differences do demand scrutiny. By making the same academic and behavioral requirements of each student, schools can force many students who are only slightly different from most into roles of academic failures or social deviants. Through inflexibility and stultifying insistence on sameness, schools can create conditions that inhibit or punish healthy expression of individuality. In an atmosphere of regimentation and repression, many students will respond with resentment, hostility, vandalism, or passive resistance to the system (see Keogh, 2003, and case of Esther P. Rothman in accompanying case book).

For students unfortunate enough to differ more than slightly from the norm in learning or behavior, the message in some classrooms is clear: To be yourself is to be bad, inadequate, or unacceptable. These students' self-perceptions are likely to become negative, their perceptions of social situations distorted, and their intellectual efficiency and motivation weakened. They can become caught in a self-perpetuating cycle of conflict and negative influence.

Insensitivity to individuals does not, of course, emanate from the school as an abstraction. Administrators, teachers, and other pupils are the people who are sensitive or insensitive to expressions of individuality. School administrators can create a reasonably tolerant or a repressive mood in the way they deal with students and adults. Teachers are primarily responsible for the classroom emotional climate and for how restrictive or permissive, individualized or regimented the student's school day will be. Peers may demand strict conformity regarding dress, speech, or deportment for social acceptance, especially in the higher grades. On the other hand, peers may be an easygoing, open group in which a fellow student can find acceptance even though he or she is quite different from the group.

Teachers and administrators who are sensitive to students but have clear and positive expectations for academic performance seem to foster appropriate behavior. We should not assume, however, that a positive and productive school climate is fostered merely by an emphasis on talking to students about their family and emotional problems. Teachers must not abandon their role as adult authority figures in attempts to develop better relationships with their students: "When teachers who have difficulty in maintaining basic order in the classroom treat pupils as peers, they may worsen an already bad situation" (Kasen, Johnson, & Cohen, 1990, p. 175). A critical key to generally improved student behavior is a clear, consistent plan for schoolwide discipline (Lewis & Sugai, 1999; Lewis, Sugai, & Colvin, 1998; Liaupsin, Jolivette, & Scott, 2004; Martella, Nelson, & Marchand-Martella, 2003; Rosenberg & Jackman, 2003; Walker et al., 2004).

In classic developmental studies, Thomas and Chess (1984) and Thomas et al. (1968) showed that the growth of emotional or behavioral disorders is accelerated by adults' failure to treat youngsters in accordance with their temperamental individuality (see the case of Richard, involving temperament in school, and Keogh, 2003). Little experimental evidence suggests that emotional or behavioral disorders are caused by insensitivity alone. However, we can readily find anecdotal evidence that insensitivity may be a feature of many students' school experience (Epstein, 1981; see also case descriptions in Kauffman, Mostert, et al., 2006). Unfortunately, insensitivity and rigidity in school environments are not relics of the past. They have always been problematic, and they remain a bane of education. Such environments appear to be a breeding ground for antisocial behavior.

The foregoing discussion is decidedly not intended as an indictment of all rules, regulations, or demands for conformity in the classroom or school. Certainly, reasonable rules must be maintained for the safety and well-being of all. No social institution can exist without some requirements of conformity, and one cannot interpret an appeal for tolerance of individual expression to mean that *anything* should be accepted. Nevertheless, insensitivity to students as individuals and needless repression of their uniqueness can contribute to emotional or behavioral problems. Students like to have a piece of the action, and allowing them to participate in self-determination of their classroom lives often results in improved behavior and academic performance (Clarke et al., 1995; Lovitt, 1977; Walker, 1995; Walker et al., 2004).

Inappropriate Expectations for Students

The expectations teachers *do* hold for their students, and the expectations they *should* hold, are continuing sources of controversy in American education (see Kauffman, 2002; Kauffman, Mostert, et al., 2006; Keogh, 2003). Two facets of the problem of expectations are the effects of what teachers are led to believe about their students (especially the possible biasing effects of diagnostic or administrative labels) and teachers' classroom standards of behavior and academic performance.

Effects of Labels

Concern about labeling is decades old, and probably older than special education itself. Some claim that many of the problems of exceptional children originate with and are perpetuated by the labels we use to designate them (see Kauffman, 1999c, 2002, 2003a, 2005a; Lilly, 1992). Some have assumed that a label such as "emotionally disturbed" carries with it an expectation of misbehavior and lower academic performance. The teacher's lower expectation for students labeled *exceptional* will be communicated in subtle ways to the students, and they will indeed fulfill this expectation. Moreover, there is concern about the stigma that goes with receiving a label denoting exceptionality, especially disability. Students' own expectations may also influence their performance.

Ultimately, we must face the fact that labels of some type are necessary for communication (Burbach, 1981; Kauffman & Konold, 2007). They simply cannot be avoided unless we refuse to discuss students' problems (Kauffman, 1999c, 2003a, 2003b, 2005a, 2007c). The issues, then, should be how we understand and use labels and how we work with the larger problem—our perceptions of the people whose characteristics we refer to when we use labels.

A popular assumption is that receiving special education services destroys students' self-esteem and social status, regardless of the particular label under which they are served. Research suggests that this assumption may be unfounded for children with learning disabilities and emotional or behavioral disorders. Studies indicate that students receiving special education for learning or behavioral disorders—students receiving these labels—may have lower self-concepts or social status than do students without learning or behavioral problems. They have not, however, been found to have lower self-perceptions and status than do nonlabeled students who have academic or behavioral problems (Coleman, McHam, & Minnett, 1992; Patterson, Kupersmidt, & Griesler, 1988; Sale & Carey, 1995). Students appear to suffer damage to self-esteem and social status as a consequence of learning and behavior problems, not as a result of being labeled; the label follows the problem, not vice versa (Hallahan, Kauffman, & Pullen, 2009; see also Singer, 1988). In fact, a label for their difficulties appears to give many people with disabilities a sense of relief and to provide others with an understandable reason for differences that, unlabeled, result in social rejection. Besides, high self-esteem has not been shown to cause better academic performance, interpersonal success, or happiness (Baumeister, Campbell, Krueger, & Vohs, 2003).

Effects of Classroom Standards

The early 21st century is marked by an emphasis on higher academic and social standards in American public schools. For students with disabilities and serious academic or social problems, these increased expectations, if interpreted as universal standards demanded of all students, create the certainty of failure without extraordinary supports and a high probability of failure even with the most effective interventions known (see Hallahan, Kauffman, & Pullen, 2009; Hockenbury, Kauffman, & Hallahan, 1999; Kauffman, 1999e, 2002, 2005b). Especially for students with emotional and behavioral disorders, alternative placements in which the expectations are adjusted to fit the students' prior learning and abilities are essential if their education is to be appropriate (see Kauffman, Bantz, & McCullough, 2002).

The research and speculation on effects of teacher bias do not lead logically to the conclusion that simply expecting normal behavior will help students with emotional or behavioral disorders improve. After all, it is quite clear that most such students are lower in tested intelligence, academic achievement, and social adjustment than are average students. Many are far below their age-mates in numerous areas of development, and expecting normal performance from them is unrealistic.

For many years, we have had good reason to suspect that a discrepancy between the child's ability and adults' expectations for performance contributes directly to the development of disordered behavior (Center, Deitz, & Kaufman, 1982; Kauffman, Mostert, et al., 2006; Kirk, 1972). If the expectations are too high or too low, the student may become disinterested, dispirited, and disruptive. We do know that students with emotional or behavioral disorders often are motivated by negative reinforcement—by behaving in ways that allow them to escape or avoid expectations for performance (Cipani & Spooner, 1997; Gunter, Denny, Jack, Shores, & Nelson, 1993).

If expectations that are too low become self fulfilling prophecies, and if expectations that are too high are frustrating and depressing and prompt attempts to avoid them, then what level of expectation will avoid the risk of contributing to development of disordered behavior? Expectations of improvement are always in order—assuming, of course, that the teacher knows the student's current level of academic performance or adequate social behavior and can specify a reasonable level of improvement along a measurable dimension. If pupil and teacher define *reasonable* together, then the expectations should be neither too low nor too high.

Research does not suggest that teachers' expectations and demands are well attuned to students' abilities and characteristics (Gunter et al., 1993, 1998). Investigating the standards and expectations of regular and special education teachers for students' academic performance and social–interpersonal behavior, Walker and Rankin (1983) found that teachers' expectations could be described as narrow, intense, and demanding. These findings suggest that teachers' expectations can be a significant problem for students with emotional or behavioral disorders, regardless of whether they are in a special or general education class and regardless of whether they are elementary or secondary students.

The top behavioral characteristics said by teachers to be critical for success in the studies by Kerr and Zigmond (1986) and Hersh and Walker (1983) were

1. Follows established classroom rules
2. Listens to teacher instructions
3. Complies with teacher commands
4. Does in-class assignments as directed
5. Avoids breaking classroom rule(s) even when encouraged by a peer
6. Produces work of acceptable quality given his or her skill level.

The top characteristics considered by classroom teachers to be intolerable in a regular classroom were

1. Engages in inappropriate sexual behavior
2. Steals
3. Behaves inappropriately in class when corrected
4. Damages others' property
5. Refuses to obey teacher-imposed classroom rules
6. Is self-abusive
7. Makes lewd or obscene gestures
8. Ignores teacher warnings or reprimands.

Given teachers' standards and expectations, it should not be surprising that students with emotional or behavioral disorders and their teachers frequently disappoint each other, thus setting the stage for conflict and coercion. We should not inappropriately generalize to *all* teachers or assume that high standards and low tolerance for misbehavior are undesirable. Some teachers apparently make few demands and have great tolerance for deviance, and others are just the opposite (Kauffman, Lloyd, & McGee, 1989; Kauffman, Wong, Lloyd, Hung, & Pullen, 1991; Walker, 1986). Compared to regular classroom teachers, special education teachers may be somewhat more tolerant of misbehavior and judge students' behavior as less deviant (Fabre & Walker, 1987; Safran & Safran, 1987; Walker, 1986). Teachers' expressed tolerance for troublesome behavior may be affected by several factors, including their self-perceived competence, the availability and quality of technical assistance, and the difficulty of the particular group of students they are teaching (Safran & Safran, 1987). Teachers who have higher standards and lower tolerance for disorderly behavior may also provide more effective instruction (Gersten, Walker, & Darch, 1988). The teacher's temperament in interaction with the child's seems to be the critical factor in many school problems (Keogh, 2003).

Inconsistent Management of Behavior

A major hypothesis underlying a structured approach to educating students with emotional or behavioral disorders is that a lack of structure or order in their daily lives contributes to their difficulties. When youngsters cannot predict adults' responses to their behavior, they become anxious, confused, and unable to choose appropriate behavioral alternatives. If at one time they are allowed to engage in a certain misbehavior without penalty and at another time are punished for the same misconduct, the unpredictability of the consequences of their behavior encourages them to act inappropriately. If they cannot depend on favorable consequences following good behavior, they have little incentive to perform well.

We find strong support in the child development literature for the contention that inconsistent behavior management fosters disordered behavior (Kerr & Nelson, 2006; Landrum & Kauffman, 2006; Reid & Eddy, 1997). If one can extrapolate from the findings that inconsistent parental discipline adversely affects children's behavioral development, then it seems highly likely that inconsistent behavior-management techniques in the school will also have negative effects. Capricious, inconsistent discipline in the classroom will contribute nothing toward helping students learn appropriate conduct. School-based studies of antisocial behavior such as vandalism also indicate a connection between punitive, inconsistent discipline and problem behavior (Mayer, Nafpaktitis, Butterworth, & Hollingsworth, 1987; see also Kauffman, Mostert, et al., 2006; Walker et al., 2004). Even though inconsistent management may not be the root of all behavioral disorders, it obviously contributes to the perpetuation of behavioral difficulties.

Instruction in Nonfunctional and Irrelevant Skills

One way in which a school increases the probability that students will misbehave or be truant is in offering instruction for which pupils have no real or imagined use. Not only does this kind of education fail to engage pupils, but it also hinders their social adaptation by wasting their time and substituting trivial information for knowledge that would allow them to pursue rewarding activities, thus increasing the likelihood that they will drop out of school (Rylance, 1997; Witt, VanDerHayden, & Gilbertson, 2004).

The problem of making education relevant to students' lives has plagued teachers for a long time. The question we need to ask is more than whether the teacher or other adults know that instruction is important for the student's future. To resolve the question, the youngster must be convinced that the learning he or she is asked to do is or will be important. The teacher must convince the student that the instruction is in some ways worthwhile; otherwise, the classroom will be merely a place for the pupil to avoid or to disrupt. For some students with a history of school problems, convincing them will require provision of artificial reasons to learn, such as extrinsic rewards for behavior and performance (see Kauffman, Conroy, Gardner, & Oswald, in press, for discussion of cultural sensitivity and instruction).

Ineffective Instruction in Critical Skills

Social acceptance and positive self-perceptions are greatly enhanced by academic competence and skills in interacting with one's peers and authority figures. Thus, the classroom must be a place in which all class members learn critical academic skills and the social skills critical for success in general education. Ineffective instruction in either area—academic or social learning—dooms many students to academic or social failure or both. Nevertheless, many classrooms are not places where students are taught effectively but places where they are left to fend for themselves instructionally, to pick up whatever skills they might acquire through incidental learning or self-discovery (Kauffman, Conroy, et al., in press).

We cannot overemphasize the importance of academic learning to emotional well-being and behavioral development (cf. Coleman & Vaughn, 2000; Gunter et al., 1998; Kauffman, Mostert, et al., 2006; Lane, 2004; Mooney, Epstein, Reid, & Nelson, 2003; Rhode, Jenson, & Reavis, 1992; Walker, 1995). For everyone, not just children and youth, being able to meet everyday expectations is critical to mental health. Faced with constant failure and unfavorable comparisons to peers, nearly anyone will succumb to feelings of frustration, worthlessness, irritability, and rage. Competence on the job is an elixir; incompetence compared to one's peers is an emotional and behavioral poison. The job of students is academic learning, and teachers who are not as effective as they could be in helping students achieve academic competence are contributing to students' emotional and behavioral problems.

Unfortunately, most of general public education has adopted instructional practices that are not effective, especially for students who come to school without the skills that most economically privileged students acquire outside school (Heward, 2003; Heward & Silvestri, 2005). Child-directed, "holistic," "discovery learning" approaches and heterogeneous grouping, for example, are instructional practices virtually certain to fail with students at risk of failure (see Dixon, 1994; Grossen, 1993; Heward, 2003; Heward & Silvestri, 2005; Kauffman, Conroy, et al., in press). Special education classes are also too often places in which effective academic instruction is not provided (Colvin, Greenberg, & Sherman, 1993; Knitzer, Steinberg, & Fleisch, 1990). Direct instruction is effective in helping students with disabilities acquire academic skills, and using such instruction could improve the learning of students in both general and special education (Bender, 1993; Engelmann, 1997; Hallahan et al., 2009; Kauffman, 2002; Stichter, Conroy, & Kauffman, 2008).

Also unfortunate is the fact that most of general public education often has failed to adopt explicit programs for teaching social skills and rewarding desirable behavior. Specific social skills need to be assessed and taught explicitly and systematically to many individuals and groups if they are to learn the basic skills needed for positive interaction with others (Kavale et al., 2004; Mayer, 1995; Meadows, Melloy, & Yell, 1996; Walker et al., 2004). Yet few schools provide such assessment or instruction. Moreover, classrooms need to be places where desirable conduct is explicitly, frequently, and effectively rewarded (Lloyd & Kauffman, 1995). Yet most classrooms are characterized by very low rates of positive consequences for appropriate behavior (Shores et al., 1993). Popularization of the notion that rewards undermine intrinsic motivation and that positive reinforcement amounts to bribes (e.g., Kohn, 1993) has further impeded the adoption of positive behavioral strategies for managing classroom behavior (Maag, 2001). However, overwhelming empirical evidence indicates that rewards do not undermine intrinsic motivation and that rewards are essential for effective, positive classroom management, especially of difficult students (see Alberto & Troutman, 2006; Cameron & Pierce, 1994; Kazdin, 2001; Kerr & Nelson, 2006; Lewis, Lewis-Palmer, Stichter, & Newcomer, 2004; McGinnis, Friman, & Carlyon, 1999; Rhode et al., 1992; Walker, 1995; Walker et al., 2004; Walker, Forness, et al., 1998).

Destructive Contingencies of Reinforcement

From the viewpoint of behavioral psychology, the school can contribute to the development of emotional or behavioral disorders in several obvious ways:

- Providing positive reinforcement for inappropriate behavior
- Failing to provide positive reinforcement for desirable behavior
- Providing negative reinforcement for behavior that allows students to avoid their work.

The following section defines positive and negative reinforcement and gives examples of how each may work in a classroom environment. We recognize that in the behavior analysis research community the distinction between positive and negative reinforcement is a matter of debate (e.g., Baron & Galizio, 2005, 2006; Chase, 2006; Sidman, 2006). In our opinion, the distinction is helpful in thinking about what happens in teaching–learning interactions in classrooms.

Positive and Negative Reinforcement: A Dynamic Duo

Reinforcement—especially negative reinforcement—is often misunderstood. Many teachers do not understand how positive and negative reinforcement typically work together and how both may be involved in maintaining either desirable or troublesome classroom behavior. In many interactions, students with emotional or behavioral disorders get a double dose of reinforcement, one positive and one negative, and often for the wrong behavior.

Reinforcement, whether positive or negative, is a reward or consequence that makes the behavior it follows more likely to recur. The "reward" may be something one gets (i.e., a positive reinforcer) or something one gets rid of or avoids (i.e., a negative reinforcer). It may be helpful to think of people looking for work and having signs stating what they want. Some signs might say, "Will work FOR___." Other signs might say, "Will work TO GET OUT OF___." Still others might say, "Will work FOR___ AND TO AVOID___." What someone will work *for* provides positive reinforcement; what someone will work *to get out of or avoid* provides negative reinforcement. Most of us will work for money, and most of us will work to get out of debt or to avoid losing our job. Most of us will work for course credit and, at the same time, work to avoid embarrassment or a bad grade. In fact, in most cases our behavior is motivated by two consequences at once: (1) something we *get,* and (2) something we *avoid* (or at least escape temporarily). We work for money and also to get out of work (the negative reinforcement—escape from work—that we call vacations).

We all experience both positive and negative reinforcement in everyday life, and both types of reinforcement play important roles in motivating our adaptive behavior. However, positive and negative reinforcement become problematic rather than helpful in the classroom or any other environment when they are misused or poorly arranged. Misuse or poor application may be the result of either of two major mistakes:

- *Misidentification.* A teacher may believe that criticisms or reprimands are negative reinforcers that a student will work to avoid, when they are actually positive reinforcers. Being reprimanded is something the student will work to get because of the attention it brings from the teacher and classroom peers (for many of us, attention is something we crave, whether it is criticism or praise; being ignored is what we will work hardest to avoid). A teacher may also fail to see that academic assignments are negative reinforcers for a student who exhibits disruptive classroom behavior: Academic work may be something the student will misbehave to get out of. Whatever behavior allows this student to escape from the work (or postpone it) will be reinforced; the student will misbehave so that he or she does not have to do the work (see Moore & Edwards, 2003).
- *Malcontingency.* The contingencies in a classroom are destructive if they result in either positive reinforcement or negative reinforcement for undesirable behavior. Students may learn this: I get lots of attention when I misbehave (positive reinforcement, even if the attention is in the form of intended punishment such as scolding); in addition, I get out of my academic work (negative reinforcement).

The dynamic duo of positive and negative reinforcement can be harnessed to give desirable behavior a double boost (see Landrum & Kauffman, 2006). Students get a double good deal when the classroom contingencies involving both positive and negative reinforcement are constructive: attention for desirable behavior (positive reinforcement) and little vacations from work (negative reinforcement) as a reward for work done promptly and well.

How Things Often Go Wrong

Destructive rather than constructive contingencies of reinforcement are in place in many classrooms, both in general education and in special education. Appropriate conduct typically goes unrewarded, whereas both positive and negative reinforcement for misconduct are frequent (Gunter et al., 1993, 1998; Kauffman, Mostert, et al., 2006; Kerr & Nelson, 2006; Shores et al., 1993; Shores & Wehby, 1999; Strain, Lambert, Kerr, Stagg, & Lenkner, 1983; Webber & Scheuermann, 1991). A great deal of evidence suggests that constructive reinforcement contingencies can be arranged to teach appropriate behavior even to students whose behavior is seriously disordered. In study after study over the past several decades, experimental studies have shown that providing teacher attention during appropriate behavior but withholding it during undesirable behavior results in improvement (see Hoff & DuPaul, 1998; Landrum & Kauffman, 2006; Pullen, 2004; Walker, 1995; Walker et al., 2004; West et al., 1995).

In many classrooms, the contingencies of reinforcement are inadvertently arranged to promote the very behavior the teacher deems undesirable. The use of constructive consequences for adaptive behavior is consistent with a conceptual model that assumes interactive effects of students' and teachers' responses. An interactional or transactional model suggests that youngsters and adults exert reciprocal influence on each other. It is reasonable to believe that teachers' and problem students' mutual praise and criticism become important factors in the maintenance of behavior and that mutual hostility could be defused beginning with either teacher or pupil. Thus, in some cases, children with developmental disabilities and problem behavior have been taught to help their teachers provide positive reinforcement for their desirable behavior (e.g., Blake et al., 2000). Too often, classroom peers are allowed to provide additional reinforcement for misconduct.

Peer tutoring is another strategy designed to provide more positive reinforcement for desired behavior in the typical classroom (Tournaki & Criscitiello, 2003). Whether involving only specific pairs of students (one of whom tutors the other) or classwide peer tutoring (in which all members of the class are engaged in tutoring one another), the strategy has been shown to benefit many students whose behavior is problematic by increasing their engagement in academics and the positive interactions they have with their peers (e.g., DuPaul, Ervin, Hook, & McGoey, 1998; Gumpel & Frank, 1999). Moreover, a skillfully implemented program of peer tutoring could be a key strategy in teaching social skills to all students and teaching students nurturing responses to others, which would help make schools and the larger society kinder and gentler places in which to live. In too many cases, students are abusive of each other and their teacher, instead of helpful or nurturing.

Abundant empirical evidence shows that students' classroom behavior can be altered by manipulating the contingencies of reinforcement, even when the reinforcement is as natural a part of the classroom as teacher and peer attention (see Alberto & Troutman, 2006; Cullinan, 2002; Kerr & Nelson, 2006). It is easy to see the potential implications of this evidence in the school's contributions to the development of emotional or behavioral disorders. Students whose behavior is a problem often receive abundant attention for misbehavior but little or no attention for appropriate conduct. Even though the attention they receive for misbehavior is often in the form of criticism or punishment, it is still attention and is likely to reinforce whatever they are doing at the time it is dispensed. The effect of attention for misbehavior and nonattention for good deportment is likely to be perpetuation of the miscreant's deeds, regardless of the intentions of the teacher or another adult.

Undesirable Models of School Conduct

Children and youth are great imitators. Much of their learning is the result of watching others and mimicking their behavior. Youngsters are particularly likely to imitate the behavior modeled by people who are socially or physically powerful, attractive, and in command of important reinforcers (Bandura, 1986). Unless the modeling process is carefully controlled, students who act out and disrupt the classroom are likely to gravitate toward other peers who are disruptive. Teachers must find ways to call attention to and reward the appropriate behavior of high-status peers (Hallenbeck & Kauffman, 1995; Walker, 1995; Walker et al., 2004).

Exemplary behavior on the part of the teacher encourages like conduct in pupils. Maltreatment by the teacher of any student in the class is very likely to encourage students to treat each other with hostility or disrespect. Teachers whose attitude toward their work is cavalier or who are disorganized may foster similar carelessness and disorganization in their students. Corporal punishment—still used in some schools and classrooms—is a horrid example of aggressive misconduct by adults that may be mimicked by students in their relationships with others. A teacher's lack of self-awareness is likely to encourage a lack of self-awareness on the part of pupils (Richardson & Shupe, 2003).

Peers exert considerable social pressure on students' behavior in school, particularly at the high school level. Schools in which high-status students either refuse to perform academic tasks or exhibit serious misbehavior with impunity are likely to see the spread of academic failure and social misconduct (see Arnold & Brungardt, 1983; Farmer, 2000; Rutter, Maughan, Mortimer, Ouston, & Smith, 1979; Walker et al., 2004).

IMPLICATIONS FOR EDUCATORS

The teacher of students with emotional or behavioral disorders must be prepared to work with pupils who are below average intellectually and academically as well as deviant in their social behavior. Some of these students are superior intellectually and academically, but not most. Teaching these students demands not only the ability to instruct pupils across an extremely wide range of intellectual and academic levels but also the ability to teach social and other nonacademic behaviors that make scholastic success possible, such as good work habits, attention strategies, and independence (Meadows & Stevens, 2004). The most crucial tasks of the teacher as a preventive agent are to foster academic success and to lessen the student's antisocial conduct. Academic failure and antisocial behavior limit future opportunities and make future maladjustment likely.

The teacher's primary task is to modulate the school environment in ways that will contribute to adaptive, prosocial behavior and academic growth. The first requirement of appropriate education for students with emotional and behavioral disorders is that they be provided with effective instruction in academic skills (Bateman, 2004; Lane, 2004; Witt et al., 2004). In addition, every special education classroom should be characterized by the strategies of teachers who are also effective in preventing discipline problems and promoting self-control. Such characteristics are listed in Table 11.1.

Regrettably, many teachers of students with emotional or behavioral disorders are poorly prepared for the task. Moreover, the effectiveness of many special education programs is undercut by lack of support from administrators and parents. The challenge we face is not just preparing more and better teachers but also providing the supports that will facilitate their success and keep the best in the field longer (see cases in accompanying case book for further discussion).

Table 11.1 Strategies Used by Effective Classroom Managers to Create Classroom Climates that Prevent Discipline Problems and Promote Self-Discipline

---

In general, effective classroom teachers

☐ Work hard to develop a classroom environment that is caring, pleasant, relaxed, and friendly, yet orderly and productive
☐ Show a sincere interest in the life of each individual student (e.g., knows their interests, family, pets)
☐ Model the behaviors they desire in their students and convey that such behaviors are truly important
☐ Encourage active student participation in decision making
☐ Strive to not only teach prosocial behavior and to reduce undesirable behavior, but also to develop cognitions and emotions related to prosocial behavior
☐ Work to develop both peer acceptance, peer support, and close friendship among students
☐ Appreciate and respect diversity
☐ Appreciate and respect students' opinions and concerns
☐ Emphasize fairness by allowing for flexibility in application of consequences for rule violations
☐ Use cooperative learning activities
☐ Discourage competition and social comparisons
☐ Avoid producing feelings of shame (focusing more on pride and less on guilt)
☐ Reinforce acts of kindness in the school and community
☐ Communicate often with each child's home
☐ Provide frequent and positive feedback, encouragement, and praise, characterized by
  • Sincerity and credibility
  • Special suggestions and opportunities for good behavior
  • Highlighting the importance and value of the student's social and academic achievement
  • Attributing success to effort and ability, which implies that similar successes can be expected in the future
  • Encouraging students to believe that they behave well because they are capable and desire to do so, not because of consequences
  • A focus on both the process and the product of good behavior
  • Reference to prior behavior when commenting on improvement
  • Specification of what is being praised
  • Praise that is contingent on good behavior
☐ Establish clear rules, beginning during the first few days of school, which are characterized by
  • Clear and reasonable expectations
  • "Dos" and "Do nots" regarding classroom behavior
  • Attempts to develop student understanding of rules and their consequences
  • Highlighting the importance of a small number of important rules
  • Fairness and developmental appropriateness
  • Explanations and discussions of the rationale for each rule
  • Student input during their development
  • Clear examples of appropriate and inappropriate behavior related to each rule and direct teaching of appropriate behavior if necessary
  • Clear consequences for rule infractions
  • Distributing of a copy of rules and consequences to children and parents
  • Their consistency with school rules
  • Frequent reminders of rules and expected behaviors
  • Their nondisturbance of the learning process—the rules do not discourage healthy peer interactions such as cooperative learning or appropriate peer discussions

---

Source: Bear, G. G. (1998). School discipline in the United States: Prevention, correction, and long-term social development. *School Psychology Review, 27,* 20. © 1998 by the National Association of School Psychologists. Reprinted by permission of the publisher.

SUMMARY

The role of the school in causing emotional or behavioral disorders is a particularly important consideration for educators. In our society, school failure is tantamount to personal failure. The school environment is not only critically important for social development but is also the factor over which educators have direct control.

As a group, students with emotional or behavioral disorders score below average on intelligence tests and are academic underachievers. Many of them lack specific social skills. The behavior they exhibit is inimical to school success. Disordered behavior and underachievement appear to influence each other reciprocally; in an individual case, which causes the other is not as important as recognizing that they are interrelated. Academic failure and low intelligence, when combined with antisocial behavior or conduct disorder, portend social adjustment problems in adulthood. The school may contribute to the development of emotional or behavioral disorders in children in several ways:

- School administrators, teachers, and other pupils may be insensitive to the student's individuality.
- Teachers may hold inappropriate expectations of students.
- Teachers may be inconsistent in managing students' behavior.
- Instruction may be offered in nonfunctional (that is, seemingly irrelevant) skills.
- Ineffective instruction may be offered in skills that are critical for school success.
- School personnel may arrange destructive contingencies of reinforcement.
- Peers and teachers may provide models of undesirable conduct.

Teachers of students with emotional or behavioral disorders must be prepared to teach youngsters who are underachieving and difficult to instruct, and instruction must be provided in both academics and social skills.

CASE FOR DISCUSSION

You Had Better Get on Them
Bob Winters

Bob Winters had been prepared to teach preschoolers with disabilities, but he accepted a job teaching a special class of students with mild mental disabilities in a middle school. When he was hired, the principal, Mr. Dudley, had told him, "You're the expert. We'll give you a lot of leeway for making decisions about these students because you're the one who's trained to work with difficult students. Mr. Arter, the teacher last year, had lots of trouble with these kids. You'll have to come down on them hard."

Bob struggled to develop appropriate instructional programs for his students. Other teachers were coming to him for advice, but he had little or nothing to offer. He ended up assigning lots of worksheets emphasizing basic skills. He tried to keep the kids busy, but as the days and weeks rolled by, his class became more and more rowdy, and he felt his classroom control slipping away. The students raced through their assignments and then wandered around the room laughing and joking in small groups and verbally abusing each other. Poor grades did not bother them. In fact, they bragged about getting bad grades and were particularly glad to show off a paper that had the lowest score in the class.

Bob's class became so unruly and noisy that Mr. Dudley occasionally came down the hall to open the classroom door and glare or shout at Bob's students. The students laughed and joked about Mr. Dudley after he left. "He thinks he's bad," one would say, and the others would shake their heads in agreement. Bob was determined to get tougher. He simply had to get control over this class. He began trying Mr. Dudley's shouted directions. As punishment, he began requiring students to copy pages out of the dictionary, something they seemed to dread. But one Thursday he invoked this punishment when Ronnie disrupted the class as he returned from the restroom. Ronnie grinned impishly and declared, "Okay, I *love* copying the dictionary." He copied more pages than Bob had assigned. But the next day Ronnie flatly refused to copy any pages at all, and Bob eventually ordered him to the office.

Eventually, Bob decided to arrange the students' desks facing the classroom walls. Maybe this way they wouldn't distract each other so much and would get more work done, he reasoned. But then they began moving their desks together without permission. They met his reprimands with saucy comments such as "Oh, big man!" and "Yeah, he thinks he's going to do something!" When Gerald jumped out of his seat and ran over to whack Mike playfully on the back of the head, Bob lashed out. "Get your ass in the chair!" he bellowed. Gerald froze. The others stared silently at Bob as he went on, "I don't give a damn what you all want to do. You're going to do as I say." Cathy nudged Ronnie, who sat beside her, and they began to giggle. Bob descended on Cathy immediately, shouting, "Go to the office!" With flashing, angry eyes, Cathy stalked out and slammed the door. Her classmates shook their heads and exchanged scowls.

Ten minutes later, Mr. Dudley was at Bob's door. "Mr. Winters, may I see you outside?" As he walked to the door, Bob heard Amber say, "He's going to be in trouble." Bob guessed she was right.

Note: *This case was adapted from the following source: Kauffman, J. M., Mostert, M. P., Trent, S. C., Nuttycombe, D. J., & Hallahan, D. P. (1993).* Managing classroom behavior: A reflective case-based approach. *Boston: Allyn & Bacon.*

Questions About the Case

1. How do Bob's teaching and management strategies illustrate the concepts presented in this section? What was Mr. Dudley's role in contributing to the problems with this class?

2. If you were Bob's friend and colleague, what advice would you give him about improving his teaching performance?

3. Where does the responsibility lie for preventing situations like the one depicted here?

PERSONAL REFLECTIONS

School Factors

Rudolph E. Ford, Ph.D., is principal of the Onslow W. Minnis, Sr., Middle School, in Richmond, Virginia.

What behavioral characteristics do at-risk students exhibit in school?

At-risk students often exhibit behaviors designed to draw attention to themselves. One may attribute some of this attention-grabbing conduct to students' natural tendency to seek acceptance. This is a universal trait among all youth. However, when students are at risk, they often try to compensate for their feelings of academic inadequacy by succeeding at the popularity game. In transitions between classes, these children are often loud, obnoxious, defiant, ill-mannered, and overanimated in their social interactions. They communicate in profound verbal and nonverbal ways. They may suck their teeth, roll their eyes, mouth words as if talking to themselves, or turn away from someone who approaches them. These are only a few of the gestures I often observe.

Middle and high school students seem to be more overtly interested in pursuing the opposite sex. They may dress in a more provocative way, often with the full knowledge that their dress will mean trouble with school officials. The immediate, powerful gratification that sex promises simply has more appeal to them than does avoiding trouble. Locker room talk among boys and intercepted notes of girls often reveal a level of sexual awareness or activity that surprises teachers who hold middle-class values. A male student in my school was so determined to walk his girlfriend to class and kiss her good-bye that he quickly reached the point of being a habitual offender for tardiness. In subsequent conversations with this student, he admitted to me that his girlfriend mattered more than promptness to class. He clearly and unabashedly coveted the immediate gratification of her hug, and he valued being seen with her more than any academic goal. Passing to the next grade just did not matter in his culture at home, and he had brought this culture to school. Educational pursuits did not hold much value in his world.

At-risk students often cannot see the value in education. Frequently, they do not know anyone outside of the school who has an advanced education, so they acquire an "us against them" mentality. At-risk student peer groups will sometimes socially reject those who dare to achieve. Those who strive to achieve become social pariahs who "think they are better than us," according to their peers. The social conditioning of their peer group teaches them to believe they cannot achieve. Too often, those students who are at risk but want to succeed come to believe that they are not expected to achieve. Ironically, educators often contribute to these self-doubts through negative relationships with students. These self-doubts produce low effort, which then produces low achievement. The cycle of failure becomes a self-fulfilling prophecy. These students frequently do not understand the mores of middle-class, mainstream peers.

How would you characterize teachers who are likely to have special difficulty with behavior management or have negative effects on students' behavior?

Teachers who take things personally often struggle with behavior management. Predictably, these are teachers who negatively influence students' behavior. They have a low tolerance for behaviors that are dissimilar to the behaviors they learned as children. They often will not admit to being flawed themselves because they think that will reveal weakness. They rarely make apologies. Failed teachers *tell* more often than they *listen*. They rarely obtain or use feedback. They do not value what students think.

Economically deprived students and at-risk students are often the same, and they often exhibit the behaviors I have described. Teachers experiencing difficulty confuse any tolerance of such behaviors as a sign of weakness and are convinced that the strong stand they take against these behaviors is in students' long-term best interests. They do not strive to guide at-risk students toward more socially acceptable behaviors through successive approximations. These teachers believe they should immediately suppress the behavior with punishment, lest they be weak. Struggling teachers establish an adversarial relationship with students. When these teachers see an unacceptable behavior, such as loud talking, they misinterpret the negative behavior as a conscious affront to their authority. In reality, students may be displaying coping mechanisms they have learned in their socioeconomically deprived subcultures at home. Teachers may be the furthest thing from their minds.

Teachers who do not understand students' modes of communication, motivation, neighborhood culture, unspoken rules, methods of giving and receiving respect, and varieties of learning styles often struggle. Teachers in at-risk schools, by design, are asked to establish relationships with students who come from subcultures different from their own. Students at risk are not regularly exposed to successful college graduates. However, all teachers must be at least minimally successful college graduates to be qualified to teach. After graduation, teachers are sorted and selected through the application process. The most civil, intelligent, poised, and charming applicants are the successful candidates for teaching positions. This process reinforces, in the mind of teachers, that how they conduct themselves is the key to success. They are appalled on the first day of school to learn that their students do not share their understanding of right and wrong. Attributes such as civility, achievement, manners, and consideration of others' feelings are not part of the rules of the street. Teachers and students must recognize the rules necessary to diffuse the dissonance that occurs when two sets of standards for behavior are in effect in the same environment. If teachers will acknowledge this duality, then they can move past it and direct students toward appropriate behaviors.

However, the importance of students learning mainstream mores cannot be overstated if they are to experience success in the workplace. Successful teachers describe for students the acceptable behavioral norm and teach students that they must learn the mainstream way of behaving to live comfortably in our society. When teachers frame this message in the context of excellent relationships with students,

the odds for productive teaching and learning are increased. Teachers must gain the trust of students if they hope to direct them toward higher achievement. The teacher who is snide and sarcastic will rarely successfully establish a good rapport with students. Teachers themselves must model behaviors they expect from students. If teachers respond to students in a steady, calm, and respectful manner, then students will eventually return the favor. Teachers who bark commands, telling students what they must do rather than being a model of what they expect, often struggle with bad pupil–teacher relationships.

What do you do as a principal to try to establish a positive and supportive school climate?

The establishment of a positive and supportive school climate is paramount to the success of any school. The principal must be constantly vigilant to make sure he or she considers how decisions will affect the school climate. The stakeholders of public schools are parents, students, teachers, and administrators. Each one of these groups must feel it is a vital part of the school for the school to be successful. As a principal, the most important thing I can do is to promote positive relationships between and among all of the stakeholder groups. I must have a highly visible presence. I must exude confidence, high energy, and a "can-do" attitude with everything I do. I must model my belief in the students, faculty, and parents. I must work hard at building positive relationships with every single person with whom I come into contact— even in difficult situations such as disciplinary hearings or employee reprimands.

I ask my teachers and students and parents about their families and listen attentively until they are done telling me about them. If I am not willing to hear about Sandra hitting a home run during last Saturday's Little League game, then I should not ask. In asking, however, I show teachers, students, and parents that I care about them as individuals. I have enjoyed some very supportive and loyal colleagues as well as trusting, happy parents and students. Although I know I may not be able to establish a positive conversational rapport with everybody, I believe it is my duty to try.

As principal, I must seize each moment of each day and tweak it for all it's worth. I must embrace accountability and resist making excuses for a lack of performance, focusing instead on maximizing performance. I must convince teachers, students, and parents that we are better off with standards. I must show them that standards are a way to improve the lives of all stakeholders in our school. I must show them that standards give us a tool to measure our performances. I must ensure that the curriculum is no mystery to teachers and that they have a clear and concise understanding of what they should teach. Teachers are a hardworking group of professionals who generally have an abundance of energy and hope. I must ensure that the daily grind does not wear them down and demoralize them into becoming pessimists. Teachers must be included in decision making throughout the school. In positive school climates, all stakeholders feel ownership of the mission. This ownership is built through group decision making. I have witnessed better-quality decisions in general when the group is involved in making that decision. The cliché "Two heads are better than one" usually holds true. As principal, I have noticed that I can feel far more confident in the decision being accepted by all stakeholders when I have included them in the decision-making process.

To build a positive school climate, I must make sure there are abundant opportunities for everyone to have fun. I must smile and ensure that everyone knows that seriousness of purpose and having a good time are not mutually exclusive. People need to have the idea that they are free to initiate an idea or program to foster a positive school climate. They must feel that creativity is welcome. They must revel in the idea that a risk that might result in better teaching and learning is worth taking. If the principal focuses his or her dialogue on what is right about the institution, then a positive climate can be established and maintained. My goal is for everyone to be familiar with my vigor, enthusiasm, and faith in the mission, joy, and love of my profession and the people at school. I believe I am always onstage, so I must always show my very best. If I strive every day to do the things I have outlined, a positive school climate will be the eventual result or will be successfully maintained.

School climate is greatly influenced by the level of support teachers feel from the administration. Teachers have to be shown in a variety of ways how much they are valued, both individually and collectively. I accomplish this through one-on-one conversational relationship building and through a variety of enjoyable schoolwide activities designed to show appreciation. I hold a monthly teachers' coffee morning social, have monthly "goody days," give ice cream sundae treats, give single roses to teachers, hand out candy bar treats for various holidays, buy birthday corsages, go to wedding and baby showers, attend socials at various staffers' homes, and try numerous other positive, climate-boosting activities.

What do you think are the most important aspects of a student's experience at school that contribute to behavioral problems?

Lack of success is one of most important contributors to behavioral problems. When a student's life is devoid of success, he or she is certain to shut down, tune out, and rebel. The unsuccessful student will turn away from the painful failure experiences and toward social pursuits. Often, negative, attention-grabbing behaviors emerge. Therefore, opportunities for students to succeed must permeate instruction throughout the day.

When teachers lecture, do not engage students actively, do not allow students to touch anything during the lesson, focus on knowledge that is not relevant to students' real world and not connected to something students want, then students are not likely to tune in. Teachers who waste time getting started with a lesson often lose students. Students must be actively engaged as soon as they walk in the door—sometimes even before that. I recently observed a successful teacher meeting students on the sidewalk with a handout of written instructions to proceed with the lesson on entering the room. The activity had a time limit and required an oral report in just 5 minutes. The teacher handed the sheet to them without saying a word. As soon as students looked at it, they sprang into action—hurrying to their seats, swiftly unpacking, and getting to work. This was a teacher who only 1 year earlier had contemplated quitting at midyear. She says the higher level of structure she provides this year is the difference for her. She is a much happier professional now. If you are teaching fractions the day after Halloween, why not make candy the object of the fractions? Let students manipulate the candy.

Impoverished students use particular mechanisms of survival in their neighborhoods. However, teachers who refuse to recognize and control these differences often create negative tensions that contribute to behavioral problems. Schools with predominantly at-risk populations must control these tendencies through careful policies designed to teach students the right way to behave—meeting them where they are. Educators must demonstrate to at-risk students that they are advocates, not foes. At-risk students must believe their teachers are advocates. This perception is paramount for the steady academic progress that standards-based educational policy demands. I do not advocate that we create new and special knowledge for any subgroup. The Ebonics fiasco in California was an example of the futility of that approach. To the contrary, I believe that standards are good for students. However, teachers who understand that students who exhibit unacceptable behaviors may be doing things the only way they know how experience more joy, gratification, and success. Teachers must free themselves from feelings of resentment toward students for their actions and view misbehavior as an opportunity to teach them yet another usable skill for success in life.

Do you have any other reflections on your role in the school?

The principal must be a reflective practitioner who has a vision for the school that transcends its current efficacy. I must accept this responsibility: My leadership will steer the school to ultimate success or failure. I define success as sustained, continuous improvement. Every decision I make as principal must have this goal as its driving force. The vision I have for where we can go must be as clear in my mind as if I were looking at a sharply focused picture.

To achieve this, I must work very hard to get the best, most competent staff possible. The staff must be given an abundance of development activities to build their confidence and focus their efforts on exactly what will be tested and therefore what must be taught. For a school to be known as high performing, mediocrity must become scarce or extinct. Effective principals acquire the vision and then use the team decision-making approach to create the plans for success. Once these plans are formulated, they should be put into writing as a schoolwide improvement plan. This plan should clearly define the roles and expectations of all stakeholders, including teachers, parents, students, and administrators.

I must deliver and facilitate the delivery of service. If we develop raving fans instead of just satisfied customers, then we will have succeeded as a service organization. Traditionally, principals have not approached community relations as a marketing challenge. Too often, excellence can be observed in classrooms, but the public is not aware of the quality of the instruction students are receiving. I must seek opportunities to market our school. With the current national debate about school choice as an option, marketing our school may be more important than ever.

QUESTIONS FOR FURTHER REFLECTION

1. As a teacher, how can you make sure that you are aware of how you might be contributing to a student's problems?
2. If your school administrators are not supportive of what you consider to be essential or best practices, what are your best options for trying to change things?
3. How would you describe your most important goals for the students you teach, and what rationale can you provide for choosing those goals?

SECTION 12
CULTURAL FACTORS

As you read this section, keep these guiding questions in mind:

- How do conflicts between cultures create stress for children and youth?

- What steps can educators take to avoid the problems of bias and discrimination against students whose cultures differ from their own?

- Besides family and school, what major cultural factors may contribute to behavioral

deviance? Why is it difficult to evaluate the effects of these factors?

- What relationships have been established between TV viewing and children's antisocial and prosocial behavior?

- How would you characterize a neighborhood that provides support for development of children's appropriate social behavior?

APPEAL OF CULTURAL FACTORS AS CAUSAL EXPLANATIONS

Neither families nor schools include all the social influences that determine how youngsters behave. Children, families, and teachers are part of a larger culture that molds their behavior. Parents and teachers tend to hold values and set behavioral standards and expectations that are consistent with those of the cultures in which they live and work. Children's attitudes and behavior gravitate toward the cultural norms of their families, peers, and communities. We must therefore evaluate family factors in the context of cultural differences and changes. Family relationships change across time and are different in different cultures. Although we may find certain patterns or characteristics of successful child rearing that are the same across time and in all cultures, it is also clear that the same specific behaviors that are adaptive in one circumstance may not be in another (e.g., inner city versus affluent suburb; time of peace versus time of war; economic stability and growth versus economic depression; rearing by parents versus rearing by grandparents; one-parent versus two-parent families). Therefore, the findings of studies in 2010 or 2015 or 2020 may tell us less than we might imagine about American families by 2030 or later because of changing conditions and demographics.

Culture involves behavioral expectations, but it is more than that (see Banks & Banks, 2007). Culture may include values, typical or acceptable behavior, languages and dialects, patterns of nonverbal communication, awareness of cultural identity, and worldviews or general perspectives. Nations and other large social entities have a shared culture or national culture. Within the larger society are many smaller groups with unique values, styles, languages, dialects, ways of communicating nonverbally, awareness, frames of reference, and identification (often called subcultures, not because they are dominated or of lesser importance but because they are only a part of the whole). How do we maintain American culture and at the same time respect the subcultures that form it? The answer is neither obvious nor easy (see Hallahan, Kauffman, & Pullen, 2009; Kauffman, 1999b, 1999g, 2002, 2005; Kauffman, Bantz, & McCullough, 2002; Kauffman, Conroy, Gardner, & Oswald, in press, for further discussion of multiculturalism and education).

The United States has often been called a cultural melting pot—an amalgam of various nationalities and cultures. We have come to believe that its diversity of citizens makes the United States strong and good. But we realize that if we do not make a true alloy of the diverse ingredients of our culture—if we do not amalgamate our diverse elements into a single, uniquely American identity—we can be neither strong nor good as a society. *E pluribus unum* (out of many, one), a slogan stamped on our coins, seems to present an increasing paradox (see Hallahan, Kauffman, & Pullen, 2009; Hodgkinson, 1995; Ogbu, 1990; Osher et al., 2004; Singh, 1996; Singh, Ellis, Oswald, Wechsler, & Curtis, 1997). We value cultural diversity, but common cultural values hold our society together. The tension between our separateness and our togetherness—our distinctiveness and our oneness—obviously can set the stage for disordered emotions and behavior, as well as conflicts among groups on nearly every issue. But it is togetherness, oneness, unity, and commonality that provide the glue holding any society together. An emphasis on differences to the exclusion of seeing the common sets the stage for cultural conflicts, racism, hatred, and war (see Britt, 1999; Kauffman, 2002; Raspberry, 1999; Singh, 1996). Moreover, the same fundamental principles of behavior and instruction seem to apply to all cultures (Kauffman, Conroy, et al., in press).

When the child's, family's, school's, or teacher's values or expectations conflict with other cultural norms, emotional or behavioral development may be adversely affected or school behavior may become a difficult issue (see Cartledge, Kea, & Ida, 2000; Osher et al., 2004; Fisher, 2003; Nakamura, 2003). To the extent that different cultural forces tug a youngster's behavior in different directions, they create conflicting expectations and increase the probability that he or she will violate cultural norms and be labeled deviant.

Comer (1988) noted that "differences between home and school—whether of class, race, income, or culture—always create potential conflict" (p. 37). It is not surprising, therefore, that researchers have given a great deal of attention to cultural factors that contribute to disordered behavior (see Evertson & Weinstein, 2006, for discussion of multicultural issues in behavior management). "Race" is not a scientifically defensible biological fact. Rather, "the concept of race is a cultural invention, a culturally and historically specific way of thinking about, categorizing, and treating human beings" (Mukhopadhyay & Henze, 2003, p. 673). This is not to say that the cultural construct of race is unimportant, only that it has no basis in biology.

CONFLICTING CULTURAL VALUES AND STANDARDS

It is easy to find examples of conflicting cultural values and standards and the stress they create for children and youth. Television shows, movies, and magazines glamorize the behavior and values of high-status models that are incompatible with the standards of many children's families; youngsters' imitation of these models results in disapproval from parents. Religious groups may proscribe certain behaviors that are normative in the larger community (such as dancing, attending movies, dating, masturbating). Youngsters who conform to these religious teachings may be rejected by peers, stigmatized, or socially isolated, whereas those who violate the proscriptions may feel extreme guilt. The values children attach to certain possessions or behavior because they are highly regarded by their peers or teachers (such as wearing particular items of clothing or achieving at school) may be incomprehensible to their parents. Differences between parents' and children's values may become the focus of parental nattering.

Hitting and aggression are generally considered unacceptable in our society. However, "corporal punishment has been an integral part of how parents discipline their children throughout the history of the United States," and data suggest that almost 95% of American parents spank their young children (Gershoff, 2002, p. 539; see also Kauffman, Conroy, et al., in press, for a discussion of this issue). Although some nations of the world have outlawed the corporal punishment of children, the

United States has not. Attitudes among various cultural groups toward corporal punishment and knowledge of the effects of spanking remain matters of considerable controversy (Gershoff, 2002).

Children of interracial marriages may have difficulty developing a sense of identity, particularly during adolescence. They may have major problems reconciling their dual racial identifications into a single, personal identity that affirms the positive aspects of each heritage and acknowledges society's ambivalence toward biracial persons. At the same time, the demographic trends in America are toward a mixing of national, ethnic, and racial categories (Glazer, 1997; Hodgkinson, 1995), and just how or when someone takes on a particular cultural identity is not known (see Kauffman, Conroy, et al., in press).

Conflicting cultural influences on behavior are sometimes perverse; the culture provides both inducements for a given type of behavior and severe penalties for engaging in it. This kind of temptation or pressure with one hand and punishment with the other is especially evident in the areas of violent behavior and sexuality (see case of Teri Leigh in the accompanying case book). Our society fosters violence through its glorification of high-status, violent models in the mass media, yet it seeks severe punishment for youngsters' imitative social aggression. Consider teenage pregnancy—the cultural forces that foster it and society's responses to it. During the past several decades, sexual mores have changed so that adolescents now have much greater freedom and added responsibilities for preventing pregnancy. Our society tempts adolescents, offering them freedoms and responsibilities they are not equipped to handle, yet it does nothing to help them deal with these freedoms and responsibilities and in fact punishes them for abusing freedom and behaving irresponsibly. Motion pictures, MTV, and commercials highlight sex appeal and sexual encounters, providing models of behavior that are incompatible with efforts to encourage sexual abstinence and avoid pregnancy. Teenagers often pressure their peers to become sexually active; at the same time, conservative politicians have attempted to restrict sex education and make contraceptives less available to teens. Education for family life and child rearing is often inadequate.

MULTICULTURAL PERSPECTIVE

Besides the conflicts that differing cultural standards create, children's and adults' own cultural values may bias their perceptions of others. A full discussion of cultural bias in education is far beyond the scope of this section, but it is important to note that problems of bias and discrimination carry serious implications for evaluating youngsters' behavior.

Ultimately, nearly all behavioral standards and expectations—and therefore nearly all judgments regarding behavioral deviance—are culture-bound; value judgments cannot be entirely culture-free. In our pluralistic society, which values multicultural elements, the central question for educators is whether they have made sufficient allowance in their judgments for behavior that is a function of a child's particular cultural heritage (see Cartledge et al., 2000; Council for Children with Behavioral Disorders, 1996; Coutinho & Oswald, 1998; Osher et al., 2004). Cultural differences that do not put the youngster at risk in the larger society should be accepted; only values and behaviors that are incompatible with achieving the larger goals of education (self-actualization, independence, and responsibility) should be modified.

Who determines the larger goals of society? We all tend to view our own cultural orientation as the standard against which others should be judged. Because the United States has been dominated by European subcultures, the focus of multicultural concerns has been on non-European minority cultures.

It is not easy to establish rules for applying a multicultural perspective. Teachers and school administrators must make daily decisions about which standards of conduct represent their personal value systems and which represent justifiable demands for adaptation to the larger society. For example, is it really necessary for students to remove their hats in the classroom? What is "polite" English, and is it necessary that students use it to address adults in school? What values and behaviors are inconsistent with a youngster's success and happiness in society at large? When do the values of a particular culture place a student at risk for school failure? Under what conditions is risk of school failure a fault of the school itself—how it is organized and the demands it makes of students?

These and similar questions have no ready answers. They will continue to be part of our struggle for fairness and justice in a multicultural society. At the same time, we note that the greatest fairness to students is achieved by offering them instruction that is evidence based (Kauffman, Mock, Tankeresley, & Landrum, 2008; see also Morris & Mather, 2008). Kauffman, Conroy, et al. (in press) stated:

> All things considered, we believe that we can be passionately committed to education as a science while maintaining sensitivity to the cultural differences of individual children and their families. However, first and foremost we must recognize that the most culturally responsive practices are empirically validated instructional strategies.

PROBLEMS IN EVALUATING THE EFFECTS OF CULTURAL FACTORS

Besides the family and the school, which are topics of separate sections, the most frequently researched cultural factors include the mass media, peer group, neighborhood, ethnic origin, social class, religious institutions, urbanization, and health and welfare services. Evaluating the role of these factors in emotional or behavioral disorders is extremely difficult, primarily for three reasons.

First, the interrelationships among the many cultural influences are so strong that untangling the effects of most of the individual factors is impossible. Decades ago, Farrington (1986) noted the interaction of culture with other variables, a problem reiterated by Coutinho and Oswald (1998). Hodgkinson (1995) observed that concern with racial and ethnic differences has diverted our attention from the more pervasive effects of poverty. Although poverty may be correlated with racial or ethnic identities, the best strategy for improving the lives of children who are members of racial or ethnic minorities and those with disabilities may be to focus on poverty itself (see Park, Turnbull, & Turnbull, 2002):

> To some extent, race diverted our attention from the most urgent issue: *poverty reduces the quality of the lives of all children, regardless of race or ethnicity*. Had we spent the 40 years since the *Brown* [1954 school desegregation] decision systematically seeking to lower the poverty level for *all* American children, we would be in a different, and probably better, condition today. (emphasis in original; Hodgkinson, 1995, pp. 178–179)

Second, research related to several of the factors is limited or nearly nonexistent. Religious beliefs and institutions, for example, probably have a strong influence on family life and child behavior, yet there is little research on the effects of religion on child behavior and family life (see Kauffman, Conroy, et al., in press).

Third, culture and temperament are interrelated in ways that make identification of problem behavior difficult. Is the problem in the child's behavior, the teacher's expectations, or the lack of fit between the two? Keogh (2003) summarized the problem succinctly:

> The idea of culturally related differences in how temperament is viewed is especially relevant to school. Classrooms are filled with students from many different cultural and ethnic backgrounds. They come to school from homes with particular expectations about what is acceptable or unacceptable behavior, about the meaning and importance of particular temperamental characteristic. Teachers, too, come with unique temperaments that reflect their own cultural beliefs and values. In some cases, the two will mesh well; in other cases, the two will be discrepant, leading to misunderstandings and stress. (p. 35)

Despite these difficulties in understanding cultural factors, available research does suggest relationships between certain cultural characteristics and the development of behavioral deviance. For example, violence in the media and the ready availability of guns, two prominent features of contemporary American culture, are consistently linked to aggressive conduct of children and youth (Huesmann, Moise-Titus, Podolski, & Eron, 2003; Stoff, Breiling, & Maser, 1997; Walker, Ramsey, & Gresham, 2004). The challenge is to understand and sustain cultural diversity that enhances the human condition while modifying cultural patterns of behavior that destroy the human spirit (see Kauffman, Bantz, & McCullough, 2002).

Biology, Family, School, and Culture: A Tangled Web of Causal Influences

When we think of cultural factors, we think of social institutions—nations, ethnic groups, religions, schools, and families. These and other social institutions are interconnected in ways that defy simple explanations of causal influences on children's behavior. For each possible combination of social institutions, we must ask how one affects the other. To what extent does the nation make its schools, and to what extent do its schools make that nation? To what degree can schools succeed without the support of families, and to what degree can families be successful without schools that teach what their children need to learn? What are the cultural factors, other than families and schools, that shape children's behavior, and how do families and schools create, enhance, or counteract these other influences? The answers to these questions are neither simple nor obvious, but they are critical to our understanding of the roles of schools and teachers in our society.

The role of schools in American culture—the extent to which schools merely reflect our national character and the extent to which they are responsible for creating it—is frequently a matter for discussion. Perhaps the increasing use of guns in the United States is peculiarly American. If it is a part of American culture, then it is no wonder it has invaded our schools. Researchers have found that Southeast Asian refugee families adopting an orientation to certain American values—acquisition of material possessions and pursuit of fun and excitement—have children whose academic performance is lower than that of children from families maintaining traditional Southeast Asian values: persistence, achievement, and family support (Caplan, Choy, & Whitmore, 1992). From one vantage point, then, it appears that schools and teachers face a task at which they cannot succeed unless changes occur in other aspects of social context or culture. "It is clear that the U.S. educational system can work—if the requisite familial and social supports are provided for the students outside school" (Caplan et al., 1992, p. 36).

We cannot, however, ignore the fact that schools and teachers have a special responsibility to influence the families and communities for which they exist—the other parts of our culture that they also reflect. True, parents must be involved with and support the work of teachers if the schools are to succeed. "Yet we cannot expect the family to provide such support alone. Schools must reach out to families and engage them meaningfully in the education of their children" (Caplan et al., 1992, p. 42). And meaningful engagement can occur only if schools offer instruction that addresses the concerns of families and communities. Delpit (1995) noted that many poor minority children have been shortchanged by an exclusive focus on "progressive" methods of instruction that cater to the learning of middle-class White students: "I have come to believe that the 'open-classroom movement,' despite its progressive intentions, faded in large part because it was not able to come to terms with the concerns of poor and minority communities" (p. 20). Yet the affection of the public and educators for "progressive" methods seem to other writers to continue to stymie the progress of many students, especially ethnic minorities and children with disabilities or other disadvantages (see Heward, 2003; Heward & Silvestri, 2005; Hirsch, 1996; Kauffman, 2002). There is great irony in the fact that many advocates of so-called culturally sensitive instruction embrace constructivist ideas that are inimical to the success of students whose cultures and languages are different from those of the larger society (see Kauffman, Conroy, et al., in press).

Many see the role of schools in American culture changing, in large measure because of the increasingly troublesome behavior, attitudes, and social needs of students. American culture itself is shaped in significant ways by the distribution of wealth among its citizens, and increasing economic disparities are a troublesome part of American culture. Poverty is a part of American culture that we obviously have not addressed effectively (Park et al., 2002). The cultural context of American public schools in the 21st century includes widespread poverty among children and the deterioration of families and other social institutions that previously offered more support for schools. The role of special education for children and youth with emotional or behavioral disorders in this context will likely be a matter for increasingly hot debate because it is clear that special education has not adequately addressed the problems our society wants to see solved (see Walker, Forness, et al., 1998).

As if this were not complicated enough, genes and environments have considerable influence on behavior and the creation of culture (cf. Diamond, 1997; Pinker, 2002; Weiner, 1999; Wilson, 1998). Thus, cultures, including families, schools, and other features of societies, are partly a result of social learning and partly a result of biological fates. Wilson (1998) captured the perspective on biological and social determinants of behavior succinctly:

> All biologists speak of the interaction between heredity and environment. They do not, except in laboratory shorthand, speak of a gene "causing" a particular behavior, and they never mean it literally. That would make no more sense than its converse, the idea of behavior arising from culture without the intervention of brain activity. The accepted explanation of causation from genes to culture, as from genes to any other product of life, is not heredity alone. It is not environment alone. It is interaction between the two. (p. 149)

Genetic influences on behavior and culture seem at first consideration to suggest that cultures will always evolve so that those that are most "fit," in a Darwinian sense, will survive. Ultimately, perhaps, this is so, but "culture can indeed run wild for a while, and even destroy the individuals that foster it" (Wilson, 1998, p. 171). Cultures are neither immutable nor immortal (Pinker, 2002).

Mass Media

Mass media include printed materials, radio, television, motion pictures, and electronic information now available on the Internet. Societal concern for the effects of mass media on the behavior of children and youth began when books and magazines became widely available (Donelson, 1987). A few generations ago, concerns about the effects of radio programs and comic books were frequently expressed. Present controversies rage over the effects of textbooks, pornographic magazines, novels, motion pictures, electronic games, and information and pornography available on the World Wide Web on the thinking and behavior of the young.

That what people read, see, and hear influences their behavior is hardly questionable; yet relatively little sound research is available to explain how—with the exception of advertising material. Publishers and broadcasters do market research to show the effectiveness of sponsors' ads; they know a lot about what sells and what influences the buying habits of specific segments of their audiences, including children and adolescents. Nevertheless, the influence of the media on youngsters' social behavior is often dubious or hotly disputed. Ironically, the same individuals (television network executives) who express confidence in the behavioral effects of television commercials argue that the effects of television violence on children's social behavior is negligible (Eron & Huesmann, 1986).

Today, the effects of television on behavioral development is by far the most serious media issue. Watching lots of television appears to have adverse effects on the cognitive abilities of young children (Zimmerman & Chistakis, 2005) and to be associated in adolescence with risk for development of problems in attention, learning, and schooling (Johnson, Cohen, Kasen, & Brook, 2007). Moreover, researchers and policy makers are interested in how watching television may increase children's aggression and their prosocial behavior (for example, helping, sharing, cooperation). Research clearly links watching television to increases in aggression, but the link is a statistical probability, not a one-to-one correspondence. Some highly aggressive children do not watch much television, and some children who watch television almost incessantly are not aggressive. Yet television viewing is clearly a contributing factor in some children's antisocial conduct, and it is important to understand how television viewing can be involved in causation. One obvious way in which television violence can facilitate aggressive conduct is through observational learning; youngsters imitate what they see. This explanation is probably a gross oversimplification; however, research now suggests that much more complicated processes are involved.

The most likely explanation of the effects of television viewing fits Bandura's (1986) social cognitive model. The effects involve reciprocal influence among three components: person variables (thoughts and feelings), the social environment, and behavior. In the case of television violence and aggression, Bandura's triadic reciprocality involves the child's thoughts and feelings about aggression and the television characters who perform it, the child's environment (including school, home, and community), and the child's selection of violent television programs and aggressive responses to problem situations. But general social circumstance—the social ecology in which aggression is exhibited, including friendship patterns and school performance—must also be considered (Eron & Huesmann, 1986).

Sprafkin, Gadow, and Adelman (1992) and Gadow and Sprafkin (1993) reviewed decades of research on the effects of television viewing on exceptional children. They found little evidence that watching television programs showing prosocial acts causes children with emotional or behavioral disorders to engage in more appropriate social interaction. Their review also indicated that high levels of television viewing, whether the shows contained much violence or not, have negative effects on children's behavior.

Huesmann, Moise, and Podolski (1997) reviewed research on the relationship between antisocial behavior (particularly aggression) and media violence, including dramatic violence, music videos, video games, and news violence. Their conclusions are straightforward:

> Over the past four decades, a large body of scientific literature has emerged that overwhelmingly demonstrates that exposure to media violence does indeed relate to the development of violent behavior. The emerging theories and data suggest that multiple processes are involved, but that the most important seem to involve the observational learning of attitudes, beliefs, attributional biases, and scripts that promote aggressive behavior. Desensitization of emotional processes may also play a role in long-term effects as may a cognitive justification process in which the more aggressive children use media violence to justify their acts. At the same time, powerful

shorter term effects of media violence may be engendered by excitation transfer from media violence to real life and by the tendency of media violence to cue well-learned aggressive habits. These processes would seem to place children most at-risk who already live in a "culture of violence" in which there are few norms against aggressive behavior, in which there are ethnic or nationalistic forces that support violence against dehumanized targets, and in which there is little family or educational intervention to moderate the effects of media violence. (p. 190)

More recent research by Huesmann et al. (2003) has added confirmatory evidence that watching a lot of TV violence dramatically increases the risk that a child will grow up to exhibit violent interpersonal behavior in adulthood. Violent media action appears to instigate antisocial acts in some cases, to desensitize children to acts of aggression (i.e., make them more apathetic to displays of aggression and less likely to help others), and to perceive their environment as a more aggressive and dangerous place. Some violent video games appear to provide effective training in violent acts through emotional preparation and behavioral rehearsal. Although research may not indicate clearly that watching television violence consistently causes children (including those with emotional or behavioral disorders) to be violent, there are good reasons to limit children's television viewing and direct their attention toward more constructive activities. The American Psychological Association (1993) and Walker et al. (2004) concluded that decreasing the violence depicted on television and in movies would help lower the level of violent behavior among children and youth.

The role of the mass media (not just television but all print, film, video, and broadcast media) in the development of emotional or behavioral disorders is a concern to those who wish to construct a more prosocial and humane society. For example, teenage suicidal behavior appears to increase following media coverage of teen suicides (Eisenberg, 1984; Hawton, 1986). Motion pictures that glorify violent solutions to problems may add to the effects of television violence. It is difficult to conclude that print materials featuring violence and pornography play any *positive* role in behavioral development or conduct.

Perhaps decreasing portrayal of undesirable behavior and increasing prosocial programming and reporting of prosocial acts would make our culture less self-destructive and more humane. Yet the solution to the media problem is not apparent; censorship is not compatible with the principles of a free society. Personal choice and responsibility in patronage may be the only acceptable way to approach the problem. How to increase responsible personal choice in media production and viewing remains unknown.

Peer Group

The peer group is a possible contributing factor to emotional or behavioral disorders in two ways. First, the establishment of positive, reciprocal peer relationships is critical for normal social development. Children who are unable to establish positive relationships with their classmates are at high risk because the peer group is an important link to social learning (LeBlanc, Sautter, & Dore, 2006). Second, some children and youth are socially skilled and have high social status but are enmeshed in a peer group that exerts pressure toward maladaptive patterns of behavior (Farmer, 2000; Farmer, Rodkin, Pearl, & Van Acker, 1999; Walker et al., 2004).

Absence of Positive Peer Relationships

Peer relationships are extremely important for behavioral development, especially during middle childhood and early adolescence, yet until the early 1980s, research tended to focus more on family relationships than on socialization to the peer group (J. R. Harris, 1995; Hops, Finch, & McConnell, 1985). We can now identify problematic relations with peers in children as young as 5 years of age, and these problems tend to persist over time (Ialongo, Vaden-Kiernan, & Kellam, 1998; Loeber, Green, Lahey, Christ, & Frick, 1992; Walker et al., 2004). Behavioral characteristics associated with emergence and maintenance of social status in the peer group and relationships between peer status and later behavioral problems are becoming clearer (Farmer, 2000; Farmer, Farmer, & Gut, 1999; Walker & Sprague, 2007).

Research indicates that, in general, high status or social acceptance is associated with helpfulness, friendliness, and conformity to rules—to prosocial interaction with peers and positive attitudes toward others. Low status or social rejection is associated with hostility, disruptiveness, and aggression in the peer group. To complicate matters, aggressive youngsters, compared to nonaggressive, seem more likely to attribute hostile intentions to their peers' behavior, and they are more likely to respond aggressively even when they interpret their peers' intentions as nonhostile. Low social status among peers is also associated with academic failure and a variety of problems in later life, including suicide and delinquency. In fact, poor peer relations, academic incompetence, and low self-esteem are among the primary factors in an empirically derived model of the development of antisocial behavior (Dishion, 1990; Patterson, 1986b; Patterson, Reid, & Dishion, 1992; Walker et al., 2004).

The evidence that antisocial children and youth are typically in conflict with their peers as well as with adult authorities is overwhelming, as is the evidence that antisocial youngsters tend to gravitate toward deviant peers (see Farmer, 2000; Farmer, Farmer, & Gut, 1999; Farmer, Rodkin, et al., 1999; Walker et al., 2004). Youngsters who do not learn about cooperation, empathy, and social reciprocity from their peers are at risk for inadequate relationships later in life. They are likely to have problems developing the intimate, enduring friendships that are necessary for adequate adjustment throughout life. Thus, the peer group is a critical factor in creating social deviance.

These generalizations do not do justice to the complexity of the research on relationships between social status among peers and children's behavioral characteristics (Farmer, Rodkin, et al., 1999). Social status can be measured using peer nominations, teacher ratings, or direct behavioral observations. Depending on the source of data, different pictures of social acceptance or rejection emerge. Normal or expected behavior in the peer group differs with age and sex, so the same type of behavior can have different implications for peer relations depending on age and sex. The social processes that lead to social rejection may be quite different from those that lead to social isolation or neglect (Coie, Dodge, & Kupersmidt, 1990; Farmer, 2000). The same classroom conditions can produce different effects on social status and friendship patterns for students of different races, and bias in peers' social perceptions can produce different outcomes in terms of social acceptability for two individuals who exhibit similar behavior.

All sources of information regarding children's social acceptance indicate that better-liked youngsters are those who are considerate, helpful, and able to appeal to group norms or rules without alienating their peers. Social rejection is related to opposite characteristics—violating rules, hyperactivity, disruption, and aggression—although the antisocial behavior that characterizes rejected youngsters changes with age. As children grow older, they tend to exhibit less overt physical aggression. The ways in which they irritate others, and so become rejected, become more complex, subtle, and verbal. Physical aggression is more often a factor leading to rejection in boys' groups than in girls'.

Social withdrawal is often associated with peer rejection, but the causal relationship is not always clear. Apparently, social withdrawal is not as prominent as aggression in young children's thinking about relations with their peers. As children grow older, however, withdrawal correlates more closely with rejection, perhaps because rejected children are acquiring a history of unsuccessful attempts to join social groups. This correlation suggests that withdrawal is the result of rejection, a way of dealing with repeated social rebuffs. Youngsters who withdraw following repeated rejection may become the targets of taunts and abuse, perpetuating a cycle of further withdrawal and further rejection.

We know less about the behavior of socially neglected children than about those who are actively rejected, partly because it is difficult to study the characteristics of children who are all but invisible to their peers. Nevertheless, it appears that their peers see them as shy and withdrawn, that they engage in solitary play more frequently than most children, and that they are less aggressive and higher achieving than even popular youngsters (Wentzel & Asher, 1995). Neglected children sometimes appear to exhibit relatively high levels of prosocial behavior and conformity to teacher expectations, but their general lack of assertiveness may result in their peers' not perceiving them as socially competent.

Given that we have identified social skills in which rejected, withdrawn, and neglected youngsters are deficient, programs to teach those skills are logical interventions. Social skills training programs are now readily available. Nevertheless, social skills training often yields equivocal results, perhaps in part because training programs are typically implemented poorly or inconsistently (Kavale, Mathur, & Mostert, 2004; Maag, 2006; Quinn, Kavale, Mathur, Rutherford, & Forness, 1999; Sridhar & Vaughn, 2001; Vaughn et al., 2003).

Moreover, we often do not know exactly what skills need to be taught. The notion that we can easily identify critical social skill deficits without careful assessment is a deceptive oversimplification (Walker et al., 2004). Research increasingly reveals that social competence is much more complex than previously thought. Social competence may relate to the ability to display specific skills in specific situations, but precise identification of skills and exact specifications of performance in given situations are extremely difficult to determine (see Pearl, 2002). Moreover, identifying social skill deficits that cause youngsters to have problems with their peers is not always possible; the causes of peer rejection or neglect are typically multiple and complex.

An important aspect of the analysis of peer relations and social skills training, and one that has not always been considered in research, is the development of expectations that bias youngsters' perceptions of their peers' behavior. If, for example, a youngster acquires a reputation among his or her peers for aggression or for popularity, others respond to this reputation. They expect behavior that is consistent with their attributions of the motives of an individual whose reputation they accept as valid, and they interpret behavioral incidents accordingly. If one child throws a ball that hits another child on the head, peers are likely to interpret the incident in terms of their beliefs about the motives of the child who threw the ball. If the child is popular and does not have a reputation for aggression, they are likely to interpret the incident as an accident; if the child has a reputation for aggression, they are likely to interpret it as aggressive. The reciprocal interaction of biased perceptions and actual behavior must be taken into account in trying to understand why some youngsters are rejected, whereas others who behave similarly are not.

Effective social skills interventions must, therefore, include provisions for dealing with peer-group response to the youngster with emotional or behavioral disorders as well as teaching skills that enhance social acceptance (Vaughn et al., 2003; Walker et al., 2004). Only when the social ecology of the peer group can be altered to support appropriate behavioral change are social skills likely to result in improved status of the target child. Knowing that a youngster lacks specific social skills necessary for social acceptance and being able to teach those skills is not enough; one must also change the youngster's reputation—the perceptions and attributions of peers.

Undesirable Peer Socialization

An important causal factor in some emotional or behavioral disorders, especially antisocial behavior and delinquency, is peer pressure and socialization to deviant peer groups. The assumption that students who exhibit antisocial tendencies will observe and imitate the desirable behavior of their regular classroom peers appears to be based on myth rather than facts about observational learning (Hallenbeck & Kauffman, 1995). Antisocial students often reject prosocial models and gravitate toward a deviant peer group (Farmer, 2000). J. R. Harris (1995) has been credited with bringing attention to the primacy of peer influences on social development, but the recognition of the importance of peers does not mean that parents have no influence on their children's socialization (Kauffman, 1999a).

Peer pressure toward rejection of academic tasks, as well as toward antisocial behavior, appears to be a serious problem in many communities. Consider the observations of R. Leon Churchill, Jr., an African American who, at the time of the following comments, was 33 years of age and the assistant city manager of Charlottesville, Virginia. He recalled that as a boy in school in Williamsburg, his good study habits cost him friends. "I remember being teased constantly for getting good grades. . . . One of the major issues that Charlottesville and most schools have to deal with is the gauntlet that African-American males have to run through for achievement" (Zack, 1995, B1, B2; see also McWhorter, 2000; Williams, 2007).

Pressure of the peers of some African American students toward academic failure and classroom disruption may involve not wanting to act or be accused of acting White, but racial and ethnic perceptions are not the only factors in such peer pressure, nor are African American students the only ones to experience peer pressure toward marginal or failing performance at school. In any ethnic or racial group and in any social stratum, we may find groups of peers who express disdain for those who are studious, high achieving, and tractable (see Farmer, Rodkin, et al., 1999; Miller-Johnson, Coie, Maumary-Gamaud, Lochman, & Terry, 1999; Williams, 2007).

In some schools, regardless of the ethnicity of the students, a high proportion of students exhibit behavior that is seriously, persistently maladaptive and incompatible with learning. The stressors or risk factors that students in these schools experience "may combine to create a school culture in which noncompliance is the norm and where peer reinforcement leads to students' acceptance and expectation of disruptive behavior in their peers" (Warren et al., 2003, p. 82).

Teachers must thus be aware of how their efforts to induce and maintain appropriate behavior in their students can be undermined by negative peer pressure. More important, teachers need to find ways, perhaps through peer tutoring or other means, to build a peer culture that supports kindness and achievement. Research suggests that this may be accomplished for most students when they are given regular opportunities to learn, with proper training and supervision, to nurture and teach younger children (see Farmer, Stuart, Lorch, & Fields, 1993; Strayhorn, Strain, & Walker, 1993). Moreover, special classroom settings may be required for the most effective instruction in desirable social behavior for youngsters with emotional or behavioral disorders (Farmer, 2000; Kauffman, Bantz, and McCullough, 2002; Kauffman, Mock, et al., 2008; Stage & Quiroz, 1998).

Neighborhood and Urbanization

Neighborhood refers not only to residents' social class and the quality of physical surroundings but also to the available psychological support systems as well. Loeber, Farrington, Stouthamer-Loeber, and Van Kammen (1998a) drew the connection between antisocial behavior and neighborhood factors explicitly:

> Externalizing problems, unlike internalizing problems, were associated with neighborhood factors. Most of the externalizing problems we studied, and particularly physical aggression and delinquency, were more prevalent in the worse neighborhoods. Therefore, interventions for externalizing problems will need to take neighborhood into account. (p. 268)

Separating the neighborhood from other causal factors in social deviance, particularly social class, has proved difficult, if not impossible (Farrington, 1986, 1995). The neighborhood and community may play important roles in the prevention of certain types of highly visible behavioral deviance, such as conduct disorder and juvenile crime (Hawkins, Arthur, & Olson, 1997; Lorion, Brodsky, Flaherty, & Holland, 1995; Short, 1997). For example, a community sense of moral order, social control, safety, and solidarity may be extremely difficult to achieve in a neighborhood in which crime rates are high. Interventions aimed at individuals will probably not succeed because of the lack of neighborhood monitoring and mutual support. Students who carry weapons to school have been found to perceive less social support from parents, teachers, classmates, and friends (Malecki & Demaray, 2003). Group-oriented community interventions that promote a shared sense of being able to cope with deviance may be more likely to help prevent juvenile delinquency and crime in high-crime neighborhoods (Lorion et al., 1995). A neighborhood in which violence is "normative" may, actually, foster the use of violence among children and youths (see Ng-Mak, Salzinger, Feldman, & Stueve, 2002).

The belief that city life is not conducive to mental health has persisted for well over a century despite a lack of evidence that this is the case (cf. Jarvis, 1852). Achenbach, Howell, Quay, and Conners (1991), in a national study of behavior problems, found no differences between rural and urban settings in parental ratings of children's behavior problems. However, higher behavioral problem ratings were found in areas of intermediate urbanization (i.e., urban areas of fewer than one million people).

Compared with rural areas, higher rates of delinquency are sometimes found to occur in urban areas, but a major difficulty in establishing urban environments as a causal factor in social deviance is that urbanization cannot be easily separated from other factors, such as crowding, quality of housing, community or neighborhood supports, social class, and so on (see Farrington, 1986, 1995). However, it is also clear that family functioning and child rearing are often quite difficult in today's urban environment.

Some people express enthusiasm for the virtues and healing powers of rural retreats and agrarian cultures, but there is not much evidence that they are superior to urban environments in producing mentally healthy and high-achieving children. The overriding factors associated with deviance appear to be low socioeconomic status and the breakdown of family and community ties. Recent reports of economic and social conditions in rural America leave no doubt that inner cities are not our only disaster areas for families and children. If rural ever meant "safe," "healthful," or "educationally superior" for children, it is clear that it does not necessarily mean those things in the present era (see the case of John in the accompanying case book, pp. 82–83).

More recently, there has been considerable concern for the health (including the mental health) of children because many are spending so little time outdoors and so much time indoors playing computer games and otherwise avoiding engagement with "nature" (St. George, 2007). In fact, Louv (2005) wrote of what he termed "nature deficit disorder." He considers children's gravitation toward indoor pursuits, such as computers, computer games, and television, to be related to increases in obesity, depression, and attention-deficit disorder. Whether outdoor pursuits are more conducive to mental health than are indoor activities is no doubt something that will be answered by future research.

Ethnicity

Ethnicity has been the focus of much contemporary concern for understanding cultural diversity and forging multicultural education. Nevertheless, ethnic identity is increasingly difficult for many Americans to define, and we must be careful to separate ethnic influences on behavior from those of other factors such as economic deprivation, social class, the peer group, and so on (see National Research Council, 2002; Roberts, Roberts, & Xing, 2006).

In one of the largest and most carefully controlled studies of prevalence of behavioral problems in children and adolescents, Achenbach and Edelbrock (1981) found very few racial differences. They did, however, find substantial differences in behavioral ratings from different social classes, with children of lower class exhibiting higher problem scores and lower social competence scores than did those from higher class. Cullinan and Kauffman (2005) did not find that teacher judgment of emotional or behavioral problems was biased by ethnicity of students or that bias in referral explained the disproportional representation of African American students in special education for students with EBD. Roberts et al. (2006) did not find differences among psychiatric disorders among African, European, and Mexican American adolescents. Neighbors et al. (2007) did find that African Americans tend to underuse mental health services.

When the effects of social class are controlled, ethnicity apparently has little or no relationship to emotional or behavioral disorders. The risk factors that may appear to accompany ethnicity are probably a function of the poverty of many ethnic minority families (Garmezy, 1987; Hodgkinson, 1995; Park et al., 2002; Short, 1997).

Ethnicity is often suggested as a factor in juvenile delinquency because studies show higher delinquency rates among Black than among White youngsters, but we must question the meaning of differences in rate for at least two reasons. First, discrimination in processing may account for higher official delinquency rates among students of African descent. Second, ethnic origin is difficult or impossible to separate from other causal factors, including family, neighborhood, and social class. Thus, it is not clear that ethnicity is related to delinquency independently of other factors (Dinges, Atlis, & Vincent, 1997; Farrington, 1986; Yung & Hammond, 1997).

Our tendency has been to make sweeping judgments regarding ethnic groups without taking individual backgrounds and experiences into account. This leads to stereotypes based on ethnic identity alone (see Tores, Solberg, & Carlstrom, 2002). Ethnic identity plays a part in how youngsters, particularly adolescents, are treated in our society (National Research Council, 2002; Osher et al., 2004; Peterson & Ishii-Jordan, 1994; Spencer, 1997).

The issues surrounding ethnicity are complex because the values, standards, and expectations of ethnic groups are shaped not only internally by members of these groups but also by external pressures from the larger culture of which they are a part. Thus, we must be careful in analyses of the effects of ethnicity to separate the influences of ethnic background from the effects of the dominant cultural groups' treatment of other ethnic groups.

Given the long history of maltreatment of ethnic groups with relatively little power by the dominant American ethnic groups, we should not be surprised to find that membership in an ethnic minority that has comparatively little political or social power presents barriers to the achievement of academic competence, economic security, and mental health. Moreover, it is important to recognize that most ethnic minority youngsters do not succumb to the risk factors they experience:

> The majority of ethnic minority youths are not members of gangs, do not abuse alcohol or other drugs, do not commit acts of violence, and do not indulge in other problem behaviors. This includes many disadvantaged youngsters who are subject to comparable individual, family, or community-based risks that have influenced antisocial behavior in their similarly exposed peers. (Yung & Hammond, 1997, p. 491)

An important point is that the disproportionality of ethnic groups in special education or juvenile justice does not mean that a very high percentage of youngsters from an ethnic group are in special education or juvenile justice. For example, it is an egregious error to conclude that half of all African American students are emotionally disturbed because half of the students in special education for students with emotional disturbance are African Americans. This is the kind of logical and mathematical error that fosters stereotypes.

Social Class and Poverty

One ordinarily measures children's social class in terms of parental occupation, with children of laborers and domestic workers representing one of the lower classes and children of professional or managerial workers representing one of the higher classes. Although lower social class is often associated with psychopathology, the meaning of this finding is controversial.

The relationship between social class and specific types of disordered behavior does not hold up as well as the relationship to emotional and behavioral problems in general. Furthermore, family discord and disintegration, low parental intelligence, parental criminality, and deteriorated living conditions seem to be much more influential than does parents' occupational prestige in accounting for children's behavior. Although it is true that many parents in low-prestige occupations may be described by the characteristics just cited, it is not clear that low social class in itself is a contributing factor in children's social deviance; social class may be a factor only in the context of these other parental and family characteristics (see Roberts et al., 2006).

Economic disadvantage—poverty, with all its deprivations and stress—is apparently a factor in the development of disordered behavior, but social class, at least as measured by occupational prestige of parents, probably is not (cf. Delpit, 1995; Hart & Risley, 1995; Hodgkinson, 1995; Park et al., 2002; Qi & Kasiser, 2003; Roberts et al., 2006). Merely being poor does not make people inadequate or destroy families or account for children's school failure or emotional and behavioral problems. However, we do know that many of the conditions that often are part of poverty, especially in its extreme, are strong negative influences on children's cognitive and social development: inadequate shelter, food, and clothing; exposure to chaotic living conditions and violence; and lack of opportunities to learn from nurturant, attentive adults. Nevertheless, poverty itself is the best predictor of school failure, as Hodgkinson (1995) pointed out in a conclusion that is still valid:

> If there is one universal finding from educational research, it is that poverty is at the core of most school failures. And this is as true for white children from Appalachia as for black and Hispanic children from inner-city slums. . . .
>
> Consider the issue of relative deprivation. Is a child with dark skin more likely to be disadvantaged in terms of life chances than a child born into poverty? Today, the answer is clearly no; poverty is a more pervasive index of social disadvantage than is minority status.
>
> This emphatically does *not* mean that we can ignore poor minority children; it means that a successful strategy will have to lift the largest number of children out of poverty, regardless of their race. . . .
>
> There is clear evidence from the U.S. Government Accounting Office and from other sources that a number of social programs are effective in mitigating the effects of poverty. Head Start, WIC (Women, Infants, and Children feeding program), AFDC (Aid to Families with Dependent Children), and Upward Bound are programs that reduce the effects of poverty and help reduce the number of America's youngsters who remain in poverty. In addition, the prevention agenda—ensuring that bad things do not happen to young children—is "color blind" in its effectiveness for all poor children. We have at our disposal a set of proven programs for reducing poverty for *all* children from birth to age 18. Why is this agenda not fully implemented? (pp. 176–178, emphasis on original)

Occasionally, poverty is glorified, or at least its ravages are denied and the right to be poor is defended, usually by those who have not experienced poverty or seen it up close. One middle class man with a physical disability recalls the following in his autobiography.

> I remember one night that we were at Mr. Peshkin's [the history teacher's] house. . .and we were talking about the various rights of speech and thought. And Mr. Peshkin, our very own sly Socrates, asked if we thought we had the right to be poor, and, of course, privileged middle-class youths that we were, never having seen a right we didn't like, we said yes. And we were debating this right to be poor, with great eloquence, when Mr. Lombardo, the high school Spanish teacher, dropped by the house. Mr. Lombardo, who was from South America, had been dirt poor; and he laced into this group of privileged middle-class white boys with the passion and pain of his whole life. Having silenced us, shamed us, with this dose of reality, he went on to argue for the right not to be poor. He persuaded me. (Mee, 1999, pp. 193–194)

IMPLICATIONS FOR EDUCATORS

Educators should be aware of how cultural factors may be contributing to their students' emotional or behavioral problems and of the possibility of cultural bias in evaluating behavioral problems. We can seldom untangle the effects of isolated factors from the mix of circumstances and conditions associated with disordered behavior. Parental attitudes toward behavior and its correction cannot be understood without reference to cultural and community norms, especially for such controversial issues as corporal punishment (Gershoff, 2002) and touching students (Fisher, 2003).

Sometimes, the difference between teacher and students in culture or ethnicity is jarring, and teachers are caught completely by surprise. For example, Nakamura (2003) described his surprise at the contempt students showed for him in a Japanese high school, where he found that "Just as in America, a large number of students are being left behind" (p. 31). The story of two volunteers for Teach for America (Fisher, 2003) is a tale of success and failure in a District of Columbia elementary school. The story includes this observation of one of the teachers about Josh, who was unsuccessful:

> "Josh's disciplinary methods were pretty much what I do," says Vest [another teacher], "but I'm an African American woman in my mid-fifties, older than many of these children's grandmothers, and I get a different kind of respect. I'm sorry, but in many of those cases, there was nothing Josh could have done differently except be born a different color. We complain a lot about it when it's the reverse, but this was the same things we face—racism. Children called the white teachers bitches and MFs, parents could threaten them, and it was okay." (Fisher, 2003, pp. 42–43)

However, this view of racism as the root problem might be challenged. Another teacher who had taught in the same school saw things differently. "Other white teachers were able to overcome the race issue. . . .However, because Josh was having a tough time, race became an issue" (Fisher, 2003, p. 43). Teachers with well-honed skills in instruction and behavior management are usually successful, regardless of their personal identity or that of their students (see Kauffman, Conroy, et al., in press; Landrum & Kauffman, 2006).

Research on specific factors that may give rise to disorders has important implications for prevention, especially if intervention can be aimed at improving children's individual circumstances. Strong evidence now suggests a basis for corrective action in many cases. Reducing television violence and providing more prosocial television programming, for example, would probably help reduce the level of aggression in our society, as would simply reducing the amount of time many children spend watching television.

Much could be done to address the needs of children reared under adverse conditions in which their health and safety, not to mention intellectual stimulation and emotional development, are at stake. These kinds of social changes demand large-scale efforts that educators cannot achieve alone; indeed, the politicization of issues regarding the physical and mental health risks of children and youth calls for all Americans to speak out. Programs to serve children and youth living in poverty will have enormous consequences for the nation's future. An open question is the extent to which local, state, and national governments will ask taxpayers to fund programs for poor and disadvantaged children and youth (see in accompanying case book, "The Health and Welfare of Children: How Important Are They in American Culture?").

Of the causal factors discussed in this section, the peer relations of rejected and neglected students is perhaps the most important consideration for the daily work of educators. Although we now recognize the great significance of students' poor peer relations or socialization to deviant peers, we know relatively little about the most effective means of intervening to improve their status or change their social affiliations once patterns of maladaptive behavior have become well established. Developing school-based, early interventions for target children and their peers should be a priority for researchers and teachers. These interventions may play an important role in the prevention of social adjustment problems (see Evertson & Weinstein, 2006; Martella, Nelson, & Marchand-Martella, 2003).

A FINAL NOTE ON CAUSAL FACTORS

When we think about the causes of emotional or behavioral disorders, oversimplifications and overgeneralizations are great temptations. We are inclined to assume that highly inappropriate behavior is simply a result of inadequate parenting or teaching, physiological problems, or cultural influences. We are too often tempted to believe that ____ is destiny, whether the ____ stands for biology, culture, or anything else. Keogh (2003) noted how biological factors do not always have the negative consequences for human relationships that we might expect. She described watching preschoolers' social interactions with peers and teachers:

> One of [the] students with the most severe physical limitations was a 4-year-old boy with cerebral palsy who had no speech and only minimal locomotion. Yet he was a magnet for the other children and the staff. He was an exceptionally responsive, cheerful, and outgoing child who thrived on interactions with others and who, despite serious physical limitations, was the most popular child in the class. Other children with milder disabilities were less sought after and had fewer and less satisfactory personal relationships. The differences in these children's temperaments were striking. (pp. xiv–xv)

But it is easy to miss Keogh's message, too. Her message is not that temperament is destiny, simply that temperament must be considered for the complex role it plays in children's development—and not just the temperament of the child, but the temperament of parents and teachers as well. Oswald (2003) stated, "Causality in the world of emotional and behavioral disorders is rarely linear; it rarely proceeds unambiguously from event A to outcome B" (p. 202).

Physiology, parenting, teaching, and culture can be significant causal factors, but we must be extremely cautious in drawing conclusions about the individual case. Before concluding that a student's undesirable classroom behavior is a result of the teacher's ineptitude or that the child's disorder is caused by poor parenting, we must examine carefully what transpires in the interactions between student and teacher or child and parent. However, even if we observe these interactions and find that the adult clearly is behaving toward the child in a less-than-admirable manner, we must be careful not to jump to the conclusion that we have found the root of the problem. A child with a serious emotional or behavioral disorder may be extremely difficult for anyone to live with; he or she may be highly effective in frustrating and bringing out the worst in just about anyone.

Recognizing that causal effects are not so simple or unidirectional as they first appear should help us maintain a reasonable level of humility in evaluating our own work with children and youth and give us caution in placing blame on the other adults who work with them as well.

We know more today about some of the origins of emotional or behavioral disorders than we knew 25 or even 10 years ago, but researchers now realize that causal mechanisms are far more complex than previously assumed. At the same time that research is revealing the incredible complexity and interconnectedness of causal factors, it is opening up new possibilities for intervention. Old ideas that the course of psychopathology is set by early life experiences or biology and is impervious to intervention have given way to more hopeful attitudes for most disorders. At the same time, newer ideas about the positive influences of therapeutic environments are being tempered by the realization that many patterns of behavior reflect genetics and other biophysical processes and that teachers and parents should not be blamed for them or held responsible for correcting these problems solely through interpersonal interventions.

Mark Twain said, "It is wiser to find out than to suppose" (Mark Twain Foundation, 1966, p. 943). Pinker (2002) and Tavris (2003) have reminded us also of the importance of skepticism in trying to find out why people behave as they do. The scientific frame of mind is critically important. We need also to remember Polsgrove's maxim, "Just because you *think* it doesn't make it true" (Polsgrove, 2003, p. 223), as well as the bumper sticker saying, "Don't believe everything you think."

SUMMARY

Children, families, and teachers are influenced by the standards and values of the larger cultures in which they live and work. Conflicts among cultures can contribute to youngsters' stress and to their problem behavior. Not only conflicts among different cultures, but mixed messages from the same culture can be a negative influence on behavior. Cultures sometimes both encourage and punish certain types of behavior; for example, youngsters may be tempted or encouraged by the media to engage in sexual behavior, yet our society creates penalties for teenage pregnancy.

We must guard against bias and discrimination in our pluralistic, multicultural society. Cultural differences in behavior that do not put the child or youth at risk in the larger society must be accepted. Educators should seek to change only behavior that is incompatible with achievement of the larger goals of education. However, clear rules for applying a multicultural perspective have not been established. Teachers and school administrators must continue to struggle with decisions about what behavior puts a child at risk in society at large.

Besides family and school, cultural factors that influence behavior include mass media, peer group, neighborhood, urbanization, ethnicity, and social class. A major difficulty in assessing most of these and other cultural factors is that they are so intimately intertwined. It is difficult, for example, to untangle the factors of social class, ethnicity, neighborhood, urbanization, and peer groups. Social class, ethnicity, the neighborhood, and urbanization have not been shown to be, in themselves, significant causal factors in emotional and behavioral disorders. They are apparently significant only in the context of economic deprivation and family conflict.

Other cultural factors are more clearly involved in causing disordered behavior. Watching television causes rising levels of aggression among children who are already aggressive. Rejection by peers also increases the upward spiral of aggression among youngsters who are uncooperative, unhelpful, disruptive, and aggressive. Socialization to deviant peers also may be a significant factor in antisocial behavior. In both cases—television violence and peer rejection or social gravitation to bad companions—youngsters' behavior, their environments (including others' reactions to their behavior), and their perceptions are factors in the development of increasing social deviance.

The literature on peer relations and social skills training has the clearest and most direct implications for educators. Teachers must be concerned about teaching the social skills deviant students need, but they must also be concerned with the responses and perceptions of the peer group and the deviant social networks that students with behavioral disorders may establish.

We have a lot to learn about how causal factors work together. We must guard against oversimplifications and overgeneralizations.

CASE FOR DISCUSSION

What Would You Have Done?
Contributed by Shannon Fitzsimmons

I hop on the train going toward my house and make my way past a group of kids near the door. I sit down next to a woman my age and look around me. The group of youths at the door becomes the primary focus of my attention. There are six or seven of them—one girl. I'd say they range from 10 to 13 years old. Two of the boys are engaged in a game of some sort; there is no distracting them. The language the others are using with each other is pretty coarse for public talk. As the train grows more full at each stop, the youth remain sprawled, as if the car were empty. New passengers step over their legs that are extended into the aisle.

Given the range of behaviors that one can reasonably expect from individuals in this age range, the kids that I can hear are skirting its edges. Perhaps for this reason, no one is issuing those warm smiles that adults so readily cast onto children. Perhaps for this reason also, a middle aged woman, sitting just behind the group and across from me, stands up and moves to a seat farther back.

At this point, I notice the boy directly in front of me has an odd posture: almost a fetal position, slouched far, far down. New passengers walking by eye him curiously. After this happens several times, I lean forward to see what he is doing. He backs up, standing now, but hunched over—and resumes his activity of drawing on the seat in thick, dark ink. As I have obviously seen him, and he has obviously seen me see him, I must call him out—he's vandalizing a full train, after all.

"What are you doing?" I ask in a tone I think is curious but stern.

"I'm drawing [expletive]. What does it look like I'm doing?"

I freeze, redden. He looks up now. He is staring at me hard. I hold the stare, but I have no idea how to respond. He must be—what?—11?

"You can't do that," I say finally, and while we are not speaking loudly, everyone near us is taking note.

No one says anything.

"Listen, [expletive], if you don't want me to rob you, you'd better shut the [expletive] up."

"Excuse me?"

"I said, if you wanna keep your stuff, you'd better shut the [expletive] up."

This exchange goes on for one or two more rounds. I say nothing substantial. The 11-year-old continues to threaten me. I realize we have reached my stop. The woman beside me, who has obviously witnessed the entire event, stands up and says, "Excuse me," as she would normally to make her way out of our seat and off the train. I pick up my things. I can feel all eyes on me as I leave.

I have no idea what happened when I exited the train and began walking down the street. Maybe someone said or did something firm about the child's language or his action and got results. Maybe the kid kept on drawing in a car full of immobile adults while a handful of adolescents learned that intimidation is an effective means of achieving objectives.

After replaying the incident a number of times in my mind, I'm still not sure what I could have done or said to get the desired outcome—cessation of vandalism. I know my approach was not successful. I also know, for me, this event illuminated greater societal problems: that some children have experienced this kind of threatening dialogue enough times in their own lives to replicate it confidently with a stranger in public and that a group of adults allowed, for what ever reason, such an event to transpire.

Questions About the Case

1. What are some ways that immediate presence of the group of peers of the vandalizing youth could have affected his behavior?

2. Of the many cultural factors discussed in section 12, which do you feel are most likely to have influenced the encounter described in the story?

3. What cultural bias do you think the narrator brought to her interpretation of the encounter? What cultural biases do you bring to your reading of the case?
   Note: See the accompanying case book for more questions about this case.

■ PERSONAL REFLECTIONS

Cultural Factors

Jose Luis Alvarado, Ph.D., is an associate professor in the Department of Special Education at San Diego State University. His research interests include effective instruction and behavior support for culturally and linguistically diverse students with disabilities. Currently he is project director of two Office of Special Education Programs personnel preparation grants focusing on training special education teachers in a high-poverty, rural, and diverse area of Southern California. Prior to his current position, he was a behavior specialist for a regional special education agency and was responsible for wide-scale implementation of positive behavior supports in public schools. As a special education teacher, he taught elementary students with emotional and behavioral disorders.

Angela S. McIntosh, Ph.D., is an assistant professor of special education at San Diego State University. Her research and professional activities seek to advance quality and equity in the delivery of special education services to culturally diverse students, both through the recruitment and training of culturally competent service providers and through a focus on the use of appropriate and research-validated assessment and instructional practices. She taught students with autism and emotional and behavioral disorders at the elementary level, and served on the faculty of Hampton University in Virginia prior to her appointment at SDSU.

Which aspects of culture do you think are of most significance for instruction of students with emotional or behavioral disorders, and which aspects do you think are of least importance?

The term *culture* is so heavily steeped in ideas, perceptions, expectations, understandings, and misunderstandings, that it is essentially impossible to dichotomize aspects of culture as significant or insignificant for instruction of students with emotional or behavioral disorders. Essentially, one's culture is the product of genetic or biologically based characteristics (e.g., gender, race, age), social and familial influences (e.g., language, nationality, religious preference, socioeconomic status), and individual life choices, opportunities, and experiences (e.g., level of education, marital status, geographic area of residence, type of employment). The presence, degree of development and influence, and various interactions among these heterogeneous

and complicated variables constitute an individual's culture. We often make the mistake of forming assumptions and developing expectations based on only one or a few of the many variables present in the equation that defines culture. In those cases, mistakes can be at least misguided, at worst, reflective of racism or ethnocentrism. Students with emotional or behavioral disorders need instruction in skills and behaviors that foster success in school, community, and home environments. Therefore, what matters most is whether or not behaviors that have developed within a student's cultural framework support or impede positive educational and life outcomes

What is the difference between behavior that indicates an emotional or behavioral problem and behavior that merely reflects a cultural difference?

This distinction can only be made when parents, teachers, or behavior interventionists accept the responsibility to investigate and examine thoroughly the range of

variables that influence culture and serve to predispose, occasion, and maintain behaviors, thoughts, and feelings that are considered indicative of emotional or behavioral disorder in American society.

As we evaluate students to determine whether the behaviors in question are merely different or whether they are problematic violations of the norms of the student's cultural/ethnic group, we must consider cultural contexts. Culturally and linguistically diverse students may be reared in traditional contexts of their culture or ethnic group, and these may differ from the behavioral expectations of the majority group. This difference, at times, may appear to be easy to detect. However, one must be careful not to make such judgments based on partial or faulty information. For example, a student may have been reared with the belief that making eye contact with adults is disrespectful. This same behavior may be perceived by a teacher as shyness, withdrawal, and in some instances as defiance because the student refuses to make eye contact. Reaching conclusions based on faulty evidence or misconceptions may lead to inappropriately targeting behavior that is different rather than problematic and may perpetuate negative cultural stereotypes.

We strive for professional practices that are as expansive and all-encompassing as possible. When we are thorough in gathering data/information about behaviors and the environmental variables that influence those behaviors, we automatically gather information about the student's culture and differences that may only seem to be problem behaviors. It is for this reason that we must realize that the assessment process is conducted within a context that is invariably tainted with cultural overtones. However, a thorough functional behavioral assessment (FBA) can identify variables that exhibit the most influence over behaviors and will reveal the function of those behaviors so that instruction on positive replacement behaviors that serve the same function can take place. Proceeding with the knowledge of how cultural variables affect a student's behavior can only result in more effective and efficient practices that ultimately lead to better outcomes for all students.

When is it appropriate to ask a student to learn about cultures other than their own or things they have not experienced themselves?

The very nature of education suggests that students should be exposed to new ideas and be provided with opportunities to develop knowledge and understandings based on experiences other than those that are inherently a part of their individual cultures. In order to understand how to function within American society, our students must gain knowledge and experiences that go beyond what their individual cultural perspective can offer. However, this is quite different from imposing foreign cultural views on students from a perspective of dominance. Appropriate educational approaches to teaching about culture are not the same as devaluing cultural views or favoring one over another without attention to social validity.

Expanded knowledge of cultures is valuable for both teachers in training as well as the students that they will ultimately serve. Teachers must be mindful of the experiences that students bring with them into the classroom and how these experiences may differ from the experiences that are the basis for the behaviors that we might expect these students to perform. Eventually, teachers should consider the purpose of learning about cultures other than the students' and ultimately the social validity of the behavioral expectations for these students. To be different is not necessarily inappropriate, yet as teachers come to a better understanding and support for cultural diversity, their goal should be to improve the human condition while seeking alternative ways of changing behaviors that do not damage the human spirit.

Under what conditions is it appropriate to ask students to ignore differences between themselves and those who teach them or provide models for them to emulate?

If we are to empower students to achieve equity in American society, which is becoming increasingly diverse, then we must reverse the focus on differences and replace it with a focus on commonalities among individuals and groups in American society. The challenge to all education professionals is to identify links with the students they serve. These links will serve as bridges, allowing for the reciprocal exchange, acceptance, and value of cultural differences.

Given the rich cultural and linguistic diversity within the United States, it is important that special education teachers understand the influence of culture and language on the development of students in general as well as students with disabilities. Working in collaboration with families from diverse cultural and linguistic backgrounds is enhanced if special educators approach these relationships with cultural awareness and an attitude of cultural reciprocity. Our communications and interactions should emphasize competence and communicate acceptance of individual differences as we strive to provide an adapted learning environment. It is within this adapted environment that teachers will be able to support integration, participation, and growth to maximize students' abilities.

Additionally, it is an advantage for culturally and linguistically diverse children to have teachers who are culturally responsive and ensure that best practices are implemented. Culturally responsive teachers are professionals who make connections with their students as individuals, while understanding the sociocultural-historical contexts that influence who these students are and how they interact with the environment. Differences between teacher and student become far less important when effective educa-

tion occurs in supportive environments. At San Diego State University, our preservice teachers are trained in classrooms that provide opportunities to practice effective teaching within culturally and linguistically diverse student populations. For example, our teacher candidates must come to understand that children who are English language learners deal with issues that are quite different from those who are native English speakers. These are students who may have to communicate in their native language at home, yet are expected to acquire and become fluent in English at school.

Differences are not just unavoidable but desirable in our pluralistic society. Given that some racial and ethnic minorities experience a higher rate of classroom failure and a higher rate of identification as emotionally or behaviorally disordered, it is incumbent upon every educator to respond positively to cultural differences rather than to ignore them.

QUESTIONS FOR FURTHER REFLECTION

1. What cultural biases and preferences do *you* bring to thinking about children's behavior in school, and what can you do to minimize or eliminate your biases?
2. Under what circumstances do you see making assumptions about a student's behavior

because of his or her ethnic identity becoming a stereotype?
3. In your judgment, what are the most important aspects of culture of which teachers should be aware, and how do you think teachers can best be made aware of them?

SECTION 13
ATTENTION AND ACTIVITY DISORDERS

As you read this section, keep these guiding questions in mind:

- Why do we not define *hyperactivity* simply as being highly active?

- What types of behavior are most closely associated with attention deficit–hyperactivity disorder (ADHD)?

- Why are students with attention and activity disorders typically unpopular with their peers?

- What behavioral interventions are frequently used to manage hyperactivity and related problems?

- What general conclusions have been reached regarding the use of self-monitoring to manage off-task behavior and improve academic performance?

DEFINITION AND PREVALENCE

We said that youngsters with emotional or behavioral disorders often induce negative feelings and behavior in others. Among the many characteristics that are bothersome or irritating to others and induce others to respond negatively are disorders of attention and activity. During the past several decades, individuals with these disorders have been described by a variety of terms, including *hyperactive* and *hyperkinetic*. Severe and chronic problems in regulating attention and activity are now commonly known as *attention deficit–hyperactivity disorder*. The inability to control one's attention has replaced hyperactivity as the core problem of concern. The prevailing opinion is that hyperactivity usually, but not always, accompanies attention deficits. ADHD is a term about which there is still much uncertainty and controversy (see Hallahan, Kauffman, & Pullen, 2009; Hallahan, Lloyd, Kauffman, Weiss, & Martinez, 2005; Weyandt, 2007).

In this section, we use the term ADHD because we are concerned primarily with children and youth who have attention and activity disorders, and who have problems that are more severe than most. These youngsters with extreme attention and activity problems may also be categorized as having emotional or behavioral disorders or learning disabilities. Youngsters whose attention deficits are accompanied by hyperactivity and *impulsivity* are more likely to have conduct disorders than are those who show attention deficits and disorganization without hyperactivity. Our concern here is with youngsters who have serious social or emotional problems, whether related to hyperactivity or other manifestations of attention deficits, in addition to problems attending to their schoolwork. The varied nature of the social problems of children with disorders of attention and activity was summarized well by Whalen and Henker (1991):

> There are two truisms regarding the interpersonal difficulties of children with . . . ADHD. . . . The first is that the vast majority of these youngsters have serious social problems that pervade their everyday lives and spur frequent conflicts and confrontations. The second is that their patterns and styles of social exchange display marked heterogeneity in form as well as intensity. Many hyperactive children show a curious combination of social busyness and clumsiness, frequently initiating contact with others but in a manner perceived as immature, intrusive, or inept. A smaller number of these children show less interpersonal interest, appearing aloof and at times even oblivious as they skirt the periphery of social action. Still other hyperactive youngsters are highly aggressive, but even in this realm, heterogeneity is the rule rather than the exception. Some may engage in aggressive acts that appear planned, instrumental, and at times even hostile. For others, aggression seems to be more explosive than exploitative, linked to emotional volatility and difficulties dealing with frustration. (p. 231)

ADHD is among the most controversial disorders. Like learning disability, ADHD is seen by some people as a real and serious disability and by others as an attempt to legitimize teachers' or parents' inadequacies, or as "a fancy excuse for getting undeserved special consideration" (Bateman, 1992, p. 29). Good teaching and good discipline at home and school would, according to some skeptics, resolve the problem of ADHD in all but a small percentage of cases. Others see ADHD as a true developmental disability for which there is no cure. Professional disagreement and public confusion have been found at almost every point of research and practice (Hallahan & Cottone, 1997; Hallahan et al., 2005).

We believe that ADHD does exist and that a consensus among professionals regarding its nature and treatment is gradually emerging. Contrary to much popular opinion, the emerging consensus, based on decades of research, is that ADHD is neither a minor problem nor a temporary characteristic of childhood that is typically outgrown. It is a distinctive set of problems, a real disorder, a real disability (Barkley, 1998, 2003; Hallahan, Kauffman, & Pullen, 2009; Hallahan et al., 2005; Levy & Hay, 2001; Wasserstein, Wolf, & Lefever, 2001).

Most definitions of ADHD suggest that it is a developmental disorder of attention and activity, is evident relatively early in life (before the age of 7 or 8), persists throughout the life span, involves both academic and social skills, and is frequently accompanied by other disorders.

The difficulties in focusing and sustaining attention, controlling impulsive action, and showing appropriate motivation that characterize ADHD can make a person with the disorder—regardless of his or her age—a trial for parents, siblings, teachers, classroom peers, or coworkers. Hyperactive, distractible, impulsive youngsters upset their parents and siblings because they are difficult to live with at home; at school they often drive their teachers to discomposure. They are often unpopular with their peers, and they do not typically make charming playmates or helpful workmates. Incessant movement, impulsiveness, noisiness, irritability, destructiveness, unpredictability, flightiness, and other similar characteristics of students with ADHD are not endearing to anyone—parents, siblings, teachers, and schoolmates included. The following classic description illustrates how unpleasant children with ADHD can be to those around them:

> A hyperactive child's mother might report that he has difficulty remembering not to trail his dirty hand along the clean wall as he runs from the front door to the kitchen. His peers may find that he spontaneously changes the rules while playing Monopoly or soccer. His teacher notes that he asks what he is supposed to do immediately after detailed instructions were presented to the entire class. He may make warbling noises or other strange sounds that inadvertently disturb anyone nearby. He may seem to have more than his share of accidents—knocking over the "tower" his classmates are erecting, spilling his cranberry juice on the linen tablecloth, or tripping over the television cord while retrieving the family cat, thereby disconnecting the set in the middle of the Superbowl game. A hyperactive child is all too frequently "in trouble"—with his peers, his teachers, his family, his community. His social faux pas do not seem to stem from negativism and maliciousness. In fact, he is often quite surprised when his behaviors elicit anger and rejection from others. (Whalen, 1983, pp. 151–152)

Teachers need to be aware of the developmental aspects of attention and understand what distinguishes the student with ADHD from one who exhibits normal levels of inattention and impulsivity. We frequently see a high level of seemingly undirected activity, short attention span, and impulsive behavior in normally developing young children. As children grow older, however, they gradually become better able to direct their activity into socially constructive channels, to pay attention for longer periods and more efficiently, and to consider alternatives before responding. Thus, only when attentional skills, impulse control, and motoric activity level are markedly discrepant from those expected at a particular age is the child's behavior considered to require intervention. Children with ADHD stand out from their age peers, often from an early age (DuPaul & Stoner, 2002). Moreover, the characteristics of ADHD are not typically subtle; they tend to be "in your face" behaviors that make most of the child's peers and most adults want to exclude the child from their environment or resort to "in your face" reprisals. In fact, it is becoming more and more apparent that ADHD is frequently a component of other disorders.

Relationship to Other Disorders

Disorders of attention and activity are very frequently seen in children and youth with a wide variety of other disorders (Dulcan, 1997; Gershon, 2002; Satterfield et al., 2007; Schaeffer & Ross, 2002; Tankersley & Landrum, 1997). Nearly all teachers, parents, and clinicians agree that many youngsters with other types of emotional or behavioral disorders—conduct disorders or autism, for example—have difficulty controlling their attention to academic and social tasks and are disruptive.

Figure 13.1 shows the central role that not paying attention and disruptive behavior play in a variety of emotional and behavioral disorders, not just ADHD. When we observe the core symptoms of inattention and disruptive behavior, therefore, we need to look further to know whether these behaviors are part of ADHD, conduct disorders, mood disorders (e.g., depression), anxiety and related disorders (e.g.,

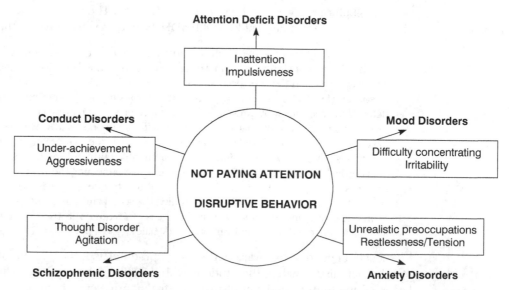

Figure 13.1   Core classroom symptoms and their possible relationships to psychiatric disorders

Source: Forness, S. R., Kavale, K. A., King, B. H., & Kasari, C. (1994). Simple versus complex conduct disorders: Identification and phenomenology. *Behavioral Disorders,* 19, 308.

obsessions, compulsions), or thought disorders such as schizophrenia. As Forness, Kavale, King, and Kasari (1994) have explained, not paying attention may be related to aggressiveness, impulsiveness, irritability, restlessness and emotional tension, or agitation, each of which is associated with a particular set of symptoms or diagnostic category. To complicate the picture further, a given child may have multiple disorders. Inattention may thus be part of the complex, multiple problems of an individual child.

In combination with other developmental problems such as conduct disorders or juvenile delinquency, ADHD greatly increases the risk of school failure and severity of symptoms, especially in boys (Gershon, 2002; Hallahan & Cottone, 1997; Siegel & Welsh, 2005). In fact, hyperactivity, inattention, and impulsiveness appear to play a key role in the development of antisocial behavior, at least for boys (Flory, Milich, Lynam, Leukefeld, & Clayton, 2003; Loeber et al., 1998a).

Nearly all researchers who recognize that disorders of attention and activity exist conclude that although ADHD is a separate, distinctive disorder in its own right, there is great overlap between ADHD and other diagnostic categories (Barkley, 1998, 2003; Dulcan, 1997; Gershon, 2002; Satterfield et al., 2007). Whether ADHD should become a separate category under the Individuals with Disabilities Education Act and regulations has been a matter for hot debate.

Whether there are unique features of ADHD and, if so, where the boundaries between ADHD and other disorders should be drawn are points of considerable controversy. Most experts believe that a significant percentage (perhaps about 30%) of the children with ADHD have not been served under any category of special education and that a high percentage (perhaps 50% to 70%) of those with specific learning disabilities or "emotional disturbance" (emotional or behavioral disorders) also have ADHD (cf. Bloomingdale, Swanson, Barkley, & Satterfield, 1991; Dulcan, 1997; Fletcher, Morris, & Francis, 1991; Hallahan et al., 2005; Schnoes, Reid, Wagner, & Marder, 2006). The confusion about the nature of ADHD and its relationship to other disorders is heightened by the fact that the children referred for mental health services often are those with extreme attention problems, with or without hyperactivity. Children and youth with emotional or behavioral disorders typically have difficulty relating to their peers, often being actively rejected by peers because of their inappropriate social behavior. Although many children with attention deficits do not have problems with peers, some are rejected. If they have extreme attention deficits, their peer problems may be understandable: people (children or adults) do not usually prefer as companions those who are extremely "flighty." We may conclude the following:

- Many children and youth with ADHD will not be found to have emotional or behavioral disorders.
- A sizable percentage of those with extreme ADHD will be identified as having emotional or behavioral disorders.
- Many of those receiving special education because of other emotional or behavioral disorders will have ADHD.
- Learning disabilities may accompany any combination of disabilities.

We might speculate that the relationships among the populations of individuals having ADHD, emotional or behavioral disorders, and learning disabilities, are

Figure 13.2 Hypothetical relationships among the populations having attention deficit–hyperactivity disorder (ADHD), emotional or behavioral disorders (EBDs), and learning disabilities (LDs)

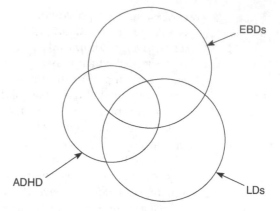

approximately those shown in Figure 13.2. EBDs and LDs may occur alone or in combination with each other and with ADHD.

Prevalence

Controversy regarding definition makes the prevalence of a disorder extremely hard to estimate. Most authorities estimate the prevalence of ADHD at 3% to 5% of the school-age population, making it one of the most common disorders of children and youth and putting it among the most common reasons for referral (Hallahan et al., 2005). Moreover, ADHD is not merely an American phenomenon (Wilens, Biederman, & Spencer, 2002). Among those referred for ADHD and related disorders, boys far outnumber girls. Gender bias may be a partial explanation for the predominance of boys, but the size of the disparity suggests that there may also be biological gender differences that contribute to the disorder (Barkley, 1998, 2003; Gershon, 2002).

CAUSAL FACTORS AND PREVENTION

Historically, brain dysfunction has been the presumed cause of what is now known as ADHD (Hallahan, Kauffman, & Pullen, 2009; Hallahan et al., 2005). Today, researchers are investigating biological causes through more sophisticated anatomical and physiological tests involving blood flow to the brain, neurotransmitters, and so on (e.g., electrical potentials in brain tissue, magnetic resonance imaging). As yet, no reliable evidence shows precisely what neurological problem is the basis of ADHD, although many researchers suspect an underlying biological cause of most cases (Nigg, 2006).

Various food substances (e.g., dyes, sugars, preservatives), environmental toxins (e.g., lead), and allergens have been suggested as causes of hyperactivity and related disorders. None of these has been demonstrated to be a frequent cause of ADHD, although evidence does suggest that such factors may be a cause in a very small number of cases. Claims that foods, toxins, or allergies are frequent causes are not substantiated by credible research (Barkley, 1998; DuPaul & Barkley, 1998; McLoughlin & Nall, 1994; Wolraich, Wilson, & White, 1995).

Genetic factors appear to increase risk for ADHD, although the genetics of the disorder are very poorly understood. We do know that ADHD is more common among the biological relatives of children who have the disorder than in the general population, suggesting that ADHD is genetically organized in some way. It is plausible that genetic factors may give some individuals a predisposition toward attention problems and impulse control and that it leads to ADHD in combination with other biological or psychological factors (see DuPaul & Barkey, 1998; Pinker, 2002).

A difficult temperament—an inborn behavioral style characterized by irritability, high activity level, short attention span, distractibility, and so on—has been suggested as a possible starting point for ADHD. Children with ADHD are often identifiable as toddlers or preschoolers (Barkley, 1998, 2003). Temperamentally, they fit the description of the "difficult child." They are children who "in the early preschool years show a mixture of problems in attention, impulse control, noncompliance, and aggression" (Campbell, Breaux, Ewing, & Szumowski, 1986, p. 232; see also Keogh, 2003). Yet temperament alone does not explain all the problems of these youngsters. In short, evidence does not clearly and consistently link any particular biological factor to ADHD. It is plausible, however, that biological factors are involved in most cases, but precisely what they are and how they operate remain unknown (Hallahan et al., 2005).

Hypothesized psychological causes of ADHD range from psychoanalytic explana tions to those involving social learning theory. For instance, numerous studies of modeling and imitation illustrate how children could acquire deviant behavior patterns through observation of frenetically active parents or siblings. The literature is replete with examples of how children's inappropriate behavior can be manipulated by social attention, suggesting that parents and teachers could inadvertently teach youngsters to behave in the manner that characterizes ADHD. Nevertheless, research has not demonstrated that ADHD is primarily a matter of undesirable social learning, and therefore it is inappropriate for us to lay responsibility for the creation of ADHD on parents or teachers (Barkley, 1998, 2003; Braswell & Bloomquist, 1991; DuPaul & Barkley, 1998; Hallahan et al., 2005).

To summarize what we know about causes, we do not know exactly why children have ADHD. There does not appear to be a single cause. In the vast majority of cases, we suspect that neurological or genetic factors launch the child toward ADHD and that these factors, in combination with other influences in the child's physical and social environment, produce the inattentive or hyperactive behavior (Nigg, 2006).

We know more about how to control the problems related to this disorder once it has appeared than we know about its origins, so prevention is largely a matter of intervening early in the families and classrooms of youngsters who are difficult to manage (see Kauffman, 2003b, 2005). Effective primary prevention—keeping ADHD from emerging during the child's development—would require knowledge of neurology and genetics that we do not presently have, in addition to training in child care and management that would eliminate possible environmental causes. Secondary prevention—reduction and management of problems that have emerged—is the most feasible approach (see Kauffman, 1999c, 2003b, 2005, for further discussion of primary versus secondary prevention).

Much of the responsibility for secondary prevention falls on educators, who must manage the child's behavior in school and provide instructional programs that will foster academic success and social adjustment (Hallahan et al., 2005). ADHD appears to be a persistent set of problems that follows children into adolescence and adulthood (Barkley, 1998; Wilens et al., 2002). It interferes with academic achievement and peer relations. Lack of achievement, feelings of failure, social isolation or rejection, and low motivation make for high rates of socially inappropriate behavior. The student with ADHD becomes trapped in a self-perpetuating pattern of negative self-perceptions, inappropriate behavior, and negative interactions with others. Prevention of later and more serious difficulties depends on breaking this cycle.

ASSESSMENT

Assessment of ADHD usually involves a medical examination, a clinical interview by a psychologist or psychiatrist, and parent and teacher ratings of behavior (Barkley, 1998, 2003; Dulcan, 1997; Hallahan et al., 2005; Rapport, Timko, & Wolfe, 2006). The clinical assessment of ADHD by a psychologist or psychiatrist and the educational assessment of ADHD by teachers or other school personnel may differ considerably. Clinicians will likely be interested primarily in determining whether the child meets certain diagnostic criteria; teachers will be more interested in devising a plan for management of classroom behavior and instruction. Parents will want to know why their child behaves as he or she does and how they should respond.

Although the characteristics of ADHD may be noticed by parents or others before the child enters school, it is often not until the child is confronted by the demands of the classroom that someone—usually a teacher—becomes aware of the seriousness of the child's problems. In the context of school, ADHD often becomes intolerable, and the child's behavior is perceived as provoking a crisis. Children with ADHD often exhibit social behavior about which teachers are understandably upset. Teachers' concerns about their students' academic performance apparently most often leads them to refer students for special education (Abidin & Robinson, 2002; Lloyd, Kauffman, Landrum, & Roe, 1991). However, many pupils with ADHD present both behavioral and academic concerns.

The primary means of assessment of ADHD that are useful in school settings are teacher and peer rating scales, direct observation, and interviews. A wide variety of rating scales have been used; some are intended to be specific to ADHD, whereas others are the broader. The value of any of these scales is that they allow someone to organize and quantify teachers' and peers' perceptions of the student's academic and social behavior. These perceptions are important, but they may not correspond well to direct observation of the student's behavior. One of the problems in assessing ADHD is determining whether the youngster shows problems related to attention deficits, aggression, or both. ADHD may be distinguished by disrupting the classroom, exhibiting problems in daily academic performance, being unprepared for class, not having required materials, and so on. These problems may or may not be accompanied by aggressive behavior or other indications of additional emotional or behavioral disorders. The distinction may be important in judging the seriousness of the student's problems and designing an intervention plan.

Direct observation of the youngster's behavior in various school settings—classroom, playground, lunchroom, hallways—and careful daily records (as opposed to teacher ratings) of academic performance are critical aspects of assessment. These can pinpoint the behavioral aspects of the problem of ADHD and serve as an objective measure of the effectiveness of interventions. Both objective records of behavior and performance and subjective judgments regarding the nature and acceptability of the student's behavior and performance are important in managing ADHD.

INTERVENTION AND EDUCATION

In most cases, ADHD involves a cluster of related behavioral characteristics, including problems in regulating attention, motivation, hyperactivity, and socially inappropriate responses. Consequently, many different intervention techniques have been tried in both home and classroom settings. The two most common and successful approaches have been medication and training parents and teachers how to manage the student's behavior (psychosocial interventions). The vast majority of cases require multiple interventions involving both parents and teachers (Barkley, 1998, 2003; Hallahan et al., 2005).

Medication

No method of dealing with ADHD has been so controversial as medication (DeGrandpre, 1999; Hallahan, Kauffman, & Pullen, 2009; Hallahan et al., 2005; Weyandt, 2007). The medications usually given are psychostimulants, such as Ritalin, Dexedrine, Cylert, or Adderall, or a nonstimulant drug called Strattera. Opponents of medication have described the drugs' possible negative side effects, unknown long-term effects on growth and health, possible negative effects on perceptions of personal responsibility and self-control, and possibility of encouraging drug abuse. The statements of some of the opponents of medication have been unfounded and hysterical; others have been thoughtful and cautious, based on reliable evidence that stimulant drugs are not a panacea and do, like all medications, carry risks as well as benefits. You might consider the case of John in the accompanying case book and the thoughts of his mother and her acquaintances about the management of ADHD.

Research now clearly indicates that the right dosage of the right drug results in remarkable improvement in behavior and facilitates learning (makes the student more teachable) in about 90% of youngsters with ADHD (Crenshaw, Kavale, Forness, & Reeve, 1999; Forness, Kavale, Sweeney, & Crenshaw, 1999; Spencer, Biederman, & Wilens, 2002). It is important to recognize that a higher-than-optimal dosage may impair learning rather than facilitate it, that a medication may not have effects on all the youngster's problem behaviors (e.g., it may improve hyperactivity but have little or no effect on aggression), and that the effects of medication may be different in different settings (e.g., more improvement in school than at home). Children with other disorders in addition to ADHD, such as anxiety or depression, may not respond well to stimulant drugs (Tannock, Ickowicz, & Schachar, 1995).

Research clearly points to medication as the single most effective treatment of ADHD (see Forness, Freeman, & Papparella, 2006; Jensen et al., 2001). However, there is absolutely no reason to choose between medication and other interventions. As is the case with virtually all emotional and behavioral disorders, both medication and other treatments can be used to best advantage. A combination of medication and behavior management provides even better outcomes for children with ADHD than medication alone (Gully et al., 2003). In fact, stimulant drugs may improve the effects of good behavior management strategies, and good behavior management may improve the effects of medication (Kolko, Bukstein, & Barron, 1999; Northrup et al., 1999).

When reasonable precautions are taken in their use and the dosage and effects are carefully monitored, stimulant drugs are a safe and sane way of augmenting parents' and teachers' other strategies for managing ADHD (Jensen et al., 2001; Spencer et al., 2002), but good psychopharmacology demands careful monitoring of the effects of medication. Teachers should offer parents and physicians their observations about the effects (or noneffects) and side effects of medications on the behavior and learning of a medicated student who is in their class.

Psychosocial Training Involving Parents and Teachers

Medication alone is not the most effective means of bringing the behavior of children with ADHD under control. Parents typically have serious difficulty managing these children at home, and teachers often have difficulty managing these children in school. Consequently, systematic training of parents and teachers in behavior management skills is an approach frequently used by psychologists who serve children with ADHD and their families (Alberto & Troutman, 2006; Barkley, 1998, 2003; Jensen et al., 2001). The objective of this training is not to cure or eliminate ADHD but to help parents and teachers learn how to manage children's behavior more effectively. The training is organized around principles of behavioral psychology and involves teaching parents and teachers to interact more positively with their children during ordinary activities, avoiding the coercive interactions that are hallmarks of families with aggressive and hyperactive children and adolescents. The procedures parents and teachers are taught to use may include a token reinforcement system for encouraging appropriate behavior and response cost (withdrawing some part of an earned reward) or time-out (brief social isolation or temporary suspension of the opportunity to earn reinforcers) for misbehavior.

Ultimately, parents may be taught techniques for managing behavior in public places and generalizing the training to new problems and settings (Barkley, 2000). This type of training is not possible with all parents, nor is it always successful when parents are receptive to it. However, it has been used successfully with many parents. The psychologist working with parents will typically involve teachers as well in a behavior management plan because little change is likely in school unless similar behavior management procedures are used in the classroom. Parents may also need suggestions for how to manage everyday events for families, such as an adolescent learning to drive (Snyder, 2001).

The problems of students with ADHD are usually most evident in the classroom, where compliance and focused attention to task are essential for success. Teachers should be helped to understand the likely functions of ADHD and related behavioral problems in the classroom, which they may discover through functional behavioral assessment.

> The most likely function for ADHD-related behavior in school is to *escape effortful tasks,* particularly those that involve independent writing activity (e.g., seatwork) or an extended sequence of chores. This is based on the assumption that presenting independent work or a chore is an antecedent for inattention, which is then followed by a lack of work completion. A second possible function is to *gain adult and/or peer attention.* A frequent consequent event for inattention and disruption is a verbal reprimand from the adult as well as nonverbal (e.g., smiles) and verbal reactions (e.g., laughter) from the student's classmates. An additional possible function is for the ADHD-related behavior to result in *sensory stimulation* that appears more reinforcing than the stimuli that the child is expected to attend to. For example, when presented with a set of written math problems to complete, the student begins playing with a toy that was kept in his pocket. (DuPaul & Barkley, 1998, p. 152, emphasis in original)

Behavioral interventions and cognitive strategy training are the two most widely recommended approaches to managing the problems of ADHD (Barkley, 1998; Hallahan et al., 2005). Teachers must be trained in how to use these approaches if they are to have a reasonable chance of success; they are not intuitive methods or ones that every teacher learns.

Behavioral Intervention

A basic behavioral principle is that behavior is affected by its antecedents and consequences (see Alberto & Troutman, 2006; DuPaul & Barkley, 1998; Landrum & Kauffman, 2006). Behavioral intervention is not likely to be successful unless the person who is trying to use it both understands the principles that make it work and is attuned to the student's individual characteristics and preferences. It is a powerful tool—but a good one only in the hands of a perceptive and sensitive teacher. Adept use of behavioral interventions results in warm, caring relationships between students and teachers (Cullinan, 2002; Kauffman et al., 2002, 2004; Kerr & Nelson, 2006; Landrum & Kauffman, 2006; Walker, 1995; Walker, Ramsey, & Gresham, 2004).

Behavioral intervention means making certain that rewarding consequences follow desirable behavior and that either no consequences or punishing consequences follow undesirable behavior. As is true with parents, rearranging consequences to support desirable behavior and not support undesirable behavior may be as simple as shifting attention from inappropriate to appropriate behavior. More powerful consequences such as *token reinforcement, response cost,* and *time-out* may be needed as well. Coles et al. (2005) demonstrated the use of this very combination to improve the behavior of four students with ADHD in a summer treatment program on such outcomes as rule violations in both recreational and classroom settings and disruptions (which decreased), and assignment completion and following activity rules (which increased).

In many cases, it is helpful to make the contingencies of reinforcement and punishment more explicit by writing a *contingency contract* (see section 14). In addition to the procedures used in the classroom, the parents may be involved in a home–school behavior modification program in which behavior at school earns the pupil rewards provided by the parents at home (see Hallahan et al., 2005). The emphasis must be on positive consequences for appropriate behavior, but prudent negative consequences for misbehavior may be necessary (DuPaul & Barkley, 1998; DuPaul & Stoner, 2002; Northrup et al., 1999; see also section 14).

Other behavioral intervention procedures involve altering classroom conditions or instruction to make them more attractive to students. These procedures do not in any way make consequences unimportant. They are simply an additional means of putting behavior principles to work in helping students with ADHD behave more appropriately and learn more. For example, Powell and Nelson (1997) compared the undesirable behavior of a student with ADHD under two conditions: no choice, when the teacher simply gave the student, Evan, an assignment, and a choice condition in which "the teacher presented Evan with three different language arts assignments taken from the class curriculum, and he chose one to complete" (p. 182). Figure 13.3 shows that under the choice condition, Evan's undesirable behavior was much lower. Other researchers have also found that giving students with ADHD and other

Figure 13.3 Percentage of intervals rated as containing undesirable behaviors across conditions

Source: Powell, S., & Nelson, B. (1997). Effects of choosing academic assignments on a student with attention deficit hyperactivity disorder. *Journal of Applied Behavior Analysis, 30,* 181–183.

emotional or behavioral disorders a say in their work (not, of course, whether to work, but perhaps which assignment to do) is helpful (e.g., Bennett, Zentall, French, & Giorgetti-Borucki, 2006; Mithaug & Mithaug, 2003).

Recall the quotation (p. 265) of DuPaul and Barkley (1998) about why children may exhibit ADHD-related behavior. It is important to understand what maintains undesirable behavior—attention from others versus escape from effortful tasks, for example. If undesirable behavior is maintained by escape from effortful tasks, then giving a student choices of assignments may be helpful. However, if the undesirable behavior is maintained by attention from others, then giving the student choices may have no effect at all (Romaniuk et al., 2002).

Behavioral interventions are not foolproof for controlling problems of ADHD or any other emotional or behavioral disorder, but research has demonstrated that noisy, destructive, disruptive, and inattentive behavior can usually be changed for the better by controlling the contingencies of reinforcement. Like medication or any other intervention, behavioral interventions can be abused and misused. Even when used skillfully, they can have unanticipated or undesirable outcomes, and they will not necessarily make a student with ADHD appear normal. Nonetheless, behavioral interventions may be the best tool available to teachers and parents.

Cognitive Strategy Training

The interventions falling under the general rubric of cognitive training or cognitive strategy training include self-instruction, self-monitoring, self-reinforcement, and cognitive–interpersonal problem solving (see Reid, Trout, & Schartz, 2005). All have the goal of helping individuals become more aware of their responses to academic tasks and social problems and actively engage in the control of their own responses. We describe just three strategies—mnemonics, self-instruction, and self-monitoring—because they are the most widely used in classroom settings. However, other strategies that involve students cognitively and actively in their self-management, such as goal setting, are also valuable in working with ADHD (Bicard & Neef, 2002; Hallahan & Cottone, 1997; Hallahan et al., 2005; Hoff & DuPaul, 1998).

Mnemonic strategies are ways of helping students remember things. These methods include teaching students with memory problems to use first-letter strategies, key words, and peg words. For example, a teacher might use the acronym HOMES to help a student remember the names of the five Great Lakes of North America by associating the acronym with the first letters of the lakes: Huron, Ontario, Michigan, Erie, and Superior. Using key words involves choosing a picture and a phonetically similar word to retrieve a definition. For example, a teacher might help a student picture a bear acting as a lawyer to remember the meaning of the word barrister. Peg words use rhyming. For example, Washington might be remembered by thinking of (or picturing) a gun being washed, with wash and gun being the rhyming elements remembering the first president of the United States. Mnemonic strategies have been found to be effective in helping students with learning, emotional, and behavioral disorders remember important information (Kleinheksel & Summy, 2003; Lloyd, Forness, & Kavale, 1998).

Self-instruction involves teaching students to talk to themselves about what they are doing and what they should do. Teaching students to label stimuli and to rehearse the instructions or tasks they have been given appears to have merit as an instructional strategy in many cases. For example, a student may be told to verbalize each arithmetic problem or its operation sign while working a problem, to say each letter of a word aloud while writing it, or to rehearse a reading passage before reading it aloud to the teacher.

Typically, self-instruction training requires a series of steps in which verbal control of behavior is first modeled by an adult, then imitated by the student, and finally used independently by the student. On a given task or in a given social situation, the adult first performs the task or response while verbalizing thoughts about the task requirements or social circumstance. The adult may talk about relevant stimuli or cues, planning a response, performing as expected, coping with feelings, and evaluating performance. Then the adult and student might run through the task or response to the social situation together, with the student shadowing the adult's verbal and nonverbal behavior. Eventually, the student tries it alone while verbalizing aloud and finally with subvocal self-instruction. Teaching students to use their own language to regulate behavior has been a successful approach with some impulsive children and youth in academic or social situations. Telling impulsive students to slow down and be careful before responding may not work, yet if these same students can be taught to tell themselves in some way to stop and think before they respond, they might improve their behavior considerably.

Self-monitoring has been widely used for helping students who have difficulty staying on task in the classroom, particularly during independent seat-work time. A tape recorder is used to produce tones (prerecorded to sound at random intervals ranging from 10 to 90 seconds, with an average interval of about 45 seconds) that cue the student to ask, "Was I . . . [usually, paying attention]?" and self-record the response on a form. This simple procedure has been found effective in increasing the on-task behavior of many students, ranging from children as young as 5 years to adolescents, who have ADHD and a variety of other disorders. Variations on the procedure have been used to improve academic productivity, accuracy of work, and social behavior (Harris, Friedlander, Saddler, Frizzelle, & Graham, 2005; Lloyd, Hallahan, Kauffman, & Keller, 1998; Mathes & Bender, 1997; Shapiro, Durnan, Post, & Levinson, 2002).

Figure 13.4 shows an example of a simple recording sheet that might be used with a student who is self-monitoring his or her attention to a task (or to the teacher) during a lesson. Figure 13.5 shows examples of broader self-monitoring activities that might be used to help students remember various academic-related skills that are necessary if they are to be successful in typical classroom instruction. Self-monitoring can be adapted to a variety of circumstances and types of behavior. For example, Hoff and DuPaul (1998) used a combination of token reinforcement, explicit feedback to students about rule following, matching self-evaluation with teacher evaluation of behavior, and self-evaluation alone to lower the disruptive behavior of several students with ADHD and related problems. The students were gradually moved from more extrinsic, teacher-determined rewards to self-management. These procedures were successful for several students in general education across different classroom

Was I Paying Attention?					
	Yes	No		Yes	No
1			11		
2			12		
3			13		
4			14		
5			15		
6			16		
7			17		
8			18		
9			19		
10			20		

Figuro 13.4 Examplo of a oolf monitoring form

settings and activities. Research on self-monitoring has led to the following general conclusions:

1. Self-monitoring procedures are simple and straightforward, but they cannot be implemented without preparing the students. Brief training is necessary, in which the teacher talks with the student about the nature of off-task and appropriate behavior, explains the procedure, role-plays the procedure, and has the student practice.
2. Self-monitoring of on-task behavior increases time on task in most cases.
3. Self-monitoring of on-task behavior also typically increases academic productivity.
4. Improvement in on-task behavior and performance usually lasts for several months after the procedure is discontinued.

Daily Assignment Recording Sheet				
Name:		**Class:**	**Date:**	
Did I remember to:			yes	no
1. Bring all materials to class (notebook, textbook, pen or pencil)				
2. Complete my homework and place it in the homework folder				
3. Copy down today's homework assignment in my planner				
4. Raise my hand before asking a question or giving an answer				
5. Listen quietly while others were speaking				

Figure 13.5 Example of a recording sheet for broader self-monitoring activities

5. The beneficial effects of self-monitoring are usually achieved without the use of backup reinforcers; extrinsic rewards, such as tokens or treats for improved behavior, are seldom necessary.
6. The tape-recorded tones (cues) prompting self-monitoring are a necessary part of the initial training procedure and implementation, although they can usually be discontinued after a period of successful self-monitoring.
7. Students' self-recording—marking answers to their self-questioning—is a necessary element of initial training and implementation but can be discontinued after a period of successful self-monitoring.
8. Accuracy in self-monitoring is not critically important; some students will be in close agreement with the teacher's assessment of their on-task behavior, but others will not be.
9. The cueing tones and other aspects of the procedure are usually minimally disruptive to other students in the class.

Notwithstanding the enthusiasm with which development of cognitive strategies was greeted and the many reports of their success in dealing with a wide variety of problems, they have not produced the generalized changes in behavior and cognition in ADHD that researchers and others had hoped for. Cognitive training in all its various forms clearly is not a panacea for the problems presented by disorders of attention and activity. Moreover, cognitive training is not as simple as it might first appear. The teacher who wishes to use any of the techniques effectively must understand their theoretical basis and carefully construct procedures to fit the individual case (Hallahan et al., 2005; Shapiro et al., 2002).

A PERSPECTIVE ON INTERVENTION

Nearly every type of intervention that has been used with any kind of troublesome behavior has been tried with ADHD (cf. Barkley, 1998; Neuwirth, 1994). Perhaps that in itself is a commentary on the seriousness with which adults approach the problem. Psychotherapy, providing an optimal level of sensory stimulation, biofeedback, relaxation training, dietary control—you name it, and it has probably been experimented with or even touted as a breakthrough, a revolutionary treatment, or an outright cure.

The lure of the idea that we should be able to find a way to "fix" this common and perplexing malady of children and youth is strong, perhaps irresistible. Over the past several decades, various intervention strategies have been devised by leading scholars and researchers, investigated with initial excitement, adopted widely, and endorsed enthusiastically by many as a solution, if not the cure, for the problems we now call ADHD. Each strategy eventually has been found not to be the fix. This initial overenthusiasm for an intervention—one said to be so powerful that the developmental disorder disappears—and the eventual disappointment it leads to has been the history of our approach to every developmental disability, including mental retardation, autism, cerebral palsy, and other developmental disorders. Leading researchers now suggest that ADHD is, indeed, a developmental disability for which we have no cure, and we are not likely to find one soon (Barkley, 1998, 2003; Hallahan & Cottone, 1997; Hallahan et al., 2005).

Recognition of the fact that we have no cure for ADHD should not deter us from seeking and implementing the most effective interventions possible. We do have interventions and approaches to education that will help us reach important goals. We know that medication can be extremely helpful, especially in combination with psychological interventions. For teachers, the most important tools are a highly structured classroom where the student's attention is clearly and consistently focused, behavioral interventions are consistently and explicitly implemented, and self-management procedures are taught systematically.

Given our present level of understanding, our goal should not be to eliminate the disability known as ADHD but to manage it as effectively as possible, recognizing that it is a chronic, disabling condition.

SUMMARY

Attention deficit–hyperactivity disorder is now the most widely used term for disorders of attention and activity. There is still considerable controversy and confusion regarding terminology and definition. However, most definitions suggest that ADHD is a developmental disorder of attention and activity level that is evident before the age of 7 or 8, persists throughout the life span, involves both academic and social problems, and is frequently accompanied by other disorders. The core problems of concern are regulation of attention, cognition, motivation, and social behavior. ADHD, learning disabilities, and emotional and behavioral disorders are overlapping, interrelated categories. About 3% to 5% of the school-aged population is diagnosed with ADHD, with boys greatly outnumbering girls.

Brain injury or dysfunction has long been suspected as a cause of ADHD. Many other biological causes, including food substances, environmental toxins, genetic factors, and temperament have been researched. Various psychological causes have also been suggested, but as yet research does not clearly and reliably point to any specific biological or environmental cause. Leading researchers suggest that poorly understood neurological factors instigate the problem, which is then exacerbated by a variety of factors in the physical and social environment. Prevention of ADHD and related disorders consists primarily of managing problems once they are evident.

Assessment for teaching and assessment for clinical treatment may differ considerably. School personnel and parents are interested primarily in assessment that helps them design an intervention program. Teacher and peer rating scales and direct observation of troublesome behavior in various school settings are most useful to educators.

The most widely used and successful approaches to intervention and education with ADHD and related disorders are medication, parent training, and teacher training. Medication is very controversial, but research clearly indicates its value when it is properly managed, and alternative approaches have not been as successful as medication or medication in combination with behavioral interventions. Medication cannot teach skills or resolve all problems, but it can make the youngster more teachable. Parent and teacher training typically involves instruction in behavior management skills. Teacher training usually involves implementing behavioral interventions (e.g., token reinforcement, response cost, contingency contracts) or cognitive training strategies (e.g., self-instruction or self-monitoring). It may be important to articulate classroom behavior modification with a home-school program involving contingencies managed by parents.

Nearly every known type of intervention has been suggested and attempted with ADHD and related disorders. None has provided a cure. The goal of intervention should be to manage the youngster's problems as successfully as possible, realizing that a cure is not available and that coping strategies for parents and teachers are important for dealing with this chronic, disabling condition.

◢ PERSONAL REFLECTIONS

Attention and Activity Disorders

Cleo L. Holloway, Ed. S., is an assistant principal at Huntington Middle School in Newport News, Virginia. She wrote this feature when she was a classroom teacher at the same school.

Describe the school in which you teach and your particular role in the school.

I work in an inner-city middle school (grades 6 through 8) with a population of 873 students. There are 17 special-education classes at Huntington: three for mild mental retardation, one for severe mental retardation, two for emotional and behavioral disorders (EBDs), nine learning disabilities (LDs) self-contained classrooms, and two LD resource classes. I am one of the two LD resource teachers, but some of my students exhibit emotional and behavioral disorders, as well as learning disabilities.

Think of a particular student with an attention disorder. How does this student manifest the disorder?

Marvin was diagnosed with ADHD as a third grader and prescribed Ritalin. Now he's one of my eighth graders. He consistently complied with his medication regimen during the sixth, seventh, and now the eighth grade, but the medication has had an inconsistent effect on his behavior.

When he entered school, Marvin had difficulty maintaining self-control and following directions, behaviors that are usually disruptive to the learning environment. He is often confrontational in a loud and aggressive manner toward peers and adults. However, in a very small, highly structured instructional setting, he displays the ability and willingness to follow directions and apply himself to academic tasks. Marvin is perceived by others as extremely oppositional and determined to have things his way. He avoids, dislikes, or is reluctant to engage in tasks that require sustained mental effort; fails to give close attention to details; has difficulty organizing tasks and activities; and will not tolerate constructive correction from anyone outside the resource setting. He apparently feels threatened by their suggestions and becomes argumentative. To say the

least, Marvin has difficulty respecting those in authority.

Marvin's problem behaviors have escalated, and now he has been suspended as a consequence of behaviors such as using obscene language, failing to comply with requests from adults in authority and showing disrespect for them, and throwing a roll of tissue paper in the face of another student. Eventually, he was suspended in May for the remainder of the school year.

What procedures have you found most useful in working with Marvin?

My experience in working with kids who have ADHD was quite limited until I met Marvin. He is academically strong, yet his hyperactivity and impulsivity are alarming. I did for Marvin what I have always done for my students, regardless of their disability. I established rules and expectations that were clear and consistent, and I set forth consequences ahead of time and delivered them immediately, depending on behavior. A highly structured environment alleviated a lot of Marvin's inappropriate behaviors. Marvin knew what to expect and realized I would not permit him to give me excuses about why he was out of control.

My ultimate goal was to establish an environment that would nurture Marvin. I wanted to establish a routine and help him learn a habit of mind that would allow him to control his behavior and succeed academically as well as socially. I found out that Marvin was dynamic with Legos. He loved working with them. So we built every school experience around the assembling of Legos as a consequence for his doing his work. This proved to be very helpful. He would enter class, work feverishly on assignments, and then be allowed to construct whatever he wanted.

Marvin was also an avid reader, and his comprehension skills were great. I used his talents and made him the class helper. He tutored fellow classmates in literature. This improved his self-esteem and social skills. As a result, other students in the resource room changed their impressions of him. He became part of the team. However, this behavior did not transfer or generalize to regular education settings. One factor was that regular classroom peers were not as tolerant of his behavior as were the kids in the resource room.

I also found it helpful to work with Marvin's mother, a social worker, and other community agencies to plan healthy relationships at home, in the school, and in the community. This way we achieved consistency and clear expectations—a structured and predictable environment for Marvin that would help him maintain balance in his life. I emphasize that family counseling and parenting classes really facilitated this process.

What do you see as the prospects for Marvin's educational progress in the coming year?

If Marvin's behavior does not improve, I believe he will be referred to the eligibility committee, which will consider placing him in a more restrictive environment or a modified or cross-categorical program. His repeated acts of noncompliance, characterized by behaviors such as defiance of directives, use of profanity, and aggressive outbursts, have greatly impaired his ability to learn and have interfered with the learning of his classmates. He will probably receive academic support from the LD teacher as well as help in learning adolescent social skills from the EBD teacher. It is becoming increasingly difficult to request that regular education teachers make accommodations to address his needs. More support from the special educators may help Marvin have a successful school year. Thus, my recommendation is that we have discussions to address placement issues and to determine the setting best suited to Marvin's needs.

What do you see as the biggest long-term problems Marvin will face?

Marvin is a highly anxious, insecure young man whose needs for support, stability, and nurturance are considerable. Although he demonstrates notable tendencies toward aggressive, acting-out behaviors, he possesses a great longing to obtain the approval of significant others. However, as a consequence of his past behavioral patterns, coupled with a pervasive sense of inadequacy, he views himself as unable and unworthy to garner the acceptance he seeks. The latter circumstance is exacerbated by his compelling compensatory drives, aimed at gaining attention and response from others, however negative or unacceptable such attention and responses may be.

Marvin's impulsivity means that he is inclined to act without giving serious thought to the consequences of his behaviors. He became involved in the juvenile court during the summer and was eventually placed in detention. He and his family are now receiving in-home counseling services. I hope that this intervention will help Marvin conform to rules at every level.

Cleo Holloway Interviews Marvin

Ms. H: Marvin, what has been your experience at school?

M: Okay, but it could have been better.

Ms. H: Why do you think it could have been better?

M: Because of my behavior. When somebody says something to me, I just take off. I have a quick temper.

Ms. H: What is the most difficult task for you?

M: Managing my temper.

Ms. H: What do you normally do when your temper goes off?

M: I get mad. I be ready to fight. I don't want nobody to say nothing to me. I want everybody to get along.

Ms. H: At this point, do you see yourself as successful in school?

M: Sometimes. I try, but sometimes I end up messing up.

Ms. H: How would we know when you're about to have a bad day?

M: I talk back. Get smart. Blurt out. Act up.

Ms. H: What kinds of things can we do to make you more successful in school?

M: When I get mad, you can have me be by myself or let me help y'all.

Ms. H: What do you think you need the most help in?

M: Controlling my temper. The medicine don't help.

Ms. H: When do you take your medicine?

M: In the morning when I first come to school. And it take about 30 minutes to start working.

Ms. H: If you don't take your medicine, what happens?

M: I can be bad without it, and I can be good without it.

Ms. H: Is there anything we can do about managing your behavior and getting your work done?

M: Not about my behavior.

Ms. H: Can you get your work done?

M: I try. Sometimes.

Ms. H: Name some behaviors that you do that you know keep you from having a good day.

M: Fighting, skip class. When I get here in the morning, I go to the cafeteria and take my medicine. Then I'm supposed to go to class, but I don't. When I go to class, I make jokes and people laugh.

Ms. H: How does it make you feel when people laugh at your jokes?

M: I be breaking up and liking it. I start rankin' on my friends.

Ms. H: And this is during instructional time, right?

M: Yeah. [Marvin expresses dislike for teachers and describes getting into a fight in the neighborhood before school, then resuming the fight at school and being physically restrained by a counselor.]

Ms. H: When you came in yesterday morning, none of us knew what had happened in the neighborhood. We didn't know you had a fight, and we were trying to keep you in school. And that's what we want to do because we know you're very bright. I know you have a hard time ignoring people who are saying things to you, and you feel you have to defend yourself, but how is that going to help you in school if you play into that kind of stuff every single day?

M: I didn't want to fight, but I couldn't back down because he hit me first. I know kids shouldn't fight, but sometimes you have to. But I could ignore it. But if he hits me, I'll hit him back.

Ms. H: Can you ignore him, then?

M: I can. All I gotta do is walk away.

Ms. H: What types of goals do you have for yourself?

M: Get out of this bad class. I don't care who knows I'm in the bad class.

Ms. H: How can you get out of classes that are labeled? What do you need to do?

M: Do my work. Stay out of trouble. Get to school on time every day. Stop ranking.

Ms. H: Yes, stop ranking. That's a big one. 'Cause you like to rank.

M: Yeah, I be doing stuff too, but I ain't gonna blame it all on me. It could be teachers quick to say, "Oh, he's got problems, don't pay him no mind." They're quick to say that. Or, "He's a problem child. You know, he didn't take his meds yet." You know, teachers try to put me down.

Ms. H: We need to encourage you so you can get your work done. . . . If you think about your life five years from now, in five years you'll be . . .

M: In college. I'll be 18 and on my way to college.

Ms. H: So what do you want to be or do then?

M: I want to be a cop.

QUESTIONS FOR FURTHER REFLECTION

1. How would you explain to parents the difference between a child being very active and a child having ADHD?
2. At what point, or after what acts on your part as a teacher, should you request a student's evaluation for possible ADHD?
3. What evidence would you need before arguing with a school psychologist or other school personnel or parents that a particular student's ADHD (already identified as such) was not merely ADHD but an indication of other problems or disorders as well?

SECTION 14
CONDUCT DISORDER
OVERT AGGRESSION AND COVERT
ANTISOCIAL BEHAVIOR

As you read this section, keep these guiding questions in mind:

- What distinguishes aggressive antisocial behavior from normal development?

- If we conceptualize overt and covert antisocial behavior as different ends of a single dimension or continuum, what type of behavior is shared by both?

- How and why is aggression a multicultural issue?

- What environmental conditions are associated with high risk for conduct disorder?

- What type of prevention programs are particularly relevant for children with covert antisocial behavior?

DEFINITION, PREVALENCE, AND CLASSIFICATION

Definition

Normally developing children and adolescents occasionally exhibit antisocial behavior of various descriptions. They may throw temper tantrums, fight with their siblings or peers, cheat, lie, be physically cruel to animals or other people, refuse to obey their parents, or destroy their own or others' possessions. Normally developing youngsters do not, however, perform antisocial acts in most social contexts, nor with such frequency as to become pariahs among their peers or excessively burdensome to their parents and teachers.

A child or youth who has a conduct disorder (CD) exhibits a persistent pattern of antisocial behavior that significantly impairs everyday functioning at home or school or leads others to conclude that the youngster is unmanageable (Hinshaw & Lee, 2003; Kazdin, 1994, 1998; Walker, 1995; Walker, Ramsey, & Gresham, 2004). Many of these children are known as bullies (Tattum & Lane, 1989; Walker et al., 2004). Kazdin (1998) summarized the essential features of CD:

> Conduct disorder encompasses a broad range of antisocial behavior such as aggressive acts, theft, vandalism, firesetting, lying, truancy, and running away. Although these behaviors are diverse, their common characteristic is that they tend to violate major social rules and expectations. Many of the behaviors often reflect actions against the environment, including both persons and property. Antisocial behaviors emerge in some form over the course of normal development. Fighting, lying, stealing, destruction of property, and noncompliance are relatively common at different points in childhood and adolescence. For the most part, these behaviors diminish over time, do not interfere with everyday functioning, and do not predict untoward consequences in adulthood.
>
> The term conduct disorder is usually reserved for a pattern of antisocial behavior that is associated with significant impairment in everyday functioning at home or school, and concerns of significant others that the child or adolescent is unmanageable. (p. 199)

Two broad forms of conduct disorder are often distinguished: overt aggression, typically characterized by acting out toward others verbally or physically; and covert antisocial behavior, manifested in antisocial acts such as vandalism or fire setting that are intentionally concealed from others. Awareness of different forms of conduct disorder has existed for decades, but reliable empirical evidence of the different forms emerged from large-scale studies since the 1980s (Eddy, Reid, & Curry, 2002; Loeber & Schmaling, 1985a, 1985b; Quay 1986b). These studies are based on statistical probabilities. Thus, a particular child is not necessarily characterized by behavior at one end of the continuum (overt or covert antisocial behavior). Indeed, some children are versatile in their antisocial conduct, showing both overt and covert forms.

Youngsters who show versatile antisocial behavior generally have more and more severe problems, and their prognosis is usually poorer compared to those who exhibit only one type of antisocial behavior (Kazdin, 1998, 2001; Loeber & Schmaling, 1985a;

Loeber et al., 1993; Loeber, Farrington, Stouthamer-Loeber & Van Kammen, 1998a). Versatility is a matter of degree; some individuals are much more versatile or exclusive in their antisocial conduct than others are.

Conduct disorder of both types is often difficult to distinguish from other disorders, especially juvenile delinquency. In fact, the socialized (covert) form typically involves delinquent activities, often with bad companions or gangs and often involving alcohol or other drug use. *Delinquency* is a legal term, however, and connotes behavior that is the topic of section 15.

As may be obvious, assessment and management of overt and covert forms of antisocial behvaior present different challenges to educators. Whereas overt antisocial behavior is easy to see—indeed it is hard to miss—covert antisocial behavior is by definition difficult to observe and assess. Covert antisocial behavior includes untrustworthiness and manipulation of others, running away, and concealment of one's acts. Loeber and Schmaling (1985a) suggested that overt and covert antisocial behavior may represent different ends of a single behavioral dimension, with noncompliance—sassy, negative, persistent disobedience—as the most common or keystone characteristic of both extremes (see also Loeber et al., 1993; Loeber et al., 1998a, 1998b; Patterson, Reid, & Dishion, 1992; and the case of George in the accompanying case book).

The children about whom we are concerned here—particularly those displaying overt antisocial behavior—perform noxious behaviors at a much higher rate and at a much later age than do normally developing children (see Loeber et al., 1998a, 1998b). A youngster with aggressive conduct disorder may match the noxious behaviors of the normally developing child 2 to 1 or more; and whereas the normally developing child exhibits social aggression at a decreasing rate as he or she grows older, the youngster with conduct disorder usually does not.

In a now classic study, Patterson and his colleagues spent many hours observing in the homes of both normally developing children and aggressive children (Patterson et al., 1975). They identified noxious behaviors, measuring the rates at which they were performed by normally developing children and contrasting them to the rates at which they were performed by aggressive children whose behavior might fit the definition of CD. They found, for example, that an aggressive child can be expected to be noncompliant about every 10 minutes, as well as to hit and to tease about every half hour. In contrast, a nonaggressive child might be expected to be noncompliant once in 20 minutes, to tease once in about 50 minutes, and to hit once in a couple of hours. Patterson's description of Don (see the accompanying case book) illustrates the type of behavior that extremely socially aggressive young children exhibit at home and school. Don's interactions with his family are characterized by coercive exchanges. Without effective intervention to break the coercive cycle at home and school, Don seems virtually certain to experience a high rate of failure in school and continuing conflict in the community.

CD must be judged with reference to chronological age. Ordinarily, children tend to exhibit less overt aggression as they grow older. Compared to nonaggressive youngsters, children and youth with CDs typically show age-inappropriate aggression from an earlier age, develop a larger repertoire of aggressive acts, exhibit aggression across a wider range of social situations, and persist in aggressive behavior for a longer time (Patterson et al., 1992; Walker et al., 2004). A significant percentage of children and adolescents with CDs showed earlier the characteristics of oppositional defiant disorder (ODD). That is, they showed a pattern of negativistic, hostile, and defiant behavior uncharacteristic of normally developing children of the same age. Representative characteristics include having frequent temper tantrums and often arguing with adults, refusing to obey adults, deliberately annoying other people, and acting angry and resentful (Eddy et al., 2002; Hinshaw & Lee, 2003; Kazdin, 1998).

CD is often comorbid with other disorders, such as attention deficit–hyperactivity disorder (ADHD). ODD, ADHD, and CD are known to be closely linked, although having one of these disorders does not necessarily mean that a youngster will have the other. In fact, several subtypes of CD are now well established, and all types of CD may be comorbid with ADHD, depression, anxiety, delinquency, substance abuse, and sexual acting out (see Kessler, Bergland, Demler, Jin, & Walters, 2005; Kessler, Chiu, Demler, & Walters, 2005).

Prevalence

Estimates of the prevalence of CD range from 6% to 16% of boys and 2% to 9% of girls under age 18. The preponderance of boys with CD may reflect a combination of biological susceptibilities and socialization processes involving social roles, models, expectations, and reinforcement (see Costello et al., 2005, 2006).

The prevalence of each subtype of conduct disorder has not been estimated precisely, but some generalities are evident; these include evidence of gender differences (Talbott, Celinska, Simpson, & Coe, 2002; Talbott & Thiede, 1999). For example, boys with CD tend to exhibit fighting, stealing, vandalism, and other overtly aggressive, disruptive behavior; girls are more likely to exhibit lying, truancy, running away, substance abuse, prostitution, and other less overtly aggressive behavior (Robins, 1986). Others have corroborated these different patterns of antisocial behavior among samples of boys and girls (e.g., Farmer, Rodkin, Pearl, & Van Acker, 1999; Talbott & Callahan, 1997; Talbott & Thiede, 1999).

Talbott and Callahan (1997) noted that measurement, prediction, and comorbidity are the critical issues in studying the antisocial behavior of girls. Moreover, "it appears that the aggressive and disruptive behavior of girls is both similar and different from that of boys, depending on the developmental period during which it is measured" (Talbott & Callahan, 1997, p. 307). Much remains to be learned about gender differences in antisocial conduct, particularly the way in which biological and social factors influence the developmental course of antisocial behavioral patterns of boys and girls.

The consensus among researchers is not only that the problem affects at least the officially estimated percentage of children and youth but also that the prevalence is increasing. Moreover, the severity of the disorder is perceived as increasing, and a delay of years in treatment after the onset of the disorer is common (see Hinshaw & Lee, 2003; Kazdin, 1998; Steiner, 1997; Wang et al., 2005).

Classification

One way of classifying CD is by age of onset. Researchers have frequently found that children with early onset of CD and delinquency (before age 10 or 12) typically show more severe impairment and have a poorer prognosis than do those with later onset (see Dinitz, Scarpitti, & Reckless, 1962; Eddy et al., 2002; Patterson et al., 1992; Walker, 1995; Walker et al., 2004). CD may be classified as mild (resulting in only minor harm to others), moderate, or severe (causing considerable harm to others).

CD may also be classified as undersocialized or socialized (Quay, 1986a, 1986b). *Undersocialized conduct disorder* includes characteristics such as hyperactivity, impulsiveness, irritability, stubbornness, demandingness, arguing, teasing, poor peer relations, loudness, threatening and attacking others, cruelty, fighting, showing off, bragging, swearing, blaming others, sassiness, and disobedience. *Socialized conduct disorder* is characterized by more covert antisocial acts such as negativism, lying, destructiveness, stealing, setting fires, associating with bad companions, belonging to a gang, running away, truancy, and abuse of alcohol or other drugs. However, some youngsters are described as *versatile* because they show both overt and covert forms of antisocial conduct (Loeber & Schmaling, 1985a, 1985b). As we shall see, however, antisocial behavior of all types is closely linked to delinquency and substance abuse, which we discuss in section 15.

Undersocialized aggressive CD is closely associated with violent behavior. The level of violence in our society, particularly among youth, is a widespread and long-standing concern, especially to educators and others concerned with children's development (Flannery, 1999; Flannery & Huff, 1999; Furlong & Morrison, 1994; Walker & Shinn, 2002; Walker et al., 2004). Our discussion in this section thus addresses both CD and the problem of violence among children and youth, including school violence.

AGGRESSION AND VIOLENCE IN SOCIAL CONTEXT

Aggression has been a common feature of American life for a long time (Goldstein, Carr, Davidson, & Wehr, 1981). In fact, this now old reference seems all the more apropos in the early decades of the 21st century. Aggression is not new to American children, their homes and families, or their schools. Even a cursory examination of *Children and Youth in America* (Bremner, 1970, 1971) and other similar histories quickly reveals that coercion, violence, and brutality have been practiced by and toward children and youth since the founding of the United States.

Recognizing the historical presence of violence does not in any way, however, reduce the unacceptable level of aggression in the present-day lives of American children. Through the media, children are exposed to brutal acts of aggression at a rate unprecedented in the history of civilization (Huesmann, Moise-Titus, Podolski, & Eron, 2003; Sprafkin, Gadow, & Adelman, 1992). Assaultive behavior, disruptiveness, and property destruction in schools have grown commonplace. Violence and weapons in schools are problems now apparent in small towns as well as big cities, in small schools as well as big ones, and in affluent as well as poor schools (Flannnery, 1999; Flannery & Huff, 1999). Incivility has become a pervasive issue in schools (Kauffman & Burbach, 1997).

Aggression as a Multicultural Issue

Aggression and violence are multicultural issues in that all subcultural groups in the United States are affected, and stereotypes regarding cultural minorities are common. African American and Latino cultures are frequently miscast as tolerant of it, and violence among Native American and Asian–Pacific island American youth is poorly understood. Particularly vulnerable populations are often overlooked in discussions of violence, including children with disabilities and groups of every description.

Without ignoring the special vulnerabilities and needs of any group, it is important to recognize the commonalities of sociocultural conditions and needs for nurturing among all children and youth, regardless of color or ethnic background. Hill, Soriano, Chen, and LaFromboise (1994) noted that "the developmental mandates of all youth during adolescence are similar. But the resources for achieving developmental milestones are significantly fewer for economically disadvantaged ethnic minority youth, particularly in inner cities and particularly if they have not had the opportunity to internalize the values of their own ethnic culture that can protect against violence" (p. 86). In fact, the same risk factors for socialization appear to be operative among African American youths as among other ethnic groups (see Loeber et al., 1998a; Miller-Johnson, Coie, Maumary-Gremaud, Lochman, & Terry, 1999; Xie, Cairns, & Cairns, 1999).

Intervention programs designed for particular groups of aggressive students, such as African American males or Latino students, have been suggested (e.g., Hudley & Graham, 1995; Middleton & Cartledge, 1995; Vasquez, 1998). However, Hudley and Graham (1995) concluded that "although it has been asserted that African American children have distinct learning styles and preferred modes of instruction, in truth the data in support of these assertions are scant" (p. 193). Cultural sensitivity and multicultural competence are important, but they are no substitute for effective interventions that transcend ethnic and gender identity (Kauffman, 1999b; Kauffman, Conroy, Gardner, & Oswald, in press; National Research Council, 2002).

Regardless of color, ethnicity, gender, and other personal characteristics, children and youth are placed at risk by common factors such as poverty, family disruption, abuse, neglect, racism, poor schools, lack of employment opportunities, and other social blights. Likewise, the most effective remedies for these risk factors and the protective factors that increase children's resilience are essentially the same across all cultural groups.

Still, the definitions of psychopathologies are grounded in cultures. Moreover, it is important to recognize the special considerations that must be made in assessing and treating psychopathology:

> Perhaps the most important factor to consider is that the families of minority children and adolescents are not only adjusting to the general influences that affect mainstream society but also are facing the transitional stress generated by the necessary

adjustment of a minority culture into American society. This process is complicated by poverty at home, lack of familiarity with English, poor schools, racism, and a community ecology that generates existential frustration, fear, and violence. (Yamamoto, Silva, Ferrari, & Nukariya, 1997, p. 51)

Cultural factors are not simply a matter of racial identity, ethnic identity, or social class but a combination of these factors:

In American society there is an important interrelationship among ethnicity, race, and social class, with high status associated with membership in white, Anglo-Saxon, middle-class families and low status associated with membership in nonwhite, ethnic, minority, lower-class families. . . . It follows that children and adolescents in many Asian, black, Hispanic, and American Indian families are triply stigmatized in American society because they differ from the norm in three major respects: they are nonwhite by race (except for white Hispanics), non–Anglo-Saxon by ethnicity, and predominantly non–middle-class by socioeconomic status. (Gibbs & Huang, 1998, p. 11)

Knowing the difference between pathological behavior and behavior that is simply an expression of cultural heritage is no easy matter. It is a problem of enormous consequence, however, because racism includes both (a) cultural bias in the attribution of pathology and (b) the dismissal of truly pathological behavior as a mere indication of cultural convention. More research is needed to help us make definitive statements about the differences between behavior that is merely cultural and behavior that represents pathological aggression.

Aggression in the Context of School

General education teachers must be prepared to deal with aggression, for it is likely that at least one of their students will be highly disruptive, destructive, or assaultive toward other students or the teacher. Teachers of students with emotional or behavioral disorders must be ready to handle an especially large dose of aggression, for conduct disorder is one of the most common forms of exasperating deportment and psychopathology that brings students into special education.

The prospective special education teacher who expects most students to be withdrawn or who believes that students with CD will quickly learn to reciprocate a kindly social demeanor will be shocked. Without effective means for controlling aggression, the teacher of students with emotional or behavioral disorders must develop a superhuman tolerance for interpersonal nastiness.

Observations in schools and studies of school records suggest that we may expect highly problematic, disruptive classroom behaviors from aggressive youngsters. These behaviors are frequently accompanied by academic failure. Not surprisingly, students who exhibit aggressive conduct disorder are often rejected by their peers and perceive their peers as hostile toward them. When children exhibit aggressive antisocial behavior and academic failure beginning in the early grades, the prognosis is particularly grim, unless effective early intervention is provided (Cullinan, 2002; Eddy et al., 2002; Flannery & Huff, 1999; Loeber et al., 1998a, 1998b; Walker & Shinn, 2002; Walker et al., 2004; Walker, Shinn, O'Neill, & Ramsey, 1987).

The high rates of antisocial behavior and the significant impairment of everyday functioning of youngsters with undersocialized aggressive conduct disorder do not bode well for their futures. Such youngsters tend to exhibit a relatively stable pattern of aggressive behavior over time; their problems do not tend to dissipate but continue into adulthood, especially when the onset is early and the child's problem are multiple and complex (Eddy et al., 2002; Kazdin, 1995, 1998; Loeber et al., 1998a, 1998b; McMahon & Wells, 1998; Odgers et al., 2007; Olweus, 1979; Patterson et al., 1992; Robins, 1986; Satterfield et al., 2007; Walker et al., 2004). Consequently, the prognosis for later adjustment is poor, and the pattern of antisocial conduct is often transmitted over generations. Because aggressive antisocial behavior tends to keep people in contact with mental health and criminal justice systems, and because the behavior inflicts considerable suffering on victims of physical assault and property loss, the cost to society is enormous.

Although for boys a history of serious antisocial conduct before age 15 increases the chances of externalizing psychopathology (aggression, criminal behavior, alcohol and drug abuse) in adulthood, for girls this kind of childhood history increases the later life probability of both externalizing disorders and internalizing disorders (depression, phobias; Robins, 1986). We have known this for many years: "Clearly, no other disorder of childhood and adolescence is so widespread and disruptive of the lives of those who suffer it and the lives of others" (Quay, 1986b, p. 64). Thus, finding effective interventions for conduct disorder is a priority among social scientists and educators (Eddy et al., 2002; Eron, Gentry, & Schlegel, 1994; Walker et al., 2004; Walker, Forness, et al., 1998).

Antisocial behavior, especially when it is characterized by violent aggression, is rightfully a critical concern of all teachers. It is especially of concern to special educators who teach students with emotional or behavioral disorders.

CAUSAL FACTORS

In general, the same causal factors seem to underlie covert aggression and aggressive antisocial conduct, and many of these factors influence both boys and girls in very similar ways (see Eddy et al., 2002). The contextual variables and determinants found by Patterson et al. (1992) are shown in Figure 14.1. The personal, family, and social contexts are the background for poor behavior management skills of the parents, who are unskilled in monitoring and disciplining their children and fail to use positive reinforcement and problem solving in family interactions. The outcome is social incompetence and antisocial behavior of the child. To be sure, this parental inadequacy in child rearing is not always the cause of antisocial behavior, either overt or covert. However, it is characteristic of the environments of the great majority of children and youth who exhibit antisocial behavior.

In some studies comparing overt to covert antisocial children, families of those who exhibited covert antisocial behavior are characterized by lower rates of aversive, coercive behavior on the part of parents and children and less supervision or monitoring on the part of parents. Other studies, however, have found no

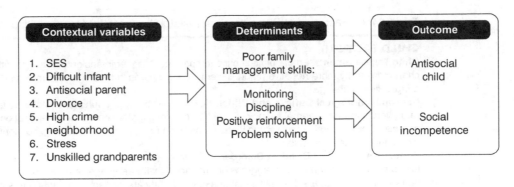

Figure 14.1 The effect of context on child adjustment

Source: From *Antisocial Boys* by Gerald R. Patterson, John B. Reid, and Thomas J. Dishion, © 1992 by Castalia Publishing Company. Reprinted by permission.

differences between overtly and covertly antisocial youngsters on family process variables such as parental rejection. A fairly consistent finding is that youngsters with versatile antisocial behavior come from the most disturbed families in which child-rearing practices are the most inadequate (Loeber & Schmaling, 1985a; Patterson et al., 1992).

As perhaps the most common defining characteristic of overt antisocial behavior, aggression has historically been an object of study for scientists in many disciplines, and many alternative explanations have been offered for it.

Psychoanalytic theories, drive theories, and simple conditioning theories have not led to effective intervention strategies, and they have been largely discounted by alternative explanations based on scientific research (Pepler & Slaby, 1994). Biological and social learning theories are supported by more reliable evidence (Dodge & Pettit, 2003). In some cases, medication for aggressive behavior may be helpful, particularly when aggression is related to ADHD (see Connor, Boone, Steingard, Lopez, & Melloni, 2003; Connor, Glatt, Lopez, Jackson, & Melloni, 2002; Konopasek & Forness, 2004; Lynn & King, 2002).

Although genetic and other biological factors apparently contribute to the most severe cases of conduct disorder, their role in milder cases of aggression is not clear; in both severe and mild forms of conduct disorder, the social environment obviously contributes to the problem (Eddy et al., 2002; Webster-Stratton & Dahl, 1995; Wells & Forehand, 1985). Furthermore, it is now apparent that there is not a single cause of conduct disorder and related problems (Burke, Loeber, & Birmaher, 2002).

Sociobiology is an intriguing and controversial topic (Pinker, 2002; Wright, 1995a, 1995b), but it has little to offer developmental psychologists who are seeking more immediate causes of aggression (Loeber et al., 1998a, 1998b). In fact, decades of research by numerous scientists strongly suggest that an individual's social environment is a powerful regulator of neurobiological processes and behavior; social learning may be the most important determinant of aggression and prosocial behavior (Eddy et al., 2002; Pepler & Slaby, 1994; Walker et al., 2004).

Table 14.1   Factors that Place Youth at Risk for the Onset of Conduct Disorder

CHILD FACTORS

Child Temperament. A more difficult child temperament (on a dimension of "easy-to-difficult"), as characterized by more negative mood, lower levels of approach toward new stimuli, and less adaptability to change.

Neuropsychological Deficits and Difficulties. Deficits in diverse functions related to language (e.g., verbal learning, verbal fluency, verbal IQ), memory, motor coordination, integration of auditory and visual cues, and "executive" functions of the brain (e.g., abstract reasoning, concept formation, planning, control of attention).

Subclinical Levels of Conduct Disorder. Early signs (e.g., elementary school) of mild ("subclinical") levels of unmanageability and aggression, especially with early age of onset, multiple types of antisocial behaviors, and multiple situations in which they are evident (e.g., at home, school, the community).

Academic and Intellectual Performance. Academic deficiencies and lower levels of intellectual functioning.

PARENT AND FAMILY FACTORS

Prenatal and Perinatal Complications. Pregnancy and birth-related complications including maternal infection, prematurity and low birth weight, impaired respiration at birth, and minor birth injury.

Psychopathology and Criminal Behavior in the Family. Criminal behavior, antisocial personality disorder, and alcoholism of the parent.

Parent–Child Punishment. Harsh (e.g., severe corporal punishment) and inconsistent punishment increase risk.

Monitoring of the Child. Poor supervision, lack of monitoring of whereabouts, and few rules about where children can go and when they can return.

Quality of the Family Relationships. Less parental acceptance of their children, less warmth, affection, and emotional support, and less attachment.

Marital Discord. Unhappy marital relationships, interpersonal conflict and aggression of the parents.

Family Size. Larger family size, that is, more children in the family.

Sibling With Antisocial Behavior. Presence of a sibling, especially an older brother, with antisocial behavior.

Socioeconomic Disadvantage. Poverty, overcrowding, unemployment, receipt of social assistance ("welfare"), and poor housing.

SCHOOL-RELATED FACTORS

Characteristics of the Setting. Attending schools where there is little emphasis on academic work, little teacher time spent on lessons, infrequent teacher use of praise and appreciation for school work, little emphasis on individual responsibility of the students, poor working conditions for pupils (e.g., furniture in poor repair), unavailability of the teacher to deal with children's problems, and low teacher expectancies.

Source: Kazdin, A. E. (1998). Conduct disorder. In R. J. Morris & T. R. Kratochwill (Eds.), *The practice of child therapy* (3rd ed., pp. 199–230). Boston: Allyn & Bacon, p. 202.

The many factors that place children and youth at risk for development of a conduct disorder are shown in Table 14.1.

Among the several psychological explanations of aggression, one that stands out as most clearly supported by careful, systematic, scientific research is the *social learning theory*. Particularly relevant to our discussion here is the coercive process model constructed after decades of research by Gerald Patterson and his colleagues (e.g., Eddy et al., 2002; Patterson et al., 1992). Consequently, we focus on these social learning explanations for aggression and its prevention. We first summarize the general findings of social learning research and then highlight personal, family, school, peer group, and other cultural factors and review Patterson's model of the coercive process that produces and sustains aggression.

General Conclusions from Social Learning Research

A social learning (or social cognitive) analysis of aggression includes three major controlling influences: the environmental conditions that set the occasion for behavior or that reinforce or punish it, the behavior itself, and cognitive-affective (person) variables (Bandura, 1986; Bandura & Locke, 2003). Whether or not a person exhibits aggressive behavior depends on the reciprocal effects of these three factors and the individual's social history. Social learning theory suggests that aggression is learned through the direct consequences of aggressive and nonaggressive acts and through observation of aggression and its consequences. Research in social learning supports several generalizations about how aggression is learned and maintained (see Eddy et al., 2002; Goldstein, 1983a, 1983b; McMahon & Wells, 1998; Patterson, 1986a, 1986b; Patterson et al., 1992; Pepler & Slaby, 1994; Walker et al., 2004):

- Children learn many aggressive responses by observing models or examples. The models may be family members, members of the child's subculture (friends, acquaintances, peers, and adults in the community), or individuals portrayed in the mass media (including real and fictional, human and nonhuman).
- Children are more likely to imitate aggressive models when the models are of high social status and when they see that the models receive reinforcement (positive consequences or rewards) or do not receive punishment for their aggression.
- Children learn aggressive behavior when, given opportunities to practice aggressive responses, they experience either no aversive consequences or succeed in obtaining rewards by harming or overcoming their victims.
- Aggression is more likely to occur when children experience aversive conditions (perhaps physical assault, verbal threats, taunts, or insults) or decreases in or termination of positive reinforcement. Children may learn through observation or practice that they can obtain rewarding consequences by engaging in aggressive behavior. The probability of aggression under such circumstances is especially high when alternative (appropriate) means of obtaining reinforcement are not readily available or have not been learned and when aggression is sanctioned by social authorities.
- Factors that maintain aggression include three types of reinforcement: *external reinforcement* (tangible rewards, social status rewards, removal of aversive conditions, expressions of injury or suffering by the victim), *vicarious reinforcement* (gratification obtained by observing others gain rewards through aggression), and *self-reinforcement* (self-congratulation or increased self-esteem following successful aggression).
- Aggression may be perpetuated by cognitive processes that justify hostile action: comparing one's deeds advantageously to more horrific deeds of others, appealing to higher principles (such as protection of self or others), placing responsibility on

others (the familiar "I didn't start it" and "He made me do it" ploys), and dehumanizing the victims (perhaps with demeaning labels such as *nerd, dweeb, trash, pig, drooler*).

- Punishment may also serve to heighten or maintain aggression when it causes pain, when there are no positive alternatives to the punished response, when punishment is delayed or inconsistent, or when punishment provides a model of aggressive behavior. When counterattack against the punisher seems likely to succeed, punishment maintains aggression. The adult who punishes a child by striking out not only causes pain, which increases the probability of aggression, but provides a model of aggression as well.

A social learning analysis of aggression generates testable predictions about environmental conditions that foster aggressive behavior. Research over several decades has led to the following empirically confirmed predictions about the genesis of aggression:

- Viewing televised aggression may increase aggressive behavior, especially in males and in children who have a history of aggressiveness.
- Delinquent subcultures, such as deviant peer groups or street gangs, will maintain aggressive behavior in their members by modeling and reinforcing aggression.
- Families of aggressive children are characterized by high rates of aggression on the part of all members, by coercive exchanges between the aggressive child and other family members, and by parents' inconsistent, punitive control techniques and lack of supervision.
- Aggression begets aggression. When one person presents an aversive condition for another (hitting, yelling, whining), the affronted individual is likely to reply by presenting a negative condition of his or her own, resulting in a coercive process. The coercive interaction will continue until one individual withdraws his or her aversive condition, providing negative reinforcement (escape from aversive stimulation) for the victor.

Family, school, and cultural factors involving social learning were discussed in previous sections. These factors undoubtedly play a major role in the development of aggressive conduct disorders. By providing models of aggression and supplying reinforcement for aggressive behavior, families, schools, and the larger society teach youngsters (albeit inadvertently) to behave aggressively. This insidious teaching process is most effective for youngsters who are already predisposed to aggressive behavior by their biological endowment or their previous social learning. And the process is maintained by reciprocity of effects among the behavior, the social environment, and the child's cognitive and affective characteristics. The teaching-learning process involved in aggression includes reciprocal effects such as these:

- The social environment provides aversive conditions (noxious stimuli), including social disadvantage, academic failure, peer rejection, and rejection by parents and other adults.
- The youngster perceives the social environment as both threatening and likely to reward aggression.

- The youngster's behavior is noxious to others, who attempt to control it by threats and punitive responses.
- The youngster develops low self-concept and identifies himself or herself in primarily negative terms.
- In coercive bouts, the youngster is frequently successful in overcoming others by being more aversive or persistent, thereby obtaining reinforcement for aggression and confirming his or her perceptions of the social environment as threatening and controlled by aggressive behavior.

All of these factors contribute to the development of antisocial behavior and, over time, cement it into a pattern very resistant to change. Patterson et al. (1992) depicted the major causal factors that contribute to antisocial behavior, as shown in Figure 14.2. We next examine major contributing factors and how they are interrelated in a coercive process.

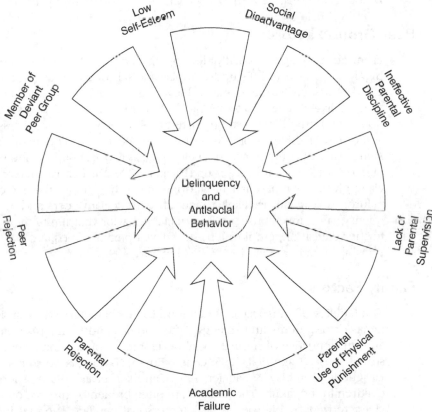

Figure 14.2   The causal wheel

Source: Patterson, G. R., Reid, J. B., & Dishion, T. J. (1992). *Antisocial Boys.* Eugene, OR: Castalia. Copyright © 1992 by Castalia Publishing Company. Reprinted by permission.

Personal Factors

As discussed in section 9, children are born with dispositions or temperaments that, although modifiable, tend to be fairly consistent over a period of years (see Caspi, Henry, McGee, Moffitt, & Silva, 1995; Keogh, 2003; Smith & Prior, 1995). Many children with difficult, irritable temperaments are at risk for developing antisocial behavior (Center & Kemp, 2003). Their difficult temperaments as infants may evolve through social interaction with their caretakers into high rates of noncompliance and oppositional behavior in the early childhood years. These children are likely to develop low self-esteem and depressed affect as well as to have major problems in peer relations and academic achievement. In short, they may begin life with personal attributes that make social rejection likely, and these characteristics may be exacerbated by cycles of negative interaction with caretakers, peers, and teachers. Although demographic factors such as low socioeconomic status and family factors such as parental substance abuse are important, the personal characteristics of attention problems and especially fighting are predictive of the early onset of conduct disorder in boys (Keogh, 2003; Loeber et al., 1998a, 1998b; Loeber, Green, Keenan, & Lahey, 1995).

Peer Group Factors

From an early age, normally developing peers tend to reject their peers who are highly aggressive and disruptive of play and school activities (Guevremont & Dumas, 1994). Antisocial students may achieve high status among a subgroup of peers, but they are likely to be rejected by most of their nonantisocial peers. Further, peer rejection in childhood may also be related to the persistence of aggressive behavior into adulthood (Rabiner, Coie, Miller-Johnson, Boykin, & Lochman, 2005). To achieve some sense of competence and belonging, antisocial children and youths often gravitate toward a deviant peer group (Farmer, 2000; Farmer, Farmer, & Gut, 1999). Especially given poor parental monitoring and other family risk factors and academic failure, adolescents are likely to identify with deviant peers and be drawn into delinquency, substance abuse, and antisocial behavior that limits their opportunities for further education, employment, and development of positive and stable social relationships (Loeber et al., 1998a, 1998b; Short, 1997).

Family Factors

The families of antisocial children tend to be characterized by antisocial or criminal behavior of parents and siblings. Often homes and family relationships are chaotic and unsupportive of normal social development or are characterized by physical or sexual abuse (Campbell, 1995; Green, Russo, Navratil, & Loeber, 1999; Kazdin, 1998; Lavigueur, Tremblay, & Saucier, 1995; Patterson et al., 1992). There are often many children in the family. The families are often broken by divorce or abandonment and characterized by high levels of interpersonal conflict. Parental monitoring of children's behavior tends to be lax or almost nonexistent, and discipline tends to be unpredictable but harsh—precisely the opposite of that suggested by those well versed in the topic of rearing well-socialized children (e.g., Dishion & Patterson,

1996). Often many generations live together, and grandparents or other relatives living in the home also typically lack child-rearing skills. As discussed in section 10, the children and parents often become enmeshed in a coercive cycle of interaction in which parent and child increase the pain they cause the other until one party "wins." We should be careful not to assume that all families of antisocial children can be so characterized. However, these are the typical family characteristics of children who are antisocial. Domestic violence, poverty, poor parental education, family members' criminality, and other adverse conditions increase the risk (i.e., chances) that a child will be aggressive or exhibit other emotional or behavioral disorders, such as depression (Yamamoto et al., 1997).

The growth, development, and perpetuation of antisocial behavior is pictured in Figure 14.3. Patterson et al. (1992) described the stages of growth of the "vile weed" of antisocial behavior. Their coercive model begins in Stage 1 with the contextual variables shown in the underground level of the diagram: difficult child temperament, stressors such as poverty and family conflict, poor discipline and monitoring by parents and grandparents, and parental antisocial behavior and substance abuse. This social context is likely to produce an antisocial child with low self-esteem. In Stage 2, school failure, parental rejection, peer rejection, and depression all contribute to one another and further strengthen the child's antisocial tendencies. In Stage 3, the youngster becomes oriented toward antisocial peers and engages in delinquency and substance abuse. Now the youth has become enmeshed in social relationships and behavioral patterns that often lead to Stage 4, in which the antisocial youth becomes an antisocial adult who is unable to hold a job and is at high risk for incarceration or other institutionalization and a disrupted marriage. Clearly, any offspring of someone in Stage 4 of this model is likely to drop into similar ground (social context) and grow through the same stages. So antisocial behavior can be passed from one generation to the next, perhaps in part through genetics but also through the conditions of the home and community. Eddy et al. (2002) depicted similar coercive interactions and conditions as causes of antisocial behavior.

School Factors

Most antisocial students experience academic failure and rejection by peers and adults in school. In many cases, they attend schools that are in deteriorated or crowded buildings. The discipline they experience in school is often little better than the parental discipline they experience at home: highly punitive, erratic, escalating, with little or no attention to their nonaggressive behavior or efforts to achieve. The academic work they are given is often not consistent with their achievement level or relevant to their eventual employment, forcing them to face failure and boredom every day they attend school (Jones & Jones, 1995; Walker et al., 2004). As for family factors, we must be careful not to accuse all teachers and school administrators of failing to teach and manage difficult students well. However, the typical school experience of antisocial students is highly negative, contributing to further maladjustment, as discussed in section 11.

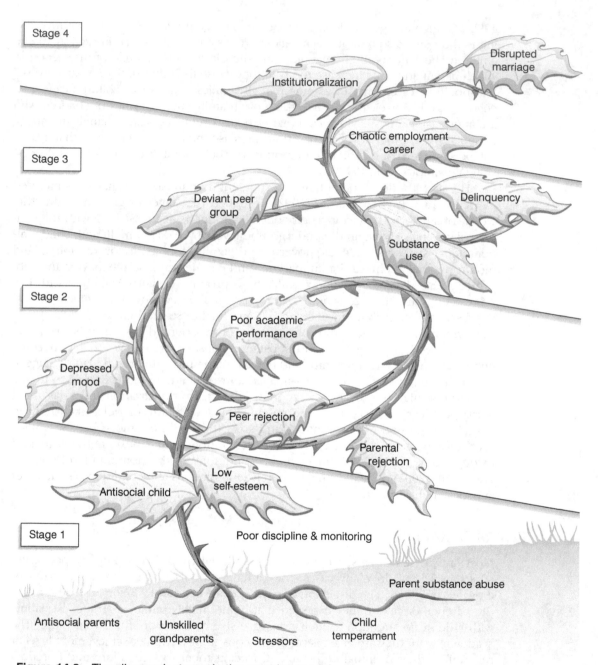

Figure 14.3 The vile weed: stages in the coercion model

Source: Patterson, G. R., Reid, J. B., & Dishion, T. J. (1992). *Antisocial Boys*. Eugene, OR: Castalia. Copyright © 1992 by Castalia Publishing Company. Reprinted by permission.

ASSESSMENT

The antisocial behavior characterizing conduct disorder is included on nearly all behavior problem checklists and behavior rating scales. Moreover, a variety of instruments have been designed specifically to measure the antisocial behavior of children and adolescents through self-reports or ratings of parents, teachers, or peers. These measures of antisocial behavior are often helpful, but they must always be supplemented by direct observation of the children or youth in several different settings to obtain more precise information about the problem (Freeman & Hogansen, 2006).

The instruments and practices described apply to the assessment of CD. The following suggestions for assessing CD build on our prior discussion (see Kazdin, 1993, 1998, 2001):

1. Use rating scales that have multiple dimensions, because children with CD are likely to have other problems as well.
2. Make sure you assess prosocial skills (behavioral strengths or appropriate behavior) as well as CD.
3. Compare the child to norms for others of the same age and sex.
4. Assess the social contexts, including family, community, and school.
5. Make provisions for periodic reassessment to measure progress of intervention.

It is important to know what social skills a student has and what his or her standing is in peer groups (see Kavale, Mathur, & Mostert, 2004; Vaughn et al., 2003). Another aspect of assessment is functional behavioral assessment or functional analysis: finding out what purpose the student's behavior serves, what consequences, gains, or benefits it provides (see Fox & Gable, 2004). A functional analysis can provide guidance for making alterations in the environment (e.g., tasks, commands, reinforcement) that will prevent or ameliorate problems. Unfortunately, the behavior of many disruptive students is motivated in large measure by negative reinforcement—escape from academic demands (see Kauffman et al., 2006; Kerr & Nelson, 2006).

Recall from our discussion of ADHD in section 13 that "the most likely function for ADHD-related behavior is to escape *effortful tasks*, particularly those that involve independent writing activity (e.g., seatwork) or an extended sequence of chores" (DuPaul & Barkley, 1998, p. 152). Gunter et al. (1998), Kyger (1999), Shores and Wehby (1999), and other researchers have found that neutral and negative teacher commands dominate the typical classrooms of students with behavioral problems. Teachers seldom give students work at which they can succeed and provide immediate and frequent positive reinforcement for behaving as expected. Teaching teachers to change this pattern is not easy (see Kyger, 1999). However, teachers must begin by asking questions related to their instruction and how their students are responding to it as well as their own (teacher's) responses to students.

As mentioned in our discussion of prevention, precorrection strategies are based on the premise that assessment of the context in which antisocial behavior is likely to occur will help teachers find ways of short-circuiting misbehavior and coercive struggles. Ultimately, assessment is of little value unless it suggests the variables that could be changed to alter antisocial behavior (Kauffman et al., 2006; Walker et al., 2004).

INTERVENTION AND EDUCATION

Prevention

Prediction and social control of violent behavior are among the most controversial and critical issues involving American youths. Prediction—anticipation—of antisocial behavior is essential to prevention, simply because no one can prevent what they do not anticipate (Kauffman, 2003a, 2005a). Research during the past two decades has yielded a bonanza of evidence about community, family, school, peer, and personal characteristics that place children and youth at high risk of adopting antisocial behavior patterns. Nevertheless, most individuals in our society are hesitant to intervene early to prevent later problems (Kauffman, 1999c, 2003a, 2004, 2005a; Walker & Sprague, 2007). This is an unproductive if not maddening denial of realities that others have observed:

> Small children often exhibit the "soft" signs of antisocial behavior that are relatively trivial (e.g., noncompliance, arguing, lying) and gradually progress to much more severe "hard" signs (e.g., cruelty, aggression, bullying, harassment, violence, theft, arson) as they mature. . . .Thus, it is important to address these early signs and less serious acts while we still have a chance to affect them. Far too often, we wait until it's too late to turn around vulnerable children before we define their problem behavior as in need of intervention. (Walker et al., 2004, p. 55)
>
> Preschool children, particularly boys, often engage in oppositional, overly active, and pestering behavior that may not seem serious at this developmental level. However, the manifestations of this behavior pattern in adolescence are very different and can be quite destructive. . . .The myth that preschoolers will outgrow their antisocial behavior is pervasive among many teachers and early educators. Unfortunately, this belief leads many professionals to do nothing early on, when the problem can often be addressed successfully. (Walker et al., 2004, pp. 57–58)

We can now make more recommendations regarding the prevention of aggressive behavior with considerable confidence, based on research like the work we have just reviewed (see Biglan, 1995; Conduct Problems Prevention Research Group, 1999; Eddy et al., 2002; Flannery & Huff, 1999; Hester & Kaiser, 1998; Kauffman, 1994b, 1999c, 2003b; Mayer, 1995; Strain & Timm, 2001; Walker et al., 2004; Walker & Sprague, 2007). However, as Biglan (1995) noted, "It is ironic that we have such high rates of serious antisocial behavior at the same time that the behavioral sciences are making so much progress in understanding and intervening in the contextual conditions that contribute to the development of antisocial behavior" (p. 479). Clearly, we need to address antisocial behavior at all levels of prevention, as Walker and Shinn (2002) suggested: *primary* (to prevent serious antisocial behavior from emerging), *secondary* (to remediate or ameliorate antisocial behavior once it is established), and *tertiary* (to accommodate or attenuate the negative effects of antisocial behavior that is unlikely to be changed).

Many members of our society, including professional practitioners in education and related disciplines as well as politicians and policy makers, have been reluctant to take the steps that we have good reason to believe would prevent or attenuate antisocial behavior (Kauffman, 1999c, 2003b, 2005a). Although all may agree that the level of antisocial behavior and violence in our society is unacceptable, many are opposed to the coherent, sustained, and costly programs of government at all levels that are necessary to address the problem effectively.

The steps research suggests we should take might be summarized as follows (see Kauffman, 1994b):

1. *Provide effective consequences to deter aggression.* Antisocial behavior is less likely to recur if it is followed by consequences that are nonviolent but immediate, certain, and proportional to the seriousness of the offense. Violence as a means of controlling aggression engenders counteraggression, setting the stage for further coercion. Aggression is reduced in the long term if the consequences are swift, assured, and restrictive of personal preferences rather than harsh or physically painful. Antisocial children and youth are typically punished capriciously and severely; the consequences of their behavior are often random, harsh, and unfair, cementing the pattern of counteraggression. The belief that harsher punishment is more effective is a deeply ingrained superstition. If teachers, parents, and others dealing with antisocial behavior learn to use effective nonviolent consequences, then the level of violence in our society will decline.

2. *Teach nonaggressive responses to problems.* Aggressive behavior is, to a significant degree, learned. So is nonaggressive behavior. Teaching youngsters how to solve personal conflicts and other problems nonaggressively is not easy, nor will teaching nonaggression help them solve all problems. A school curriculum including nonaggressive conflict resolution and problem solving could lower the level of violence, but that effect would be multiplied many times were the media, community leaders, and high-profile role models to join forces with educators in teaching that nonviolence is a better way.

3. *Stop aggression early before it takes root.* Aggression begets aggression, particularly when it is successful in obtaining desired ends and when it has become well practiced. Aggression often escalates from relatively minor noncompliance and belligerence to appalling acts of violence. Nonviolent consequences are more effective when applied early in the sequence. We need intervention that is early in two ways: first, early in that we intervene with young children; second, early in that we intervene from first instances of antisocial behavior, the earliest behaviors in a chain of aggressive interactions.

4. *Restrict access to the instruments of aggression.* Aggressors use the most efficient tools available to damage their targets. True, some will show aggression with whatever tools are available. The more important truth is that having more efficient weapons (e.g., guns) enables aggressors to accomplish violent ends with less immediate risk to themselves and to escalate the level of violence easily. More effective restriction of access to the most efficient tools of aggression would help to check the rise in violence: restrictions on the manufacture, distribution, and possession of both the tools themselves and of the parts that make the most efficient weapons of violence operable.

5. *Restrain and reform public displays of aggression.* The behavior one observes affects one's own thinking and overt behavior. Much of the fare marketed by the entertainment industry is saturated with aggressive acts, desensitizes observers to aggression and its consequences, and disinhibits expressions of aggression. Broadcasts of admired athletes and other public figures often depict them bragging, intimidating their opponents, bullying, or fighting. They are often portrayed

as swaggering winners or sore losers, in either case as very bad role models. Reducing the amount and type of antisocial behavior purveyed to the public as entertainment and requiring that the realistic consequences of aggression be depicted would contribute to the goal of a less-violent society. Sports figures who eschew both violence and braggadocio could add immeasurably to this effect.

6. *Correct the conditions of everyday life that foster aggression.* People tend to be more aggressive when they are deprived of basic necessities, experience aversive conditions, or perceive that there is no path to their legitimate goals other than aggression. Poverty and its attendant deprivations and aversive conditions affect an enormous proportion of American children and youth, and these conditions of everyday life provide fertile ground for aggressive conduct. Social programs that address poverty, unemployment, and related social inequities would help to remove the conditions that breed aggression. Opportunities for supervised recreation offer alternatives to antisocial behavior. A reasonably supportive society cannot abolish poverty or remove all of life's dangers, but it can keep many children from living in abject fear, misery, and hopelessness. We must have more effective social programs involving government, the private sector, local communities, religious groups, families, and individuals.

7. *Offer more effective instruction and more attractive educational options in public schools.* Achieving academic success and engaging in study that they see as interesting and useful in their lives reduces the likelihood that youngsters will behave aggressively. By adopting instructional methods known to produce superior results—putting instruction on a solid scientific footing—schools could ensure that more students achieve success in the basic skills needed to pursue any educational option. By offering highly differentiated curricula, school systems could help more students find options that interest them and prepare them for life after high school.

Prevention of covert antisocial behavior in many ways parallels prevention of overt aggression. Character training or moral education seems to the casual observer particularly relevant to the prevention of stealing, lying, vandalism, and so on. The effects of typical moral and character education, however, have been nil or very slight. Moral behavior often does not match moral judgment. Children and youth, as well as adults, often do wrong even though they know what is right. Moral behavior tends to be controlled at least as much by situational factors as by moral or character traits; youngsters are honest or altruistic at some times and in some situations but not in others (Walker, de Vries, & Trevethan, 1987). Teachers' talk about classroom conventions, procedures, and moral issues has little effect on children's reasoning about morals. For schools to have much influence in teaching prosocial values, they must develop coherent and pervasive programs of character education that include discussion, role-playing, and social-skills training to help students recognize moral dilemmas, adopt moral values, and select moral behavioral alternatives. This training may be particularly important for students with emotional or behavioral disorders (Walker et al., 2004).

Although preventive efforts may have a significant effect if implemented in only one social context (e.g., school or family), they will have maximum effect only if implemented as a coherent package of interventions involving multiple facets of the problem (see Conduct Problems Prevention Research Group, 1999; Strain & Timm, 2001). This knowledge should not deter educators or any other professionals from implementing preventive practices immediately, regardless of what happens in spheres outside their immediate responsibility or direct influence.

Most important for educators is understanding how instruction is a key tool for prevention (cf. Kauffman et al., 2006). Being confronted daily, if not hourly, by academic and social tasks at which they are failures is known to contribute directly to students' tendency to exhibit antisocial behavior. Many antisocial students do not know how to do the academic tasks and do not have the social coping skills to be successful in the typical classroom, and each failure increases the probability of future antisocial responses to problems (Gunter et al., 1998).

The most effective approaches to school-based prevention of antisocial behavior are *proactive* and *instructive:* planning ways to avoid failure and coercive struggles regarding both academic and social behavior and actively teaching students more adaptive, competent ways of behaving. Antisocial behavior should prompt teachers to ask what prosocial skills the student needs to learn as a replacement for aggression and to devise an explicit instructional strategy for teaching those skills.

Major Features of Social Learning Interventions

Many conceptual approaches to intervention in a CD once it has emerged have been suggested. These have included psychodynamic therapies, biological treatments, and behavioral interventions. Parent management training, problem-solving training, family therapy based on systems theory and behaviorism, and treatments addressing multiple social systems (family, school, community) as well as the individual are among the most promising approaches. Interventions based on social learning principles have generally been more successful than have those based on other conceptual models (Dean, Duke, George, & Scott, 2007; Eddy et al., 2002; Kazdin, 1994; Walker, 1995; Walker & Sprague, 2007; Walker et al., 2004; Webster-Stratton & Dahl, 1995). Furthermore, a social learning approach offers the most direct, practical, and reliable implications for the work of teachers. Consequently, we confine discussion here to interventions based on social learning concepts.

A *social learning approach* to the control of aggression includes three primary components: specific behavioral objectives, strategies for changing behavior by altering the social environment, and precise measurement of behavioral change. These components allow us to judge the outcome of intervention quantitatively as well as qualitatively against an objective goal.

Social learning interventions sometimes appear quite simple, but the apparent simplicity is deceptive because it is often necessary to make subtle adjustments in technique to make them work. An exquisite sensitivity to human communication is necessary to become a virtuoso in the humane and effective application of behavior principles. The range of possible techniques for an individual case is extensive, calling for a high degree of creativity to formulate an effective and ethical plan of action.

School-based social learning interventions designed to reduce aggression may include a wide variety of strategies or procedures (Kauffman et al., 2006; Landrum & Kauffman, 2006). Walker (1995) discussed 12 intervention techniques for managing the acting-out student, providing guidelines for correct application, special issues, and advantages and disadvantages of each. These 12 techniques (and others) may be used individually or in combination. The following thumbnail sketches of the 12 techniques provide a beginning point for understanding how effective interventions for conduct disorder may be constructed:

- *Rules*—clear, explicit statements defining the teacher's expectations for classroom conduct. Clarity of expectations is a hallmark of corrective or therapeutic environments for students with conduct disorder. A few clear rules let students know how they should behave and what is prohibited; they are important guidelines for classroom conduct and teacher behavior as well. Positively stated rules, which should predominate, guide the teacher's praise, approval, and other forms of positive reinforcement. Negatively stated rules, which should be kept to a minimum, guide the teacher's use of punishment.
- *Teacher praise*—positive verbal, physical, gestural, or other affective indications of approval. Teacher praise for desirable, nonaggressive student conduct is one of the key ingredients in successful behavioral management. Many teachers neglect this aspect of instruction or use praise too sparingly or unskillfully. Yet it is perhaps the most important element in a program of positive reinforcement. Moreover, rules alone are much less effective than are rules combined with frequent, skillful teacher praise for following them.
- *Positive reinforcement*—presentation of a rewarding consequence that increases the future probability or strength of the behavior it follows. Such consequences can be extremely varied in form. Rhode, Jenson, and Reavis (1992) suggested that to be most effective, praise and other forms of positive reinforcement should be given (a) immediately after appropriate behavior, (b) frequently, (c) with enthusiasm, (d) with eye contact from the teacher, (e) after or with description of the behavior that earned the reward, (f) in ways that build excitement and anticipation for obtaining them, and (g) in great variety. Sometimes, token reinforcers are given that can be exchanged later for desired objects or privileges (much like any other economic exchange or monetary system). The effective use of positive reinforcement requires differential responding to the student's behavior. That is, the desired behavior is to be reinforced; undesirable behavior is to be ignored (not reinforced). The basic idea of positive reinforcement is very simple; its skillful implementation is not, especially with difficult antisocial students.
- *Verbal feedback*—information about the appropriateness or inappropriateness of academic or social behavior. Teachers' responses to students' academic performance and conduct (the content, emotional tone, and timing of what they say and do in reaction to students' behavior) are crucial factors in how students learn to behave. Giving clear feedback, keeping it primarily positive, steering clear of arguments, and finding the most effective pace and timing are critical issues. Using verbal feedback effectively requires much experience, training, and reflection.
- *Stimulus change*—alteration of antecedent events or conditions that set the stage for behavior. Sometimes antecedents can be changed easily, resulting in a marked decrease in problem behavior. For example, making instructions or assignments shorter and clearer may result in greatly improved levels of compliance. Presenting

tasks or commands in a different way may also defuse resistance to them. Increasing attention is being given to the effects of the context in which aggression occurs, and modification of the context is often found to be both feasible and effective in reducing aggression.

- *Contingency contract*—a written performance agreement between a student and teacher (or parents, or both teacher and parents), specifying roles, expectations, and consequences. Contracts must be written with the student's age and intelligence in mind. They should be simple, straightforward statements. Successful contracts are clearly written, emphasize the positive consequences for appropriate conduct, specify fair consequences to which all parties agree, and are strictly adhered to by the adults who sign the document. Contracts are not generally successful if they are used as the only or primary intervention strategy. They are useful primarily for individuals and carefully delimited problem behaviors.
- *Modeling plus reinforcing imitation*—showing or demonstrating the desired behavior and providing positive reinforcement for matching responses. Learning through watching models and imitating them—*observational learning*—is a basic social learning process. The models may be adults or peers, but it is critical that the student who is to learn more appropriate behavior be taught whom to watch, what to look for, and what to match; models without explicit instruction are not typically effective in remediating academic or social problems (see Hallenbeck & Kauffman, 1995). Effective modeling and reinforcement often must be done in private one-on-one sessions with the teacher, and procedures must be used to help students exhibit in everyday circumstances the improved behavior they learn through observational learning.
- *Shaping*—a process of building new responses by beginning with behavior the student already exhibits at some level and reinforcing successive approximations of the desired behavior. The key factor in shaping is identifying and reinforcing small increments of improvement. This typically requires careful attention to the student's current behavior in relation to a behavioral goal. It also requires ignoring behavior that does not represent progress toward the goal. As is true of positive reinforcement, the basic idea is simple, but the skillful implementation is not.
- *Systematic social skills training*—a curriculum in which the skills taught are those that help students (a) initiate and maintain positive social interactions, (b) develop friendships and social support networks, and (c) cope effectively with the social environment. Social skills involve getting along with authority figures such as teachers and parents, relating to peers in a variety of activities, and solving social problems in constructive, nonaggressive ways. They involve both skill deficits (the student does not have the skill) and performance deficits (the student has but does not use the skill). A useful social skills training program must not only be intensive and systematic but also aimed at demonstration and practice of the skills in natural or everyday environments in which they are needed to avoid coercive struggles and aggressive behavior.
- *Self-monitoring and self-control training*—consistent tracking, recording, and evaluating of specific behaviors of one's own with the intention of changing those behaviors. These procedures many involve not only keeping track of one's own behavior but also prompting oneself or applying consequences to oneself. These procedures require explicit training and rehearsal, as well as the motivation to use

them. As discussed in section 13, self-monitoring is a strategy frequently used with students who have ADHD. Self-monitoring may be an inappropriate strategy for serious aggressive behavior and for students who do not have the cognitive awareness or social maturity to carry out the procedures.

- *Time-out*—the removal, for a specified period of time and contingent on a specific misbehavior, a student's opportunity to obtain positive reinforcement. Time-out may involve removing a student from the group or classroom, although that is not always necessary (e.g., it may involve the teacher's turning away and refusing to respond or a time during which the student cannot earn points or other rewards). Time-out should be reserved for serious behavioral problems. Like any punishment procedure, it is easily misunderstood, misused, and abused. Used knowledgeably and skillfully and in combination with other positive procedures, it is an important nonviolent tool for reducing aggressive behavior.

- *Response cost*—the removal of a previously earned reward or reinforcer (or a portion thereof) contingent on a specific misbehavior. Response cost is a fine or penalty incurred for each instance of an inappropriate behavior. Minutes of recess, free time, or access to another preferred activity or points toward earning a reinforcing item or activity may be lost for each misbehavior. Like any other punishment procedure, response cost is subject to misunderstanding and misuse. Moreover, it is ineffective without a strong program of positive reinforcement. However, of all types of punishment procedures, it is probably the least likely to engender strong emotional side effects and resistance.

The Uses and Misuses of Punishment

Many people in the United States appear to embrace corporal punishment and other highly punitive approaches to child discipline (e.g., Evans & Richardson, 1995; Gershoff, 2002; Hyman, 1995). Indeed, numerous studies have confirmed the low rates of positive reinforcement for appropriate behavior and high rates of aversive conditions for students in typical U.S. classrooms, as discussed in section 11 (see Bear, 1998; Gunter et al., 1998; Maag, 2001). In reaction to excessive and ineffective punishment, some have advocated a ban on all manner of punishment, arguing that positive measures alone are sufficient, and punishment in any form is unethical. Research does not support a complete abandonment of punishment as a means of child management, but it does suggest great care in the use of punishment procedures (see Cullen & Mudford, 2005; Mulick & Butter, 2005; Newsom & Kroeger, 2005).

Although teaching appropriate behavior is important in social learning interventions, some behaviors may require punishment because they are intolerable or dangerous and unresponsive to alternative positive interventions (Kazdin, 1998; Newsom & Kroeger, 2005; Walker, 1995; Walker et al., 2004). It may be difficult or impossible to establish adequate classroom control, particularly with students who have learning and behavioral problems, without using negative consequences for misbehavior in addition to positive reinforcement of appropriate conduct. Judicious use of negative consequences for misconduct can even enhance the effectiveness of positive consequences (Lerman & Vorndran, 2002; Pfiffner & O'Leary, 1987; Pfiffner, Rosen, & O'Leary, 1985).

We must be extremely careful in the use of punishment, however, because ill-timed, vengeful, and capricious punishment, especially in the absence of incentives for appropriate behavior, provides a vicious example for youngsters and encourages their further misbehavior. Harsh punishment provokes counteraggression and coercion. Punishment is a seductive, easily abused approach to controlling behavior. Harsh punishment has an immediate effect; because it frequently results in immediate cessation of the individual's irritating or inappropriate behavior, it provides a powerful negative reinforcement for the punisher. Thus, it is often the beginning point of a coercive style of interaction in which the punished and the punisher vie for the dubious honor of winning an aversive contest. And because people mistakenly believe that punishment makes the individual suffer, physical punishment is frequently thought to be more effective than milder forms. These dangers, misconceptions, and abuses of punishment appear to underlie the coercive relationships that characterize families of aggressive antisocial children (cf. Patterson et al., 1992). Consequently, it is crucial to carefully consider punishment in educational settings to avoid having the school become another battleground for aversive control.

A pervasive misconception about punishment is that it requires inflicting physical pain, psychological trauma, or social embarrassment. None of these is required; punishment can be defined as any consequence that results in a decline in the rate or strength of the punished behavior. Thus, a mild, quiet reprimand, temporary withdrawal of attention, or loss of a small privilege may often be an effective punishment. For persistent and serious misbehavior, stronger punishment may be necessary, but mild forms of social punishment such as restrictions or loss of rewards are most effective if the youngster's environment also provides many opportunities for positive reinforcement of appropriate behavior.

The social learning literature clearly supports the assertion that punishment, if carefully and appropriately administered, is a humane and effective tool for controlling serious misbehavior (Lerman & Vorndran, 2002; Newsom & Kroeger, 2005; Walker, 1995; Walker et al., 2004). Effective punishment may actually be necessary to rear a nonaggressive, socialized child (Dishion & Patterson, 1996; Patterson, 1982; Patterson et al., 1992). However, clumsy, vindictive, or malicious punishment is the teacher's or parent's downfall. And it is a mistake not to offer positive reinforcement for desired alternative behavior when punishment is employed (Maag, 2001; Newsom & Kroeger, 2005; Thompson, Iwata, Conners, & Roscoe, 1999). We also must first give attention to what types of behavior may be legitimately punished. Punishment that is out of proportion to the seriousness of the offense has no place in humane treatment. Before using punishment procedures, educators must be sure that a strong program of teaching and positive consequences for appropriate behavior is in place, and they must carefully consider the types of behavior that are priorities for punishment. Teachers should study the use of punishment procedures in depth before implementing them in the classroom. Following are general guidelines for humane and effective punishment:

• Punishment should be reserved for serious misbehavior that is associated with significant impairment of the youngster's social relationships and behaviors that positive strategies alone have failed to control.

- Punishment should be instituted only in the context of ongoing behavioral management and instructional programs that emphasize positive consequences for appropriate conduct and achievement.
- Punishment should be used only by people who are warm and loving toward the individual when his or her behavior is acceptable and who offer ample positive reinforcement for nonaggressive behavior.
- Punishment should be administered matter-of-factly, without anger, threats, or moralizing.
- Punishment should be fair, consistent, and immediate. If the youngster is able to understand descriptions of the contingency, punishment should be applied only to behavior that he or she has been warned is punishable. In short, punishment should be predictable and swift, not capricious or delayed.
- Punishment should be of reasonable intensity. Relatively minor misbehavior should evoke only mild punishment, and more serious offenses or problems should generally result in stronger punishment.
- Whenever possible, punishment should involve response cost (loss of privileges or rewards or withdrawal of attention) rather than aversives.
- Whenever possible, punishment should be related to the misbehavior, enabling the youngster to make restitution or practice a more adaptive alternate behavior.
- Punishment should be discontinued if it is not quickly apparent that it is effective. Unlike positive reinforcement, which may not have an immediate effect on behavior, effective punishment usually results in an almost immediate decline in misbehavior. It is better not to punish than to punish ineffectively, because ineffective punishment may merely increase the individual's tolerance for aversive consequences. Punishment will not necessarily be more effective if it becomes harsher or more intense; using a different type of punishment, making the punishment more immediate, or making the punishment more consistent may make it more effective.
- There should be written guidelines for using specific punishment procedures. All concerned parties—students, parents, teachers, and school administrators—should know what punishment procedures will be used. Before implementing specific punishment procedures, especially those involving time out or other aversive consequences, they should be approved by school authorities.

As we have discussed, children and youth with CD have typically experienced lax monitoring and inconsistent, harsh punishment with little positive reinforcement for appropriate behavior. Their discipline has typically contributed to their CD, not because it has included punishment per se but because it has included too little positive reinforcement for the right kind of behavior and punishment that is not appropriate. Effective intervention in CDs may often require punishment, but of a different kind.

THE ACTING-OUT BEHAVIOR CYCLE AND PRECORRECTION

Social learning interventions are increasingly focused on stepping in early to prevent the escalation of aggression and the blowups in which it often terminates. One clear presentation of this approach is provided by Colvin (1992). He describes the phases

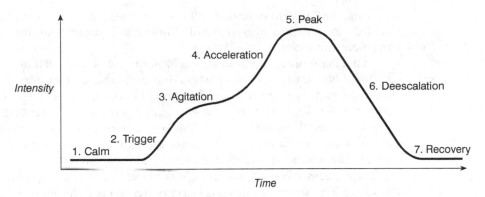

Figure 14.4   Phases of acting-out behavior
Source: Colvin, G. (1992). Managing acting-out behavior: *Behavior Associates.* Copyright © 1992 by Behavior Associates Reprinted by permission.

children and youth typically go through in a cycle of acting-out behavior. Figure 14.4 is a graphic depiction of the seven phases.

A highly significant feature of the acting-out cycle is that it begins with a *calm* phase in which the student is behaving in ways that are expected and appropriate. The student is cooperative, compliant, and task oriented. Most students with CD exhibit appropriate behavior at least some of the time, but this behavior is typically ignored by teachers. Major emphasis should be placed on recognizing and showing approval of students in the calm phase.

An unresolved problem in school or outside school may *trigger* the first stage in moving toward a major blowup. At this point, teachers may avert further escalation if they recognize the triggering events or conditions and move quickly to help the student resolve the problem.

If triggering problems are not resolved, the student may move into a state of *agitation,* in which overall behavior is unfocused and off task. If the teacher recognizes indications of agitation, further escalation of aggressive behavior may be prevented by altering teacher proximity, engaging the student in alternative activities, involving the student in a plan of self-management, or using other strategies designed to help the student avoid a blowup.

Agitation may lead to *acceleration,* a phase in which the student engages the teacher in a coercive struggle. Acceleration is characterized by attempts to draw the teacher into arguments or demand teacher attention through noncompliant, highly disruptive, abusive, or destructive behavior. At this point, it is extremely important for the teacher to avoid getting drawn in, to use crisis-prevention strategies to extricate himself or herself from the struggle. By the time the student gets to this point, it is very difficult to deescalate the behavior. Clear consequences for such behavior need to be established and communicated to the student beforehand so that at this point the teacher can deliver the needed information to the student matter-of-factly and allow him or her a few seconds to make a decision (e.g., "Roger, you must stop throwing stuff around now, or I will call the principal. Take a couple of seconds to decide"). Prompt and unequivocal follow-through in applying the consequence is extremely important.

In the *peak* phase, the student's behavior is out of control. It may be necessary to call the police or the student's parents or remove the student from the classroom or school. Preparation for such out-of-control behavior is essential so that the involved adults are as calm, systematic, and effective as possible in preventing injury or damage so that the deescalation phase can be entered as quickly as possible. Frequent out-of-control behavior should be a signal to educators to examine the environment and schoolwork for conditions that need to be changed.

During *deescalation* following a peak phase, the student typically is beginning to disengage from the struggle and is in a confused state. Behavior may range from withdrawal, to denial and blaming others for what happened, to wanting to make up, to responsiveness to directions and willingness to engage in simple tasks. It is important to take measures to help the student cool down, restore the environment as much as possible (e.g., pick up books and chairs, clean up a mess), and get back to routine activities. This is not yet the time to talk to the student about his or her behavior. Debriefing at this point in the cycle is likely to be counterproductive; the student is likely to be reluctant to talk at all or may not be able to think clearly about the incident, what led to it, and how similar problems might be avoided.

Finally, the student enters a *recovery* phase in which he or she is eager for busywork and a semblance of ordinary classwork but still reluctant to discuss what happened. It is important to provide strong reinforcement for normal routines and to avoid negotiations about the negative consequences that may have been applied to the serious misbehavior. However, it is very important at this point to *debrief* the student, to review what led up to the problem and what alternative behaviors the student might have chosen (Sugai & Colvin, 1997). Any effort of the student to problem-solve should be acknowledged, and the student should be helped to devise a step-by-step plan for avoiding repetitions of the blowup. The student needs reassurance that he or she can succeed and avoid such out-of-control incidents with help.

Educators often place a great deal of emphasis on Phases 4 and 5 of the acting-out behavior cycle, virtually ignoring the first three phases, particularly Phase 1 (calm). Walker et al. (2004) noted that this is counterproductive. The opposite emphasis is recommended by decades of research: Focus attention on the earlier phases of the cycle, on attention to and reinforcement of calm behavior, removing or ameliorating triggers, and intervening early and nonthreateningly when students begin showing signs of agitation. One systematic way of focusing attention and effort on earlier phases of the cycle is the precorrection plan described by Colvin, Sugai, and Patching (1993). Strong reinforcement for appropriate behavior is important, but precorrection begins with examination of the context in which misbehavior is likely and how conditions might be altered and instructional (as opposed to correctional) procedures used to prevent the misbehavior from occurring—how triggers and agitation can be avoided. Figure 14.5 shows a precorrection checklist and plan devised by a sixth-grade teacher for Jimmy, a student in her class.

A Completed Precorrection Plan

Teacher: <u>Pat Puller</u>   Student: <u>Jimmy Ott (six grade)</u>   Date: <u>Oct. 11, 2002</u>

1. Context [where and when; situation, circumstances, or conditions in which predictable behavior occurs]

   Upon entering the classroom in the morning, when at least one other student is in the room

---

   Predictable Behavior [the error or misbehavior that you can anticipate in the context]

   Jimmy describes his deviant behavior or deviant intentions (e.g., how he drank or did drugs or got into a fight or stole something or is going to "take someone out")

---

2. Expected Behavior [what you want the student to do instead of the predictable behavior]

   Jimmy will talk about appropriate topics when he enters the class

---

3. Context Modification [how you can change the situation, circumstances, or conditions to make the predictable behavior less likely and the expected behavior more likely to occur]

   Meet Jimmy at the door and immediately ask a question demanding appropriate talk as an answer

---

4. Behavior Rehearsal [practice; dry run; try out; drill]

   Practice with Jimmy coming into class and responding to my question, then talking about appropriate topics

---

5. Strong Reinforcement [special reward for doing the expected behavior]

   Praise for appropriate talk on coming into the classroom, plus 5 min to talk with his choice of me, principal, cook, or custodian if no inappropriate talk before first period assignment is given (principal, cook, and custodian agreed and trained in how to handle conversation)

---

6. Prompts [gestures or other signals indicating "remember; do it now"]

   Hand signal to Jimmy when I first see him in the morning, worked out in advance to indicate "appropriate talk"

---

7. Monitoring Plan [record of performance; indicator of success that you can show someone]

   Jimmy and I to record daily successful school entry talk

Figure 14.5 Precorrection checklist and plan for Jimmy
Source: Kauffman, J. M., Mostert, M. P., Trent, S. C., & Hallahan, D. P. (2002). *Managing classroom behavior: A reflective case based approach* (3rd ed.). Boston: Allyn & Bacon, p. 63. Copyright © 2002. Reprinted by permission of the publisher.

In section 10, we cited Patterson's (1986b) research. He observed that many of the characteristics of CD emerge from "the prosaic daily round of parental mismanagement . . . something as inherently banal as family coercive exchanges. What leads to things getting out of hand may be a relatively simple affair, whereas the process itself, once initiated, may be the stuff of which novels are made" (p. 442). It is highly probable that a similar process characterizes the emergence of conduct disorder in school. Astute teachers perceive the potential for triggers and agitation and move quickly and positively to help students learn to avoid them, not just to deal appropriately with the early stages of acting out (see Kauffman, Bantz, & McCullough, 2002). Many of the most effective interventions involve expert management of ordinary events.

School Violence and Schoolwide Discipline

There is strong consensus among those who study schools and behavioral deviance that the problems of student misconduct have increased enormously in seriousness and pervasiveness during the past two decades. Such episodes will not be managed well or lessened without a coherent schoolwide plan of behavior management in addition to strategies designed for individuals and classroom groups (Liaupsin, Jolivette, & Scott, 2004; Martella, Nelson, & Marchand-Martella, 2003).

In many schools today, especially middle schools, students are concerned about the violent behavior of their peers. Teaching peace and conflict-resolution skills has been suggested as an effective strategy for reducing violence (e.g., Lantieri, 1995), and perhaps such instruction can contribute to safer, less-violent schools. However, it is possible that the most effective approach to school violence is focused primarily on the more ordinary, routine interactions that characterize classrooms and other school environments and that are natural extensions or refinements of basic educational practices rather than special curricula. In fact, schoolwide discipline plans may be universal interventions that help to prevent severe disorders.

An important concept in the prevention of violence is that violent acts, like the more mundane acts of aggression that characterize CD, typically follow a pattern of escalating conflict. The most effective strategies for controlling school violence, therefore, are those that modify the conditions under which lower levels of aggressive acts are most likely to occur, deal quickly and nonviolently with the earliest indications that aggressive behavior is on an escalating path, and organize the school staff to support consistent, schoolwide implementation of discipline procedures. With a good schoolwide plan, the entire school staff functions as a team to set clear behavioral expectations, establish a positive school climate in which desirable behavior is frequently recognized and reinforced, monitor student behavior continuously, apply consistent and planned consequences for unacceptable behavior, provide collegial support, and maintain clear communication about both behavioral expectations and problem incidents (see Lewis & Sugai, 1999; Liaupsin et al., 2004; Martella et al., 2003; Walker et al., 2004).

Much of the problem of antisocial behavior in schools is in the form of bullying—coercion, intimidation, and threats that often start as mean-spirited teasing and progress to extortion and physical attack. Bullying is now recognized as a serious problem in the schools of many nations throughout the world (cf. Sheras, 2002; Walker et al., 2004). It is a serious problem that is often a precursor to school violence. Antisocial students are typically the bullies, not the victims, although they sometimes suffer the same fate as those they bully. Any student who is particularly passive, submissive, or provocative is a potential victim of bullies. Effective intervention in bullying typically requires a schoolwide, if not communitywide, effort, as well as individual intervention, because much of the bullying occurs outside the presence of any one adult. The general features of effective antibullying interventions include the following (see Olweus, 1991; Walker et al., 2004, for further discussion):

- A school climate characterized by a warm, positive, supportive school atmosphere in which adults set clear and firm limits on unacceptable behavior

- Nonhostile, nonphysical sanctions applied immediately and consistently to violations of behavioral expectations
- Continuous monitoring and surveillance of student activities in and around the school
- Adult mediation of student interactions and assumption of authority to stop bullying when it is observed
- Discussion of the issue of bullying with bullies, victims, parents, and neutral students (nonparticipants) to clarify school values, expectations, procedures, and consequences

We would like to think that all schools are responsible for all children and that no child should be excluded from a school because of his or her disability. However, some students with severe conduct disorder are disabled in ways that make their inclusion in regular classrooms and neighborhood schools inadvisable on ethical grounds, if not a mockery of social justice (see Brigham & Kauffman, 1998; Farmer, 2000; Kauffman, Bantz, & McCullough, 2002; Kauffman, Lloyd, Baker, & Riedel, 1995; Mock & Kauffman, 2003, for further discussion). Violent behavior cannot and must not be tolerated in schools if nonviolent students and their teachers are to maintain a viable social and instructional environment.

Interventions Specific to Covert Antisocial Behavior

Because of similarities in the nature and causes of the problems, intervention and education in overt and covert forms of conduct disorder share many features, but they also have important differences (cf. Eddy et al., 2002; Loeber et al., 1998a, 1998b; Walker et al., 2004). Consequently, the particular problems, as well as the approaches to intervention, may differ somewhat for specific types of covert antisocial acts. Families of children who steal, more often than families of aggressive children who do not steal, are extremely difficult treatment targets (Patterson, 1982; Patterson et al., 1992). Sometimes family therapy or parent discipline training is simply unfeasible or ineffective. Vandalism is often a particular problem in schools, and some intervention programs may therefore be primarily school based. Fire setting may be only tangentially related to school programs, but schools may be targets of arson by students with academic difficulties. Truancy is by definition an educational problem, although it is associated with delinquency, and programs to encourage school attendance may involve both the school and other community agencies.

Stealing

A common behavior problem that parents of young children report is that they do not recognize and respect the property rights of others. Many young children simply take what they want when they see it, without regard for ownership; in short, they steal. If this behavior persists beyond the age of 5 or 6, the child may become known as a stealer and get into trouble with peers and adults. The most useful analyses of the origins and management of stealing come from a behavioral or social learning perspective (Eddy et al., 2002; McMahon & Wells, 1998; Miller & Prinz, 1991; Sprick & Howard, 1995).

Reid and Patterson and their associates (see Eddy et al., 2002; Loeber et al., 1993; Moore, Chamberlain, & Mukai, 1979; Patterson, 1982; Patterson, Reid, Jones, & Conger, 1975; Reid & Hendricks, 1973; Reid & Patterson, 1976) have systematically researched the characteristics and behavior modification of aggressive children who steal. These generalizations have emerged:

- Stealers exhibit lower rates of observable out-of-control (negative–coercive and antisocial) behavior than do aggressive children who do not steal.
- Families of stealers demonstrate lower rates of both positive–friendly and negative–coercive behaviors than do families of aggressive children who do not steal.
- The differences in positive–friendly and negative–coercive behavior rates are almost completely because of the mothers' behavior.

Many stealers appear to exhibit high rates of antisocial behavior only away from home or at home when no observers are present. Many stealers are likely to confine their antisocial behavior to settings outside the home, disturbing the community rather than their parents by their theft and leaving their parents with little motivation to work on the problem. Parents of stealers tend to blame the stealing on someone else, thus refusing to recognize the problem and failing to follow through on intervention plans (see Eddy et al., 2002; Patterson, 1982; Patterson et al., 1975; Reid & Patterson, 1976).

Families of stealers appear to be loosely structured and characterized by lack of parental supervision or emotional attachment to the children (Patterson, 1982; Reid & Patterson, 1976). The stealer may, therefore, learn that taking others' possessions is acceptable behavior, that no one will care what he or she takes, and that no adverse consequences will follow theft. The child who learns to steal may be motivated to seek stimulation and reinforcement outside the family.

Despite the difficult and destructive family interaction patterns of stealers, relatively successful behavioral interventions have been devised. Patterson et al. (1975) believed that a behavioral antistealing program has several essential components. Before instituting the actual antistealing program, however, one must resolve a fundamental problem: parental definition of stealing. Parents of stealers are usually hesitant to accuse the child of theft and are loath to take disciplinary action. Because they are unlikely to observe the child in the act of taking something, the parents feel obliged to accept their child's explanation for how something came into his or her possession. Many parents blindly accept the child's claims of finding, borrowing, trading, winning, or receiving as payment whatever item was stolen. When their child is accused by teachers, peers, or police, parents of stealers argue that the child is being unjustly attacked. By blaming others—making it somebody else's problem—the parents avoid having to deal with the problem themselves. Even when the behavior occurs at home, parents often do not adequately define *stealing*. Some parents consider it theft to take food from the refrigerator without specific permission, whereas others view all family possessions as common property. The value of an item is also an issue because many parents of stealers cannot bring themselves to apply consequences for stealing something they consider to be worth very little.

The first step in dealing with theft is to recognize that the child is in difficulty because he or she steals more than other children of the same age do, may steal valuable objects, and has been labeled by others as a thief. The antitheft strategy must include steps to help the child stop being accused of theft and being viewed with suspicion. The child will not lose the stigma associated with the label until he or she learns to avoid even the appearance of wrongdoing. Following is the recommended strategy of parents (see Patterson et al., 1975, 1992):

1. Agree to define *stealing* as the child's possession of anything that does not belong to him or her or taking anything he or she does not own.
2. Only the parents decide whether a theft has occurred. They may base their judgment on either their own observation or on the report of a reliable informant.
3. When it is determined that the child has stolen, the parents state that, according to the rules, the child has taken the item and then apply the consequences. The parents must not shame or counsel the child at the time they discover the theft and apply the consequences, but they are encouraged to discuss the theft with him or her at another time.
4. Every instance of stealing must receive consequences.
5. Parents are advised to keep their eyes open and ask about "new" property rather than use detective tactics such as searching the child's room or clothing.
6. Consequences for stealing are either a specified interval of useful work or a period of grounding or restriction. Stealing more expensive items receives more severe consequences. Harsh consequences, such as humiliation or beating, are prohibited.
7. No positive reinforcement is given for periods of nonstealing because it is impossible to know that successful covert stealing has not occurred.
8. The program should stay in effect for at least 6 months following the last episode of stealing.

If the child steals both at home and at school, parents and teachers must implement consistent antitheft programs in both environments (Williams, 1985). Effective and early management of stealing is particularly important; the younger the age at which children begin stealing and the longer they persist, the more likely they are to become chronic stealers and adjudicated delinquents (Loeber et al., 1993). In general, the more severe the conduct disorder, the less likely it is that intervention will be successful (Webster-Stratton & Dahl, 1995). Management of stealing at school can present legal problems, particularly with older students, and the school must avoid illegal searches and seizures.

Lying

Parents and teachers consistently rate lying as a serious problem behavior of childhood, yet there has been little research on the subject (see Mash & Barkley, 2003; Shinn, Walker, & Stoner, 2002). In fact, McMahon and Wells (1998) stated, "To our knowledge, there have been no reports of formalized interventions to deal with lying" (p. 159). This apparently remains the case.

Developmental changes clearly occur in the understanding of lies and liars, but the relationship of these changes to the development of pathological lying is not understood. Apparently, children often lie in attempts to escape punishment. Adults consider lying a serious problem not only because it is an attempt at concealment but also because it is associated with other antisocial behaviors such as stealing and truancy. In the classroom, lying and cheating are functionally similar behaviors.

As one might expect, lying is related to the same sort of family process variables, especially lack of parental monitoring or supervision, that characterize stealing (Stouthamer-Loeber & Loeber, 1986). Although lying is a serious problem and may be a stepping-stone to the development of other conduct problems (Loeber et al., 1993), only a small body of research is available to guide intervention. However, "the cornerstone of effective management of honest behavior is the monitoring of work in progress and its subsequent verbal and written products to accurately identify occurrences of lying and cheating" (Stokes & Osnes, 1991, p. 619). In addition to careful monitoring, providing reinforcement for honest behavior and punishment of lying and cheating is necessary. It is important to determine whether the student can discriminate truth from nontruth, to find the probable reason for the student's telling untruths (e.g., to avoid consequences or work), and to avoid getting caught up in arguments about the veracity of what the student has said (see Sprick & Howard, 1995).

Fire Setting

The fires that children set frequently cause injury, loss of life, and property damage. In fact, youthful arsonists account for more than half of all set fires. Although fire setting has been a behavior of scientific interest for more than 150 years (Wooden & Berkey, 1984), we still do not understand very well the causes and management of this behavior in children (Kolko, 2002). Fanciful psychodynamic explanations that connect fire setting to sexual excitement have only recently begun to give way to conceptualizations grounded in reliable empirical evidence. Kolko and Kazdin (1986) proposed a social learning model for conceptualizing risk factors of fire play and fire setting that consists of three primary factors: learning experiences and cues, personal repertoires (cognitive, behavioral, and motivational), and parent and family influences and stressors. Kolko and Kazdin noted that children learn attitudes and behaviors from early experiences, such as watching parents or older siblings working or playing with fire. Children of fire fighters, furnace stokers, smokers, and adults who otherwise model behavior dealing with fire may be more likely to set fires.

We see interest in fire and playing with fire in a high percentage of young children. The ready availability of incendiary materials to children who are interested in fire and observe models who set or manage fires may set the stage for fire setting. Another major factor, however, is the personal repertoires that may heighten the risk of fire setting. Children may be more likely to set fires if any of the following are true:

- They do not understand the danger of fire or the importance of fire safety.
- They do not have the necessary social skills to obtain gratification in appropriate ways.

- They engage in other antisocial behaviors.
- They are motivated by anger and revenge.

Finally, stressful life events; parental psychopathology; and lack of parental supervision, monitoring, and involvement can increase the chances that a child will set fires (see Kolko, 2002; Kolko & Kazdin, 1989). Although research does not clearly distinguish different types of fire setters, all fires obviously are not set under the same conditions or for the same reasons. Some fires are set accidentally by children playing with matches or lighters, some by angry children who are seeking revenge but do not understand the awful consequences, others by delinquents who know full well the consequences of arson and are seeking to conceal another crime they have committed, some in response to deviant peer pressure, some in attempts to injure the fire setters themselves, and still others by youngsters whose behavior is related to anxiety and obsessions or compulsions.

Most school-aged youngsters who set fires have a history of school failure and multiple behavioral problems. Schools are sometimes their targets, so educators are among those who have an interest in identifying and treating fire setters. Fire safety education and cognitive-behavioral treatment are among the more frequent interventions used with fire setters and their families, but research on the outcomes of these approaches is scant (Kolko, Herschell, & Scharf, 2006). Thus, at this point, we can make few research-based recommendations for intervention or prevention. Both intervention and prevention will probably require efforts similar to those suggested for managing other covert antisocial behaviors such as stealing, vandalism, and truancy (McMahon & Wells, 1998). However, educators may have a unique role to play in finding out about the motivations and behavior of fire setters and finding interventions that work (Pinsonneault, Richardson, & Pinsonneault, 2002).

Vandalism

Deliberate destruction of school property costs hundreds of millions of dollars each year, and vandalism in other community settings results in much higher costs. Destructiveness and violence against people are often linked, and both are on the increase (Mayer & Sulzer-Azaroff, 2002; Walker et al., 2004). It appears to increase dramatically in antisocial boys after age 7 and to peak in the middle school years. The typical response of school administrators and justice officials to violence and vandalism is to tighten security measures and provide harsher punishment. Unfortunately, punitive measures may only aggravate the problems.

Vandalism in schools appears to be, at least in part, a response to aversive environments. More specifically, students tend to be disruptive and destructive when school rules are vague, discipline is punitive, punishment is rigidly applied regardless of students' individual differences, relationships between students and school personnel are impersonal, the school curriculum is mismatched with students' interests and abilities, and students receive little recognition for appropriate conduct or achievement. Decreasing the aversiveness of the school environment by adjusting school rules, teachers' expectations, and consequences for desirable and undesirable behavior might be more effective in preventing vandalism than increasing security and making punishment more severe (see Mayer & Sulzer-Azaroff, 1991, 2002; Sprick & Howard, 1995; Walker et al., 2004).

Truancy

Truancy becomes a greater problem in higher grades, and it is a major factor in school failure and delinquency (see Loeber et al., 1998a). Attendance at school certainly does not guarantee academic success, but chronic unexcused absence virtually ensures failure. Frequent truancy is serious not only because of probable school failure but because chronic truants are at risk for later unemployment or employment failure, criminal convictions, substance abuse, and a variety of other difficulties. Dissatisfaction with school programs and failure to attend school regularly are important signals that the student may drop out (Edgar & Siegel, 1995; Walker et al., 2004).

The problem of truancy is not new, and neither are the most effective approaches to reducing it. Interventions based on social learning principles continue to produce better results than do other approaches (see Kerr & Nelson, 2006; Walker et al., 2004). These interventions are intended to make school more attractive by recognizing and praising attendance, setting up systems in which attendance earns special rewards or privileges, giving the student work that is more interesting to him or her and at which he or she can be successful, connecting school and work or later education that is important to the student, stopping harassment by peers or other social punishment in school, and, if possible, decreasing the satisfaction or fun the student has outside school during school hours. It is often necessary to have the cooperation of the student's parents to make school more attractive and alternatives less attractive.

SUMMARY

Conduct disorder is characterized by persistent antisocial behavior that violates the rights of others as well as age-appropriate social norms. It includes aggression to people and animals, destruction of property, deceitfulness and theft, and serious violation of rules. We distinguish youngsters with conduct disorder from those who are developing normally by their higher rates of noxious behaviors and by the persistence of such conduct beyond the age at which most children have adopted less aggressive behavior. CD is often comorbid with other disorders. It is one of the most prevalent psychopathological disorders of childhood and youth, estimated to affect 6% to 16% of males and 2% to 9% of females under the age of 18. CD may be classified by age of onset, and those with early onset typically show more serious impairment and have a worse prognosis. Other subtypes include overt aggressive (undersocialized); covert antisocial (socialized), such as theft, lying, and arson; and versatile (socialized and undersocialized).

Aggressive behavior has long been a common phenomenon in American culture, but aggression and violence have become a much greater concern in schools during the past two decades. Aggression and violence are multicultural issues, although most contributing factors and interventions appear to apply equally across all subgroups. Both general and special education teachers must be prepared to deal with the aggressive behavior of students.

Many contributing causes of aggression have been identified, but social learning theory provides the best supported and most useful conceptualizations for educators. We know that aggression may be learned through processes of modeling, reinforcement of aggression, and ineffective punishment. The risk of aggressive behavior is increased by a wide variety of personal, family, school, peer, and other cultural factors. These factors are often combined in a coercive process leading to aggressive behavior that is passed from one generation to the next.

Steps likely to be effective in preventing CD include consequences that deter aggression, instruction in nonaggressive responses to problems, early intervention, restriction of the tools of aggression, restraint of public displays of aggression, correction of everyday living conditions, and more effective and attractive school options. A proactive, instructional approach to prevention is of greatest value to educators.

A variety of rating scales are of value in assessing CD, but direct observation of behavior in various settings must supplement the ratings. Assessment requires evaluation of a variety of domains, including both academic and social problems and behavior at home and school. Assessment must include prosocial skills as well as social deficits. Ongoing assessment to monitor progress is essential. Social skills must be assessed to guide instruction. Functional assessment of behavior to determine what consequences, gains, or benefits it provides the student will help guide intervention.

Interventions based on social learning are the most reliable and useful for teachers. These may include strategies such as rules, teacher praise, positive reinforcement, verbal feedback, stimulus change, contingency contracts, modeling and reinforcement of imitation, shaping, systematic social skills instruction, self-monitoring and self-control training, time-out, and response cost. Particular care must be taken in the use of punishment because it is seductive and easily misused. The focus must be on positive strategies. The concepts of the acting-out cycle and pre-correction help keep the focus of intervention on positive strategies applied early in the sequence. The acting-out cycle includes the phases *calm, trigger, agitation, acceleration, peak, deescalation,* and *recovery*. Greatest emphasis should be placed on intervention in the first three phases of the cycle. Precorrection plans help to keep the focus on earlier phases in the cycle. Schoolwide discipline plans may help decrease the level of violence in schools by focusing efforts on positive attention to appropriate behavior, clear expectations and monitoring of student behavior, staff communication and support, and consistent consequences for unacceptable behavior.

Covert antisocial behavior consists of acts such as stealing, lying, fire setting, vandalism, and truancy. These also are best addressed by application of social learning principles to problem reduction or resolution.

■ PERSONAL REFLECTIONS

Aggressive Conduct Disorder

Lisa Funk is originally from Ohio and earned her bachelor of arts and single-subject credential from Cleveland State University. She spent a year teaching high school social studies before moving to California, where she has spent the past six years educating high school students in a day treatment program for students with emotional and behavioral disorders.

Think of a particular student who exhibits a conduct disorder. How does this student manifest the disorder?

Marko is an 18-year-old Hispanic male who receives his education in a non–public school setting, which is the most resrictive environment next to home schooling and hospitalization available in California. Beginning in the fourth grade, Marko began arguing with peers, which quickly escalated to routine violence toward peers. Although the primary manner in which Marko's conduct disorder manifests in his behavior is through the use of violence and fighting, it is not limited to such.

Other areas affected by the conduct disorder include his relationship with his mother, to authority, and with the law. He has been arrested several times in the past two years for fighting with his mother. Consequently, their relationship has become so strained that she currently questions whether she can continue to live with him and support him. Additionally, he has recently been hospitalized following a fight involving several known gang members. Marko suffered extensive injuries, including stitches in his mouth, eye, cheek, and staples in his head. This incident did nothing to lessen his propensity toward fighting, and immediately after discharge Marko went looking for the people involved. Finally, Marko routinely breaks the law by driving without a license, among other things. Most of the behaviors within the classroom associated with his diagnosis relate to his difficulty being told "no." Despite these challenging aspects of his personality, he has successfully earned a high school diploma.

What procedures have you found most useful in working with this student?

One of the most effective tools I used while working with Marko for the past two years was one-on-one emotional processing. This means that when he entered the classroom visibly upset, I would make it a point to pull him aside or directly address the difference in his demeanor. I would later follow up when time permitted to give him an opportunity to let me know what was going on. This was not possible in the beginning of his time in my classroom, as it takes months (or more) to build the necessary trust to implement such an intervention. Knowing this, in the beginning I would have him journal his thoughts/emotions and turn them in at the end of the day.

Another method that worked well with Marko was giving him constant praise. Although this may seem obvious to some, it isn't always regularly implemented. Students who regularly receive attention for negative reasons need exponentially more praise due to this fact. He would always respond with a warm thank-you when acknowledged for progress in his impulse control and decision making. Although it was difficult, it was imperative that I build a relationship with his mother as well. We even attempted a home-school contract which rewarded Marko for following his mother's directions at home and treating her respectfully with privileges in the classroom that were important to him. This contract helped to improve the communication between the home and school, which helped to stabilize Marko's behavior. Another method that proved effective with Marko was to have him evaluate his own behavior after each academic period and at the end of each day. This tool helped Marko to begin looking at his behavior honestly and forced him both to take credit for his positive behavior and responsibility for his negative behavior throughout the day.

What do you see as the biggest long-term problems this student will face?

As mentioned earlier, Marko has received his high school diploma. He plans to attend vocational school or a community college to enhance his skills in the area of musical engineering and production. I believe that if he finds early success in his classes or has professors that take an interest in guiding him, he will complete his goal of augmenting his talents with education. I do believe that although he has the potential to succeed, many factors could potentially prevent his success. Some of my fears for him include his mother deciding that she has had enough and withdrawing financial and housing support. I also fear his getting in trouble for a serious offense, leading him to jail. In addition to the difficulty he may have finishing school without a mentor or guiding adult, he will need this too in terms of making decisions in relationships and in working. One of Marko's greatest strengths has been his ability to listen to adults whom he trusts and heed their advice to the best of his ability. If he continues in therapy or is taken under the wing of a stable adult figure, I have no doubt that he can accomplish what he sets out to do positive in this world.

Ms. Funk Interviews Marko

Ms. Funk: Tell me about the Linden Center.

Marko: Do you want me to say what I tell other people?

Ms. F: Just describe what kind of a school it is.

Marko: It's like a probation school; everyone that got in trouble is in this school. It's a school for kids that are messed up and are all in one place. It's a little school with a bunch of rules. You get help with the things you need there.

Ms. F: Is there anything you'd like to add?

Marko: It's a cool school, too.

Ms. F: What are some of the things you liked about attending school there?

Marko: I liked that everyone accepted everyone. No one was judged by their appearance, everyone knew that everyone had problems there and was cool to each other. There was a lot less fighting and drama between people. The teachers were more caring at the Linden Center; in public schools the teachers didn't really care. The teachers were more sincere about what they said.

Ms. F: I'm a little afraid to ask, but . . . what were some of the things you didn't like?

Marko: Ha-ha-ha. I didn't like Leave the Groups.

Ms. F: No one will know what that means; so what didn't you like about the Leave the Groups?

Marko: I felt at times we were being treated as children, and in public schools you can get away with a lot more.

Ms. F: Could you be more specific?

Marko: We couldn't mention anything sexual or gang-related, which you could get away with in a public school. I also would get bored being in one class for the whole day. I didn't like eating in my classroom either. There was no place for the kids to get together and socialize, like a patio.

Ms. F: What are the things the school has helped you with in terms of behavior?

Marko: I learned to take cool-outs instead of acting on my anger.

Ms. F: What are some ways you have changed in the past six years, since being at the school?

Marko: I don't gangbang anymore and I have calmed down a lot. I'm not into fighting as much anymore. I've learned to not be like that.

Ms. F: What do you mean?

Marko: I don't want that future anymore, because there is too much stress when I am always getting in trouble. I also want to set a good example for my little cousin.

Ms. F: What helped make this change?

Marko: At school I learned how to talk out my problems rather than fight and also to resolve conflicts. I learned you could be mad at someone and work it out.

Ms. F: Even though I already know, what are some of the things you feel you do well?

Marko: I rap very well, I have a quick mind; and I can come up with lyrics really quick. I am what you say, musically inclined.

Ms. F: What does that mean to you?

Marko: That means anything to do with music I am good at. This includes making beats, writing lyrics, everything.

Ms. F: Other than music, are there other things you are good at?

Marko: I am easy to get along with.

Ms. F: What are some of the things you struggle with or are currently struggling with?

Marko: I am having trouble getting along with my mom and am also having trouble finding employment.

Ms. F: Are the two related?

Marko: No, with my mom we just don't click, we argue about everything and she trips on me about basically everything. In terms of getting a job, the problem is I've applied to a bunch of jobs, followed up, and get nothing. I think it's because of the way I look with my shaved head and my style of clothes.

Ms. F: What do you see as obstacles to your success in the future?

Marko: I think that in the music industry it is going to take a lot of things to prove myself. I will have trouble doing that because I am going to have to be patient and I am going to have to get to know how the industry works, do things that no one else is doing and step up to the plate in terms of competition.

Ms. F: Do you foresee any other difficulties you may encounter down the road?

Marko: Other than music I will probably have problems with money. I don't see myself having a stable life or living with consistent money. It will take a long time for me to make any money, which may cause me to have more stress with my mom.

Ms. F: Do you foresee any problems in your education or academically at junior college or trade school?

Marko: Academically I don't see any problems in a music school because this is what I like, this is want I want to do.

Ms. F: How will you handle the obstacles you mentioned, such as being patient and getting along with your mom?

Marko: I will keep my mind busy so that I don't focus on my frustrations, like hanging out with my friends and going to parties.

Ms. F: What about your mom?

Marko: I'll have to move out; I think for the first few months to a year it will be tough living on my own and being responsible for bills. I think that once I get the hang of it, it will be all right, though.

Ms. F: Is there anything else you want to add?

Marko: No, that's it.

QUESTIONS FOR FURTHER REFLECTION

1. How would you argue with someone who insisted that overt conduct disorder is not an emotional disturbance but an indication of social maladjustment that should not be included in special education?
2. What level of aggression or violence, if any, would you argue justifies removal of a student from a regular classroom or from a typical neighborhood school?
3. What are the things you can do as a teacher to keep acting-out, aggressive behavior in your classroom to a minimum, and how are these related to cultural diversity?

SECTION 15
PROBLEM BEHAVIORS OF ADOLESCENCE
DELINQUENCY, SUBSTANCE ABUSE, AND EARLY SEXUAL ACTIVITY

As you read this section, keep these guiding questions in mind:

- What are the similarities and differences between conduct disorder and delinquency?

- What arguments support the view that most or all incarcerated youngsters have disabilities and need special education?

- What are the primary causes and prevention strategies related to substance abuse?

- What are the primary reasons for concern about early sexual activity?

- Which substances do children and youth most commonly abuse, and why are they not the focus of most concern about drugs?

In this section, we focus on delinquency, early sexual activity, and substance abuse because these particular problem behaviors often have been found to occur together (see Siegel & Welsh, 2005). Bear in mind that the concept of adolescence continues to evolve, as do the definitions of problem behaviors associated with adolescence.

PROBLEM BEHAVIORS IN ADOLESCENCE AND EARLY ADULTHOOD

Juvenile delinquents rarely display only one isolated problem behavior. More often, they engage in a constellation of a number of interrelated problem behaviors, including delinquency, sexual precocity, and substance abuse (Jessor, 1998; Jessor, Van Den Bos, Vanderryn, Costa, & Turbin, 1995; Siegel & Welsh, 2005). These different problem behaviors tend to overlap with each other. That is, youngsters who are delinquent, abuse substances, and engage in early sexual behavior often participate in other antisocial activities and possess similar personality and contextual characteristics (Ensminger & Juon, 1998).

Most adolescents engage in some risky behaviors, but most stop short of serious involvement (e.g., drug addiction) and reduce the intensity of or stop such behaviors altogether by the time they are adults (Donovan & Jessor, 1985; Siegel & Welsh, 2005). Attention deficit–hyperactivity disorder (ADHD), lack of guilt, poor communication with parents, low achievement, and anxiety are all characteristics of adolescents who exhibit escalating levels of problem behavior that are likely to continue into adulthood (Chang, Chen, & Brownson, 2003; Chassin, Ritter, Trim, & King, 2003; Siegel & Welsh, 2005; Silbereisen, 1998). That is, adolescents with those characteristics are predicted to have the highest levels of problem behaviors. The presence of problem behaviors in adolescence is the strongest predictor of problem behaviors in adulthood (Brigham, Weiss, & Jones, 1998; Jessor, Donovan, & Costa, 1991).

Loeber, Farrington, Stouthamer–Loeber, and Van Kammen (1998a, 1998b) found that measures of eight forms of problem behaviors were all highly related to each other: delinquency, substance abuse, ADHD, conduct problems, physical aggression, covert behavior such as lying and manipulation, depressed mood, and shyness or being withdrawn. That is, high scores in one area of problem behavior were often accompanied by high scores in the other seven areas. Externalizing behaviors were more interrelated to each other than they were to internalizing behaviors so that physical aggression was strongly related to substance abuse, but shyness and being withdrawn were not. Boys with high levels of problem behaviors were also characterized by high levels of delinquency, sexual precocity, and substance abuse. Forness, Kavale, and Walker (1999) suggested that such behaviors are often a symptom of more complex psychiatric disorders. Although many of these disorders are detected after a series of punitive interventions aimed at the most superficial aspects of the problem (Forness et al., 1999), researchers have been able to identify groups of variables that reliably predict the development of these complex disorders (Leech, Day, Richardson, & Goldschmidt, 2003). ADHD, for example, seems to put adolescents at particularly high risk for substance abuse problems (Flory, Milich, Lynam, Leukefeld, & Clayton, 2003; Weyandt, 2007).

Research supports the importance and plausibility of early identification. Although the remainder of this section is organized around different categories of problem behaviors, it is highly unlikely that any individual will display one and only one element of problem behavior. Problem behavior theory (Jessor & Jessor, 1977; Siegel & Welsh, 2005) and observations of comorbidity of problem behaviors with complex psychiatric disorders suggest that addressing only one or a few aspects of the problem behaviors described in this section will be of limited use. Rather, these problems are likely to respond only to more complex interventions that unite educational, mental health, and psychopharmocologic interventions (Forness et al., 1999).

JUVENILE DELINQUENCY

Definition

When someone who is not legally an adult (i.e., a juvenile) commits an act that could result in apprehension by police, he or she is said to have committed a *delinquent* act. Because many delinquent acts do not result in arrests, the extent of juvenile delinquency is difficult to determine. Some laws are vague or loosely worded so that *delinquency* is not clearly defined. Some acts are illegal if committed by a juvenile but not if they are committed by an adult (such as buying or drinking alcoholic beverages). Other delinquent acts are clearly criminal; they are considered morally wrong and punishable by law regardless of the age of the person who commits them (such as assault or murder; see cases in the accompanying case book). Many aggressive children's behavior just skirts legal delinquency. Much of the behavior of delinquents, including incarcerated youth and those at risk of incarceration, is irritating, threatening, or disruptive but not delinquent in a legal sense. Delinquent behavior may bring juveniles into contact with law enforcement.

It is important that we distinguish between delinquent behavior and official delinquency. Any act that has legal constraints on its occurrence may be considered delinquent behavior. Juveniles may commit *index crimes*—crimes that are illegal regardless of a person's age and that include the full range of criminal offenses, from misdemeanors to first-degree murder. Common index crimes committed by juveniles are vandalism, shoplifting, and various other forms of theft such as auto theft, armed robbery, and assault. Other illegal behavior may be against the law only because of the offender's age. Acts that are illegal only when committed by a minor are called *status offenses*. Status offenses include truancy, running away from home, buying or possessing alcoholic beverages, and sexual promiscuity. They also include a variety of ill-defined behaviors described by labels such as *incorrigible, unmanageable,* or *beyond parental control*. Status offenses are a grab bag category that can be abused in determining whether or not a child is a juvenile delinquent; it is a category that encompasses serious misdeeds but that adult authorities can expand to include mere suspicion or the appearance of misconduct (Blackburn, 1993; see also Sims & Preston, 2006).

The differences between official delinquency and delinquent behavior are significant. Surveys in which children and adolescents report whether they engage in specific delinquent acts indicate that the vast majority (80% to 90%) have done so. Self-reports appear to be by far the best way to estimate the true extent of delinquent behavior (Siegel & Senna, 1994; Siegel & Welsh, 2005). Research studies have provided data indicating that self-reported delinquent behavior correlates positively with depressed mood (Beyers & Loeber, 2003) and negatively with parental awareness of a child's delinquent behavior (Laird, Pettit, Bates, & Dodge, 2003). Only about 20% of all minors are at some time officially delinquent; in a given year, approximately two million youths are arrested (Siegel & Welsh, 2005). We find a disproportionate number of official delinquents among lower socioeconomic classes and ethnic minorities (Laub & Lauritsen, 1998; Loeber, Farrington, Stouthamer-Loeber, and Van Kammen, 1998a; Penn, Greene, & Gabbidon, 2006; Siegel & Welsh, 2005).

Delinquent behavior, conduct disorder, and official delinquency are overlapping phenomena. Although data support a positive correlation between conduct disorder and delinquent behaviors (Vermeiren, Schwab-Stone, Ruchkin, De Clippele, & Deboutte, 2002), a youngster with conduct disorder of either the overt or covert variety may or may not engage in delinquent behavior and may or may not become an official delinquent.

Few delinquents begin their criminal behavior with extreme behaviors such as violent crime. Rather, they ease into their delinquency through a series of minor offenses. The earlier the series of behaviors begins, the more likely it is that the individual will eventually show more serious examples of problem behavior and violence. Therefore, educators must not be lulled into a sense of false security that a young misbehaving youngster will outgrow his or her behavior patterns. Quite the opposite is implied by the research conducted to date. Rather than growing out of their misbehavior, children who exhibit problem behaviors at an early age very often grow into more serious problem behaviors.

Types of Delinquents

Researchers have attempted to delineate homogeneous groups of delinquents based on behavioral characteristics, types of offenses, and membership in subcultural groups (e.g., Achenbach, 1982; Quay, 1986a; see also Siegel & Welsh, 2005; Sims & Preston, 2006). However, it may be more helpful to distinguish between those who commit one or a few delinquent acts and those who are serious repeat offenders, especially those who commit violent crimes against persons. Some have argued that because a majority of adolescents commit delinquent acts, the differences between those who are convicted and those who are not are largely a reflection of police or court biases, but "this view can be firmly rejected" (Farrington, 1995, p. 956). Farrington argued that the correspondence between official arrest records and self-reports of delinquent and criminal acts, plus the ability of self-reports to predict future convictions, indicates that both self-reports and convictions are valid measures that distinguish the worst offenders. This view is supported by the finding that a prior arrest for a violent crime and a history of family violence and criminality are the best predictors (e.g., better than prior gang involvement or heavy alcohol and drug use) of a youth's likelihood of committing a violent crime (Lattimore, Visher, & Linster, 1995; see also Siegel & Welsh, 2005).

Another useful way of thinking about different types of delinquents is the age at which they commit their first offense. Prior research has indicated that the prognosis for those who begin a delinquent pattern of behavior before the age of 12 is much worse than it is for those who are late starters (Dinitz, Scarpitti, & Reckless, 1962; see also Sayre-McCord, 2007). This pattern apparently typifies the trajectories of boys more so than girls (see Bryant et al., 1995; Kratzer & Hodgins, 1999). The data appear to be consistent with the observation that more serious delinquent behavior is associated with a coercive family process that trains children in antisocial behavior from an early age (Patterson, Reid, & Dishion, 1992). In addition, research seems to indicate a correlation between parental dysfunction and child delinquency that is not explained by observational learning (Tapscott, Frick, Wootton, & Kruh, 1996).

Prevalence

We have pointed out that most children and youth commit at least one delinquent act. But because authorities do not detect most illegal acts, hidden delinquency remains a major problem. About half of the juveniles who become official delinquents are adjudicated for only one offense before they become adults. Juveniles who commit repeated offenses (*recidivists*) account for the majority of official delinquency. Recidivists commit more serious offenses, begin performing delinquent acts at an earlier age (usually before they are 12 years old), and tend to continue their antisocial behavior as adults (Farrington, 1995; Tolan, 1987; Tolan & Thomas, 1995).

Males commit most juvenile offenses, particularly serious crimes against people and property. Females may be increasingly involved in major offenses, but males still outnumber females in official delinquency statistics (Schaffner, 2006; Siegel & Senna, 1994; Siegel & Welsh, 2005). Race, drug use, poor school performance, truancy, risk-seeking, and conflicts with parents, in addition to gender, are all factors associated with delinquency recidivism (Chang et al., 2003). Delinquency rates rise and fall, and although the early years of the 21st century saw a decline for boys in many types of offenses, the rates for girls have continued to increase (Schaffner, 2006; Siegel & Welsh, 2005).

The peak ages for juvenile delinquency are ages 15 to 17, after which delinquency rates decline. Orientation to drugs and delinquency related to drugs, especially alcohol abuse, are pervasive concerns of parents, educators, and other adults for this age group.

Causal Factors and Prevention

Delinquency is not just law-violating behavior but also involves the responses of adult authority to it (Farrington, 1995, 2007). Incarceration and other forms of punishment have failed to control delinquency. Many social-cultural factors, including our society's failure to control access to firearms, contribute to delinquency. The problem is not merely young people's criminal behavior but adult responses that tend to exacerbate rather than reduce delinquency. The scope of the problem is great, and the issues in delinquency have complex legal, moral, psychological, and sociological implications.

Criminologists have constructed a variety of theories of crime that include social–environmental, biological, familial, and personal causal factors (see Blackburn, 1993; Siegel & Senna, 1994; Siegel & Welsh, 2005). We focus here on explanations of the origins of delinquency that have the greatest implications for educators.

Longitudinal research in England and New Zealand, as well as the United States, has led to remarkably consistent findings and hypotheses about the risk factors for delinquency and suggestions for prevention (Farrington, 1995; Forness, Kavale, & Walker, 1999; Loeber et al., 1998a, 1998b; Loeber & Farrington, 2000). Research consistently reveals that the following characteristics put preadolescents at high risk for later delinquency:

- History of child abuse
- Hyperactivity, impulsivity, and problems in paying attention
- Low intelligence and low academic achievement, as well as a general pattern of disengagement from school
- Lax parental supervision and harsh authoritarian discipline
- A family history of criminality and family conflict, including aggression between siblings
- Poverty, large family size, densely populated neighborhood, poor housing
- Antisocial behavior or conduct disorder, including especially aggressive behavior and stealing.

Researchers have formed hypotheses about how these and related factors work in leading to delinquency. Three general models of influence appear in the delinquency literature: (a) delinquent behavior is the result of stable antisocial personality traits located within the delinquent individual, (b) delinquent behavior is mostly the product of external environmental factors and circumstances, and (c) delinquent behavior is primarily the result of interactions between the personal characteristics of the individual (e.g., hyperactivity, ability) and the environment (Loeber & Stouthamer-Loeber, 1998). Most researchers endorse the third option and suggest that no single factor can account for delinquent behavior (Siegel & Welsh, 2005).

Steinberg and Avenevoli (1998) found that children at risk for delinquent behavior are often disengaged from school and that school disengagement appeared to precede engagement in other problem behaviors. However, their results suggested that engagement in school was more important as a protective factor than disengagement was as a risk factor. According to them, engaged students' strong bond to school (a conventional institution) serves to maintain conventional behavior and inhibit deviant behavior by increasing the costs of deviance (e.g., suspension or expulsion from school). That is, students who are engaged in school have more to lose (e.g., positive peer group, good education, entrance into college, a job) if they become involved in deviant behavior. For these reasons, "school engagement may be an important domain for delinquency prevention" (p. 420). Note that these authors do not claim that suspension and expulsion are effective deterrents to delinquency for youth who are already disengaged from school. It is only to the extent that individuals can be reengaged in schooling or prevented from becoming disengaged that such punitive processes are likely to work as deterrents to delinquency.

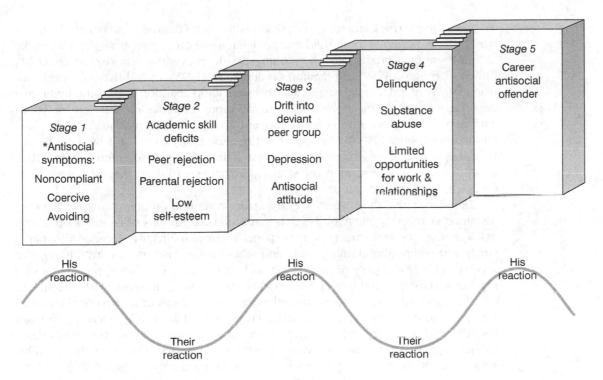

*The defining characteristics for that stage.

Figure 15.1 A concatenation of actions and reactions
Source: Patterson, G. R., Reid, J. B., & Dishion, T. J. (1992). *Antisocial Boys.* Eugene, OR: Castalia. Reprinted by permission.

As we saw in section 14, the parents of youngsters with conduct disorder typically do not monitor their children's behavior appropriately. Fridrich and Flannery (1995) found that parental monitoring and susceptibility to antisocial peer influence characterized early adolescent delinquents regardless of their ethnicity. These risk factors appear to be what Patterson et al. (1992) have called "a concatenation of actions and reactions"—a series of interconnected, interdependent events and conditions leading through several stages to a criminal career. These stages and their defining characteristics, as described by Patterson et al. (1992), are shown in Figure 15.1. Not only the stages and their descriptions but also the coercive process involving the exchange of mutually aversive reactions are depicted by the wavelike "his reaction, their reaction" sequence. You may recall from the discussion in section 14 that this "my turn, your turn" sequence is part and parcel of the acting-out cycle that we see in school. Patterson et al. (1992) see it as the essence of the coercive process leading to antisocial behavior and, left unchecked, eventually to a criminal career. It is important to note that this model does not suggest that delinquent behaviors are learned solely through parental modeling. Although such an explanation holds intuitive appeal, data do not necessarily support this conclusion (Frick & Loney, 2002).

Given these risk factors, can we predict with a high degree of accuracy which students who experience them will become delinquent? More specifically, can we make accurate enough predictions to warrant specific prevention efforts? Leech et al., (2003), Farrington (1995), and Sampson and Laub (1993) argued that we can; Lundman (1993) argued that we cannot and that we should abandon at least the traditional delinquency-prevention efforts and focus on more effective intervention for youth who have been apprehended for delinquent acts (as we discuss later). Loeber and Stouthamer-Loeber (1998) also argued that because many forms of delinquent behavior, particularly aggression, often appear first in the home and community before they appear at school, interventions must include strategies to deal with the behaviors in each setting where they occur.

Hamburg (1998) and others who argue for prevention programs suggest that they be aimed at relieving many of the disadvantageous conditions of life associated with delinquency: unemployment, poverty, poor housing, ineffective parental discipline, family and community disintegration, and school failure. However, currently popular approaches rely primarily on incapacitation by incarceration—earlier, more adultlike, harsher, and longer punishment. Research shows that these strategies are ineffective, at least for youth who have not committed index crimes against other people (Lundman, 1993). In addition, some crimes committed by juveniles have predictors and recidivism patterns that are quite different from those of adults committing the same crimes (Miner, 2002). Popular as they may be with social policy makers, highly punitive approaches are seen by many researchers as counterproductive (Siegel & Welsh, 2005).

Delinquency, Disabling Conditions, and the Need for Special Education

Educating juvenile delinquents presents difficult problems for public schools and correctional institutions because of unclear definitions of disabling conditions (see Nelson, Leone, & Rutherford, 2004). Are juvenile delinquents disabled and therefore included under the Individuals with Disabilities Education Act (IDEA)? We might contend that most or all incarcerated delinquents logically fall into the IDEA category of "emotionally disturbed." Unfortunately, the decision is not that clear-cut. The current federal definition specifically excludes youngsters who are "socially maladjusted but not emotionally disturbed." Thus, when delinquent behaviors are attributed to social maladjustment rather than emotional disturbance, students are denied the protections and services mandated by IDEA—unless they have mental retardation, learning disabilities, physical or sensory impairments, or mental illness as determined by a psychiatrist (see Leone, Rutherford, & Nelson, 1991; Nelson et al., 2004).

Researchers have consistently found that disabilities are common in delinquents, with learning disability the most prevalent disabling condition (Jarvelin, Daara, Rantakallio, Moilanen, & Ishohanni, 1995; Murphy, 1986; Nelson et al., 2004; Preston, 2006; Siegel & Senna, 1994; Zabel & Nigro, 1999). This finding seems reasonable given the high degree of comorbidity of emotional or behavioral disorders with learning disabilities (Glassberg, Hooper, & Mattison, 1999). Nevertheless, the ambiguous wording of the law precludes using adjudication or assignment to a correctional facility as the basis for identifying an emotional or behavioral disability. It requires curious turns of logic, however, to conclude that many incarcerated youths do not have emotional or behavioral disorders and are not entitled to special education under the law. If behavioral disorders include both overt and covert antisocial behavior, then finding incarcerated youth who do not have behavioral disorders is a logical impossibility (except, of course, children or youth who are held unjustly).

We know that mentally ill youngsters are often incarcerated and that a diagnosis of conduct disorder is often used as a rationale for incarcerating rather than providing mental health services to children and youth (see Ginsburg & Demeranville, 1999; Preston, 2006). We also know that conduct disorder is frequently accompanied by emotional or behavioral disorders of other types (Forness et al., 1999; Kazdin, 1994; Pullis, 1991; Webster–Stratton & Dahl, 1995). If higher levels of delinquent conduct indicate higher levels of psychopathology, and if youth who commit more frequent and more serious delinquent acts are more likely to be incarcerated, then the argument that all or nearly all incarcerated youth are disabled is supported. Finally, if behavioral disorders are not defined as disabling conditions under the law, then logically indefensible distinctions are drawn between emotional disturbance and social maladjustment. Wolf, Braukmann, and Ramp (1987) stated long ago that "evidence and consensus are growing that delinquent behavior, especially when persistent and serious, may often be part of a durable, significantly handicapping condition that is composed of multiple antisocial and dysfunctional behaviors, and that sometimes appears to be familially transmitted" (p. 350). The evidence and the consensus have grown that Wolf and his colleagues were correct.

Assessment of Delinquents' Educational Needs

Delinquents' disruptive behavior, bravado, and lack of cooperation often make them inaccessible, and they may be successful in covering up their academic deficits. However, the assessment of their educational needs does not differ in any essential way from the assessment of other students' needs; evaluation should focus directly on the skills in which instruction is to be offered (see Merrell, 1994; Nelson et al., 2004; Overton, 2003). Because many delinquents have cognitive and academic deficits in addition to social and vocational skills deficits, their assessment must often be multifaceted. Disabilities make their assessment, treatment, and transition back to the community after incarceration all the more difficult (Unruh & Bullis, 2005). Assessment must often be done hurriedly and without relevant background information because delinquents are often in detention centers or special facilities where student populations are transient, educational records unavailable, and communication with other agencies difficult. Finally, because there is little agreement about the most important skills for delinquents—social, academic, or vocational—the focus of assessment is often questionable.

Intervention in Juvenile Delinquency

Juvenile delinquency—antisocial behavior that crosses the line into the illegal or criminal—presents one of the most difficult challenges for effective intervention.

There are no easy or surefire solutions for any facet of the problem of delinquency, and the issues in treating violent juvenile delinquents are particularly complex (Hamburg, 1998; Nelson et al., 2004; Sims & Preston, 2006). The cyclic history of interventions and the failures of our legal system to deal with the problems of crime and violence, including delinquency of minors, seems characterized by a recurrent pattern of enthusiasm for proposed solutions having a scant research base followed by failure to win support sufficient for success (Achenbach, 1975; Lundman, 1993; Silberman, 1978; Sims & Preston, 2006; Spergel, 1995). Little wonder that there are those who would abandon the very notion of juvenile justice (see Caeti & Fritsch, 2006).

The 1990s were a period of pessimism regarding government social programs and enthusiasm for harsher punishment (cf. Baker, 1996). Although an exclusive reliance on harsher punishment is clearly inadvisable on scientific grounds (cf. Tate, Reppucci, & Mulvey, 1995), some have argued that we need to lower our typical expectations when working with persistent antisocial behavior. Individuals have argued that human behavior of this type is very hard to change; thus, many objectives short of a cure are worthy (Etzioni, 1994).

Effective intervention, like prevention, must include the astute, persistent, multi-faceted efforts of a variety of individuals and agencies, focusing not only on risk factors but also on those factors that have demonstrated protective effects (Arthur, Hawkins, Pollard, Catalano, & Baglioni, 2002; Gavazzi, Wasserman, Partridge, & Sheridan, 2000). We make brief mention here of intervention in families and the juvenile court and corrections systems but concentrate attention on schooling.

Families

Make no mistake: Parents who are loving, nurturing, and skilled in child rearing *can* have delinquent children. Still, neglectful parents with poor discipline skills are far more likely to have delinquent children. In fact, parent–child relationships have been linked to the quality of children's social interaction into adulthood (Doyle & Markiewicz, 1996; Ford, 2006; Sayre-McCord, 2007).

The typical parents of chronic delinquents do not monitor and nurture their children closely. They punish aggressive, delinquent behavior unpredictably, harshly, and ineffectively. They often show little concern when their children offend the community by stealing or fighting outside the home. As long as they do not have to deal with the misbehavior, they choose not to see their children as a serious problem. Within the home, they show little motivation to change their own behavior to decrease the coercion and violence that characterize their interactions with their children (Dishion, 1990; Patterson, 1982, 1986b; Patterson et al., 1992). Other parents may not believe that they have the ability to make a difference in the lives of their children (Bandura, 1995a, 1995b).

Intervention in the families of chronic offenders is extremely difficult. Changing long-standing patterns of coercion may be impossible in families in which parents are unmotivated and have few cognitive and social skills. Patterson and his colleagues reported success in significantly reducing aggressive behavior and stealing in many families of aggressive children; however, the long-term outcome for stealers and chronic adolescent delinquents is guarded. Although delinquent behavior may be significantly reduced during behavioral intervention, research does not show that the improvement will persist after treatment is terminated (Patterson et al., 1992). Follow-up of juvenile offenders who were placed in group homes that used a *teaching-family method* (a behaviorally oriented program designed to provide an appropriate family atmosphere) also shows that behavioral improvement during treatment is not maintained (Kirigin, Braukman, Atwater, & Wolf, 1982; Wolf et al., 1987). At this time, there appears to be no effective substitute for a family social system that has failed—at least when the criterion for effectiveness is "cure," or permanent behavioral change that requires no further treatment. Researchers have suggested that serious antisocial behavior and delinquency should be considered a social disability requiring long-term treatment (Hamburg, 1998; Walker, Ramsey, & Gresham, 2004; Wolf et al., 1987). Studies of early intervention programs with preschoolers, particularly those with parental training, consistently demonstrated that the participating children had more positive school outcomes and lower rates of violence and crime well into adolescence (Hawkins, Farrington, & Catalano, 1998). However, findings of intervention studies with older children yield less optimistic results. Unless effective child-rearing skills can be taught to the parents of a delinquent youth, effective long-term intervention in this disability may require placing the youth with a foster or surrogate family in which trained parents provide appropriate behavioral controls, models, and supports throughout adolescence and into adulthood.

Juvenile Courts and Corrections

Juvenile courts were instituted in the United States in about 1900 to offer more humane treatment of juvenile offenders than the 19th-century reform schools had provided. Judges were empowered to use their discretion in determining the consequences of a child's misconduct. Although the intent was good, the institution has become mired in an overload of cases, and the rights of children—if children are considered to have constitutional rights equal to those of all other citizens—have been blatantly abridged. Consequently, the juvenile court system and the question of children's rights have come under close scrutiny (see Bazemore & Umbreit, 1995; Siegel & Senna, 1994; Siegel & Welsh, 2005; Sims & Preston, 2006; Warboys & Shauffer, 1990).

Although we frequently hear proposals for drastic reform, the juvenile court system is likely to remain as it is for a considerable time. A sizable proportion of children and youth will make appearances before a juvenile court during their school years, and teachers could profit from familiarity with the court's workings. Whatever the failures in the social systems of families and schools, one can find equal disasters in the procedures and institutions devised by lawyers and judges.

Under the juvenile justice system, juvenile court judges have wide discretion in handling cases. They may release juveniles to the custody of their parents, refer youngsters to social service agencies, or assign them to a variety of correctional programs ranging from probation to restitution to community attention homes to state detention centers or even to private, less-monitored wilderness-challenge experiences or boot camps. The effectiveness of the various juvenile justice and corrections options are widely and hotly debated (see Caeti & Fritsch, 2006; Siegel & Senna, 1994), and abuses seem widespread. Most researchers conclude that harsher punishment is counterproductive in the vast majority of cases, contrary to the opinions of many holding political office.

Lundman (1993) argued persuasively for community-based intervention for all juveniles who have committed property crimes, reserving incarceration or other institutional treatment only for those who have committed index crimes against persons. (Nearly everyone agrees that juveniles who commit violent crimes against people must be placed in correctional facilities for some period of time.) Lundman (1993) suggested that *diversion* should be the standard juvenile justice response to minor property offenses and other relatively nonserious delinquency (see also Marsh & Patrick, 2006; Siegel & Welsh, 2005). *Diversion* means that the juvenile is referred for services (e.g., family services, counseling) rather than sent to juvenile court. For moderately delinquent juveniles who are convicted of index crimes against property, Lundman recommended probation as the first and most frequent sentencing option. He also recommended abandoning efforts to scare delinquents straight through prison visits, informational seminars, and so on. Community-based interventions, including intensive monitoring and supervision, are the best approaches for most chronic property offenders, Lundman concluded.

The *restorative justice model* is a response to delinquency that is in keeping Lundman's principals. In this model, the response to crime and delinquency focuses on accountability for illegal behavior and the development of competencies that prevent reoffending (see Umbreit, Greenwood, & Coates, 2000; White, 2006). In this way, offenses are responded to on individual bases, focusing not on punishment, but on compensation for the victim(s).

Schooling

A substantial proportion of all juvenile crime occurs in school buildings or on school grounds (Nelson et al., 2004; Siegel & Senna, 1994). Each month during the academic year, thousands of teachers and millions of children in U.S. schools are assaulted or otherwise victimized. Theft, assault, drug and alcohol abuse, extortion, sexual promiscuity, and vandalism occur all too frequently, not just in deteriorated inner-city schools but in affluent suburban and rural communities as well.

Punishment and increased focus on security are schools' usual responses to delinquent behavior. The typical punishment (detention) or exclusion (office referral, suspension, disciplinary transfer, or expulsion) is usually ineffective in reducing the problem behavior and improving the student's academic progress. In short, the typical school's response to disruptive behavior is woefully inadequate and does little more than maintain a semblance of order and prevent total abandonment of its traditional programs (Mayer, Nofpoktitis, Butterworth, & Hollingsworth, 1987; Walker et al., 2004).

In section 14, we discussed schoolwide discipline and positive, nonpunitive procedures designed to reduce antisocial behavior. Those strategies apply also to delinquent behavior in school (see also Butler & Watkins, 2006).

One approach to dealing with problems of students at risk for a variety of undesirable outcomes (e.g., dropping out, delinquency) is the establishment of alternative schools. In a review of research, Cox, Davidson, and Bynum (1995) found that alternative schools have had a small overall positive effect on school performance, attitude toward school, and self-esteem but not on delinquency. Alternative programs that target specific populations, such as those at risk for delinquency or low achievers, generally produced larger positive effects than did those with open admissions.

Education of children and youth with disabilities in detention is governed by the same federal laws and regulations as is education of youngsters in public schools (Nelson et al., 2004). Those in detention facilities are guaranteed all the procedural protections and requirements for nonbiased individualized assessment, individualized education programs, and so on afforded under IDEA and related laws and regulations. Ideally, therefore, assessment of students in detention is functionally related to an appropriate curriculum, and the instruction of students is data based and prepares them with critical life skills. Nevertheless, incarcerated children and youth often do not receive assessment and education. Given the following difficulties, it is not surprising that many delinquent youngsters' needs are not met:

- Criminal justice officials and the public often take the attitude that delinquent and criminal young people are not entitled to the same educational opportunities as are law-abiding citizens.
- Some psychologists, psychiatrists, and educators take the position that many incarcerated youths are not disabled.
- There is a shortage of qualified personnel to staff good special education programs in correction facilities.
- Some of the provisions of IDEA, such as regulations requiring education in the least-restrictive environment and parental involvement in educational planning, are particularly difficult to implement in correctional facilities.
- The student population of correctional facilities is transient, making educational assessment and planning especially difficult.
- Interagency cooperation and understanding are often limited, which hampers obtaining student records, designating responsibility for specific services, and working out transition from detention to community.
- Administrators of correction facilities often consider security and institutional rules more important than education.
- Funds for educational programs in correction facilities are limited.

Street Gangs

An increasing problem related to delinquency is gang activities. Gangs have proliferated across the world, and now most cities and towns have problems with gangs and gang violence (Delaney, 2006; Short & Hughes, 2006a, 2006b; Hagedorn, 2007; Spergel, 2007). Gang activity is also prevalent in many schools. And gang activity now includes "'Preppie Gangs,' . . . composed of teens from rich, gated communities or upper-middle-class backgrounds" (Crews, Purvis, & Hjelm, 2006, p. 193).

Misconceptions about gangs and gang activities abound; misunderstandings are often created or perpetuated by distorted media coverage, misinformed profession-als, or both, and research on gangs is difficult (Klein, 1995, 2006; Sims & Preston, 2006). Among the most egregious misimpressions is that most youth street gangs are organized to distribute drugs. Drug involvement by street gangs has increased, but the drug trade is not the primary activity of most street gangs.

Gangs have been an object of serious study for several decades, and here we summarize only a small part of the extensive and complex literature on gangs that is most relevant to educators. The definition of *gang* is difficult and controversial. Although there are many different kinds of gangs organized for different purposes, we are concerned here primarily with what are known as *street gangs,* which Klein (1995) defined as aggregations of youth who recognize themselves as a group and are oriented toward delinquent acts. It is important to recognize that some gang mem-bers are not delinquents and some delinquents are not gang members.

Gang membership is a means of obtaining affiliation, protection, excitement, and money, objects, or substances that members desire (Fagan & Wilkinson, 1998). The two characteristics that most clearly set an aggregation of youth apart as a gang are (a) commitment to a criminal orientation and (b) self-recognition as a gang, as signi-fied by special vocabulary, clothing, signs, colors, and graffiti-marked territory (Klein, 1995). Gang members are overwhelmingly male, mostly adolescent, and predomi-nantly homogeneous groups of ethnic minorities. Minority groups differ in the nature or focus of their gang activities (Klein, 1995; Spergel, 1995). However, increases in younger and older members, female members, and White supremacist gangs were seen in the 1990s (see Delaney, 2006; Short & Hughes, 2006). Early research in this area indicated that members of gangs tend to come from families that place less impor-tance on intrafamilial socialization, youth supervision, and outward expressions of affection. The typical gang member is now thought to exhibit one or more of the following characteristics, according to Klein (1995):

- A notable set of personal deficiencies—perhaps difficulty in school, low self-esteem, lower impulse control, inadequate social skills, a deficit in useful adult contacts
- A notable tendency toward defiance, aggressiveness, fighting, and pride in physical prowess
- A greater-than-normal desire for status, identity, and companionship that can be at least partly satisfied by joining a special group like a gang
- A boring, uninvolved lifestyle, in which the occasional excitement of gang exploits or rumored exploits provides a welcome respite. (p. 76)

Street gangs spend most of their time just hanging out together. Contrary to popular perception, researchers who have spent decades studying street gangs portray them as inactive most of the time:

> Street gangs through the years have done nothing more often than they have done something exciting. Their customary activities are sleeping, eating, and hanging around. Criminal acts are a minority of the activities they engage in, and violent acts are a minority of those. We must remember that despite the drama and lethality of gang violence, its prevalence does not deserve using the label *violent gang.* This only

feeds a stereotype that needs no help from scholars. To repeat, most gang members' behavior is not criminal, and most gang members' crimes are not violent. And of course, most violent people are not gang members, so it's not very useful to define gangs in terms of violent crime alone. (Klein, 1995, pp. 28–29)

It is interesting that researchers have found few differences between gang-related homicides and nongang homicides (Rosenfield, Bray, & Egley, 1999). In fact, both of these types of crimes were highly concentrated in disadvantaged, racially isolated neighborhoods—suggesting more powerful predictors of violence than gang affiliation.

A variety of causal models have been constructed to explain the formation and maintenance of gangs. As Klien (1995) saw it, social and economic conditions that create an underclass are partly to blame for creating gangs. The underclass is created by industrial withdrawal from an area (typically an inner-city area), creating an absence of jobs. The failure of the educational system further contributes to jobless-ness in the area. Segregation of ethnic minorities also plays a role, as do other forms of racism. Opportunities for individuals in the middle class to migrate out of the depressed area result in the absence of alternative social and employment-related activities and the absence of social controls provided by important vibrant, active institutions that are necessary to maintain the social fabric. Churches, children's ser-vice agencies, business clubs, and so on suffer the loss of talented leaders, and many of those left in the community have poor skills in parental discipline and few practical skills in maintaining community organizations that control social behavior.

The onset of gang organizations may be fostered by these conditions, but they are not necessary for the organization of gangs (Short & Hughes, 2007b; Crews et al., 2006). Gang behavior may exacerbate crime, minority segregation, and other negative community conditions, but gangs are maintained by things that threaten members, legitimize the need for the gang, and increase the cohesiveness of the group. These maintaining factors include institutions that oppose the gangs (e.g., police); gang rivalries that threaten personal safety, possessions, or status; perceived barriers to alternatives to gang membership and activities; and gang intervention programs that inadvertently strengthen the gang's cohesion—for example, attempts to use the gang structure to redirect members toward noncriminal activities.

Laub and Lauristsen (1998) noted that gang influence can also be spread by stu-dent transfer and busing programs. In less-mobile student populations, gang influ-ence tends to be restricted to a turf, but more mobile student populations appear to allow for spread of gang influence into a school or from a school back into a student's neighborhood.

Interventions designed to reduce gang membership and gang-related delinquent behavior are matters of considerable controversy (Nelson et al., 2004; Short & Hughes, 2006b). Gang members have extensive contact with like-minded individuals with similar behavioral, educational, and socioeconomic backgrounds (Fagan & Wilkinson, 1998; see also Hagedorn, 2007). This pattern of association exacerbates the problems associated with gang memberships (e.g., exposure to violence) and insulates many gang members from interventions designed to assist them in creating more favorable life circumstances. Intervention programs typically have lacked inten-sity and comprehensiveness or have relied primarily on punitive measures (e.g., a crackdown by law enforcement) or other approaches that exacerbate the problem. Truly effective programs to stem the tide of gangs and gang violence would require an unlikely scenario given the current political climate. Such programs would need to include massive and sustained efforts that accomplish the following: (a) reduce poverty, (b) provide job training and well-paid jobs for youth, (c) provide decent housing in inner cities, (d) rebuild and reform deteriorated schools and their instructional programs, and (e) reduce racism and other social blights.

The Problems of Overreaction and Punitive Responses

Public misconceptions about delinquency, violence, and gangs have led to major problems, especially overreaction and punitive responses. Many schools, Klein (1995) observed, are running scared, approaching problems primarily through scare tactics, tightened security, and punitive measures, often with the help of law enforcement. Overreaction of the public, under the misimpression that there is a juvenile crime wave or that juveniles are becoming extremely violent, is a major problem, and harsh punishment makes the problem worse. Miller, Potter, and Kappeler (2006) concluded

> No evidence exists to indicate that the nation is under attack by a violent body of young superpredators. The fear of young people fueled by media accounts of juvenile violence has led to the metamorphosis of our rehabilitative juvenile justice system into a punitive mini-adult system. We are treating more juveniles as adults than ever before, incarcerating them for longer periods of time and housing them with adults. This has all occurred during a time when the juvenile delinquency and crime rate has decreased. It has even occurred during a period when the arrest rate of juveniles has decreased. (p. 187)

Although school safety is an important and legitimate concern, schools should put their primary efforts into positive schoolwide discipline plans and restructured programs designed to meet more of the social and educational needs of students (Liaupsin, Jolivette, & Scott, 2004; Martella, Nelson, & Marchand-Martella, 2003; Spergel, 1995; Walker et al., 2004). In their obsession with college-bound youth, schools fail to provide the work-oriented high school programs that keep youth in school and help them find employment (Edgar & Siegel, 1995; Spergel, 1995, 2007). Schools could play a major role in reduction of delinquency and gang membership if they focused on positive discipline, effective instruction and remediation, a differentiated curriculum with courses leading directly to work for those who are not headed for college, coordination of efforts with other community agencies, and an array of extracurricular activities designed to attract all students into meaningful alternatives.

SUBSTANCE ABUSE

We use the term *substance abuse* rather than *drug abuse* because not all abused chemicals are drugs. Abused substances other than drugs include gasoline, cleaning fluids, glue, and other chemicals that can cause psychological effects. Loeber et al. (1998a) added cigarettes to the list of substances associated with problem behavior patterns in adolescents. The substances under discussion here are those deliberately used to induce physiological or psychological effects (or both) for other than therapeutic purposes. *Abuse* usually is defined as use that contributes to health risks, disruption of psychological functioning, adverse social consequences, or some combination of these.

As Newcomb and Richardson (1995) noted, substance abuse disorders cannot exist without the availability of the substance and a willing user. Many substances are readily available, and many people are willing or anxious to use or abuse them. These facts imbue much of the discussion of substance abuse with a moralistic tone (the notion that substance abusers are simply evil or weak willed) and encourage the assumption that interdiction of supply will be effective in reducing use and abuse.

Definition and Prevalence

"Use of psychoactive substances is the norm for adolescents" (Baer, MacLean, & Marlatt, 1998, p. 183). Although the illicit use of alcohol and drugs may have declined in recent years, the prevalence remains relatively high (Donohue, Karmely, & Strada, 2006). Prevalence studies suggest that the use of psychoactive substances is more likely to be experimental or episodic for most adolescents. What is the difference between experimentation and abuse? Does a single episode of use by a child or adolescent constitute abuse? At what level of use should an adolescent be considered to have a substance abuse disorder? It is clear that most adolescents take or use substances but that only a minority of them (perhaps 6% to 10% of users) become chronic abusers (Newcomb & Richardson, 1995).

Adolescent substance abuse is in many ways similar to substance abuse in adulthood, but it is not exactly the same. Many adolescents who use or abuse substances do not become adults with substance abuse disorders. The definition of *substance abuse* is clouded by controversy regarding specific criteria, changing social attitudes, and political use of the issue (Bukstein, 1995; Donohue et al., 2006). Baer et al. (1998) suggested that one aspect of substance use that differentiates abuse from less problematic use is the accumulation of negative consequences related to use. However, this definition is unsatisfactory because adults and adolescents face different laws, customs, and consequences related to substance use.

The topic of drug use is especially prone to distortion of fact and hysterical rhetoric because the definition of adolescent substance abuse is anchored in cultural tradition, social fad, and political positioning as well as scientific evidence. Moreover, controversy regarding definition makes many prevalence figures suspect. Nevertheless, nearly all authorities on the topic agree that substance use and abuse are alarmingly high among American children and youth and that effective measures to reduce both use and abuse of substances are needed.

A common misperception is that substance abuse has to do primarily with illegal drugs such as cocaine, marijuana, and heroin or with illicit use of prescription medications such as barbiturates; but as Werry (1986b) noted more than a generation ago, "alcohol and tobacco are, as ever, the real drug problem" (p. 228).

Alcohol and tobacco are *still* the largest problems because they are readily available to adults, they are advertised for sale, most people view their use by adults as socially acceptable, and children usually receive their first exposure to and first experiment with these substances in the home (Severson & James, 2002). The earlier the child's first experience with alcohol and tobacco, the more likely he or she will become a regular user. Early use of alcohol and tobacco, as well as other substances, correlates with family problems, low socioeconomic status, school failure, and psychiatric disorders, especially conduct disorder (Upadhyaya, Brady, Wharton, & Liao, 2003).

Because the negative health consequences of alcohol and tobacco are staggering, preventing children and adolescents from beginning to smoke and drink seems wise. Indeed, the most common cause of death among teenagers in the United States is auto accidents, whereas driving under the influence of alcohol and disease caused by smoking cigarettes are the leading mortality factors among the general population of the United States (see Roll, 2005). Thus, the "war on drugs" has not been focused on what likely should be its primary targets.

Another common misperception is that substance abuse is disproportionately a problem of ethnic minorities. This mistaken impression is likely an artifact of data collection procedures and intervention programs. "We may conclude that, nationwide, there are no real differences in overall patterns of use as a function of ethnicity. Nonetheless, ethnic minorities (particularly African Americans and Hispanics) are currently far *more* likely than other adolescent groups to be targeted for attention from law enforcement officials as a function of drug involvement" (Newcomb & Richardson, 1995, p. 414, emphasis in original). Contrary to many racial stereotypes, the drug ecstasy (3,4-methylenedioxymethamphetamine; MDMA) has actually been found to have higher abuse rates among White adolescents (Yacoubian, 2003). Despite racial targeting, researches have found that among individuals arrested for drug offenses, White arrestees were found more than 20 times as likely to be guilty of an ecstasy offence than non-White arrestees (Urbach, Reynolds, & Yacoubian, 2002).

Some youngsters, primarily adolescents age 15 or older, do abuse substances other than alcohol and tobacco. Following is a list of several major types of drugs of abuse, along with a few examples of each. Some of these drugs are prescribed for therapeutic purposes, so they have legitimate purposes as well as potential for abuse. We also list some of the most typical effects or symptoms of serious intoxication with the drug and of drug withdrawal:

- Depressants: alcohol, Phenobarbital, Valium, Quaalude
  Signs of intoxication: drowsiness, irritability, disinhibition, extreme relaxation or sedation
  Signs of withdrawal: tremors, fever, anxiety, hallucinations
- Stimulants: nicotine, caffeine, cocaine, amphetamines and methamphetamines
  Signs of intoxication: dilated pupils, restlessness, loss of appetite, paranoia, hallucinations
  Signs of withdrawal: fatigue, mental and physical slowness or depression
- Stimulant hallucinogens: phencyclidine (PCP), MDMA (Ecstasy), Ketamine
  Signs of intoxication: agitation, irritability, grandiosity, dilated pupils, fine tremors, sweating, rapid speech and movement, hallucinations, dry mouth and throat, uncontrolled jaw movements, repetitive movements

Signs of withdrawal: anxiety, agitation, depression, fatigue, sleeplessness, panic attacks, increased appetite, psychosis, suicidal thoughts

- Narcotics: morphine, methadone, codeine, Darvon
  Signs of intoxication: drowsiness, slurred speech, constricted pupils, poor physical coordination, analgesia (insensitivity to pain)
  Signs of withdrawal: vomiting, cramps, fever, chills, "goose flesh"
- Inhalants: glues, aerosols, paint thinners, cleaning fluids, fuels
  Signs of intoxication: confusion, hallucinations, exhilaration or depression, poor balance
  Signs of withdrawal: inconsistent
- Marijuana: cigarettes or forms taken by mouth
  Signs of intoxication: sleepiness, poor concentration, confusion, anxiety, paranoia, distorted perceptions
  Signs of withdrawal: psychological distress
- Hallucinogens: mescaline, psilocybin, lysergic acid diethylamide (LSD)
  Signs of intoxication: dilated pupils, hallucinations, altered perceptions of body or time, problems focusing attention, emotional lability
  Signs of withdrawal: not well established.

As we mentioned earlier, the substances that become popular or receive intensive media attention in any given period of time are highly variable and affected by fads and other social phenomena. For example, in the mid-1990s, Ritalin became a popular drug of abuse, and national media attention heightened concern about its prescription and control. In the late 1990s, media attention shifted to ecstasy abuse, especially among adolescents and young adults attending raves. Much of what we know about the effects of this drug is based on anecdotal evidence; clinical research has been plagued with problems including an unethical risk of neural brain injury to participants in such studies (Ricaurte, Yuan, Hatzidimitriou, Cord, & McCann, 2003) Despite varying trends in media attention, marijuana is the most widely used illicit drug in Western societies (Iversen, 1999). In addition to those we have listed, people may abuse many other preparations, including *designer drugs*—new concoctions made up in illegal laboratories and represented as well-known drugs or touted to produce euphoria. The street names of various drugs are numerous, and new names are constantly being invented.

Baer et al. (1998) reported two consistent patterns of substance abuse over time. First, experimentation with alcohol and other substances begins in adolescence and declines significantly for most individuals with transition to young adulthood. Prosocial processes associated with marriage and employment are consistently associated with declines in substance use across the early adult years. However, the second pattern suggests that there are risks for adult adjustment based on adolescent behavior. The adolescent substance abuser who becomes a substance-abusing adult typically abuses multiple substances. In addition, adolescent problem behavior and patterns of nonconformity predict adult substance abuse better than level of substance use does.

The emotional and behavioral problems associated with substance abuse include both the effects produced by using the substance and the effects of abstinence after a period of use (i.e., withdrawal). Terms commonly used in discussion of substance use include the following:

- *Intoxication* indicates symptoms of a toxic amount of substance in the bloodstream (enough to have physiological or psychological effects).
- *Tolerance* refers to physiological adaptation to a substance so that an increasing amount is required to produce the same effects; tolerance typically increases with repeated use and decreases after a period of abstinence.
- *Addiction* indicates compulsive use of a substance and that obtaining and using the substance has become a central concern and pattern of behavior.
- *Dependence* refers to the need to continue using a substance to avoid physical or emotional discomfort or both.
- *Withdrawal* designates physical or emotional discomfort associated with a period of abstinence.

An important feature of advanced substance abuse is its insidious onset, progressing through various stages. A substance abuser rarely becomes a habitual user immediately; rather, experimentation, perhaps under peer pressure, is followed by occasional social or recreational use, then use in certain circumstances or situations (perhaps to relax after a stressful event, to stay awake to perform a demanding task, or to sleep). Situational use may intensify and become part of daily routine; eventually, the substance can become the individual's central focus. Clearly, substance use and abuse do not always progress to the obsessive-dependent addiction stage (Newcomb & Richardson, 1995). However, teachers and other adults should be aware of the danger signals of the transitions from experimentation to social–recreational and to situational–circumstantial use. Teachers may first observe changes in social behavior and academic performance at the point of transition to situational use (Severson & James, 2002).

An additional concern regarding substance abuse since the 1980s is contracting the human immunodeficiency virus (HIV) through unprotected sex or the use of contaminated needles for intravenous injection of drugs. The probability of sexual activity, including sexual intercourse without a condom, is greatly increased by the use of alcohol and other substances that alter mood and cognitive control. Adolescents who are runaways, homeless, or substance abusers are a particularly high-risk group for sexual promiscuity and for contracting HIV.

It is difficult to estimate the extent of substance abuse among children and adolescents. Students with emotional or behavioral disorders are at higher risk than is the general population of students (Genaux, Morgan, & Friedman, 1995; Donohue et al., 2006). The level of use and abuse of specific substances by adolescents reflects adult patterns and is affected by fads, social attitudes, and prohibitions (Bukstein, 1995; Newcomb & Richardson, 1995). Use of hallucinogenic drugs was lower in the 1980s than in the previous two decades, but in the 1980s cocaine became a major concern, and marijuana use, which in previous decades caused much alarm and sometimes resulted in legal penalties of absurd proportions, was considered comparatively safe (cf. Miksic, 1987). Beginning in the mid-1980s, there was a steady decrease in the use of most illicit drugs (Bukstein, 1995). The trends or fads that will appear during the next decade are impossible to predict.

Causal Factors and Prevention

A variety of theories have been offered to explain adolescent substance abuse, including models that view it as a disease (metabolic or genetic abnormality), a moral issue (lack of willpower), a spiritual problem (needing the help of a higher power), or a psychological disorder (learned maladaptive behavior or intrapsychic conflicts; Bukstein, 1995; Newcomb & Richardson, 1995). Most researchers have concluded that no single cause has been or is likely to be found and that substance abuse has multiple causes. The focus is on assessing factors that heighten risk or tend to protect against risk (Severson & James, 2002).

Family factors known to increase risk are poor and inconsistent parental discipline, family conflict, and lack of emotional bonding of family members. Family members may provide models of substance abuse and introduce children to the use of substances. Undoubtedly, genetic factors contribute risk, perhaps by making some individuals more susceptible to the physiological and psychological effects of drugs (Newcomb & Richardson, 1995).

Socialization with a deviant peer group may play a major role in substance abuse, as may media exposure to substance use and abuse. All aspects of the culture in which the youngster is embedded may have a substantial influence on initiation to substance use (Kaminer, 1994).

Community conditions of joblessness and deteriorated living conditions are also risk factors. Certainly, substance abuse is no stranger to middle-class and upscale communities. Still, the lack of socioeconomic opportunity, hopelessness, crowding, and violence that characterize many poor urban communities are very significant risk factors (Bukstein, 1995).

Age of onset of substance use is a known risk factor. The earlier the age at which a youngster has his or her first experience with substance use, the greater the risk of later abuse. Risk of polydrug use, use of more than one substance within a four-week period, seems to increase with age during adolescence (Smit, Monshouwer, & Verdurmen, 2002).

Substance abuse disorders often occur with a variety of other disorders or psychiatric illnesses. Externalizing behavior problems (aggression and other characteristics of conduct disorder) are especially likely to increase risk (Lewinsohn, Gotlib, & Seeley, 1995; Steele, Forehand, Armistead, & Brody, 1995). The polysubstance abuser typically has multiple disorders, all of which are intertwined and need to be addressed. It is important to note the reciprocal influences of substance use and other disorders. Some disorders, such as schizophrenia and depression, may be precipitated by substance use. A variety of disorders may both contribute to substance abuse and be exacerbated by it (Severson & James, 2002).

Baer et al. (1998) reported that different factors were associated with drinking level compared with drinking problems. Across a number of studies, the results suggested that drinking level is more closely tied to peer group, whereas drinking problems are associated with familial and psychological problems. People who are problem drinkers experience difficulties compared to nonproblem drinkers, even at the same level of consumption. "Adolescents who experience problems [in this domain] come from more aversive familial environments, associate with deviant, heavy-drinking peers, have an under-controlled behavioral style, are more heavily engaged in deviant behaviors, experience more negative affect, and are more poorly adjusted than those who drink but do not experience problems" (Baer et al., 1998, p. 190).

Protective factors include not only the opposite of family characteristics associated with high risk but personality characteristics, perhaps extending from early temperament, such as low anger and aggression, school achievement, compliance, and responsibility (Brook, Whiteman, Cohen, Shapiro, & Balka, 1995; Jessor et al., 1995; Werner, 1999). Researchers have also found that factors associated with resilience and safe sex attitudes, such as HIV/AIDS knowledge, self-esteem, and hopefulness, were in fact negatively related to drug and alcohol use among adolescents (Chang, Bendel, Koopman, McGarvey, & Canterbury, 2003). Thus, the very same strengths that may work to prevent incarceration and HIV/AIDS infection may also serve to prevent substance abuse.

Social and cultural influences such as peer support and societal disapproval can help influence children and youth to avoid substance use during adolescence or at least delay the age at which they have their first experience with substance use. Communities in which there are jobs and alternative activities to substance abuse are also protective.

Bukstein (1995) noted that a variety of targets for prevention have been suggested, including prevention of use (especially early onset of use), abuse, the consequences of use, and the risk factors associated with use and abuse. Prevention can also be aimed at increasing the protective factors that lower risk. The most effective prevention efforts we can devise will address all of these concerns. Moreover, prevention strategies should encompass and be matched with all risk factors, including peer-related factors, individual factors (e.g., poor academic and social skills, conduct disorder), family factors (e.g., parental discipline), biological factors (e.g., use of medications), and community factors (e.g., socioeconomic conditions; Baer et al., 1998). Interventions can be classified according to whether they target individuals or the larger environment. Simplistic prevention programs such as teaching children to "just say no" are doomed because alcohol and drug experimentation has become a largely normative behavior in adolescent development (Baer et al., 1998). Adolescents who break the "just say no" taboo and find no immediate negative consequences may disregard all subsequent substance abuse warnings. Clearly, a more intensive and reasoned approach to prevention is called for. General recommendations for prevention strategies are that they should be developmentally appropriate, focused on high-risk populations, comprehensive (address multiple risk factors), coordinated with changes in social policies in the community, and long term.

Most relevant for discussion here are the skills-based interventions that form educational efforts to prevent adolescent substance abuse—interventions aimed at helping students understand the effects and consequences of substance use and abuse. Bukstein (1995) discussed curricula designed to help students learn a variety of skills that allow them to do the following things:

- Resist peer pressure
- Change attitudes, values, and behavioral norms related to substance use
- Recognize and resist adult influences toward substance use
- Use problem-solving strategies such as self-control, stress management, and appropriate assertiveness

- Set goals and improve self-esteem
- Communicate more effectively

Prevention is preferable to intervention after substance abuse has become a reality; but if it is to be effective, it must be intensive, comprehensive, and sustained, focusing on high-risk youth in high-risk neighborhoods, especially on improving the social and economic conditions in the communities of youth at highest risk (Bukstein, 1995). Unfortunately, public sentiment and social policy in the United States indicates less willingness to support effective prevention programs of the type Bukstein (1995) recommended (Kauffman, 2004).

Intervention and Education

Substance abuse prevention programs are highly desirable, but they do little to help those who are already using drugs (Baer et al., 1998). A wide range of intervention approaches and combinations of treatments are employed in treating adolescent substance abuse, including medication (see Mirza, 2002) and behavioral approaches (see Roll, 2005). Traditional methods include 12-step programs such as those suggested by Alcoholics Anonymous and Narcotics Anonymous. Group therapy, family therapy (either single families or groups of families), cognitive-behavior modification, and psychopharmacological treatment are alternatives frequently employed. Family involvement and programs that are consistent with cultural traditions are critical features of prevention and intervention efforts (Bukstein, 1995; Ross, 1994; Severson & James, 2002). Some programs provide a comprehensive approach to prevention and intervention involving the entire spectrum of intervention agents: schools, peer groups, families, the media, communities, law enforcement, and the business sector (e.g., Wodarski & Feit, 1995). It is important that treatment be designed for the individual case and that careful consideration be given to inpatient versus outpatient treatment (Bukstein, 1995; Newcomb & Richardson, 1995).

Our primary concern here is educational intervention. One important feature of successful substance abuse education programs is getting accurate and useful information into the hands of teachers, parents, and students in an accessible, abbreviated form. Table 15.1 is an example of the type and amount of information that can be made available.

Information alone does not necessarily change behavior, and it is therefore necessary to take more specific action. More specific action might include: (a) clear, well-defined policies for teachers and students spelling out how drug use or possession will be handled; (b) basic, simple drug education at all grade levels; (c) increased teacher awareness about local drug problems and community service agencies; (d) group discussions about topics such as adolescent development and drug use; (e) one-to-one and group counseling using community resources such as community counseling centers and drop-in centers within the school; and (f) peer-group approaches with positive role models for group or individual support.

Many students with substance abuse problems have belief systems that lead to either increased risk of substance abuse or decreased ability to respond to intervention

Table 15.1 Commonly Abused Drugs

Substance category and name	Commercial or street names	Intoxification effects	Potential health consequences
Cannabinoids			
Marijuana	dope, grass, herb, joints, pot, reefer, weed	Euphoria, slowed thinking and reaction time, confusion, impaired balance and coordination	Cough, frequent respiratory infections, impaired memory and learning, increased heart rate, anxiety, panic attacks; tolerance, addiction
Hashish	boom, hash, hash oil, hemp		
Depressants			
Barbiturates	*Amytal, Nembutal, Seconal, Phenobarbitol;* barbs, reds, red birds, phennies, tooies, yellows, yellow jackets	For all depressants— reduced anxiety; feeling of well-being; lowered inhibitions; slowed pulse and breathing; lowered blood pressure; poor concentration	For all depressants— fatigue; confusion; impaired coordination, memory, judgment; addiction; respiratory depression and arrest; death
Benzodiazepines (other than flunitrazepam)	*Ativan, Halcion, Librium, Valium, Xanax;* candy, downers, sleeping pills, tranks		
Flunitrazepam	*Rohypnol;* forget-me pill, Mexican Valium, R2, Roche, roofies, roofinol, rope, rophies	Also, for barbiturates— sedation, drowsiness	Also, for barbiturates— depression, unusual excitement, fever, irritability, poor judgment, slurred speech, dizziness, life-threatening withdrawal
GHB	*gamma-hydroxybutyrate:* G, Georgia home boy, grievous bodily harm, liquid ecstasy	for benzodiazepines— sedation, drowsiness for GHB—drowsiness, nausea	for benzodiazepines— dizziness
Methaqualone	*Quaalude, Sopor, Parest:* ludes, mandrex, quad, quay	for methaqualone— euphoria	for flunitrazepam—visual and gastrointestinal disturbances, urinary retention, memory loss for the time under the drug's effects for GHB— vomiting, headache, loss of consciousness, loss of reflexes, seizures, coma, death for methaqualone— depression, poor reflexes, slurred speech, coma
Dissociative anesthetics			
Ketamine	*Ketalar SV;* cat Valiums, K, Special K, vitamin K	For all dissociative anesthetics—increased heart rate and blood pressure, impaired motor function Also, for ketamine—at high doses, delirium, depression, respiratory depression and arrest for PCP and analogs— possible decrease in blood pressure and heart rate, panic, aggression, violence	For all dissociative anesthetics—memory loss; numbness; nausea/ vomiting for PCP and analogs—loss of appetite, depression
PCP and analogs	*phencyclidine:* angel dust, boat, hog, love boat, peace pill		

Substance category and name	Commercial or street names	Intoxification effects	Potential health consequences
Hallucinogens			
LSD	*lysergic acid diethylamide*: acid, blotter, boomers, cubes, microdot, yellow sunshines	For all hallucinogens— altered states of perception and feeling; nausea Also, for LSD and	For all hallucinogens— persisting perception disorder (flashbacks) Also, for LSD and
Mescaline	mescaline buttons, cactus, mesc, peyote l/swallowed, smoked	mescaline—increased body temperature, heart rate, blood pressure; loss of	mescaline—increased body temperature, heart rate, blood pressure; loss of
Psilocybin	magic mushroom, purple passion, shrooms	appetite, sleeplessness, numbness, weakness, tremors for LSD—persistent mental disorders for psilocybin—nervous- ness, paranoia	appetite, sleeplessness, numbness, weakness, tremors for LSD—persistent mental disorders for psilocybin—nervousness, paranoia
Opiates and morphine derivatives			
Codeine	*Empirin with Codeine, Fiorinal with Codeine, Robitussin A-C, Tylenol with Codeine*: Captain Cody, Cody, schoolboy; (with glutethimide) doors & fours, loads, pancakes and syrup	For all opiates and morphine derivatives— pain relief, euphoria, drowsiness Also, for codeine—less analgesia, sedation, and respiratory depression than Morphine for heroin—staggering gait	For all opiates and morphine derivatives— nausea, con- stipation, confusion, seda- tion, respiratory depression and arrest, tolerance, addiction, unconscious- ness, coma, death
Fentanyl and fentanyl analogs	*Actiq, Duragesic, Sublimaze;* apache, China girl, China white, dance fever, friend, goodfella, jackpot, murder 8, TNT, Tango and Cash		
Heroin	*Diacetylmorphine;* brown sugar, dope, H, horse, junk, skag, skunk, smack, white horse		
Morphine	*Roxanol, Duramorph;* M, Miss Emma, monkey, white stuff		
Opium	*laudanum, paragoric;* big O, black stuff, block, gum, op		
Oxycodone HCL	*OxyContin;* Oxy, O.C., killer		
Hydrocodone bitartrate, acetaminophen	*Vicodin;* vike, Watson-387		
Stimulants			
Amphetamine	*Biphetamine, Dexedrine:* bennies, black beauties, crosses, hearts, LA turn- around, speed, truck dri- vers, uppers	For all stimulants— increased heart rate, blood pressure, metabolism; feel- ings of exhilaration, energy, increased mental alertness	For all stimulants— rapid or irregular heart beat; reduced appetite, weight loss, heart failure, nervousness, insomnia

(Continued)

Table 15.1 *Continued*

Substance category and name	Commercial or street names	Intoxification effects	Potential health consequences
Cocaine	*Cocaine hydrochloride:* blow, bump, C, candy, Charlie, coke, crack, flake, rock, snow, toot	Also, for amphetamine— rapid breathing for cocaine—increased temperature	Also, for amphetamine— tremor, loss of coordination; irritability, anxiousness, restlessness, delirium, panic, paranoia, impulsive behavior, aggressiveness, tolerance, addiction, psychosis for cocaine—chest pain, respiratory failure, nausea, abdominal pain, strokes, seizures, headaches, malnutrition, panic attacks
MDMA (methylene-dioxymethamphetamine) Methamphetamine Methylphenidate (safe and effective for treatment of ADHD) nicotine	Adam, clarity, ecstasy, Eve, lover's speed, peace, STP, X, XTC *Desoxyn:* chalk, crank, crystal, fire, glass, go fast, ice, meth, speed *Ritalin:* JIF, MPH, R-ball, Skippy, the smart drug, vitamin R cigarettes, cigars, smoke-less tobacco, snuff, spit tobacco, bidis, chew	for MDMA—mild hallucino-genic effects, increased tactile sensitivity, empathic feelings for methamphetamine— aggression, violence, psy-chotic behavior	for MDMA—impaired memory and learning, hyperthermia, cardiac toxicity, renal failure, liver toxicity for methamphetamine— memory loss, cardiac and neurological damage; impaired memory and learning, tolerance, addiction for nicotine—additional effects attributable to tobacco exposure: adverse pregnancy outcomes; chronic lung disease, cardiovascular disease, stroke, cancer; tolerance, addiction
Other compounds Anabolic steroids	*Anadrol, Oxandrin, Durabolin, Depo-Testosterone, Equipoise:* roids, juice	No intoxification effects	Hypertension, blood clotting and cholesterol changes, liver cysts and cancer, kid-ney cancer, hostility and aggression, acne; in adolescents, premature stop-page of growth; in males, prostate cancer, reduced sperm production, shrunk-en testicles, breast enlarge-ment; in females, menstrual irregularities, development of beard and other mascu-line characteristics

Substance category and name	Commercial or street names	Intoxification effects	Potential health consequences
Dextromethorphan (DXM)	Found in some cough and cold medications; Robotripping, Robo, Triple C	Dissociative effects, distorted visual perceptions to complete dissociative effects	For effects at higher doses see 'dissociative anesthetics'
Inhalants	Solvents (paint thinners, gasoline, glues), gases (butane, propane, aerosol propellants, nitrous oxide), nitrites (isoamyl, isobutyl, cyclohexyl): laughing gas, poppers, snappers, whippets	Stimulation, loss of inhibition; headache; nausea or vomiting; slurred speech, loss of motor coordination; wheezing	Unconsciousness, cramps, weight loss, muscle weakness, depression, memory impairment, damage to cardiovascular and nervous systems, sudden death

Source: National Institute on Drug Abuse (http://www.drugabuse.gov/DrugPages/DrugsofAbuse.html), retrieved July 16, 2007

efforts. Individuals who are at the greatest risk for initial substance abuse problems are more likely to report beliefs that they are unable to avoid using substances or to resist peer pressure. After becoming involved with drug use, problem substance users more often report beliefs that they are unable to control their drug use or minimize the harmful effects of drug use. For such individuals, treatment must involve more than information and admonitions to abstain from drug use. Supportive environments that help individuals reinterpret environmental cues and develop more positive belief systems over time, although difficult to realize, are clearly necessary. Without such supports, individuals with maladaptive efficacy beliefs who are learning to manage their substance abuse are likely to interpret minor setbacks and difficulties as additional evidence of their inability to effect change in their own lives. Consequently, they may abandon their efforts to limit their substance use and its damaging effects. Treatments affecting efficacy beliefs are, for the most part, rare in schools and other public institutions. However, the high rates of relapse associated with substance abuse interventions suggest that this element is a promising addition to existing interventions.

Teachers need to know how to manage suspected substance abuse episodes and suspected intoxication or withdrawal crises in school. Their role is to manage and refer students appropriately, not to become investigators or counselors. Although educators must be aware of indications of substance abuse, they should not automatically assume that certain physical or psychological symptoms are the result of intoxication or withdrawal. Referral to counselors or medical personnel is appropriate to determine the cause. A clear school policy regarding detection and management helps teachers and administrators respond correctly to suspected abuse and crisis situations. In the event of an emotional–behavioral crisis, the teacher should remain calm and nonconfrontational. We have known for a long time that safety is more important than demonstrating disciplinary control (Miksic, 1987).

EARLY SEXUAL ACTIVITY AND TEEN PARENTHOOD

Delinquency, substance abuse, and sexual activity are often linked. Sexual activity itself may be defined as a juvenile status offense (Udry & Bearman, 1998), but some juveniles commit index sex crimes such as rape, sodomy, or molestation (see Dwyer & Laufersweiler–Dwyer, 2006; Morenz & Becker, 1995). However, most early sexual intercourse is a concern because it is associated with a high risk of teenage pregnancy and premature parental responsibility, contracting sexually transmitted diseases (STDs), and a wide variety of psychological and health risks (Botvin, Schinke, & Orlandi, 1995). In earlier times, sexuality was less often discussed and assumed to be a feature of adult life. However, "sexuality is no longer relegated to adulthood by cultural definition and is clearly part of adolescent behavior; yet, at the same time, increases in both teen pregnancy and sexually transmitted diseases observed with the lowering of the age of first intercourse have led to continued reluctance to accept sexual behavior in adolescents" (Graber, Brooks–Gunn, & Galen, 1998, p. 279). Sexual intercourse itself is of much less concern when it is engaged in by an 18-year-old than by a 13-year-old; the level of concern is inversely proportional to the age of the child or youth (cf. Gordon & Schroeder, 1995).

Adolescents with psychological problems are at particularly high risk for contracting acquired immunodeficiency syndrome (AIDS) and other STDs through casual sexual encounters, which are often linked with substance abuse. Sexual activity of young teenagers is also associated with social and emotional maladjustment and inadequate child-care skills (Thomas & Rickel, 1995). Many adolescents have distorted perceptions of their own high-risk behavior; they see having sex as relatively low in risk and high in benefit for them (Siegel et al., 1994). Students with emotional or behavioral disorders tend to have distorted ideas about sexual behavior that put them at high risk of contracting AIDS (Singh, Zemitzsch, Ellis, Best, & Singh, 1994). Teenage pregnancy and parenthood present enormous problems for young people, particularly those who may already be penalized by our society's responses to ethnicity (Benson & Torpy, 1995). The problems encountered by the children of teenage mothers and fathers are often overwhelming (Scott-Jones, 1993).

The sexual behavior of teens may be motivated by a variety of factors other than physiological urges. The social and psychological conditions that encourage early sexual activity are many and complex; they include the family and cultural factors we discussed in part 3. Sexual abuse by older individuals may initiate the sexual activity of some teenagers, and they may suffer long-term psychological stress or dysfunction as a result (Gordon & Schroeder, 1995). Many sexually active teenagers appear to be seeking a sense of belonging, emotional closeness, or importance that they are unable to achieve in other ways. They may romanticize parenthood, believing that their child will give them the love they have not found from others. Some appear to be addicted to sex and love (Griffin–Shelley, 1994). In a study of approximately 200 adolescents aged 12 to 19 years of age, Donenberg, Bryant, Emerson, Wilson, and Pasch (2003) found that three variables enabled the researchers to predict which girls initiated sexual activity at or before 14 years of age: hostile parental control, peer influence, and externalizing psychopathology. The psychological and physical risks are grave for these young teenagers. The realities and personal costs of teenage parenthood—to the teenagers and to their children—are staggering.

There are also differences in the reasons that adolescents engage in sexual intercourse that are related to the sex of the individual as well as the culture in which he or she lives. Eyre and Millstein (1999) asked 83 adolescents between the ages of 16 and 20 to list the qualities they preferred in a sexual partner as well as the reasons to have or abstain from having sexual intercourse. A core of beliefs related to reasons to have sex emerged across all of the groups included in the study. They included familiarity with the partner and the partner's sexual history, the partner's overall level of intelligence, and ease of communication as positive factors. The absence of these factors was associated with reasons not to have sex with a person. This study also found variations in attitudes and sexual behavior between males and females, as well as between African Americans and White adolescents. Males of both races described sexual arousal as a reason for engaging in intercourse, whereas females more often described concerns regarding personal respect and the individual's prospects for the future as reason to have sex. African American adolescents who were sexually active more often reported association of such activity with love, marriage, and parenthood, whereas White adolescents (particularly males) more often reported sexual activity in relation to drinking.

Clearly, suggesting that all males, females, African Americans, or White adolescents express the same views on sexuality is inappropriate. However, the findings of this report suggest that several general social motivational as well as group specific factors may be harnessed to reduce the impact of risky sexual behavior.

The facts of teenage sexual activity and parenthood are often assumed to imply a need for education about sexuality, family life, and parenting. However, education and other interventions designed to decrease teen sexual activity have yet to demonstrate their effectiveness. Benson and Torpy (1995) studied the sexual behavior of students in grades 6 through 8 in Chicago schools, finding that none of the following variables was related to loss of virginity: church attendance, religious affiliation, school grade-point average, type of housing, marital status of the child's natural parents, self-esteem, knowledge related to sex education, or school attendance. They concluded that most school-based efforts to reduce sexual activity and pregnancy among young teenagers are unlikely to be effective. Research on how to lower the prevalence of early sexual activity has lagged behind research on the prevention of substance abuse (Botvin et al., 1995).

Because early sexual activity and premature parenthood are often accompanied by emotional or behavioral disorders of both teenagers and their children, special educators are often involved in planning and implementing the curriculum. In addition, special educators must work with other professionals who provide supportive services to families and children in distress.

SUMMARY

Children and adolescents with emotional or behavior disorders often engage in delinquency, substance abuse, and precocious sexual behavior. These behaviors rarely occur in isolation from each other. Rather, troubled adolescents more often display a constellation of interrelated behavioral difficulties. The behaviors discussed in this section are related to the persistence and aggravation of such problems in adult life.

Juvenile delinquency is a legal term indicating violation of the law by an individual who is not yet an adult. Acts that are illegal only if committed by a minor are *status offenses; index crimes* are illegal regardless of the individual's age. The vast majority of youngsters commit delinquent acts; a small percentage are apprehended. Delinquent children and youth often have other emotional or behavioral disorders, especially conduct disorder. However, not all delinquents are identified as having conduct disorder, and not all youngsters with conduct disorder are delinquents. The most important distinctions are probably between those who commit few delinquent acts and those who are chronic offenders, especially those who repeat violent offenses against persons.

About 20% of all children and youth are at some time officially delinquent, and about 3% are adjudicated each year. About half of all official delinquents commit only one offense before reaching adulthood. Recidivists account for the majority of official delinquency. Peak ages for juvenile delinquency are ages 15 to 17. Most adjudicated delinquents are male.

Causal factors in delinquency are numerous and include antisocial behavior, hyperactivity and impulsivity, low intelligence and school achievement, family conflict and criminality, poverty, and poor parental discipline. Delinquency appears to grow from environmental disadvantages, weakened social bonds (to family, school, and work), and disrupted social relationships between youths and social institutions in the community. Effective prevention would have to address all the conditions that increase risk of delinquency.

We might logically take the position that nearly all incarcerated delinquents have emotional or behavioral disorders requiring special education. Assessment of delinquents' educational needs is extremely difficult because of the behavioral characteristics of delinquents and the social agencies that serve them.

Intervention in delinquency, if it is to be successful, must involve families, juvenile justice, schools, and communities. Parents need training to monitor and discipline their children more effectively. Juvenile justice may involve a variety of strategies, ranging from diversion to incarceration. The recommendations of researchers are typically for interventions that keep all but violent offenders in the community. Schools typically respond to disruptive and delinquent behavior with heightened punishment and a focus on security, but schoolwide discipline and emphasis on attention to appropriate behavior are more successful. Education in the corrections system should include functional assessment of students' needs, a curriculum that teaches important life skills, vocational training, supportive transition back to the community, and a full range of educational and related services from collaborating agencies.

Street gangs are an increasing problem in many cities, but misperceptions of these gangs are common. Street gangs are aggregations of youth who define themselves as a group and are committed to a criminal orientation. Most do not have drug distribution as a primary focus, and most of gang members' time is spent doing noncriminal and nonviolent acts. Gang members typically have notable personal deficiencies, are antisocial, desire status and companionship, and lead mostly boring lives. The causes and approaches to prevention of gangs are similar to those for delinquency, and many of the same intervention strategies apply, especially addressing problems of poverty and joblessness. However, gangs are maintained by perceived external threats and interventions that strengthen their cohesiveness. Many schools are running scared and approach gangs in ways that are counterproductive. A particular educational need is a differentiated curriculum that includes programs for noncollege-bound youth.

Substance abuse is not easy to define. However, a substance may be considered abused when it is deliberately used to induce physiological or psychological effects (or both) for other than therapeutic purposes and when its use contributes to health risks, impaired psychological functioning, adverse social consequences, or some combination of these. The most pervasive substance abuse problems involve alcohol and tobacco. Substance abuse typically progresses through several stages: from experimentation to social–recreational use to circumstantial–situational use, which may become intensified and lead to obsessional dependency. Teachers are most likely to observe the first indications of substance use during the transition from experimentation to social–recreational or to circumstantial–situational use. The causes of substance abuse are varied and include family, peer, community, and biological factors. Substance abuse is often accompanied by other disorders. Effective prevention programs are expensive, multifaceted, and controversial. Intervention in substance abuse must be designed for the individual case. School-based interventions require clear school policies regarding drugs, systematic efforts to provide information, referral to other agencies, and involvement of families and peers. In addition, interventions related to substance abuse may need to target the individual's beliefs that they actually can effect change in their patterns of substance use.

Early sexual activity is of concern primarily because of the risk of pregnancy, sexually transmitted diseases, and psychological and health problems. The sexual activity of juveniles may be motivated by a variety of factors, but the risk of negative consequences is always high. Teachers may be involved in educational programs, but current school-based intervention programs may be ineffective.

Problem Behaviors
of Adolescence

Michele M. Brigham, M.Ed., has been teaching for over 30 years. She has been a high school special education resource teacher and music teacher and works with general education teachers. She has also been the choral director for her school and directed its musicals. She has been an adjunct faculty member for the University of Virginia, teaching special education courses in Falls Church, Virginia.

How would you describe the academic needs of most of the high school students you teach?

Most of the high school students I teach face three sources of tension in dealing with their academic needs. First, my students have severe deficits in basic skills. Schools are reluctant to provide direct remediation of basic skills because to do so would mean setting up specialized treatments which would remove students from some inclusive environments and some elements of the standards-based curriculum delivered to their age mates. Second, they are not passing their classes so any time you could provide remediation is spent tutoring them on class assignments. Even with this tutorial assistance, many students still have trouble passing their classes and the state proficiency examinations. Consequently, many of them will not earn a standard high school diploma. Third, one of the results of the standards-based curriculum reform is a drastic reduction in vocational educational opportunities. In addition to it being unlikely my students can graduate with a standard high school diploma, they are unlikely to leave schools with the skills required for entry into the skilled or semiskilled labor force.

The students I work with are far behind their peers in reading and writing skills. For example, it is very common for seniors in my Practical English classes to have standard scores in the low 50s to mid-80s or third- to eighth-grade reading levels. They lack decoding skills to enable them to read fluently, and poor comprehension is the direct result of that lack of fluency. Their reading skills are so deficient that they don't consider reading a pleasurable activity or a viable way of gaining information about the world. They resist reading aloud, which is the best way to gain accuracy, and long before they get to high school

most of their teachers have refrained from requiring them to read aloud. As a result, they have been unable to make much progress in their fluency and comprehension. As reading is a primary access skill for the general curriculum, core content classes present tremendous challenges for these students.

One would expect people with poor reading skills to be deficient in writing skills also, and this is certainly the case for my students. They have difficulty in grammar, syntax, and pragmatic language. Their problems with written language include basic mechanics difficulties such as spelling and punctuation. They require training in forming complete sentences and organizing ideas into complex sentences and paragraphs. Their compositions lack elaboration and provide only sketchy information about their content knowledge or the topic on which they are writing. Writing is a slow and laborious task for them, and they often have poor handwriting and keyboarding skills. Therefore, it's easy to see that skills that are automatic for most students at this level are causing distraction from the type of cognitive skills required to craft both expository and narrative prose. One of the major ways that high school students are expected to demonstrate competency in the core content classes is through writing. The writing deficiencies that characterize my students further exacerbate the problems caused by their reading difficulties as they face the demands of core content classes.

There is a complex interaction between these skill deficits and general verbal abilities. My students lack the confidence in their ability to understand other people and to express themselves. Consequently, they often mask their confusion with the appearance of belligerence or nonchalance. Many teachers base their informal judgments about what students know or students' interest level in the class on their participation in classroom discussions. Many of my students who believe they lack the ability to interact in the complex exchange of ideas may behave in ways that cause the teacher to see them as disruptive, incompetent, or aloof. Although some of them are disruptive, many of them are using these behaviors to mask their insecurity or their inability to participate competitively with their peers. These skills are rarely explicitly taught at this level in the general education curriculum. Consequently, students who have failed to acquire them before they reach high school are unlikely to extrapolate them from immediate experience or profit substantially from mere exposure to the general curriculum.

The interaction of these skill deficits leads to an even larger problem for my students, which is a deficient store of background knowledge. Their background knowledge deficits make it difficult for them to participate meaningfully in many aspects of general education classes. Put simply, they just don't understand what their teachers and peers are talking about. Consequently, many of my students dismiss the general education curriculum as "stupid" or irrelevant. Although the relevance of the curriculum is debatable, I am convinced that these problems make the curriculum far more difficult for my students than it is for most of their peers.

Most of my direct teaching is with language arts. However, in my work with students in remedial settings, I have observed similar deficits in their ability to keep up with their peers in mathematics, science, and social studies. It is easy to see how their skill deficits in reading and writing cause similar problems in these areas.

To what extent do the youngsters you teach need social skills training?

Most of the students I work with have serious problems in the social domain. However, the extent to which they would profit from direct social skills training is somewhat questionable. To many educators, social skills training means instruction in specific interactional skills such as making eye contact, shaking hands, and polite conversation. At the high school level, social skills intervention probably should be more about the students' belief that appropriate behavior is worth the effort rather than remediation of skill deficits. There is a difference between knowing the skills and using them. Most of my students know the appropriate behaviors and have the skills to

employ them, but they behave in a maladaptive way because they have found that to be more effective and efficient in attaining their immediate goals. Their previous interactions have led them to believe they will never achieve competence in the skills prized in the academic domain, so the reward structure for them has become focused on escape and avoidance.

Many of the psychologists and guidance officials who are in supportive roles construct anger management plans for my students that allow them to leave the instructional environment anytime they become upset rather than teaching them strategies to cope with demands that are difficult for them. I am not always convinced that this is the best way to support my students in reaching their long-term goals because it (a) deprives them of the instruction they need to succeed academically and (b) keeps them from learning coping skills that will allow them to achieve independence and success in employment. For example, one of the young men who was supported by such a plan was unsuccessful in work-study during his senior year and has yet to hold down a job in the 3 years since he has graduated. Whenever he is provided with negative feedback by a supervisor, he uses the same strategy he was taught in school and walks off his job. This inability to meet the demands of the working world leads me to doubt his ability to successfully meet the commitment of marriage, parenting, and other social relationships that enhance quality of life. By the time they are seniors, most of my students have experienced repeated failure in holding jobs, and I suspect that their lack of coping ability rather than deficits in specific social skills is directly related to this problem. Social skills training at the high school level would probably be better accomplished through a set of coping strategies taught through clearly established rules, expectations, and consequences that are consistently enforced, with parallels drawn to the working world.

What advice would you offer to teachers of typical high school students who are likely to have trouble with the law or need special education because of emotional or behavioral disorders?

Interestingly enough, many teachers already know the techniques that would be most successful with my students. Teacher effectiveness has been studied in depth, and teacher and lesson effectiveness variables have been identified that are crucial to students with emotional and behavioral disorders. Teachers need to consciously use the good teaching techniques that have been identified through empirical research. These include maximizing engaged time on task, with students actively participating in instructional activities; making sure the content is covered with appropriate pacing, well-defined and prioritized objectives, and structured delivery of information that includes a statement of the objectives, review and repetition of the important points, ample opportunities for practice, and frequent and explicit feedback using techniques such as curriculum-based measurement. It is important for my students to have a much higher density of feedback to allow them to see and acknowledge for themselves that they are making steps toward competency. Structure and consistency in the classroom are important for my students to feel secure enough to make attempts at learning material that has been difficult or impossible for them to learn in past attempts.

What are the most important things a teacher can do to help students who have begun to abuse substances?

Dealing with substance abuse is a bigger problem than most teachers should handle by themselves because our training prepares us for instructional–behavioral issues within the classroom. We should respect the limits as well as the competencies of our training.

Unless a teacher is trained to deal with this type of problem, the first step should always be to refer the student to the appropriate professionals. In my school, our guidance professionals, school nurse, and school psychologist are the front line for working with students with substance abuse problems. However, in thinking about things that can be done in the classroom, it's hard to imagine that the kinds of good teaching methods that help students with disabilities would be completely ineffective with students who have begun to abuse substances. Clear and explicit feedback, focus on accomplishments, high density of reinforcement for accomplishment, and helping students to understand the relationship between effective effort and successful outcome are tools teachers can use effectively with students engaging in substance abuse. It is important that the reinforcement is for legitimate accomplishment. Too often we provide reinforcement for inconsequential behaviors in our attempt to promote self-esteem. My students see

through this immediately, which breaks the bond of trust required for successful instruction and creates even more concern regarding their own potential. It is vital to provide students with the skills to allow them to experience self-esteem through success.

What are the most common behavioral problems that you must deal with in your classroom?

The major problems that I have with my students are refusal to participate, truancy, and tardiness. Refusal to participate takes many forms, including gestures and language that some see as the problem instead of as serving the function of escape. I believe that whatever form the refusal to participate takes, the real problem that we should deal with is the attempt to withdraw from the instruction. I see my students in two very controlled settings outside of the core content classes—a resource–tutorial setting and a dedicated practical English class. Although many people prefer the word *segregated,* that implies involuntary separation. Most of my students are terrified that they will be forced to return to the general education settings, where they are well aware that their skill level will keep them from success, and they will perceive their failure as personal humiliation. Even within these homogeneous settings, I experience high levels of resistance to instruction from many students. Task avoidance behaviors such as refusal to participate in instruction, refusal to attempt to do assignments or otherwise participate in classroom activities, tardiness, and truancy have been inadvertently rewarded in both regular and special education settings.

When students present teachers with the choice of ignoring their disengagement or dealing with the disruption that is likely to result from intervening with these behaviors, teachers who are overwhelmed by the size of their classes and the amount of material to be covered can ill afford to devote substantial amounts of instructional time to that student at the expense of the rest of the class. These teachers understandably opt for the former, teaching our students that those behaviors are both effective and efficient to obtain their goals. Support staff, parents, and IEP teams too often excuse students from instructional demands rather than provide them with the requisite skills to benefit from instruction. By the time they get to high school, many of these students are so overwhelmed by their cycle of failure they are no longer willing to take the risks or make the effort required for success in learning.

What are the kids you teach actually like? Give us a thumbnail sketch of several of them.

Carrie is a sophomore, but still considered a freshman because she hasn't passed enough classes or SOLs (state exams called Standards of Learning). She is living with her grandmother. Carrie has had a lot of difficulty in her classes and has lost a job she really liked because of her inability to control her temper, work with people she doesn't like, and tell the truth. She has an emotional or behavioral disorder and a behavior plan, and she is being considered for placement in a special school but has not been placed yet because of inadequate documentation of her problems.

Kate is a junior with a learning disability (LD) and has become quite successful in her practical level classes. She takes classes half the school day and has been placed for work-study in a job she really enjoys. Though she's very proud of her job, it is currently in jeopardy because she has been unable to pass her driver's test and needs transportation (not provided by the school).

Larry is also a junior with an LD. He is probably the most successful of the three in understanding and working with his disability. He will take standard-level classes during his senior year. He is involved with his community and is active in a theater company. Larry is a very talented artist as well. Though he describes himself as a former "hoodlum," Larry has mastered the social skills he needs to be successful in school.

Michele Brigham Interviews Carrie, Kate, and Larry (individual interviews, different responses)

Ms. B.: If there was one thing you could change about school, what would it be?

Carrie: The group situation. I don't like how people are classified into different groups. You've got the Goths, the preps, the rednecks. I don't like that. I think everybody should get along. . .You see a lot of them hang out, and you still classify them into different groups.

Ms. B.: If there was anything you could change about yourself to make school easier, what would you change?

C: I don't really think I'd actually change anything about myself. I know I have an attitude problem, and I'm working on that. But I don't think I'd change anything. Because I don't think my schooling is about me. It's my attitude, and that's just about it, and I'm working on that one.

Ms. B.: If you actually made that change, how do you think it would affect you outside of school, after you're done with school?

C: I think it would help me a whole lot if I changed my attitude, because I sometimes open my mouth about things that I really shouldn't. And I think it'd make life a little bit more easier for me.

Ms. B.: What do you think you want to be doing when you get out of school?

C: I definitely want to go to college. I either want to go and be a lawyer or a doctor. I like the whole doctor scene. I want to do something with helping people. I definitely want to do that. I'm a hands-on person helping people. I definitely want to do something like that.

Ms. B.: Is there anything in school that's helping you toward that goal?

C: Well, not at this point, but next year I'm taking a nurses class over at [the vocational–technical school] that'll give me a little feel for what I'm doing, what I'm getting into.

Ms. B.: Is there anything in school that's keeping you from that goal?

C: Not to my knowledge. No.

Ms. B.: Have you ever thought about dropping out?

C: No. I've told my father it doesn't matter how many years I'm in high school, I'm going to graduate.

Kate: No. Not ever.

Larry: Well, I'm 18 now. I became 18 last month. Pretty much no. But one of my teachers gave me the idea that maybe I could, because I'm 18, drop out and get a GED [general equivalency diploma] and completely skip my senior year and go straight to college. And I thought about that, and I asked some people, and everyone seems to agree that it's a bad idea.

Ms. B.: And you're comfortable with that?

L: Yeah. I'm a year older than I should be because I got held back in first grade. Because I was a little hoodlum back then. Caused a lot of trouble. And I really wish that hadn't happened because I won't have many friends next year. Because almost all of my friends are seniors.

Ms. B.: What's made you decide to stay in school?

C: I have a boyfriend now who didn't finish school, and he regrets it. And my father and mother dropped out of school, too. And they regret it to this day. And they tell me, "You need to finish school," but I've always promised my grandparents and everyone I'm going to make something of myself, and I am. I don't care how many years it takes me just to graduate high school, I'm going to make something of myself.

K: I don't know. It's just my goal to graduate and be with my brother. He's the only one to graduate [from high school] from my biological family.

Ms. B.: Think about the way you want to be 5 years from now. Is there anything about yourself you want to work on to get to that goal?

C: I want to work on accepting me for who I am. I really have a bad problem with doing that. Whether it's like in choir and I can't sing or, like, it's beauty pageants I go to and I don't win or something, I need to accept myself for who I am, because I really can't change myself. Wish I could, but it'd be a little silly I think. But I need to work on that.

K: Have a better attitude about things. I seem to get mad if I don't understand something. They say I have attention disorder or something.

Ms. B.: When you get mad, what problems does that cause you?

K: I get frustrated and just want to stop doing whatever it is I'm doing right there at that second and start cleaning. That's the only way I can take my frustration out.

Ms. B.: Why do you have an IEP?

C: I think it's because of my. . .I call it a learning disability, I really don't know what you would call it. I think it's because of my level of reading and the way I comprehend things.

K: I have ADD.

Ms. B.: What does that mean?

K: Attention deficit disorder.

Ms. B.: Do you take medication for that?

K: No. I quit taking it because, I was taking Ritalin and it didn't help at all, and they found I was better off of it.

L: Well, the teachers, back when I was little, you know, they used to say I had ADD. My dad didn't want to believe it. And they gave me a test to check. And it turns out I didn't have ADD. I had short-term memory loss. So, you know, I have a hard time

remembering things. But I think I worked things out in a way so it's not such a big problem anymore.

Ms. B.: Do you write things down?

L: No, I just. . .I don't know. It's still there, but it's not as big a problem anymore. It's something you work to overcome.

Ms. B.: How do you feel about that—having an IEP?

C: It doesn't bother me. It used to really bother me, because over at [middle school] I had two Englishes and then I was always in a study hall here, and it kind of bothered me to begin with, but then again it really didn't because I see that I needed the help. But I had to want to do it for myself. I couldn't let somebody else help me.

K: I think it's fine. I mean, it's not a regular diploma. It's not a standard or advanced, but it's a diploma.

Ms. B.: So you're going to get an IEP diploma?

K: Yeah. But it's a diploma. And it's just like a regular one. It doesn't have the word IEP on it.

Ms. B.: Do you think your IEP is helpful to you?

C: I think it is if I'd use it. Sometimes I won't use it, as you found out. I've got to want to ask for help.

K: Yes, I do.

L: Yeah. It gives me resource to get stuff done. And often times in, like, math—and math is my weak point—I'll need help, a lot of help. And that gives me help.

Ms. B.: Some people say that we should do away with special education altogether and everyone should be in a regular class. How do you feel about that?

C: I think that's a little silly, because not everybody learns the same way as somebody else would, because I definitely don't catch on to what people are saying quickly. I think we should have the special education thing because, if everybody learned at the same level school would go by so much faster, but, you know, it doesn't. And everybody comprehends things at a different pace, and we all need somebody to teach us differently.

K: I think they're wrong when they say that, because. . . Take me and [another student] who are in special education, and put them in regular classes with regular people. They're going to get made fun of if they don't know the answers. Because I'm going through that now in one of my regular classes.

L: I disagree. Because some kids are smarter, and some kids are not as smart. That's just the way things are. People like to believe that everyone's equal, but in reality they're not.

Ms. B.: Why do you think some kids abuse drugs and alcohol?

C: I think some say it has to do with their parents or peer pressure and things like that. I can honestly say, and I know you've probably heard this from a lot of kids, but I've never really done drugs. I have drank, I'll admit to that. I've been scared because my father used to do alcohol and used to do weed and stuff like that, and I've always been ascared that I'd get addicted to it, and I don't really want to ruin my life like that. I just don't understand why you would waste your life. . . . But some people, they'll start off with a little weed and then it goes to worse things, and then they really realize what they did, but it's peer pressure. [This school] definitely has a lot of that, because there are parties and the parties aren't directly chaperoned. There are a lot of parties that are illegal and have so much stuff, and freshmen go to them, and, they're like, "I'm gonna be cool" and the little freshmen want to fit in with the big seniors. So they try something . . . and then it leads to something worse.

K: Because they think it's something that's going to help them, and it's not.

Ms. B.: Why do you think that?

K: Because. . .it just makes your mind light-headed. The only reason that I know that is my brother was in a bad accident a couple years ago. He had been drinking and got behind the wheel of a car, and I vowed I'd never do it.

L: It's kind of like an escape, probably. Some kids do it because it makes them feel older, it makes them feel. . .I don't know. I don't do drugs or alcohol. I've drunk before, but not often, and it's not that big a deal, and I don't do it at all anymore. I've never done drugs, and I never will. And that's because of my sister. The problem with things like drugs or weed or any of that stuff is that when you're a teenager, part of being a teenager is having these ups and downs on an emotional scale. When you're a teenager you cry a lot and laugh a lot at the same time. And what drugs do is dull that, and you go through your whole teenage life without that experience. So you don't develop like a normal person does. So you can be 34 or 40 and still be 17 mentally, because you never went through that whole stage in your life, because you dulled it. I just look at it as a complete waste of time, you know. They spend hundreds of dollars on this habit, and they just sit around with each other and smoke their weed or whatever . . . and the feelings are artificial. I believe in the good feelings that I already have. Some people get a buzz off the chemical the brain produces when you exercise a lot, they get addicted to it, and that's a good addiction. . . . Sometimes I've even gotten a buzz off music, just getting good feelings, I just felt so happy, and it's uplifting. Some people get a buzz off skiing. It just depends on what part of life your drug is. I don't believe in these other things.

Ms. B.: We just finished our state testing program. Some kids will pass and some won't. Do you think these tests are good for the school and for students?

C: I think people will see them as good for the school, because they can see if teachers are doing their job. Which I don't believe. I don't think any kid really likes the SOLs. Technically, if they do, well. . .they like tests. I don't like them because I don't think they're fair to students, because students like me, I know I freak out when you have a big test coming up . . . I don't deal too well with pressure. It's not fair, because you don't really know how the teacher's teaching, because you don't know if the teacher taught you all you should know. . . . If you don't pass the SOLs, then you can't graduate, and I don't think that's too fair. It's too much pressure on us.

L: I don't really care. SOLs are a joke to me. They're so easy. If you don't pass them then you really don't deserve to pass the school, because they're so pathetically easy. They don't even mention them in advanced and honors classes. They know the kids are more than prepared to crush the tests.

Ms. B.: Do you have siblings?

L: I have an older sister. She's 4 years older than me, she's 23.

Ms. B.: Do you think school was harder for you than it was for your sister?

L: At first, she was better at school. She used to get straight As. And I used to be the one that did poorly in school. And then, ever since she hit a certain age she started mixing in with the wrong people and her grades dropped, you know, she started getting into really bad stuff, and then she had a baby and then she dropped out of school. So it was, like, for a while she was the better one, and it switched all of a sudden, and then she became the rotten apple.

Ms. B.: So, do you think you learned something from that? From seeing her get mixed up with the wrong people?

L: Oh, yes, absolutely. Because she did that, I am very firm in the belief that I'll never do any of the stuff she did, like drugs. She's completely irresponsible, and she made the worst possible choices and got with the worst people you can imagine. Like, my nephew's father is in prison right now. And I just don't ever want to become her.

Ms. B.: How about your parents and grandparents—do you know anything about how school was for them?

L: My Brazilian grandparents, I don't know them very well at all. I hardly ever see them. And I only met my grandma once, and she wasn't really my grandma. She's my step-grandmother, I suppose. My Brazilian grandpa died. . .I probably met him, but I was too young to remember. . .I don't know what the deal was with her. They probably didn't go to school much at all. My American grandparents, I know my grandmother, she only has a middle school education. So, from there, she dropped out and married my grandpa. And I'm not really sure about his education. He joined the military.

QUESTIONS FOR FURTHER REFLECTION

1. What are the things you can do as a teacher to help steer students away from the most serious problems of adolescence?

2. What should you do, and how should you do it, if you become aware that one of your students (of any age) is abusing substances?

3. As a teacher, how would you talk to a student who comes to you with accounts of early sexual experience? What would you ask? What would you say, and how would you say it?

SECTION 16
ANXIETY AND RELATED DISORDERS

As you read this section, keep these guiding questions in mind:

- How is anxiety related to a variety of emotional and behavioral disorders?

- Under what conditions should educators and others be concerned when a youngster exhibits behavior that is characteristic of anxiety?

- What are the most effective intervention strategies in anxiety disorders, including school phobia?

- What kinds of obsessive-compulsive behavior are most often seen in children and adolescents?

- What role can the peer group play in effective intervention in social isolation?

Sections 13 through 15 dealt mostly with problems that fall under the general dimension of *externalizing disorders*. This section turns to problems designated generally as *internalizing*. Although the broadband classification of *internalizing* is well established in empirical studies of behavioral dimensions, most of the specific categories and disorders that fall under it are not. In short, there is more confusion and controversy over terminology and classification for internalizing problems than for externalizing problems. Therefore, grouping internalizing problems for discussion presents unavoidable difficulties.

Regardless of how internalizing problems are grouped for discussion, it is important to recognize that they may occur along with externalizing problems. Externalizing and internalizing are not mutually exclusive, and when they occur together, the child is at particularly high risk. In fact, Loeber, Farrington, Stouthamer-Loeber, and Van Kammen (1998a) found in their longitudinal work evidence of a connection between internalizing problems and delinquency in some cases.

Anxiety, social withdrawal, and other internalizing behavior problems often occur together and sometimes are comorbid—coexisting—with externalizing behavioral problems (Albano, Chorpita, & Barlow, 2003; Brigham & Cole, 1999; Gresham & Kern, 2004; Kazdin, 2001; Tankersley & Landrum, 1997), although this is not always the case (Bagwell, Molina, Kashdan, Pelham, & Hoza, 2006). Eating disorders and reluctant speech may both involve specific fears or anxieties, stereotyped movement disorders may involve obsessions or compulsions or both, and so on. Anxiety is a frequent component of other disorders, and anxiety disorders of all types may be comorbid with a variety of other disorders. "In general, it is important to keep in mind that comorbidity is the rule—not the exception in abnormal child psychology" (Rabian & Silverman, 1995, p. 236).

The relationships among the various problems involving anxiety and other internalizing problems are tenuous. We will not attempt to summarize definition, prevalence, causal factors, prevention, assessment, intervention, or education for the general case or for all specific disorders because these disorders are so varied and loosely related. The problems we discuss are representative of those most frequently described in the literature. We begin with anxiety disorders because they are the broadest category; anxiety appears to be a significant component of all the others.

ANXIETY DISORDERS

Anxiety—the distress, tension, or uneasiness that goes with fears and worries—is part of the normal development of young children (Albano et al., 2003; Dadds, 2002; Hintze, 2002; Morris & Kratochwill, 1998; Stevenson-Hinde & Shouldice, 1995; Woodruff-Borden & Leyfer, 2006). At birth, infants have a fear of falling and of loud noise; fear of other stimuli (strange persons, objects, situations) ordinarily develops during the first few months. These fears probably have survival value, and they are considered normal and adaptive, not deviant. As children grow into the middle childhood years they develop additional fears, especially about imaginary creatures or events. Unless the fears become excessive or debilitative and prevent the child from engaging in normal social interaction, sleep, school attendance, or exploring the environment, they are not maladaptive. Indeed, a child who has no fears at all is not only highly unusual but also likely to be hurt or killed because of inappropriate brashness.

Children's anxieties or fears may be mild and short-lived enough that they do not seriously interfere with social growth. In fact, "study of the *prevalence of anxiety* in childhood has focused on subclinical fears and school phobia" (Strauss, 1993, p. 240, emphasis in original). Most studies show that about 7% or 8% of children experience intense anxieties at some time, although not all of these anxieties require clinical intervention (see Anderson, 1994; Woodruff-Borden & Leyfer, 2006). When fear unnecessarily restricts the child's activity, however, intervention is called for. A child or youth may be in a chronic state of anxiety about a broad range of things, in which case he or she may be described as having a generalized anxiety disorder. However, a youngster may also have a more specific anxiety. It may be an extreme irrational fear that is out of proportion to reality and leads to automatic avoidance of the feared situation, which is often called a phobia. The child who shows extreme anxiety and social withdrawal (often labeled *neurosis* in psychodynamic literature) has traditionally been assumed to be more disturbed and to have a worse prognosis for adult adjustment than does the hostile, acting-out child with an externalizing disorder. Research does not bear out this assumption.

Characteristics associated with anxiety and withdrawal are usually more transitory and amenable to treatment than are those associated with conduct disorder, and anxiety does not put a child at risk for later development of schizophrenia or other major psychiatric disorders in adulthood (Klein & Last, 1989; Quay & La Greca, 1986; Robins, 1966, 1986). Compared to their awareness of peers' aggressive and disruptive behavior, children's awareness of their peers' anxiety and withdrawal is not as keen or as early to develop. At least among normal children, those with high levels of anxiety appear to see themselves in more negative terms than do those whose anxiety is lower (Muris, Merckelbach, Mayer, & Snieder, 1998).

Anxiety-withdrawal in its typical form is not the greatest concern to knowledgeable professionals who work with children and youth who have emotional or behavioral disorders. Nevertheless, in their extreme forms, anxiety and related disorders *do* result in serious impairment of functioning. Extreme social isolation, extreme and persistent anxiety, and persistent extreme fears, for example, can seriously endanger social and personal development and demand effective intervention. Some children and adolescents experience severe attacks of panic: "the unexpected occurrence of episodes of intense distress. . .[consisting of] a constellation of four or more cognitive and somatic symptoms (e.g., sweating, pounding heart, rapid breathing, tingling sensations, racing thoughts over losing control) and may or may not be triggered by a situational cue" (Barrios & O'Dell, 1998, p. 253). Moreover, anxiety is frequently comorbid with depression, conduct disorder, learning disabilities, and other disorders discussed later in this section (see Barrios & O'Dell, 1998; Newcomer, Barenbaum, & Pearson, 1995; Rabian & Silverman, 1995).

Quay and La Greca (1986) estimated that persistent anxiety may characterize 2% of the child population and that about 5% may be affected by such behavior problems at one time or another. Anxiety may be part of the problems of 20% to 30% of youngsters referred to clinics for treatment of behavioral disorders. The prevalence of anxious-withdrawn behavior appears to be approximately the same as that of conduct disorder, placing it among the most common emotional or behavioral disorders of childhood (Anderson & Werry, 1994; Woodruff-Borden & Leyfer, 2006). Boys and girls are referred for these problems in about equal percentages, but these are only rough estimates because there have been no extensive studies done of prevalence in children.

Evidence suggests that much anxiety is learned but that biological factors also may contribute to anxiety disorders. Humans learn fears in a variety of ways (see Herbert, 1994; Morris & Kratochwill, 1983, 1998; Siegel & Ridley-Johnson, 1985, for detailed analyses of fear acquisition). Infants and young children especially may learn fear through classical or respondent conditioning. If an already fright-producing stimulus is paired with another object or event, the child may come to fear that object or event. Comments, remonstrations, and other verbal communications of parents (especially the mother) and other adults about objects, activities, places, persons, or situations induce fearfulness in children who have acquired language skills (see Turner, Beidel, Roberson-Nay, & Tervo, 2003). Adults' and other children's nonverbal behavior can also have a powerful influence on a child's learning fear. A child who is overly fearful of dogs may have acquired the fear in one or a combination of ways: A dog may have frightened the child by barking or growling, jumping, knocking the child down, biting, and so on; the parents or someone else may have warned the child in an emotional way about the dangers of dogs, or the child may have heard people talk about a dog's meanness and dangerousness; or the child may have seen a parent, sibling, or other child (or someone in a movie or on television) attacked or frightened by dogs.

In addition to social learning, anxiety appears in some cases to be affected by physiological factors (Harden, Pihl, Vitaro, Gendreau, & Tremblay, 1995; Morris & Kratochwill, 1998). Anxiety disorders of various types tend to run in families, and it is suspected that genetic or other physiological factors may be involved in the origins of these disorders as well as social learning. However, "at the present time, causes of anxiety and phobic disorders in childhood are not well understood and appear to be multifaceted" (Rabian & Silverman, 1995, p. 248).

Some children develop fears or phobias about separation, and leaving home or their parents—even for a short time—may be extremely traumatic for them. Some are extremely anxious about going to school. School phobia may more appropriately be called social phobia in some cases because it is a fear of the social interactions that are an expected part of school attendance (Beidel & Turner, 1998). Of course, a student may have extreme anxiety about both separation from home or parents and social interaction in school.

Social learning principles can help resolve both children's and adults' excessive or irrational anxieties and fears. Three approaches, which can be used in combination, have been particularly successful: modeling, desensitization, and self-control training. With these techniques, clinicians have helped children and youth overcome a wide array of fears and phobias (see Barrios & O'Dell, 1998; Dadds, 2002; Kendall & Gosch, 1994; King, Heyne, & Ollendick, 2005; March, 1995; Morris & Kratochwill, 1998). Teachers may be asked to assist in implementing these procedures in school settings. Medications to reduce anxiety may also be helpful (Garland, 2002; Konopasek & Forness, 2004).

Having fearful children watch movies in which other youngsters are having fun (at a party or playing games) while approaching the feared object without hesitation (for example, the youngsters in the movie may be handling dogs or snakes while playing) reduces fear in the observers and makes them more willing to approach the thing they fear. Having individuals with phobias watch several different peer models unanxiously approach several different feared objects and showing films that display the actual feared object (rather than a replica) have increased the effectiveness of this method of fear reduction. Positive reinforcement of the fearful person's approach to the feared object adds to the fear-reducing effects of watching models. Filmed modeling procedures have been highly effective in preventing children from acquiring maladaptive fears of medical and dental procedures, as well as in dealing with children who have already become fearful (see Dadds, 2002; King, Hamilton, & Murphy, 1983).

Procedures variously referred to as systematic desensitization, reciprocal inhibition, and counterconditioning have also been effective in lowering fears of children and adults. The central feature of these procedures involves the individual's gradual and repeated exposure to the fear-provoking stimuli (either in real life or in purposeful fantasy of them), while the person remains unanxious and perhaps engaged in an activity that is incompatible with or inhibits anxiety (such as eating a favorite treat or relaxing comfortably in a chair). The gradual approach to the feared object, repeated exposure to it, and maintenance of an unanxious state during exposure are thought to weaken the conditioned or learned bond between the object and the fear response it elicits (Barrios & O'Dell, 1998; Beidel & Turner, 1998; Dadds, 2002; Morris & Kratochwill, 1998; Rabian & Silverman, 1995; Wolpe, 1975).

In self-control training, fearful individuals learn to talk through a variety of techniques for managing anxiety. They may learn relaxation, self-reinforcement, self-punishment, self-instruction, visual imagery, or problem-solving strategies. The trainer might help the individual develop mental images that represent calm or pleasant feelings that are incompatible with anxiety and that the subject can recall when he or she encounters anxiety-provoking circumstances.

Interventions based on behavioral principles have been quite successful in remediating the problem of school phobia and other social fears (Beidel & Turner, 1998; King, Ollendick, & Tonge, 1995). Specific techniques vary from case to case, but general procedures include one or more of the following:

- Desensitization of the child's fear through role playing or in vivo (real-life) approximations of attending school for an entire day
- Reinforcement for attending school even for a brief period, gradually lengthening the time the child is required to stay in school
- Matter-of-fact parental statements that the child will go back to school, avoiding lengthy or emotional discussion
- Removal of reinforcers for staying home (such as being allowed to watch television, play a favorite game, stay close to their mother, or engage in other pleasurable activities).

Albano et al. (2003) and King et al. (1983) suggested that many maladaptive fears in the school setting are preventable. Prevention involves desensitizing young children to school by introducing future teachers, school routines, play activities, and so on. Transitions to middle school and senior high school similarly can be made less anxiety provoking by preparing students for their new environments and new expectations. Although many schools attempt to provide orientation experiences, they are often not carefully planned. Individual students may need to learn coping skills to deal with irrational thoughts and to learn adaptive behavior (such as asking a teacher or a peer for assistance) through modeling, rehearsal, feedback, and reinforcement.

Obsessive-Compulsive Disorders

Obsessions are repetitive, persistent, intrusive impulses, images, or thoughts about something, not worries about real-life problems. *Compulsions* are repetitive, stereotyped acts the individual feels he or she must perform to ward off a dreaded event, although these acts are not really able to prevent it. Sometimes the obsessions or compulsions are seen as bizarre, as when a young person is obsessed with the idea that he or she might turn into someone or something else (e.g., become a "transformer") or take on some undesired characteristic (Volz & Heyman, 2007).

Both obsessions and compulsions may be part of ritualistic behavior by which an individual attempts to reduce anxiety. When such behavior causes marked distress, is inordinately time-consuming, or interferes with a person's routine functioning in home, school, or job, it is considered an obsessive-compulsive disorder (OCD). Children with OCD often do not understand that their behavior is excessive and unreasonable, although adults with OCD typically do.

OCD affects perhaps as many as 1 in 200 children and adolescents, making it a relatively rare disorder (see Albano et al., 2003; Johnston & March, 1992). It may involve many types of ritualistic thoughts or behaviors, such as:

- Washing, checking, or other repetitive motor behavior
- Cognitive compulsions consisting of words, phrases, prayers, sequence of numbers, or other forms of counting
- Obsessional slowness, taking excessive time to complete simple everyday tasks
- Doubts and questions that elevate anxiety.

Many children and adolescents with this disorder are not diagnosed, in part because they are often secretive about their obsessional thoughts or rituals. However, OCD can result in significant impairment in social and academic impairment. Johnston and March (1992) described a case in point:

> Betsy, an 11-year-old girl, was referred to our clinic by a local psychologist. During the initial telephone contact, Betsy's mother explained that their situation seemed desperate, as Betsy had been unable to attend school for the 2 preceding weeks. Her mother explained that Betsy repeatedly dressed and undressed and then dressed again, over and over, and was unable to stop until she was nearly exhausted. (p. 118)

Betsy's dressing rituals had begun 7 months earlier. Psychodynamic therapy was ineffective, and her symptoms worsened. Her schoolwork suffered, and her teachers reported that she was not turning in homework or completing assignments. When her parents asked her why she was having trouble, she was evasive but eventually said that it was because "she had to read each sentence three times, 'just the right way'" (Johnston & March, 1992, p. 119). After more probing by her mother, Betsy admitted that she thought if she did not "get it right" her parents would feel hurt. Later, Betsy began repeating phrases and sentences and performing other rituals, including washing her hands up to 30 times a day to avoid contracting AIDS.

The most effective interventions are based on social learning principles, particularly strategies employed for reduction of anxiety (Albano et al., 2003; March & Mulle, 1998; Milby, Robinson, & Daniel, 1998). Medications to reduce anxiety may also be helpful (Beer, Karitani, Leonard, March, & Sweda, 2002; Garland, 2002; Johnston & March, 1992; Quintana & Birmaher, 1995). Teachers may play an important role in detecting OCD, especially when the student is secretive about thoughts or rituals and careful observation and questioning are necessary to discover why the student is having socialization or academic difficulties. Special educators may be expected to assist in intervention by implementing features of anxiety-reduction procedures in the classroom.

Posttraumatic Stress Disorder

Posttraumatic stress disorder (PTSD) refers to prolonged, recurrent emotional and behavioral reactions following exposure to an extremely traumatic event (or multiple events) involving threatened death or serious injury to oneself or others. The person's response at the time of experiencing the event(s) must include intense fear, helplessness, or horror (children may show disorganized or agitated behavior). Although very traumatic events are experienced by many children before they are 16 years of age, most of them do not develop PTSD (Copeland, Keeler, Angold, & Costello, 2007). However, some children experience multiple traumatic events, and some do develop PTSD. Traumatic childhood events, whether they result in PTSD or not, are generally related to a variety of forms of psychopathology, especially anxiety disorders and depression (Copeland et al., 2007).

PTSD is characterized by persistent cognitive, perceptual, emotional, or behavioral problems related to the event. For example, people with PTSD may reexperience the traumatic event in a variety of ways, such as through recurrent and intrusive thoughts, images, or dreams. They may avoid stimuli associated with the event or experience a general emotional numbing or unresponsiveness. Their symptoms may also include increased arousal (e.g., difficulty sleeping or concentrating; see Fletcher, 2003; Mindell & Owens, 2003; Saigh, 1998).

Until relatively recently, children's delayed emotional and behavioral reactions to extreme stress were largely ignored. PTSD was seldom studied unless the traumatic stress occurred in adulthood. Since the mid-1980s, however, mental health workers have recognized that extremely traumatic experiences can cause delayed emotional or behavioral disorders in children as well as adults (Copeland et al., 2007; Fletcher, 2003; Terr, 1995; Yule, 1994). By the mid-1990s, it was well recognized that extreme stress or life-threatening experiences can produce not only depression, anxiety, fears, and other reactions in children but also can result in PTSD (Barrios & O'Dell, 1998;

Saigh, 1998; Wolfe, 1998). Terr (1995) concluded that four characteristics are common to extreme childhood trauma:

- Visualized or otherwise repeatedly perceived memories of the trauma
- Repetitive behaviors that may be similar to obsessions or compulsions
- Fears linked specifically to the traumatic event
- Altered attitudes toward people, life, or the future, reflecting feelings of vulnerability.

Individuals respond to traumatic events in tremendously different ways. However, researchers are finding that accidents, wars, natural disasters such as earthquakes or hurricanes, terrorism, and the domestic and community violence commonly experienced in contemporary urban life may often produce PTSD in children and adolescents.

Treatment of these disorders may involve a variety of approaches, such as group discussion and support activities, crisis counseling, and individual treatment to reduce anxiety and improve coping strategies. Prevention involves not only efforts to reduce accidents and violence but also planning for the traumas that are likely if not inevitable.

Events producing PTSD may occur in school or the community. Sexual and physical abuse or school shootings, for example, may give rise to PTSD. As more immigrant children from war-torn countries enter our schools, we will no doubt see an increase in the number of children showing posttraumatic stress. Meese (2005) reported that more than 80% of foreign-born children adopted by U.S citizens in the decade prior to 2002 had lived for one or more years in institutions. Although the nature and quality of care in foreign orphanages varies tremendously, Meese suggested that a number of factors, including the reasons that children were placed in orphanages in the first place, puts them at heightened risk for PTSD in addition to cognitive delays and behavioral difficulties. Regardless of the location at which the traumatic event occurs, the student with PTSD is likely to have serious problems in school. Anxiety and related responses to the trauma may make it very difficult for the student to concentrate on academic work or engage in typical social activities. Consequently, it is important that teachers be aware of the indicators of possible PTSD, refer students for evaluation, and participate in efforts to reduce anxiety to manageable levels.

Historically, recognition and treatment of disabilities in civilians has followed the return of injured soldiers. Because PTSD is one of the major problems of soldiers returning from the wars in Iraq and Afghanistan, perhaps the public will become more aware of and demand better treatment of youngsters with PTSD.

Stereotyped Movement Disorders

Stereotyped movements are involuntary, repetitious, persistent, and nonfunctional acts over which the individual can exert at least some voluntary control under some circumstances but not total control in all circumstances. Stereotyped movements include self-stimulation and self-injury, as we discuss in section 18. However, they may also include repetitive movements related to anxiety (Albano et al., 2003; Himle, Flessner, Bonow, & Woods, 2006; Milby et al., 1998; Werry, 1986c).

Most stereotyped movements that are not labeled self-stimulation or self-injury are referred to as tics. Tics that involve only the facial muscles and last only a short time are common; nearly one fourth of all children will at some time during their development display these tics, and it is best to ignore them. Tics involving the entire head, neck, and shoulders, however, typically require intervention. Tics may be vocal as well as motor; the individual may make a variety of noises or repeat words or word sounds, with or without accompanying motor tics.

Chronic motor tics that last more than a year and involve at least three muscle groups simultaneously are more serious than those involving fewer muscles or lasting a shorter time. There are a variety of tic disorders, but the most severe variety and the one on which most research has been done is Tourette's disorder or Tourette's syndrome (TS, Spencer, Biederman, Harding, Wilens, & Faraone, 1995). The fourth edition of the *Diagnostic and Statistical Manual of Mental Disorders* (American Psychiatric Association, 2000) defines TS as a disorder with onset before age 18 in which the person has both multiple motor and one or more verbal tics occurring many times a day (usually in clusters) nearly every day or intermittently for more than a year. TS occurs in about 4 or 5 individuals per 10,000, across diverse racial and ethnic groups, and about 1.5 to 3 times more often in males than in females.

In the 1990s, TS became a focus for much research on obsessive-compulsive and anxiety disorders. Because it has been so misunderstood until recently, TS has carried extraordinary social stigma. The symptoms of TS may be very mild and not readily apparent to the casual observer. However, a person with severe symptoms may find that others respond with fear, ridicule, or hostility to their bizarre behavior (e.g., twitching, grunting, shouting obscenities or words inappropriate to the circumstances). The diagnosis of TS in two high profile athletes (baseball player Jim Eisenreich and basketball player Mohmoud Abdul-Rauf, formerly Chris Jackson), the brilliant writing of neurologist Oliver Sacks for the popular press (see "A Surgeon's Life" in Sacks, 1995, the story of a surgeon and pilot with TS), and the work of the Tourette Syndrome Association have done much to dispel ignorance, discrimination, and cruelty shown toward children and adults with TS.

We now know that TS is a neurological disorder, although the cause and precisely what is wrong neurologically are not known. TS is a multifaceted problem with social and emotional as well as neurological features (Coffey, Miguel, Savage, & Rauch, 1994; Kerbeshian & Burd, 1994; Linet, 1995). It may have a genetic component. It can vary greatly in severity and nature of symptoms, and it is often a comorbid condition with a variety of other disorders, especially attention deficit–hyperactivity disorder (ADHD) and OCD. In fact, some researchers suggest that TS is a specific form of attentional or obsessive-compulsive disorder and that OCD in children with TS may become more severe with age (Bloch et al., 2006). Some symptoms of TS may involve ticlike ritualistic behavior (e.g., stereotyped touching or arrangement of objects, repetition of words or phrases). In some cases, the person with TS has difficulty inhibiting aggression, and TS can be mistaken for or comorbid with conduct disorder (Riddle, Hardin, Ort, Leckman, & Cohen, 1988). The symptoms of TS may become more severe under specific conditions, especially with the experience of anxiety, trauma, or social stress (Silva, Munoz, Barickman, & Friedhoff, 1995).

TS is becoming better understood as diagnosis becomes more accurate and research reveals more about its nature and treatment. The most effective treatments are cognitive-behavioral therapies and medications or a combination of the two (March, 1995; Walkup, 2002). Many individuals with TS do not like the side effects of neuroleptics and other medications that may be prescribed to attenuate their symptoms. Management of tics by other means, including allowing them to occur under many circumstances and educating others to understand and accept them, are often the preferred strategies (see the report of Kane in the accompanying case book).

Special educators are likely to encounter students with TS because it is often comorbid with other disorders and because misunderstanding of TS often leads to stigma and social rejection or isolation. Effective intervention often requires involvement of the family and school as well as the student with TS (see Albano et al., 2003; Milby et al., 1998; Riddle et al., 1988). A major aspect of the educator's role is understanding and communicating to others the nature of TS, ignoring the tics that cannot be controlled, and focusing on the student's capabilities.

Selective Mutism

Children who are extremely reluctant to speak, although they know how to converse normally, are said to exhibit *selective mutism* (SM): They choose to speak only to a certain individual or small groups of people and refuse to talk to all others. Other terms used to describe their problems include *elective mutism, speech inhibition, speech avoidance, speech phobia,* and *functional mutism.* These children present a puzzling behavior problem to teachers (Brigham & Cole, 1999; Dow, Sonies, Scheib, Moss, & Leonard, 1995; Hultquist, 1995; Rogers-Adkinson, 1999). Brigham and Cole (1999) noted that most children with SM are first identified by educators when they enter school, but "because SM is rare, it is unlikely that many individuals have much experience on which they can rely when working with children with SM. . . .Additionally, the resistance to treatment demonstrated by many children with SM can lead to feelings of ineptitude or anger on the part of the child's teacher" (p. 184).

Because the selectively mute youngster does not need to acquire normal speech but merely to learn to use speech under ordinary circumstances, remediation is often considerably easier than that of the mute or echolalic child. The selectively mute child is, at least to some degree, socially withdrawn, although he or she may be withdrawn only from adults or only from peers. Selective mutism may sometimes be a response to trauma or abuse (Jacobsen, 1995), but it appears to be a result of social anxiety in most cases, a specific fear of talking to certain individuals or groups of people (Bergman, Piacentini, & McCracken, 2002; Black & Uhde, 1995). The causes of selective mutism are apparently diverse, however, and many children who exhibit this behavior have multiple behavior problems and dysfunctional families (Brigham & Cole, 1999; Cunningham, Cataldo, Mallion, & Keyes, 1984; Hultquist, 1995). Nevertheless, parents may often assist in the assessment and treatment of selective mutism (Schill & Kratochwill, 1996). Psychopharmacological treatment may be an important adjunct of other interventions.

As with other fears, social learning principles have been the basis for the most successful approaches to treating selective mutism. Strategies involve alteration of the demands or conditions under which the child is expected to speak, desensitization to the fear of speaking, and reinforcement for gradual approximations of speaking freely to the person(s) in whose presence the child has been mute (see Beidel & Turner, 1998; Brigham & Cole, 1999).

Selective mutism is, as Brigham and Cole (1999) noted, poorly understood (even mysterious) and an extremely rare condition, but it can be an extraordinarily challenging problem for teachers. In some cases, the child simply starts talking more normally without treatment. Therefore, the first decision of concerned adults must be whether to implement intervention—whether the child's behavior is such a serious problem that intervention should be attempted. Evidence to date suggests that it is better to intervene than to wait for spontaneous resolution (Bergman et al., 2002; Pionck Stone, Kratochwill, Sladezcek, & Serlin, 2002). If intervention is initiated, then it is important for the teacher to work with other professionals, especially speech-language pathologists and those involved with the student's family. It is also important to implement a nonpunitive, behavioral approach to encouraging speech in the classroom and to realize that in many cases successful intervention requires long term treatment (Beidel & Turner, 1998; Dow et al., 1995; Harris, 1996; Hultquist, 1995).

EATING DISORDERS

Eating disorders receive much attention in the press because the nation's affluence makes it acceptable to waste food and because of the near obsession many people—particularly of high social status—have with slenderness (Siegel, 1998). Among eating disorders, anorexia nervosa (or simply *anorexia*), bulimia (sometimes called *bulimarexia* or *bulimia nervosa*), binge eating, and obesity garner the most attention (Macera & Mizes, 2006; Wilson, Becker, & Heffernan, 2003). Bulimia and anorexia are primarily, but not exclusively, problems of females, especially adolescent girls, and they appear to be more prevalent among White than among Black women (Robb & Dadson, 2002; Striegel-Moore et al., 2003). Medication is one possible treatment of such disorders (Kotler, Devlin, & Walsh, 2002; Roerig, Mitchell, Myers, & Glass, 2002).

Anorexia (literally, loss of appetite) is a misnomer, for those with the disorder do not report absence of hunger, and the problem is clearly a refusal to eat a proper diet. Individuals with anorexia are obsessively concerned with losing weight and extremely anxious about getting fat. They starve themselves down to an abnormally low weight, often exercising compulsively as well as severely restricting caloric intake. They endanger their health, sometimes dying of self-starvation. Anorexia occurs most often in females (by a ratio of about 10 to 1), usually in the early adolescent to young adult age range.

Bulimia involves binge eating followed by behavior designed to offset the food intake, such as self-induced vomiting, using laxatives or enemas, or extra exercise. People with bulimia often try to keep their eating binges and related behavior a secret. They often feel depressed and unable to control their eating habits.

Despite public fascination with anorexia and bulimia and the relatively high estimates of prevalence of these disorders among high school and college females, we have relatively little understanding of the causes or effective treatment, especially when the onset of these disorders is in childhood. Researchers now recognize that the problems are multidimensional and require multimodal treatment approaches. The cultural ideal of thinness may be a factor in precipitating some cases of eating disorders (Adams, Katz, Beauchamp, Cohen, & Zavis, 1993). Family conflicts about eating and difficulty in communicating with other family members are known to be associated with adolescents' maladaptive attitudes toward food and eating (Eme & Danielak, 1995; Mueller et al., 1995). However, genetic predisposition to eating problems is increasingly recognized by researchers (Mizes, 1995; Wilson et al., 2003). Behavioral analyses of causes and behavioral or cognitive-behavioral interventions have been encouraging in the short run, but long-term follow-up evaluations indicate the need for more comprehensive assessment and treatment approaches (Mizes, 1995). Effective intervention requires consideration of the eating behaviors themselves and the thoughts and feelings associated with anorexia and bulimia, plus the social environment in which the patterns have developed and are maintained.

Other eating disorders include pica (eating inedible substances such as paint, hair, cloth, or dirt), rumination (self-induced vomiting, which usually begins in infancy), highly exclusive food preferences, and obesity (Foreyt & Kondo, 1985; Johnson & Hinkle, 1993; Siegel, 1998; Werry, 1986c). These problems severely limit a child's social acceptability and endanger health.

Childhood and adolescent obesity is a growing problem in most Western cultures and carries significant health risks, usually results in a poor self-image, contributes to poor social relations and may be exacerbated by social relationships, and tends to persist into adulthood (Boodman, 1995; Christakis & Fowler, 2007; Johnson & Hinkle, 1993; Peterson, Reach, & Grabe, 2003; Siegel, 1998; Wilson et al., 2003). Obese children often pay a heavy price in social rejection or neglect. Although causes of obesity include genetic, physiological, and environmental factors, "the basic problem is a negative imbalance between caloric intake and energy expenditure, resulting in the storage of fat in adipose cells" (Spence, 1986, p. 447). Successful management of obesity therefore requires not only changing eating habits but also increasing physical activity (Johnson & Hinkle, 1993). Obesity has often been thought to be a result of the individual's learning undesirable eating patterns and poor nutritional habits, but socialization to accept obesity undoubtedly plays a critical role (Christakis & Fowler, 2007). However, the discovery in 1995 of a gene that controls obesity in mice spurred public perceptions that morbid obesity in humans is often caused by genetic factors (Weiss, 1995). It is important to remember that avoidance of obesity requires a combination of proper diet and exercise—a regimen harder for some than for others but possible for nearly everyone. José Caro, chairman of the Department of Medicine at Thomas Jefferson Medical College, is quoted as saying, "Obesity is a disease. . .but it is exacerbated by a social and cultural environment that encourages consumption while minimizing physical exertion" (Weiss, 1996, p. 11; see also Christakis & Fowler, 2007).

Special educators will often deal with students who have eating disorders. These disorders are not to be addressed by special educators alone, and teachers should not independently assume responsibility for eating problems. Students with anorexia and other eating disorders may display high levels of anxious or obsessive-compulsive behavior in the classroom. The role of special education in such disorders is to provide instruction and support for proper nutrition and exercise as needed and to work with other disciplines in managing students' food intake.

ELIMINATION DISORDERS

Attitudes toward toileting vary widely among cultures and within social groups. In Western culture, toilet training is considered very important and is generally begun at a young age. Although the extreme practice of beginning toilet training in the first few weeks of life is ill advised, behavioral research shows that most children can be taught by 16 or 18 months (see O'Leary & Wilson, 1975). When children continue to wet or soil themselves after the age of 5 or 6, they are considered to have a problem that demands intervention. *Enuresis* may be either diurnal (wetting during waking hours) or nocturnal (bed-wetting). About twice as many boys as girls are enuretic, and 2% or 3% of children are enuretic at age 14. At the time they begin first grade, approximately 13% to 20% of children are enuretic. *Encopresis,* or soiling, usually occurs during the day and is a rarer problem than is enuresis.

Toilet training is usually a gradual process, and stress and illness have an effect on bowel and bladder control. Thus, the younger the child and the more stressful the circumstances, the more one can expect accidents to occur. Enuresis and encopresis are not matters of infrequent accidents; the child has a chronic problem, after the age at which children are expected to be continent of urine and feces, in retaining urine or feces and releasing it only in the toilet (Peterson et al., 2003; Siegel, 1992, 1998).

Psychodynamic ideas attribute enuresis and encopresis to underlying emotional conflicts, usually conflicts involving the family. Although these psychodynamic ideas are not supported by reliable evidence, family factors obviously play an important role if the family is inconsistent or unreasonable in toilet training. At the least, wetting and soiling can sour parent–child relationships regardless of the cause of the problem. Not many parents can face these problems with complete equanimity, and rare is the child who is completely unaffected by adults' reactions to misplaced excrement. Thus, one must recognize that negative feelings about the problem often run high in families of children with elimination disorders. Treatment must be planned to avoid further parental anger and abuse of the child.

Enuresis is seldom the child's only problem; the child with enuresis often has other difficulties—perhaps stealing, overeating, or underachievement (Siegel, 1998; Vivian, Fischel, & Liebert, 1986). Nearly all children with encopresis have multiple problems, often of a severe nature. Diurnal enuresis and encopresis at school are intolerable problems for teachers and result in peer rejection (Walker & Rankin, 1983). Understandably, most youngsters with elimination disorders have low self-esteem.

In a few cases, elimination disorders have physiological causes that can be corrected by surgery or medication, but the vast majority of cases have no known anatomical defect, and medication is not particularly helpful. These disorders are in the vast majority of cases a matter of failure to learn how to control the bladder or bowels, and the effective methods of treating them involve habit training or practice. Intervention may thus involve training the child in urine retention, rapid awakening, and practice in toileting as well as reward for appropriate toileting or mild punishment for wetting. For many children, a urine alarm system in the bed or pants has successfully eliminated enuresis (Mountjoy, Ruben, & Bradford, 1984; Siegel, 1998; Taylor & Turner, 1975).

Although many approaches to enuresis have been tried and many behavioral techniques have been highly successful, no single approach has been successful for every child, and combinations of techniques are often used. Encopresis is sometimes treated by training children in biofeedback so that they learn to control their sphincters more deliberately. Those who soil themselves may be required to clean themselves rather than receive solicitous attention and cleaning from an adult. Selecting a successful technique for enuresis or encopresis depends on careful assessment of the individual case (Siegel, 1992).

Special educators who work with students having more severe disorders are particularly likely to encounter those who have elimination disorders. These disorders can be extremely troublesome in school, making students unwelcome to adults and peers alike and becoming the central issue in behavior management. Special educators need to work with professionals from other disciplines, particularly psychology and social work, to address the problems created by elimination disorders in the classroom.

SEXUAL PROBLEMS

Promiscuous sexual conduct is often thought to connote moral misjudgment, and promiscuity is often involved in delinquency. Early sexual intercourse and teenage pregnancy are serious problems for teenagers and their children, as discussed in section 15. Dating and related heterosexual relationships are of great concern to teens and their adult caretakers. Sexual relationships and sexual behavior can be sources of enormous anxiety and obsessive-compulsive behavior for children and teens. Scarcely anyone condones exhibitionism, sadomasochism, incest, prostitution, fetishism, and sexual relations involving children; and these behaviors usually carry serious social penalties. American social mores do not condone all sex practices—some sexual behavior is clearly taboo, and incest is taboo in nearly every society (see Becker & Bonner, 1998; Wilson, 1998). However, most people now recognize the wide variety of normal sexual expression that is a matter of preference or biological determination. Graziano and Dorta (1995) noted types of behavior that bring children and youth to therapy:

> Intense, excessive, and inappropriate masturbation (e.g., public), cross-sex dressing and other behavior, sexual promiscuity in young adolescents, homosexuality, and paraphilia (bizarre/perverted sexual behavior) are examples of sex-related child/youth problems treated in behavior therapy. Unlike most of the others listed, homosexuality in children is defined as a problem based largely on parents' personal values and whether the child or adolescent feels the homosexual urges are threatening. (pp. 174–175)

Autoerotic activity is not inherently maladaptive, although it is viewed as undesirable or prohibited by some religious groups. When carried to excess or done publicly, sexual self-stimulation is considered disordered behavior by nearly everyone. Although many or most teachers have observed children masturbating publicly, little research has been done on the problem of children's public masturbation, perhaps because masturbation has for so long been looked upon as evil (Hare, 1962; Stribling, 1842) and is still condemned by some religions, as is homosexuality.

Classifying gender-related behavior of any kind as a disorder raises serious questions of cultural bias and discrimination. The consensus is that some forms of sexual expression are deviant and should be prevented—incest, sexual sadism or masochism, pedophilia, and public masturbation, for example. Today, however, many people feel there is nothing deviant about other sex-related behaviors, such as preference for clothing styles, stereotypical masculine or feminine mannerisms, and homosexuality. Clothing styles and accepted sex roles have changed dramatically since about 1970. *Androgyny* (having the characteristics of both sexes) is apparent in many fashions and in role models. Problems related to sexual preference may be seen as primarily a matter of cultural or personal intolerance, so we must be sensitive to the possibility of cultural and personal bias in judging sex-related behavior, just as we must be aware of personal biases toward racial and ethnic identity. In children, *gender identity disorder* may be manifested by an insistent desire to be the opposite sex, strong preference for or insistence on dressing like the other sex or adopting the opposite sex role, strong preference for playmates of the other sex, and persistent wishes to have the physical features of the opposite sex. If such characteristics cause significant distress or impairment of social functioning, then they may be considered a disorder (see American Psychiatric Association, 2000; Gordon & Schroeder, 1995; Zucker & Bradley, 1995).

Sexual behavior that involves intimidation, harassment, and other forms of aggression are, as noted in prior sections, more accurately associated with conduct disorder and delinquency. However, many individuals who exhibit sexual aggression may experience high levels of anxiety as a comorbid condition (Araji, 1997).

Special educators, especially those who deal with adolescents, are certain to be confronted by students' sexual behavior and knowledge (or lack of it) that are of great concern. Maintaining an open mind about sexual preferences and alternative modes of sexual expression is important; so is an understanding of pathological behavior and the necessity of addressing it. Teachers must be ready to work with psychologists, psychiatrists, social workers, and other professionals in identifying and managing deviant sexual behavior (see Soutter, 1996).

SOCIAL ISOLATION AND INEPTITUDE

Social isolation may result from excessive behavior, such as hyperactivity or aggression, that drives others away, or it may result from deficiencies in behavior, such as lack of social initiative (see Farmer, 2000; McClelland & Scalzo, 2006; McFadyen-Ketchum & Dodge, 1998; Rubin, Burgess, Kennedy, & Stewart, 2003). Some socially isolated youngsters lack social approach skills, such as looking at, initiating conversation with, asking to play with, and appropriately touching their peers or adults. Usually, they also lack responsiveness to others' initiations of social contact. Others may be neglected by their peers for reasons that are not well understood. However, rejected, socially isolated children do not engage in the *social reciprocity* (exchange of mutual and equitable reinforcement between pairs of individuals) that is characteristic of normal social development. The isolated or neglected student usually lacks specific social skills for making and keeping friends and may be rejected by peers.

Social isolation is not an all-or-nothing problem. All children and youth sometimes exhibit withdrawn behavior and are socially inept. This behavior may occur with any degree of severity, ranging along a continuum from a normal social reticence in new situations to the profound isolation of psychosis. In nearly any classroom, from preschool through adulthood, however, some individuals are distinguished by their lack of social interaction. Their social isolation is often accompanied by immature or inadequate behavior that makes them targets of ridicule or taunts. They are friendless loners who are apparently unable to avail themselves of the joy and satisfaction of social reciprocity. Unless their behavior and that of their peers can be changed, they are likely to remain isolated from close and frequent human contact and the attendant developmental advantages afforded by social interaction. Their prognosis, then, is not good without intensive intervention (McEvoy & Odom, 1987).

Causal Factors and Prevention

Social learning theory predicts that some children, particularly those who have not been taught appropriate social interaction skills and those who have been punished for attempts at social interaction, will be withdrawn. A mildly or moderately withdrawn youngster is likely to be anxious and have a low self-concept, but the conclusion that anxiety and low self-concept cause withdrawal and social isolation is not justifiable. It is more plausible that anxiety and low self-concept result from the child's lack of social competence.

Parental overrestrictiveness or social incompetence, lack of opportunity for social learning, and early rebuffs in social interaction with peers may contribute to a child's learning to play in isolation from others and to avoid social contact. Parents who are socially obtuse are likely to have children whose social skills are not well developed, probably because socially awkward parents provide models of undesirable behavior and are unable to teach their children the skills that will help them become socially attractive (Dadds, 2002; Putallaz & Heflin, 1990). Aversive social experiences, including abuse by parents or siblings, may indeed produce anxious children who have little self-confidence and evaluate themselves negatively. Anxiety and self-derogation may thereafter contribute to reticence in social situations and help to perpetuate social incompetence. Nevertheless, the child's temperamental characteristics, in combination with early socialization experiences and the nature of the current social environment, probably account for the development of social isolation (Keogh, 2003; Kochanska, 1995). The social learning view of isolate behavior, which focuses on the factors of reinforcement, punishment, and imitation, carries direct implications for intervention and suggests ways in which to remediate isolation by teaching social skills. Effective prevention of social isolation, however, involves more than teaching youngsters how to approach and respond to others; it requires arranging a social environment that is conducive to positive interactions.

Assessment

The definition of *social isolation* includes active rejection by peers or neglect of peers. Measurement of rejection and acceptance frequently includes use of a questionnaire or sociometric game that asks youngsters to choose or nominate classmates for various roles. Students may be asked to indicate which of their peers they would most like to play, sit, or work with, or invite to a party, and with whom they would least like to interact. The results of this procedure are then analyzed to see which individuals have high social status in the group (to whom many peers are attracted), those who are isolates (not chosen as playmates or workmates by anyone), and those who are rejected (with whom peers want to avoid social contact). More precise measurement of social interaction may be obtained by direct daily observation and recording of behavior. We can thus define *social isolates* as children who have a markedly lower number of social interactions than do their peers.

Sociometric status and direct measurement of social interactions, although both are valuable in assessment, do not necessarily reveal what causes a youngster to experience social isolation. A student could, for example, have a relatively high rate of positive social interaction and still be a relative social isolate; his or her interactions might involve relatively few peers and be characterized by a superficial or artificial quality (Hundert, 1995; Walker, Ramsey, & Gresham, 2004). Consequently, assessment should also include teacher ratings and self-reports. Thus, adequate measurement of social skills or social isolation requires attention to the rate of interactive behaviors, qualitative aspects of social interaction, and children's perceptions of social status (see Cartledge & Milburn, 1995).

As social skills research becomes more sophisticated, the nuances of appropriate social interaction become more difficult to capture. Much of our knowledge about the nature of children's social skills is superficial. Children's social intentions (*why* as well as *what* they do) may be an important area to research; we may need to assess their pragmatic reasons for interacting with peers in specified ways to fully understand social isolation and social acceptance.

Intervention and Education

One approach to the problem of withdrawal is to try to improve the youngster's self-concept, on the assumption that this will result in a tendency to engage more often in social interactions. We can encourage children to express their feelings about their behavior and social relationships in play therapy or in therapeutic conversations with a warm, accepting adult. As they come to feel accepted and able to express their feelings openly, their self-concepts will presumably become more positive. The incidence of positive social interactions should then increase as well. Attempts to remediate social isolation without teaching specific social skills or manipulating the social environment are usually ineffectual, however. Few data show that self-concept can be improved without first improving behavior. If youngsters' appraisals of their own behavior are unrealistic, then bringing self-perceptions into line with reality is, to be sure, a worthy goal. If youngsters are indeed socially isolated, then attempting to convince them of their social adequacy without first helping them learn the skills for social reciprocity may be misleading. After their behavior has been improved, however, there is a foundation for improving self-image.

Arranging appropriate environmental conditions helps teach socially isolated youngsters to reciprocate positive behavior with their peers. Situations that are conducive to social interaction contain toys or equipment that promote social play and bring the isolated youngster into proximity with others who have social interaction skills or who require social interaction from the target child. Specific intervention strategies based on social learning principles include these:

- Reinforcing social interaction (perhaps with praise, points, or tokens)
- Providing peer models of social interaction
- Providing training (models, instruction, rehearsal, and feedback) in specific social skills
- Enlisting peer confederates to initiate social interactions and reinforce appropriate social responses.

Of course, all four strategies may be used together, and experimental research shows the effectiveness of these procedures in modifying certain behaviors (Walker, Schwarz, Nippold, Irvin, & Noell, 1994). Social learning strategies for defining, measuring, and changing disabled youngsters' deficient social behavior show great promise. Nevertheless, current social skills training methods do not adequately address the problems of producing behavioral changes that actually make disabled children and youth more socially acceptable, that generalize across a variety of social situations, and that are maintained after intervention is terminated. As Strain, Odom, and McConnell (1984) noted, social skills involve *reciprocity*—an exchange of behavior between two people. Interventions that focus exclusively on changing the isolated individual's behavior miss that vital aspect of social adaptation: social interaction. The goal of intervention must be to help the socially isolated individual become enmeshed or entrapped in positive, reciprocal, self-perpetuating social exchanges, which can be done only by carefully choosing the target skills. One must select target skills with these questions in mind:

- Are the particular social behaviors likely to be maintained after intervention is terminated?
- Are the skills likely to generalize across different settings (as in different areas of the school and during different types of activities)?
- Do the target skills relate to peers' social behavior so that peer behavior prompts and reinforces performance of the skill (that is, are the skills part of naturally occurring, positive social interactions)?

If these questions generate affirmative answers, then social skills training is more likely to last (McConnell, 1987).

Some children and youth are not social isolates but still do not fit in well with their peers and are hampered by inadequate social sensitivity or ineptness in delicate social situations. Children whose previous social experience is at odds with the majority of their peers, adolescents making their first approaches to members of the opposite sex, and adolescents interviewing for their first jobs are often quite tactless or unskilled in the social graces demanded for acceptance. Some individuals have irritating personal habits that detract from social adequacy. The results of social ineptitude may be negative self-image, anxiety, and withdrawal.

One can often eliminate or avoid bungling social behaviors by teaching important social cues and appropriate responses. Offering group and individual counseling, showing the youngster videotaped replays of his or her own behavior, modeling appropriate behavior, and providing guided practice (or some combination of these strategies) have been used to teach social skills (see Blake, Wang, Cartledge, & Gardner, 2000; Gresham, 2000; Kavale, Mathur, & Mostert, 2004). A social learning view of the origin and remediation of interpersonal ineptness is clearly a functional view for the special educator, for it implies that direct instruction is most effective.

The design of intervention strategies depends partly on the age of the student and the nature of the student's relationship to peers. Older students with a long history of socialization difficulties and victimization by peers may need a safe haven, such as a special school or class, in which to learn new skills (as illustrated by the case of Pauline in the accompanying case book).

SUMMARY

Grouping anxiety and related disorders for discussion is problematic because the disorders are loosely interrelated. Subcategories of anxiety disorders are not well defined, and anxiety disorders are frequently comorbid with a variety of other disorders.

Anxiety—uneasiness, fears, and worries—is part of normal development. However, extreme anxiety and fears (phobias) can be seriously debilitating. Anxiety disorders are generally more transient and are associated with lower risk for adulthood psychiatric disorder than are behaviors related to externalizing disorders. Excessive anxiety may characterize 2% to 5% of the child population and 20% to 30% of youngsters referred to clinics for behavior problems. Boys and girls are affected about equally. Anxiety disorders appear to have both social and biological causes and to be most amenable to social learning approaches to intervention, sometimes combined with medication.

Anxiety appears to play a significant role in a variety of related disorders. Obsessive-compulsive disorder involves ritualistic thinking or behavior intended to ward off feared events. It may take many forms and is potentially a serious detriment to school attendance and performance. Posttraumatic stress disorder is now recognized as a disorder of children and adolescents as well as adults. The anxiety and other problems associated with PTSD can seriously impede students' progress in school. Stereotyped movement disorders include Tourette's syndrome, a disorder involving multiple motor and vocal tics and now recognized as a neurological problem. TS is often comorbid with other disorders and appears to be particularly closely associated with anxiety, attention disorders, and obsessive-compulsive disorders. *Selective mutism* is extreme, persistent anxiety about speaking in the presence of certain individuals. Intervention is typically designed to reduce anxiety in situations demanding speech.

Eating disorders include anorexia, bulimia, and compulsive overeating, which often involve anxiety about food, eating, and body weight. Elimination disorders include enuresis and encopresis. These disorders are extremely problematic in school settings and must be resolved if children are to develop normal peer relations. Sexual problems are difficult to define because of societal attitudes toward sexual behavior. However, some types of sexual behavior, such as public masturbation, incest, and masochism, are clearly taboo.

Socially isolated children and youth do not have the social approach and response skills necessary to develop reciprocally reinforcing relationships. They may lack these skills because of inappropriate models of social behavior at home, inadequate instruction or opportunity to practice social skills, or other circumstances that inhibit social development. Intervention and prevention call for teaching social skills that are assumed important for social development, but there is a great deal of controversy concerning which are the most appropriate skills and the most effective instructional methods. In general, social skills training involves modeling, rehearsal, guided practice, and feedback, either for individual students or for groups. Peer-mediated interventions that alter both the socially isolated youngster's behaviors and those of peers in naturally occurring interactions may be the most effective strategies.

PERSONAL REFLECTIONS

Anxiety and Related Disorders

Anastacio T. Vazquez, Jr., M.Ed., is an intervention specialist at Shaker Heights High School in Shaker Heights, Ohio. Mr. Vazquez teaches students in grades 9 to 12 who have cross-catagorical special education needs. He was formerly a behavior specialist and classroom teacher at the Positive Education Program (PEP) in Cleveland, Ohio, which is a day treatment program for students with behavioral, cognitive, and emotional disorders.

Describe the school in which you work and your professional role in the school.

The Shaker Heights school district is consistently ranked as one of the best school districts in the nation. The district is an inner-ring suburb that is culturally and socioeconomically diverse. The school's population is balanced racially and economically. Shaker Heights High School enrolls about 1,800 students in grades 9 through 12. About 48% of the students are Caucasian, and about 52% are of minority ethnicity.

Think of a particular student in your school who exhibits severe anxiety. How does the student's behavior demonstrate anxiety?

John comes from an upper middle-class, intact family. His parents have advanced degrees and both are employed, and he has two younger siblings. The behaviors that prompted John's referral for evaluation for possible special education services included severe anxiety and depression when he entered the high school as a freshman. John is a tall, good-looking young adult who always greets others with a smile. John becomes extremely anxious, however, when he has to go to physical education class. He will initially attempt to get out of P.E. class by claiming he needs to go to the school nurse, to speak with his counselor, or to meet with his assistant principal. He will also often resort to causing a commotion in order to be removed from class when he feels the need to take a break, and he will typically make efforts to extend the time he is out of class so that he misses the entire P.E. period. John perceives that going to P.E. will put him in danger of being physically or verbally assaulted by someone. It is very difficult to figure out the reason for this anxiety, but the level of stress that it causes him is very obvious. He has been observed to cry or have tantrums if he is requested simply to sit out and watch the class from the bleachers. Other demonstrated behaviors include claims of physical pain in various parts of his body, and he often states that he is extremely dizzy and that he cannot stand due to having "weak legs." These behaviors become more intense and frequent, and this is later defined as panic attacks.

What strategies have you found most helpful in working with John?

A number of strategies have been used successfully with John, including many typical behavioral or cognitive-behavioral strategies for dealing with challenging behavior. Discussing his feelings and thoughts, fears and perceptions concerning not wanting to participate in P.E. class seemed to have positive effects at times. All members of John's IEP team provided positive reassurance and emotional support when he displayed the observed behavior. We would role-play and model positive and appropriate social skills to help him learn strategies for dealing with "possible situations" that could come up in P.E. class. In addition to teaching John strategies to avoid or minimize the occurrence of anxiety, we as staff had to learn how to deal with John during anxiety attacks. During any periods of extreme anxiety, staff would remain calm and attempt to calm him with consistent, clear, and understandable directions. We would also take him to a "safe area" (usually an area near an outside door to provide fresh air). He perceived this as a safe and quiet environment where he was able to relax and release his anxiety appropriately and safely, under staff supervision.

Following incidents of extreme anxiety, we would encourage John to discuss and record his feelings and what he did that helped him calm down, using a portable tape recorder. This was very helpful because it gave him a reference point on how to deal with his anxiety issues in the future.

What are your biggest concerns about John's future?

Some of the main concerns I have are that I don't think that his anxiety issues will ever disappear. He may with consisent therapy learn to handle the disability better and to identify triggers before severe anxiety attacks occur, but sadly his anxiety may limit his ability to function fully and successfully as an adult. He will always be liked by his peers, but I fear that his personal strengths will be ignored or overlooked by those who focus more on his anxiety and related behaviors. Because of the anxiety, I fear that he will struggle to maintain interpersonal relationships and his weaknesses in social skills may alienate him from others socially.

Mr. Vazquez interviews John

Mr. V: John, tell me about your feelings about your high school.

J: I don't really like the school because it is so large but I do like my friends and teachers. . .most of them. I also do enjoy being able to eat lunch in the classroom instead of the cafeteria. Too many people, that I don't know.

Mr. V: What are some of the things that you would like to change about the school?

J: I would like to be able to only have one class for everything. I mean I would like to stay in one area and not have to worry about if something is going to happen.

Mr. V: Have you always felt like "something" was going to happen to you that was bad before you came to the high school?

J: I really don't think that wanting to know what is going to happen is a problem. I don't feel that I ever had a problem before I came to the high school. No one told me about this problem.

Mr. V: So you don't feel like you have a problem?

J: I think sometimes I am just overreacting. My parents and you teachers feel like I have a problem.

QUESTIONS FOR FURTHER REFLECTION

1. What indications would lead you to believe that a student of yours is anxious to the point of having an emotional or behavioral disorder?
2. Given your information to this point, what possible changes in behavior might you anticipate if a student who is taking medication for an anxiety-related disorder discontinues taking it?
3. If a student of yours were socially inept, how would you approach this student (what would you try to accomplish, and what would you say to him or her)?

SECTION 17
DEPRESSION AND SUICIDAL BEHAVIOR

As you read this section, keep these guiding questions in mind:

- How does the federal definition of "emotionally disturbed" include internalizing disorders and depression?

- How do comorbidity and the episodic nature of mood disorders complicate the assessment of depression?

- What are the major theories or models of depression that guide intervention?

- What is the relationship between age, gender, ethnicity, and suicide rates?

- How can teachers help reduce suicide risk, and how should they manage students following a suicide threat or attempt?

One of the five distinguishing characteristics of children defined in federal regula-tions as having serious emotional disturbance is "a general, pervasive mood of unhappiness or depression". Just which youngsters federal officials meant to identify by this characteristic is not clear (Cullinan, 2004; Duncan, Forness, & Hartsough, 1995; Forness, 1988b; Forness & Kavale, 1997). A general, pervasive mood of unhappiness or depression is more narrow and restrictive than the broadband behavioral dimen-sion of *internalizing,* yet it does not correspond exactly with narrower dimensions, such as social withdrawal (see section 16). Neither is it consistent with the clinical cri-teria for a major depressive episode but approximates a less-severe condition referred to by clinicians as *dysthymia.* However, depressed mood might be consid-ered the prototypical internalizing disorder (Reynolds, 1992, 2006). A reasonable con-clusion is that the federal definition of "emotionally disturbed" should be interpreted to include a wide range of internalizing disorders such as anxiety-withdrawal and clin-ical depression.

Depression has been relatively neglected in special education research, yet its close relationship to a variety of other disorders and to academic and social difficul-ties is now clear. It is recognized as an important disorder of childhood and adoles-cence that increases in prevalence with age, often coexists with other disorders, and is associated with long-term risks of mental illness and suicide (Carr, 2002; Geller & DelBello, 2003; Kaslow, Morris, & Rehm, 1998; Kazdin & Marciano, 1998; Shaffer & Waslick, 2002; Spirito & Overholser, 2003). The relationship between depression and suicidal behavior—a concern of all educators but especially those who work with psy-chologically disturbed students—makes these important related topics.

DEPRESSION

Definition and Prevalence

Childhood depression has been a controversial topic for several decades. Traditional psychoanalytic theory suggests that depression cannot occur in childhood because psychological self-representation is not sufficiently developed. Some scholars suggest that children's depression is masked by other symptoms—expressed indirectly through symptoms such as enuresis, temper tantrums, hyperactivity, learning disabil-ities, truancy, and so on. However, most researchers now agree that depression in childhood parallels adult depression in many ways, but the specific types of behavior the depressed person exhibits will be developmentally age appropriate (Kaslow et al., 1998; Kazdin & Marciano, 1998; Stark, Ostrander, Kurowski, Swearer, & Bowen, 1995). Both children and adults can thus be characterized by depressed mood and loss of interest in productive activity, but adults may develop problems around work and marriage, whereas children may have academic problems and exhibit a variety of inappropriate conduct such as aggression, stealing, social withdrawal, and so forth.

The assumption that depression in childhood is similar to depression in adult-hood is evident in the fourth edition of the *Diagnostic and Statistical Manual of Mental Disorders* (*DSM–IV;* American Psychiatric Association, 2000). Depression is not listed among the disorders that are usually first diagnosed in infancy, childhood, or adolescence, but special notes on depression in children are included under the section on adults' mood disorders. To some extent, however, the assumption that depression is the same phenomenon in children and adults may be misleading. We must remember that children are not merely scaled-down versions of adults, that childhood depression may be accompanied by other disorders (attention deficit–hyperactivity disorder, conduct disorder, anxiety disorders, learning disabilities, school failure, and so on), and that children's limited experience and cognitive capacity may give them perceptions of depression that differ from adults'.

Childhood depression was at one time looked on as just a normal part of human development, an idea we now realize is erroneous. After the abnormality of childhood depression had been recognized, it was seen by some as the underlying problem behind all other childhood disorders, another view that clearly is not tenable. If aggression, hyperactivity, noncompliance, learning disabilities, school failure, and other problems of nearly any sort are all attributed to underlying depression in the absence of core features of depressed behavior (depressed mood, loss of interest in most or all normal activities), then depression becomes meaningless as a concept and diagnostic category. A more defensible perspective is that childhood depression is a serious disorder in its own right that may or may not be accompanied by other maladaptive behavior or be comorbid with other disorders (Hammen & Rudolph, 2003; Seeley, Rohde, Lewinsohn, & Clarke, 2002; Waslick, Kandel, & Kakouros, 2002).

Depression is part of a larger category of *mood disorders* delineated in the *DSM–IV*. One's mood may be elevated or depressed, and mood disorders may involve different levels of severity of symptoms in both directions (or toward both poles). Depressed mood is characterized by *dysphoria,* feelings of unhappiness or unwellness not consistent with one's circumstances. In children and adolescents, dysphoria may be shown as irritability as well as by unhappiness. Elevated mood is characterized by the opposite—*euphoria,* a feeling of extraordinary and often unrealistic happiness or wellness. Dysphoric mood or irritability that lasts for a protracted period of time (a year or more for children and adolescents) but does not reach an intense level is called *dysthymia*. Euphoria and frenetic activity are known as *mania*.

Some mood disorders are *unipolar,* such as depressive disorder in which mood varies between normal and extreme dysphoria (depression) or normal and extreme euphoria (mania). Others are *bipolar,* in which mood swings from one extreme to the other (Geller & DelBello, 2003). (*Bipolar* has largely replaced the earlier terminology, *manic-depressive*.) Whether children with bipolar disorder are typically appropriately diagnosed remains quite controversial (Groopman, 2007).

Although the *DSM–IV* sets out detailed diagnostic criteria for the clinical diagnosis of various mood disorders in adults and makes notes regarding diagnosis in children and adolescents, considerable uncertainty remains about just how these criteria should apply to children and adolescents. The same general characteristics apply to adults and children, but the exact characterization of these disorders in children awaits much more research. Generally speaking, the symptoms one looks for in depression and related mood disorders in children and adolescents include the following:

- Anhedonia (inability to experience pleasure in all or nearly all activities)
- Depressed mood or general irritability

- Disturbance of appetite and significant weight gain or loss
- Disturbance of sleep (insomnia or hypersomnia)
- Psychomotor agitation or retardation
- Loss of energy, feelings of fatigue
- Feelings of worthlessness, self-reproach, excessive or inappropriate guilt, or hopelessness
- Diminished ability to think or concentrate; indecisiveness
- Ideas of suicide, suicide threats or attempts, recurrent thoughts of death.

These symptoms indicate depression only if several are exhibited over a protracted period of time and if they are not temporary, reasonable responses to life circumstances (e.g., as a consequence of a death in the family, we would expect several symptoms associated with depression during a period of grieving; see the case of Bryan in the accompanying case book for an example of childhood depression).

Depression and other mood disorders tend to be episodic and of long duration. People tend to have repeated bouts with depression and related disorders, and those who have a major episode are at high risk for more. Children and adolescents with long-standing depression (2 years or longer) have been found to have more significant impairments, greater anxiety, and lower self-esteem and to show more acting-out behavior (Dubois, Felner, Bartels, & Silverman, 1995). Depressive behavior may result in peer rejection, particularly if it is exhibited under conditions of low stress and there is no apparent reason for depressive behavior (Little & Garber, 1995).

Depression affects a substantial percentage of children and adolescents, and many young people who are depressed remain untreated for the disorder (Kazdin & Marciano, 1998; Seeley, Rohde, Lewinsohn, & Clarke, 2002). In prepubescent children, the prevalence of these disorders is about the same in boys and girls, with prepubescent boys being perhaps even slightly more likely than girls the same age to be depressed. By age 15, however, girls are twice as likely as boys to be depressed, and this high female–male ratio of about 2 to 1 remains constant for the next 35 to 40 years (Seeley et al., 2002; Stark et al., 1995). Although there is still considerable uncertainty about the definition and diagnosis of many mood disorders, bipolar disorder is increasingly diagnosed in adolescents with major mental health problems and recognized as a topic needing research. Also, the comorbidity of depressive disorders with other disorders, particularly conduct disorder and attention deficit–hyperactivity disorder, is increasingly recognized (Kazdin & Marciano, 1998; Papolos, 2003; Seeley et al., 2002). Depression has also been found to affect some children diagnosed with autism or other forms of pervasive developmental disorder (DeJong & Frazier, 2003; Ghaziuddin & Greden, 1998).

Assessment

The diagnosis of depression and other mood disorders in children and adolescents is generally left to psychologists or psychiatrists. However, educators can play a key role in aiding the assessment of these disorders (Cullinan, 2004). Competent assessment requires a multimodal approach in which several sources of information are tapped: self-reports, parental reports, peer nominations, observation, and clinical interviews.

A substantial number of devices are available for assessing depression, including rating scales and structured interviews (Kaslow et al., 1998; Merrell, 1994; Reynolds, 2006). However, the most important contribution of teachers to assessment may be careful observation of students' behavior that may reflect depression.

The types of behavior indicating possible depression include four categories of problems: affective, cognitive, motivational, and physiological. We may expect the depressed student to show depressed affect—to act unusually sad, lonely, and apathetic. Cognitive characteristics may include negative comments about oneself that indicate low self-esteem, excessive guilt, and pessimism. Depressed students often avoid demanding tasks and social experiences, show little interest in normal activities, and seem not to be motivated by ordinary or special consequences. Finally, depressed students often have physical complaints of fatigue or illness or problems with sleeping or eating. If a student exhibits such characteristics frequently for a period of weeks, the teacher should consider the possibility that the student is suffering from a mood disorder and refer him or her for evaluation. However, it is important not to overlook the possibility that other behaviors, such as general irritability or acting out, are also sometimes signs of depression, especially in children and adolescents. Difficulty in expressing anger appropriately is one characteristic associated with depression (Kashani, Dahlmeier, Borduin, Soltys, & Reid, 1995), so a student's behavior might be mistakenly thought to reflect an externalizing disorder.

Comorbidity of depression with other disorders sometimes makes assessment particularly difficult, as does the episodic nature of mood disorders and the fact that an individual can have more than one mood disorder. If the student exhibits conduct disorder or attention deficit–hyperactivity disorder, for example, it may be easy to overlook indications of depression. When an individual is recovering a more normal mood after a depressive episode, it is easy to assume that the depression was not serious or that the risk of another episode is nil. If the student has a dysthymic disorder but is going through a major depressive episode, the low-grade depression may be misinterpreted as normal.

CAUSAL FACTORS, RELATIONSHIP TO OTHER DISORDERS, AND PREVENTION

In most cases, we do not know exactly what causes depression. Some cases are evidently *endogenous* (a response to unknown genetic, biochemical, or other biological factors); other cases are apparently *reactive* (a response to environmental events, such as death of a loved one or academic failure). Predictably, child abuse, parental psychopathology, and family conflict and disorganization are frequently linked to children's depression. Research provides some suggestion that childhood depression and adult religiosity may be related (Miller, Weissman, Gur, & Greenwald, 2002).

Evidence is accumulating that there is a significant correlation between parents' depression and a variety of problems in their children, including depression (see Beardslee, Versage, Van de Velde, Swatling, & Hoke, 2002; Joiner & Coyne, 1999; Kaslow et al., 1998; Kazdin & Marciano, 1998; Ohannessian et al., 2005; Seeley et al.,

2002). Despite this evidence, it would be erroneous to conclude that all children of depressed mothers develop serious psychopathology. In a study of the psychosocial outcomes for children of mothers with depression or bipolar disorder, although there was a general trend for the parents' grown children to have received a psychiatric diagnosis and to have accessed mental health services, significant variability was observed in the adult outcomes these children experienced (Mowbray & Mowbray, 2006). This relationship undoubtedly reflects genetic influences on behavior. However, the fact that depression runs in families may reflect family interactions as well. Depressed parents may provide models of depressed behavior (which their children imitate), reinforce depressive behaviors in their children, or create a home environment that is conducive to depression (by setting unreasonable expectations, providing few rewards for achievement or initiative, emphasizing punishment, or providing noncontingent rewards and punishments). Depressed mothers are known to lack parenting skills, which could account for at least some of their children's behavioral and affective problems. Cummings and Davies (1999) noted: "On the one hand, in comparison to nondepressed parents, depressed parents are more inconsistent, lax, and generally ineffective in child management and discipline. On the other hand, when they are not yielding to the child's demands, they are more likely to engage in direct, forceful control strategies and are less likely to end disagreements in compromise" (p. 307).

Educators are in a particularly good position to identify depression and should give special attention to the ways in which a student's depression may affect and be affected by school performance (Seeley et al., 2002). Young children who are depressed engage in less play and exhibit more undirected activity than do typical children (Lous, de Wit, De Bruyn, & Riksen-Walraven, 2002). Depression appears to be associated with lowered performance on some cognitive tasks, lowered self-esteem, lowered social competence, deficits in self-control, and a depressive attributional style in which children tend to believe that bad outcomes are a result of their own unmodifiable and global inadequacies. There is an inverse relationship between depressive symptoms and problem-solving abilities: Better problem solvers tend to show fewer depressive symptoms (Goodman, Gravitt, & Kaslow, 1995), and depression appears to be related to poor academic self-image (Masi et al., 2000).

These findings suggest that school failure and depression may be reciprocal causal factors: depression makes the student less competent and less confident, both academically and socially; failing academically and socially makes the student feel and act more depressed and reinforces the attribution of failure to unalterable personal characteristics (Patterson & Capaldi, 1990). Depression and failure may thus become a vicious cycle that is hard to break. This cycle may often be a part of conduct disorder and, to a lesser extent, learning disabilities. Yet teachers and other school personnel have been slow to recognize the signs of depression and even slower to provide intervention. Kazdin and Marciano (1998) noted in discussion of the underidentification of depression:

> In school settings, for example, it is likely that teachers may not view withdrawal and moodiness as possible signs of serious dysfunction. Also, because depression is so often comorbid with externalizing disorders (e.g., Conduct Disorder, Substance

Abuse), it is likely to be overshadowed in the clinical picture. Even when systematically assessed and identified, the depression may not receive much explicit attention. (p. 240)

Preventing depression is important because childhood depression, at least in its severe and chronic form, is linked to adult maladjustment and sometimes to suicidal behavior. However, research provides little guidance for preventive efforts (Kazdin & Marciano, 1998). We might guess that an accumulation of major stressful life events is an important factor in some youngsters' depression and suicide. However, more typical daily hassles can also put adolescents at risk for depression, particularly in the late childhood and early adolescent years (Lewinsohn, Gotlib, & Seeley, 1995). Primary prevention may therefore involve efforts to reduce all manner of stressful life events for all children, but such broad-based, unfocused efforts are unlikely to receive much political or fiscal support. There is a better chance for support and success if efforts focus on relieving stress for abused and neglected youngsters and others whose lives are obviously extremely stressful. Another approach to primary prevention, somewhat more focused and feasible, is parenting training for depressed parents (Beardslee et al., 2002). Secondary and third-level prevention are still more focused and feasible, giving depressed youngsters behavioral or cognitive-behavioral training in overcoming their specific difficulties. This training is preventive in that it keeps the child's current situation from worsening and may forestall the development of long-term negative outcomes and recurrent episodes of depression.

Intervention and Education

Antidepressant drugs are often prescribed for childhood depression, although there has been inadequate research on their effectiveness, and the side effects can be problematic (Hammen & Rudoph, 2003; Kaslow et al., 1998; Konopasek & Forness, 2004; Kusumakar, Lazier, MacMaster, & Santor, 2002; Ryan, 2002). A number of recent studies have compared behavioral to psychopharmacologic treatments for depression, and early evidence suggests that a combined approach—one using both behavioral interventions and medication—may be most efficacious (Forness, Freeman, & Paparella, 2006). When medications are prescribed, teachers need to carefully monitor the effects on behavior and learning. As is the case in nearly every type of disorder, successful intervention requires collaborative, multimodal treatment involving a variety of professionals.

A very controversial treatment of depression for adults is electroconvulsive treatment (ECT, sometimes called electroshock treatment) (Wang, 2007). At one time, ECT was frequently used for depression, but it is now used rarely because of its history of abuse. It is now used only in cases in which depression is severe and not responsive to drug therapies, and it is extremely unlikely to be used with adolescents.

Teachers are most likely to be directly involved in interventions that are behavioral or cognitive-behavioral. These interventions are based on theories of depression that highlight the roles of social skills, productive and pleasurable activity, causal attributions, cognitive assertions, and self-control (see Kaslow et al., 1998; Kazdin & Marciano, 1998; Maag & Swearer, 2005; Seeley et al., 2002).

Kaslow et al. (1998) outlined a general decision-making model for approaching the treatment of depression. First, if a student appears to be depressed, it is important to ask whether there are associated disorders. If so, then interventions should be implemented to address them first because depression might be relieved if the other disorders are ameliorated; if not, then intervention for depression is necessary. In designing interventions for depression, Kaslow et al. suggested assessing the student's problems in the following order and providing intervention if significant problems of that type are found:

1. Low activity level
2. Social skills deficits
3. Self-control deficits
4. Depressive attributional style
5. Low self-esteem and feelings of hopelessness
6. Limited self-awareness and interpersonal awareness.

In their schema, the priority for assessment and intervention is activity level and the second target for intervention is social skills. Teachers can be extremely helpful, if not the key players, in implementing both of these strategies.

SUICIDAL BEHAVIOR

Definition and Prevalence

The definition of *completed suicide* is straightforward: to kill oneself intentionally. However, determining that a death was a suicide is often difficult because the circumstances, particularly the intentions of the deceased, are in question. Suicide is socially stigmatizing, so the label *suicide* is likely to be avoided if death can be attributed to accident (Madge & Harvey, 1999). Accidents are the leading cause of death among adolescents in the 15 to 24 age bracket, and many researchers suspect that, in this age group, many deaths attributed to accident are disguised or misreported suicides (e.g., Madge & Harvey, 1999).

The term *parasuicide* sometimes refers to unsuccessful or uncompleted suicidal behavior. *Attempted suicide* is difficult to define because studies often differ in distinctions between suicidal gestures (suicidal behavior that is interpreted as not serious in intent), thoughts of suicide, threats of suicide, and self-inflicted injury requiring medical treatment (see Spirito & Overholser, 2003).

Regardless how we define them, suicide and suicide attempts of adolescents (and, to a lesser extent, younger children) have increased dramatically during the past several decades (Spirito, 2003). Only accidents and homicides are more often the cause of death among youth between the ages of 15 and 24. Suicidal behavior among children and adolescents is a major public health problem, not only in this country but also in many countries of the world (Spirito & Overholser, 2003). Adolescent males have a higher suicide rate than do females, and this sex difference becomes more marked with age. Among older adolescents and young adults, parasuicides are more common for females than for males. Among children, the gender difference is reversed, with suicide attempts more common for boys than for girls. In the United States, until recently, Black males have had significantly lower suicide rates than did White males; rates for Native American youth are higher than are rates for Whites (Wyche & Rotheram-Borus, 1990). However, suicide rates for Black males have increased markedly since 1986, and it may no longer be accurate to say that Black males are at lower risk of suicide than are White males (Shaffer, Gould, & Hicks, 1994). The accurate assessment of suicide risk may require particular sensitivity to specific minority populations (Goldston, 2003). Suicide rates are higher for married than for unmarried teenagers. Suicide methods appear to relate to the availability of means; firearms are more commonly used in the United States than they are in most other countries.

Although suicide is rarely reported in children under 10 years old and is relatively infrequent even in prepubertal children (Shaffer & Hicks, 1994; Smith, 1992), we do occasionally encounter reports of suicide attempts and successful suicides of very young children (e.g., Rosenthal & Rosenthal, 1984). However, rising suicidal behavior among young people and the high rate at which children and youth kill or attempt to kill themselves are alarming. "It appears . . . that by late adolescence, teenagers' tendency toward self-destructiveness has mushroomed from a rare event to a phenomenon that is at least passingly considered by most teens and is acted on by 1 out of 12 of them" (Smith, 1992, p. 257). Greater understanding of the causes and more effective prevention programs must be priorities. We also need better means of dealing with suicidal individuals after an attempted suicide and with survivors after a completed suicide.

Causal Factors and Prevention

Most authorities agree that biological and nonbiological factors interact in complex ways in the causation of suicide and depression. There appear to be genetic and other physiological contributions to depressive behavior, as we have already noted, and these factors may increase risk for suicidal behavior as well. However, educators focus primarily on the environmental factors involved. The many complex factors that contribute to children's and adolescents' suicidal behavior include major psychiatric problems, feelings of hopelessness, impulsivity, naive concepts of death, substance abuse, social isolation, abuse and neglect by parents, family conflict and disorganization, a family history of suicide and parasuicide, and cultural factors, including stress caused by the educational system and attention to suicide in the mass media. Youth with emotional or behavioral disorders, especially those who use alcohol or illicit drugs, are at particularly high risk of suicidal behavior (Carr, 2002; Spirito & Overholser, 2003).

The common thread among all causal factors is that suicidal individuals believe they have little impact on the world around them. They often do not know that help is available for dealing with their problems, believing that no one cares and that they must deal with their problems alone. Culp, Clyman, & Culp (1995) studied 220 students in grades 6 through 12. Nearly half of those who reported feelings of depression did not ask for help, most often because they did not know about services available to them in the school or, if they did, believed they had to take care of their problems by themselves. Feelings of loneliness and especially hopelessness appear to be among the best predictors of suicidal thoughts and intentions (Spirito & Overholser, 2003).

Hopelessness has long been recognized as a primary characteristic of the thinking of those prone to suicide (Esposito, Johnson, Wolfsdorf, & Spirito, 2003). Hopelessness and intent to commit suicide correlate more highly than do depression and suicide intent. Apparently, all individuals who feel hopeless are depressed, but not all who are depressed feel hopeless. Those who feel hopeless are convinced that things will not get better, cannot get better, so they might as well give up hope. Hopelessness may represent the final stage of depression that tends to precede suicidal intent, the stage at which an individual concludes that suicide is justified.

Many children and adolescents who commit suicide or parasuicide have a history of emotional or behavioral disorders and school failure. In fact, school performance of adolescents who show suicidal behavior is almost uniformly poor, and most teenagers' suicides and parasuicides occur in the spring months, when school problems (grades, graduation, college admission) are highlighted.

Other factors increasing the likelihood of suicide attempts, besides mood disorders, include high levels of stress related to parents (e.g., having been physically hurt by a parent, running away, living apart from both parents), sexuality (e.g., concerns regarding pregnancy, sexually transmitted diseases, and pressure to become sexually active), police contacts, and lack of adult support outside the home (Flisher, 1999; Wolfe, 1998). Some have suspected that social stress related to homosexuality is a factor in suicide, but research has found no reliable connection between sexual orientation and suicide (Shaffer et al., 1994). Unsurprisingly, suicidal behavior appears to be learned, at least in part, through observation of the behavior of others in family and social contexts. Families that do not form emotional bonds and parents whose discipline style is chaotic are also factors increasing the risk for suicidal behavior (Bush & Pargament, 1995). Outbreaks of suicide attempts are particularly likely to occur in institutional settings and psychiatric hospitals, probably partly as a result of imitation or competitive bids for attention and status.

Ordinarily, we think of depression as the primary disorder associated with suicidal behavior. However, the role of aggressive behavior is increasingly recognized (Spirito & Overholser, 2003). Primary suicide prevention presents enormous problems of identifying individuals who are at risk because, in any attempt to make predictions, the number of false positives is extremely high and the consequences of false negatives are extremely severe. Because only a relatively small percentage of the population commits or attempts suicide, and because suicidal and nonsuicidal individuals have many common characteristics, any general screening procedure turns up many false positives—individuals who are not actually at high risk. But the consequence of identifying as "not at risk" those who are in fact likely to attempt or commit suicide (the false negatives) are obviously grim. Consequently, most primary prevention programs are aimed at entire school populations.

Assessment

Suicidal behavior is not always preceded by recognizable signals, although some characteristics and circumstances are danger signals for which educators and other adults should be on the lookout. Adults' and peers' awareness of indications that a child or youth might be at risk for suicidal behavior is an important aspect of assessing the general school population (Carr, 2002; Popenhagen & Qualley, 1998; Spirito & Overholser, 2003). These are some indications of risk in the general school population:

- Sudden changes in usual behavior or affect
- Serious academic, social, or disciplinary problems at school
- Family or home problems, including parental separation or divorce, child abuse, or running away from home
- Disturbed or disrupted peer relations, including peer rejection and breakup of romantic relationships or social isolation
- Health problems, such as insomnia, loss of appetite, sudden weight change, and so on
- Substance abuse
- Giving away possessions or talk of not being present in the future
- Talk of suicide or presence of a suicide plan
- Situational crisis such as death of a family member or close friend, pregnancy or abortion, legal arrest, loss of employment of self or family member.

Part of any assessment of risk involves systematic evaluation of the characteristics of individuals who are thought to be at higher than usual risk. A personal characteristic associated with most suicides, parasuicides, and thoughts of suicide is depression, so it is important to assess depression. However, depression may be accompanied by aggressive behavior, conduct disorder, or a variety of other problems.

Intervention and Education

Adults should do the following:

- Take all suicide threats and attempts seriously
- Seek to reestablish communication
- Provide emotional support or sustenance that relieves alienation.

Although dealing adequately with the problem of suicidal behavior requires a complex, multifaceted effort, the general notion is that the suicidal individual must be helped to establish and maintain as many points of contact as possible with significant others, including adults and peers. The child or adolescent must be shown ways that are not self-destructive to solve problems and get attention from others. Teachers can aid in suicide prevention by realizing that they can identify students who are at risk; school systems can play a part in prevention by providing curricula that acquaint students with others' experience of normal physical and social development (Seeley et al., 2002; Spirito & Overholser, 2003).

The educator's role in intervention is primarily to provide information about suicide and refer students who appear at risk to other professionals. A comprehensive program of suicide awareness and prevention has several parts: administrative guidelines specifying school policy, faculty inservice to obtain support of teachers and provide them with basic information and skills in dealing with students, and curricular programs for students. In addition, hotlines, peer counseling, and programs designed to reduce and manage stress may be implemented.

Managing children and adolescents after their suicide attempts or threats is the joint responsibility of counselors or other mental health personnel and teachers. Although teachers should not attempt to offer counseling or therapy themselves, they can provide critical support by encouraging students and families to obtain help from qualified counselors or therapists. Teachers can also help by reducing unnecessary stress on students and being willing and empathic listeners.

SUMMARY

The federal definition of "emotionally disturbed" suggests that youngsters with internalizing problems, including depression, should be eligible for special education, although the definition describes depression and related disorders ambiguously. Childhood depression has only recently become a topic of serious research. Consensus is emerging that depression is a major disorder of childhood that parallels adult depression in many respects, but particular behaviors exhibited in response to depressed affect will be developmentally age appropriate. Both adults and children who are depressed experience depressed moods and lose interest in productive activity. Depressed children may exhibit a variety of inappropriate behavior, and depression is often comorbid with other conditions.

Depression is part of the larger category of mood disorders, which includes unipolar and bipolar disorders involving elevated or depressed mood. Indications of depression include anhedonia, depressed mood or irritability, disturbances of sleep or appetite, psychomotor agitation or retardation, loss of energy or fatigue, feelings of self-derogation or hopelessness, difficulty thinking or concentrating, and suicidal ideation or attempts. Several of these symptoms are exhibited for a protracted period and are not a reasonable response to life events. Prevalence of depression is higher among older adolescents than young children, and girls are more affected at older ages. Depression may be found in 2% to 8% of the child population, and researchers suspect that many cases are not identified.

Assessment of depression must be multifaceted and should include self-reports, parental reports, peer nominations, observations, and clinical interviews. The judgments of teachers should not be overlooked.

Teachers should be on the lookout for four categories of problems: affective, cognitive, motivational, and physiological.

Some cases of depression clearly result from unknown biological factors, but the causal factors in most cases are indeterminable. In some cases, depression represents a reaction to stressful or traumatic environmental events. We find significant correlations between parents' depression and problems of their children, including depression. Educators should give special attention to how depression and school failure can be reciprocal causal factors. Prevention of depression is important because severe chronic depression is associated with adult maladjustment and suicidal behavior. Prevention may involve reducing stress, training in parenting, or teaching specific cognitive or behavioral skills.

Antidepressant drugs may be useful in some cases of depression, but their effects and side effects should be monitored carefully. Interventions are based on theories that attribute depression to inadequate social skills, maladaptive thought patterns, and lack of self-control. Selecting intervention strategies depends on analyzing the depressed individual's specific cognitive and social characteristics. Teachers can play a major role in teaching social skills and engaging students in higher levels of productive activities as well as assisting in other approaches.

Suicide and suicidal behavior (parasuicide) of children and youth, especially of adolescents and young adults, have increased dramatically in the past several decades. Factors increasing the risk of suicidal behavior include biological and environmental factors, especially a history of difficulty or failure in school, stress related to family dysfunction or abuse, substance abuse, family members or acquaintances who have completed suicide, depression and feelings of hopelessness, and aggressive behavior.

Prevention of suicide is extremely difficult because of the problems associated with false positives and false negatives. Prevention programs are typically aimed at entire school populations and consist of guidelines for teaching, in-service for teachers, and instructional programs for students and parents. Assessment of suicide risk involves recognizing danger signals and evaluating the individual's sense of hopelessness. Evaluation of statistically based risk factors and the student's ability to perform specific coping tasks are required to determine whether a suicide attempt is imminent.

Teachers and other adults should take all suicide threats and attempts seriously, seek to reestablish communication with students who feel alienated and help them establish as many points of contact as possible with significant others, and provide emotional sustenance and support. Schools should have a plan for follow-up intervention when a suicide occurs.

Depression and Suicidal Behavior

Tezella G. Cline, B.S., Winston-Salem State University, works with the professional development team as a full-time, senior mentor with the Charlotte–Mecklenburg New Teacher Program and is enrolled in the school administration master's program at Gardner-Webb University. She taught at the Spaugh Middle School of Math, Science, and Technology in Charlotte, North Carolina, when she wrote this feature.

Describe the school in which you teach and your particular role in the school.

I teach in an inner-city magnet school that focuses on math, science, and technology. The technology-rich curriculum is designed to stimulate student interest and enhance student learning. The school's population is balanced racially. We have about 700 students enrolled in grades 6 through 8. Our school population is 63% male, 44% Black, and 56% other ethnicities (Asian, Hispanic, Native American, multiracial, or White). About 45% of the students receive free or reduced-cost lunch, 18% are identified as gifted and talented, and 11% receive resource services or are in special classes. Students identified as "exceptional" number about 70, with 20 of these being classified as behaviorally and emotionally handicapped. The exceptional classes at my school include two resource classes and two self-contained classes. The resource classes serve mostly the learning disabled students, and the self-contained classes serve behaviorally and emotionally disabled students.

I am presently teaching sixth- and seventh-grade students in a self-contained setting. My eight students (five boys and three girls) have behavioral and emotional disorders. I also serve as team leader for our department as well as mentor for new special education teachers. I am a part of the Charlotte–Mecklenburg School Division's Teacher Leader Program, which works with the staff development department to offer training sessions for professional growth for all teachers. This year, I was awarded an Impact II grant.

Think of a particular student who exhibits depression or suicidal behavior. How does this student manifest the disorder?

I want to preface my answer with some general observations about teaching. A classroom teacher has a very important responsibility: to teach all students. Another important part of this responsibility is to observe each student for possible behavioral, emotional, academic, or social difficulties. This task means that teachers must be willing to establish one-to-one as well as group relationships with students. The better the teacher knows individuals and their families, the better he or she can serve the student. Careful daily observation and analysis of behaviors is essential. Another vital part of a successful educational program is communication. The teacher must communicate what has been observed with the parent or caretaker and with other professionals. This will allow us to better meet the needs of the student with behavioral or emotional difficulties.

George, one of my students who exhibits depression and suicidal behaviors, has the following five characteristics. First, he lacks appropriate social skills. This child has difficulty presenting himself in a socially acceptable way. When placed in a positive situation, he acts out—behaves in a negative, inappropriate way. When those around him react to his behavior, he usually responds with negative verbal statements about himself or others. He then blames others for being "stupid" enough to think that he could perform in that particular situation. Additional negative verbal responses from him include "I don't care," "So?" and "Nobody cares." Whenever he is faced with a challenge (good or bad), he seems to become frightened and tries to avoid the challenge by being so negative that he will have to be removed from the situation. He seems to try to push friends, loved ones, and those who care away. He tries to isolate himself. Once this is done, however, he experiences depressed feelings.

Second, George becomes aggressive. He tries to create conflict situations, at times simply to have an excuse to become aggressive and avoid the challenge of the moment. For example, he will lie about someone hitting him or complain that other students are looking at him or making threats toward him. He often puts himself in conflict situations and then complains that no one ever helps him.

Third, George withdraws from or avoids social activity with his peers. Even when he's with a group, he will isolate himself by doing something to irritate others in the group. I have seen this occur even during fun, seemingly nonthreatening activities. At the beginning of the activity or event he will be overly excited and anxious to participate. Then, as he gets more involved, he becomes progressively negative and finally withdraws by giving up. Once this has occurred, his anger sets in.

Fourth, George exhibits mood swings. Within moments, this student can go from being happy, excited, and cheerful to being sad, angry, and aggressive. For example, recently we were having our classroom project presentations for parents and other adult visitors. George had presented successfully for the principal, teachers, and his parent. It was the last day of school before the winter holiday. He had been given gifts and food during class, and everyone seemed to be having fun and smiling. George even shared a gift with teachers and explained that the gift was something that he had made himself, especially for the teachers. His mom was proud of his success, and she told him so as they kissed each other good-bye. Less than 30 minutes later his mood changed drastically. He became very active and disruptive to students around him. He was angry and cursing and on the verge of fighting with another student. The fact that other adults and a school administrator were in the room did not matter. Although I reminded him of what a great day he was having and how proud we all were of him, he proceeded to tell me that he did not care about any of this stuff. He also informed me that he wanted his gifts back. He continued making threats of aggression and arguing with staff. When we sent him to the time-out area in the room, he rolled on the floor and made loud noises. Later, when calm, he appeared sad and lonely. He made negative statements about himself and asked to go home, stating that he was tired.

Fifth, George picks friends and activities that are dangerous. He makes poor decisions about most things. He knows what's right, but he does the opposite. He often lies to himself and others about his choices. There are times when George will do anything to get peers to like him. He will also try to "buy" friendships.

What procedures have you found most useful in working with this student?

I have found that George responds best when he gets additional one-on-one attention. This attention can come from me or from our security officer. I believe that this male influence sometimes reaches him in a way that I cannot.

I believe it is important for students with emotional or behavioral disorders to build positive relationships with a variety of adults in their school or community environment. These relationships may prove helpful in crisis situations. When I notice a mood swing or an aggressive episode coming on, I try to ask another significant adult in the child's life to take the student for a walk to talk to him. This strategy has been most effective because it removes the student from the environment that he or she is having difficulty with. In addition, it removes the audience (the other students). Both (environment and audience) are factors that can prolong or intensify a problem. When a student is removed, he or she is no longer the center of peer attention yet has the attention that he or she is seeking.

Another way that I have been successful with George is by keeping up my daily communication with his mother. I believe that this gives him a feeling of family and consistency. He feels secure when he knows that what happens at home will be communicated to me and that all events from school will be shared with his mother. This also lets him know how important he is.

In addition, I also plan special, exciting, fun activities at least every 2 weeks. Also, my daily instruction includes activities that allow students to interact with each other as they use hands-on materials and engage themselves in discovery learning. I build in choices for students, and this gives them all a feeling of control and something to look forward to. We have special events or snacks at the end of the school day. Doing this helps to address feelings of hopelessness and encourages students to be motivated to stay focused on their tasks and to try to get the reward at the end of the day. Another benefit of planning special events is that they may relieve some of the stress that middle school students feel, especially those dealing with depression.

Another strategy I use with George is to listen when he asks to talk. Often, he comes to me and says, "I need to talk to you outside." I always set aside a time during the day to just listen to his concerns or ideas. The information that he shares is usually very helpful and enlightening. My role here is to support him by listening.

What are the prospects for this student's educational progress in the coming year?

Academically, George is average. He enjoys math and has just been mainstreamed into a regular math class on a trial basis. If he can be successful in this class, I will work toward placing him into another mainstream class. This depends, of course, on how well he adjusts and how consistent he can be. The challenge for me is to monitor him closely. Because I know his pattern of behavior, I expect that after the second week he will probably feel the pressure and will begin doing things to get himself put out of the class. He will then develop an "I don't care" attitude and begin to make negative statements about going to the class. I will be proactive by establishing a reward system and by communicating with the home to get his mother to do the same. This will, I hope, assist in keeping his interest and motivation level high.

George's prospects for the future are good if he continues to get support from parents, teachers, and other professionals. He does not deal well with changes in his environment, especially if he feels neglected. Academically, he is able to succeed, but he will need continued emotional support to progress. He presently gets professional counseling weekly with an outside agency (not in school). This will need to continue if progress is to occur.

What are the biggest long-term problems this student faces?

It is difficult for George to be consistent because of his mood swings. This will probably cause continued difficulty for him. Also, a major area of concern is his lack of appropriate social skills needed to obtain reinforcement from his social environment. He functions within the controlled environment of the special classroom, but my concern is how he will make it when out on his own.

George must be able to deal with changes in his environment and in relationships to the point that he can manage and control his negative responses to those changes. He must deal with changes in his world without giving up.

Tezella Cline Interviews George

Ms. C: How are you feeling today?

G: Good.

Ms. C: How would you describe yourself?

G: Trapped up in feelings.

Ms. C: Can you tell me about any of those?

G: Like, different ones. Like, wanting to go home, but my mom hadn't came yet.

Ms. C: Name and describe things that make you feel the best about yourself.

G: I like working alone. And . . . when I'm doing a good job and the teacher says that I'm doing a good job.

Ms. C: Describe your personality.

G: I think I'm a nice guy. When you get to know me a good bit. And generous.

Ms. C: Tell me about your life.

G: There have been ups and downs all through it. I had to go to Alexander.

Ms. C: What's Alexander?

G: Children's' Center . . . and then I had to go back home to live with my mom. I was in regular classes, then I went to BEH [behaviorally and emotionally handicapped classes], and that's all. There have been ups and downs in my life.

Ms. C: How do you feel about those ups and downs?

G: Well, when I went to Alexander, I didn't like it. It was a childrens' center where they kept me overnight for 60 days.

Ms. C: When did you go there?

G: I think when I was like 4 or 5. I was out of control.

Ms. C: Out of control? What do you mean by that?

G: I was, like, being too bad to stay at home.

Ms. C: And at school? What was it like there?

G: I was in a regular class, and I didn't do very good in school. I got suspended a lot.

Ms. C: How often do you think you got suspended?

G: I got in trouble with the teacher, like, more than once every day.

Ms. C: Can you describe for me some of the types of things that you did?

G: I would not follow directions and not respect the teachers. I would mostly talk to my peers. Not listen to the teacher.

Ms. C: But all kids do that sometimes, right?

G: Yeah.

Ms. C: But what made you different?

G: I was doing it constantly.

Ms. C: Tell me the best thing about your life right now.

G: That I have a loving family that cares about me.

Ms. C: Do you have friends?

G: Yeah! I do!

Ms. C: Tell me about your friends.

G: They're fun, and I talk to them.

Ms. C: You don't have to name them, but describe your friends.

G: Some of them are bad, and some of them are good.

Ms. C: Which ones do you like to be with the most? Be honest.

G: Sometimes the bad.

Ms. C: What makes you say that they are bad?

G: Their actions are bad.

Ms. C: For example. . . .

G: Like they do bad things when they know it's wrong. Then they try to cover up for it.

Ms. C: What kinds of things?

G: Like, they throw spit balls or something like that.

Ms. C: What do you like best about being in school?

G: The math.

Ms. C: Why?

G: Because that's my favorite subject.

Ms. C: How do you feel when you're doing your favorite subject?

G: It makes me feel good 'cause I know what I'm doing most of the time.

Ms. C: What kinds of expressions do you have when you're doing math?

G: Like algebra and stuff like that?

Ms. C: No, I mean what kinds of emotions?

G: I'm feeling good because I know that I know how to do this and it's fun.

Ms. C: What do you like best about being at home?

G: All the privileges that I get, and I know I can't do that in a group home or something like that.

Ms. C: So you do think about that sometimes?

G: Yes, when my mom reminds me about it a lot.

Ms. C: How do you feel when you have to do subjects that you do not want to do?

G: I feel mad sometimes at the teacher, but I try to do it the best I can.

Ms. C: When you do those subjects that you don't like, tell me what you might be thinking.

G: I'm thinking that I don't want to do it, but I've got to 'cause I want to learn.

Ms. C: How do you handle those feelings when you feel them coming?

G: I try to ignore them because I need to do my work.

Ms. C: Do you talk to yourself?

G: Yes.

Ms. C: What do you say?

G: I can do it. I give myself strategies saying that I can do it and stuff like that.

Ms. C: What kind of strategies have you learned through the years?

G: That if you talk to yourself enough that you will convince yourself that you can do it.

Ms. C: Tell me the things that you say, specifically.

G: I can do it, and you're the one that can do it.

Ms. C: Now, think about when you are angry and you're not saying those things to yourself. What kinds of things are you saying?

G: When I'm angry, I'm mostly angry at somebody and it gets me really mad. And I'm not thinking about nothing, and I just say things that I don't really mean.

Ms. C: Right. What kinds of things come out?

G: Sometimes I curse.

Ms. C: After you've said things that you don't really mean, then what are you feeling? Do you feel good, or do you feel bad?

G: I feel bad because I've blown up at my mom a lot, and then at the end I'm really sad that I did that, and I can't live with myself sometimes doing that. So I need to stop doing it.

Ms. C: You have a lot of emotions going on there. Think now specifically about how you feel when you're getting angry or upset. What's usually the first feeling on up to where it's the top feeling?

G: That I'm really getting mad at somebody . . . like I'm saying I can cool down a little bit. Whenever I get to the top of it, I get really, really mad, and then I get like saying, "*Rurrrr*," and I get, like, shaking all over and my face starts to turn red and stuff like that.

Ms. C: When you reach that point, what are you thinking?

G: That I should, like, sometimes I think that I need to hit the person, but I know in myself that I shouldn't because I'll get suspended from school.

Ms. C: So what do you do?

G: I tell myself that you shouldn't hit 'cause it's not the right thing to do.

Ms. C: Have you ever told yourself the right thing but then done the other?

G: Yeah. I do that a lot. Then I think I know the right thing, then whenever I be bad I think it's a little more funner, sometimes.

Ms. C: So it makes you feel. . . .

G: Happy sometimes when I be bad, but whenever I get the consequences, it don't make sense to me.

Ms. C: Okay. Think about when you're angry. You told me what you're telling yourself. What ways do you show others that you're angry?

G: I really have a high temper. I mean, I yell a lot. Sometimes I throw things.

Ms. C: So explain this to me. Are you saying that it's not always when you have to do work, or you have to do things that other people tell you to do that get you angry?

G: No, it's not like that. It's like almost every day I try to deal with it to a certain extent.

Ms. C: So sometimes, even when you're doing something that you like to do, you get mad?

G: Yeah, I get angry then, too.

Ms. C: Do you ever get mad at yourself?

G: Yeah. I get mad at myself 'cause I can't do it myself, sometimes. That makes me mad at myself.

Ms. C: When you get mad at yourself, how does that make you feel toward yourself? Do you ever do things to yourself or say negative things to yourself?

G: Yeah, like right after I get done yelling at my mom when we have a big fight, I say, I tell it to myself, I say, "Why did you do that? You shouldn't have done that 'cause she's your mom. And you shouldn't say those kind of things to your mom." And I get real mad at myself sometimes.

Ms. C: Do you ever feel like hurting yourself or something like that?

G: At one point in my life I did. I thought I couldn't live with myself doing this. And I thought that I should kill myself, but I didn't.

Ms. C: Do you remember how old you were when you thought that?

G: I think I was around 6 or 5.

Ms. C: That young?

G: Yeah.

Ms. C: Since then, have you ever tried to hurt yourself in any way?

G: Well, there was this one time I was sitting in a car and I had a knife. I cut my finger. Right across here.

Ms. C: Have you ever felt just really, really low or really sad?

G: Yes.

Ms. C: Have you ever felt, would you say, depressed?

G: Yes. I felt that way a lot when I was really young.

Ms. C: Can you use any words to describe how that feels?

G: It feels like you can't go any lower than you go. You're, like, real low and you're saying to yourself, "Why can't I go on? What have I done?" And I just got so low, and it's hard to like, do stuff 'cause you're so depressed and you don't know what to do next.

Ms. C: What do teachers do that makes you feel this way sometimes?

G: When they tell you to do something over and over. They keep doing that over and over, and that gets me mad.

Ms. C: What do teachers do sometimes that makes you feel depressed or sad or low?

G: Whenever a teacher makes fun of me, it makes me feel sad or low.

Ms. C: What could teachers do to help make you feel better or feel lifted or happy once you're feeling depressed or sad or low?

G: Like, do my favorite subject, like math or something like that.

Ms. C: Name some things that you do at school that seem to get you into trouble.

G: I tend to hang with some bad people, bad friends. I shouldn't do that. I should know better.

Ms. C: Anything else that you do at school that gets you into trouble? What about in the classroom?

G: Yeah. I talk back, and I don't follow the teacher's directions.

Ms. C: What happens when you talk back or don't follow the teacher's directions? What comes after that?

G: I usually lose points or I get, like, a time-out.

Ms. C: How do you feel when that happens?

G: I feel angry at myself along with them [bad friends] because I didn't follow directions. And with them because they made me have to do it.

Ms. C: So even though you understand the rules and you know what is expected, then when you don't do what is expected and you get the consequence you still feel angry when you get the consequence?

G: Yes.

Ms. C: Now, is that anger directed to the teacher, do you think, or is it to yourself?

G: Mostly toward myself and also a little bit toward the teacher.

Ms. C: How do you react when you get caught doing something wrong?

G: Most of the time I say, "I didn't do it" or "It wasn't me."

Ms. C: Do you accept responsibility for your own behavior?

G: Sometimes. But I do not accept it more than I do accept it.

Ms. C: Do you tell the truth?

G: Sometimes.

Ms. C: Do you tell the truth about serious things?

G: Yes.

Ms. C: What kinds of things do you think you do not tell the truth about?

G: My behavior or something I did wrong.

Ms. C: Do you do your homework?

G: Sometimes, when I feel like it.

Ms. C: What makes you feel like doing it?

G: I want to get it over with so I can have time to play.

Ms. C: How do you feel about your school?

G: I feel like the school has lived up to its potential because it's been here so long and I think it's done good in all subjects. It teaches kids how to do good.

Ms. C: How do you feel about your class right now? The situation in your [self-contained] class right now?

G: I think we're not doing too good toward making the school's name that it's already got. Because we have a lot of problems in class. Behavior problems.

Ms. C: Describe the problems. What kinds of problems?

G: Behavior problems and temper moods. Tempers fly up, and we get mad at each other and mad at the teachers and stuff like that.

Ms. C: What do you think the teacher should do when the moods and tempers fly up?

G: The teacher should give them consequences and redirect them.

Ms. C: What are the things about your class that help you the most?

G: That some people in my class help me do my work. Group work.

Ms. C: What are some things in your class that upset you or make you angry?

G: When their tempers fly up at me and they think I did something and I didn't.

Ms. C: Do you have a routine in your class?

G: Yes. It's on our point system where we have to do math or social studies.

Ms. C: Do you think that's good for you?

G: Yeah. I like to know what is after each other so I can prepare for it. I think that's a good routine.

Ms. C: When you're feeling sad or depressed, how long does that feeling usually last?

G: Feeling angry and depressed, well, I'm never like that for a long period of time. For some reason my feelings never stay the same. They never keep going on and on and on like some people. They last 5 minutes or less.

Ms. C: Do you always know what makes you sad or depressed? Or does it just sometimes come upon you?

G: It sometimes just comes on me at different times of the day.

Ms. C: When do you think you're the most up or happy?

G: In the morning.

Ms. C: Then when does that feeling of lowness or depression come on you?

G: In the afternoon. Especially after lunch 'cause that's when I have to take my medicine.

Ms. C: How does that make you feel?

G: It makes me feel not good 'cause I know I can't control my behavior without it. Makes me feel kind of depressed because I can't do it without it. It makes me feel not good at all.

Ms. C: How can teachers or other adults help you when you feel like hurting yourself or becoming aggressive?

G: Probably restrain the person.

Ms. C: How does that make you feel?

G: Angry.

Ms. C: How do you think it makes the teacher feel when they have to restrain you?

G: They are probably thinking the same thing.

Ms. C: What would you say to a person who was feeling hopeless and trying to hurt themselves?

G: You shouldn't do that because you have a life to live and God put you on this earth so you could live this life.

Ms. C: Think about a time when you were having a great day and then suddenly everything changed within you and you began feeling angry or sad. Can you explain why or how that happened?

G: Yeah. Like, when I was all happy and then I thought about my rabbit died 'cause my dog killed it. I started to feel sad, and then I got all angry at everybody and I took my anger out on them.

Ms. C: So, sounds like what causes you to have sad or depressed feelings is sometimes on the outside, but sometimes they are on the inside too. And they have the same effect on you just like it's happening now. So it sounds like it's important to talk about your feelings before . . . to let people know what's going on.

G: Yeah, I think it is because you can let people know before you explode. So they'll know what to expect.

Ms. C: Is talking to your teacher important?

G: Yes, I think it is because you can let your feelings out and you can express to them how you feel.

Ms. C: Name three things that you love about school.

G: Math, science, and technology.

Ms. C: Name three things that you really dislike about school.

G: Social studies and reading.

Ms. C: How do rules make you feel?

G: Feels like we are trapped. You can do this, but you can't do that. It makes you feel like you're restricted to certain things.

Ms. C: And then, as a result of that feeling, what other feelings come? What do you feel like doing if you feel trapped?

G: It feels like you can't get out of here, you can't move, and stuff like that.

QUESTIONS FOR FURTHER REFLECTION

1. How would you tell the difference between depression and other problems that one of your students is experiencing?

2. In your opinion, what are the kinds of events that would cause your students to legitimately experience a depressed mood?

3. What are the most helpful things you could do as a teacher to prevent depression and suicide attempts among your students?

SECTION 18
SCHIZOPHRENIA AND OTHER SEVERE DISORDERS

As you read this section, keep these guiding questions in mind:

- What does *psychotic* mean, and how might schizophrenia fit or not fit a definition?

- What are the signs or symptoms of schizophrenia, and how might they be mistaken for other disorders in children?

- What is the prognosis for a child with schizophrenia?

- Why is a full range of educational interventions required for students with schizophrenia?

- What are the primary causes of and interventions for stereotypies?

We have already sketched major features of schizophrenia, primarily in section 9. This section briefly recaps information regarding the nature and causes of schizophrenia and other severe disorders but focuses primarily on the educational implications of several characteristics common to many individuals who have schizophrenia or disabilities that are severe, either in their own right or because they are found in combination with other disorders. Some texts on severe disabilities do not include discussion of schizophrenia and related disorders (e.g., Snell & Brown, 2006). However, researchers and clinicians increasingly recognize that psychopathology, including schizophrenia and related disorders, occur across the full spectrum of intellectual ability and co-occur with mental retardation (Lee, Moss, Friedlander, Donnelly, & Honer, 2003; Matson & Laud, 2007).

Schizophrenia is explicitly included in the federal category "emotionally disturbed". Schizophrenia is typically referred to as a psychotic disorder, and many pervasive developmental disabilities (PDD) have often been called psychoses as well. However, the term *psychotic* has had many definitions, none of which is universally accepted. Usually, a psychotic disorder includes delusions (ideas that are not grounded in reality) and/or hallucinations (imaginary sensory experiences, such as hearing voices or noises that do not exist or seeing imaginary objects or events). In the words of Cepeda (2007), ". . . psychosis has traditionally referred to the presence of hallucinations and delusions" (p. 1).

Schizophrenia is usually diagnosed by a psychiatrist. Several subtypes of schizophrenia may be named, including paranoid type, disorganized type, catatonic type, and so on. Sometimes a particular form of schizophrenia is diagnosed, such as schizophreniform disorder (like schizophrenia, but shorter in duration, usually just 1 to 6 months in duration; a relatively short episode of schizophrenia) or schizoaffective disorder (schizophrenia that includes an affective or mood disorder, such as bipolar disorder or depression, as well).

A variety of disorders other than schizophrenia may fall under the general heading of "psychotic." These might include such diagnoses as delusional disorder, substance-induced psychotic disorder, and so on. The major feature of these psychotic disorders in all cases is an inability to distinguish reality from unreality.

Pervasive developmental disorders (PDD) affect multiple aspects of a child's development (Schreibman, Stahmer, & Akshoomoff, 2006). These disorders include autism spectrum disorders (ASD, not included in the federal definition of emotional disturbance), *Rett's disorder* (normal development for 5 months to 4 years followed by regression and retardation), and *childhood disintegrative disorder* (normal development for at least 2 and up to 10 years followed by significant loss of skills; see Schopler, Mesibov, & Kunce, 1998; Zwaigenbaum & Szatmati, 1999). Most youngsters with schizophrenia have multiple problems, and most of those with pervasive developmental disorders could be included in the federal category of severe and multiple disabilities.

Much controversy has surrounded the inclusion of autism in special education categories (see Sweeney & Hoffman, 2004). Autism has been excluded from the category "emotionally disturbed" and has been made a separate category of its own under federal special education regulations. Nevertheless, some of the behaviors that are severely problematic and may be considered emotional or behavioral disorders in their own right (e.g., mutism, extreme self-stimulation, or self-injury) are sometimes seen in children with autism as well as other pervasive developmental disabilities. Moreover, some students with various forms of ASD are served in special education for those with EBD (see, for example, the personal reflections feature at the end of this section). Therefore we include discussion of some of the more severe problems associated with PDD and ASD in particular.

An important point about the emotional and behavioral problems associated with schizophrenia and related disabilities is that they are now recognized as having their origins primarily in biological factors, as noted in section 9. Although researchers are increasingly finding a biological basis for many types of emotional and behavioral disorders, the scientific evidence of biological factors is stronger for more severe disorders.

We first discuss schizophrenia. Then we turn our attention to behavior often seen in youngsters with severe disabilities, regardless of their diagnostic labels: socialization problems, communication disorders, and stereotypy (abnormal repetitive behavior), especially self-stimulation and self-injury. Behavior of these types is severely debilitating and often presents persistent challenges to teachers and others who work with children and youth who have schizophrenia, autism, severe mental retardation, or other severe developmental disabilities.

SCHIZOPHRENIA

Definition, Prevalence, and Characteristics

Schizophrenia is a disorder in which people usually have two or more of the following symptoms:

- Delusions
- Hallucinations
- Disorganized speech (e.g., they may frequently get derailed or be incoherent)
- Grossly disorganized or catatonic behavior
- Negative symptoms such as lack of affect, inability to think logically, or inability to make decisions (American Psychiatric Association, 2000; see also Asarnow & Asarnow, 2003)

The definition of schizophrenia is not simple. "Schizophrenia is a complex, multifaceted disorder (or group of disorders), which has escaped precise definition after almost a century of study" (Russell, 1994, p. 631; see also Caplan, Guthrie, Tang, Komo, & Asarnow, 2000; Cepeda, 2007). Defining schizophrenia in children is even more problematic than defining it in adults (the usual age of onset is between ages 18 and 40 years) because children usually have more difficulty explaining themselves (see Erlenmeyer-Kimling et al., 1998). Nevertheless, "there is no longer any question that schizophrenia can be reliably diagnosed in children using the same criteria used with adults" (Asarnow & Asarnow, 1994, p. 595; see also Asarnow & Asarnow, 2003). Moreover, children can have schizophrenia and another disability, including mental retardation (Lee et al., 2003; Matson & Laud, 2007).

Table 18.1 Examples of Psychotic Symptoms

Hallucinations

Unrelated to affective state

A 7-year-old boy stated, "Everything is talking, the walls, the furniture, I just know they're talking."

Command

An 11-year-old boy heard both "good" and "bad" voices. The bad voices tell him to hit others and that they will kill the good voices if he does not obey. The "good" voices say things like "Help your mom with dinner."

Conversing

An 8-year-old boy stated, "I can hear the devil talk—God interrupts him and the devil says 'shut up' to God. God and the devil are always fighting."

Religious

An 11-year-old boy heard God's voice saying, "Sorry D., but I can't help you now, I am helping someone else." He also reported hearing Jesus and the devil.

Persecutory

A 9-year-old boy reported voices calling him bad names, and threatening that if he doesn't do what he is told something bad will happen to him.

Commenting

An 8-year-old girl reported an angel saying things like "You didn't cry today" and "You've been a very nice girl today."

Visual

A 9-year-old girl reported, "If I stare at the wall I see monsters coming toward me. If I stop staring, they'll come faster."

Tactile

An 5-year-old boy felt snakes and spiders on his back (and was so convincing he was taken to the emergency room by his parents).

Somatic

An 8-year-old girl reported feeling an angel, babies, and devil inside her arm, and that she could feel them fighting.

Schizophrenia affects about 1 in 100 adults, but it is rare in ages lower than 18. Delusional thinking is uncommon in children, but sometimes young children are convinced of the reality of their fantasies or the delusions of other people. They may engage in fantasies during play, and these fantasies may interfere with their socialization or academic learning. The case of Wanda (see the accompanying case book) illustrates the extent to which children with schizophrenia can become caught up in their fantasies.

Table 18.1 shows examples of the hallucinations, delusions, and thought disorders seen in children. The hallucinations and delusions take a wide variety of forms. The delusions of children and adolescents frequently have sexual or religious content.

Table 18.1 *Continued*

Delusions

Bizarre

A 7-year-old boy believed that there were "memory boxes" in his head and body and reported that he could broadcast his thoughts from his memory boxes with a special computer using radar tracking.

Persecutory

A girl believed that the "evil one" was trying to poison her orange juice.

Somatic

One 7-year-old boy believed that there were boy and girl spirits living inside his head: "They're squishing on the whole inside, they're touching the walls, the skin."

Reference

An 8-year-old girl believed that people outside of her house were staring and pointing at her trying to send her a message to come outside. She also believed that people on the TV were talking to her because they used the word "you."

Grandiose

An 11-year-old boy had the firm belief that he was "different" and able to kill people. He felt that when "God zooms through me [him]" he became very strong and developed big muscles.

Thought Disorder

"I used to have a Mexican dream. I was watching TV in the family room. I disappeared outside of this world and then I was in a closet. Sounds like a vacuum dream. It's a Mexican dream. When I was close to that dream earth, I was turning upside down. I don't like to turn upside down. Sometimes I have Mexican dreams and vacuum dreams. It's real hard to scream in dreams."

Source: Russell, A. T. (1994). The clinical presentation of childhood-onset schizophrenia. *Schizophrenia Bulletin, 20,* 634–635.

Children having delusions and hallucinations are not always diagnosed as having schizophrenia. They may be diagnosed as having bipolar disorder (Isaac, 1995), or they may have comorbid disorders, such as schizophrenia along with conduct disorder, attention deficit–hyperactivity disorder (ADHD), depression or bipolar disorder, or another diagnosable psychiatric disorder (Asarnow & Asarnow, 2003).

In many cases, the diagnosis of schizophrenia is difficult because the onset is insidious–slow, perhaps beginning with conduct problems, anxiety disorders, or ADHD. Symptom patterns may go unrecognized or be confused (Asarnow, Thompson, & Goldstein, 1994; Russell, 1994). Sometimes, children who show violent aggression and have serious school problems are later found to have schizophrenia (Schaeffer & Ross, 2002).

Some children who are diagnosed with autism or other pervasive developmental disorders are later diagnosed as having schizophrenia, but this is not typically the case. Most children with schizophrenia never lose their symptoms completely, although some do (Asarnow & Asarnow, 1994, 2003).

Causes and Prevention

As discussed in section 9, the causes of schizophrenia are known to be in large measure biological, but the exact biological mechanisms responsible for the illness are not known (Asarnow, Asamen, et al., 1994; Asarnow & Asarnow, 2003; Gottesman, 1991; Lenzenweger & Dworkin, 1998). Genetic factors are known to play a critical role, but which genes are involved and how they work is not understood. It is quite likely that schizophrenia is not a single disease entity but a cluster of highly similar disorders in the same way that cancer is not a single disease.

The same causal factors seem to operate whether schizophrenia is first diagnosed in childhood or adulthood (Asarnow & Asarnow, 1995, 2003). However, onset of schizophrenia in childhood or adolescence seems to carry a worse prognosis than adult-onset schizophrenia, particularly when the symptoms of the disease are severe (Eggers, Bunk, & Drause, 2000; Lay, Blanz, Hartmann, & Schmidt, 2000).

We know that in the vast majority of cases, if not all, biological and environmental factors work together to cause schizophrenia. Families in which the parents exhibit deviant behavior may contribute to the development of schizophrenia (Asarnow, Thompson, & Goldstein, 1994). Primary prevention consists of assessing genetic risks and avoiding behavior that may trigger schizophrenia in vulnerable persons, especially substance abuse and extreme stress (Gottesman, 1987). Secondary prevention consists mainly of psychopharmacological treatment and structured environments in which symptoms can be managed most effectively.

Education and Related Interventions

Educational intervention for children and youth with schizophrenia is nearly impossible to describe because the symptoms and educational needs of these students vary so greatly. We are safe in saying that education will be only one of several interventions because pharmacological treatment and social work with the family will be critical as well (see Forness, Kavale, Sweeney, & Crenshaw, 1999; Konopasek & Forness, 2004; Sweeney, Forness, Kavale, & Levitt, 1997). When special education is necessary, it appears that a highly structured, individualized program provides a feeling of safety and allows the student to keep symptoms in check as much as possible.

The outcomes for children and youth with schizophrenia are extremely variable. A substantial proportion of these students do not make a good overall adjustment as they progress into adulthood. Some cases, however, turn out quite well (as illustrated by the case of Bill in the accompanying case book). Schizophrenia is nearly always treated with antipsychotic drugs (neuroleptics) such as Haldol (haloperidol) or Mellaril (thioridazine), which are designed to reduce hallucinations and other symptoms (see Figure 6.1). "Children with schizophrenia show a positive treatment response to some of the same pharmacologic treatments that have demonstrated efficacy with adults with schizophrenia" (Asarnow & Asarnow, 1995, p. 595). However, these drugs do not work well for all children and youth (or adults), and they may have serious side effects (Asarnow & Asarnow, 2003).

In summary, schizophrenia is a rare and disabling disorder of childhood. The onset is often insidious and confused with other disorders. Intervention nearly always involves psychopharmacology, along with social and educational interventions (Forness, Walker, & Kavale, 2003). A structured, individualized educational program is often necessary. With appropriate intervention, some children and youth with schizophrenia lose many or most of their symptoms.

SOCIALIZATION PROBLEMS

As we have noted, socialization depends to a great extent on competence in communication. However, children and youth with schizophrenia or related disorders may fail to develop other social skills besides language (see McClelland & Scalzo, 2006; Schreibman et al., 2006). Their odd, unresponsive, and rejecting patterns of behavior may disable them in learning to play with, befriend, and be befriended by others. Teaching self-control (Polsgrove & Smith, 2004), social skills (Kavale, Mathur, & Mosteri, 2004), and appropriate alternative behavior (Meadows & Stevens, 2004) to youngsters with any type of emotional or behavioral disorder is difficult. Teaching these to students with intellectual deficits is even more complicated (Sukhodolsky & Butter, 2007)

Most children with pervasive developmental disorders have extreme problems with social skills of nearly every type. Many critical social skills cannot be taught one-on-one by an adult teacher or with a group of other equally unskilled children, so it is not surprising that most intervention requires interaction with normally developing peers. Peers may be trained to serve as models, to initiate interactions, and to respond appropriately to the student with severe disorders in home, classroom, or community settings.

As discussed previously, students with schizophrenia and pervasive developmental disorders exhibit a wide range of emotional and behavioral problems and often have comorbid disorders. Consequently, the full range of interventions used with disorders discussed in other sections, including attention deficit disorder, hyperactivity, conduct disorder, depression, and so on, may be needed.

COMMUNICATION DISORDERS

Teaching children with pervasive developmental disorders to use communication effectively is one of the greatest challenges in their education. Enormous progress has been made since the 1960s, when the first systematic attempts were made in teaching language to children with autism.

Educational programs of the 1960s and 1970s used an operant conditioning approach to teach, step-by-step, approximations of functional language. The child's responses at each step in the sequence were rewarded, typically with praise, hugs, and food given by the teacher immediately following the child's performance of the desired behavior. For example, at the earliest step in the sequence, a child might be reinforced for establishing eye contact with the teacher. The next step might be making any vocalization while looking at the teacher, next making a vocalization approximating a sound made by the teacher, then imitating words spoken by the teacher, and finally replying to the teacher's questions. Of course, this description is a great simplification of the procedures that were employed, but through such methods nonverbal children were taught basic oral language skills.

A disappointing outcome of early language training was that few of the children acquired truly useful or functional language, even after intensive and prolonged training. Their speech tended to have a mechanical quality, and they often did not learn to use their language for many social purposes. A current trend in language intervention is emphasis on pragmatics (making language more functional in social interaction) and motivating children to communicate (see Hallahan, Kauffman, & Pullen, 2009). Instead of training children to imitate words in isolation or to use syntactically and grammatically correct forms, we might train them to use language to obtain a desired result. For example, the child might be taught to say, "I want juice" (or a simplified form: "juice" or "want juice") to get a drink of juice. Increasingly, language intervention in autism involves structuring opportunities to use language in natural settings. For example, the teacher may set up opportunities for children to make requests by using a missing item strategy (e.g., give the child a coloring book but not crayons, prompting a request for the crayons), interrupting a chain of behavior (e.g., stopping the child on her way out to play, prompting a request to go out), or delaying assistance with tasks (e.g., waiting to help a child put on his coat until he asks for assistance).

Progress in teaching functional communication skills comes slowly through careful, programmatic research. Claims of breakthrough interventions are almost always misleading and disappointing. In the early 1990s, there were claims of the discovery of normal or extraordinary intelligence and communicative ability in children and adults with autism using a procedure called facilitated communication (e.g., Biklen, 1990; Biklen & Schubert, 1991). However, by the mid-1990s, researchers had accumulated overwhelming evidence that facilitated communication is not a reliable and efficient means of communication. In the vast majority of cases, research has shown that facilitated communication is a complete hoax in which the facilitator, not the person with a developmental disability, does the communicating. If not an outright fraud, facilitated communication has been found to be very limited and inefficient (Gardner, 2001; Kauffman & Sasso, 2006a; Mostert, 2001; Shane, 1994).

The language training procedures based on operant conditioning applied to natural language contexts have not led to dramatic breakthroughs or a cure. However, research over a period of decades now supports the use of these procedures in most cases. Table 18.2 summarizes recommendations on teaching communication skills. Thorough evaluation of speech and language skills is necessary before these teaching practices are used (Gerenser & Forman, 2007; Justice, 2006).

Table 18.2 Recommendations for Teaching Communication Skills

1. Early intervention is important. Teaching should begin as soon as it is evident that communication skills are lacking.
2. Involve parents and other family members, and provide instruction in as normal or natural an environment as possible.
3. Make the most important information in communication as obvious as possible by using highlighting.
4. Be highly organized and use a lot of repetition; better to repeat too much than not enough.

Source: Adapted from Gerenser & Forman (2007).

STEREOTYPY (ABNORMAL REPETITIVE MOVEMENT)

Children and adults with severe emotional, behavioral, or cognitive disabilities may engage in persistent, repetitive, seemingly meaningless behavior. Their stereotypical patterns of behavior, or *stereotypy*, may or may not result in serious self-injury. "The term 'stereotyped behavior' or 'repetitive behavior' is an umbrella term used to refer to the broad and often disparate class of behaviors linked by repetition, rigidity, invariance, inappropriateness, and lack of adaptability" (Bodfish, 2007, p. 484). Such repetitive movement may have been caused by biological or environmental factors or both.

Often repetitive movement seems to serve the primary or sole purpose of providing sensory feedback, and it is therefore called self-stimulation. In its most severe and troubling form, it results in physical injury to the individual who does it. We briefly discuss both noninjurious self-stimulation and self-injury.

Self-Stimulation

Self-stimulation can take an almost infinite variety of forms, such as staring blankly into space, body rocking, hand flapping, eye rubbing, lip licking, or repeating the same vocalization over and over. Depending on the *topography* (particular movements) of self-stimulation and the rate or intensity, it can result in physical injury—for example, eye rubbing at a high rate and pressure.

Self-stimulation is apparently a way to obtain self-reinforcing or self-perpetuating sensory feedback (Rapp, Miltenberger, Galensky, Ellingson, & Long, 1999). It is not likely to stop for long unless demands for other incompatible responses are made or it is actively suppressed. This appears to be true of some self-stimulatory behavior (such as nail biting) of ordinary people. As Sroufe, Steucher, and Stutzer (1973) suggested long ago, we could probably find some form of self-stimulation in everyone's behavior, varying only in subtlety, social appropriateness, and rate. It is a pervasive characteristic of normally developing infants, and nearly everyone engages in higher rates of self-stimulatory behavior when bored or tired. Thus, like most behaviors, self-stimulation is considered normal or pathological depending on its social context, intensity, and rate.

High rates of self-stimulation sometimes require highly intrusive, directive intervention procedures because students are unlikely to learn academic or social tasks when engaged in such behavior. Many procedures have been researched, among them using self-stimulation or alternative sensory stimulation as a reinforcer for appropriate behavior, medications, and changing the environmental conditions in which it occurs (see Bodfish, 2007). As we learn more about the nature of self-stimulation and related behavior, we are coming to understand that the context in which it occurs (e.g., highly structured tasks or relatively unstructured recreation) has much to do with the success of the procedures used to control it (Haring & Kennedy, 1990; Newsom, 1998; Scheuermann & Webber, 2002).

The best method of controlling self-stimulation varies according to the individual. Intervention is not always justified; for some, reducing self-stimulation may serve no therapeutic purpose. When self-stimulation does not result in physical injury or deformity, interfere significantly with learning, or prevent participation in normal activities, then intervention may not be justified. Whether to intervene depends on the topography, rate, duration, and typical social consequences of the behavior. Intervention should attempt to find the function that the repetitive behavior serves (i.e., the reason or reasons the person does it) and provide positive support for appropriate behavior.

Self-Injury

Like self-stimulation, some types of self-injury may occur in people whose behavior is considered normal. For example, body piercing and tattooing, although typically performed by others at the request of an individual, may be considered deliberate self-injury. Only the social context and rate or level of most behavior distinguish what is acceptable from what is unacceptable. Nearly any behavior is maladaptive and considered socially inappropriate when it is engaged in at a very high level, but normal and acceptable at a lower level or under certain conditions.

However, some youngsters injure themselves repeatedly and deliberately in the most brutal and socially unacceptable fashion. We find this kind of *self-injurious behavior* (SIB) in some individuals with severe intellectual disability (mental retardation), but it is a characteristic often associated with multiple disabilities—for example, mental retardation and autism or schizophrenia and another disorder. Very rarely does an individual with SIB have well-developed oral language. Most people who show SIB of the type we are discussing here are either mute or have very limited language abilities. In fact, one frequent approach to SIB is to try to figure out what function such behavior has, what it communicates, and what noninjurious consequences it produces (e.g., attention or escape from adults' demands, sensory stimulation; see Bodfish, 2007; Scheuermann & Webber, 2002).

Nevertheless, some children and youth with normal intelligence and language skills deliberately injure themselves without the intent of killing themselves. The prevalence of such behavior may be as high as 2% to 3% of adolescents (Garrison et al., 1993). Such behavior may include "skin cutting, skin burning, self-hitting, interfering with wound healing, severe skin scratching, hair pulling and bone breaking"

(Garrison et al., 1993, p. 343). As noted in section 17, such behavior is closely associated with depression and thoughts of suicide.

Whatever their causes or functions, the atavistic (primitive) behaviors known as SIBs take a variety of forms, but if left unchecked, they share the consequence of bodily injury. Without physical restraint, protective gear, or effective intervention, there is risk that the youngster will permanently disfigure, incapacitate, or kill himself or herself.

The deviant aspects of SIBs are its rate, intensity, and persistence. Perhaps 10% of young, nondisabled children under the age of 5 occasionally engage in some form of self-injurious behavior (Zirpoli & Lloyd, 1987). It is considered normal, for example, for young children in fits of temper to bang their heads or hit themselves. Deviant self-injury, however, occurs so frequently and is of such intensity and duration that the youngster cannot develop normal social relationships or learn self-care skills and is in danger of becoming even more severely disabled.

Evidence indicates that SIBs could in some cases be a result of deficiencies in biochemicals required for normal brain functioning, inadequate development of the central nervous system, early experiences of pain and isolation, sensory problems, insensitivity to pain, or the body's ability to produce opiatelike substances in response to pain or injury. But no single biological explanation is now supported by research (Bodfish, 2007; Iwata, Zarcone, Vollmer, & Smith, 1994; Oliver, 1995). However, biological factors need not, and probably usually do not, operate independently of social factors in causing SIBs. Perhaps, in many cases, biological factors cause initial self-injury, but social learning factors exacerbate and maintain the problem. Self-injury, like other types of behavior, may be reinforced by social attention. This notion has important implications for intervention because it suggests ways of teaching alternatives to self-injury.

Some children appear to use SIBs as a means of getting adults to withdraw demands for performance, which the children experience as aversive. When presented with a task that demands their attention and performance, these children begin to injure themselves; the demands are then withdrawn. The social interaction and attention involved in teaching and learning is reinforcing for some children, and withdrawal of attention contingent upon SIBs is, for some, an effective extinction or punishment procedure. The same type of interaction and attention is apparently aversive for other children, and withdrawal of attention contingent on SIBs is negatively reinforcing for them; it makes the problem worse instead of better (see Oliver, 1995).

The assessment of self-injury is at once straightforward and complex. It is straightforward in that assessment involves direct observation and measurement: self-injurious behaviors should be defined, observed, and recorded daily in the different environments in which they occur. It is complex in that the causes are not well understood, and care must be taken to assess possible biological and subtle environmental causes (see Bodfish, 2007; Iwata et al., 1994; Lerman, Iwata, Zarcone, & Ringdahl, 1994). Possible biological causes include genetic anomalies and factors such as ear infections and sensory deficits. SIBs may occur more often in some environments than in others, and a change in environmental conditions (such as demands for performance) may dramatically alter the problem. It is thus important to assess the quality of the youngster's surroundings and social environment as well as the behavior itself, and it is particularly important to assess the social consequences of SIBs (Belcher, 1995; Scheuermann & Webber, 2002).

Many different approaches to reducing SIBs have been tried. No approach has been entirely successful, although some show much better results than others do. Among the least successful have been various forms of psychotherapy, "sensory-integration therapy," and "gentle teaching," approaches that are nonaversive (i.e., do not involve punishment) but are supported by very little scientific evidence that they reduce SIBs (see Scheuermann & Webber, 2002, for a succinct listing of controversial treatments and evidence of their effectiveness). The most effective nonaversive strategies yet devised involve functional analysis (to find the purpose the behavior serves) and arranging an environment in which alternative behaviors are taught or SIB is less likely to occur (see Bodfish, 2007; Klinger, Dawson, & Renner, 2003; Scheuermann & Webber, 2002). The emphases of research and practice in the early 21st century are on functional analysis, nonaversive procedures, and pharmacological treatments.

Some have suggested that all behavioral problems are resolvable without the use of punishment or aversive consequences (e.g., LaVigna & Donnellan, 1986). However, nonaversive approaches are not always successful, and in some cases punishing consequences have been quickly and highly effective in reducing self-injury (see Iwata et al., 1994; Schreibman, 1994). Controversy continues regarding the use of aversives, partly because *aversive* and *successful treatment* are difficult to define. Although everyone agrees that the use of nonaversive interventions is preferable, not everyone agrees that aversive interventions should be strictly and totally prohibited (Lerman & Vorndran, 2002).

SUMMARY

In the federal category "serious emotional disturbance," schizophrenia is explicitly included and autism is excluded (it is now a separate category under the Individuals with Disabilities Education Act [IDEA]). Schizophrenia and pervasive developmental disorders are rare, severe disorders of children and youth in which emotional and behavioral disorders are manifested.

Schizophrenia is a major psychiatric disorder falling under the general category of "psychotic disorders." Symptoms include hallucinations, delusions, and grossly aberrant behavior or thinking. It affects about 1 in 100 adults. Schizophrenia is unusual in individuals under 18 years of age, especially in preteens. The onset is often insidious and may be confused with other disorders. However, schizophrenia seems to be essentially the same disorder in children and adults. The causes appear to be primarily biological, although they are not well understood. Effective education is usually highly structured and individualized. Psychopharmacological treatment is essential. Some children with schizophrenia recover, although many make little improvement and continue to have major symptoms in adulthood.

The socialization problems of children and youth with schizophrenia and pervasive developmental disorders are extremely varied. Schizophrenia may be comorbid with a wide variety of other disorders, such as conduct disorder, ADHD, depression, or intellectual disability (mental retardation).

A full range of intervention strategies is needed to address the socialization problems of these children and youth. Communication disorders are a central feature of many severe disorders. Language interventions now focus on naturalistic applications of operant conditioning principles in communication training.

Stereotypy consists of repetitive, stereotyped acts that seem to provide reinforcing sensory feedback. Stereotypies may be merely self-stimulatory or self-injurious. Self-stimulation may interfere with learning. The best method of control depends on its topography and function. Self-injurious behavior appears to have multiple causes, both biological and social. It may serve the function of getting attention from others or allowing the individual to escape from demands. Current trends in research and intervention emphasize functional analysis, nonaversive procedures, and psychopharmacological treatment.

Schizophrenia and Other Severe Disorders

Ruth Ballinger, Ph.D., is a special education teacher on the island of Maui, Hawaii. She has experience teaching children from birth through the age of 20. She is currently an autism consulting teacher and works with students who have an autism spectrum disorder and their educational teams through the Maui District Department of Education.

Describe the school in which you teach and your particular role in the school.

I am an "autism consulting teacher" for one of the school districts here in Hawaii. My role is to provide support to the teams of students with autism spectrum disorders (ASD). I assist in the development, implementation, and monitoring of educational programs for students with ASD for over a dozen different schools. I help teams write IEPs and provide training to school personnel and the community. I also respond to crisis situations, such as when a student develops aggressive behaviors. In addition, I help facilitate disagreements among team members, in particular disputes that may arise between the family and the school.

Think of a particular student with a pervasive developmental disorder. How does this student manifest the disorder?

Mike is currently 6 years old and has just finished his kindergarten year. He is nonverbal and uses a picture exchange system to communicate. He primarily uses it when he wants a cookie or some juice, but sometimes he will ask for a particular ABC puzzle or another of his favorite toys.

Mike relies on routines and is good at following his visual schedule, which is a set of pictures arranged so that he knows what activity is coming next. If his daily routine is changed, he typically becomes upset and drops to the floor, starts to cry, and pushes or hits any adult who tries to move him toward the unexpected activity. I have observed him behave this way even when the upcoming event is one of his preferred activities.

Mike finds it difficult to pay attention in a group situation. Thus, he does most of his schoolwork in a small section of the classroom with one adult, either his teacher or his full-time aide. The area is blocked off with room dividers as he is easily visually distracted, and this helps him focus on the task at hand.

Mike is excellent at matching pictures, colors, and shapes, but has difficulty with receptive language, which is the ability to identify an object when given the name of the item. Mike is also learning to draw vertical and horizontal lines, use a pair of scissors, and manipulate buttons and zippers. He still wears pull-ups, but is learning to use the toilet.

Mike enjoys "sensory play." He likes two types of sensory play. One type involves movement. For example, he loves to sit and be bounced on a large therapy ball, to lie on and be dragged on a "magic carpet," and to sit on a "sit 'n spin" and be spun around. The other type of sensory play that he likes provides tactile input. He likes the feel of birdseed, uncooked rice and beans, lotion, and water. For the most part, Mike does not play with toys in the way that typically developing children do. For example, he lines up toys and markers or continuously taps toys on hard surfaces.

Mike enjoys eating bread, chicken, and tuna. He also likes chocolate chip cookies and potato chips. He seldom eats anything else and will not drink water. Although his teacher and parents are aware of his nutritional needs, they have decided to focus on other aspects of his program and not to tackle that issue at this time.

Mike is beginning to become interested in other children his own age. In the past couple of months, he has started to go over to other children who are playing. He will observe them for a few minutes, but does not try to join them. Even his desire to be with adults is inconsistent and depends on the activity they are doing. During movement sensory play he makes strong eye contact and, if the adult pauses the play, he holds out his hands or vocalizes to indicate he wants the play to resume. During other activities he often looks away from others' faces unless he is expecting an edible treat.

Mike can exhibit challenging behaviors and even aggression when he does not want to do what is expected of him. He will drop to the ground, whine, hit, kick, scratch, and attempt to bite when he is really unhappy about something. We have found that ignoring his behavior and giving him the opportunity to ask for a break with a "break card" reduces these behaviors.

What procedures have you found most useful in working with this student?

I have implemented a diverse program for Mike that targets a number of different skill areas. Use of pictures for communication—providing a way for Mike to express his wants and allowing the adult to tell Mike what is happening next in his day—is crucial. I contrive opportunities for Mike to communicate by putting his favorite toys and foods within sight but out of reach. In addition, whenever he does not want to do what is being asked of him, he can hand a break card to the adult and get a 2-minute break from the activity. Of course, he doesn't get to do anything fun during that time or earn reinforcers such as potato chips. However, this is the only way he can let us know when he really needs a break. Over the next year, as Mike becomes more familiar with the pictures associated with his routines, I will periodically change the order of activities slightly to give him practice at handling changes in routine. To promote preacademic skills as well as receptive language, his team uses a method called "discrete trial training."

Discrete trial training is a highly structured teaching strategy in which the adult gives an instruction, the child is expected to perform a specific behavior, and the adult provides reinforcement for successful completion of the instruction. For example, Mike is presented with three objects and instructed to "Give me cup." If he gives his partner the cup, then he receives a tiny piece of potato chip. These trials are presented over and over until he learns the concept.

Mike's social program consists of several components. As a precursor, he is taught how to play with toys. The adult plays with him, modeling conventional ways of playing with toys and then verbally and physically prompting Mike to imitate. In addition, he is given daily opportunities to observe his peers and encouraged to imitate them. This year I plan to create a "lunch bunch" for Mike. This will consist of inviting a couple of his peers to eat lunch with him in the classroom and then play some structured games with him. An adult will assist Mike by choosing games that he will likely enjoy, coaching the peers on how best to get him to interact with them, and prompting Mike to respond.

The sensory play is another aspect of his program that teaches him to make better eye contact and to want to interact with other people. In addition, sensory play tends to be calming and regulating for Mike. By incorporating it at different points in his day, Mike is better able to sit and concentrate on the task at hand.

Finally, I plan to add a functional life skills component to his educational program. I would like him to learn to do chores such as setting the lunch table, washing his dishes, assisting with simple food preparation, watering plants, and wiping the table. Besides these being useful skills, I think that Mike would learn to enjoy these activities.

What do you see as the prospects for this student's educational progress in the coming year?

I expect slow, but steady progress in the coming year. Mike has "good" days in which he can focus more easily and work more consistently. There are also days, which have sometimes stretched into weeks, when he asks for breaks frequently and exhibits challenging behaviors. During these times his progress in terms of skill development has slowed considerably. Nevertheless, I am excited about the fact that he is showing an interest in peers and hope that by the end of the year he will be reliably approaching them and wanting to initiate more interaction. With regard to language, I expect him to understand and use more pictures, but I do not anticipate him developing functional spoken language.

What do you see as the biggest long-term problems this student will face?

The fact that Mike is now 6 years old and still has no intelligible spoken language will be a major obstacle for him. If he does not develop spoken language, he is unlikely to become a reader and writer, which means he will remain dependent on using a picture-based communication system. He may never move beyond communicating only concrete wants and needs to abstract ideas and feelings.

Given Mike's unconventional interests, challenging behaviors, and difficulty with social interactions, he will struggle in many areas. He will have difficulty developing friendships and may never have an intimate relationship outside his family. He will most likely have difficulty finding suitable employment that will allow him to live independently. A reasonable goal for his adulthood may be for him to be successful in a group living situation or with family and to follow a regular routine that involves functional daily living skills, supported or volunteer work situations, and recreational opportunities.

(Author note: Because Mike is nonverbal, we do not provide the transcript of an interview.)

QUESTIONS FOR FURTHER REFLECTION

1. What behavioral characteristics would indicate to you as a teacher that a student might be developing schizophrenia?
2. If you are going to teach students with schizophrenia or autistic spectrum disorder, what kinds of behavior should you be prepared to deal with, and how would you characterize your best preparation for the task?
3. Under what circumstances, if any, do you believe punishment is justified with students who have schizophrenia or pervasive developmental disorders?

GLOSSARY

Adjustment disorders Maladaptive reactions to an identifiable and stressful life event or circumstance. Includes impairment of social and/or occupational functioning. Maladaptive behavior is expected to change when stress is removed.

Affective disorders *See* Mood disorders.

Amnesia Chronic or severe inability to remember; loss of memory that is general or more than temporary.

Anorexia nervosa Severe self-starvation and marked weight loss that may be life threatening. Occurs most often in adolescent girls.

Anoxia; hypoxia Deprivation of oxygen for a long enough time to result in brain trauma.

Anxiety disorders Disorders in which anxiety is the primary feature. Anxiety may focus on specific situations, such as separation or social contact with strangers, or it may be generalized and pervasive.

Anxiety withdrawal Behavior characterized by anxiety, feelings of inadequacy, embarrassment, shyness, and withdrawal from social contact.

Asperger's syndrome Impairment of social behavior (e.g., eye-to-eye gaze, facial expression, peer relationships, sharing of experience, social reciprocity) and restricted, repetitive, stereotyped patterns of behavior or interests but without significant delay in language or cognitive development.

Athetoid movement Involuntary, jerky, writhing movements (especially of the fingers and wrists) associated with athetoid cerebral palsy.

Attentional strategies Use of verbal labeling, rehearsal, self-instruction, or other techniques to improve a child's ability to attend efficiently to appropriate stimuli.

Attention deficit and disruptive behavior disorders Includes attention deficit–hyperactivity disorder, conduct disorder, oppositional defiant disorder, and disruptive behavior disorder.

Attention deficit–hyperactivity disorder (ADHD) A disorder that includes inattention, impulsivity, and hyperactivity, beginning before age 7 and of sufficient severity and persistence to result in impairment in two or more settings (e.g., home and school) in social, academic, or occupational functioning. May be primarily hyperactive–impulsive type or primarily inattentive type.

Autism; autistic *See* Autism spectrum disorder.

Autism spectrum disorder Autism is a pervasive developmental disorder with onset before age 3 in which there is qualitative impairment of social interaction and communication and restricted, repetitive, stereotyped patterns of behavior, interests, and activities. Autism spectrum disorder includes the full range of autism symptoms, from classic autism as just defined, to a generally milder form known as Asperger's syndrome and autisticlike behavior.

Aversive conditioning A form of punishment; presenting an aversive (painful or unpleasant) consequence following a behavior to reduce the frequency or probability of its recurrence.

Behavior intervention plan (BIP) A plan for changing a problem behavior.

Behavior modification Systematic control of environmental events, especially of consequences, to produce specific changes in observable responses. May include reinforcement, punishment, modeling, self-instruction, desensitization, guided practice, or any other technique for strengthening or eliminating a particular response.

Behavioral model Assumptions that emotional or behavioral disorders result primarily from inappropriate learning and that the most effective preventive actions and therapeutic interventions involve controlling the child's environment to teach appropriate responses.

Biological model Assumptions that emotional or behavioral disorders result primarily from dysfunction of the central nervous system (because of brain lesions, neurochemical irregularities, or genetic defects) and that the most effective preventive actions and therapeutic interventions involve prevention or correction of such biological defects.

Bipolar disorder Major mood disorder characterized by both manic and depressive episodes. *See also* Depression, Manic.

Brain syndrome *See* Organic brain syndrome.

Bulimia Recurrent episodes of binge eating followed by purging (by vomiting or enemas) or other compensatory behavior (e.g., fasting or excessive exercise) intended to prevent weight gain, accompanied by preoccupation with body shape or weight.

Case An example. A story describing a problem and information relevant to understanding it.

Catatonic behavior Characterized by muscular rigidity and mental stupor, sometimes alternating with periods of extreme excitement; inability to move or interact normally; "frozen" posture or affect.

Catharsis In psychoanalytic theory, the notion that it is therapeutic to express one's feelings freely under certain conditions (e.g., that aggressive drive can be reduced by free expression of aggression in a safe way, such as hitting a punching bag or a doll).

Cerebral palsy   A developmental disability resulting from brain damage before, during, or soon after birth and having as a primary feature weakness or paralysis of the extremities. Often accompanied by mental retardation, sensory deficiencies, and/or behavioral disorders.

Cerebral trauma   *See* Traumatic brain injury.

Character disorder   Acting-out, aggressive behavior with little or no indication of associated anxiety or guilt.

Childhood disintegrative disorder   Normal development followed by significant loss, after age 2 but before age 10, of previously acquired social, language, self-care, or play skills with qualitative impairment in social interaction or communication and stereotyped behavior.

Childhood psychosis   Used to denote a wide range of severe and profound disorders of children, including autism, schizophrenia, and symbiotic psychosis.

Choreoathetoid movement   Involuntary, purposeless, uncontrolled movement characteristic of some types of neurological disorders.

Comorbid condition   A condition or disorder occurring simultaneously with another.

Comorbidity   Two or more disorders occurring together, as in comorbidity of depression and conduct disorder.

Conceptual model   A theory. In emotional or behavioral disorders, a set of assumptions regarding the origins and nature of the problem and the nature of therapeutic mechanisms; a set of assumptions guiding research and practice.

Conduct disorder; conduct problem   Repetitive, persistent pattern of behavior violating basic rights of others or age-appropriate social norms or rules, including aggression toward people and animals, destruction of property, deceitfulness or theft, and serious violation of family or school rules. Onset may be in childhood or adolescence, and severity may range from mild to severe.

Contingency contract   In behavior modification, a written agreement between a child and an adult (or adults) specifying the consequences for specific behavior.

Counterconditioning   Behavior therapy that teaches, by means of classical and operant conditioning, adaptive responses that are incompatible with maladaptive responses.

Countertheorists   *See* Humanistic education.

Craniocerebral trauma   *See* Traumatic brain injury.

Criterion referenced   Assessment or testing based on a standard or criterion that the student should be able to reach rather than an average or norm.

Curriculum-based evaluation; curriculum-based assessment; curriculum-based measurement   Evaluation or assessment based on the student's performance in the actual curriculum with the materials (texts, problems) that the teacher is using for instruction. Requires frequent, brief measurement of the student's performance using regular instructional materials.

Cyclothymia; cyclothymic disorder   Fluctuation of mood alternating between depression and mania but with symptoms not severe enough to be considered bipolar disorder. *See also* Bipolar disorder; Depression; Manic.

Delinquency   The illegal behavior of a minor.

Delusion   Abnormal mental state in which something is falsely believed.

Delusional disorder   Disorder characterized by non-bizarre (i.e., potentially true) delusions without schizophrenia.

Depression; depressive episode   Depressed mood and loss of interest or pleasure in nearly all normal activities; episode lasting for at least 2 weeks.

Desensitization; systematic desensitization   Elimination of fears or phobias by gradually subjecting the fearful individual to successively more anxiety-provoking stimuli (real or imagined) while the individual remains relaxed and free of fear.

Developmental disorders   Disorders apparently caused by the child's failure to develop at a normal rate or according to the usual sequence.

Diagnostic and Statistical Manual of the American Psychiatric Association (DSM)   Editions designated by Roman numerals, as *DSM–IV* for the fourth edition. Revised third edition is referred to as *DSM–III–R*. The most recent edition released in 2000 involved a "text revision"; and is often referred to as *DSM–IV–TR*.

Distractibility   Inability to direct and sustain attention to the appropriate or relevant stimuli in a given situation. *See also* Selective attention.

Down syndrome   A genetic defect in which the child is born with an extra chromosome (number 21 in the 22 pairs; hence, trisomy 21) in each cell; a syndrome associated with mental retardation.

Dynamic psychiatry   The study of emotional processes, mental mechanisms, and their origins; study of evolution, progression, or regression in human behavior and its motivation. Distinguished from *descriptive psychiatry,* in which focus is on static clinical patterns, symptoms, and classification.

Dysphoria   General feeling of unhappiness or unwellness, especially when disproportionate to its cause or inappropriate to one's life circumstances. Opposite of *euphoria.*

Dysthymia   Feeling of depressed mood on most days for at least 2 years but not of the severity required for diagnosis of a major depressive episode or clinical depression.

Echolalia; echolalic   The parroting repetition of words or phrases either immediately after they are heard or later. Typical in very young children who are learning to talk. Among older children and adults, usually observed only in individuals with schizophrenia or autism.

Ecobehavioral analysis A procedure in which naturally occurring, functional events are identified and employed to improve instruction and behavior management.

Ecological model Assumptions that emotional or behavioral disorders result primarily from flaws in a complex social system in which various elements of the system (e.g., child, school, family, church, community) are highly interdependent and that the most effective preventive actions and therapeutic interventions involve changes in the entire social system.

Educateur An individual broadly trained to enhance social development of children and youth in various community contexts. Someone trained in education and related disciplines to intervene in the social ecology of troubled children and youth.

Ego The conscious mind. In Freudian psychology, the volitional aspect of behavior.

Ego psychology Psychological theories or models emphasizing the ego.

Elective mutism *See* Selective mutism.

Electroencephalogram (EEG) A graphic record of changes in the electrical potential of the brain. Used in neurological and psychiatric research.

Emotional intelligence Adeptness in assessing and managing emotions, including skills in awareness of one's own emotions, recognition of others' emotional states, regulation of one's own emotions and motivation, and management of interpersonal relationships.

Emotional lability Unstable or rapidly shifting emotional states.

Encephalitis Inflammation of the brain, usually as a result of infection and often accompanied by behavioral manifestations such as lethargy.

Encopresis Incontinence of feces, which may consist of passing feces into the clothing or bed at regular intervals or leaking mucus and feces into the clothing or bed almost continuously.

Endogenous depression Depression apparently precipitated by biological factors rather than adverse environmental circumstances.

Enuresis; enuretic Incontinence of urine, which may be diurnal (wetting oneself during the day) or nocturnal (bed-wetting).

Epilepsy Recurrent abnormal electrical discharges in the brain that cause seizures. A person is not considered to have epilepsy unless repeated seizures occur.

Ethology Scientific comparative study of animal and human behavior, especially study of the development of human character.

Eugenics Belief that human qualities can be improved through selective mating. A science dealing with improving inherited characteristics of a race or breed.

Euphoria Feeling of elation. Extreme and unrealistic happiness.

Externalizing behavior Acting-out behavior, such as fighting. Sometimes called conduct disorder.

Facilitated communication A procedure said to allow persons who are unable to communicate through speech to communicate by using a keyboard. A facilitator assists communication by giving emotional and physical support as the disabled person types.

Feeding disorder of infancy or early childhood Feeding disturbance, occurring before age 6, characterized by persistent failure to eat adequately and gain weight but not due to gastrointestinal or other general medical conditions.

Follow-back studies Studies in which adults with a given disorder are "followed back" in time in an attempt to find the antecedents of their condition in their medical, educational, or social histories.

Fragile X syndrome A genetic disorder, associated primarily with mental retardation but also a variety of other mental or behavioral problems, in which part of the X chromosome shows variations, such as breaks or gaps.

Frustration–aggression hypothesis Hypothesis that frustration always produces aggression and that aggression is always the result of frustration.

Functional analysis Assessment of behavior to determine the purposes, goals, or function of behavior.

Functional behavioral assessment (FBA) Procedures designed to find out why a student exhibits problem behavior, including assessment of the antecedents and consequences of behavior and the apparent purpose of the problem behavior.

General intelligence The totality of skills and knowledge that enable a person to solve problems and meet social expectations. The theory that intelligence consists of general problem-solving abilities rather than abilities to perform specific tasks.

Heightened risk A higher chance or risk than is true for the general population that an individual will experience an event or condition (e.g., use drugs, acquire a traumatic head injury, become delinquent, fail in school, be diagnosed with schizophrenia, etc.).

Holistic education An approach emphasizing individuals' construction of their own realities based on personal experience and rejecting traditional analytic and quantitative views of reality.

Humanistic education Education suggested by countertheorists, who call for radical school reform and/or greater self-determination by the child. Education in which freedom, openness, innovation, self-direction, and self-evaluation by students and mutual sharing between students and teachers are practiced.

Hyperactivity; hyperactive High level of motor activity accompanied by socially inappropriate behavior, often including conduct disorder, distractibility, and impulsivity.

Hyperkinesis   Excessive motor activity.

Hyperthyroidism   Enlargement of and excessive secretion of hormones from the thyroid gland that may result in nervousness, weakness, and restless overactivity.

Hypoglycemia   Abnormally low level of blood sugar that may produce behavioral symptoms such as irritability, fretfulness, confusion, negativism, or aggression. May be associated with diabetes.

Hypomanic   *See* Manic.

Hypoxia   Severely reduced supply of oxygen. *See* Anoxia.

Immaturity–inadequacy   Disorder characterized by social incompetence, passivity, daydreaming, and behavior typical of younger children.

Impulsivity   Tendency to react quickly and inappropriately to a situation rather than take time to consider alternatives and choose carefully.

Incidence   The rate of occurrence (as new cases) of a specific disorder in a given population during a given period of time (e.g., 25 per 1,000 per year).

Incontinence; incontinent   The release of urine or feces at inappropriate times or places. Lack of control of bladder or bowel function.

Index crime   An act that is illegal regardless of the person's age. Crimes for which the FBI keeps records, including the range from misdemeanors to murder.

Individuals with Disabilities Education Act (IDEA)   The federal special education law, enacted in 1990, that amended the Education for All Handicapped Children Act of 1975 (which was also known as Public Law 94–142), most recently reauthorized in 2004. The 2004 reauthorization changed the name of the law to the Individuals with Disabilities Education Improvement Act; sometimes referred to as IDEIA or IDEIA 2004, the original acronym IDEA is still more commonly used even when referring to the most recent reauthorization.

Induction approach   Use of reasoning, explanation, modeling, and expressions of love and concern in discipline, especially in teaching or enforcing moral standards.

Infantile autism   *See* Autistic spectrum disorder.

Interactional–transactional model   Assumptions that emotional or behavioral disorders result primarily from the mutual influence of the child and other people on each other and that the most effective preventive actions and therapeutic interventions involve changing the nature of interactions and transactions between the child and others.

Interim alternative educational setting (IAES)   A placement that may be used for students with disabilities when they commit disciplinary infractions resulting in temporary suspension or expulsion from school for more than 10 days. Special education must be continued in the IAES.

Internalizing behavior   Behavior typically associated with social withdrawal, such as shyness, anxiety, or depression.

Intervention   Method or strategy used in treatment of an emotional or behavioral disorder.

Intrapsychic; intrapsychic causal factors   Having to do with the mind; in the mind itself. Conflict or disequilibrium between parts of the mind (in psychoanalytic theory, the id, the ego, and the superego), especially conflict in the unconscious.

Kanner's syndrome; early infantile autism   Originally described by Leo Kanner in 1943. *See also* Autistic spectrum disorder.

Lability   *See* Emotional lability.

Life-impact curriculum   A special curriculum intended to change students' thinking about their experiences and choices. A curriculum based on humanistic or holistic philosophy.

Life space crisis intervention   Ways of talking with children based on psychoeducational theory to help them understand and change their behavior through reflection and planning. *See also* Life space interview.

Life space interview (LSI)   Therapeutic way of talking with disturbed children about their behavior. A set of techniques for managing behavior by means of therapeutic communication.

Locus of control   Belief that one's behavior is under internal or external control. Individuals have an internal locus to the extent that they believe they are responsible for their actions, an external locus to the extent that they believe chance or others' actions determine their behavior.

Macroculture   A nation or other large social entity with a shared culture.

Mania   Excessive excitement or enthusiasm, usually centered on a particular activity or object.

Manic; manic episode   Persistently elevated, expansive, or irritable mood. Episode of such mood lasting at least 1 week.

Manifestation determination   A school-based process used to determine whether a student's misbehvaior is due to his or her disability, usually in the process of determining appropriate disciplinary action for serious behavioral offenses.

Megavitamin therapy   Administration of extremely large doses of vitamins in the hope of improving or curing behavior disorders.

Metacognition; metacognitive   Thinking about thinking. Awareness and analysis of one's thought processes. Controlling one's cognitive processes.

Microculture   A smaller group existing within a larger cultural group and having unique values, style, language, dialect, ways of communicating nonverbally, awareness, frame of reference, and identification.

Minimal brain dysfunction; minimal brain damage   Term applied to children who exhibit behavioral characteristics (e.g., hyperactivity, distractibility) thought to be associated with brain damage, in the absence of other evidence that their brains have been damaged.

Minimal cerebral dysfunction   *See* Minimal brain dysfunction.

Modeling   Providing an example to imitate. Behavior modification technique in which a clear model of the desired behavior is provided. (Typically, reinforcement is given for imitation of the model.)

Mood disorders   Disorders of emotion that color outlook on life. Usually characterized by either elation or depression. May be episodic or chronic, manic or depressive.

Moral therapy; moral treatment   Treatment provided in the late 18th and early 19th centuries characterized by humane and kindly care, therapeutic activity, and consistent consequences for behavior.

Multiaxial assessment   A system used in the *DSM–IV* in which the client is rated on five axes: clinical disorders, personality disorders or mental retardation, general medical conditions, psychosocial and environmental problems, and global assessment of functioning.

Multiple intelligences   Highly specific types of problem-solving abilities (e.g., analytical, synthetic, and practical abilities) or intelligence in specific areas (e.g., linguistic, musical, spatial, interpersonal, intrapersonal, bodily–kinesthetic, or logical–mathematical). The theory that persons do not have a general intelligence but specific intelligences in various areas of performance.

Negative reinforcement   Withdrawal or postponement of a negative reinforcer (aversive event or stimulus) contingent upon a behavior, which increases the probability that the behavior will be repeated.

Neologism   A coined word that is meaningless to others. A meaningless word in the speech of a person with a psychotic disorder or a pervasive developmental disorder.

Neuroleptics   Antipsychotic drugs. Drugs that suppress or prevent symptoms of psychosis. Major tranquilizers.

Neurosis; neurotic behavior   Emotional or behavioral disorder characterized by emotional conflict but not loss of contact with reality.

No Child Left Behind Act (NCLB)   Major federal legislation enacted in 2001 with emphasis on increased accountability for schools; greater choice for parents of children attending schools that do not demonstrate "adequate yearly progress" (AYP); and increased flexibility for states and local schools in how they spend federal education money.

Normative   Based on a norm, a sample assumed to provide a normal distribution of scores. Based on comparison to a statistical average for a representative sample of individuals.

Operant conditioning   Changing behavior by altering its consequences. Altering the future probability of a response by providing reinforcement or punishment as a consequence.

Oppositional defiant disorder (ODD)   A pattern of negativistic, hostile, and defiant behavior that is unusual for the individual's age and developmental level, lasting at least 6 months and often characterized by fits of temper, arguing with adults, refusing to comply with adults' requests or rules, and deliberately annoying others and resulting in significant impairment of social, academic, or occupational functioning.

Organic brain syndrome; organic psychosis   Disorder caused by brain damage.

Organic mental disorders   Disorders caused by transient or permanent brain dysfunction, often resulting from *anoxia,* ingestion of drugs or other toxic substances, or injury to brain tissue.

Organicity   Behavioral indications of brain damage or organic defects.

Orthomolecular therapy   Administration of chemical substances, vitamins, or drugs on the assumption that they will correct a basic chemical or molecular error that causes emotional or behavioral disorders.

Overcorrection   Set of procedures designed to overcorrect behavioral errors. May be *positive practice* overcorrection (requiring the individual to practice a more adaptive or appropriate form of behavior) or *restitution* overcorrection (requiring the individual to restore the environment to a condition better than its status before the misbehavior occurred).

Overselective attention   *See* Selective attention.

Parasuicide   Attempted suicide.

Permissive approach to education   Allowing children to behave as they wish within broad or loosely defined limits, on the assumption that it is therapeutic to allow them to act out their feelings (unless they endanger someone) and that the teacher must be permissive to build a sound relationship with children. Derived mostly from psychoanalytic theory.

Personal agency   The assumption, based on social learning theory, that a person is self-conscious and can make predictions and choices.

Person variables   Thoughts, feelings, and perceptions. Private events or states.

Personality disorders   Deeply ingrained, inflexible, maladaptive patterns of relating to, perceiving, and thinking about the environment and oneself that impair adaptive functioning or cause subject distress.

Personality problem   Disorder characterized by neurotic behavior, depression, and withdrawal.

Pervasive developmental disorder   Distortion of or lag in all or most areas of development, as in autism. *See also* Asperger's syndrome; Childhood disintegrative disorder; Rett's disorder.

Phenomenological model   Assumptions that emotional or behavioral disorders result primarily from inadequate or distorted conscious experience with life events and that the most effective preventive actions and therapeutic interventions involve helping individuals examine their conscious experience of the world.

Phobia   Irrational and debilitating fear.

Pica   Persistent eating of nonnutritional substances (e.g., paint, plaster, cloth).

Play therapy   Therapeutic treatment in which the child's play is used as the theme for communication between therapist and child.

Positive behavior support (PBS)/Positive behavioral intervention and supports (PBIS)   Interchangeable terms referring to a model of behavioral intervention that involves the systematic application of behavior analysis to solve behavior problems. Emphasis is on positive procedures and focus on enviornmental and contextual variables that influence behavior in different settings. Although the terms PBS and PBIS are often used interchangeably, PBS sometimes refers to a belief in behavior management without the use of punishment under any circumstances.

Positive practice   *See* Overcorrection.

Positive reinforcement   Presentation of a positive reinforcer (reward) contingent upon a behavior, which increases the probability that the behavior will be repeated.

Postencephalitic behavior syndrome   Abnormal behavior following encephalitis (inflammation of the brain).

Posttraumatic stress disorder (PTSD)   Disorder in which after experiencing a highly traumatic event the individual persistently reexperiences the event, avoids stimuli associated with the event, becomes generally unresponsive, or has persistent symptoms of arousal (e.g., hypervigilant, irritable, difficulty concentrating, difficulty sleeping), resulting in significant impairment of everyday functioning.

Pragmatics   The practical use of language in social situations. The functional use rather than the mechanics of language.

Precorrection   The strategy of anticipating and avoiding misbehavior by identifying and modifying the context in which it is likely to occur. Using proactive procedures to teach desired behavior rather than focusing on correction of misbehavior.

Premorbid; premorbid personality   Condition or personality characteristics predictive of later onset of illness or disorder.

Prevalence   The total number of individuals with a specific disorder in a given population (e.g., 2%).

Primary prevention   Procedures designed to keep a disorder (or disease) from occurring.

Primary process thinking   Psychoanalytic concept that disorganized or primitive thought or activity represents direct expression of unconscious mental processes. Distinguished from *secondary process* (rational, logical) thinking.

Prosocial behavior   Behavior that facilitates or maintains positive social contacts. Desirable or appropriate social behavior.

Pseudoretardation   Level of functioning associated with mental retardation that increases to normal level of functioning when environmental factors are changed. Falsely diagnosed mental retardation.

Psychoactive substance use disorders   Disorders involving abuse of mood-altering substances (e.g., alcohol or other drugs).

Psychoanalytic model   Assumptions that emotional or behavioral disorders result primarily from unconscious conflicts and that the most effective preventive actions and therapeutic interventions involve uncovering and understanding unconscious motivations.

Psychodynamic model   *See* Psychoanalytic model.

Psychoeducational model   Approach to education that takes into account psychodynamic concepts such as unconscious motivation but focuses intervention on the ego processes by which the child gains insight into his or her behavior.

Psychoneurosis; psychoneurotic   *See* Neurosis.

Psychopath; psychopathic   An individual who exhibits mostly amoral or antisocial behavior and is usually impulsive, irresponsible, and self-gratifying without consideration for others. Also called *sociopath* or *sociopathic*.

Psychopathology   Mental illness. In psychiatry, the study of significant causes and development of mental illness. More generally, emotional or behavioral disorder.

Psychophysiological   Physical disorder thought to be caused by psychological (emotional) conflict.

Psychosexual disorder   Disorders involving sexual functioning or sex-typed behavior.

Psychosis   A major mental illness in which thought processes are disordered (e.g., schizophrenia).

Psychosomatic; psychosomaticization   *See* Psychophysiological.

Psychotherapy   Any type of treatment relying primarily on verbal and nonverbal communication between patient and therapist rather than on medical procedures. Not typically defined to include behavior modification. Typically administered by a psychiatrist or a clinical psychologist.

Psychotic disorder; psychotic behavior   Emotional or behavioral disorder characterized by major departure from normal patterns of acting, thinking, and feeling (e.g., schizophrenia). *See also* Schizophrenic disorder; Substance-induced psychotic disorder.

Punishment   Consequences that reduce future probability of a behavior. May be *response cost* (removal of a valued object or commodity) or *aversive conditioning* (presentation of an aversive stimulus such as a slap or an electric shock).

Rave   An all-night dance party frequented by adolescents and young adults, generally involving electronic dance music and abuse of the drug Ecstasy and other controlled substances.

Reactive attachment disorder of infancy or early childhood   Markedly disturbed and developmentally inappropriate social behavior beginning before age 5 and assumed to be caused by neglect of the child's basic emotional and physical needs or by repeated changes in primary caregiver (e.g., frequent changes in foster placement).

Reactive depression Depression apparently precipitated by a specific event. Depression that is a reaction to adverse circumstances.

Reactive disorders Emotional or behavioral disorders apparently caused by reaction to stressful circumstances.

Reciprocal inhibition *See* Desensitization.

Reinforcement Presenting or removing stimuli following a behavior to increase its future probability. *Positive reinforcement* refers to presenting positive stimuli (rewards). *Negative reinforcement* refers to removing negative stimuli (punishers) contingent on a response. Both positive and negative reinforcement increase the rate or strength of the response.

Respondent behavior An elicited response. Reflexive behavior elicited automatically by presenting a stimulus (e.g., pupillary contraction elicited by shining a light in the eye).

Respondent conditioning Process by which a previously neutral stimulus comes to elicit a respondent behavior after the neutral stimulus has been paired with presentation of another stimulus (an unconditioned stimulus that already elicits a response) on one or more trials.

Response cost Punishment technique consisting of taking away a valued object or commodity contingent on a behavior. A fine. Making an inappropriate response "cost" something to the misbehaving child.

Response topography The particular movements that comprise a response. How the response looks to an observer as opposed to the effect of the response on the environment.

Restitution *See* Overcorrection.

Rett's disorder Apparently normal development through at least age 5 months, followed by deceleration of head growth between ages 5 months and 48 months, loss of psychomotor skills, and severe impairment of expressive and receptive language. Usually associated with severe mental retardation.

Risk The chance or probability that a specified outcome or set of outcomes will occur. A risk factor is an event or condition increasing the probability of a specified outcome.

Rumination; mercyism Regurgitation with loss of weight or failure to thrive.

Schizoaffective disorder An episode of mood disorder concurrent with schizophrenia.

Schizoid; schizophrenic spectrum behavior *See* Schizophreniform disorder.

Schizophrenia *See* Schizophrenic disorder.

Schizophrenic disorder Psychotic disorder characterized by distortion of thinking, abnormal perception, and bizarre behavior and emotions lasting at least 6 months.

Schizophreniform disorder Behavior like that seen in schizophrenia but not as long in duration or accompanied by decline in functioning. *See also* Schizophrenic disorder.

Schizophrenogenic Someone (in psychoanalytic theory, typically the mother) or something that causes schizophrenia.

School phobia Fear of going to school, usually accompanied by indications of anxiety about attendance, such as abdominal pain, nausea, or other physical complaints just before leaving for school in the morning.

Secondary prevention Procedures implemented soon after a disorder (or disease) has been detected. Designed to reverse or correct a disorder or prevent it from becoming worse.

Selective attention Ability to direct and sustain one's attention to the appropriate and relevant stimuli in a given situation. Disorders of selective attention include *underselective attention* (inability to focus attention only on relevant stimuli or to disregard irrelevant stimuli) and *overselective attention* (inability to attend to all the relevant stimuli or tendency to focus on an irrelevant stimulus).

Selective mutism Consistent failure to speak in specific social circumstances in which speaking is expected, such as school (and despite speaking in other situations, e.g., home) but not due to lack of knowledge of or ability to use language.

Self-instruction Telling oneself what to do or how to perform. Technique for teaching children self-control or how to improve their performance by talking to themselves about what they are doing.

Self-stimulation Any repetitive, stereotyped activity that seems only to provide sensory feedback.

Sensitization approach Use of harsh punishment, threats, and overpowering force in discipline, especially in teaching or enforcing moral standards.

Separation anxiety disorder Developmentally inappropriate and excessive anxiety about separation from home or those to whom the individual is attached lasting at least 4 weeks, beginning before age 18, and causing significant distress or impairment of social or academic functioning.

Sequela Something that follows. A consequence. The lingering effect of an injury or disease (pl. *sequelae*).

Social-cognitive theory *See* Social learning theory.

Social learning theory Assumptions that antecedent or setting events (e.g., models, instructions), consequences (rewards and punishments), and cognitive processes (perceiving, thinking, feeling) influence behavior. Includes features of behavioral model or behavior modification with additional consideration of cognitive factors.

Social validity The acceptability and significance of a treatment procedure as judged by parents or other consumers.

Socialized delinquency; Subcultural delinquency Delinquent behavior in the context of an antisocial peer group.

Sociological model Approximate equivalent of *ecological model*.

Sociopath; sociopathic *See* Psychopath.

Soft neurological signs Behavioral indications, such as uncoordination, distractibility, impulsivity, perceptual problems, and certain patterns of nerve reflexes, that may occur in individuals who are not brain damaged as well as in those who are. Signs that an individual may be brain damaged but that cannot be said to indicate the certainty of brain damage.

Somatic   Physical. Of or relating to the body.

Somatoform disorders   Physical symptoms suggesting a physical disorder, in the absence of demonstrable organic findings to explain the symptoms.

Status offense   An act that is illegal only if committed by a minor (e.g., buying or drinking alcohol).

Stereotype   A simplified, standardized concept or image with particular meaning in describing a group. A routine or persistently repeated behavior.

Stereotypic behavior   Persistent repetition of speech or motor activity.

Stereotypic movement disorder   Repetitive, seemingly driven, nonfunctional motor behavior that markedly interferes with normal activities or results in self-inflicted injury requiring medical treatment.

Stereotypy   A persistent, repetitive behavior or vocalization associated with self-stimulation, self-injury, or tic.

Strauss syndrome   Group of emotional and behavioral characteristics, including hyperactivity, distractibility, impulsivity, perceptual disturbances, no family history of mental retardation, and medical history suggestive of brain damage. Named after Alfred A. Strauss.

Structured approach to education   Making the classroom environment highly predictable by providing clear directions for behavior, firm expectations that students will behave as directed, and consistent consequences for behavior. Assumes that children lack order and predictability in everyday life and will learn self-control in a highly structured (predictable) environment. Derives primarily from learning theory.

Substance-induced psychotic disorder   Delusions or hallucinations caused by intoxication with or withdrawal from drugs or other substances.

Systematic desensitization   See Desensitization.

Target assessment   Definition and direct measurement (counting) of behaviors that are considered to be a problem (as opposed to administering psychological tests designed to measure behavioral traits or mental characteristics).

Temperament   Inborn emotional or behavioral style, including general level of activity, regularity or predictability, approach or withdrawal, adaptability, intensity of reaction, responsiveness, mood, distractibility, and persistence.

Tertiary prevention   Procedures designed to keep a severe or chronic disorder (or disease) from causing complications or overwhelming the individual or others.

Therapeutic milieu   Total treatment setting that is therapeutic. Environment that includes attention to therapeutic value of both physical and social surroundings.

Tic   Sudden, rapid, recurrent, nonrhythmic, stereotyped movement or vocalization.

Tic disorder   Stereotyped movement disorder in which there is disregulation of gross motor movement. Recurrent, involuntary, repetitive, rapid, purposeless movement. May be transient or chronic.

Time out   Technically, time out from positive reinforcement. Interval during which reinforcement (rewards) cannot be earned. In classroom practice, usually a brief period of social isolation during which the child cannot receive attention or earn rewards.

Token economy; token reinforcement; token system   System of behavior modification in which tangible or token reinforcers, such as points, plastic chips, metal washers, poker chips, or play money, are given as rewards and later exchanged for backup reinforcers that have value in themselves (e.g., food, trinkets, play time, books). A miniature economic system used to foster desirable behavior.

Topography   See Response topography.

Tourette's disorder   Multiple motor and vocal tics occurring many times daily (not necessarily together), with onset before age 18 and causing marked distress or significant impairment of social or occupational functioning.

Tourette's syndrome (TS)   See Tourette's disorder.

Transactions   Exchanges.

Transference   Unconscious redirection of feelings toward a different person (e.g., responding to teacher as if to parent). In psychoanalytic theory, responding to the therapist as if to another person, usually a parent.

Traumatic brain injury (TBI)   Injury to the brain caused by an external force, not caused by a degenerative or congenital condition, and resulting in a diminished or altered state of consciousness and neurological or neurobehavioral dysfunction.

Traumatic head injury   See Traumatic brain injury.

Triadic reciprocality   The mutual influences of environment, person variables (thoughts, feelings), and behavior in social development.

Underselective attention   See Selective attention.

Unipolar   In psychology, feelings characterized by mood swings in one direction (e.g., swings from normal feelings to feelings of depression without swings to manic behavior or feelings of euphoria).

Unsocialized aggression   Unbridled aggressive behavior characterized by hostility, impulsivity, and alienation.

Vicarious extinction   Extinction of a fear response by watching someone else engage in an anxiety-provoking activity without apparent fear. Loss of fear (or other response) by observing others' behavior.

Vicarious reinforcement   Reinforcement obtained by watching someone else obtain reinforcers (rewards) for a particular response.